Single Volume Edition of Better Reading

REPERTORY

SINGLE VOLUME EDITION OF *Better Reading*

REPERTORY

introduction to essays and articles, biography

and history, short stories, drama, and poetry

Walter Blair

UNIVERSITY OF CHICAGO

John Gerber

STATE UNIVERSITY OF IOWA

Scott, Foresman and Company

CHICAGO   ATLANTA   DALLAS   PALO ALTO   FAIR LAWN, N.J.

The *Single Volume Edition of Better Reading: Repertory* is composed principally of the two volumes *Better Reading 1: Factual Prose*, copyright 1959 by Scott, Foresman and Company, and *Better Reading 2: Literature*, copyright 1959 by Scott, Foresman and Company.

Specific acknowledgment of the courtesy of those who have made possible the reprinting of selections from their publications is made on the first pages where the selections appear. *Bound East for Cardiff* from *The Long Voyage Home: Seven Plays of the Sea*, by Eugene O'Neill. Copyright 1919 and renewed 1946 by Eugene O'Neill. Reprinted by permission of Random House, Inc. "Ransom's 'Bells for John Whiteside's Daughter'" from *Selected Essays of Robert Penn Warren*. Copyright 1943 by Robert Penn Warren. Reprinted by permission of Random House, Inc. "Musée des Beaux Arts" from *The Collected Poetry of W. H. Auden*. Copyright 1940 by W. H. Auden. Reprinted by permission of Random House, Inc. "The Express" from *Collected Poems 1928-1953*, by Stephen Spender. Copyright 1934 by The Modern Library, Inc. Reprinted by permission of Random House, Inc. "Auto Wreck" from *Poems 1940-1953*, by Karl Shapiro. Copyright 1941 by Karl Shapiro. Reprinted by permission of Random House, Inc.

The illustrations appearing on the following pages are the work of Seymour Fleishman: 428, 697, 702, 703, 841, 842, 907, 942, 943.

Art direction, Hal Kearney. Design, Catherine Hinkle.

CONTENTS

Part Two

FACTUAL PROSE: TYPES

Part Three

....

IMAGINATIVE LITERATURE: TYPES

Part Four

....

STUDENT'S HANDBOOK

The following titles were given by the editors to excerpts from longer works or to untitled selections: "My First Encounters with Politics," "The Limits of Government Interference," "Three Aims for Writers," and "The Assassination of Lincoln."

Introduction

Repertory, the Single Volume Edition of *Better Reading*, is first of all a full collection of what we believe are exceptionally interesting essays, articles, histories, biographies, criticisms, short stories, dramas, and poems, ranging in time from the distant past to the present and exhibiting markedly different and even clashing views of life.

It should provide ample readings for the first course in college English. The essays and articles in Parts One and Two have been selected not only to stimulate discussion but also to suggest interesting topics for papers. Most of them should, furthermore, furnish models which students will find valuable as they confront problems as writers. The stories, plays, and poetry in Part Three have been selected to provide an introduction to literature and help develop insights and critical standards.

The selections in Part One include considerations of a variety of important problems. They are grouped under these headings: Society and the Individual, Government, College Education, Language and Its Use, Mass Media, Literature and the Fine Arts, Science, and Religion and Ethics. The discussions differ from one another in purpose, in form, and in the attitudes they express. In the first group of selections, for example, E. B. White, George Orwell, William H. Whyte, and Vance Packard are all concerned in various ways with the inability of the individual to resist the pressure of society, while Plato in *Crito* and Thoreau in *Civil Disobedience* proclaim the necessity for the individual to live up to his own convictions despite imprisonment or death.

The selections in Part Two are organized according to types: Essays and Articles (including works by Bacon, Hazlitt, Stevenson, Woolf, Cowley, Wilson, and Podhoretz, and providing perspective on the variety and development of the essay); History (exhibiting five different approaches to the writing of history, including the consideration by one historian of another historian's thesis); and Biography (treating widely different personalities—a general, a president, a congressman, and a poet—and representing different biographical methods). Although criticisms are not grouped under a separate heading, there are many examples throughout the book, including criticisms of literature in general, criticisms of types of literature, and criticisms of specific pieces.

Part Three deals with the types of imaginative literature—short stories, drama, and poetry. Introductory discussions point out the main characteristics of each type, and headnotes for particular works or groups of works are provided when needed. Because of the ways contemporaneous audiences and theaters shape plays, most of the dramas are preceded by a relevant historical discussion and by illustrations designed to help the student visualize the production of the play in its own period. Twenty-five short stories, eight plays, and over one hundred poems are included and the selections range in time from Sophocles' *Oedipus* to Paddy Chayefsky's television play *Marty*.

The anthology proper contains relatively little editorial material. However, in addition to the introductions and headnotes, a Student's Handbook containing helpful suggestions for reading factual prose and imaginative literature and an Index of Authors and Titles with brief biographical information are given at the end of the book. Thus while *Repertory* is essentially an anthology of factual prose and imaginative literature, it also contains editorial aids for those instructors and students who wish to use them.

To our colleagues and to the many teachers and students who have used editions of *Better Reading 1* and *2*, we give our sincere thanks for helpful suggestions. We also wish to thank the many authors and publishers who have permitted us to include selections from their works.

W.B.   *J.G.*

Factual Prose:

Representative Selections

The selections in Part One of this book deal with important problems and issues of the world today. You will find that these articles vary in excellence according to any of the evaluative tests which you can apply to factual prose (pp. 1118-1127). They embody varied forms; in literary excellence they range from competent to superb; and each group sets forth contrasting or conflicting attitudes. In an important sense, therefore, they typify the range of the factual reading available to anyone interested in current affairs.

A word about the arrangement of these selections: The divisions treat in turn social and individual problems, government, college education, language, mass media, literature and the fine arts, science, and religion and ethics. Each of these divisions is introduced by an autobiographical passage which tells of the personal discovery by some writer of the matter dealt with in that group. Some of these contacts are shocking, some are full of delight, some are a mingling of pain and pleasure, one is comical. All, however, show insights into experience of the sort that makes problems important to us as individuals. Thereafter, in each division, authors argue for or explain varying points of view.

Society and the Individual

One of man's most persistent and perplexing problems involves his relationship to the group. How can a man be a useful and cooperative member of society and yet keep his individuality and integrity? There is no neat answer, and the problem seems to be growing more difficult to solve rather than easier. Indeed, some contemporary scientists feel that we are losing our individuality altogether, that we are not only willing but eager to conform to outside social pressures in the belief that only by so doing can we gain security. The essays in this section take up some facets of this complex problem.

George Orwell describes the problem from the standpoint of the man in authority. In "Shooting an Elephant" he tells of the discovery he made while a minor British civil servant in lower Burma: that one loses his independence of action and must compromise his principles the moment he becomes a symbol of authority. In "The Family Which Dwelt Apart" E. B. White relates the problem to the family, showing how society invades family privacy even on a remote island in the lower reaches of Barnetuck Bay. The incident is funny, but its point is not. William H. Whyte's "A Generation of Bureaucrats" relates the problem to college seniors. His essay is not a flattering one, since he argues that most seniors are now looking for jobs with big corporations, happy to surrender their independence for the security—and conformity—of the corporation. Vance Packard relates the problem to the public as a whole when in "The Growing Power of Admen" he charges that the mass media, in this case advertising, are pushing us toward conformity and passivity.

For the most rousing statements in defense of individuality we must go back to past centuries. Thoreau's "Civil Disobedience" can still disturb our apathy even if it seems dated in some respects. For the greatest statement of them all, perhaps, we must go back 2400 years to Socrates and his arguments against knuckling under to the crowd. Socrates was put to death by the crowd, but his dialog with Crito as related by Plato lives on as one of the great documents in human history.

George Orwell

SHOOTING AN ELEPHANT

A personal discovery

In Moulmein, in Lower Burma, I was hated by large numbers of people—the only time in my life that I have been important enough for this to happen to me. I was sub-divisional police officer of the town, and in an aimless, petty kind of way anti-European feeling was very bitter. No one had the guts to raise a riot, but if a European woman went through the bazaars alone somebody would probably spit betel juice over her dress. As a police officer I was an obvious target and was baited whenever it seemed safe to do so. When a nimble Burman tripped me up on the football field and the referee (another Burman) looked the other way, the crowd yelled with hideous laughter. This happened more than once. In the end the sneering yellow faces of young men that met me everywhere, the insults hooted after me when I was at a safe distance, got badly on my nerves. The young Buddhist priests were the worst of all. There were several thousands of them in the town and none of them seemed to have anything to do except stand on street corners and jeer at Europeans.

All this was perplexing and upsetting. For at that time I had already made up my mind that imperialism was an evil thing and the sooner I chucked up my job and got out of it the better. Theoretically—and secretly, of course—I was all for the Burmese and all against their oppressors, the British. As for the job I was doing, I hated it more bitterly than I can perhaps make clear. In a job like that you see the dirty work of Empire at close quarters. The wretched prisoners huddling in the stinking cages of the lock-ups, the grey, cowed faces of the long-term convicts, the scarred buttocks of the men who had been flogged with bamboos—all these oppressed me with an intolerable sense of guilt. But I could get nothing into perspective. I was young and ill educated and I had had to think out my problems in the utter silence that is imposed on every Englishman in the East. I did not even know that the British Empire is dying, still less did I know that it is a great deal better than the younger empires that are going to supplant it. All I knew was that I was stuck between my hatred of the empire I served and my rage against the evil-spirited little beasts who tried to make my job impossible. With one part of my mind I thought of the British Raj as an unbreakable tyranny, as something clamped down, in *saecula saeculorum*, upon the will of prostrate peoples; with another part I thought that the greatest joy in the world would be to drive a bayonet into a Buddhist priest's guts. Feelings like these are the normal by-products of imperialism; ask any Anglo-Indian official, if you can catch him off duty.

One day something happened which in a roundabout way was enlightening. It was a tiny incident in itself, but it gave me a better glimpse than I had had before of the real nature of imperialism—the real motives for which despotic governments act. Early one morning the sub-inspector at a police station the other end of the town rang me up on the 'phone and said that an elephant was ravaging the bazaar. Would I please come and do something about it? I did not know what I could do, but I wanted to see what was happening and I got on to a pony and started out. I took my rifle, an old .44 Winchester and much too small to kill an elephant, but I thought the noise might be useful *in terrorem*. Various Burmans stopped me on the way and told me about the elephant's doings. It was not, of course, a wild elephant, but a tame one which had gone "must." It had been chained up, as tame elephants always are when their attack of "must" is due, but on the previous night it had broken its chain and escaped. Its mahout, the only person who could manage it when it was in that state, had set out in pursuit, but had taken the wrong direction and was now twelve hours' journey away, and in the morning the elephant had suddenly reappeared in the town. The Burmese population had no weapons and were quite helpless against it. It had already destroyed somebody's bamboo hut, killed a cow and raided some fruit-stalls and devoured the stock; also it had met the municipal rubbish van and, when the driver jumped out and took to his heels, had turned the van over and inflicted violences upon it.

The Burmese sub-inspector and some Indian constables were waiting for me in the quarter where the elephant had been seen. It was a very poor quarter, a labyrinth of squalid bamboo huts, thatched with palm-leaf, winding all over a steep hillside. I remember that it was a cloudy, stuffy morning at the beginning of the rains. We began questioning the people as to where the elephant had gone and, as usual, failed to get any definite information. That is invariably the case in the East; a story always sounds clear enough at a distance, but the nearer you get to the scene of events the vaguer it becomes. Some of the people said that the elephant had gone in one direction, some said that he had gone in another, some professed not even to have heard of any elephant. I had almost made up my mind that the whole story was a pack of lies, when we heard yells a little distance away. There was a loud, scandalized cry of "Go away, child!

Go away this instant!" and an old woman with a switch in her hand came round the corner of a hut, violently shooing away a crowd of naked children. Some more women followed, clicking their tongues and exclaiming; evidently there was something that the children ought not to have seen. I rounded the hut and saw a man's dead body sprawling in the mud. He was an Indian, a black Dravidian coolie, almost naked, and he could not have been dead many minutes. The people said that the elephant had come suddenly upon him round the corner of the hut, caught him with its trunk, put its foot on his back and ground him into the earth. This was the rainy season and the ground was soft, and his face had scored a trench a foot deep and couple of yards long. He was lying on his belly with arms crucified and head sharply twisted to one side. His face was coated with mud, the eyes wide open, the teeth bared and grinning with an expression of unendurable agony. (Never tell me, by the way, that the dead look peaceful. Most of the corpses I have seen looked devilish.) The friction of the great beast's foot had stripped the skin from his back as neatly as one skins a rabbit. As soon as I saw the dead man I sent an orderly to a friend's house nearby to borrow an elephant rifle. I had already sent back the pony, not wanting it to go mad with fright and throw me if it smelt the elephant.

The orderly came back in a few minutes with a rifle and five cartridges, and meanwhile some Burmans had arrived and told us that the elephant was in the paddy fields below, only a few hundred yards away. As I started forward practically the whole population of the quarter flocked out of the houses and followed me. They had seen the rifle and were all shouting excitedly that I was going to shoot the elephant. They had not shown much interest in the elephant when he was merely ravaging their homes, but it was different now that he was going to be shot. It was a bit of fun to them, as it would be to an English crowd; besides they wanted the meat. It made me vaguely uneasy. I had no intention of shooting the elephant—I had merely sent for the rifle to defend myself if necessary —and it is always unnerving to have a crowd following you. I marched down the hill, looking and feeling a fool, with the rifle over my shoulder and an ever-growing army of people jostling at my heels. At the bottom, when you got away from the huts, there was a metalled road and beyond that a miry waste of paddy fields a thousand yards across, not yet ploughed but soggy from the first rains and dotted with coarse grass. The elephant was standing eight yards from the road, his left side towards us. He took not the slightest notice of the crowd's approach. He was tearing up bunches of grass, beating them against his knees to clean them and stuffing them into his mouth.

I had halted on the road. As soon as I saw the elephant I knew with perfect certainty that I ought not to shoot him. It is a serious matter to shoot a working elephant—it is comparable to destroying a huge and costly piece of machinery —and obviously one ought not to do it if it can possibly be avoided. And at that distance, peacefully eating, the elephant looked no more dangerous than a cow. I thought then and I think now that his attack of "must" was already passing off; in which case he would merely wander harmlessly about until the mahout came back and caught him. Moreover, I did not in the least want to shoot him.

I decided that I would watch him for a little while to make sure that he did not turn savage again, and then go home.

But at that moment I glanced round at the crowd that had followed me. It was an immense crowd, two thousand at the least and growing every minute. It blocked the road for a long distance on either side. I looked at the sea of yellow faces above the garish clothes—faces all happy and excited over this bit of fun, all certain that the elephant was going to be shot. They were watching me as they would watch a conjurer about to perform a trick. They did not like me, but with the magical rifle in my hands I was momentarily worth watching. And suddenly I realized that I should have to shoot the elephant after all. The people expected it of me and I had got to do it; I could feel their two thousand wills pressing me forward, irresistibly. And it was at this moment, as I stood there with the rifle in my hands, that I first grasped the hollowness, the futility of the white man's dominion in the East. Here was I, the white man with his gun, standing in front of the unarmed native crowd—seemingly the leading actor of the piece, but in reality I was only an absurd puppet pushed to and fro by the will of those yellow faces behind. I perceived in this moment that when the white man turns tyrant it is his own freedom that he destroys. He becomes a sort of hollow, posing dummy, the conventionalized figure of a sahib. For it is the condition of his rule that he shall spend his life in trying to impress the "natives," and so in every crisis he has got to do what the "natives" expect of him. He wears a mask, and his face grows to fit it. I had got to shoot the elephant. I had committed myself to doing it when I sent for the rifle. A sahib has got to act like a sahib; he has got to appear resolute, to know his own mind and do definite things. To come all that way, rifle in hand, with two thousand people marching at my heels, and then to trail feebly away, having done nothing—no, that was impossible. The crowd would laugh at me. And my whole life, every white man's life in the East, was one long struggle not to be laughed at.

But I did not want to shoot the elephant. I watched him beating his bunch of grass against his knees, with that preoccupied grandmotherly air that elephants have. It seemed to me that it would be murder to shoot him. At that age I was not squeamish about killing animals, but I had never shot an elephant and never wanted to. (Somehow it always seems worse to kill a *large* animal.) Besides, there was the beast's owner to be considered. Alive, the elephant was worth at least a hundred pounds; dead, he would only be worth the value of his tusks, five pounds, possibly. But I had got to act quickly. I turned to some experienced-looking Burmans who had been there when we arrived, and asked them how the elephant had been behaving. They all said the same thing: he took no notice of you if you left him alone, but he might charge if you went too close to him.

It was perfectly clear to me what I ought to do. I ought to walk up to within, say, twenty-five yards of the elephant and test his behavior. If he charged, I could shoot; if he took no notice of me, it would be safe to leave him until the mahout came back. But also I knew that I was going to do no such thing. I was a poor shot with a rifle and the ground was soft mud into which one would sink at every step. If the elephant charged and I missed him, I should have about as much chance as a toad under a steam-roller. But even then I was not thinking particularly of my own skin, only of the watchful yellow faces behind. For at that moment, with the crowd watching me, I was not afraid in the ordinary sense, as I would have been if I had been alone. A white man mustn't be frightened in front of "natives"; and so, in general, he isn't frightened. The sole thought in my mind was that if anything went wrong those two thousand Burmans would see me pursued, caught, trampled on and reduced to a grinning corpse like that Indian up the hill. And if that happened it was quite probable that some of them would laugh. That would never do. There was only one alternative. I shoved the cartridges into the magazine and lay down on the road to get a better aim.

The crowd grew very still, and a deep, low, happy sigh, as of people who see the theatre curtain go up at last, breathed from innumerable throats. They were going to have their bit of fun after all. The rifle was a beautiful German thing with cross hair sights. I did not then know that in shooting an elephant one would shoot to cut an imaginary bar running from ear-hole to ear-hole. I ought, therefore, as the elephant was sideways on, to have aimed straight at his ear-hole: actually I aimed several inches in front of this, thinking the brain would be further forward.

When I pulled the trigger I did not hear the bang or feel the kick—one never does when a shot goes home—but I heard the devilish roar of glee that went up from the crowd. In that instant, in too short a time, one would have thought, even for the bullet to get there, a mysterious, terrible change had come over the elephant. He neither stirred nor fell, but every line of his body had altered. He looked suddenly stricken, shrunken, immensely old, as though the frightful impact of the bullet had paralyzed him without knocking him down. At last, after what seemed a long time—it might have been five seconds, I dare say—he sagged flabbily to his knees. His mouth slobbered. An enormous senility seemed to have settled upon him. One could have imagined him thousands of years old. I fired again into the same spot. At the second shot he did not collapse but climbed with desperate slowness to his feet and stood weakly upright, with legs sagging and head drooping. I fired a third time. That was the shot that did for him. You could see the agony of it jolt his whole body and knock the last remnant of strength from his legs. But in falling he seemed for a moment to rise, for as his hind legs collapsed beneath him he seemed to tower upward like a huge rock toppling, his trunk reaching skywards like a tree. He trumpeted, for the first and only time. And then down he came, his belly towards me, with a crash that seemed to shake the ground even where I lay.

I got up. The Burmans were already racing past me across the mud. It was obvious that the elephant would never rise again, but he was not dead. He was breathing very rhythmically with long rattling gasps, his great mound of a side painfully rising and falling. His mouth was wide open—I could see far down into caverns of pale pink throat. I waited a long time for him to die, but his breathing did not weaken. Finally I fired my two remaining shots into the spot where I thought his heart must be. The thick blood welled out of him like red velvet, but still he did not die. His body did not even jerk when the shots hit him, the tortured breathing continued without a pause. He was dying, very slowly and in great agony, but in some world remote from me where not even a bullet could damage him further. I felt that I had got to put an end to that dreadful noise. It seemed dreadful to see the great beast lying there, powerless to move and yet powerless to die, and not even to be able to finish him. I sent back for my small rifle and poured shot after shot into his heart and down his throat. They seemed to make no impression. The tortured gasps continued as steadily as the ticking of a clock.

In the end I could not stand it any longer and went away. I heard later that it took him half an hour to die. Burmans were bringing dahs and baskets even before I left, and I was told they had stripped his body almost to the bones by the afternoon.

Afterwards, of course, there were endless discussions about the shooting of the elephant. The owner was furious, but he was only an Indian and could do nothing. Besides, legally I had done the right thing, for a mad elephant has to be killed, like a mad dog, if its owner fails to control it. Among the Europeans opinion was divided. The older men said I was right, the younger men said it was a damn shame to shoot an elephant for killing a coolie, because an elephant was worth more than any damn Coringhee coolie. And afterwards I was very glad that the coolie had been killed; it put me legally in the right and it gave me a sufficient pretext for shooting the elephant. I often wondered whether any of the others grasped that I had done it solely to avoid looking a fool.

E. B. White

THE FAMILY WHICH DWELT APART

On a small, remote island in the lower reaches of Barnetuck Bay there lived a family of fisherfolk by the name of Pruitt. There were seven of them, and they were the sole inhabitants of the place. They subsisted on canned corn, canned tomatoes, pressed duck, whole-wheat bread, terrapin, Rice Krispies, crabs, cheese, queen olives, and homemade wild-grape preserve. Once in a while Pa Pruitt made some whiskey and they all had a drink.

They liked the island and lived there from choice. In winter, when there wasn't much doing, they slept the clock around, like so many bears. In summer they dug clams and set off a few pinwheels and salutes on July 4th. No case of acute appendicitis had ever been known in the Pruitt household, and when a Pruitt had a pain in his side he never even noticed whether it was the right side or the left side, but just hoped it would go away, and it did.

One very severe winter Barnetuck Bay froze over and the Pruitt family was marooned. They couldn't get to the mainland by boat because the ice was too thick, and they couldn't walk ashore because the ice was too treacherous. But inasmuch as no Pruitt had anything to go ashore for, except mail (which was entirely second class), the freeze-up didn't make any difference. They stayed indoors, kept warm, and ate well, and when there was nothing better to do, they played crokinole. The winter would have passed quietly enough had not someone on the mainland remembered that the Pruitts were out there in the frozen bay. The word got passed around the county and finally reached the Superintendent of State Police, who immediately notified Pathé News and the United States Army. The Army got there first, with three bombing planes from Langley Field, which flew low over the island and dropped packages of dried apricots and bouillon cubes, which the Pruitts didn't like much. The newsreel plane, smaller than the bombers and equipped with skis, arrived next and landed on a snow-covered field on the north end of the island. Meanwhile, Major Bulk, head of the state troopers, acting on a tip that one of the Pruitt children had appendicitis, arranged for a dog team to be sent by plane from Laconia, New Hampshire, and also dispatched a squad of troopers to attempt a crossing of the bay. Snow began falling at sundown, and during the night three of the rescuers lost their lives about half a mile from shore, trying to jump from one ice cake to another.

The plane carrying the sled dogs was over southern New England when ice began forming on its wings. As the pilot circled for a forced landing, a large meat bone which one of the dogs had brought along got wedged in the socket of the main control stick, and the plane went into a steep dive and crashed against the side of a powerhouse, instantly killing the pilot and all the dogs, and fatally injuring Walter Ringstead, 7, of 3452 Garden View Avenue, Stamford, Conn.

Shortly before midnight, the news of the appendicitis reached the Pruitt house itself, when a chartered autogiro from Hearst's International News Service made a landing in the storm and reporters informed Mr. Pruitt that his oldest boy, Charles, was ill and would have to be taken to Baltimore for an emergency operation. Mrs. Pruitt remonstrated, but Charles said his side did hurt a little, and it ended by his leaving in the giro. Twenty minutes later another plane came in, bearing a surgeon, two trained nurses, and a man from the National Broadcasting Company, and the second Pruitt boy, Chester, underwent an exclusive appendectomy in the kitchen of the Pruitt home, over the Blue Network. This lad died, later, from eating dried apricots too soon after his illness, but Charles, the other boy, recovered after a long convalescence and returned to the island in the first warm days of spring.

He found things much changed. The house was gone, having caught fire on the third and last night of the rescue when a flare dropped by one of the departing planes lodged in a bucket of trash on the piazza. After the fire, Mr. Pruitt had apparently moved his family into the emergency shed which the radio announcers had thrown up, and there they had dwelt under rather difficult conditions until the night the entire family was wiped out by drinking a ten-per-cent solution of carbolic acid which the surgeon had left behind and which Pa Pruitt had mistaken for grain alcohol.

Barnetuck Bay seemed a different place to Charles. After giving his kin decent burial, he left the island of his nativity and went to dwell on the mainland.

William H. Whyte, Jr.

A GENERATION OF BUREAUCRATS

When I was a college senior in 1939, we used to sing a plaintive song about going out into the "cold, cold world." It wasn't really so very cold then, but we did enjoy meditating on the fraughtness of it all. It was a big break we were facing, we told ourselves, and those of us who were going to try our luck in the commercial world could be patronizing toward those who were going on to graduate work or academic life. We were taking the leap.

Seniors still sing the song, but somehow the old note of portent is gone. There is no leap left to take. The union between the world of organization and the college has been so cemented that today's seniors can see a continuity between the college and the life thereafter that we never did. Come graduation, they do not go outside to a hostile world; they transfer.

For the senior who is headed for the corporation it is almost as if it were part of one master scheme. The locale shifts; the training continues, for at the same time that the colleges have been changing their curriculum to suit the corporation, the corporation has responded by setting up its own campuses and classrooms. By now the two have been so well molded that it's difficult to tell where one leaves off and the other begins.

The descent, every spring, of the corporations' recruiters has now become a built-in feature of campus life. If the college is large and its placement director efficient, the processing operation is visibly impressive. I have never been able to erase from my mind the memory of an ordinary day at Purdue's placement center. It is probably the largest and most effective placement operation in the country, yet, much as in a well-run group clinic, there seemed hardly any activity. In the main room some students were quietly studying company literature arranged on the tables for them; others were checking the interview timetables to find what recruiter they would see and to which cubicle he was assigned; at the central filing desk college employees were sorting the hundreds of names of men who had registered for placement. Except for a murmur from the row of cubicles there was little to indicate that scores of young men were, every hour on the half hour, making the decisions that would determine their whole future life.

Someone from a less organized era might conclude that the standardization of this machinery—and the standardized future it portends—would repel students. It does not. For the median senior this is the optimum future; it meshes so closely with his own aspirations that it is almost as if the corporation was planned in response to an attitude poll.

Because they are the largest single group, the corporation-bound seniors are the most visible manifestation of their generation's values. But in essentials their contemporaries headed for other occupations respond to the same urges. The lawyers, the doctors, the scientists—their occupations are also subject to the same centralization, the same trend to group work and to bureaucratization. And so are the young men who will enter them. Whatever their many differences, in one great respect they are all of a piece: more than any generation in memory, theirs will be a generation of bureaucrats.

They are, above all, conservative. Their inclination to accept the status quo does not necessarily mean that in the historic sweep of ideas they are con-servative—in the more classical sense of conservatism, it could be argued that the seniors will be, in effect if not by design, agents of revolution. But this is a matter we must leave to later historians. For the immediate present, at any rate, what ideological ferment college men exhibit is not in the direction of basic change.

This shows most clearly in their attitude toward politics. It used to be axiomatic that young men moved to the left end of the spectrum in revolt against their fathers and then, as the years went on, moved slowly to the right. A lot of people still believe this is true, and many businessmen fear that twenty years of the New Deal hopelessly corrupted our youth into radicalism. After the election of 1952 businessmen became somewhat more cheerful, but many are still apprehensive, and whenever a poll indicates that students don't realize that business makes only about 6 per cent profit, there is a flurry of de-mands for some new crusade to rescue our youth from socialistic tendencies.

If the seniors do any moving, however, it will be from dead center. Liberal groups have almost disappeared from the campus, and what few remain are anemic. There has been no noticeable activity at the other end of the spectrum either. When William Buckley, Jr., produced *God and Man at Yale*, some people thought this signaled the emergence of a strong right-wing movement among the young men. The militancy, however, has not proved particularly contagious; when the McCarthy issue roused and divided their elders, undergraduates seemed somewhat bored with it all.

Their conservatism is passive. No cause seizes them, and nothing so exuber-ant or willfully iconoclastic as the Veterans of Future Wars has reappeared. There are Democrats and Republicans, and at election time there is the usual flurry of rallies, but in comparison with the agitation of the thirties no one seems to care too much one way or the other. There has been personal unrest— the suspense over the prospect of military service assures this—but it rarely gets resolved into a thought-out protest. Come spring and students may start whacking each other over the head or roughing up the townees and thereby cause a rush of concern over the wild younger generation. But there is no real revolution in them, and the next day they likely as not will be found with their feet firmly on the ground in the recruiters' cubicles.

Some observers attribute the disinterest to fear. I heard one instructor tell his colleagues that in his politics classes he warned students to keep their noses clean. "I tell them," he said, "that they'd better realize that what they say might be held against them, especially when we get to the part about Marx and Engels. Someday in the future they might find their comments bounced back at them in an investigation."

The advice, as his colleagues retorted, was outrageously unnecessary. The last thing students can be accused of now is dangerous discussion; they are not interested in the kind of big questions that stimulate heresy and whatever the subject—the corporation, government, religion—students grow restive if the talk tarries on the philosophical. Most are interested in the philosophical only to the extent of finding out what the accepted view is in order that they may accept it and get on to the practical matters. This spares the bystander from the lofty bulling and the elaborate pose of unorthodoxy that my contemporaries often used to affect, but it does make for a rather stringent utilitarianism.

Even in theological seminaries, this impatience to be on with the job has been evident. Writes Norman Pittenger, professor at General Theological Seminary:

It is a kind of authoritarianism in reverse. Theological students today, in contrast to their fellows of twenty years ago, want "to be told." I have gone out of my way to ask friends who teach in seminaries of other denominations whether they have recognized the new tendency. Without exception they have told me that they find the present generation of students less inquiring of mind, more ready to accept an authority, and indeed most anxious to have it "laid on the line."

In the seminary this means that the lecturer or teacher must be unusually careful lest his opinion, or what "the Bible says" or "the church teaches," shall be taken as the last word. . . . What troubles many of us is that students today are not willing enough to think things through for themselves. If this is what the Bible says, then how does it say it and why, and how do we know that this is indeed the teaching of Scripture? If this is what the church teaches, why does it teach it, what evidence can be given for the teaching and what right has the church to teach at all? Or if a professor says that such-and-such a view is correct, why does he say it and what real evidence can he produce that his statement is true? It would be better and healthier if the new respect for authority were more frequently found in combination with a spirit of inquiry, a ready willingness to think through what is authoritatively declared, and a refusal ever to accept anything simply because some reputable expert makes the statement.

In judging a college generation, one usually bases his judgment on how much it varies from one's own, and presumably superior, class, and I must confess that I find myself tempted to do so. Yet I do not think my generation has any license to damn the acquiescence of seniors as a weakening of intellectual fiber. It is easy for us to forget that if earlier generations were less content with society, there was a great deal less to be contented about. In the intervening years the economy has changed enormously, and even in retrospect the senior can hardly be expected to share former discontents. Society is not out of joint for him, and if he acquiesces it is not out of fear that he does so. He does not want to rebel against the status quo because he really likes it—and his elders, it might be added, are not suggesting anything bold and new to rebel *for*.

Perhaps contemporaryism would be a better word than conservatism to describe their posture. The present, more than the past, is their model; while they share the characteristic American faith in the future also, they see it as more of same. As they paraphrase what they are now reading about America, they argue that at last we have got it. The big questions are all settled; we know the direction, and while many minor details remain to be cleared up, we can be pretty sure of enjoying a wonderful upward rise.

While the degree of their optimism is peculiarly American, the spirit of acquiescence, it should be noted, is by no means confined to the youth of this country. In an Oxford magazine, called, aptly enough, *Couth*, one student writes this of his generation:

> It is true that over the last thirty years it has been elementary good manners to be depressed. . . . But . . . we are not, really, in the least worried by our impending, and other people's present, disasters. This is not the Age of Anxiety. What distinguishes the comfortable young men of today from the uncomfortable young men of the last hundred years . . . is that for once the younger generation is not in revolt against anything. . . . We don't want to rebel against our elders. They are much too nice to be rebellable-against. Old revolutionaries as they are, they get rather cross with us and tell us we are stuffy and prudish, but even this can't provoke us into hostility. . . . Our fathers . . . brought us up to see them not as the representatives of ancient authority and unalterable law but as rebels against our grandfathers. So naturally we have grown up to be on their side, even if we feel on occasion that they were a wee bit hard on their fathers, or even a little naïve.[1]

More than before, there is a tremendous interest in techniques. Having no quarrel with society, they prefer to table the subject of ends and concentrate instead on means. Not what or why but *how* interests them, and any evangelical strain they have they can sublimate; once they have equated the common weal with organization—a task the curriculum makes easy—they will let the organization worry about goals. "These men do not question the sys-

---

1. Similar tendencies have been noticed among German youth. In *Der Junge Arbeiter von Heute*, Karl Bednarik, a former leader in the socialist youth movement, has commented on the "bourgeoisification" of younger workers as a response to the postwar situation.

tem," an economics professor says of them, approvingly. "They want to get in there and lubricate and make them run better. They will be technicians of the society, not innovators."

The attitude of men majoring in social science is particularly revealing on this score. Not so very long ago, the younger social scientist was apt to see his discipline as a vehicle for protest about society as well as the study of it. The seniors that set the fashion for him were frequently angry men, and many of the big studies of the twenties and thirties—Robert and Helen Lynd's *Middletown*, for example—did not conceal strong opinions about the inequities in the social structure. But this is now old hat: it is the "bleeding-heart" school to the younger men (and to some not so young, too), for they do not wish to protest; they wish to collaborate. Reflecting the growing reconciliation with middle-class values that has affected all types of intellectuals, they are turning more and more to an interest in methodology, particularly the techniques of measurement. Older social scientists who have done studies on broad social problems find that the younger men are comparatively uninterested in the problems themselves. When the discussion period comes, the questions the younger men ask are on the technical points; not the what, or why, but the how.

The urge to be a technician, a collaborator, shows most markedly in the kind of jobs seniors prefer. They want to work for somebody else. Paradoxically, the old dream of independence through a business of one's own is held almost exclusively by factory workers—the one group, as a number of sociologists have reported, least able to fulfill it. Even at the bull-session level college seniors do not affect it, and when recruiting time comes around they make the preference clear. Consistently, placement officers find that of the men who intend to go into business—roughly one half of the class—less than 5 per cent express any desire to be an entrepreneur. About 15 to 20 per cent plan to go into their fathers' business. Of the rest, most have one simple goal: the big corporation.

And not just as a stopgap either. When I was a senior many of us liked to rationalize that we were simply playing it smart; we were going with big companies merely to learn the ropes the better to strike out on our own later. Today, seniors do not bother with this sort of talk; once the tie has been established with the big company, they believe, they will not switch to a small one, or, for that matter, to another big one. The relationship is to be for keeps.[2]

2. One reason why seniors prefer big business is that the big companies go after them and the small ones don't. Of the 450,000 incorporated firms in the U. S., only about 1,000 actually recruit on the campuses, and it is these active 1,000 firms—generally the biggest—that get the cream. Sometimes college placement directors do line up the small company position, but even then they find the students apathetic. "Frankly," says one placement director, echoing many another, "the only kind I can interest in the small company job is the dynamic sort—the one type that is least likely to get lost in a big company. I would sooner interest the other kind; I point out to the shy, diffident fellows that in a small outfit they'd be something of a jack-of-all-trades, that they'd get a better chance to express themselves, to grow out of their shell. They still don't want it."

It is not simply for security that they take the vows. Far more than their predecessors they understand bigness. My contemporaries, fearful of anonymity, used to talk of "being lost" in a big corporation. This did not prevent us from joining corporations, to be sure, but verbally, at least, it was fashionable to view the organization way with misgivings. Today this would show a want of sophistication. With many of the liberals who fifteen years ago helped stimulate the undergraduate distrust of bigness now busy writing tracts in praise of bigness, the ideological underpinnings for the debate have crumbled.

The fact that a majority of seniors headed for business shy from the idea of being entrepreneurs is only in part due to fear of economic risk. Seniors can put the choice in moral terms also, and the portrait of the entrepreneur as a young man detailed in postwar fiction preaches a sermon that seniors are predisposed to accept. What price bitch goddess Success? The entrepreneur, as many see him, is a selfish type motivated by greed, and he is, furthermore, unhappy. The big-time operator as sketched in fiction eventually so loses stomach for enterprise that he finds happiness only when he stops being an entrepreneur, forsakes "21," El Morocco, and the boss's wife and heads for the country. Citing such fiction, the student can moralize on his aversion to entrepreneurship. His heel quotient, he explains, is simply not big enough.

Not that he is afraid of risk, the senior can argue. Far from being afraid of taking chances, he is simply looking for the *best* place to take them in.[3] Small business is small because of nepotism and the roll-top desk outlook, the argument goes; big business, by contrast, has borrowed the tools of science and made them pay off. It has its great laboratories, its market-research departments, and the time and patience to use them. The odds, then, favor the man who joins big business. "We wouldn't hesitate to risk adopting new industrial techniques and products," explains a proponent of this calculated-risk theory, "but we would do it only after we had subjected it to tests of engineers, pre-testing in the market and that kind of thing." With big business, in short, risk-taking would be a cinch.

In turning their back on the Protestant Ethic they are consistent; if they do not cherish venture, neither do they cherish what in our lore was its historic reward. They are without avarice. Reflecting on the difference between the postwar classes and his own class of 1928, an erstwhile Yale history professor confessed that the former were so unmercenary he was almost a little homesick for his own. "We were a terrible class. It was the days of the roasted lark, Hell's entries, of the white-shoe boys. Everyone was playing the stock market—they even had a ticker down at the Hotel Taft—and I wound up for a while in a bucket shop down in Wall Street. But today you don't hear that kind of talk. They don't want a million. They are much more serious, much more worth while." He shook his head nostalgically.

3. A Youth Institute Survey of 4,660 young men indicated that only 20 per cent felt they could not achieve all their economic desires by working for someone else.

Others have been similarly impressed. One recruiter went through three hundred interviews without one senior's mentioning salary, and the experience is not unusual. Indeed, sometimes seniors react as if a large income and security were antithetical. As some small companies have found to their amazement, the offer of a sales job netting $15,000 at the end of two years is often turned down in favor of an equivalent one with a large company netting $8,000. Along with the $8,000 job, the senior says in justification, goes a pension plan and other benefits. He could, of course, buy himself some rather handsome annuities with the extra $7,000 the small company offers, but this alternative does not suggest itself readily.

When seniors are put to speculating how much money they would like to make twenty or thirty years hence, they cite what they feel are modest figures. Back in forty-nine it was $10,000. Since then the rising cost of living has taken it up higher, but the median doesn't usually surpass $15,000.[4] For the most part seniors do not like to talk of the future in terms of the dollar—on several occasions I have been politely lectured by someone for so much as bringing the point up.

In popular fiction, as I will take up later, heroes aren't any less materialistic than they used to be, but they are decidedly more sanctimonious about it. So with seniors. While they talk little about money, they talk a great deal about the good life. This life is, first of all, calm and ordered. Many a senior confesses that he's thought of a career in teaching, but as he talks it appears that it is not so much that he likes teaching itself as the sort of life he associates with it— there is a touch of elms and quiet streets in the picture. For the good life is equable; it is a nice place out in the suburbs, a wife and three children, one, maybe two cars (you know, a little knock-about for the wife to run down to the station in), and a summer place up at the lake or out on the Cape, and, later, a good college education for the children. It is not, seniors explain, the money that counts.

They have been getting more and more relaxed on the matter each year. In the immediate postwar years they were somewhat nervous about the chances for the good life. They seemed almost psychotic on the subject of a depression, and when they explained a preference for the big corporation, they did so largely on the grounds of security. When I talked to students in 1949, on almost every campus I heard one recurring theme: adventure was all very well, but it was smarter to make a compromise in order to get a depression-proof sanctuary. "I don't think A T & T is very exciting," one senior put it, "but that's the company I'd like to join. If a depression comes there will always be an A T & T." (Another favorite was the food industry: people always have to eat.) Corporation recruiters were unsettled to find that seniors seemed primarily interested in such things as pension benefits and retirement programs.

4. The figures depend a great deal on the college. In the study done by the Youth Research Institute on a cross section of college seniors the median figure is about $8,000. At Princeton and Williams, by contrast, the figure is almost double.

Seven years of continuing prosperity have made a great difference. Students are still interested in security but they no longer see it as a matter of security *versus* opportunity. Now, when they explain their choice, it is that the corporation is security *and* opportunity both. If the questionnaires that I have been giving groups of college seniors over the past six years are any indication, students aiming for the big corporation expect to make just as much money as those who say they want to start their own business or join a small one.[5]

Who is to blame them for being contented? If you were a senior glancing at these ad headlines in the *Journal of College Placement*, how much foreboding would you feel?

A WORLD OF EXPANDING OPPORTUNITY

OPPORTUNITY UNLIMITED

CAREERS UNLIMITED

THE HORIZONS ARE UNLIMITED FOR COLLEGE GRADUATES AT UNION CARBIDE

A GATEWAY TO LIFETIME SECURITY

A WISE CHOICE TODAY PUTS YOU AHEAD OF YOUR FUTURE

WHY THEY'RE SURE THEY'RE IN THE RIGHT JOB AT HARNSCHFEGER

TO THE YOUNG MAN BENT ON CONQUERING THE UNKNOWN

A SECOND EDUCATION

GROWTH COMPANY IN A GROWTH INDUSTRY

"BRAIN BOX" NEEDS BRAINS

SO YOU WANT TO GO INTO BUSINESS

WHY COLLEGE GRADUATES SHOULD CONSIDER UNION CARBIDE

A MAN CAN GROW AND KEEP ON GROWING WITH OWENS-ILLINOIS GLASS CO.

A BRIGHT FUTURE WITH RCA

DOW OFFERS THE GRADUATE A BRIGHT FUTURE

MORE AND BETTER JOBS

EXCEPTIONAL OPPORTUNITIES FOR COLLEGE MAN IN TEXTILE SALES

AN EQUITABLE LIFE INSURANCE MAN IS "A MAN ON HIS WAY UP"

GROUND-FLOOR OPPORTUNITIES IN TRANSISTORS

VITRO OFFERS YOUR GRADUATES THE ENGINEERS OF TOMORROW!

YOUR OPPORTUNITY FOR A LIFETIME CAREER

OPPORTUNITY FOR YOUR COLLEGE GRADUATES

OPPORTUNITIES FOR MATH MAJORS

AN UNUSUAL OPPORTUNITY FOR OUTSTANDING MATH MAJORS

THE SKY IS OUR WORLD

THE SKY IS THE LIMIT!

5. This faith in the beneficence of the corporate salary is fairly universal. In the Youth Research Institute study previously mentioned this question was put to 4,660 high-school seniors, college seniors, recent graduates and veterans: "Do you feel that you will be able to achieve all of your economic desires by working for someone else?" 61.1 per cent said yes; 20.4 per cent said no; and 18.5 per cent couldn't make up their minds. There were no significant differences in optimism among any of the four groups.

It would be enough to make a man cynical. But the students are not a cynical lot. When they talk about security they like to make the point that it is the psychic kind of security that interests them most. They want to be of service. Occasionally, their description of service borders on the mawkish, as though the goal was simply to defend the little people, but underneath there is real concern. Seniors want to do something *worth while*.

This worth-whileness needs some qualification. To listen to seniors talk, one would assume that there has been an upsurge of seniors heading toward such service careers as the ministry. There is no evidence of such a rush. The public variety of service doesn't attract either. Seniors scarcely mention politics as a career and even for the more aseptic forms of public service they show little enthusiasm; the number aiming for the foreign services or the civil services has been declining, and this decline was well under way before the Washington investigations.

If they are going to be worth while, seniors want to be worth while with other people. Their ideal of service is a gregarious one—the kind of service you do others right in the midst of them and not once removed. A student at a round-table discussion on the pursuit of happiness put it this way: "People who are just selfish and wrapped up in themselves have the most trouble. And people who are interested in other people . . . are the type of person that is not too much concerned with security. Somehow the security is provided in the things they do, and they are able to reach out beyond themselves."

The kind of work that students want to do within the corporation illumines the character of this concept of worth-whileness. What the preferences show is a strong inclination toward the staff rather than the line. In a check I made of two hundred corporation-bound students of the classes of '55 and '56, only 12 per cent said they were aiming for production work, while roughly a third indicated a staff job.

Of these, the personnel slot is the glamour one. When seniors first expressed this yen for personnel work right after the war, many people thought it was simply a temporary phenomenon. The veterans of the postwar classes labored under the idea that because they had "handled people" in the services they were ideally suited for personnel work, and the advice given them by Veterans Administration counselors further confirmed them in the belief. But the years have gone by, and the quest has persisted. Wearily, placement directors explain that the work is semiprofessional, that there are few openings in it, and that in any event they are rarely open to recruits. It still doesn't seem to make much difference. With a phrase that has become a standing joke in placement circles, the senior explains that it is the job for him just the same—he *likes people*.

His vision of the job is a mirage. The actual work is connected more with time study, aptitude testing, and stop watches than adjusting people, but to the senior it seems to promise the agreeable role of a combination YMCA worker, office Solomon, and father confessor to the men at the lathes. It promises also to be somewhat out of the main stream. Much like life in the services, it seems to offer a certain freedom from competition; it is a technician's job, the job of one who services others. For a class intent on the happy mean, it is the all-round package: not only does it promise economic security, it promises spiritual security as well.

Because the quest has been so long unrequited, seniors have been turning to public relations. In some colleges it has already outdistanced personnel work as a choice. But it is really the same job they are thinking about. The senior does not see himself worrying about seating lists for banquets, ghostwriting speeches, or the like; in his vision he sees the universal man of the future, testing the pulse of the workers to see that they are happy, counseling with educators and clergymen for better inter-group communication, spellbinding the mossbacks with advocacy of the common man. As in personnel work, he will be nice to everybody on company time.

When seniors check such ostensibly line occupations as sales, they still exhibit the staff bias. For they don't actually want to sell. What they mean by sales is the kind of work in which they will be technical specialists helping the customer, or, better yet, master-minding the work of those who do the helping. They want to be sales engineers, distribution specialists, merchandising experts—the men who back up the men in the field.

If they must sell in the old, vulgar sense of the word, they want to do it as a member of a group and not as a lone individual. And most definitely, they do not want to sell on commission. This has been made quite clear in the reception given life insurance recruiters. Except when they have home office jobs to offer, insurance recruiters have always had fairly rough going in the colleges, but it's now so difficult that sometimes they sit in the interview room a whole day without a senior once coming near them. Mainly out of commiseration for the recruiters, one placement director uses a stratagem to force students into signing up for insurance interviews. "I tell them it's good for the practice," he explains. "I also tell them that if they don't turn up for these interviews I won't let them have a crack later at those nice big corporations."

Those who mark down finance as a choice are also staff-minded. Few ever mention speculating or investing in stocks and bonds. Their interest in finance is administrative rather than accumulative; they are primarily interested in credit, mortgage loan work, trust and estate work, and financial analysis.

A distinction is in order. While the fundamental bias is for staff work, it is not necessarily for a staff job. If the choice is offered them, a considerable number of students will vote for "general managerial" work, and many who choose personnel or public relations do so with the idea that it is the best pathway to the top line jobs. Seniors see no antithesis; in their view the line and staff have become so synonymous that the comfortable pigeonhole and the ladder, to mix some favorite metaphors, are one and the same. Their concept of the manager subsumes the two. As older executives are so fond of telling them, the "professionalization" of the executive is making a new kind of man, and more literally than the older men know, the younger ones believe every word of it. In fact, of course, as well as in the senior's fancy, the manager's work has been shifted more to the administrative. But not half so much as seniors would like to see it. In this respect, as so many business-school people hopefully say, seniors are way ahead of everybody else.

But not so very much. The bureaucrat as hero is new to America, and older, conventional dreams of glory do linger on—the lawyer brilliantly turning the tables in cross-examination. the young scientist discovering the secret in the microscope late at night. Even in corporations' institutional advertising there is some cultural lag—many an ad still shows us the young man dreaming by himself of new frontiers as he looks up at a star or a rainbow or a beautiful hunk of alto-cumulus clouds. But slowly the young man at the microscope is being joined by other young men at microscopes; instead of one lone man dreaming, there are three or four young men. Year by year, our folklore is catching up with the needs of organization man.

In *Executive Suite* we catch a glimpse of the hero in mid-passage. In clean-cut Don Walling, the hitherto junior executive, what senior could not feel that there, with the grace of God, would go he? In Walling have been resolved all the conflicts of organization life; he puts everything he has into his work and plays baseball with his boy; he cares little about money and his ranch house is beautiful; he is a loyal subordinate and gets to be president. He is not fully the new model—he is too pushy, he plays too rough in the clinches for that—but he could almost be the class valedictorian as he electrifies his elders with his ringing, if somewhat hazy, statement of belief. Management man does not work to make money for himself and the company. Business is *people*, and when you help people to rise to their fullest you make them fulfill themselves, you create more and better goods for more people, you make happiness.

While the trust in organization is very strong among the majority group of college seniors headed for a business career, it is less so with a smaller group who say, at least, that they prefer a small firm. In the course of sessions during the past few years I have had with different undergraduate groups, to get the discussion rolling I have asked the students to answer several hypothetical questions on the "ideal" relationship between an individual and the demands of organization. I attach no great statistical significance to the actual figures, but I have kept the terms the same with each group, and I have noticed that consistently there is a difference between the answers of those headed for big organization and those not. As is brought out more forcefully by the kind of questions that the students themselves later asked, the big-corporation men are more inclined to the group way than the others.

Here is how a total of 127 men answered the two chief questions: on the question of whether research scientists should be predominantly the team player type, 56 per cent of the men headed for a big corporation said yes, versus 46 per cent of the small-business men. On the question of whether the key executive should be basically an "administrator" or a "bold leader," 54 per cent of the big-corporation men voted for the administrator, verus only 45 per cent of the small-business men. Needless to say, the weightings varied from college to college, and often the influence of a particular teacher was manifest —in one class the students complained that they probably seemed so chary of big business because they had been "brain-washed" by a liberal instructor. Whatever the absolute figures, however, there was generally the same relative difference between the big-business and the small-business men.

These differences raise an interesting question. It is possible that the majority group might be less significant than the minority—that is to say, the more venturesome may become the dominant members of our society by virtue of their very disinclination to the group way. As a frankly rapacious young salesman put it to me, the more contented his run-of-the-mill contemporaries, the freer the field for the likes of him.

While this can only be a matter of opinion at this date, I doubt that our society, as it is now evolving, will suffer such a double standard. The corporation-bound man may be an exaggeration of his generation's tendencies but only in degree, not in character. Other occupations call for different emphases, but on the central problem of collective versus individual work, young men going into other fields, such as teaching or law or journalism, show the same basic outlook.

Seniors do not deny that the lone researcher or the entrepreneur can also serve others. But neither do they think much about it. Their impulses, their training, the whole climate of the times, incline them to work that is tangibly social. Whether as a member of a corporation, a group medicine clinic, or a law factory, they see the collective as the best vehicle for service.

To a degree, of course, this is a self-ennobling apologia for seeking the comfortable life—and were they thoroughly consistent they would more actively recognize that public service is social too. But it is not mere rationalization; the senior is quite genuine in believing that while all collective effort may be worth while, some kinds are more so. The organization-bound senior can argue that he is going to the main tent, the place where each foot pound of his energy will go the farthest in helping people. Like the young man of the Middle Ages who went off to join holy orders, he is off for the center of society.

Vance Packard

THE GROWING POWER OF ADMEN

America's advertising industry is moving into a commanding role in our society. Its executives are becoming masters of our economic destiny, the engineers behind some of our most successful political campaigns, major patrons of our social scientists, dictators of the content of most of the radio and television programs we hear, judges with life-and-death power over most of our mass-circulation magazines. Also, they have become our most powerful taste makers. In 1957 they made millions of Americans suddenly feel somehow inadequate because they did not own high-tailed automobiles.

They have, in short, become major wielders of social control in America in this second half of the twentieth century. Their power to do good or non-good is becoming massive, and many are using their power irresponsibly.

The growth of their power is seen in the amount of money entrusted to them to spend. In 1940 they had at their disposal $2 billion to conduct campaigns of persuasion. Today they have $10 billion. If you divide that figure by the total U. S. population, you come up with a fairly startling statistic. Approximately $60 is now being spent each year on *each* man, woman, and child in America solely to coax him or her to use products the admen are promoting.

This growing power of advertising men derives from the dominant role that selling plays in the dynamics of our economy. In the executive suites of thousands of corporations the main preoccupation is no longer with production problems but rather with selling problems.

The most obvious explanation for this shift of emphasis is the fabulous productivity of our automated factories. Since 1940 our gross national product has soared more than 400 per cent. In 1954 it was predicted that our GNP would hit the long-dreamed-of mark of $400 billion by 1958. Actually it shot past that figure in 1956 and is expected to reach $600 billion within the coming decade.

To absorb this fantastic outpouring of goods we shall have to step up our personal consumption of goods by almost 50 per cent. As the chairman of America's leading advertising agency proclaimed recently: "We have to expand our levels of consumption in the next ten years by an amount nearly equal to the entire growth of the country in the two hundred years from colonial days up to 1940." The big problem we face, he said, is to cut down the "time lag" in the process by which we ordinarily learn to expand our wants and needs, in order to "absorb this production." Advertising men are the experts who can overcome this lag.

The real needs of most of us were satisfied long ago. About 40 per cent of the things we buy today are unnecessary in terms of any real need. Even our wants are pretty well satisfied. It has become a question of creating in our minds new, unrealized wants and needs.

Happily for the marketers, Americans by nature seem to relish learning to want new things. We are a restless people who like continually to hear of new things to do and buy. (Note the recent popularity of bejeweled fly swatters and mousetraps.) Emerson commented on this trait in Americans when he said that they, unlike Europeans, exhibit "an uncalculated, headlong expenditure." This makes them the world's prize consumers.

Recently the president of the Institute for Motivational Research (which conducts psychological studies for marketers) noted with satisfaction "our increasing willingness to give vent to our whims and desires" and offered the opinion that America is "experiencing a revolution in self-indulgence."

A corollary problem of marketers in moving their goods into our homes is that of making us discontented with what we already have, since most of us already own perfectly serviceable automobiles, washing machines, refrigerators, and clothing. We must be persuaded that the old product has become hopelessly inadequate to meet our needs or desired style of living. Advertising men call this "creating psychological obsolescence."

Another development adding to the power, glory, and prosperity of advertising men is the increased standardization of competing products. Perhaps connoisseurs can still detect significant differences in gasolines, whiskeys, cigarettes, beer, tires, cake mixes, and detergents, but most of us no longer can. Reports on blindfold tests conducted with cigarette smokers and whiskey and beer drinkers consistently reveal an inability of people to spot their favorite brand. A few days ago I heard a gathering of advertising men being advised that in blindfold tests people can't even tell the difference between Coca-Cola and Pepsi-Cola!

It used to startle me to hear advertising men make casual statements that in many fields such as gasoline and cigarettes the products are "all the same." Now it becomes apparent why they can be so complacent. It is the advertising man's genius that makes products seem compellingly different in our minds.

A third reason for the increasing influence of admen is the growth of self-service selling at supermarkets, vending machines, and so on. More and more, machines or systems are replacing people at the selling counter. The product maker can no longer rely on word-of-mouth selling by a clerk, merchant, or attendant. Thus the customer must be pre-sold, through advertising, so that he will have the product's image firmly etched in his mind as he enters the market place.

II

In the face of all these crying needs for more effective selling, America's 3300 advertising agencies have come to constitute "a great sociological battering ram," to use a phrase current with admen. Individually, advertising men have become "merchants of discontent."

As advertising men by the tens of thousands bring their wiles to bear to stimulate sales of products, we are seeing a massive straining for greater impact. Some months ago a distiller sent a photographic team to the edges of the Sahara Desert in order to obtain a photograph of a martini-filled glass in a setting which would suggest dryness. The photographers faced a crisis when, in searching the fruit markets of Cairo for a sliver of yellow lemon peel to go with the drink, they discovered that lemons sold in Egypt are green. This problem was solved when they arranged for a yellow lemon to be flown over from Italy.

Advertising men now ponder the advisability of making the "entertainment" portion of their TV sponsored programs a little dull so that the commercials will seem more exciting by contrast. In pictorial presentations one trend has been to the absurdly incongruous, to catch our eye as we search for reading matter amid a jungle of ads. Men sell whiskey while seated sideways on white horses, men with beards sell tonic water, shaggy dogs sell rum, kangaroos sell airline tickets. Meanwhile one advertising man complained: "We are suffering from fatigue of believability."

The advertising agencies, in their straining to become more persuasive, have been spending millions of dollars in research designed to learn more about the consumer. Batten Barton Durstine & Osborn has set up a division which it refers to grandiosely as "The National Panel of Consumer Opinion." It consists of several thousand housewives carefully chosen to constitute a "scale model" of the American female populace. These women can earn merchandise premiums by answering questionnaires about products and about their daily habits. Meanwhile Dr. George Gallup, long a researcher for admen, inaugurated a method of probing the consumer which he called "activation research." He set up a "sample bank" of people which he called "Mirror of America," and began probing the people in order to isolate just what triggers the sale of a product.

The most commotion in advertising circles in recent years, however, has centered on a probing technique called "motivation research," which promises to put deeper impact into sales messages. This "depth approach" to consumers involves the use of psychiatry and the social sciences to get inside the consumers' subconscious in order to discover the "psychological hook" which will impel consumers by the millions to buy a certain product.

Most of the leading advertising agencies now have psychologists, psychiatrists, or both on their payrolls. McCann-Erickson recently spent $3 million on a single monumental study of consumer psychology. A Chicago advertising agency rounded up eight leading social scientists in the Midwest (two psychoanalysts, a cultural anthropologist, a social psychologist, two sociologists, and two professors of social science) and had them spend a twelve-hour day in a hotel room watching television programs in order to glean new insights into the appeal of the sponsored programs and the commercials.

Meanwhile several dozen research firms have sprung up, all promising proficiency in depth research. The most famous, the Institute for Motivational Research, commanded by a psychoanalyst from Austria, Dr. Ernest Dichter, occupies a mountaintop castle on the Hudson. The room where local children observe television programs is equipped with hidden tape recorders, one-way viewing screens, and so on, to catch their reactions. Several hundred residents of the area constitute a "psycho-panel." They have been depth-probed and card-indexed as to their hidden anxieties, hostilities, and so forth. If you want to know how much impact a sales message will have on hypochondriacs, for example, Dr. Dichter has a group of bona fide hypochondriacs on call for a trial run.

So far much of the depth-probing of consumers is more hunch than science, but still most of the nation's largest producers of consumer products have been turning to it in an effort to increase their sales penetration. Giant corporations are raiding each other's customers with campaigns mapped by doctors of psychology.

One of the nation's largest advertising agencies now gives every single product it handles a motivational checkup. The merchandising journal *Tide* predicts that within ten years "few national marketers will launch an advertising campaign or introduce a new product without first conducting a thorough study of consumer motivations."

III

Some of the techniques used to probe consumer motives have been borrowed straight from psychiatric clinics and sociological laboratories: the depth interview (a miniature psychoanalysis without the couch), projective picture and word association tests, galvanometers (lie detectors), hypnosis, and social-layer analysis. When our motives are fathomed the experts then shape and bait psychological hooks which will bring us flopping into their corporate boats.

Among the more common strategies devised to lure us are: building self-images of ourselves into their product (playful gasolines for playful people); reminding us that their product can fill one of our hidden needs (security, self-esteem); playing upon our anxiety feelings; offering us ways, through products, to channel our aggressive feelings; selling us sexual reassurance; encouraging impulse buying; conditioning the young; selling us status symbols; making us style-conscious and then switching styles.

Several of the uses to which the insights are put strike me as constructive, or at least non-objectionable. The technique of gearing appeals to the social class most likely to enjoy your product would seem to be a step toward rationality in marketing. One of the notable cases of ill-considered selling occurred in Chicago when one of the leading brewers developed social pretensions for its brew, which had long been popular with the tavern-type clientele. The brewer's advertising men, in an effort to give the brew more class, began showing it being sipped by fox hunters, concert pianists, and drawing-room socialites. Sales did pick up slightly in the better residential areas but began falling disastrously with old customers. The boys in the taverns found the brew didn't taste right any more, though the formula was unchanged.

Social Research, Inc., looked into this fiasco when it depth-probed several hundred typical beer drinkers for the *Chicago Tribune*. It found that beer drinking in America is accepted as an informal, predominantly middle-class custom. So the brewers' foundation in its ads has recently been stressing the back-fence character of beer drinking.

The recent history of beer marketing reveals another way in which motivational analysts can produce constructive, or at least more rational, results. You may recall that in the mid-fifties many beer producers started to proclaim that their beer was particularly low-caloried and hence relatively non-fattening. The campaign was inspired by the mania for weight reduction which was particularly feverish then. Reportedly there were some impressive gains in sales as a result, but the motivational analysts viewed the low-calorie campaigns for beer with misgivings. Dr. Dichter's depth-probers, in testing the thoughts which sprang into people's minds when they say the words "low calorie," found people thought of self-deprivation, discomfort. He admonished brewers to play up beer as a pleasure, not a medicine.

Motivational analysts have also performed a constructive service by showing advertising men how to conquer unreasonable prejudice against a product. A classic job in this respect was performed on the prune by Dr. Dichter's institute and advertising men of the prune industry. Prunes simply were not selling, and Dr. Dichter was asked to find why. His depth-probers found the prune, in our society, had become ridden with a host of connotations, all unfortunate. We thought of prunes in terms of dried-up old maids, boarding-houses, constipation, even witches. Under Dr. Dichter's guidance the prune has now been "rediscovered" as the "California wonder fruit," and admen now almost always show it in gay, zestful, youthful, colorful settings. The laxative angle is now mentioned in small type; and the prune industry, at last reports, is showing a hearty revival.

Still another way that the depth approach can perform a valid service is to help people achieve a feeling of self-worth through advertising. A producer of steam shovels found sales lagging. When a motivation study was made of prospective customers, it was discovered that steam-shovel operators play a large role in influencing the decisions of purchasing agents, and shovel operators did not like the shovel in question. A study of the ads that had been used to promote the shovel suggested a clue.

The shovel was always shown at work in all its monumental glory. Its operator was depicted as a barely visible figure inside the distant cab. The operators subconsciously felt their role was belittled. When the advertising men were advised of this source of irritation they began taking their pictures over the shoulder of the operator, with the operator shown as the confident master of the machine. This new approach reportedly brought a marked mellowing in the attitude of operators toward the shovel advertised.

IV

Several of the techniques being used on us by certain of the advertising men (and their scientific allies), however, do give cause for concern. These are the techniques designed to catch us when our conscious guard is down. Here are some of the types of operation I have in mind.

1. Appeals designed to play upon our hidden weaknesses. At one of America's largest advertising agencies, staff psychologists have been exploring the subconscious of sample humans in order to find how to shape messages that will have maximum impact with people of high anxiety, body consciousness, hostility, passiveness, and so on.

In Chicago a smaller agency has conducted a psychiatric study of women's menstrual cycle and the emotional states which go with each stage of the cycle in order to learn how to sell cake mixes to women more effectively. The aim was to learn how to incorporate within one ad a double-barreled message which would appeal to women in the high phase of their cycle (creative, sexually excitable, narcissistic, outgoing, loving) and also at the same time to women who happened to be in their low phase (want attention, affection, things done for them). This could be achieved, the agency concluded, by offering the high-phase woman something new and the low-phase woman an easy-does-it meal.

2. Strategies involving the manipulation of children. The agency just mentioned also conducted a study of the psyche of straight-haired small girls to find how best to persuade them and their mothers that the girls might feel doomed to ugliness and unhappiness if they were not somehow provided with curly hair. The agency was trying to promote the use of home permanents on children and used many psychiatric techniques in probing the little girls.

The most inviting opportunity to manipulate children for profit, of course, is via television. Five-year-old children, admen have learned, make mighty fine amplifiers of singing jingles (beer or cigarettes included). They can be taught to sing them endlessly with gusto around the house all day long and, unlike the TV set, they can't be turned off.

3. The use of subthreshold effects to slip messages past our conscious guard. Some advertising men have been investigating, very quietly, the possibility of inserting "flash" sales messages in TV and movie film. The bits of film flash by so fast they are not "seen" by the conscious eye, but are reportedly seen by the subconscious eye. In late 1956 the London *Sunday Times* charged that advertisers had produced a notable rise in ice cream consumption at a cinema in New Jersey during experiments with subthreshold effects. The use of such surreptitious appeals on any substantial basis will raise an ethical question of the most serious nature, particularly if such hidden appeals are used to put across political candidates or points of view.

4. The deliberate sale of products for their status-enhancement value. Automotive advertisers have hammered so long and loud on the theme of bigness that many Americans feel socially insecure in a small or medium-sized car (unless it is their second car or a chic foreign-made car). Although the times cry for more compact cars for our crowded highways and traffic-clogged metropolitan centers, most U. S. car makers stress, in their ads, the luxurious bigness of their cars. A TV commercial for one of the medium-priced cars stressed how Big it was and then, in a bit of theatrics, the announcer exclaimed: "People are getting smart about car buying nowadays!" With that, the screen showed a crowd of "people" chanting, "We're everybody. . . . We want a Big Car and style too."

5. The creation of illogical, irrational loyalties. This occurs most conspicuously in the promotion of gasolines, cigarettes, whiskeys, detergents. The research director of a leading advertising agency which has made a study in depth of cigarette smoking states that 65 per cent of all smokers are absolutely loyal to one brand of cigarette, even to the extent of walking down five flights of stairs to buy their own brand rather than accept another brand offered by a friend. About 20 per cent are relatively loyal. Yet he found in tests where cigarettes were masked that people could identify their brand by only 2 per cent better than chance. He concluded: "They are smoking an image completely."

In the building of images, cylinders of tobacco shreds wrapped in white paper have been invested with a variety of "exciting" personalities, to use one researcher's phrase. One smoke may have an image of elegance, another is daintily feminine, still another has an image of hair-on-your-chest virility. One cigarette company deliberately changed its image to almost a teen-age personality—even though most of the heavy smokers are in the thirty-to-forty age group. The aim reportedly was to recruit more beginner smokers and develop loyalty in them which would pay off on a long-term basis.

6. The exploitation of our deepest sexual sensitivities. According to the Institute of Motivational Research the admen who conceived the cigarette slogan "Like Your Pleasures Big?" were not unaware that the phrase was a *double entendre* with "latent sexual meaning" The same institute counseled motorboat builders that men could be appealed to on the fact that power boats can be used to express a sense of power in "almost a sexual way." A Midwestern advertising agency has discovered that men can be persuaded to buy a new car by the implied promise that the new, more powerful car offers them a renewal of potency.

7. The application of the insights of depth-selling to politics. In 1956 many political candidates, including the heads of the ticket, were counseled by admen to present an attractive image to the public. The most popular models were father images and courageous young Davids. At one quite important level the presidential campaign settled into a battle between advertising agencies. Batten Barton Durstine & Osborn for the Republicans and the smaller agency Norman Craig & Kummel for the Democrats.

The advertising man's approach to politics was perhaps best summed up by ad executive Rosser Reeves, who conceived the ceaseless barrage of half-minute spots on TV and radio in 1952 for the GOP. He said, "I think of a man in a voting booth who hesitates between two levers as if he were pausing between competing tubes of toothpaste in a drugstore. The brand that has made the highest penetration on his brain will win his choice."

The Democratic candidate, Adlai Stevenson (who reportedly became very unhappy about some of the strategies conceived for him by admen late in the campaign), voiced his irritation at the symbol manipulators' approach to politics (at least the GOP variety) by saying: "The idea that you can merchandise candidates for high office like breakfast cereal . . . is the ultimate indignity to the democratic process."

To sum up, I feel that while advertising in general is a constructive—and indispensable—force in our economy, its practitioners are becoming uncomfortably powerful and many of them need to exhibit more responsibility in their use of their new power than they have been doing. This particularly applies to their use of the depth approach to consumers.

The responsible leaders of the industry should, I believe, review the current trends in advertising and admonish practitioners to proceed with greater consideration for the public's welfare in certain areas. As a start they might consider the following broad trends which I believe should be viewed uneasily by thoughtful citizens:

Advertising men are pushing us toward conformity and passivity. Americans by the millions respond to their signals. Perhaps the trend to passivity is more serious than the trend to conformity. Max Lerner, in commenting on the implications he saw in some of the depth persuasion activites I described in my book, made one of the most perceptive and disquieting remarks I have encountered concerning the trend in selling. He wrote: "In motivation research . . . the consumer is always passive. He is analyzed, dissected, acted upon, bought and sold. He is a commodity to be trafficked in. The human being as a commodity, that is the disease of our age."

Many of the efforts of the advertising men provoke lasting anxieties. Economist Robert Lekachman recently speculated that we could only guess at the tensions and anxieties generated by the relentless pursuit of the emblems of success being encouraged in our society today.

The advertising men frequently are encouraging irrationality, as when they persuade us to buy products on the basis of images they have skillfully devised rather than on the merits of the physical product inside the package.

They are tending to demean many scientists who have been lured into serving them. Some of the social scientists collaborating with the advertising men maintain their standards of investigation; others strive to please, and often lay before their employers insights into our vulnerabilities which the advertising men do not hesitate to exploit.

Many of them are encouraging an attitude of wastefulness on the part of the public toward the nation's fast-shrinking resources. One conspicuous way they do this is by deliberately striving to make us dissatisfied with the serviceable products we already own.

Finally they often seek to invade the privacy of the mind. They want to know too much about us, and the inner workings of our emotions, for comfort. We should be able to be a little irrational and neurotic at times without having to fear that we thus become vulnerable to outside manipulation.

If advertising is to represent progress rather than regress for man in his struggle for self-mastery, then these considerations must be honestly faced.

Henry David Thoreau

CIVIL DISOBEDIENCE

I heartily accept the motto,—"That government is best which governs least;" and I should like to see it acted up to more rapidly and systematically. Carried out, it finally amounts to this, which also I believe,—"That government is best which governs not at all;" and when men are prepared for it, that will be the kind of government which they will have. Government is at best but an expedient; but most governments are usually, and all governments are sometimes, inexpedient. The objections which have been brought against a standing army, and they are many and weighty, and deserve to prevail, may also at last be brought against a standing government. The standing army is only an arm of the standing government. The government itself, which is only the mode which the people have chosen to execute their will, is equally liable to be abused and perverted before the people can act through it. Witness the present Mexican war, the work of comparatively a few individuals using the standing government as their tool; for, in the outset, the people would not have consented to this measure.

This American government,—what is it but a tradition, though a recent one, endeavoring to transmit itself unimpaired to posterity, but each instant losing some of its integrity? It has not the vitality and force of a single living man; for a single man can bend it to his will. It is a sort of wooden gun to the people themselves. But it is not the less necessary for this; for the people must have some complicated machinery or other, and hear its din, to satisfy that idea of government which they have. Governments show thus how successfully men can be imposed on, even impose on themselves, for their own advantage. It is excellent, we must all allow. Yet this government never of itself furthered any enterprise, but by the alacrity with which it got out of its way. *It* does not keep the country free. *It* does not settle the West. *It* does not educate. The character inherent in the American people has done all that has been accomplished; and it would have done somewhat more, if the government had not sometimes got in its way. For government is an expedient by which men would fain succeed in letting one another alone; and, as has been said, when it is most expedient, the governed are most let alone by it. Trade and commerce, if they were not made of India-rubber, would never manage to bounce over the obstacles which legislators are continually putting in their way; and, if one were to judge these men wholly by the effects of their actions and not partly by their intentions, they would deserve to be classed and punished with those mischievous persons who put obstructions on the railroads.

But, to speak practically and as a citizen, unlike those who call themselves no-government men, I ask for, not at once no government, but *at once* a better government. Let every man make known what kind of government would command his respect, and that will be one step toward obtaining it.

After all, the practical reason why, when the power is once in the hands of the people, a majority are permitted, and for a long period continue, to rule is not because they are most likely to be in the right, nor because this seems fairest to the minority, but because they are physically the strongest. But a government in which the majority rule in all cases cannot be based on justice, even as far as men understand it. Can there not be a government in which majorities do not virtually decide right and wrong, but conscience?—in which majorities decide only those questions to which the rule of expediency is applicable? Must the citizen ever for a moment, or in the least degree, resign his conscience to the legislator? Why has every man a conscience, then? I think that we should be men first, and subjects afterward. It is not desirable to cultivate a respect for the law, so much as for the right. The only obligation which I have a right to assume is to do at any time what I think right. It is truly enough said, that a corporation has no conscience; but a corporation of conscientious men is a corporation *with* a conscience. Law never made men a whit more just; and, by means of their respect for it, even the well-disposed are daily made the agents of injustice. A common and natural result of an undue respect for law is, that you may see a file of soldiers, colonel, captain, corporal, privates, powder-monkeys, and all, marching in admirable order over hill and dale to the wars, against their wills, ay, against their common sense and consciences, which makes it very steep marching indeed, and produces a palpitation of the heart. They have no doubt that it is a damnable business in which they are concerned; they are all peaceably inclined. Now, what are they? Men at all? or small movable forts and magazines, at the service of some unscrupulous man in power? Visit the Navy-Yard, and behold a marine, such a man as an American government can make, or such as it can make a man with its black arts,—a mere shadow and reminiscence of humanity, a man laid out alive and standing, and already, as one may say, buried under arms with funeral accompaniments, though it may be,—

> "Not a drum was heard, not a funeral note,
>   As his corse to the rampart we hurried;
> Not a soldier discharged his farewell shot
>   O'er the grave where our hero we buried."

The mass of men serve the state thus, not as men mainly, but as machines, with their bodies. They are the standing army, and the militia, jailors, constables, posse comitatus, etc. In most cases there is no free exercise whatever of the judgment or of the moral sense; but they put themselves on a level with wood and earth and stones; and wooden men can perhaps be manufactured that will serve the purpose as well. Such command no more respect than men of straw or a lump of dirt. They have the same sort of worth only as horses and dogs. Yet such as these even are commonly esteemed good citizens. Others—as most legislators, politicians, lawyers, ministers, and office-holders—serve the state chiefly with their heads; and, as they rarely make any moral distinctions, they are as likely to serve the Devil, without *intending* it, as God. A very few, as heroes, patriots, martyrs, reformers in the great sense, and *men*, serve the state with their consciences also, and so necessarily resist it for the most part; and they are commonly treated as enemies by it. A wise man will only be useful as a man, and will not submit to be "clay," and "stop a hole to keep the wind away," but leave that office to his dust at least:—

> "I am too high-born to be propertied,
>   To be a secondary at control,
>   Or useful serving-man and instrument
> To any sovereign state throughout the world."

He who gives himself entirely to his fellow-men appears to them useless and selfish; but he who gives himself partially to them is pronounced a benefactor and philanthropist.

How does it become a man to behave toward this American government to-day? I answer, that he cannot without disgrace be associated with it. I cannot for an instant recognize that political organization as *my* government which is the *slave's* government also.

All men recognize the right of revolution; that is, the right to refuse allegiance to, and to resist, the government, when its tyranny or its inefficiency are great and unendurable. But almost all say that such is not the case now. But such was the case, they think, in the Revolution of '75. If one were to tell me that this was a bad government because it taxed certain foreign commodities brought to its ports, it is most probable that I should not make an ado about it, for I can do without them. All machines have their friction; and possibly this does enough good to counterbalance the evil. At any rate, it is a geat evil to make a stir about it. But when the friction comes to have its machine, and oppression and robbery are organized, I say, let us not have such a machine any longer. In other words, when a sixth of the population of a nation which has undertaken to be the refuge of liberty are slaves, and a whole country is unjustly overrun and con-quered by a foreign army, and subjected to military law, I think that it is not too soon for honest men to rebel and revolutionize. What makes this duty the more urgent is the fact that the country so overrun is not our own, but ours is the invading army.

Paley, a common authority with many on moral questions, in his chapter on the "Duty of Submission to Civil Government," resolves all civil obligation into expediency; and he proceeds to say, "that so long as the interest of the whole society requires it, that is, so long as the established government cannot be resisted or changed without public inconveniency, it is the will of God that the established government be obeyed, and no longer. . . . This principle being admitted, the justice of every particular case of resistance is reduced to a com-putation of the quantity of the danger and grievance on the one side, and of the probability and expense of redressing it on the other." Of this, he says, every man shall judge for himself. But Paley appears never to have contemplated those cases to which the rule of expediency does not apply, in which a people, as well as an individual, must do justice, cost what it may. If I have unjustly wrested a plank from a drowning man, I must restore it to him though I drown myself. This, according to Paley, would be inconvenient. But he that would save his life, in such a case, shall lose it. This people must cease to hold slaves, and to make war on Mexico, though it cost them their existence as a people.

In their practice, nations agree with Paley; but does any one think that Massachusetts does exactly what is right at the present crisis?

> "A drab of state, a cloth-o'-silver slut,
>   To have her train borne up, and her soul trail in the dirt."

Practically speaking, the opponents to a reform in Massachusetts are not a hundred thousand politicians at the South, but a hundred thousand merchants and farmers here, who are more interested in commerce and agriculture than they are in humanity, and are not prepared to do justice to the slave and to Mexico, *cost what it may*. I quarrel not with far-off foes, but with those who, near at home, coöperate with, and do the bidding of, those far away, and without whom the latter would be harmless. We are accustomed to say, that the mass of men are unprepared; but improvement is slow, because the few are not materially wiser or better than the many. It is not so important that many should be as good as you, as that there be some absolute goodness somewhere; for that will leaven the whole lump. There are thousands who are *in opinion* opposed to slavery and to the war, who yet in effect do nothing to put an end to them; who, esteeming themselves children of Washington and Franklin, sit down with their hands in their pockets, and say that they know not what to do, and do nothing; who even postpone the question of freedom to the question of free-trade, and quietly read the prices-current along with the latest advices from Mexico, after dinner, and, it may be, fall asleep over them both. What is the price-current of an honest man and patriot to-day? They hesitate, and they regret, and sometimes they petition; but they do nothing in earnest and with effect. They will wait, well disposed, for others to remedy the evil, that they may no longer have it to regret. At most, they give only a cheap vote, and a feeble countenance and God-speed, to the right, as it goes by them. There are nine hundred and ninety-nine patrons of virtue to one virtuous man. But it is easier to deal with the real possessor of a thing than with the temporary guardian of it.

All voting is a sort of gaming, like checkers or backgammon, with a slight moral tinge to it, a playing with right and wrong, with moral questions; and betting naturally accompanies it. The character of the voters is not staked. I cast my vote, perchance, as I think right; but I am not vitally concerned that that right should prevail. I am willing to leave it to the majority. Its obligation, therefore, never exceeds that of expediency. Even voting *for the right* is *doing* nothing for it. It is only expressing to men feebly your desire that it should prevail. A wise man will not leave the right to the mercy of chance, nor wish it to prevail through the power of the majority. There is but little virtue in the action of masses of men. When the majority shall at length vote for the abolition of slavery, it will be because they are indifferent to slavery, or because there is but little slavery left to be abolished by their vote. *They* will then be the only slaves. Only *his* vote can hasten the abolition of slavery who asserts his own freedom by his vote.

I hear of a convention to be held at Baltimore, or elsewhere, for the selection of a candidate for the Presidency, made up chiefly of editors, and men who are politicians by profession; but I think, what is it to any independent, intelligent, and respectable man what decision they may come to? Shall we not have the advantage of his wisdom and honesty, nevertheless? Can we not count upon some independent votes? Are there not many individuals in the country who do not attend conventions? But no: I find that the respectable man, so called, has immediately drifted from his position, and despairs of his country, when his country has more reason to despair of him. He forthwith adopts one of the candidates thus selected as the only *available* one, thus proving that he is himself *available* for any purposes of the demagogue. His vote is of no more worth than that of any unprincipled foreigner or hireling native, who may have been bought. O for a man who is a *man*, and, as my neighbor says, has a bone in his back which you cannot pass your hand through! Our statistics are at fault: the population has been returned too large. How many *men* are there to a square thousand miles in this country? Hardly one. Does not America offer any inducement for men to settle here? The American has dwindled into an Odd Fellow,—one who may be known by the development of his organ of gregariousness, and a manifest lack of intellect and cheerful self-reliance; whose first and chief concern, on coming into the world, is to see that the Almshouses are in good repair; and, before yet he has lawfully donned the virile garb, to collect a fund for the support of the widows and orphans that may be; who, in short, ventures to live only by the aid of the Mutual Insurance company, which has promised to bury him decently.

It is not a man's duty, as a matter of course, to devote himself to the eradication of any, even the most enormous wrong; he may still properly have other concerns to engage him; but it is his duty, at least, to wash his hands of it, and, if he gives it no thought longer, not to give it practically his support. If I devote myself to other pursuits and contemplations, I must first see, at least, that I do not pursue them sitting upon another man's shoulders. I must get off him first, that he may pursue his contemplations too. See what gross inconsistency is tolerated. I have heard some of my townsmen say, "I should like to have them order me out to help put down an insurrection of the slaves, or to march to Mexico;—see if I would go;" and yet these very men have each, directly by their allegiance, and so indirectly, at least, by their money, furnished a substitute. The soldier is applauded who refuses to serve in an unjust war by those who do not refuse to sustain the unjust government which makes the war; is applauded by those whose own act and authority he disregards and sets at naught; as if the state were penitent to that degree that it hired one to scourge it while it sinned, but not to that degree that it left off sinning for a moment. Thus, under the name of Order and Civil Government, we are all made at last to pay homage to and support our own meanness. After the first blush of sin comes its indifference; and from immoral it becomes, as it were, *un*moral, and not quite unnecessary to that life which we have made.

The broadest and most prevalent error requires the most disinterested virtue to sustain it. The slight reproach to which the virtue of patriotism is commonly liable, the noble are most likely to incur. Those who, while they disapprove of the character and measures of a government, yield to it their allegiance and support are undoubtedly its most conscientious supporters, and so frequently the most serious obstacles to reform. Some are petitioning the state to dissolve the Union, to disregard the requisitions of the President. Why do they not dissolve it themselves,—the union between themselves and the state,—and refuse to pay their quota into its treasury? Do not they stand in the same relation to the state that the state does to the Union? And have not the same reasons prevented the state from resisting the Union which have prevented them from resisting the state?

How can a man be satisfied to entertain an opinion merely, and enjoy *it?* Is there any enjoyment in it, if his opinion is that he is aggrieved? If you are cheated out of a single dollar by your neighbor, you do not rest satisfied with knowing that you are cheated, or with saying that you are cheated, or even with petitioning him to pay you your due; but you take effectual steps at once to obtain the full amount, and see that you are never cheated again. Action from principle, the perception and the performance of right, changes things and relations; it is essentially revolutionary, and does not consist wholly with anything which was. It not only divides states and churches, it divides families; ay, it divides the *individual,* separating the diabolical in him from the divine.

Unjust laws exist: shall we be content to obey them, or shall we endeavor to amend them, and obey them until we have succeeded, or shall we transgress them at once? Men generally, under such a government as this, think that they ought to wait until they have persuaded the majority to alter them. They think that, if they should resist, the remedy would be worse than the evil. But it is the fault of the government itself that the remedy *is* worse than the evil. *It* makes it worse. Why is it not more apt to anticipate and provide for reform? Why does it not cherish its wise minority? Why does it cry and resist before it is hurt? Why does it not encourage its citizens to be on the alert to point out its faults, and *do* better than *it* would have them? Why does it always crucify Christ, and excommunicate Copernicus and Luther, and pronounce Washington and Franklin rebels?

One would think, that a deliberate and practical denial of its authority was the only offense never contemplated by government; else, why has it not assigned its definite, its suitable and proportionate penalty? If a man who has no property refuses but once to earn nine shillings for the state, he is put in prison for a period unlimited by any law that I know, and determined only by the discretion of those who placed him there; but if he should steal ninety times nine shillings from the state, he is soon permitted to go at large again.

If the injustice is part of the necessary friction of the machine of government, let it go, let it go: perchance it will wear smooth,—certainly the machine will wear out. If the injustice has a spring, or a pulley, or a rope, or a crank, exclusively for itself, then perhaps you may consider whether the remedy will not be worse than the evil; but if it is of such a nature that it requires you to be the agent of injustice to another, then, I say, break the law. Let your life be a counter friction to stop the machine. What I have to do is to see, at any rate, that I do not lend myself to the wrong which I condemn.

As for adopting the ways which the state has provided for remedying the evil, I know not of such ways. They take too much time, and a man's life will be gone. I have other affairs to attend to. I came into this world, not chiefly to make this a good place to live in, but to live in it, be it good or bad. A man has not everything to do, but something; and because he cannot do *everything*, it is not necessary that he should do *something* wrong. It is not my business to be petitioning the Governor or the Legislature any more than it is theirs to petition me; and if they should not hear my petition, what should I do then? But in this case the state has provided no way: its very Constitution is the evil. This may seem to be harsh and stubborn and unconciliatory; but it is to treat with the utmost kindness and consideration the only spirit that can appreciate or deserves it. So is all change for the better, like birth and death, which convulse the body.

I do not hesitate to say, that those who call themselves Abolitionists should at once effectually withdraw their support, both in person and property, from the government of Massachusetts and not wait till they constitute a majority of one, before they suffer the right to prevail through them. I think that it is enough if they have God on their side, without waiting for that other one. Moreover, any man more right than his neighbors constitutes a majority of one already.

I meet this American government, or its representative, the state government, directly, and face to face, once a year—no more—in the person of its tax-gatherer; this is the only mode in which a man situated as I am necessarily meets it; and it then says distinctly, Recognize me; and the simplest, most effectual, and, in the present posture of affairs, the indispensablest mode of treating with it on this head, of expressing your little satisfaction with and love for it, is to deny it then. My civil neighbor, the tax-gatherer, is the very man I have to deal with,—for it is, after all, with men and not with parchment that I quarrel,—and he has voluntarily chosen to be an agent of the government. How shall he ever know well what he is and does as an officer of the government, or as a man, until he is obliged to consider whether he shall treat me, his neighbor, for whom he has respect, as a neighbor and well-disposed man, or as a maniac and disturber of the peace, and see if he can get over this obstruction to his neighborliness without a ruder and more impetuous thought or speech corresponding with his action. I know this well, that if one thousand, if one hundred, if ten men whom I could name,—if ten *honest* men only,—if *one* HONEST man, in this State of Massachusetts, *ceasing to hold slaves*, were actually to withdraw from this copartnership, and be locked up in the county jail therefor, it would be the abolition of slavery in America. For it matters not how small the beginning may seem to be: what is once well done is done forever. But we love better to talk about it: that we say is our mission. Reform keeps many scores of newspapers in its service, but not one man. If my esteemed neighbor, the State's ambassador, who will devote his days to the settlement of the question of human rights in the Council Chamber, instead of being threatened with the prisons of Carolina, were to sit down the prisoner of Massachusetts, that State which is so anxious to foist the sin of slavery upon her sister,—though at present she can discover only an act of inhospitality to be the ground of a quarrel with her,—the Legislature would not wholly waive the subject the following winter.

Under a government which imprisons any unjustly, the true place for a just man is also a prison. The proper place to-day, the only place which Massachu-

setts has provided for her freer and less desponding spirits, is in her prisons,
to be put out and locked out of the State by her own act, as they have already put
themselves out by their principles. It is there that the fugitive slave, and the
Mexican prisoner on parole, and the Indian come to plead the wrongs of his
race should find them; on that separate, but more free and honorable ground,
where the State places those who are not *with* her, but *against* her,—the only
house in a slave State in which a free man can abide with honor. If any think
that their influence would be lost there, and their voices no longer afflict the
ear of the State, that they would not be as an enemy within its walls, they do not
know by how much truth is stronger than error, nor how much more eloquently
and effectively he can combat injustice who has experienced a little in his own
person. Cast your whole vote, not a strip of paper merely, but your whole influence. A minority is powerless while it conforms to the majority; it is not even a
minority then; but it is irresistible when it clogs by its whole weight. If the
alternative is to keep all just men in prison, or give up war and slavery, the
State will not hesitate which to choose. If a thousand men were not to pay their
tax-bills this year, that would not be a violent and bloody measure, as it would
be to pay them, and enable the State to commit violence and shed innocent
blood. This is, in fact, the definition of a peaceable revolution, if any such is
possible. If the tax-gatherer, or any other public officer, asks me, as one has
done, "But what shall I do?" my answer is, "If you really wish to do anything,
resign your office." When the subject has refused allegiance, and the officer
has resigned his office, then the revolution is accomplished. But even suppose
blood should flow. Is there not a sort of blood shed when the conscience is
wounded? Through this wound a man's real manhood and immortality flow
out, and he bleeds to an everlasting death. I see this blood flowing now.

I have contemplated the imprisonment of the offender, rather than the
seizure of his goods,—though both will serve the same purpose,—because they
who assert the purest right, and consequently are most dangerous to a corrupt
State, commonly have not spent much time in accumulating property. To such
the State renders comparatively small service, and a slight tax is wont to appear
exorbitant, particularly if they are obliged to earn it by special labor with their
hands. If there were one who lived wholly without the use of money, the State
itself would hesitate to demand it of him. But the rich man—not to make any
invidious comparison—is always sold to the institution which makes him rich.
Absolutely speaking, the more money, the less virtue; for money comes between
a man and his objects, and obtains them for him; and it was certainly no great
virtue to obtain it. It puts to rest many questions which he would otherwise be
taxed to answer; while the only new question which it puts is the hard but
superfluous one, how to spend it. Thus his moral ground is taken from under
his feet. The opportunities of living are diminished in proportion as what are
called the "means" are increased. The best thing a man can do for his culture
when he is rich is to endeavor to carry out those schemes which he entertained
when he was poor. Christ answered the Herodians according to their condition.
"Show me the tribute-money," said he;—and one took a penny out of his

pocket;—if you use the money which has the image of Cæsar on it and which he has made current and valuable, that is, *if you are men of the State*, and gladly enjoy the advantages of Cæsar's government, then pay him back some of his own when he demands it. "Render therefore to Cæsar that which is Cæsar's, and to God those things which are God's,"—leaving them no wiser than before as to which was which; for they did not wish to know.

When I converse with the freest of my neighbors, I perceive that, whatever they may say about the magnitude and seriousness of the question, and their regard for the public tranquillity, the long and the short of the matter is, that they cannot spare the protection of the existing government, and they dread the consequences to their property and families of disobedience to it. For my own part, I should not like to think that I ever rely on the protection of the State. But, if I deny the authority of the State when it presents its tax-bill, it will soon take and waste all my property, and so harass me and my children without end. This is hard. This makes it impossible for a man to live honestly, and at the same time comfortably, in outward respects. It will not be worth the while to accumulate property; that would be sure to go again. You must hire or squat somewhere, and raise but a small crop, and eat that soon. You must live within yourself, and depend upon yourself always tucked up and ready for a start, and not have many affairs. A man may grow rich in Turkey even, if he will be in all respects a good subject of the Turkish government. Confucius said: "If a state is governed by the principles of reason, poverty and misery are subjects of shame; if a state is not governed by the principles of reason, riches and honors are the subjects of shame." No: until I want the protection of Massachusetts to be extended to me in some distant Southern port, where my liberty is endangered, or until I am bent solely on building up an estate at home by peaceful enterprise, I can afford to refuse allegiance to Massachusetts, and her right to my property and life. It costs me less in every sense to incur the penalty of disobedience to the State than it would to obey. I should feel as if I were worth less in that case.

Some years ago, the State met me in behalf of the Church, and commanded me to pay a certain sum toward the support of a clergyman whose preaching my father attended, but never I myself. "Pay," it said, "or be locked up in the jail." I declined to pay. But, unfortunately, another man saw fit to pay it. I did not see why the schoolmaster should be taxed to support the priest, and not the priest the schoolmaster; for I was not the State's schoolmaster, but I supported myself by voluntary subscription. I did not see why the lyceum should not present its tax-bill, and have the State to back its demand, as well as the Church. However, at the request of the selectmen, I condescended to make some such statement as this in writing:—"Know all men by these presents, that I, Henry Thoreau, do not wish to be regarded as a member of any incorporated society which I have not joined." This I gave to the town clerk; and he has it. The State, having thus learned that I did not wish to be regarded as a member of that church, has never made a like demand on me since; though it said that it must adhere to its original presumption that time. If I had known how to name them, I should then have signed off in detail from all the societies which I never signed on to; but I did not know where to find a complete list.

I have paid no poll-tax for six years. I was put into a jail once on this account, for one night; and, as I stood considering the walls of solid stone, two or three feet thick, the door of wood and iron, a foot thick, and the iron grating which strained the light, I could not help being struck with the foolishness of that institution which treated me as if I were mere flesh and blood and bones, to be locked up. I wondered that it should have concluded at length that this was the best use it could put me to, and had never thought to avail itself of my services in some way. I saw that, if there was a wall of stone between me and my towns-men, there was a still more difficult one to climb or break through before they could get to be as free as I was. I did not for a moment feel confined, and the walls seemed a great waste of stone and mortar. I felt as if I alone of all my townsmen had paid my tax. They plainly did not know how to treat me, but behaved like persons who are underbred. In every threat and in every compliment there was a blunder; for they thought that my chief desire was to stand the other side of that stone wall. I could not but smile to see how industriously they locked the door on my meditations, which followed them out again without let or hindrance, and *they* were really all that was dangerous. As they could not reach me, they had resolved to punish my body; just as boys, if they cannot come at some person against whom they have a spite, will abuse his dog. I saw that the State was half-witted, that it was timid as a lone woman with her silver spoons, and that it did not know its friends from its foes, and I lost all my remaining respect for it, and pitied it.

Thus the State never intentionally confronts a man's sense, intellectual or moral, but only his body, his senses. It is not armed with superior wit or honesty, but with superior physical strength. I was not born to be forced. I will breathe after my own fashion. Let us see who is the strongest. What force has a multitude? They only can force me who obey a higher law than I. They force me to become like themselves. I do not hear of *men* being *forced* to live this way or that by masses of men. What sort of life were that to live? When I meet a government which says to me, "Your money or your life," why should I be in haste to give it my money? It may be in a great strait, and not know what to do: I cannot help that. It must help itself; do as I do. It is not worth the while to snivel about it. I am not responsible for the successful working of the machin-ery of society. I am not the son of the engineer. I perceive that, when an acorn and a chestnut fall side by side, the one does not remain inert to make way for the other, but both obey their own laws, and spring and grow and flourish as best they can, till one, perchance, overshadows and destroys the other. If a plant cannot live according to its nature, it dies; and so a man.

The night in prison was novel and interesting enough. The prisoners in their shirt-sleeves were enjoying a chat and the evening air in the doorway, when I entered. But the jailer said, "Come, boys, it is time to lock up;" and so they dis-persed, and I heard the sound of their steps returning into the hollow apartments. My roommate was introduced to me by the jailer as "a first-rate fellow and a clever man." When the door was locked, he showed me where to hang my hat, and how he managed matters there. The rooms were whitewashed once a month; and this one, at least, was the whitest, most simply furnished, and probably the neatest apartment in the town. He naturally wanted to know where I came from, and what brought me there; and, when I had told him, I asked him in my turn how he came there, presuming him to be an honest man, of course; and, as the world goes, I believe he was. "Why," said he, "they accuse me of burning a barn; but I never did it." As near as I could discover, he had probably gone to bed in a barn when drunk, and smoked his pipe there; and so a barn was burnt. He had the reputation of being a clever man, had been there some three months waiting for his trial to come on, and would have to wait as much longer; but he was quite domesticated and contented, since he got his board for nothing, and thought that he was well treated.

He occupied one window, and I the other; and I saw that if one stayed there long, his principal business would be to look out the window. I had soon read all the tracts that were left there, and examined where former prisoners had broken out, and where a grate had been sawed off, and heard the history of the various occupants of that room; for I found that even here there was a history and a gossip which never circulated beyond the walls of the jail. Probably this is the only house in the town where verses are composed, which are afterward printed in a circular form, but not published. I was shown quite a long list of verses which were composed by some young men who had been detected in an attempt to escape, who avenged themselves by singing them.

I pumped my fellow-prisoner as dry as I could, for fear I should never see him again; but at length he showed me which was my bed, and left me to blow out the lamp.

It was like traveling into a far country, such as I had never expected to behold, to lie there for one night. It seemed to me that I never had heard the town-clock strike before, nor the evening sounds of the village; for we slept with the windows open, which were inside the grating. It was to see my native village in the light of the Middle Ages, and our Concord was turned into a Rhine stream, and visions of knights and castles passed before me. They were the voices of old burghers that I heard in the streets. I was an involuntary spectator and auditor of whatever was done and said in the kitchen of the adjacent village-inn,—a wholly new and rare experience to me. It was a closer view of my native town. I was fairly inside of it. I never had seen its institutions before. This is one of its peculiar institutions; for it is a shire town. I began to comprehend what its inhabitants were about.

In the morning, our breakfasts were put through the hole in the door, in small oblong-square tin pans, made to fit, and holding a pint of chocolate, with brown bread, and an iron spoon. When they called for the vessels again, I was green enough to return what bread I had left; but my comrade seized it, and said that I should lay that up for lunch or dinner. Soon after he was let out to work at haying in a neighboring field, whither he went every day, and would not be back till noon; so he bade me good-day, saying that he doubted if he should see me again.

When I came out of prison,—for some one interfered, and paid that tax,—I did not perceive that great changes had taken place on the common, such as he observed who went in a youth and emerged a tottering and gray-headed man; and yet a change had to my eyes come over the scene,—the town, and State, and country,—greater than any that mere time could effect. I saw yet more distinctly the State in which I lived. I saw to what extent the people among whom I lived could be trusted as good neighbors and friends; that their friendship was for summer weather only; that they did not greatly propose to do right; that they were a distinct race from me by their prejudices and superstitions, as the Chinamen and Malays are; that in their sacrifices to humanity they ran no risks, not even to their property; that after all they were not so noble but they treated the thief as he had treated them, and hoped, by a certain outward observance and a few prayers, and by walking in a particular straight though useless path from time to time, to save their souls. This may be to judge my neighbors harshly; for I believe that many of them are not aware that they have such an institution as the jail in their village.

It was formerly the custom in our village, when a poor debtor came out of jail, for his acquaintances to salute him, looking through their fingers, which were crossed to represent the grating of a jail window, "How do ye do?" My neighbors did not thus salute me, but first looked at me, and then at one another, as if I had returned from a long journey. I was put into jail as I was going to the shoemaker's to get a shoe which was mended. When I was let out the next morning, I proceeded to finish my errand, and, having put on my mended shoe, joined a huckleberry party, who were impatient to put themselves under my conduct; and in half an hour,—for the horse was soon tackled,—was in the midst of a huckleberry field, on one of our highest hills, two miles off, and then the State was nowhere to be seen.

This is the whole history of "My Prisons."

I have never declined paying the highway tax, because I am as desirous of being a good neighbor as I am of being a bad subject; and as for supporting schools, I am doing my part to educate my fellow-countrymen now. It is for no particular item in the tax-bill that I refuse to pay it. I simply wish to refuse allegiance to the State, to withdraw and stand aloof from it effectually. I do not care to trace the course of my dollar, if I could, till it buys a man or a musket to shoot with,—the dollar is innocent,—but I am concerned to trace the effects of my allegiance. In fact, I quietly declare war with the State, after my fashion, though I will still make what use and get what advantage of her I can, as is usual in such cases.

If others pay the tax which is demanded of me, from a sympathy with the State, they do but what they have already done in their own case, or rather they abet injustice to a greater extent than the State requires. If they pay the tax from a mistaken interest in the individual taxed, to save his property, or prevent his going to jail, it is because they have not considered wisely how far they let their private feelings interfere with the public good.

This, then, is my position at present. But one cannot be too much on his guard in such a case, lest his action be biased by obstinacy or an undue regard for the opinions of men. Let him see that he does only what belongs to himself and to the hour.

I think sometimes, Why, this people mean well, they are only ignorant; they would do better if they knew how: why give your neighbors this pain to treat you as they are not inclined to? But I think again, This is no reason why I should do as they do, or permit others to suffer much greater pain of a different kind. Again, I sometimes say to myself, When many millions of men, without heat, without ill will, without personal feeling of any kind, demand of you a few shillings only, without the possibility, such is their constitution, of retracting or altering their present demand, and without the possibility, on your side, of appeal to any other millions, why expose yourself to this overwhelming brute force? You do not resist cold and hunger, the winds and the waves, thus obstinately; you quietly submit to a thousand similar necessities. You do not put your head into the fire. But just in proportion as I regard this as not wholly a brute force, but partly a human force, and consider that I have relations to those millions as to so many millions of men, and not of mere brute or inanimate things, I see that appeal is possible, first and instantaneously, from them to the Maker of them, and, secondly, from them to themselves. But if I put my head deliberately into the fire, there is no appeal to fire or to the Maker of fire, and I have only myself to blame. If I could convince myself that I have any right to be satisfied with men as they are, and to treat them accordingly, and not according, in some respects, to my requisitions and expectations of what they and I ought to be, then, like a good Mussulman and fatalist, I should endeavor to be satisfied with things as they are, and say it is the will of God. And, above all, there is this difference between resisting this and a purely brute or natural force, that I can resist this with some effect; but I cannot expect, like Orpheus, to change the nature of the rocks and trees and beasts.

I do not wish to quarrel with any man or nation. I do not wish to split hairs, to make fine distinctions, or set myself up as better than my neighbors. I seek rather, I may say, even an excuse for conforming to the laws of the land. I am but too ready to conform to them. Indeed, I have reason to suspect myself on this head; and each year, as the tax-gatherer comes round, I find myself disposed to review the acts and position of the general and State governments, and the spirit of the people, to discover a pretext for conformity.

> "We must affect our country as our parents,
> And if at any time we alienate
> Our love or industry from doing it honor,
> We must respect effects and teach the soul
> Matter of conscience and religion,
> And not desire of rule or benefit."

I believe that the State will soon be able to take all my work of this sort out of my hands, and then I shall be no better a patriot than my fellow-countrymen. Seen from a lower point of view, the Constitution, with all its faults, is very good; the law and the courts are very respectable; even this State and this American government are, in many respects, very admirable, and rare things, to be thankful for, such as a great many have described them; but seen from a point of view a little higher, they are what I have described them; seen from a higher still, and the highest, who shall say what they are, or that they are worth looking at or thinking of at all?

However, the government does not concern me much, and I shall bestow the fewest possible thoughts on it. It is not many moments that I live under a government, even in this world. If a man is thought-free, fancy-free, imagination-free, that which *is not* never for a long time appearing *to be* to him, unwise rulers or reformers cannot fatally interrupt him.

I know that most men think differently from myself; but those whose lives are by profession devoted to the study of these or kindred subjects content me as little as any. Statesmen and legislators, standing so completely within the institution, never distinctly and nakedly behold it. They speak of moving society, but have no resting-place without it. They may be men of a certain experience and discrimination, and have no doubt invented ingenious and even useful systems, for which we sincerely thank them; but all their wit and usefulness lie within certain not very wide limits. They are wont to forget that the world is not governed by policy and expediency. Webster never goes behind government, and so cannot speak with authority about it. His words are wisdom to those legislators who contemplate no essential reform in the existing government; but for thinkers, and those who legislate for all time, he never once glances at the subject. I know of those whose serene and wise speculations on this theme would soon reveal the limits of his mind's range and hospitality. Yet, compared with the cheap professions of most reformers, and the still cheaper wisdom and eloquence of politicians in general, his are almost the only sensible and valuable words, and we thank Heaven for him. Comparatively, he is always strong, original, and, above all, practical. Still, his quality is not wisdom, but prudence. The lawyer's truth is not Truth, but consistency or a consistent expediency. Truth is always in harmony with herself, and is not concerned chiefly to reveal the justice that may consist with wrong-doing. He well deserves to be called, as he has been called, the Defender of the Constitution. There are really no blows to be given by him but defensive ones. He is not a leader, but a follower. His leaders are the men of '87. "I have never made an effort," he says, "and never propose to make an effort; I have never countenanced an effort, and never mean to countenance an effort, to disturb the arrangement as originally made, by which the various States came into the Union." Still thinking of the sanction which the Constitution gives to slavery, he says, "Because it was a part of the original compact,— let it stand." Notwithstanding his special acuteness and ability, he is unable to take a fact out of its merely political relations, and behold it as it lies absolutely to be disposed of by the intellect,—what, for instance, it behooves a man to do here in America to-day with regard to slavery,—but ventures, or is driven to make some such desperate answer as the following, while professing to speak absolutely, and as a private man,—from which what new and singular code of social duties might be inferred? "The manner," says he, "in which the governments of those States where slavery exists are to regulate it is for their own consideration, under their responsibility to their constituents, to the general laws of propriety, humanity, and justice, and to God. Associations formed elsewhere, springing from a feeling of humanity, or other cause, have nothing whatever to do with it. They have never received any encouragement from me, and they never will."

They who know of no purer sources of truth, who have traced up its stream no higher, stand, and wisely stand, by the Bible and the Constitution, and drink at it there with reverence and humility; but they who behold where it comes trickling into this lake or that pool, gird up their loins once more, and continue their pilgrimage toward its fountain-head.

No man with a genius for legislation has appeared in America. They are rare in the history of the world. There are orators, politicians, and eloquent men, by the thousand; but the speaker has not yet opened his mouth to speak who is capable of settling the much-vexed questions of the day. We love eloquence for its own sake, and not for any truth which it may utter, or any heroism it may inspire. Our legislators have not yet learned the comparative value of free-trade and of freedom, of union, and of rectitude, to a nation. They have no genius or talent for comparatively humble questions of taxation and finance, commerce and manufactures and agriculture. If we were left solely to the wordy wit of legislators in Congress for our guidance, uncorrected by the seasonable experience and the effectual complaints of the people, America would not long retain her rank among the nations. For eighteen hundred years, though perchance I have no right to say it, the New Testament has been written; yet where is the legislator who has wisdom and practical talent enough to avail himself of the light which it sheds on the science of legislation?

The authority of government, even such as I am willing to submit to,—for I will cheerfully obey those who know and can do better than I, and in many things even those who neither know nor can do so well,—is still an impure one: to be strictly just, it must have the sanction and consent of the governed. It can have no pure right over my person and property but what I concede to it. The progress from an absolute to a limited monarchy, from a limited monarchy to a democracy, is a progress toward a true respect for the individual. Even the Chinese philosopher was wise enough to regard the individual as the basis of the empire. Is a democracy, such as we know it, the last improvement possible in government? Is it not possible to take a step further towards recognizing and organizing the rights of man? There will never be a really free and enlightened State until the State comes to recognize the individual as a higher and independent power, from which all its own power and authority are derived, and treats him accordingly. I please myself with imagining a State at last which can afford to be just to all men, and to treat the individual with respect as a neighbor; which even would not think it inconsistent with its own repose if a few were to live aloof from it, not meddling with it, nor embraced by it, who fulfilled all the duties of neighbors and fellowmen. A State which bore this kind of fruit, and suffered it to drop off as fast as it ripened, would prepare the way for a still more perfect and glorious State, which also I have imagined, but not yet anywhere seen.

Plato was a pupil of Socrates from 407 B.C. until the latter's death in 399. In this dialog Plato relates what presumably was the final attitude of Socrates upon the subject of the state. Socrates has been condemned to death by the Athenians for subversive teaching. His friend Crito visits him in prison.

CRITO

SOCRATES. Why have you come at this hour, Crito? it must be quite early?

CRITO. Yes, certainly.

SOCRATES. What is the exact time?

CRITO. The dawn is breaking.

SOCRATES. I wonder that the keeper of the prison would let you in.

CRITO. He knows me, because I often come, Socrates; moreover I have done him a kindness.

SOCRATES. And are you only just come?

CRITO. No, I came some time ago.

SOCRATES. They why did you sit and say nothing, instead of awakening me at once?

CRITO. Why, indeed, Socrates, I myself would rather not have all this sleeplessness and sorrow. But I have been wondering at your peaceful slumbers, and that was the reason why I did not awaken you, because I wanted you to be out of pain. I have always thought you happy in the calmness of your temperament; but never did I see the like of the easy, cheerful way in which you bear this calamity.

SOCRATES. Why, Crito, when a man has reached my age he ought not to be repining at the prospect of death.

CRITO. And yet other old men find themselves in similar misfortunes, and age does not prevent them from repining.

SOCRATES. That may be. But you have not told me why you come at this early hour.

CRITO. I come to bring you a message which is sad and painful; not, as I believe, to yourself, but to all of us who are your friends, and saddest of all to me.

SOCRATES. What! I suppose that the ship has come from Delos, on the arrival of which I am to die?

CRITO. No, the ship has not actually arrived, but she will probably be here to-day, as persons who have come from Sunium tell me that they left her there; and therefore to-morrow, Socrates, will be the last day of your life.

SOCRATES. Very well, Crito; if such is the will of God, I am willing; but my belief is that there will be a delay of a day.

CRITO. Why do you say this?

SOCRATES. I will tell you. I am to die on the day after the arrival of the ship?

CRITO. Yes; that is what the authorities say.

SOCRATES. But I do not think that the ship will be here until to-morrow; this I gather from a vision which I had last night, or rather only just now, when you fortunately allowed me to sleep.

CRITO. And what was the nature of the vision?

SOCRATES. There came to me the likeness of a woman, fair and comely, clothed in white raiment, who called to me and said: "O Socrates, the third day hence to Phthia shalt thou go."

CRITO. What a singular dream, Socrates!

SOCRATES. There can be no doubt about the meaning, Crito, I think.

CRITO. Yes; the meaning is only too clear. But, Oh! my beloved Socrates, let me entreat you once more to take my advice and escape. For if you die I shall not only lose a friend who can never be replaced, but there is another evil: people who do not know you and me will believe that I might have saved you if I had been willing to give money, but that I did not care. Now, can there be a worse disgrace than this—that I should be thought to value money more than the life of a friend? For the many will not be persuaded that I wanted you to escape, and that you refused.

SOCRATES. But why, my dear Crito, should we care about the opinion of the many? Good men, and they are the only persons who are worth considering, will think of these things truly as they happened.

CRITO. But do you see, Socrates, that the opinion of the many must be regarded, as is evident in your own case, because they can do the very greatest evil to any one who has lost their good opinion.

SOCRATES. I only wish, Crito, that they could; for then they could also do the greatest good, and that would be well. But the truth is, that they can do neither good nor evil: they can not make a man wise or make him foolish; and whatever they do is the result of chance.

CRITO. Well, I will not dispute about that; but please to tell me, Socrates, whether you are not acting out of regard to me and your other friends: are you not afraid that if you escape hence we may get into trouble with the informers for having stolen you away, and lose either the whole or a great part of our property; or that even a worse evil may happen to us? Now, if this is your fear, be at ease; for in order to save you we ought surely to run this, or even a greater risk; be persuaded, then, and do as I say.

SOCRATES. Yes, Crito, that is one fear which you mention, but by no means the only one.

CRITO. Fear not. There are persons who at no great cost are willing to save you and bring you out of prison; and as for the informers, you may observe that they are far from being exorbitant in their demands; a little money will satisfy them. My means, which, as I am sure, are ample, are at your service, and if you have a scruple about spending all mine, here are strangers who will give you the use of theirs; and one of them, Simmias the Theban, has brought a sum of money for this very purpose; and Cebes and many others are willing to spend their money too. I say therefore, do not on that account hesitate about making your escape, and do not say, as you did in the court, that you will have a difficulty in knowing what to do with yourself if you escape. For men will love you in other places to which you may go, and not in Athens only; there are friends of mine in Thessaly, if you like to go to them, who will value and protect you, and no Thessalian will give you any trouble. Nor can I think that you are justified, Socrates, in betraying your own life when you might be saved; this is playing into the hands of your enemies and destroyers; and moreover I should say that you were betraying your children; for you might bring them up and educate them; instead of which you go away and leave them, and they will have to take their chance; and if they do not meet with the usual fate of orphans, there will be small thanks to you. No man should bring children into the world who is unwilling to per-severe to the end in their nurture and education. But you are choosing the easier part, as I think, not the better and manlier, which would rather have become one who professes virtue in all his actions, like yourself. And indeed, I am ashamed not only of you, but of us who are your friends, when I reflect that this entire business of yours will be attributed to our want of courage. The trial need never have come on, or might have been brought to another issue; and the end of all, which is the crowning absurdity, will seem to have been permitted by us, through cowardice and baseness, who might have saved you, as you might have saved yourself, if we had been good for anything (for there was no difficulty in escaping); and we did not see how disgrace-ful, Socrates, and also miserable all this will be to us as well as to you. Make your mind up then, or rather have your mind already made up, for the time of deliberation is over, and there is only one thing to be done, which must be done, if at all, this very night, and which any delay will render all but im-possible; I beseech you therefore, Socrates, to be persuaded by me, and to do as I say.

SOCRATES. Dear Crito, your zeal is invaluable, if a right one; but if wrong, the greater the zeal the greater the evil; and therefore we ought to consider whether these things shall be done or not. For I am and always have been one of those natures who must be guided by reason, whatever the reason may be which upon reflection appears to me to be the best; and now that this fortune has come upon me, I can not put away the reasons which I have before given: the principles which I have hitherto honored and revered I still honor, and unless we can find other and better principles on the instant, I am certain not to agree with you; no, not even if the power of the multitude could inflict many more imprisonments, confiscations, deaths, frightening us like children with hobgoblin terrors. But what will be the fairest way of considering the question? Shall I return to your old argument about the opinions of men? some of which are to be regarded, and others, as we were saying, are not to be regarded. Now were we right in maintaining this before I was condemned? And has the argument which was once good now proved to be talk for the sake of talking;—in fact an amusement only, and altogether vanity? That is what I want to consider with your help, Crito:—whether, under my present circumstances, the argument appears to be in any way different or not; and is to be allowed by me or disallowed. That argument, which, as I believe, is maintained by many who assume to be authorities, was to the effect, as I was saying, that the opinions of some men are to be regarded, and of other men not to be regarded. Now you, Crito, are a dis-interested person who are not going to die to-morrow—at least, there is no human probability of this, and you are therefore not liable to be deceived by the circumstances in which you are placed. Tell me then, whether I am right in saying that some opinions, and the opinions of some men only, are to be valued, and other opinions, and the opinions of other men, are not to be valued. I ask you whether I was right in maintaining this?

CRITO. Certainly.

SOCRATES. The good are to be regarded, and not the bad?

CRITO. Yes.

SOCRATES. And the opinions of the wise are good, and the opinions of the unwise are evil?

CRITO. Certainly.

SOCRATES. And what was said about another matter? Was the disciple in gym-nastics supposed to attend to the praise and blame and opinion of every man, or of one man only—his physician or trainer, whoever that was?

CRITO. Of one man only.

SOCRATES. And he ought to fear the censure and welcome the praise of that one only, and not of the many?

CRITO. That is clear.

SOCRATES. And he ought to live and train, and eat and drink in the way which seems good to his single master who has understanding, rather than accord-ing to the opinion of all other men put together?

CRITO. True.

SOCRATES. And if he disobeys and disregards the opinion and approval of the one, and regards the opinion of the many who have no understanding, will he not suffer evil?

CRITO. Certainly he will.

SOCRATES. And what will the evil be, whither tending and what affecting, in the disobedient person?

CRITO. Clearly, affecting the body; that is what is destroyed by the evil.

SOCRATES. Very good; and is not this true, Crito, of other things which we need not separately enumerate? In the matter of just and unjust, fair and foul, good and evil, which are the subjects of our present consultation, ought we to follow the opinion of the many and to fear them; or the opinion of the one man who has understanding, and whom we ought to fear and reverence more than all the rest of the world: and whom deserting we shall destroy and injure that principle in us which may be assumed to be improved by justice and deteriorated by injustice;—is there not such a principle?

CRITO. Certainly there is, Socrates.

SOCRATES. Take a parallel instance:—if, acting under the advice of men who have no understanding, we destroy that which is improvable by health and deteriorated by disease—when that has been destroyed, I say, would life be worth having? And that is—the body?

CRITO. Yes.

SOCRATES. Could we live, having an evil and corrupted body?

CRITO. Certainly not.

SOCRATES. And will life be worth having, if that higher part of man be depraved, which is improved by justice and deteriorated by injustice? Do we suppose that principle, whatever it may be in man, which has to do with justice and injustice, to be inferior to the body?

CRITO. Certainly not.

SOCRATES. More honored, then?

CRITO. Far more honored.

SOCRATES. Then, my friend, we must not regard what the many say of us: but what he, the one man who has understanding of just and unjust, will say, and what the truth will say. And therefore you begin in error when you suggest that we should regard the opinion of the many about just and unjust, good and evil, honorable and dishonorable.—Well, some one will say, "but the many can kill us."

CRITO. Yes, Socrates; that will clearly be the answer.

SOCRATES. That is true: but still I find with surprise that the old argument is, as I conceive, unshaken as ever. And I should like to know whether I may say the same of another proposition—that not life, but a good life, is to be chiefly valued?

CRITO. Yes, that also remains.

SOCRATES. And a good life is equivalent to a just and honorable one—that holds also?

CRITO. Yes, that holds.

SOCRATES. From these premises I proceed to argue the question whether I ought or ought not to try and escape without the consent of the Athenians: and if I am clearly right in escaping, then I will make the attempt; but if not, I will abstain. The other considerations which you mention, of money and loss of character and the duty of educating children, are, as I fear, only the doctrines of the multitude, who would be as ready to call people to life, if they were able, as they are to put them to death—and with as little reason. But now, since the argument has thus far prevailed, the only question which remains to be considered is, whether we shall do rightly either in escaping or in suffering others to aid in our escape and paying them in money and thanks, or whether we shall not do rightly; and if the latter, then death or any other calamity which may ensue on my remaining here must not be allowed to enter into the calculation.

CRITO. I think that you are right, Socrates; how then shall we proceed?

SOCRATES. Let us consider the matter together, and do you either refute me if you can, and I will be convinced, or else cease, my dear friend, from repeating to me that I ought to escape against the wishes of the Athenians: for I am extremely desirous to be persuaded by you, but not against my own better judgment. And now please to consider my first position, and do your best to answer me.

CRITO. I will do my best.

SOCRATES. Are we to say that we are never intentionally to do wrong, or that in one way we ought and in another way we ought not to do wrong, or is doing wrong always evil and dishonorable, as I was just now saying, and as has been already acknowledged by us? Are all our former admissions which were made within a few days to be thrown away? And have we, at our age, been earnestly discoursing with one another all our life long only to discover that we are no better than children? Or are we to rest assured, in spite of the opinion of the many, and in spite of consequences whether better or worse, of the truth of what was then said, that injustice is always an evil and dishonor to him who acts unjustly? Shall we affirm that?

CRITO. Yes.

SOCRATES. Then we must do no wrong?

CRITO. Certainly not.

SOCRATES. Nor when injured injure in return, as the many imagine; for we must injure no one at all?

CRITO. Clearly not.

SOCRATES. Again, Crito, may we do evil?

CRITO. Surely not, Socrates.

SOCRATES. And what of doing evil in return for evil, which is the morality of the many—is that just or not?

CRITO. Not just.

SOCRATES. For doing evil to another is the same as injuring him?

CRITO. Very true.

SOCRATES. Then we ought not to retaliate or render evil for evil to any one, whatever evil we may have suffered from him. But I would have you consider, Crito, whether you really mean what you are saying. For this opinion has never been held, and never will be held, by any considerable number of persons; and those who are agreed and those who are not agreed upon this point have no common ground, and can only despise one another when they see how widely they differ. Tell me, then, whether you agree with and assent to my first principle, that neither injury nor retaliation nor warding off evil by evil is ever right. And shall that be the premiss of our argument? Or do you decline and dissent from this? For this has been of old and is still my opinion; but, if you are of another opinion, let me hear what you have to say. If, however, you remain of the same mind as formerly, I will proceed to the next step.

CRITO. You may proceed, for I have not changed my mind.

SOCRATES. Then I will proceed to the next step, which may be put in the form of a question:—Ought a man to do what he admits to be right, or ought he to betray the right?

CRITO. He ought to do what he thinks right.

SOCRATES. But if this is true, what is the application? In leaving the prison against the will of the Athenians, do I wrong any? or rather do I not wrong those whom I ought least to wrong? Do I not desert the principles which were acknowledged by us to be just? What do you say?

CRITO. I can not tell, Socrates; for I do not know.

SOCRATES. Then consider the matter in this way:—Imagine that I am about to play truant (you may call the proceeding by any name which you like), and the laws and the government come and interrogate me: "Tell us, Socrates," they say; "what are you about? are you going by an act of yours to overturn us—the laws and the whole state, as far as in you lies? Do you imagine that a state can subsist and not be overthrown, in which the decisions of law have no power, but are set aside and overthrown by individuals?" What will be our answer, Crito, to these and the like words? Any one, and especially a clever rhetorician, will have a good deal to urge about the evil of setting aside the law which requires a sentence to be carried out; and we might reply, "Yes; but the state has injured us and given an unjust sentence." Suppose I say that?

CRITO. Very good, Socrates.

SOCRATES. "And was that our agreement with you?" the law would say; "or were you to abide by the sentence of the state?" And if I were to express astonishment at their saying this, the law would probably add: "Answer, Socrates, instead of opening your eyes: you are in the habit of asking and answering questions. Tell us what complaint you have to make against us which justifies you in attempting to destroy us and the state? In the first place did we not bring you into existence? Your father married your mother by our aid and begat you. Say whether you have any objection to urge against those of us who regulate marriage?" None, I should reply. "Or against those of us who regulate the system of nurture and education of children in which you were trained? Were not the laws, who have the charge of this, right in commanding your father to train you in music and gymnastic?" Right, I should reply. "Well then, since you were brought into the world and nurtured and educated by us, can you deny in the first place that you are our child and slave, as your fathers were before you? And if this is true you are not on equal terms with us; nor can you think that you have a right to do to us what we are doing to you. Would you have any right to strike or revile or do any other evil to a father or to your master, if you had one, when you have been struck or reviled by him, or received some other evil at his hands?—you would not say this? And because we think right to destroy you, do you think that you have any right to destroy us in return, and your country as far as in you lies? And will you, O professor of true virtue, say that you are justified in this? Has a philosopher like you failed to discover that our country is more to be valued and higher and holier far than mother or father or any ancestor, and more to be regarded in the eyes of the gods and of men of understanding? also to be soothed, and gently and reverently entreated when angry, even more than a father, and if not persuaded, obeyed? And when we are punished by her, whether with imprisonment or stripes, the punishment is to be endured in silence; and if she lead us to wounds or death in battle, thither we follow as is right; neither may any one yield or retreat or leave his rank, but whether in battle or in a court of law, or in any other place, he must do what his city and his country order him; or he must change their view of what is just: and if he may do no violence to his father or mother, much less may he do violence to his country." What answer shall we make to this, Crito? Do the laws speak truly, or do they not?

CRITO. I think that they do.

SOCRATES. Then the laws will say: "Consider, Socrates, if this is true, that in your present attempt you are going to do us wrong. For, after having brought you into the world, and nurtured and educated you, and given you and every other citizen a share in every good that we had to give, we further proclaim and give the right to every Athenian, that if he does not like us when he has come of age and has seen the ways of the city, and made our acquaintance, he may go where he pleases and take his goods with him; and none of us laws will forbid him or interfere with him. Any of you who does not like us and the city, and who wants to go to a colony or to any other city, may go where he likes, and take his goods with him. But he who has experience of the manner in which we order justice and administer the state, and still remains, has entered into an implied contract that he will do as we command him. And he who disobeys us is, as we maintain, thrice wrong; first, because in disobeying us he is disobeying his parents; secondly, because we are the authors of his education; thirdly, because he has made an agreement with us that he will duly obey our commands; and he neither obeys them nor convinces us that our commands are wrong; and we do not rudely impose them, but give them the alternative of obeying or convincing us;—that is what we offer, and he does neither. These are the sort of accusations to which, as we were saying, you, Socrates, will be exposed if you accomplish your intentions; you, above all other Athenians." Suppose I ask, why is this? they will justly retort upon me that I above all other men have acknowledged the agreement. "There is clear proof," they will say, "Socrates, that we and the city were not displeasing to you. Of all Athenians you have been the most constant resident in the city, which, as you never leave, you may be supposed to love. For you never went out of the city either to see the games, except once when you went to the Isthmus, or to any other place unless when you were on military service; nor did you travel as other men do. Nor had you any curiosity to know other states or their laws: your affections did not go beyond us and our state; we were your special favorites, and you acquiesced in our government of you; and this is the state in which you begat your children, which is proof of your satisfaction. Moreover, you might, if you had liked, have fixed the penalty at banishment in the course of the trial—the state which refuses to let you go now would have let you go then. But you pretended that you preferred death to exile, and that you were not grieved at death. And now you have forgotten these fine sentiments, and pay no respect to us the laws, of whom you are the destroyer; and are doing what only a miserable slave would do, running away and turning your back upon the compacts and agreements which you made as a citizen. And first of all answer this very question: Are we right in saying that you agreed to be governed according to us in deed, and not in word only? Is that true or not?" How shall we answer that, Crito? Must we not agree?

CRITO. There is no help, Socrates.

SOCRATES. Then will they not say: "You, Socrates, are breaking the covenants and agreements which you made with us at your leisure, not in any haste or under any compulsion or deception, but having had seventy years to think of them, during which time you were at liberty to leave the city, if we were not to your mind, or if our covenants appeared to you to be unfair. You had your choice, and might have gone either to Lacedaemon or Crete, which you often praise for their good government, or to some other Hellenic or foreign state. Whereas you, above all other Athenians, seemed to be so fond of the state, or, in other words, of us her laws (for who would like a state that has no laws), that you never stirred out of her; the halt, the blind, the maimed were not more stationary in her than you were. And now you run away and forsake your agreements. Not so, Socrates, if you will take our advice; do not make yourself ridiculous by escaping out of the city.

"For just consider, if you transgress and err in this sort of way, what good will you do either to yourself or to your friends? That your friends will be driven into exile and deprived of citizenship, or will lose their property, is tolerably certain; and you yourself, if you fly to one of the neighboring cities, as, for example, Thebes or Megara, both of which are well-governed cities, will come to them as an enemy, Socrates, and their government will be against you, and all patriotic citizens will cast an evil eye upon you as a subverter of the laws, and you will confirm in the minds of the judges the justice of their own condemnation of you. For he who is a corruptor of the laws is more than likely to be corruptor of the young and foolish portion of mankind. Will you then flee from well-ordered cities and virtuous men? and is existence worth having on these terms? Or will you go to them without shame, and talk to them, Socrates? And what will you say to them? What you say here about virtue and justice and institutions and laws being the best things among men. Would that be decent of you? Surely not. But if you go away from well-governed states to Crito's friends in Thessaly, where there is a great disorder and license, they will be charmed to have the tale of your escape from prison, set off with ludicrous particulars of the manner in which you were wrapped in a goatskin or some other disguise, and metamorphosed as the fashion of runaways is—that is very likely; but will there be no one to remind you that in your old age you violated the most sacred laws from a miserable desire of a little more life. Perhaps not, if you keep them in a good temper; but if they are out of temper you will hear many degrading things; *you will live, but how?*—as the flatterer of all men, and the servant of all men; and doing what?—eating and drinking in Thessaly, having gone abroad in order that you may get a dinner. And where will be your fine sentiments about justice and virtue then? Say that you wish to live for the sake of your *children*, that you may bring them up and educate them—will you take them into Thessaly and deprive them of Athenian citizenship? Is that the benefit which you would confer upon them? Or are you under the impression that they will be better cared for and educated here if you are still alive, although absent from them; for that your friends will take care of them? Do you fancy that if you are an inhabitant of Thessaly they will take care of them, and if you are an inhabitant of the other world they will not take care of them? Nay; but if they who call themselves friends are truly friends, they surely will.

"Listen, then, Socrates, to us who have brought you up. Think not of life and children first, and of justice afterwards, but of justice first, that you may be justified before the princes of the world below. For neither will you nor any that belong to you be happier or holier or juster in this life, or happier in another, if you do as Crito bids. Now you depart in innocence, a sufferer and not a doer of evil; a victim, not of the laws, but of men. But if you go forth, returning evil for evil, and injury for injury, breaking the covenants and agreements which you have made with us, and wronging those whom you ought least to wrong, that is to say, yourself, your friends, your country, and us, we shall be angry with you while you live, and our brethren, the laws in the world below, will receive you as an enemy; for they will know that you have done your best to destroy us. Listen, then, to us and not to Crito."

This is the voice which I seem to hear murmuring in my ears like the sound of the flute in the ears of the mystic; that voice, I say, is humming in my ears, and prevents me from hearing any other. And I know that anything more which you may say will be vain. Yet speak, if you have anything to say.

CRITO. I have nothing to say, Socrates.

SOCRATES. Then let me follow the intimations of the will of God.

Government

The passages in this section deal with a problem that began when men first agreed to surrender certain of their personal liberties for the sake of mutual protection and betterment. It is the problem of the individual and his relation to both a national and an international organization. The section begins with the personal discovery made by Fiorello H. La Guardia, who was a congressman, later a mayor of New York City, and still later an administrator of postwar relief overseas. He tells in his account how he first became aware of the importance of the state even to a boy living in an army post in Arizona. The selections which follow range from the distant past to the present. The first three selections (by an early Hebrew, a nineteenth-century Englishman, and a twentieth-century American) present widely varying points of view on the relation of the individual to his national government. The concluding selection in this section (by a federal judge) takes up the problem of international law and organization.

Fiorello H. La Guardia

MY FIRST
ENCOUNTERS WITH POLITICS

A personal discovery

What I saw and heard and learned in my boyhood days in Arizona made lasting impressions on me. Many of the things on which I have such strong feelings—feelings which some of my opponents have regarded as unreasonable obsessions—were first impressed on my mind during those early days, and the knowledge I acquired then never left me. On some of those things I believe I am so right in my attitude that I remain uncompromising.

For instance, there is the professional politician. Though I have been in politics for well over forty years, I loathe the professional politician. I have never been a regular. I have fought political machines and party politics at every opportunity. This attitude had its origin in the loudly dressed, slick and sly Indian agents, political appointees, I saw come into Arizona. The first time I ever heard the word politician was at Fort Huachuca, when I was still a small child. The word was applied to those Indian agents. I learned afterwards that they got the jobs because they were small-fry ward heelers. I saw hungry Indians, and the little Indian kids watched us while we munched a Kansas apple or ate a cookie Mother baked. I knew, even as a child, that the government in Washington provided food for all those Indians, but that the "politicians" sold the rations to miners and even to general stores, robbing the Indians of the food the government provided for them. That was my first contact with "politicians."

I had my first experience with a lobby when I was about twelve. My father received a letter from someone in Washington stating that the pay of band leaders could be increased to $100 a month. The pay was then $60 a month. The letter also stated that band leaders could become commissioned officers. I can see the gleam in Dad's eye to this day as he fancied himself adorned with shoulder straps. It all seemed so easy; just sign the agreement to pay one month's salary when the bill became the law, and no further obligation except to send $50 for necessary expenses.

Even as a kid I could not understand this. Why the expenses? There were hints in the letter that it was necessary to see certain Representatives and Senators, and that there were disbursements to be met. It was rather crude. But this technique of the 'nineties didn't differ so much from the technique of our own 'forties. I don't know why, but I felt instinctively that it was wrong. And Mother was on my side. I figured it out that if the men in the various regiments at our post sent in this money, it would amount to $2,250. That was a lot of money in those days. "It's a fake, a swindle," I shouted, and when I ran out of adjectives in denouncing the scheme to my father, I resorted to what to me has always been the most odious thing you could say about people: "They're a bunch of politicians." Father, a musician, who never bothered with politics, was soon talked out of joining the plan. The band leaders of the Army are still waiting for those shoulder straps some of them sent their money to get. . . .

. . . It was during my boyhood in Arizona that I first learned about corrupt local government, and I got my political education from Pulitzer's New York *World*. We had two newspapers in Prescott, the *Journal Miner* and the Prescott *Courier*. These were typical Bret Harte Western newspapers, devoted mostly to local news. When the Sunday edition of the New York *World* arrived in Prescott on the following Friday or Saturday, I would rush to Ross's drugstore where it was on display. There I had looked at the first funny sections I had ever seen, featuring the Yellow Kid. From that comic strip came the expression "yellow journalism." I have enjoyed the comics ever since.

When I got home with the Sunday *World*, I would carefully read every word of the *World*'s fight against the corrupt Tammany machine in New York. That was the period of the lurid disclosures made by the Lexow investigation of corruption in the Police Department that extended throughout the political structure of the city. The papers then were filled with stories of startling crookedness on the part of the police and the politicians in New York. Unlike boys who grew up in the city and who hear from childhood about such things as graft and corruption, the amazing disclosures hit me like a shock. I could not understand how the people of the greatest city in the country could put up with the vice and crime that existed there. A resentment against Tammany was created in me at that time, which I admit is to this day almost an obsession. But I did not become cynical or lose faith in government. I was certain that good people could eliminate bad people from public office. But as I grew older, my hatred of corrupt politicians and my feeling against dishonest and inefficient government increased with the years in proportion with my experience of it.

When I went to live in New York again after my return from Europe in 1906, Tammany was once more all-powerful. It was the era of "honest graft." When

I had to choose a political party, my choice was easy. I joined the Republican Party. I was young and innocent. A party in the minority cannot help being good and pure. That seemed the only avenue I could choose at the time in order to carry out my boyhood dreams of going to work against corrupt government.

There was, of course, great excitement at Whipple Barracks in Prescott when the news reached us that the U. S. battleship *Maine* had been blown up in the harbor of Havana, Cuba, on the fifteenth of February 1898. The Postal Telegraph operator in Prescott pasted up Associated Press bulletins on the *Maine* disaster as soon as they came in, and along with the other children of Army men, as well as the parents, I watched and waited eagerly for the latest news. We expected war momentarily, especially after the news came that two hundred and fifty American lives had been lost.

Within about ten days, orders came for our regiment to get itself ready for war. Inventories were taken. The equipment of some other regiments and of National Guard units was not up to date, but our regiment had the modern Krag-Jörgensen rifles. Some of our noncommissioned officers had seen service in the Civil War.

As the weeks passed and there was still no declaration of war, there was a feeling in our military circles that President McKinley was hesitating too long. But it finally came on April twenty-fifth, and our regiment was soon sent to Jefferson Barracks, St. Louis, Missouri. It remained there for a few days and then went into camp at Mobile, Alabama, but the families of the officers and enlisted men remained in quarters at Jefferson Barracks.

Though I was only fifteen years old, I was restless and wanted to join the Army. My age, and the fact that I was short and under the required weight, made that impossible. But I persuaded the St. Louis *Post-Dispatch* to pay my fare to the camp at Mobile where my father was stationed. I did a couple of articles for the *Post-Dispatch* from the camp.

As an Army child I was familiar with drill and other training courses. I noticed at that time that it was very difficult to train Army officers quickly, though it was easy to train a large body of men in a hurry once you had the officers to do the job. This knowledge was very useful to me later when I was a legislator, and particularly when I became a member of the House Committee on Military Affairs. I also noticed at that time that the Medical Corps was both inefficient and unsufficient in the Spanish-American War. During the first world war the Medical Corps brought its technique and efficiency almost to perfection. In the second world war it surpassed anything that had been attained previously in this and, perhaps, in any other country. But the government's record as a whole during the Spanish-American War was not up to the heroism of our men who took part in that war.

My particular Spanish-American War hero was "Bucky" O'Neil. I remember that he came to our school soon after the declaration of war and told us what that declaration meant, and what war meant. He expressed the opinion that when we won this war, no other nation would ever again attempt to dominate territory in the Western Hemisphere. When Arizona provided a troop for

Colonel Theodore Roosevelt's Rough Riders, "Bucky" O'Neil became a member of that troop. I felt he should have commanded it. He was killed in action during the famous charge on San Juan Hill.

One of the worst scandals of our entire military history occurred during this short Spanish-American War and made a lasting impression upon me, for my father was one of its victims. Corrupt contractors supplied the Army with diseased beef. My father became so ill as a result of eating some of this diseased beef that he had to be discharged from the service on account of disability. Though we did not know it then, he had only a few years to live because of the work of crooked Army contractors.

That experience never left my mind. When I became a Congressman during World War I, the first measure I introduced in the House was a bill providing the death penalty for contractors who supplied defective food or other supplies and equipment in time of war, and a heavy jail sentence, if they sold such stuff in time of peace. I introduced that measure on April 3, 1917, a few days before Congress declared war on Germany. It was referred to the Committee on Judiciary, where it was allowed to languish. But I still think it is a good idea. It might prevent other families from losing their fathers.

After Father's discharge from the Army, our family returned to New York City, where we renewed old acquaintances. Then the family went to Trieste, to live with my mother's family. It was while we were in Trieste that my father died in 1901, a victim of condemned Army meat.

In these chapters the ancient scribe outlines the more general regulations ordained by God for the conduct of the Israelites. Though bound by the fairly rigid code of the patriarchal system, the people still recognize God as the ultimate power in their government. That they do not necessarily act according to His desires is abundantly evident.

The Bible

SELECTIONS FROM EXODUS

In the third month, when the children of Israel were gone forth out of the land of Egypt, the same day came they into the wilderness of Sinai. For they were departed from Rephidim, and were come to the desert of Sinai, and had pitched in the wilderness; and there Israel camped before the mount.

And Moses went up unto God, and the Lord called unto him out of the mountain, saying, Thus shalt thou say to the house of Jacob, and tell the children of Israel;

Ye have seen what I did unto the Egyptians, and how I bare you on eagles' wings, and brought you unto myself.

Now therefore, if ye will obey my voice indeed, and keep my covenant, then ye shall be a peculiar treasure unto me above all people: for all the earth is mine:

And ye shall be unto me a kingdom of priests, and an holy nation. These are the words which thou shalt speak unto the children of Israel.

And Moses came and called for the elders of the people, and laid before their faces all these words which the Lord commanded him.

And all the people answered together, and said, All that the Lord hath spoken we will do. And Moses returned the words of the people unto the Lord.

And the Lord said unto Moses, Lo, I come unto thee in a thick cloud, that the people may hear when I speak with thee, and believe thee for ever. And Moses told the words of the people unto the Lord.

And the Lord said unto Moses, Go unto the people, and sanctify them to day and to morrow, and let them wash their clothes.

And be ready against the third day: for the third day the Lord will come down in the sight of all the people upon mount Sinai.

And thou shalt set bounds unto the people round about, saying, Take heed to yourselves, that ye go not up into the mount, or touch the border of it: whosoever toucheth the mount shall be surely put to death:

There shall not an hand touch it, but he shall surely be stoned, or shot through; whether it be beast or man, it shall not live: when the trumpet soundeth long, they shall come up to the mount.

And Moses went down from the mount unto the people, and sanctified the people; and they washed their clothes.

And he said unto the people, Be ready against the third day: come not at your wives.

And it came to pass on the third day in the morning, that there were thunders and lightnings, and a thick cloud upon the mount, and the voice of the trumpet exceeding loud; so that all the people that was in the camp trembled.

And Moses brought forth the people out of the camp to meet with God; and they stood at the nether part of the mount.

And mount Sinai was altogether on a smoke, because the Lord descended upon it in fire: and the smoke thereof ascended as the smoke of a furnace, and the whole mount quaked greatly.

And when the voice of the trumpet sounded long, and waxed louder and louder, Moses spake, and God answered him by a voice.

And the Lord came down upon mount Sinai, on the top of the mount: and the Lord called Moses up to the top of the mount; and Moses went up.

And the Lord said unto Moses, Go down, charge the people, lest they break through unto the Lord to gaze, and many of them perish.

And let the priests also, which come near to the Lord, sanctify themselves, lest the Lord break forth upon them.

And Moses said unto the Lord, The people cannot come up to mount Sinai: for thou chargedst us, saying, Set bounds about the mount, and sanctify it.

And the Lord said unto him, Away, get thee down, and thou shalt come up, thou, and Aaron with thee: but let not the priests and the people break through to come up unto the Lord, lest he break forth upon them.

So Moses went down unto the people, and spake unto them.—Exodus 19

And God spake all these words, saying,

I am the Lord thy God, which have brought thee out of the land of Egypt, out of the house of bondage.

Thou shalt have no other gods before me.

Thou shalt not make unto thee any graven image, or any likeness of any thing that is in heaven above, or that is in the earth beneath, or that is in the water under the earth:

Thou shalt not bow down thyself to them, nor serve them: for I the Lord thy God am a jealous God, visiting the iniquity of the fathers upon the children unto the third and fourth generation of them that hate me;

And shewing mercy unto thousands of them that love me, and keep my commandments.

Thou shalt not take the name of the Lord thy God in vain; for the Lord will not hold him guiltless that taketh his name in vain.

Remember the sabbath day, to keep it holy.

Six days shalt thou labour, and do all thy work:

But the seventh day is the sabbath of the Lord thy God: in it thou shalt not do any work, thou, nor thy son, nor thy daughter, thy manservant, nor thy maidservant, nor thy cattle, nor thy stranger that is within thy gates:

For in six days the Lord made heaven and earth, the sea, and all that in them is, and rested the seventh day: wherefore the Lord blessed the sabbath day, and hallowed it.

Honour thy father and thy mother: that thy days may be long upon the land which the Lord thy God giveth thee.

Thou shalt not kill.

Thou shalt not commit adultery.

Thou shalt not steal.

Thou shalt not bear false witness against thy neighbour.

Thou shalt not covet thy neighbour's house, thou shalt not covet thy neighbour's wife, nor his manservant, nor his maidservant, nor his ox, nor his ass, nor any thing that is thy neighbour's.

And all the people saw the thunderings, and the lightnings, and the noise of the trumpet, and the mountain smoking: and when the people saw it, they removed, and stood afar off.

And they said unto Moses, Speak thou with us, and we will hear: but let not God speak with us, lest we die.

And Moses said unto the people, Fear not: for God is come to prove you, and that his fear may be before your faces, that ye sin not.

And the people stood afar off, and Moses drew near unto the thick darkness where God was.—Exodus 20:1-21

And when the people saw that Moses delayed to come down out of the mount, the people gathered themselves together unto Aaron, and said unto him, Up, make us gods, which shall go before us; for as for this Moses, the man that brought us up out of the land of Egypt, we wot not what is become of him.

And Aaron said unto them, Break off the golden earrings, which are in the ears of your wives, of your sons, and of your daughters, and bring them unto me.

And all the people brake off the golden earrings which were in their ears, and brought them unto Aaron.

And he received them at their hand, and fashioned it with a graving tool, after he had made it a molten calf: and they said, These be thy gods, O Israel, which brought thee up out of the land of Egypt.

And when Aaron saw it, he built an altar before it; and Aaron made proclamation, and said, To morrow is a feast to the Lord.

And they rose up early on the morrow, and offered burnt offerings, and brought peace offerings; and the people sat down to eat and to drink, and rose up to play.

And the Lord said unto Moses, Go, get thee down: for thy people, which thou broughtest out of the land of Egypt, have corrupted themselves:

They have turned aside quickly out of the way which I commanded them: they have made them a molten calf, and have worshipped it, and have sacrificed thereunto, and said, These be thy gods, O Israel, which have brought thee up out of the land of Egypt.

And the Lord said unto Moses, I have seen this people, and, behold, it is a stiffnecked people:

Now therefore let me alone, that my wrath may wax hot against them, and that I may consume them: and I will make of thee a great nation.

And Moses besought the Lord his God, and said, Lord why doth thy wrath wax hot against thy people, which thou hast brought forth out of the land of Egypt with great power, and with a mighty hand?

Wherefore should the Egyptians speak, and say, For mischief did he bring them out, to slay them in the mountains, and to consume them from the face of the earth? Turn from thy fierce wrath, and repent of this evil against thy people.

Remember Abraham, Isaac, and Israel, thy servants, to whom thou swarest by thine own self, and saidst unto them, I will multiply your seed as the stars of heaven, and all this land that I have spoken of will I give unto your seed, and they shall inherit it for ever.

And the Lord repented of the evil which he thought to do unto his people.

And Moses turned, and went down from the mount, and the two tables of testimony were in his hand: the tables were written on both their sides; on the one side and on the other were they written.

And the tables were the work of God, and the writing was the writing of God, graven upon the tables.

And when Joshua heard the noise of the people as they shouted, he said unto Moses, There is a noise of war in the camp.

And he said, It is not the voice of them that shout for mastery, neither is it the voice of them that cry for being overcome: but the noise of them that sing do I hear.

And it came to pass, as soon as he came nigh unto the camp, that he saw the calf, and the dancing: and Moses' anger waxed hot, and he cast the tables out of his hands, and brake them beneath the mount.

And he took the calf which they had made, and burnt it in the fire, and ground it to powder, and strawed it upon the water, and made the children of Israel drink of it.

And Moses said unto Aaron, What did this people unto thee, that thou hast brought so great a sin upon them?

And Aaron said, Let not the anger of my lord wax hot: thou knowest the people, that they are set on mischief.

For they said unto me, Make us gods, which shall go before us: for as for this Moses, the man that brought us up out of the land of Egypt, we wot not what is become of him.

And I said unto them, Whosoever hath any gold, let them break it off. So they gave it me: then I cast it into the fire, and there came out this calf.

And when Moses saw that the people were naked; (for Aaron had made them naked unto their shame among their enemies:)

Then Moses stood in the gate of the camp, and said, Who is on the Lord's side? let him come unto me. And all the sons of Levi gathered themselves together unto him.

And he said unto them, Thus saith the Lord God of Israel, Put every man his sword by his side, and go in and out from gate to gate throughout the camp, and slay every man his brother, and every man his companion, and every man his neighbour.

And the children of Levi did according to the word of Moses: and there fell of the people that day about three thousand men.

For Moses had said, Consecrate yourselves to day to the Lord, even every man upon his son and upon his brother; that he may bestow upon you a blessing this day.

And it came to pass on the morrow, that Moses said unto the people, Ye have sinned a great sin: and now I will go up unto the Lord; peradventure I shall make an atonement for your sin.

And Moses returned unto the Lord, and said, Oh, this people have sinned a great sin, and have made them gods of gold.

Yet now, if thou wilt forgive their sin—; and if not, blot me, I pray thee, out of thy book which thou hast written.

And the Lord said unto Moses, Whosoever hath sinned against me, him will I blot out of my book.

Therefore now go, lead the people unto the place of which I have spoken unto thee: behold, mine Angel shall go before thee: nevertheless in the day when I visit I will visit their sin upon them.

And the Lord plagued the people, because they made the calf, which Aaron made.—Exodus 32

John Stuart Mill

THE LIMITS OF GOVERNMENT INTERFERENCE

I have reserved for the last place [in this discussion] a large class of questions respecting the limits of government interference. . . . These are cases in which the reasons against interference do not turn upon the principle of liberty: the question is not about restraining the actions of individuals, but about helping them: it is asked whether the government should do, or cause to be done, something for their benefit. instead of leaving it to be done by themselves, individually, or in voluntary combination.

The objections to government interference, when it is not such as to involve infringement of liberty, may be of three kinds.

The first is, when the thing to be done is likely to be better done by individuals than by the government. Speaking generally, there is no one so fit to conduct any business, or to determine how or by whom it shall be conducted, as those who are personally interested in it. This principle condemns the interferences, once so common, of the legislature, or the officers of government, with the ordinary processes of industry. But this part of the subject has been sufficiently enlarged upon by political economists, and is not particularly related to the principles of this Essay.

The second objection is more nearly allied to our subject. In many cases, though individuals may not do the particular thing so well, on the average, as the officers of government, it is nevertheless desirable that it should be done by them, rather than by the government, as a means to their own mental education—a mode of strengthening their active faculties, exercising their judgment, and giving them a familiar knowledge of the subjects with which they are thus left to deal. This is a principal, though not the sole, recommendation of jury trial (in cases not political); of free and popular local and municipal institutions; of the conduct of industrial and philanthropic enterprises by voluntary associations. These are not questions of liberty, and are connected with that subject only by remote tendencies; but they are questions of development. It belongs to a different occasion from the present to dwell on these things as parts of national education; as being, in truth, the peculiar training of a citizen, the practical part of the political education of a free people, taking them out of the narrow circle of personal and family selfishness, and accustoming them to the comprehension of joint interests, the management of joint concerns—habituating them to act from public or semi-public motives, and guide their conduct by aims which unite instead of isolating them from one another. Without these habits and powers, a free constitution can neither be worked nor preserved; as is exemplified by the too-often transitory nature of political freedom in countries where it does not rest upon a sufficient basis of local liberties. The management of purely local business by the localities, and of the great enterprises of industry by the union of those who voluntarily supply the pecuniary means, is further recommended by all the advantages which have been set forth in this Essay as belonging to individuality of development, and diversity of modes of action. Government operations tend to be everywhere alike. With individuals and voluntary associations, on the contrary, there are varied experiments, and endless diversity of experience. What the State can usefully do is to make itself a central depository, and active circulator and diffuser, of the experience resulting from many trials. Its business is to enable each experimentalist to benefit by the experiments of others; instead of tolerating no experiments but its own.

The third, and most cogent reason for restricting the interference of government is the great evil of adding unnecessarily to its power. Every function superadded to those already exercised by the government causes its influence over hopes and fears to be more widely diffused, and converts, more and more, the active and ambitious part of the public into hangers-on of the government, or of some party which aims at becoming the government. If the roads, the railways, the banks, the insurance offices, the great joint-stock companies, the universities, and the public charities, were all of them branches of the government; if, in addition, the municipal corporations and local boards, with all that now devolves on them, became departments of the central administration; if the employees of all these different enterprises were appointed and paid by the government, and looked to the government for every rise in life; not all the freedom of the press and popular constitution of the legislature would make this or any other country free otherwise than in name. And the evil would be greater, the more efficiently and scientifically the administrative machinery was constructed—the more skilful the arrangements for obtaining the best qualified hands and heads with which to work it. In England it has of late been proposed that all the members of the civil service of government should be selected by competitive examination, to obtain for these employments the most intelligent and instructed persons procurable; and much has been said and written for and against this proposal. One of the arguments most insisted on by its opponents, is that the occupation of a permanent official servant of the State does not hold out sufficient prospects of emolument and importance to attract the highest talents, which will always be able to find a more inviting career in the professions, or in the service of companies and other public bodies. One would not have been surprised if this argument had been used by the friends of the proposition, as an answer to its principal difficulty. Coming from the opponents it is strange enough. What is urged as an objection is the safety-valve of the proposed system. If indeed all the high talent of the country *could* be drawn into the service of the government, a proposal tending to bring about that result might well inspire uneasiness. If every part of the business of society which required organized concert, or large and comprehensive views, were in the hands of the government, and if government offices were universally filled by the ablest men, all the enlarged culture and practised intelligence in the country, except the purely speculative, would be concentrated in a numerous bureaucracy, to whom alone the rest of the community would look for all things: the multitude for direction and dictation in all they had to do; the able and aspiring for personal advancement. To be admitted into the ranks of this bureaucracy, and when admitted, to rise therein, would be the sole objects of ambition. Under this régime, not only is the outside public ill-qualified, for want of practical experience, to criticize or check the mode of operation of the bureaucracy, but even if the accidents of despotic or the natural working of popular institutions occasionally raise to the summit a ruler or rulers of reforming inclinations, no reform can be effected which is contrary to the interest of the bureaucracy. Such is the melancholy condition of the Russian empire, as shown in the accounts of those who have had sufficient opportunity of observation. The Czar himself is powerless against the bureaucratic body; he can send any one of them to Siberia, but he cannot govern without them, or against their will. On every decree of his they have a tacit veto, by merely refraining from carrying it into effect. In countries of more advanced civilization and of a more insurrectionary spirit, the public, accustomed to expect everything to be done for them by the State, or at least to do nothing for themselves without asking from the State not only leave to do it, but even how it is to be done, naturally hold the State responsible for all evil which befalls them, and when the evil exceeds their amount of patience, they rise against the government, and make what is called a revolution; whereupon somebody else, with or without legitimate authority from the nation, vaults into the seat, issues his orders to the bureaucracy, and everything goes on much as it did before; the bureaucracy being unchanged, and nobody else being capable of taking their place.

A very different spectacle is exhibited among a people accustomed to transact their own business. In France, a large part of the people, having been engaged in military service, many of whom have held at least the rank of non-commissioned officers, there are in every popular insurrection several persons competent to take the lead, and improvise some tolerable plan of action. What the French are in military affairs, the Americans are in every kind of civil business; let them be left without a government, every body of Americans is able to improvise one, and to carry on that or any other public business with a sufficient amount of intelligence, order, and decision. This is what every free people ought to be: and a people capable of this is certain to be free; it will never let itself be enslaved by any man or body of men because these are able to seize and pull the reins of the central administration. No bureaucracy can hope to make such a people as this do or undergo anything that they do not like. But where everything is done through the bureaucracy, nothing to which the bureaucracy is really adverse can be done at all. The constitution of such countries is an organization of the experience and practical ability of the nation into a disciplined body for the purpose of governing the rest; and the more perfect that organization is in itself, the more successful in drawing to itself and educating for itself the persons of greatest capacity from all ranks of the community, the more complete is the bondage of all, the members of the bureaucracy included. For the governors are as much the slaves of their organization and discipline as the governed are of the governors. A Chinese mandarin is as much the tool and creature of a despotism as the humblest cultivator. An individual Jesuit is to the utmost degree of abasement the slave of his order, though the order itself exists for the collective power and importance of its members.

It is not, also, to be forgotten, that the absorption of all the principal ability of the country into the governing body is fatal, sooner or later, to the mental activity and progressiveness of the body itself. Banded together as they are—working a system which, like all systems, necessarily proceeds in a great measure by fixed rules—the official body are under the constant temptation of sinking into indolent routine, or, if they now and then desert that mill-horse round, of rushing into some half-examined crudity which has struck the fancy of some leading member of the corps: and the sole check to these closely allied, though seemingly opposite, tendencies, the only stimulus which can keep the ability of the body itself up to a high standard, is liability to the watchful criticism of equal ability outside the body. It is indispensable, therefore, that the means should exist, independently of the government, of forming such ability, and furnishing it with the opportunities and experience necessary for a correct judgment of great practical affairs. If we would possess permanently a skilful and efficient body of functionaries—above all, a body able to originate and willing to adopt improvements; if we would not have our bureaucracy degenerate into a pedantocracy, this body must not engross all the occupations which form and cultivate the faculties required for the government of mankind.

To determine the point at which evils, so formidable to human freedom and advancement, begin, or rather at which they begin to predominate over the benefits attending the collective application of the force of society, under its recognized chiefs, for the removal of the obstacles which stand in the way of its well-being; to secure as much of the advantages of centralized power and intelligence as can be had without turning into governmental channels too great a proportion of the general activity—is one of the most difficult and complicated questions in the art of government. It is, in a great measure, a question of detail, in which many and various considerations must be kept in view, and no absolute rule can be laid down. But I believe that the practical principle in which safety resides, the ideal to be kept in view, the standard by which to test all arrangements intended for overcoming the difficulty, may be conveyed in these words: the greatest dissemination of power consistent with efficiency; but the greatest possible centralization of information, and diffusion of it from the centre. Thus, in municipal administration, there would be, as in the New England States, a very minute division among separate officers, chosen by the localities, of all business which is not better left to the persons directly interested; but besides this, there would be, in each department of local affairs, a central superintendence, forming a branch of the general government. The organ of this superintendence would concentrate, as in a focus, the variety of information and experience derived from the conduct of that branch of public business in all the localities, from everything analogous which is done in foreign countries, and from the general principles of political science. This central organ should have a right to know all that is done, and its special duty should be that of making the knowledge acquired in one place available for others. Emancipated from the petty prejudices and narrow views of a locality by its elevated position and comprehensive sphere of observation, its advice would naturally carry much authority; but its actual power, as a permanent institution, should, I conceive, be limited to compelling the local officers to obey the laws laid down for their guidance. In all things not provided for by general rules, those officers should be left to their own judgment, under responsibility to their constituents. For the violation of rules, they should be responsible to law, and the rules themselves should be laid down by the legislature; the central administrative authority only watching over their execution, and if they were not properly carried into effect, appealing, according to the nature of the case, to the tribunals to enforce the law, or to the constituencies to dismiss the functionaries who had not executed it according to its spirit. Such, in its general conception, is the central superintendence which the Poor Law Board is intended to exercise over the administrators of the Poor Rate throughout the country. Whatever powers the Board exercises beyond this limit were right and necessary in that peculiar case, for the cure of rooted habits of maladministration in matters deeply affecting not the localities merely, but the whole community; since no locality has a moral right to make itself by mismanagement a nest of pauperism, necessarily overflowing into other localities, and impairing the moral and physical condition of the whole labouring community. The powers of administrative coercion and subordinate legislation possessed by the Poor Law Board (but which, owing to the state of opinion on the subject, are very scantily exercised by them), though perfectly justifiable in a case of first-rate national interest, would be wholly out of place in the superintendence of interests purely local. But a central organ of information and instruction for all the localities would be equally valuable in all departments of administration. A government cannot have too much of the kind of activity which does not impede, but aids and stimulates, individual exertion and development. The mischief begins when, instead of calling forth the activity and powers of individuals and bodies, it substitutes its own activity for theirs; when, instead of informing, advising, and, upon occasion, denouncing, it makes them work in fetters, or bids them stand aside and does their work instead of them. The worth of a State, in the long run. is the worth of the individuals composing it; and a State which postpones the interest of *their* mental expansion and elevation to a little more of administrative skill. or of that semblance of it which practice gives. in the details of business; a State which dwarfs its men. in order that they may be more docile instruments in its hands even for beneficial purposes—will find that with small men no great thing can really be accomplished; and that the perfection of machinery to which it has sacrificed everything will in the end avail it nothing. for want of the vital power which. in order that the machine might work more smoothly, it has preferred to banish.

Franklin Delano Roosevelt

PROGRESSIVE GOVERNMENT

My friends: I count it a privilege to be invited to address the Commonwealth Club. It has stood in the life of this city and State. and it is perhaps accurate to add, the Nation. as a group of citizen leaders interested in fundamental problems of Government, and chiefly concerned with achievement of progress in Government through non-partisan means. The privilege of addressing you. therefore. in the heat of a political campaign. is great. I want to respond to your courtesy in terms consistent with your policy.

I want to speak not of politics but of Government. I want to speak not of parties, but of universal principles. They are not political, except in that larger sense in which a great American once expressed a definition of politics. that nothing in all of human life is foreign to the science of politics.

I do want to give you, however, a recollection of a long life spent for a large part in public office. Some of my conclusions and observations have been deeply accentuated in these past few weeks. I have traveled far—from Albany to the Golden Gate. I have seen many people, and heard many things, and today, when in a sense my journey has reached the half-way mark, I am glad of the opportunity to discuss with you what it all means to me.

Sometimes, my friends, particularly in years such as these, the hand of discouragement falls upon us. It seems that things are in a rut, fixed, settled, that the world has grown old and tired and very much out of joint. This is the mood of depression, of dire and weary depression.

But then we look around us in America, and everything tells us that we are wrong. America is new. It is in the process of change and development. It has the great potentialities of youth, and particularly is this true of the great West, and of this coast, and of California.

From *The Public Papers and Addresses of Franklin D. Roosevelt*, Volume I, Random House, Inc. This speech was made before the Commonwealth Club in San Francisco, during the 1932 campaign for the presidency and in the midst of a nation-wide depression.

I would not have you feel that I regard this as in any sense a new community. I have traveled in many parts of the world, but never have I felt the arresting thought of the change and development more than here, where the old, mystic East would seem to be near to us, where the currents of life and thought and commerce of the whole world meet us. This factor alone is sufficient to cause man to stop and think of the deeper meaning of things, when he stands in this community.

But more than that, I appreciate that the membership of this club consists of men who are thinking in terms beyond the immediate present, beyond their own immediate tasks, beyond their own individual interests. I want to invite you, therefore, to consider with me in the large, some of the relationships of Government and economic life that go deeply into our daily lives, our happiness, our future and our security.

The issue of Government has always been whether individual men and women will have to serve some system of Government or economics, or whether a system of Government and economics exists to serve individual men and women. This question has persistently dominated the discussion of Government for many generations. On questions relating to these things men have differed, and for time immemorial it is probable that honest men will continue to differ.

The final word belongs to no man; yet we can still believe in change and in progress. Democracy, as a dear old friend of mine in Indiana, Meredith Nicholson, has called it, is a quest, a never-ending seeking for better things, and in the seeking for these things and the striving for them, there are many roads to follow. But, if we map the course of these roads, we find that there are only two general directions.

When we look about us, we are likely to forget how hard people have worked to win the privilege of Government. The growth of the national Governments of Europe was the struggle for the development of a centralized force in the Nation, strong enough to impose peace upon ruling barons. In many instances the victory of the central Government, the creation of a strong central Government, was a haven of refuge to the individual. The people preferred the master far away to the exploitation and cruelty of the smaller master near at hand.

But the creators of national Government were perforce ruthless men. They were often cruel in their methods, but they did strive steadily toward something that society needed and very much wanted, a strong central State able to keep the peace, to stamp out civil war, to put the unruly nobleman in his place, and to permit the bulk of individuals to live safely. The man of ruthless force had his place in developing a pioneer country, just as he did in fixing the power of the central Government in the development of Nations. Society paid him well for his services and its development. When the development among the Nations of Europe, however, had been completed, ambition and ruthlessness, having served their term, tended to overstep their mark.

There came a growing feeling that Government was conducted for the benefit of a few who thrived unduly at the expense of all. The people sought a balancing—a limiting force. There came gradually, through town councils, trade guilds, national parliaments, by constitution and by popular participation and control, limitations on arbitrary power.

Another factor that tended to limit the power of those who ruled, was the rise of the ethical conception that a ruler bore a responsibility for the welfare of his subjects.

The American colonies were born in this struggle. The American Revolution was a turning point in it. After the Revolution the struggle continued and shaped itself in the public life of the country. There were those who because they had seen the confusion which attended the years of war for American independence surrendered to the belief that popular Government was essentially dangerous and essentially unworkable. They were honest people, my friends, and we cannot deny that their experience had warranted some measure of fear. The most brilliant, honest and able exponent of this point of view was Hamilton. He was too impatient of slow-moving methods. Fundamentally he believed that the safety of the republic lay in the autocratic strength of its Government, that the destiny of individuals was to serve that Government, and that fundamentally a great and strong group of central institutions, guided by a small group of able and public spirited citizens, could best direct all Government.

But Mr. Jefferson, in the summer of 1776, after drafting the Declaration of Independence turned his mind to the same problem and took a different view. He did not deceive himself with outward forms. Government to him was a means to an end, not an end in itself; it might be either a refuge and a help or a threat and a danger, depending on the circumstances. We find him carefully analyzing the society for which he was to organize a Government. "We have no paupers. The great mass of our population is of laborers, our rich who cannot live without labor, either manual or professional, being few and of moderate wealth. Most of the laboring class possess property, cultivate their own lands, have families and from the demand for their labor, are enabled to exact from the rich and the competent such prices as enable them to feed abundantly, clothe above mere decency, to labor moderately and raise their families."

These people, he considered, had two sets of rights, those of "personal competency" and those involved in acquiring and possessing property. By "personal competency" he meant the right of free thinking, freedom of forming and expressing opinions, and freedom of personal living, each man according to his own lights. To insure the first set of rights, a Government must so order its functions as not to interfere with the individual. But even Jefferson realized that the exercise of the property rights might so interfere with the rights of the individual that the Government, without whose assistance the property rights could not exist, must intervene, not to destroy individualism, but to protect it.

You are familiar with the great political duel which followed; and how Hamilton, and his friends, building toward a dominant centralized power were at length defeated in the great election of 1800, by Mr. Jefferson's party. Out of that duel came the two parties, Republican and Democratic, as we know them today.

So began, in American political life, the new day, the day of the individual against the system, the day in which individualism was made the great watchword of American life. The happiest of economic conditions made that day long and splendid. On the Western frontier, land was substantially free. No one, who did not shirk the task of earning a living, was entirely without opportunity to do so. Depressions could, and did, come and go; but they could not alter the fundamental fact that most of the people lived partly by selling their labor and partly by extracting their livelihood from the soil, so that starvation and dislocation were practically impossible. At the very worst there was always the possibility of climbing into a covered wagon and moving west where the untilled prairies afforded a haven for men to whom the East did not provide a place. So great were our natural resources that we could offer this relief not only to our own people, but to the distressed of all the world; we could invite immigration from Europe, and welcome it with open arms. Traditionally, when a depression came a new section of land was opened in the West; and even our temporary misfortune served our manifest destiny.

It was in the middle of the nineteenth century that a new force was released and a new dream created. The force was what is called the industrial revolution, the advance of steam and machinery and the rise of the forerunners of the modern industrial plant. The dream was the dream of an economic machine, able to raise the standard of living for everyone; to bring luxury within the reach of the humblest; to annihilate distance by steam power and later by electricity, and to release everyone from the drudgery of the heaviest manual toil. It was to be expected that this would necessarily affect Government. Heretofore, Government had merely been called upon to produce conditions within which people could live happily, labor peacefully, and rest secure. Now it was called upon to aid in the consummation of this new dream. There was, however, a shadow over the dream. To be made real, it required use of the talents of men of tremendous will and tremendous ambition, since by no other force could the problems of financing and engineering and new developments be brought to a consummation.

So manifest were the advantages of the machine age, however, that the United States fearlessly, cheerfully, and, I think, rightly, accepted the bitter with the sweet. It was thought that no price was too high to pay for the advantages which we could draw from a finished industrial system. The history of the last half century is accordingly in large measure a history of a group of financial Titans whose methods were not scrutinized with too much care, and who were honored in proportion as they produced the results, irrespective of the means they used. The financiers who pushed the railroads to the Pacific were always ruthless, often wasteful, and frequently corrupt; but they did build railroads, and we have them today. It has been estimated that the American investor paid for the American railroad system more than three times over in the process; but despite this fact the net advantage was to the United States. As long as we had free land; as long as population was growing by leaps and bounds; as long as our industrial plants were insufficient to supply our own needs, society chose to give the ambitious man free play and unlimited reward provided only that he produced the economic plant so much desired.

During this period of expansion, there was equal opportunity for all, and the business of Government was not to interfere but to assist in the development of industry. This was done at the request of business men themselves. The tariff was originally imposed for the purpose of "fostering our infant industry," a phrase I think the older among you will remember as a political issue not so long ago. The railroads were subsidized, sometimes by grants of money, oftener by grants of land; some of the most valuable oil lands in the United States were granted to assist the financing of the railroad which pushed through the Southwest. A nascent merchant marine was assisted by grants of money, or by mail subsidies, so that our steam shipping might ply the seven seas. Some of my friends tell me that they do not want the Government in business. With this I agree; but I wonder whether they realize the implications of the past. For while it has been American doctrine that the Government must not go into business in competition with private enterprises, still it has been traditional, particularly in Republican administrations, for business urgently to ask the Government to put at private disposal all kinds of Government assistance. The same man who tells you that he does not want to see the Government interfere in business—and he means it, and has plenty of good reasons for saying so—is the first to go to Washington and ask the Government for a prohibitory tariff on his product. When things get just bad enough, as they did two years ago, he will go with equal speed to the United States Government and ask for a loan; and the Reconstruction Finance Corporation is the outcome of it. Each group has sought protection from the Government for its own special interests, without realizing that the function of Government must be to favor no small group at the expense of its duty to protect the rights of personal freedom and of private property of all its citizens.

In retrospect we can now see that the turn of the tide came with the turn of the century. We were reaching our last frontier; there was no more free land and our industrial combinations had become great uncontrolled and irresponsible units of power within the State. Clear-sighted men saw with fear the danger that opportunity would no longer be equal; that the growing corporation, like the feudal baron of old, might threaten the economic freedom of individuals to earn a living. In that hour, our anti-trust laws were born. The cry was raised against the great corporations. Theodore Roosevelt, the first great Republican Progressive, fought a Presidential campaign on the issue of "trust busting" and talked freely about malefactors of great wealth. If the Government had a policy it was rather to turn the clock back, to destroy the large combinations and to return to the time when every man owned his individual small business.

This was impossible; Theodore Roosevelt, abandoning the idea of "trust busting," was forced to work out a difference between "good" trusts and "bad" trusts. The Supreme Court set forth the famous "rule of reason" by which it seems to have meant that a concentration of industrial power was permissible if the method by which it got its power, and the use it made of that power, were reasonable.

Woodrow Wilson, elected in 1912, saw the situation more clearly. Where Jefferson had feared the encroachment of political power on the lives of individuals, Wilson knew that the new power was financial. He saw, in the highly centralized economic system, the despot of the twentieth century, on whom great masses of individuals relied for their safety and their livelihood, and whose irresponsibility and greed (if they were not controlled) would reduce them to starvation and penury. The concentration of financial power had not proceeded so far in 1912 as it has today; but it had grown far enough for Mr. Wilson to realize fully its implications. It is interesting, now, to read his speeches. What is called "radical" today (and I have reason to know whereof I speak) is mild compared to the campaign of Mr. Wilson. "No man can deny," he said, "that the lines of endeavor have more and more narrowed and stiffened; no man who knows anything about the development of industry in this country can have failed to observe that the larger kinds of credit are more and more difficult to obtain unless you obtain them upon terms of uniting your efforts with those who already control the industry of the country, and nobody can fail to observe that every man who tries to set himself up in competition with any process of manufacture which has taken place under the control of large combinations of capital will presently find himself either squeezed out or obliged to sell and allow himself to be absorbed." Had there been no World War—had Mr. Wilson been able to devote eight years to domestic instead of to international affairs— we might have had a wholly different situation at the present time. However, the then distant roar of European cannon, growing ever louder, forced him to abandon the study of this issue. The problem he saw so clearly is left with us as a legacy; and no one of us on either side of the political controversy can deny that it is a matter of grave concern to the Government.

A glance at the situation today only too clearly indicates that equality of opportunity as we have known it no longer exists. Our industrial plant is built; the problem just now is whether under existing conditions it is not overbuilt. Our last frontier has long since been reached, and there is practically no more free land. More than half of our people do not live on the farms or on lands and cannot derive a living by cultivating their own property. There is no safety valve in the form of a Western prairie to which those thrown out of work by Eastern economic machines can go for a new start. We are not able to invite the immigration from Europe to share our endless plenty. We are now providing a drab living for our own people.

Our system of constantly rising tariffs has at last reacted against us to the point of closing our Canadian frontier on the north, our European markets on the east, many of our Latin-American markets to the south, and a goodly proportion of our Pacific markets on the west, through the retaliatory tariffs of those countries. It has forced many of our great industrial institutions which exported their surplus production to such countries, to establish plants in such countries, within the tariff walls. This has resulted in the reduction of the operation of their American plants, and opportunity for employment.

Just as freedom to farm has ceased, so also the opportunity in business has narrowed. It still is true that men can start small enterprises, trusting to native shrewdness and ability to keep abreast of competitors; but area after area has been preempted altogether by the great corporations, and even in the fields which still have no great concerns, the small man starts under a handicap. The unfeeling statistics of the past three decades show that the independent business man is running a losing race. Perhaps he is forced to the wall; perhaps he cannot command credit; perhaps he is "squeezed out," in Mr. Wilson's words, by highly organized corporate competitors, as your corner grocery man can tell you. Recently a careful study was made of the concentration of business in the United States. It showed that our economic life was dominated by some six hundred odd corporations who controlled two-thirds of American industry. Ten million small business men divided the other third. More striking still, it appeared that if the process of concentration goes on at the same rate, at the end of another century we shall have all American industry controlled by a dozen corporations, and run by perhaps a hundred men. Put plainly, we are steering a steady course toward economic oligarchy, if we are not there already.

Clearly, all this calls for a re-appraisal of values. A mere builder of more industrial plants, a creator of more railroad systems, an organizer of more corporations, is as likely to be a danger as a help. The day of the great promoter or the financial Titan, to whom we granted anything if only he would build, or develop, is over. Our task now is not discovery or exploitation of natural resources, or necessarily producing more goods. It is the soberer, less dramatic business of administering resources and plants already in hand, of seeking to reestablish foreign markets for our surplus production, of meeting the problem of underconsumption, of adjusting production to consumption, of distributing wealth and products more equitably, of adapting existing economic organizations to the service of the people. The day of enlightened administration has come.

Just as in older times the central Government was first a haven of refuge, and then a threat, so now in a closer economic system the central and ambitious financial unit is no longer a servant of national desire, but a danger. I would draw the parallel one step farther. We did not think because national Government had become a threat in the 18th century that therefore we should abandon the principle of national Government. Nor today should we abandon the principle of strong economic units called corporations, merely because their power is susceptible of easy abuse. In other times we dealt with the problem of an unduly ambitious central Government by modifying it gradually into a constitutional democratic Government. So today we are modifying and controlling our economic units.

As I see it, the task of Government in its relation to business is to assist the development of an economic declaration of rights, an economic constitutional order. This is the common task of statesman and business man. It is the minimum requirement of a more permanently safe order of things.

Happily, the times indicate that to create such an order not only is the proper policy of Government, but it is the only line of safety for our economic structures as well. We know, now, that these economic units cannot exist unless prosperity is uniform, that is, unless purchasing power is well distributed throughout every group in the Nation. That is why even the most selfish of corporations for its own interest would be glad to see wages restored and unemployment ended and to bring the Western farmer back to his accustomed level of prosperity and to assure a permanent safety to both groups. That is why some enlightened industries themselves endeavor to limit the freedom of action of each man and business group within the industry in the common interest of all; why business men everywhere are asking a form of organization which will bring the scheme of things into balance, even though it may in some measure qualify the freedom of action of individual units within the business.

The exposition need not further be elaborated. It is brief and incomplete, but you will be able to expand it in terms of your own business or occupation without difficulty. I think everyone who has actually entered the economic struggle—which means everyone who was not born to safe wealth—knows in his own experience and his own life that we have now to apply the earlier concepts of American Government to the conditions of today.

The Declaration of Independence discusses the problem of Government in terms of a contract. Government is a relation of give and take, a contract, perforce, if we would follow the thinking out of which it grew. Under such a contract rulers were accorded power, and the people assented to that power on consideration that they be accorded certain rights. The task of statesmanship has always been the re-definition of these rights in terms of a changing and growing social order. New conditions impose new requirements upon Government and those who conduct Government.

I held, for example, in proceedings before me as Governor, the purpose of which was the removal of the Sheriff of New York, that under modern conditions it was not enough for a public official merely to evade the legal terms of official wrong-doing. He owed a positive duty as well. I said in substance that if he had acquired large sums of money, he was when accused required to explain the sources of such wealth. To that extent this wealth was colored with a public interest. I said that in financial matters, public servants should, even beyond private citizens, be held to a stern and uncompromising rectitude.

I feel that we are coming to a view through the drift of our legislation and our public thinking in the past quarter century that private economic power is, to enlarge an old phrase, a public trust as well. I hold that continued enjoyment of that power by any individual or group must depend upon the fulfillment of that trust. The men who have reached the summit of American business life know this best; happily, many of these urge the binding quality of this greater social contract.

The terms of that contract are as old as the Republic, and as new as the new economic order.

Every man has a right to life; and this means that he has also a right to make a comfortable living. He may by sloth or crime decline to exercise that right; but it may not be denied him. We have no actual famine or dearth; our industrial and agricultural mechanism can produce enough and to spare. Our Government, formal and informal. political and economic, owes to everyone an avenue to possess himself of a portion of that plenty sufficient for his needs, through his own work.

Every man has a right to his own property; which means a right to be assured, to the fullest extent attainable, in the safety of his savings. By no other means can men carry the burdens of those parts of life which, in the nature of things, afford no chance of labor; childhood, sickness, old age. In all thought of property, this right is paramount; all other property rights must yield to it. If, in accord with this principle, we must restrict the operations of the speculator, the manipulator, even the financier, I believe we must accept the restriction as needful, not to hamper individualism but to protect it.

These two requirements must be satisfied, in the main, by the individuals who claim and hold control of the great industrial and financial combinations which dominate so large a part of our industrial life. They have undertaken to be, not business men, but princes of property. I am not prepared to say that the system which produces them is wrong. I am very clear that they must fearlessly and competently assume the responsibility which goes with the power. So many enlightened business men know this that the statement would be little more than a platitude, were it not for an added implication.

This implication is, briefly, that the responsible heads of finance and industry instead of acting each for himself, must work together to achieve the common end. They must, where necessary, sacrifice this or that private advantage; and in reciprocal self-denial must seek a general advantage. It is here that formal Government—political Government, if you choose—comes in. Whenever in the pursuit of this objective the lone wolf, the unethical competitor, the reckless promoter, the Ishmael or Insull whose hand is against every man's, declines to join in achieving an end recognized as being for the public welfare, and threatens to drag the industry back to a state of anarchy, the Government may properly be asked to apply restraint. Likewise, should the group ever use its collective power contrary to the public welfare, the Government must be swift to enter and protect the public interest.

The Government should assume the function of economic regulation only as a last resort, to be tried only when private initiative, inspired by high responsibility, with such assistance and balance as Government can give, has finally failed. As yet there has been no final failure, because there has been no attempt; and I decline to assume that this Nation is unable to meet the situation.

The final term of the high contract was for liberty and the pursuit of happiness. We have learned a great deal of both in the past century. We know that individual liberty and individual happiness mean nothing unless both are ordered in the sense that one man's meat is not another man's poison. We know that the old "rights of personal competency," the right to read, to think, to speak, to choose and live a mode of life, must be respected at all hazards. We know that liberty to do anything which deprives others of those elemental rights is outside the protection of any compact; and that Government in this regard is the maintenance of a balance, within which every individual may have a place if he will take it; in which every individual may find safety if he wishes it; in which every individual may attain such power as his ability permits, consistent with his assuming the accompanying responsibility.

All this is a long, slow talk. Nothing is more striking than the simple innocence of the men who insist, whenever an objective is present, on the prompt production of a patent scheme guaranteed to produce a result. Human endeavor is not so simple as that. Government includes the art of formulating a policy, and using the political technique to attain so much of that policy as will receive general support; persuading, leading, sacrificing, teaching always, because the greatest duty of a statesman is to educate. But in the matters of which I have spoken, we are learning rapidly, in a severe school. The lessons so learned must not be forgotten, even in the mental lethargy of a speculative upturn. We must build toward the time when a major depression cannot occur again; and if this means sacrificing the easy profits of inflationist booms, then let them go; and good riddance.

Faith in America, faith in our tradition of personal responsibility, faith in our institutions, faith in ourselves demand that we recognize the new terms of the old social contract. We shall fulfill them, as we fulfilled the obligation of the apparent Utopia which Jefferson imagined for us in 1776, and which Jefferson, Roosevelt and Wilson sought to bring to realization. We must do so, lest a rising tide of misery, engendered by our common failure, engulf us all. But failure is not an American habit; and in the strength of great hope we must all shoulder our common load.

John J. Parker

LAW IN THE WORLD COMMUNITY[1]

I esteem it a great honor that you have invited me to speak before this group interested in international law and the law of international relationships. The occasion suggests the subject on which I should like to talk, Law in the World

"Law in the World Community" by John J. Parker, originally published in *Vital Speeches of the Day*, June 1, 1958, © 1958 by City News Publishing Co.
1. This speech was prepared for delivery at the annual conference dinner of the United Nations League of Lawyers, Washington, D. C., March 18, 1958. Parker, who was Chief Judge of the U. S. Court of Appeals for the Fourth Judicial Circuit, died March 17, 1958.

Community. The thing that stands out in the history of the last quarter of a century is that within that period this world of ours really has become one community. Any part of it can be reached from any other part in a few hours' time. Communication is a matter of seconds. Strife anywhere is fraught with real danger that the whole world may be involved and the whole fabric of our civilization destroyed. Never in the history of the human race has there been greater need for men of good will to stand and work together for the preservation of those ideals and standards upon which our civilization is built.

In this period of unprecedented crisis and danger, the first duty that confronts us of the free world is to make ourselves strong—strong enough to resist any aggregation of power that may come against us—so strong that no aggregation of power will dare to come. It is true today as it has always been that to be prepared for war is the surest guaranty of peace. Disarmament and appeasement are not the way to peace. They are the way to war and slavery. There is need for scientific education and the development of scientific instruments of welfare. I would not for an instant discount the supreme importance of this and of our duty to make any sacrifice necessary to maintain our strength. While we maintain it, however, we, as lawyers, must not forget that peace will ultimately rest, not upon scientific achievement, but upon the establishment of law in the world community and that the establishment of law is essentially the work of the lawyer.

I have been especially impressed with this recently by three outstanding speeches. One was by Attorney General Brownell in Westminster Hall, London, when standing before the representatives of the bars of England and America he pleaded for the development of law in international relationships. Another was the speech of the Lord Chancellor of England at the same meeting in which he spoke of the natural law which underlies all organized life of man or nations. The third was the speech of Charles S. Rhyne, president of the American Bar Association, at Los Angeles, in which he urged the lawyers of America to lead in the development of legal machinery by which the principles of law could be interpreted and applied in international affairs. These were practical men. They were talking sense. And their message is one which I would echo here this evening.

What is law? Law is not a mere collection of rules and forms and precedents. Law is the life principle of organized society—the categorical imperative which prescribes how organized society must live. It is not imposed from without, but arises from within the social organism. As Cicero put it, "Law arises out of the nature of things." The Lord Chancellor referring to this law of nature as one of the noblest conceptions in the history of jurisprudence, quoted the following eloquent statement of Lord Bryce, regarding it:

It is simple and rational, as opposed to that which is artificial or arbitrary. It is universal, as opposed to that which is local or national. It is superior to all other law because it belongs to mankind as mankind, and is the expression of the purpose of the Deity or of the highest reason of man. It is therefore natural, not so much in the sense of belonging to man in his primitive and uncultured condition, but rather as corresponding to and regulating his fullest and most perfect social development in communities, where they have ripened through the teachings of reason.

When this noble concept of law is accepted, it follows that the development of international law is natural and necessary. When men deal with each other across international boundaries or travel into foreign countries for the purpose of trade and commerce or for other reasons, relationships are established, customs arise and reason prescribes rights and duties in numberless situations. Without any international legislature, there arise rules and standards which are enforced by the common consent of civilized peoples. They are evidenced by the decisions of courts, by treaties between nations and by the writings of the wise and the learned. This is international law; and the real purpose of any world order must be to develop and give expression to this law and to enforce it fairly and justly among men and nations. In no other way is it possible to establish an enduring foundation for world peace.

We must never forget that peace is not a negative but a positive thing. Peace connotes, not mere absence of conflict, but the orderly functioning of life in accordance with the laws of life. I have peace within my body when all the members function in accordance with the laws of the body. We have peace within a city when all elements live in accordance with the laws of the city. And we shall have peace within the world only when the life of the world functions in accordance with the laws which reason prescribes for the functioning of world life. This is the great challenge to the lawyer today. Of the three learned professions, says Ruskin, it pertains to the minister to teach, to the physician to heal and to the lawyer to give peace and order to society. The lawyer has performed this function as the family has developed into the tribe and the tribe into the Nation. If civilization is to live, he must perform it as nations merge into the world community. His duty is to develop legal institutions which will give form and content to the rules which arise out of international relationships and provide for their enforcement in such way as to preserve the peace and order of the international society which has come into being. The time is ripe for the effort. The world is growing weary of the strife and bickering in international affairs. with the ever-present threat of terrible calamity upon the breaking out of international strife.

While we were engaged in the great World War and were standing on the mountain peaks of heroic achievement, it was generally assumed that the ending of the war was to be followed, as a matter of course, by the building of an international organization for the establishment of a world order based on law. When the danger passed, however, and peace had come, many who should have led in the movement lost their enthusiasm for it; and among those who lack vision and understanding the feeling has arisen that international organization is not practical. I believe not only that it is practical but that it is the only practical approach to the problems which confront us. Such organization does not mean the building of a superstate as the world federalists advocate, but it does require three things, which, I submit, are eminently practical, viz.: (1) adequate judicial machinery for the settlement, on the basis of reason, of disputes of an international character; (2) adequate legislative machinery for bringing to bear the intelligence of mankind upon the solution of international problems; and (3) adequate organization of force for the preservation of peace and the enforcement of law.

There is no reason why disputes of states should not be subjected to judicial settlement, as is required by the Constitution of the United States in the case of disputes between the several States of our Union. I remember that some years ago there was a dispute between my State and the State of Tennessee over a boundary line, just the sort of dispute that has so often led to war; but did we call out the militia and declare war on Tennessee? We did not: We brought suit against her in the Supreme Court of the United States and the Court had a commission run and established the boundary. Back in the seventies, North Carolina repudiated some bonds that she had issued. Some of them came into the possession of the State of South Dakota and she demanded that we pay them. We refused to do so on the ground that the bonds were fraudulent. South Dakota did not declare war on us. She sued us in the Supreme Court; and the Court gave judgment against us; and we paid the judgment, and now we have forgotten all about the matter. There is no reason in God's world, why the controversies plaguing the Middle East should not be settled on the basis of reason by some sort of international tribunal.

The permanent Court of International Justice set up pursuant to article 14 of the League of Nations functioned successfully in the judicial settlement of international controversies. It was manned by judges of outstanding character, including, among others, Mr. John Bassett Moore, Chief Justice Hughes, Secretary Kellogg and Prof. Manley O. Hudson, and made a real contribution to the law of the world. It has been succeeded by the International Court of Justice created under the charter of the United Nations; and the jurisdiction of that court has been accepted by practically all the civilized nations of the world including our own country. There is no reason why justiciable disputes between nations should not be settled by this court.

As President Rhyne pointed out in his Los Angeles speech, however, the International Court of Justice should hold sessions in different parts of the world, so that the people can see it in action and become familiar with its jurisdiction. And in this connection I would make another suggestion. I believe it would be well to create a system of inferior international courts with appeal to the International Court of Justice, to hear cases arising between citizens of different countries involving large amounts or delicate international questions. One of the fertile sources of international conflict is alleged injustice to nationals, as where contracts are not properly enforced or property is confiscated by unjust decisions. It seems to me that such a system of international courts would command the confidence and respect of those who trade, travel, or invest their money in foreign countries, and would thus do much to extend commerce and unify commercial and business law, as well as avoid some of the most fruitful sources of international conflict.

The jurisdiction of these courts would correspond in a general way to the diversity jurisdiction exercised by our Federal courts where the parties litigant are citizens of different states. It finds analogy also in the jurisdiction formerly exercised by extraterritorial courts such as the United States Court for China or the Mixed Court of Egypt. Such courts were recommended in a report of a committee of the American Bar Association composed of some of the ablest lawyers of the country, among others Mr. John W. Davis, former Senator George Wharton Pepper, and former Attorney General William H. Mitchell.

The latest example of a provision for peaceful settlement of international disputes under law is in the treaty creating the European Economic Community, where a seven-member court is created to decide disputes between members of that community.

The Charter of the Organization of American States provides that "every American State has the duty to respect the rights enjoyed by every other state in accordance with international law." But there is no court such as the new European Court to decide disputes. There is an Inter-American Council of Jurists which now serves as an advisory body and could easily be transformed into a court. As Mr. Rhyne has pointed out, "Here is a chance for the Americas to show leadership in the search for machinery to maintain peace by creating such a regional court as a part of the Organization of American States. Such a step could well be a historic breakthrough of momentous proportions because of the example it would offer to the world."

Provision should be made, also, for the setting up of criminal courts for trying war crimes and other criminal offenses against international law. In the past, persons accused of such crimes have been tried, *ex necessitate*, in national courts; but it is highly desirable that an international court be created for trying crimes of this character, or at least that provision be made for the setting up of such a court if occasion for the exercise of its jurisdiction should arise. Through lack of such a court, those charged with having committed the most heinous war crimes during the First World War were allowed to escape punishment and the world was deprived of the salutary influence that their trial would have had upon world opinion. Crimes committed in the Second World War were brought to trial and punished before the International Military Tribunal and military courts established by the several victorious nations; but much bitter controversy would have been avoided and the results would have been more readily acceptable, certainly by the conquered nations, and possibly by the world at large, if the courts which conducted the trials had been set up by an existing international institution such as the International Court of Justice.

Adequate machinery for the judicial settlement of justiciable disputes between nations and their nationals, with arbitration of disputes that are not of a justiciable character, and with machinery for the trial of criminals who commit offences against the law of nations will not only help preserve the world's peace but will also lead to the healthy growth and expansion of international law. Every lawyer knows that the most important developments of the law have come, not from action by a legislature, but from court decisions—from the application of reason to the settlement of actual controversies.

While adequate machinery for the settlement of disputes is one of the first essentials in world organization based on law, it is not the only essential. There must also be adequate legislative machinery for bringing to bear the intelligence of mankind upon the settlement of international problems. There have been many of these growing out of the last world war and the postwar developments, and they will increase rather than diminish as time goes on and the life of the world grows more interrelated and complex—problems affecting international trade, travel, and communication, problems arising out of the use of the air and the seas for the purposes of commerce, problems arising out of the exchange of goods and commodities, problems of international finance and credit, international labor problems, etc. The settlement of these cannot be left to the individual action of nations nor allowed to await the judicial action of courts or councils or arbitrators. Rules for their solution must in some way be laid down in advance by the legislative process; and this means that an assembly must be provided in which representatives of the constituent nations may be heard and may take action or make recommendations with respect to the problems that confront them.

The assembly of the United Nations provides just the sort of legislative assembly that the world must have; and it is no objection that it has not the power to enact laws by majority vote as does Congress or a State legislature. In the assembly and in the economic and social council the world's problems are debated and explored in the view of all mankind, and world public opinion is formed with regard to them. When the adoption of new and binding rules is necessary, this can be accomplished by the negotiation of multilateral treaties based on the conclusions which have been reached in the assembly with regard thereto.

Of tremendous importance is the functioning of commissions set up to make studies and recommendations as to matters which are important to the development of world life—commissions such as the International Law Commission, the International Labor Organization, UNESCO and others, which can and do make recommendations with respect to a myriad of matters many of which are entirely within the sphere of national control. Studies and recommendations with respect to education, labor conditions, currency stabilization and exchange, agricultural development, production and development of food and raw materials, public health and control of disease, regulation of the traffic in narcotics, etc.—recommendations of this sort are being made under the authority of the United Nations and are of the greatest value to the progress of mankind. While the United Nations does not attempt to exercise legislative power on the reports of these commissions, the reports serve as a basis of international agreements or legislation by the member countries. In this way, law grows by the legislative as well as by the judicial process for the preservation of peace and the betterment of living conditions throughout the world community.

Our American Union furnishes a fine illustration of cooperation for the purposes of collective security. No one of our States would be able to protect itself effectively against foreign aggression but collectively they possess a power that is today greater than that of any other nation in the world. This power is used to preserve the peace and enforce the law throughout the Union as well as to protect against dangers from without. Some such pooling of force for purposes of collective security and to enforce the rules of international law and the decrees of international tribunals is essential to the success of any international organization. Order rests upon reason and force. Force without reason is tyranny but reason without force to make it effective is anarchy. Most people will obey the rules of law willingly, but, unless others are forced to obey, the rules fall into disrepute. We do not expect peace in domestic affairs without force to preserve it; and it is idle to think that we can have peace in international relationships on any other basis. We did not leave Capone or Dillinger or Touhy to be dealt with by their victims, nor did we content ourselves with preaching sermons to them. We brought to bear the force of organized society and put an end to their criminal conduct. When Germany and Italy and Japan started out on a course of international brigandage, however, there was no adequate organization of the world's force to stop them. If the League of Nations had had such force available, Japan would never have dared invade Manchuria, Hitler would never have marched into the Rhineland, Mussolini would not have dreamed of seizing Ethiopia, and the great World War might never have come. And if the force had been available, there probably would have been no need to use it; for the mere presence of available force, without more, generally serves as a sufficient restraint upon those who would otherwise violate the law.

The great superiority of the United Nations over the old League of Nations is that in the Security Council we have a more effective pooling of the world's force for the preservation of world law and order. In Korea, in Suez, and in many other situations its value has been amply demonstrated. We have reached the point, however, where there must be an even greater pooling of force for the purposes of collective security. Suez has demonstrated the importance of providing the United Nations with a police force and how such a force can be maintained. NATO has demonstrated the importance to the preservation of liberty and law of defense alliances for the purposes of collective security. The organization of American States is another illustration of the pooling of force for collective security in the international field. It is not too much to hope that along these lines we will eventually be able to secure a pooling of the world's force for the preservation of the peace and the enforcement of law in the world community.

The establishment of a world order based on law is an undertaking fraught with great difficulties, as every great undertaking always is, but these must be approached realistically and with courage; and we are approaching them in that way. The veto power has prevented the use of world force as it might have been used for the maintenance of peace; but within the framework of the United Nations we are building defensive alliances like the North Atlantic Pact for the preservation of freedom under law. If that pact had been in existence at the time of the seizure of Czechoslovakia, that outrage, in all probability, would not have occurred. We have been faced with the intransigence of Russia; but the presence of Soviet representatives in the United Nations has enabled Russia to get the full impact of the powerful public opinion of the world, and the indications are that this is beginning to have its effect and Russia is evidencing at least an apparent willingness to cooperate with other nations for the establishment of peace. If Russia is willing to cooperate, world organization for peace will be a thing of the immediate future. If she is unwilling to go along with us, she will eventually get out or be put out of the United Nations; and thus freed from her opposition, we should proceed to strengthen the organization among the nations that remain, making it a defensive alliance of the free nations as well as an instrumentality for preserving law and order among men.

Order in human affairs can be achieved only by organization and such organization must be commensurate with the life for which peace and order is desired. Organization which was sufficient for the tribe or the State is not sufficient for the larger world community. That community must be organized on the basis of world law and it is being so organized through the structure of the United Nations. We should rally to the United Nations, therefore, with confident hope and firm purpose that it shall succeed. For myself I feel that it is succeeding. It has not brought the millennium, of course, but I shudder to think what might have happened to the civilization of the world if it had not been in existence. It has, at least given us over the years since the ending of the war a world forum in which the desperate problems threatening the peace and safety of mankind have been brought out into the light where we could see them and take measures for their solution. It has set up an international court for the juridical settlement of international disputes, which has had its compulsory jurisdiction accepted by the most powerful nations now existing. It has effected a certain pooling of the world's force which has preserved a measure of peace in Israel and Indonesia, has brought the free nations of the world to the defense of the liberties of Korea, and has prevented the outbreak of war over Suez.

We are told that the League of Nations failed and that the United Nations must go the way of the League. I do not accept either premise. The League was a good beginning and it accomplished a very great deal. It brought 63 of the 73 nations of the world together around a common conference table; it found solution for many troublesome international problems; it brought into being the World Court; it furnished the world the best example that it had had up to that time of how to govern conquered territory; it unquestionably averted a number of wars; and who can say what it might or might not have accomplished if American statesmen like Root and Baker and Hughes had sat in its councils and this great, rich and powerful Nation had given it unstinted support in the stormy years following the First World War?

Rome was not built in a day; our own Federal Union required many years in coming to maturity; and I have an abiding faith that given proper support, the United Nations will grow in power and influence with the passage of time and will eventually give us a stable world order based on law and embodying the fundamental principles of human freedom. The forces of science and commerce have brought the world to the position where its life must be given unity. It is unthinkable that the strife and conflict which have attended recent years should continue. If unity is not achieved on the basis of reason and law, it will eventually be achieved through force; and the only hope of defeating those who would unify the world on the basis of force is for those who believe in the reign of law to rise above the narrow limitations of nationalism and support an intelligent organization of world life based upon law and righteousness.

This, if I may repeat, is the challenge that comes to the lawyers of today. May we go forward together, not merely today and tomorrow, but in all the years that lie ahead, leading the free world toward the attainment, not merely of world order, but of world order based on law and on those eternal principles of human liberty which are the chief glory of the Western World.

College Education

In 1786, Thomas Jefferson wrote, "I think by far the most important bill in our whole code is that for the diffusion of knowledge among the people. No other sure foundation can be devised for the preservation of freedom and happiness." Thomas Jefferson expressed an attitude with which Americans still enthusiastically agree. But there always have been, and probably always will be, arguments about the precise means and ends of "the diffusion of knowledge." The passage which introduces this section tells how Lincoln Steffens, a well-known journalist and commentator on American politics, made a very important personal discovery about education. The two discussions which follow are concerned with one of the greatest problems in American education today: "What is to be done about the vast number of students who are, or who will be, attempting to get an education?" Terry Ferrer approaches the problem by considering the social orientation of today's college students and the effects of this upon college education. Douglas Bush argues that the only solution to the problem is a selected college enrollment. The problem of liberal arts training versus vocational training is discussed by Ernest Earnest. The final selection in this section is Emerson's famous address, sometimes called "our intellectual Dec·laration of Independence."

Lincoln Steffens

I BECOME A STUDENT

A personal discovery

It is possible to get an education at a university. It has been done; not often, but the fact that a proportion, however small, of college students do get a start in interested, methodical study, proves my thesis, and the two personal ex·periences I have to offer illustrate it and show how to circumvent the faculty, the other students, and the whole college system of mind-fixing. My method might lose a boy his degree, but a degree is not worth so much as the capacity and the drive to learn, and the undergraduate desire for an empty baccalaureate is one of the holds the educational system has on students. Wise students some day will refuse to take degrees, as the best men (in England, for instance) give, but do not themselves accept, titles.

My method [used at the University of California, 1885-1889] was hit on by accident and some instinct. I specialized. With several courses prescribed, I concentrated on the one or two that interested me most, and letting the others go, I worked intensively on my favorites. In my first two years, for example, I worked at English and political economy and read philosophy. At the begin·ning of my junior year I had several cinches in history. Now I liked history; I had neglected it partly because I rebelled at the way it was taught, as positive knowledge unrelated to politics, art, life, or anything else. The professors gave us chapters out of a few books to read, con, and be quizzed on. Blessed as I was with a "bad memory," I could not commit to it anything that I did not under·stand and intellectually need. The bare record of the story of man, with names, dates, and irrelative events, bored me. But I had discovered in my readings of literature, philosophy, and political economy that history had light to throw upon unhistorical questions. So I proposed in my junior and senior years to specialize in history, taking all the courses required and those also that I had flunked in. With this in mind I listened attentively to the first introductory talk of Professor William Cary Jones on American constitutional history. He was a dull lecturer, but I noticed that, after telling us what pages of what books we must be prepared in, he mumbled off some other references "for those that may care to dig deeper."

When the rest of the class rushed out into the sunshine, I went up to the pro·fessor and, to his surprise, asked for this memorandum. He gave it to me. Up in the library I ran through the required chapters in the two different books, and they differed on several points. Turning to the other authorities, I saw that they disagreed on the same facts and also on others. The librarian, appealed to, helped me search the book-shelves till the library closed, and then I called on Professor Jones for more references. He was astonished, invited me in, and began to approve my industry, which astonished me. I was not trying to be a good boy; I was better than that: I was a curious boy. He lent me a couple of his books, and I went off to my club to read them. They only deepened the mystery, clearing up the historical question, but leaving the answer to be dug for and written.

The historians did not know! History was not a science, but a field for research, a field for me, for any young man, to explore, to make discoveries in and write a scientific report about. I was fascinated. As I went on from chapter to chapter, day after day, finding frequently essential differences of opinion and of fact, I saw more and more work to do. In this course, American constitutional history, I hunted far enough to suspect that the Fathers of the Republic who wrote our sacred Constitution of the United States not only did not, but did not want to, establish a democratic government, and I dreamed for a while —as I used as a child to play I was Napoleon or a trapper—I promised myself to write a true history of the making of the American Constitution. I did not do it; that chapter has been done or well begun since by two men: Smith of the University of Washington and Beard (then) of Columbia (afterward forced out, perhaps for this very work). I found other events, men, and epochs waiting for students. In all my other courses, in ancient, in European, and in modern history, the disagreeing authorities carried me back to the need of a fresh search for (or of) the original documents or other clinching testimony. Of course I did well in my classes. The history professor soon knew me as a student and seldom put a question to me except when the class had flunked it. Then Professor Jones would say, "Well, Steffens, tell them about it."

Fine. But vanity wasn't my ruling passion then. What I had was a quickening sense that I was learning a method of studying history and that every chapter of it, from the beginning of the world to the end, is crying out to be rewritten. There was something for Youth to do; these superior old men had not done anything, finally.

Years afterward I came out of the graft prosecution office in San Francisco with Rudolph Spreckels, the banker and backer of the investigation. We were to go somewhere, quick, in his car, and we couldn't. The chauffeur was trying to repair something wrong. Mr. Spreckels smiled; he looked closely at the defective part, and to my silent, wondering inquiry he answered: "Always, when I see something badly done or not done at all, I see an opportunity to make a fortune. I never kick at bad work by my class: there's lots of it and we suffer from it. But our failures and neglects are chances for the young fellows coming along and looking for work."

Nothing is done. Everything in the world remains to be done or done over. "The greatest picture is not yet painted, the greatest play isn't written (not even by Shakespeare), the greatest poem is unsung. There isn't in all the world a perfect railroad, nor a good government, nor a sound law." Physics, mathematics, and especially the most advanced and exact of the sciences, are being fundamentally revised. Chemistry is just becoming a science; psychology, economics, and sociology are awaiting a Darwin, whose work in turn is awaiting an Einstein. If the rah-rah boys in our colleges could be told this, they might not all be such specialists in football, petting parties, and unearned degrees. They are not told it, however; they are told to learn what is known. This is nothing, philosophically speaking.

Somehow or other in my later years at Berkeley, two professors, Moses and Howison, representing opposite schools of thought, got into a controversy, probably about their classes. They brought together in the house of one of them a few of their picked students, with the evident intention of letting us show in conversation how much or how little we had understood of their respective teachings. I don't remember just what the subject was that they threw into the ring, but we wrestled with it till the professors could stand it no longer. Then they broke in, and while we sat silent and highly entertained, they went at each other hard and fast and long. It was after midnight when, the debate over, we went home. I asked the other fellows what they had got out of it, and their answers showed that they had seen nothing but a fine, fair fight. When I laughed, they asked me what I, the D.S.,[1] had seen that was so much more profound.

I said that I had seen two highly-trained, well-educated Masters of Arts and Doctors of Philosophy disagreeing upon every essential point of thought and knowledge. They had all there was of the sciences; and yet they could not find any knowledge upon which they could base an acceptable conclusion. They had no test of knowledge; they didn't know what is and what is not. And they have no test of right and wrong; they have no basis for even an ethics.

Well, and what of it? They asked me that, and that I did not answer. I was stunned by the discovery that it was philosophically true, in a most literal sense, that nothing is known; that it is precisely the foundation that is lacking for science; that all we call knowledge rested upon assumptions which the scientists did not all accept; and that, likewise, there is no scientific reason for saying, for example, that stealing is wrong. In brief: there was no scientific basis for an ethics. No wonder men said one thing and did another; no wonder they could settle nothing either in life or in the academies.

I could hardly believe this. Maybe these professors, whom I greatly respected, did not know it all. I read the books over again with a fresh eye, with real interest, and I could see that, as in history, so in other branches of knowledge, everything was in the air. And I was glad of it. Rebel though I was, I had got the religion of scholarship and science; I was in awe of the authorities in the academic world. It was a release to feel my worship cool and pass. But I could

1. "Damned Stinker," a nickname given by the other students to Steffens because of his activities as commander of the cadet corps in the military department.

not be sure. I must go elsewhere, see and hear other professors, men these California professors quoted and looked up to as their high priests. I decided to go as a student to Europe when I was through with Berkeley, and I would start with the German universities.

My father listened to my plan, and he was disappointed. He had hoped I would succeed him in his business; it was for that that he was staying in it. When I said that, whatever I might do, I would never go into business, he said, rather sadly, that he would sell out his interest and retire. And he did soon after our talk. But he wanted me to stay home and, to keep me, offered to buy an interest in a certain San Francisco daily paper. He had evidently had this in mind for some time. I had always done some writing, verse at the poetical age of puberty, then a novel which my mother alone treasured. Journalism was the business for a boy who liked to write, he thought, and he said I had often spoken of a newspaper as my ambition. No doubt I had in the intervals between my campaigns as Napoleon. But no more. I was now going to be a scientist, a philosopher. He sighed; he thought it over, and with the approval of my mother, who was for every sort of education, he gave his consent.

Terry Ferrer

OUR EGOCENTRIC COLLEGE YOUTH

A few months ago the Rev. Alvin L. Kershaw, the Protestant Episcopal minister who rose to fame as a jazz expert on TV quiz shows, was visiting a large Midwestern university with Louis Armstrong, the great jazz trumpeter. After the Armstrong concert the students and guests adjourned to the nearby students' union for a discussion of jazz. Ten minutes later a girl jumped up and said: "Excuse me, Mr. Kershaw, but I have to leave now. Thinking makes my head hurt."

This honest young lady may not be completely typical of today's college students—but neither is she completely atypical. Take the senior from one of the best Ivy League institutions who says: "I have my own Golden Rule: Do unto others as they do unto me." Or the sophomore from one of the great scientific university colleges who cheerfully admits that he does not subscribe to any newspaper and never reads one if he can help it.

It is always a temptation to label succeeding college generations—the "jazz-age kids" of the Twenties, the "Depression" youngsters of the Thirties, and, more recently, the "silent generation" or the "cautious generation." If a tag must be found for today's collegians, I should dub them the "egocentric generation."

For those who find this indictment too harsh, let me quickly add that on the whole it isn't all their fault. Going to college used to be something that was

Reprinted from the *Saturday Review*, September 14, 1957.

only for the few. In 1900, for example, only one of every twenty-five youngsters made it to the nation's campuses. By 1930, the figure had jumped to only one out of twelve. This means that the coon-skinned, flask-carrying boys and girls of the Twenties were indeed some kind of elite. Most of them went to college because their parents could afford to send them and bragged about it. The more serious plunged into artistic and intellectual turmoil. F. Scott Fitzgerald and Nathanael West were their gods; their heaven the Left Bank of Paris. President Nathan M. Pusey of Harvard, who graduated in 1928, recalls: "We were concerned with the narrowness of big business and the insensitiveness of American culture. Life seemed to be better understood on the Left Bank of Paris."

The collegians of twenty years ago were a far more serious breed. Caught in the financial depression of the Thirties they realized that many of their parents had made a deep sacrifice to send them to college. The League of Nations was an ideological rallying point.

Little "peace clubs" blossomed on many a campus, as Adolf Hitler slowly began to consolidate his power. The Young Communist League started to grow, and even if its numbers were small on most campuses, its misguided members readily made up for size with strength—hefty and occasionally noisy enthusiasm. Still, no one thought the YCL's any odder than those who joined the Young Democratic and Young Republican Clubs. All of the young politicos were more likely to be found reading *The New York Times* than *The Daily Worker*.

It was not until the late Forties that the seeds of today's college attitudes were really sown. Under the GI bill, thousands of veterans invaded the campus. The vast majority studied hard; many professors still say they were the best students the colleges have had in fifty years.

The impact of the veteran was thus the most jarring to hit the nation's 1,900 institutions of higher learning in this century. Its results are evident now: In 1957, one out of every three young people is in college. With the present college population of about 3,500,000 expected almost to double by 1970, and probably double again by 1977, the ratio may even go beyond one of every two boys and girls in higher education. Paradoxically, in a society which is basically anti-intellectual and anti-egghead, a college degree has become the *ne plus ultra*. Some eager statisticians have even supplied its monetary value: $100,000 more earnings per lifetime with an A.B.

It should be no surprise, then, that the young people in college now are not the greatest students. It follows that with more and more boys and girls in college, the intellectual level is not inclined to rise. College faculties complain bitterly that freshmen today cannot write or do simple mathematics—some still cannot read. A charitable college dean from the Northwest said the other day: "They're much worse prepared, but they've got a good spirit. A college freshman bragged to me recently that the average grade in his chemistry course (200 members) was between 20 and 23 per cent. (One guy did get 97 per cent.)"

Since he knows that many of his fellow students are in the same intellectual boat, the college boy isn't too upset or drastically concerned about his studies. His parents want him to go to college, he has to go for prestige's sake, and he's firmly convinced that somehow he'll make out.

Dr. Philip E. Jacob, professor of political science at the University of Pennsylvania, recently published the findings of fifteen years of study of college student attitudes on fifty of the nation's campuses. Jacob said that college student values today are "remarkably homogeneous, and in many ways appear quite different from earlier generations. . . . A dominant characteristic of the current student generation is that they are *gloriously contented* both in regard to their present day-to-day activity and their outlook for their future. Few of them are worried—about their health, their prospective careers, their family relations, the state of national or international society, or the likelihood of their enjoying secure and happy lives. They are supremely confident that their destinies lie within their own control rather than in the grip of external circumstances."

Further, Jacob decided that "the great majority of students appear unabashedly *self-centered*. They aspire for material gratifications for themselves and their families. They intend to look out for themselves first and expect others to do likewise.

"But this is not the individualistic self-centeredness of the pioneer," Jacob continues. "American students fully accept the conventions of the contemporary business society as the context within which they will realize their personal desires. They cheerfully expect to conform to the economic status quo and to receive ample rewards for dutiful and productive effort. They anticipate no die-hard struggle for survival of the fittest as each seeks to gratify his own desires, but rather an abundance for all as each one teams up with his fellow self-seeker in appointed places on the American assembly-line."

Certainly today's students shouldn't have any complaints about contemporary business society. They have little trouble getting a job. Most of them work summers to pick up extra pocket money whether they need it or not. On graduation, they are likely to have five or six good job offers (even if they're not engineers), or they may even have agreed to work for a certain firm before starting their senior year (a new business twist for tying up the best prospects in advance of the competition). A good many of the men expect to be a vice president within ten years at the most. One can only regret that so many of them will be disappointed.

Jacob also found that a great number of today's students are "politically irresponsible and often politically illiterate as well. . . . Students predict another major war within a dozen years, yet international problems are the least of [their] concerns." After visiting a number of campuses which cannot support either Young Democratic or Young Republican Clubs because of lack of interest, this writer must agree. Needless to say, there are virtually no United Nations or UNESCO clubs.

What, then, does interest today's college generation? He is not much of a "cause" man, although he is likely to be tolerant of those racially or economically different from him. Studies are not of principal concern; Jacob found that to get through college many students employ "systematic cheating" (although they admire moral virtues like loyalty and honesty).

What interests the collegian most is himself. When the war and later the shadow of the draft hung heavy over the nation's teenagers, their dating habits began to change. A girl knew she had to snare a boy before he entered the services—or she probably wouldn't get him at all. Going steady, followed by earlier marriage, became the custom. Now, with the draft drastically slowed down and college deferrals the rule, young college boys and girls continue the pattern. They want to get married, so why wait? Permissive parents are inclined to agree. As a result, 16 per cent of today's collegians are married—many with working wives. At some campuses, the married percentage is as high as twenty-seven out of every 100. Some twenty-five years ago, students were expelled for marrying while at college. Now the larger universities are scrambling to put up married-student developments, complete with playground and nursery school. Once again, the students' personal preference outweighs their supposed quest for knowledge. Often parents have to help not only the student financially, but his whole family as well.

There is some consolation in the growing numbers of married students, however. Married boys—and sometimes girls—take their work more seriously. John A. Hannah, president of Michigan State University (which last year had 3,300 married students), is all for them: "We believe that the married student is not a liability, as was once believed, but an asset which lends quality, stability, and admirable strength of purpose to the student body as a whole."

Perhaps the only college boys and girls who escape the egocentric pattern are those who go to the smaller or denominational institutions. (Professor Jacob also cites these colleges as notable exceptions to his general conclusions.) But it is these smaller colleges of liberal arts which will have the hardest time surviving in the next twenty years. They have neither the funds nor the buildings to expand very much; besides, many of them do not want to. They do not want and will not get monies from state or Federal funds. The state universities, which are prepared to double or triple their enrolments, are expected in the future to absorb as much as 75 per cent of all those in college. This leaves a bare quarter who can be expected to achieve notable standards in respect for learning and political and moral values.

This does not mean that only morons will go to Harvard or the University of California. But it does mean that citizens and parents might well take a good deal more notice of what's going on in the nation's colleges, and of what's going on inside their children—or isn't. As a rule, children reflect the beliefs and attitudes of their parents. Hence today's egocentrics cannot be made to take all the blame. But mental apathy and easy-does-it values should hardly be the hallmarks of so-called educated men and women. Just thinking about it, as the Midwestern coed said, is enough to make the head hurt.

Douglas Bush

THE HUMANITIES

No one would ever speak of "the plight of the natural sciences," or of "the plight of the social sciences," but it is always proper to speak of "the plight of the humanities," and in the hushed, melancholy tone of one present at a perpetual death bed. For something like twenty-five hundred years the humanities have been in more or less of a plight, not because they are themselves weak, but because their war is not merely with ignorance but with original sin; and as civilization has advanced, the means of stultifying the head and heart have multiplied in variety and power. As a sample of cultural leadership, or of a common attitude, I should like to read a declaration of faith delivered some years ago by the chairman of the department of humanities in a well-known technological institution. We will call him Professor X. This is most of the report, from the *New York Times*, of his speech to a convention of engineers:

> Professor X . . . asserted last night that it would be "morally wrong" for him to advise the reading of the literary classics in this fast-moving age of television, radio and movies. . . .
>
> One should read for the purpose of doing something with what one reads, he asserted: not of polishing one's mind like a jewel, but of improving the world around.
>
> Take up a book because it will tell you something of the world . . . ; read what you want to read, not what you think you should read. "This is the frame of mind that makes reading worthwhile and often deeply rewarding.
>
> "For example, it would be morally wrong of me to urge you to take up a classic like 'David Copperfield' and to settle yourselves in easy chairs for winter evenings' reading. If you tried 'David Copperfield' you would grow restive; you would think of all the other things you might be doing more consistent with your daily environment—looking at television, listening to the radio, going to the movies.
>
> "Moreover, you would wonder why you should spend so much time laboriously reading 'David Copperfield' when you could see the book as a film, should it return some time to the neighborhood movie." . . . .
>
> "The single prescription for adult reading," he added, "should be to read something different, something that will change your mind. Herein lies compensation for the loss of the purely reflective life."

Engineers are not, to be sure, in common repute the most cultivated branch of mankind, but did even they deserve such counsel, and from such a source?

From *The Educational Record*, January 1955 and *The Key Reporter*, February 1955. Reprinted by permission of Douglas Bush, American Council on Education, and *The Key Reporter*.

The humanities, as I said, have always had to contend with the crude urges of the natural man, with his resistance to higher values than his own, but the speech I just quoted from reminds us of the many new ways there are of escaping from active thought and feeling into a state of lazy collapse, of passive surrender to unthinking action or external sensation. Many people would endorse our oracle's view that one should not read to polish one's mind like a jewel but for the sake of improving the world around. The humanistic tradition has always stood for improvement of the world, but it has always insisted that a man must make himself worthy of such an enterprise; one of our perennial troubles is that improvement of the world is undertaken by so many unpolished minds. Then our touching faith in machinery is illustrated by the quaint assumption that a movie is the same thing as a great book. And that *Ersatz* doctrine extends down through television to the comics, which have now joined the march of mind by reducing literary classics to capsule form. That sort of thing, by the way, was done, and done much better, a dozen centuries ago, and has been commonly labeled a symptom of the Dark Ages. But this is only a reminder; there is no need of enlarging upon such powerful elements in our popular civilization. The opposition to such elements comes from the humanities.

Negative terms, however, are not enough. The "humanities," in the original meaning of this and kindred words, embraced chiefly history, philosophy, and literature. These were the studies worthy of a free man, that ministered to *homo sapiens*, man the intellectual and moral being, and not to *homo faber*, the professional and technical expert. And these, with divinity, completed the central circle of human knowledge and understanding. Divinity went overboard long ago; history, which once was literature, is now a social science; and philosophy, though still grouped with the humanities, has become a branch of mathematics. Thus in common usage the humanities mean literature and the fine arts. That is an unfortunate narrowing but we may take things as we find them and concentrate on literature, which is central and representative.

One plain fact nowadays is that the study of literature, which in itself is comprehensive and complex, has had to take over the responsibilities that used to be discharged by philosophy and divinity. Most young people now get their only or their chief understanding of man's moral and religious quest through literature. Anyone who has been teaching literature for twenty-five or thirty years, as I have, can testify to the marked change there has been in the spiritual climate during that time. (A rigorously scientific colleague of mine, in psychology, will not permit the use of the word "spiritual," but I use it anyhow.) I am speaking mainly of the higher order of college students, but it would be hard to imagine even the better students of twenty-five or thirty years ago reading Dante and George Herbert and Milton and Hopkins and Eliot with the real sympathy that many now show. For the more intelligent and sensitive young people of today, and there are very many of that kind, are a serious and a conservative lot. They not only live in our unlovely world, they have no personal experience of any other. They are aware of hollowness and confusion all around them, and, what is still more real, of hollowness and confusion in themselves. They feel adrift in a cockboat on an uncharted sea, and they want a sense of direction, of order and integration. And in literature they find, as countless people have found before them, that their problems are not new, that earlier generations have been lost also. Most of the young people I see find in literature, literature of the remote past as well as of the present, what they cannot find in textbooks of psychology and sociology, the vision of human experience achieved by a great spirit and bodied forth by a great artist.

I apologize for elaborating what may be called clichés, but those familiar lists of courses in catalogues make one forget that the frigid label "English 10" or "French 20" may represent an illumination and a rebirth for John or Betty Doe. Not that courses are the only or even the main road to enriched experience and sensitivity, but they are one road; and a teacher can help as a guide or catalyst. Josiah Royce is said to have complained that a philosopher was expected to spiritualize the community. The modern philosopher is expected only to semanticize the community; the other function, as I said, falls upon the teacher of literature. I do not of course mean inspirational gush. I mean that teachers, conducting a critical discussion of a piece of great literature, necessarily deal not only with the artistic use of words and materials but with the moral and spiritual experience that are its subject matter. That is why, as President Pusey has said, the humanities must be the cornerstone of a liberal education. Naturally teachers will have their methods under constant scrutiny, but their material, the world's great literature, can hardly be improved; all it needs is a chance to work upon responsive minds and characters.

While I cannot guess the temper of this gathering, and while all the administrators present may, for all I know, regard the humanities as a pearl of great price, that is not their general reputation. Administrators are commonly said to prize the solid and tangible virtues of the natural and social sciences and to look upon the humanities as a nice luxury for the carriage trade. How far that general reputation is true or false I wouldn't know, but, just in case it has a modicum of truth, I have been insisting that the humanities are not a luxury; they are the most practical of necessities if men and women are to become fully human. The humanities commonly suffer in esteem because they do not lend themselves to statistical reports of achievement. You cannot demonstrate with graphs and charts that John or Betty Doe, through reacting to a piece of literature, became a person of richer moral and imaginative insight, of finer wisdom and discrimination and stability. For the experience of literature is an individual experience, and nothing that is really important can be measured.

When we look at the American educational scene, the diversity of standards is so great that generalizations about this or that part of it may be violently contradictory. At any rate educational history of the past fifty years seems to furnish a pretty good forecast of the bad effects of the deluge to be expected in the next fifteen. In school, college, and university, the results of the huge increase in the student body suggest that the principle of education for all, however fine in theory, in practice leads ultimately to education for none. An editorial in the *New York Times* of September 13, 1954, takes the usual line of defense. The principle of education for all, it says, forces us "to accept the principle, also, that the function of education is primarily social and political rather than purely intellectual." "It cannot be denied," the *Times* proceeds, "that this means a down-grading of the learning process. We are adjusting to an 'average' that must be spread so widely that it comes down automatically. Education is no longer the intellectual privilege of the gifted few. It is held to be the democratic right of all." The *Times* does go a little beyond this orthodox assent to express uneasiness over the sacrifice, in elementary and secondary schools, of quality to quantity.

To mention one of many results, there has been an appalling growth of illiteracy at all levels, even in the graduate school. (Somehow stenographers are still literate, even if their college-bred employers are not.) At every orgy of Commencements one wonders how many of the hordes of new bachelors of arts can speak and write their own language with elementary decency, or read it with understanding. After all, the polished mind is suspect, whether in a student, a professor, or a Presidential candidate. And illiteracy, and content-ment with illiteracy, are only symptoms of general shoddiness.

Obviously one main cause of this state of things has been the sheer pressure of numbers, along with a deplorable shrinkage in the number of qualified teachers. But the situation would not be so bad as it has been if the downward pressure of numbers had not been powerfully strengthened by misguided doc-trine and practice. The training of teachers and the control of school curricula have been in the hands of colleges of education and their products, and these have operated on principles extracted from John Dewey's philosophy of bar-barism. (If that phrase seems unduly harsh, I may say that I have in mind Dewey's hostility to what he regarded as leisure-class studies; his anti-historical attitude, his desire—intensified in his followers—to immerse students in the contemporary and immediate; and his denial of a hierarchy of studies, his doc-trine that all kinds of experience are equally or uniquely valuable; and it would not be irrelevant to add his notoriously inept writing.) The lowest common denominator has been, not an evil, but an ideal. The substantial disciplines have been so denuded of content that multitudes of students, often taught by uneducated teachers, have been illiterate, uninformed, and thoroughly im-mature. There is no use in priding ourselves on the operation of the dem-ocratic principle if education loses much of its meaning in the process. When we think, for instance, of education for citizenship, which has been the cry of modern pedagogy, we may think also of the volume and violence of popular support given to the anti-intellectual demagoguery of the last few years. Mass education tends to reflect mass civilization, instead of opposing it. Even if education were everywhere working on the highest level, it would still face tremendous odds.

The great problem has been, and will be, first, the preservation of minority culture against the many and insidious pressures of mass civilization, and, secondly, the extension of that minority culture through wider and wider areas.

The rising flood of students is very much like the barbarian invasions of the early Middle Ages, and then the process of education took a thousand years. We hope for something less overwhelming, and for a less protracted cure, but the principle is the same; Graeco-Roman-Christian culture not only survived but triumphed, and with enrichment. If we think of our problem in the light of that one, we shall not be disheartened but recognize both as phases of man's perennial growing pains.

Throughout history it has been a more or less small minority that has created and preserved what culture and enlightenment we have, and, if adverse forces are always growing, that minority is always growing too. In spite of the low standards that have commonly prevailed in public education during the last fifty years, I think the top layer of college students now are proportionately more numerous than they were thirty years ago and are more generally serious and critical. There is a growing nucleus of fine minds, and teachers are concerned with the enlargement of that all-important group. At the same time, without retreating from that position, one wonders what it is in our educational process or in our culture at large that often causes a liberal education to end on Commencement Day.

I have no novel and dramatic remedy for the evils that have shown themselves so clearly already and will become more formidable still. But I might mention a few things of varying importance which do not seem utopian. Of course I represent no one but myself, and I cannot even say, like a member of the House of Lords, that I enjoy the full confidence of my constituents.

In the first place, I see no reason why the flood of students should be allowed to pour into college, why automatic graduation from school should qualify anyone for admission. We ought to recognize, and make people in general recognize, that a desire for economic or social advantage, or for merely four years of idle diversion, is not enough. Under such pressure as is coming, surely the state universities have the strength to set up bars and select their student body, instead of admitting all who choose to walk in the front door and then, with much trouble and expense, trying to get rid of some through the back door. Doubtless such procedure would require a campaign of enlightenment and persuasion, but legislators always have an alert ear for the cry of economy, and the public must be convinced that higher education, or what passes for that, is neither a birthright nor a badge of respectability, and that useful and happy lives can be led without a college degree. As things are, we have an army of misfits, who lower educational standards and increase expense, and no branch of a university staff has grown more rapidly of late years than the psychiatric squad.

Secondly, many people have grounds for the belief that the multiplying junior colleges can and will drain off a large number of the young who for various reasons are unfitted for a really strenuous four-year course. Junior colleges, however, should not be recreational centers for the subnormal.

Thirdly, I think the need for formal education beyond high school would be much lessened, and the quality of both secondary and higher education obviously improved, if the colleges and universities, getting the public behind them, made a concerted and effectual demand that the schools do their proper work and do it better than a great many schools have been doing it. Quite commonly, a distressing proportion of a college course now consists of high school work. We have grown so accustomed to a battalion of instructors teaching elementary composition to freshmen that we take it as a normal part of college education, whereas it is a monstrosity. Imagine a European university teaching the rudiments of expression! If high school graduates are illiterate, they have no business in college. For a long time, and for a variety of reasons, we have had slackness all along the line; somehow, some time, strictness and discipline have got to begin.

Increased enrollments have almost inevitably led to increased reliance upon large lecture courses. There are administrators who assume that there is no limit to the effectiveness of a lecture course except the size of the auditorium, and there are also teachers who see positive virtues in lectures and can themselves display them. Perhaps because I never remember anything I hear in a lecture, I do not share that faith. I favor classes small enough to allow discussion, and that is expensive. But there are possible economies that would be highly desirable in themselves. We do not need to maintain the naive doctrine that there has to be a course in anything in which anyone ever has been or might be interested. Many catalogues list courses that can only be called fantastic, and I don't think I am guilty of partisan prejudice if I say that these are rarely found among the humanities. If we had fewer and less specialized courses, and if we did not have our armies of composition teachers, a considerable number of man-hours would be released for smaller classes.

One thing that has suffered grievously and conspicuously in this last generation has been the study of foreign languages. The usual reason given is again the pressure of numbers, the numbers who are not going beyond high school, but again a positive reason has been open or quiet hostility. Languages have been pretty well crowded out of the school curriculum, and of course there has been a corresponding decline in college study. Nothing has been commoner in recent decades than the applicant for admission to a graduate school who has had little or no acquaintance with any foreign language except possibly a year or two of Spanish. Serious study of a foreign language means work, and a first principle of modern pedagogy has been the elimination of work. Thus, during the years in which we have all become conscious of one small world, and in which this country has become the leader of that world, educational theory and practice have retreated into cultural parochialism. There is no need to argue how necessary for the ordinary citizen is some knowledge of a foreign language and a foreign people. In the last few years a good many parents have been aroused, and the Modern Language Association has been putting on a vigorous campaign, so that progress has been made; but there is a long way to go. It is encouraging that in some cities successful experiments have been made in the teaching of languages in elementary schools, where, for good psychological reasons, they ought to begin. I wish there were something en-

couraging to be said about the ancient languages, but we are concerned with
actualities.

Finally, since I touched on the large number of young people who are in
college and shouldn't be, I might mention those who are not and should be, and
who may be lost in the oncoming flood. Educators and others are more conscious than they once were of our failure to recognize and foster promising
students who cannot afford college, and increasing efforts are being made in
that direction; but we are still very far behind England, where bright students
are picked out at the age of ten or eleven and brought along on scholarships.
If we spent on exceptional students a fraction of the time and money we have
spent on nursing lame ducks, there would be a considerable change in the
quality of education.

One last word on a different matter. Like everything else, the Ph.D. has
been cheapened by quantitative pressure, and it might be earnestly wished
that it were not a union card for the teaching profession. There are plenty of
young men and women who would be good teachers without such a degree,
and the degree itself ought to mean something more than it does. Along
with that may go another earnest wish, that both administrators and members
of departments would abandon the principle of "publish or perish." Socrates
would never have had a chance at an assistant professorship.

Ernest Earnest

EVEN A.B.'S MUST EAT

There is considerable current alarm about the future of the Liberal Arts
College. Naturally this emotion is felt most keenly by persons whose livelihood
depends upon the continued existence of that type of institution. They usually
defend their bread and butter by eloquent pleas for the non-material values.
Thus the many articles in academic journals are likely to be labeled "A Defense
of Humanism," or "The Humanities and the Opportunity of Peace." And the
discussions are filled with phrases like: "stimulating . . . a critical and aesthetic
taste"; "an appreciative love for what is truly and enduringly beautiful"; "teach
hope, love, and courage"; "recognize or retrieve those eternal truths which are
above the stream of evolution and change"; ". . . true education is but a continuous process of re-examining, re-appraising, and re-vitalizing the interrelationships of existence." And of course there is always the old stand-by: education
for democracy.

Now I have no quarrel with any or all of these objectives except, perhaps, with
their vagueness. There is always the suspicion that when a use cannot be found
for something, it will be asserted to have "higher values"—like an impractical

From *The American Scholar*, Autumn 1944. Reprinted by permission of *The American Scholar*.

coffee urn kept in the china closet as an *objet d'art*. Our Victorian ancestors were more prone to that sort of thing than we are—though the whatnot has come back in decorator-designed interiors. The magazines are beginning to speak of "the revival of the style of a more leisurely and comfortable age." There is a suspicious parallel between the advertising of Victorian reproductions of furniture and the arguments of the humanists. Please don't ask for a definition of humanist or humanity; there seems to be no agreement on that point. A working definition might be *humanist:* a person who teaches some subject other than science or a vocation; and *humanity:* a subject that students must be *required* to take along with the ones they really want.

Now I, for one, do not believe that a college course in Lunchroom Management or Clothing Selection is preferable to one in aesthetics or Greek history. I am not at all sure that the first two are the more practical. But I do not believe that any number of eloquent pleas for recapturing the "lost soul" of society is going to entice students into the Colleges of Liberal Arts. In fact any students who are attracted by the grandiloquent phrases are likely to be aesthetes, impractical idealists, or potential school teachers. Boys and girls from wealthy homes may come also, but they come for very practical reasons: four years of pleasant life, social polish, and a certificate of culture useful in certain social circles. As a rule the Liberal Arts College is very efficient in supplying these requirements. Certainly more efficient than a school offering training in lunchroom management or methods of teaching shorthand.

It is quite another matter to educate one to appreciate "what is truly and enduringly beautiful" or to "recognize or retrieve . . . eternal truths." Too often it is assumed that these things can be taught as entities unrelated to other considerations—that there is a world in which morality, truth, and beauty exist apart from the ethics of business, or the truth of a scientific or social theory, or the beauty of a particular poem or office building.

The advocates of liberal arts training will deny this. They will argue that a knowledge of philosophy helps one to understand the values in contemporary life (or more often the alleged lack of values); that mathematics trains the accurate use of the reason (an idea long since exploded by psychologists); that history helps in an understanding of today's politics; and that literature and art give one standards of judgment to apply to contemporary literature or art, or that they do something or other for one's personality—something very fine, of course.

Students often pay lip service to these doctrines: they say that they want college to give them "culture." But that is almost always a secondary aim. The vast majority of students are in college to become engineers, accountants, physicians, social workers, teachers—or even chiropodists and undertakers. If at the same time they can acquire the mystic quality called culture by taking a few courses in language, history, and literature they are willing to spare a little time from their real purpose. But few pre-meds will elect Fine Arts 1 if it conflicts with Biology 127; and fewer civil engineers will study Chaucer when they can get Strength of Materials instead.

All this may be simply an indication of mistaken values, the symptoms of a materialistic national culture, the worship of false gods. I believe that it is rather an indication of faulty methods. Two deeply religious men may both desire the kingdom of heaven; one may try to reach it by praying continually, wearing a hair shirt, and refusing to bathe; the other by ministering to the sick. It is quite possible that the second man will find very little time to examine his soul or clarify points of theology. He therefore spends less time on his "specialty" than does the ascetic, but he may be more fully obtaining his objective.

The analogy may apply to a liberal education. It is quite possible that extreme specialization is not the best preparation for most professions or intellectual occupations. It is impossible in a paper of this sort to support this point of view in detail. But it is a point of view almost universal among believers in a liberal education.

However, I venture upon two assertions: one, that the liberal arts colleges fail to implement this point of view; and two, that they fail to demonstrate its validity. To put the case more specifically: I believe that the liberal arts college fails to relate its work to the world the students must face, and that it fails to make the student understand its aims. In colloquial phraseology, the liberal arts college high-hats the vocational phases of education, and it fails to sell itself to its customers.

Almost all the defenders of a liberal education use a tone of moral superiority. The phrases quoted at the beginning of this essay suggest an out-of-this-world point of view. Yet if the liberal arts college is to survive, it must function in this world and must make that function clear. In a democratic society, the primary function demanded of a college or university is that it prepare its students to earn a living. The point of view stated by Jacques Barzun: "Vocational training has nothing to do with education," implies that education is only for a leisure class or a scholarly elite. Only at their peril can liberal arts colleges cater to a Brahmin caste. Most students and parents are certainly not going to be less materialistic about their bread and butter than are the defenders of a liberal education.

It may seem that this premise denies any possibility of preserving the liberal arts. Not at all. I have already pointed out that the arts colleges insist on the superior value of their training as preparation for an intellectual vocation or profession. I agree with this point of view. In the rapidly changing world of business, technology, and social order, a narrowly specialized training is often obsolete before the student graduates. Many of my former college mates are in fields of activity which did not exist twenty years ago. No vocational training then offered could have helped them. A contemporary radio news analyst would certainly find his college work in European history more valuable than his course in News Story Write-Up. History, language, literature, philosophy have vocational value. More obvious is the vocational aspect of social science and psychology. All these are elements in a liberal arts program.

Specifically I suggest that the liberal arts colleges integrate their programs with vocational fields. For instance: what courses should be elected by a student interested in entering the diplomatic field, or social security, or a host of other governmental activities for which the A.B. course is the best preparation? Few faculty advisers have this information. Students themselves are often unaware that certain of these fields exist; more have no idea how to prepare for them. So, instead, they take a degree in marketing or dentistry or advertising—anything with a label indicating possible usefulness. Students are often amazed to find that they can enter law school with an A.B. in history and literature instead of a B.S. in "pre-law."

This brings us to my second recommendation: a better publicizing of the vocational usefulness of a liberal arts education. Bulletins and catalogs of vocational schools often have much to say about opportunities in the fields they train for; those of liberal arts colleges are extremely reticent on this point. Except for occasional listings of requirements for medical school or teaching, there is almost no discussion of so crass a topic as preparing for a job. For instance, in a recent study of training for the field of social security, Karl de Schweinitz states that the best possible background is the academic discipline and a cultural education. It is significant that this study was made for the Social Security Board and not under the auspices of the colleges.

All this may seem to imply that the liberal arts colleges should turn themselves into vocational schools. The answer is that they are vocational schools and always have been. Harvard College was founded specifically to train ministers of the gospel. The classical education of the nineteenth century was regarded as the best possible training for the law and the church. Today students in liberal arts colleges are preparing to become biologists, psychologists, sociologists, teachers, and lawyers.

What I suggest, then, is not a revision of the curriculum: no addition of gadget courses to attract uncritical customers. It is simply that the colleges accept the fact that they have a vocational function and that they exercise that function intelligently. That means vocational guidance for students, not in a haphazard way, but by trained counselors with adequate budgets for research; it means well run placement bureaus; it means making vocational information readily available to students; and it means a constant and intelligent study of the changing needs of the community. It is shortsighted if not unethical to turn out thousands more pre-meds than the medical schools will accept; to produce English teachers far in excess of demand, and at the same time to ignore fields where educated persons are desperately needed.

But what happens to "culture" in all this? Does it mean that we forget all about the permanently true and beautiful? My answer is that "culture" is always a by-product of something else. Shakespeare's plays are now studied chiefly for their cultural value; they were written to attract patrons to the box office. Architects have always designed their buildings for specific utilitarian purposes. Stiegel produced his famous glass for a market; he went bankrupt when he overestimated the market. The arts have always been closely linked with the business of living. It is only when they become art for art's sake that they wither. Similarly, culture for culture's sake becomes exotic and unreal.

If literature and history and philosophy cannot be related to the life of the community, they have no very important values. In other words, if a psychologist is not a better psychologist because he knows something about the development of human thought and the expression of human nature through art, then there is little hope for philosophy, history, and literature.

Many of the defenders of a liberal education emphasize its broader social values: the making of intelligent citizens; the training for life rather than making a living; the understanding of ethical and moral values. But a member of a democratic society functions in that society chiefly through his occupation. A man's contribution to his age is above all his contribution as a physician, a manufacturer, a chemist, a writer, a publisher. A physician's knowledge or lack of knowledge of sociology will appear during dinner table conversations and at the polls. But it is vastly more important in his work as a physician and member of a medical association. It is there that his knowledge or lack of knowledge chiefly affects society.

Culture does not function in a vacuum. The "lost soul" of society will be found not in college courses, but in the market place and the laboratory and the court of law. The liberal arts college cannot educate some sort of mythical men of vision; it must educate chemists and sociologists and journalists with vision. When it fully accepts this function, it will no longer be troubled by falling enrollments. The professors can cease to worry about their own bread and butter when they recognize that even an A.B. must eat.

Ralph Waldo Emerson

THE AMERICAN SCHOLAR[1]

Mr. President and Gentlemen, I greet you on the recommencement of our literary year. Our anniversary is one of hope, and, perhaps, not enough of labor. We do not meet for games of strength or skill, for the recitation of histories, tragedies, and odes, like the ancient Greeks; for parliaments of love and poesy, like the Troubadours; nor for the advancement of science, like our contemporaries in the British and European capitals. Thus far, our holiday has been simply a friendly sign of the survival of the love of letters amongst a people too busy to give to letters any more. As such it is precious as the sign of an indestructible instinct. Perhaps the time is already come when it ought to be, and will be, something else; when the sluggard intellect of this continent will look from under its iron lids and fill the postponed expectation of the world with something better than the exertions of mechanical skill. Our day of dependence, our long apprenticeship to the learning of other lands, draws to a close. The

1. An oration delivered before the Phi Beta Kappa Society at Cambridge, August 31, 1837.

millions that around us are rushing into life, cannot always be fed on the sere remains of foreign harvests. Events, actions arise, that must be sung, that will sing themselves. Who can doubt that poetry will revive and lead in a new age, as the star in the constellation Harp, which now flames in our zenith, astronomers announce, shall one day be the pole-star for a thousand years?

In this hope I accept the topic which not only usage but the nature of our association seem to prescribe to this day,—the AMERICAN SCHOLAR. Year by year we come up hither to read one more chapter of his biography. Let us inquire what light new days and events have thrown on his character and his hopes.

It is one of those fables which out of an unknown antiquity convey an unlooked-for wisdom, that the gods, in the beginning, divided Man into men, that he might be more helpful to himself; just as the hand was divided into fingers, the better to answer its end.

The old fable covers a doctrine ever new and sublime; that there is One Man, —present to all particular men only partially, or through one faculty; and that you must take the whole society to find the whole man. Man is not a farmer, or a professor, or an engineer, but he is all. Man is priest, and scholar, and states-man, and producer, and soldier. In the *divided* or social state these functions are parcelled out to individuals, each of whom aims to do his stint of the joint work, whilst each other performs his. The fable implies that the individual, to possess himself, must sometimes return from his own labor to embrace all the other laborers. But, unfortunately, this original unit, this fountain of power, has been so distributed to multitudes, has been so minutely subdivided and peddled out, that it is spilled into drops, and cannot be gathered. The state of society is one in which the members have suffered amputation from the trunk, and strut about so many walking monsters,—a good finger, a neck, a stomach, an elbow, but never a man.

Man is thus metamorphosed into a thing, into many things. The planter, who is Man sent out into the field to gather food, is seldom cheered by any idea of the true dignity of his ministry. He sees his bushel and his cart, and nothing beyond, and sinks into the farmer, instead of Man on the farm. The tradesman scarcely ever gives an ideal worth to his work, but is ridden by the routine of his craft, and the soul is subject to dollars. The priest becomes a form; the attorney a statute-book; the mechanic a machine; the sailor a rope of the ship.

In this distribution of functions the scholar is the delegated intellect. In the right state he is *Man Thinking*. In the degenerate state, when the victim of society, he tends to become a mere thinker, or still worse, the parrot of other men's thinking.

In this view of him, as Man Thinking, the theory of his office is contained. Him Nature solicits with all her placid, all her monitory pictures; him the past instructs; him the future invites. Is not indeed every man a student, and do not all things exist for the student's behoof? And, finally, is not the true scholar the only true master? But the old oracle said, "All things have two handles: beware of the wrong one." In life, too often, the scholar errs with mankind and forfeits his privilege. Let us see him in his school, and consider him in reference to the main influences he receives.

I. The first in time and the first in importance of the influences upon the mind is that of nature. Every day, the sun; and, after the sunset, Night and her stars. Ever the winds blow; ever the grass grows. Every day, men and women, conversing, beholding and beholden. The scholar is he of all men whom this spectacle most engages. He must settle its value in his mind. What is nature to him? There is never a beginning, there is never an end, to the inexplicable continuity of this web of God, but always circular power returning into itself. Therein it resembles his own spirit, whose beginning, whose ending, he never can find,—so entire, so boundless. Far too as her splendors shine, system on system shooting like rays, upward, downward without centre, without circumference,—in the mass and in the particle, Nature hastens to render account of herself to the mind. Classification begins. To the young mind every thing is individual, stands by itself. By and by, it finds how to join two things and see in them one nature; then three, then three thousand; and so, tyrannized over by its own unifying instinct, it goes on tying things together, diminishing anomalies, discovering roots running under ground whereby contrary and remote things cohere and flower out from one stem. It presently learns that since the dawn of history there has been a constant accumulation and classifying of facts. But what is classification but the perceiving that these objects are not chaotic, and are not foreign, but have a law which is also a law of the human mind? The astronomer discovers that geometry, a pure abstraction of the human mind, is the measure of planetary motion. The chemist finds proportions and intelligible method throughout matter; and science is nothing but the finding of analogy, identity, in the most remote parts. The ambitious soul sits down before each refractory fact; one after another reduces all strange constitutions, all new powers, to their class and their law, and goes on forever to animate the last fibre of organization, the outskirts of nature, by insight.

Thus to him, to this schoolboy under the bending dome of day, is suggested that he and it proceed from one root; one is leaf and one is flower; relation, sympathy, stirring in every vein. And what is that root? Is not that the soul of his soul? A thought too bold; a dream too wild. Yet when this spiritual light shall have revealed the law of more earthly natures,—when he has learned to worship the soul, and to see that the natural philosophy that now is, is only the first groupings of its gigantic hand, he shall look forward to an ever expanding knowledge as to a becoming creator. He shall see that nature is the opposite of the soul, answering to it part for part. One is seal and one is print. Its beauty is the beauty of his own mind. Its laws are the laws of his own mind. Nature then becomes to him the measure of his attainments. So much of nature as he is ignorant of, so much of his own mind does he not yet possess. And, in fine, the ancient precept, "Know thyself," and the modern precept, "Study nature," become at last one maxim.

II. The next great influence into the spirit of the scholar is the mind of the Past,—in whatever form, whether of literature, of art, of institutions, that mind is inscribed. Books are the best type of the influence of the past, and perhaps we shall get at the truth,—learn the amount of this influence more conveniently, —by considering their value alone.

The theory of books is noble. The scholar of the first age received into him the world around; brooded thereon; gave it the new arrangement of his own mind, and uttered it again. It came into him life; it went out from him truth. It came to him short-lived actions; it went out from him immortal thoughts. It came to him business; it went from him poetry. It was dead fact; now, it is quick thought. It can stand, and it can go. It now endures, it now flies, it now inspires. Precisely in proportion to the depth of mind from which it issued, so high does it soar, so long does it sing.

Or, I might say, it depends on how far the process had gone, of transmuting life into truth. In proportion to the completeness of the distillation, so will the purity and imperishableness of the product be. But none is quite perfect. As no air-pump can by any means make a perfect vacuum, so neither can any artist entirely exclude the conventional, the local, the perishable from his book, or write a book of pure thought, that shall be as efficient, in all respects, to a remote posterity, as to contemporaries, or rather to the second age. Each age, it is found, must write its own books; or rather, each generation for the next succeeding. The books of an older period will not fit this.

Yet hence arises a grave mischief. The sacredness which attaches to the act of creation, the act of thought, is transferred to the record. The poet chanting was felt to be a divine man: henceforth the chant is divine also. The writer was a just and wise spirit: henceforward it is settled the book is perfect; as love of the hero corrupts into worship of his statue. Instantly the book becomes noxious: the guide is a tyrant. The sluggish and perverted mind of the multitude, slow to open to the incursions of Reason, having once so opened, having once received this book, stands upon it, and makes an outcry if it is disparaged. Colleges are built on it. Books are written on it by thinkers, not by Man Thinking; by men of talent, that is, who start wrong, who set out from accepted dogmas, not from their own sight of principles. Meek young men grow up in libraries, believing it their duty to accept the views which Cicero, which Locke, which Bacon, have given; forgetful that Cicero, Locke, and Bacon were only young men in libraries when they wrote these books.

Hence, instead of Man Thinking, we have the bookworm. Hence the book-learned class, who value books, as such; not as related to nature and the human constitution, but as making a sort of Third Estate with the world and the soul. Hence the restorers of readings, the emendators, the bibliomaniacs of all degrees.

Books are the best of things, well used; abused, among the worst. What is the right use? What is the one end which all means go to effect? They are for nothing but to inspire. I had better never see a book than to be warped by its attraction clean out of my own orbit, and made a satellite instead of a system. The one thing in the world, of value, is the active soul. This every man is entitled to; this every man contains within him, although in almost all men obstructed, and as yet unborn. The soul active sees absolute truth and utters truth, or creates. In this action it is genius; not the privilege of here and there a favorite, but the sound estate of every man. In its essence it is progressive. The book, the college, the school of art, the institution of any kind, stop with some past utterance of genius. This is good, say they,—let us hold by this. They pin me down. They look backward and not forward. But genius looks forward: the eyes of man are set in his forehead, not in his hindhead: man hopes: genius creates. Whatever talents may be, if the man create not, the pure efflux of the Deity is not his;—cinders and smoke there may be, but not yet flame. There are creative manners, there are creative actions, and creative words; manners, actions, words, that is, indicative of no custom or authority, but springing spontaneous from the mind's own sense of good and fair.

On the other part, instead of being its own seer, let it receive from another mind its truth, though it were in torrents of light, without periods of solitude, inquest, and self-recovery, and a fatal disservice is done. Genius is always sufficiently the enemy of genius by over-influence. The literature of every nation bears me witness. The English dramatic poets have Shakspearized now for two hundred years.

Undoubtedly there is a right way of reading, so it be sternly subordinated. Man Thinking must not be subdued by his instruments. Books are for the scholar's idle times. When he can read God directly, the hour is too precious to be wasted in other men's transcripts of their readings. But when the intervals of darkness come, as come they must,—when the sun is hid and the stars withdraw their shining,—we repair to the lamps which were kindled by their ray, to guide our steps to the East again, where the dawn is. We hear, that we may speak. The Arabian proverb says, "A fig tree, looking on a fig tree, becometh fruitful."

It is remarkable, the character of the pleasure we derive from the best books. They impress us with the conviction that one nature wrote and the same reads. We read the verses of one of the great English poets, of Chaucer, of Marvell, of Dryden, with the most modern joy,—with a pleasure, I mean, which is in great part caused by the abstraction of all *time* from their verses. There is some awe mixed with the joy of our surprise, when this poet, who lived in some past world, two or three hundred years ago, says that which lies close to my own soul, that which I also had well-nigh thought and said. But for the evidence thence afforded to the philosophical doctrine of the identity of all minds, we should suppose some pre-established harmony, some foresight of souls that were to be, and some preparation of stores for their future wants, like the fact observed in insects, who lay up food before death for the young grub they shall never see.

I would not be hurried by any love of system, by any exaggeration of instincts, to underrate the Book. We all know, that as the human body can be nourished on any food, though it were boiled grass and the broth of shoes, so the human mind can be fed by any knowledge. And great and heroic men have existed who had almost no other information than by the printed page. I only would say that it needs a strong head to bear that diet. One must be an inventor to read well. As the proverb says, "He that would bring home the wealth of the Indies, must carry out the wealth of the Indies." There is then creative reading as well as creative writing. When the mind is braced by labor and invention, the page of whatever book we read becomes luminous with manifold allusion. Every sentence is doubly significant, and the sense of our author is as broad as the world. We then see, what is always true, that as the seer's hour of vision is short and rare among heavy days and months, so is its record, perchance, the least part of his volume. The discerning will read, in his Plato or Shakspeare, only that least part,—only the authentic utterances of the oracle;—all the rest he rejects, were it never so many times Plato's and Shakspeare's.

Of course there is a portion of reading quite indispensable to a wise man. History and exact science he must learn by laborious reading. Colleges, in like manner, have their indispensable office,—to teach elements. But they can only highly serve us when they aim not to drill, but to create; when they gather from far every ray of various genius to their hospitable halls, and by the concentrated fires, set the hearts of their youth on flame. Thought and knowledge are natures in which apparatus and pretension avail nothing. Gowns and pecuniary foundations, though of towns of gold, can never countervail the least sentence or syllable of wit. Forget this, and our American colleges will recede in their public importance, whilst they grow richer every year.

III. There goes in the world a notion that the scholar should be a recluse, a valetudinarian,—as unfit for any handiwork, or public labor as a penknife for an axe. The so-called "practical men" sneer at speculative men, as if, because they speculate or *see*, they could do nothing. I have heard it said that the clergy, —who are always, more universally than any other class, the scholars of their day,—are addressed as women; that the rough, spontaneous conversation of men they do not hear, but only a mincing and diluted speech. They are often virtually disfranchised; and indeed there are advocates for their celibacy. As far as this is true of the studious classes, it is not just and wise. Action is with the scholar subordinate, but it is essential. Without it he is not yet man. Without it thought can never ripen into truth. Whilst the world hangs before the eye as a cloud of beauty, we cannot even see its beauty. Inaction is cowardice, but there can be no scholar without the heroic mind. The preamble of thought, the transition through which it passes from the unconscious to the conscious, is action. Only so much do I know, as I have lived. Instantly we know whose words are loaded with life, and whose not.

The world,—this shadow of the soul, or *other me*,—lies wide around. Its attractions are the keys which unlock my thoughts and make me acquainted with myself. I run eagerly into this resounding tumult. I grasp the hands of those next me, and take my place in the ring to suffer and to work, taught by an instinct that so shall the dumb abyss be vocal with speech. I pierce its order; I dissipate its fear; I dispose of it within the circuit of my expanding life. So much only of life as I know by experience, so much of the wilderness have I vanquished and planted, or so far have I extended my being, my dominion. I do not see how any man can afford, for the sake of his nerves and his nap, to spare any action in which he can partake. It is pearls and rubies to his discourse. Drudgery, calamity, exasperation, want, are instructors in eloquence and wisdom. The true scholar grudges every opportunity of action past by, as a loss of power. It is the raw material out of which the intellect moulds her splendid products. A strange process too, this by which experience is converted into thought, as a mulberry leaf is converted into satin. The manufacture goes forward at all hours.

The actions and events of our childhood and youth are now matters of calmest observation. They lie like fair pictures in the air. Not so with our recent actions,—with the business which we now have in hand. On this we are quite unable to speculate. Our affections as yet circulate through it. We no more feel or know it than we feel the feet, or the hand, or the brain of our body. The new deed is yet a part of life,—remains for a time immersed in our unconscious life. In some contemplative hour it detaches itself from the life like a ripe fruit, to become a thought of the mind. Instantly it is raised, transfigured; the corruptible has put on incorruption. Henceforth it is an object of beauty, however base its origin and neighborhood. Observe too the impossibility of antedating this act. In its grub state, it cannot fly, it cannot shine, it is a dull grub. But suddenly, without observation, the self-same thing unfurls beautiful wings, and is an angel of wisdom. So is there no fact, no event, in our private history, which shall not, sooner or later, lose its adhesive, inert form, and astonish us by soaring from our body into the empyrean. Cradle and infancy, school and playground, the fear of boys, and dogs, and ferules, the love of little maids and berries, and many another fact that once filled the whole sky, are gone already; friend and relative, profession and party, town and country, nation and world, must also soar and sing.

Of course, he who has put forth his total strength in fit actions has the richest return of wisdom. I will not shut myself out of this globe of action, and transplant an oak into a flower-pot, there to hunger and pine; nor trust the revenue of some single faculty, and exhaust one vein of thought, much like those Savoyards, who, getting their livelihood by carving shepherds, shepherdesses, and smoking Dutchmen, for all Europe, went out one day to the mountain to find stock, and discovered that they had whittled up the last of their pine trees. Authors we have, in numbers, who have written out their vein, and who, moved by a commendable prudence, sail for Greece or Palestine, follow the trapper into the prairie, or ramble round Algiers, to replenish their merchantable stock.

If it were only for a vocabulary, the scholar would be covetous of action. Life is our dictionary. Years are well spent in country labors; in town; in the insight into trades and manufactures; in frank intercourse with many men and women; in science; in art; to the one end of mastering in all their facts a language by which to illustrate and embody our perceptions. I learn immediately from any speaker how much he has already lived, through the poverty or the splendor of his speech. Life lies behind us as the quarry from whence we get tiles and copestones for the masonry of to-day. This is the way to learn grammar. Colleges and books only copy the language which the field and the work-yard made.

But the final value of action, like that of books, and better than books, is that it is a resource. The great principle of Undulation in nature, that shows itself in the inspiring and expiring of the breath; in desire and satiety; in the ebb and flow of the sea; in day and night; in heat and cold; and, as yet more deeply ingrained in every atom and every fluid, is known to us under the name of Polarity,—these "fits of easy transmission and reflection," as Newton called them, are the law of nature because they are the law of spirit.

The mind now thinks, now acts, and each fit reproduces the other. When the artist has exhausted his materials, when the fancy no longer paints, when thoughts are no longer apprehended and books are a weariness,—he has always the resource *to live*. Character is higher than intellect. Thinking is the function. Living is the functionary. The stream retreats to its source. A great soul will be strong to live, as well as strong to think. Does he lack organ or medium to impart his truth? He can still fall back on this elemental force of living them. This is a total act. Thinking is a partial act. Let the grandeur of justice shine in his affairs. Let the beauty of affection cheer his lowly roof. Those "far from fame," who dwell and act with him, will feel the force of his constitution in the doings and passages of the day better than it can be measured by any public and designed display. Time shall teach him that the scholar loses no hour which the man lives. Herein he unfolds the sacred germ of his instinct, screened from influence. What is lost in seemliness is gained in strength. Not out of those on whom systems of education have exhausted their culture, comes the helpful giant to destroy the old or to build the new, but out of unhandselled savage nature; out of terrible Druids and Berserkers come at last Alfred and Shakspeare.

I hear therefore with joy whatever is beginning to be said of the dignity and necessity of labor to every citizen. There is virtue yet in the hoe and the spade, for learned as well as for unlearned hands. And labor is everywhere welcome; always we are invited to work; only be this limitation observed, that a man shall not for the sake of wider activity sacrifice any opinion to the popular judgments and modes of action.

I have now spoken of the education of the scholar by nature, by books, and by action. It remains to say somewhat of his duties.

They are such as become Man Thinking. They may all be comprised in self-trust. The office of the scholar is to cheer, to raise, and to guide men by showing them facts amidst appearances. He plies the slow, unhonored, and unpaid task of observation. Flamsteed and Herschel, in their glazed observatories, may catalogue the stars with the praise of all men, and the results being splendid and useful, honor is sure. But he, in his private observatory, cataloguing obscure and nebulous stars of the human mind, which as yet no man has thought of as such,—watching days and months sometimes for a few facts; correcting still his old records;—must relinquish display and immediate fame. In the long period of his preparation he must betray often an ignorance and shiftlessness in popular arts, incurring the disdain of the able who shoulder him aside. Long he must stammer in his speech; often forego the living for the dead. Worse yet, he must accept—how often!—poverty and solitude. For the ease and pleasure of treading the old road, accepting the fashions, the education, the religion of society, he takes the cross of making his own, and, of course, the self-accusation, the faint heart, the frequent uncertainty and loss of time, which are the nettles and tangling vines in the way of the self-relying and self-directed; and the state of virtual hostility in which he seems to stand to society, and especially to educated society. For all this loss and scorn, what offset? He is to find consolation in exercising the highest functions of human nature. He is one who raises himself from private considerations and breathes and lives on public and illustrious thoughts. He is the world's eye. He is the world's heart. He is to resist the vulgar prosperity that retrogrades ever to barbarism, by preserving and communicating heroic sentiments, noble biographies, melodious verse, and the conclusions of history. Whatsoever oracles the human heart, in all emergencies, in all solemn hours, has uttered as its commentary on the world of actions,—these he shall receive and impart. And whatsoever new verdict Reason from her inviolable seat pronounces on the passing men and events of to-day,—this he shall hear and promulgate.

These being his functions, it becomes him to feel all confidence in himself, and to defer never to the popular cry. He and he only knows the world. The world of any moment is the merest appearance. Some great decorum, some fetish of a government, some ephemeral trade, or war, or man, is cried up by half mankind and cried down by the other half, as if all depended on this particular up or down. The odds are that the whole question is not worth the poorest thought which the scholar has lost in listening to the controversy. Let him not quit his belief that a popgun is a popgun, though the ancient and honorable of the earth affirm it to be the crack of doom. In silence, in steadiness, in severe abstraction, let him hold by himself; add observation to observation, patient of neglect, patient of reproach, and bide his own time,—happy enough if he can satisfy himself alone that this day he has seen something truly. Success treads on every right step. For the instinct is sure, that prompts him to tell his brother what he thinks. He then learns that in going down into the secrets of his own mind he has descended into the secrets of all minds. He learns that he who has mastered any law in his private thoughts, is master to that extent of all men whose language he speaks, and of all into whose language his own can be translated. The poet, in utter solitude remembering his spontaneous thoughts and recording them, is found to have recorded that which men in crowded cities find true for them also. The orator distrusts at first the fitness of his frank confessions, his want of knowledge of the persons he addresses, until he finds that he is the complement of his hearers;—that they drink his words because he fulfils for them their own nature; the deeper he dives into his privatest, secretest presentiment, to his wonder he finds this is the most acceptable, most public, and universally true. The people delight in it; the better part of every man feels, This is my music; this is myself.

In self-trust all the virtues are comprehended. Free should the scholar be,— free and brave. Free even to the definition of freedom, "without any hindrance that does not arise out of his own constitution." Brave; for fear is a thing which a scholar by his very function puts behind him. Fear always springs from ignorance. It is a shame to him if his tranquillity, amid dangerous times, arise from the presumption that like children and women his is a protected class; or if he seek a temporary peace by the diversion of his thoughts from politics or vexed questions, hiding his head like an ostrich in the flowering bushes, peeping into microscopes, and turning rhymes, as a boy whistles to keep his courage up. So is the danger a danger still; so is the fear worse. Manlike let him turn and face it. Let him look into its eye and search its nature, inspect its origin,—see the whelping of this lion,—which lies no great way back; he will then find in himself a perfect comprehension of its nature and extent; he will have made his hands meet on the other side, and can henceforth defy it and pass on superior. The world is his who can see through its pretension. What deafness, what stone-blind custom, what overgrown error you behold is there only by sufferance,—by your sufferance. See it to be a lie, and you have already dealt it its mortal blow.

Yes, we are the cowed,—we the trustless. It is a mischievous notion that we are come late into nature; that the world was finished a long time ago. As the world was plastic and fluid in the hands of God, so it is ever to so much of his attributes as we bring to it. To ignorance and sin, it is flint. They adapt themselves to it as they may; but in proportion as a man has any thing in him divine, the firmament flows before him and takes his signet and form. Not he is great who can alter matter, but he who can alter my state of mind. They are the kings of the world who give the color of their present thought to all nature and all art, and persuade men by the cheerful serenity of their carrying the matter, that this thing which they do is the apple which the ages have desired to pluck, now at last ripe, and inviting nations to the harvest. The great man makes the great thing. Wherever Macdonald sits, there is the head of the table. Linnæus makes botany the most alluring of studies, and wins it from the farmer and the herb-woman; Davy, chemistry; and Cuvier, fossils. The day is always his who works in it with serenity and great aims. The unstable estimates of men crowd to him whose mind is filled with a truth, as the heaped waves of the Atlantic follow the moon.

For this self-trust, the reason is deeper than can be fathomed,—darker than can be enlightened. I might not carry with me the feeling of my audience in stating my own belief. But I have already shown the ground of my hope, in adverting to the doctrine that man is one. I believe man has been wronged; he has wronged himself. He has almost lost the light that can lead him back to his prerogatives. Men are become of no account. Men in history, men in the world of to-day, are bugs, are spawn, and are called "the mass" and "the herd." In a century, in a millennium, one or two men; that is to say, one or two approximations to the right state of every man. All the rest behold in the hero or the poet their own green and crude being,—ripened; yes, and are content to be less, so *that* may attain to its full stature. What a testimony, full of grandeur, full of pity, is borne to the demands of his own nature, by the poor clansman, the poor partisan, who rejoices in the glory of his chief. The poor and the low find some amends to their immense moral capacity, for their acquiescence in a political and social inferiority. They are content to be brushed like flies from the path of a great person, so that justice shall be done by him to that common nature which it is the dearest desire of all to see enlarged and glorified. They sun themselves in the great man's light, and feel it to be their own element. They cast the dignity of man from their downtrod selves upon the shoulders of a hero, and will perish to add one drop of blood to make that great heart beat, those giant sinews combat and conquer. He lives for us, and we live in him.

Men such as they are, very naturally seek money or power; and power because it is as good as money,—the "spoils," so called, "of office." And why not? for they aspire to the highest, and this, in their sleep-walking, they dream is highest. Wake them and they shall quit the false good and leap to the true, and leave governments to clerks and desks. This revolution is to be wrought by the gradual domestication of the idea of Culture. The main enterprise of the world for splendor, for extent, is the upbuilding of a man. Here are the materials strewn along the ground. The private life of one man shall be a more illustrious monarchy, more formidable to its enemy, more sweet and serene in its influence to its friend, than any kingdom in history. For a man, rightly viewed, comprehendeth the particular natures of all men. Each philosopher, each bard, each actor has only done for me, as by a delegate, what one day I can do for myself. The books which once we valued more than the apple of the eye, we have quite exhausted. What is that but saying that we have come up with the point of view which the universal mind took through the eyes of one scribe; we have been that man, and have passed on. First, one, then another, we drain all cisterns, and waxing greater by all these supplies, we crave a better and more abundant food. The man has never lived that can feed us ever. The human mind cannot be enshrined in a person who shall set a barrier on any one side to this unbounded, unboundable empire. It is one central fire, which, flaming now out of the lips of Etna, lightens the capes of Sicily, and now out of the throat of Vesuvius, illuminates the towers and vineyards of Naples. It is one light which beams out of a thousand stars. It is one soul which animates all men.

But I have dwelt perhaps tediously upon this abstraction of the Scholar. I ought not to delay longer to add what I have to say of nearer reference to the time and to this country.

Historically, there is thought to be a difference in the ideas which predominate over successive epochs, and there are data for marking the genius of the Classic, of the Romantic, and now of the Reflective or Philosophical age. With the views I have intimated of the oneness or the identity of the mind through all individuals, I do not much dwell on these differences. In fact, I believe each individual passes through all three. The boy is a Greek; the youth, romantic; the adult, reflective. I deny not, however, that a revolution in the leading idea may be distinctly enough traced.

Our age is bewailed as the age of Introversion. Must that needs be evil? We, it seems, are critical; we are embarrassed with second thoughts; we cannot enjoy any thing for hankering to know whereof the pleasure consists; we are lined with eyes; we see with our feet; the time is infected with Hamlet's unhappiness,—

> "Sicklied o'er with the pale cast of thought."

It is so bad then? Sight is the last thing to be pitied. Would we be blind? Do we fear lest we should outsee nature and God, and drink truth dry? I look upon the discontent of the literary class as a mere announcement of the fact that they find themselves not in the state of mind of their fathers, and regret the coming state as untried; as a boy dreads the water before he has learned that he can swim. If there is any period one would desire to be born in, is it not the age of Revolution; when the old and the new stand side by side and admit of being compared; when the energies of all men are searched by fear and by hope; when the historic glories of the old can be compensated by the rich possibilities of the new era? This time, like all times, is a very good one, if we but know what to do with it.

I read with some joy of the auspicious signs of the coming days, as they glimmer already through poetry and art, through philosophy and science, through church and state.

One of these signs is the fact that the same movement which effected the elevation of what was called the lowest class in the state, assumed in literature a very marked and as benign an aspect. Instead of the sublime and beautiful, the near, the low, the common, was explored and poetized. That which had been negligently trodden under foot by those who were harnessing and provisioning themselves for long journeys into far countries, is suddenly found to be richer than all foreign parts. The literature of the poor, the feelings of the child, the philosophy of the street, the meaning of household life, are the topics of the time. It is a great stride. It is a sign—is it not?—of new vigor when the extremities are made active, when currents of warm life run into the hands and the feet. I ask not for the great, the remote, the romantic; what is doing in Italy or Arabia; what is Greek art, or Provençal minstrelsy; I embrace the common, I explore and sit at the feet of the familiar, the low. Give me insight into to-day, and you may have the antique and future worlds. What would we really know the meaning of? The meal in the firkin; the milk in the pan; the ballad in the street; the news of the boat; the glance of the eye; the form and the gait of the body;—show me the ultimate reason of these matters; show me the sublime presence of the highest spiritual cause lurking, as always it does lurk, in these suburbs and extremities of nature; let me see every trifle bristling with the polarity that ranges it instantly on an eternal law; and the shop, the plough, and the ledger referred to the like cause by which light undulates and poets sing;—and the world lies no longer a dull miscellany and lumber room, but has form and order; there is no trifle, there is no puzzle, but one design unites and animates the farthest pinnacle and the lowest trench.

This idea has inspired the genius of Goldsmith, Burns, Cowper, and in a newer time, of Goethe, Wordsworth, and Carlyle. This idea they have differently followed and with various success. In contrast with their writing, the style of

Pope, of Johnson, of Gibbon, looks cold and pedantic. This writing is blood-warm. Man is surprised to find that things near are not less beautiful and won-drous than things remote. The near explains the far. The drop is a small ocean. A man is related to all nature. This perception of the worth of the vulgar is fruitful in discoveries. Goethe, in this very thing the most modern of the moderns, has shown us, as none ever did, the genius of the ancients.

There is one man of genius who has done much for this philosophy of life, whose literary value has never yet been rightly estimated;—I mean Emanuel Swedenborg. The most imaginative of men, yet writing with the precision of a mathematician, he endeavored to engraft a purely philosophical Ethics on the popular Christianity of his time. Such an attempt of course must have difficulty which no genius could surmount. But he saw and showed the con-nection between nature and the affections of the soul. He pierced the emblem-atic or spiritual character of the visible, audible, tangible world. Especially did his shade-loving muse hover over and interpret the lower parts of nature; he showed the mysterious bond that allies moral evil to the foul material forms, and has given in epical parables a theory of insanity, of beasts, of unclean and fearful things.

Another sign of our times, also marked by an analogous political movement, is the new importance given to the single person. Every thing that tends to in-sulate the individual,—to surround him with barriers of natural respect, so that each man shall feel the world is his, and man shall treat with man as a sovereign state with a sovereign state,—tends to true union as well as greatness. "I learned," said the melancholy Pestalozzi, "that no man in God's wide earth is either willing or able to help any other man." Help must come from the bosom alone. The scholar is that man who must take up into himself all the ability of the time, all the contributions of the past, all the hopes of the future. He must be an university of knowledges. If there be one lesson more than another which should pierce his ear, it is, The world is nothing, the man is all; in yourself is the law of all nature, and you know not yet how a globule of sap ascends; in yourself slumbers the whole of Reason; it is for you to know all; it is for you to dare all. Mr. President and Gentlemen, this confidence in the unsearched might of man belongs, by all motives, by all prophecy, by all preparation, to the American Scholar. We have listened too long to the courtly muses of Europe. The spirit of the American freeman is already suspected to be timid, imitative, tame. Public and private avarice make the air we breathe thick and fat. The scholar is decent, indolent, complaisant. See already the tragic consequence. The mind of this country, taught to aim at low objects, eats upon itself. There is no work for any but the decorous and the complaisant. Young men of the fairest promise, who begin life upon our shores, inflated by the mountain winds, shined upon by all the stars of God, find the earth below not in unison with these, but are hindered from action by the disgust which the principles on which business is managed inspire, and turn drudges, or die of disgust, some of them suicides. What is the remedy? They did not yet see, and thousands of young men as hopeful now crowding to the barriers for the career do not yet see, that if the single man plant himself indomitably on his instincts. and there abide, the huge world will come round to him. Patience,—patience; with the shades of all the good and great for company; and for solace the perspective of your own infinite life; and for work the study and the communication of principles, the making those instincts prevalent, the conversion of the world. Is it not the chief disgrace in the world, **not** to be an unit;—not to be reckoned one character;—not to yield that peculiar fruit which each man was created to bear, but to be reckoned in the gross, in the hundred, or the thousand, of the party, the section, to which we belong; and our opinion predicted geographically. as the north, or the south? Not **so**, brothers and friends,—please God. ours shall not be so. We will walk on **our** own feet; we will work with our own hands; we will speak our own minds. The study of letters shall be no longer a name for pity, for doubt, and for sensual indulgence. The dread of man and the love of man shall be a wall of defence and a wreath of joy around all. A nation of men will for the first time exist, because each believes himself inspired by the Divine Soul which also inspires all men.

Language and Its Use

This section, which deals with language. takes up a subject that must be an immediate and fundamental concern of all students in college English courses. The writers represented here approach the subject variously. Robert Benchley simply reports humorously on the kind of experience we have all had with the irregularities of English word forms. Charlton Laird claims that the traditional English grammar does not explain the language and argues that it should be replaced with a modern, workable grammar. Jacques Barzun strikes out against what he terms the "infinite duplication of dufferism" and calls for greater purity in the use of language. Irving Lee is particularly concerned about people's tendency to "talk past each other," and urges greater attention to the exact communication of ideas. Finally, Somerset Maugham tells us what he has come to believe are the important achievements in expression for a good writer.

Robert Benchley

WORD TORTURE

A personal tribulation

In his column a short time ago Mr. O. O. McIntyre asked who could tell, without looking it up, the present tense of the verb of which "wrought" is the past participle. That was, let us say, of a Thursday. Today my last finger-nail went.

At first I thought that it was so easy that I passed it by. But, somewhere in the back of that shaggy-maned head of mine, a mischievous little voice said: "All right—what is it?"

"What is what?" I asked, stalling.

"You know very well what the question was. What is the present tense of the verb from which the word 'wrought' comes?"

I started out with a rush. "I *wright,*" I fairly screamed. Then, a little lower: "I wrught." Then, very low: "I wrouft." Then silence.

From that day until now I have been muttering to myself: "I wright—I wraft —I wronjst. You wruft—he wragst—we wrinjsen." I'll be darned if I'll look it up, and it looks now as if I'll be incarcerated before I get it.

People hear me murmuring and ask me what I am saying.

"I wrujhst," is all that I can say in reply.

"I know," they say, "but what were you *saying* just now?"

"I wringst."

This gets me nowhere.

While I am working on it, however, and just before the boys come to get me to take me to the laughing academy, I will ask Mr. McIntyre if he can help me out on something that has almost the same possibilities for brain seepage. And no fair looking *this* up, either.

What is a man who lives in Flanders and speaks Flemish? A Flem? A Flan? A Floom? (This is a lot easier than "wrought," but it may take attention away from me while I am writhing on the floor.) And, when you think you have got it the easy way, remember there is another name for him, too, one that rhymes with "balloon." I finally looked that one up.

At present I'm working on "wrought."

Charlton Laird

THE SPEECH THAT BLOOMS
ON THE TONGUE, TRA-LA,
HAS LITTLE TO DO WITH CASE

Grammar Is Not a Pigeonhole Desk

The previous chapter has suggested that our traditional grammar and our actual grammar bear little resemblance to each other. Many people to whom this

From *After 1903—What?* by Robert Benchley. Copyright, 1938, by Robert Benchley. Reprinted by permission of Harper & Brothers.
From *The Miracle of Language* by Charlton Laird. Reprinted by permission of World Publishing Company.

statement may be unwelcome would reply, however, that whatever the theory may be, the practice of modern grammar is sound. They will say that although applying grammatical rules may be a little difficult, because grammar is a difficult and complicated subject, grammatical rules do explain the language. These people are likely to feel that they themselves can explain most of the language, and would be able to explain the remainder if they knew their grammar a little better.

This I have not found to be true. For years I have taught a college course in the nature of language through which have passed a considerable number of persons who were sure that the grammatical rules had been worked out and that they knew these rules. During this time I have maintained a standing challenge to anybody to make the following simple experiment. Pick up a book at random, open to a page at random, and put your finger on a sentence. Then explain the meaning of the sentence by conventional grammar. I have never found anyone who could do so. Some day I will. Some day I will lose because somebody will be lucky enough to put his finger on *Ouch!* He will say "Interjection," and I shall have lost, at least by his rules of the game. In reality, to explain the grammar of *Ouch!* we should need to examine adjacent sentences, but the conventional grammarian would never concede I was being fair in expecting that of him, and accordingly I should lose. As yet, however, this has not happened, and nobody has explained a sentence for me on the basis of Latin grammar.

People who think the conventional grammar makes sense usually do so because they are not examining the grammar at all. They are doing one, and usually all, of the following:

(1) They restrict their examination of language to sentences made up to fit rules, and they do not examine these sentences further than to notice that they do fit. This of course is nonsense. If grammar will not explain ordinary prose— to say nothing of sentences made up *not* to fit the rules—there is something wrong with the grammatical rules.

(2) They expect to save any rule which gets into trouble by assuming, in any example which will not fit it, that additional words or a different order is "understood." The sentence is accordingly changed so that it does fit. Let us see how this works. Since I have recommended taking a sentence at random from a book, I will take one from a book which happens to be lying open on the table. It is Josephine Tey's *The Daughter of Time* (New York; Macmillan, 1952), opened to page 80. Running my eye down the page—since I am now looking for an example, not trying to explain any piece of prose—I find that one character says "Oh!" unexpectedly, and the hero asks, "What was the 'Oh' for?" Let us endeavor to parse this last sentence. *What* is an interrogative pronoun, subject of the sentence. *Was* is the verb. *Oh* is the complement. What is *for?* The *New International Dictionary*, second edition, which embodies a good compendium of conventional but relatively liberal grammatical opinion, gives *for* as a conjunction or a preposition. (Lest I be accused of treating dictionaries unkindly—and I am very far from wishing to do so—let me say once for all that I am citing dictionaries partly for my own convenience, and partly be-

cause the makers of widely used dictionaries have generally been more liberal than the makers of widely used grammars.) But *for* in this sentence cannot be a conjunction; it has nothing to join. It cannot be a preposition; it has no object.

Obviously, *for* must be something. Accordingly a conventional grammarian would be likely to start by changing the sentence to another which is "understood." He might substitute "What was the 'Oh' intended for?" *Intended* can modify *oh*, and if *for* can be an adverb, it can modify the past participle *intended*. This is possible, for although the *New International* does not enter *for* as an adverb, doubtless some other authority does so. Or the grammarian could change the sentence to "For what was the 'Oh' intended?" *For* has now become a preposition. Other additions are possible, for instance, "For what remark which you suppressed was the 'Oh' intended to substitute?" and "What does the 'Oh' stand for?" The conventional grammarian also changes the order, although, if order is the basis of English grammar, one wonders what right he has to change it. He might say that the sentence is understood to be "For what was the 'Oh'?" No one would talk such nonsense, but let us pass that. Is *for what* the subject? Obviously not, for whatever a *for what* is, it is not and was not an *Oh*. Nor does the sentence improve if we try to make *for what* the complement and *Oh* the subject. Can *for what* be a modifier of *is?* Surely not; it does not qualify the is-ness of *is*. Unless *is* means *serves, substitutes,* or something else it does not mean, *for what* can scarcely modify it.

This sort of grammatical juggling might warrant several comments, but here are two obvious ones. First, these additions of words and changes of structure are not "understood." If they are understood, how are we to know which of the various possibilities we are to understand? I suspect that Miss Tey would have been outraged were we to suggest that she had meant any of these words or structures to be understood in place of the words and structure she used.

Now for a second comment. If we are to discuss the grammar of this sentence, we must discuss the sentence as it is. Obviously it has grammar. It was written by a reputable writer; it is put into the mouth of a presumably well-educated man and one who is highly intelligent; the man is at the moment discussing a subject seriously. Certainly Miss Tey thought the sentence had grammar when she wrote it. Any competent reader of English would know at once what the sentence was intended to mean. Therefore, Miss Tey is right; the sentence has grammar, and any grammatical statement which will not account for "What was the 'Oh' for?" without changing it in any particular is an inadequate statement. Our grammatical rules, not Miss Tey's grammar, are at fault.

(3) The people who defend conventional grammar are not concerned with understanding the grammar, but with putting words into pigeonholes. This is a harmless diversion, but it has little to do with English grammar, particularly since there are no pigeonholes into which grammatical concepts in English can be assorted so as to form anything like a classification. On what basis does the conventionally accepted grammar classify words? Not on form. Most of the so-called parts of speech have no connection with form, and those which do

have some have not much. Adverbs end in *-ly*, but *fast* and *well* are adverbs (unless you call them verbs, modifiers, or adjectives, which of course they can be) and *homely* and *family* are supposedly not adverbs, although they end in *-ly*. Neither does traditional grammar classify words on meaning. Supposedly nouns are determined on meaning, and within limits the division is valid, but the presence of nouns determined by meaning among other pigeonholed objects determined on other bases only confuses the classification. And last, the conventional grammarians do not use function as a means of classification, although this is the most commonly supposed basis. Most of the supposed functions do not exist, and those that do, do not fit the categories.

For instance, where does the verb in the following sentence begin and end? *You'd better start doing something about getting the tire blown up. You* is the subject. *Had* (contracted to *'d*) is part of the verb, but part of what verb: *had start, had doing, had start doing?* None of these makes any sense. Unless the verb includes *better* the sentence has no meaning, and yet no conventional grammarian can admit, and no conventional authority I have consulted does admit, that *better* in this sense can be part of a verb. (Just in case anyone should suggest that this sentence is not "good grammar," notice E. B. White's "I better get them today" [*One Man's Meat*, p. 261]. I assume that most modern writers would agree that if *better* as a verb is good enough for White it is good enough for them.) Is the verb *better start doing?* This still has no meaning. *Had better start doing something* has meaning, but not the meaning of the sentence. Clearly the verb must include *doing something about*; it must also include *getting*, and *blown up* if the words in the sentence are to have their meanings. *The tire*, by all conventional statements, is a noun with its article and presumably is a complement. But observe what happens if we remove it: *You'd better start doing something about getting blown up.* Can we say that even a noun is not somehow involved in the verb if the entire meaning of the verb changes when the noun is removed? Pretty clearly we have one idea which develops all the way from *had* to *blown up*; it cannot be broken up into little chunks which can be filed in pigeonholes unless we are willing to ignore the meanings of words and the whole meaning of the sentence.

But perhaps this sentence is exceptional. Suppose we try *Grandma was peeling apples by the window.* This is certainly a simple, ordinary sentence which should fit conventional rules if any sentence will. The conventional statement would be as follows: *Grandma* is a noun, subject of the verb; *was peeling* is a verb made up of present participle *peeling* and auxiliary *was*; *apples* is a noun, direct object of *peeling*; *by the window* is an adverbial prepositional phrase, made up of the preposition *by*, which introduces the object of the preposition, *window*, modified by the article *the*, and the whole prepositional phrase modifies the verb, *was peeling*. This sounds objective, learned, even final. But does it make much sense? *By the window* is said to modify *was peeling*, but it must also modify *grandma* and *apples*. They must all have been by the window or grandma could not have been peeling the apples. But to say this is heresy, for *grandma* and *apples* are both nouns, and modifiers of nouns are adjectives, not adverbs. That is, it is completely impossible to decide whether *by the window* is an adjective or an adverb. It is a modifier, but pretty clearly it modifies the whole sentence. Now for *apples;* it is said to be the direct object, because it receives the action of the verb. But it also determines the action of the verb. Remove it, and the action becomes quite different: *Grandma was peeling by the window.* Grandma has now become scrofulitic, or perhaps, like Gypsy Rose Lee, ecdysiastic.

And these, of course, are not the difficult grammatical categories. They are the common ones. Even a concept like *pronoun* will stand no analysis. "A pronoun is a word used in place of a noun." Consider the following:

> Johnny is my nephew.
> He is a brat.

Conventional grammarians would say something like this of the pair of sentences: *He* in the second sentence is a pronoun because it is used in the place of the noun *Johnny*. To simplify:

> *Johnny = he* .·. *he* is a pronoun because it is used in place of *Johnny*,
>   a noun.

Now substitute another word for *he* in the second sentence.

> Johnny is my nephew.
> The boy is a brat.

Follow the same procedure with this pair of sentences.

> *Johnny = the boy* .·. *boy* is a pronoun because it is used in place of
>   *Johnny*, a noun.

If *boy* is a pronoun, and it must be, by the logic of conventional grammar, then what has become of the concept of nouns and pronouns? Why cannot all nouns be pronouns?

For is called a co-ordinating conjunction and *because* a sub-ordinating conjunction, but are they not identical in use in *I honor Brutus, for he is an honorable man; I honor Brutus because he is an honorable man?*

And so it goes. Any careful examination of the conventional categories of the parts of speech will reveal that they mean very little; they do not include what they should include, they do not exclude all words outside their category, and they do not reveal the functioning of Modern English. Usually they are unworkable, and when they can be made to include the words we use, most of them tell very little about what gives the words meaning. In short, the conventional grammar is not much more revealing of the actual grammar of Modern English than one would expect it to be when we consider what has happened: The grammar of an inflected language, Latin, has been forced upon a distributive language, English, which has been wrenched in an attempt to make it fit the alien grammar. A large number of intelligent people have labored for generations to make sense of this forced wrenching, this set of rules which is fundamentally wrong. That the conventional grammar makes as much sense as it does is a high tribute to the patience and intelligence of our grammarians.

The Grammatical System We Do Not Have

According to the traditionalists, the core of our grammar is nouns which have gender, number, and case, and verbs which occur in certain tenses and moods. Let us examine these assumptions. Most nouns have number, expressed in form; except for certain borrowed words and some words which retain archaic characteristics, the plural is formed by adding -s, or -es. We have developed other plurals by distributive means (*many a man, person after person*), but on the whole, declension provides number in the noun.

Of gender there remain scraps, such fragmentary scraps that most Americans do not know what gender is. With us it has become a synonym for sex, which it is not, because distinction on the basis of sex is the only bit of gender we have left, and that appears only in the third person singular pronoun (*he, she, it*), unless one excepts forms like *comedian, comedienne, actor, actress.* Gender is a much broader concept, which can include any sort of classification of objects, and in Indo-European must have included a considerable number, distinguished by different sets of case endings. So in other languages. Certain North American Indian languages have gender which requires with any noun the use of syllables which indicate one of the following: that the object mentioned is in the immediate possession of the speaker; that it is not in his possession, but can be reached by sight, sound, smell, or touch; that it is not within reach of his senses, but is supposedly not far away; that it is at a remote or unknown place.

Of case, also, almost nothing remains. Of the seven cases in Indo-European, only one, the so-called possessive, can now be recognized. It is steadily being replaced by forms with *of*, and of course it often does not indicate possession. Consider the following:

> Please keep *your* seats while I introduce *your* candidate for sheriff. From *his* earliest childhood he has been a staunch supporter of *our* party; he has been a noble servant of *his* constituents in *his* previous offices, promoting *their* best interests in *our* country as, prior to *his* entry into public life, he promoted the interests of *his* company, distributing *their* products in *your* community.

The italicized words are all "possessives," although most of them do not show possession in the capitalistic sense. *Your seats* are yours only because you are sitting in them; they belong to whoever owns the hall. *Your candidate* is yours only in the sense that you are expected to vote for him. *His childhood* is his only in the sense that he experienced it. *Our party* is ours not because it belongs to us but because we belong to it. The candidate did not own *his offices, his constituents,* or *his company;* and the company, although it owns its products, would still call them *their* products after they have sold them.

Such are the remnants of declension in the noun. Most of the relationships within a sentence which involve names for things are now made clear by order or by relationship words. Anybody who tries to talk about nouns on the conventional basis is not talking about much.

With verbs the situation is no better. The following are the commonly recognized tenses:

Present:	I drive
Past:	I drove
Perfect:	I have driven
Pluperfect:	I had driven
Future:	I shall (will) drive
Future Perfect:	I shall (will) have driven

But these are not the tenses they profess to be. *I drive* is not simple present. No one would say, "I drive an automobile," meaning that he is now at this moment in process of operating a vehicle. If he wishes to say that he would probably say "I'm driving an automobile," which is supposedly a progressive form. One says, "I drive to work every morning," thereby implying a past, a present, and a probable future. Similarly, the past is not usually the past, and the perfect is not usually the perfect since it does not represent a "perfected" or completed action. The past is most commonly used for the perfect (I *drove* into the yard and *stopped* at the front door), and the perfect is commonly used for the past (I *have driven* all my life; I *have been driving* all my life). Curiously enough, the pluperfect is actually used for the pluperfect. The future can be the future, but the approved form *I shall drive* is certainly less common than *I'm going to drive.* The future perfect also exists, but is a rare form which might well be removed from a simplified paradigm in favor of some of the common uses of the verb which we do not recognize.

The supposed uses of the verb, then, are not the uses they are supposed to be. But do these forms give us any notion of the English verb, even though the uses are misnamed? They do not. Consider, for instance, the following list, which by no means exhausts the forms which we use constantly as futures:

I shall (will) drive (I'll drive)
I am going to drive (I'm going to drive)
I drive tomorrow
I am just about to drive
I am just going to drive
I am off to drive
I am on the verge of driving
I am now in a position to drive
I expect to drive
I am considering driving
I am scheduled to drive

I am determined (have decided) to drive
This requires me to drive
It would seem best to drive
I am bound to drive
There will be the drive
And then there is the drive
I have to plan on driving

This is only a beginning. One might notice that although the simple present *I drive* is not a simple present, it can be a future. One might notice, also, something about the nature of the future tense. The future is always uncertain, and Modern English, since it builds its verbs mainly by distributive means, is uncommonly rich in devices for expressing degrees of future uncertainty. The list above includes futures which allow for doubt in the speaker's mind and for the unpredictability of events. The following forms provide for a still wider latitude of uncertainty:

If I am able to drive
If I could drive
If I were able to drive
If only I were able to drive
Could I drive
Were I in a position to drive
If I could manage to drive
If it were possible to drive
If the road were drivable
I should like to drive
I should like to be able to drive
I wish I could drive
If I were in a position to drive
If the driving conditions were other than they are

The list omits many of the strongly subjunctive forms, expressing a wish, like *Oh, that I could drive;* the passive forms like *I'm going to be driven, I am about to be driven,* and the imperative and interrogative forms.

Furthermore, we have ignored the concept of aspect, one of the most important qualities of a verb, but one so neglected that until recently it did not even appear in dictionaries as a grammatical term, and it still does not occur in many grammars. It might be called the attitude of the speaker toward time. For instance, *I keep falling into mudholes; I am forever getting into debt* are iterative; they imply a repeated action. *I walk to work whenever it is not raining* and *Rain usually accompanies a moist front of air* imply habitual or routine actions. *I am just going to start making payments* is inceptive, implying beginning, and *I have only now finished the inventory* is conclusive, implying ending. By combining aspect with tense and mood, and by combining the resulting verbs with modifiers and complements, verb forms can be devised which permit extremely exact expression: *We used to go to the beach every Sunday, but this summer we haven't felt like bothering except now and then.*

The English verb, and especially the American verb, can become extremely complicated. Early in this chapter we observed a verb which seemed to be so amorphous that it was taking unto itself various supposed nouns, pronouns, and modifiers. But let us not complicate the situation so much. Let us now use a verb which is made of nothing but recognizable verb forms:

> I should like to go
> I should like to be able to go
> I should have liked to be able to go

These are acceptable forms. Furthermore, they represent slight variations in meaning, so that the writer of English can vary his statement with extreme exactitude if he wishes. But what are the names of these forms? Do we have paradigms for them?

On the whole, no. No book which has gained any currency contains anything like a description of the Modern American verb. If anyone has as yet made a genuinely serious effort to collect and classify the forms of the American verb I have not heard of it—although I admit that this may be going on and I do not know about it. There is a good beginning in Harold Whitehall's *The Structural Essentials of Written English* (Indiana University, 1951), and Professor Whitehall would be the first to point out that his paradigms provide only a beginning. Margaret Bryant's *A Functional English Grammar* (Boston, 1945) contains a sound survey of verbs. I say with admiration that much excellent work in the study of modern language, including grammar, is now going forward in this country. The fact remains, however, that as yet nothing like a full description of Modern English has been published; and only recently have we begun to become aware of the fantastic depths of our ignorance.

Grammar Is Slippery Stuff

Grammar is somewhat like a freshly caught fish. Take it in your hand to wash it in the stream; two wriggles, and it is gone. So with grammar, and I speak as one who has gone through the chastening experience of asking himself quite soberly what our grammar is. I have tried to divest myself of old grammatical prejudices beaten into me at an early age, and acquired later with the profligate expenditure of midnight electricity. I have at times thought I had drawn from the deceptive grammatical waters a fine, trim, grammatical fact. I grasped him firmly by the tail, and meant only to clean him up a bit. Two flips, and he was gone.

And thus it is in all humility that I point out that we have not as yet described our grammar. Grammatical concepts are not easy to deal with. Grammatical phenomena are extremely numerous, extremely varied, and bafflingly shifty. Part of our trouble is that we have no precedent. Except English, Chinese is the only great distributive language, and the Chinese have apparently done no more than we to understand their grammar. At least, if there is any adequate Chinese analysis of language it has gained no currency in this country to provide students of English with anything like a pilot job. Apparently, if we are to understand our language we shall have to think, and observe, and argue our way through the exploration ourselves.

We have a start. In fact, we have an excellent start. All grammarians now concede—even those who still think as though Latin grammar is the basis of grammar—that the grammar of any language must be derived from the language itself. All grammarians now concede that the source of English grammar is to be sought in Anglo-Saxon, and in the changes which the English language has undergone since Anglo-Saxon days. They all concede that in studying language we must take account of both written and oral language, and that of the two, oral language is probably the more significant, although the more difficult to deal with.

It is hard to see how this new understanding of the revealing ways to work with language can be wrong. It is also hard to see how any work on the old basis, a basis that is fundamentally wrong, could produce entirely valid conclusions. But we have now changed our approach to one which seems basically right. We now think we know how to work with English grammar and we are working.

We have acquired this new approach neither easily nor quickly. Apparently the new attitudes grew out of the study of Anglo-Saxon and Middle English. It is interesting to observe that linguistic truth came as a sort of handmaiden of literary love. Early English was not much studied before the last century; *Beowulf* was not known, and nobody knew how to pronounce Chaucer's English. Only a smattering of early writing had been printed, and that smattering mostly in poor editions. Even universities did not teach the study of early English languages; Latin, Greek, and Hebrew were either the marks of a gentleman or the tools of a divine, but relatively few scholars bothered with Anglo-Saxon or Middle English. Partly the change came about through the Romantic Movement, which made old things, especially bizarre, primitive, and "Gothic" things popular. Partly the change is due to German philologists who started studying language, especially all dialects of Germanic language, with patience, competence, and objectivity.

Then love took a hand. Scholars discovered that the ancient and medieval Germanic writings constituted an entrancing body of literature. *Beowulf*, for instance, appeared no longer as the crude product of a barbarous time, but as a highly wrought, powerful, and in some ways sophisticated poem. Chaucer was obviously a literary craftsman of very high order, as well as one of the most engaging human beings who ever harbored a sly smile. Since *Beowulf* and the *Canterbury Tales* had become works of art, their grammar became subjects of scholarly study. Gradually, students who had gone to the older literatures for love of the literatures saw in these works evidence that English grammar was a native thing, that it existed before Anglo-Saxons knew anything about Latin, and that English seemed quite capable of living on its own resources, using a grammar that differed sharply from Latin.

While all this was going on, a philosophical background was growing for a new linguistic approach. Brilliant grammatical thinkers, mostly German and Scandinavian, had broken loose from traditional limitations. The whole concept of language families, which appeared with the knowledge of the relationships of languages like Sanskrit, Gothic, Greek, and Anglo-Saxon, suggested that grammatical notions needed revision, that linguistic truths might be much broader, deeper, and more significant than the older writers upon language had been aware. Men like Bopp and Rask, Max Müller and the Grimm brothers produced most fruitful researches and most pregnant thought, although, as a matter of course, these men were wrong much of the time. Their conclusions have required revision. Nevertheless, they shook Western linguistic study loose from its old classic complacency, and in a general way they laid out the lines which modern thinking about language has followed.

The New Look in Language

This is not the place for a history of modern linguistic thought. Among the results of this growth, however, are bodies of careful linguistic study, and in this century several efforts to approach Modern English grammar objectively. The Danish grammarian, Otto Jespersen, endeavored to salvage the terminology of conventional grammar while superimposing upon it a system of ranks in words. He started with the noun as the name of an object, and a use as subject or complement; this noun became primary, its modifiers secondary, and the modifiers of modifiers tertiary. Thus in the combination, *slightly aching head*, *head* is primary, *aching* is secondary, and *slightly* is tertiary. This ranking he maintained in the face of the older conceptions; *father* would normally be considered a noun, but in the combination *father's aching head*, *father's* would become tertiary. There is much to be said for this system; it certainly has some logic behind it. But it provides us with two schemes of grammar, where one is baffling us already, and it has never received the subsequent careful working over which would be required in a satisfactory grammatical statement—assuming that a statement could be worked out with this system.

Some grammarians, recognizing that speakers of English make themselves understood by naming a subject and then modifying this subject, have tried to reduce the parts of speech to two, subjects and modifiers. This would seem to be simplicity itself, and certainly as far as it goes it is hard to find out what is wrong with it. In the sentence *John runs*, *runs*, although it is commonly called a verb, certainly modifies our conception of John. Or expand the sentence as follows: *John, being as stubborn as a mule and as conceited as a peacock, runs every four years for President of the United States, having himself nominated by the No-Cigarettes-for-Women Party*. We still have *John*, the subject, modified in our minds by all that comes after it. But assuming that this description is valid, does it help much? In effect, this approach provides us with a new term for the old grammatical tenet that a sentence is made up of a subject and a predicate. If we accept this statement, the fact remains that the modifier (or predicate) can be an extremely complicated agglomeration, which would seem to need some breaking down before we can hope to grasp it very well.

I. A. Richards suggested that the study of grammar be based entirely upon meaning, but understandably did not care to spend the remainder of his life trying to do so. No systematic study of English grammar has been founded exclusively upon meaning, but since grammarians have usually assumed that the "use" of a word—that is, its function in composition—was to reveal meaning, the whole idea of function rests upon meaning. Other grammarians have forsaken both meaning and function as a starting point for the study of English grammar, and have tried to study it upon the basis of speech rhythm, upon word patterns, or upon something which can be approached with relative objectivity. Studying meaning objectively has proved very difficult, because meaning is highly varied and shifting.

The most elaborate recent attempt is embodied in *The Structure of English* by Professor Charles Carpenter Fries of the University of Michigan. Professor Fries has long been an independent thinker and indefatigable worker in language. During the late war he was able to acquire some fifty hours of transcribed conversation. By studying the conversation he constructed a theory of grammar which makes but limited use of meaning. He relies upon sentence patterns and accepts as a part of speech any word which can fall into a certain position within the pattern. The results are extremely interesting, and they will certainly be worked over carefully by other grammarians. Obviously Professor Fries is right about many things, and his book will deeply affect our thinking about Modern English grammar. Whether the book will be accepted as the standard statement no one can as yet safely predict—it was published while this manuscript was being written—but it suggests the degree to which modern grammar is at last being studied, in and for itself.

Another interesting recent treatment appears in *The Structural Essentials of Written English* mentioned above. Professor Whitehall employs sentence pattern, as indeed anyone must, for if modern grammar has demonstrated one fact it is that a distributive grammar relies upon patterns of words as an inflected language relies upon forms of words. He also makes use of the phoneme, a relatively recent concept in language, which may be defined as all the sound within a spread of sound which hearers would recognize as part of the same word. For instance, the [l] in *lean* differs from the [l] in *hill*, but the two sounds constitute one phoneme because they convey one meaning. Similarly, some speakers will pronounce the [ɪ] in *hill* lower or farther back than other speakers do, but so long as this vowel does not go so far back or down that the word becomes *hull* or *hell*, all of these sounds of [ɪ] constitute one phoneme. In his use of pattern and the phoneme Professor Whitehall is modern, although not startlingly new; but in resting grammar and grammatical analysis mainly upon the rising and falling tone of the spoken voice, he is pioneering. He asserts (the italics are his): "Remember that *English sentences are not sentences merely by virtue of the kind of constructions they represent or the kind of words they contain: they are sentences because they possess one or other of the final tone patterns characteristic of English."*

At this writing Modern English grammar is a lively if confusing subject. We do not understand our grammar, but apparently it has become something distinctive enough to intrigue our interest and warrant our understanding. And we may yet solve its mystery.

Jacques Barzun

ENGLISH AS SHE'S NOT TAUGHT

At an educational conference held in Vancouver last summer, leaders of the Canadian school system generally agreed that from half to three quarters of their students in the first year of college were incompetent in grammar, syntax, and analysis of thought. What was notable in the discussion was that nearly every participant used the English language with uncommon force and precision. Any looseness or jargon heard there came from the three American guests, of whom I was one. Most of our hosts—Canadian teachers, principals, supervisors, and university instructors—had obviously gone through the mill of a classical education; the chairman made a mild pun involving Latin and was rewarded with an immediate laugh. Yet they declared themselves unable to pass on their linguistic accomplishment to the present school generation, and they wanted to know why.

In the United States the same complaint and inquiry has been endemic, commonplace, for quite a while. You come across it in the papers. You hear parents, school people, editors and publishers, lawyers and ministers, men of science and of business, lamenting the fact that their charges or their offspring or their employees can neither spell nor write "decent English." The deplorers blame the modern progressive school or the comics or TV; they feel that in school and outside, something which they call discipline is lacking, and they vaguely connect this lack with a supposed decline in morality, an upsurge of "crisis." Like everything else, bad English is attributed to our bad times, and the past (which came to an end with the speaker's graduation from college) is credited with one more virtue, that of literary elegance.

The facts seem to me quite different, the causes much more tangled, and the explanation of our linguistic state at once more complex and less vague. For many years now I have been concerned with the art of writing and kept busy at the invidious task of improving other people's utterance, and I cannot see that performance has deteriorated. The level is low but it has not fallen. As a reader of history I am steadily reminded that the writing of any language has always been a hit-and-miss affair. Here is Amos Barrett, our chief source on the battles of Concord and Lexington: "It wont long before their was other minit Compneys . . . We marched Down about a mild or a mild half and we see them acomming . . ." and so on. An illiterate New England farmer? Not so, since he could write; he had been taught and in some way represents "the past." The question he poses is, how do people write who are not professionals or accomplished amateurs? The answer is: badly, at all times.

Writing is at the very least a knack, like drawing or being facile on the piano. Because everybody can speak and form letters, we mistakenly suppose that good, plain, simple writing is within everybody's power. Would we say this of good, straightforward, accurate drawing? Would we say it of melodic sense and correct, fluent harmonizing at the keyboard? Surely not. We say these are "gifts." Well, so is writing, even the writing of a bread-and-butter note or a simple public notice; and this last suggests that something has happened within the last hundred years to change the relation of the written word to daily life.

Whether it is the records we have to keep in every business and profession or the ceaseless communicating at a distance which modern transport and industry require, the world's work is now unmanageable, unthinkable, without *literature.* Just see how many steps you can take without being confronted with something written or with the necessity of writing something yourself. Having been away for a couple of weeks during the summer, I find a bill from the window washer, who luckily came on a day when the cleaning woman was in the apartment. He has therefore scribbled below the date: "The windows have been cleaned Wed. 12:30 P.M. Your maid was their to veryfey the statement"— perfectly clear and adequate. One can even appreciate the change of tenses as his mind went from the job just finished to the future when I would be reading this message from the past.

Call this bad writing if you like, it remains perfectly harmless. The danger to the language, if any, does not come from such trifles. It comes rather from the college-bred millions who regularly write and who in the course of their daily work circulate the prevailing mixture of jargon, cant, vogue words, and loose syntax that passes for prose. And the greater part of this verbiage is published, circulated, presumably read. A committee won't sit if its drivelings are not destined for print. Even an interoffice memo goes out in sixteen copies and the schoolchildren's compositions appear verbatim in a mimeographed magazine. Multiply these cultural facts by the huge number of activities which (it would seem) exist only to bombard us with paper, and you have found the source of the belief in a "decline" in writing ability—no decline at all, simply the infinite duplication of dufferism. This it is which leads us into false comparisons and gloomy thoughts.

The apparent deterioration of language is a general phenomenon which is denounced throughout Western Europe. One had only to read the Catalogue of the British Exhibition of 1951 to see the common symptoms in England. Sir Ernest Gowers's excellent little book of a few years earlier, *Plain Words,* was an attempt to cure the universal disease in one congested spot, the Civil Service, which is presumably the most highly educated professional group in Britain.

In France, the newspapers, the reports of Parliamentary debates, and the literary reviews show to what extent ignorance of forms and insensitivity to usage can successfully compete against a training obsessively aimed at verbal competence. And by way of confirmation, M. Jean Delorme, a native observer of the language in French Canada, recently declared the classic speech "infected" on this side of the Atlantic too. As for Germany, a foreign colleague and correspondent of mine, a person of catholic tastes and broad judgment, volunteers the opinion that "people who cultivate good pure German are nowadays generally unpopular, especially among the devotees of newspaper fiction and articles. The universal barbarism of language has already gone well into the grotesque."

So much for the democratic reality. But great as has been the effect of enlarged "literacy," it does not alone account for what is now seen as linguistic decadence. The educated, in fact the leaders of modern thought, have done as much if not more to confuse the judgment. For what is meant by the misnomer "pure speech" is simply a habit of respect toward usage, which insures a certain fixity in vocabulary, forms, and syntax. Language cannot stand still, but it can change more or less rapidly and violently. During the last hundred years, nearly every intellectual force has worked, in all innocence, against language. The strongest, science and technology, did two damaging things: they poured quantities of awkward new words into the language and this in turn persuaded everybody that each new thing must have a name, preferably "scientific." These new words, technical or commercial, were fashioned to impress, an air of profundity being imparted by the particularly scientific letters k, x, and $o =$ Kodak, Kleenex, Sapolio. The new technological words that came in were sinful hybrids like "electrocute" and "triphibian," or misunderstood phrases like "personal equation," "nth degree," or "psychological moment"—brain addlers of the greatest potency.

The passion for jargon was soon at its height, from which it shows no sign of descending. Every real or pseudo science poured new verbiage into the street, every separate school or -ism did likewise, without shame or restraint. We can gauge the result from the disappearance of the Dictionary properly so called. Consult the most recent and in many ways the best of them, *Webster's New World Dictionary*, and what you find is a miniature encyclopedia filled with the explanation of initials, proper names, and entries like "macrosporangium" or "abhenry," which are not and never will be words of the English language.

Under the spate of awe-inspiring vocables, the layman naturally felt that he too must dignify his doings and not be left behind in the race for prestige. Common acts must suggest a technical process. Thus we get "contact" and "funnel" as workaday verbs—and "process" itself: "we'll process your application"— as if it were necessary to name the steps or choices of daily life with scientific generality. I know a young businessman who makes jottings of his business thoughts; when he has enough on one topic he *folderizes* them.

What is wrong with all this is not merely that it is new, heedless, vulgar, and unnecessary (all signs of harmful vice in a language) but that jargon swamps thought. The habit of talking through cant words destroys the power of seeing things plain. "I'll contact you to finalize the agreement." What does it mean? The drift is plain enough, but compare: "I'll call at your office to sign the contract." The former raises no clear image or expectation, the latter does. Moreover, the former smells of inflated ego, it fills the mouth in a silly bumptious way.

But who cares? Why fuss?—good questions both. Nobody cares much because —we all think—it's the deed (or the thing) that counts, not the words. This conviction, too, is a product of modern technology, and its effect is great though unremarked. The power of words over nature, which has played such a role in human history, is now an exploded belief, a dead emotion. Far from words controlling things, it is now things that dictate words. As soon as science was able to chop up the physical world and recombine it in new forms, language followed suit; and this not only among scientists making up new vocables, but among the supposed guardians of the language, the poets and men of letters. It is highly significant that around 1860 writers deliberately began to defy usage and turn syntax upside down. Lewis Carroll and Edward Lear made good fun with it; "obscure" poets such as Rimbaud sought new depths of meaning. There was in this a strong impulse to destroy all convention, for Victorian moralism had made the idea of conventionality at once suspect and hateful. The revolt succeeded and its spirit is still alive; novelty-hunting is now a linguistic virtue, or to express it differently, a common influence is at work in Jabberwocky and James Joyce, in the scientist's lingo and in the advertiser's "Dynaflow," "Hydramatic," or "Frigidaire"—which end by becoming household words. In short, modern man is feeling his oats as the manipulator of objects and he shows it in his manhandling of words.

This helps to explain why the predominant fault of the bad English encountered today is not the crude vulgarism of the untaught but the blithe irresponsibility of the taught. The language is no longer regarded as a common treasure to be hoarded and protected as far as possible. Rather, it is loot from the enemy to be played with, squandered, plastered on for one's adornment. Literary words imperfectly grasped, meanings assumed from bare inspection, monsters spawned for a trivial cause—these are but a few of the signs of squandering. To give examples: the hotel clerk giving me a good room feels bound to mention the well-known person whom "we last hospitalized in that room." Not to lag behind Joyce, the advertiser bids you "slip your feet into these easy-going *leisuals* and breathe a sigh of real comfort."

Undoubtedly these strange desires are often born of the need to ram an idea down unwilling throats. We all fear our neighbor's wandering attention and try to keep him awake by little shocks of singularity, or again by an overdose of meaning. Unfortunately, novelty-hunting proceeds from the known to the unknown by a leap of faith. "It was pleasant," writes the author of very workmanlike detective stories, "to watch her face and find his resentment *vitiate* as he made excuses for her."

The notable fact is that all this occurs in printed books, written by writers, published (usually) by first-rate firms that employ editors. In speech, the same blunders and distortions come from educated people. It is all very well to say, as one expert has confidently done, that "what certain words really mean is moving toward what they seem to mean," the implication being that after a while everything will be in place. Actually, this leaves meaning nowhere, if only because we're not all moving in step. The *New Yorker* spotted a movie theater sign on which "adultery" was used to mean "adulthood." From an English periodical I learn that some new houses "*affront* the opposite side of the street." If Mrs. Malaprop is going to become the patron saint of English, what is going to prevent "contention" from meaning the same thing as "contentment" or the maker of woodcuts from being called a woodcutter?

There is no getting around it: meaning implies convention, and the discovery that meanings change does not alter the fact that when convention is broken misunderstanding and chaos are close at hand. Mr. Churchill has told how Allied leaders nearly came to blows because of the single word "table," a verb which to the Americans meant dismiss from the discussion, whereas to the English, on the contrary, it meant put on the agenda. This is an extraordinary instance, and the vagaries of those who pervert good words to careless misuse may be thought more often ludicrous than harmful. This would be true if language, like a great maw, could digest anything and dispose of it in time. But language is not a kind of ostrich. Language is alive only by a metaphor drawn from the life of its users. Hence every defect in the language is a defect in somebody.

For language is either the incarnation of our thoughts and feelings or a cloak for their absence. When the ordinary man who has prepared a report on sales up to June 30 rumbles on about "the frame of reference in which the co-ordination campaign was conceived," he is filling the air with noises, not thoughts.

For self-protection, no doubt, the contemporary mind is opposed to all this quibbling. It speaks with the backing of popular approval when it says: "Stop it! You understand perfectly well what all these people mean. Don't be a dirty purist looking under the surface and meddling with democratic self-expression." To haggle over language *is* quibbling, of course. All precision is quibbling, whether about decimals in mathematics or grains of drugs in prescriptions—fairly important quibbles. The question is whether in language the results justify the quibble. Well, the public is here the best judge, and it is evident that as a consumer of the written word, the public is always complaining that it cannot understand what it is asked to read: the government blanks, the instructions on the bottle or gadget, the gobbledygook of every trade, the highbrow jargon of the educators, psychiatrists, and social workers, and—one must also add—the prose of literary critics. The great cry today is for improved communication, mass communication, the arts of communication, and yet under the pretext of being free and easy and above quibbling, those who do the most talking and writing indulge themselves in the very obscurities and ambiguities that cause the outcry.

They are abetted, moreover, by another offspring of the scientific spirit, the professional student of language. In his modern embodiment, the linguist takes the view that whatever occurs in anybody's speech is a fact of language and must not be tampered with, but only caught in flight and pinned on a card. This is "scientific detachment," and it has gone so far that under its influence in many schools all the categories of grammar, syntax, and rhetoric have been discarded. The modern way to learn English or a foreign language is to absorb a phrase-by-phrase enumeration of all that might conceivably be said in ordinary talk—a directory instead of a grammar.

This brings us back to our first difficulty, how to teach the millions the use of their mother tongue *in composition*. We have made nearly everybody literate in the sense of able to read and write words. But that is not writing. Even those who profess disdain for the literary art and the literary quibbles respond automatically to good writing, which they find unexpectedly easy to read and retain, mysteriously "pleasant" as compared with their neighbors' matted prose. The linguists themselves pay lip service to "effective" speech, approving the end while forbidding discrimination among the means.

Now many thousands of people in the United States today exercise this discrimination; there is amid the garbage a steady supply of good writing, modestly done and published—in every newspaper and magazine, over TV and radio, in millions of ads and public notices, in railroad timetables, travel booklets, and printed instructions on objects of daily use. Good writing is good writing wherever it occurs, and some of the impugned comics which are supposed to defile the native well of English in our young are far better than acceptable.

It is therefore idle and erroneous to condemn "the newspapers" or "the radio" en masse. Here too one must discriminate, and the failure to do so is one cause of the trouble—the strange cultural trait whose origin I have sketched and which makes us at once indifferent to our language, full of complaints about it, and irresponsible about mangling it still more. In these conditions people who write well learn to do so by virtue of a strong desire, developed usually under necessity: their job requires lucidity, precision, brevity. If they write advertising copy they must not only make it fit the space but make the words yield the tone.

Tone—that is the starting point of any teaching in composition. What effect are you producing and at what cost of words? The fewer the words, and the more transparent they are, the easier they will be to understand. The closer the ideas they stand for and the more natural their linkage, the more easily will the meaning be retained. Simple in appearance, this formula is yet extremely difficult to apply, and even more arduous to teach. You cannot work on more than one pupil at a time and you must be willing to observe and enter into his mind. On his part, the discipline calls for a thorough immersion in the medium. He must form the habit of attending to words, constructions, accents, and etymologies in everything he reads or hears—just as the painter unceasingly notes line and color and the musician tones. The would-be writer has the harder task because words are entangled with the business of life and he must stand off from it to look at them, hearing at the same time their harmonies and discords. It is an endless duty, which finally becomes automatic. The ideal writer would mentally recast his own death sentence as he was reading it—if it was a bad sentence.

Now such a discipline cannot be imposed from without, and not everybody needs it in full. But its principle, which suffices for ordinary purposes, should be made clear to every beginner, child or adult. Unfortunately, the school system, even when progressive, makes writing an irrational chore approached in the mood of rebellion. The school does this in two ways: by requiring length and by concentrating on correctness. I know very well that correctness was supposedly given up long ago. The modern teacher does not mention it. But if the teacher marks spelling and grammatical errors and speaks of little else, what is a child to think? He gets a mark with the comment "imaginative" or "not imaginative enough" and most often: "too short," and he is left with no more idea of composition than a cow in a field has of landscape painting. How *does* one judge the right length and get it out of a reluctant brain? Nobody answers, except perhaps with the word "creative," which has brought unmerited gloom to many a cheerful child. Who can be creative on demand, by next Tuesday, and in the requisite amount? In all but a few chatterboxes, mental frostbite is the only result.

Meanwhile the things that are teachable, the ways of translating the flashes of thought into consecutive sentences, are neglected. They have been, most often, neglected in the teachers themselves. How do *they* write or speak, what do *they* read? If they read and write educational literature, as they often must for advancement, are they fit to teach composition? And what of the teachers of other subjects, whose professional jargon also infects their speech, what is their countervailing effect on a child to whom a good English teacher has just imparted a notion of the writer's craft? Suppose the teacher of a course on family life has just been reading *Social Casework* and his mind is irradiated with this: "Familial societality is already a settled question biologically, structured in our inherited bodies and physiology, but the answer to those other questions are not yet safely and irrevocably anatomized." Unless this is immediately thrown up like the nux vomica it is, it will contaminate everybody it touches from pupil to public—in fact the whole blooming familial societality.

The cure is harsh and likely to be unpopular, for it must start with self-denial. It can be initiated by the school but it must not stop there. As many of us as possible must work out of our system, first, all the vogue words that almost always mean nothing but temporary vacancy of mind—such words as "basic," "major," "over-all," "personal," "values," "exciting" (everything from a new handbag to a new baby); then all the wormy expressions indicative of bad conscience, false modesty, and genteelism, as in: "Frankly, I don't know too much about it"—a typical formula which tries through candor and whining to minimize ignorance while claiming a kind of merit for it; finally, all the tribal adornments which being cast off may disclose the plain man we would like to be: no frames of reference, field theories, or apperception protocols; no texture, prior to, or in terms of; and the least amount of coördination, dynamics, and concepts.

After the vocabulary has been cleansed, the patient is ready for what our Canadian friends at the Vancouver conference deplored the lack of in the modern undergraduate: analysis of thought. To show what is meant and let criticism begin at home, I choose an example from a New York City report of 1952 entitled "The English Language Arts." It begins: "Because language arts or English is so—" Stop right there! What are language arts?—A perfectly unnecessary phrase of the pseudo-scientific kind which tries to "cover." Besides, "language arts or English" is nonsense: ever hear of another language? Moreover, "language arts . . . is" doesn't sound like a happy opening for a report by and to English teachers. Let us go on: English is so what? Well, "language arts or English is so intimately connected with all knowledge and all living, it is the subject which most often bursts the dikes separating it from others." What do you mean, language is *connected* with living? And how does English connect with *all* knowledge and *all* living? Is the practical knowledge of the Russian engineer intimately connected with English? Do the amoebas speak English? And if this intimacy does exist, then what are these dikes that separate English from other subjects? Are these subjects not part of "all knowledge" with which English is connected—or rather, of which it too is a part?

Cruel work, but necessary if anything akin to thought is to arise from the written word. The Neanderthal glimmer from which the quoted sentence sprang is irrecoverable but its developed form should run something like this: "English, being a medium of communication, cannot be confined within set limits like other subjects; to the peoples whose speech it is, all theoretical knowledge, and indeed most of life, is inseparable from its use."

And this is so true that it justifies the operation just performed on the specimen of non-thought. For although it is possible to think without words and to communicate by signs, our civilization depends, as I said before, on the written word. Writing is embodied thought, and the thought is clear or muddy, graspable or fugitive, according to the purity of the medium. Communication means one thought held in common. What could be more practical than to try making that thought unmistakable?

As for the receiver, the reader, his pleasure or grief is in direct proportion to the pains taken by the writer; to which one can add that the taking of pains brings its special pleasure. I do not mean the satisfaction of vanity, for after a bout of careful writing one is too tired to care; I mean the new perceptions—sensuous or intellectual or comic—to be had all day long in one's encounters with language. Imagine the fun people miss who find nothing remarkable in the sentence (from Sax Rohmer): "The woman's emotions were too tropical for analysis"; or who, trusting too far my disallowance of "contact" as a verb, miss the chance of using it at the hottest, stickiest time of year: "On a day like this, I wouldn't contact anybody for the world."

Irving Lee

THEY TALK PAST EACH OTHER

"It takes," says Thoreau, in the noblest and most useful passage I remember to have read in any modern author, "two to speak truth—one to speak and another to hear."—Robert Louis Stevenson, "Truth of Intercourse," *Virginibus Puerisque*, J. M. Dent & Sons, 1925, p. 32.

How Misunderstanding Happens

The one thing people tend to take for granted when talking to others is that they understand each other. It is rare, indeed, in a meeting to have someone hold up his own argument long enough to say, "I think you said. . . . Did you?" or "Was I right in thinking you meant . . . ?" We found people ever so eager to parry what a man says without ever wondering whether *that* is what the man said.

In the give-and-take of talk things go fast, and one is so busy organizing his reply that he doesn't take the time to make sure he knows what he is replying to. This is unfortunate because it often means that, instead of talking with others, people talk past or by-pass each other.

Note some by-passings.

1. The British Staff prepared a paper which they wished to raise as a matter of urgency, and informed their American colleagues that they wished to "table it." To the American staff "tabling" a paper meant putting it away in a drawer and forgetting it. A long and even acrimonious argument ensued before both parties realised that they were agreed on the merits and wanted the same thing.[1]

2. I remember a worrisome young man who, one day, came back from the X-ray room wringing his hands and trembling with fear. "It is all up with me," he said. "The X-ray man said I have a hopeless cancer of the stomach." Knowing that the roentgenologist would never have said such a thing, I asked, "Just what did he say?" and the answer was on dismissing him, the roentgenologist said to an assistant, "N.P." In Mayo clinic cipher this meant "no plates," and indicated that the X-ray man was so satisfied with the normal appearance of the stomach on the X-ray screen that he did not see any use in making films. But to the patient, watching in an agony of fear for some portent of disaster, it meant "nothing possible": in other words that the situation was hopeless![2]

From *How to Talk with People* by Irving Lee, Harper & Brothers. Copyright, 1952, by Harper & Brothers.

1. Winston Churchill, "The Second World War," Vol. III, Book II, *The New York Times*, February 28, 1950, p. 31.
2. Walter C. Alvarez, *Nervousness, Indigestion and Pain*, Paul B. Hoeber, Inc., 1943, p. 74.

3. A foreman told a machine operator he was passing: "Better clean up around here." It was ten minutes later when the foreman's assistant phoned: "Say, boss, isn't that bearing Sipert is working on due up in engineering pronto?"

"You bet your sweet life it is. Why?"

"He says you told him to drop it and sweep the place up. I thought I'd better make sure."

"Listen," the foreman flared into the phone, "get him right back on that job. It's got to be ready in twenty minutes."

. . . What [the foreman] had in mind was for Sipert to gather up the oily waste, which was a fire and accident hazard. This would not have taken more than a couple of minutes, and there would have been plenty of time to finish the bearing. Sipert, of course, should have been able to figure this out for himself—except that something in the foreman's tone of voice, or in his own mental state at the time, made him misunderstand the foreman's intent. He wasn't geared to what the foreman had said.[3]

4. Lady recently ordered some writing paper at a department store and asked to have her initials engraved thereon. The salesgirl suggested placing them in the upper right-hand corner or the upper left-hand corner, but the customer said no, put them in the center. Well, the stationery has arrived, every sheet marked with her initials equidistant from right and left and from top and bottom.[4]

5. In a private conversation with Mr. Molotov, it became apparent that another difficult misunderstanding in language had arisen between ourselves and the Russians. At the San Francisco Conference when the question of establishing a trusteeship system within the United Nations was being considered, the Soviet delegation had asked Mr. Stettinius what the American attitude would be toward the assumption by the Soviet Union of a trusteeship. Mr. Stettinius replied in general terms, expressing the opinion that the Soviet Union was "eligible" to receive a territory for administration under trusteeship. Mr. Molotov took this to mean we would support a Soviet request for a trusteeship.[5]

In each case a word or phrase or sentence was used one way by the speaker and interpreted in another way by the listener. This is possible because words are versatile. Except for those intended for highly specialized purposes (like tetrasporangium, icosahedron, bisulfite), it is not unusual to find most words put to rather varied uses. A seventh-grade class in English was able to make up thirty sentences in which the word "set" was used differently each time. Even "word" is listed in sixteen different ways in *The American College Dictionary*.

3. *The Foreman's Letter*, National Foreman's Institute, Inc., February 8, 1950, p. 3.
4. "The Talk of the Town," *The New Yorker*, January 28, 1950, p. 21. Reprinted by permission. Copyright, 1950, The New Yorker Magazine, Inc.
5. James F. Byrnes, *Speaking Frankly*. Harper & Brothers, 1947, p. 96.

The naïve speaker of a language usually has the feeling that, in general, words have a meaning, and he is seldom conscious of the great "area" of meaning for all except highly technical words. It is in this respect that the student's observation first needs widening and sharpening. Frequently we have tried to "build vocabularies" by adding more units or words. But to push first the addition of more vocabulary units in order to increase the number of words may interfere with, rather than help, effective mastery of language. This is the process that produces a Mrs. Malaprop. Most frequently the student needs first to know well the various areas of use of the units he is already familiar with; he needs to be made conscious of the great diversity of uses or meanings for commonly used words. He must be made aware, for example, that the statement "The children did not *count*" can mean that they did not *utter the words* for the numbers in a series, or that the children *were not considered*. Ordinarily we just don't believe without considerable careful examination that for the five hundred most used words in English (according to the Thorndike *Word Book*) the Oxford Dictionary records and illustrates from our literature 14,070 separate meanings.[6]

At different times the same words may be used differently.

When Francis Bacon referred to various people in the course of his *Essays* as *indifferent, obnoxious,* and *officious,* he was describing them as "impartial," "submissive," and "ready to serve." When King James II observed that the new St. Paul's Cathedral was *amusing, awful,* and *artificial,* he implied that Sir Christopher Wren's recent creation was "pleasing, awe-inspiring, and skilfully achieved." When Dr. Johnson averred that Milton's *Lycidas* was "*easy, vulgar,* and therefore *disgusting*," he intended to say that it was "effortless, popular, and therefore not in good taste."[7]

A role of experience also affects the varieties of usage. Brander Matthews provided an example from a dinner-party conversation:

The second topic . . . was a definition of the image called up in our several minds by the word *forest*. Until that evening I had never thought of forest as clothing itself in different colors and taking on different forms in the eyes of different men; but I then discovered that even the most innocent word may don strange disguises. To Hardy forest suggested the sturdy oaks to be assaulted by the woodlanders of Wessex; and to Du Maurier it evoked the trim and tidy avenues of the national domain of France. To Black the word naturally brought to mind the low scrub of the so-called deer-forests of Scotland; and to Gosse it summoned up a view of the green-clad mountains that towered up from the Scandinavian fiords. To Howells it recalled the thick woods that in his youth fringed the rivers of Ohio; and to me

6. Charles C. Fries, "Using the Dictionary," *Inside the ACD,* October 1948, p. 1.
7. Simeon Potter, *Our Language,* Pelican Books, 1950, p. 116.

there came back swiftly the memory of the wild growths bristling up unrestrained by man, in the Chippewa Reservation which I had crossed fourteen years before in my canoe trip from Lake Superior to the Mississippi. Simple as the word seemed, it was interpreted by each of us in accord with his previous personal experience.[8]

This conclusion about the range and possible uses of a word is easily verified. When it is forgotten, a listener just as easily comes to believe that (1) there is but one way to use a word—*his*—and (2) the speaker is doing with his words what the listener would were the listener doing the talking.

Can you see these beliefs at work in the examples given above?

In short, what *you* understand by any word or statement may not be what someone else intends to say. In a way, this is so obvious that most of us feel no obligation to think more about it. However, when one is aware of the fact it does not necessarily follow that he will act in terms of it. And there is some evidence that, unless people can be made sensitive to the possibility of bypassing, they make only meager efforts to stop it.

It Takes Two to Make Communication

I have no wish here to give comfort to the bore who gets so much pleasure squelching discussions with his defiant "Define your terms." His maneuver results in shifting the burden in communication to the other fellow. Both must be brought into the act. We would have the listener work just a bit, too. So we urge him to state his notion of what was being said. Incidentally, that bore may sometimes be routed with this: "What definition of my words have you in mind? Perhaps we are thinking together after all."

The "plain-talk" and "say-it-in-simple-words" teachers have been in vogue but they haven't been especially helpful. They, too, tend to put the emphasis on one side of the communication line. Putting the burden for understanding on the speaker is a kind of implied invitation to the listener to sit back and contentedly assume he has nothing to do but wait his turn. And besides, even the simple words have uses which too frequently vary between man and man.

We once observed eight meetings of a group of nine men, who functioned as a standing committee in a corporation having wide public responsibilities. Five had taken one or more courses and had studied some of the books on "talking plainly." One of the items checked had to do with "the assumption of understanding." Can men be differentiated according to their readiness to believe they know what the other fellow is referring to? We looked in their replies for such indications as *questions* for assurance that the asker is "with" the speaker, *qualifications* like "If I understand what you say" or "If

8. Brander Matthews, *These Many Years: Recollections of a New Yorker*, Charles Scribner's Sons, 1917, pp. 287–288. Quoted from the essay by Allen Walker Read, "Linguistic Revision as a Requisite for the Increasing of Rigor in Scientific Method," read at the Third Congress on General Semantics, July 22, 1949.

I knew what you mean. . . ," *invitations* like "Correct me if I'm off the beam" or "Tell me whether I answered what you intended to say. . . . "

We were hardly prepared to find that four of the "plain-talk students" did the least amount of questioning, qualifying, inviting, etc. This may, of course, be an accident. Before a conclusion worth much can be drawn we should have a broader sampling of the population. And before a cause can be assigned with confidence much more investigation would be needed. Nevertheless, *these particular men*, knowing the ways to "plainness" and using them, tended to think they had done enough when they spoke so. They seemed to focus attention on *their* talking. They made no comparable effort to look to the character of what they heard.

I am not at all arguing that this finding in these particular cases means that training in plain talking makes for poor listening. I am trying to suggest only that training in the explicit effort at understanding may be a difficult sort of thing and may not automatically carry over from other training.

Cardinal Manning once said something relevant:

> I have no doubt that I will hear that I am talking of what I do not understand; but in my defence I think I may say, I am about to talk of what I do not understand for this reason: I cannot get those who talk about it to tell me what they mean. I know what I mean by it, but I am not at all sure that I know what they mean by it; and those who use the same words in different senses are like men that run up and down the two sides of a hedge, and so can never meet.

It is helpful to think of the radio in this. The performer in the studio can talk his heart out, but if the man in the easy chair is tuned in elsewhere it really makes no difference what is being said. Unless the receiver is on the same wave length, the character of what is sent out hardly governs the communication process.[9]

This is not to imply that a speaker cannot help by putting what he has to say in clear, listenable language. Anything he does to define, simplify, amplify, illustrate, is all to the good. But it is only part of the process. The listener has a job to do, too. He must make the effort to come to terms with the speaker to keep from assuming that he inevitably knows what the speaker has in mind. At the very least he might temper his arrogance with a question now and then just to make sure.

It takes two to make communication.

Are You on His Communication Line?

The preceding pages of this chapter were mimeographed and given to three groups, one meeting for study of the Bible, one considering matters of policy in a business corporation, and one working on problems in the administration

9. This image is well developed in the article by Charles T. Estes, "Speech and Human Relations in Industry," *The Quarterly Journal of Speech*, April 1946, pp. 160–169.

of a college fraternity. Every member of each group read a portion out loud. We then talked about the main point—it takes two to make communication. We agreed that this was rather simple stuff and that we would try to talk with the possibility of by-passing in mind. We agreed, further, that no one of us would be insulted if asked to clarify or "talk some more" on any doubtful point. Nor would anyone feel hesitant about trying to get on the same wave length with anyone else. We gave each a small card with the inscription, "Are you on *his* communication line?"

What happened?

In each case the business of the meeting was slowed down. Only half as many items on the agenda could be covered. There was a certain amount of unfruitful wrangling about small points. Some members became tongue-tied in the face of so much freedom. Others became impatient with what seemed a waste of time, this trying to get to the speaker. The first sessions were always the worst. Most members felt comfortable only after the second or third.

And then we came upon something interesting. A man was being listened to. He found that others were actually waiting until he finished. He felt flattered in turn by the fact that another was trying to reach him rather than argue at him. He found himself trying to make his points so that his hearers would have less trouble with them. They were trying harder to read the cards he was putting on the table. The ornery member, normally so quick to doubt, stayed to question. The timid member found that the social pressure about the participation was all on his side.

We are inclined to think that the long-run results were worth the time and trouble.

The Purist's Dogma

In a number of experimental discussion groups generous enough to submit to such instruction there was a curious resistance to this seemingly obvious doctrine. I would be asked questions like these: Do you mean to say that a word doesn't have some definite, accurate meaning of its own regardless of the person who uses it? Isn't there a right or correct use for each word? If somebody fails to use a word exactly isn't he violating some rule in rhetoric or grammar?

How did these people come under the spell of the purist's dogma? Were they remembering some menacing drillmaster with a word list asking "what is *the* meaning of ——?" Or had they been badgered by vocabulary tests with entries like *glabrous heads: bald, over-sized, hairy, square, round; his stilted manner: irresolute, improper, cordial, stiffly formal* with instructions to circle the meaning? Or maybe they grew up when Alexander Woollcott was campaigning against certain current usage. He fought the use of "alibi" as a synonym for excuse; he wanted it saved for its "elsewhere" sense. He sneered when "flair" was used in the sense of knack or aptitude. He wanted it reserved for "capacity to detect." He and the traditional handbooks had a long list of such "reservations."

Or maybe they got their moorings from the pronouncements of Richard Grant White, who once said, "There is a misuse of words that can be justified by no authority, however great, and by no usage, however general." Or maybe they got no further in *Through the Looking Glass* than

> ". . . How old did you say you were?"
> Alice made a short calculation, and said, "Seven years and six months."
> "Wrong!" Humpty Dumpty exclaimed triumphantly. "You never said a word like it!"
> "I thought you meant 'How old *are* you?'" Alice explained.
> "If I'd meant that, I'd have said it," said Humpty Dumpty.

Regardless of the source, they used this dogma as the basis for a theory of their own about the cause of misunderstanding. If a speaker didn't use a word correctly it was only natural if a listener who did know the exact meaning was misled. Just get people to use words in their right meaning and then everyone will understand everyone else.

Indeed, this might be a way—but how can we do it? Who has the authority to declare *the* correct use and who has the time to learn it? There are more than 600,000 words in the Merriam-Webster unabridged dictionary and perhaps half as many more in the technical vocabularies of medicine, engineering, law, etc. And when the dictionary gives several meanings, which is *the* one? And just how is anyone going to curb those who, like Humpty Dumpty, would have their own ways with words:

> ". . . Impenetrability! That's what I say!"
> "Would you tell me please," said Alice, "what that means?"
> "Now you talk like a reasonable child," said Humpty Dumpty, looking very much pleased. "I meant by 'impenetrability' that we've had enough of that subject, and it would be just as well if you'd mention what you mean to do next, as I suppose you don't mean to stop here all the rest of your life."
> "That's a great deal to make one word mean," Alice said in a thoughtful tone.
> "When I make a word do a lot of work like that," said Humpty Dumpty, "I always pay it extra."

And what is more crucial, why do we look at words alone? Are words not most often used with other words in phrases, clauses, sentences? May not the setting affect the word?

We tried to get around this ill-advised zeal for exactness by suggesting that a word might be compared with a tool which can be used in a variety of ways. Thus, a screwdriver might be designed to drive screws, but once available it can be used to stir paint, jimmy a tight window, or, lacking any other weapon, to defend oneself with. You might, if you wish, insist that the screw function is the "right" or "correct" one and that a pistol is a much more effective weapon. But your insistence will hardly stop me from using the screwdriver in these other ways if I find it convenient or necessary to do so. A carpenter with a full rack of tools may have good reason for reserving each for but one use, but if some other purpose is served there is nothing in the nature of the tool which could prevent that other use. The desire for the restriction, then, is personal rather than functional.

Within limits, especially in technical disciplines, it is possible to standardize word usage. One is usually safe in assuming that the workers in specialized areas will conform to some established, stipulated word usages. In the military establishment and in legal affairs, for example, it is often possible as well as necessary to insist that particular words be used in particular ways.

Once outside the range of the specialist's interests, however, we are wise if we expect words to be used variously. A speaker's concern at any moment is not to use a word but to make a statement. In his eagerness to speak his piece he is more concerned with his continuous expression than with his total effect. If he happens to range outside his listeners' conventional usage, they will get nowhere lamenting his lexicographical heresy. And if they do not get to his usage they are likely to assume that he said what he never intended to.

We have come to see wisdom in this advice: Never mind what words mean. What did *he* mean?

It may take time to find out what a man means. It may demand a patient listening and questioning. It may be an unexciting effort. But it should help to bring people into an area of awareness which they are too often on the outside of. Mr. Justice Jackson's experience in a situation more momentous than anything we were exposed to adds to our confidence in the advice:

> It was my experience with the Soviet lawyers at Nurnberg that the most important factor in collaboration with the Soviet was patiently and persistently to make sure, when a proposition is first advanced, that it is thoroughly understood and that both sides are using their words to express the same sense. When this was done, the Soviet lawyers kept their agreements with us quite as scrupulously as American lawyers would. They may or may not regard that as a compliment, but my intentions are good. But it was my experience that it took infinite patience with them, as they thought it took infinite patience with us, to get to a point where there was a real meeting of minds as distinguished from some textual abstract formula which both could accept only because concretely it meant nothing or meant different things to each. And I have sometimes wondered how much misunderstanding could have been avoided if arrangements between the two countries had not often been concluded so hurriedly, in the stress of events, that this time-consuming and dreary process of reducing generalities to concrete agreements was omitted.[10]

10. Excerpt from address by Mr. Justice Robert H. Jackson at the Bar Dinner of the New York County Lawyers' Association, December 8, 1949.

W. Somerset Maugham

THREE AIMS FOR WRITERS

I knew that I should never write as well as I could wish, but I thought with pains I could arrive at writing as well as my natural defects allowed. On taking thought it seemed to me that I must aim at lucidity, simplicity and euphony. I have put these three qualities in the order of the importance I assigned to them.

I have never had much patience with the writers who claim from the reader an effort to understand their meaning. You have only to go to the great philosophers to see that it is possible to express with lucidity the most subtle reflections. You may find it difficult to understand the thought of Hume, and if you have no philosophical training its implications will doubtless escape you; but no one with any education at all can fail to understand exactly what the meaning of each sentence is. Few people have written English with more grace than Berkeley. There are two sorts of obscurity that you find in writers. One is due to negligence and the other to wilfulness. People often write obscurely because they have never taken the trouble to learn to write clearly. This sort of obscurity you find too often in modern philosophers, in men of science, and even in literary critics. Here it is indeed strange. You would have thought that men who passed their lives in the study of the great masters of literature would be sufficiently sensitive to the beauty of language to write if not beautifully at least with perspicuity. Yet you will find in their works sentence after sentence that you must read twice to discover the sense. Often you can only guess at it, for the writers have evidently not said what they intended.

Another cause of obscurity is that the writer is himself not quite sure of his meaning. He has a vague impression of what he wants to say, but has not, either from lack of mental power or from laziness, exactly formulated it in his mind and it is natural enough that he should not find a precise expression for a confused idea. This is due largely to the fact that many writers think, not before, but as they write. The pen originates the thought. The disadvantage of this, and indeed it is a danger against which the author must be always on his guard, is that there is a sort of magic in the written word. The idea acquires substance by taking on a visible nature, and then stands in the way of its own clarification. But this sort of obscurity merges very easily into the wilful. Some writers who do not think clearly are inclined to suppose that their thoughts have a significance greater than at first sight appears. It is flattering to believe that they are too profound to be expressed so clearly that all who run may read, and very naturally it does not occur to such writers that the fault is with their own minds which have not the faculty of precise reflection. Here again the magic of the written word obtains. It is very easy to persuade oneself that a phrase that one does not quite understand may mean a great deal more than one realizes. From this there is only a little way to go to fall into the habit of setting down one's impressions in all their original vagueness. Fools can always be found to discover a hidden sense in them. There is another form of wilful obscurity that masquerades as aristocratic exclusiveness. The author wraps his meaning in mystery so that the vulgar shall not participate in it. His soul is a secret garden into which the elect may penetrate only after overcoming a number of perilous obstacles. But this kind of obscurity is not only pretentious; it is short-sighted. For time plays it an odd trick. If the sense is meagre time reduces it to a meaningless verbiage that no one thinks of reading. This is the fate that has befallen the lucubrations of those French writers who were seduced by the example of Guillaume Apollinaire. But occasionally it throws a sharp cold light on what had seemed profound and thus discloses the fact that these contortions of language disguised very commonplace notions. There are few of Mallarmé's poems now that are not clear; one cannot fail to notice that his thought singularly lacked originality. Some of his phrases were beautiful; the materials of his verse were the poetic platitudes of his day.

Simplicity is not such an obvious merit as lucidity. I have aimed at it because I have no gift for richness. Within limits I admire richness in others, though I find it difficult to digest in quantity. I can read one page of Ruskin with delight, but twenty only with weariness. The rolling period, the stately epithet, the noun rich in poetic associations, the subordinate clauses that give the sentence weight and magnificence, the grandeur like that of wave following wave in the open sea; there is no doubt that in all this there is something inspiring. Words thus strung together fall on the ear like music. The appeal is sensuous rather than intellectual, and the beauty of the sound leads you easily to conclude that you need not bother about the meaning. But words are tyrannical things, they exist for their meanings, and if you will not pay attention to these, you cannot pay attention at all. Your mind wanders. This kind of writing demands a subject that will suit it. It is surely out of place to write in the grand style of inconsiderable things. No one wrote in this manner with greater success than Sir Thomas Browne, but even he did not always escape this pitfall. In the last chapter of *Hydriotaphia* the matter, which is the destiny of man, wonderfully fits the baroque splendour of the language, and here the Norwich doctor produced a piece of prose that has never been surpassed in our literature; but when he describes the finding of his urns in the same splendid manner the effect (at least to my taste) is less happy. When a modern writer is grandiloquent to tell you whether or no a little trollop shall hop into bed with a commonplace young man you are right to be disgusted.

But if richness needs gifts with which everyone is not endowed, simplicity by no means comes by nature. To achieve it needs rigid discipline. So far as I know ours is the only language in which it has been found necessary to give a name to the piece of prose which is described as the purple patch; it would not

have been necessary to do so unless it were characteristic. English prose is
elaborate rather than simple. It was not always so. Nothing could be more racy,
straightforward and alive than the prose of Shakespeare; but it must be remembered that this was dialogue written to be spoken. We do not know how he
would have written if like Corneille he had composed prefaces to his plays.
It may be that they would have been as euphuistic as the letters of Queen
Elizabeth. But earlier prose, the prose of Sir Thomas More, for instance, is
neither ponderous, flowery nor oratorical. It smacks of the English soil. To my
mind King James's Bible has been a very harmful influence on English prose.
I am not so stupid as to deny its great beauty. It is majestical. But the Bible is an
oriental book. Its alien imagery has nothing to do with us. Those hyperboles,
those luscious metaphors, are foreign to our genius. I cannot but think that not
the least of the misfortunes that the Secession from Rome brought upon the
spiritual life of our country is that this work for so long a period became the
daily, and with many the only, reading of our people. Those rhythms, that
powerful vocabulary, that grandiloquence, became part and parcel of the national sensibility. The plain, honest English speech was overwhelmed with ornament. Blunt Englishmen twisted their tongues to speak like Hebrew prophets.
There was evidently something in the English temper to which this was
congenial, perhaps a native lack of precision in thought, perhaps a naïve
delight in fine words for their own sake, an innate eccentricity and love of embroidery, I do not know; but the fact remains that ever since, English prose
has had to struggle against the tendency to luxuriance. When from time to time
the spirit of the language has reasserted itself, as it did with Dryden and the
writers of Queen Anne, it was only to be submerged once more by the pomposi-
ties of Gibbon and Dr. Johnson. When English prose recovered simplicity with
Hazlitt, the Shelley of the letters and Charles Lamb at his best, it lost it again
with De Quincey, Carlyle, Meredith and Walter Pater. It is obvious that the
grand style is more striking than the plain. Indeed many people think that a
style that does not attract notice is not style. They will admire Walter Pater's,
but will read an essay by Matthew Arnold without giving a moment's attention
to the elegance, distinction and sobriety with which he set down what he had
to say.

The dictum that the style is the man is well known. It is one of those aphorisms
that say too much to mean a great deal. Where is the man in Goethe, in his bird-
like lyrics or in his clumsy prose? And Hazlitt? But I suppose that if a man has
a confused mind he will write in a confused way, if his temper is capricious
his prose will be fantastical, and if he has a quick, darting intelligence that is
reminded by the matter in hand of a hundred things he will, unless he has
great self-control, load his pages with metaphor and simile. There is a great
difference between the magniloquence of the Jacobean writers, who were intoxicated with the new wealth that had lately been brought into the language,
and the turgidity of Gibbon and Dr. Johnson, who were the victims of bad
theories. I can read every word that Dr. Johnson wrote with delight, for he
had good sense, charm and wit. No one could have written better if he had not

wilfully set himself to write in the grand style. He knew good English when he saw it. No critic has praised Dryden's prose more aptly. He said of him that he appeared to have no art other than that of expressing with clearness what he thought with vigour. And one of his Lives he finished with the words: "Whoever wishes to attain an English style, familiar but not coarse, and elegant but not ostentatious, must give his days and nights to the volumes of Addison." But when he himself sat down to write it was with a very different aim. He mistook the orotund for the dignified. He had not the good breeding to see that simplicity and naturalness are the truest marks of distinction.

For to write good prose is an affair of good manners. It is, unlike verse, a civil art. Poetry is baroque. Baroque is tragic, massive and mystical. It is elemental. It demands depth and insight. I cannot but feel that the prose writers of the baroque period, the authors of King James's Bible, Sir Thomas Browne, Glanville, were poets who had lost their way. Prose is a rococo art. It needs taste rather than power, decorum rather than inspiration and vigour rather than grandeur. Form for the poet is the bit and the bridle without which (unless you are an acrobat) you cannot ride your horse; but for the writer of prose it is the chassis without which your car does not exist. It is not an accident that the best prose was written when rococo with its elegance and moderation, at its birth attained its greatest excellence. For rococo was evolved when baroque had become declamatory and the world, tired of the stupendous, asked for restraint. It was the natural expression of persons who valued a civilized life. Humour, tolerance and horse sense made the great tragic issues that had preoccupied the first half of the seventeenth century seem excessive. The world was a more comfortable place to live in and perhaps for the first time in centuries the cultivated classes could sit back and enjoy their leisure. It has been said that good prose should resemble the conversation of a well-bred man. Conversation is only possible when men's minds are free from pressing anxieties. Their lives must be reasonably secure and they must have no grave concern about their souls. They must attach importance to the refinements of civilization. They must value courtesy, they must pay attention to their persons (and have we not also been told that good prose should be like the clothes of a well-dressed man, appropriate but unobtrusive?), they must fear to bore, they must be neither flippant nor solemn, but always apt; and they must look upon "enthusiasm" with a critical glance. This is a soil very suitable for prose. It is not to be wondered at that it gave a fitting opportunity for the appearance of the best writer of prose that our modern world has seen, Voltaire. The writers of English, perhaps owing to the poetic nature of the language, have seldom reached the excellence that seems to have come so naturally to him. It is in so far as they have approached the ease, sobriety and precision of the great French masters that they are admirable.

Whether you ascribe importance to euphony, the last of the three characteristics that I mentioned, must depend on the sensitiveness of your ear. A great many readers, and many admirable writers, are devoid of this quality. Poets as we know have always made a great use of alliteration. They are persuaded that the repetition of a sound gives an effect of beauty. I do not think it does so in prose. It seems to me that in prose alliteration should be used only for a special reason; when used by accident it falls on the ear very disagreeably. But its accidental use is so common that one can only suppose that the sound of it is not universally offensive. Many writers without distress will put two rhyming words together, join a monstrous long adjective to a monstrous long noun, or between the end of one word and the beginning of another have a conjunction of consonants that almost breaks your jaw. These are trivial and obvious instances. I mention them only to prove that if careful writers can do such things it is only because they have no ear. Words have weight, sound and appearance; it is only by considering these that you can write a sentence that is good to look at and good to listen to.

I have read many books on English prose, but have found it hard to profit by them; for the most part they are vague, unduly theoretical, and often scolding. But you cannot say this of Fowler's Dictionary of Modern English Usage. It is a valuable work. I do not think anyone writes so well that he cannot learn much from it. It is lively reading. Fowler liked simplicity, straightforwardness and common sense. He had no patience with pretentiousness. He had a sound feeling that idiom was the backbone of a language and he was all for the racy phrase. He was no slavish admirer of logic and was willing enough to give usage right of way through the exact demesnes of grammar. English grammar is very difficult and few writers have avoided making mistakes in it. So heedful a writer as Henry James, for instance, on occasion wrote so ungrammatically that a school-master, finding such errors in a schoolboy's essay, would be justly indignant. It is necessary to know grammar, and it is better to write grammatically than not, but it is well to remember that grammar is common speech formulated. Usage is the only test. I would prefer a phrase that was easy and unaffected to a phrase that was grammatical. One of the differences between French and English is that in French you can be grammatical with complete naturalness, but in English not invariably. It is a difficulty in writing English that the sound of the living voice dominates the look of the printed word. I have given the matter of style a great deal of thought and have taken great pains. I have written few pages that I feel I could not improve and far too many that I have left with dissatisfaction because, try as I would, I could do no better. I cannot say of myself what Johnson said of Pope: "He never passed a fault unamended by indifference, nor quitted it by despair." I do not write as I want to; I write as I can.

But Fowler had no ear. He did not see that simplicity may sometimes make concessions to euphony. I do not think a far-fetched, an archaic or even an affected word is out of place when it sounds better than the blunt, obvious one or when it gives a sentence a better balance. But, I hasten to add, though I think you may without misgiving make this concession to pleasant sound, I think you should make none to what may obscure your meaning. Anything is better than not to write clearly. There is nothing to be said against lucidity, and against simplicity only the possibility of dryness. This is a risk that is well worth taking when you reflect how much better it is to be bald than to wear a curly wig. But there is in euphony a danger that must be considered. It is very likely to be monotonous. When George Moore began to write, his style was poor; it gave you the impression that he wrote on wrapping paper with a blunt pencil. But he developed gradually a very musical English. He learnt to write sentences that fall away on the ear with a misty languor and it delighted him so much that he could never have enough of it. He did not escape monotony. It is like the sound of water lapping a shingly beach, so soothing that you presently cease to be sensible of it. It is so mellifluous that you hanker for some harshness, for an abrupt dissonance, that will interrupt the silky concord. I do not know how one can guard against this. I suppose the best chance is to have a more lively faculty of boredom than one's readers so that one is wearied before they are. One must always be on the watch for mannerisms and when certain cadences come too easily to the pen ask oneself whether they have not become mechanical. It is very hard to discover the exact point where the idiom one has formed to express oneself has lost its tang. As Dr. Johnson said: "He that has once studiously formed a style, rarely writes afterwards with complete ease." Admirably as I think Matthew Arnold's style was suited to his particular purposes, I must admit that his mannerisms are often irritating. His style was an instrument that he had forged once for all; it was not like the human hand capable of performing a variety of actions.

If you could write lucidly, simply, euphoniously and yet with liveliness you would write perfectly: you would write like Voltaire. And yet we know how fatal the pursuit of liveliness may be: it may result in the tiresome acrobatics of Meredith. Macaulay and Carlyle were in their different ways arresting; but at the heavy cost of naturalness. Their flashy effects distract the mind. They destroy their persuasiveness; you would not believe a man was very intent on ploughing a furrow if he carried a hoop with him and jumped through it at every other step. A good style should show no sign of effort. What is written should seem a happy accident. I think no one in France now writes more admirably than Colette, and such is the ease of her expression that you cannot bring yourself to believe that she takes any trouble over it. I am told that there are pianists who have a natural technique so that they can play in a manner that most executants can achieve only as the result of unremitting toil, and I am willing to believe that there are writers who are equally fortunate. Among them I was much inclined to place Colette. I asked her. I was exceedingly surprised to hear that she wrote everything over and over again. She told me that she would often spend a whole morning working upon a single page. But it does not matter how one gets the effect of ease. For my part, if I get it at all, it is only by strenuous effort. Nature seldom provides me with the word, the turn of phrase, that is appropriate without being far-fetched or commonplace.

Mass Media

The mass media are the means of communication, such as television, moving pictures, radio, and the press, which reach vast numbers of Americans. Members of the great audiences to which they appeal are tremendously influenced by them in their ways of thinking and looking at things. In a democracy, therefore, these media are of great importance. Their audiences have the responsibility of knowing them for what they are, of gauging them, of judging them. Those in control of them have the responsibility of using them wisely and fairly. The first passage in this section, a part of the autobiography of Eric Sevareid, journalist and radio and television commentator, tells how Sevareid, working on a newspaper when he was eighteen, became aware of some of the problems of the press. Edgar Dale's "The Effects of the Mass Media" notes the significant effects of mass media in general, and suggests some practical ways of assuring that these forces for good or evil will be put to the best use. T. S. Matthews' "What Makes News" sets forth some challenging ideas about the role and the power of newspapers. Arthur Knight's "Types, Stereotypes, and Acting in Films" discusses some of the special demands of movie acting and the development of that phenomenon, the Hollywood star. Martin Mayer's "What Happens to the Talent?" describes the work that went into developing a television documentary series and also points out the difficulty the television industry has in holding talent.

Eric Sevareid

CUB REPORTER

A personal discovery

If a young man goes directly from secondary school to the university, and completes the study of his profession in theory and principle before entering his first office, everything is quite different. The faces, the titles, the very arrangement of the desks and departments he sees as a functional pattern. He has his mind on the end product of the concern; he knows how and why his product came about in modern society; he knows its present status in terms of history, and he no doubt understands the relationship of himself and his work to the times in which he lives. It must be a great advantage to begin that way, but it also means missing a brief period of complete enchantment. The old Minneapolis *Journal*, no longer extant, was an imposing and venerable institution in that northwest country, identified with the permanent structures of the landscape—the original buildings of Fort Snelling, the first dam on the upper Mississippi, the first roadbed laid by Jim Hill, the Empire Builder. It spoke with authority in the land, if not with wisdom, and it was an interconnecting cog in the social machinery of a widely scattered civilization. I was unaware that its directors were in, hand and glove, with the potentates of railroad, timber, and milling who for a very long time dictated, as if by kingly right, the political and economic affairs of this civilization. I was unaware that the men who wrote its pages *were* aware, bitterly so, of the paper's true function. To me at eighteen it was that most remarkable, most fascinating of all human institutions, a daily newspaper, peopled with those glamorous, incomparable men known as reporters and editors, actually there, alive, touchable, knowable. The ceremony of the "ghost walking" with the pay envelopes on Saturday afternoon was merely one of the more delightful moments of the week, a necessary bit of the engrossing ritual that preceded the ceremony of drinking beer down below at the "Greasy Spoon." The pay check of course was not really essential, these superhuman creatures being above anything so prosaic as the need for food, but was merely a kind of token and badge to signify that one Belonged. There was a positive sensual pleasure when one hurried from below-zero weather, so early it was scarcely light, into the warmth and smells of the city room where the telegraph editor was already waiting for the first yellow strips from the press association machines, into the warmer, noisier, greasier composing room upstairs where the limp, moist galley proofs of overset matter were piled and waiting for distribution below. The movement and noise built up with every hour, with the ordered cacophony of improvised symphony to the thundering finale by the great presses below the street, followed by the quiet aftermath of triumph when I would stagger into the city room with fifty fresh, pungent copies in my arms for the relaxing virtuosi who waited there, feet upon their instruments, gifted fingers lighting cigarettes.

This was my entry into the world of private enterprise in which most Americans pass their earthly existence. Surely, this was the best of all possible systems of life, where one simply chose the thing he most wanted to do, and, because he loved it, worked as hard as he could, and, because he worked hard, steadily rose from position to position, until he had "arrived," when the world would hold no more secrets or problems, and life gracefully leveled out on a plane of confidence, security, and happiness. I was convinced of the truth of this when after only six weeks as a copy runner I was made a reporter, with a desk of my own, admission to the Saturday night poker game around the copy desk, and fifteen dollars a week. Up to that time I had never made an enemy, never known anyone to feel that I was a threat to him, nor felt that anyone else was a threat to me. When I broke the great news that I was to become a reporter, to a rewrite man I worshiped, I received the first shock and hurt and began to learn. I expected warm congratulations and perhaps admiring predictions of future greatness. Instead, the Godlike journalist looked at me coldly and said: "For Christ's sake. The bastards." It was some time before I realized that experienced reporters, family men who required more than fifteen dollars a week, were being rebuffed each day in their search for employment.

My one regular chore on the paper, the inescapable heritage of the newest and rawest cub, was to spend each Friday as "religious editor," which meant putting together a page of copy with a summed-up story of Sunday's events, followed by several columns of "church notices" in six-point type. It meant interviewing a few visiting clerics of distinction, who never turned down the request. One of these was Billy Sunday, the evangelist, then in his last days. In his case, no questions were needed. He bounded about the hotel room, now peering intently out the window with one foot on the sill, now grasping the dressing table firmly in both hands while lecturing his reflection in the mirror. I never opened my mouth after introducing myself and scarcely remembered a word of what he said. Suddenly he ceased talking and darted out of the room, whereupon "Ma" Sunday unhooked a half-dozen typewritten sheets from a loose-leaf folder and handed them to me. This was the interview, all prepared, his emphasis marked by capitalized words and phrases in red ink with many exclamation marks. When I first took over this task on the paper I mentioned it one day to a Protestant pastor I happened to know rather well. He clasped his hands together, cast a brief glance upwards, and said: "Thank God for that! I have been grieving over the lack of publicity for our little church." He gripped my shoulder in a brotherly manner and said: "I hope this will be the answer to my prayers." I was quickly to learn that of all the citizens who rang the newspaper or came to the lobby seeking publicity, the men of the church were the most demanding and insatiable. I was frequently embroiled in controversy with pastors who would demand why I had not run the photographs of themselves which they had just sent in, whereas Pastor X had had *his* picture in the paper twice in the last three months. The rabbis were equally desirous, but generally more clever about it, while the important Catholic priests simply let their assistants handle the publicity question and rarely entered the negotiations in person. I learned that the newspaper was frightened of the preachers. The city desk could tell a vaudeville press agent to go to hell when his demands overreached the decent limit, but nobody ever spoke anything but soft words to the press agent of a church. I could see why nobody else wanted my task, but no doubt it was good training in basic diplomacy.

I was firmly convinced that a newspaper reporter "saw life" as did no one else in current society. (He sees no more of life than the iceman does, but he is compelled to note down and comment and thus acquires some habit of observation, if not reflection. That's all the difference there is.) I wanted to observe "human nature" and for some reason did not believe preachers exhibited any manifestations of human nature. So I seized any other kind of assignment anybody else was too lazy or too wise to want: interviews with the drinkers of canned heat who lived, and often died, in the caves and shacks along the riverbed, with movie stars of more majestic condescension than any bishop. Once I dressed as a waiter and served Katharine Hepburn her breakfast in bed after she had kept the reporters waiting in bitter cold for two hours at the station, then refused to see them. I have a vivid memory of knocking at apartment doors in the dead of night, to inform a young wife that her husband had just been killed in an accident or a police shooting, and did she have a photograph of him? Usually she turned white and ran to grab up the baby from its crib. These experiences left me limp and shaking. But somehow these wretched people— if they were poor, with poor people's belief that newspapers are powerful things with unquestioned rights—would find a photograph, would, between sobs, answer my questions. It was a surprise to find that the rich did not react the same way. When I went to ask questions of the wife of a manufacturer who had killed a man in disgraceful circumstances, she waited until I had spoken, then coolly requested me to leave the premises before she called the police. I spent three weeks in police headquarters, in Washington Avenue saloons, in the parlors of innumerable citizens, trying to solve the celebrated local mystery of the missing baby, stolen from the bed of its fifteen-year-old "unwed mother" in the city hospital. I worked morning, noon, and night, un- covered various bits of evidence, and finally located a youthful suspect who the police were convinced was the kidnapper, but whom they were unable to con- vict. I had always had the normal citizen's respect for the police, but during this experience discovered to my surprise that we reporters were frequently hours and days ahead of them unraveling the mystery.

One became, at that age, aware of social structure but not of social forces. One knew that certain individuals represented certain levels of the structure, in the city and inside the office, but one was scarcely aware that these individ- uals themselves were pushed and pulled by invisible pressures of a class allegiance, in society and business. It took me a long time to understand that the publisher had far more in common with, far more loyalty to, the bankers or grain merchants with whom he lunched at the Minneapolis Club than to the editors and reporters who worked with him to produce the paper. I began work with an idealistic view of the newspaper as the mounted knight of society, pure in heart, its strength as the strength of ten, owing no favor, fearing no man. I did not know that, while many great organs had begun that way (a few retained their integrity) with rugged, incorruptible founders, they had been handed down to sons and grandsons who were less interested in the true social function of the institution than in its money-making capacities which secured their position in the luxury class to which they, unlike their fathers and grand- fathers, were born. You learned. You learned by listening to the servile voices of the women who wrote the society pages as they asked the great ladies of Lowry Hill to be so very kind as to give them the names of their reception guests. You learned by discovering that if you became involved in controversy with an important businessman about the handling of a given story, you were always wrong and the businessman was always right. You learned by finding that if a picture were published of a Negro, however distinguished, and one of the great ladies, who happened to be from Georgia, telephoned to protest that she was offended, profuse apologies would be offered the sensitive creature.

With this general discovery of the structure of community life came the simultaneous discovery that nearly all men, working in a large American concern, did their daily work under the tyranny of fear. It varied in intensity from man to man, from prosperity to depression, but it was always there. The reporters were afraid of the city editor, the assistant city editor was afraid of the city editor, and the city editor, worried about his job, was afraid of his assistant. All were afraid of the managing editor, who in turn was afraid of the publisher. None of them wanted to feel that way, few were really "after" another's position, but each understood the pressures on the other which might at any moment cause the latter in self-protection to bear down upon the former. I might have learned all this much earlier, as most boys do from their fathers, who come home at night and relate to their wives at dinner the latest move in their "office politics." But my father had been an independent operator most of his life, and even when he did join a large establishment his sense of personal dignity and honor forbade him to discuss his superiors or inferiors, even with his family. And so I had begun working life in the simple faith that one's rise or fall was a matter solely of one's own capacities.

There was a charming old man who lived like an office hermit in a musty room in the interior labyrinths of the *Journal*. He was a scholar of some distinction, in love with the history of the northwest country, and he wrote graceful essays and homilies for the Sunday edition. I was charmed by his style and occasionally would take my portable lunch and bottle of milk at noon to eat with him. I assumed that with his literary attainments he was an important and respected person in the establishment. Once I stayed longer than usual; we were both spellbound with his own fascinating account of a vanished village. He looked suddenly at his watch. He became extremely agitated, grabbed up his copy in trembling fingers, and said: "Excuse me, excuse me. The editors. They will be very rough with me. I am very late." His bent figure shuffled rapidly from the room. He had spent his life on that newspaper.

The financial editor worked at a desk directly behind my own. One night when I was working exceptionally late, he came in slightly unsteady from drinking. He emptied into a suitcase the contents of his locker, a few books, a batch of clippings, a pair of golf shoes. I asked in surprise if he was leaving. He said: "I've been on this paper eighteen years, son. I've just been fired by a guy I used to teach where to put commas." He staggered out, leaving me with a sick, hollow feeling in the pit of my stomach and a dark light dawning in my head. Innocence departed. Life, it seemed, was a relentless, never-ending battle; one never "arrived"; loyalty, achievement, could be forgotten in a moment; a single man's whim could ruin one. I began to take stock of the situation and discovered that the men who got to the top, no matter how long they stayed here, were nearly all men who had studied in universities, who knew something besides the routine of their own desks. It was fear as much as anything else that drove me to college, purely personal ambition as much as curiosity about the world I lived in and what had made it the way I found it to be.

Edgar Dale

THE EFFECTS OF THE MASS MEDIA

Mayor Jimmy Walker of New York City once challenged the censors by pointing out that he had never heard of any girl being ruined by a book. Morris Ernst, noted exponent of civil liberties, asked members of an audience whether any of them had ever been morally injured by reading any book, or seeing a play or motion picture. The inference in both cases was that no girl was ever ruined by a book or that no individual was ever hurt by the mass media.

Are these men saying that books, or movies, or plays have no effects—good or bad? Morris Ernst would hardly have written *The First Freedom* just for his own pleasure. If books have no effect, then why concern ourselves about the censorship of such books? It seems to me that those who argue against censorship on the ground that the mass media have no significant effects on behavior are on shaky ground. We oppose censorship of books, newspapers, films, or television precisely because these media *do* have significant effects.

Further, we are for free and open discussion of ideas because this is one way of trying to figure out just what effects such ideas may have. It is also a way of changing the effects, as I shall point out later. We prohibit the communication of ideas only when they are obscene or when harmful action may follow the communication so closely that there will be no time for discussing and evaluating the ideas. You can go to jail for yelling "Fire!" in a theater only because the immediate effect is likely to be panic. You can yell "Fire!" in a park to your heart's content—even though there is no fire. Listeners may conclude that you are either crazy or a congenital liar. We see, then, that the situation helps determine what the effect will be.

But let us look a little more closely at the word "effect." One of our problems in discussing the effects of the mass media is one of definition. If we use the word "effect" as meaning only a precipitating event, the last event in a chain of related events, the final triggering action, we would have to admit that a book, a film, a letter, or many communication devices can finally trigger off an action.

Thus, if a boy commits a robbery by imitating a specific method shown in a movie or TV program, we must first ask what kind of boy he was. Was he ready to rob in any of another half dozen ways? If he had not seen the movie, is it likely he would have made no other attempt? Did the movie "load the gun," or merely pull the trigger?

We could hardly expect that television and other media could refrain from portrayal of all actions which might be imitated with disastrous effects. A playmate of mine seeing a circus acrobat dive into a net decided after reaching

From *The News Letter*, November 1953, edited by Edgar Dale, Professor of Education, Bureau of Educational Research, Ohio State University.

home to dive out of the haymow onto a spring mattress, thus permanently injuring his spine. But we could hardly argue that high diving should not be permitted in circuses because little boys may imitate it with dangerous results.

When we talk about the mass media, therefore, we must distinguish between those immediate triggering effects which might also be set off by other activities exclusive of mass media and those influences which have "a persistent, shaping effect upon the thought and behavior of human beings, singly or collectively," as noted by Louis Gottschalk in his book *Understanding History*.

What are some of these possible shaping effects upon our ways of using leisure time? At least five thousand motion picture theaters have closed in the last few years. This has an effect on the way former patrons will now use their leisure time. Perhaps they now attend a larger movie theater, but more than likely they are spending the movie time looking at television. They have changed their habits, but whether for good or ill is an extraordinarily difficult question to answer. But a truly massive effect has already been made upon the way they spend their leisure time.

Do the mass media have a persistent shaping effect upon specific behavior? Some maintain that the mass media do influence behavior but only on the good side of the ledger. The mass media can reinforce good, they say, but not the bad. However, if it is reasonable to assume that a medium can have "beneficial" effects, then we must also assume that it can produce "harmful" effects. Consequent behavior can move in socially disapproved or socially approved directions.

As one reads the literature on the effects of the mass media, he notes the hardly debatable conclusion that it is much easier to reinforce present values than to change values. It will obviously be easier to bring about more learning in a particular field than to get unlearning plus relearning. Thus it is usually less difficult to interest a man in improving his golf game than it is to persuade him to quit it and learn another sport. One may also conclude that transfer of learning will occur under certain conditions. It took twenty years of work with mass media and demonstration to get Iowa farmers to accept hybrid corn. But the introduction of hybrid oats, following hybrid corn, took only three years.

What about the effect of the mass media upon the shaping of specific attitudes? On this point Joseph T. Klapper in *The Effects of Mass Media* says: "Thousands of experiments have established beyond reasonable doubt that persuasion can be achieved by the planned, or even unplanned presentation of appropriate content through mass media."

One finds this specifically documented in the Payne Fund studies of Thurstone and Peterson, *Motion Pictures and Attitudes of Children*. Their major conclusion was "that motion pictures have definite, lasting effects on the social attitudes of children and that a number of pictures pertaining to the same issue may have a cumulative effect on attitude."

The fact that films or radio programs or written material can be used to change attitudes does not mean that it is easy to do it. About half of the films selected by Thurstone and Peterson to study for possible effects did not produce the expected effect. One film brought about the exact opposite of what had been predicted. Carefully laid public relations programs sometimes boomerang. As noted above, it is easier to produce an effect which means merely giving increased momentum to one's attitudes than it is to decelerate and reverse the attitude.

What about the use of the mass media in shaping erroneous ideas about people, in causing them to accept false information as true? Here again, the findings are like those relating to attitudes. There is a tendency to accept as true what is seen on the screen unless it is patently false or unless the person already has sound information with which to evaluate it. Thus if you don't know what college is like, you are likely to accept the picture presented in a movie. If you have good sense about what the world is like, nonsense can take care of itself. It will be seen as foolish, or funny, or fantastic. But when the truth is not known, the inaccurate is accepted as truth and the dream is seen as reality.

One of the most illuminating findings about effects of mass media relates to latency. Thus in the studies in the armed forces it was discovered that some expected effects were not found just after the film exposure but that they did appear several months later.

The mass media, then, do have significant effects. Some are merely triggers to set off a gun that somebody else, some other agency of communication, has loaded and cocked. But the mass media play their own role, too, and influence the ideas, the attitudes, and the stock of information which people have about the real world.

What can we do about it? First, we must try to convince people that they are not immune to the symbolic world as brought to us through movies, television, radio, and the press. It is subtly influencing our ways of thinking.

Second, we reject the idea that the free flow of ideas should be impeded either by censorship or by monopoly control. There is no simple answer to the problem of one-newspaper towns, newspaper chains, four television networks, concentration of film production. Some argue cogently that large-scale operation is a necessity and that competition among the various media makes monopoly difficult.

We need to make certain that the mass media are not monopolized by persons who have the same ideas about labor, capital, religion, taxation, or whatever the field may be. Perhaps we need some more *Christian Science Monitors* or labor dailies. There should be competition of ideas in the market-place of opinion. In all the shouting of the mass media there must be room for the opposing voices to be heard.

Third, we must bend every effort to develop the discriminating viewer, listener, and reader. There are so many falsehoods presented through the mass media (e.g., the toothpaste ads), so many accusations, so many divergent claims, that we must develop some rough yardsticks as to whom to believe. The remedy for this avalanche of claims and counterclaims is not to doubt everything but to learn how to tell what is true and what is false, a truly tough job.

Our schools must give students contact with excellence wherever it appears in the mass media. Provision must be made in colleges, for example, for students to see the best in films—theatrical, documentary, and educational films. This association with excellence is good vaccination against what is phony. Students should have an opportunity somewhere in their English or social studies curriculum to become acquainted with excellent magazines and daily newspapers.

Certainly we can expect that there will be discriminating teaching in reference to television. Students can be asked to report on programs best and least liked and to give reasons for their choices. They can sample programs recommended by fellow students or by teachers. They can contrast and evaluate styles of news commentators. They can discuss which ones seem to appeal primarily to one's emotions and which depend upon facts and reasoning for their judgments.

If mass media are having a persistent shaping effect upon our information, our outlook, our attitudes, then parents, schools, and colleges have an obligation to help children and young people to think through what these effects are and whether they are good or bad. If the effects are deemed desirable, then we ask how such effects may be accelerated. If the effects are contrary to sound parental teachings or to public policy, then we must ask how harmful effects can be minimized or eliminated. We must work with national organizations which are constructively trying to improve taste in television. Perhaps more than anything else, the consumer of the mass media should not think of them as "out of this world." They are in the same world he is, and he should make the most of it.

T. S. Matthews

WHAT MAKES NEWS

The main business of the press, supposedly, is news, as the main business of banks is money. It might surprise the public to discover how incurious many bankers are about the real nature of money and how unclear they are about it. In just the same way, and perhaps to a greater extent, most journalists are incurious about the real nature of news and just as unclear about it.

Perhaps the neatest as well as the most generally accepted definition of news is "what happened yesterday." I remember once toting up the front-page news stories in a good provincial newspaper in America. Of the eleven stories on the page, seven had not happened at all. Some of the speculations about the future, and there were many, might have come true, but so far they were just speculations. If news is what happened yesterday, the newspapers print an awful lot of phony news.

Most of the world's "news" is manufactured by the press itself: interviews with important men, reports on grave situations, press conferences, press investigations, political surveys, "informed speculation." An amusing example of manufactured news appeared last winter in the New York *Herald Tribune's* Paris edition. On

From *The Atlantic Monthly*, December 1957. Reprinted by permission of the author.

February 6, 1957, the main headline on the front page read: "Dulles Believes Israel, Egypt Will Obey Resolutions of UN" and the following day the main headline was: "Eisenhower Believes Israel Will Withdraw." For two days the biggest news the paper could find was what an official *said* he thought!

Most "hard news" falls into the press's lap like meteorites or manna from heaven: murder and suicide, rape, war, pestilence, famine, catastrophes of all kinds. This bad news is the best news to the press: it is not only exciting to read but it comes ready-made. Mongers of sensational news, like the London *Daily Mirror*, admitting that the supply of this sort of news is unsteady, meet the daily demand for sensation in two ways: by dressing up small news to look big and by ballyhooing daily features. There is no essential difference between the inevitable screaming front-page headline of the *Mirror* and the "running story" of a diplomatic conference from Reuter's News Agency. Both are manufactured news. They are said to have happened big; actually, they either didn't happen at all or they only happened a little.

Some of the more exacting followers of C. P. Scott, the famous editor of the *Manchester Guardian*, still insist that their paper deals in sacredly regarded facts. That is probably true in spots, although they conveniently overlook the other spots in the paper that are profanely opinionated rather than sacredly factual. A large part of the British and American press has in effect abandoned the pretense of dealing exclusively with facts or the pretense that their source is invariably as pure as the Pierian spring. A great many newspapers, for example, make no bones about printing gossip. They still, officially at least, exclude rumor (except from the gossip columns or unless it can be attributed to a "hitherto unimpeachable source," when it rises from "rumor" to "speculation" or "inside information").

Actually, news includes a great deal of rumor. A journalist friend of mine, on assignment in Central America, once had occasion to hire a "stringer" (a local correspondent) in a small town there. Since there was no newspaper in the town, the most likely candidate was one of the few English-speaking inhabitants who seemed to know his way around. He was duly hired and his duties explained to him. A few days later my friend looked up the new stringer to see how he was getting on. As yet he had found nothing to report, but he had prepared himself for any emergency by buying a large notebook which he had divided into two sections; the first was headed "Rumors," the second "False Rumors."

Claud Cockburn, once a prized London *Times* correspondent, during the last war put out a brilliant weekly news sheet that was read by the small number of people who constituted "everybody" in London. His views on the nature of news were also unorthodox:

> I went about saying that rumours were just as important, just as significant, just as—in the last analysis—"valid" as "facts."
>
> This shocked people horribly, although if you pressed them and asked whether it was not true that ninety percent of "information received" by such serious persons as Ambassadors and Chiefs of Police really consists in

significant rumours and rumours which can be interpreted by the person who knows enough rumours, they were usually bound to admit that this is indeed the case. . . . Unless one is God, how on earth can one tell truth from rumour in less than perhaps fifty years? And fifty years is too long to wait if one is in the business of issuing a weekly newspaper.

Cockburn was honest enough—or cynical enough, if you prefer—to include rumor in his definition of news. Few editors would agree with him without wincing, but whatever they may say, their practice follows his precept. The only journalists who are consistently successful in keeping rumor and gossip out of the news are the Communists. The Communist press, an avowed instrument of government, is dedicated to the proposition that facts equal propaganda equals truth. The facts are chosen, the propaganda ordered, and the truth announced. It's much simpler than with us. And the Russians have a great contempt for the confusions of the Western press, which all stem from this inadmissible *search* for news. News in Russia is issued as a valuable, state-controlled ration.

When Ilya Ehrenbourg, one of the dark stars of Communist journalism, visited the United States a few years ago, he was much bothered by reporters who pried into what he considered irrelevant personal questions. The one that moved him to most sardonic mirth was whether a suit he was having made at a New York tailor's was to have trousers with a buttoned fly or with a zipper. There, he said triumphantly, you have a picture of the Western press, which concerns itself with gossip: buttons or zipper, that is all it cares to know about. In the doctrinaire Communist view, our free press makes too little distinction between public news (which is the press's only business) and private news (which is none of its business). Moreover, say the Communists, nobody but they knows what news is fit to publish, or what news really is.

Our answer to this is apt to be, "The truth shall make you free"—by which we mean that if everybody talks continuously at the top of his lungs, somebody from time to time will probably say something true, somebody else may hear it, and it may have some good effect, by and large. Nevertheless, we have an uneasy suspicion that there should be some distinction between public and private news, and that the press doesn't make the distinction clear—no doubt because of the general confusion about what news really is. Public or private, the news must affect our individual lives, it must be translatable into our personal terms, before we will pay attention to it. Even the news in Russian papers, which couldn't be more public, can be so translated, I should imagine. Everything *Pravda* or *Izvestia* publishes means some action or threat of action by the government; the trick is to figure out, "How is that going to affect *me?*" We read the newspapers that way in time of war, when all governments are gray. In peacetime, public news for most of us is just something to quack about, and it rolls off our backs; the news that really concerns us comes by word of mouth or by mail. The opening door, the doctor's verdict, the expected letter, the telegram that says "death" or "life": each of these is the kind of news that comes home to us. Perhaps it is the only real news there is.

Nevertheless, we feel that there should be bigger news than this, and the press continually assures us that indeed there is. The press keeps on telling it, in big headlines; big good news and big bad news. The big good news is mainly manufactured, not so much because the press is sanguine by nature as because it is committed to the encouraging notion of progress. The big bad news is what has actually happened. When our candidate is elected or the war ends, we may call the news both big and good; but what will it be called by the people who voted for the other man, or who lost the war? No really good news, in the public sense, is either incredible or beyond our understanding. And yet we crave it, its absence seems wrong, we want it to be.

The press, which is as human as the rest of us, shares this craving and gropes for big good news—however incredible or beyond our understanding. When the New York *Times* printed the text of Einstein's theory, it was in this mystical and groping spirit. It's rather like the poem in which Thomas Hardy said that if someone asked him on Christmas Eve to come with him to the stable to see the oxen kneel before the Christ child, he would go along, "Hoping it might be so." The hope was that Einstein had found a large piece of truth even if nobody, or almost nobody, could understand it; and in that hope the New York *Times* editor was willing to bow his uncomprehending head and take the whole congregation of the *Times* to their knees with him.

In less than two generations science has become untranslatable, and its speculations about the world come to us more and more faintly. The news that it sends back to us (with the press as messenger) often seems contradictory of earlier bulletins; the gist of it comes across as a progressive disillusionment with accepted facts and an immense widening and deepening of the unknowable. But this is depressing and therefore unacceptable to our optimistic habit of mind—as if, with all our advantages, we were just catching up with Socrates. So the press continues to hail every scientific "discovery" (the substitution of a new theory for an abandoned one) as if it were real news, big news, and good news. And the public, official view of science's search for knowledge is one of untiring hope and faith. In private, however, there is skepticism and doubt, and not just among illiterate peasants, either.

The only big news, private and public, that human beings are really concerned about is news of life and death. There has been no new news on either subject for some time—nearly 2000 years, in fact. The Resurrection was tremendous good news, if true; the best news ever reported. But though it has been told wherever Christian missionaries have gone, and a large proportion of the earth's population must have heard it, it is still widely disbelieved or believed only in a poetic or mystical sense, as an honorable thought or an incomprehensible symbol.

The press is only a reflection of the world it reports, and, like the world, it is quite unable to recognize or accept really good news—a saint for the ages, a lasting hero, a revelation of permanent truth; it can only exaggerate or minimize, ignore, misreport, or doubt, just like the rest of us. Big bad news it can't miss; big good news it never sees, though it pretends a lot of little good news is big, and manufactures all the big good news it can. What keeps the press going is mainly snippets: some news, much gossip, loads of rumors—not to speak of all the features, extras, special acts, and entertaining etceteras.

The biggest piece of claptrap about the press is that it deals exclusively, or even mainly, with news. And the next biggest piece of claptrap is that the press has enormous power. This delusion is persistent and widespread. It is taken for granted by the public-at-large, who are apt to be impressed by anything that is said three times; it is continually advertised by the press itself; and it is cherished by press lords, some of whom, at least, should know better.

In what way is the press supposed to be so powerful? The general notion is that the press can form, control, or at least strongly influence public opinion. Can it really do any of these things? Hugh Cudlipp, editorial director of the London *Daily Mirror,* and a man who should know something about the effect of newspapers on public opinion, doesn't share this general notion about their power. He thinks newspapers can echo and stimulate a wave of popular feeling, but that's all: "A newspaper may successfully accelerate but never reverse the popular attitude which common sense has commended to the public." In short, it can jump aboard the bandwagon, once the bandwagon is under way, and exhort others to jump aboard too; but it can't start the bandwagon rolling or change its direction once it has started.

Like other habit-forming pills, the press can stimulate or depress, but it cannot cure. It can fan fear and hatred of another nation when the fear and hatred are there waiting to be fanned, but it cannot make peace. William Randolph Hearst, in his day the biggest of American press tycoons, deliberately used his papers to embroil the United States with Spain in 1898. In the process of fomenting war fever, he sent correspondents to Cuba, then in halfhearted revolt against Spain, to get propaganda photographs and inflammatory stories. When one of them protested that he could find no suitable photographs, Hearst cabled him in a fury: "You furnish the pictures and I'll furnish the war."

As more and more people have painful reason to know, the press has a nasty kind of power, the same kind of power a bully has; that of hurting somebody smaller and weaker than himself. An individual's only defense against the press is the law of libel, but considerable harm and much pain can be caused without going so far as to commit an actionable libel. Journalists themselves generally have a horror of being interviewed, "written up," or even noticed by the press; they know too well from their own experience how inept and cruel a distortion the result is likely to be—even in photographs—which, in the lying phrase, "cannot lie." They can be made to lie (for example, to bolster a point of propaganda, as Northcliffe was one of the first to discover. When he was using the *Daily Mail* to try to get Asquith out as Prime Minister and Lloyd George in, he once issued this order: "Get a smiling picture of Lloyd George, and underneath put the caption 'Do It Now,' and get the worst possible picture of Asquith and label it 'Wait and See.'" Since Northcliffe's day this technique has been developed much further). In spite of the reluctance of picture editors to admit it, the camera can also distort. In the office where I worked there used to be a saying: "The camera distorts. The TV camera distorts absolutely."

Nine times out of ten, ineptness is to blame rather than conscious cruelty; but there is always that tenth case. And a blundering friendly hand can be as heavy as an unfriendly fist. The press is often like a clumsy giant who gives you a pat on the back and knocks the wind out of you, if he doesn't cause internal injuries. I remember once coming upon an elderly professor from my university who had just been "written up" by the paper I worked on. When he saw me, tears came into his eyes, and he said: "What have I done to them? What have I done to deserve this?" He was deeply wounded by the article and regarded it as an extremely unkind caricature. Knowing that it had been written by one of his former students who liked and admired the professor, I tried to reassure him that it was at least kindly meant. I don't think I succeeded.

The press has a negative power—to titillate, alarm, enrage, amuse, humiliate, annoy, even to drive a person out of his community or his job. But of the positive power to which it pretends and of which the press lords dream—to make and break governments, to swing an election, to stop a war or start a revolution—there is no tangible evidence. Its vaunted might is a gigantic spoof. Professor David Mitrany, speaking in 1932 on "The Press and International Relations," put the case with delicate irony: "There is no need to spend time in an attempt to show how great is the influence of the press. It is greater in certain fields than in others. It is greater, one could say, in any field in which the knowledge and interest of the man in the street is lesser. For in that case the reading public is apt to think that the press speaks with the voice of Authority; while the authorities are apt to assume that the press is speaking with the voice of the People. . . ."

Everyone has heard of the "power of the press"; no one has seen it. The greatest believers in this exaggerated power and the loudest promoters of it are, naturally, the press lords themselves. One of the most deluded of these, not even excepting Northcliffe or Beaverbrook, was Robert McCormick, publisher of the Chicago *Tribune* (still emblazoned with his modest motto, "The world's greatest newspaper"). McCormick and, of course, his paper were always in bitter opposition to the Roosevelt Democrats as well as to the liberal element in his own Republican Party. A story used to be told about the Chicago *Tribune*, no doubt apocryphal but in essence true: that one of the janitors in the *Tribune* building always bet against any political candidate the paper supported, and gave odds to boot; and that he found this side line so profitable that he was able to buy two sizable apartment houses. The men in the street are better able than the press lords to judge the power of the press; in spite of all the kowtowing and brass bands, they can see that the Emperor has no clothes on.

During the twenty years (1932-1952) of Democratic Party government in America under Roosevelt and Truman, something like 85 per cent of the American press was owned or controlled by Republicans: the majority of American newspaper readers were being continually exhorted to vote Republican but continued to vote Democrat. The people in Chicago who bought the *Tribune* didn't buy it to find out how to cast their votes: they bought it in spite of its advice and its bias, because on the whole they liked its personality and found it entertaining.

Does this seem to argue a too shrewd, calm, and sensible attitude on the part of the ordinary newspaper reader? The press is generally appreciated by the public for what it is rather than for what it pretends to be; they don't feel it as a power in their lives but as a perquisite in their working day.

Arthur Knight

TYPES, STEREOTYPES, AND ACTING IN FILMS

Incredible as it may seem, there was a time when the movies existed without stars. For more than a decade after films were born, pictures were recognized by the companies that produced them—Biograph, Vitagraph, Edison—or, by the more discerning, through their directors—Griffith, Porter, even the French Georges Méliès. The players themselves remained anonymous, some by choice (a motion-picture appearance was considered degrading by most professional actors—a last resort when all else failed), more importantly because the producers calculated that any effort spent in building up a name might endanger the price structure of their industry. They might have to pay their actors more than the customary $5.00 a day.

It was the public itself that created the star system. Audiences began to discover that most Biographs featured a pretty little girl with long golden curls. They called her "Little Mary," after the name generally given her in the stories. The buxom beauty in the Vitagraph productions became, quite simply, "The Vitagraph Girl." And "Broncho Billy" was singled out by young and old alike as the first Western hero. Gradually, out of the repertory companies that each studio established for itself, types began to emerge—the handsome leading man, the flat-footed comic, the villain with his fine airs, the golden-haired heroine. But the public soon wanted to know who its heroes were, the names of the pretty girls who won its heart week after week in their ten- or twenty-minute melodramas. The companies were barraged by letters of inquiry into the identity of the new favorites. The letters went unanswered.

One shrewd showman, however—Carl Laemmle, who directed the destinies of Universal Pictures for so many years—guessed that this public interest in personalities could be turned to advantage. He engaged the services of the anonymous "Biograph Girl" and, amid suitable publicity, introduced her as Florence Lawrence. The star system was born (and, it might be noted, the word

Reprinted by permission of *The English Journal* and Arthur Knight, author of *The Liveliest Art, a Panoramic History of the Movies.*

itself was born almost simultaneously). Miss Lawrence made her debut under her own name in 1910. By 1913 few of the companies had not acceded to popular demand—prodded by their own actors who threatened to work elsewhere if they could not drink the heady, profitable mead of personal publicity at their own studios. Two years later, the star was a dominant factor in the film industry, a position that has been but slightly altered since that time. "Famous Players in Famous Plays," one successful company called itself and forthwith began to ransack the stage for names and properties to live up to its grandiose title. The enterprising Samuel Goldwyn brought from the operatic stage Mary Garden and Geraldine Farrar to star in his silent spectacles.

The odd thing is that the great names of the theater meant little to the movies. Some doting parents in the nickelodeon era, when movies were still considered déclassé, exposed their children to culture by taking them to see Sarah Bernhardt in *Queen Elizabeth* and similar uplifting enterprises; but the true movie star was created by the audiences, not by the producers. Between 1915 and 1920 virtually every great name on the stage—Mrs. Fiske, Pavlova, even Caruso—flirted with immortality through celluloid only to withdraw, sadder but richer, to their proper element. On the other hand, this great dragnet that the early film producers had flung over the theater did scrape up a number of relatively obscure young actors who, lured by the promise of a modest but regular weekly pay check, went to work for the movie companies. Among the more successful of these was a sad-faced young actor in Shakespearean repertory, leading man to Julia Arthur and Modjeska, who was quickly transformed into that prototype of all strong, silent Western heroes, William S. Hart. The comedian in a touring British music hall turn was offered $125.00 a week to join the Keystone Company—but the management wasn't certain whether his name was Caplan or Chaplin. A breezy juvenile from the Broadway stage, Douglas Fairbanks, was signed by the Triangle Corporation, distinctly a lesser plum in a pie that also contained Sir Herbert Beerbohm Tree, Weber and Fields, DeWolf Hopper, Billie Burke, and Frank Keenan.

What happened, of course, is that Hart, Chaplin, and Fairbanks, and all the others who permanently deserted the stage for the studio, discovered that there was a very special kind of acting required by the camera, a technique quite different from anything they had ever known before. The successful were those who modified and adapted their styles to movie requirements. But the great ones, the established names in the theater, persisted in performing as if they were still behind the footlights at the Empire or the Lyceum. Even granting the relatively uninhibited acting permissible in the movies of those days, their gestures were still too broad and emphatic, their facial contortions too absurd, their manner too grand for the average movie patron. They were playing for the gallery instead of the little black box a few feet away. And, it must be admitted, there were some few aging juveniles and matronly ingenues who failed to pass the searching scrutiny of the camera lens. By 1920 the noble experiment of importing famous players in wholesale lots had been abandoned by the studios, and most of the importees had returned to their legitimate bailiwicks. Not until 1929, with the advent of sound, did the studios again raid Broadway with such reckless abandon.

Two fundamental differences set movie-acting apart from acting in the theater: one is the manner in which movies are produced, and the other is film technique itself. Although the two are closely related, it might be well to consider them apart for the moment. A play is presented, and generally rehearsed, all of a piece. At any rate, before too many days have passed, each actor knows his part in relation to the play as a whole. Rehearsals pass from Act I to Act II to Act III before touchups are applied to individual scenes. When the play is finally presented, the actor may be called upon to sustain his characterization for two or three hours a night, but there is a continuity to his work; it has a beginning, a middle, and an end, a logical progression that he follows and feels at each performance. For those few hours he builds his role, even lives his part. But once the curtain comes down, the character disappears completely until the next show.

Movies, of course, are made quite differently. Their actual shooting time may extend over a month or more. And never are they shot in orderly progression from the first fade-in to the final clinch. No one in Hollywood feels that this might not be an ideal way to make a picture, but to produce a film economically any number of additional factors must be taken into consideration. It is the job of the assistant director to juggle all these factors—star availability, the allocations of studio time, how to group the crowd scenes most economically, and, if possible, how to get through all the scenes with the higher-priced players in the least number of days. He breaks down the script, not in terms of the actor's problem, but in terms of the most efficient production schedule. And if $500,000 —or even $5,000—can be saved by shooting first the middle, then the ending, then the opening scene, that is the way the schedule is arranged. In actual practice, the scrambling is far more intense than this, with separate fragments of even the same scene being taken days or even weeks apart. And there have been instances where no one, not even the writer, knew precisely what the ending would be when the initial sequences were already before the camera.

Naturally, this creates a certain difficulty for the actor. He is called upon to play a scene, or a fragment of a scene, often with only the sketchiest knowledge of its relation to the completed picture. He is called upon to create a characterization on occasions when the details of that character have yet to be clarified in the author's own mind. In any case, almost invariably it is the director who carries about the complete knowledge of how everything fits together. Rare indeed is the film—so rare as to make news—that is rehearsed before it goes on the floor, the film in which at least the principals are completely familiar with their characters and their relation one to the other.

Something more than acting, in the theater's sense of building and sustaining a character, is clearly called for in motion pictures. And part of that extra quality is to be found in film technique itself. As early film theoreticians like Eisenstein and Pudovkin pointed out years ago, the film actor is no more than one element in the completed picture. His image, photographed on a strip of film, is commingled by the editor with hundreds of others—a flower, a busy street, a steamboat departing, a cocktail glass. The emotion associated with the inanimate object colors, even clarifies, the mood of the actor as conveyed on the strips immediately preceding and following the insert.

To illustrate this, Pudovkin once conducted an interesting experiment. From a completed film he extracted a strip containing a practically immobile closeup of the actor Mozhukhin. He inserted this into another film, followed immediately by a closeup of a plate of soup. Later in the film he used the same shot of Mozhukhin joined to a scene of a dead woman in her coffin; and still later he joined it to a shot of a little girl playing with a teddy bear. The audience marveled at the virtuosity of Mozhukhin's performance, his range and subtlety —his pensive glance at the soup, his deep sorrow over the dead woman, the little smile that touched his lips as he gazed at the child. The public acclaimed the acting; Pudovkin went on experimenting with the techniques of putting a film together. He searched for what he called "plastic material," the most appropriate visual references to create and sustain the emotional content of a scene. The actor to him was no more than incidental.

Indeed, so very incidental is the actor that the director can decompose him at will, concentrating solely on the cigarette held nervously between his fingers, the slump of his shoulders as seen from the rear, his stumbling footsteps on an icy sidewalk, if these will more fully project the emotional tone of a scene than a grimacing closeup and a line of dialogue. The camera's unique ability to frame off the most significant detail of a scene and present it from its most significant aspect often reduces the actor in this way to a mere thing, simply another object to be manipulated by the director and his editor, another bit of "plastic material." Alfred Hitchcock once summarized, inelegantly but expressively, the typical director's point of view: "Actors are cattle," he said.

Naturally, the director likes to believe that the final picture is his creation alone. Yet few are so utterly egoistic as to believe that their name on the credit sheets is what brings audiences into moviehouses across the nation—or across the world. Perhaps a dozen directors are known by name to the average moviegoer; of them less than half actually mean anything when it comes to selling tickets at the box office. But their actors—their "cattle"—are known, loved, and revered wherever movies are shown. In our democratic United States stars are treated like royalty. Elsewhere they become veritable gods. A Chaplin, a Garbo, today even a Marilyn Monroe, can so affect audiences as to induce a mass hysteria. The characters that they have created on the screen become accepted as an extension of their true personalities. And woe betide the artist who would disabuse his public of that fact! No small part of Chaplin's recent troubles are due less to the unpopularity of his political views than to the one-time popularity of the man himself. Audiences did not want their favorite funny man to think. Ingrid Bergman, the screen's epitome of pure love, lost vast sections of her fans after her sensational affair with Roberto Rossellini, the noted Italian director. But Rita Hayworth, the screen's epitome of *im*pure love, lost none of her following after her no less sensational affair with Aly Khan—nor its equally sensational denouement.

It is here that we find a most significant clue to the nature of film-acting. Technique to one side, the successful actor is the one who can suggest on the screen a complete, living personality. Out of the thousands of individual shots that together make up a single feature-length film, shots lasting an average of only twenty seconds, there must emerge a single, integrated, recognizable human being. It is scarcely an accident, considering how movies are made, that this character tends to be the same in picture after picture. No matter what the director may choose to believe, a Clark Gable film *is* a Clark Gable film. Gable's self-confidence, his virility, his brusque humor, are evident in every role he plays. The unsuccessful Clark Gable picture is the one in which the starring role has not been written to capitalize fully on Gable's screen personality.

One can examine each of the box-office favorites over the years and find the same law in operation. Each star has a handful of adjectives to describe the kind of role he plays best: Bing Crosby—genial, folksy, sentimental; Gary Cooper—easy-going, even shy, until he is pushed; Greer Garson—lady-like, intelligent, true-blue; Humphrey Bogart—tough, devil-may-care, a clouded past; Joan Crawford—hard, sophisticated, but a sufferer. Given a script that utilizes these highly specific character traits, each can turn in a capable enough performance. When the script utilizes them naturally and to full advantage, an outstanding performance often results—Crosby's in *Going My Way*, Cooper's in *High Noon*, Garson's in *Mrs. Miniver*, Bogart's in *The African Queen*, Crawford's in *Mildred Pierce*. Unfortunately, the studios are also aware of this fact. If they have a story that might make a good Gary Cooper picture, they may very well change the central character a bit—or a good bit—to make it fit more snugly to Cooper's special qualities. The result is stereotype, deadly to both actors and the film itself.

But this abuse of type-casting, prevalent though it be, does not alter the basic correctness of the process for motion-picture purposes. Documentary directors have repeatedly demonstrated that no actor makes as convincing a steelworker as a real steelworker; and today in Hollywood men like Elia Kazan and Fred Zinnemann—and in Italy, De Sica and Rossellini—make it a practice to cast subsidiary roles with nonprofessional types. The stars, as *professional* types, are similarly incorporated by the skilled director into his narrative. They become "plastic material" which he can shape and mold at his discretion. Considering the basic ability of many a star performer, this is an especially sound procedure. It is also a partial explanation of why so many of our actors will shine in the hands of one director and appear completely wooden when handled by others. The director with a reputation of being "good with actors" is generally the director who knows how much he can elicit from his performers and how much he must suggest by artifice, by the use of film technique.

In addition to the star performer, however, the motion-picture medium over the years has developed a handful of highly skilled virtuoso players sufficiently protean in their abilities to rise above both type and stereotype. Garbo, Chaplin, Bette Davis, Alec Guinness, and, of the younger crop, Richard Widmark and Jean Simmons—each seems able to suggest a life that extends beyond whatever film he is appearing in, a life that began before the introductory titles and will go on after the film is over. The parts they play are surcharged with emotional overtones, frequently suggesting depths in the character untouched by the screen-play. And though type-casting inevitably has claimed them all from time to time, pictures fitted to the stars instead of the other way around, the mediocrity of a role is invariably accepted as a challenge by these performers, an opportunity to add new feathers to an old hat.

Certainly, few stars have had more old hats handed to them than Bette Davis. Yet throughout her long career (she entered films in 1930) she has waged a constant, and generally successful, struggle against being typed. True, she has repeated more than a few times her cold, self-centered Mildred in *Of Human Bondage*, the role that brought the first full revelation of her talents. But always there were new insights into the character, new facets to be explored, as in *Bordertown, Jezebel*, and, more recently, *Beyond the Forest*. It is never Bette Davis playing the same old role, but a new personality being created from the ground up by Bette Davis. And in between these roles have come a great gallery of memorable portraits—the mad Carlotta of *Juarez*, the courageous wife of *Watch on the Rhine*, the calculating Regina of *The Little Foxes*, the mercuric Margo Channing of *All about Eve*. In each of these the actress has submerged herself, even transformed herself physically in the process of developing a new identity. (Chaplin strikingly displayed this same rare ability in the series of guises he invented for his *Monsieur Verdoux*.) An act of creative imagination that must be sustained over a long period of time, it is only possible where the star's influence and control over a picture approximate that of the director.

Alec Guinness is another whose ability to transform himself physically to meet the demands of virtually any script is little short of extraordinary. His gnarled, malevolent Fagin in *Oliver Twist* was no less remarkable than the exuberant youthfulness of his Denry Machin in *The Promoter*, or his prissy, middle-aged bank clerk in *The Lavender Hill Mob*. But in Guinness we discover always, disturbingly, the personality of the performer peeping out through the character he has created. Disturbing not because the personality is in conflict with the role, but because Guinness himself always seems to promise more than the character he is playing. There is mischief in the man, a mischief that springs from profound sources, something almost otherworldly. It touches every role he plays; but only once to date—in the early, relatively unsuccessful J. B. Priestley film, *Last Holiday*—has the character portrayed itself embraced this elusive quality. For Guinness, of course, it was a triumph of acting over material, yet particularly memorable because here the material came so supernaturally close to the actor. More than any other film star, however,

Guinness has the ability to merge his identity with whatever role he is perform-ing—but it is a process of merging, not submerging.

In the work of such true artists as these, screen-acting may be seen at its best, the creation and projection of a complete personality, a believable human being that is not the personality of the star himself—not lovable old Spencer Tracy, not rugged Burt Lancaster, not pouty Lana Turner—but an equally vivid "Denry Machin" or "Sidney Stratton," a "Regina Giddens" or "Margo Channing," a "Monsieur Verdoux." Pudovkin spoke of this quality as "trans-mutation of self," in contrast to the "direct manifestation of self" that charac-terizes most film-acting. The "direct manifestation of self," or at least of a recognizable film personality recurring in picture after picture, is something nurtured by most film companies today. They call it "building a star," and they see to it that their star's virtues and graces are buttressed both by the stories in which he appears and by the stories that appear about him in fan magazines, the daily press, and radio and television interviews. Even the products that he indorses so enthusiastically in the advertisements must be "suitable," in keep-ing with his screen character. A photogenic face, an attractive physique, an agreeable speaking voice—these are appurtenances enough for a star buildup, should the studio be so inclined.

But "transformation of self" is the work of the individual actor. He under-takes it alone, often against the expressed wishes of his studio. It is a kind of non-conformism, a break with the pattern that may even result in the actor's being branded as "difficult" and refused work. "Difficult" the actor is who believes that simply by exchanging one type for another he can become a better actor. For great film-acting is achieved only by those few who, once they have mastered the actor's art, are then prepared to master the art of the film, to participate fully in the creative effort of breathing life into moving shadows on a white sheet.

Martin Mayer

WHAT HAPPENS TO THE TALENT?[1]

Of all the industries which use publicly owned water, land, and air to pro-duce private profits, one alone is specifically licensed to operate "in the public interest": broadcasting. All the others are regulated in the prices they may charge and the quantity of service they must give. From the broadcaster alone the law demands a *quality* of service, a balanced schedule which provides in-formation as well as entertainment.

From *Television's Lords of Creation* by Martin Mayer. Reprinted by permission of the author. Copyright © 1956 by Harper & Brothers.
. This is the second of two articles published in *Harper's Magazine* titled "Television's Lords of Creation."

"We function," says Sig Mickelson, CBS Vice President in charge of Public Affairs, "as the conscience of the network. The big problem in this business is to strike a balance between showmanship and the objectives of public enlightenment. There's a red line somewhere, separating the two, and we stay on the educational side of the line. We think of our programs in terms of good will, proof of the public-spiritedness of the officials of the network."

Mickelson is a large, square-faced Midwesterner in his early forties who came to broadcasting from newspaper work in Sioux Falls and Minneapolis. As a vice president of the parent CBS (which has a separate executive structure from CBS Television), he has considerable independent authority. His department is supposed to lose money, and to produce programs which will please the more discriminating members of the television audience. The measure of his success is that despite broadcasting profits two or three times as great as those of NBC—a most suspicious circumstance—CBS has far greater acceptance than NBC in the intellectual community.

CBS has not yet been known to turn down a sponsor's money for a public-affairs program, and will make minor changes in any show to meet a sponsor's desires. But it is particularly proud of the programs which are, from the book-keeper's point of view, pure public service. Defending his business against a scouting party from the Senate, CBS President Frank Stanton cited nine public-affairs programs as an example of what a network can do; not one of them was a sponsored show.

At NBC the charitable aspect of public affairs is far less heavily played. The department itself is busier, producing feature spots for "Today," "Home," and "Tonight," as well as the usual educational and religious shows, news and documentaries; and revenues attributable to its work account for more than one-sixth of NBC's gross sales.

"NBC," says Davidson Taylor, who is Mickelson's opposite number and speaks in rounded periods, "is not interested in public-affairs shows that do not get sponsored. Good ones will be sponsored. It is to the self-interest of the American advertiser to become identified with projects that enlarge the American horizon."

The advertiser usually acquires this identification after the fact. Sometimes an attempt is made to sell him an idea (NBC asked General Dynamics for $4,250,000 to finance a proposed series of programs on the forthcoming International Geophysical Year—and was turned down), but more often the show is filmed and in the can before the advertiser is approached. On NBC's "Project 20," "documentaries of contemporary life," the producer's deadline is at least ten weeks earlier than the proposed broadcast time, so that potential advertisers can see the show before committing the money. The customary budget for these hour-long shows is $100,000, and NBC wants a sponsor to pick up the entire bill.

Some of the department's work, of course, is done without considering advertising. NBC has a producer assigned full-time to the production of filmed obituaries, with the co-operation of the eventual obituees. Negotiations with the Soviet government have been in progress for more than a year, and if satisfactory arrangements can be made NBC will gladly fork over $150.000 to make a documentary film on the daily life of the Russian people—not a subject particularly attractive to advertisers. And even without General Dynamics, NBC went ahead with its plans to send a cameraman down to the Antarctic last winter, and presented without sponsorship two hours of the film he took. These programs were extremely well received, but NBC does not like to talk about them—they can't have been as good as people say or else, by definition, they would have been sponsored.

This doctrinaire optimism about advertisers, a reflection of former NBC Chairman Pat Weaver's complete confidence in all the people with whom he did business, limits to some extent the work of the department. Staff producer Ted Mills, after the success of "Assignment: India," was anxious as only a young producer can be to do a serious film about the postwar crises of France. But Chester LaRoche, who owns one of the nation's prominent advertising agencies, had suggested that the "Assignment: India" team move on to Southeast Asia generally. So NBC in gratitude for Mills' accomplishments gave him $100,000 to produce a film about "Maurice Chevalier's Paris"—on condition that he would then do Southeast Asia.

Planning a Major Series

CBS relies much more heavily on its own judgment. Confronted with a crisis in its plans for "Air Power," perhaps the most expensive film documentary series ever attempted, the network promptly gave the job to Perry Wolff, a young poet and novelist who in seven years of broadcasting had never written or produced a sponsored program.

"Air Power" is a series of twenty-six films which tells the story of the airplane as a military weapon from the primitive strut-and-canvas devices of the early years to the newest jets. The first of the films, an hour-long examination of present American preparedness, was broadcast as a special Armistice Day feature; the others, each half an hour long, will be appearing every Sunday until May on 154 CBS affiliated television stations.

It is a true documentary series, composed almost entirely of film shot on the spot; its production was a joint venture by CBS, which put into it approximately $1,000,000, and the U. S. Air Force, which contributed most of the film, a certain amount of laboratory work, transportation, and technical guidance.

The Air Force brought the idea for "Air Power" to CBS in 1952, when it became apparent that both parties could use an answer to NBC's "Victory at Sea." But it was not until late 1953—when the Air Force Association submitted twenty-six fifteen-minute training films which it hoped could be used as the basis for the series—that CBS became seriously interested. In 1954 a staff producer was assigned to work up the training films from a quarter to half an hour, and a skeleton staff was hired to help him. By the end of the year it was clear that the training films would have to be junked if anything of any distinction was to be accomplished, and that the producer was not the man to start so large a project from scratch.

Perry Wolff was then producing, with the help of the staff of the American Museum of Natural History, the highly imaginative, prize-winning "Adventure"; the network asked him to switch. Wolff accepted, with the understanding that he was to produce something more significant than just another series of heavy-action war films.

"It may be," Wolff explained, "that I've been spending too much time with anthropologists, but I see modern man with the airplane the way stone-age man is with metal. You give metal to stone-age people, and for a while they try to use it as stone; then it revolutionizes their culture. Today we're in a crisis period; we're suffering a cultural lag, adjusting to the airplane.

"You can tell a lot about people by the way they use their airplanes. You remember the Japanese Kamikazes? When the Japanese were hard-pressed, they built planes without landing gear, without escape gear. We never built such planes, and neither did the Germans. And—I think it's one of the most hopeful signs—neither did the Russians.

"What you do with the airplane is always the key. In the 1930s, when the United States committed itself to the B-17, it couldn't be isolationist any more. The B-17 was an *attacking* weapon.

"These are the points I want to make in the series—these and one more: I'd like to see the show called 'Peace Through Air Power,' because the more I see the more convinced I am there mustn't be another war. The films won't directly *say* all this, of course, but I like to think it's what will come through to people as they're watching."

Wolff shook his head and gave a typical shy grin. "Well," he concluded, "everybody takes his own work too seriously."

Fifty Thousand Miles of Pictures

Wolff was born in Chicago the same day Skeezix was born to the residents of Gasoline Alley; his father and his friends have never called him anything but Skee. He got out of college just in time to serve four years in the infantry, two of them fighting in France and Germany. After the war he spent some time in France, in the Gertrude Stein ménage, published a book of poetry ("*not* paid for by me"), and went to work for WBBM in Chicago as a writer and producer of radio documentaries; his programs on juvenile delinquency and racial discrimination won Peabody Awards in 1947 and 1950. While with WBBM he wrote a novel about the war, *The Friend*, which sold several thousand copies in hard covers and several hundred thousand in a pocket reprint under the title *Attack*. Like many other Americans who saw considerable combat, he has never been able to shake the war from the front of his consciousness; he took on "Air Power" partly for the opportunity "to live with the war again, nine hours a day."

CBS set him up in a suite of eight rooms in a minor office building off Broadway, and to these rather dingy offices, every business day for two full years

—and every night the last few months—came the staff of fifteen which put together "Air Power." Its two senior members were James Faichney and Peter Poor, who had been hired as supervising editor and film editor by Wolff's predecessor; Wolff made Faichney Associate Producer ("He's been co-producer, really," Wolff says) and Poor, Senior Editor.

Faichney, a cheerful, very steady man in his late thirties, was in charge of censoring and releasing all combat film taken by the U. S. Army and Army Air Force during the war; after the war he was for several years head of the film division of the U. S. Information Service. Poor, a fairly recent Harvard graduate who studied cinema in Rome on a two-year Fulbright scholarship, did miscellaneous movie and television jobs for independent producers before signing up with "Air Power."

In October 1954, Poor and Faichney went together to the Air Force film depository in Dayton, Ohio, to look at movies. Eight to ten hours a day, six days a week, for five weeks ("Our wives loved our new jobs") they stood at adjacent tables, cranking film through a viewer by hand. Between them, they looked at nearly ten million feet of film (1,800 hours' worth at normal running time) and noted down what "Air Power" would need. The film included captured German footage, and non-military newsreel aviation photography given to the Air Force by the newsreel companies, as well as material taken by Air Force cameramen. "But," said Faichney, who is a walking archive of all the film that has ever passed across his desk, "some of the stuff I remember we haven't found yet. A lot of film was lost toward the end of the war—it was shipped out to Culver City, where it sat around for a couple of years on open flat cars, convenient for any larceny. Some of my friends at Culver City have the best Kodachromes the Air Force ever took."

For the Japanese view of the war there was the Japanese film depository, seized by the Americans during the Occupation and subsequently rejected by the Pentagon, the Signal Corps, and others before finding a home at the Library of Congress. Its only catalogue was the original Japanese list, a succession of flowery titles; the film itself, after ten years in untouched cans, had seriously deteriorated. Some of it had disintegrated into clouds of gaseous nitrogen, which filled the room and choked the intrepid editors; even the best of it had shrunk and wouldn't fit into the sprockets of ordinary film machines. But from the nitrogen vapor descended tens of thousands of feet of war photography never before shown outside Japan—including a complete, twenty-reel documentation of the attack on Pearl Harbor.

While in Washington, Faichney spoke to the Air Attaché at the British Embassy, who cleared the way for him to go to London in the spring of 1955. There the RAF opened its archives at Stanmore Park to him, releasing certain secret material for the first time, and put its information officers and historians at his disposal.

From London Faichney went on to Germany, where CBS correspondent Dick Hottelet had dug up, among other things, a terrifying 16-mm. film on the bombing of Hamburg, which the Germans had put together for civil-defense instruction purposes. At the American High Commissioner's office in Munich. Faichney found thousands of feet of film about the Berlin airlift. And he made contact with a mysterious type who, for a consideration, smuggled Soviet film about the Red Air Force from the East to the West Zone.

At the end, Faichney, Poor, and their assistants had spun through 50,000 miles of film, representing 50,000 hours of normal running time. All that was left to do was boil it down to two dozen half-hour shows.

From Rough Cut to Script

Every picture starts with a story line. The story line for each of the "Air Power" films was hammered out in conference by Wolff and Faichney, with a writer sitting in on the few occasions when Wolff did not do the script himself. Then either Wolff or Faichney would write a "treatment," a sequential list, two to eight pages long, of what pictures the film should contain. This was turned over to one of "Air Power's" three film editors, who went looking in the files for the film that would make the written treatment a movie.

"Sometimes it isn't there," Poor said, "and then the treatment changes. The treatment ought to be defined as what you'd *like* to do if you could find the stuff."

The three editors worked in one square room, each editor at a "Moviola," a green, upright machine which shows pictures on a small glass plate. Behind each Moviola was a cardboard barrel, into which the film disappeared as it ran off the machine. When they found a scene immediately useful, the editors clipped the strip of film and hung it on a rack; useless sections they stuffed back in the can. In a matter of minutes an editor could take a thousand-foot reel of film and convert it to fifty pieces, some hanging straight on racks, some curled up in the bottom of the barrel for further examination, some stacked in neat cylinders back in the film can.

From these short strips of film—perhaps as many as 600 of them—the editor made up a "rough cut," which might run as long as an hour and a half for a 26½-minute show. The rough cut often included more than the treatment demanded.

"Half of a film editor's job," Poor says, "is spotting something good; you can't just say, 'It's not in the treatment.' "

During the work for "The Conquest of the Air," a researcher picked up from the Signal Corps several miles of film about preparations for the Normandy invasion. Running through it Poor spotted what could only be—even without a sound track—an impromptu French lesson given from the hatch of a tank by an educated GI. This brief scene—the soldier saying *"Boire,"* his companions attempting the strange sound, the soldier shaking his head and repeating, *"Boire"*—established in thirty seconds the mood of the Army awaiting the call to invasion.

Wolff, Faichney, Poor, and the individual editor—if it wasn't Poor himself, who put together about half the films—went over the rough cut on the more elaborate Westrex Moviola in Wolff's office. Wolff perched on a high stool over the Moviola's ground-glass screen, studying the film for technical quality, asking where individual shots came from. whether Faichney had sound effects, whether the locality shown was *really* Bastogne. Sometimes he recognized the source of the shot and the locality: "Mm-hmm." he said as the screen showed assault boats allegedly crossing the Rhine, "the Roer."

A rough cut exists to be changed; suggestions for change were made continuously. At the end there was an hour's conference. or more. Then the editor went back to work. patching. revising. cutting. adding; and the scene in Wolff's office was repeated.

Eight or nine rough cuts were par for the course, and even then the whole job might be scratched. The film on the 1930s. for example. was done over entirely.

"I put it together myself." Faichney said. grinning under his mustache, "because I had my first job in the 'thirties, as an editor for Pathé News. I went back over my own work—the big steel strike. the dust bowl—and I thought, 'Gee, I was awfully good when I was a kid.' So I used all my own stuff. and now somebody else will have to redo it."

Finally the rough cut was pared down and reassembled into a film exactly 2,370 feet long, running 26 minutes and 20 seconds, with its own dramatic unity; and Wolff sat down at his typewriter, with the Moviola beside him, to express that unity in words.

"You can't write a script like this away from the film. because talk goes one way, film goes another," Wolff explains. "Whenever I say that. Faichney always says, 'Not if you know what you're doing.' But it's the way I have to work."

If Wolff were to criticize "Victory at Sea." it would be to say that the NBC films had too much narration, emotionally overcharged. "The film has all the emotion," he said, "the film and the score. The narration ought to explain what's happening. not tell you how you should feel about it."

Where the scene called for words of emotional content. Wolff tried to give it to actors, voices for the airmen in the picture, rather than to the narrator. Sometimes he could find out what the men were saying by lip-reading the film, and in a few instances "Air Power" had sound film containing actual dialogue. Where he had to write his own dialogue, Wolff hunted—with that Tom Sawyer imagination which made "Adventure" a Peabody Award winner—for ways to make sure he was right.

One film. the story of the deep-penetration raid on the ball-bearing factories at Schweinfurt, from which one-third of the American planes failed to return, Wolff wanted to do without narration. He had an introduction from the Amherst War Memorial, which includes a memorial stone to the Schweinfurt raid, and opening scenes lifted bodily from "Target for Today," a never-issued Air Force documentary, complete with dialogue. Most of the rest of the film showed the men in the planes, going ahead without fighter escort to meet the Luftwaffe. During these scenes he wanted the sounds of the intercom. the airmen talking back and forth with each other as the German fighters attacked. He asked the Air Force for a man who had been on the Schweinfurt raid, and they sent him a Major who had flown the mission.

"He came over here," Wolff recalls, "all jaunty and gay, not taking it very seriously, and I showed him the film. When it was over, his hands were as wet as if he'd been keeping them in a bucket of warm water. He was trembling. I turned on the tape recorder, and asked him what guys said to each other during this sort of run. Sometimes he was crying as it came back to him, he lived it again on the film; I felt as though I were an analyst, putting him on the couch. And all the dialogue in those scenes comes off that tape."

Like the rough cut, the script usually went through half a dozen drafts or more. When Wolff had more or less satisfied himself, seven or eight people gathered in his office to hear him read the script against the film as it ran through the Moviola. Criticism was expected—on all grounds from artistry to veracity: a researcher was supposed to find a document supporting every statement. Wolff listened carefully to all objections and often stopped the film for a discussion, which might end with Faichney's serio-comic, "You're outvoted, boss."

"They call it democracy," Wolff said, "I call it anarchy. But I can't remember a time—not since the early days, anyway, when we were just getting to know each other—when I ever said, 'I'm the producer and this is the way it's got to be.' We've hammered everything out. When I wrote the script I needed someone to tell me, this stinks, because I was, in a way, abandoning my function as producer to write it. There were some films which Faichney edited and I wrote, and when we'd finished we'd run it for Poor, and we'd be hanging on his frown or smile, because he was the only one of us who could judge it."

Words and Music

Next to the film itself, Wolff considered the musical score the most important part of each show, and budgeted more money for music than for script (which is one of the reasons he wound up writing the scripts himself). NBC had hired Richard Rodgers to do the music for "Victory at Sea," with Robert Russell Bennett turning Rodgers' effort into a usable score. Wolff ran a competition among three widely respected American composers. The winner was Norman Dello Joio, whose orchestral scores have been played by most of the nation's major symphonies and whose opera, "The Trial at Rouen," was presented last year by the NBC Television Opera Theater.

Dello Joio had his own room in the "Air Power" offices, furnished with a desk, a Moviola, and an unlovely upright piano at which he could be heard picking and then pounding as he watched the film spin by. Since his score was not to run throughout the film, but to accentuate the impact of certain scenes, he couldn't get to work until editing and script were final. He and Wolff and Faichney would sit over the Westrex, choosing the scenes which wanted music to heighten their effect or establish their continuity. Music cannot be written in seven-second bursts, and Dello Joio would fight for time to "get in," time to "get out." He had to be very exact, because the music was to be recorded without his presence. Sometimes scenes would be recut or rearranged to give him development time.

Narrator for all the films was CBS announcer Walter Cronkite, who worked mostly in a New York studio, but was also ferried around Europe and Africa to appear before backgrounds appropriate to the films he would introduce. Wolff never let Cronkite see a film until after he had recorded the narration: "I wanted to be sure his tone would be completely neutral, he wouldn't be influenced by what went with the words."

The roars of sound for "Air Power" were contracted out to a young engineer supervised by Faichney and Poor. Voices for the airmen were recorded separately by actors, some of them quite prominent, gathered at minimum Equity rates from among Wolff's friends. Then, when all the separate sound tracks were done, Wolff, Faichney, Poor, and Dello Joio gathered in a big, lavish screening room at Reeves' Sound Studios to see what they had accomplished and to make a "mix" of the six or seven sound tracks, a final lock-up of the film.

Until this point, changes were relatively easy and relatively cheap to make; after the mix, any change would involve doing over almost the entire technical and laboratory job. Often it took an entire day for a half-hour film. And then the film was finished.

Satisfying the Brass

Except that a higher power might intervene. As a joint production of the United States Air Force and the Columbia Broadcasting System, each final film had to be approved *in toto* and in detail by high brass in both organizations. At the beginning there were liaison men from both in the "Air Power" offices. Not long after Wolff took over, the Air Force representative was transferred to London ("as far away," Faichney explained, "as we could decently arrange to have him sent"), but the CBS liaison man continued throughout the work, supervising the budget and making himself useful on the business end.

Political considerations were vital to the Air Force. Each film when finished had to be taken down to Washington, to be reviewed for accuracy by an Air Force historian, and for policy by a committee of thirteen colonels. Even if the colonels liked it, there might still be trouble with a general. Wolff remembers the Pentagon screening of "Strangle," a film about the Italian campaign. Wolff sat behind a general who had brought his wife to see the free movie. At the end, the general got up shaking his head and said, "It completely misrepresents the strategic spirit of the war in Italy." His wife had been crying through most of the film; she said, "Shut up, you son of a bitch."

The one serious altercation with the Air Force came at the very beginning, with the film about the raids on the oil refineries at Ploesti, the first show "Air Power" put in the can. Wolff had titled his original script "Ploesti—The Defeat of the American Air Force." It had not previously occurred to the Air Force that any of their television shows might be tragedies, and they shot "Ploesti" back with bitter comments. An objection of such gravity was outside Wolff's competence. He and his staff sat on the sidelines—collecting their salaries and planning for the future, but finishing no films—until CBS and the Air Force had reached a new agreement, which gave Wolff the desired freedom plus the co-operation of a sympathetic combat airman with a strong sense of public relations, Colonel John C. Pitchford, who became chairman of the review board.

Pitchford came to New York one day a week, and called up three or four times a week, keeping steadily in touch with all developments.

With CBS relations were more formal. Wolff at the beginning had submitted a budget, which was accepted with some anguish. ("You know," said Sig Mickelson, with the air of a child who has been told over and over again that the world is round, not flat, "it's surprising, but it costs more to make a film from stock than to go out and shoot something new.") Thereafter his only regular contact with his employers was through the liaison man on his staff.

CBS did, of course, want to know what it was getting for its $1,000,000. When Wolff had finished his first four films he began showing them to executives of the public-affairs department, and to the salesmen who would try to find a sponsor for the series. Then, one morning when Wolff and Faichney were in Washington, the CBS telephone rang in the "Air Power" offices, and Peter Poor, as officer of the day, was ordered to bring the films to a studio that afternoon. William S. Paley, Chairman of the Board, wanted to see them.

Top television executives do not go to screening rooms to look at films; they sit in their own offices watching their television sets, on which the films appear via closed-circuit transmission. Poor crouched in the studio, alone with the engineers, and when all the films had been shown he had not the vaguest notion of their reception.

Soon, however, reactions began to appear, delivered by messengers. Wolff was told to watch out for his openings, because the television audience, according to the best research reports, decides whether to stay with a program or move on to another station during the first three minutes. The titles, which originally appeared against banks of clouds, were to have a new background; and the voices of soldiers and airmen on which Wolff had relied to tell much of his story were to be eliminated; Mr. Paley didn't like them.

Wolff was willing to change the title backgrounds, and to put as much zip as possible into his openings; but the use of voices rather than narration was basic to his conception of the series. He knew that the word passed finally to the creative personnel always represents some garbling of the original executive statement, because each subordinate must protect his superior and nobody dares request an explanation (for fear that the boss doesn't have one). He fought to find out what Paley had really said. It turned out that the criticism was specific rather than general. Paley had disliked the use of voices in a single scene in "The Winning of France."

"And, of course," Wolff said, shortly after the case had been marked Closed in everybody's files, "Paley was right. He was saying that I had overwritten the film. I probably could have accepted it more easily if it wasn't that everybody—Faichney, Poor, the guy who sweeps up the film from the workroom—had been telling me all along that I was overwriting. It's the writer's essential vice—he always feels he's got to express in words what the picture is expressing very well all by itself."

While Wolff was putting together his films, the CBS Sales Department was preparing a printed brochure about "Air Power"—its national importance, the enormous audience it could be expected to draw, its wonderful scenes, the amount of money it would cost an advertiser. (The brochure was full of pictures of Navy planes, which outraged the Air Force.) And in July of this year, a long, thin CBS salesman named Bob Livingston, who had been trying to sell a Skee Wolff show since the days when they were both with WBBM, Chicago, sold "Air Power" to the Prudential Life Insurance Company, to be slotted in the "You Are There" time at 6:30 Sunday nights, beginning on November 11.

Prudential paid about $675,000 for the twenty-six films, and CBS can count on recovering the rest of its costs by re-releasing the series—selling it to independent stations or even another network after the first run. Everyone was off the hook. Most important of all, the fear that "Air Power" might not make a splash commensurate with the work that had gone into it was removed. With the program presented weekly on 154 stations, thousands of Prudential agents spreading the word through their communities, CBS and Air Force public relations pulling in harness on the groaning chariot of publicity, "Air Power" would surely receive more attention than anything on TV—except a high-stake quiz show.

CBS has paid "Air Power" the ultimate compliment: it has budgeted another million dollars for another series of documentary films made from stock footage. And the "Air Power" films themselves will receive a kind of acclaim which has been given to nothing since "Victory at Sea," for war is one of the few subjects that fascinate intellectuals and the large audience alike. "Air Power" is inevitably better, as a job of documentary-making, than "Victory at Sea": Wolff says, "I built on what they did, and some day somebody else will build on me." Henry Salomon, producing "Victory at Sea," had established the clichés of the medium; Wolff could thereupon reject them.

In addition to his benefits from Salomon's pioneer work, Wolff had a more photogenic subject with a greater variety of incident to describe. But his task was more subtle. "Victory at Sea" was frankly a propaganda series for the Navy, produced by a man who had worked under Rear Admiral Samuel Eliot Morison in the naval historian's office. Wolff was an infantryman in the war, and his attitude toward the Air Force is essentially civilian, a mixture of admiration and anxiety.

The message he hoped to convey, under the straight narrative of the films themselves, was a delicate one; and his success in conveying it is a delicate question—one that can be answered only by the viewer who will see the films without hearing the message personally from their producer.

Exit the Talent

Wolff has been offered the production of the new documentary series but has turned it down; he is leaving television, at least temporarily, taking his family to Italy, where he hopes to sit still for a while, write one or more novels, and generally contemplate the world.

"I've given four years to television," he said recently, "and I'm not sure whether either television or myself has got much out of it. I'm not complaining about anything. But I remember Gertrude Stein saying that the problem with the movies was, there wasn't any garret. I was pretty impressed with that at the time, until I found out she hadn't seen a movie since 1926. But it's true of television—all those flat-roofed studios, no garret at all. No place for experimental work. They were still calling 'Adventure' experimental after I'd been producing it a year and a half, and I'd run out of ideas completely." Wolff stopped and thought for a moment.

"They make so much money in this business," he said.

Wolff's departure is a symbol of television's besetting difficulty: the growing shortage of talent. Among them, the three networks are on the air more than 12,000 hours a year. They use more copy than all the nation's mass-circulation magazines put together, more film than the movie industry, more actor-hours than the Broadway stage. They offer to talent—with considerable good will, too—an unapproachable opportunity and very good money. But they have failed to hold the allegiances of first-rate people. Hardly anybody says proudly, "I work in television"; the writers are novelists or playwrights, the actors are hanging on until a part opens up in a show, the producers and directors have their eyes on Hollywood.

The reasons for leaving are as varied as the individuals who leave. Some are offended by the ephemeral nature of the medium, by the fact that the result of their work is a single, brief appearance before an invisible audience. Some find it hard to be a cog in so large a wheel as a television network—even "Air Power," a major project, will represent only one per cent of CBS program production during the six months of its run. Some resent the restraints of advertising, or of the artificial code which says what can and what can't be put on a television screen, or of the rigid time limits (thirty, sixty, ninety minutes) into which their thoughts must be squeezed or stretched.

What drives away most of the talent that touches television, though, is the nature of the medium itself.

"My people," Wolff said, "are film people, not television people, and I've had to teach them that you can't put as many ideas per minute into a television film as you can into a film for a theater. People pay money to get into a movie house, they sit in a dark room and they come to give something; people who watch television just have a box in a corner, and all they want to do is take. They won't concentrate."

The television audience is amorphous, composed not of people interested in the subject but of people with nothing better to do at the moment; the television artist feels that the eyes watching him are essentially hostile.

Such an audience is inevitable when a show is aimed at so vast a public. A hit movie reaches perhaps twelve million Americans; a television show with twice that audience is only fairly successful. Only the pressure of a developing art form could make serious people seriously interested in presenting their talents before so neutral a mass. And since it has no garret, television has no place where such pressure can be generated.

Public-affairs programs have been generally better than entertainment programs because they have been able to attract, on a full-time basis, a higher grade of talent. There is no other paying market for documentary films. But even here the blight is on the vine. Ed Murrow's commercial "Person to Person" has deprived the lesser ranks at CBS of their feeling that there was a man up top who cared deeply about the informational functions of television; Pat Weaver's dismissal from NBC is seen throughout the industry as a lowering of the relative prestige of imagination as against money. As the public-affairs departments become more important in network schedules there is a greater executive feeling that the programs should be made failure-proof in the commercial sense, by using old, well-tested ideas or employing "big names," whether or not their talents are suited to the subject. Nothing could be more depressing to the people who do the work.

Beneath this depression lies a fundamental philosophical failure: the inability of the networks to decide what the medium can add to the sum of human production. There has been much nonsense spoken about Frank Costello's hands or television's exposure of phoniness, much complaint that programs are somehow not "good" enough; but the only constructive theory offered from within the industry was that of Pat Weaver, who saw television as a "communications instrument." In Weaver's mind, television's highest value is that it can communicate all the products of all the arts, to an audience previously deprived of such stimuli.

This philosophy is widely admired in the industry, even by those who devoted years to fighting Weaver, and those who put in several days getting him to resign. But it has little appeal for talent. If television is merely a communications instrument, then the men who work in it are mere communicators; and you cannot get highly talented people to man a telephone switchboard, whatever wages you pay.

Literature and the Fine Arts

The writers of this section draw on their own experiences for their discussion of some important questions regarding literature and the arts. First H. L. Mencken describes his early formative experiences as a reader. The following three writers are concerned in part with attitudes toward literature and the arts. Sylvia Wright is concerned with the attitudes of the general public. Art, she argues, is not susceptible of statistical analysis or of second-hand explanation. Politicians, propagandists, all of us, must let art speak for itself. William Faulkner is concerned with the attitudes of the artist. The writer, he feels, must not be content simply to report but must "help man endure by lifting his heart." Theodore Morrison is concerned with the attitudes of the critics. His "story" shows a series of critics each making his approach to a particular work of art—a poem. Implicit in the selections by Faulkner and Morrison are ideas about the nature of literature. In the two articles which follow, Alfred H. Barr, Jr., discusses the problem of understanding and appreciating modern painting, and Aaron Copland describes the process involved in creating music.

H. L. Mencken

LARVAL STAGE OF A BOOKWORM

A personal discovery

The first long story I ever read was "The Moose Hunters," a tale of the adventures of four half-grown boys in the woods of Maine, published in *Chatterbox* for 1887. *Chatterbox*, which now seems to be pretty well forgotten, was an English annual that had a large sale, in those days, in the American colonies, and "The Moose Hunters" seems to have been printed as a sort of sop or compliment to that trade, just as an English novelist of today lards his narrative with such cheery native bait as "waal, pardner," "you betcha" and "geminy-crickets." The rest of the 1887 issue was made up of intensely English stuff; indeed, it was so English that, reading it and looking at the woodcuts, I sucked in an immense mass of useless information about English history and the English scene, so that to this day I know more about Henry VIII and Lincoln Cathedral than I know about Millard Fillmore or the Mormon Temple at Salt Lake City.

"The Moose Hunters," which ran to the length of a full-length juvenile, was not printed in one gob, but spread through *Chatterbox* in installments. This was an excellent device, for literary fans in the youngest brackets do their reading slowly and painfully, and like to come up frequently for air. But writing down to them is something else again, and that error the anonymous author of "The Moose Hunters" avoided diligently. Instead, he wrote in the best journalese of the era, and treated his sixteen-year-old heroes precisely as if they were grown men. So I liked his story very much, and stuck to it until, in a series of perhaps twenty sessions, I had got it down.

This was in the Summer of 1888 and during hot weather, for I remember sitting with the volume on the high marble front steps of our house in Hollins street, in the quiet of approaching dusk, and hearing my mother's warnings that reading by failing light would ruin my eyes. The neighborhood apprentices to gang life went howling up and down the sidewalk, trying to lure me into their games of follow-your-leader and run-sheep-run, but I was not to be lured, for I had discovered a new realm of being and a new and powerful enchantment. What was follow-your-leader to fighting savage Canucks on the Little Magalloway river, and what was chasing imaginary sheep to shooting real meese? I was near the end of the story, with the Canucks all beaten off and two carcasses of gigantic meese hanging to trees, before the author made it clear to me that the word *moose* had no plural, but remained unchanged *ad infinitum*.

Such discoveries give a boy a considerable thrill, and augment his sense of dignity. It is no light matter, at eight, to penetrate suddenly to the difference between *to, two* and *too*, or to that between *run* in baseball and *run* in topographical science, or *cats* and *Katz*. The effect is massive and profound, and at least comparable to that which flows, in later life, out of filling a royal flush or debauching the wife of a major-general of cavalry. I must have made some effort to read *Chatterbox* at the time my Grandmother Mencken gave it to me, which was at Christmas, 1887, but for a while it was no go. I could spell out the shorter pieces at the bottoms of columns, but the longer stories were only jumbles of strange and baffling words. But then, as if by miracle, I found suddenly that I could read them, so I tackled "The Moose Hunters" at once, and stuck to it to the end. There were still, of course, many hard words, but they were no longer insurmountable obstacles. If I staggered and stumbled somewhat, I nevertheless hung on, and by the Fourth of July, 1888, I had blooded my first book.

An interval of rough hunting followed in Hollins street and the adjacent alleys, with imaginary Indians, robbers and sheep and very real tomcats as the quarry. Also, I was introduced to chewing tobacco by the garbageman, who passed me his plug as I lay on the roof of the ash-shed at the end of the backyard, watching him at his public-spirited work. If he expected me to roll off the roof, clutching at my midriff, he was fooled, for I managed to hold on until he was out of sight, and I was only faintly dizzy even then. Again, I applied myself diligently to practicing leap-frog with my brother Charlie, and to mastering the rules of top-spinning, catty and one-two-three. I recall well how it impressed me to learn that, by boys' law, every new top had to have a license burned into it with a red-hot nail, and that no strange boy on the prowl for loot, however blackhearted, would venture to grab a top so marked. That discovery gave me a sense of the majesty of the law which still sustains me, and I always take off my hat when I meet a judge—if, of course, it is in any place where a judge is not afraid to have his office known.

But pretty soon I was again feeling the powerful suction of beautiful letters— so strange, so thrilling, and so curiously suggestive of the later suction of amour—, and before Chistmas I was sweating through the translation of Grimms' Fairy Tales that had been bestowed upon me, "for industry and good deportment," at the closing exercises of F. Knapp's Institute on June 28. This volume had been put into lame, almost pathological English by a lady translator, and my struggles with it awoke in me the first faint gutterings of the critical faculty. Just what was wrong with it I couldn't, of course, make out, for my gifts had not yet flowered, but I was acutely and unhappily conscious that it was much harder going than "The Moose Hunters," and after a month or so of unpleasantly wrestling with it I put it on the shelf. There it remained for more than fifty years. Indeed, it was not until the appearance of "Snow White" as a movie that I took it down and tried it again, and gagged at it again.

The second experiment convinced me that the fault, back in 1888, must have been that of either the brothers Grimm or their lady translator, but I should add that there was also some apparent resistant within my own psyche. I was born, in truth, without any natural taste for fairy tales, or, indeed, for any other writing of a fanciful and unearthly character. The fact explains, I suppose, my lifelong distrust of poetry, and may help to account for my inability to memorize even a few stanzas of it at school. It probably failed to stick in my mind simply because my mind rejected it as nonsense—sometimes, to be sure, very jingly and juicy nonsense, but still only nonsense. No doubt the same infirmity was responsible for the feebleness of my appetite for the hortatory and incredible juvenile fiction fashionable in my nonage—the endless works of Oliver Optic, Horatio Alger, Harry Castlemon and so on. I tried this fiction more than once, for some of the boys I knew admired it vastly, but I always ran aground in it. So far as I can recall, I never read a single volume of it to the end, and most of it finished me in a few pages.

What I disliked about it I couldn't have told you then, and I can account for my aversion even now only on the theory that I appear to have come into the world with a highly literal mind, geared well enough to take in overt (and usually unpleasant) facts, but very ill adapted to engulfing the pearls of the imagination. All such pearls tend to get entangled in my mental *vibrissae,* and the effort to engulf them is as disagreeable to me as listening to a sermon or reading an editorial in a second-rate (or even first-rate) newspaper. I was a grown man, and far gone in sin, before I ever brought myself to tackle "Alice in Wonderland," and even then I made some big skips, and wondered sadly how and why such feeble jocosity had got so high a reputation. I am willing to grant that it must be a masterpiece, as my betters allege—but not to *my* taste, not for *me.* To the present moment I can't tell you what is in any of the other juvenile best-sellers of my youth, of moral and sociological hallucination all compact, just as I can't tell you what is in the Bhagavad-Gita (which Will Levington Comfort urged me to read in 1912 or thereabout), or in the works of Martin Tupper, or in the report of Vassar Female College for 1865. I tried dime-novels once, encouraged by a boy who aspired to be a train-robber, but they only made me laugh. At a later time, discovering the pseudo-scientific marvels of Jules Verne, I read his whole canon, and I recall also sweating through a serial in a boys' weekly called *Golden Days,* but this last dealt likewise with *savants* and their prodigies, and was no more a juvenile, as juveniles were then understood, than "Ten Thousand Leagues Under the Sea."

But before you set me down a prig, let me tell you the rest of it. That rest of it is my discovery of "Huckleberry Finn," probably the most stupendous event of my whole life. The time was the early part of 1889, and I wandered into

Paradise by a kind of accident. Itching to exercise my newly acquired art of reading, and with "The Moose Hunters" exhausted and Grimms' Fairy Tales playing me false, I began exploring the house for print. The Baltimore *Sun-paper* and *Evening News*, which came in daily, stumped me sadly, for they were full of political diatribes in the fashion of the time, and I knew no more about politics than a chimpanzee. My mother's long file of *Godey's Lady's Book* and her new but growing file of the *Ladies' Home Journal* were worse, for they dealt gloomily with cooking, etiquette, the policing of children, and the design and construction of millinery, all of them sciences that still baffle me. Nor was there any pabulum for me in the hired girl's dog's-eared files of *Bow Bells* and the *Fireside Companion*, the first with its ghastly woodcuts of English milkmaids in bustles skedaddling from concupiscent baronets in frock-coats and cork-screw mustaches. So I gradually oscillated, almost in despair, toward the old-fashioned secretary in the sitting-room, the upper works of which were full of dismal volumes in the black cloth and gilt stamping of the era. I had often eyed them from afar, wondering how long it would be before I would be ripe enough to explore them. Now I climbed up on a chair, and began to take them down.

They had been assembled by my father, whose taste for literature in its purer states was of generally low order of visibility. Had he lived into the days of my practice as a literary critic, I daresay he would have been affected almost as unpleasantly as if I had turned out a clergyman, or a circus clown, or a labor leader. He read every evening after dinner, but it was chiefly newspapers that he read, for the era was one of red-hot politics, and he was convinced that the country was going to Hell. Now and then he took up a book, but I found out long afterward that it was usually some pamphlet on the insoluble issues of the hour, say "Looking Backward," or "If Christ Came to Chicago," or "Life Among the Mormons." These works disquieted him, and he naturally withheld them from his innocent first-born. Moreover, he was still unaware that I could read —that is, fluently, glibly, as a pleasure rather than a chore, in the manner of grown-ups.

Nevertheless, he had managed somehow to bring together a far from con-temptible collection of books, ranging from a set of Chambers' Encyclopedia in five volumes, bound in leather like the Revised Statutes, down to "Atlantis: the Antediluvian World," by Ignatius Donnelly, and "Around the World in the Yacht *Sunbeam*." It included a two-volume folio of Shakespeare in em-bossed morocco, with fifty-odd steel plates, that had been taken to the field in the Civil War by "William H. Abercrombie, 1st Lieut. Company H, 6th Regiment, Md. Vol. Inftr.," and showed a corresponding dilapidation. Who this gallant officer was I don't know, or whether he survived the carnage, or how his cherished text of the Bard ever fell into my father's hands. Also, there were Dickens in three thick volumes, George Eliot in three more, and William Carleton's Irish novels in a third three. Again, there were "Our Living World," by the Rev. J. G. Woods; "A History of the War For the Union," by E. A. Duyckinck; "Our Country," by Benson J. Lossing, LL.D., and "A Pictorial History of the World's Great Nations From the Earliest Dates to the Present Time," by

Charlotte M. Yonge—all of them likewise in threes, folio, with lavish illustrations on steel, stone and wood, and smelling heavily of the book-agent. Finally, there were forty or fifty miscellaneous books, among them, as I recall, "Peculiarities of American Cities," by Captain Willard Glazier; "Our Native Land," by George T. Ferris; "A Compendium of Forms," by one Glaskell; "Adventures Among Cannibals" (with horrible pictures of missionaries being roasted, boiled and fried), "Uncle Remus," "Ben Hur," "Peck's Bad Boy," "The Adventures of Baron Münchhausen," "One Thousand Proofs That the Earth Is Not a Globe" (by a forgotten Baltimore advanced thinker named Carpenter), and a deadly-looking "History of Freemasonry in Maryland," by Brother Edward T. Schultz, 32°, in five coal-black volumes.

I leave the best to the last. All of the above, on my first exploration, repelled and alarmed me; indeed, I have never read some of them to this day. But among them, thumbing round, I found a series of eight or ten volumes cheek by jowl, and it appeared on investigation that the whole lot had been written by a man named Mark Twain. I had heard my father mention this gentleman once or twice in talking to my mother, but I had no idea who he was or what he had done: he might have been, for all I knew, a bartender, a baseball-player, or one of the boozy politicoes my father was always meeting in Washington. But here was evidence that he was a man who wrote books, and I noted at once that the pictures in those books were not of the usual funereal character, but light, loose and lively. So I proceeded with my inquiry, and in a little while I had taken down one of them, a green quarto, sneaked it to my bedroom, and stretched out on my bed to look into it. It was, as smarties will have guessed by now, "Huckleberry Finn."

If I undertook to tell you the effect it had upon me my talk would sound frantic, and even delirious. Its impact was genuinely terrific. I had not gone further than the first incomparable chapter before I realized, child though I was, that I had entered a domain of new and gorgeous wonders, and thereafter I pressed on steadily to the last word. My gait, of course, was still slow, but it became steadily faster as I proceeded. As the blurbs on the slip-covers of murder mysteries say, I simply couldn't put the book down. After dinner that evening, braving a possible uproar, I took it into the family sitting-room, and resumed it while my father searched the *Evening News* hopefully for reports of the arrest, clubbing and hanging of labor leaders. Anon, he noticed what I was at, and demanded to know the name of the book I was reading. When I held up the green volume his comment was "Well, I'll be durned!"

I sensed instantly that there was no reproof in this, but a kind of shy rejoicing. Then he told me that he had once been a great reader of Mark Twain himself —in his younger days. He had got hold of all the volumes as they came out—"The Innocents" in 1869, when he was still a boy himself; "Roughing It" in 1872, "The Gilded Age" in 1873, "Tom Sawyer" in 1876, "A Tramp Abroad" in 1880, the year of my birth, and so on down to date. (All these far from pristine firsts are still in the Biblioteca Menckeniana in Hollins street, minus a few that were lent to neighbor boys and never returned, and had to be replaced.) My father read them in the halcyon days before children, labor troubles and Grover Cleveland had begun to frazzle him, and he still got them down from the shelf on quiet evenings, after the first-named were packed off to bed. But a man of advancing years and cares had to consider also the sorrows of the world, and so he read in Mark less than aforetime.

As for me, I proceeded to take the whole canon at a gulp—and presently gagged distressfully. "Huckleberry Finn," of course, was as transparent to a boy of eight as to a man of eighty, and almost as pungent and exhilarating, but there were passages in "A Tramp Abroad" that baffled me, and many more in "The Innocents," and a whole swarm in "A Gilded Age." I well recall wrestling with the woodcut by W. F. Brown on page 113 of the "Tramp." It shows five little German girls swinging on a heavy chain stretched between two stone posts on a street in Heilbronn, and the legend under it is "Generations of Bare Feet." That legend is silly, for all the girls have shoes on, but what puzzled me about it was something quite different. It was a confusion between the word *generation* and the word *federation*, which latter was often in my father's speech in those days, for the American Federation of Labor had got under way only a few years before, and was just beginning in earnest to harass and alarm employers. Why I didn't consult the dictionary (or my mother, or my father himself) I simply can't tell you. At eight or nine, I suppose, intelligence is no more than a small spot of light on the floor of a large and murky room. So instead of seeking help I passed on, wondering idiotically what possible relation there could be between a gang of little girls in pigtails and the Haymarket anarchists, and it was six or seven years later before the "Tramp" became clear to me, and began to delight me.

It then had the curious effect of generating in me both a great interest in Germany and a vast contempt for the German language. I was already aware, of course, that the Mencken family was of German origin, for my Grandfather Mencken, in his care for me as *Stammhalter,* did not neglect to describe eloquently its past glories at the German universities, and to expound its connections to the most remote degrees. But my father, who was only half German, had no apparent interest in either the German land or its people, and when he spoke of the latter at all, which was not often, it was usually in sniffish terms. He never visited Germany, and never signified any desire to do so, though I recall my mother suggesting, more than once, that a trip there would be swell. It was "A Tramp Abroad" that made me German-conscious, and I still believe that it is the best guidebook to Germany ever written. Today, of course, it is archaic, but it was still reliable down to 1910, when I made my own first trip. The uproarious essay on "The Awful German Language," which appears at the end of it as an appendix, worked the other way. That is to say, it confirmed my growing feeling, born of my struggles with the conjugations and declensions taught at F. Knapp's Institute, that German was an irrational and even insane tongue, and not worth the sufferings of a freeborn American. These diverse impressions have continued with me ever since. I am still convinced that Germany, in the intervals of peace, is the most pleasant country to travel in ever heard of, and I am still convinced that the German language is of a generally preposterous and malignant character.

"Huck," of course, was my favorite, and I read it over and over. In fact, I read it regularly not less than annually down to my forties, and only a few months ago I hauled it out and read it once more—and found it as magnificent as ever.

Sylvia Wright

SELF-CONSCIOUSNESS, CULTURE, AND THE CARTHAGINIANS

During the war, when writers in the Office of War Information had to explain the difficulties of supplying our armies, they used the following statistic: "It takes one ton of equipment to land an American soldier in the European battle zone, and seven tons a month to keep him fighting."

This compact and handy fact soon came so trippingly from various typewriters that one editor used to comment somberly, "Here comes old one-ton-seven-tons again." Old one-ton-seven-tons was one of many, including "One-third of America's manpower is woman power" (war production) and "From Guadalcanal to Tokyo is six times the distance from Paris to Berlin."

In recent months I have been working for the State Department as an editor of a booklet called *The Arts in the United States,* for distribution overseas under the information program. Again I tapped a mine of neat, self-contained facts that come easily to the typewriter—this time not about war but about American culture. In the field of music, for example: "Since 1936, there has been an enormous increase in the number of summer music schools and music festivals in the United States." (I am ashamed to say that the word "burgeon" often creeps in.) "During twenty years at the Eastman School Festival of American Music, 900 orchestral works by more than 400 American composers have been played."

The elemental and classic quote in this galaxy was used by Frederick Lewis Allen in an article called "The Spirit of the Times" in the July issue of *Harper's:* "In 1900 there were only a handful of symphony orchestras in the country; by May 1951 there were 659 'symphonic groups'—including 52 professional, 343 community, 231 college, and a scattering of miscellaneous amateur groups. Fifteen hundred American cities and towns now support annual series of concerts."

I could give you similar meaningful facts about American literature, painting, and the other arts.

If you write propaganda you need facts like these, and it can't be helped if they become clichés. It can't be helped either if things are always entering the

Reprinted from *The Reporter,* November 25, 1952, by permission of the author.

main stream of American culture or some American art form is always coming of age. American literature has come of age at least four separate times—which reminds me again of the old OWI, where there were four different turning points for the Second World War.

In putting together a booklet on the arts in the United States, the Division of Publications of the State Department was moved by the worthy ambition of correcting some false impressions and convincing the outside world that we *are* a cultured people—traditional European belief, the wails of our avant-garde, and the general appearance of things to the contrary notwithstanding. What more natural than to describe an increasing interest in the arts all over the country, the huge new audience for classic ballet, the new audience for artistic films, and even, on the basis of Gian-Carlo Menotti's television opera "Amahl and the Night Visitors," to hold out hope for television as the source of a huge new audience for opera?

This is the "659-symphonic-groups" approach to American culture. I think it's just, it's dignified, it's worthy, and I don't like it.

At one point when my colleagues and I despaired of producing a booklet that would be anything but boring in the face of this approach, we decided to be Frenchmen producing a propaganda booklet on the arts in France. It was a breeze. Outside pressure prevented us from arriving at a complete table of contents, but it contained something like the following: at least one article on the philosophy of fashion; a hitherto unpublished and startling set of limericks from recently unearthed notebooks of a late great French savant; a lyrically written article called "The Morality of Evil," on the beauty of early morning in the red-light district of Paris (this was composed by a new fifteen-year-old writer in the jail where he was serving a term for peddling dope and was illustrated by Brassai or Cartier-Bresson photographs); somewhere in the book there was, of course, a full-page photograph of Jean Cocteau's hands; the lead article, by Sartre and entitled *"L'Etre, ce n'est pas moi,"* announced that Sartre had ceased to exist and was therefore repudiating existentialism.

You see what I mean. There were no statistics, nothing about how the population loved art, nothing about little orchestras sawing away in remote *départements*. The French booklet took for granted that France had culture and dealt with specific products—the work of artists.

Mr. Allen of *Harper's*, like the State Department, prefers the symphonic approach. He takes a comparison from the late President A. Lawrence Lowell of Harvard between the civilization of Greece, which influenced the whole world because the Greeks respected learning, philosophy, and the arts, and Carthage, which had no influence at all because its civilization was purely commercial. Mr. Allen sets out to prove that the United States is not a Carthage, that although we are not as religious as our ancestors, we have a new sort of morality that is not entirely to be sneezed at, and that many of us Americans are constantly busy with cultural activities of all kinds.

Now, about the Carthaginians. They were deeply religious in their own peculiar way—probably more so than we are—and there were a number of well-educated and able Carthaginians like Hannibal. But as a whole they concentrated their energy on trading all over the Mediterranean, and their education, designed to promote money-making, emphasized handwriting, arithmetic, and bookkeeping. In short, they had no culture.

But the real reason Carthage made little mark on history is not that the Carthaginians were a money-grubbing lot, but that in seven hundred years they produced only three or four good writers—and the magnum opus of one of these was a twenty-eight-volume work on animal husbandry. My own hunch is that most of the people who could write spent their time turning out propaganda pamphlets for the Romans, the Libyans, and the Numidians: "It takes one elephant to get a Carthaginian soldier to Italy, and seven elephants a month to keep him fighting"; "Carthaginians attend at least three hundred lectures on cultural subjects every year"; "Fifty thousand Carthaginians study the lyre and the flute"; "Although respect for the gods isn't as great as it was in the time of Hanno, still, during the past year twenty-seven new temples were built and four thousand aristocratic children under the age of six were sacrificed to Moloch."

The Roman reaction to this kind of thing was to announce at regular intervals that Carthage must be destroyed.

Leaving the Carthaginians out of it, it is something new to describe a country's civilization in terms of the number of people engaged in cultural activities. I've never heard how many Elizabethans sang in amateur madrigal groups or put on experimental masques in small community theaters all over England. When I went to college, we learned about the great artists of the Elizabethan period. We did hear that Shakespeare always drew large audiences, but I don't remember figures on the study groups of farmers and workers who met to discuss the plays. In fact, from some of the descriptions, Shakespeare's audiences sound pretty uncultured.

How do you determine how cultured a population at large is, and who cares? Worrying about your culture is dangerous: You can get sacred and mystical, and then you are in the soup. (See Germany.) The only other country I can think of which gets so upset about its culture is the Soviet Union, where, as various commentators have pointed out, everyone rushes to clean up washrooms, speak politely, and produce more tanks if his behavior is criticized as "*nyet kulturni.*" I could make out an argument (but I won't) that in emphasizing our culture, the State Department is being un-American.

In a thousand or two thousand or three thousand years, what historian of civilization will care that we played in 659 "symphonic groups," in one year, bought 231 million pocket books (including 350,000 copies of the Odyssey), and visited art museums fifty million strong, if he possesses one recording of *Appalachian Spring*, one copy of *The Wild Palms*, a Cummings poem, or a Marin water color?

Propaganda writers are supposed to project American democracy, so perhaps it is natural that they should talk about the arts in terms of the largest group of people involved—the audience. But this is like talking about swimming the English Channel in terms of the number of minnows frightened by the swimmer. Art has nothing to do with large groups of people. It is lonely, ruthless, and ademocratic. We have a tradition that any American boy can be President. We should call a halt before we find ourselves believing that any American boy can be Hemingway. One is plenty.

But it is true that if he is called on to talk about the artists themselves, the propaganda writer is in trouble. "What are their politics?" demands a Congressman or one of the several security agencies set up to screen material before it gets to the point where Congress can leap on it. While those Congressmen who get artists—particularly abstract ones—mixed up with Communists are relatively few, their influence, which is out of all proportion to their number, permeates the minds of government workers with doubt and fear, and forces them to confine American art to those artists who have never signed a petition, made an ill-advised statement, written an ill-advised letter to the newspapers, or loved a doubtful friend.

Artists who have never done any of these things are either half dead or wholly dead, in which case they are considered O.K. to write about. For example, it is much easier to compose a State Department booklet on American painting of the nineteenth century than that of the twentieth. Thomas Eakins never had a chance to belong to an organization on the Attorney General's list, or Albert Ryder to sign a petition for sending aid to Loyalist Spain. The mind boggles at what Whitman, if he were alive today, might have involved himself in. But he's dead, so he can be the father of modern American poetry. It is obvious why propaganda writers head for those "symphonic groups" like homing pigeons. (Query from the State Department editor: "Could you change the pigeons? In translation, it might come out as a reference to That Dove.")

But in the end even the Congressman will not be soothed or enlightened by reading about how cultured we are as a nation. If you give him statistics, he will say, "Fine, we have all the culture Europe has, and we have a lot of other things besides." He will be quite happy until he hears the community symphonic group playing something by Henry Cowell or John Cage, and then he will start looking up the conductor in a list of subversives. All that can be done about him is to throw as much straight art as possible at him. In time he may realize that it is profoundly more subversive than even he thought, but perhaps he will also realize that in a free country it doesn't matter.

When I suggest that we should talk more about our artists and less about our cultured population, it is clear that I think our artists are doing all right, and that some of them are superb. A good many better-qualified people don't agree. Artists today in America, they say, are in despair. The gilt is off the gingerbread and there is no God. Well, artists are frequently in despair, usually because they can't get on with the next chapter, and a cheery, cultured attitude on the part of the rest of the population isn't going to make them do anything but snarl. Besides, while despair may not be a fruitful state for a non-artist, it can be fruitful for an artist, who must know as much as possible about all emotions.

The strongest argument against what I am saying is that a cultured population is important because it is the seed bed for artists. A learned and brilliant case could be made for this, but I am not sure that it is valid. Many critics have outlined the conditions under which art can and does blossom. Yet the arrival of an artist remains something unpredictable. He is an inexplicable and unexpected gift of God, a man of unusual talent and insight, of course, but, perhaps more important, of unusual energy, for this makes him able to carry through the most heartbreakingly difficult work in the world. Symphonic groups cannot distract him nor mass culture harm, for he is looking in another direction, into himself for the thing which is peculiarly his and which he must draw painfully up, like a heavy anchor out of a sea fathoms deep. There is no way the rest of us can help him except by leaving him alone, and yet we must ceaselessly hunt him down in order to find out what he has to tell us. In the modern world, there may be no God visible, but if He is here, the artist will see Him.

What the artist produces is particular to his time and place, and yet it is also what all the propaganda writers are looking for and wish were theirs, a true Esperanto, the only language which crosses national boundaries and which can be understood by men in all countries. From it the rest of the world will learn far more about the United States than from statistics about symphonic groups. Let us export our music, our painting, and our literature and forget about the advertising leaflets and preliminary selling copy. It is both logical and practical to do so, because, being international, our art is the most easily exportable product we manufacture. The thread gauges of art are the same all over the world. Artists use only one system of measurement.

William Faulkner

....

THE WRITER'S DUTY

I feel that this award was not made to me as a man but to my work—a life's work in the agony and sweat of the human spirit, not for glory and least of all for profit, but to create out of the materials of the human spirit something which did not exist before. So this award is only mine in trust. It will not be difficult to find a dedication for the money part of it commensurate with the purpose and significance of its origin. But I would like to do the same with the acclaim too, by using this moment as a pinnacle from which I might be listened

Upon receiving the Nobel Prize, Stockholm, December 10, 1950. Courtesy of Random House, Inc.

to by the young men and women already dedicated to the same anguish and travail, among whom is already that one who will someday stand here where I am standing.

Our tragedy today is a general and universal physical fear so long sustained by now that we can even bear it. There are no longer problems of the spirit. There is only the question: When will I be blown up? Because of this, the young man or woman writing today has forgotten the problems of the human heart in conflict with itself which alone can make good writing because only that is worth writing about, worth the agony and the sweat.

He must learn them again. He must teach himself that the basest of all things is to be afraid; and, teaching himself that, forget it forever, leaving no room in his workshop for anything but the old verities and truths of the heart, the old universal truths lacking which any story is ephemeral and doomed—love and honor and pity and pride and compassion and sacrifice. Until he does so he labors under a curse. He writes not of love but of lust, of defeats in which nobody loses anything of value, of victories without hope and worst of all without pity or compassion. His griefs grieve on no universal bones, leaving no scars. He writes not of the heart but of the glands.

Until he relearns these things he will write as though he stood among and watched the end of man. I decline to accept the end of man. It is easy enough to say that man is immortal simply because he will endure; that when the last ding-dong of doom has clanged and faded from the last worthless rock hanging tideless in the last red and dying evening, that even then there will still be one more sound: that of his puny inexhaustible voice, still talking. I refuse to accept this. I believe that man will not merely endure: he will prevail. He is immortal, not because he alone among creatures has an inexhaustible voice, but because he has a soul, a spirit capable of compassion and sacrifice and endurance. The poet's, the writer's, duty is to write about these things. It is his privilege to help man endure by lifting his heart, by reminding him of the courage and honor and hope and pride and compassion and pity and sacrifice which have been the glory of his past. The poet's voice need not merely be the record of man, it can be one of the props, the pillars to help him endure and prevail.

Matthew Arnold

DOVER BEACH[1]

> The sea is calm tonight,
> The tide is full, the moon lies fair
> Upon the straits;—on the French coast the light

1. This poem is the subject of the literary criticisms presented in the article which follows.

Gleams and is gone; the cliffs of England stand,
Glimmering and vast, out in the tranquil bay.   5
Come to the window, sweet is the night-air!
Only, from the long line of spray
Where the sea meets the moon-blanched land,
Listen! you hear the grating roar
Of pebbles which the waves draw back, and fling,   10
At their return, up the high strand,
Begin, and cease, and then again begin,
With tremulous cadence slow, and bring
The eternal note of sadness in.

Sophocles long ago   15
Heard it on the Aegean, and it brought
Into his mind the turbid ebb and flow
Of human misery; we
Find also in the sound a thought,
Hearing it by this distant northern sea.   20

The Sea of Faith
Was once, too, at the full, and round earth's shore
Lay like the folds of a bright girdle furled.
But now I only hear
Its melancholy, long, withdrawing roar,   25
Retreating, to the breath
Of the night-wind, down the vast edges drear
And naked shingles of the world.

Ah, love, let us be true
To one another! for the world, which seems   30
To lie before us like a land of dreams,
So various, so beautiful, so new,
Hath really neither joy, nor love, nor light,
Nor certitude, nor peace, nor help for pain;
And we are here as on a darkling plain   35
Swept with confused alarms of struggle and flight,
Where ignorant armies clash by night.

Told though it is in the form of a story, this interesting magazine article is in fact
a shrewd commentary upon different kinds of literary criticism. Because it is at times
less explicit than magazine articles usually are, the reader needs to note particularly
its implications.

Theodore Morrison

DOVER BEACH REVISITED

Early in the year 1939 a certain Professor of Educational Psychology, occupying a well-paid chair at a large endowed university, conceived a plot. From his desk in the imposing Hall of the Social Sciences where the Research Institute in Education was housed he had long burned with resentment against teachers of literature, especially against English departments. It seemed to him that the professors of English stood square across the path of his major professional ambition. His great desire in life was to introduce into the study, the teaching, the critical evaluation of literature some of the systematic method, some of the "objective procedure" as he liked to call it, some of the certainty of result which he believed to be characteristic of the physical sciences. "You make such a fetish of science," a colleague once said to him, "why aren't you a chemist?"—a question that annoyed him deeply.

If such a poem as Milton's "Lycidas" has a value—and most English teachers, even to-day, would start with that as a cardinal fact—then that value must be measurable and expressible in terms that do not shift and change from moment to moment and person to person with every subjective whim. They would agree, these teachers of literature, these professors of English, that the value of the poem is in some sense objective; they would never agree to undertake any objective procedure to determine what that value is. They would not clearly define what they meant by achievement in the study of literature, and they bridled and snorted when anyone else attempted to define it. He remembered what had happened when he had once been incautious enough to suggest to a professor of English in his own college that it might be possible to establish norms for the appreciation of Milton. The fellow had simply exploded into a peal of histrionic laughter and then had tried to wither him with an equally histrionic look of incredulity and disgust.

He would like to see what would happen if the teachers of English were forced or lured, by some scheme or other, into a public exposure of their position. It would put them in the light of intellectual charlatanism, nothing less . . . and suddenly Professor Chartly (for so he was nicknamed) began to see his way.

It was a simple plan that popped into his head, simple yet bold and practical. It was a challenge that could not be refused. A strategically placed friend in one of the large educational foundations could be counted on: there would be money for clerical expenses, for travel if need be. He took his pipe from his pocket, filled it, and began to puff exultantly. Tomorrow he must broach the

From *Harper's Magazine*, February 1940. Reprinted by permission of Theodore Morrison.

scheme to one or two colleagues; to-night, over cheese and beer, would not be too soon. He reached for the telephone.

The plan that he unfolded to his associates that evening aroused considerable skepticism at first, but gradually they succumbed to his enthusiasm. A number of well-known professors of literature at representative colleges up and down the land would be asked to write a critical evaluation of a poem prominent enough to form part of the standard reading in all large English courses. They would be asked to state the criteria on which they based their judgment. When all the answers had been received the whole dossier would be sent to a moderator, a trusted elder statesman of education, known everywhere for his dignity, liberality of intelligence, and long experience. He would be asked to make a preliminary examination of all the documents and to determine from the point of view of a teacher of literature whether they provided any basis for a common understanding. The moderator would then forward all the documents to Professor Chartly, who would make what in his own mind he was frank to call a more scientific analysis. Then the jaws of the trap would be ready to spring.

Once the conspirators had agreed on their plot their first difficulty came in the choice of a poem. Suffice it to say that someone eventually hit on Arnold's "Dover Beach," and the suggestion withstood all attack. "Dover Beach" was universally known, almost universally praised; it was remote enough so that contemporary jealousies and cults were not seriously involved, yet near enough not to call for any special expertness, historical or linguistic, as a prerequisite for judgment; it was generally given credit for skill as a work of art, yet it contained also, in its author's own phrase, a "criticism of life."

Rapidly in the days following the first meeting the representative teachers were chosen and invited to participate in the plan. Professional courtesy seemed to require the inclusion of an Arnold expert. But the one selected excused himself from producing a value judgment of "Dover Beach" on the ground that he was busy investigating a fresh clue to the identity of "Marguerite." He had evidence that the woman in question, after the episode hinted at in the famous poems, had married her deceased sister's husband, thus perhaps affecting Arnold's views on a social question about which he had said a good deal in his prose writings. The expert pointed out that he had been given a half-year's leave of absence and a research grant to pursue the shadow of Marguerite through Europe, wherever it might lead him. If only war did not break out he hoped to complete this research and solve one of the vexing problems that had always confronted Arnold's biographers. His energies would be too much engaged in this special investigation to deal justly with the more general questions raised by Professor Chartly's invitation. But he asked to be kept informed, since the results of the experiment could not fail to be of interest to him.

After a few hitches and delays from other quarters, the scheme was ripe. The requests were mailed out, and the Professor of Educational Psychology sat back in grim confidence to await the outcome.

II

It chanced that the first of the representative teachers who received and answered Professor Chartly's letter was thought of on his own campus as giving off a distinct though not unpleasant odor of the ivory tower. He would have resented the imputation himself. At forty-five Bradley Dewing was handsome in a somewhat speciously virile style, graying at the temples, but still well-knit and active. He prided himself on being able to beat most of his students at tennis; once a year he would play the third or fourth man on the varsity and go down to creditable defeat with some elegiac phrases on the ravages of time. He thought of himself as a man of the world; it was well for his contentment, which was seldom visibly ruffled, that he never heard the class mimic reproducing at a fraternity house or beer parlor his manner of saying: "After all, gentlemen, it is pure poetry that lasts. We must never forget the staying power of pure art." The class mimic never represents the whole of class opinion, but he can usually make everyone within earshot laugh.

Professor Dewing could remember clearly what his own teachers had said about "Dover Beach" in the days when he was a freshman in college himself, phrases rounded with distant professional unction: faith and doubt in the Victorian era; disturbing influence of Darwin on religious belief; Browning the optimist; Tennyson coming up with firm faith after a long struggle in the waters of doubt; Matthew Arnold, prophet of skepticism. How would "Dover Beach" stack up now as a poem? Pull Arnold down from the shelf and find out.

Ah, yes, how the familiar phrases came back. The sea is calm, the tide is full, the cliffs of England stand. . . . And then the lines he particularly liked:

> Come to the window, sweet is the night air!
> Only, from the long line of spray
> Where the sea meets the moon-blanch'd land,
> Listen! you hear the grating roar
> Of pebbles which the waves draw back, and fling,
> At their return, up the high strand,
> Begin, and cease, and then again begin,
> With tremulous cadence slow . . .

Good poetry, that! No one could mistake it. Onomatopoeia was a relatively cheap effect most of the time. Poe, for instance: "And the silken sad uncertain rustling of each purple curtain." Anyone could put a string of s's together and make them rustle. But these lines in "Dover Beach" were different. The onomatopoeia was involved in the whole scene, and it in turn involved the whole rhythmical movement of the verse, not the mere noise made by the consonants or vowels as such. The pauses—only, listen, draw back, fling, begin, cease—how they infused a subdued melancholy into the moonlit panorama at the same time that they gave it the utmost physical reality by suggesting the endless iteration of the waves! And then the phrase "With tremulous cadence slow" coming as yet one more touch, one "fine excess," when it seemed that every phrase and pause the scene could bear had already been lavished on it: that was Miltonic, Virgilian.

But the rest of the poem?

> The Sea of Faith
> Was once, too, at the full, and round earth's shore
> Lay like the folds or a bright girdle furl'd . . .

Of course Arnold had evoked the whole scene only to bring before us this metaphor of faith in its ebb-tide. But that did not save the figure from triteness and from an even more fatal vagueness. Everything in second-rate poetry is compared to the sea: love is as deep, grief as salty, passion as turbulent. The sea may look like a bright girdle sometimes, though Professor Dewing did not think it particularly impressive to say so. And in what sense is *faith* a bright girdle? Is it the function of faith to embrace, to bind, to hold up a petticoat, or what? And what is the faith that Arnold has in mind? The poet evokes no precise concept of it. He throws us the simple undifferentiated word, unites its loose emotional connotations with those of the sea, and leaves the whole matter there. And the concluding figure of "Dover Beach":

> . . . we are here as on a darkling plain
> Swept with confused alarms of struggle and flight,
> Where ignorant armies clash by night.

Splendid in itself, this memorable image. But the sea had been forgotten now; the darkling plain had displaced the figure from which the whole poem tacitly promised to evolve. It would not have been so if John Donne had been the craftsman. A single bold yet accurate analogy, with constantly developing implications, would have served him for the whole poem.

Thus mused Professor Dewing, the lines of his verdict taking shape in his head. A critic of poetry of course was not at liberty to pass judgment on a poet's thought; he could only judge whether in treating of the thought or sensibility he had received from his age, the poet had produced a satisfactory work of art. Arnold, Professor Dewing felt, had not been able to escape from the didactic tone or from a certain commonness and vagueness of expression. With deep personal misgivings about his position in a world both socially and spiritually barbarous, he had sought an image for his emotion, and had found it in the sea —a natural phenomenon still obscured by the drapings of conventional beauty and used by all manner of poets to express all manner of feelings. "Dover Beach" would always remain notable, Professor Dewing decided, as an expression of Victorian sensibility. It contained lines of ever memorable poetic skill. But it could not, he felt, be accepted as a uniformly satisfactory example of poetic art.

III

It was occasionally a source of wonder to those about him just why Professor Oliver Twitchell spent so much time and eloquence urging that man's lower nature must be repressed, his animal instincts kept in bounds by the exertion of the higher will. To the casual observer, Professor Twitchell himself did not seem to possess much animal nature. It seemed incredible that a desperate struggle with powerful bestial passions might be going on at any moment within his own slight frame, behind his delicate white face in which the most prominent feature was the octagonal glasses that focused his eyes on the outside world. Professor Twitchell was a good deal given to discipleship but not much to friendship. He had himself been a disciple of the great Irving Babbitt, and he attracted a small number of disciples among his own more earnest students. But no one knew him well. Only one of his colleagues, who took a somewhat sardonic interest in the mysteries of human nature, possessed a possible clue to the origin of his efforts to repress man's lower nature and vindicate his higher. This colleague had wormed his way sufficiently into Oliver Twitchell's confidence to learn about his family, which he did not often mention. Professor Twitchell, it turned out, had come of decidedly unacademic stock. One of his brothers was the chief salesman for a company that made domestic fire-alarm appliances. At a moment's notice he would whip out a sample from his bag or pocket, plug it into the nearest electric outlet, and while the bystanders waited in terrified suspense, would explain that in the dead of night, if the house caught fire, the thing would go off with a whoop loud enough to warn the soundest sleeper. Lined up with his whole string of brothers and sisters, all older than he, all abounding in spirits, Professor Twitchell looked like the runt of the litter. His colleague decided that he must have had a very hard childhood, and that it was not his own animal nature that he needed so constantly to repress, but his family's.

Whatever the reasons, Professor Twitchell felt no reality in the teaching of literature except as he could extract from it definitions and illustrations of man's moral struggle in the world. For him recent history had been a history of intellectual confusion and degradation, and hence of social confusion and degradation. Western thought had fallen into a heresy. It had failed to maintain the fundamental grounds of a true humanism. It had blurred the distinction between man, God, and nature. Under the influence of the sciences, it had set up a monism in which the moral as well as physical constitution of man was included within nature and the laws of nature. It had, therefore, exalted man as naturally good, and exalted the free expression of all his impulses. What were the results of this heresy? An age, complained Professor Twitchell bitterly, in which young women talked about sexual perversions at the dinner table; an age in which everyone agreed that society was in dissolution and insisted on the privilege of being dissolute; an age without any common standards of value in morals or art; an age, in short, without discipline, without self-restraint in private life or public.

Oliver Twitchell when he received Professor Chartly's envelope sat down with a strong favorable predisposition toward his task. He accepted wholeheartedly Arnold's attitude toward literature: the demand that poetry should be serious, that it should present us with a criticism of life, that it should be measured by standards not merely personal, but in some sense *real*.

"Dover Beach" had become Arnold's best-known poem, admired as his masterpiece. It would surely contain, therefore, a distillation of his attitude. Professor Twitchell pulled down his copy of Arnold and began to read; and as he read he felt himself overtaken by surprised misgiving. The poem began well enough. The allusion to Sophocles, who had heard the sound of the retreating tide by the Aegean centuries ago, admirably prepared the groundwork of high seriousness for a poem which would culminate in a real criticism of human experience. But did the poem so culminate? It was true that the world

> Hath really neither joy, nor love, nor light,
> Nor certitude, nor peace, nor help for pain

if one meant the world as the worldling knows it, the man who conducts his life by unreflective natural impulse. Such a man will soon enough encounter the disappointments of ambition, the instability of all bonds and ties founded on nothing firmer than passion or self-interest. But this incertitude of the world, to a true disciple of culture, should become a means of self-discipline. It should lead him to ask how life may be purified and ennobled, how we may by wisdom and self-restraint oppose to the accidents of the world a true human culture based on the exertion of a higher will. No call to such a positive moral will, Professor Twitchell reluctantly discovered, can be heard in "Dover Beach." Man is an ignorant soldier struggling confusedly in a blind battle. Was this the culminating truth that Arnold the poet had given men in his masterpiece? Professor Twitchell sadly revised his value-judgment of the poem. He could not feel that in his most widely admired performance Arnold had seen life steadily or seen it whole; rather he had seen it only on its worldly side, and seen it under an aspect of terror. "Dover Beach" would always be justly respected for its poetic art, but the famous lines on Sophocles better exemplified the poet as a critic of life.

IV

As a novelist still referred to in his late thirties as "young" and "promising," Rudolph Mole found himself in a curious relation toward his academic colleagues. He wrote for the public, not for the learned journals; hence he was spared the necessity of becoming a pedant. At the same time the more lucrative fruits of pedantry were denied to him by his quiet exclusion from the guild. Younger men sweating for promotion, living in shabby genteel poverty on yearly appointments, their childless wives mimicking their academic shop-talk in bluestocking phrases, would look up from the stacks of five-by-three cards on which they were constantly accumulating notes and references, and would say to him, "You don't realize how lucky you are, teaching composition. You aren't expected to know anything." Sometimes an older colleague, who had passed through several stages of the mysteries of preferment, would belittle professional scholarship to him with an elaborate show of graciousness and envy. "We are all just pedants," he would say. "You teach the students what they really want and need." Rudolph noticed that the self-confessed pedant went busily on publishing monographs and being promoted, while he himself remained, year by year, the English Department's most eminent poor relation.

He was not embittered. His dealings with students were pleasant and interesting. There was a sense of reality and purpose in trying to elicit from them a better expression of their thoughts, trying to increase their understanding of the literary crafts. He could attack their minds on any front he chose, and he could follow his intellectual hobbies as freely as he liked, without being confined to the artificial boundaries of a professional field of learning.

Freud, for example. When Professor Chartly and his accomplices decided that a teacher of creative writing should be included in their scheme and chose Rudolph Mole for the post, they happened to catch him at the height of his enthusiasm for Freud. Not that he expected to psychoanalyze authors through their works; that, he avowed, was not his purpose. You can't deduce the specific secrets of a man's life, he would cheerfully admit, by trying to fit his works into the text-book patterns of complexes and psychoses. The critic, in any case, is interested only in the man to the extent that he is involved in his work. But everyone agrees, Rudolph maintained, that the man is involved in his work. Some part of the psychic constitution of the author finds expression in every line that he writes. We can't understand the work unless we can understand the psychic traits that have gained expression in it. We may never be able to trace back these traits to their ultimate sources and causes, probably buried deep in the author's childhood. But we need to gain as much light on them as we can, since they appear in the work we are trying to apprehend, and determine its character. This is what criticism has always sought to do. Freud simply brings new light to the old task.

Rudolph was fortunate enough at the outset to pick up at the college bookstore a copy of Mr. Lionel Trilling's recent study of Matthew Arnold. In this volume he found much of his work already done for him. A footnote to Mr. Trilling's text, citing evidence from Professors Tinker and Lowry, made it clear that "Dover Beach" may well have been written in 1850, some seventeen years before it was first published. This, for Rudolph's purposes, was a priceless discovery. It meant that all the traditional talk about the poem was largely null and void. The poem was not a repercussion of the bombshell that Darwin dropped on the religious sensibilities of the Victorians. It was far more deeply personal and individual than that. Perhaps when Arnold published it his own sense of what it expressed or how it would be understood had changed. But clearly the poem came into being as an expression of what Arnold felt to be the particular kind of affection and passion he needed from a woman. It was a love poem, and took its place with utmost naturalness, once the clue had been

given, in the group of similar and related poems addressed to "Marguerite."
Mr. Trilling summed up in a fine sentence one strain in these poems, and the
principal strain in "Dover Beach," when he wrote that for Arnold "fidelity is a
word relevant only to those lovers who see the world as a place of sorrow and
in their common suffering require the comfort of constancy."

> Ah, love, let us be true
> To one another! for the world . . .
> Hath really neither joy, nor love, nor light . . .

The point was unmistakable. And from the whole group of poems to which
"Dover Beach" belonged, a sketch of Arnold as an erotic personality could
be derived. The question whether a "real Marguerite" existed was an idle
one, for the traits that found expression in the poems were at least "real"
enough to produce the poems and to determine their character.

And what an odd spectacle it made, the self-expressed character of Arnold
as a lover! The ordinary degree of aggressiveness, the normal joy of conquest
and possession, seemed to be wholly absent from him. The love he asked for
was essentially a protective love, sisterly or motherly; in its unavoidable in-
gredient of passion he felt a constant danger, which repelled and unsettled him.
He addressed Marguerite as "My sister!" He avowed and deplored his own
womanish fits of instability:

> I too have wish'd, no woman more,
> This starting, feverish heart, away.

He emphasized his nervous anguish and contrary impulses. He was a "teas'd
o'erlabour'd heart," "an aimless unallay'd Desire." He could not break through
his fundamental isolation and submerge himself in another human soul, and
he believed that all men shared this plight:

> Yes: in the sea of life enisl'd,
> With echoing straits between us thrown,
> Dotting the shoreless watery wild,
> We mortal millions live *alone*.

He never "without remorse" allowed himself "To haunt the place where passions reign," yet it was clear that whether he had ever succeeded in giving himself up wholeheartedly to a passion, he had wanted to. There could hardly be
a more telltale phrase than "Once-long'd-for storms of love."

In short much more illumination fell on "Dover Beach" from certain other
verses of Arnold's than from Darwin and all his commentators:

> Truth—what is truth? Two bleeding hearts
> Wounded by men, by Fortune tried,
> Outwearied with their lonely parts,
> Vow to beat henceforth side by side.

The world to them was stern and drear;
Their lot was but to weep and moan.
Ah, let them keep their faith sincere,
For neither could subsist alone!

Here was the nub. "Dover Beach" grew directly from and repeated the same emotion, but no doubt generalized and enlarged this emotion, sweeping into one intense and far-reaching conviction of insecurity not only Arnold's personal fortunes in love, but the social and religious faith of the world he lived in. That much could be said for the traditional interpretation.

Of course, as Mr. Trilling did not fail to mention, anguished love affairs, harassed by mysterious inner incompatibilities, formed a well-established literary convention. But the fundamental sense of insecurity in "Dover Beach" was too genuine, too often repeated in other works, to be written off altogether to that account. The same sense of insecurity, the same need for some rock of protection, cried out again and again, not merely in Arnold's love poems but in his elegies, reflective pieces, and fragments of epic as well. Whenever Arnold produced a genuine and striking burst of poetry, with the stamp of true self-expression on it, he seemed always to be in the dumps. Everywhere dejection, confusion, weakness, contention of soul. No adequate cause could be found in the events of Arnold's life for such an acute sense of incertitude; it must have been of psychic origin. Only in one line of effort this fundamental insecurity did not hamper, sadden, or depress him, and that was in the free play of his intelligence as a critic of letters and society. Even there, if it did not hamper his efforts, it directed them. Arnold valiantly tried to erect a barrier of culture against the chaos and squalor of society, against the contentiousness of men. What was this barrier but an elaborate protective device?

The origin of the psychic pattern that expressed itself in Arnold's poems could probably never be discovered. No doubt the influence that Arnold's father exercised over his emotions and his thinking, even though Arnold rebelled to the extent at least of casting off his father's religious beliefs, was of great importance. But much more would have to be known to give a definite clue—more than ever could be known. Arnold was secure from any attempt to spy out the heart of his mystery. But if criticism could not discover the cause, it could assess the result, and could do so (thought Rudolph Mole) with greater understanding by an attempt, with up-to-date psychological aid, to delve a little deeper into the essential traits that manifested themselves in that result.

v

In 1917 Reuben Hale, a young instructor in a Western college, had lost his job and done time in the penitentiary for speaking against conscription and for organizing pacifist demonstrations. In the twenties he had lost two more academic posts for his sympathies with Soviet Russia and his inability to forget his Marxist principles while teaching literature. His contentious, eager, lovable, exasperating temperament tried the patience of one college administration after another. As he advanced into middle age, and his growing family suffered repeated upheavals, his friends began to fear that his robust quarrels with established order would leave him a penniless outcast at fifty. Then he was invited to take a flattering post at a girls' college known for its liberality of views. The connection proved surprisingly durable; in fact it became Professor Hale's turn to be apprehensive. He began to be morally alarmed at his own security, to fear that the bourgeois system which he had attacked so valiantly had somehow outwitted him and betrayed him into allegiance. When the C.I.O. made its initial drive and seemed to be carrying everything before it, he did his best to unseat himself again by rushing joyfully to the nearest picket lines and getting himself photographed by an alert press. Even this expedient failed, and he reconciled himself, not without wonder, to apparent academic permanence.

On winter afternoons his voice could be heard booming out through the closed door of his study to girls who came to consult him on all manner of subjects, from the merits of Plekhanov as a Marxist critic to their own most personal dilemmas. They called him Ben; he called them Smith, Jones, and Robinson. He never relaxed his cheerful bombardment of the milieu into which they were born, and of the larger social structure which made bourgeois wealth, bourgeois art, morals, and religion possible. But when a sophomore found herself pregnant it was to Professor Hale that she came for advice. Should she have an abortion or go through with it and heroically bear the social stigma? And it was Professor Hale who kept the affair from the Dean's office and the newspapers, sought out the boy, persuaded the young couple that they were desperately in love with each other, and that pending the revolution a respectable marriage would be the most prudent course, not to say the happiest.

James Joyce remarks of one of his characters that she dealt with moral problems as a cleaver deals with meat. Professor Hale's critical methods were comparably simple and direct. Literature, like the other arts, is in form and substance a product of society, and reflects the structure of society. The structure of society is a class structure: it is conditioned by the mode of production of goods, and by the legal conventions of ownership and control by which the ruling class keeps itself in power and endows itself with the necessary freedom to exploit men and materials for profit. A healthy literature, in a society so constituted, can exist only if writers perceive the essential economic problem and ally themselves firmly with the working class.

Anyone could see the trouble with Arnold. His intelligence revealed to him the chaos that disrupted the society about him; the selfishness and brutality of the ruling class; the ugliness of the world which the industrial revolution had created, and which imperialism and "liberalism" were extending. Arnold was at his best in his critical satire of this world and of the ignorance of those who governed it. But his intelligence far outran his will, and his defect of will finally blinded his intelligence. He was too much a child of his class to disown it and fight his way to a workable remedy for social injustice. He caught a true vision of himself and of his times as standing between "two worlds, one dead, one powerless to be born." But he had not courage or stomach enough to lend

his own powers to the birth struggle. Had he thrown in his sympathies un-
reservedly with the working class, and labored for the inescapable revolution,
"Dover Beach" would not have ended in pessimism and confusion. It would
have ended in a cheerful, strenuous, and hopeful call to action. But Arnold
could not divorce himself from the world of polite letters, of education, of
culture, into which he had been born. He did his best to purify them, to make
them into an instrument for the reform of society. But instinctively he knew
that "culture" as he understood the term was not a social force in the world
around him. Instinctively he knew that what he loved was doomed to defeat.
And so "Dover Beach" ended in a futile plea for protection against the hideous-
ness of the darkling plain and the confused alarms of struggle and flight.

Professor Chartly's envelope brought Reuben Hale his best opportunity
since the first C.I.O. picket lines to vindicate his critical and social principles.
He plunged into his answer with complete zest.

VI

When Peter Lee Prampton agreed to act as moderator in Professor Chartly's
experiment he congratulated himself that this would be his last great academic
chore. He had enjoyed his career of scholarship and teaching, no man ever
more keenly. But now it was drawing to an end. He was loaded with honors
from two continents. The universities of Germany, France, and Britain had
first laid their formative hands on his learning and cultivation, then given their
most coveted recognition to its fruits. But the honor and the glory seemed a little
vague on the June morning when the expressman brought into his library the
sizable package of papers which Professor Chartly had boxed and shipped to
him. He had kept all his life a certain simplicity of heart. At seventy-four he
could still tote a pack with an easy endurance that humiliated men of forty.
Now he found himself giving in more and more completely to a lust for trout.
Half a century of hastily snatched vacations in Cape Breton or the Scottish
Highlands had never allowed him really to fill up that hollow craving to find a
wild stream and fish it which would sometimes rise in his throat even in the
midst of a lecture.

Well, there would be time left before he died. And meanwhile here was this
business of "Dover Beach." Matthew Arnold during one of his American lecture
tours had been entertained by neighbors of the Pramptons. Peter Lee Prampton's father had dined with the great man, and had repeated his conversation
and imitated his accent at the family table. Peter himself, as a boy of nineteen
or so, had gone to hear Arnold lecture. That, he thought with a smile, was
probably a good deal more than could be said for any of these poor hacks who
had taken Professor Chartly's bait.

At the thought of Arnold he could still hear the carriage wheels grate on
the pebbly road as he had driven, fifty odd years ago, to the lecture in town, the
prospective Mrs. Prampton beside him. His fishing rod lay under the seat. He
chuckled out loud as he remembered how a pound-and-a-half trout had jumped
in the pool under the clattering planks of a bridge, and how he had pulled up
the horse, jumped out, and tried to cast while Miss Osgood sat scolding in the

carriage and shivering in the autumn air. They had been just a little late reaching the lecture, but the trout, wrapped in damp leaves, lay safely beside the rod.

It was queer that "Dover Beach" had not come more recently into his mind. Now that he turned his thoughts in that direction the poem was there in its entirety, waiting to be put on again like a coat that one has worn many times with pleasure and accidentally neglected for a while.

> The Sea of Faith was once, too, at the full.

How those old Victorian battles had raged about the Prampton table when he was a boy! How the names of Arnold, Huxley, Darwin, Carlyle, Morris, Ruskin had been pelted back and forth by the excited disputants! *Literature and Dogma, God and the Bible, Culture and Anarchy*. The familiar titles brought an odd image into his mind: the tall figure of his father stretching up to turn on the gas lamps in the evening as the family sat down to dinner; the terrific pop of the pilot light as it exploded into a net of white flame, shaped like a little beehive; the buzz and whine of a jet turned up too high.

> Ah, love, let us be true
> To one another! for the world, which seems
> To lie before us like a land of dreams,
> So various, so beautiful, so new,
> Hath really neither joy, nor love, nor light,
> Nor certitude, nor peace, nor help for pain . . .

Peter Lee Prampton shivered in the warmth of his sunny library, shivered with that flash of perception into the past which sometimes enables a man to see how all that has happened in his life, for good or ill, turned on the narrowest edge of chance. He lived again in the world of dreams that his own youth had spread before him, a world truly various, beautiful, and new; full of promise, adventure, and liberty of choice, based on the opportunities which his father's wealth provided, and holding out the prospect of a smooth advance into a distinguished career. Then, within six months, a lavish demonstration that the world has neither certitude, nor peace, nor help for pain: his mother's death by cancer, his father's financial overthrow and suicide, the ruin of his own smooth hopes and the prospect instead of a long, hampered, and obscure fight toward his perhaps impossible ambition. He lived again through the night hours when he had tramped out with himself the youthful question whether he could hold Miss Osgood to her promise in the face of such reversals. And he did not forget how she took his long-sleepless face between her hands, kissed him, and smiled away his anxiety with unsteady lips. Surely everyone discovers at some time or another that the world is not a place of certitude; surely everyone cries out to some other human being for the fidelity which alone can make it so. What more could be asked of a poet than to take so profound and universal an experience and turn it into lines that could still speak long after he and his age were dead?

The best of it was that no one could miss the human feeling, the cry from the heart, in "Dover Beach"; it spoke so clearly and eloquently, in a language everyone could understand, in a form classically pure and simple. Or did it? Who could tell what any job-lot of academicians might be trusted to see or fail to see? And this assortment in Chartly's package might be a queer kettle of fish! Peter Lee Prampton had lived through the *Yellow Book* days of Art for Art's sake; he had read the muckrakers, and watched the rise of the Marxists and the Freudians. Could "Dover Beach" be condemned as unsympathetic with labor? Could a neurosis or a complex be discovered in it? His heart sank at the sharp sudden conviction that indeed these and worse discoveries about the poem might be seriously advanced. Well, he had always tried to go on the principle that every school of criticism should be free to exercise any sincere claim on men's interest and attention which it could win for itself. When he actually applied himself to the contents of Professor Chartly's bale he would be as charitable as he could, as receptive to light from any quarter as he could bring himself to be.

But the task could wait. He felt the need of a period of adjustment before he could approach it with reasonable equanimity. And in the meanwhile he could indulge himself in some long-needed editorial work on his dry-fly book.

Alfred H. Barr, Jr.

WHAT IS MODERN PAINTING?

What is modern painting? It is not easy to answer this question in writing, for writing is done with words while paintings are made of shapes and colors. The best words can do is to give you some information, point out a few things you might overlook, and if, to begin with, you feel that you don't like modern painting anyway, words may help you to change your mind. But in the end you must look at these works of art with your own eyes and heart and head. This may not be easy, but most people who make the effort find their lives richer, more worth living.

What is modern painting? Stop reading a few minutes, turn the pages of this selection and look at the pictures, keeping in mind that these small reproductions represent paintings which actually are very different in size and color.[1]

What is your first impression? Bewildering variety? Yes, that is true. The variety of modern art reflects the complexity of modern life; though this may

Reprinted by permission from *What Is Modern Painting?* by Alfred H. Barr, Jr., The Museum of Modern Art, 1952.
1. The book from which this selection is taken includes a number of reproductions of modern painting. On pages 389-392 you will find eight interesting examples from this larger collection.

give us mental and emotional indigestion, it does offer each of us a wide range to choose from.

But it is important not to choose too quickly. The art which makes a quick appeal or is easy to understand right away may wear thin like a catchy tune which you hear twice, whistle ten times and then can't stand any more.

It is just as important not to fool yourself. Don't pretend to like what you dislike or can't understand. Be honest with yourself. We don't all have to like the same things. Some people have no ear for music; a few have no eye for painting—or say they haven't because they are timid or don't want to make the effort.

Yet everybody who can see has an eye for pictures. Most of us see hundreds, maybe thousands, of pictures every week, some of them very good ones too—photographs in newspapers and magazines, cartoons, illustrations and comics, advertising in buses and subways: Joe Palooka Happy Atom Scientists Buy Sweetie Pie Soap Buck Rogers Vote For McLevy Dallam Scores in Third Wreck Near Trenton Zowie The Pause That Refreshes—pictures which try to get you to buy this or that, tell you something you may forget tomorrow or give you a moment's lazy entertainment. (And do you remember the pictures on the walls of your home?)

When you look at the pictures in this selection you may be upset because you can't understand them all at first glance. These paintings are not intended to sell you anything or tell you yesterday's news, though they may help you to understand our modern world.

Some of them may take a good deal of study, for although we have seen a million pictures in our lives we may never have learned to look at painting as an art. For the art of painting, though it has little to do with words, is like a language which you have to learn to read. Some pictures are easy, like a primer, and some are hard with long words and complex ideas; and some are prose, others are poetry, and others still are like algebra or geometry. But one thing is easy, there are no foreign languages in painting as there are in speech; there are only local dialects which can be understood internationally, for painting is a kind of visual Esperanto. Therefore it has a special value in this riven world.

The greatest modern artists are pioneers just as are modern scientists, inventors and explorers. This makes modern art both more difficult and often more exciting than the art we are already used to. Galileo, Columbus, the Wright brothers suffered neglect, disbelief, even ridicule. Read the lives of the modern artists of seventy years ago, Whistler or van Gogh for instance, and you will keep an open mind about the art you may not like or understand today. Unless you can look at art with some spirit of adventure, the pioneer artists of our own day may suffer too. This might be your loss as well as theirs.

Perhaps you feel that these pictures have little to do with our everyday lives. This is partly true; some of them don't, and that is largely their value—by their poetry they have the power to lift us out of humdrum ruts. But others have a lot to do with ordinary life: vanity and devotion, joy and sadness, the beauty of landscape, animals and people, or even the appearance of our houses

DAVIS: *Summer Landscape*. 1930. Oil, 29 x 42″. Museum of Modern Art. *Stuart Davis*, American, born 1894.
Photograph of the original scene upon which Davis based his painting *Summer Landscape*.

FAUSETT: *Derby View.* 1939. Oil 24⅛ x 40″. Museum of Modern Art. *Dean Fausett, American, born 1913.*
EURICH: *Withdrawal from Dunkirk.* 1940. Oil, 30 x 40″. Owned by the British Government. *Richard Eurich (Yurik), British, born 1903.*

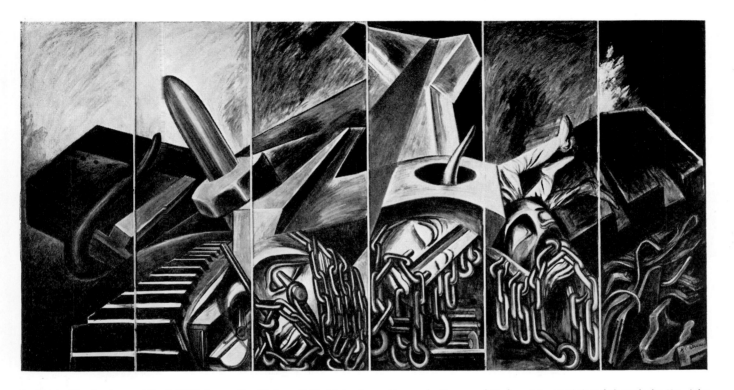

OROZCO: *Dive Bomber and Tank.* 1940. Fresco, 9 x 18 feet, divided into 6 movable panels. Museum of Modern Art, commissioned through the Mrs. John D. Rockefeller, Jr., Purchase Func. *José Clemente Orozco, Mexican, 1883-1949.*

WHISTLER: *Arrangement in Grey and Black (Portrait of the Artist's Mother).* c. 1871. Oil, 56 x 64". The Louvre Museum, Paris. *James Abbott McNeill Whistler,* American, born Lowell, Mass., 1834; died in London, 1903.

MONDRIAN: *Composition in White, Black and Red.* 1936. Oil, 40¼ x 41". Museum of Modern Art, gift of the Advisory Committee. *Piet Mondrian,* born The Netherlands, 1872; worked in Paris; died New York, 1944.

DOVE: *Grandmother.* 1925. Shingles, needle-point, printed paper, pressed flowers, 20 x 21¼". Museum of Modern Art, gift of Philip L. Goodwin. *Arthur G. Dove,* American, 1880-1946.

and our kitchen floors. And still others have to do with the crucial problems of our civilization: war, the character of democracy and tyranny, the effects of industrialization, the exploration of the subconscious mind, the survival of religion, the liberty and restraint of the individual.

The artist is a human being like the rest of us. He cannot solve these problems except as one of us; but through his art he can help us see and understand them, for artists are the sensitive antennae of society.

Beyond these comparatively practical matters art has another more important function: the work of art is a symbol, a visible symbol of the human spirit in its search for truth, for freedom and for perfection.

Contrasts: Two Landscapes

It is good to rest the eye on Dean Fausett's peaceful Vermont valley. The style of *Derby View* (p. 212), the way it is painted, is as relaxed and free from strain as the subject. The artist has spread before you the panorama of green hills with broad, easy brush strokes. The paint itself has a fresh beauty of color and texture which unobtrusively enhances the pictured beauty of the landscape.

Fausett, though he is a young American, paints his summer scene in a manner handed down from English artists of over a hundred years ago. Stuart Davis is older than Fausett but he works in a more "modern" style. Davis' *Summer Landscape* (p. 211) does not depend for its chief interest upon what the artist saw in nature but upon how he has changed what he saw.

The photograph, although it was taken in winter with no leaves on the trees, shows the scene on which Davis based his picture. Comparing it with the painting we can see how the artist has transformed a prosaic, commonplace view into a lively, decorative composition.

How did he go about it? First he drew the forms in simple outlines, leaving out unimportant or confusing details and reducing board fences, clouds and ripples to a lively linear shorthand. By omitting all shadows he lets you see these essential shapes and patterns more clearly. He moves houses around and even keeps half the house to the left of the telephone pole while throwing the other half away—probably without your noticing it. But with all these omissions and simplifications and rearrangements Davis has given a clearer and more complete idea of the village than does the snapshot. And when you see the original painting you may agree that he has not only created a crisp, vivacious, gayly colored design but has even caught the lighthearted spirit of a summer day.

Perhaps when you compare Fausett's *Derby View* and Davis' *Summer Landscape* you will find it hard to choose between them, but it is not hard to decide which shows the more imagination, the greater will to select, control, arrange and organize.

Contrasts: Two War Pictures

To help us not to forget World War II, its glory and its agony, we have these two paintings, one of them by a young English artist, the other by a famous

Mexican. Both were painted in 1940 but they are so unlike that they seem done in different centuries, even in different worlds.

In the foreground of Richard Eurich's *Withdrawal from Dunkirk* (p. 212) British troops, thick as ants, are ferried out through the surf to embark on small steamers and fishing craft. At the right a destroyer swings away toward England; and in the distance beyond the lighthouse rises a vast, black umbrella of smoke. The painter has recorded all this patiently, with exact detail and British reticence. His picture is as calm as the blue sky above the scene, clearer than a photograph and almost as impersonal. From the way he paints you would not guess that his subject was one of the crucial and overwhelmingly dramatic moments of the entire War.

Orozco's mural *Dive Bomber and Tank* (p. 213) was painted two months after Dunkirk. His mind, like ours, was full of the shock of the mechanical warfare which had just crushed western Europe. But instead of picturing an actual incident with technically accurate details he makes us feel the essential horror of modern war—the human being mangled in the crunch and grind of grappling monsters "that tear each other in their slime." We can see suggestions of the bomber's tail and wings, of tank treads and armor plate and human legs dangling from the jaws of shattered wreckage. Beneath emerge three great sightless masks weighted with chains which hang from pierced lips or eyes. The ancient symbols of dramatic agony and doom are fused with the shapes of modern destruction to give the scene a sense of timeless human tragedy.

As you can see, Orozco makes full use of the modern artist's freedom: he combines real and unreal objects, employs the cubist technique of breaking up nature into half-abstract, angular planes and uses emphatic, emotional, expressionist drawing.

Eurich's technique was developed five hundred years ago. Orozco's belongs to the twentieth century. Stop a moment and look at them both again. Subject matter aside, which style, which way of painting means more to you? Or do both have value?

Contrasts: Two Portraits

In 1877 John Ruskin, the renowned art critic, visited an exhibition where he saw several paintings by Whistler, who had for years been the storm center of art in London. Ruskin was outraged, called Whistler impudent and accused him of "flinging a pot of paint in the public's face." Whistler brought suit for libel but the trial was a farce; the public and the court sided with Ruskin, and Whistler, although he won half a cent damages, was forced into bankruptcy by legal expenses.

It was really the freedom of the artist which had been on trial. Ruskin and the public insisted that painting should be an exact, detailed, realistic picture of some object, scene or event. Whistler answered—but let him use his own words:

"The vast majority of folk cannot and will not consider a picture as a picture, apart from any story which it may be supposed to tell . . . . As music is the poetry of sound, so is painting the poetry of sight, and the subject matter has nothing to do with harmony of sound or of color.

"Take the picture of my mother, exhibited at the Royal Academy as an *Arrangement in Grey and Black* (p. 214). Now that is what it is. To me it is interesting as a picture of my mother; but what can or ought the public to care about the identity of the portrait?"

Whistler's *Mother* did not actually figure in the trial. It was painted six years before and, though this is hard to believe now, it had been rejected when Whistler sent it to the annual national exhibition at the Royal Academy. Only after one of the more open-minded members threatened to resign was it finally exhibited. For the next twenty years it remained unsold, even traveling to America, where no one offered to buy it. Ultimately the French Government acquired it for eight hundred dollars. Forty years later, in 1932, when it was again brought to America for exhibition by the Museum of Modern Art, it was insured for $500,000.

Looking back on the astonishing story of Whistler, we can see that the public was blind and intolerant. To them the *Mother* seemed dull in color, unpleasantly flat and simplified in style. And they resented the artist's calling it an "arrangement." But Whistler was mistaken too in asking the public to ignore the human interest of his painting, the quality which has made it one of the world's most popular pictures.

Whistler's ideas were not only ahead of his time—they were actually ahead of his own art. He wanted people to look at his paintings as "harmonies" or "arrangements" without paying attention to the subject matter. Therefore if he had followed his principles to a logical conclusion he might have made his intention clearer by leaving out the figure of his mother entirely from his *Arrangement in Grey and Black*—since he had already asked us to ignore her emotionally. We would then have had left a composition of rectangles, as in the diagram below. And this diagram is not very different from the abstract *Composition in White, Black and Red* (p. 214) painted by Mondrian in 1936, many years after Whistler died. (Of course Whistler would have pointed out

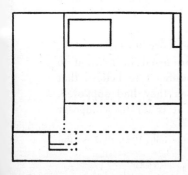

Diagram showing the main lines of Whistler's composition (p. 214) with the figure omitted. Compare the Mondrian, page 214.

quite justly that by omitting his mother's silhouette his design had been spoiled —so let us put her back in again so that we can distinguish her from Dove's *Grandmother* [p. 214].)

If you like you can also look at Arthur Dove's composition called *Grandmother* as an arrangement of rectangles and irregular forms, an arrangement made all the more interesting to the eye because the forms are not painted but are actual textures formed by cloth, wood, paper. But if you do look at it simply as an arrangement you will miss half the point of the picture, for the artist in making his composition has taken a page from an old Bible concordance, some pressed ferns and flowers, a piece of faded needlepoint embroidery and a row of weathered shingles turned silvery grey with age; these he has combined into a visual poem, each element, each metaphor of which suggests some aspect of the idea of grandmother: her age, her fragility, her silvery hair, her patience, her piety.

So we find Whistler calling his portrait of his mother an *Arrangement in Grey and Black* and, fifty years later, Dove naming his arrangement of assorted textures and shapes *Grandmother*. During those fifty years many things happened in the history of art which help to explain how this paradox came about. But the important matter here and now is not history but the relation between yourself and these two pictures, no matter whether you prefer to look at them as compositions or portraits of old ladies or both. And the same is true of the two landscapes and the two battle pictures. Each pair has shown you two very different ways of treating a similar subject. Actually there are a hundred ways, a thousand—as many as there are pictures. Have you open eyes and a free mind?

Aaron Copland

THE CREATIVE PROCESS IN MUSIC

Most people want to know how things are made. They frankly admit, however, that they feel completely at sea when it comes to understanding how a piece of music is made. Where a composer begins, how he manages to keep going—in fact, how and where he learns his trade—all are shrouded in impenetrable darkness. The composer, in short, is a man of mystery to most people, and the composer's workshop an unapproachable ivory tower.

One of the first things most people want to hear discussed in relation to composing is the question of inspiration. They find it difficult to believe that composers are not as preoccupied with that question as they had supposed. The layman always finds it hard to realize how natural it is for the composer

Reprinted from *What to Listen for in Music*, by Aaron Copland. Copyright, 1939, 1957, by the McGraw-Hill Company, Inc., New York, New York.

to compose. He has a tendency to put himself into the position of the composer and to visualize the problems involved, including that of inspiration, from the perspective of the layman. He forgets that composing to a composer is like fulfilling a natural function. It is like eating or sleeping. It is something that the composer happens to have been born to do; and, because of that, it loses the character of a special virtue in the composer's eyes.

The composer, therefore, confronted with the question of inspiration, does not say to himself: "Do I feel inspired?" He says to himself: "Do I feel like composing today?" And if he feels like composing, he does. It is more or less like saying to himself: "Do I feel sleepy?" If you feel sleepy, you go to sleep. If you don't feel sleepy, you stay up. If the composer doesn't feel like composing, he doesn't compose. It's as simple as that.

Of course, after you have finished composing, you hope that everyone, including yourself, will recognize the thing you have written as having been inspired. But that is really an idea tacked on at the end.

Someone once asked me, in a public forum, whether I waited for inspiration. My answer was: "Every day!" But that does not, by any means, imply a passive waiting around for the divine afflatus. That is exactly what separates the professional from the dilettante. The professional composer can sit down day after day and turn out some kind of music. On some days it will undoubtedly be better than on others; but the primary fact is the ability to compose. Inspiration is often only a by-product.

The second question that most people find intriguing is generally worded thus: "Do you or don't you write your music at the piano?" A current idea exists that there is something shameful about writing a piece of music at the piano. Along with that goes a mental picture of Beethoven composing out in the fields. Think about it a moment and you will realize that writing away from the piano nowadays is not nearly so simple a matter as it was in Mozart or Beethoven's day. For one thing, harmony is so much more complex than it was then. Few composers are capable of writing down entire compositions without at least a passing reference to the piano. In fact, Stravinsky in his *Autobiography* has even gone so far as to say that it is a bad thing to write music away from the piano because the composer should always be in contact with *la matière sonore.* That's a violent taking of the opposite side. But, in the end, the way in which a composer writes is a personal matter. The method is unimportant. It is the result that counts.

The really important question is: "What does the composer start with; where does he begin?" The answer to that is, Every composer begins with a musical idea—a *musical* idea, you understand, not a mental, literary, or extra-musical idea. Suddenly a theme comes to him. (Theme is used as synonymous with musical idea.) The composer starts with his theme; and the theme is a gift from Heaven. He doesn't know where it comes from—has no control over it. It comes almost like automatic writing. That's why he keeps a book very often and writes themes down whenever they come. He collects musical ideas. You can't do anything about that element of composing.

The idea itself may come in various forms. It may come as a melody—just a one-line simple melody which you might hum to yourself. Or it may come to the composer as a melody with an accompaniment. At times he may not even hear a melody; he may simply conceive an accompanimental figure to which a melody will probably be added later. Or, on the other hand, the theme may take the form of a purely rhythmic idea. He hears a particular kind of drumbeat, and that will be enough to start him off. Over it he will soon begin hearing an accompaniment and melody. The original conception, however, was a mere rhythm. Or, a different type of composer may possibly begin with a contrapuntal web of two or three melodies which are heard at the same instant. That, however, is a less usual species of thematic inspiration.

All these are different ways in which the musical idea may present itself to the composer.

Now, the composer has the idea. He has a number of them in his book, and he examines them in more or less the way that you, the listener, would examine them if you looked at them. He wants to know what he has. He examines the musical line for its purely formal beauty. He likes to see the way it rises and falls, as if it were a drawn line instead of a musical one. He may even try to retouch it, just as you might in drawing a line, so that the rise and fall of the melodic contour might be improved.

But he also wants to know the emotional significance of his theme. If all music has expressive value, then the composer must become conscious of the expressive values of his theme. He may be unable to put it into so many words, but he feels it! He instinctively knows whether he has a gay or a sad theme, a noble or diabolic one. Sometimes he may be mystified himself as to its exact quality. But sooner or later he will probably instinctively decide what the emotional nature of his theme is, because that's the thing he is about to work with.

Always remember that a theme is, after all, only a succession of notes. Merely by changing the dynamics, that is, by playing it loudly and bravely or softly and timidly, one can transform the emotional feeling of the very same succession of notes. By a change of harmony a new poignancy may be given the theme; or by a different rhythmic treatment the same notes may result in a war dance instead of a lullaby. Every composer keeps in mind the possible metamorphoses of his succession of notes. First he tries to find its essential nature, and then he tries to find what might be done with it—how that essential nature may momentarily be changed.

As a matter of fact, the experience of most composers has been that the more complete a theme is the less possibility there is of seeing it in various aspects. If the theme itself, in its original form, is long enough and complete enough, the composer may have difficulty in seeing it in any other way. It already exists in its definitive form. That is why great music can be written on themes that in themselves are insignificant. One might very well say that the less complete, the less important, the theme the more likely it is to be open to new connotations. Some of Bach's greatest organ fugues are constructed on themes that are comparatively uninteresting in themselves.

The current notion that all music is beautiful according to whether the theme is beautiful or not doesn't hold true in many cases. Certainly the composer does not judge his theme by that criterion alone.

Having looked at his thematic material, the composer must now decide what sound medium will best fit it. Is it a theme that belongs in a symphony, or does it seem more intimate in character and therefore better fitted for a string quartet? Is it a lyrical theme that would be used to best advantage in a song; or had it better be saved, because of its dramatic quality, for operatic treatment? A composer sometimes has a work half finished before he understands the medium for which it is best fitted.

Thus far I have been presupposing an abstract composer before an abstract theme. But actually I can see three different types of composers in musical history, each of whom conceives music in a somewhat different fashion.

The type that has fired public imagination most is that of the spontaneously inspired composer—the Franz Schubert type, in other words. All composers are inspired of course, but this type is more spontaneously inspired. Music simply wells out of him. He can't get it down on paper fast enough. You can almost always tell this type of composer by his prolific output. In certain months, Schubert wrote a song a day. Hugo Wolf did the same.

In a sense, men of this kind begin not so much with a musical theme as with a completed composition. They invariably work best in the shorter forms. It is much easier to improvise a song than it is to improvise a symphony. It isn't easy to be inspired in that spontaneous way for long periods at a stretch. Even Schubert was more successful in handling the shorter forms of music. The spontaneously inspired man is only one type of composer, with his own limitations.

Beethoven symbolizes the second type—the constructive type, one might call it. This type exemplifies my theory of the creative process in music better than any other, because in this case the composer really does begin with a musical theme. In Beethoven's case there is no doubt about it, for we have the notebooks in which he put the themes down. We can see from his notebooks how he worked over his themes—how he would not let them be until they were as perfect as he could make them. Beethoven was not a spontaneously inspired composer in the Schubert sense at all. He was the type that begins with a theme; makes it a germinal idea; and upon that constructs a musical work, day after day, in painstaking fashion. Most composers since Beethoven's day belong to this second type.

The third type of creator I can only call, for lack of a better name, the traditionalist type. Men like Palestrina and Bach belong in this category. They both exemplify the kind of composer who is born in a particular period of musical history, when a certain musical style is about to reach its fullest development. It is a question at such a time of creating music in a well-known and accepted style and doing it in a way that is better than anyone has done it before you.

Beethoven and Schubert started from a different premise. They both had serious pretensions to originality! After all, Schubert practically created the song form singlehanded; and the whole face of music changed after Beethoven

Literature and the Fine Arts
....

222

lived. But Bach and Palestrina simply improved on what had gone before them.

The traditionalist type of composer begins with a pattern rather than with a theme. The creative act with Palestrina is not the thematic conception so much as the personal treatment of a well-established pattern. And even Bach, who conceived forty-eight of the most varied and inspired themes in his *Well Tempered Clavichord*, knew in advance the general formal mold that they were to fill. It goes without saying that we are not living in a traditionalist period nowadays.

One might add, for the sake of completeness, a fourth type of composer— the pioneer type: men like Gesualdo in the seventeenth century, Moussorgsky and Berlioz in the nineteenth, Debussy and Edgar Varese in the twentieth. It is difficult to summarize the composing methods of so variegated a group. One can safely say that their approach to composition is the opposite of the traditionalist type. They clearly oppose conventional solutions of musical problems. In many ways, their attitude is experimental—they seek to add new harmonies, new sonorities, new formal principles. The pioneer type was the characteristic one at the turn of the seventeenth century and also at the beginning of the twentieth century, but it is much less evident today.[1]

But let's return to our theoretical composer. We have him with his idea— his musical idea—with some conception of its expressive nature, with a sense of what can be done with it, and with a preconceived notion of what medium is best fitted for it. Still he hasn't a piece. A musical idea is not the same as a piece of music. It only induces a piece of music. The composer knows very well that something else is needed in order to create the finished composition.

He tries, first of all, to find other ideas that seem to go with the original one. They may be ideas of a similar character, or they may be contrasting ones. These additional ideas will probably not be so important as the one that came first— usually they play a subsidiary role. Yet they definitely seem necessary in order to complete the first one. Still that's not enough! Some way must be found for getting from one idea to the next, and it is generally achieved through use of so-called bridge material.

There are also two other important ways in which the composer can add to his original material. One is the elongation process. Often the composer finds that a particular theme needs elongating so that its character may be more clearly defined. Wagner was a master at elongation. I referred to the other way when I visualized the composer's examining the possible metamorphoses of his theme. That is the much written-about development of his material, which is a very important part of his job.

All these things are necessary for the creation of a full-sized piece—the germinal idea, the addition of other lesser ideas, the elongation of the ideas, the bridge material for the connection of the ideas, and their full development.

---

1. Recent experiments with electronically produced music, however, point to a new species of scientifically trained composer as the pioneer type of our time.

Now comes the most difficult task of all—the welding together of all that material so that it makes a coherent whole. In the finished product, everything must be in its place. The listener must be able to find his way around in the piece. There should be no possible chance of his confusing the principal theme with the bridge material, or vice versa. The composition must have a beginning, a middle, and an end; and it is up to the composer to see to it that the listener always has some sense of where he is in relation to beginning, middle, and end. Moreover, the whole thing should be managed artfully so that none can say where the soldering began—where the composer's spontaneous invention left off and the hard work began.

Of course, I do not mean to suggest that in putting his materials together the composer necessarily begins from scratch. On the contrary, every well-trained composer has, as his stock in trade, certain normal structural molds on which to lean for the basic framework of his compositions. These formal molds I speak of have all been gradually evolved over hundreds of years as the combined efforts of numberless composers seeking a way to ensure the coherence of their compositions. . . .

But whatever the form the composer chooses to adopt, there is always one great desideratum: The form must have what in my student days we used to call *la grande ligne* (the long line). It is difficult adequately to explain the meaning of that phrase to the layman. To be properly understood in relation to a piece of music, it must be felt. In mere words, it simply means that every good piece of music must give us a sense of flow—a sense of continuity from first note to last. Every elementary music student knows the principle, but to put it into practice has challenged the greatest minds in music! A great symphony is a man-made Mississippi down which we irresistibly flow from the instant of our leave-taking to a long foreseen destination. Music must always flow, for that is part of its very essence, but the creation of that continuity and flow—that long line—constitutes the be-all and end-all of every composer's existence.

Science

The impact of science on modern life is hard to overestimate. Commencement speakers have made the statement platitudinous, but it is nevertheless profoundly true that "we live in a scientific age." The following essays explore some of the facets of that age.

Joseph Wood Krutch in "Machinery for Evolution" shows the excitement of scientific discovery—not only the excitement of the discovery itself but also the excitement of the reflections that for a thoughtful person inevitably follow hard upon discovery. Thomas Henry Huxley describes how scientific discovery can be systematized and tested. First delivered as a speech in 1866 to an audience of unread workingmen in England, Huxley's "The Method of Scientific Research" still remains one of the clearest explanations of the scientific method. The two essays that follow deal with some of the effects and implications of scientific knowledge. In "Science and Human Life" Bertrand Russell declares that science offers humanity either unprecedentedly glorious achievement or utter disaster. Albert Einstein in "Science and Religion" asserts epigrammatically that "science without religion is lame, religion without science is blind."

Joseph Wood Krutch

MACHINERY FOR EVOLUTION

A personal discovery

On the second of January 1700 Anthony van Leeuwenhoek, draper of Delft and self-taught Columbus of the littlest world, was writing to the Royal Society of London one of the many letters in which he described his voyages of discovery within a drop of water.

To William Dampier and other such rovers he left the exploration of the terrestrial globe. To another contemporary he left those equally adventurous voyages "through strange seas of thought, alone" which took Newton across abysses of space to spheres much larger but not so little known as those to which Leeuwenhoek devoted his long life.

These worlds of his were not lifeless but teeming with life; and his discoveries, unlike those of Columbus, were discoveries in an absolute sense. He saw what no man, not merely no European man, had ever seen before. He had every right to be—he probably was—more amazed than Balboa.

The draper of Delft was already just short of seventy when he wrote:

> I had got the aforesaid water taken out of the ditches and runnels on the 30th of August: and on coming home, while I was busy looking at the multifarious very little animalcules a-swimming in this water, I saw floating in it, and seeming to move of themselves, a great many green round particles, of the bigness of sand-grains.
>
> When I brought these little bodies before the microscope [actually a single very small lens which he had ground himself and fixed between two perforated metal plates] I saw that they were not simply round, but that their outermost membrane was everywhere beset with many little projecting particles, which seemed to me to be triangular, with the end tapering to a point: and it looked to me as if, in the whole circumference of that little ball, eight such particles were set, all orderly arranged and at equal dis-

tances from one another: so that upon so small a body there did stand a full two thousand of the said projecting particles.

This was for me a pleasant sight, because the little bodies aforesaid, how oft soever I looked upon them, never lay still; and because too their progression was brought about by a rolling motion. . . .

Each of these little bodies had enclosed within it 5, 6, 7, nay some even 12, very little round globules, in structure like to the body itself wherein they were contained.

There is no mistaking the fact that what had just swum into Leeuwenhoek's ken was that very original and inventive organism, Volvox. Through hundreds of millions of years it had waited in countless places for man to become aware of its existence and, ultimately, to guess how important a step it had taken in the direction of both consciousness and that curiosity which was leading the Dutch draper to seek out in the ditches of Delft. The "little projecting particles" are the peripheral cells which enclose the watery jelly in Volvox's interior. The "5, 6, 7, nay some even 12, very little round globules, in structure like to the body itself" are the vegetative "daughter cells" produced by a sort of virgin birth between the sexual generations, much as in some of the higher plants "offsets" as well as seeds are produced. Nor did Leeuwenhoek's observation stop there:

While I was keeping watch, for a good time on one of the biggest round bodies . . . I noticed that in its outermost part an opening appeared, out of which one of the enclosed round globules, having a fine green color, dropped out; and so one after another till they were all out, and each took on the same motion in the water as the body out of which it came. Afterwards, the first round body remained lying without any motion: and soon after a second globule, and presently a third, dropped out of it; and so one after another till they were all out and each took its proper motion.

After the lapse of several days, the first round body became as it were, again mingled with the water; for I could perceive no sign of it.

In other words Leeuwenhoek saw both the liberation of the daughter colonies and also, though he did not realize its importance, something even more remarkable. He saw Volvox yielding to one of its two remarkable inventions—natural (or inevitable) Death. The other half of the strange story eluded him completely. He did not know that after a few generations have been vegetatively reproduced by the process he observed there comes a generation that will produce eggs which must be fertilized by sperm before they can develop.

Nearly three hundred years later and more than five thousand miles from Delft, I, in my late turn, have also been looking at Volvox still rolling along in his gracefully expert way. Like most of the free-living protozoa, he has established himself pretty well over the whole earth outside the regions of eternal ice and there is no use speculating how the cosmopolitan distribution was achieved or how he got to America. During the vast stretches of time which have been his, routes were open at one time or another from every part of the earth to every other part.

Historical plant geographers come almost to blows over the question how, for instance, the sweet potato got to the South Sea islands. But Volvox's history goes back too far for even speculation or contention to reach. If only the fit survive and if the fitter they are the longer they survive, then Volvox must have demonstrated its superb fitness more conclusively than any higher animal ever has.

My equipment is as much superior to Leeuwenhoek's as his originality, ingenuity, and persistence were superior to mine. Instead of a single blob of glass fixed in front of a tiny tube holding water and held up to sun or candlelight, I use the compound microscope, which was not brought to its present state until the second half of the nineteenth century. Light passes from a mirror through a complicated set of lenses designed to place it at exactly the right spot. An image is formed by another series of lenses, cunningly designed to correct one another's faults and then form an image in a black tube, this image again magnified by another set of lenses. I can confine Volvox to a hanging drop of water; I can light him from below, from the side, or even from the top. I can slow him down with sticky substances introduced into the drop; and I keep a supply of his species thriving in an artificial culture medium prepared for me by a biological supply house dealing in all sorts of improbable things. But though the beauty of Volvox must be even clearer to me than it was to Leeuwenhoek I have seen only what he saw and described in unmistakable terms.

Under a magnification of no more than a hundred diameters—called by microscopists "very low power"—Volvox looks about the size of a marble and when motionless less like a plant-animal than like some sort of jeweler's work intended, perhaps, as an earring. The surface of the crystal sphere is set with hundreds of tiny emeralds; its interior contains five or six larger emeralds disposed with careless effectiveness.

But Volvox is seldom motionless when alive and in good health. Bright as a jewel, intricate as a watch, and mobile as a butterfly, his revolutions bring one emerald after another into a position where they sparkle in the light. Though he is called the Roller, he actually *revolves* rather than *rolls*, because he seems to turn on an invisible axis, much as the planets do, and he moves forward with this axis pointing in the direction of his motion. His speed varies and he frequently changes direction but I once counted the seconds it took him to cross the field of the microscope and calculated that his speed, in proportion to his size, is comparable to that of a man moving at a fast trot. Volvox, however, suggests nothing so undignified as a trot. There is something majestic and, one might almost imagine, irresistible about his revolutions—again like those of a planet. One half expects to hear some music of the spheres.

Because the microscope has temporarily abolished the barrier of size which separates the universe of Volvox from my own, I enter temporarily into a dreamlike relationship with him, though he is unaware of my world and per-

aps equally unaware of his own. Nevertheless there is an easy purposefulness
n his movements and from what I have learned from the careful research of
thers I know that it is all much more complex and astonishing than I would
ver have guessed or than Leeuwenhoek did guess.

When I lift my head from the microscope the dream vanishes. But it is man
nd his consciousness which is really the fleeting dream. Volvox, or something
ery much like him, was leading his surprisingly complex life millions of years
efore man's dream began and may well continue to do so for millions of years
fter the dream ends. Harder to realize is the fact that the enterprise and ad-
entures of Volvox typify certain of the innovations and inventions which are
asually summed up in the word "evolution" and hence constituted some of the
arliest and most essential steps toward making possible our dream.

Such acquaintance with Volvox as I have gained from my own casual obser-
ations is as superficial as what one gets from a moment's examination of a
ower or from peering with mild curiosity at some strange animal behind the
ars of a zoo. Yet even so casual an examination will lead one to guess at some
f the significant facts.

The predominant color of Volvox is green; the green looks like chlorophyl,
nd so it is. Moreover Volvox can be "cultured" in a purely chemical solution.
ll of this suggests a plant rather than an animal, but biologists have decided
hat the classification is meaningless at this level. Both textbooks of zoology
nd textbooks of botany usually claim Volvox, and there are no hard feelings
ecause zoologists and botanists agree that Volvox represents a stage of evolu-
ion at which plants have not diverged from animals. He is either the one or the
ther. Or, more properly, he is neither. He is not a plant or an animal; he is
imply something which is alive.

Concerning another ambiguity the observer is likely to make an even better
uess. The walls separating one cell from another are clearly marked out and
ach of the cells which lie upon the periphery of the sphere is exactly like the
ther peripheral cells. Every one of them looks like a complete one-celled
reature, lashing its two flagella precisely as many such one-celled creatures
o—although, as was mentioned a few pages back, it is easy to see that Volvox's
ells do not crack their whips independently because they are co-ordinated in
uch a way that the organism as a whole moves purposefully forward in a
iven direction as though the individual flagella were controlled by a central
ntelligence.

Yet the individual cells not only look like separate animals but are in fact
morphologically all but indistinguishable from a certain very common specific
ree-living organism that occurs by the millions in stagnant rain water and is
ne of the usual causes why such water takes on a green color. Like this creature
ach of Volvox's peripheral cells has a nucleus, two flagella, and an "eye spot."
ny observer might easily suppose that a number of such tiny creatures had
ecently got together and formed a ball; or, that the one-celled creatures were
he result of the dissolution of Volvoxes. But if the one-celled creatures did
orm aggregates which then became cooperative, all that happened millions

of years ago and for a very long time Volvox has been much more than a mere casual grouping. One of his peripheral cells cannot live without the others. He is at least as much one creature as many and he must live or die as a whole. He can no longer dissolve into the myriad of individuals of which, long ago, his ancestors were no doubt composed.

If you want to call him a multicelled animal you have to admit that the peripheral cells have retained a good deal of their original equipment for independent life. On the other hand if you want to call him a mere aggregation you have to concede that the individuals composing the colony have been co-ordinated, disciplined, and socialized to a degree no human dictator has yet even hoped to achieve in his "monolithic" state. But in any event the guess that Volvox represents a stage in the development of the "higher" multicellular animals and suggests how the transition was made is more immediately persuasive than many of the other guesses biology finds itself compelled to make.

Without comment I pass over the suggestion made sometimes with horror and sometimes with approval that our present-day society is in the process of taking a step analogous to that once taken by Volvox; that just as the one-celled animal cooperated until he was no longer an individual but part of a multicelled body, so perhaps the highest of the multicelled animals is now in the process of uniting to make a society in which he will count for as much and as little as an individual cell counts for in the human body.

Now comes the most powerful argument of all for calling Volvox a unified individual rather than even a tight social group and it has to do with three different sorts of cells sometimes found within his central jelly. The least remarkable of the groups of special cells are those composing the "daughter colonies" which Leeuwenhoek saw and which in time will break out of the parent colony to start life on their own. About them there is nothing so very surprising, since "budding" of one kind or another is not uncommon among microscopic organisms. The other two groups of specialized cells are much more interesting because they seem to represent the first appearance of sexual differentiation.

One group is of spindle-shaped cells very much like the sperm of the higher animals. The other is a sort of egg considerably larger than the sperm because, like most eggs, it contains a rich store of reserve food to nourish a growing "embryo." Sooner or later a sperm cell will seek out an egg, the two will fuse, and thus they will pool the hereditary characteristics carried by the sperm and by the egg. Thus Volvox introduces a method of procedure almost universal among the higher plants and animals. Moreover, there is even the beginning of the distinction between Male and Female *individuals* as well as a distinction in the sex cells themselves, because, in the species which I have been observing, a given individual usually produces either eggs only or sperm only. The cynic who said that the two great errors in creation were the inclination of the earth's axis and the differentiation of the sexes probably had no idea how long ago the second error was made. To eliminate it we would not have to wipe the slate quite clean but we would have to go back at least as far as Volvox.

Being the inventor of sex would seem to be a sufficient distinction for a creature just barely large enough to be seen by the naked eye. But as we have already said, Volvox brought Natural Death as well as Sex into the world. The amoeba and the paramecium are potentially immortal. From time to time each divides itself into two, but in the course of this sort of reproduction no new individual is ever produced—only fragments of the original individuals, whose life has thus been continuous back to the time when life itself was first created. Though individuals can be killed there is no apparent reason why amoeba should ever die.

Individuals have been kept alive in laboratories for years by carefully isolating one-half of the organism after each division. What memories an amoeba would have, if it had any memories at all! How fascinating would be its firsthand account of what things were like in Protozoic or Paleozoic times! But for Volvox, death seems to be as inevitable as it is in a mouse or in a man. Volvox must die as Leeuwenhoek saw it die because it has had children and is no longer needed. When its time comes it drops quietly to the bottom and joins its ancestors. As Hegner, the Johns Hopkins zoologist, once wrote: "This is the first advent of inevitable natural death in the animal kingdom and all for the sake of sex." And as he asked: "Is it worth it?"

Nature's answer during all the years which have intervened between the first Volvox and quite recent times has been a pretty steady *Yes*. Sex plays an essential part in the vast majority of all the forms of life presumably more recent than Volvox. In your very back yard, if you have one, there is on the other hand evidence that she may be reconsidering her momentous decision—though for the moment we shall say no more about this startling fact.

Suppose we look instead a little more deeply into the meaning and purpose of that sexual love for the sake of which Volvox consented to die.

No small part of all fiction and poetry is concerned with the various ways in which a member of one sex has "proposed" to a member of the other— with the terms in which he (and sometimes she) has made the proposal, with the reasons given why the proposal should be accepted, and with the consequences that were supposed to follow if it was.

Arranged in an ascending series, such typical "proposals" have been: "Let us share a delight," "Let us commit ourselves to one another for ever," and "Let us unite our souls." Occasionally it has even been "Let us create a new life since we ourselves must die." But never, I imagine, has it ever been "Let us exchange our chromosomes." Yet that, if you insist upon equating everything with its origins, is what sex is really about.

These chromosomes are something with which all the higher plants and animals, as well as the majority of all the protozoa, come equipped. One of the reasons why the latter are not mere "blobs of undifferentiated protoplasm" is that embedded in the protoplasm is a little nodule of material quite different from the rest of the protoplasmic mass. This nucleus, as it is called, is so tremendously important that the very secret of life seems to reside within it.

A somewhat similar nucleus is found within every living-tissue cell of the human body and our nuclei are like those of many protozoa in another important respect. Both contain within themselves a number of little threads called chromosomes which seem to be the nucleus' Holy of Holies just as the nucleus is the cell's. The number of chromosomes a protozoan has is not the same as the number we have. In fact every plant and animal has a number specific for that organism and every single cell (except the sex cells) composing the tissue of any multicellular organism has the number characteristic of it.

When a typical protozoan decides that it would rather be two protozoa instead of one—when, in other words, it reproduces by fission—the first thing it does is precisely what a cell in your body does when any one of your tissues grows. No new cell would be any good without a nucleus or without a nucleus provided with chromosomes. What happens in order that it should have one is extremely complicated, but it may be simplified thus: before the cell itself begins to divide the chromosomes move about until they are arranged in a sort of spindle-shaped group. Each chromosome, already split lengthwise, cuts itself in two near the middle; two groups are formed; when the whole cell divides, one-half of each chromosome is found within the two cells existing where only one existed before.

Thus it is that the protozoan reproduces itself and that a bit of your tissue grows. The new protozoan or the new cell does not differ from the old one. What you have is merely a pair of identical twins.

Most of the cells in your body reproduce indefinitely in just that fashion. But most protozoa "conjugate" as well as divide. From time to time two meet, their bodies either completely fuse or, in the case of many, their mouths are pressed together for a considerable time in a sort of soul kiss during which each gives up to the other a portion of its nucleus. Presently each individual combines the gift portion with the retained portion of his original nucleus to make a new one. And when the time comes for division it is this new nucleus that will be shared between the two halves of itself. Hence the new individual will, like the offspring of one of the higher animals, "inherit" from each of its conjugationed parents; and because of the combination of inherited traits it will be a unique individual.

Should we, then, say that sex already exists in a large number of protozoa? The answer to that question is yes and no. It is yes because a mingling of heredities—which is the grand purpose of all sexual processes—is to some extent accomplished. Though there are no parents in the usual sense because the parent splits in two, the fact remains that the two individuals resulting from a division after a conjugation are both different from what they would have been if no conjunction had taken place. And for that reason such reproduction is commonly called "sexual," to distinguish it from either a division or a budding not preceded by any form of conjugation.

Yet the answer is no if you are thinking in terms of the complete sexual process as it occurs in the higher plants and animals. The most obvious incompleteness is in the absence of any differentiation of the sexes. No detectable difference in structure exists between two conjugating protozoa. There are no males and no females. Neither are there any specific sex cells—no eggs and no sperm. It is in respect to these two facts that Volvox takes a great step toward sexuality as it is commonly known.

Volvox never indulges in the kind of conjugation we have been describing. Neither does it ever divide into two halves. Instead it produces what may properly be called "children"—sometimes by the vegetative process which Leeuwenhoek described and sometimes by a more surprising method which no free-living, single-celled animal ever practices.

Somewhere inside its sphere appear certain groups of small cells which might at first sight be mistaken for vegetative buds. But they develop quite differently in either one of two ways. Sometimes they become quite large. Sometimes on the other hand they split up into a great number of extremely small mobile cells. The first are eggs; the second sperm. Neither is good for anything by itself. But each is ready to do what the egg and the sperm of all the higher animals do. The egg waits. The sperm seeks it out. Then the two fuse and the fertilized egg is endowed with the hereditary traits contributed by the sperm as well as with those originally its own. Some species of Volvox are hermaphroditic as many lower organisms are. A single individual, that is to say, produces both male and female cells. But Volvox is also inventing the sexual differentiation of the whole organism. Certain species are commonly either male or female; the one producing only eggs, the other only sperm.

In what ways, one is bound to wonder, is this differentiation of sex cells and the further differentiation of male and female organisms superior to the simpler arrangement which the protozoa have managed to get along with during millions of years?

It has been, as satirists have so frequently pointed out, the cause of a lot of trouble in the world. Yet there must be compensating advantages, because as one moves upward along the evolutionary scale sexuality becomes universal and even hermaphroditism tends to disappear.

That sexual differentiation provides a richer emotional experience is a reason that few biologists are likely to admit as relevant and indeed it would be hard to prove that Volvox finds life more colorful than a paramecium does. Hence the biologist has to fall back upon such things as the superior viability of an egg, which can be heavy with reserve food resources because it does not have to be active when a small mobile sperm is there to seek it out. Possibly another fact is even more important. In all the higher animals sperm and egg cells differ from every other cell in the body of that organism in that they have only half the normal number of chromosomes and that the normal number is reëstablished when the sperm's half-number is added to the egg's half-number— which arrangement certainly shuffles hereditary characteristics more thoroughly than when the offspring has the whole inheritance from both sides of the family. In any event (and to repeat) there must be some advantage, since every animal above the protozoan level tends to adopt the novel arrangement first observable in Volvox.

Having reminded myself of all this, I cannot resist the temptation to push the typewriter aside to stare again at Volvox, quietly revolving in the beam of light concentrated from below and directed upward through my microscope. He (or she, for there are no sex cells visible at the moment) revolves steadily like some planet; and at a magnification of one hundred diameters looks as large as Mars through the largest telescope. But no more than Mars will Volvox abide my question. Over and over again I catch myself referring to him as "simple." Yet though his organism as a whole may reasonably be called relatively simple his sexual processes are not simple, either comparatively or absolutely. In many respects they seem quite as involved as those in a human being, although his chromosomes are no doubt far less complex. Something unimaginably complicated and subtle goes on when his sex cells isolate the hereditary uniqueness of the one organism and then, later, unite it with the uniqueness of an individual of the opposite sex.

Is, I wonder, the difference between Volvox and a human being as great as the difference between it and any theoretical, half-living blob of undifferentiated protoplasm would be?

Suppose that some biochemist should realize his dream and synthesize in his laboratory something which is undeniably protoplasm and is alive. How long would it take that protoplasm, either with or without the chemist's aid, to get a nucleus with chromosomes and to acquire the habit of sexual reproduction? Is it as easy to imagine how the simple product of "an improbable chemical reaction" could invent sex as it is to imagine how something which had once got as far as Volvox has might go on to become a man?

Even for the sake of picturesqueness and drama I would hesitate to say that Volvox invented Love as well as Sex. What he invented was perhaps at most only the possibility of Love. But in even the simplest creature Death—either accidental as it always is in one-celled creatures or sometimes natural as it may be in Volvox—is all too plainly like death in every other creature up to man. It is something we have not been able to change or complicate any more than we have been able to abolish it. Volvox may not love as we love, but he seems to die as we die.

A drop of water suspended in the intense beam of a microscope is not a very favorable environment for any organism, and several times I have seen a Volvox die. Usually his activity slows down and then stops. There comes the moment when he gives up his little ghost, though the body, like a human corpse, may seem hardly different from what it was before. A tiny spark is extinguished as suddenly and as irrevocably as the larger spark in any larger animal. What was alive is dead. The immeasurable, indescribable difference between the animate and the inanimate has been produced in a single instant. The spark can no more be revived in Volvox than in man. He was rounder than Humpty-Dumpty but not all the king's horses or all the king's men. . . .

It is no wonder, I say to myself, that so many men in so many different places and at so many different times have assumed that some soul must at the moment of death fly the body and betake itself elsewhere. It is the most natural of all possible theories, even if it is not the current one. The dead body of even a Volvox seems suddenly to have been vacated. Something intangible seems to have departed from it. What, on the contrary, I do find surprising is not the assumption that men have souls, but that it should ever have come to be commonly assumed that no other creature has. The sense that something which was there is gone is almost as strong in the one case as in the other and nothing suggests that the death of one is radically different from the death of the other. The very word "inanimate" means "without a soul" and the fact that we still use it testifies to its appropriateness.

I assume that the biologists are right when they tell me that Volvox, having got as far as it did, seems to have got no farther. Perhaps some other creature independently paralleled his inventions—which would make the whole thing at least twice as remarkable.

Looking again at the Roller I console him thus: At least you were on the right track. Like many others in the history of invention, like, to take a very minor example, Langley and his airplane—you were on the right track even though something stopped you before ultimate success. Once you had transformed a colony into an integrated individual you showed how it was possible for living creatures to achieve more than merely microscopic size. Once you had invented the differentiation of the sexes you had started on the way to poetry as well as to rich variability.

It may also be true that none of your other inventions was more important than Death, without which none of the others could have been fully effective. As a certain multicellular, mortal and sexually-differentiated individual called Bernard Shaw has argued, nature would not have been able to experiment very freely with new forms if the earlier experiments were not removed after a reasonable time. The potentially immortal amoeba got nowhere. Only mortal creatures evolved.

Thomas Henry Huxley

THE METHOD OF
SCIENTIFIC INVESTIGATION

The method of scientific investigation is nothing but the expression of the necessary mode of working of the human mind. It is simply the mode at which all phenomena are reasoned about, rendered precise and exact. There is no more difference, but there is just the same kind of difference, between the mental operations of a man of science and those of an ordinary person, as there is be-

From *Darwiniana* by Thomas H. Huxley. Reprinted by permission of D. Appleton-Century Company.

tween the operations and methods of a baker or of a butcher weighing out his goods in common scales, and the operation of a chemist in performing a difficult and complex analysis by means of his balance and finely graduated weights. It is not that the action of the scales in the one case, and the balance in the other, differ in the principles of their construction or manner of working; but the beam of one is set on an infinitely finer axis than the other, and of course turns by the addition of a much smaller weight.

You will understand this better, perhaps, if I give you some familiar example. You have all heard it repeated, I dare say, that men of science work by means of induction and deduction, and that by the help of these operations. they, in a sort of sense, wring from Nature certain other things, which are called natural laws, and causes, and that out of these, by some cunning skill of their own, they build up hypotheses and theories. And it is imagined by many, that the operations of the common mind can be by no means compared with these processes, and that they have to be acquired by a sort of special apprenticeship to the craft. To hear all these large words, you would think that the mind of a man of science must be constituted differently from that of his fellow men; but if you will not be frightened by terms, you will discover that you are quite wrong, and that all these terrible apparatus are being used by yourselves every day and every hour of your lives.

There is a well-known incident in one of Molière's plays, where the author makes the hero express unbounded delight on being told that he has been talking prose during the whole of his life. In the same way, I trust that you will take comfort, and be delighted with yourselves, on the discovery that you have been acting on the principles of inductive and deductive philosophy during the same period. Probably there is not one here who has not in the course of the day had occasion to set in motion a complex train of reasoning, of the very same kind, though differing of course in degree, as that which a scientific man goes through in tracing the causes of natural phenomena.

A very trivial circumstance will serve to exemplify this. Suppose you go into a fruiterer's shop, wanting an apple—you take one up, and, on biting, you find it is sour; you look at it, and see that it is hard, and green. You take up another one and that too is hard, green, and sour. The shopman offers you a third; but, before biting it, you examine it, and find that it is hard and green, and you immediately say that you will not have it, as it must be sour, like those that you have already tried.

Nothing can be more simple than that, you think; but if you will take the trouble to analyse and trace out into its logical elements what has been done by the mind, you will be greatly surprised. In the first place, you have performed the operation of induction. You found, that, in two experiences, hardness and greenness in apples went together with sourness. It was so in the first case, and it was confirmed by the second. True, it is a very small basis, but still it is enough to make an induction from; you generalize the facts, and you expect to find sourness in apples where you get hardness and greenness. You found upon that a general law, that all hard and green apples are sour; and that, so far as it goes, is a perfect induction. Well, having got your natural law in this way, when you are offered another apple which you find is hard and green, you say, "All hard and green apples are sour; this apple is hard and green, therefore this apple is sour." That train of reasoning is what logicians call a syllogism, and has all its various parts and terms—its major premise, its minor premise, and its conclusion. And, by the help of further reasoning, which, if drawn out, would have to be exhibited in two or three other syllogisms, you arrive at your final determination. "I will not have that apple." So that, you see, you have, in the first place, established a law by induction, and upon that you have founded a deduction, and reasoned out the special conclusion of the particular case. Well now, suppose, having got your law, that at some time afterwards, you are discussing the qualities of apples with a friend: you will say to him, "It is a very curious thing—but I find that all hard and green apples are sour!" Your friend says to you, "But how do you know that?" You at once reply, "Oh, because I have tried them over and over again, and have always found them to be so." Well, if we were talking science instead of common sense, we should call that an experimental verification. And, if still opposed, you go further, and say, "I have heard from the people in Somersetshire and Devon-shire, where a large number of apples are grown, that they have observed the same thing. It is also found to be the case in Normandy, and in North America. In short, I find it to be the universal experience of mankind wherever attention has been directed to the subject." Whereupon your friend, unless he is a very unreasonable man, agrees with you, and is convinced that you are quite right in the conclusion you have drawn. He believes, although perhaps he does not know he believes it, that the more extensive verifications are—that the more frequently experiments have been made, and results of the same kind arrived at—that the more varied the conditions under which the same results are attained, the more certain is the ultimate conclusion, and he disputes the question no further. He sees that the experiment has been tried under all sorts of conditions, as to time, place, and people, with the same result; and he says with you, therefore, that the law you have laid down must be a good one, and he must believe it.

In science we do the same thing;—the philosopher exercises precisely the same faculties, though in a much more delicate manner. In scientific inquiry it becomes a matter of duty to expose a supposed law to every possible kind of verification, and to take care, moreover, that this is done intentionally, and not left to a mere accident, as in the case of the apples. And in science, as in common life, our confidence in a law is in exact proportion to the absence of variation in the result of our experimental verifications. For instance, if you let go your grasp of an article you may have in your hand, it will immediately fall to the ground. That is a very common verification of one of the best established laws of nature—that of gravitation. The method by which men of science establish the existence of that law is exactly the same as that by which we have established the trivial proposition about the sourness of hard and green apples. But we believe it in such an extensive, thorough, and unhesitating manner because the universal experience of mankind verifies it, and we can verify it ourselves at any time; and that is the strongest possible foundation on which any natural law can rest.

So much, then, by way of proof that the method of establishing laws in science is exactly the same as that pursued in common life. Let us now turn to another matter (though really it is but another phase of the same question), and that is, the method by which, from the relations of certain phenomena, we prove that some stand in the position of causes toward the others.

I want to put the case clearly before you, and I will therefore show you what I mean by another familiar example. I will suppose that one of you, on coming down in the morning to the parlor of your house, finds that a teapot and some spoons which had been left in the room on the previous evening are gone—the window is open, and you observe the mark of a dirty hand on the windowframe, and perhaps, in addition to that, you notice the impress of a hobnailed shoe on the gravel outside. All these phenomena have struck your attention instantly, and before two seconds have passed, you say, "Oh, somebody has broken open the window, entered the room, and run off with the spoons and the teapot!" That speech is out of your mouth in a moment. And you will probably add, "I know there has; I am quite sure of it!" You mean to say exactly what you know; but in reality you are giving expression to what is, in all essential particulars, an hypothesis. You do not *know* it at all; it is nothing but an hypothesis rapidly framed in your own mind. And it is an hypothesis founded on a long train of inductions and deductions.

What are those inductions and deductions, and how have you got at this hypothesis? You have observed in the first place, that the window is open; but by a train of reasoning involving many inductions and deductions, you have probably arrived long before at the general law—and a very good one it is— that windows do not open of themselves; and you therefore conclude that something has opened the window. A second general law that you have arrived at in the same way is that teapots and spoons do not go out of a window spontaneously, and you are satisfied that, as they are now not where you left them, they have been removed. In the third place, you look at the marks on the window sill and the shoe marks outside, and you say that in all previous experience the former kind of mark has never been produced by anything else but the hand of a human being; and the same experience shows that no other animal but man at present wears shoes with hobnails in them such as would produce the marks in the gravel. I do not know, even if we could discover any of those "missing links" that are talked about, that they would help us to any other conclusion! At any rate the law which states our present experience is strong enough for my present purpose. You next reach the conclusion that, as these kinds of marks have not been left by any other animals than men, or are liable to be formed in any other way than by a man's hand and shoe, the marks in question have been formed by a man in that way. You have, further, a general law, founded on observation, and experience, and that, too, is, I am sorry to say, a very universal and unimpeachable one—that some men are thieves; and you assume at once from all these premises—and that is what constitutes your hypothesis—that the man who made the marks outside and on the window sill, opened the window, got into the room, and stole your teapot and spoons. You have now arrived at a *vera causa;*—you have assumed a cause which, it is plain, is competent to produce all the phenomena you have observed. You can explain all these phenomena only by the hypothesis of a thief. But that is a hypothetical conclusion, of the justice of which you have no absolute proof at all; it is only rendered highly probable by a series of inductive and deductive reasonings.

I suppose your first action, assuming that you are a man of ordinary common sense, and that you have established this hypothesis to your own satisfaction, will very likely be to go off for the police, and set them on the track of the burglar, with the view to the recovery of your property. But just as you are starting with this object, some person comes in, and on learning what you are about, says "My good friend, you are going on a great deal too fast. How do you know that the man who really made the marks took the spoons? It might have been a monkey that took them, and the man may have merely looked in afterwards." You would probably reply, "Well, that is all very well, but you see it is contrary to all experience of the way teapots and spoons are abstracted; so that, at any rate, your hypothesis is less probable than mine." While you are talking the thing over in this way, another friend arrives, one of that good kind of people that I was talking of a little while ago. And he might say, "Oh, my dear sir, you are certainly going on a great deal too fast. You are most presumptuous. You admit that all these occurrences took place when you were fast asleep, at a time when you could not possibly have known anything about what was taking place. How do you know that the laws of Nature are not suspended during the night? It may be that there has been some kind of supernatural interference in this case." In point of fact, he declares that your hypothesis is one of which you cannot at all demonstrate the truth, and that you are by no means sure that the laws of Nature are the same when you are asleep as when you are awake.

Well, now, you cannot at the moment answer that kind of reasoning. You feel that your worthy friend has you somewhat at a disadvantage. You will feel perfectly convinced in your own mind, however, that you are quite right, and you say to him, "My good friend, I can only be guided by the natural probabilities of the case, and if you will be kind enough to stand aside, and permit me to pass, I will go and fetch the police." Well, we will suppose that your journey is successful, and that by good luck you meet with a policeman; that eventually the burglar is found with your property on his person, and the marks correspond to his hand and to his boots. Probably any jury would consider those facts a very good experimental verification of your hypothesis, touching the cause of the abnormal phenomena observed in your parlor, and would act accordingly.

Now, in this supposititious case, I have taken phenomena of a very common kind, in order that you might see what are the different steps in an ordinary process of reasoning, if you will only take the trouble to analyse it carefully. All the operations I have described, you will see, are involved in the mind of any man of sense in leading him to a conclusion as to the course he should take in order to make good a robbery and punish the offender. I say that you are led, in that case, to your conclusion by exactly the same train of reasoning as that which a man of science pursues when he is endeavoring to discover the origin and laws of the most occult phenomena. The process is, and always must be, the same; and precisely the same mode of reasoning was employed by Newton and Laplace in their endeavors to discover and define the causes of the movements of the heavenly bodies, as you, with your own common sense, would employ to detect a burglar. The only difference is, that the nature of the inquiry being more abstruse, every step has to be most carefully watched, so that there may not be a single crack or flaw in your hypothesis. A flaw or crack in many of the hypotheses of daily life may be of little or no moment as affecting the general correctness of the conclusions at which we may arrive; but, in a scientific inquiry, a fallacy, great or small, is always of importance, and is sure to be in the long run constantly productive of mischievous if not fatal results.

Do not allow yourselves to be misled by the common notion that an hypothesis is untrustworthy simply because it is an hypothesis. It is often urged, in respect to some scientific conclusion, that, after all, it is only an hypothesis. But what more have we to guide us in nine-tenths of the most important affairs of daily life than hypotheses, and often very ill-based ones? So that in science, where the evidence of an hypothesis is subjected to the most rigid examination, we may rightly pursue the same course. You may have hypotheses, and hypotheses. A man may say, if he likes, that the moon is made of green cheese: that is an hypothesis. But another man, who has devoted a great deal of time and attention to the subject, and availed himself of the most powerful telescope and the results of the observations of others, declares that in his opinion it is probably composed of materials very similar to those of which our own earth is made up: and that is also only an hypothesis. But I need not tell you that there is an enormous difference in the value of the two hypotheses. That one which is based on sound scientific knowledge is sure to have a corresponding value; and that which is mere hasty random guess is likely to have but little value. Every great step in our progress in discovering causes has been made in exactly the same way as that which I have detailed to you. A person observing the occurrence of certain facts and phenomena asks, naturally enough, what process, what kind of operation known to occur in Nature applied to the particular case, will unravel and explain the mystery? Hence you have the scientific hypothesis; and its value will be proportionate to the care and completeness with which its basis has been tested and verified. It is in these matters as in the commonest affairs of practical life: the guess of the fool will be folly, while the guess of the wise man will contain wisdom. In all cases, you see that the value of the result depends on the patience and faithfulness with which the investigator applies to his hypothesis every possible kind of verification.

Bertrand Russell

SCIENCE AND HUMAN LIFE

Science and the techniques to which it has given rise have changed human life during the last hundred and fifty years more than it had been changed since men took to agriculture, and the changes that are being wrought by science continue at an increasing speed. There is no sign of any new stability to be attained on some scientific plateau. On the contrary, there is every reason to think that the revolutionary possibilities of science extend immeasurably beyond what has so far been realized. Can the human race adjust itself quickly enough to these vertiginous transformations, or will it, as innumerable former species have done, perish from lack of adaptability? The dinosaurs were, in their day, the lords of creation, and if there had been philosophers among them not one would have foreseen that the whole race might perish. But they became extinct because they could not adapt themselves to a world without swamps. In the case of man and science, there is a wholly new factor, namely that man himself is creating the changes of environment to which he will have to adjust himself with unprecedented rapidity. But, although man through his scientific skill is the cause of the changes of environment, most of these changes are not willed by human beings. Although they come about through human agencies, they have, or at any rate have had so far, something of the inexorable inevitability of natural forces. Whether Nature dried up the swamps or men deliberately drained them, makes little difference as regards the ultimate result. Whether men will be able to survive the changes of environment that their own skill has brought about is an open question. If the answer is in the affirmative, it will be known some day; if not, not. If the answer is to be in the affirmative, men will have to apply scientific ways of thinking to themselves and their institutions. They cannot continue to hope, as all politicians hitherto have, that in a world where everything has changed, the political and social habits of the eighteenth century can remain inviolate. Not only will men of science have to grapple with the sciences that deal with man, but—and this is a far more difficult matter—they will have to persuade the world to listen to what they have discovered. If they cannot succeed in this difficult enterprise, man will destroy himself by his halfway cleverness. I am told that, if he were out of the way, the future would lie with rats. I hope they will find it a pleasant world, but I am glad I shall not be there.

But let us pass from these generalities to more specific questions.

One of the most obvious problems raised by a scientific technique is that of the exhaustion of the soil and of raw materials. This subject has been much discussed, and some governments have actually taken some steps to prevent the denudation of the soil. But I doubt whether, as yet, the good done by these measures is outweighing the harm done in less careful regions. Food, however, is such an obvious necessity that the problem is bound to receive increasing attention as population pressure makes it more urgent. Whether this increased attention will do good or harm in the long run is, I fear, questionable. By a spendthrift use of fertilizers, food production in the present can be increased at the cost of food production in the future. Can you imagine a politician going to his constituents and saying: "Ladies and gentlemen, it is in your power to have abundance of food for the next thirty years, but the measures that will give you this abundance will cause scarcity for your grandchildren. I am therefore proposing measures to insure frugality in the present in order to avoid famine in the somewhat distant future." Is it possible to believe that a politician who said this would win elections against one less addicted to foresight? I hardly think so, unless the general level of political intelligence and virtue can be very considerably increased.

The question of raw materials is more difficult and complex than the question of food. The raw materials required at one stage of technique are different from those required at another. It may be that by the time the world's supply of oil is exhausted, atomic power will have taken its place. But to this sort of process there is a limit, though not an easily assignable one. At present there is a race for uranium, and it would seem likely that before very long there will be no easily accessible source of uranium. If, when that happens, the world has come to depend upon nuclear energy as its main source of power, the result may be devastating. All such speculations are of course very questionable, since new techniques may always make it possible to dispense with formerly necessary raw materials. But we cannot get away from the broad fact that we are living upon the world's capital of stored energy and are transforming the energy at a continually increasing rate into forms in which it cannot be utilized. Such a manner of life can hardly be stable, but must sooner or later bring the penalty that lies in wait for those who live on capital.

In primitive times, when the human population of the globe was small, such problems did not arise. Agriculture, it is true, was practiced in ways that exhausted the soil for a time, but there were usually new vacant lands available; and if there were not, the corpses of enemies sufficed as fertilizers. The system was "conservative" in the physicists' sense. That is to say, energy on the whole accumulated as fast as it was used. Now, this is not the case; and, so far as one can see, it will never be the case while scientific technique continues.

All this however, you may say, is distant and doubtful; we have more pressing matters to consider. This is true, and I will proceed to consider some of them.

The problem which most preoccupies the public mind at the present moment is that of scientific warfare. It has become evident that, if scientific skill is allowed free scope, the human race will be exterminated, if not in the next war, then in the next but one or the next but two—at any rate at no very distant date. To this problem there are two possible reactions: there are those who say, "let us create social institutions which will make large-scale war impossible"; there are others who say, "let us not allow war to become *too* scientific. We can not perhaps go back to bows and arrows, but let us at any rate agree with our enemies that, if we fight them, both sides will fight inefficiently." For my part, I favor the former answer, since I cannot see that either side could be expected to observe an agreement not to use modern weapons if once war had broken out. It is on this ground that I do not think that there will long continue to be human beings unless methods are found of permanently preventing large-scale wars. But this is a serious question as to which I will say no more at the moment. I shall return to it presently.

The substitution of machines for human labor raises problems which are likely to become acute in the not very distant future. These problems are not new. They began with the Industrial Revolution, which ruined large numbers of skilled and industrious handicraftsmen, inflicting upon them hardships that they had in no way deserved and that they bitterly resented. But their troubles were transitory: they died; and such of their children as survived sought other occupations. The sufferers had no political power and were not able to offer any effective resistance to "progress." Nowadays, in democratic countries, the political situation is different and wage earners cannot be expected to submit tamely to starvation. But if we are to believe Norbert Wiener's book on cybernetics—and I see no reason why we should not—it should soon be possible to keep up the existing level of production with a very much smaller number of workers. The more economical methods, one may suppose, would be introduced during a war while the workers were at the front, if such a war were not quickly ended by H-bomb extermination, and when the survivors returned their former jobs would no longer be available. The social discontent resulting from such a situation would be very grave. It could be dealt with in a totalitarian country, but a democracy could only deal with it by radical changes in its social philosophy and even in its ethics. Work has been thought to be a duty, but in such a situation there would be little work to do and duty would have to take new forms.

Changes in political philosophy are necessary for several reasons. One of the most important is that modern techniques make society more organic in the sense that its parts are more interdependent and an injury to one individual or group is more likely than it formerly was to cause injury to other individuals or groups. It is easier to kill a man than to kill a sponge because he is more highly organized and more centralized. In like manner it is easier to inflict vital damage upon a scientific community than upon a community of nomads or scattered peasants. This increase of interdependence makes it necessary to limit freedom in various ways which liberals in the past considered undesirable. There are two spheres in which such limitation is especially necessary: the one is in economics; and the other, in the relations between states.

Take economics first. Suppose, as is not improbable, that most of the power used in industry comes to be distributed from a fairly small number of atomic power-stations, and suppose that the men working in these stations retained the right to strike. They could completely paralyze the industrial life of a nation and could levy almost unlimited blackmail in the form of demands for higher wages. No community would tolerate such a state of affairs. The workers in power-stations would have to have understudies like actors in a theater, and the forces of the state would have to be employed if necessary to enable the understudies to replace workers on strike. Another example, which war has already brought to the fore, is the supply and use of raw materials. Whenever raw materials are scarce their distribution has to be controlled and not left to the free play of unfettered economic forces. Scarcity of this sort has hitherto been thought of as a transitory phenomenon due to the needs and ravages of war. But it is likely to remain, in regard to many essentials, a normal condition of highly developed industry. Some central authority for the allocation of raw materials must therefore be expected as a necessary limitation of economic freedom. Another unavoidable limitation comes from the vastness of some obviously desirable enterprises. To bring fertility to the interior of Australia and to parts of Siberia is almost certainly possible, but only by an expenditure far beyond the capacity of private enterprise. One may expect that the progress of science will increase the number of such possible enterprises. Perhaps it will be possible in time to make the Sahara rainy, or even to make northern Canada warm. But, if such things become possible, they will be possible only for whole communities and not for private corporations.

Even more important than the limitations of economic liberty are the limitations on the liberty of states. The liberal doctrine of nationality, which was preached by liberals before 1848 and embodied in the Treaty of Versailles by President Wilson, had its justification as a protest against alien domination. But to allow *complete* liberty to any national state is just as anarchic as it would be to allow complete liberty to an individual. There are things which an individual must not do because the criminal law forbids them. The law and the police are in most cases strong enough to prevent such things from being done: murderers are a very small percentage of the population of any civilized country. But the relations between states are not governed by law and cannot be until there is a supranational armed force strong enough to enforce the decisions of a supranational authority. In the past, although the wars resulting from international anarchy caused much suffering and destruction, mankind was able to survive them, and, on the whole, the risks of war were thought less irksome than the controls that would be necessary to prevent it. This is ceasing to be true. The risks of war have become so great that the continued existence of our species either has become or soon will become incompatible with the new methods of scientific destruction.

The new dangers resulting from our more organic society call for certain changes in the kind of character that is admired. The bold buccaneer, or the great conqueror such as Alexander or Napoleon, has been admired and is still admired although the world can no longer afford this type of character. We come

here upon a difficulty. It is a good thing that people should be adventurous
and that there should be scope for individual enterprise; but the adventure and
enterprise, if they are not to bring total disaster, must steer clear of certain
fields in which they were formerly possible. You may still, without harm to
your fellow men, wish to be the first man to reach the moon. You may wish to be
a great poet or a great composer or a man who advances the boundaries of
scientific knowledge. Such adventure injures no one. But if Napoleon is your
ideal, you must be restrained. Certain kinds of anarchic self-assertion, which
are splendid in the literature of tragedy, have come to involve too much risk.
A motorist alone on an empty road may drive as he pleases, but in crowded
traffic he must obey the rules. More and more the lives of individuals come to
resemble the motorist in traffic rather than the lonely driver in an empty desert.

I come at last to a question which is causing considerable concern and perplexity to many men of science, namely: what is their social duty toward this
new world that they have been creating? I do not think this question is easy or
simple. The pure man of science, as such, is concerned with the advancement
of knowledge, and in his professional moments he takes it for granted that the
advancement of knowledge is desirable. But inevitably he finds himself casting
his pearls before swine. Men who do not understand his scientific work can
utilize the knowledge that he provides. The new techniques to which it gives
rise often have totally unexpected effects. The men who decide what use shall
be made of the new techniques are not necessarily possessed of any exceptional
degree of wisdom. They are mainly politicians whose professional skill consists
in knowing how to play upon the emotions of masses of men. The emotions
which easily sway masses are very seldom the best of which the individuals
composing the masses are capable. And so the scientist finds that he has un-
intentionally placed new powers in the hands of reckless men. He may easily
come to doubt, in moments of depression or overwork, whether the world
would not be a happier place if science did not exist. He knows that science
gives power and that the power which it gives could be used to increase human
welfare; but he knows also that very often it is used, not so, but in the very
opposite direction. Is he on this account to view himself as an unintentional
malefactor?

I do not think so. I think we must retain the belief that scientific knowledge
is one of the glories of man. I will not maintain that knowledge can never do
harm. I think such general propositions can almost always be refuted by well-
chosen examples. What I will maintain—and maintain vigorously—is that
knowledge is very much more often useful than harmful and that fear of knowledge is very much more often harmful than useful. Suppose you are a scientific
pioneer and you make some discovery of great scientific importance, and suppose you say to yourself, "I am afraid this discovery will do harm": you know
that other people are likely to make the same discovery if they are allowed
suitable opportunities for research; you must therefore, if you do not wish the
discovery to become public, either discourage your sort of research or control

publication by a board of censors. Nine times out of ten, the board of censors will object to knowledge that is in fact useful—e.g., knowledge concerning contraceptives—rather than to knowledge that would in fact be harmful. It is very difficult to foresee the social effects of new knowledge, and it is very easy from the sheer force of habit to shrink from new knowledge such as might promote new kinds of behavior.

Apart from the more general duties of scientists toward society, they have a quite special and exceptional duty in the present critical condition of the world. All men of science who have studied thermonuclear warfare are aware of two superlatively important facts: first, that whatever agreements may have been reached to the contrary, thermonuclear weapons will certainly be employed by both sides in a world war; second, that if such weapons are employed there can be no hope of victory for either side, but only of universal destruction involving, quite possibly, the end of all human and animal life and almost certainly, failing that, a complete reversion to barbarism. A great war with thermonuclear weapons will not produce a universal victory of communism. It will also not produce the sort of world desired by the Western Powers. Nor will it give opportunity for the independent flourishing of Southeast Asia or Africa. Radioactive clouds, borne by the wind, will not respect frontiers and will ignore the legal rights of neutrals. In view of this prospect, there is one matter upon which the interests of the whole world coincide. Whether you are a Communist or an anti-Communist, an inhabitant of Asia or Europe or America, a white, brown, yellow or black man, your interests are exactly the same as those of the rest of the human race. Your paramount interest, if you are aware of the situation, must be to preserve the existence of mankind by preventing a great war. It is clearly the duty of men of science to bring the facts home, as far as lies in their power, to the governments and peoples of both East and West. This is no easy task. The governments of both East and West, whether from ignorance or from motives of prestige, are engaged in trying to persuade their populations that thermonuclear weapons will destroy the enemy but not themselves. *The Red Star,* the official military organ of the Soviet government, published several articles on methods of defense against thermonuclear weapons. These articles were so absurd that one could hardly believe their authors to be sincere. It seemed obvious that the purpose of the articles was to deceive people in Russia as to the perils to which they would be exposed. I am afraid that the schemes for civil defense put forward in America and Britain are equally misleading. I hope that this is because the authorities are ignorant and not because they are dishonest.

Clearly, scientists both of the East and of the West have an imperative duty: namely, the duty of bringing home to the protagonists the fact that the time is past for swashbuckling and boasting and campaigns of bluff which, if the bluff is called, can end only in utter disaster. I have been glad to see a lead given by a small number of men of science of the highest eminence, representing many countries and all creeds, Americans, Western Europeans, Poles and Japanese.

I have rejoiced to see these men issue a clear statement as to what is likely to happen in a great war; and I should wish them to invite all other men of science, in all countries, to subscribe to this statement.

I am aware that this will involve a certain degree of heroism and self-sacrifice. But there will be a reward which brave men should find sufficient: the reward of preserving uprightness and self-respect in the face of danger. These virtues are common in battle, and men of science should be able to show them also in a conflict with ignorance and ferocity. Science has fought great fights in former centuries against the embattled forces of obscurantism. In the nineteenth century it seemed as though science were victorious, but the victory is in danger of proving illusory. If science is to do its duty by mankind, men of science must once again face martyrdom and obloquy and the accusation of indifference to moral values. Perhaps their prestige may suffice to save them from the worst penalties for their courage, but of this we cannot be confident. What we can say with confidence is that it is not worth while to prolong a slavish and cowardly existence for a few miserable years while those who know the magnitude of the impending catastrophe wait for that radioactive death that is in store for them as well as for others.

A difficult readjustment in the scientists' conception of duty is imperatively necessary. As Lord Adrian said in his address to the British Association, "Unless we are ready to give up some of our old loyalties, we may be forced into a fight which might end the human race." This matter of loyalty is the crux. Hitherto, in the East and in the West alike, most scientists, like most other people, have felt that loyalty to their own state is paramount. They have no longer a right to feel this. Loyalty to the human race must take its place. Everyone in the West will at once admit this as regards Soviet scientists. We are shocked that Kapitza, who was Rutherford's favorite pupil, was willing, when the Soviet government refused him permission to return to Cambridge, to place his scientific skill at the disposal of those who wished to spread communism by means of H-bombs. We do not so readily apprehend a similar failure of duty on our own side. I do not wish to be thought to suggest treachery, since that is only a transference of loyalty to another national state; I am suggesting a very different thing: that scientists the world over should join in enlightening mankind as to the perils of a great war and in devising methods for its prevention. I urge with all the emphasis at my disposal that this is the duty of scientists in East and West alike. It is a difficult duty, and one likely to entail penalties for those who perform it. But, after all, it is the labors of scientists which have caused the danger and on this account, if on no other, scientists must do everything in their power to save mankind from the madness which they have made possible.

Science from the dawn of history, and probably longer, has been intimately associated with war. I imagine that when our ancestors descended from the trees they were victorious over the arboreal conservatives because flints were sharper than coconuts. To come to more recent times, Archimedes was respected for his scientific defense of Syracuse against the Romans; Leonardo obtained employment under the Duke of Milan because of his skill in fortification, though he did mention in a postscript that he could also paint a bit; Galileo similarly derived an income from the Grand Duke of Tuscany because of his skill in calculating the trajectories of projectiles. In the French Revolution, those scientists who were not guillotined devoted themselves to making new explosives. There is therefore no departure from tradition in the present-day scientists' manufacture of A-bombs and H-bombs. All that is new is the extent of their destructive skill.

I do not think that men of science can cease to regard the disinterested pursuit of knowledge as their primary duty. It is true that new knowledge and new skills are sometimes harmful in their effects, but scientists cannot profitably take account of this fact since the effects are impossible to foresee. We cannot blame Columbus because the discovery of the Western Hemisphere spread throughout the Eastern Hemisphere an appallingly devastating plague. Nor can we blame James Watt for the Dust Bowl, although if there had been no steam engines and no railways the West would not have been so carelessly or so quickly cultivated. To see that knowledge is wisely used is primarily the duty of statesmen, not of men of science; but it is part of the duty of men of science to see that important knowledge is widely disseminated and is not falsified in the interests of this or that propaganda.

Scientific knowledge has its dangers; but so has every great thing. And over and beyond the dangers with which it threatens the present, it opens up as nothing else can the vision of a possible happy world, a world without poverty, without war, with little illness. And, what is perhaps more than all, when science has mastered the forces which mold human character, it will be able to produce populations in which few suffer from destructive fierceness and in which the great majority regard other people, not as competitors to be feared, but as helpers in a common task. Science has only recently begun to apply itself to human beings, except in their purely physical aspect. Such science as exists in psychology and anthropology has hardly begun to affect political behavior or private ethics. The minds of men remain attuned to a world that is fast disappearing. The changes in our physical environment require, if they are to bring well-being, correlative changes in our beliefs and habits. If we cannot effect these changes, we shall suffer the fate of the dinosaurs who could not live on dry land. I think it is the duty of science—I do not say of every individual man of science—to study the means by which we can adapt ourselves to the new world. There are certain things that the world quite obviously needs: tentativeness, as opposed to dogmatism, in our beliefs; an expectation of co-operation, rather than competition, in social relations; a lessening of envy and collective hatred. These are things which education could produce without much difficulty. They are not things adequately sought in the education of the present day.

It is to progress in the human sciences that we must look to undo the evils which have resulted from a knowledge of the physical world hastily and superficially acquired by populations unconscious of the changes in themselves that the new knowledge has made imperative. The road to a happier world than any known in the past lies open before us if atavistic destructive passions can be kept in leash while the necessary adaptations are made. Fears are inevitable in our time, but hopes are equally rational and far more likely to bear good fruit. We must learn to think rather less of the dangers to be avoided than of the good that will lie within our grasp if we can believe in it and let it dominate our thoughts. Science, whatever unpleasant consequences it may have by the way, is in its very nature a liberator, a liberator of bondage to physical nature and, in time to come, a liberator from the weight of destructive passions. We are on the threshold of utter disaster or unprecedentedly glorious achievement. No previous age has been fraught with problems so momentous; and it is to science that we must look for a happy issue.

Albert Einstein

SCIENCE AND RELIGION

It would not be difficult to come to an agreement as to what we understand by science. Science is the century-old endeavor to bring together by means of systematic thought the perceptible phenomena of this world into as thoroughgoing an association as possible. To put it boldly, it is the attempt at the posterior reconstruction of existence by the process of conceptualization. But when asking myself what religion is, I cannot think of the answer so easily. And even after finding an answer which may satisfy me at this particular moment, I still remain convinced that I can never under any circumstances bring together, even to a slight extent, all those who have given this question serious consideration.

At first, then, instead of asking what religion is, I should prefer to ask what characterizes the aspirations of a person who gives me the impression of being religious: a person who is religiously enlightened appears to me to be one who has, to the best of his ability, liberated himself from the fetters of his selfish desires and is preoccupied with thoughts, feelings, and aspirations to which he clings because of their super-personal value. It seems to me that what is important is the force of this super-personal content and the depth of the conviction concerning its overpowering meaningfulness, regardless of whether any attempt is made to unite this content with a Divine Being, for otherwise it would not be possible to count Buddha and Spinoza as religious personalities. Accordingly, a religious person is devout in the sense that he has no doubt of the significance and loftiness of those super-personal objects and goals which

From *Science, Philosophy and Religion* by Albert Einstein. Reprinted by permission of the Conference on Science, Philosophy and Religion and Albert Einstein.

neither require nor are capable of rational foundation. They exist with the same necessity and matter-of-factness as he himself. In this sense religion is the age-old endeavor of mankind to become clearly and completely conscious of these values and goals and constantly to strengthen and extend their effects. If one conceives of religion and science according to these definitions then a conflict between them appears impossible. For science can only ascertain what *is*, but not what should be, and outside of its domain value judgments of all kinds remain necessary. Religion, on the other hand, deals only with evaluations of human thought and action; it cannot justifiably speak of facts and relationships between facts. According to this interpretation, the well-known conflicts between religion and science in the past must all be ascribed to a misapprehension of the situation which has been described.

For example, a conflict arises when a religious community insists on the absolute truthfulness of all statements recorded in the Bible. This means an intervention on the part of religion into the sphere of science; this is where the struggle of the Church against the doctrines of Galileo and Darwin belongs. On the other hand, representatives of science have often made an attempt to arrive at fundamental judgments with respect to values and ends on the basis of scientific method, and in this way have set themselves in opposition to religion. These conflicts have all sprung from fatal errors.

Now, even though the realms of religion and science in themselves are clearly marked off from each other, nevertheless there exist between the two, strong reciprocal relationships and dependencies. Though religion may be that which determines the goal, it has, nevertheless, learned from science, in the broadest sense, what means will contribute to the attainment of the goals it has set up. But science can only be created by those who are thoroughly imbued with the aspiration towards truth and understanding. This source of feeling, however, springs from the sphere of religion. To this there also belongs the faith in the possibility that the regulations valid for the world of existence are rational, that is comprehensible to reason. I cannot conceive of a genuine scientist without that profound faith. The situation may be expressed by an image: science without religion is lame, religion without science is blind.

Though I have asserted above, that in truth a legitimate conflict between religion and science cannot exist, I must nevertheless qualify this assertion once again on an essential point, with reference to the actual content of historical religions. This qualification has to do with the concept of God. During the youthful period of mankind's spiritual evolution, human fantasy created gods in man's own image, who, by the operations of their will were supposed to determine, or at any rate to influence, the phenomenal world. Man sought to alter the disposition of these gods in his own favor by means of magic and prayer. The idea of God in the religions taught at present is a sublimation of that old conception of the gods. Its anthropomorphic character is shown, for instance, by the fact that men appeal to the Divine Being in prayers and plead for the fulfilment of their wishes.

Nobody, certainly, will deny that the idea of the existence of an omnipotent, just and omnibeneficent personal God is able to accord man solace, help, and guidance; also, by virtue of its simplicity the concept is accessible to the most undeveloped mind. But, on the other hand, there are decisive weaknesses attached to this idea in itself, which have been painfully felt since the beginning of history. That is, if this Being is omnipotent, then every occurrence, including every human action, every human thought, and every human feeling and aspiration is also His work; how is it possible to think of holding men responsible for their deeds and thoughts before such an Almighty Being? In giving out punishment and rewards He would to a certain extent be passing judgment on Himself. How can this be combined with the goodness and righteousness ascribed to Him?

The main source of the present-day conflicts between the spheres of religion and of science lies in this concept of a personal God. It is the aim of science to establish general rules which determine the reciprocal connection of objects and events in time and space. For these rules, or laws of nature, absolutely general validity is required—not proven. It is mainly a program, and faith in the possibility of its accomplishment in principle is only founded on partial success. But hardly anyone could be found who would deny these partial successes and ascribe them to human self-deception. The fact that on the basis of such laws we are able to predict the temporal behavior of phenomena in certain domains with great precision and certainty, is deeply embedded in the consciousness of the modern man, even though he may have grasped very little of the contents of those laws. He need only consider that planetary courses within the solar system may be calculated in advance with great exactitude on the basis of a limited number of simple laws. In a similar way, though not with the same precision, it is possible to calculate in advance the mode of operation of an electric motor, a transmission system, or of a wireless apparatus, even when dealing with a novel development.

To be sure, when the number of factors coming into play in a phenomenological complex is too large, scientific method in most cases fails us. One need only think of the weather, in which case prediction even for a few days ahead is impossible. Nevertheless no one doubts that we are confronted with a causal connection whose causal components are in the main known to us. Occurrences in this domain are beyond the reach of exact prediction because of the variety of factors in operation, not because of any lack of order in nature.

We have penetrated far less deeply into the regularities obtaining within the realm of living things, but deeply enough nevertheless to sense at least the rule of fixed necessity. One need only think of the systematic order in heredity, and in the effect of poisons, as for instance alcohol on the behavior of organic beings. What is still lacking here is a grasp of connections of profound generality, but not a knowledge of order in itself.

The more a man is imbued with the ordered regularity of all events, the firmer becomes his conviction that there is no room left by the side of this ordered regularity for causes of a different nature. For him neither the rule of human nor the rule of Divine Will exists as an independent cause of natural events. To be sure, the doctrine of a personal God interfering with natural events could never be *refuted*, in the real sense, by science, for this doctrine can always take refuge in those domains in which scientific knowledge has not yet been able to set foot.

But I am persuaded that such behavior on the part of the representatives of religion would not only be unworthy but also fatal. For a doctrine which is able to maintain itself not in clear light but only in the dark, will of necessity lose its effect on mankind, with incalculable harm to human progress. In their struggle for the ethical good, teachers of religion must have the stature to give up the doctrine of a personal God, that is, give up that source of fear and hope which in the past placed such vast power in the hands of priests. In their labors they will have to avail themselves of those forces which are capable of cultivating the Good, the True, and the Beautiful in humanity itself. This is, to be sure, a more difficult but an incomparably more worthy task.[1] After religious teachers accomplish the refining process indicated, they will surely recognize with joy that true religion has been ennobled and made more profound by scientific knowledge.

If it is one of the goals of religion to liberate mankind as far as possible from the bondage of egocentric cravings, desires, and fears, scientific reasoning can aid religion in yet another sense. Although it is true that it is the goal of science to discover rules which permit the association and foretelling of facts, this is not its only aim. It also seeks to reduce the connections discovered to the smallest possible number of mutually independent conceptual elements. It is in this striving after the rational unification of the manifold that it en-counters its greatest successes, even though it is precisely this attempt which causes it to run the greatest risk of falling a prey to illusions. But whoever has undergone the intense experience of successful advances made in this domain, is moved by profound reverence for the rationality made manifest in existence. By way of the understanding he achieves a far-reaching emancipation from the shackles of personal hopes and desires, and thereby attains that humble attitude of mind towards the grandeur of reason incarnate in existence, which, in its profoundest depths, is inaccessible to man. This attitude, however, appears to me to be religious, in the highest sense of the word. And so it seems to me that science not only purifies the religious impulse of the dross of its anthropomorphism, but also contributes to a religious spiritualization of our understanding of life.

The further the spiritual evolution of mankind advances, the more certain it seems to me that the path to genuine religiosity does not lie through the fear of life, and the fear of death, and blind faith, but through striving after rational knowledge. In this sense I believe that the priest must become a teacher if he wishes to do justice to his lofty educational mission.

1. This thought is convincingly presented in Herbert Samuel's book, *Belief and Action*.

Religion and Ethics

From time immemorial, one of the unceasing quests of man has been for a satisfactory religion, a satisfactory pathway to virtue. The autobiographical passage by the essayist Agnes Repplier which opens this section tells a touching story of a little girl's first serious encounter with ethical problems. The three selections which follow offer a series of contrasting answers, given by men with different attitudes, to the questions, "What should a man believe?" and "How is a man to live?" They are arranged chronologically. The first sets forth the doctrines of the founder of the Christian religion. The second states the beliefs of an American mystic, Henry David Thoreau, who wrote a literary and philosophical masterpiece, the book *Walden*, in the middle of the nineteenth century. The third gives a twentieth-century viewpoint, one by C. S. Lewis, an essayist, novelist, and Oxford professor. (In connection with the problems raised in this section, Albert Einstein's essay "Science and Religion," page 247, presents another important twentieth-century attitude.)

Agnes Repplier

SIN

A personal discovery

I was twelve years old, and very happy in my convent school. I did not particularly mind studying my lessons, and I sometimes persuaded the less experienced nuns to accept a retentive memory as a substitute for intelligent understanding, with which it has nothing to do. I "got along" with other children, and I enjoyed my friends; and of such simple things is the life of a child composed.

Then came a disturbing letter from my mother, a letter which threatened the heart of my content. It was sensible and reasonable, and it said very plainly and very kindly that I had better not make an especial friend of Lilly Milton; "not an exclusive friend," wrote my mother, "not one whom you would expect to see intimately after you leave school."

I knew what all that meant. I was as innocent as a kitten; but divorces were not common in those conservative years, and Mrs. Milton had as many to her credit as if she were living—a highly esteemed and popular lady—to-day.

From *The Atlantic Monthly*, June 1938. Reprinted by permission of *The Atlantic Monthly* and Agnes Repplier.

I regretted my mother's tendency to confuse issues with unimportant details (a mistake which grown-up people often made), and I felt sure that if she knew Lilly—who was also as innocent as a kitten, and was blessed with the sweetest temper that God ever gave a little girl—she would be delighted that I had such an excellent friend. So I went on happily enough until ten days later, when Madame Rayburn, a nun for whom I cherished a very warm affection, was talking to me upon a familiar theme—the diverse ways in which I might improve my classwork and my general behavior. The subject did not interest me deeply,—repetition had staled its vivacity,—until my companion said the one thing that had plainly been uppermost in her mind: "And Agnes, how did you come to tell Lilly Milton that your mother did not want you to go with her? I never thought you could have been so deliberately unkind."

This brought me to my feet with a bound. "Tell Lilly!" I cried. "You could not have believed such a thing. It was Madame Bouron who told her."

A silence followed this revelation. The convent discipline was as strict for the nuns as for the pupils, and it was not their custom to criticize their superiors. Madame Bouron was mistress general, ranking next to the august head, and of infinitely more importance to us. She was a cold, severe, sardonic woman, and the general dislike felt for her had shaped itself into a cult. I had accepted this cult in simple good faith, having no personal grudge until she did this dreadful thing; and I may add that it was the eminently unwise custom of reading all the letters written to or by the pupils which stood responsible for the trouble. The order of nuns was a French one, and the habit of surveillance, which did not seem amiss in France, was ill-adapted to America. I had never before wasted a thought upon it. My weekly home letter and the less frequent but more communicative epistles from my mother might have been read in the market place for all I cared, until this miserable episode proved that a bad usage may be trusted to produce, sooner or later, bad results.

It was with visible reluctance that Madame Rayburn said after a long pause: "That alters the case. If Madame Bouron told Lilly, she must have had some good reason for doing so."

"There was no good reason," I protested. "There couldn't have been. But it doesn't matter. I told Lilly it wasn't so, and she believed me."

Madame Rayburn stared at me aghast. "You told Lilly it was not so?" she repeated.

I nodded. "I could not find out for two days what was the matter," I explained; "but I got it out of her at last, and I told her that my mother had never written a line to me about her. And she believed me."

"But my dear child," said the nun, "you have told a very grievous lie. What is more, you have borne false witness against your neighbor. When you said to Lilly that your mother had not written that letter, you made her believe that Madame Bouron had lied to her."

"She didn't mind believing that," I observed cheerfully, "and there was nothing else that I could say to make her feel all right."

"But a lie is a lie," protested the nun. "You will have to tell Lilly the truth."

I said nothing, but my silence was not the silence of acquiescence. Madame Rayburn must have recognized this fact, for she took another line of attack. When she spoke next. it was in a low voice and very earnestly. "Listen to me," she said. "Friday is the first of May. You are going to confession on Thursday. You will tell Father O'Harra the whole story just as you have told it to me, and whatever he bids you do, you must do it. Remember that if you go to confession and do not tell this you will commit the very great sin of sacrilege; and if you do not obey your confessor you will commit the sin of open disobedience to the Church."

I was more than a little frightened. It seemed to me that for the first time in my life I was confronted by grown-up iniquities to which I had been a stranger. The thought sobered me for two days. On the third I went to confession, and when I had finished with my customary offenses—which, as they seldom varied, were probably as familiar to the priest as they were to me—I told my serious tale. The silence with which it was received bore witness to its seriousness. No question was asked me; I had been too explicit to render questions needful. But after two minutes (which seemed like two hours) of thinking my confessor said: "A lie is a lie. It must be retracted. To-morrow you will do one of two things. You will tell your friend the truth, or you will tell Madame Bouron the whole story just as you told it to me. Do you understand?"

"Yes." I said in a faint little voice, no louder than a sigh.

"And you will do as I bid you?"

"Yes," I breathed again.

"Then I will give you absolution, and you may go to Communion. But remember, no later than to-morrow. Believe me, it will get no easier by delay."

Of that I felt tolerably sure, and it was with the courage of desperation that I knocked the next morning at the door of Madame Bouron's office. She gave me a glance of wonderment (I had never before paid her a voluntary call), and without pause or preamble I told my tale, told it with such bald uncompromising verity that it sounded worse than ever. She listened at first in amazement, then in anger. "So Lilly thinks I lied to her," she said at last.

"Yes," I answered.

"And suppose I send for her now and undeceive her."

"You can't do that," I said. "I should tell her again my mother did not write the letter, and she would believe me."

"If you told another such lie, you would be sent from the school."

"If I were sent home, Lilly would believe me. She would believe me all the more."

The anger died out of Madame Bouron's eyes, and a look of bewilderment came into them. I am disposed to think that despite her wide experience as nun and teacher, she had never before encountered an *idée fixe*, and found out that the pyramids are flexible compared to it. "You know," she said uncertainly, "that sooner or later you will have to do as your mother desires."

I made no answer. The "sooner or later" did not interest me at all. I was living now.

There was another long pause. When Madame Bouron spoke again it was in a grave and low voice. "I wish I had said nothing about your mother's letter," she said. "I thought I could settle matters quickly that way, but I was mistaken, and I must take the consequences of my error. You may go now. I will not speak to Lilly, or to anyone else about this affair."

I did not go. I sat stunned, and asking myself if she knew all that her silence would imply. Children seldom give adults much credit for intelligence. "But," I began feebly—

"But me no buts," she interrupted, rising to her feet. "I know what you are going to say; but I have not been the head of a school for years without bearing more than one injustice."

Now when I heard these words sadly spoken something broke up inside of me. It did not break gently, like the dissolving of a cloud; it broke like the bursting of a dam. Sobs shook my lean little body as though they would have torn it apart. Tears blinded me. With difficulty I gasped out three words. "You are good," I said.

Madame Bouron propelled me gently to the door, which I could not see because of my tears. "I wish I could say as much for you," she answered, "but I cannot. You have been very bad. You have been false to your mother, to whom you owe respect and obedience; you have been false to me; and you have been false to God. But you have been true to your friend."

She put me out of the door, and I stood in the corridor facing the clock. I was still shaken by sobs, but my heart was light as a bird. And, believe it or not, the supreme reason for my happiness was—not that my difficulties were over, though I was glad of that; and not that Lilly was safe from hurt, though I was glad of that; but that Madame Bouron, whom I had thought bad, had proved herself to be, according to the standards of childhood, as good as gold. My joy was like the joy of the blessed saints in Paradise.

THE SERMON ON THE MOUNT

And seeing the multitudes, he went up into a mountain: and when he was set, his disciples came unto him. And he opened his mouth, and taught them, saying: Blessed are the poor in spirit: for theirs is the kingdom of heaven.

Blessed are they that mourn: for they shall be comforted.

Blessed are the meek: for they shall inherit the earth.

Blessed are they which do hunger and thirst after righteousness: for they shall be filled.

Blessed are the merciful: for they shall obtain mercy.

Blessed are the pure in heart: for they shall see God.

Blessed are the peacemakers: for they shall be called the children of God.

Blessed are they which are persecuted for righteousness' sake: for theirs is the kingdom of heaven.

Blessed are ye, when men shall revile you, and persecute you, and shall say all manner of evil against you falsely, for my sake.

Rejoice and be exceeding glad: for great is your reward in heaven: for so persecuted they the prophets which were before you.

Ye are the salt of the earth: but if the salt have lost his savour, wherewith shall it be salted? it is thenceforth good for nothing, but to be cast out, and to be trodden under foot of men.

Ye are the light of the world. A city that is set on an hill cannot be hid. Neither do men light a candle, and put it under a bushel, but on a candlestick; and it giveth light unto all that are in the house. Let your light so shine before men, that they may see your good works, and glorify your Father which is in heaven.

Think not that I am come to destroy the law, or the prophets: I am not come to destroy, but to fulfil. For verily I say unto you, Till heaven and earth pass, one jot or one tittle shall in no wise pass from the law, till all be fulfilled. Whosoever therefore shall break one of these least commandments, and shall teach men so, he shall be called the least in the kingdom of heaven: but whosoever shall do and teach them, the same shall be called great in the kingdom of heaven. For I say unto you, That except your righteousness shall exceed the righteousness of the scribes and Pharisees, ye shall in no case enter into the kingdom of heaven.

Ye have heard that it was said by them of old time, Thou shalt not kill; and whosoever shall kill shall be in danger of the judgment. But I say unto you, That whosoever is angry with his brother without a cause shall be in danger of the judgment: and whosoever shall say to his brother, Raca, shall be in danger of the council: but whosoever shall say, Thou fool, shall be in danger of hell fire. Therefore if thou bring thy gift to the altar, and there rememberest that thy brother hath ought against thee; leave there thy gift before the altar, and go thy way; first be reconciled to thy brother, and then come and offer thy gift. Agree with thine adversary quickly, whiles thou art in the way with him; lest at any time the adversary deliver thee to the judge, and the judge deliver thee to the officer, and thou be cast into prison. Verily I say unto thee, Thou shalt by no means come out thence, till thou hast paid the uttermost farthing.

Ye have heard that it was said by them of old time, Thou shalt not commit adultery. But I say unto you, That whosoever looketh on a woman to lust after her hath committed adultery with her already in his heart.

And if thy right eye offend thee, pluck it out, and cast it from thee: for it is profitable for thee that one of thy members should perish, and not that thy whole body should be cast into hell. And if thy right hand offend thee, cut it off, and cast it from thee: for it is profitable for thee that one of thy members should perish, and not that thy whole body should be cast into hell.

It hath been said, Whosoever shall put away his wife, let him give her a writing of divorcement, but I say unto you, That whosoever shall put away his wife, saving for the cause of fornication, causeth her to commit adultery: and whosoever shall marry her that is divorced committeth adultery.

Again, ye have heard that it hath been said by them of old time, Thou shalt not forswear thyself, but shalt perform unto the Lord thine oaths, but I say unto you, Swear not at all; neither by heaven; for it is God's throne; nor by the earth; for it is his footstool: neither by Jerusalem; for it is the city of the great King. Neither shalt thou swear by thy head, because thou canst not make one hair white or black. But let your communication be, Yea, yea; Nay, nay: for whatsoever is more than these cometh of evil.

Ye have heard that it hath been said, An eye for an eye, and a tooth for a tooth: but I say unto you, That ye resist not evil: but whosoever shall smite thee on thy right cheek, turn to him the other also. And if any man will sue thee at the law, and take away thy coat, let him have thy cloke also. And whosoever shall compel thee to go a mile, go with him twain. Give to him that asketh thee, and from him that would borrow of thee turn not thou away.

Ye have heard that it hath been said, Thou shalt love thy neighbour, and hate thine enemy. But I say unto you, Love your enemies, bless them that curse you, do good to them that hate you, and pray for them which despitefully use you, and persecute you that ye may be the children of your Father which is in heaven: for he maketh his sun to rise on the evil and on the good, and sendeth rain on the just and on the unjust. For if ye love them which love you, what reward have ye? do not even the publicans the same? And if ye salute your brethren only, what do ye more than others? do not even the publicans so?

Be ye therefore perfect, even as your Father which is in heaven is perfect.

Take heed that ye do not your alms before men, to be seen of them: otherwise ye have no reward of your Father which is in heaven. Therefore when thou doest thine alms, do not sound a trumpet before thee, as the hypocrites do in the synagogues and in the streets, that they may have the glory of men. Verily I say unto you, they have their reward.

But when thou doest alms, let not thy left hand know what thy right hand doeth that thine alms may be in secret: and thy Father which seeth in secret himself shall reward thee openly.

And when thou prayest, thou shalt not be as the hypocrites are: for they love to pray standing in the synagogues and in the corners of the streets, that they may be seen of men. Verily I say unto you, They have their reward. But thou, when thou prayest, enter into thy closet, and when thou hast shut thy door, pray to thy Father which is in secret; and thy Father which seeth in secret shall reward thee openly. But when ye pray, use not vain repetitions, as the heathen do: for they think that they shall be heard for their much speaking. Be not ye therefore like unto them: for your Father knoweth what things ye have need of, before ye ask him.

After this manner therefore pray ye: Our Father which art in heaven, Hallowed be thy name. Thy kingdom come. Thy will be done in earth, as it is in heaven. Give us this day our daily bread. And forgive us our debts, as we forgive our debtors. And lead us not into temptation, but deliver us from evil: For thine is the kingdom, and the power, and the glory, for ever. Amen.

For if ye forgive men their trespasses, your heavenly Father will also forgive you. But if ye forgive not men their trespasses, neither will your Father forgive your trespasses.

Moreover when ye fast, be not, as the hypocrites, of a sad countenance: for they disfigure their faces, that they may appear unto men to fast. Verily I say unto you, They have their reward. But thou, when thou fastest, anoint thine head, and wash thy face; that thou appear not unto men to fast, but unto thy Father which is in secret: and thy Father, which seeth in secret shall reward thee openly.

Lay not up for yourselves treasures upon earth, where moth and rust doth corrupt, and where thieves break through and steal. But lay up for yourselves treasures in heaven, where neither moth nor rust doth corrupt, and where thieves do not break through nor steal. For where your treasure is, there will your heart be also. The light of the body is the eye: if therefore thine eye be single, thy whole body shall be full of light. But if thine eye be evil, thy whole body shall be full of darkness. If therefore the light that is in thee be darkness, how great is that darkness!

No man can serve two masters: for either he will hate the one, and love the other; or else he will hold to the one, and despise the other. Ye cannot serve God and mammon. Therefore I say unto you, Take no thought for your life, what ye shall eat, or what ye shall drink; nor yet for your body, what ye shall put on. Is not the life more than meat, and the body than raiment?

Behold the fowls of the air: for they sow not, neither do they reap, nor gather into barns; yet your heavenly Father feedeth them. Are ye not much better than they? Which of you by taking thought can add one cubit unto his stature?

And why take ye thought for raiment? Consider the lilies of the field, how they grow; they toil not, neither do they spin: And yet I say unto you, That even Solomon in all his glory was not arrayed like one of these.

Wherefore, if God so clothe the grass of the field, which today is, and tomorrow is cast into the oven, shall he not much more clothe you, O ye of little faith?

Therefore take no thought, saying, What shall we eat? or, What shall we drink? or, Wherewithal shall we be clothed?

For after all these things do the Gentiles seek. For your heavenly Father knoweth that ye have need of all these things.

But seek ye first the kingdom of God, and his righteousness; and all these things shall be added unto you.

Take therefore no thought for the morrow: for the morrow shall take thought for the things of itself. Sufficient unto the day is the evil thereof.

Judge not, that ye be not judged. For with what judgment ye judge, ye shall be judged: and with what measure ye mete, it shall be measured to you again. And why beholdest thou the mote that is in thy brother's eye, but considerest not the beam that is in thine own eye? Or how wilt thou say to thy brother, Let me pull out the mote out of thine eye; and, behold, a beam is in thine own eye? Thou hypocrite, first cast out the beam out of thine own eye; and then shalt thou see clearly to cast out the mote out of thy brother's eye.

Give not that which is holy unto the dogs, neither cast ye your pearls before swine, lest they trample them under their feet, and turn again and rend you.

Ask and it shall be given you; seek, and ye shall find; knock, and it shall be opened unto you: for every one that asketh receiveth; and he that seeketh findeth; and to him that knocketh it shall be opened. Or what man is there of you, whom if his son ask bread, will he give him a stone? Or if he ask a fish, will he give him a serpent? If ye then, being evil, know how to give good gifts unto your children, how much more shall your Father which is in heaven give good things to them that ask him?

Therefore all things whatsoever ye would that men should do to you, do ye even so to them: for this is the law and the prophets.

Enter ye in at the strait gate: for wide is the gate, and broad is the way, that leadeth to destruction, and many there be which go in thereat, because strait is the gate, and narrow is the way, which leadeth unto life, and few there be that find it.

Beware of false prophets, which come to you in sheep's clothing, but inwardly they are ravening wolves. Ye shall know them by their fruits. Do men gather grapes of thorns, or figs of thistles? Even so every good tree bringeth forth good fruit; but a corrupt tree bringeth forth evil fruit. A good tree cannot bring forth evil fruit, neither can a corrupt tree bring forth good fruit. Every tree that bringeth not forth good fruit is hewn down, and cast into the fire. Wherefore by their fruits ye shall know them.

Not every one that saith unto me, Lord, Lord, shall enter into the kingdom of heaven; but he that doeth the will of my Father which is in heaven. Many will say to me in that day, Lord, Lord, have we not prophesied in thy name? and in thy name have cast out devils? and in thy name done many wonderful works? And then will I profess unto them, I never knew you: depart from me, ye that work iniquity.

Therefore whosoever heareth these sayings of mine, and doeth them, I will liken him unto a wise man, which built his house upon a rock. And the rain descended, and the floods came, and the winds blew, and beat upon that house; and it fell not: for it was founded upon a rock.

And every one that heareth these sayings of mine, and doeth them not, shall be likened unto a foolish man, which built his house upon the sand. And the rain descended, and the floods came, and the winds blew, and beat upon that house; and it fell: and great was the fall of it.

And it came to pass, when Jesus had ended these sayings, the people were astonished at his doctrine. For he taught them as one having authority, and not as the scribes.

Henry David Thoreau

HIGHER LAWS

As I came home through the woods with my string of fish, trailing my pole, it being now quite dark, I caught a glimpse of a woodchuck stealing across my path, and felt a strange thrill of savage delight, and was strongly tempted to seize and devour him raw; not that I was hungry then, except for that wildness which he represented. Once or twice, however, while I lived at the pond, I found myself ranging the woods, like a half-starved hound, with a strange abandonment, seeking some kind of venison which I might devour, and no morsel could have been too savage for me. The wildest scenes had become unaccountably familiar. I found in myself, and still find, an instinct toward a higher, or, as it is named, spiritual life, as do most men, and another toward a primitive, rank and savage one, and I reverence them both. I love the wild not less than the good. The wildness and adventure that are in fishing still recommended it to me. I like sometimes to take rank hold on life and spend my day more as the animals do. Perhaps I have owed to this employment and to hunting, when quite young, my closest acquaintance with Nature. They early introduce us to and detain us in scenery with which otherwise, at that age, we should have little acquaintance. Fishermen, hunters, woodchoppers, and others, spending their lives in the fields and woods, in a peculiar sense a part of Nature themselves, are often in a more favorable mood for observing her, in the intervals of their pursuits, than philosophers or poets even, who approach her with expectation. She is not afraid to exhibit herself to them. The traveller on the prairie is naturally a hunter, on the head waters of the Missouri and Columbia a trapper, and at the Falls of St. Mary a fisherman. He who is only a traveller learns things at second-hand and by the halves, and is poor authority. We are most interested when science reports what those men already know practically or instinctively, for that alone is a true *humanity*, or account of human experience.

They mistake who assert that the Yankee has few amusements, because he has not so many public holidays, and men and boys do not play so many games as they do in England, for here the more primitive but solitary amusements of hunting, fishing, and the like have not yet given place to the former. Almost every New England boy among my contemporaries shouldered a fowling-piece between the ages of ten and fourteen; and his hunting and fishing grounds were not limited, like the preserves of an English nobleman, but were more boundless even than those of a savage. No wonder, then, that he did not oftener stay to play on the common. But already a change is taking place, owing, not to an increased humanity, but to an increased scarcity of game, for perhaps the hunter is the greatest friend of the animals hunted, not excepting the Humane Society.

Moreover, when at the pond, I wished sometimes to add fish to my fare for variety. I have actually fished from the same kind of necessity that the first fishers did. Whatever humanity I might conjure up against it was all factitious, and concerned my philosophy more than my feelings. I speak of fishing only now, for I had long felt differently about fowling, and sold my gun before I went to the woods. Not that I am less humane than others, but I did not perceive that my feelings were much affected. I did not pity the fishes nor the worms. This was habit. As for fowling, during the last years that I carried a gun my excuse was that I was studying ornithology, and sought only new or rare birds. But I confess that I am now inclined to think that there is a finer way of studying ornithology than this. It requires so much closer attention to the habits of the birds, that, if for that reason only, I have been willing to omit the gun. Yet notwithstanding the objection on the score of humanity, I am compelled to doubt if equally valuable sports are ever substituted for these; and when some of my friends have asked me anxiously about their boys, whether they should let them hunt, I have answered, yes,—remembering that it was one of the best parts of my education,—*make* them hunters, though sportsmen only at first, if possible, mighty hunters at last, so that they shall not find game large enough for them in this or any vegetable wilderness,—hunters as well as fishers of men. Thus far I am of the opinion of Chaucer's nun, who

> "yave not of the text a pulled hen
> That saith that hunters ben not holy men."

There is a period in the history of the individual, as of the race, when the hunters are the "best men," as the Algonquins called them. We cannot but pity the boy who has never fired a gun; he is no more humane, while his education has been sadly neglected. This was my answer with respect to those youths who were bent on this pursuit, trusting that they would soon outgrow it. No humane being, past the thoughtless age of boyhood, will wantonly murder any creature which holds its life by the same tenure that he does. The hare in its extremity cries like a child. I warn you, mothers, that my sympathies do not always make the usual phil*anthropic* distinctions.

Such is oftenest the young man's introduction to the forest, and the most original part of himself. He goes thither at first as a hunter and fisher, until at last, if he has the seeds of a better life in him, he distinguishes his proper objects, as a poet or naturalist it may be, and leaves the gun and fish-pole behind. The mass of men are still and always young in this respect. In some countries a hunting parson is no uncommon sight. Such a one might make a good shepherd's dog, but is far from being the Good Shepherd. I have been surprised to consider that the only obvious employment, except woodchopping, ice-cutting, or the like business, whichever to my knowledge detained at Walden Pond for a whole half-day any of my fellow-citizens, whether fathers or children of the town, with just one exception, was fishing. Commonly they did not think that they were lucky, or well paid for their time, unless they got a long string of fish, though they had the opportunity of seeing the pond all the

while. They might go there a thousand times before the sediment of fishing
would sink to the bottom and leave their purpose pure; but no doubt such a
clarifying process would be going on all the while. The Governor and his Council faintly remember the pond, for they went a-fishing there when they were
boys; but now they are too old and dignified to go a-fishing, and so they know it
no more forever. Yet even they expect to go to heaven at last. If the legislature regards it, it is chiefly to regulate the number of hooks to be used there;
but they know nothing about the hook of hooks with which to angle for the
pond itself, impaling the legislature for a bait. Thus, even in civilized communities, the embryo man passes through the hunter stage of development.

I have found repeatedly, of late years, that I cannot fish without falling a
little in self-respect. I have tried it again and again. I have skill at it, and, like
many of my fellows, a certain instinct for it, which revives from time to time,
but always when I have done I feel that it would have been better if I had not
fished. I think that I do not mistake. It is a faint intimation, yet so are the first
streaks of morning. There is unquestionably this instinct in me which belongs
to the lower orders of creation; yet with every year I am less a fisherman, though
without more humanity or even wisdom; at present I am no fisherman at all.
But I see that if I were to live in a wilderness I should again be tempted to become a fisher and hunter in earnest. Beside, there is something essentially unclean about this diet and all flesh, and I began to see where housework com-
mences, and whence the endeavor, which costs so much, to wear a tidy and
respectable appearance each day, to keep the house sweet and free from all ill
odors and sights. Having been my own butcher and scullion and cook, as well
as the gentleman for whom the dishes were served up, I can speak from an
unusually complete experience. The practical objection to animal food in my
case was its uncleanness; and besides, when I had caught and cleaned and
cooked and eaten my fish, they seemed not to have fed me essentially. It was insignificant and unnecessary, and cost more than it came to. A little bread or a
few potatoes would have done as well, with less trouble and filth. Like many
of my contemporaries, I had rarely for many years used animal food, or tea, or
coffee, etc.; not so much because of any ill effects which I had traced to them,
as because they were not agreeable to my imagination. The repugnance to
animal food is not the effect of experience, but is an instinct. It appeared more
beautiful to live low and fare hard in many respects; and though I never did so,
I went far enough to please my imagination. I believe that every man who has
ever been earnest to preserve his higher or poetic faculties in the best condition
has been particularly inclined to abstain from animal food, and from much
food of any kind. It is a significant fact stated by entomologists,—I find it in
Kirby and Spence,—that "some insects in their perfect state, though furnished
with organs of feeding, make no use of them;" and they lay it down as "a general
rule, that almost all insects in this state eat much less than in that of larvae.
The voracious caterpillar when transformed into a butterfly . . . and the gluttonous maggot when become a fly" content themselves with a drop or two of
honey or some other sweet liquid. The abdomen under the wings of the butter-

fly still represents the larva. This is the tidbit which tempts his insectivorous fate. The gross feeder is a man in the larva state; and there are whole nations in that condition, nations without fancy or imagination, whose vast abdomens betray them.

It is hard to provide and cook so simple and clean a diet as will not offend the imagination; but this, I think, is to be fed when we feed the body; they should both sit down at the same table. Yet perhaps this may be done. The fruits eaten temperately need not make us ashamed of our appetites, nor interrupt the worthiest pursuits. But put an extra condiment into your dish, and it will poison you. It is not worth the while to live by rich cookery. Most men would feel shame if caught preparing with their own hands precisely such a dinner, whether of animal or vegetable food, as is every day prepared for them by others. Yet till this is otherwise we are not civilized, and, if gentlemen and ladies, are not true men and women. This certainly suggests what change is to be made. It may be vain to ask why the imagination will not be reconciled to flesh and fat. I am satisfied that it is not. Is it not a reproach that man is a carnivorous animal? True, he can and does live, in a great measure, by preying on other animals; but this is a miserable way,—as any one who will go to snaring rabbits, or slaughtering lambs, may learn,—and he will be regarded as a benefactor of his race who shall teach man to confine himself to a more innocent and wholesome diet. Whatever my own practice may be, I have no doubt that it is a part of the destiny of the human race, in its gradual improvement, to leave off eating animals, as surely as the savage tribes have left off eating each other when they came in contact with the more civilized.

If one listens to the faintest but constant suggestions of his genius, which are certainly true, he sees not to what extremes, or even insanity, it may lead him; and yet that way, as he grows more resolute and faithful, his road lies. The faintest assured objection which one healthy man feels will at length prevail over the arguments and customs of mankind. No man ever followed his genius till it misled him. Though the result were bodily weakness, yet perhaps no one can say that the consequences were to be regretted, for these were a life in conformity to higher principles. If the day and the night are such that you greet them with joy, and life emits a fragrance like flowers and sweet-scented herbs, is more elastic, more starry, more immortal,—that is your success. All nature is your congratulation, and you have cause momentarily to bless yourself. The greatest gains and values are farthest from being appreciated. We easily come to doubt if they exist. We soon forget them. They are the highest reality. Perhaps the facts most astounding and most real are never communicated by man to man. The true harvest of my daily life is somewhat as intangible and indescribable as the tints of morning or evening. It is a little star-dust caught, a segment of the rainbow which I have clutched.

Yet, for my part, I was never unusually squeamish; I could sometimes eat a fried rat with a good relish, if it were necessary. I am glad to have drunk water so long, for the same reason that I prefer the natural sky to an opium-eater's heaven. I would fain keep sober always; and there are infinite degrees of drunkenness. I believe that water is the only drink for a wise man; wine is not so noble a liquor; and think of dashing the hopes of a morning with a cup of warm coffee, or of an evening with a dish of tea! Ah, how low I fall when I am tempted by them! Even music may be intoxicating. Such apparently slight causes destroyed Greece and Rome, and will destroy England and America. Of all ebriosity, who does not prefer to be intoxicated by the air he breathes? I have found it to be the most serious objection to coarse labors long continued, that they compelled me to eat and drink coarsely also. But to tell the truth, I find myself at present somewhat less particular in these respects. I carry less religion to the table, ask no blessing; not because I am wiser than I was, but, I am obliged to confess, because, however much it is to be regretted, with years I have grown more coarse and indifferent. Perhaps these questions are entertained only in youth, as most believe of poetry. My practice is "nowhere," my opinion is here. Nevertheless I am far from regarding myself as one of those privileged ones to whom the Ved refers when it says, that "he who has true faith in the Omnipresent Supreme Being may eat all that exists," that is, is not bound to inquire what is his food, or who prepares it; and even in their case it is to be observed, as a Hindoo commentator has remarked, that the Vedant limits this privilege to "the time of distress."

Who has not sometimes derived an inexpressible satisfaction from his food in which appetite had no share? I have been thrilled to think that I owed a mental perception to the commonly gross sense of taste, that I have been inspired through the palate, that some berries which I had eaten on a hillside had fed my genius. "The soul not being mistress of herself," says Thsengtseu, "one looks, and one does not see; one listens, and one does not hear; one eats, and one does not know the savor of food." He who distinguishes the true savor of his food can never be a glutton; he who does not cannot be otherwise. A puritan may go to his brown-bread crust with as gross an appetite as ever an alderman to his turtle. Not that food which entereth into the mouth defileth a man, but the appetite with which it is eaten. It is neither the quality nor the quantity, but the devotion to sensual savors; when that which is eaten is not a viand to sustain our animal, or inspire our spiritual life, but food for the worms that possess us. If the hunter has a taste for mud-turtles, muskrats, and other such savage tidbits, the fine lady indulges a taste for jelly made of a calf's foot, or for sardines from over the sea, and they are even. He goes to the mill-pond, she to her preserve-pot. The wonder is how they, how you and I, can live this slimy, beastly life, eating and drinking.

Our whole life is startlingly moral. There is never an instant's truce between virtue and vice. Goodness is the only investment that never fails. In the music of the harp which trembles round the world it is the insisting on this which thrills us. The harp is the travelling patterer for the Universe's Insurance Company, recommending its laws, and our little goodness is all the assessment that we pay. Though the youth at last grows indifferent, the laws of the universe are not indifferent, but are forever on the side of the most sensitive. Listen to every zephyr for some reproof, for it is surely there, and he is unfortunate who does not hear it. We cannot touch a string or move a stop but the charming moral transfixes us. Many an irksome noise, go a long way off, is heard as music, a proud, sweet satire on the meanness of our lives.

We are conscious of an animal in us, which awakens in proportion as our higher nature slumbers. It is reptile and sensual, and perhaps cannot be wholly expelled; like the worms which, even in life and health, occupy our bodies. Possibly we may withdraw from it, but never change its nature. I fear that it may enjoy a certain health of its own; that we may be well, yet not pure. The other day I picked up the lower jaw of a hog, with white and sound teeth and tusks which suggested that there was an animal health and vigor distinct from the spiritual. This creature succeeded by other means than temperance and purity. "That in which men differ from brute beasts," says Mencius, "is a thing very inconsiderable; the common herd lose it very soon; superior men preserve it carefully." Who knows what sort of life would result if we had attained to purity? If I knew so wise a man as could teach me purity I would go to seek him forthwith. "A command over our passions, and over the external senses of the body, and good acts, are declared by the Ved to be indispensable in the mind's approximation to God." Yet the spirit can for the time pervade and control every member and function of the body, and transmute what in form is the grossest sensuality into purity and devotion. The generative energy, which, when we are loose, dissipates and makes us unclean, when we are continent invigorates and inspires us. Chastity is the flowering of man; and what are called Genius, Heroism, Holiness, and the like, are but various fruits which succeed it. Man flows at once to God when the channel of purity is open. By turns our purity inspires and our impurity casts us down. He is blessed who is assured that the animal is dying out in him day by day, and the divine being established. Perhaps there is none but has cause for shame on account of the inferior and brutish nature to which he is allied. I fear that we are such gods or demigods only as fauns and satyrs, the divine allied to beasts, the creatures of appetite, and that, to some extent, our very life is our disgrace.—

"How happy's he who hath due place assigned
To his beasts and disafforested his mind! . . .
Can use his horse, goat, wolf, and ev'ry beast,
And is not ass himself to all the rest!
Else man not only is the herd of swine,
But he's those devils too which did incline
Them to a headlong rage, and made them worse."

All sensuality is one, though it takes many forms; all purity is one. It is the same whether a man eat, or drink, or cohabit, or sleep sensually. They are but one appetite, and we only need to see a person do any one of these things to know how great a sensualist he is. The impure can neither stand nor sit with purity. When the reptile is attacked at one mouth of his burrow, he shows himself at another. If you would be chaste, you must be temperate. What is chastity? How shall a man know if he is chaste? He shall not know it. We have heard of this virtue, but we know not what it is. We speak conformably to the rumor which we have heard. From exertion come wisdom and purity; from sloth ignorance and sensuality. In the student sensuality is a sluggish habit of mind. An unclean person is universally a slothful one, one who sits by a stove, whom the sun shines on prostrate, who reposes without being fatigued. If you would avoid uncleanness, and all the sins, work earnestly, though it be at clean-ing a stable. Nature is hard to be overcome, but she must be overcome. What avails it that you are Christian, if you are not purer than the heathen, if you deny yourself no more, if you are not more religious? I know of many systems of religion esteemed heathenish whose precepts fill the reader with shame, and provoke him to new endeavors, though it be to the performance of rites merely.

I hesitate to say these things, but it is not because of the subject—I care not how obscene my *words* are,—but because I cannot speak of them without betraying my impurity. We discourse freely without shame of one form of sensuality, and are silent about another. We are so degraded that we cannot speak simply of the necessary functions of human nature. In earlier ages, in some countries, every function was reverently spoken of and regulated by law. Nothing was too trivial for the Hindoo lawgiver, however offensive it may be to modern taste. He teaches how to eat, drink, cohabit, void excrement and urine, and the like, elevating what is mean, and does not falsely excuse himself by calling these things trifles.

Every man is the builder of a temple, called his body, to the god he worships, after a style purely his own, nor can he get off by hammering marble instead. We are all sculptors and painters, and our material is our own flesh and blood and bones. Any nobleness begins at once to refine a man's features, any meanness or sensuality to imbrute them.

John Farmer sat at his door one September evening, after a hard day's work, his mind still running on his labor more or less. Having bathed, he sat down to re-create his intellectual man. It was a rather cool evening, and some of his neighbors were apprehending a frost. He had not attended to the train of his thoughts long when he heard some one playing on a flute, and that sound harmonized with his mood. Still he thought of his work; but the burden of his thought was, that though this kept running in his head, and he found himself planning and contriving it against his will, yet it concerned him very little. It was no more than the scurf of his skin, which was constantly shuffled off. But the notes of the flute came home to his ears out of a different sphere from that he worked in, and suggested work for certain faculties which slumbered in him. They gently did away with the street, and the village, and the state in which he lived. A voice said to him, Why do you stay here and live this mean moiling life, when a glorious existence is possible for you? Those same stars twinkle over other fields than these.—But how to come out of this condition and actually migrate thither? All that he could think of was to practice some new austerity, to let his mind descend into his body and redeem it, and treat himself with ever increasing respect.

C. S. Lewis

from MERE CHRISTIANITY[1]

1. The Law of Human Nature

Everyone has heard people quarrelling. Sometimes it sounds funny and sometimes it sounds merely unpleasant; but however it sounds, I believe we can learn something very important from listening to the kind of things they say. They say things like this: "How'd you like it if anyone did the same to you?"— "That's my seat, I was there first"—"Leave him alone, he isn't doing you any harm"—"Why should you shove in first?"—"Give me a bit of your orange, I gave you a bit of mine"—"Come on, you promised." People say things like that every day, educated people as well as uneducated, and children as well as grown-ups.

Now what interests me about all these remarks is that the man who makes them is not merely saying that the other man's behaviour does not happen to please him. He is appealing to some kind of standard of behaviour which he expects the other man to know about. And the other man very seldom replies: "To hell with your standard." Nearly always he tries to make out that what he has been doing does not really go against the standard, or that if it does there is some special excuse. He pretends there is some special reason in this particular case why the person who took the seat first should not keep it, or that things were quite different when he was given the bit of orange, or that something has turned up which lets him off keeping his promise. It looks, in fact, very much as if both parties had in mind some kind of Law or Rule of fair play or decent behaviour or morality or whatever you like to call it, about which they really agreed. And they have. If they had not, they might, of course, fight like animals, but they could not *quarrel* in the human sense of the word. Quarrelling means trying to show that the other man is in the wrong. And there would be no sense in trying to do that unless you and he had some sort of agreement as to what Right and Wrong are; just as there would be no sense in saying that a footballer had committed a foul unless there was some agreement about the rules of football.

Now this Law or Rule about Right and Wrong used to be called the Law of Nature. Nowadays, when we talk of the "laws of nature" we usually mean things like gravitation, or heredity, or the laws of chemistry. But when the older

1. The contents of this book were first presented by Mr. Lewis in the form of radio broadcasts over the BBC and then published in three separate parts as *The Case for Christianity* (1943), *Christian Behavior* (1943), and *Beyond Personality* (1945). In the printed versions he made a few additions to what he had said at the microphone, but otherwise left the text much as it had been.

thinkers called the Law of Right and Wrong "the Law of Nature," they really meant the Law of *Human* Nature. The idea was that, just as all bodies are governed by the law of gravitation and organisms by biological laws, so the creature called man also had *his* law—with this great difference, that a body could not choose whether it obeyed the law of gravitation or not, but a man could choose either to obey the Law of Human Nature or to disobey it.

We may put this in another way. Each man is at every moment subjected to several different sets of law but there is only one of these which he is free to disobey. As a body, he is subjected to gravitation and cannot disobey it; if you leave him unsupported in mid-air, he has no more choice about falling than a stone has. As an organism, he is subjected to various biological laws which he cannot disobey any more than an animal can. That is, he cannot disobey those laws which he shares with other things; but the law which is peculiar to his human nature, the law he does not share with animals or vegetables or inorganic things, is the one he can disobey if he chooses.

This law was called the Law of Nature because people thought that every one knew it by nature and did not need to be taught it. They did not mean, of course, that you might not find an odd individual here and there who did not know it, just as you find a few people who are colour-blind or have no ear for a tune. But taking the race as a whole, they thought that the human idea of decent behaviour was obvious to every one. And I believe they were right. If they were not, then all the things we said about the war were nonsense. What was the sense in saying the enemy were in the wrong unless Right is a real thing which the Nazis at bottom knew as well as we did and ought to have practised? If they had had no notion of what we mean by right, then, though we might still have had to fight them, we could no more have blamed them for that than for the colour of their hair.

I know that some people say the idea of a Law of Nature or decent behaviour known to all men is unsound, because different civilisations and different ages have had quite different moralities.

But this is not true. There have been differences between their moralities, but these have never amounted to anything like a total difference. If anyone will take the trouble to compare the moral teaching of, say, the ancient Egyptians, Babylonians, Hindus, Chinese, Greeks and Romans, what will really strike him will be how very like they are to each other and to our own. Some of the evidence for this I have put together in the appendix of another book called *The Abolition of Man;* but for our present purpose I need only ask the reader to think what a totally different morality would mean. Think of a country where people were admired for running away in battle, or where a man felt proud of double-crossing all the people who had been kindest to him. You might just as well try to imagine a country where two and two made five. Men have differed as regards what people you ought to be unselfish to—whether it was only your own family, or your fellow countrymen, or everyone. But they have always agreed that you ought not to put yourself first. Selfishness has never been admired. Men have differed as to whether you should have one wife or four. But they have always agreed that you must not simply have any woman you liked.

But the most remarkable thing is this. Whenever you find a man who says he does not believe in a real Right and Wrong, you will find the same man going back on this a moment later. He may break his promise to you, but if you try breaking one to him he will be complaining "It's not fair" before you can say Jack Robinson. A nation may say treaties do not matter; but then, next minute, they spoil their case by saying that the particular treaty they want to break was an unfair one. But if treaties do not matter, and if there is no such thing as Right and Wrong—in other words, if there is no Law of Nature—what is the difference between a fair treaty and an unfair one? Have they not let the cat out of the bag and shown that, whatever they say, they really know the Law of Nature just like anyone else?

It seems, then, we are forced to believe in a real Right and Wrong. People may be sometimes mistaken about them, just as people sometimes get their sums wrong; but they are not a matter of mere taste and opinion any more than the multiplication table. Now if we are agreed about that, I go on to my next point, which is this. None of us are really keeping the Law of Nature. If there are any exceptions among you, I apologise to them. They had much better read some other work, for nothing I am going to say concerns them. And now, turning to the ordinary human beings who are left:

I hope you will not misunderstand what I am going to say. I am not preaching, and Heaven knows I do not pretend to be better than anyone else. I am only trying to call attention to a fact; the fact that this year, or this month, or, more likely, this very day, we have failed to practise ourselves the kind of behaviour we expect from other people. There may be all sorts of excuses for us. That time you were so unfair to the children was when you were very tired. That slightly shady business about the money—the one you have almost forgotten—came when you were very hard up. And what you promised to do for old So-and-so and have never done—well, you never would have promised if you had known how frightfully busy you were going to be. And as for your behaviour to your wife (or husband) or sister (or brother) if I knew how irritating they could be, I would not wonder at it—and who the dickens am I, anyway? I am just the same. That is to say, I do not succeed in keeping the Law of Nature very well, and the moment anyone tells me I am not keeping it, there starts up in my mind a string of excuses as long as your arm. The question at the moment is not whether they are good excuses. The point is that they are one more proof of how deeply, whether we like it or not, we believe in the Law of Nature. If we do not believe in decent behaviour, why should we be so anxious to make excuses for not having behaved decently? The truth is, we believe in decency so much—we feel the Rule or Law pressing on us so—that we cannot bear to face the fact that we are breaking it, and consequently we try to shift the responsibility. For you notice that it is only for our bad behaviour that we find all these explanations. It is only our bad temper that we put down to being tired or worried or hungry; we put our good temper down to ourselves.

Those, then, are the two points I wanted to make. First, that human beings, all over the earth, have this curious idea that they ought to behave in a certain way, and cannot really get rid of it. Secondly, that they do not in fact behave in that way. They know the Law of Nature; they break it. These two facts are the foundation of all clear thinking about ourselves and the universe we live in.

2. Some Objections

If they are the foundation, I had better stop to make that foundation firm before I go on. Some of the letters I have had show that a good many people find it difficult to understand just what this Law of Human Nature, or Moral Law, or Rule of Decent Behaviour is.

For example, some people wrote to me saying, "Isn't what you call the Moral Law simply our herd instinct and hasn't it been developed just like all our other instincts?" Now I do not deny that we may have a herd instinct: but that is not what I mean by the Moral Law. We all know what if feels like to be prompted by instinct—by mother love, or sexual instinct, or the instinct for food. It means that you feel a strong want or desire to act in a certain way. And, of course, we sometimes do feel just that sort of desire to help another person: and no doubt that desire is due to the herd instinct. But feeling a desire to help is quite different from feeling that you ought to help whether you want to or not. Supposing you hear a cry for help from a man in danger. You will probably feel two desires—one a desire to give help (due to your herd instinct), the other a desire to keep out of danger (due to the instinct for self-preservation). But you will find inside you, in addition to these two impulses, a third thing which tells you that you ought to follow the impulse to help, and suppress the impulse to run away. Now this thing that judges between two instincts, that decides which should be encouraged, cannot itself be either of them. You might as well say that the sheet of music which tells you, at a given moment, to play one note on the piano and not another, is itself one of the notes on the keyboard. The Moral Law tells us the tune we have to play: our instincts are merely the keys.

Another way of seeing that the Moral Law is not simply one of our instincts is this. If two instincts are in conflict, and there is nothing in a creature's mind except those two instincts, obviously the stronger of the two must win. But at those moments when we are most conscious of the Moral Law, it usually seems to be telling us to side with the weaker of the two impulses. You probably *want* to be safe much more than you want to help the man who is drowning; but the Moral Law tells you to help him all the same. And surely it often tells us to try to make the right impulse stronger than it naturally is? I mean, we often feel it our duty to stimulate the herd instinct, by waking up our imaginations and arousing our pity and so on, so as to get up enough steam for doing the right thing. But clearly we are not acting *from* instinct when we set about making an instinct stronger than it is. The thing that says to you, "Your herd instinct is asleep. Wake it up," cannot itself *be* the herd instinct. The thing that tells you which note on the piano needs to be played louder cannot itself be that note.

Here is a third way of seeing it. If the Moral Law was one of our instincts, we ought to be able to point to some one impulse inside us which was always what we call "good," always in agreement with the rule of right behaviour. But you cannot. There is none of our impulses which the Moral Law may not sometimes tell us to suppress, and none which it may not sometimes tell us to encourage. It is a mistake to think that some of our impulses—say mother love or patriotism—are good, and others, like sex or the fighting instinct, are bad. All we mean is that the occasions on which the fighting instinct or the sexual desire need to be restrained are rather more frequent than those for restraining mother love or patriotism. But there are situations in which it is the duty of a married man to encourage his sexual impulse and of a soldier to encourage the fighting instinct. There are also occasions on which a mother's love for her own children or a man's love for his own country have to be suppressed or they will lead to unfairness towards other people's children or countries. Strictly speaking, there are no such things as good and bad impulses. Think once again of a piano. It has not got two kinds of notes on it, the "right" notes and the "wrong" ones. Every single note is right at one time and wrong at another. The Moral Law is not any one instinct or any set of instincts: it is something which makes a kind of tune (the tune we call goodness or right conduct) by directing the instincts.

By the way, this point is of great practical consequence. The most dangerous thing you can do is to take any one impulse of your own nature and set it up as the thing you ought to follow at all costs. There is not one of them which will not make us into devils if we set it up as an absolute guide. You might think love of humanity in general was safe, but it is not. If you leave out justice you will find yourself breaking agreements and faking evidence in trials "for the sake of humanity," and become in the end a cruel and treacherous man.

Other people wrote to me saying, "Isn't what you call the Moral Law just a social convention, something that is put into us by education?" I think there is a misunderstanding here. The people who ask that question are usually taking it for granted that if we have learned a thing from parents and teachers, then that thing must be merely a human invention. But, of course, that is not so. We all learned the multiplication table at school. A child who grew up alone on a desert island would not know it. But surely it does not follow that the multiplication table is simply a human convention, something human beings have made up for themselves and might have made different if they had liked? I fully agree that we learn the Rule of Decent Behaviour from parents and teachers, and friends and books, as we learn everything else. But some of the things we learn are mere conventions which might have been different—we learn to keep to the left of the road, but it might just as well have been the rule to keep to the right—and others of them, like mathematics, are real truths. The question is to which class the Law of Human Nature belongs.

There are two reasons for saying it belongs to the same class as mathematics. The first is, as I said in the first chapter, that though there are differences between the moral ideas of one time or country and those of another, the differences are not really very great—not nearly so great as most people imagine—and you can recognise the same law running through them all: whereas mere conventions, like the rule of the road or the kind of clothes people wear, may differ to any extent. The other reason is this. When you think about these differences between the morality of one people and another, do you think that the morality of one people is ever better or worse than that of another? Have any of the changes been improvements? If not, then of course there could never be any moral progress. Progress means not just changing, but changing for the better. If no set of moral ideas were truer or better than any other, there would be no sense in preferring civilised morality to savage morality, or Christian morality to Nazi morality. In fact, of course, we all do believe that some moralities are better than others. We do believe that some of the people who tried to change the moral ideas of their own age were what we would call Reformers or Pioneers—people who understood morality better than their neighbours did. Very well then. The moment you say that one set of moral ideas can be better than another, you are, in fact, measuring them both by a standard, saying that one of them conforms to that standard more nearly than the other. But the standard that measures two things is something different from either. You are, in fact, comparing them both with some Real Morality, admitting that there is such a thing as a real Right, independent of what people think, and that some people's ideas get nearer to that real Right than others. Or put it this way. If your moral ideas can be truer, and those of the Nazis less true, there must be something—some Real Morality—for them to be true about. The reason why your idea of New York can be truer or less true than mine is that New York is a real place, existing quite apart from what either of us thinks. If when each of us said "New York" each meant merely "The town I am imagining in my own head," how could one of us have truer ideas than the other? There would be no question of truth or falsehood at all. In the same way, if the Rule of Decent Behaviour meant simply "whatever each nation happens to approve," there would be no sense in saying that any one nation had ever been more correct in its approval than any other; no sense in saying that the world could ever grow morally better or morally worse.

I conclude then, that though the differences between people's ideas of Decent Behaviour often make you suspect that there is no real natural Law of Behaviour at all, yet the things we are bound to think about these differences really prove just the opposite. But one word before I end. I have met people who exaggerate the differences, because they have not distinguished between differences of morality and differences of belief about facts. For example, one man said to me, "Three hundred years ago people in England were putting witches to death. Was that what you call the Rule of Human Nature or Right Conduct?" But surely the reason we do not execute witches is that we do not believe there are such things. If we did—if we really thought that there were people going about who had sold themselves to the devil and received supernatural powers from him in return and were using these powers to kill their neighbours or drive them mad or bring bad weather, surely we would all agree that if anyone deserved the death penalty, then these filthy quislings did. There is no difference of moral principle here: the difference is simply about matter of fact. It may be a great advance in knowledge not to believe in witches: there is no moral advance in not executing them when you do not think they are there. You would not call a man humane for ceasing to set mousetraps if he did so because he believed there were no mice in the house.

3. The Reality of the Law

I now go back to what I said at the end of the first chapter, that there were two odd things about the human race. First, that they were haunted by the idea of a sort of behaviour they ought to practise, what you might call fair play, or decency, or morality, or the Law of Nature. Second, that they did not in fact do so. Now some of you may wonder why I called this odd. It may seem to you the most natural thing in the world. In particular, you may have thought I was rather hard on the human race. After all, you may say, what I call breaking the Law of Right and Wrong or of Nature, only means that people are not perfect. And why on earth should I expect them to be? That would be a good answer if what I was trying to do was to fix the exact amount of blame which is due to us for not behaving as we expect others to behave. But that is not my job at all. I am not concerned at present with blame; I am trying to find out truth. And from that point of view the very idea of something being imperfect, of its not being what it ought to be, has certain consequences.

If you take a thing like a stone or a tree, it is what it is and there seems no sense in saying it ought to have been otherwise. Of course you may say a stone is "the wrong shape" if you want to use it for a rockery, or that a tree is a bad tree because it does not give you as much shade as you expected. But all you mean is that the stone or tree does not happen to be convenient for some purpose of your own. You are not, except as a joke, blaming them for that. You really know, that, given the weather and the soil, the tree could not have been any different. What we, from our point of view, call a "bad" tree is obeying the laws of its nature just as much as a "good" one.

Now have you noticed what follows? It follows that what we usually call the laws of nature—the way weather works on a tree for example—may not really be *laws* in the strict sense, but only in a manner of speaking. When you say that falling stones always obey the law of gravitation, is not this much the same as saying that the law only means "what stones always do"? You do not really think that when a stone is let go, it suddenly remembers that it is under orders to fall to the ground. You only mean that, in fact, it does fall. In other words, you cannot be sure that there is anything over and above the facts themselves, any law about what ought to happen, as distinct from what does happen. The laws of nature, as applied to stones or trees, may only mean "what Nature, in fact, does." But if you turn to the Law of Human Nature, the Law of Decent Behaviour, it is a different matter. That law certainly does not mean "what human beings, in fact, do"; for as I said before, many of them do not obey this law at all, and none of them obey it completely. The law of gravity tells you what stones do If you drop them; but the Law of Human Nature tells you what human beings ought to do and do not. In other words, when you are dealing with humans, something else comes in above and beyond the actual facts. You have the facts (how men do behave) and you also have something else (how they ought to behave). In the rest of the universe there need not be anything but the facts. Electrons and molecules behave in a certain way, and certain results follow, and that may be the whole story.[2] But men behave in a certain way and that is not the whole story, for all the time you know that they ought to behave differently.

Now this is really so peculiar that one is tempted to try to explain it away. For instance, we might try to make out that when you say a man ought not to act as he does, you only mean the same as when you say that a stone is the wrong shape; namely, that what he is doing happens to be inconvenient to you. But that is simply untrue. A man occupying the corner seat in the train because he got there first, and a man who slipped into it while my back was turned and removed my bag, are both equally inconvenient. But I blame the second man and do not blame the first. I am not angry—except perhaps for a moment before I come to my senses—with a man who trips me up by accident; I am angry with a man who tries to trip me up even if he does not succeed. Yet the first has hurt me and the second has not. Sometimes the behaviour which I call bad is not inconvenient to me at all, but the very opposite. In war, each side may find a traitor on the other side very useful. But though they use him and pay him they regard him as human vermin. So you cannot say that what we call decent behaviour in others is simply the behaviour that happens to be useful to us. And as for decent behaviour in ourselves, I suppose it is pretty obvious that it does not mean the behaviour that pays. It means things like being content with thirty shillings when you might have got three pounds, doing school work honestly when it would be easy to cheat, leaving a girl alone when you would like to make love to her, staying in dangerous places when you could go somewhere safer, keeping promises you would rather not keep, and telling the truth even when it makes you look a fool.

Some people say that though decent conduct does not mean what pays each particular person at a particular moment, still, it means what pays the human race as a whole; and that consequently there is no mystery about it. Human beings, after all, have some sense; they see that you cannot have real safety or happiness except in a society where every one plays fair, and it is because they see this that they try to behave decently. Now, of course, it is perfectly true that safety and happiness can only come from individuals, classes, and nations being honest and fair and kind to each other. It is one of the most important truths in the world. But as an explanation of why we feel as we do about Right and Wrong it just misses the point. If we ask: "Why ought I to be unselfish?" and you reply "Because it is good for society," we may then ask, "Why should I care what's

2. I do not think it *is* the whole story, as you will see later. I mean that, as far as the argument has gone up to date, it *may* be.

good for society except when it happens to pay *me* personally?" and then you will have to say, "Because you ought to be unselfish"—which simply brings us back to where we started. You are saying what is true, but you are not getting any further. If a man asked what was the point of playing football, it would not be much good saying "in order to score goals," for trying to score goals is the game itself, not the reason for the game, and you would really only be saying that football was football—which is true, but not worth saying. In the same way, if a man asks what is the point of behaving decently, it is no good replying, "in order to benefit society," for trying to benefit society, in other words being unselfish (for "society" after all only means "other people"), is one of the things decent behaviour consists in; all you are really saying is that decent behaviour is decent behaviour. You would have said just as much if you had stopped at the statement, "Men ought to be unselfish."

And that is where I do stop. Men ought to be unselfish, ought to be fair. Not that men are unselfish, nor that they like being unselfish, but that they ought to be. The Moral Law, or Law of Human Nature, is not simply a fact about human behaviour in the same way as the Law of Gravitation is, or may be, simply a fact about how heavy objects behave. On the other hand, it is not a mere fancy, for we cannot get rid of the idea, and most of the things we say and think about men would be reduced to nonsense if we did. And it is not simply a statement about how we should like men to behave for our own convenience; for the behaviour we call bad or unfair is not exactly the same as the behaviour we find inconvenient, and may even be the opposite. Consequently, this Rule of Right and Wrong, or Law of Human Nature, or whatever you call it, must somehow or other be a real thing—a thing that is really there, not made up by ourselves. And yet it is not a fact in the ordinary sense, in the same way as our actual behaviour is a fact. It begins to look as if we shall have to admit that there is more than one kind of reality; that, in this particular case, there is something above and beyond the ordinary facts of men's behaviour, and yet quite definitely real—a real law, which none of us made, but which we find pressing on us.

4. What Lies Behind the Law

Let us sum up what we have reached so far. In the case of stones and trees and things of that sort, what we call the Laws of Nature may not be anything except a way of speaking. When you say that nature is governed by certain laws, this may only mean that nature does, in fact, behave in a certain way. The so-called laws may not be anything real—anything above and beyond the actual facts which we observe. But in the case of Man, we saw that this will not do. The Law of Human Nature, or of Right and Wrong, must be something above and beyond the actual facts of human behaviour. In this case, besides the actual facts, you have something else—a real law which we did not invent and which we know we ought to obey.

I now want to consider what this tells us about the universe we live in. Ever since men were able to think, they have been wondering what this universe really is and how it came to be there. And, very roughly, two views have been held. First, there is what is called the materialist view. People who take that view think that matter and space just happen to exist, and always have existed, nobody knows why; and that the matter, behaving in certain fixed ways, has just happened, by a sort of fluke, to produce creatures like ourselves who are able to think. By one chance in a thousand something hit our sun and made it produce the planets; and by another thousandth chance the chemicals necessary for life, and the right temperature, occurred on one of these planets, and so some of the matter on this earth came alive; and then, by a very long series of chances, the living creatures developed into things like us. The other view is the religious view.[3] According to it, what is behind the universe is more like a mind than it is like anything else we know. That is to say, it is conscious, and has purposes, and prefers one thing to another. And on this view it made the universe, partly for purposes we do not know, but partly, at any rate, in order to produce creatures like itself—I mean, like itself to the extent of having minds. Please do not think that one of these views was held a long time ago and that the other has gradually taken its place. Wherever there have been thinking men both views turn up. And note this too. You cannot find out which view is the right one by science in the ordinary sense. Science works by experiments. It watches how things behave. Every scientific statement in the long run, however complicated it looks, really means something like, "I pointed the telescope to such and such a part of the sky at 2:20 A.M. on January 15th and saw so-and-so," or, "I put some of this stuff in a pot and heated it to such-and-such a temperature and it did so-and-so." Do not think I am saying anything against science: I am only saying what its job is. And the more scientific a man is, the more (I believe) he would agree with me that this is the job of science—and a very useful and necessary job it is too. But why anything comes to be there at all, and whether there is anything behind the things science observes—something of a different kind—this is not a scientific question. If there is "Something Behind," then either it will have to remain altogether unknown to men or else make itself known in some different way. The statement that there is any such thing, and the statement that there is no such thing, are neither of them statements that science can make. And real scientists do not usually make them. It is usually the journalists and popular novelists who have picked up a few odds and ends of half-baked science from textbooks who go in for them. After all, it is really a matter of common sense. Supposing science ever became complete so that it knew every single thing in the whole universe. Is it not plain that the questions, "Why is there a universe?" "Why does it go on as it does?" "Has it any meaning?" would remain just as they were?

Now the position would be quite hopeless but for this. There is one thing, and only one, in the whole universe which we know more about than we could learn from external observation. That one thing is Man. We do not merely observe men, we *are* men. In this case we have, so to speak, inside information; we are in the know. And because of that, we know that men find themselves

3. See Note at the end of this chapter.

under a moral law, which they did not make, and cannot quite forget even when they try, and which they know they ought to obey. Notice the following point. Anyone studying Man from the outside as we study electricity or cabbages, not knowing our language and consequently not able to get any inside knowledge from us, but merely observing what we did, would never get the slightest evidence that we had this moral law. How could he? for his observations would only show what we did, and the moral law is about what we ought to do. In the same way, if there were anything above or behind the observed facts in the case of stones or the weather, we, by studying them from outside, could never hope to discover it.

The position of the question, then, is like this. We want to know whether the universe simply happens to be what it is for no reason or whether there is a power behind it that makes it what it is. Since that power, if it exists, would be not one of the observed facts but a reality which makes them, no mere observation of the facts can find it. There is only one case in which we can know whether there is anything more, namely our own case. And in that one case we find there is. Or put it the other way round. If there was a controlling power outside the universe, it could not show itself to us as one of the facts inside the universe— no more than the architect of a house could actually be a wall or staircase or fireplace in that house. The only way in which we could expect it to show itself would be inside ourselves as an influence or a command trying to get us to behave in a certain way. And that is just what we do find inside ourselves. Surely this ought to arouse our suspicions? In the only case where you can expect to get an answer, the answer turns out to be Yes; and in the other cases, where you do not get an answer, you see why you do not. Suppose someone asked me, when I see a man in a blue uniform going down the street leaving little paper packets at each house, why I suppose that they contain letters? I should reply, "Because whenever he leaves a similar little packet for me I find it does contain a letter." And if he then objected, "But you've never seen all these letters which you think the other people are getting," I should say, "Of course not, and I shouldn't expect to, because they're not addressed to me. I'm explaining the packets I'm not allowed to open by the ones I am allowed to open." It is the same about this question. They only packet I am allowed to open is Man. When I do, especially when I open that particular man called Myself, I find that I do not exist on my own, that I am under a law; that somebody or something wants me to behave in a certain way. I do not, of course, think that if I could get inside a stone or a tree I should find exactly the same thing, just as I do not think all the other people in the street get the same letters as I do. I should expect, for instance, to find that the stone had to obey the law of gravity —that whereas the sender of the letters merely tells me to obey the law of my human nature, He compels the stone to obey the laws of its stony nature. But I should expect to find that there was, so to speak, a sender of letters in both cases, a Power behind the facts, a Director, a Guide.

Do not think I am going faster than I really am. I am not yet within a hundred miles of the God of Christian theology. All I have got to is a Something which is directing the universe, and which appears in me as a law urging me to do right and making me feel responsible and uncomfortable when I do wrong. I think we have to assume it is more like a mind than it is like anything else we know—because after all the only other thing we know is matter and you can hardly imagine a bit of matter giving instructions. But, of course, it need not be very like a mind, still less like a person. In the next chapter we shall see if we can find out anything more about it. But one word of warning. There has been a great deal of soft soap talked about God for the last hundred years. That is not what I am offering. You can cut all that out.

NOTE.—In order to keep this section short enough when it was given on the air, I mentioned only the Materialist view and the Religious view. But to be complete I ought to mention the In-between view called Life-Force philosophy, or Creative Evolution, or Emergent Evolution. The wittiest expositions of it come in the works of Bernard Shaw, but the most profound ones in those of Bergson. People who hold this view say that the small variations by which life on this planet "evolved" from the lowest forms to Man were not due to chance but to the "striving" or "purposiveness" of a Life-Force. When people say this we must ask them whether by Life-Force they mean something with a mind or not. If they do, then "a mind bringing life into existence and leading it to perfection" is really a God, and their view is thus identical with the Religious. If they do not, then what is the sense in saying that something without a mind "strives" or has "purposes"? This seems to me fatal to their view. One reason why many people find Creative Evolution so attractive is that it gives one much of the emotional comfort of believing in God and none of the less pleasant consequences. When you are feeling fit and the sun is shining and you do not want to believe that the whole universe is a mere mechanical dance of atoms, it is nice to be able to think of this great mysterious Force rolling on through the centuries and carrying you on its crest. If, on the other hand, you want to do something rather shabby, the Life-Force, being only a blind force, with no morals and no mind, will never interfere with you like that troublesome God we learned about when we were children. The Life-Force is a sort of tame God. You can switch it on when you want, but it will not bother you. All the thrills of religion and none of the cost. Is the Life-Force the greatest achievement of wishful thinking the world has yet seen?

5. *We Have Cause to Be Uneasy*

I ended my last chapter with the idea that in the Moral Law somebody or something from beyond the material universe was actually getting at us. And I expect when I reached that point some of you felt a certain annoyance. You may even have thought that I had played a trick on you—that I had been carefully wrapping up to look like philosophy what turns out to be one more "religious jaw." You may have felt you were ready to listen to me as long as you thought I had anything new to say; but if it turns out to be only religion, well, the world has tried that and you cannot put the clock back. If anyone is feeling that way I should like to say three things to him.

First, as to putting the clock back. Would you think I was joking if I said that you can put a clock back, and that if the clock is wrong it is often a very sensible thing to do? But I would rather get away from that whole idea of clocks. We all want progress. But progress means getting nearer to the place where you want to be. And if you have taken a wrong turning, then to go forward does not get you any nearer. If you are on the wrong road, progress means doing an about-turn and walking back to the right road; and in that case the man who turns back soonest is the most progressive man. We have all seen this when doing arithmetic. When I have started a sum the wrong way, the sooner I admit this and go back and start over again, the faster I shall get on. There is nothing progressive about being pigheaded and refusing to admit a mistake. And I think if you look at the present state of the world, it is pretty plain that humanity has been making some big mistake. We are on the wrong road. And if that is so, we must go back. Going back is the quickest way on.

Then, secondly, this has not yet turned exactly into a "religious jaw." We have not yet got as far as the God of any actual religion, still less the God of that particular religion called Christianity. We have only got as far as a Somebody or Something behind the Moral Law. We are not taking anything from the Bible or the Churches, we are trying to see what we can find out about this Somebody on our own steam. And I want to make it quite clear that what we find out on our own steam is something that gives us a shock. We have two bits of evidence about the Somebody. One is the universe He has made. If we used that as our only clue, then I think we should have to conclude that He was a great artist (for the universe is a very beautiful place), but also that He is quite merciless and no friend to man (for the universe is a very dangerous and terrifying place). The other bit of evidence is that Moral Law which He has put into our minds. And this is a better bit of evidence than the other, because it is inside information. You find out more about God from the Moral Law than from the universe in general just as you find out more about a man by listening to his conversation than by looking at a house he has built. Now, from this second bit of evidence we conclude that the Being behind the universe is intensely interested in right conduct—in fair play, unselfishness, courage, good faith, honesty and truthfulness. In that sense we should agree with the account given by Christianity and some other religions, that God is "good." But do not let us go too fast here. The Moral Law does not give us any grounds for thinking that God is "good" in the sense of being indulgent, or soft, or sympathetic. There is nothing indulgent about the Moral Law. It is as hard as nails. It tells you to do the straight thing and it does not seem to care how painful, or dangerous, or difficult it is to do. If God is like the Moral Law, then He is not soft. It is no use, at this stage, saying that what you mean by a "good" God is a God who can forgive. You are going too quickly. Only a Person can forgive. And we have not yet got as far as a personal God—only as far as a power, behind the Moral Law, and more like a mind than it is like anything else. But it may still be very unlike a Person. If it is pure impersonal mind, there may be no sense in asking it to make allowances for you or let you off, just as there is no sense in asking the multiplication table to let you off when you do your sums wrong. You are bound to get the wrong answer. And it is no use either saying that if there is a God of that sort—an impersonal absolute goodness—then you do not like Him and are not going to bother about Him. For the trouble is that one part of you is on His side and really agrees with His disapproval of human greed and trickery and exploitation. You may want Him to make an exception in your own case, to let you off this one time; but you know at bottom that unless the power behind the world really and unalterably detests that sort of behaviour, then He cannot be good. On the other hand, we know that if there does exist an absolute goodness it must hate most of what we do. That is the terrible fix we are in. If the universe is not governed by an absolute goodness, then all our efforts are in the long run hopeless. But if it is, then we are making ourselves enemies to that goodness every day, and are not in the least likely to do any better tomorrow, and so our case is hopeless again. We cannot do without it, and we cannot do with it. God is the only comfort, He is also the supreme terror: the thing we most need and the thing we most want to hide from. He is our only possible ally, and we have made ourselves His enemies. Some people talk as if meeting the gaze of absolute goodness would be fun. They need to think again. They are still only playing with religion. Goodness is either the great safety or the great danger—according to the way you react to it. And we have reacted the wrong way.

Now my third point. When I chose to get to my real subject in this roundabout way, I was not trying to play any kind of trick on you. I had a different reason. My reason was that Christianity simply does not make sense until you have faced the sort of facts I have been describing. Christianity tells people to repent and promises them forgiveness. It therefore has nothing (as far as I know) to say to people who do not know they have done anything to repent of and who do not feel that they need any forgiveness. It is after you have realised that there is a real Moral Law, and a Power behind the law, and that you have broken that law and put yourself wrong with that Power—it is after all this, and not a moment sooner, that Christianity begins to talk. When you know you are sick, you will listen to the doctor. When you have realised that our position is nearly desperate you will begin to understand what the Christians are talking about. They offer an explanation of how we got into our present state of both hating goodness and loving it. They offer an explanation of how God can be this impersonal mind at the back of the Moral Law and yet also a Person. They tell you how the demands of this law, which you and I cannot meet, have been met on our behalf, how God Himself becomes a man to save man from the disapproval of God. It is an old story and if you want to go into it you will no doubt consult people who have more authority to talk about it than I have. All I am doing is to ask people to face the facts—to understand the questions which Christianity claims to answer. And they are very terrifying facts. I wish it was possible to say something more agreeable. But I must say what I think true. Of course, I quite agree that the Christian religion is, in the long run, a thing of unspeakable comfort. But it does not begin in comfort; it begins in the dismay I have been describing, and it is no use at all trying to go on to that comfort without first going through that dismay. In religion, as in war and everything else, comfort is the one thing you cannot get by looking for it. If you look for truth, you may find comfort in the end: if you look for comfort you will not get either comfort or truth—only soft soap and wishful thinking to begin with and, in the end, despair. Most of us have got over the pre-war wishful thinking about international politics. It is time we did the same about religion.

PART TWO

Factual Prose: Types

Essays and Articles

In 1580 Montaigne published his *Essais*. *Essai* is a French word meaning an attempt or a trial, and his essays were, Montaigne said, the trials or testing out of his beliefs and philosophy. They were experiments in the composition of prose. From them, essays in English derived—literary compositions, as a rule in prose, each dealing with some topic or some aspect of a topic, though the treatment is seldom exhaustive.

Since British writers adopted the form, essays have gone through many phases and variations. Some early British essays—those of Francis Bacon, for instance—were in the dry, aphoristic style of Montaigne. Later, when they became increasingly personal in both subject and style, essays were admired not only as interesting and perhaps enlightening commentaries but also as expressions of the personalities of their creators—those of Charles Lamb, of William Hazlitt, and still later of Robert Louis Stevenson are examples.

Recently, the term *essay* has been used less than it was through the early years of the twentieth century; but the essay clearly has descendants in the form of magazine articles.

Following are some of the older essays and some of the more recent magazine articles which clearly are related to them. They are all to be judged for the ideas and the personalities which they express and for the effectiveness with which they express them. In order that they may be at least broadly comparable in subject matter, those presented here have been chosen from many which deal with certain aspects of reading.

Francis Bacon

OF STUDIES

Studies serve for pastimes, for ornaments, and for abilities. Their chief use for pastime is in privateness and retiring; for ornament is in discourse, and for ability is in judgment. For expert men can execute, but learned men are fittest to judge or censure.

To spend too much time in them is sloth; to use them too much for ornament is affectation; to make judgment wholly by their rules is the humor of a scholar.

They perfect nature, and are perfected by experience.

Crafty men contemn them, simple men admire them, wise men use them, for they teach not their own use, but that there is a wisdom without them and above them, won by observation.

Read not to contradict, nor to believe, but to weigh and consider.

Some books are to be tasted, others to be swallowed, and some few to be chewed and digested; that is, some books are to be read only in parts; others to be read but cursorily, and some few to be read wholly, and with diligence and attention.

Reading maketh a full man, conference a ready man, and writing an exact man. And therefore if a man write little, he had need have a great memory; if he confer little, he had need have a present wit; and if he read little, he had need have much cunning, to seem to know that he doth not.

Histories make men wise, poets witty, the mathematics subtle, natural philosophy deep, moral grave, logic and rhetoric able to contend.

William Hazlitt

ON READING OLD BOOKS

I hate to read new books. There are twenty or thirty volumes that I have read over and over again, and these are the only ones that I have any desire ever to read at all. It was a long time before I could bring myself to sit down to the *Tales of My Landlord*, but now that author's works have made a considerable addition to my scanty library. I am told that some of Lady Morgan's are good, and have been recommended to look into *Anastasius*; but I have not yet ventured upon that task. A lady, the other day, could not refrain from expressing her surprise to a friend who said he had been reading *Delphine*: she asked if it had not been published some time back. Women judge of books as they do of fashions or complexions, which are admired only "in their newest gloss." That is not my way. I am not one of those who trouble the circulating libraries much, or pester the booksellers for mail-coach copies of standard periodical publications. I cannot say that I am greatly addicted to black-letter, but I profess myself well versed in the marble bindings of Andrew Millar, in the middle of the last century; nor does my taste revolt at Thurloe's *State Papers* in Russia leather, or an ample impression of Sir William Temple's *Essays*, with a portrait after Sir Godfrey Kneller in front. I do not think altogether the worse of a book for having survived the author a generation or two. I have more confidence in the dead than the living. Contemporary writers may generally be divided into two classes—one's friends or one's foes. Of the first we are compelled to think too well, and of the last we are disposed to think too ill, to receive much genuine pleasure from the perusal or to judge fairly of the merits of either. One candidate for literary fame, who happens to be of our acquaintance, writes finely and like a man of genius, but unfortunately has a foolish face, which spoils a delicate passage; another inspires us with the highest respect for his personal talents and character, but does not quite come up to our expectations in print. All these contradictions and petty details interrupt the calm current of our reflections. If you want to know what any of the authors were who lived before our time and are still objects of anxious inquiry, you have only to look into their works. But the dust and smoke and noise of modern literature have nothing in common with the pure, silent air of immortality.

When I take up a work that I have read before (the oftener the better), I know what I have to expect. The satisfaction is not lessened by being anticipated. When the entertainment is altogether new, I sit down to it as I should to a strange dish—turn and pick out a bit here and there, and am in doubt what to think of the composition. There is a want of confidence and security to second appetite. New-fangled books are also like made dishes in this respect, that they are generally little else than hashes and *rifaccimentos*[1] of what has been served up entire, and in a more natural state, at other times. Besides, in thus turning to a well-known author there is not only an assurance that my time will not be thrown away, or my palate nauseated with the most insipid or vilest trash, but I shake hands with and look an old, tried, and valued friend in the face, compare notes, and chat the hours away. It is true we form dear friendships with such ideal guests—dearer, alas, and more lasting than those with our most intimate acquaintance. In reading a book which is an old favorite with me (say the first novel I ever read) I not only have the pleasure of imagination and of a critical relish of the work, but the pleasures of memory added to it. It recalls the same feelings and associations which I had in first reading it and which I can never have again in any other way. Standard productions of this kind are links in the chain of our conscious being. They bind together the different scattered divisions of our personal identity. They are landmarks and guides in our journey through life. They are pegs and loops on which we can hang up, or from which we can take down, at pleasure, the wardrobe of a moral imagination, the relics of our best affections, the tokens and records of our happiest hours. They are "for thoughts and for remembrance." They are like Fortunatus's wishing-cap—they give us the best riches, those of fancy, and transport us, not over half the globe, but (which is better) over half our lives, at a word's notice.

My father Shandy solaced himself with *Bruscambille*. Give me for this purpose a volume of *Peregrine Pickle* or *Tom Jones*. Open either of them anywhere—at the *Memoirs of Lady Vane*, or the adventures at the masquerade with Lady Bellaston, or the disputes between Thwackum and Square, or the escape of Molly Seagrim, or the incident of Sophia and her muff, or the edifying prolixity of her aunt's lecture,—and there I find the same delightful, busy, bustling scene as ever, and feel myself the same as when I was first introduced into the midst of it. Nay, sometimes the sight of an odd volume of these good old English authors on a stall, or the name lettered on the back among others on the shelves of a library, answers the purpose, revives the whole train of ideas, and sets "the puppets dallying." Twenty years are struck off the list, and I am

1. Reworkings.

a child again. A sage philosopher, who was not a very wise man, said that he should like very well to be young again if he could take his experience along with him. This ingenious person did not seem to be aware, by the gravity of his remark, that the great advantage of being young is to be without this weight of experience, which he would fain place upon the shoulders of youth and which never comes too late with years. O what a privilege to be able to let this hump, like Christian's burthen, drop from off one's back, and transport oneself, by the help of a little musty duodecimo, to the time when "ignorance was bliss," and when we first got a peep at the raree-show of the world through the glass of fiction, gazing at mankind, as we do at wild beasts in a menagerie, through the bars of their cages, or at curiosities in a museum, that we must not touch! For myself, not only are the old ideas of the contents of the work brought back to my mind in all their vividness, but the old associations of the faces and persons of those I then knew, as they were in their lifetime—the place where I sat to read the volume, the day when I got it, the feeling of the air, the fields, the sky— return, and all my early impressions with them. This is better to me—those places, those times, those persons, and those feelings that come across me as I retrace the story and devour the page, are to me better far than the wet sheets of the last new novel from the Ballantyne press, to say nothing of the Minerva press in Leadenhall Street. It is like visiting the scenes of early youth. I think of the time "when I was in my father's house, and my path ran down with butter and honey"—when I was a little thoughtless child, and had no other wish or care but to con my daily task and be happy. *Tom Jones*, I remember, was the first work that broke the spell. It came down in numbers once a fortnight, in Cooke's pocket-edition, embellished with cuts. I had hitherto read only in school-books and a tiresome ecclesiastical history (with the exception of Mrs. Radcliffe's *Romance of the Forest*); but this had a different relish with it— "sweet in the mouth," though not "bitter in the belly." It smacked of the world I lived in and in which I was to live, and showed me groups, "gay creatures" not "of the element" but of the earth, not "living in the clouds" but travelling the same road that I did—some that had passed on before me, and others that might soon overtake me. My heart had palpitated at the thoughts of a boarding-school ball, or gala-day at midsummer or Christmas; but the world I had found out in Cooke's edition of the *British Novelists* was to me a dance through life, a perpetual gala-day. The sixpenny numbers of this work regularly contrived to leave off just in the middle of a sentence and in the nick of a story. . . . With what eagerness I used to look forward to the next number, and open the prints! Ah, never again shall I feel the enthusiastic delight with which I gazed at the figures, and anticipated the story and adventures of Major Bath and Commodore Trunnion, of Trim and my Uncle Toby, of Don Quixote and Sancho and Dapple, of Gil Blas and Dame Lorenza Sephora, of Laura and the fair Lucretia, whose lips open and shut like buds of roses. To what nameless ideas did they give rise, with what airy delights I filled up the outlines, as I hung in silence over the page. Let me still recall them, that they may breathe fresh life into me and

that I may live that birthday of thought and romantic pleasure over again! Talk
of the ideal! This is the only true ideal—the heavenly tints of fancy reflected in
the bubbles that float upon the spring-tide of human life.

> "O Memory, shield me from the world's poor strife,
> And give those scenes thine everlasting life!"

The paradox with which I set out is, I hope, less startling than it was; the
reader will, by this time, have been let into my secret. Much about the same
time, or I believe rather earlier, I took a particular satisfaction in reading
Chubb's *Tracts*, and I often think I will get them again to wade through. There
is a high gusto of polemical divinity in them; and you fancy that you hear a club
of shoemakers at Salisbury debating a disputable text from one of St. Paul's
epistles in a workmanlike style, with equal shrewdness and pertinacity. I cannot say much for my metaphysical studies, into which I launched shortly after
with great ardor, so as to make a toil of a pleasure. I was presently entangled
in the briers and thorns of subtle distinctions—of "fate, free-will, fore-knowledge
absolute," though I cannot add that "in their wandering mazes I found no end,"
for I did arrive at some very satisfactory and potent conclusions; nor will I go
so far, however ungrateful the subject might seem, as to exclaim with Mar-
lowe's Faustus, "Would I had never seen Wittenberg, never read book"—that
is, never studied such authors as Hartley, Hume, Berkeley, etc. Locke's *Essay
on the Human Understanding* is, however, a work from which I never derived
either pleasure or profit; and Hobbes, dry and powerful as he is, I did not read
till long afterwards. I read a few poets, which did not much hit my taste—for
I would have the reader understand I am deficient in the faculty of imagination; but I fell early upon French romances and philosophy, and devoured them
tooth-and-nail. Many a dainty repast have I made of the *New Eloise*—the description of the kiss; the excursion on the water; the letter of St. Preux, recalling
the time of their first loves; and the account of Julia's death: these I read over
and over again with unspeakable delight and wonder. Some years after, when I
met with this work again, I found I had lost nearly my whole relish for it (except some few parts), and was, I remember, very much mortified with the change
in my taste, which I sought to attribute to the smallness and gilt edges of the
edition I had bought, and its being perfumed with rose leaves. Nothing could
exceed the gravity, the solemnity, with which I carried home and read the dedication to the *Social Contract*, with some other pieces of the same author, which
I had picked up at a stall in a coarse leathern cover. Of the *Confessions* I have
spoken elsewhere, and may repeat what I have said: "Sweet is the dew of their
memory, and pleasant the balm of their recollection." Their beauties are not
"scattered like stray gifts o'er the earth," but sown thick on the page, rich and
rare. I wish I had never read the *Emilius*, or read it with less implicit faith. I had
no occasion to pamper my natural aversion to affectation or pretence, by
romantic and artificial means. I had better have formed myself on the model
of Sir Fopling Flutter. There is a class of persons whose virtues and most shin-

ing qualities sink in, and are concealed by, an absorbent ground of modesty and reserve; and such a one I do, without vanity, profess myself. Now, these are the very persons who are likely to attach themselves to the character of Emilius, and of whom it is sure to be the bane. This dull, phlegmatic, retiring humor is not in a fair way to be corrected, but confirmed and rendered desperate, by being in that work held up as an object of imitation, as an example of simplicity and magnanimity, by coming upon us with all the recommendations of novelty, surprise, and superiority to the prejudices of the world, by being stuck upon a pedestal, made amiable, dazzling, a *leurre de dupe*.[2] The reliance on solid worth which it inculcates, the preference of sober truth to gaudy tinsel, hangs like a millstone round the neck of the imagination—"a load to sink a navy,"—impedes our progress, and blocks up every prospect in life. A man, to get on, to be successful, conspicuous, applauded, should not retire upon the centre of his conscious resources, but be always at the circumference of appearances. He must envelope himself in a halo of mystery—he must ride in an equipage of opinion—he must walk with a train of self-conceit following him—he must not strip himself to a buff-jerkin, to the doublet and hose of his real merits, but must surround himself with a *cortège* of prejudices, like the signs of the Zodiac —he must seem anything but what he is, and then he may pass for anything he pleases. The world loves to be amused by hollow professions, to be deceived by flattering appearances, to live in a state of hallucination, and can forgive everything but the plain, downright, simple, honest truth—such as we see it chalked out in the character of Emilius.—To return from this digression, which is a little out of place here.

Books have in a great measure lost their power over me, nor can I revive the same interest in them as formerly. I perceive when a thing is good, rather than feel it. It is true,

> "Marcian Colonna is a dainty book";

and the reading of Mr. Keats's *Eve of St. Agnes* lately made me regret that I was not young again. The beautiful and tender images there conjured up "come like shadows—so depart." The "tiger-moth's wings," which he has spread over his rich poetic blazonry, just flit across my fancy; the gorgeous twilight window which he has painted over again in his verse, to me "blushes" almost in vain "with blood of queens and kings." I know how I should have felt at one time in reading such passages; and that is all. The sharp, luscious flavor, the fine aroma, is fled, and nothing but the stalk, the bran, the husk of literature is left. If anyone were to ask me what I read now, I might answer with my Lord Hamlet in the play, "Words, words, words." "What is the matter?" "Nothing"—they have scarce a meaning. But it was not always so. There was a time when to my thinking every word was a flower or a pearl, like those which dropped from the mouth of the little peasant-girl in the fairy tale, or like those that fall from the

2. Lure for a fool.

great preacher in the Caledonian Chapel. I drank of the stream of knowledge
that tempted but did not mock my lips, as of the river of life, freely. How eagerly
I slaked my thirst of German sentiment, "as the hart that panteth for the
water-springs"; how I bathed and revelled, and added my floods of tears to
Goethe's *Sorrows of Werter* and to Schiller's *Robbers*.

"Giving my stock of more to that which had too much."

I read and assented with all my soul to Coleridge's fine sonnet beginning,

"Schiller, that hour I would have wished to die,
If through the shuddering midnight I had sent,
From the dark dungeon of the tow'r, time-rent,
That fearful voice, a famish'd father's cry!"

I believe I may date my insight into the mysteries of poetry from the commencement of my acquaintance with the authors of the *Lyrical Ballads;* at
least, my discrimination of the higher sorts, not my predilection for such
writers as Goldsmith or Pope: nor do I imagine they will say I got my liking
for the novelists or the comic writers, for the characters of Valentine, Tattle,
or Miss Prue, from them. If so, I must have got from them what they never had
themselves. In points where poetic diction and conception are concerned, I
may be at a loss and liable to be imposed upon; but in forming an estimate of
passages relating to common life and manners I cannot think I am a plagiarist
from any man. I there "know my cue without a prompter." I may say of such
studies, "intus et in cute."[3] I am just able to admire those literal touches of
observation and description which persons of loftier pretensions overlook and
despise. I think I comprehend something of the characteristic part of Shakespeare; and in him, indeed, all is characteristic, even the nonsense and poetry.
I believe it was the celebrated Sir Humphrey Davy who used to say that Shakespeare was rather a metaphysician than a poet. At any rate, it was not ill said. I
wish that I had sooner known the dramatic writers contemporary with Shakespeare, for in looking them over, about a year ago, I almost revived my old
passion for reading and my old delight in books, though they were very nearly
new to me. The periodical essayists I read long ago. *The Spectator* I liked extremely, but *The Tatler* took my fancy most. I read the others soon after—
The Rambler, The Adventurer, The World, The Connoisseur; I was not sorry
to get to the end of them, and have no desire to go regularly through them again.
I consider myself a thorough adept in Richardson. I like the longest of his novels
best, and think no part of them tedious; nor should I ask to have anything better
to do than to read them from beginning to end, to take them up when I chose
and lay them down when I was tired, in some old family mansion in the country,
till every word and syllable relating to the bright Clarissa, the divine Clemen-

---

3. Literally, "within and inside the skin."

tina, the beautiful Pamela, "with every trick and line of their sweet favor," were once more "graven in my heart's table." I have a sneaking kindness for Mackenzie's *Julia de Roubigné*—for the deserted mansion, and straggling gilli-flowers on the mouldering garden wall; and still more for his *Man of Feeling* —not that it is better, nor so good, but at the time I read it I sometimes thought of the heroine, Miss Walton, and of Miss —— together, and "that ligament, fine as it was, was never broken."—One of the poets that I have always read with most pleasure, and can wander about in forever with a sort of voluptuous indolence, is Spenser; and I like Chaucer even better. The only writer among the Italians I can pretend to any knowledge of is Boccaccio, and of him I cannot express half my admiration. His story of the hawk I could read and think of from day to day, just as I would look at a picture of Titian's.

I remember, as long ago as the year 1798, going to a neighboring town (Shrewsbury, where Farquhar has laid the plot of his *Recruiting Officer*) and bringing home with me, "at one proud swoop," a copy of Milton's *Paradise Lost* and another of Burke's *Reflections on the French Revolution*—both which I have still; and I still recollect, when I see the covers, the pleasure with which I dipped into them as I returned with my double prize. I was set up for one while. That time is past, "with all its giddy raptures"; but I am still anxious to preserve its memory, "embalmed with odors." With respect to the first of these works, I would be permitted to remark here, in passing, that it is a sufficient answer to the German criticism which has since been started against the character of Satan (viz., that it is not one of disgusting deformity, or pure, def-ecated malice) to say that Milton has there drawn, not the abstract principle of evil, not a devil incarnate, but a fallen angel. This is the Scriptural account, and the poet has followed it. We may safely retain such passages as that well-known one,

> "His form had not yet lost
> All her original brightness; nor appear'd
> Less than archangel ruin'd, and the excess
> Of glory obscur'd,"

for the theory which is opposed to them "falls flat upon the grunsel edge and shames its worshippers." Let us hear no more, then, of this monkish cant and bigoted outcry for the restoration of the horns and tail of the devil. Again, as to the other work, Burke's *Reflections*, I took a particular pride and pleasure in it, and read it to myself and others for months afterwards. I had reason for my prejudice in favor of this author. To understand an adversary is some praise; to admire him is more. I thought I did both; I knew I did one. From the first time I ever cast my eyes on anything of Burke's (which was an extract from his *Letter to a Noble Lord*, in a three-times-a-week paper, *The St. James's Chronicle*, in 1796) I said to myself, "This is true eloquence: this is a man pouring out his mind on paper." All other style seemed to me pedantic and impertinent. Dr. Johnson's was walking on stilts; and even Junius's (who was at that time a favorite with me), with all his terseness, shrunk up into little antithetic points and well-trimmed sentences. But Burke's style was forked and playful as the lightning, crested like the serpent. He delivered plain things on a plain ground; but when he rose, there was no end of his flights and circum-gyrations—and in this very *Letter* "he, like an eagle in a dove-cot, fluttered *his* Volscians" (the Duke of Bedford and the Earl of Lauderdale) "in Corioli." I did not care for his doctrines. I was then, and am still, proof against their contagion; but I admired the author, and was considered as not a very staunch partisan of the opposite side, though I thought myself that an abstract proposi-tion was one thing, a masterly transition, a brilliant metaphor, another. I conceived, too, that he might be wrong in his main argument, and yet deliver fifty truths in arriving at a false conclusion. I remember Coleridge assuring me, as a poetical and political set-off to my sceptical admiration, that Wordsworth had written an *Essay on Marriage* which, for manly thought and nervous ex-pression, he deemed incomparably superior. As I had not, at that time, seen any specimens of Mr. Wordsworth's prose style, I could not express my doubts on the subject. If there are greater prose-writers than Burke, they either lie out of my course of study or are beyond my sphere of comprehension. I am too old to be a convert to a new mythology of genius. The niches are occupied, the tables are full. If such is still my admiration of this man's misapplied powers, what must it have been at a time when I myself was in vain trying, year after year, to write a single essay, nay, a single page or sentence; when I regarded the wonders of his pen with the longing eyes of one who was dumb and a change-ling; and when to be able to convey the slightest conception of my meaning to others in words was the height of an almost hopeless ambition. But I never measured others' excellences by my own defects, though a sense of my own incapacity and of the steep, impassable ascent from me to them made me re-gard them with greater awe and fondness.

I have thus run through most of my early studies and favorite authors, some of whom I have since criticised more at large. Whether those observations will survive me I neither know nor do I much care; but to the works themselves, "worthy of all acceptation," and to the feelings they have always excited in me since I could distinguish a meaning in language, nothing shall ever prevent me from looking back with gratitude and triumph. To have lived in the cultivation of an intimacy with such works, and to have familiarly relished such names, is not to have lived quite in vain.

There are other authors whom I have never read, and yet whom I have frequently had a great desire to read from some circumstance relating to them. Among these is Lord Clarendon's *History of the Grand Rebellion,* after which I have a hankering from hearing it spoken of by good judges, from my interest in the events and knowledge of the characters from other sources, and from having seen fine portraits of most of them. I like to read a well-penned character, and Clarendon is said to have been a master in this way. I should like to read Froissart's *Chronicles,* Holinshed and Stowe, and Fuller's *Worthies.* I intend, whenever I can, to read Beaumont and Fletcher all through. There are fifty-two f their plays, and I have only read a dozen or fourteen of them. *A Wife for a Month* and *Thierry and Theodoret* are, I am told, delicious, and I can believe it. I should like to read the speeches in Thucydides, and Guicciardini's *History of Florence*, and *Don Quixote* in the original. I have often thought of reading *The Loves of Persiles and Sigismunda* and the *Galatea* of the same author. But I somehow reserve them, like "another Yarrow." I should also like to read the last new novel (if I could be sure it was so) of the author of *Waverley*; no one would be more glad than I to find it the best.

Robert Louis Stevenson

THE LANTERN-BEARERS

These boys congregated every autumn about a certain easterly fisher-village, where they tasted in a high degree the glory of existence. The place was created seemingly on purpose for the diversion of young gentlemen. A street or two of houses, mostly red and many of them tiled; a number of fine trees clustered about the manse and the kirkyard, and turning the chief street into a shady alley; many little gardens more than usually bright with flowers; nets a-drying, and fisher-wives scolding in the backward parts; a smell of fish, a genial smell of seaweed; whiffs of blowing sand at the street-corners; shops with golf-balls and bottled lollipops; another shop with penny pickwicks (that remarkable cigar) and the *London Journal*, dear to me for its startling pictures, and a few novels, dear for their suggestive names: such, as well as memory serves me, were the ingredients of the town. These, you are to conceive posted on a spit between two sandy bays, and sparsely flanked with villas—enough for the boys to lodge in with their subsidiary parents, not enough (not yet enough) to cocknify the scene: a haven in the rocks in front: in front of that, a file of gray islets: to the left, endless links and sand wreaths, a wilderness of hiding-holes, alive with popping rabbits and soaring gulls: to the right, a range of seaward crags, one rugged brow beyond another; the ruins of a mighty and ancient fortress on the brink of one; coves between—now charmed into sunshine quiet, now whistling with wind and clamorous with bursting surges; the dens and sheltered hollows redolent of thyme and southernwood, the air at the cliff's edge brisk and clean and pungent of the sea—in front of all, the Bass Rock, tilted seaward like a doubtful bather, the surf ringing it with white, the solan-geese hanging round its summit like a great and glittering smoke. This choice piece of seaboard was sacred, besides, to the wrecker; and the Bass, in the eye of fancy, still flew the colours of King James; and in the ear of fancy the arches of Tantallon still rang with horseshoe iron, and echoed to the commands of Bell-the-Cat.

There was nothing to mar your days, if you were a boy summering in that part, but the embarrassment of pleasure. You might golf if you wanted; but I seem to have been better employed. You might secrete yourself in the Lady's Walk, a certain sunless dingle of elders, all mossed over by the damp as green as grass, and dotted here and there by the streamside with roofless walls, the cold homes of anchorites. To fit themselves for life, and with a special eye to acquire the art of smoking, it was even common for the boys to harbour there; and you might have seen a single penny pickwick, honestly shared in lengths with a blunt knife, bestrew the glen with these apprentices. Again, you might join our fishing parties, where we sat perched as thick as solan-geese, a covey of little anglers, boy and girl, angling over each other's heads, to the much entanglement of lines and loss of podleys and consequent shrill recrimination—shrill as the geese themselves. Indeed, had that been all, you might have done this often; but though fishing be a fine pastime, the podley is scarce to be regarded as a dainty for the table; and it was a point of honour that a boy should eat all that he had taken. Or again, you might climb the Law, where the whale's jawbone stood landmark in the buzzing wind, and behold the face of many counties, and the smoke and spires of many towns, and the sails of distant ships. You might bathe, now in the flaws of fine weather, that we pathetically call our summer, now in a gale of wind, with the sand scourging your bare hide, your clothes thrashing abroad from underneath their guardian stone, the froth of the great breakers casting you headlong ere it had drowned your knees. Or you might explore the tidal rocks, above all in the ebb of springs, when the very roots of the hills were for the nonce discovered; following my leader from one group to another, groping in slippery tangle for the wreck of ships, wading in pools after the abominable creatures of the sea, and ever with an eye cast backward on the march of the tide and the menaced line of your retreat. And then you might go Crusoeing, a word that covers all extempore eating in the open air: digging perhaps a house under the margin of the links, kindling a fire of the sea-ware, and cooking apples there—if they were truly apples, for I sometimes suppose the merchant must have played us off with some inferior and quite local fruit, capable of resolving, in the neighbourhood of fire, into mere sand and smoke and iodine; or perhaps pushing to Tantallon, you might lunch on sandwiches and visions in the grassy court, while the wind hummed in the crumbling turrets; or clambering along the coast, eat geans (the worst, I must suppose, in Christendom) from an adventurous gean tree that had taken root under a cliff, where it was shaken with an ague of east wind, and silvered after gales with salt, and grew so foreign among its bleak surroundings that to eat of its produce was an adventure in itself.

There are mingled some dismal memories with so many that were joyous. Of the fisher-wife, for instance, who had cut her throat at Canty Bay; and of how I ran with the other children to the top of the Quadrant, and beheld a posse of silent people escorting a cart, and on the cart, bound in a chair, her throat bandaged, and the bandage all bloody—horror!—the fisher-wife herself, who continued thenceforth to hag-ride my thoughts, and even to-day (as I recall the scene) darkens daylight. She was lodged in the little old jail in the chief street; but whether or no she died there, with a wise terror of the worst, I never in-

quired She had been tippling; it was but a dingy tragedy; and it seems strange
and hard that, after all these years, the poor crazy sinner should be still pilloried
on her cart in the scrap-book of my memory. Nor shall I readily forget a certain
house in the Quadrant where a visitor died, and a dark old woman continued
to dwell alone with the dead body; nor how this old woman conceived a hatred
to myself and one of my cousins, and in the dread hour of the dusk, as we were
clambering on the garden-walls, opened a window in that house of mortality and
cursed us in a shrill voice and with a marrowy choice of language. It was a pair
of very colourless urchins that fled down the lane from this remarkable experience! But I recall with a more doubtful sentiment, compounded out of fear
and exultation, the coil of equinoctial tempests; trumpeting squalls, scouring
flaws of rain; the boats with their reefed lugsails scudding for the harbour
mouth, where danger lay, for it was hard to make when the wind had any east
in it; the wives clustered with blowing shawls at the pier-head, where (if fate was
against them) they might see boat and husband and sons—their whole wealth
and their whole family—engulfed under their eyes; and (what I saw but once)
a troop of neighbours forcing such an unfortunate homeward, and she squall-
ing and battling in their midst, a figure scarcely human, a tragic Maenad.

These are things that I recall with interest; but what my memory dwells
upon the most, I have been all this while withholding. It was a sport peculiar
to the place, and indeed to a week or so of our two months' holiday there. Maybe
it still flourishes in its native spot; for boys and their pastimes are swayed by
periodic forces inscrutable to man; so that tops and marbles reappear in their
due season, regular like the sun and moon; and the harmless art of knucklebones has seen the fall of the Roman empire and the rise of the United States.
It may still flourish in its native spot, but nowhere else, I am persuaded; for I
tried myself to introduce it on Tweedside, and was defeated lamentably; its
charm being quite local, like a country wine that cannot be exported.

The idle manner of it was this:—

Toward the end of September, when school-time was drawing near and the
nights were already black, we would begin to sally from our respective villas,
each equipped with a tin bull's-eye lantern. The thing was so well known that it
had worn a rut in the commerce of Great Britain; and the grocers, about the
due time, began to garnish their windows with our particular brand of luminary.
We wore them buckled to the waist upon a cricket belt, and over them, such
was the rigour of the game, a buttoned top-coat. They smelled noisomely of
blistered tin; they never burned aright, though they would always burn our
fingers; their use was naught; the pleasure of them merely fanciful; and yet a
boy with a bull's-eye under his top-coat asked for nothing more. The fishermen
used lanterns about their boats, and it was from them, I suppose, that we had got
the hint; but theirs were not bull's-eyes, nor did we ever play at being fishermen.
The police carried them at their belts, and we had plainly copied them in that;
yet we did not pretend to be policemen. Burglars, indeed, we may have had
some haunting thoughts of; and we had certainly an eye to past ages when
lanterns were more common, and to certain story-books in which we had found

them to figure very largely. But take it for all in all, the pleasure of the thing was substantive; and to be a boy with a bull's-eye under his top-coat was good enough for us.

When two of these asses met, there would be an anxious "Have you got your lantern?" and a gratified "Yes!" That was the shibboleth, and very needful too; for, as it was the rule to keep our glory contained, none could recognize a lantern-bearer, unless (like the pole-cat) by the smell. Four or five would sometimes climb into the belly of a ten-man lugger, with nothing but the thwarts above them—for the cabin was usually locked, or choose out some hollow of the links where the wind might whistle overhead. There the coats would be unbuttoned and the bull's-eyes discovered; and in the chequering glimmer, under the huge windy hall of the night, and cheered by a rich steam of toasting tinware, these fortunate young gentlemen would crouch together in the cold sand of the links or on the scaly bilges of the fishing-boat, and delight themselves with inappropriate talk. Woe is me that I may not give some specimens—some of their foresights of life, or deep inquiries into the rudiments of man and nature, these were so fiery and so innocent, they were so richly silly, so romantically young. But the talk, at any rate, was but a condiment; and these gatherings themselves only accidents in the career of the lantern-bearer. The essence of this bliss was to walk by yourself in the black night; the slide shut, the top-coat buttoned; not a ray escaping, whether to conduct your footsteps or to make your glory public: a mere pillar of darkness in the dark; and all the while, deep down in the privacy of your fool's heart, to know you had a bull's-eye at your belt, and to exult and sing over the knowledge.

II

It is said that a poet has died young in the breast of the most stolid. It may be contended, rather, that this (somewhat minor) bard in almost every case survives, and is the spice of life to his possessor. Justice is not done to the versatility and unplumbed childishness of man's imagination. His life from without may seem but a rude mound of mud; there will be some golden chamber at the heart of it, in which he dwells delighted; and for as dark as his pathway seems to the observer, he will have some kind of a bull's-eye at his belt.

It would be hard to pick out a career more cheerless than that of Dancer, the miser, as he figures in the *Old Bailey Reports*, a prey to the most sordid persecutions, the butt of his neighbourhood, betrayed by his hired man, his house beleaguered by the impish school-boy, and he himself grinding and fuming and impotently fleeing to the law against these pin-pricks. You marvel at first that any one should willingly prolong a life so destitute of charm and dignity; and then you call to memory that had he chosen, had he ceased to be a miser, he could have been freed at once from these trials, and might have built himself a castle and gone escorted by a squadron. For the love of more recondite joys, which we cannot estimate, which, it may be, we should envy, the man had willingly forgone both comfort and consideration. "His mind to him a kingdom was"; and sure enough, digging into that mind, which seems at first a dust-heap, ve unearth some priceless jewels. For Dancer must have had the love of power nd the disdain of using it, a noble character in itself; disdain of many pleasures, chief part of what is commonly called wisdom; disdain of the inevitable end, hat finest trait of mankind; scorn of men's opinions, another element of virtue; nd at the back of all, a conscience just like yours and mine, whining like a cur, windling like a thimble-rigger, but still pointing (there or thereabout) to some onventional standard. Here were a cabinet portrait to which Hawthorne per- aps had done justice; and yet not Hawthorne either, for he was mildly minded, nd it lay not in him to create for us that throb of the miser's pulse, his fretful nergy of gusto, his vast arms of ambition clutching in he knows not what: nsatiable, insane, a god with a muck-rake. Thus, at least, looking in the bosom f the miser, consideration detects the poet in the full tide of life, with more, ndeed, of the poetic fire than usually goes to epics; and tracing that mean man bout his cold hearth, and to and fro in his discomfortable house, spies within im a blazing bonfire of delight. And so with others, who do not live by bread lone, but by some cherished and perhaps fantastic pleasure; who are meat alesmen to the external eye, and possibly to themselves are Shakespeares, Napoleons, or Beethovens; who have not one virtue to rub against another in ae field of active life, and yet perhaps, in the life of contemplation, sit with the aints. We see them on the street, and we can count their buttons; but heaven nows in what they pride themselves! heaven knows where they have set their reasure!

There is one fable that touches very near the quick of life: the fable of the nonk who passed into the woods, heard a bird break into song, hearkened for trill or two, and found himself on his return a stranger at his convent gates; or he had been absent fifty years, and of all his comrades there survived but one recognise him. It is not only in the woods that this enchanter carols, though erhaps he is native there. He sings in the most doleful places. The miser hears im and chuckles, and the days are moments. With no more apparatus than n ill-smelling lantern I have evoked him on the naked links. All life that is not nerely mechanical is spun out of two strands: seeking for that bird and hear- ng him. And it is just this that makes life so hard to value, and the delight of ach so incommunicable. And just a knowledge of this, and a remembrance f those fortunate hours in which the bird has sung to us, that fills us with such vonder when we turn the pages of the realist. There, to be sure, we find a picture f life in so far as it consists of mud and of old iron, cheap desires and cheap ears, that which we are ashamed to remember and that which we are careless vhether we forget; but of the note of that time-devouring nightingale we hear o news.

The case of these writers of romance is most obscure. They have been boys nd youths; they have lingered outside the window of the beloved, who was hen most probably writing to some one else; they have sat before a sheet of aper, and felt themselves mere continents of congested poetry, not one line f which would flow; they have walked alone in the woods, they have walked in ities under the countless lamps; they have been to sea, they have hated, they have feared, they have longed to knife a man, and maybe done it; the wild taste of life has stung their palate. Or, if you deny them all the rest, one pleasure at least they have tasted to the full—their books are there to prove it—the keen pleasure of successful literary composition. And yet they fill the globe with volumes, whose cleverness inspires me with despairing admiration, and whose consistent falsity to all I care to call existence, with despairing wrath. If I had no better hope than to continue to revolve among the dreary and petty businesses, and to be moved by the paltry hopes and fears with which they surround and animate their heroes, I declare I would die now. But there has never an hour of mine gone quite so dully yet; if it were spent waiting at a railway junction, I would have some scattering thoughts, I could count some grains of memory, compared to which the whole of one of these romances seems but dross.

These writers would retort (if I take them properly) that this was very true; that it was the same with themselves and other persons of (what they call) the artistic temperament; that in this we were exceptional, and should apparently be ashamed of ourselves; but that our works must deal exclusively with (what they call) the average man, who was a prodigious dull fellow, and quite dead to all but the paltriest considerations. I accept the issue. We can only know others by ourselves. The artistic temperament (a plague on the expression!) does not make us different from our fellow-men, or it would make us incapable of writing novels; and the average man (a murrain on the word!) is just like you and me, or he would not be average. It was Whitman who stamped a kind of Birmingham sacredness upon the latter phrase; but Whitman knew very well, and showed very nobly, that the average man was full of joys and full of a poetry of his own. And this harping on life's dulness and man's meanness is a loud profession of incompetence; it is one of two things: the cry of the blind eye, *I cannot see*, or the complaint of the dumb tongue, *I cannot utter*. To draw a life without delights is to prove I have not realized it. To picture a man without some sort of poetry—well, it goes near to prove my case, for it shows an author may have little enough. To see Dancer only as a dirty, old, small-minded, impotently fuming man, in a dirty house, besieged by Harrow boys, and probably beset by small attorneys, is to show myself as keen an observer as . . . the Harrow boys. But these young gentlemen (with a more becoming modesty) were content to pluck Dancer by the coat-tails; they did not suppose they had surprised his secret or could put him living in a book: and it is there my error would have lain. Or say that in the same romance—I continue to call these books romances, in the hope of giving pain—say that in the same romance, which now begins really to take shape, I should leave to speak of Dancer, and follow instead the Harrow boys; and say that I came on some such business as that of my lantern-bearers on the links; and described the boys as very cold, spat upon by flurries of rain, and drearily surrounded, all of which they were; and their talk as silly and indecent, which it certainly was. I might upon these lines, and had I Zola's genius, turn out, in a page or so, a gem of literary art, render the lantern-light with the touches of a master, and lay on the indecency with the ungrudging hand of love; and when all was done, what a triumph would my picture be of shallowness and dulness! how it would have missed the point! how it would have belied the boys! To the ear of the stenographer, the talk is merely silly and indecent; but ask the boys themselves, and they are discussing (as it is highly proper they should) the possibilities of existence. To the eye of the observer they are wet and cold and drearily surrounded; but ask themselves, and they are in the heaven of a recondite pleasure, the ground of which is an ill-smelling lantern.

III

For, to repeat, the ground of a man's joy is often hard to hit. It may hinge at times upon a mere accessory, like the lantern; it may reside, like Dancer's, in the mysterious inwards of psychology. It may consist with perpetual failure, and find exercise in the continued chase. It has so little bond with externals (such as the observer scribbles in his note-book) that it may even touch them not; and the man's true life, for which he consents to live, lie altogether in the field of fancy. The clergyman, in his spare hours, may be winning battles, the farmer sailing ships, the banker reaping triumph in the arts: all leading another life, plying another trade from that they chose; like the poet's housebuilder, who, after all is cased in stone,

> By his fireside, as impotent fancy prompts,
> Rebuilds it to his liking.

In such a case the poetry runs underground. The observer (poor soul, with his documents!) is all abroad. For to look at the man is but to court deception. We shall see the trunk from which he draws his nourishment; but he himself is above and abroad in the green dome of foliage, hummed through by winds and nested in by nightingales. And the true realism were that of the poets, to climb up after him like a squirrel, and catch some glimpse of the heaven for which he lives. And the true realism, always and everywhere, is that of the poets: to find out where joy resides and give it a voice far beyond singing.

For to miss the joy is to miss all. In the joy of the actors lies the sense of any action. That is the explanation, that the excuse. To one who has not the secret of the lanterns, the scene upon the links is meaningless. And hence the haunting and truly spectral unreality of realistic books. Hence, when we read the English realists, the incredulous wonder with which we observe the hero's constancy under the submerging tide of dulness, and how he bears up with his jibbing sweetheart, and endures the chatter of idiot girls, and stands by his whole unfeatured wilderness of an existence, instead of seeking relief in drink or foreign travel. Hence, in the French, in that meat-market of middle-aged sensuality, the disgusted surprise with which we see the hero drift sidelong, and practically quite untempted, into every description of misconduct and dishonour. In each, we miss the personal poetry, the enchanted atmosphere, that rainbow work of fancy that clothes what is naked and seems to ennoble what is base; in each, life falls dead like dough, instead of soaring away like a balloon into the colours of the sunset; each is true, each inconceivable; for no man lives in the external truth, among salts and acids, but in the warm, phantasmagoric chamber of his brain, with the painted windows and the storied walls.

Of this falsity we have had a recent example from a man who knows far better —Tolstoi's *Powers of Darkness*. Here is a piece full of force and truth, yet quite untrue. For before Mikita was led into so dire a situation he was tempted, and temptations are beautiful at least in part; and a work which dwells on the ugliness of crime and gives no hint of any loveliness in the temptation, sins against the modesty of life, and even when a Tolstoi writes it, sinks to melodrama. The peasants are not understood; they saw their life in fairer colours; even the deaf girl was clothed in poetry for Mikita, or he had never fallen. And so, once again, even an Old Bailey melodrama, without some brightness of poetry and lustre of existence, falls into the inconceivable and ranks with fairy tales.

IV

In nobler books we are moved with something like the emotions of life; and this emotion is very variously provoked. We are so moved when Levine labours in the field, when André sinks beyond emotion, when Richard Feverel and Lucy Desborough meet beside the river, when Antony, "not cowardly, puts off his helmet," when Kent has infinite pity on the dying Lear, when, in Dostoieffsky's *Despised and Rejected*, the uncomplaining hero drains his cup of suffering and virtue. These are notes that please the great heart of man. Not only love, and the fields, and the bright face of danger, but sacrifice and death and unmerited suffering humbly supported, touch in us the vein of the poetic. We love to think of them, we long to try them, we are humbly hopeful that we may prove heroes also.

We have heard, perhaps, too much of lesser matters. Here is the door, here is the open air. *Itur in antiquam silvam.*[1]

Virginia Woolf

HOW SHOULD ONE READ A BOOK?

In the first place, I want to emphasise the note of interrogation at the end of my title. Even if I could answer the question for myself, the answer would apply only to me and not to you. The only advice, indeed, that one person can give another about reading is to take no advice, to follow your own instincts, to use your own reason, to come to your own conclusions. If this is agreed between us, then I feel at liberty to put forward a few ideas and suggestions because you will not allow them to fetter that independence which is the most important quality that a reader can possess. After all, what laws can be laid down about books? The battle of Waterloo was certainly fought on a certain day; but is

1. Here is the road to the virgin forest.—Virgil, Æneid, vi, 179.

Hamlet a better play than *Lear?* Nobody can say. Each must decide that question for himself. To admit authorities, however heavily furred and gowned, into our libraries and let them tell us how to read, what to read, what value to place upon what we read, is to destroy the spirit of freedom which is the breath of those sanctuaries. Everywhere else we may be bound by laws and conventions —there we have none.

But to enjoy freedom, if the platitude is pardonable, we have of course to control ourselves. We must not squander our powers, helplessly and ignorantly, squirting half the house in order to water a single rose-bush; we must train them, exactly and powerfully, here on the very spot. This, it may be, is one of the first difficulties that faces us in a library. What is "the very spot"? There may well seem to be nothing but a conglomeration and huddle of confusion. Poems and novels, histories and memoirs, dictionaries and blue-books; books written in all languages by men and women of all tempers, races, and ages jostle each other on the shelf. And outside the donkey brays, the women gossip at the pump, the colts gallop across the fields. Where are we to begin? How are we to bring order into this multitudinous chaos and so get the deepest and widest pleasure from what we read?

It is simply enough to say that since books have classes—fiction, biography, poetry—we should separate them and take from each what it is right that each should give us. Yet few people ask from books what books can give us. Most commonly we come to books with blurred and divided minds, asking of fiction that it shall be true, of poetry that it shall be false, of biography that it shall be flattering, of history that it shall enforce our own prejudices. If we could banish all such preconceptions when we read, that would be an admirable beginning. Do not dictate to your author; try to become him. Be his fellow-worker and accomplice. If you hang back, and reserve and criticise at first, you are preventing yourself from getting the fullest possible value from what you read. But if you open your mind as widely as possible, then signs and hints of almost imperceptible fineness, from the twist and turn of the first sentences, will bring you into the presence of a human being unlike any other. Steep yourself in this, acquaint yourself with this, and soon you will find that your author is giving you, or attempting to give you, something far more definite. The thirty-two chapters of a novel—if we consider how to read a novel first—are an attempt to make something as formed and controlled as a building: but words are more impalpable than bricks; reading is a longer and more complicated process than seeing. Perhaps the quickest way to understand the elements of what a novelist is doing is not to read, but to write; to make your own experiment with the dangers and difficulties of words. Recall, then, some event that has left a distinct impression on you—how at the corner of the street, perhaps, you passed two people talking. A tree shook; an electric light danced; the tone of the talk was comic, but also tragic; a whole vision, an entire conception, seemed contained in that moment.

But when you attempt to reconstruct it in words, you will find that it breaks into a thousand conflicting impressions. Some must be subdued; others emphasized; in the process you will lose, probably, all grasp upon the emotion itself. Then turn from your blurred and littered pages to the opening pages of some great novelist—Defoe, Jane Austen, Hardy. Now you will be better able to appreciate their mastery. It is not merely that we are in the presence of a different person—Defoe, Jane Austen, or Thomas Hardy—but that we are living in a different world. Here, in *Robinson Crusoe*, we are trudging a plain high road; one thing happens after another; the fact and the order of the fact is enough. But if the open air and adventure mean everything to Defoe they mean nothing to Jane Austen. Hers is the drawing-room, and people talking, and by the many mirrors of their talk revealing their characters. And if, when we have accustomed ourselves to the drawing-room and its reflections, we turn to Hardy, we are once more spun round. The moors are round us and the stars are above our heads. The other side of the mind is now exposed—the dark side that comes uppermost in solitude, not the light side that shows in company. Our relations are not towards people, but towards Nature and destiny. Yet different as these worlds are, each is consistent with itself. The maker of each is careful to observe the laws of his own perspective, and however great a strain they may put upon us they will never confuse us, as lesser writers so frequently do, by introducing two different kinds of reality into the same book. Thus to go from one great novelist to another—from Jane Austen to Hardy, from Peacock to Trollope, from Scott to Meredith—is to be wrenched and uprooted; to be thrown this way and then that. To read a novel is a difficult and complex art. You must be capable not only of great fineness of perception, but of great boldness of imagination if you are going to make use of all that the novelist—the great artist—gives you.

But a glance at the heterogeneous company on the shelf will show you that writers are very seldom "great artists"; far more often a book makes no claim to be a work of art at all. These biographies and autobiographies, for example, lives of great men, of men long dead and forgotten, that stand cheek by jowl with the novels and poems, are we to refuse to read them because they are not "art"? Or shall we read them, but read them in a different way, with a different aim? Shall we read them in the first place to satisfy that curiosity which possesses us sometimes when in the evening we linger in front of a house where the lights are lit and the blinds not yet drawn, and each floor of the house shows us a different section of human life in being? Then we are consumed with curiosity about the lives of these people—the servants gossiping, the gentlemen dining, the girl dressing for a party, the old woman at the window with her knitting. Who are they, what are they, what are their names, their occupations, their thoughts, and adventures?

Biographies and memoirs answer such questions, light up innumerable such houses; they show us people going about their daily affairs, toiling, failing, succeeding, eating, hating, loving, until they die. And sometimes as we watch, the house fades and the iron railings vanish and we are out at sea; we are hunting, sailing, fighting; we are among savages and soldiers; we are taking part in great campaigns. Or if we like to stay here in England, in London, still the scene changes; the street narrows; the house becomes small, cramped, diamond-paned, and malodorous. We see a poet, Donne, driven from such a house because the walls were so thin that when the children cried their voices cut through them. We can follow him, through the paths that lie in the pages of books, to Twickenham; to Lady Bedford's Park, a famous meeting-ground for nobles and poets; and then turn our steps to Wilton, the great house under the downs, and hear Sidney read the *Arcadia* to his sister; and ramble among the very marshes and see the very herons that figure in that famous romance; and then again travel north with that other Lady Pembroke, Anne Clifford, to her wild moors, or plunge into the city and control our merriment at the sight of Gabriel Harvey in his black velvet suit arguing about poetry with Spenser. Nothing is more fascinating than to grope and stumble in the alternate darkness and splendour of Elizabethan London. But there is no staying there. The Temples and the Swifts, the Harleys and the St. Johns beckon us on; hour upon hour can be spent disentangling their quarrels and deciphering their characters; and when we tire of them we can stroll on, past a lady in black wearing diamonds, to Samuel Johnson and Goldsmith and Garrick; or cross the channel, if we like, and meet Voltaire and Diderot, Madame du Deffand; and so back to England and Twickenham—how certain places repeat themselves and certain names!—where Lady Bedford had her Park once and Pope lived later, to Walpole's home at Strawberry Hill. But Walpole introduces us to such a swarm of new acquaintances, there are so many houses to visit and bells to ring that we may well hesitate for a moment, on the Miss Berrys' doorstep, for example, when behold, up comes Thackeray; he is the friend of the woman whom Walpole loved; so that merely by going from friend to friend, from garden to garden, from house to house, we have passed from one end of English literature to another and wake to find ourselves here again in the present, if we can so differentiate this moment from all that have gone before. This, then, is one of the ways in which we can read these lives and letters; we can make them light up the many windows of the past; we can watch the famous dead in their familiar habits and fancy sometimes that we are very close and can surprise their secrets, and sometimes we may pull out a play or a poem that they have written and see whether it reads differently in the presence of the author. But this again rouses other questions. How far, we must ask ourselves, is a book influenced by its writer's life—how far is it safe to let the man interpret the writer? How far shall we resist or give way to the sympathies and antipathies that the man himself rouses in us—so sensitive are words, so receptive of the character of the author? These are questions that press upon us when we read lives and letters, and we must answer them for ourselves, for nothing can be more fatal than to be guided by the preferences of others in a matter so personal.

But also we can read such books with another aim, not to throw light on literature, not to become familiar with famous people, but to refresh and exercise our own creative powers. Is there not an open window on the right hand of the bookcase? How delightful to stop reading and look out! How stimulating the scene is, in its unconsciousness, its irrelevance, its perpetual movement—

the colts galloping round the field, the woman filling her pail at the well, the donkey throwing back his head and emitting his long, acrid moan. The greater part of any library is nothing but the record of such fleeting moments in the lives of men, women, and donkeys. Every literature, as it grows old, has its rubbish-heap, its record of vanished moments and forgotten lives told in faltering and feeble accents that have perished. But if you give yourself up to the delight of rubbish-reading you will be surprised, indeed you will be overcome, by the relics of human life that have been cast out to moulder. It may be one letter—but what a vision it gives! It may be a few sentences—but what vistas they suggest! Sometimes a whole story will come together with such beautiful humour and pathos and completeness that it seems as if a great novelist had been at work, yet it is only an old actor, Tate Wilkinson, remembering the strange story of Captain Jones; it is only a young subaltern serving under Arthur Wellesley and falling in love with a pretty girl at Lisbon; it is only Maria Allen letting fall her sewing in the empty drawing-room and sighing how she wishes she had taken Dr. Burney's good advice and had never eloped with her Rishy. None of this has any value; it is negligible in the extreme; yet how absorbing it is now and again to go through the rubbish-heaps and find rings and scissors and broken noses buried in the huge past and try to piece them together while the colt gallops round the field, the woman fills her pail at the well, and the donkey brays.

But we tire of rubbish-reading in the long run. We tire of searching for what is needed to complete the half-truth which is all that the Wilkinsons, the Bunburys, and the Maria Allens are able to offer us. They had not the artist's power of mastering and eliminating; they could not tell the whole truth even about their own lives; they have disfigured the story that might have been so shapely. Facts are all that they can offer us, and facts are a very inferior form of fiction. Thus the desire grows upon us to have done with half-statements and approximations; to cease from searching out the minute shades of human character, to enjoy the greater abstractness, the purer truth of fiction. Thus we create the mood, intense and generalised, unaware of detail, but stressed by some regular, recurrent beat, whose natural expression is poetry; and that is the time to read poetry when we are almost able to write it.

> Western wind, when wilt thou blow?
> The small rain down can rain.
> Christ, if my love were in my arms,
> And I in my bed again!

The impact of poetry is so hard and direct that for the moment there is no other sensation except that of the poem itself. What profound depths we visit then—how sudden and complete is our immersion! There is nothing here to catch hold of; nothing to stay us in our flight. The illusion of fiction is gradual; its effects are prepared; but who when they read these four lines stops to ask who wrote them, or conjures up the thought of Donne's house or Sidney's sec-

etary; or enmeshes them in the intricacy of the past and the succession of generations? The poet is always our contemporary. Our being for the moment is
centred and constricted, as in any violent shock of personal emotion. Afterwards,
it is true, the sensation begins to spread in wider rings through our minds; remoter senses are reached; these begin to sound and to comment and we are
aware of echoes and reflections. The intensity of poetry covers an immense range
of emotion. We have only to compare the force and directness of

> I shall fall like a tree, and find my grave,
>   Only remembering that I grieve,

with the wavering modulation of

> Minutes are numbered by the fall of sands,
> As by an hour glass; the span of time
> Doth waste us to our graves, and we look on it;
> An age of pleasure, revelled out, comes home
> At last, and ends in sorrow; but the life,
> Weary of riot, numbers every sand,
> Wailing in sighs, until the last drop down,
> So to conclude calamity in rest,

or place the meditative calm of

> whether we be young or old,
> Our destiny, our being's heart and home,
> Is with infinitude, and only there;
> With hope it is, hope that can never die,
> Effort, and expectation, and desire,
> And something evermore about to be,

beside the complete and inexhaustible loveliness of

> The moving Moon went up the sky,
> And no where did abide:
> Softly she was going up,
> And a star or two beside—

or the splendid fantasy of

> And the woodland haunter
> Shall not cease to saunter
>   When, far down some glade,
> Of the great world's burning,
> One soft flame upturning
> Seems, to his discerning,
>   Crocus in the shade.

to bethink us of the varied art of the poet; his power to make us at once actors and spectators; his power to run his hand into character as if it were a glove, and be Falstaff or Lear; his power to condense, to widen, to state, once and for ever.

"We have only to compare"—with those words the cat is out of the bag, and the true complexity of reading is admitted. The first process, to receive impressions with the utmost understanding, is only half the process of reading; it must be completed, if we are to get the whole pleasure from a book, by another. We must pass judgment upon these multitudinous impressions; we must make of these fleeting shapes one that is hard and lasting. But not directly. Wait for the dust of reading to settle; for the conflict and the questioning to die down; walk, talk, pull the dead petals from a rose, or fall asleep. Then suddenly without our willing it, for it is thus that Nature undertakes these transitions, the book will return, but differently. It will float to the top of the mind as a whole. And the book as a whole is different from the book received currently in separate phrases. Details now fit themselves into their places. We see the shape from start to finish; it is a barn, a pig-sty, or a cathedral. Now then we can compare book with book as we compare building with building. But this act of comparison means that our attitude has changed; we are no longer the friends of the writer, but his judges; and just as we cannot be too sympathetic as friends, so as judges we cannot be too severe. Are they not criminals, books that have wasted our time and sympathy; are they not the most insidious enemies of society, corrupters, defilers, the writers of false books, faked books, books that fill the air with decay and disease? Let us then be severe in our judgments; let us compare each book with the greatest of its kind. There they hang in the mind the shapes of the books we have read solidified by the judgments we have passed on them—*Robinson Crusoe, Emma, The Return of the Native*. Compare the novels with these—even the latest and least of novels has a right to be judged with the best. And so with poetry—when the intoxication of rhythm has died down and the splendour of words has faded a visionary shape will return to us and this must be compared with *Lear*, with *Phèdre*, with *The Prelude*; or if not with these, with whatever is the best or seems to us to be the best in its own kind. And we may be sure that the newness of new poetry and fiction is its most superficial quality and that we have only to alter slightly, not to recast, the standards by which we have judged the old.

It would be foolish, then, to pretend that the second part of reading, to judge, to compare, is as simple as the first—to open the mind wide to the fast flocking of innumerable impressions. To continue reading without the book before you, to hold one shadow-shape against another, to have read widely enough and with enough understanding to make such comparisons alive and illuminating—that is difficult; it is still more difficult to press further and to say, "Not only is the book of this sort, but it is of this value; here it fails; here it succeeds; this is bad; that is good." To carry out this part of a reader's duty needs such imagination, insight, and learning that it is hard to conceive any one mind sufficiently endowed; impossible for the most self-confident to find more than the seeds of such powers in himself. Would it not be wiser, then, to remit this part of reading and to allow the critics, the gowned and furred authorities of the library, to decide the question of the book's absolute value for us? Yet how impossible! We may stress the value of sympathy; we may try to sink our own identity as we read. But we know that we cannot sympathise wholly or immerse ourselves wholly; there is always a demon in us who whispers, "I hate, I love," and we cannot silence him. Indeed, it is precisely because we hate and we love that our relation with the poets and novelists is so intimate that we find the presence of another person intolerable. And even if the results are abhorrent and our judgments are wrong, still our taste, the nerve of sensation that sends shocks through us, is our chief illuminant; we learn through feeling; we cannot suppress our own idiosyncrasy without impoverishing it. But as time goes on perhaps we can train our taste; perhaps we can make it submit to some control. When it has fed greedily and lavishly upon books of all sorts—poetry, fiction, history, biography—and has stopped reading and looked for long spaces upon the variety, the incongruity of the living world, we shall find that it is changing a little; it is not so greedy, it is more reflective. It will begin to bring us not merely judgments on particular books, but it will tell us that there is a quality common to certain books. Listen, it will say, what shall we call *this?* And it will read us perhaps *Lear* and then perhaps the *Agamemnon* in order to bring out that common quality. Thus, with our taste to guide us, we shall venture beyond the particular book in search of qualities that group books together; we shall give them names and thus frame a rule that brings order into our perceptions. We shall gain a further and a rarer pleasure from that discrimination. But as a rule only lives when it is perpetually broken by contact with the books themselves—nothing is easier and more stultifying than to make rules which exist out of touch with facts, in a vacuum—now at last, in order to steady ourselves in this difficult attempt, it may be well to turn to the very rare writers who are able to enlighten us upon literature as an art. Coleridge and Dryden and Johnson, in their considered criticism, the poets and novelists themselves in their unconsidered sayings, are often surprisingly relevant; they light up and solidify the vague ideas that have been tumbling in the misty depths of our minds. But they are only able to help us if we come to them laden with questions and suggestions won honestly in the course of our own reading. They can do nothing for us if we herd ourselves under their authority and lie down like sheep in the shade of a hedge. We can only understand their ruling when it comes in conflict with our own and vanquishes it.

If this is so, if to read a book as it should be read calls for the rarest qualities of imagination, insight, and judgment, you may perhaps conclude that literature is a very complex art and that it is unlikely that we shall be able, even after a lifetime of reading, to make any valuable contribution to its criticism. We must remain readers; we shall not put on the further glory that belongs to those rare beings who are also critics. But still we have our responsibilities as readers and even our importance. The standards we raise and the judgments we pass steal into the air and become part of the atmosphere which writers breathe as they work. An influence is created which tells upon them even if it never finds its way into print. And that influence, if it were well instructed, vigorous and individual and sincere, might be of great value now when criticism is necessarily in abeyance; when books pass in review like the procession of animals in a shooting gallery, and the critic has only one second in which to load and aim and shoot and may well be pardoned if he mistakes rabbits for tigers, eagles for barndoor fowls, or misses altogether and wastes his shot upon some peaceful cow grazing in a further field. If behind the erratic gunfire of the press the author felt that there was another kind of criticism, the opinion of people reading for the love of reading, slowly and unprofessionally, and judging with great sympathy and yet with great severity, might this not improve the quality of his work? And if by our means books were to become stronger, richer, and more varied, that would be an end worth reaching.

Yet who reads to bring about an end however desirable? Are there not some pursuits that we practise because they are good in themselves, and some pleasures that are final? And is not this among them? I have sometimes dreamt, at least, that when the Day of Judgment dawns and the great conquerors and lawyers and statesmen come to receive their rewards—their crowns, their laurels, their names carved indelibly upon imperishable marble—the Almighty will turn to Peter and will say, not without a certain envy when He sees us coming with our books under our arms, "Look, these need no reward. We have nothing to give them here. They have loved reading."

Malcolm Cowley

WILLIAM FAULKNER'S
LEGEND OF THE SOUTH

William Faulkner is one of the writers who reward and even in a sense demand a second reading. When you return to one of his books years after its publication, the passages that had puzzled you are easier to understand and each of them takes its proper place in the picture. Moreover, you lose very little by knowing the plot in advance. Faulkner's stories are not the sort that unwind in celluloid ribbons until the last inch of them has been reflected on a flat screen, with nothing to imagine and nothing more to see except the newsreel, the animated cartoon and the Coming Repulsions; instead his books are sculptural, as if you could walk round them for different views of the same solid object. But it is not merely a statue that he presented: rather it is a whole monument or, let us say, a city buried in the jungle, to which the author wishes to guide us, but not at once or by following a single path. We start out along one road, winding between walls of jungle growth in the humid afternoon, and it is not long until we catch a glimpse of our destination. Just beyond us, however, is a swamp filled with snakes, and the guide makes us turn back. We take another road; we gain a clearer picture of the city; but this time there are other dangers in front of us, quicksands or precipices, and again the guide makes us return. By whatever road we travel, we always catch sight of our goal, always learn more about it and are always forced back; till at last we find the proper path and reach the heart of the city just as it is about to be overwhelmed by fire or earthquake. . . . Reading the same book a second time is like soaring over the jungle in a plane, with every section of the landscape falling into its proper perspective.

And there is another respect in which our judgment of the author changes when we return to not one but several of his novels in succession. On a first reading what had chiefly impressed us may have been their violence, which sometimes seemed to have no justification in art or nature. We had remembered incidents and figures like the violating of Temple Drake, in *Sanctuary;* like the pursuit and castration of Joe Christmas, in *Light in August;* like the idiot boy who fell in love and eloped with a cow, in *The Hamlet;* and like the nameless woman, in *The Wild Palms,* who bore her child unaided in the midst of a Mississippi River flood, on an Indian mound where all the snakes in the Delta had taken refuge. After a second reading, most of these nightmares retain their power to shock, but at the same time they merge a little into the background, as if they were the almost natural product of the long unbearable Mississippi summers; as if they were thunder showers brewed in the windless heat. We pay less attention to the horrors as such, and more to the old situation out of which they developed and the new disasters it seems to foreshadow.

The situation itself, and not the violence to which it leads, is Faulkner's real subject. It is, moreover, the same situation in all his books—or, let us say, in all the novels and stories belonging to his Yocknapatawpha County series. Briefly it is the destruction of the old Southern order, by war and military occupation and still more by finance capitalism that tempts and destroys it from within. "Tell about the South," says Quentin Compson's roommate at Harvard, who comes from Edmonton, Alberta, and is curious about the unknown region beyond the Ohio. "What's it like there?" Shreve McCannon goes on to ask. "What do they do there? Why do they live there? Why do they live at all?" And Quentin, whose background is a little like that of the author and who often seems to speak for him—Quentin answers, "You can't understand it. You would have to be born there." Nevertheless, he tells a long and violent story that he regards as the essence of the Deep South, which is not so much a region as it is, in Quentin's mind, an incomplete and frustrated nation trying to recover its own identity, trying to relive its legendary past.

There was a boy, Quentin says—I am giving the plot of *Absalom, Absalom!* —a mountain boy named Thomas Sutpen whose family drifted into the Virginia Tidewater. There his father found odd jobs on a plantation. One day the father sent him with a message to the big house, but he was turned away at the door by a black man in livery. The mountain boy, puzzled and humiliated, was seized upon by the ambition to which he would afterwards refer as "the design." He would own a plantation, with slaves and a livery butler; he would build a mansion as big as any of those in the Tidewater; and he would have a son to inherit his wealth.

A dozen years later, Sutpen appeared in the frontier town of Jefferson, Mississippi, and, by some transaction the nature of which is never explained —though it certainly wasn't by honest purchase—he obtained a hundred square miles of land from the Chickasaws. He disappeared again, and this time he returned with twenty wild Negroes from the jungle and a French architect. On the day of his reappearance, he set about building the largest house in northern Mississippi, with timbers from the forest and bricks that his Negroes molded and baked on the spot; it was as if his mansion, Sutpen's Hundred, had been literally torn from the soil. Only one man in Jefferson—he was Quentin's grandfather, General Compson—ever learned how and where Sutpen had acquired his slaves. He had shipped to Haiti from Virginia, worked as an overseer on a sugar plantation and married the rich planter's daughter, who had borne him a son. Then, finding that his wife had Negro blood, he had simply put her away, with her child and her fortune, while keeping the twenty slaves as a sort of indemnity. He explained to General Compson in the stilted speech he had taught himself that she could not be "adjunctive to the forwarding of the design."

"Jesus, the South is fine, isn't it," says Shreve McCannon, listening while Quentin talks, half to himself. "It's better than the theatre, isn't it. It's better than Ben Hur, isn't it. No wonder you have to come away now and then, isn't it."

Sutpen married again, Quentin continues. This time his wife belonged to a pious family of the neighborhood, and she bore him two children, Henry and Judith. He became the biggest landowner and cotton planter in the county, and it seemed that his "design" had already been fulfilled. At this moment, however—it was Christmas in 1859—Henry came home from the University of Mississippi with an older and worldlier new friend, Charles Bon, who was in reality Sutpen's son by his first marriage. Charles became engaged to Judith. Sutpen learned his identity and without making a sign of recognition, ordered him to leave the house. Henry, who refused to believe that Charles was his half-brother, renounced his birthright and followed him to New Orleans. In 1861 all the male Sutpens went off to war, and all of them survived four years of fighting. Then, in the spring of 1865, Charles suddenly decided to marry Judith, even though he was certain by now that she was his half-sister. Henry rode beside him all the way back to Sutpen's Hundred, but tried to stop him at the gate, killed him when he insisted on going ahead with his plan, told Judith what he had done, and disappeared.

"The South," Shreve McCannon says as he listens to the story. "The South. Jesus. No wonder you folks all outlive yourselves by years and years." And Quentin says, remembering his own sister with whom he was in love—just as Charles Bon, and Henry too, were in love with Judith—"I am older at twenty than a lot of people who have died."

But Quentin's story of the Deep South does not end with the war. Colonel Sutpen came home, he says, to find his wife dead, his son a fugitive, his slaves dispersed (they had run away even before they were freed by the Union army) and most of his land about to be seized for debt. But still determined to carry out "the design," he did not even pause for breath before undertaking to restore his house and plantation as nearly as possible to what they had been. The effort failed; he lost most of his land and was reduced to keeping a crossroads store. Now in his sixties, he tried again to beget a son; but his wife's younger sister, Miss Rosa Coldfield, was outraged by his proposal ("Let's try it," he had said, "and if it's a boy we'll get married."); and later poor Milly Jones, with whom he had an affair, gave birth to a baby girl. At that Sutpen abandoned hope and provoked Milly's grandfather into killing him. Judith survived her father for a time, as did the half-caste son of Charles Bon by a New Orleans octoroon. After the death of these two by yellow fever, the great house was haunted rather than inhabited by an ancient mulatto woman, Sutpen's daughter by one of his slaves. The fugitive Henry Sutpen came home to die; the townspeople heard of his illness and sent an ambulance after him; but old Clytie thought they were arresting him for murder and set fire to Sutpen's Hundred. The only survivor of the conflagration was Jim Bond, a half-witted, saddle-colored creature who was Charles Bon's grandson.

"Do you know what I think?" says Shreve McCannon after the story has ended. "I think that in time the Jim Bonds are going to conquer the western hemisphere. Of course it won't be quite in our time and of course as they spread toward the poles they will bleach out again like the rabbits and the birds do, so they won't show up so sharp against the snow. But it will still be Jim Bond; and so in a few thousand years, I who regard you will also have sprung from the loins of African kings. Now I want you to tell me just one thing more. Why do you hate the South?"

"I don't hate it," Quentin says quickly, at once. "I don't hate it," he repeats, speaking for the author as well as himself. *I don't hate it,* he thinks, panting in the cold air, the iron New England dark; *I don't. I don't! I don't hate it! I don't hate it!*

The reader cannot help wondering why this sombre and, at moments, plainly incredible story had so seized upon Quentin's mind that he trembled with excitement when telling it and felt that it revealed the essence of the Deep South. It seems to belong in the realm of Gothic romances, with Sutpen's Hundred taking the place of the haunted castle on the Rhine, with Colonel Sutpen as Faust and Charles Bon as Manfred. Then slowly it dawns on you that most of the characters and incidents have a double meaning; that besides their place in the story, they also serve as symbols or metaphors with a general application. Sutpen's great design, the land he stole from the Indians, the French architect, who built his house with the help of wild Negroes from the jungle, the woman of mixed blood whom he married and disowned, the unacknowledged son who ruined him, the poor white whom he wronged and who killed him in anger, the final destruction of the mansion like the downfall of a social order:

all these might belong to a tragic fable of Southern history. With a little cleverness, the whole novel might be explained as a connected and logical allegory, but this, I think, would be going beyond the author's intention. First of all he was writing a story, and one that affected him deeply, but he was also brooding over a social situation. More or less unconsciously, the incidents in the story came to represent the forces and elements in the social situation, since the mind naturally works in terms of symbols and parallels. In Faulkner's case, this form of parallelism is not confined to *Absalom, Absalom!* It can be found in the whole fictional framework that he has been elaborating in novel after novel, until his work has become a myth or legend of the South.

I call it a legend because it is obviously no more intended as a historical account of the country south of the Ohio than *The Scarlet Letter* is intended as a history of Massachusetts or *Paradise Lost* as a factual description of the Fall. Briefly stated, the legend might run something like this: The Deep South was settled partly by aristocrats like the Sartoris clan and partly by new men like Colonel Sutpen. Both types of planters were determined to establish a lasting social order on the land they had seized from the Indians (that is, to leave sons behind them). They had the virtue of living single-mindedly by a fixed code; but there was also an inherent guilt in their "design," their way of life, that put a curse on the land and brought about the Civil War. After the War was lost, partly as a result of their own mad heroism (for who else but men as brave as Jackson and Stuart could have frightened the Yankee into standing together and fighting back?) they tried to restore "the design" by other methods. But they no longer had the strength to achieve more than a partial success, even after they had freed their land from the carpetbaggers who followed the Northern armies. As time passed, moreover, the men of the old order found that they had Southern enemies too: they had to fight against a new exploiting class descended from the landless whites of slavery days. In this struggle between the clan of Sartoris and the unscrupulous tribe of Snopes, the Sartorises were defeated in advance by a traditional code that prevented them from using the weapons of the enemy. But the Snopeses as price of their victory had to serve the mechanized civilization of the North, which was morally impotent in itself, but which, with the aid of its Southern retainers, ended by corrupting the Southern nation. In our own day, the problems of the South are still unsolved, the racial conflict is becoming more acute; and Faulkner's characters in their despairing moments foresee or forebode some catastrophe of which Jim Bond and his like will be the only survivors.

II

This legend of Faulkner's, if I have stated it correctly, is clearly not a scientific interpretation of Southern history (if such a thing exists); but neither is it the familiar plantation legend that has been embodied in hundreds of romantic novels. Faulkner presents the virtues of the old order as being moral rather than material. There is no baronial pomp in his novels; no profusion of silk and silver, mahogany and moonlight and champagne. The big house on

Mr. Hubert Beauchamp's plantation (in *Go Down, Moses*) had a rotted floor-board in the back gallery that Mr. Hubert never got round to having fixed. Visitors used to find him sitting in the spring-house with his boots off and his feet in the water while he drank a morning toddy, which he invited them to share. Visitors to Sutpen's Hundred were offered champagne: it was the best, doubtless, and yet it was "crudely dispensed out of the burlesqued pantomime elegance of Negro butlers who (and likewise the drinkers who gulped it down like neat whiskey between flowery and unsubtle toasts) would have treated lemonade the same way." All the planters lived comfortably, with plenty of servants, but Faulkner never lets us forget that they were living on what had recently been the frontier. What he admires about them is not their wealth or their manners or their fine houses, but rather their unquestioning accept-ance of a moral code that taught them "courage and honor and pride, and pity and love of justice and of liberty." Living with single hearts, they were, says Quentin Compson's father:

> . . . . people too as we are, and victims too as we are, but victims of a dif-ferent circumstance, simpler and therefore, integer for integer, larger, more heroic and the figures therefore more heroic too, not dwarfed and involved but distinct, uncomplex, who had the gift of living once or dying once in-stead of being diffused and scattered creatures drawn blindly limb from limb from a grab bag and assembled, author and victim too of a thousand homicides and a thousand copulations and divorcements.

The old order was a moral order: briefly that was its strength and the secret lost by its heirs. I don't wish to give the impression that Faulkner is the only Southern writer to advance this principle. During the last few years, it has been stated or suggested in a considerable body of Southern fiction and poetry, in-cluding the work of Allen Tate, Robert Penn Warren, Caroline Gordon and several others. The fact is that most of the ideas embodied in Faulkner's legend are held in common by many Southern writers of the new generation; what Faulkner has done is to express them in a whole series of novels written with his own emotional intensity and technical resourcefulness. But his version of the legend also has features that set it apart: most notably its emphasis on the idea that the Southern nation (like most of his own fictional heroes) was defeated from within.

In Faulkner's reading, the old order not only had its virtues of dignity and courage and love of justice; it also bore the moral burden of a guilt so great that the War and even Reconstruction were in some sense a merited punishment. There is madness, but there is a metaphorical meaning too, in Miss Rosa Cold-field's belief that Sutpen was a demon and that his sins were the real reason ". . . . why God let us lose the War: that only through the blood of our men and the tears of our women could He stay this demon and efface his name and lineage from the earth." Quentin's father is quite sane, in his sober moments, and yet he expresses almost the same idea about Sutpen's guilt and its consequences.

He is telling the story of the Sutpens when he remarks that the Civil War was ".... a stupid and bloody aberration in the high (and impossible) destiny of the United States, maybe instigated by that family fatality which possessed, along with all circumstances, that curious lack of economy between cause and effect which is always a characteristic of fate when reduced to using human materials."

Colonel Sutpen himself has a feeling, not exactly of guilt, since he has never questioned the rightness of his design, but rather of amazement that so many misfortunes have fallen on him. Sitting in General Compson's office, he goes back over his career, trying to see where he had made his "mistake," for that is what he calls it. Sometimes the author seems to be implying that the sin for which Sutpen and his class are being punished is simply the act of cohabiting with Negroes. But before the end of *Absalom, Absalom!* we learn that miscegenation is only part of it. When Charles Bon's curious actions are explained, we find that he was taking revenge on his father for having refused to recognize him by so much as a single glance. Thus, heartlessness was the "mistake" that had ruined Sutpen, not the taking of a partly Negro wife and Negro concubines. And the point becomes clearer in a long story called "The Bear" (in *Go Down, Moses*), probably the best single piece that Faulkner has written. When Isaac McCaslin is twenty-one, he insists on relinquishing the big plantation that is his by inheritance; he thinks that the land is cursed. It is cursed in his eyes by the deeds of his grandfather: "that evil and unregenerate old man who could summon, because she was his property, a human being because she was old enough and female, to his widower's house and get a child on her and then dismiss her because she was of an inferior race, and then bequeath a thousand dollars to the infant because he would be dead then and wouldn't have to pay it." It follows that the land was cursed—and the War was part of the curse—because its owners had treated human beings as instruments; in a word, it was cursed by slavery.

All through his boyhood, Faulkner must have dreamed of fighting in the Civil War. It was a Sartoris war and not a Snopes war, like the one in which he afterwards risked his life in a foreign army. And yet his sympathies did not wholly lie with the slaveholding clan of Sartoris, even though it was his own clan. The men he most admired and must have pictured himself as resembling were the Southern soldiers—after all, they were the vast majority—who owned no slaves themselves and suffered from the institution of slavery. The men he would praise in his novels were those "who had fought for four years and lost .... not because they were opposed to freedom as freedom, but for the old reasons for which man (not the generals and politicians but man) has always fought and died in wars: to preserve a status quo or to establish a better future one to endure for his children." You might define his position as that of an anti-slavery Southern nationalist.

His attitude toward Negroes will seem surprising only to Northerners. It seems to have developed from the attitude of the slaveholders, which was often inhuman but never impersonal—that is, the slave might be treated as a domestic animal, but not as a machine or the servant of a machine. Apparently the slave-holding class had little or no feeling of racial animosity. Frederick Law Olm-stead, a sharp and by no means a friendly observer, was struck by what he called "the close cohabitation and association of black and white." In his *Journey in the Seaboard Slave States*, the record of his travels in 1853-54, he said: "Negro women are carrying black and white babies together in their arms; black and white children are playing together (not going to school together); black and white faces are constantly thrust together out of the doors, to see the train go by." He described the relation between masters and servants as having a "familiarity and closeness of intimacy that would have been noticed with astonishment, if not with manifest displeasure, in almost any chance company at the North." In Faulkner's historical novels, we find this closeness of intimacy compounded with closeness of blood, for the servants are very often the illegitimate half-brothers or sisters of their white companions—not only more often than in life, a mild way of putting it, but also more often than in any Abolitionist tract. He describes the old South as inhabited by two races that lived essentially the same life on their different levels. Thus, he says in *Absalom, Absalom!* that the young planters were

> . . . only in the surface matter of food and clothing and daily occupation any different from the Negro slaves who supported them—the same sweat, the only difference being that on the one hand it went for labor in the fields where on the other it went as the price of the spartan and meagre pleasures which were available to them because they did not have to sweat in the fields: the hard violent hunting and riding; the same pleasures: the one, gambling for worn knives and brass jewelry and twists of tobacco and buttons and garments because they happened to be easiest and quickest to hand; on the other for the money and horses, the guns and watches, and for the same reason; the same parties: the identical music from the identical instruments, crude fiddles and guitars, now in the big house with candles and silk dresses and champagne, now in dirt-floored cabins with smoking pine knots and calico and water sweetened with molasses.

"They will endure. They are better than we are." Ike McCaslin says of the Negroes, although he finds it more painful to utter this heresy than it is to surrender his plantation. "Stronger than we are," he continues. "Their vices are vices aped from white men or that white men and bondage have taught them: improvidence and intemperance and evasion—not laziness . . . and their virtues are their own: endurance and pity and tolerance and forbearance and fidelity and love of children, whether their own or not or black or not." In Faulkner's novels, the Negroes are an element of stability and endurance, just as the octoroons (like Charles Bon and Joe Christmas) are an element of tragic instability. His favorite characters are the Negro cooks and matriarchs who hold a white family together: Elnora and Dilsey and Clytie and Aunt Mollie Beauchamp. After the Compson family has gone to pieces (in *The Sound and the Fury*), it is Dilsey the cook who endures and is left behind to mourn. Looking up at the square, unpainted house with its rotting portico, she thinks, "Ise seed de first en de last"; and later in the kitchen, looking at the cold stove, "I seed de first en de last."

The increasing hatred between two races is explained in Faulkner's novels partly by the heritage of slavery and Reconstruction; partly by the coming into power of a new class which, so far as it consists of families with landless and slaveless ancestors, has a tradition of hostility to the Negroes. But Faulkner also likes to think that the lynch mobs were often led by the descendants of his old enemies, the carpetbaggers—

> . . . that race threefold in one and alien even among themselves save for a single fierce will for rapine and pillage, composed of the sons of middle-aged Quartermaster lieutenants and Army sutlers and contractors in military blankets and shoes and transport mules, who followed the battles they themselves had not fought and inherited the conquest they themselves had not helped to gain . . . and left their bones and in another generation would be engaged in a fierce economic competition of small sloven farms with the black men they were supposed to have freed and the white descendants of fathers who had owned no slaves anyway whom they were supposed to have disinherited, and in the third generation would be back once more in the little lost county seats as barbers and garage mechanics and deputy sheriffs and mill and gin hands and power-plant firemen, leading, first in mufti then later in an actual formalized regalia of hooded sheets and passwords and fiery Christian symbols, lynching mobs against the race their ancestors had come to save.

III

Faulkner's novels of contemporary Southern life continue the legend into a period that he regards as one of moral confusion and social decay. He is continually seeking in them for violent images to convey his sense of despair. *Sanctuary* is the most violent of all his novels; it is also the most popular and by no means the least important (in spite of Faulkner's comment that it was "a cheap idea . . . deliberately conceived to make money"). The story of Popeye and Temple Drake has more meaning than appears on a first hasty reading— the only reading that most of the critics have been willing to grant it. George Marion O'Donnell went over the novel more carefully and decided that it formed a coherent allegory. Writing in *The Kenyon Review* (Autumn, 1939), he said that the pattern of the allegory was something like this:

> Southern Womanhood Corrupted but Undefiled (Temple Drake), in the company of the Corrupted Tradition (Gowan Stevens, a professional Virginian), falls into the clutches of amoral Modernism (Popeye), which is itself impotent, but which with the aid of its strong ally Natural Lust ("Red") rapes Southern Womanhood unnaturally and then seduces her so satisfactorily that her corruption is total, and she becomes the tacit ally of

Modernism. Meanwhile Pore White Trash (Goodwin) has been accused of the crime which he, with the aid of the Naif Faithful (Tawmmy), actually tried to prevent. The Formalized Tradition (Horace Benbow), perceiving the true state of affairs, tries vainly to defend Pore White Trash. However, Southern Womanhood is so hopelessly corrupted that she willfully sees Pore White Trash convicted and lynched; she is then carried off by Wealth (Judge Drake) to meaningless escape in European luxury. Modernism, carrying in it from birth its own impotence and doom, submits with masochistic pleasure to its own destruction for the one crime that it has not yet committed—Revolutionary Destruction of Order (the murder of the Alabama policeman, for which the innocent Popeye is executed).

Mr. O'Donnell deserves very great credit as the first critic to discuss Faulkner as a moralist, the first to compare him in passing with Hawthorne, and almost the first to see that he is engaged in creating Southern myths. In his comments on *Sanctuary*, however, he has been entirely too ingenious. There is no doubt that his allegorical scheme can be read into the novel, but it hardly seems possible that the author intended to put it there. Faulkner tells us that *Sanctuary* was written "in about three weeks." It was completely rewritten two years later, in the effort "to make out of it something which would not shame *The Sound and the Fury* and *As I Lay Dying* too much"; but I doubt that Faulkner had or took the time to give every character a double meaning. Lee Goodwin, for example, is not Pore White Trash, capitalized, but a tough, frightened moonshiner dishonorably discharged from the Army. Tawmmy is not the Naif Faithful, capitalized; he is simply faithful and stupid. If Temple Drake has any symbolic value, she represents the South as a whole, or the younger generation in the South, rather than Southern Womanhood (a phrase that makes Faulkner wince); but it is also quite possible that she represents nothing but a rather silly co-ed. Popeye, however, is another question; and at this point Mr. O'Donnell's reading is not only ingenious but comes very close to Faulkner's conscious or unconscious intention.

Popeye is one of several characters in Faulkner's novels who stand for something that might be called "amoral Modernism," considering that they are creatures of the time and have no social morality whatever; but it might also be called—more accurately, I think—the mechanical civilization that has invaded and partly conquered the South. Popeye is always described in mechanical terms: his eyes "looked like rubber knobs"; his face "just went awry, like the face of a wax doll set too near a hot fire and forgotten"; his tight suit and stiff hat were "all angles, like a modernistic lampshade"; and in general he had "that vicious depthless quality of stamped tin." He was the son of a professional strikebreaker, from whom he inherited syphilis, and the grandson of a pyromaniac. Like two other villains in Faulkner's novels, Joe Christmas and Januarius Jones, he had spent most of his childhood in an institution. He was the man "who made money and had nothing he could do with it, spend it for, since he knew that alcohol would kill him like poison, who had no friends and had never known a woman"—in other words, he was the compendium of all the hateful qualities that Faulkner assigns to finance capitalism. *Sanctuary* is not the connected allegory that Mr. O'Donnell presents in outline (he doesn't approve of allegorical writing by novelists), but neither is it the accumulation of pointless horrors as which it has been dismissed by other critics. It is an example of the Freudian method turned backwards, being full of sexual night-mares that are in reality social symbols. In the author's mind, the novel is somehow connected with what he regards as the rape and corruption of the South.

And the descendants of the old ruling caste, in Faulkner's novels, have the wish but not the courage or the strength of will to prevent this new disaster. They are defeated by Popeye (like Horace Benbow), or they run away from him (like Gowan Stevens, who had gone to school at Virginia and learned to drink like a gentleman, but not to fight for his principles), or they are robbed and replaced in their positions of influence by the Snopeses (like old Bayard Sartoris, the president of the bank), or they drug themselves with eloquence and alcohol (like Mr. Compson), or they retire into the illusion of being inviolable Southern ladies (like Mrs. Compson, who says, "It can't be simply to flout and hurt me. Whoever God is, He would not permit that. I'm a lady."), or they dwell so much on the past that they are incapable of facing the present (like Reverend Hightower, of *Light in August*, who loses his wife and his church through living in a dream world), or they run from danger to danger (like young Bayard Sartoris) frantically seeking their own destruction. Faulkner's novels are full of well-meaning and even admirable people, not only the grand-sons of the cotton aristocracy, but also pine-hill farmers and storekeepers and sewing-machine agents and Negro cooks and sharecroppers; but they are almost all of them defeated by circumstances and they carry with them a sense of their own doom.

They also carry, whether heroes or villains, a curious sense of submission to their fate. "There is not one of Faulkner's characters," says André Gide in his dialogue on "The New American Novelists," "who, properly speaking, has a soul"; and I think he means that not one of them exercises the faculty of conscious choice between good and evil. They are haunted, obsessed, driven forward by some inner necessity. Like Miss Rosa Coldfield (in *Absalom, Absalom!*), they exist in "that dream state in which you run without moving from a terror in which you cannot believe, toward a safety in which you have no faith." Or like the slaves freed by General Sherman's army (in *The Unvanquished*), they follow the roads toward any river, believing that it will be their Jordan:

> They were singing, walking along the road singing, not even looking to either side. The dust didn't even settle for two days, because all that night they still passed; we sat up listening to them, and the next morning every few yards along the road would be the old ones who couldn't keep up any more, sitting or lying down and even crawling along, calling to the others

to help them; and the others—the young ones—not stopping, not even looking at them. "Going to Jordan," they told me. "Going to cross Jordan."

All Faulkner's characters, black and white, are a little like that. They dig for gold frenziedly after they have lost their hope of finding it (like Henry Armstid in *The Hamlet* and Lucas Beauchamp in *Go Down, Moses*); or they battle against and survive a Mississippi flood for the one privilege of returning to the state prison farm (like the tall convict in *The Wild Palms*); or, a whole family together, they carry a body through flood and fire and corruption to bury it in the cemetery at Jefferson (like the Bundrens in *As I Lay Dying*); or they tramp the roads week after week in search of men who had promised to marry them (like Lena Grove, the pregnant woman of *Light in August*); or, pursued by a mob, they turn at the end to meet and accept death (like Joe Christmas in the same novel). Even when they seem to be guided by a conscious design, like Colonel Sutpen, it is not something they have chosen by an act of will, but something that has taken possession of them: ". . . . not what he wanted to do but what he just had to do, had to do it whether he wanted to or not, because if he did not do it he knew that he could never live with himself for the rest of his life." In the same way, Faulkner himself writes, not what he wants to, but what he just has to write whether he wants to or not. And the effect produced on us by all these haunted characters, described in hypnagogic prose, is that of myths or fairy tales or dreams, where again the people act under compulsion, toward fatally predetermined ends.

In addition to being a fatalist, Faulkner is also an idealist, more strongly so than any other American writer of our time. The idealism disguises itself as its own opposite, but that is because he is deeply impressed by and tends to exaggerate the contrast between the life around him and the ideal picture in his mind. No other American writer makes such a use of negative turns of speech: his stories abound in words like "paintless," "lightless," "windowless," "notfeeling," "unvisioned." He speaks of "that *roadless* and even *pathless* waste of *unfenced* fallow and wilderness jungle—*no* barn, *no* stable, *not so much as* a hen-coop; just a log cabin built by hand and *no* clever hand either, a meagre pile of clumsily cut firewood sufficient for about one day and *not even* a gaunt hound to come bellowing out from under the house when he rode up." In the same story ("The Bear"), he speaks of ". . . the empty fields without plow or seed to work them, fenceless against the stock which did not exist within or without the walled stable which likewise was not there." He speaks of faces watching "without alarm, without recognition, without hope," and he speaks of the South under Reconstruction as "a lightless and gutted and empty land." Always in his mind he has an ideal picture of how the land and the people should be—a picture of painted, many-windowed houses, fenced fields, overflowing barns, eyes lighting up with recognition; and always, being honest, he measures that picture against the land and people he has seen. And both pictures are not only physical but moral; for always in the background of his novels is a sense of moral standards and a feeling of outrage at their being violated or simply pushed aside. Seeing little hope in the future, he turns to the past, where he hopes to discover a legendary and recurrent pattern that will illuminate and lend dignity to the world about him. So it is that Reverend Hightower, dying in the dingy ruin of his plans, sees a vision of Bedford Forrest's troopers, who lived without question by a single and universally accepted code:

> He hears above his heart the thunder increase, myriad and drumming. Like a long sighing of wind in trees it begins, then they sweep into sight, borne now upon a cloud of phantom dust. They rush past, forwardleaning in the saddles, with brandished arms, beneath whipping ribbons from slanted and eager lances; with tumult and soundless yelling they sweep past like a tide whose crest is jagged with the wild heads of horses and the brandished arms of men like the crater of the world in explosion. They rush past, are gone; the dust swirls skyward sucking, fades away into the night which has fully come. Yet, leaning forward in the window . . . it seems to him that he still hears them: the wild bugles and the clashing sabres and the dying thunder of hooves.

Edmund Wilson

THE HISTORICAL
INTERPRETATION OF LITERATURE

I want to talk about the historical interpretation of literature—that is, about the interpretation of literature in its social, economic and political aspects.

To begin with, it will be worth while to say something about the kind of criticism which seems to be furthest removed from this. There is a kind of comparative criticism which tends to be non-historical. The essays of T. S. Eliot, which have had such an immense influence in our time, are, for example, fundamentally non-historical. Eliot sees, or tries to see, the whole of literature, so far as he is acquainted with it, spread out before him under the aspect of eternity. He then compares the work of different periods and countries, and tries to draw from it general conclusions about what literature ought to be. He understands, of course, that our point of view in connection with literature changes, and he has what seems to me a very sound conception of the whole body of writing of the past as something to which new works are continually being added, and which is not thereby merely increased in bulk but modified as a whole—so that Sophocles is no longer precisely what he was for Aristotle, or Shakespeare what he was for Ben Jonson or for Dryden or for Dr. Johnson, on

"The Historical Interpretation of Literature" from *The Triple Thinkers*, by Edmund Wilson, Oxford University Press, 1948. Reprinted by permission of the author.

account of all the later literature that has intervened between them and us. Yet at every point of this continual accretion, the whole field may be surveyed, as it were, spread out before the critic. The critic tries to see it as God might; he calls the books to a Day of Judgment. And, looking at things in this way, he may arrive at interesting and valuable conclusions which could hardly be reached by approaching them in any other way. Eliot was able to see, for example—what I believe had never been noticed before—that the French Symbolist poetry of the nineteenth century had certain fundamental resemblances to the English poetry of the age of Donne. Another kind of critic would draw certain historical conclusions from these purely aesthetic findings, as the Russian D. S. Mirsky did; but Eliot does not draw them.

Another example of this kind of non-historical criticism, in a somewhat different way and on a somewhat different plane, is the work of the late George Saintsbury. Saintsbury was a connoisseur of wines; he wrote an entertaining book on the subject. And his attitude toward literature, too, was that of the connoisseur. He tastes the authors and tells you about the vintages; he distinguishes the qualities of the various wines. His palate was as fine as could be, and he possessed the great qualification that he knew how to take each book on its own terms without expecting it to be some other book and was thus in a position to appreciate a great variety of kinds of writing. He was a man of strong social prejudices and peculiarly intransigent political views, but, so far as it is humanly possible, he kept them out of his literary criticism. The result is one of the most agreeable and most comprehensive commentaries on literature that have ever been written in English. Most scholars who have read as much as Saintsbury don't have Saintsbury's discriminating taste. Here is a critic who has covered the whole ground like any academic historian, yet whose account of it is not merely a chronology but a record of fastidious enjoyment. Since enjoyment is the only thing he is looking for, he does not need to know the causes of things, and the historical background of literature does not interest him very much.

There is, however, another tradition of criticism which dates from the beginning of the eighteenth century. In the year 1725, the Neapolitan philosopher Vico published *La Scienza Nuova*, a revolutionary work on the philosophy of history, in which he asserted for the first time that the social world was certainly the work of man, and attempted what is, so far as I know, the first social interpretation of a work of literature. This is what Vico says about Homer: "Homer composed the *Iliad* when Greece was young and consequently burning with sublime passions such as pride, anger and vengeance—passions which cannot allow dissimulation and which consort with generosity; so that she then admired Achilles, the hero of force. But, grown old, he composed the *Odyssey*, at a time when the passions of Greece were already somewhat cooled by reflection, which is the mother of prudence—so that she now admired Ulysses, the hero of wisdom. Thus also, in Homer's youth, the Greek people liked cruelty, abuse, savagery, fierceness, ferocity; whereas, when Homer was old, they were already enjoying the luxuries of Alcinoüs, the delights of Calypso, the pleasures of Circe, the songs of the sirens and the pastimes of the suitors, who went no further in aggression and combat than laying siege to the chaste Penelope—all of which practices would appear incompatible with the spirit of the earlier time. The divine Plato is so struck by this difficulty that, in order to solve it, he tells us that Homer had foreseen in inspired vision these dissolute, sickly and disgusting customs. But in this way he makes Homer out to have been but a foolish instructor for Greek civilization, since, however much he may condemn them he is displaying for imitation these corrupt and decadent habits which were not to be adopted till long after the foundation of the nations of Greece, and accelerating the natural course which human events would take by spurring the Greeks on to corruption. Thus it is plain that the Homer of the *Iliad* must have preceded by many years the Homer who wrote the *Odyssey*; and it is plain that the former must belong to the northeastern part of Greece, since he celebrates the Trojan War, which took place in his part of the country, whereas the latter belongs to the southeastern part, since he celebrates Ulysses, who reigned there."

You see that Vico has here explained Homer in terms both of historical period and of geographical origin. The idea that human arts and institutions were to be studied and elucidated as the products of the geographical and climatic conditions in which the people who created them lived, and of the phase of their social development through which they were passing at the moment, made great progress during the eighteenth century. There are traces of it even in Dr. Johnson, that most orthodox and classical of critics—as, for example, when he accounts for certain characteristics of Shakespeare by the relative barbarity of the age in which he lived, pointing out, just as Vico had done, that "nations, like individuals, have their infancy." And by the eighties of the eighteenth century Herder, in his *Ideas on the Philosophy of History*, was writing of poetry that it was a kind of "Proteus among the people, which is always changing its form in response to the languages, manners, and habits, to the temperaments and climates, nay even to the accents of different nations." He said—what could still seem startling even so late as that—that "language was not a divine communication, but something men had produced themselves." In the lectures on the philosophy of history that Hegel delivered in Berlin in 1822-23, he discussed the national literatures as expressions of the societies which had produced them—societies which he conceived as great organisms continually transforming themselves under the influence of a succession of dominant ideas.

In the field of literary criticism, this historical point of view came to its first complete flower in the work of the French critic Taine, in the middle of the nineteenth century. The whole school of historian-critics to which Taine belonged—Michelet, Renan, Sainte-Beuve—had been occupied in interpreting books in terms of their historical origins. But Taine was the first of these to attempt to apply these principles systematically and on a large scale in a work devoted exclusively to literature. In the introduction to his *History of English Literature*, published in 1863, he made his famous pronouncement that works of literature were to be understood as the upshot of three interfusing factors: *the moment, the race and the milieu.* Taine thought he was a scientist and a mechanist, who was examining works of literature from the same point of view as the chemist in experimenting with chemical compounds. But the difference between the critic and the chemist is that the critic cannot first combine his elements and then watch to see what they will do; he can only examine phenomena which have already taken place. The procedure that Taine actually follows is to pretend to set the stage for the experiment by describing the moment, the race and the milieu, and then to say: "such a situation demands such and such a kind of writer." He now goes on to describe the kind of writer that the situation demands, and the reader finds himself at the end confronted with Shakespeare or Milton or Byron or whoever the great figure is—who turns out to prove the accuracy of Taine's prognosis by precisely living up to the description.

There was thus a certain element of imposture in Taine; but it was the rabbits he pulled out that saved him. If he had really been the mechanist that he thought he was, his work on literature would have had little value. The truth was that Taine loved literature for its own sake—he was at his best himself a brilliant artist—and he had very strong moral convictions which give his writing emotional power. His mind, to be sure, was an analytical one, and his analysis, though terribly oversimplified, does have an explanatory value. Yet his work was what we call creative. Whatever he may say about chemical experiments, it is evident when he writes of a great writer that the moment, the race and the milieu have combined, like the three sounds of the chord in Browning's poem about Abt Vogler, to produce not a fourth sound but a star.

To Taine's set of elements was added, dating from the middle of the century, a new element, the economic, which was introduced into the discussion of historical phenomena mainly by Marx and Engels. The non-Marxist critics themselves were at the time already taking into account the influence of the social classes. In his chapters on the Norman conquest of England, Taine shows that the difference between the literatures produced respectively by the Normans and by the Saxons was partly the difference between a ruling class, on the one hand, and a vanquished and oppressed class, on the other. And Michelet, in his volume on the Regency, which was finished the same year that the *History of English Literature* appeared, studies the *Manon Lescaut* of the Abbé Prévost as a document representing the point of view of the small gentry before the French Revolution. But Marx and Engels derived the social classes from the way that people made or got their livings—from what they called the *methods of production;* and they tended to regard these economic processes as fundamental to civilization.

The Dialectical Materialism of Marx and Engels was not really so materialistic as it sounds. There was in it a large element of the Hegelian idealism that Marx and Engels thought they had got rid of. At no time did these two famous materialists take so mechanistic a view of things as Taine began by professing;

and their theory of the relation of works of literature to what they called the *economic base* was a good deal less simple than Taine's theory of the moment, the race and the milieu. They thought that art, politics, religion, philosophy and literature belonged to what they called the *superstructure* of human activity; but they saw that the practitioners of these various professions tended also to constitute social groups, and that they were always pulling away from the kind of solidarity based on economic classes in order to establish a professional solidarity of their own. Furthermore, the activities of the superstructure could influence one another, and they could influence the economic base. It may be said of Marx and Engels in general that, contrary to the popular impression, they were tentative, confused and modest when it came down to philosophical first principles, where a materialist like Taine was cocksure. Marx once made an attempt to explain why the poems of Homer were so good when the society that produced them was from his point of view—that is, from the point of view of its industrial development—so primitive; and this gave him a good deal of trouble. If we compare his discussion of this problem with Vico's discussion of Homer, we see that the explanation of literature in terms of a philosophy of social history is becoming, instead of simpler and easier, more difficult and more complex.

Marx and Engels were deeply imbued, moreover, with the German admiration for literature, which they had learned from the age of Goethe. It would never have occurred to either of them that *der Dichter*[1] was not one of the noblest and most beneficent of humankind. When Engels writes about Goethe, he presents him as a man equipped for "practical life," whose career was frustrated by the "misery" of the historical situation in Germany in his time, and reproaches him for allowing himself to lapse into the "cautious, smug and narrow" philistinism of the class from which he came; but Engels regrets this, because it interfered with the development of the "mocking, defiant, world-despising genius," "der geniale Dichter," "der gewaltige Poet,"[2] of whom Engels would not even, he says, have asked that he should have been a political liberal if Goethe had not sacrificed to his bourgeois shrinkings his truer esthetic sense. And the great critics who were trained on Marx—Franz Mehring and Bernard Shaw—had all this reverence for the priesthood of literature. Shaw deplores the absence of political philosophy and what he regards as the middle-class snobbery in Shakespeare; but he celebrates Shakespeare's poetry and his dramatic imagination almost as enthusiastically as Swinburne did, describing even those potboiling comedies—*Twelfth Night* and *As You Like It*—the themes of which seem to him most trashy—as "the Crown Jewels of English dramatic poetry." Such a critic may do more for a writer by showing him as a real man dealing with a real world at a definite moment of time than the impressionist critic of Swinburne's type who flourished in the same period of the late nineteenth century. The purely impressionist critic approaches the whole literature

1. The poet.
2. The highly gifted poet, the mighty poet.

as an exhibit of belletristic jewels, and he can only write a rhapsodic catalogue. But when Shaw turned his spotlight on Shakespeare as a figure in the Shavian drama of history, he invested him with a new interest as no other English critic had done.

The insistence that the man of letters should play a political role, the disparagement of works of art in comparison with political action, were thus originally no part of Marxism. They only became associated with it later. This happened by way of Russia, and it was due to special tendencies in that country that date from long before the Revolution or the promulgation of Marxism itself. In Russia there have been very good reasons why the political implications of literature should particularly occupy the critics. The art of Pushkin itself, with its marvelous power of implication, had certainly been partly created by the censorship of Nicholas I, and Pushkin set the tradition for most of the great Russian writers that followed him. Every play, every poem, every story, must be a parable of which the moral is *implied*. If it were stated, the censor would suppress the book as he tried to do with Pushkin's *Bronze Horseman*, where it was merely a question of the packed implications protruding a little too plainly. Right down through the writings of Chekhov and up almost to the Revolution, the imaginative literature of Russia presents the peculiar paradox of an art that is technically objective and yet charged with social messages. In Russia under the Tsar, it was inevitable that social criticism should lead to political conclusions, because the most urgent need from the point of view of any kind of improvement was to get rid of the tsarist regime. Even the neo-Christian moralist Tolstoy, who pretended to be non-political, was to exert a subversive influence, because his independent preaching was bound to embroil him with the Church, and the Church was an integral part of the tsardom. Tolstoy's pamphlet called *What Is Art?*, in which he throws overboard Shakespeare and a large part of modern literature, including his own novels, in the interest of his intransigent morality, is the example which is most familiar to us of the moralizing Russian criticism; but it was only the most sensational expression of a kind of approach which had been prevalent since Belinsky and Chernyshevsky in the early part of the century. The critics, who were usually journalists writing in exile or for a contraband press, were always tending to demand of the imaginative writers that they should dramatize bolder morals.

Even after the Revolution had destroyed the tsarist government, this state of things did not change. The old habits of censorship persisted in the new socialist society of the Soviets, which was necessarily made up of people who had been stamped by the die of the despotism. We meet here the peculiar phenomenon of a series of literary groups that attempt, one after the other, to obtain official recognition or to make themselves sufficiently powerful to establish themselves as arbiters of literature. Lenin and Trotsky and Lunacharsky had the sense to oppose these attempts; the comrade-dictators of Proletcult or Lev or Rapp would certainly have been just as bad as the Count Benckendorff who made Pushkin miserable, and when the Stalin bureaucracy, after the death of Gorky, got control of this department as of everything else, they instituted a system of repression that made Benckendorff and Nicholas I look like Lorenzo de' Medici. In the meantime, Trotsky, who was Commissar of War but himself a great political writer with an interest in belles-lettres, attempted, in 1924, apropos of one of these movements, to clarify the situation. He wrote a brilliant and valuable book called *Literature and Revolution,* in which he explained the aims of the government, analyzed the work of the Russian writers, and praised or rebuked the latter as they seemed to him in harmony or at odds with the former. Trotsky is intelligent, sympathetic; it is evident that he is really fond of literature and that he knows that a work of art does not fulfill its function in terms of the formulas of party propaganda. But Mayakovsky, the Soviet poet, whom Trotsky had praised with reservations, expressed himself in a famous joke when he was asked what he thought of Trotsky's book—a pun which implied that a Commissar turned critic was inevitably a Commissar still;[1] and what a foreigner cannot accept in Trotsky is his assumption that it is the duty of the government to take a hand in the direction of literature.

This point of view, indigenous to Russia, has been imported to other countries through the permeation of Communist influence. The Communist press and its literary followers have reflected the control of the Kremlin in all the phases through which it has passed, down to the wholesale imprisonment of Soviet writers which has been taking place since 1935. But it has never been a part of the American system that our Republican or Democratic administration should lay down a political line for the guidance of the national literature. A recent gesture in this direction on the part of Archibald MacLeish, who seemed a little carried away by his position as Librarian of Congress, was anything but cordially received by serious American writers. So long as the United States remains happily a nontotalitarian country, we can very well do without this aspect of the historical criticism of literature.

Another element of a different order has, however, since Marx's time been added to the historical study of the origins of works of literature. I mean the psychoanalysis of Freud. This appears as an extension of something which had already got well started before, which had figured even in Johnson's *Lives of the Poets,* and of which the great exponent had been Sainte-Beuve: the interpretation of works of literature in the light of the personalities behind them. But the Freudians made this interpretation more exact and more systematic. The great example of the psychoanalysis of an artist is Freud's own essay on Leonardo da Vinci; but this has little critical interest: it is an attempt to construct a case history. One of the best examples I know of the application of Freudian analysis to literature is in Van Wyck Brooks' book, *The Ordeal of Mark Twain,* in which Mr. Brooks uses an incident of Mark Twain's boyhood as a key to his whole career. Mr. Brooks has since repudiated the method he

---

1. *The first pancake lies like a narkom* . . . (people's commissar)—a parody of the Russian saying, . . . *The first pancake lies like a lump.*

resorted to here, on the ground that no one but an analyst can ever know enough about a writer to make a valid psychoanalytic diagnosis. This is true, and it is true of the method that it has led to bad results where the critic has built a Freudian mechanism out of very slender evidence, and then given us merely a romance exploiting the supposed working of this mechanism, in place of an actual study that sticks close to the facts and the documents of the writer's life and work. But I believe that Van Wyck Brooks really had hold of something important when he fixed upon that childhood incident of which Mark Twain gave so vivid an account to his biographer—that scene at the deathbed of his father when his mother had made him promise that he would not break her heart. If it was not one of those crucial happenings that are supposed to determine the complexes of Freud, it has certainly a typical significance in relation to Mark Twain's whole psychology. The stories that people tell about their childhood are likely to be profoundly symbolic even when they have been partly or wholly made up in the light of later experience. And the attitudes, the compulsions, the emotional "patterns" that recur in the work of a writer are of great interest to the historical critic.

These attitudes and patterns are embedded in the community and the historical moment, and they may indicate its ideals and its diseases as the cell shows the condition of the tissue. The recent scientific experimentation in the combining of Freudian with Marxist method and of psychoanalysis with anthropology, has had its parallel development in criticism. And there is thus another element added to our equipment for analyzing literary works, and the problem grows still more complex.

The analyst, however, is of course not concerned with the comparative values of his patients any more than the surgeon is. He cannot tell you why the neurotic Dostoevsky produces work of immense value to his fellows while another man with the same neurotic pattern would become a public menace. Freud himself emphatically states in his study of Leonardo that his method can make no attempt to account for Leonardo's genius. The problems of comparative artistic value still remain after we have given attention to the Freudian psychological factor just as they do after we have given attention to the Marxist economic factor and to the racial and geographical factors. No matter how thoroughly and searchingly we may have scrutinized works of literature from the historical and biographical points of view, we must be ready to attempt to estimate, in some such way as Saintsbury and Eliot do, the relative degrees of success attained by the products of the various periods and the various personalities. We must be able to tell good from bad, the first-rate from the second-rate. We shall not otherwise write literary criticism at all, but merely social or political history as reflected in literary texts, or psychological case histories from past eras, or, to take the historical point of view in its simplest and most academic form, merely chronologies of books that have been published.

And now how, in these matters of literary art, do we tell the good art from the bad? Norman Kemp Smith, the Kantian philosopher, whose courses I was fortunate enough to take at Princeton twenty-five years ago, used to tell us that this recognition was based primarily on an emotional reaction. For purposes of practical criticism this is a safe assumption on which to proceed. It is possible to discriminate in a variety of ways the elements that in any given department go to make a successful work of literature. Different schools have at different times demanded different things of literature: *unity, symmetry, universality, originality, vision, inspiration, strangeness, suggestiveness, improving morality, socialist realism,* etc. But you could have any set of these qualities that any school of writing has called for and still not have a good play, a good novel, a good poem, a good history. If you identify the essence of good literature with any one of these elements or with any combination of them, you simply shift the emotional reaction to the recognition of the element or elements. Or if you add to your other demands the demand that the writer must have *talent,* you simply shift this recognition to the talent. Once people find some grounds of agreement in the coincidence of their emotional reactions to books, they may be able to discuss these elements profitably; but if they do not have this basic agreement, the discussion will make no sense.

But how, you may ask, can we identify this élite who know what they are talking about? Well, it can only be said of them that they are self-appointed and self-perpetuating, and that they will compel you to accept their authority. Imposters may try to put themselves over, but these quacks will not last. The implied position of the people who know about literature (as is also the case in every other art) is simply that they know what they know, and that they are determined to impose their opinions by main force of eloquence or assertion on the people who do not know. This is not a question, of course, of professional workers in literature—such as editors, professors and critics, who very often have no real understanding of the products with which they deal—but of readers of all kinds in all walks of life. There are moments when a first-rate writer, unrecognized or out of fashion with the official chalkers-up for the market, may find his support in the demand for his work of an appreciative cultivated public.

But what is the cause of this emotional reaction which is the critic's divining rod? This question has long been a subject of study by the branch of philosophy called esthetics, and it has recently been made a subject of scientific experimentation. Both these lines of inquiry are likely to be prejudiced in the eyes of the literary critic by the fact that the inquiries are sometimes conducted by persons who are obviously deficient in literary feeling or taste. Yet one should not deny the possibility that something of value might result from the speculations and explorations of men of acute minds who take as their given data the esthetic emotions of other men.

Almost everybody interested in literature has tried to explain to himself the nature of these emotions that register our approval of artistic works; and I of course have my own explanation.

In my view, all our intellectual activity, in whatever field it takes place, is an attempt to give a meaning to our experience—that is, to make life more pracicable; for by understanding things we make it easier to survive and get around among them. The mathematician Euclid, working in a convention of abstracions, shows us relations between the distances of our unwieldy and clutteredup environment upon which we are able to count. A drama of Sophocles also indicates relations between the various human impulses, which appear so confused and dangerous, and it brings out a certain justice of Fate—that is to say, of the way in which the interaction of these impulses is seen in the long run to work out—upon which we can also depend. The kinship, from this point of view, of the purposes of science and art appears very clearly in the case of the Greeks, because not only do both Euclid and Sophocles satisfy us by making patterns, but they make much the same kind of patterns. Euclid's *Elements* takes simple theorems and by a series of logical operations builds them up to a climax in the square on the hypotenuse. A typical drama of Sophocles develops in a similar way.

Some writers (as well as some scientists) have a different kind of explicit message beyond the reassurance implicit in the mere feat of understanding life or of moulding the harmony of artistic form. Not content with such an achievement as that of Sophocles—who has one of his choruses tell us that it is better not to be born, but who, by representing life as noble and based on law, makes its tragedy easier to bear—such writers attempt, like Plato, to think out and recommend a procedure for turning it into something better. But other departments of literature—lyric poetry such as Sappho's, for example— have *less* philosophical content than Sophocles. A lyric gives us nothing but a pattern imposed on the expression of a feeling; but this pattern of metrical quantities and of consonants and vowels that balance has the effect of reducing the feeling, however unruly or painful it may seem when we experience it in the course of our lives, to something orderly, symmetrical and pleasing; and it also relates this feeling to the more impressive scheme, works it into the larger texture, of the body of poetic art. The discord has been resolved, the anomaly subjected to discipline. And this control of his emotion by the poet has the effect at second-hand of making it easier for the reader to manage his own emotions. (Why certain sounds and rhythms gratify us more than others, and how they are connected with the themes and ideas that they are chosen as appropriate for conveying, are questions that may be passed on to the scientist.)

And this brings us back again to the historical point of view. The experience of mankind on the earth is always changing as man develops and has to deal with new combinations of elements; and the writer who is to be anything more than an echo of his predecessors must always find expression for something which has never yet been expressed, must master a new set of phenomena which has never yet been mastered. With each such victory of the human intellect, whether in history, in philosophy or in poetry, we experience a deep satisfaction: we have been cured of some ache of disorder, relieved of some oppressive burden of uncomprehended events.

This relief that brings the sense of power, and, with the sense of power, joy, is the positive emotion which tells us that we have encountered a first-rate piece of literature. But stay! you may at this point warn: are not people often solaced and exhilarated by literature of the trashiest kind? They are: crude and limited people do certainly feel some such emotion in connection with work that is limited and crude. The man who is more highly organized and has a wider intellectual range will feel it in connection with work that is finer and more complex. The difference between the emotion of the more highly organized man and the emotion of the less highly organized one is a matter of mere gradation. You sometimes discover books—the novels of John Steinbeck, for example—that seem to mark precisely the borderline between work that is definitely superior and work that is definitely bad. When I was speaking a little while back of the genuine connoisseurs who establish the standards of taste, I meant, of course, the people who can distinguish Grade A and who prefer it to the other grades.

Norman Podhoretz

THE ARTICLE AS ART

Anyone who has given much attention to postwar American fiction is likely to have noticed a curious fact. Many of our serious novelists also turn out book reviews, critical pieces, articles about the contemporary world, memoirs, sketches—all of which are produced for magazines and which these writers undoubtedly value far lower than their stories and novels.

Indeed, some novelists (and this applies to many poets too) tend to express their contempt or disdain for discursive prose in the very act of writing it. You can hear a note of condescension toward the medium they happen to be working in at the moment; they seem to be announcing in the very construction of their sentences that they have no great use for the prosy requirements of the essay or the review, that they are only dropping in from Olympus for a brief, impatient visit. But just as often—and this is the curious fact I am referring to—the discursive writing of people who think of themselves primarily as novelists turns out to be more interesting, more lively, more penetrating, more intelligent, more forceful, more original—in short, *better*—than their fiction, which they and everyone else automatically treat with greater respect.

Two examples spring immediately to mind: the late Isaac Rosenfeld and the young Negro author, James Baldwin. Rosenfeld, who died of a heart attack in Chicago two years ago at the age of thirty-seven, was immensely gifted, possibly the most gifted writer to appear in America in the last few decades. Born of immigrant parents and raised in a Yiddish-speaking milieu, he came to own the English language by an act of absolute appropriation. He could make it do anything he wanted—sprout lush flora, like a tropical landscape, or walk in

Reprinted from *Harper's Magazine*, July 1958, by permission of Harper & Brothers.

stately simplicity as though it had been designed only to express the basic emotions and the most direct and uncomplicated apprehensions of reality. Beyond that, however, he was intelligent and literate, endowed with wide curiosity and a frisky imagination. He was also prolific: for years his name was ubiquitous in the world of the little magazine, with a story here, a review there, an article yet somewhere else. Though he published only one novel, *A Passage from Home,* and a collection of short stories, *King Solomon's Mines,* he regarded himself and was regarded by others as essentially a novelist.

Yet the truth is that he never produced a piece of fiction which drew on the whole range of his talent and sensibility. You got the impression that in order to write a story, this man had to suppress half of what he knew and saw, that he was possessed of a mind and an eye and an imagination which could not get their full play in a dramatic narrative. Though banality of thought and falsity of feeling hardly ever entered his articles and reviews, his fiction frequently suffered from derivativeness, artificiality, and mere cleverness. You would scarcely have suspected even from his novel that Rosenfeld was more than a bright young man who had read Proust and Joyce and saw himself, like a thousand other bright young men, as a creature set apart by his artistic vocation. You would scarcely have suspected him capable of that marvelous posthumous piece published in *Commentary* called "Life in Chicago," in which the smell and feel of a city and its history are rendered to perfection, in which the meaning of that history is defined through a deliciously fanciful theory of the effect on a city of distance from the sea, in which the combination of love and repulsion that a "rootless" American intellectual invariably feels for his home town are superbly expressed, and in which everything—description, analysis, exhortation, and sheer kidding around—converges in the end on a declaration of faith in the supremacy of the arts and what they represent over the prevalent values of modern life. It is a declaration all the more moving for its directness and candor, and all the more powerful for coming from someone who knows that he is flying in the face of the contemporary spirit—but who also knows that a man at some point in his life has to stop agonizing over his apparent eccentricities and say, simply and without refinement or embellishment, "This is what I stand for."

This essay gives you more of Chicago, more of what it means to be an artist and an intellectual in America, and more of Rosenfeld himself than *A Passage from Home,* which, as it happens, is also about Chicago, the artist in America, and the soul of Isaac Rosenfeld.

The case of James Baldwin is no less striking. Baldwin has so far published three books—a collection of essays, *Notes of a Native Son,* and two novels, *Go Tell It on the Mountain* and *Giovanni's Room* (his third novel is coming out some time this year). The essays in *Notes of a Native Son* all appeared originally in magazines; a couple of them are literary criticism, one is a movie review, and the others are memoirs relating to various aspects of a Negro's confrontation with the white world both in America and Europe. Taken together they make up the best book I have ever read about the American Negro, a book that conveys a phenomenally keen sense of the special quality of Negro experience today. What distinguishes these pieces, even apart from the clarity, subtlety, and vividness with which they are written, is Baldwin's complex conception of the Negro as a man who is simultaneously like unto all other men and yet profoundly, perhaps irrevocably different. The nature of the sameness and the nature of the difference are the subject of the book, and he never allows himself to forget the one term while exploring the other.

But it is precisely the loss of complexity that characterizes his novels. *Go Tell It on the Mountain* is a fairly conventional first novel about a Negro boy in Harlem, and though the hero's milieu (especially the religious background of his life) is well delineated, you nevertheless feel that Baldwin is trying to persuade you that there is no real difference between the situation of John Grimes and that of any other sensitive American boy who is at odds with his environment. But there *is* a difference, and it is not merely one of degree —as any reader of *Notes of a Native Son* can tell you.

Similarly with *Giovanni's Room*, which, though it does not deal with Negroes, exhibits the same slurring over of differences in relation to homosexuality. (The white homosexual in America is in the same boat as the oppressed Negro—they are both, as it were, "black" in the eyes of their culture.) Baldwin, in writing about a young American living in Paris who discovers that he is a homosexual, tries very hard to make it appear that a love affair between two men is spiritually and psychologically indistinguishable from a heterosexual romance—which strikes me as at worst an untruth and at best an oversimplification. Here again, then, we have a writer who seems able to produce fiction only at the expense of suppressing half of what he sees and knows, whose discursive prose is richer, more imaginative, and fundamentally more honest than his novels and stories. And with proper qualifications in each case, similar points might be made of James Agee, Mary McCarthy, Elizabeth Hardwick, Randall Jarrell, Leslie Fiedler, and several others.

The Glory of Being a Novelist

Now it can, of course, be said that these examples prove nothing—and would still prove nothing even if another twenty were added to them—except that some people are better essayists than novelists. And if I asked why a first-rate essayist should feel obliged to work so hard at turning out second-rate fiction, the answer would be that the novel is to us what drama was to the Elizabethans and lyric poetry to the Romantics, so that an ambitious writer today will naturally make his bid there. In every college in the country, and probably in most of the high schools too, there are kids who want to be novelists when they grow up—who are convinced that a novelist is the most glorious of all things to be, and who are often prepared to make sacrifices in pursuit of this vocation. The aura of sanctity that used to attach to the idea of a poet has now floated over to rest on the head of the novelist—a very congenial switch when we consider that Americans tend to regard poets as sissies and novelists as ard-drinking, hard-loving, hard-fighting men of the world. (Compare the public image of T. S. Eliot and Wallace Stevens to Hemingway's or Faulkner's and you see that the poets and novelists themselves seem driven to play true to type.)

But the prestige of the novel cannot account for the fact that so much good writing about precisely those experiences which are closest to the heart of life in America and which we would suppose to be the proper province of fiction—experiences involving the quest for self-definition in a society where a man's identity is not given and fixed by birth—has been done in our day not in novels but in discursive pieces of one kind or another.

Lionel Trilling made a similar observation in a review of David Riesman's *The Lonely Crowd*:

> People of literary inclinations . . . have a natural jealousy of sociology because it seems to be in process of taking over from literature one of literature's most characteristic functions, the investigation and criticism of morals and manners. Yet it is but fair to remark that sociology has pre-empted what literature has voluntarily surrendered.

Nor is it academic sociology alone that has "pre-empted what literature has voluntarily surrendered." The reportage done in magazines by professional journalists like Dwight Macdonald, Robert Shaplen, Richard H. Rovere, John Bartlow Martin, and a good many others, has carried on a more exhaustive and more accomplished investigation of our morals and manners than the bulk of contemporary fiction.

The novel form is honored as never before, yet a feeling of dissatisfaction and impatience, irritation and boredom with contemporary serious fiction is very widespread. The general mood was well expressed by Leslie Fiedler who opened a fiction chronicle in *Partisan Review* not long ago with the complaint that the sight of a group of new novels stimulates in him "a desperate desire to sneak out to a movie. How respectable the form has become," he lamented, "how predictable!" Many other critics have tried to explain the low condition of current fiction by declaring that the novel is "dead," an exhausted genre like the epic and verse drama. But whether or not the novel is dead (and I myself don't believe that it is), one thing is certain: that a large class of readers, with or without benefit of theories about the rise and fall of literary forms, has found itself responding more enthusiastically to what is lamely called "non-fiction" (and especially to magazine articles and even book reviews) than to current fiction.

Wanted: a Name for Non-fiction

This is not, of course, a new observation. The popularity of "criticism"—a word often used as a catch-all term for any writing about literature or culture in general—has been deplored even more passionately than the dullness of post-war fiction and poetry, and has been taken as a sign of the sickness of our present condition. Some years ago, Randall Jarrell, in a famous article, christened this period "The Age of Criticism," and complained that nowadays young men were taking to their typewriters not to compose poems but to analyze and explicate the poems of others. Personally, I have never been able to understand why Mr. Jarrell was so eager to have everyone writing poetry; we can, after all, take it pretty much for granted that any young man who has it in him to become a poet *will* become a poet, even in an "Age of Criticism." And I should have thought that the danger was not that the popularity of criticism would rob us of poets but that the prestige of the "creative" would rob us of good critics, who have always been rarer, even today, than good poets.

Writing in the heyday of piety toward the divine faculty of imagination that succeeded the great flowering of English poetry during the first half of the nineteenth century, Matthew Arnold provided the best possible retort to Mr. Jarrell:

> Everybody . . . would be willing to admit, as a general proposition, that the critical faculty is lower than the inventive. But is it true that criticism is really, in itself, a baneful and injurious employment; is it true that all time given to writing critiques on the works of others would be much better employed if it were given to original composition of whatever kind this may be? Is it true that Johnson had better have gone on producing more *Irenes* instead of writing his *Lives of the Poets* . . . ?

Arnold's allusion to the distinction between the "critical faculty" and the "inventive" is one that any modern reader would pass over with automatic assent, so accustomed have we all become to thinking in terms of two radically different categories of mind—the imaginative, which is the mind that creates, and the . . . well, there is not even an adequate word for the other kind of mind. "Critical" won't do because it has too restricted a reference; nor will "philosophical" quite serve. The fact is that our attitude reveals itself beautifully in this terminological difficulty: we call everything that is not fiction or poetry "non-fiction," as though whole ranges of human thought had only a negative existence. We would all admit, if pressed, that books like Freud's *The Interpretation of Dreams* or Tocqueville's *Democracy in America* are as much works of the imagination as *Ulysses* or *The Waste Land*, but we tend in the ordinary course of things to identify "imagination" and "creativity" exclusively with the arts and, where literature is concerned, with poetry, the novel, and the drama. This idea is a legacy from nineteenth-century aesthetic theory. Throughout the eighteenth century the word "imagination" (or its synonym, "fancy") was often used pejoratively and sometimes held to be the source of lies and the enemy of reason. Reason was considered the faculty for perceiving truth, and good poetry was regarded as one of its products.

"A poet is not to leave his reason, and blindly abandon himself to follow fancy," declared the critic Thomas Rymer, "for then his fancy might be monstrous, might be singular, and please no body's maggot but his own; but reason s to be his guide, reason is common to all people, and can never carry him from what is natural."

Even before Coleridge formulated his famous theory of the poetic imagination as the highest mode of apprehending reality and credited poetry with a truth superior to the truths of reason and science, early Romantics like William Blake were pushing toward a doctrine that would justify the claims of the poet against those of the "natural philosophers." By the age of Victoria, the Coleridgean view had swept all before it; nothing is more characteristic of the Victorians than the reverence they felt toward poets and poetry (a reverence, as Mr. Jarrell should have remembered, which led to the production of more bad verse than any other period has ever foisted upon the world). The poet was a saint and a sage: the robust-minded Keats became to the Victorians a delicate aesthete languishing away for the sake of beauty and killed by the cruel barbs of the critics, while Shelley—a man up to his neck in politics and causes—was thought of as the wholly spiritual Ariel. The wicked Lord Byron only added to the charm of these images, and the somber Wordsworth was well suited to the role of Olympian wise man.

The "Fit" Theory of Creation

One of the consequences of this conception of the poetic faculty was to foster the idea that poetry could be written only in a kind of fit of divine inspiration that had nothing to do with intelligence or consciousness or concern with what was going on in the world. And a plausible relation can be traced between that notion and the decline of poetry in the latter part of the nineteenth century. It was the novelists of Victorian England, who had not yet quite achieved the status of "creative" and "imaginative" writers and to whom the smell of vulgarity that had once been associated with the novel still clung—Dickens, George Eliot, Thackeray, James—who represent their age most vitally and powerfully. What strikes one today about Victorian fiction is the scope it provided for the exercise of intelligence, the testing of ideas in the medium of experience, the examination of major contemporary problems. The novel flourished partly because it was such a free, amorphous, sprawling form in which almost anything (except, of course, explicit discussion of sex!) could go: there was no question of George Eliot's having to suppress half of what *she* knew and saw when she sat down to write fiction. And it flourished because it remained in touch with the world around it, while the poets were busy transcending the mundane and the prosaic.

By now we seem to have reached a point where the novel has taken over from poetry as the sanctified genre, and this has coincided (just as with poetry in the nineteenth century) with the aftermath of a great flowering. Proust, Joyce, Lawrence, Mann, Kafka, Hemingway, Faulkner are all behind us; in our eyes they have borne out the claims made for the "art of the novel" by Henry James and others, just as Wordsworth, Byron, Keats, and Shelley won the case for the superiority of the "poetic faculty" at the bar of Victorian judgment.

In a recent book called *The Living Novel* Granville Hicks, whose benign reviews in the *New Leader* have established him as the most promiscuous admirer of new writing since the days of Carl Van Doren, collected essays by ten well-known novelists aimed at refuting the charge that the novel is dead. Most of the essays are bad—bad thinking and bad writing—but they are interesting for what they reveal of the novelist's view of himself today. The dominant note is one of persecution. Mr. Hicks talks about the "enemies of the novel" and says that the novel has always had enemies. Almost all the contributors throw around words like "vision," "intensity," and, of course, "imagination" to distinguish the novel from other kinds of writing. There is a good deal of bitterness against the critics and a strong implication that they are resentful of "creativity." Saul Bellow (who has fared very well at the hands of the critics) says for example:

> And so we are told by critics that the novel is dead. These people can't know what the imagination is nor what its powers are. I wish I could believe in their good-natured objectivity. But I can't. I should like to disregard them, but that is a little difficult because they have a great deal of power. . . . And they can be very distracting. But the deadly earnestness with which they lower the boom! On what? after all. On flowers. On mere flowers.

You can't blame Mr. Bellow for being irritated by people who insist that the novel is dead while he is trying to write novels, but it is worth noticing that he does not answer the charge by asserting that good novels are still being produced and then trying to prove it; instead he invokes the name of "imagination" in reverent accents and identifies it with novels (apparently whether they are good or bad), while criticism is a "boom" lowered in metaphorical confusion on the "flowers" around it. Now it would be hard to think of a more infelicitous image for a novel than a flower; novels, if you like, are trees, they are robust and sturdy, not at all delicate. Why should Mr. Bellow have seized on this inept image? Partly to arouse the reader's sense of pathos, I think, but also because the idea of flowers, with its associations of sweetness, fragility, and loveliness, confers an ethereal dignity on the novel.

The idea comes out of the same sort of thinking that was applied to poetry by many Victorians: poetry was delicate, transcendent, special, inspired—anything, in short, but the measured discourse of a keen human sensibility operating on a world of men. But a new element has been added to the Victorian view. Not only does "imagination" now sprout "flowers," and not only does it (as in Coleridge) represent the highest faculty of intellection; it has also become the principle of "life" itself, while mind and consciousness are now seen as having signed a pact with the Angel of Death. The novel is valuable, we gather from Mr. Bellow and some of his colleagues, because it is the only place left in our world where imagination and its correlatives—sensitivity, responsiveness, passion—still function. (The *reductio* of all this can be found in the "spontaneous bop prosody" of Jack Kerouac.) Mr. Hicks goes so far as to say that "there is no substitute now available for the novel, and those who talk about the death of the novel are talking about the death of the imagination."

The Article Takes Over

I am not one of those who talk about the death of the novel, but I do think that it has fallen on bad days. I also think that the fault lies at least partly with these rarefied and incense-burning doctrines of the imagination, which have had the effect of surrendering the novel—to apply a remark of F. R. Leavis on Shelley's theory of inspiration—"to a sensibility that has no more dealings with intelligence than it can help." My own criticism of much contemporary fiction would be precisely that it lacks the only species of imagination worth mentioning— the kind that is vitalized by contact with a disciplined intelligence and a restless interest in the life of the times. And what the novel has abdicated has been taken over by discursive writers. Imagination has not died (how could it?) but it has gone into other channels; these channels are not by any means commensurate with the novel: they are, in fact, *channels* and not the sea. But there is living water in them nevertheless.

What I have in mind—and I cheerfully admit that the suggestion sounds preposterous—is *magazine articles*. I won't call them essays, even though to do so would make the point seem less disreputable and silly, because the type of thing I am referring to is not an essay in the old sense. Strictly speaking, the essay requires an audience that has no doubts about where the relevant subjects of discussion are to be found, and it is therefore written without any need to persuade the reader that he ought to concern himself with this particular question. The magazine article, as they say in the trade, always hangs on a peg; it takes off from an event in the news, a book recently published, a bill in Congress. And even then, with its relevance established in the most obvious way conceivable, it still has to sell itself to a reader who wants to be told why he should bother pushing his way through it when there are so many other claims on his attention. This is a tyrannical condition which can, of course, result in the reduction of all thought to the occasional and the newsworthy. But now and then a writer whose interests and talent go beyond the merely journalistic can be forced into very exciting pieces of work by the necessity to demonstrate the continuing importance of his special concerns by throwing them into the buzz and hum around him.

The Death-house Letters

To my mind, the critical pieces of Lionel Trilling offer perhaps the best example we have of discursive writing that is not only rich in imagination but animated by an uncanny sensitivity to the life from which it springs. Trilling has spent most of his time analyzing books—often remote books—but who has told us more than he about the way we feel and think today? But for the purposes of detailed illustration, I would like to take a less well-known example, an article (published in *Commentary* in 1953) called "The 'Idealism' of Julius and Ethel Rosenberg" by the late Robert Warshow who, like Isaac Rosenfeld, died suddenly at thirty-seven just when his extraordinary powers were developing into full maturity, and who—unlike Rosenfeld—never wrote any fiction.

This article began as a review of the Rosenberg death-house letters which came out around the time the convicted couple went to their execution. Since Warshow was one of those who believed that the world-wide clamor against the death sentence was largely motivated not by compassion for the Rosenbergs or a desire to see justice done, but by political anti-Americanism of one shade or another, one might have expected the review to be a pronouncement on the Communist menace. And certainly the crudity and vulgarity of the Rosenberg letters provided enough opportunity for scoring points against them and the movement to which they gave their lives. But Warshow's imagination would not permit him to turn out a simple polemical tract: what he wanted was an insight into the soul of the Rosenbergs, and it took a powerful act of imagination to find the soul of the Rosenbergs in the mass of depersonalized clichés that make up their correspondence. Considering the patent insincerity of their rhetoric, the temptation was great to deny them any human feelings at all. But again, Warshow's imagination would not allow him to fall into that trap. After quoting several particularly grotesque passages in which they discuss their children, Warshow comments:

> The fact that Julius Rosenberg can speak of a lack of toys as the "materials situation" does not in the least permit us to assume that he did not suffer for his children just as much as anyone else would have suffered. Nor does the impudence of Ethel's appeal to her "sister Americans"— whose lives she had been willing to put in danger—diminish in any way the reality of the "stab of longing for my boy." On the whole, the Rosenbergs in dealing with their children sound the authentic tone of parental love in the educated and conscientious middle class, facing each "problem" boldly and without displaying undue emotion, though "of course" not denying the existence of emotion either. . . . This is how we all deal with our children, and surely we are right to do so. If it happens that you must "prepare" the children for their parents' death in the electric chair instead of for having their tonsils out, then doubtless something better is required. But what, for God's sake? Some unique inspiration, perhaps, and the truth. But we cannot blame the Rosenbergs for their failure to achieve an inspiration, and the commitment for which they died—and by which, we must assume, they somehow fulfilled themselves—was precisely that the truth was not to be spoken. Not spoken, not whispered, not approached in the merest hint.

Warshow goes on to show how the literal truth had ceased to exist for the Rosenbergs as a result of their commitment to Communism, and he connects this brilliantly with "the awkwardness and falsity of the Rosenbergs' relations to culture, to sports, and to themselves" that is evident in their letters:

> It is as if these two had no internal sense of their own being but could see themselves only from the outside, in whatever postures their "case" seemed to demand—as if, one might say, they were only the most devoted of their thousands of "sympathizers."
> . . . But it is important to observe the dimensions of their failure, how almost nothing really belonged to them, not even their own experience; they filled their lives with the second-hand, never so much as suspecting that anything else was possible. Communism itself—the vehicle of whatever self-realization they achieved—had disappeared for them, becoming only a word to be written in quotation marks as if it represented a hallucination. . . .

In the end, we discover that "they were equally incapable of truth and of falsehood. What they stood for was not Communism as a certain form of social organization, not progress as a belief in the possibility of human improvement, but only their own identity *as* Communists or 'progressives,' and they were perfectly 'sincere' in making use of whatever catchwords seemed at any moment to assert that identity. . . ." It is this, Warshow argues, that makes the Rosenbergs truly representative of the Communism of 1953. But his piece does not really close on a note of analysis or condemnation:

> The Rosenbergs thought and felt whatever their political commitment required them to think and feel. But if they had not had the political commitment could they have thought and felt at all?
> Well, we cannot dispose of them quite so easily. They did suffer, for themselves and for their children, and though they seem never to have questioned the necessity of their "martyrdom" or the absolute rightness of all they had ever done . . . , they wept like anyone else at the approach of death. . . .

I have quoted at length from this short article in order to let the grace and beauty of Warshow's style speak for themselves. It is a beauty that comes not from ornateness or self-conscious finesse, but from a remarkable fusion of feeling and intelligence: to follow this prose is to follow a language in which analysis cannot be distinguished from emotion. When the rhetoric surges ("But what, for God's sake?") it is not for the sake of sweeping the reader away, but in response to a simultaneous movement of the mind and the heart: the heart has discovered something and the mind springs like a panther to formulate its meaning.

A six-page review of a book in a monthly magazine; a discussion of a controversial political question almost completely forgotten only five years later—

yet it turns out to be a piece of imaginative and creative writing as good as any we have seen in this gloomy period, a piece that is at once a moving expression of a man's ability to feel for two human beings who sacrificed themselves to a cause he hated and despised, a brilliant analysis of the Communist mentality, and a profound comment on the nature of sincerity. And the rest of Warshow's work—almost all of it as good as and better than the Rosenberg article—remains buried in magazines, mostly in the highly perishable form of movie reviews.

The Cult of Usefulness

Why should the magazine article, of all things, have become so important and fertile a genre in our day? Why have so many writers—both "critics" and professional journalists—found it possible to move around more freely and creatively within it than within fiction or poetry? No doubt it has something to do with the spiritual dislocations of the Cold War period, but the essence of the answer, I think, lies in an analogy with architecture. It has often been pointed out that functionalism is more an idea than a reality: the products of functional architecture aren't purely functional at all, since they always contain "useless" elements that are there for aesthetic rather than practical reasons. Yet the fact remains that our sense of beauty today is intimately connnected with the sense of usefulness: we consider a building beautiful when it seems to exist not for anyone to enjoy the sight of or to be impressed by, but solely and simply to be used. We think of those glass structures like Lever House in New York or the United Nations or the Manufacturers Trust Company building on Fifth Avenue as practical, in the sense that women call walking shoes practical; they have a kind of no-nonsense look about them, sensible, stripped down to essentials, purged of all superfluous matter.

The same is true of the way we furnish our homes—Scandinavian efficiency is our idea of handsomeness; foam rubber rather than down our idea of comfort; stainless steel rather than silver our notion of elegant cutlery. I would suggest that we have all, writers and readers alike, come to feel temporarily uncomfortable with the traditional literary forms because they don't *seem* practical, designed for "use," whereas a magazine article by its nature satisfies that initial condition and so is free to assimilate as many "useless," "non-functional" elements as it pleases. It is free, in other words, to become a work of art.

This is not, of course, an ideal situation for literature to be in, but nothing can be gained from turning one's eyes away in horror. Certainly the rigid distinction between the creative and the critical has contributed to the growth of a feeling that the creative is "useless." Curiously enough, the very concept of imagination as a special faculty—and of novels and poetry as mysteriously unique species of discourse subject to strange laws of their own—itself implies that art is of no use to life in the world. What we need, it seems to me, is a return to the old idea of literature as a category that includes the best writing on any subject in any form. This idea is the prevailing one in England today, where the best novels (for example those of C. P. Snow or of William Golding) exhibit all the qualities of intelligence and implication in contemporary problems that are so glaringly absent from current American fiction. We need a return to this idea and we need it, I should add, most urgently of all for the sake of fiction and poetry.

History

Briefly defined, written history is a record of past events. But this definition is too simple; it obscures the complexity of the historian's problem and the many differences which exist among historical accounts.

Even if a historian tries to do nothing but set down a chronological sequence of events, his task is not easy. The material he must work with includes every type of evidence imaginable: artifacts, official documents, letters, testimony, periodicals, skeletons, diaries, and so on. To complicate matters further, each bit of evidence must be weighed for relevance and reliability, for evidence is not uniformly useful. Where there is a substantial quantity of reliable evidence that agrees, the historian can feel that he can make statements of fact with assurance. Where there is little or no evidence, or where the evidence disagrees, the historian must resort to inference. Almost all written histories are combinations of fact and inference.

Most historians try to do more than simply record events in their chronological order. They try to account for events by showing what they think to be their causes. In so doing, historians do more than record history; they interpret it. And their interpretations vary widely because they are the result not only of the evidence but also of the historians' assumptions about life and the nature of things. The Declaration of Independence, for example, has been variously interpreted as being caused by God, fate, accident, the political forces of the time, the economic forces of the time, the prevailing philosophy, and a few strong-willed men like Sam Adams. It would be proper to say that to the extent that a historical account is a record of events it is an explanation; to the extent that it is an interpretation of events it is an argument. Certainly every history should be read both as an explanation and as an argument.

The following selections are a few examples of the many different approaches to the writing of history. The Breasted selection is an example of a historical account composed almost completely of inferences drawn from artifacts. The accounts of the Declaration, while based largely on fact rather than inference, show how skilled and reputable historians using the same material construct different interpretations. The Turner selection exemplifies the historical essay in which the historian's concern is primarily with the interpretation of events rather than with the recording of them. Finally, the Smith selection is a literary historian's discussion of the Turner hypothesis.

James Henry Breasted

THE GREAT ICE AGE
AND PALEOLITHIC MAN

The earth was at this time rich with animal and vegetable life, but it was destined to pass through one of the most critical periods of its history. There had been a great deal of mountain-making and earth movement in the Pliocene period, and when this was followed by extreme climatic changes, the result was almost catastrophic. Geologists and climatologists have not yet found out exactly why, but for thousands of years the climate grew steadily colder and more moist. There was, therefore, an increasing snowfall, especially on the summit of the mountains. It is supposed that ice began to accumulate around these centers of snowfall. Finally there were formed great sheets of inland ice, which, it is estimated, covered at the maximum extent about twelve million square miles of the earth's surface. During the period of severest glaciation there is evidence that the ice extended across North America, as far south as Long Island and westward along the valleys of the Ohio and the Missouri. In Europe and Asia the edges of the great northern ice sheet reached almost to the south coast of England and stretched southeastward across central Europe to about the fiftieth parallel of latitude in the Dnieper Valley, and thence northeastward to the Ural Mountains. Other areas of glaciation seem to have radiated from the Pyrenees, the Alps, the Carpathians, and the Balkans, in Europe; from the coast ranges of Asia Minor, the Lebanon, the Caucasus, the Zagros, and other Persian ranges, in Western Asia; and from the great heights of central Asia. In the southern hemisphere most of the glaciation of this period took place on the Antarctic Continent. This period of glaciation we shall call the Great Ice Age,[1] to distinguish it from the other glacial periods which occurred in earlier eras of earth history.

Geologists seek to determine the movements and extent of the ice sheets by the drift or material which these sheets deposited. Such evidences of ice-sheet movements are found in boulder-beds known as till, in banded or laminated clays known as varves, or in the striated or grooved rocky floor over which the sheet has passed. One conclusion reached from the study of the drift is that there were several glacial periods separated by warmer intervals when the ice sheets were entirely melted or considerably shrunken. At present the geologists differ as to the number of these periods of glaciation, but all are agreed as to

1. The reader must realize that this last period of glaciation may not be ended, for continental ice sheets still cover Greenland and the Antarctic Continent. The present may be, therefore, but an interglacial period.

the contrasts in climate during the Great Ice Age, and the consequent advance and recession of the ice sheets off and on for perhaps a million years.

Of course in the areas immediately surrounding the ice sheets it must have been very cold, but even during periods of extreme glaciation large parts of France, Austria, and Germany were never ice covered. Moreover, many of the deposits of the interglacial periods contain fossil remains of warm temperate or subtropical creatures such as the hippopotamus and lion in England, and the camel and tapir in the southern United States. During the intervals between periods of glaciation, therefore, the climate of Europe and North America might have been as warm as it is today. Thus great stretches of territory in North America and Europe were habitable during the whole period of the Great Ice Age, which the geologists call Pleistocene.

The invasion of the ice, nevertheless, made life very difficult for early men on the north of the Mediterranean basin, and it is probable that these earliest Europeans made greatest cultural progress during the intervals between the periods of glaciation. If we examine a map of North Africa, however, we shall see that in the region just south of the Mediterranean basin there was only one area of glaciation, and that in the extreme west in the vicinity of the Atlas Mountains. Hence the entire Southern Flatlands in North Africa, the region which we now call the Sahara Plateau, was never visited by the ice. The same atmospheric moisture which in frozen form built up the vast glaciers on the *north* side of the Mediterranean, probably fell as plentiful rain on the *south* side. The Sahara Plateau was, therefore, well watered and in many parts of it there were meadows, forests, and jungle growth. Across this fertile region the North African hunters probably pursued the same animals as exist today on the table-lands of central and southern Africa. Often these early men followed the game down into the wide and deep gorge which the Nile had already cut clear across the eastern end of the Sahara.

The Nile was at that time a much larger river than now. Like the Missouri River it sometimes shifted its bed and then never went back to the old one. One of the now dry beds of this larger early Nile, a stretch over fifty miles long, parallel with the present river, has recently been discovered. On digging into its gravels, which are sixty feet deep, the archeologists found that it contained stone weapons of the earliest hunters of the Southern Flatlands, who must have lost them there as they sought their game on the banks of the river, probably a million years ago.

The earliest well-formed stone implements made by man are known as paleoliths, and archeologists have come to call the age in which prehistoric men made such implements the Paleolithic ("Old Stone") Age. If we fit this age into the geologic periods of earth history, we shall find that in all the lands around the Mediterranean paleoliths have been discovered in Pleistocene strata. The Paleolithic Age of man, therefore, coincided with much of the period of the Great Ice Age.

Paleoliths were made of flint and were flaked to the right shape and size by two methods: the earlier by *percussion*, that is, chipping by blows with another stone; and the later by *pressure*, usually with a hard piece of bone (or horn), first on one side, and then on both sides.[1] The most typical implement among the earliest paleoliths is a kind of ax. Indeed, it seems to be the earliest of the heavy hand-tools, and is variously called *coup de poing*, fist-hatchet, or hand-ax. Specimens have been found in Paleolithic gravels all around the Mediterranean, and similar implements have been found in many other parts of the world. The fist-hatchets are thus the earliest widely distributed human devices which have survived to our day. Other later flints flaked by Paleolithic man seem to have served as awls, scrapers, knife blades, points (probably for use on hunting missiles), choppers, and hammers.

If we consider Paleolithic man from a social and industrial point of view, we find he belonged to that group which the ethnologists call food-gatherers. Among the primitive peoples the food-gatherers are those people who take what nature has to offer them and do nothing to augment or add to the natural processes of food-production. The men bring home the meat which they have taken in the chase, and the women gather the fruits and grains which they find growing. Although such people generally have no fixed habitation and usually wander in order to gather food elsewhere after they have exhausted the supply in one locality, it is most interesting to find that in Paleolithic Europe certain sites were occupied by man period after period. This was probably mainly caused by the extreme cold and the scarcity of warm dry caves or rock shelters. Another reason for the continued presence of early men in certain localities may have been the existence in those localities of particularly good beds of flint from which material for implements might be obtained. Some of the caves and rock shelters, consequently, contain in stratified layers a complete archeological record of the progress of Paleolithic man from the period when he first began to produce definitely formed flints.

In these Paleolithic sites have been found burials containing human remains, personal adornments, and weapons or tools—these last perhaps as equipment for an after life. Such burials show not only that Paleolithic man was a thinking animal, but the fossil bones disclose to us also something of his physical characteristics. That he was a representative of an earlier stage in man's slow advance is evident from his short stature (four feet eight to five feet three), his stooping posture with his head thrust forward, his short legs, his retreating forehead, the prominent ridges over his eyes, his broad nose, and his protruding jaws. He is commonly called the Neanderthal Man, after the region of Germany where one of the best specimens of his type was found in 1856. He survived probably thousands of years. Slowly but relentlessly he was displaced by a more intelligent rival, whom we call Aurignacian Man, after the cavern of Aurignac in France where seventeen bodies of his type were found. Several physical types are now included in this term. All of them are taller and with larger brain than their Neanderthal rivals; but one of the

1. When discovered by the Dutch the Tasmanians still used implements made according to Paleolithic methods.

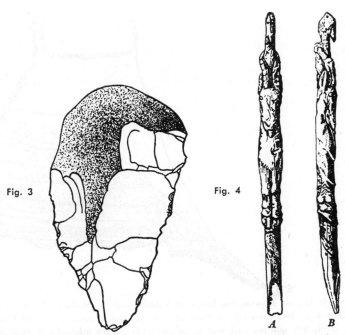

Fig. 3

Fig. 4

A   B

Fig. 3. A Flint Fist Hatchet, Found in an Ancient Bed of the Nile. This tool was usually grasped in the fist by the thicker part, and never had any handle. The original of the above illustration is about seven and one-half inches long, and was found by the Oriental Institute of the University of Chicago.

Fig. 4. Two Views of a Spear-Thrower Used by a Paleolithic Hunter (A) seen from the front; (B) seen from the side. It is carved of reindeer horn to represent the head and forelegs of an ibex. Observe the hook at the top of B for holding the butt of the spear-shaft. The spear-thrower and the bow were the earliest devices of man for hurling his weapons with speed.

Aurignacian types is not tall, always under five feet six, while another Aurignacian type, called Cro-Magnon Man after the French cavern of this name, is a magnificent specimen sometimes reaching a stature of six feet four and a half. These Aurignacians were decidedly more like modern men.

The Aurignacian hunters were also more skillful craftsmen than their Neanderthal predecessors. They learned to flake their flint implements with greater precision and symmetry than before, and they produced more highly specialized tools. The pressure-chipped edges, flaked on both sides, were sharp enough to cut and shape even bone, ivory, and especially reindeer horn. The mammoth furnished the hunters with ivory; and when they needed horn they found great herds of reindeer, driven southward by the ice. The reindeer became at this time man's greatest dependence. He used the hide for clothes, the flesh for food, and the horns and bones for weapons. Indeed, this period has sometimes been called the Reindeer Age.

With their new and keener tools, the hunters worked out barbed ivory spear-points, which they attached to long wooden shafts, and each carried at his girdle a sharp flint dagger. During this period they must have invented the bow and arrow also, for we find rock paintings which show the hunters using them. For

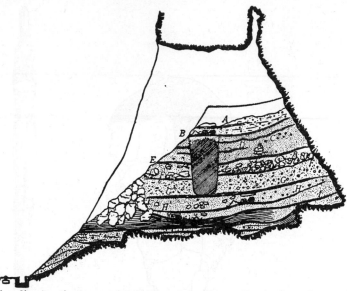

Fig. 5. A Cross Section Showing the Layers of Rubbish and the Human Remains in a Cavern of the Paleolithic Age. This cavern is at Grimaldi, on the Italian coast of the Mediterranean. The entrance is at the left, and the back wall at the right. We see the original rock floor at the bottom, and above it the layers of accumulations, 30 feet deep. The black lines A to I represent layers of ashes, etc., the remains of nine successive hearth fires, each of which must have been kept going by the natives for many years. The thicker (lightly shaded) layers consisted of the bones of animals, rubbish, and rocks which had fallen from the roof of the cavern in the course of ages. The lowermost layers (below I) contained bones of the rhinoceros (representing a warm climate), while the uppermost layers contained bones of the reindeer (indicating a cold climate). Five burials were found by the excavators in the layers B, C, H, and I; layer C contained the bodies of two children. The lowermost burial (in I) was 25 feet below the surface of the accumulations in the cave. Since the above drawing was made, excavators digging in front of the cavern have penetrated to a depth of 60 feet below the original surface of the accumulations and have continued to find flint implements and other evidences of human occupation. (After Déchelette)

straightening their wooden spear shafts and arrows they made an ingenious shaft-straightener of reindeer horn. Another clever device of horn or ivory was a spear-thrower by which a hunter could hurl his long spear much farther and with greater force than he could before. Harpoons and fish hooks indicate that Stone Age man was becoming a fisherman as well as a hunter. Fine ivory needles show that these people learned to protect themselves from cold and from the brambles of the forest wilderness with clothing made by sewing together the skins of the animals slain.

Thus equipped, the hunters of the late Paleolithic Age were much more dangerous foes of the wild creatures than were the men of the earlier period. In a single cavern in Sicily modern archeologists have dug out the bones of no less than two thousand hippopotamuses which these hunters killed. In France one group of such men slew so many wild horses for food that the bones which they tossed about their camp fires gathered in heaps, finally forming a layer in some places six feet thick and covering some 40,000 square feet, an area about equal to four modern city lots of fifty by two hundred feet. Among such deposits excavators have found even the bone whistle with which a returning hunter was able to announce his coming to his hungry family waiting in the cave. On his arrival there he found his home surrounded by revolting piles of garbage. Amid foul odors of decaying flesh this savage European crept into his cave-dwelling at night, little realizing that, many feet beneath the cavern floor on which he slept, lay the remains of his ancestors in layer upon layer, the accumulations of thousands of years.

In spite of the darkness and savagery of their daily life these primitive hunters were standing just at the breaking of the first great light that entered the souls of men. Each of these hunters, when he lay down in his cavern at night, could close his eyes and see mind-pictures of the great beasts he had been pursuing all day. He could recall likewise curious trees the shape of which sometimes reminded him of an animal, or he might turn as he lay and see a bulging mass of rock in his cavern, which looked like the form of a horse. Thus there arose slowly in his mind the idea of *resemblance:* the animal and the tree that looked like it, the horse and the rounded rock that looked like the horse. As this thought continued, he began to be aware that the resemblance of the bulging rock to a horse might be aided by his own hands; until he next discovered that he himself could imitate the form of one object by shaping another like it. In this way the possibility of *imitation* awoke in his mind. In that moment art was born, and the soul of man entered a new and beautiful world filled with a light that had never brightened his life before. For ages his *body* had been developing, but in this new realization that he might create beautiful forms out of the storehouse of his memory, his *mind* rose to a new and higher level. Sketches on small stones have been found, made by beginners just learning to draw. They are like modern studio exercises, still showing the corrections by the more skilled hand of the master.

The new and *creative* age of man's prehistoric life has been revealed to us in an amazing series of works of art discovered in Paleolithic sites. This art takes, on the one hand, the form of engravings and carvings, in relief as well as in the round, on bone, ivory, horn, or stone movable objects. Some of these are objects of utility, such as spear-throwers, lamps, harpoons, painter's palette; while others seem to be simply pictures engraved or carved on slabs of limestone or stray pieces of bone or ivory. More pretentious, although no more astounding, are the monumental engravings and paintings which adorn the walls of caves and rock shelters in France, Spain, and Italy. In North Africa related examples of this art survive on rocks under the open sky, from Algiers, across the Sahara, eastward to the upper Nile. The paintings themselves are very wonderful, but just as remarkable is Paleolithic man's knowledge of pigments. The colors used were red, yellow, and black, and the powdered pigment was kept in little tubes made of hollow bones, some of which have been found in the cave sites. Other surviving equipment of the Paleolithic artist includes pestles for grinding pigment, palettes, and a flint graver apparently *in situ* near an engraving on a cave wall.

All these remains show what a high degree of technical skill Paleolithic man had developed and how this skill had probably enabled him to get more pleasure out of life. But Paleolithic man made no further progress in civilization. In Europe, as the climate moderated and the glaciers melted away, Paleolithic man and Paleolithic industries disappeared. Perhaps after a period of great progress, the civilization simply declined, as has happened in later periods of history. On the other hand, a change of climate brought about changes in fauna and flora. In Europe the reindeer and other cold-loving animals retreated northward, and the dense oak forests, which now spread over Europe, harbored the stag, the wild ox, the boar—an entirely different group of animals. No doubt hunting was much more difficult. Perhaps, then, this was a period of great migrations, and Paleolithic men wandered away from their old haunts to begin life elsewhere as pioneers. Be that as it may, the remains of the culture of the period immediately following the Ice Age in Europe are depressing. They reveal a bare, meager life of scattered groups of people, many of which gained a livelihood by fishing rather than hunting. Perhaps the most interesting of all are the remains of the pioneer life of Scandinavia, the southern part of which was probably free of the great northern ice sheet and open to settlement by man about 10,000 years ago.[1]

While we postulate a period of migration for the men of post-glacial Europe, we have definite evidence that the men south of the Mediterranean were forced

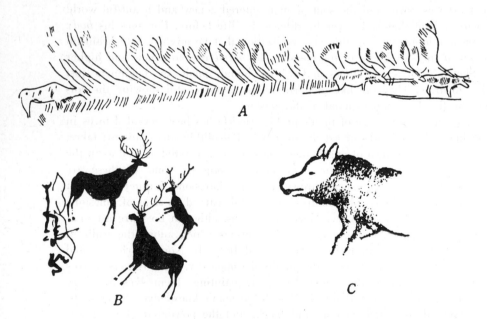

Fig. 6. Examples of Stone-Age Art. The herd of reindeer sketched in A is carved on the wing bone of an eagle. This drawing shows that the earliest artists had some ideas about composition in art and were able to draw a group of animals so as to give an impression of a great number in an almost modern way. B is a hunting scene painted on a rock shelter by Stone Age man after he had invented the bow. The painting of a wolf, C, is from a cave in France. (After Breuil)

Fig. 7. North African Rock Drawing of an Elephant Protecting Her Young from the Attack of a Tiger. The elephant mother throws her trunk around the young one to ward off the tiger, which is preparing to spring. This situation could not have lasted more than a few seconds; but the North African hunter's eye caught the scene, and he probably made a quick sketch then, which he afterward enlarged on a great rock in southern Algiers. The occurrence of such drawings, often in the most inaccessible regions of the desert, is further proof that the Sahara Plateau was, many thousands of years ago, a fertile region enjoying plentiful rains. (After Frobenius and Obermaier)

to migrate from their plateau home and seek new habitation and new ways of living. At some time in the Ice Age the rains which had long watered North Africa began to fail. The reason for this diminished rainfall is not yet clearly understood. The decreasing rainfall caused the great Sahara Plateau slowly to dry up. Its parching vegetation gradually disappeared. During a period of many thousands of years the North African plateau was changed into the waterless desert which we know today.

At this period the Nile Valley was of the greatest value to these early hunters of the Sahara Plateau. The valley is a gorge, or canyon, nowhere more than thirty miles in width, with steep rock walls varying from a few hundred to a thousand feet in height. With its great river flowing down the gorge the valley offered the Stone Age hunters a new home with plenty of water. Therefore they shifted their dwellings down into the Nile gorge and made their homes along the banks of the river. Here the bottom of the great Nile trench, although it was as rainless as the desert, was watered by the river, which was plentifully fed from the rainy regions far south of the desert. Protected on both sides by practically rainless desert and unvisited by the ice or the cold of the north side

1. Baron Gerard de Geer, the Swedish geologist, and his pupils have counted the clay varves deposited by the ice sheet as it receded northward across Scandinavia at the end of the Ice Age. It is believed that each layer, or varve, represents the mud dropped each summer by the edge of the ice sheet. It is in this manner that the above estimate of 10,000 years has been obtained.

of the Mediterranean, the great valley formed a *sheltered* home where the inhabitants were soon to advance from the stage of food-gathering to that of food-production.

Charles A. and Mary R. Beard

INDEPENDENCE
AND CIVIL CONFLICT

The second Continental Congress, which met at Philadelphia in May, 1775, soon took the path that led to revolution. It rejected Lord North's offer of peace on the ground that the right of Parliament to tax was not renounced or offending acts repealed. While it petitioned the king again for a redress of grievances, it turned resolutely to the defense of American claims with all the weapons at hand. Fate decreed that this remarkable assembly should direct the storm for many years, and that all the colonies should afford high talent for its councils. In the long course of its sessions it had among its members nearly every outstanding leader of the Revolution: such as Washington, Jefferson, Wythe, Harrison, the Lees from Virginia; Samuel and John Adams, Gerry and Hancock of Massachusetts; Franklin and Morris of Pennsylvania; Read and Rodney of Delaware; Roger Sherman and Oliver Wolcott of Connecticut.

Its delegates were nearly all citizens of substance and affairs. Of the fifty-six that signed the Declaration of Independence, eight were merchants, six were physicians, five were farmers, and twenty-five were lawyers—members of that learned and contentious profession against which Burke had warned his countrymen. Most of them were tutored in the arts of local politics; many had served in colonial legislatures; a majority had taken an active part in agitations against British policy; nearly all were plain civilians with natural talents for political management. Among them there was no restless son of an ancient family, like Julius Caesar, eager for adventure in unsettled times; no zealot like Oliver Cromwell, waiting to direct the storm in field and forum; no professional soldier, like Bonaparte, watching for a chance to ride into power; no demagogue, like Danton, marshaling the proletariat against his colleagues.

From beginning to end, the spirit of the Congress was civic rather than martial. Every debate was haunted by a dread of military power, the delegates seeming to fear a triumphant American army almost as much as they did the soldiers of George III. At no time did a dictator attempt to seize the helm of the government. Washington might have made himself master of the scene with ease, but the operation was foreign to the spirit of that Virginia gentleman.

When, upon occasion, sovereign powers were conferred upon him by the Congress, he always returned them in due time unsullied by personal ambitions. Even in the most crucial hour there arose in the Congress no tyrannical committee of public safety such as ruled France in the darkest days of her revolution.

Nor were the proceedings of the Congress especially dramatic. Usually there were not more than twenty or thirty members in attendance; and in such an assembly the stormy eloquence of a Marat would have been comic. Although the lawyers present consumed weeks and months in displaying their logical capacities, the Congress was, on the whole, more like a village debating society than the Convention which carried France through the Reign of Terror. Moreover, it met in the little town of Philadelphia, with its twenty thousand inhabitants dominated by Quakers, not in a Paris crowded by half a million people—soldiers, priests, noblemen, merchants, artisans, raging Amazons, and passionate radicals. When, in the sultry days of 1776, it discussed the Declaration of Independence, no throngs pressed into the galleries to intimidate the wavering, no tumultuous mob stormed the doors clamoring for a decision. As a rule its transactions had the air of timidity and negotiation instead of resolution and mastery, disputes, vacillation, and delays marking its operations from session to session.

Its incompetence was not all due, however, as its critics have alleged, to mere perversity of human nature. The members of the Congress labored under the gravest of difficulties. Unlike the party of Cromwell or the national assembly of France, they could not take over an administrative machine that was already organized and working. Exactly the opposite was true; they had to create everything national out of a void—a government, a treasury, an army, even a bookkeeping system, and agencies for buying supplies.

Unlike the English and French revolutionists, they had no centuries of national tradition behind them—no nation-wide class informed by a historic solidarity of interests to which they could appeal for support with assurance. Instead, they were largely dependent from the first day to the last upon the good graces of state assemblies and governors for troops, money, supplies, and the enforcement of their resolutions. And in the best of times the states were in arrears on everything; almost on the eve of Yorktown, Washington recorded that hardly one had put one-eighth of its quota of men at the service of the Revolution.

To make matters worse, the Congress itself was beset by the sectional jealousies which divided the states. Everything had to be viewed with an eye to its effect on the commercial or the planting interests. Among the members was no dominant majority invincibly united for a specific end, no single person moved to grasp large powers and enforce by sheer strength of will the acts of the Congress. All business had to be done by committees and on every important committee each state usually had at least one member.

Administration as well as legislation was controlled by commissions: foreign affairs, finance, supplies, and other matters of prime significance were entrusted to boards. Even the treasury was supervised by a committee until near the end of the struggle, when dire necessity forced the appointment of Robert Morris as superintendent of finance. Yet this is the body that gave voice to the national revolutionary movement, directed war, conducted foreign relations, made treaties, won independence, created a government, and nourished the germs of American nationality.

In view of the dogged jealousy which plagued the Congress, it was surprising that the members were able to agree upon entrusting the armed forces to the command of a single general. Here, perhaps, the divine winds of fortune favored them. Necessity hurried them into a decision and by one of the strangest ironies of history sectional discords then contributed to unity. When the second Congress met, on May 10, 1775, blows had already been struck at Lexington and Concord and thousands of militiamen had poured into the region around Boston—soldiers without supplies or organization. Confronted by the task of feeding and paying them, the Massachusetts assembly turned to the Congress for help. According to John Adams, every post brought letters from friends "urging in pathetic terms the impossibility of keeping their men together without the assistance of Congress."

But when he asked for help, Adams encountered jealousy at the very outset. More than that, there were some people unkind enough to hint that Massachusetts, having started the war, was trying to share the expenses with her neighbors. At all events, the price of united action was the choice of a Virginia soldier, George Washington, as the Commander-in-chief. Thus the hero of the Revolution, a man beyond question nobly qualified for the task of leadership, owed his selection partly to a political trade. With a certain dry humor, Washington, who was in Congress when the transaction took place, noted that his appointment was due to "the partiality of Congress joined to a political motive."

It was only by exercising the same fine arts of negotiation that the advocates of independence were able to overcome local jealousies and conservative fears and at length bring a majority of the delegates into line for the momentous decision of July 2, 1776. In fact, the idea of breaking definitely with the mother country was slow in taking form and slow in winning its way among the people. Washington and Franklin vowed that before the battle of Lexington no one had thought of revolutionary action. Even Sam Adams, though charged by the Tories with secretly harboring that motive from the beginning, was careful to conceal his opinion if he had the goal of separation always before him.

Months after the first blood was shed, strong men continued to express their affection for England and to hope for a peaceful way out of the prolonged deadlock. "Never let us lose out of sight that our interest lies in a perpetual connection with our mother country," urged a preacher of Swiss origin in his sermon before the Georgia provincial congress. "Look ye!" roared John Dickinson at John Adams, "if you don't concur with using our pacific system, I and a number of us will break off from you in New England and will carry on the opposition by ourselves in our own way."

Against this spirit of conciliation, however, opinions and facts made a steady headway in the direction of ultimate independence. The idea was advanced by discussions in newspapers and broadsides, broached in sermons, argued in taverns, covertly mentioned by the extremists in the provincial assemblies. "When one form of government is found by the majority," hinted the President of Harvard in a sermon before the local assembly of Massachusetts, on May 31, 1775, "not to answer the grand purpose in any tolerable degree, they may by common consent put an end to it and set up another." In the highways and byways, this familiar sentiment gathered from the writings of John Locke gradually became the chief topic of conversation and debate. From the thought it was but a step to action, and events were daily, hourly, hastening the movement. War was at hand. Royal governors and their retinues were fleeing from their capitals. Revolutionary committees were taking the places of the old agencies of authority in all the colonies—office holders, who had lived by the British Empire, showing a strange unwillingness to die by it at their posts.

The air was vibrant in the opening days of 1776 when Thomas Paine sent forth from the press the first of his powerful pamphlets, *Common Sense*, calling for absolute independence without fear and without apologies. Casting off the language of loyalty and humility in which the Americans had framed their petitions to the throne, brushing aside the lawyers' pleas for the chartered rights of Englishmen, Paine boldly challenged the king, the British constitution, and the policies of the British government.

In serried array he presented political and economic arguments for separation: the rights of human nature are broad enough and firm enough to support the American cause; the blood of the slain calls for separation; it is not the affair of a city, a county, a province, or a kingdom, but a continent; it is not a concern of the day but of all posterity to the end of time. "O! ye that love mankind! Ye that dare to oppose not only the tyranny but the tyrant, stand forth!" So ran the plea. "Sound doctrine and unanswerable reasons!" exclaimed Washington when he read it. Soon a hundred thousand copies were circulating to the uttermost parts of the colonies, everywhere giving heart to the timid and quickening the intrepid to action.

In the provincial assemblies the cause was also making headway. Early in that year Massachusetts informed her agents at Philadelphia that independence would be welcome. On April 13, North Carolina—the "first," says Allan Nevins, "to give explicit approval"—told her delegates that they might concur with their colleagues in separating from Great Britain. About a month later, Virginia clearly instructed her representatives in the Congress to propose independence and give their assent to that daring act. Although New York had resolved that the people were not ready for revolution, although Maryland still hoped for a happy reunion with Britain, the cords of loyalty were snapping fast. Several colonies had already cast off British authority in fact by setting up new governments of their own; General Gage had been compelled to evacuate Boston; and Washington was moving on New York. The more impatient members of the Congress openly declared that the hour had come for separation. "Is not America already independent? Why not then declare it?" asked Samuel Adams.

On June 7, Richard Henry Lee, in the name of the Virginia delegation, moved that "these united colonies are and of right ought to be free and independent states." In response a committee was chosen to draft the state paper proclaiming the Revolution and stating the reasons for that momentous stroke. Thomas Jefferson, whose facility of expression was known to his colleagues, was made chairman and assigned the delicate task of framing the document. For eighteen days he worked at it, cutting, polishing, and balancing.

When at last the great oration was finished, several suggestions by Benjamin Franklin and John Adams were incorporated and the instrument was laid before the Congress, where a caustic debate followed. While Jefferson twisted and winced, some lines were struck out, others were amended, and a few added. On July 2, the Congress went on record in favor of independence. On July 4, the final draft of Jefferson's paper was formally adopted, merely confirming the fateful step already taken. Contrary to tradition, no drama marked the roll call, no independence bell rang out the news in joyous peals, no far-seeing prophet, looking down the centuries, beheld countless generations celebrating that event with solemn reverence—and firecrackers. Three or four days later the Declaration was read in a public plaza, later known as Independence Square. Copies were spread broadcast and published in city, town and village from New Hampshire to Georgia. In New York the king's statue was pulled down; in Rhode Island it was provided that anyone guilty of praying for George III, so respectfully addressed a few months before, should be liable to a fine of a thousand pounds.

The Declaration of Independence itself falls into two principal parts. The first, containing the moral ground upon which the Revolutionists rested their cause, takes the form of "self-evident truths": all men are created equal and are endowed by their Creator with certain unalienable rights including life, liberty, and the pursuit of happiness; the purpose of government is to make such rights secure; for these reasons governments are instituted, deriving their just power from the consent of the governed; whenever any form of government becomes destructive of these ends, the people have a right to alter or abolish it and institute a new government in a form most likely to effect their safety and happiness.

These high doctrines, later called "glittering generalities" by a critical orator, were not, as sometimes fancied, French in their origin. As a matter of fact, they were essentially English, being derived, as we have hinted, from the writings of John Locke, the philosopher who supplied the rhetorical defense mechanism for the Whig revolution of 1688 which ended in the expulsion of James II. In Locke's hands the catechism of politics was short indeed: the aim of government is to protect property and when any government invades the privileges of property, the people have a right to alter or abolish the government and establish a new one. The idea was almost a century old when Jefferson artfully applied it in a modified form to the exigencies of the American Revolution. Without effect did the critics assail the creed as borrowed from England and contrary to the facts of life. Jefferson easily countered by saying that he claimed no originality for it. Neither was he oblivious to the historical objections that could be urged against it, but he was appealing to the verdict of the onrushing future, not to the sanction of heavy custom.

The second part of the Declaration contained a summary of colonial grievances launched at George III, making him the scapegoat for the Parliament and ministry of Great Britain. In a long bill of particulars, the king was accused of blocking laws passed by the local legislatures, imposing on the colonies judges independent of their will, sending upon them a swarm of royal officers to eat out their substance, quartering troops upon them, cutting off their commerce, laying taxes upon them without their consent, and sending soldiers to harry their coasts, burn their towns, and murder their people. Against these acts, petitions and warnings had been vain and fruitless. Therefore, no course was open to the colonies except to declare themselves free and independent states and take their place among the sovereign nations of the earth.

Samuel Eliot Morison
Henry Steele Commager

INDEPENDENCE AND
THE GREAT DECLARATION

Still, the idea of independence was repugnant to many members of Congress and to a large part of the American people. The ostensible purpose of the two Continental Congresses had been to get the Coercive Acts repealed, restore imperial relations as before 1763, and thus avert both war and independence. As late as the autumn of 1775 the legislatures of North Carolina, Pennsylvania, New Jersey, New York and Maryland went on record against independence. Public opinion was not yet ready for any drastic action. Yet the colonies could not forever remain half in, half out of the empire, professing allegiance while refusing obedience. Moderates persuaded themselves that they were not fighting the king or the mother country, but the "unprincipled hirelings of a venal ministry." They referred to the enemy as the "ministerial," not the British army; they hoped for a political crisis in England that would place their friends in power; as late as January 1776 the king's health was toasted nightly in the officer's mess presided over by General Washington. Radicals acquiesced in

From *The Growth of the American Republic*, by Samuel Eliot Morison and Henry Steele Commager, copyright 1930, 1937, 1942, 1950 by Oxford University Press, Inc.

this policy because they expected that it would have the contrary effect, and make Britain more uncompromising; as it did.

As the months wore on, the difficulties of prosecuting a war while still a part of the empire became more and more patent. Independence was desirable for military success; without it the colonies could scarcely expect that assistance from France upon which they based great hopes. Furthermore, it became clearer every day that the first Congress's policy of non-importation and non-exportation was a complete failure. Commercial pressure was not effective after fighting had aroused passion. It simply prevented the Americans from getting needed supplies, and hurt them more than it did the British. And after so many lives had been lost, at Bunker Hill and in the vain assault on Quebec (December 1775), there came a feeling that something of permanent value ought to be achieved.

No compromise came from England. King George, naturally regarding as insincere an "olive-branch" petition from a body that was carrying on armed rebellion, refused to receive it, and instead issued a proclamation declaring the colonies to be in a state of rebellion (23 August 1775). And on 22 December 1775, all trade and intercourse with the Thirteen Colonies was interdicted by Parliament. The triumphant comment of John Adams reveals how this Act helped the American radicals:

> I know not whether you have seen the Act of Parliament called the Restraining Act or Prohibitory Act, or Piratical Act or Act of Independency— for by all these titles it is called. I think that the most apposite is the Act of Independency; the King, Lords and Commons have united in sundering this country from that, I think forever. It is a complete dismemberment of the British Empire. It throws thirteen colonies out of the royal protection, and makes us independent in spite of supplications and entreaties.

In January 1776 Thomas Paine's pamphlet *Common Sense* was published. This book was to the American Revolution what *Uncle Tom's Cabin* was to the Civil War. Sweeping aside dialectic and sentiment, Paine stated the case for independence in a crisp, vigorous language, that appealed to the ordinary American. It presented in popular form the natural rights philosophy that was to be embodied in the Declaration of Independence. "Society in every state is a blessing, but Government, even in its best state, is but a necessary evil; in its worst, an intolerable one. Government, like dress, is the badge of lost innocence; the palaces of kings are built upon the ruins of the bowers of Paradise." With ruthless disregard for tradition and sentiment Paine attacked the monarchy, the British Constitution, and the empire. Monarchy itself, he argued, is an absurd form of government; one honest man worth "all the crowned ruffians that ever lived"; and George III, "the Royal Brute of Great Britain," the worst of monarchs. Such words were sweet music to democratic ears. How absurd, too, that a continent should be governed by an island! Such an unnatural connection merely subjected the colonies to exploitation, and involved them in every European war. Separation would not only avert these evils, but bring positive benefits—such as a world market for American trade. Anticipating the idea of isolation, Paine announced it to be "the true interest of America to steer clear of European contentions, which she can never do while, by her dependence on Great Britain, she is made the make-weight in the scale of British politics."

Thus with persuasive simplicity Paine presented the alternatives: continued submission to a tyrannous king, an outworn government, and a vicious economic system; or liberty and happiness as a self-sufficient independent republic. The loyalists he lumped together and denounced as "interested men who are not to be trusted, weak men who *cannot* see, prejudiced men who will not see, and a certain set of moderate men who think better of the European world than it deserves." And he closed with the eloquent peroration:

O! ye that love mankind! Ye that dare oppose not only the tyranny but the tyrant, stand forth! Every spot of the old world is overrun with oppression. Freedom hath been hunted round the Globe. Asia and Africa have long expelled her. Europe regards her as a stranger and England hath given her warning to depart. O! receive the fugitive and prepare in time an asylum for mankind.

The influence of this amazing pamphlet cannot well be exaggerated. Within a few months it had been read by or to almost every American. It rallied the undecided and the wavering, and proved a trumpet call to the radicals. "Every Post and every Day rolls in upon us Independence like a Torrent," observed John Adams exultantly. Among the makers of the new nation few played a more dynamic part than Thomas Paine, sometime staymaker of Norfolk in old England.

In each colony now a keen struggle was going on between conservatives and radicals for control of the delegations in Congress. As yet only a few delegations were definitely instructed for independence: it was the task of the radicals to force everyone into line. The struggle coincided with the class and sectional divisions which we have already described as present in most of the colonies. Everywhere the radicals were using the powerful lever of independence to oust the conservatives and put themselves in control, and, under cover of a popular war, push through their programs of democratic reform. The alternative that faced the conservatives in such colonies as New York, Pennsylvania, Maryland, and South Carolina was not pleasant. If they tried to stem the popular tide, they would see themselves denounced as tories, hurled out of office, and old institutions exposed to the mercies of the radical democrats. They could maintain their accustomed position and influence, and save their property, only by acquiescing in a policy of war and separation. In Pennsylvania the struggle was particularly bitter, coinciding as it did with the ancient feud of Scotch-Irish frontiersmen and the city artisans against the Quaker oligarchy and the wealthier Germans. The success of the radicals here was achieved only by overthrowing the old government, establishing a new one with full representation of the frontier counties, and drawing up a new constitution. This new revolutionary government promptly instructed the Pennsylvania delegates for independence. The effect of this radical victory upon the Congress, sitting in Philadelphia, was tremendous.

Events now moved rapidly toward independence. In January 1776 came the burning of Norfolk by the patriots to prevent it falling into the power of Lord Dunmore, and Virginia loyalists had to seek the protection of the British fleet. The next month the embattled farmers of the South repulsed royal troops and native loyalists at Moore's Creek Bridge. In March the legislature of North Carolina instructed its delegates to declare independence and form foreign alliances. Congress then threw the ports of America open to the commerce of the world, and sent an agent to France to obtain assistance. On 10 May Congress advised the states to establish independent governments, as several had done already. On 7 June Richard Henry Lee, pursuant to instructions from his native state, rose in Congress and moved "That these United Colonies are, and of right ought to be, Free and Independent States." After a terrific debate in which sturdy John Adams pled the cause of independence, Lee's motion was carried on 2 July. Meantime Congress had appointed a committee consisting of Thomas Jefferson, John Adams, Benjamin Franklin, Roger Sherman, and Robert Livingston to prepare a formal declaration "setting forth the causes which impelled us to this mighty resolution." This Declaration of Independence, written by Thomas Jefferson, was adopted 4 July 1776.

The Declaration of Independence not only announced the birth of a new nation; the philosophy which it set forth has been a dynamic force in the entire Western world throughout the nineteenth century. "Out of a decent respect for the opinions of mankind," Jefferson summed up, not only the reasons which impelled Americans to independence, but the political and social principles upon which the Revolution itself rested. The particular "abuses and usurpations" which are charged against the king, and which fill a large part of the Declaration, are not advanced as the basis for revolution, but merely as proof that George III had "in direct object the establishment of an absolute tyranny over these states." The Declaration rests, therefore, not upon particular grievances, but upon a broad basis which commanded general support not only in America but in Europe as well. The grievances are scarcely those which appeal to the student of that period as fundamental; examined in the candid light of history many seem distorted, others inconsequential, some unfair. One of the strongest, an indictment of the slave trade, was struck out at the insistence of Southern and New England delegates. But the historical accuracy of the grievances is not the yardstick by which they are to be measured. Jefferson was making history, not writing it.

Jefferson's indictment is drawn against George III, despite the fact that for twelve years the dispute between the colonies and Britain had centered on the question of parliamentary authority. The only reference to Parliament is in the clause, "He has combined with others to subject us to a jurisdiction foreign to our constitution and unacknowledged by our laws, giving his assent to their acts of pretended legislation." Entire odium of parliamentary misdeeds is transferred to the hapless George III. The reason for this shift was not that the king's influence over politics was understood, but that Congress had finally accepted the position of Adams, Jefferson, and Wilson regarding Parliament as merely the legislative body of Great Britain, each colonial legislature being a co-equal and coordinate body, having exclusive power (with the king or his representative) over that particular colony.

The political philosophy of the Declaration is set forth clearly and succinctly in the second paragraph:

> We hold these truths to be self-evident, that all men are created equal, that they are endowed by their creator with certain inalienable rights, that among these are life, liberty, and the pursuit of happiness. That to secure these rights governments are instituted among men, deriving their just powers from the consent of the governed. That whenever any form of government becomes destructive to these ends, it is the right of the people to alter or abolish it, and to institute new government, laying its foundation on such principles and organizing its powers in such form, as to them shall seem most likely to effect their safety and happiness.

"These truths" were not the creatures of Jefferson's mind; they formed a political theory "self-evident" to his generation. The obvious sources for this philosophy were Harrington and Sidney, John Locke's *Second Treatise on Government*, and the actual experience of Americans. It is unnecessary to seek further.

And what was the nature of this ideal government? It was one created by social compact. Originally, so Locke and Jefferson held, men lived equal in a state of nature. When necessity required some form of control, they got together and set up a government by popular consent. It is the function and purpose of government to protect men in their life, liberty, and property. Jefferson substituted for the term "property" the phrase "pursuit of happiness": a characteristic and illuminating stroke on the part of this social philosopher who throughout his life placed human rights first. If government fails to perform these functions, "it is the right of the people to alter or abolish it altogether, and to institute new government"—as the Americans were doing. To the troublesome charge that such popular power would lead to anarchy, Jefferson replied, "all experience hath shown that mankind are more disposed to suffer while evils are sufferable, than to right them by abolishing the forms to which they are accustomed."

It is futile and irrelevant to argue that this theory of the origin of government does not square with nineteenth-century experience and twentieth-century anthropological knowledge. Whatever the origin of government may have been in prehistoric times, in America it often arose just as Jefferson described. As in the Mayflower Compact of 1620, so in countless frontier settlements from the Watauga to the Willamette, men came together spontaneously and organized a government. Jefferson's political philosophy seemed to them merely the common sense of the matter. And the ideas of the Declaration were vital throughout in the nineteenth century. Historical facts derive their significance not as they are judged correct or incorrect by some abstract criterion, but by the place they come to hold in the minds and imaginations of men. By a curious transfer of ideas Jefferson's doctrine that all men are *created* equal has gradually come to mean that all men *are* equal, or that if not they ought to be. And although Jefferson did not mean to include slaves as men, public opinion finally came to regard slavery as inconsistent with the Declaration. Most of the great liberal reform movements of the nineteenth century—abolition, universal suffrage, labor laws, popular education; most of the nationalist movements—in Ireland, Finland, Italy, Germany in '48, Czecho-Slovakia—based their philosophy on the Declaration of Independence; and the American Union could not have been saved in 1861-65 without it. The timelessness of its doctrines and the haunting beauty of its phrasing insure immortality to the Great Declaration.

Frederick Jackson Turner

THE SIGNIFICANCE OF THE FRONTIER IN AMERICAN HISTORY

We may next inquire what were the influences [of the Frontier] on the East and on the Old World. A rapid enumeration of some of the more noteworthy effects is all that I have time for.

First, we note that the frontier promoted the formation of a composite nationality for the American people. The coast was preponderantly English, but the later tides of continental immigration flowed across to the free lands. This was the case from the early colonial days. The Scotch-Irish and the Palatine Germans, or "Pennsylvania Dutch," furnished the dominant element in the stock of the colonial frontier. With these peoples were also the freed indented servants, or redemptioners, who at the expiration of their time of service passed to the frontier. Governor Spotswood of Virginia writes in 1717, "The inhabitants of our frontiers are composed generally of such as have been transported hither as servants, and, being out of their time, settle themselves where land is to be taken up and that will produce the necessarys of life with little labour." Very generally these redemptioners were of non-English stock. In the crucible of the frontier the immigrants were Americanized, liberated, and fused into a mixed race, English in neither nationality nor characteristics. The process has gone on from the early days to our own. Burke and other writers in the middle of the eighteenth century believed that Pennsylvania was "threatened with the danger of being wholly foreign in language, manners, and perhaps even inclinations." The German and Scotch-Irish elements in the frontier of the South

ere only less great. In the middle of the present century the German element
in Wisconsin was already so considerable that leading publicists looked to the
creation of a German state out of the commonwealth by concentrating their
colonization. Such examples teach us to beware of misinterpreting the fact
that there is a common English speech in America into a belief that the stock
is also English.

In another way the advance of the frontier decreased our dependence on England. The coast, particularly of the South, lacked diversified industries, and was
dependent on England for the bulk of its supplies. In the South there was even
dependence on the Northern colonies for articles of food. Governor Glenn, of
South Carolina, writes in the middle of the eighteenth century: "Our trade with
New York and Philadelphia was of this sort, draining us of all the little money
and bills we could gather from other places for their bread, flour, beer, hams,
bacon, and other things of their produce, all which, except beer, our new town-
ships begin to supply us with, which are settled with very industrious and thriving Germans. This no doubt diminishes the number of shipping and the appearance of our trade, but it is far from being a detriment to us." Before long the
frontier created a demand for merchants. As it retreated from the coast it became
less and less possible for England to bring her supplies directly to the consumer's
wharfs, and carry away staple crops, and staple crops began to give way to
diversified agriculture for a time. The effect of this phase of the frontier action
upon the northern section is perceived when we realize how the advance of the
frontier aroused seaboard cities like Boston, New York, and Baltimore, to engage in rivalry for what Washington called "the extensive and valuable trade of
a rising empire."

The legislation which most developed the powers of the national government,
and played the largest part in its activity, was conditioned on the frontier.
Writers have discussed the subjects of tariff, land, and internal improvement,
as subsidiary to the slavery question. But when American history comes to be
rightly viewed it will be seen that the slavery question is an incident. In the
period from the end of the first half of the present century to the close of the Civil
War slavery rose to primary, but far from exclusive, importance. But this does
not justify Dr. von Holst (to take an example) in treating our constitutional
history in its formative period down to 1828 in a single volume, giving six
volumes chiefly to the history of slavery from 1828 to 1861, under the title "Constitutional History of the United States." The growth of nationalism and the
evolution of American political institutions were dependent on the advance of
the frontier. Even so recent a writer as Rhodes, in his "History of the United
States since the Compromise of 1850," has treated the legislation called out by
the western advance as incidental to the slavery struggle.

This is a wrong perspective. The pioneer needed the goods of the coast, and
so the grand series of internal improvement and railroad legislation began,
with potent nationalizing effects. Over internal improvements occurred great
debates, in which grave constitutional questions were discussed. Sectional
groupings appear in the votes, profoundly significant for the historian. Loose

construction increased as the nation marched westward. But the West was not content with bringing the farm to the factory. Under the lead of Clay—"Harry of the West"—protective tariffs were passed, with the cry of bringing the factory to the farm. The disposition of the public lands was a third important subject of national legislation influenced by the frontier.

The public domain has been a force of profound importance in the nationalization and development of the government. The effects of the struggle of the landed and the landless States, and of the Ordinance of 1787, need no discussion. Administratively the frontier called out some of the highest and most vitalizing activities of the general government. The purchase of Louisiana was perhaps the constitutional turning point in the history of the Republic, inasmuch as it afforded both a new area for national legislation and the occasion of the downfall of the policy of strict construction. But the purchase of Louisiana was called out by frontier needs and demands. As frontier States accrued to the Union the national power grew. In a speech on the dedication of the Calhoun monument Mr. Lamar explained: "In 1789 the States were the creators of the Federal Government; in 1861 the Federal Government was the creator of a large majority of the States."

When we consider the public domain from the point of view of the sale and disposal of the public lands we are again brought face to face with the frontier. The policy of the United States in dealing with its lands is in sharp contrast with the European system of scientific administration. Efforts to make this domain a source of revenue, and to withhold it from emigrants in order that settlement might be compact, were in vain. The jealousy and the fears of the East were powerless in the face of the demands of the frontiersmen. John Quincy Adams was obliged to confess: "My own system of administration, which was to make the national domain the inexhaustible fund for progressive and unceasing internal improvement, has failed." The reason is obvious; a system of administration was not what the West demanded; it wanted land. Adams states the situation as follows: "The slaveholders of the South have bought the coöperation of the western country by the bribe of the western lands, abandoning to the new Western States their own proportion of the public property and aiding them in the design of grasping all the lands into their own hands. Thomas H. Benton was the author of this system, which he brought forward as a substitute for the American system of Mr. Clay, and to supplant him as the leading statesman of the West. Mr. Clay, by his tariff compromise with Mr. Calhoun, abandoned his own American system. At the same time he brought forward a plan for distributing among all the States of the Union the proceeds of the sales of the public lands. His bill for that purpose passed both Houses of Congress, but was vetoed by President Jackson, who, in his annual message of December, 1832, formally recommended that all public lands should be gratuitously given away to individual adventurers and to the States in which the lands are situated."

"No subject," said Henry Clay, "which has presented itself to the present, or perhaps any preceding, Congress, is of greater magnitude than that of the

public lands." When we consider the far-reaching effects of the government's
land policy upon political, economic, and social aspects of American life, we
are disposed to agree with him. But this legislation was framed under frontier
influences, and under the lead of Western statesmen like Benton and Jackson.
Said Senator Scott of Indiana in 1841: "I consider the preëmption law merely
declaratory of the custom of common law of the settlers."

It is safe to say that the legislation with regard to land, tariff, and internal
improvements—the American system of the nationalizing Whig party—was
conditioned on frontier ideas and needs. But it was not merely in legislative
action that the frontier worked against the sectionalism of the coast. The
economic and social characteristics of the frontier worked against sectionalism. The men of the frontier had closer resemblances to the Middle region than
to either of the other sections. Pennsylvania had been the seed-plot of frontier
emigration, and, although she passed on her settlers along the Great Valley
into the west of Virginia and the Carolinas, yet the industrial society of these
Southern frontiersmen was always more like that of the Middle region than like
that of the tide-water portion of the South, which later came to spread its industrial type throughout the South.

The Middle region, entered by New York harbor, was an open door to all
Europe. The tide-water part of the South represented typical Englishmen,
modified by a warm climate and servile labor, and living in baronial fashion on
great plantations; New England stood for a special English movement—
Puritanism. The Middle region was less English than the other sections. It
had a wide mixture of nationalities, a varied society, the mixed town and
county system of local government, a varied economic life, many religious
sects. In short, it was a region mediating between New England and the South,
and the East and the West. It represented that composite nationality which
the contemporary United States exhibits, that juxtaposition of non-English
groups, occupying a valley or a little settlement, and presenting reflections of
the map of Europe in their variety. It was democratic and nonsectional, if not
national; "easy, tolerant, and contented"; rooted strongly in material prosperity. It was typical of the modern United States. It was least sectional, not only
because it lay between North and South, but also because with no barriers to
shut out its frontiers from its settled region, and with a system of connecting
waterways, the Middle region mediated between East and West as well as
between North and South. Thus it became the typically American region. Even
the New Englander, who was shut out from the frontier by the Middle region,
tarrying in New York or Pennsylvania on his westward march, lost the acuteness of his sectionalism on the way.

The spread of cotton culture into the interior of the South finally broke down
the contrast between the "tide-water" region and the rest of the State, and based
Southern interests on slavery. Before this process revealed its results the western
portion of the South, which was akin to Pennsylvania in stock, society, and industry, showed tendencies to fall away from the faith of the fathers into internal
improvement legislation and nationalism. In the Virginia convention of 1829-30,

called to revise the constitution, Mr. Leigh, of Chesterfield, one of the tide-water counties, declared:

> One of the main causes of discontent which led to this convention, that which had the strongest influence in overcoming our veneration for the work of our fathers, which taught us to contemn the sentiments of Henry and Mason and Pendleton, which weaned us from our reverence for the constituted authorities of the State, was an overweening passion for internal improvement. I say this with perfect knowledge, for it has been avowed to me by gentlemen from the West over and over again. And let me tell the gentleman from Albemarle (Mr. Gordon) that it has been another principal object of those who set this ball of revolution in motion, to overturn the doctrine of State rights, of which Virginia has been the very pillar, and to remove the barrier she has interposed to the interference of the Federal Government in that same work of internal improvement, by so reorganizing the legislature that Virginia, too, may be hitched to the Federal car.

It was this nationalizing tendency of the West that transformed the democracy of Jefferson into the national republicanism of Monroe and the democracy of Andrew Jackson. The West of the War of 1812, the West of Clay, and Benton and Harrison, and Andrew Jackson, shut off by the Middle States and the mountains from the coast sections, had a solidarity of its own with national tendencies. On the tide of the Father of Waters, North and South met and mingled into a nation. Interstate migration went steadily on—a process of cross-fertilization of ideas and institutions. The fierce struggle of the sections over slavery on the western frontier does not diminish the truth of this statement; it proves the truth of it. Slavery was a sectional trait that would not down, but in the West it could not remain sectional. It was the greatest of frontiersmen who declared: "I believe this Government can not endure permanently half slave and half free. It will become all of one thing or all of the other." Nothing works for nationalism like intercourse within the nation. Mobility of population is death to localism, and the western frontier worked irresistibly in unsettling population. The effect reached back from the frontier and affected profoundly the Atlantic coast and even the Old World.

But the most important effect of the frontier has been in the promotion of democracy here and in Europe. As has been indicated, the frontier is productive of individualism. Complex society is precipitated by the wilderness into a kind of primitive organization based on the family. The tendency is anti-social. It produces antipathy to control, and particularly to any direct control. The tax-gatherer is viewed as a representative of oppression. Prof. Osgood, in an able article, has pointed out that the frontier conditions prevalent in the colonies are important factors in the explanation of the American Revolution, where individual liberty was sometimes confused with absence of all effective government. The same conditions aid in explaining the difficulty of instituting a strong government in the period of the confederacy. The frontier individualism has from the beginning promoted democracy.

The frontier States that came into the Union in the first quarter of a century of its existence came in with democratic suffrage provisions, and had reactive effects of the highest importance upon the older States whose peoples were being attracted there. An extension of the franchise became essential. It was *western* New York that forced an extension of suffrage in the constitutional convention of that State in 1821; and it was *western* Virginia that compelled the tide-water region to put a more liberal suffrage provision in the constitution framed in 1830, and to give to the frontier region a more nearly proportionate representation with the tide-water aristocracy. The rise of democracy as an effective force in the nation came in with western preponderance under Jackson and William Henry Harrison, and it meant the triumph of the frontier—with all of its good and with all of its evil elements. An interesting illustration of the tone of frontier democracy in 1830 comes from the same debates in the Virginia convention already referred to. A representative from western Virginia declared:

But, sir, it is not the increase of population in the West which this gentleman ought to fear. It is the energy which the mountain breeze and western habits impart to those emigrants. They are regenerated, politically I mean, sir. They soon become *working politicians;* and the difference, sir, between a *talking* and a *working* politician is immense. The Old Dominion has long been celebrated for producing great orators; the ablest metaphysicians in policy; men that can split hairs in all abstruse questions of political economy. But at home, or when they return from Congress, they have negroes to fan them asleep. But a Pennsylvania, a New York, an Ohio, or a western Virginia statesman, though far inferior in logic, metaphysics, and rhetoric to an old Virginia statesman, has this advantage, that when he returns home he takes off his coat and takes hold of the plow. This gives him bone and muscle, sir, and preserves his republican principles pure and uncontaminated.

So long as free land exists, the opportunity for a competency exists, and economic power secures political power. But the democracy born of free land, strong in selfishness and individualism, intolerant of administrative experience and education, and pressing individual liberty beyond its proper bounds, has its dangers as well as its benefits. Individualism in America has allowed a laxity in regard to governmental affairs which has rendered possible the spoils system and all the manifest evils that follow from the lack of a highly developed civic spirit. In this connection may be noted also the influence of frontier conditions in permitting lax business honor, inflated paper currency and wild-cat banking. The colonial and revolutionary frontier was the region whence emanated many of the worst forms of an evil currency. The West in the War of 1812 repeated the phenomenon on the frontier of that day, while the speculation and wild-cat banking of the period of the crisis of 1837 occurred on the new frontier belt of the next tier of States. Thus each one of the periods of lax financial integrity coincides with periods when a new set of frontier communities had arisen, and coincides in area with these successive frontiers, for the most part. The recent Populist agitation is a case in point. Many a State that now declines any connection with the tenets of the Populists, itself adhered to such ideas in an earlier stage of the development of the State. A primitive society can hardly be expected to show the intelligent appreciation of the complexity of business interests in a developed society. The continual recurrence of these areas of paper-money agitation is another evidence that the frontier can be isolated and studied as a factor in American history of the highest importance.

The East has always feared the result of an unregulated advance of the frontier, and has tried to check and guide it. The English authorities would have checked settlement at the headwaters of the Atlantic tributaries and allowed the "savages to enjoy their deserts in quiet lest the peltry trade should decrease." This called out Burke's splendid protest:

> If you stopped your grants, what would be the consequence? The people would occupy without grants. They have already so occupied in many places. You can not station garrisons in every part of these deserts. If you drive the people from one place, they will carry on their annual tillage and remove with their flocks and herds to another. Many of the people in the back settlements are already little attached to particular situations. Already they have topped the Appalachian Mountains. From thence they behold before them an immense plain, one vast, rich, level meadow; a square of five hundred miles. Over this they would wander without a possibility of restraint; they would change their manners with their habits of life; would soon forget a government by which they were disowned; would become hordes of English Tartars; and, pouring down upon your unfortified frontiers a fierce and irresistible cavalry, become masters of your governors and your counselers, your collectors and comptrollers, and of all the slaves that adhered to them. Such would, and in no long time must, be the effect of attempting to forbid as a crime and to suppress as an evil the command and blessing of Providence, "Increase and multiply." Such would be the happy result of an endeavor to keep as a lair of wild beasts that earth which God, by an express charter, has given to the children of men.

But the English Government was not alone in its desire to limit the advance of the frontier and guide its destinies. Tide-water Virginia and South Carolina gerrymandered those colonies to insure the dominance of the coast in their legislatures. Washington desired to settle a State at a time in the Northwest; Jefferson would reserve from settlement the territory of his Louisiana Purchase north of the thirty-second parallel, in order to offer it to the Indians in exchange for their settlements east of the Mississippi. "When we shall be full on this side," he writes, "we may lay off a range of States on the western bank from the head to the mouth, and so range after range, advancing compactly as we multiply." Madison went so far as to argue to the French minister that the United States had no interest in seeing population extend itself on the right bank of the Mississippi, but should rather fear it. When the Oregon question was under debate, in 1824, Smyth, of Virginia, would draw an unchangeable line for the limits of the United States at the outer limit of two tiers of States beyond the Mississippi, complaining that the seaboard States were being drained of the flower of their population by the bringing of too much land into market. Even Thomas Benton, the man of widest views of the destiny of the West, at this stage of his career declared that along the ridge of the Rocky Mountains "the western limits of the Republic should be drawn, and the statue of the fabled god Terminus should be raised upon its highest peak, never to be thrown down." But the attempt to limit the boundaries, to restrict land sales and settlement, and to deprive the West of its share of political power were all in vain. Steadily the frontier of settlement advanced and carried with it individualism, democracy, and nationalism, and powerfully affected the East and the Old World.

The most effective efforts of the East to regulate the frontier came through its educational and religious activity, exerted by interstate migration and by organized societies. Speaking in 1835, Dr. Lyman Beecher declared: "It is equally plain that the religious and political destiny of our nation is to be decided in the West," and he pointed out that the population of the West "is assembled from all the States of the Union and from all the nations of Europe, and is rushing in like the waters of the flood, demanding for its moral preservation the immediate and universal action of those institutions which discipline the mind and arm the conscience and the heart. And so various are the opinions and habits, and so recent and imperfect is the acquaintance, and so sparse are the settlements of the West, that no homogeneous public sentiment can be formed to legislate immediately into being the requisite institutions. And yet they are all needed immediately in their utmost perfection and power. A nation is being 'born in a day.' . . . But what will become of the West if her prosperity rushes up to such a majesty of power, while those great institutions linger which are necessary to form the mind and the conscience and the heart of that vast world. It must not be permitted. . . . Let no man at the East quiet himself and dream of liberty, whatever may become of the West. . . . Her destiny is our destiny."

With the appeal to the conscience of New England, he adds appeals to her fears lest other religious sects anticipate her own. The New England preacher and school-teacher left their mark on the West. The dread of Western emancipation from New England's political and economic control was paralleled by her fears lest the West cut loose from her religion. Commenting in 1850 on reports that settlement was rapidly extending northward in Wisconsin, the editor of the *Home Missionary* writes: "We scarcely know whether to rejoice or mourn over this extension of our settlements. While we sympathize in whatever tends to increase the physical resources and prosperity of our country, we can not forget that with all these dispersions into remote and still remoter corners of the land the supply of the means of grace is becoming relatively less and less."

Acting in accordance with such ideas, home missions were established and Western colleges were erected. As seaboard cities like Philadelphia, New York, and Baltimore strove for the mastery of Western trade, so the various denominations strove for the possession of the West. Thus an intellectual stream from New England sources fertilized the West. Other sections sent their missionaries; but the real struggle was between sects. The contest for power and the expansive tendency furnished to the various sects by the existence of a moving frontier must have had important results on the character of religious organization in the United States. The multiplication of rival churches in the little frontier towns had deep and lasting social effects. The religious aspects of the frontier make a chapter in our history which needs study.

From the conditions of frontier life came intellectual traits of profound importance. The works of travelers along each frontier from colonial days onward describe certain common traits, and these traits have, while softening down, still persisted as survivals in the place of their origin, even when a higher social organization succeeded. The result is that to the frontier the American intellect owes its striking characteristics. That coarseness and strength combined with acuteness and inquisitiveness; that practical, inventive turn of mind, quick to find expedients; that masterful grasp of material things, lacking in the artistic but powerful to effect great ends; that restless, nervous energy; that dominant individualism, working for good and for evil, and withal that buoyancy and exuberance which comes with freedom—these are traits of the frontier, or traits called out elsewhere because of the existence of the frontier. Since the days when the fleet of Columbus sailed into the waters of the New World, America has been another name for opportunity, and the people of the United States have taken their tone from the incessant expansion which has not only been open but has even been forced upon them. He would be a rash prophet who should assert that the expansive character of American life has now entirely ceased. Movement has been its dominant fact, and, unless this training has no effect upon a people, the American energy will continually demand a wider field for its exercise. But never again will such gifts of free land offer themselves. For a moment, at the frontier, the bonds of custom are broken and unrestraint is triumphant. There is not *tabula rasa*. The stubborn American environment is there with its imperious summons to accept its conditions; the inherited ways of doing things are also there; and yet, in spite of environment, and in spite of custom, each frontier did indeed furnish a new field of opportunity, a gate of escape from the bondage of the past; and freshness, and confidence, and scorn of older society, impatience of its restraints and its ideas, and indifference to its lessons, have accompanied the frontier. What the Mediterranean Sea was to the Greeks, breaking the bond of custom, offering new experiences, calling out new institutions and activities, that, and more, the ever retreating frontier has been to the United States directly, and to the nations of Europe more remotely. And now, four centuries from the discovery of America, at the end of a hundred years of life under the Constitution, the frontier has gone, and with its going has closed the first period of American history.

Harry Nash Smith

THE MYTH OF THE GARDEN AND
TURNER'S FRONTIER HYPOTHESIS

By far the most influential piece of writing about the West produced during the nineteenth century was the essay on "The Significance of the Frontier in American History" read by Frederick Jackson Turner before the American Historical Association at Chicago in 1893. The "frontier hypothesis" which he advanced on that occasion revolutionized American historiography and eventually made itself felt in economics and sociology, in literary criticism, and even in politics.[1]

Turner's central contention was that "the existence of an area of free land, its continuous recession, and the advance of American settlement westward explain American development."[2] This proposition does not sound novel now because it has been worked into the very fabric of our conception of our history, but in 1893 it was a polemic directed against the two dominant schools of historians: the group interpreting American history in terms of the slavery controversy, led by Hermann Edouard von Holst, and the group headed by Turner's former teacher, Herbert B. Adams of Johns Hopkins, who explained American institutions as the outgrowth of English, or rather ancient Teutonic germs planted in the New World. Turner maintained that the West, not the proslavery South or the antislavery North, was the most important among American sections, and that the novel attitudes and institutions produced by the frontier, especially through its encouragement of democracy, had been more significant than the imported European heritage in shaping American society.

To determine whether Turner's hypothesis is or is not a valid interpretation of American history forms no part of the intention of this book.[3] The problem

Reprinted by permission of the publishers from Harry Nash Smith, *Virgin Land: The American West As Symbol and Myth*. Cambridge, Mass.: Harvard University Press, Copyright, 1950, by The President and Fellows of Harvard College.

1. *References on the Significance of the Frontier in American History*, compiled by Everett E. Edwards (United States Department of Agriculture Library, Bibliographical Contributions, No. 25, 2nd ed. [April, 1939]. Mimeographed), lists 124 items bearing on the subject, ranging in date from Franklin's "Observations on the Peopling of Countries" (1751) to 1939. A passage from a radio address by Franklin D. Roosevelt in 1935 which Dr. Edwards quotes in his excellent Introduction illustrates the political application of Turner's ideas: "Today we can no longer escape into virgin territory. We must master our environment. . . . We have been compelled by stark necessity to unlearn the too comfortable superstition that the American soil was mystically blessed with every kind of immunity to grave economic maladjustments . . ." (p. 3).

2. "The Significance of the Frontier in American History," in *The Early Writings of Frederick Jackson Turner, with a List of All His Works Compiled by Everett E. Edwards and an Introduction by Fulmer Mood* (Madison, Wisconsin, 1938), p. 186.

here is to place his main ideas in the intellectual tradition that has been examined in earlier chapters. Whatever the merits or demerits of the frontier hypothesis in explaining actual events, the hypothesis itself developed out of the myth of the garden. Its insistence on the importance of the West, its affirmation of democracy, and its doctrine of geographical determinism derive from a still broader tradition of Western thought that would include Benton and Gilpin as well, but its emphasis on agricultural settlement places it clearly within the stream of agrarian theory that flows from eighteenth-century England and France through Jefferson to the men who elaborated the ideal of a society of yeoman farmers in the Northwest from which Turner sprang. Turner's immersion in this stream of intellectual influence had an unfortunate effect in committing him to certain archaic assumptions which hampered his approach to twentieth-century social problems. But one must not forget that the tradition was richer than these assumptions, and that it conferred on him the authority of one who speaks from the distilled experience of his people.[4] If the myth of the garden embodied certain erroneous judgments made by these people concerning the economic forces that had come to dominate American life, it was still true to their experience in the large, because it expressed beliefs and aspirations as well as statistics. This is not the only kind of historical truth, but it is a kind historians need never find contemptible.

Turner's most important debt to his intellectual tradition is the ideas of savagery and civilization that he uses to define his central factor, the frontier. His frontier is explicitly "the meeting point between savagery and civilization."[5] For him as for his predecessors, the outer limit of agricultural settlement is the boundary of civilization, and in his thought as in that of so many earlier interpreters we must therefore begin by distinguishing two Wests, one beyond and one within this all-important line.

3. A growing body of scholarship is being devoted to this challenging question. George W. Pierson has called attention to inconsistencies in Turner's doctrines and has inquired into the extent of their currency among historians at the present time: "The Frontier and Frontiersman of Turner's Essays: A Scrutiny of the Foundations of the Middle Western Tradition," *Pennsylvania Magazine of History and Biography*, LXIV, 449-478 (October, 1940); "The Frontier and American Institutions: A Criticism of the Turner Theory," *New England Quarterly*, XV, 224-255 (June, 1942); "American Historians and the Frontier Hypothesis in 1941," *Wisconsin Magazine of History*, XXVI, 36-60, 170-185 (September, December, 1942). I am indebted to Professor Pierson for many ideas, especially the remark he quotes from a colleague to the effect that Turner's frontiersman closely resembles the stock eighteenth-century picture of the small farmer of Britain (*Wisconsin Magazine of History*, XXVI, 183-184) and the suggestion that Turner's "poetic interpretations" revived "the grandest ideas that had gone to make up the American legend" (*idem*).
4. James C. Malin points out that most of Turner's ideas were "in the air." He remarks that great thinkers are normally "the beneficiaries of the folk process and are probably seldom so much true creators as channels through which the folk process finds its fullest expression in explicit language . . ." ("Space and History: Reflections on the Closed-Space Doctrines of Turner and Mackinder and the Challenge of Those Ideas by the Air Age," *Agricultural History*, XVIII, 67-68, April, 1944).
5. *Early Writings*, p. 187.

From the standpoint of economic theory the wilderness beyond the frontier, the realm of savagery, is a constantly receding area of free land. Mr. Fulmer Mood has demonstrated that Turner derived this technical expression from a treatise on economics by Francis A. Walker used as a text by one of his teachers at Johns Hopkins, Richard T. Ely. In Walker's analysis Turner found warrant for his belief that free land had operated as a safety valve for the East and even for Europe by offering every man an opportunity to acquire a farm and become an independent member of society. Free land thus tended to relieve poverty outside the West, and on the frontier itself it fostered economic equality. Both these tendencies made for an increase of democracy.[6] Earlier writers from the time of Franklin had noted that the West offered freedom and subsistence to all,[7] but Turner restated the idea in a more positive form suggested by his conviction that democracy, the rise of the common man, was one of the great movements of modern history.

In an oration delivered in 1883 when he was still an undergraduate he had declared: "Over all the world we hear mankind proclaiming its existence, demanding its rights. Kings begin to be but names, and the sons of genius, springing from the people, grasp the real sceptres. The reign of aristocracy is passing; that of humanity begins."[8] Although "humanity" is a broad term, for Turner it referred specifically to farmers. He conceived of democracy as a trait of agricultural communities. About this time, for example, he wrote in his Commonplace Book that historians had long occupied themselves with "noble warriors, & all the pomp and glory of the higher class—But of the other phase, of the common people, the lowly tillers of the soil, the great mass of humanity . . . history has hitherto said but little." And he fully accepted the theory of small landholdings that underlay the cult of the yeoman. He planned to develop the idea in an "Oration on Peasant Proprietors in U. S." (by which he meant small farmers tilling their own land).

> . . . the work of the Cobden Club on Land Tenure [he wrote] giving the systems of the various countries the paper on America—opens by showing how uninteresting is the subject being as it is purely peasant proprietorship — In this simplicity of our land system lies one of the greatest factors in our progress. Enlarge on the various systems & show the value of it here —point out the fact that if our lands in the west had not been opened to &

6. Fulmer Mood, "The Development of Frederick Jackson Turner as a Historical Thinker," *Publications of the Colonial Society of Massachusetts*, XXXIV: *Transactions 1937-1942* (Boston, 1943), pp. 322-325.
7. Turner copied into a Commonplace Book that he kept in 1886, during his first year of teaching, a quotation ascribed to Franklin: "The boundless woods of America which are sure to afford freedom and subsistence to any man who can bait a hook or pull a trigger" (Commonplace Book [II], p. [1]. Turner Papers, Henry E. Huntington Library). The idea occurs often in Franklin but I have not been able to find these words.
8. "The Poet of the Future," delivered at the Junior Exhibition, University of Wisconsin, May 25, 1883, and reported in full in the Madison *University Press* (May 26, 1883), p. 4 (clipping in Turner Papers, Henry E. Huntington Library).

filled with foreign emigrant it is not unlikely that they would have fallen into the hands of capitalists & hav been made great estates—e.g. Daly-rymple farm— Show effects of great estates in Italy—in Eng.[9]

In systems of land tenure, he felt, lay the key to the democratic upsurge that had reached a climax in the nineteenth century:

> It is not by Contrat Socials that a nation wins freedom & prosperity for its people—; it is by attention to minor details—like this—it is by evolution— Show place of F. R. [French Revolution]—ring in Shelleys Prometheus this was an awakening but now—in our own age is the real revolution going on which is to raise *man* from his low estate to his proper *dignity* (enlarge from previous oration)—in this grand conception it is not an anticlimax to urge the value—the essential necessity of such institutions as the peas-ant proprietors—a moving force, all the stronger that it works quietly in the great movement.[1]

This is the theoretical background of the proposition in the 1893 essay that "democracy [is] born of free land,"[2] as well as of the celebrated pronouncement made twenty years later: "American democracy was born of no theorist's dream; it was not carried in the Susan Constant to Virginia, nor in the Mayflow-er to Plymouth. It came stark and strong and full of life out of the American forest, and it gained new strength each time it touched a new frontier."[3]

But while economic theory still underlies this later statement, the change of terminology has introduced new and rich overtones. We have been transferred from the plane of the economist's abstractions to a plane of metaphor, and even

9. Commonplace Book [I], 1883, pp. [25-27]. Turner Papers, Henry E. Huntington Library.
1. *Ibid.*, pp. [49-53].
2. *Early Writings*, p. 221.
3. "The West and American Ideals," an address delivered at the University of Washington, June 17, 1914, *Washington Historical Quarterly*, V, 245 (October, 1914). When Turner revised this address for inclusion in the volume of collected papers *The Frontier in American History* in 1920, he omitted the words "stark and strong and full of life" (New York, 1920, reprint ed., 1931, p. 293). Although Turner repudiated the "germ theory" of constitutional develop-ment in his 1893 essay (*Early Writings*, p. 188), he had accepted it for a time after he left Herbert B. Adams' seminar at Johns Hopkins. Reviewing the first two volumes of Theodore Roosevelt's *The Winning of the West* in the Chicago *Dial* in August of 1889 (X, 72), he remarked that "the old Germanic 'tun'" reappeared in the "forted village" of early Kentucky and Tennessee, the "folkmoot" in popular meetings of the settlers, and the "witenagemot" in representative assemblies like the Transylvania legislature. "These facts," he added, "carry the mind back to the warrior-legislatures in the Germanic forests, and forward to those constitutional conventions now at work in our own newly-made states in the Far West; and they make us proud of our English heritage." In an undergraduate address he had asserted that "The spirit of individual liberty slumbered in the depths of the German forest" from the time of the barbarian invasions of Rome until it burst forth in the American and French Revolutions (Madison *University Press* [May 26, 1883], p. 4). Turner's discovery of the American frontier as a force encouraging democracy may exhibit some imaginative persistence of this association between desirable political institutions and a forest.

of myth—for the American forest has become almost an enchanted wood, and the image of Antaeus has been invoked to suggest the power of the Western earth. Such intimations reach beyond logical theory. They remind us that the wilderness beyond the limits of civilization was not only an area of free land; it was also nature. The idea of nature suggested to Turner a poetic account of the influence of free land as a rebirth, a regeneration, a rejuvenation of man and society constantly recurring where civilization came into contact with the wilderness along the frontier.[4]

Rebirth and regeneration are categories of myth rather than of economic analysis, but ordinarily Turner kept his metaphors under control and used them to illustrate and vivify his logical propositions rather than as a structural principle or a means of cognition: that is, he used them rhetorically not poetically. The nonpoetic use of a vivid metaphor is illustrated in a speech he delivered in 1896:

> Americans had a safety valve for social danger, a bank account on which they might continually draw to meet losses. This was the vast unoccupied domain that stretched from the borders of the settled area to the Pacific Ocean. . . . No grave social problem could exist while the wilderness at the edge of civilizations [*sic*] opened wide its portals to all who were oppressed, to all who with strong arms and stout heart desired to hew out a home and a career for themselves. Here was an opportunity for social development continually to begin over again, wherever society gave signs of breaking into classes. Here was a magic fountain of youth in which America continually bathed and was rejuvenated.[5]

The figure of the magic fountain is merely a rhetorical ornament at the end of a paragraph having a rational structure and subject to criticism according to

4. A characteristic phrase is the reference to "this rebirth of American society" that has gone on, decade after decade, in the West (from an essay in the *Atlantic*, 1896, reprinted in *The Frontier in American History*, p. 205). In his undergraduate Commonplace Book Turner had jotted down, among notes for an oration, "See Emerson's preface to 'Nature' . . ." and had added part of a sentence: ". . . let us believe in the eternal genesis, the freshness & value of things present, act as though, just created, we stood looking a new world in the face and investigate for ourselves and act regardless of past ideas" (Commonplace Book [I], p. [3]). This is quite Emersonian; it might well be a paraphrase of the familiar first paragraph of Emerson's essay: "Why should not we also enjoy an original relation to the universe? Embosomed for a season in nature, whose floods of life stream around and through us, and invite us, by the powers they supply, to action proportioned to nature, why should we grope among the dry bones of the past, or put the living generation into masquerade out of its faded wardrobe?" (*Complete Works*, Volume I: *Nature, Addresses, and Lectures* [Boston, 1903], p. [3]). Turner said in 1919 that he had been impressed with Woodrow Wilson's emphasis on Walter Bagehot's idea of growth through "breaking the cake of custom" (Frederick Jackson Turner to William E. Dodd, Cambridge, Mass., October 7, 1919, copy in Turner Papers, Henry E. Huntington Library). The phrase appears in the *Atlantic* essay (*The Frontier in American History*, p. 205).

5. Address at the dedication of a new high school building at Turner's home town of Portage, Wisconsin, January 1, 1896, reported in the Portage *Weekly Democrat*, January 3, 1896 (clipping in Turner Papers, Henry E. Huntington Library).

recognized canons. But sometimes, especially when the conception of nature as the source of occult powers is most vividly present, Turner's metaphors threaten to become themselves a means of cognition and to supplant discursive reasoning. This seems to happen, for example, in an essay he wrote for the *Atlantic* in 1903. After quoting a clearly animistic passage from Lowell's Harvard Commemoration Ode on how Nature had shaped Lincoln of untainted clay from the unexhausted West, "New birth of our new soil, the first American," Turner builds an elaborate figurative structure:

> Into this vast shaggy continent of ours poured the first feeble tide of European settlement. European men, institutions, and ideas were lodged in the American wilderness, and this great American West took them to her bosom, taught them a new way of looking upon the destiny of the common man, trained them in adaptation to the conditions of the New World, to the creation of new institutions to meet new needs; and ever as society on her eastern border grew to resemble the Old World in its social forms and its industry, ever, as it began to lose faith in the ideal of democracy, she opened new provinces, and dowered new democracies in her most distant domains with her material treasures and with the ennobling influence that the fierce love of freedom, the strength that came from hewing out a home, making a school and a church, and creating a higher future for his family, furnished to the pioneer.[6]

It would be difficult to maintain that all these metaphors are merely ornamental. Is it wholly meaningless, for example, that the West, the region close to nature, is feminine, while the East, with its remoteness from nature and its propensity for aping Europe, is neuter?

In the passage just quoted, a beneficent power emanating from nature is shown creating an agrarian utopia in the West. The myth of the garden is constructed before our eyes. Turner is asserting as fact a state of affairs that on other occasions he recognized as merely an ideal to be striven for. Earlier in the same essay, for example, he had summarized Jefferson's "platform of political principles" and his "conception that democracy should have an agricultural basis."[7] The "should" easily becomes "did": Jefferson's agrarian ideal proves to be virtually identical with the frontier democracy that Turner believed he had discovered in the West. To imagine an ideal so vividly that it comes to seem actual is to follow the specific procedure of poetry.

The other member of the pair of ideas which defined the frontier for Turner was that of civilization. If the idea of nature in the West provided him with a rich and not always manageable store of metaphorical coloring, his use of the idea of civilization had the equally important consequence of committing him to the theory that all societies, including those of successive Wests, develop through the same series of progressively higher stages. Mr. Mood has traced

6. *The Frontier in American History*, pp. 255, 267.
7. *Ibid.*, p. 250.

this conception also to Ely and to Walker, and back of them to the German economic theorist Friedrich List.[8] But, as we have had occasion to notice earlier in this study, the idea had been imported into the United States from France soon after 1800 and by the 1820's had become one of the principal instruments for interpreting the agricultural West.

Turner's acceptance of this theory involved him in the difficulties that it had created for earlier observers of frontier society, such as Timothy Flint. For the theory of social stages was basically at odds with the conception of the Western farmer as a yeoman surrounded by utopian splendor. Instead, it implied that the Western farmer was a coarse and unrefined representative of a primitive stage of social evolution. Turner's adoption of these two contradictory theories makes it difficult for him to manage the question of whether frontier character and society, and frontier influence on the rest of the country, have been good or bad. As long as he is dealing with the origins of democracy in the West he evidently considers frontier influence good. A man who refers to "the familiar struggle of West against East, of democracy against privileged classes"[9] leaves no doubt concerning his own allegiance. This attitude was in fact inevitable as long as one maintained the doctrine that frontier society was shaped by the influence of free land, for free land was nature, and nature in this system of ideas is unqualifiedly benign. Indeed, it is itself the norm of value. There is no way to conceive possible bad effects flowing from the impact of nature on man and society.

But when Turner invokes the concept of civilization, the situation becomes more complex. His basic conviction was that the highest social values were to be found in the relatively primitive society just within the agricultural frontier. But the theory of social stages placed the highest values at the other end of the process, in urban industrial society, amid the manufacturing development and city life which Jefferson and later agrarian theorists had considered dangerous to social purity. Turner wavered between the two views. In the 1893 essay, to take a minute but perhaps significant bit of evidence, he referred to the evolution of each successive region of the West "into a higher stage"—in accord with the orthodox theory of civilization and progress. When he revised the essay for republication in 1899, he realized that such an assumption might lead him into inconsistency and substituted "a different industrial stage."[1]

But he could not always maintain the neutrality implied in this revision. For one thing, he strongly disapproved of the Western love of currency inflation, which he considered a consequence of the primitive state of frontier society. "The colonial and Revolutionary frontier," he asserted in the 1893

8. *Publications of the Colonial Society of Massachusetts*, XXXIV, 304-307. Mr. Mood says that the idea of applying the theory of evolution to social phenomena was the "fundamental, unifying concept" of Turner's early writings (p. 304), but adds that the *a priori* idea of a sequence of social stages "can be asserted to be, as a universal rule . . . fallacious. . . . It is one component element in Turner's [1893] essay that will not now stand the test of inspection" (p. 307n.).
9. *The Frontier in American History*, p. 121 (1908).
1. *Early Writings*, pp. 199, 285.

essay, "was the region whence emanated many of the worst forms of an evil currency," and he pointed out that each of the periods of lax financial integrity in American history had coincided with the rise of a new set of frontier communities. The Populist agitation for free coinage of silver was a case in point.

Many a state that now declines any connection with the tenets of the Populists [he wrote] itself adhered to such ideas in an earlier stage of the development of the state. A primitive society can hardly be expected to show the intelligent appreciation of the complexity of business interests in a developed society.[2]

In his revision of the essay in 1899 Turner noted with satisfaction that Wisconsin had borne out his principles:

Wisconsin, to take an illustration, in the days when it lacked varied agriculture and complex industrial life, was a stronghold of the granger and greenback movements; but it has undergone an industrial transformation, and in the last presidential contest Mr. Bryan carried but one county in the state.[3]

Here the evolution of society from agrarian simplicity toward greater complexity is assumed to bring about improvement.

Yet if Turner could affirm progress and civilization in this one respect, the general course of social evolution in the United States created a grave theoretical dilemma for him. He had based his highest value, democracy, on free land. But the westward advance of civilization across the continent had caused free land to disappear. What then was to become of democracy? The difficulty was the greater because in associating democracy with free land he had inevitably linked it also with the idea of nature as a source of spiritual values. All the overtones of his conception of democracy were therefore tinged with cultural primitivism, and tended to clash with the idea of civilization. In itself this was not necessarily a disadvantage; the conception of civilization had been invoked to justify a number of dubious undertakings in the course of the nineteenth century, including European exploitation of native peoples all over the world. Furthermore, as we have had occasion to observe in studying the literary interpretation of the agricultural West, the theory of social progress through a uniform series of stages was poor equipment for any observer who wished to understand Western farmers. But Turner had accepted the idea of civilization as a general description of the society that had been expanding across the continent, and with the final disappearance of free land this idea was the only remaining principle with which he could undertake the analysis of contemporary American society.

Since democracy for him was related to the idea of nature and seemed to have no logical relation to civilization, the conclusion implied by his system was that

2. *Ibid.*, p. 222.
3. *Ibid.*, p. 285.

post-frontier American society contained no force tending toward democracy. Fourierists earlier in the century, reaching a conclusion comparable to this, had maintained that civilization was but a transitory social stage, and that humanity must transcend it by advancing into the higher stage of "association." Henry George in Turner's own day had announced that progress brought poverty, that civilization embodied a radical contradiction and could be redeemed only by a revolutionary measure, the confiscation of the unearned increment in the value of natural resources. But Turner did not share the more or less revolutionary attitude that lay back of these proposals.[4] On the contrary, he conceived of social progress as taking place within the existing framework of society, that is, within civilization. Whatever solution might be found for social problems would have to be developed according to the basic principles already accepted by society. This meant that his problem was to find a basis for democracy in some aspect of civilization as he observed it about him in the United States. His determined effort in this direction showed that his mind and his standards of social ethics were subtler and broader than the conceptual system within which the frontier hypothesis had been developed, but he was the prisoner of the assumptions he had taken over from the agrarian tradition.[5] He turned to the rather unconvincing idea that the Midwestern state universities might be able to save democracy by producing trained leaders,[6] and later he placed science beside education as another force to which men might turn for aid in their modern perplexity. But these suggestions were not really satisfying to him, and he fell back at last on the faith he had confided to his Commonplace Book as an undergraduate—a faith neither in nature nor in civilization but simply in man, in the common people. In 1924, after reviewing the most urgent of the world's problems, Turner declared with eloquence and dignity:

> I prefer to believe that man is greater than the dangers that menace him; that education and science are powerful forces to change these tendencies and to produce a rational solution of the problems of life on the shrinking planet. I place my trust in the mind of man seeking solutions by intellectual toil rather than by drift and by habit, bold to find new ways of adjustment, and strong in the leadership that spreads new ideas among the common people of the world; committed to peace on earth, and ready to use the means of preserving it.[7]

4. Frederick Jackson Turner to Merle E. Curti, San Marino, Cal., January 5, 1931. Copy in Turner Papers, Henry E. Huntington Library. Turner says he had not read George before writing the 1893 essay and that he had never accepted the single-tax idea.
5. Professor Malin has emphasized the fact that in his later career Turner was "baffled by his contemporary world and had no satisfying answer to the closed-frontier formula in which he found himself involved" (*Essays on Historiography*, Lawrence, Kansas, 1946, p. 38).
6. *The Frontier in American History*, p. 285 (1910).
7. "Since the Foundation," an address delivered at Clark University, February 4, 1924, *Publications of the Clark University Library*, VII, No. 3, p. 29. After the words "dangers that menace him" Turner has indicated in his personal copy in the Henry E. Huntington

This statement is an admission that the notion of democracy born of free land, colored as it is by primitivism, is not an adequate instrument for dealing with a world dominated by industry, urbanization, and international conflicts. The First World War had shaken Turner's agrarian code of values as it destroyed so many other intellectual constructions of the nineteenth century. He continued to struggle with the grievous problems of the modern world, but his original theoretical weapons were no longer useful.

Turner's predicament illustrates what has happened to the tradition within which he worked. From the time of Franklin down to the end of the frontier period almost a century and a half later, the West had been a constant reminder of the importance of agriculture in American society. It had nourished an agrarian philosophy and an agrarian myth that purported to set forth the character and destinies of the nation. The philosophy and the myth affirmed an admirable set of values, but they ceased very early to be useful in interpreting American society as a whole because they offered no intellectual apparatus for taking account of the industrial revolution. A system which revolved about a half-mystical conception of nature and held up as an ideal a rudimentary type of agriculture was powerless to confront issues arising from the advance of technology. Agrarian theory encouraged men to ignore the industrial revolution altogether, or to regard it as an unfortunate and anomalous violation of the natural order of things. In the restricted but important sphere of historical scholarship, for example, the agrarian emphasis of the frontier hypothesis has tended to divert attention from the problems created by industrialization for a half century during which the United States has become the most powerful industrial nation in the world.[8] An even more significant consequence of the agrarian tradition has been its effect on politics. The covert distrust of the city and of everything connected with industry that is implicit in the myth of the garden has impeded coöperation between farmers and factory workers in more than one crisis of our history, from the time of Jefferson to the present.

The agrarian tradition has also made it difficult for Americans to think of themselves as members of a world community because it has affirmed that the destiny of this country leads her away from Europe toward the agricultural interior of the continent. This tendency is quite evident in Turner.[9] Although he devoted much attention to the diplomatic issues arising out of westward

Library (No. 222544) the addition of the following words: "that there are automatic adjustments in progress."

8. Charles A. Beard makes this point in what seems to me a convincing manner in "The Frontier in American History," *New Republic*, XCVII, 359-362 (February 1, 1939). Professor Malin asserts vigorously that "among other things, the frontier hypothesis is an agricultural interpretation of American history which is being applied during an industrial urban age..." ("Mobility and History," *Agricultural History*, XVII, 177, October, 1943).

9. Benjamin F. Wright has a similar comment in his review of *The Significance of Sections in American History*, *New England Quarterly*, VI, 631 (September, 1933). Professor Malin calls the frontier hypothesis "an isolationist interpretation in an international age" (*Agricultural History*, XVII, 177). "It seemed to confirm the Americans," he remarks elsewhere,

expansion, the frontier hypothesis implied that it would be a last misfortune for American society to maintain close connections with Europe. The frontier which produced Andrew Jackson, wrote Turner with approval in 1903, was "free from the influence of European ideas and institutions. The men of the 'Western World' turned their backs upon the Atlantic Ocean, and with a grim energy and self-reliance began to build up a society free from the dominance of ancient forms."[1] It was only later, when he was trying to find a theoretical basis for democracy outside the frontier, that Turner criticized the American attitude of "contemptuous indifference" to the social legislation of European countries.[2]

But if interpretation of the West in terms of the idea of nature tended to cut the region off from the urban East and from Europe, the opposed idea of civilization had even greater disadvantages. It not only imposed on Westerners the stigma of social, ethical, and cultural inferiority, but prevented any recognition that the American adventure of settling the continent had brought about an irruption of novelty into history. For the theory of civilization implied that America in general, and the West a fortiori, were meaningless except in so far as they managed to reproduce the achievements of Europe. The capital difficulty of the American agrarian tradition is that it accepted the paired but contradictory ideas of nature and civilization as a general principle of historical and social interpretation. A new intellectual system was requisite before the West could be adequately dealt with in literature or its social development fully understood.

Biography

Since biography can be thought of as simply a special type of history, almost everything that was said about the latter holds true for the former. In most respects the ends and the means are similar.

Biographers have many purposes in their writing; here are some of the most common ones: (1) to give the bare facts of the subject's life, as in the brief accounts in *Who's Who in America* and the *Dictionary of American Biography*; (2) to present an example of a virtuous and successful life for the

"in their continental isolationism. Was not their United States a unique civilization; was it not superior to that of Europe and Asia?" (*ibid.*, XVIII, 67, April, 1944).

1. *The Frontier in American History*, p. 253 (1903).

2. *Ibid.*, p. 294 (1914). In the 1903 article Turner had emphasized the contrast between American democracy, which was "fundamentally the outcome of the experiences of the American people in dealing with the West," and the "modern efforts of Europe to create an artificial democratic order by legislation" (*ibid.*, p. 266). The implication is clearly that American democracy is the opposite of artificial, i.e., natural, and that this natural origin establishes its superiority.

edification, particularly, of the young; (3) to pay tribute to a personal or popular hero; (4) to debunk a popular hero; (5) to define a class, like Americans of the nineteenth century, by describing a typical example; (6) to reinterpret the life of a man about whom several biographies have already been written; (7) to write a good story based more or less on the facts of someone's life. With one exception, these purposes can be found at the root of autobiographies, too: It is probably seldom that a man sets out to debunk his own reputation, but he might well wish to set forth the facts, interpret the facts, or offer himself as a splendid example of what all men should be.

The following selections give the reader a good opportunity to study the relation between means and ends, and to compare and contrast biographers' approaches to their subjects.

Clifford Dowdey

GENERAL LEE'S UNSOLVED PROBLEM

Long after the Civil War was over, with contemplative years for perspective, Jefferson Davis wrote that Robert E. Lee always commanded subject to *his* orders. The former Confederate president made quite a point of this overlordship, and held to the concept of Davis, the leader, manipulating armies and generals and the destinies of a people. Of course, Davis was right. As he made of the Confederate experiment a one-man show, technically he was Lee's boss.

Davis never imagined that the struggle was maintained by the extent to which Lee imposed his own ideas on him. The nature of the war in its main theater in Virginia changed in proportion to Lee's influence in three main phases. The early indecisiveness was determined by Davis' complete control before Lee emerged; the period of bold strokes and great hopes, 1862-63, reflected Lee's influence; and the nature of "the long agony" beginning in 1864 was determined by the effect of the control Davis continued until it was altogether too late to do anything about it.

For Davis got in over his head as leader of an extemporized revolutionary movement, and lacked the flexibility of character and the suppleness of mind to change with changing conditions. While he lacked also the humility to admit to his limitations, his organism revealed the unnatural strain (as it invariably did under stress) by the psychosomatic ailments that afflicted him during the war years.

Actually he brought to the war only the bureaucratic technique learned as a peace-time secretary of war, and neither magnitude nor nature of disaster

Clifford Dowdey, "General Lee's Unsolved Problem," *The American Heritage Reader*, 1956. Reprinted by permission of *American Heritage*, The Magazine of History.

could budge his grasp on the familiar details of certainty. Likewise, his leadership was from the book, an abstraction, a part of his personal concept of the aristocrat.

Under the definition of aristocrat as a member of a ruling class, Davis was synthetic. He was a *nouveau,* characterized by the personal arrogance of the self-made Bourbons of the new cotton kingdom. Davis was touchy about his dignity, while purblind about the feelings of others. He knew nothing about people, either as individuals or in the mass.

In Lee, Davis encountered the real thing, the perfected product of the ruling *class* which Davis presumably represented. Davis never quite knew what to make of him. Though in time Lee's successes caused Davis privately to admit in a cry of anguish that Lee might act as his military *equal* in the field ("Oh, if only I could take one wing and Lee the other!"), it never occurred to him that Lee was able to achieve this recognized equality only by a character which made it possible for him to work through the commander in chief for the sake of his land.

Lee's struggle in his relations with Jefferson Davis represented one of the great, undramatized achievements of the war, even though this undeclared and ceaseless struggle never reached a decision—and the president probably never realized it was happening.

The essence of Lee's character and mental cast, as related to Davis, derived from a generic aristocracy of which he was a natural product—indeed, as has been said, "a flowering." With all the nonsense about the Virginia Aristocrat, Lee's family achieved that ideal of communal responsibility which the myth attributed to all. To Lee, leadership was a moral responsibility to the people from which his class arose and not a thing of personal pride.

For Lee there was no inner conflict in fulfilling his moral obligation through the constituted authority; deference to all constituted authority was inherent in his conservative society. That Davis made it personally difficult for Lee changed nothing: this was a detail, merely another burden to be borne in performing his duty to his state.

There is no question that Davis' peremptoriness and insensitivity to others gave Lee trouble. He wrote Mrs. Lee, "Mr. Davis can be very sharp." Harder to bear even than the unconscious rudenesses of the self-aware aristocrat were the thoughtless wastes that Davis exacted of Lee's time, energies, and talents. He would call Lee in for interminable conferences, in which the soldier was used as a sounding board while his advice was never heeded, and Lee's aide mentions the harassed state in which he returned from these futile conferences.

But all this was in the realm of Lee's personal difficulties. The real, though inarticulated, struggle was over the essential differences in the military purposes of Lee and of Davis.

Davis believed that a static defense of territory (accompanied by proclamations of their rights) would cause independence to be *granted.* Lee believed that independence would be *won* in the field, by counterstrokes designed to drive the enemy away and discourage future attempts at subjugation.

So Lee had to fight two wars—the open fight against the avowed enemy and the tacit fight to achieve his ends through the constituted authority. That Lee, a superb physical specimen, aged more than any other general on either side can fairly clearly be attributed to the dual strain of the two wars he fought. Not a self-analytical or reflective man, Lee suffered the strain mutely with no faltering in the loyalty he gave the man in the office.

From first to last, Davis' policy expressed itself militarily through a system of defense in which immobilized units were placed, in bureaucratic order, to represent the territorial dominion of the Confederacy. In 1862, before Lee took command, when all the troops in Virginia would not have equalled the one main Union army in the state, Davis had seven "armies" scattered so as to form, with pins on a chart, an imposing outline of the map of the Old Dominion.

On resigning from the U. S. Army in the spring of 1861, Lee offered his services directly to Virginia, which had not then joined the Confederacy, and was offered the thankless and Herculean assignment of fortifying its many avenues of entree against the coming invasion. He was then a magnificent looking man of 54, with a strong build and fine carriage. He had not yet grown his beard, and his mustache and hair were dark. A former engineer and cavalryman who disliked paper work intensely (all during the war it tried his temper), he perceived that his task must be performed from a desk—and that was where Davis found him when the Confederacy's capital was changed to Richmond.

From Davis' arrival in Richmond, with the Virginia troops mustered into the Confederate Army, Lee was unceremoniously thrust into an anomalous position. Retained at the desk where Davis first encountered him, he became something like an unofficial executive officer of the commander in chief for the Department of Virginia. Davis used the proven soldier, not where his services would contribute to his state's defense, but where his courteous self-negation and patriotic subordination served the president personally.

To the crucial military sector at Manassas Junction, Davis had sent glory-loving P. G. T. de Beauregard, and Davis and the Creole wrote back and forth on important matters of the Virginia defense as if Lee did not exist. Then, when the first big conflict—"Manassas" to the South: "Bull Run" to the North—was fought (on the lines of defense drawn by Lee), Lee was left to cool his heels in his Richmond office, while Davis rushed off to Manassas. There he took part in the conference, of later controversy, with Beauregard and Joe Johnston, who between them managed to immobilize the victorious army then and for months to come—or until the Federals had built a larger war machine to come at them again the following spring.

During these months of inaction in Virginia, while events took a serious turn against the Confederates, Davis sent Lee on an ignominious assignment to western Virginia ("an inspector's job," a Richmond newspaper called it) to act as Davis' representative-without-authority in a squabble between political generals. After that, Lee was sent to erect coastal fortifications in the Charleston area. Then Lee was brought back to Richmond for another desk job—this time as "advisor to the commander in chief." His brother officers regarded the assignment as such a humiliation that only the elaborately courteous "Prince John" Magruder could bring himself to congratulate Lee.

Though Lee accepted this "advisory" role without complaint, and patiently trotted back and forth the block between the war office and the president's office like a glorified clerk, he was depressed by the futile, nerve-straining assignment. His change to a position of influence came about indirectly. Disaster was threatening from all sides and very close to Richmond, and Joe Johnston, the field commander in Virginia, was stubbornly refusing to confide in the president. Instead, the sprightly little general was retreating up the Peninsula before the Federal General, George B. McClellan, in defiance of the Administration's expressed wishes. Further to complicate the situation, Joe Johnston was in titular command of the troops in northern Virginia confronting McClellan's pincer under General Irvin McDowell, and of Stonewall Jackson's small, detached force in the Shenandoah Valley. With Johnston out of communication with them, the president allowed the clerical details concerning those troops to fall on Lee. This was the chance seized by the long-suffering Lee to perform as a soldier. He quietly began a correspondence with the aggressive-minded Jackson that was to change the nature of the Confederacy's struggle in Virginia, as well as Lee's relations to Davis.

At the time, the Unions had more men than the Confederates at each of three danger spots—the Peninsula toward Richmond from the east, the Piedmont toward Richmond from the north, and the supplyland of the Valley. Joe Johnston's idea was to concentrate all Confederates in front of Richmond to meet McClellan, but Lee reasoned that if the Confederates concentrated, so would the Unions. Lee perceived that he and the strange Presbyterian in the Valley were thinking along the same lines: a threat to the North from the "covered way" of the Valley (as Grant called it) would immobilize the Unions in middle Virginia and keep them away from McClellan.

Lee made no announcement of the plan, which grew in scope as it evolved between Jackson and him. In fact, with a guile unassociated with his legend, he urged Jackson to hurry. Lee knew that when Johnston, nearing Richmond, re-established communications with the distant troops, he would call off any movement that threatened to keep reinforcements away from *him*. As it worked out, Jackson's dazzling Valley campaign caused the Union authorities to withhold McDowell's troops, north of Richmond, whereupon Davis forced Joe Johnston to attack McClellan seven miles east of Richmond, at Seven Pines. There Johnston was hit by a stray bullet. By the accident of this Yankee shot, Lee was finally given field command in June, 1862, and the first phase of the war in Virginia was over—though the president did not realize it.

Lee in the field was not Lee the "advisor." From the assumption of command of the loosely-organized divisions, brigades, legions and whatnot called an army, Lee planned the strategy to effectuate his own aggressive policy. Though he deferentially cleared the plans (of the Seven Days and then the great Second Manassas Campaign) through Davis, the plans were his and the army became his as no other army in the war was identified with its leader. From the mob he inherited, Lee moulded the Army of Northern Virginia. In less than three months, Lee cleared Virginia of the enemy and was invading north!

With this success, Lee's influence over the president entered the positive phase. Lee had to beg for the release of troops from garrisons and fixed positions, and Davis always compromised; Lee was constantly thwarted by the inefficiency of supply services which fell foul of the bureaucracy; but for his strategy Lee made the plans and the president formally approved. In the field, Lee commanded without advice or interference from anyone.

In his first battle, (Mechanicsville, which opened his Seven Days Campaign), Davis had rushed to the field with a large entourage and even issued orders to a brigade of D. H. Hill without consulting anybody. When Lee saw him, he showed a tough side and, in effect, ordered Davis away. When Lee led an army on the field, *he* was the constituted authority there, and he let the president know it. Davis never ventured on another field commanded by Lee.

Within that pattern of relationship, Lee suffered a temporary decline in the extent of his power after the invasion failed at Sharpsburg, Maryland, in September, 1862. Back in Virginia, he wanted to withdraw deeper toward Richmond in order to draw the enemy after him and catch him in a counterstroke, as he had caught General John Pope at Second Manassas. This of course expressed his policy of destroying the enemy; but Davis ordered him to fight on an arbitrarily drawn line across the waist of the state, on a terrain from which no fruits of the victory were possible. The repulse of the clumsy Union attack at Fredericksburg was the most pointless important battle of the war, and Lee knew it. But Davis was pleased that his territorial defense was intact, and Lee remained chained to the line of the Rappahannock River for the coming spring. There he tried to destroy the enemy, but even the Civil War masterpiece at Chancellorsville achieved only another repulse of the Union Army.

However, the mere fact of field victories restored his influence with the president in the policy area sufficiently for him to gain a partial approval for another try for decision through invasion. Lee wanted his invasion to be part of a general advance, with immobilized units striking out from their positions and garrisons stripped to protect Virginia against raids. But the other forces remained fixed, and a number of battle-wise, war-hardened veterans of Lee's army were held in Virginia. One-fourth of Pickett's crack Virginia division was uselessly guarding a supply depot near Richmond during the attack at Gettysburg.

The Gettysburg stroke was Lee's last chance at executing his own policy. Arithmetic was overtaking his defense of his land. Yet, now that it was too late, for the last phase of the slow-coming end that began in the spring of 1864, Lee became for the first time in complete control of his whole area.

Under the massive, three-pronged Union thrust for a decision, Lee's battleground became of necessity the state of Virginia; and, against the almost overwhelming pressure of Grant, Lee defended, from day to day, with an army which revealed the ravages of attrition. While he gave a more personalized and active field generalship to his own declining army, he unofficially assumed the combined roles of commanding general and chief of staff for the theater. Had he not done so, the war would have ended (as Grant expected) in the summer.

While thwarting Grant's thrust at Richmond, always for his desperate measures Lee ceremoniously cleared through the bureaucratic structure of the president. Sick half the time, his beard and hair whitening, and with the army 24 hours a day, Lee had no time for the president's cherished conferences.

However, for Davis, Lee's communications, along with military items from the war office, served to satisfy his sense of participation as commander in chief. War clerks mention the president staggering homeward at the end of the day up the steep walks of Capitol Square burdened with the paper work he was taking home.

For Lee, the added burden of working through the inefficiency of Davis' bureaus was nerve-racking, and he revealed the strain with uncharacteristic short bursts of temper. Once Beauregard, resurrected in the East and commanding a Department within Lee's area, entered a telegraphic debate with the Old Man on the subject of proper channels to go through for reinforcements, and Lee cut loose even at the president in angry impatience.

Lee was finally forced into the strictly defensive position which he had always dreaded. Tied to Richmond and its railroad junction with the South, he was actually withstanding a siege—and he knew victory that way was hopeless.

During the spring and summer of 1864, he and Davis had perforce worked at the level of details. For the last fall, winter, and brief spring, Lee continued to work with the commander in chief on details (because for Davis by then there was nothing else) but there was time again to resume the conferences. Davis would write Lee wistfully when military duties in the lines kept him from a meeting.

They had come, full cycle, round to the first days when Davis came to Richmond, only now, when it was all over, the two men met as equals. Of course, Lee conferred with the president for the larger plans but, as in the first summer, Lee could not bring himself to express opinions outside the proper sphere of his authority. Though he knew the war was lost, and wanted peace, he continued to report dutifully on the actions that whittled away his disintegrating army.

To Davis, Lee had come to exist as an immutable abstraction: his army had never been driven from a field—therefore, it never would. Davis clung to his irrational belief in defense during that fall and winter when the country collapsed outside of Lee's area, and Lee's area dwindled to the ground he held.

So the president and Lee would meet in the little room off the White House parlor, with their boots spread on the white rug to get warmth from the slag-fire in the grate, and Mrs. Davis would bring in substitute coffee in thin china cups, and in the winter afternoons the erect gentleman and the aging aristocrat discussed the details of their defense as if they were talking about the same thing.

Lee, longing for a climax to the ordeal, consulted the president on the advisability of abandoning the Richmond area. He wanted movement in the open for one final throw, and he outlined the physical needs in minutest detail. Davis, in his memoirs, recalled how stoutly he suggested that Lee "anticipate the need" and move at once. In memory, he attributed the Old Man's remaining in the freezing trenches to Lee's reluctance to retreat. He had not heard a word Lee said about the need of subsistence for man and beast, for more horses, for more wagons—and, above all, for the drying of the muddy roads.

Even when Grant's superb army overwhelmed Lee's survivors at Petersburg, and Lee wired the war office that Richmond must be evacuated, Davis in reply asked if Lee could not delay his retreat in order that papers be removed from the capital!

When Lee, in final fulfillment of his moral obligation, suffered the last long week of the retreat that ended at Appomattox, the president still clung to his abstract defense. He was the only leader, Confederate or Union, who did not accept the end with the end of Lee. He missed the whole point of the Confederacy's struggle when, from the beginning, he missed the point of Lee.

In the first year, before Lee held any authority, the Confederacy stood on the verge of defeat; during the fifteen months of Lee's limited authority, though conditions were far less favorable than at the beginning, the Confederacy most nearly won its independence; during the last fifteen months of Lee's complete authority in his own area, a defeat which overtook the rest of the weakening Confederacy was staved off in his area only by virtue of this belated authority.

Without the authority he won through his own character, the war would have ended sooner; had this authority been granted from the beginning, clearly the war would have taken quite a different course. The end might have been the same but it definitely would not have come about through attrition which prolonged the agony and brought (as Sherman said) "ruin and misery" to a people about whom Davis never knew anything.

Carl Sandburg

THE ASSASSINATION OF LINCOLN

The play proceeds, not unpleasant, often stupid, sprinkled with silly puns, drab and aimless dialogues, forced humor, characters neither truly English nor truly American nor fetching as caricatures. The story centers around the Yankee lighting his cigar with an old will, burning the document to ashes and thereby throwing a fortune of $400,000 away from himself into the hands of an English cousin. The mediocre comedy is somewhat redeemed by the way the players are doing it. The audience agrees it is not bad. The applause and laughter say the audience is having a good time.

From *Abraham Lincoln: The War Years* by Carl Sandburg. Copyright, 1939, by Harcourt, Brace and Company, Inc. Reprinted by permission of Harcourt, Brace and Company, Inc.

Mrs. Lincoln sits close to her husband, at one moment leaning on him fondly, suddenly realizing they are not alone, saying with humor, "What will Miss Harris think of my hanging on to you so?" and hearing his: "She won't think anything about it."

From the upholstered rocking armchair in which Lincoln sits he can see only the persons in the box with him, the players on the stage, and any persons off-stage on the left. The box on the opposite side of the theatre is empty. With the box wall at his back and the closely woven lace curtains at his left arm, he is screened from the audience at his back and from the musicians in the orchestra pit, which is below and partly behind him.

The box has two doors. Sometimes by a movable cross partition it is converted into two boxes, each having its door. The door forward is locked. For this evening the President's party has the roominess and convenience of double space, extra armchairs, side chairs, a small sofa. In the privacy achieved he is in sight only of his chosen companions, the actors he has come to see render a play, and the few people who may be offstage to the left.

This privacy however has a flaw. It is not as complete as it seems. A few feet behind the President is the box door, the only entry to the box unless by a climb from the stage. In this door is a small hole, bored that afternoon to serve as a peephole—from the outside. Through this peephole it is the intention of the Outsider who made it with a gimlet to stand and watch the President, then at a chosen moment to enter the box. This door opens from the box on a narrow hallway that leads to another door which opens on the balcony of the theatre.

Through these two doors the Outsider must pass in order to enter the President's box. Close to the door connecting with the balcony two inches of plaster have been cut from the brick wall of the narrow hallway. The intention of the Outsider is that a bar placed in this cut-away wall niche and then braced against the panel of the door will hold that door against intruders, will serve to stop anyone from interference with the Outsider while making his observations of the President through the gimleted hole in the box door.

At either of these doors, the one to the box or the one to the hallway, it is the assigned duty and expected responsibility of John F. Parker to stand or sit constantly and without fail. A Ward Lamon or an Eckert on this duty would probably have noticed the gimleted hole, the newly made wall niche, and been doubly watchful. If Lincoln believes what he told Crook that afternoon, that he trusted the men assigned to guard him, then as he sits in the upholstered rocking armchair in the box he believes that John F. Parker in steady fidelity is just outside the box door, in plain clothes ready with the revolver Pendel at the White House had told him to be sure to have with him.

In such a trust Lincoln is mistaken. Whatever dim fog of thought or duty may move John F. Parker in his best moments is not operating tonight. His life habit of never letting trouble trouble him is on him this night; his motive is to have no motive. He has always got along somehow. Why care about anything, why really care? He can always find good liquor and bad women. You take your fun as you find it. He can never be a somebody, so he will enjoy himself as a nobody—though he can't imagine how perfect a cipher, how completely the little end of nothing, one John F. Parker may appear as a result of one slack easygoing hour.

"The guard . . . acting as my substitute," wrote the faithful Crook later, "took his position at the rear of the box, close to an entrance leading into the box. . . . His orders were to stand there, fully armed, and to permit no un-authorized person to pass into the box. His orders were to stand there and protect the President at all hazards. From the spot where he was thus stationed, this guard could not see the stage or the actors; but he could hear the words the actors spoke, and he became so interested in them that, incredible as it may seem, he quietly deserted his post of duty, and walking down the dimly-lighted side aisle, deliberately took a seat."

The custom was for a chair to be placed in the narrow hallway for the guard to sit in. The doorkeeper Buckingham told Crook that such a chair was provided this evening for the accommodation of the guard. "Whether Parker oc-cupied it at all, I do not know," wrote Crook. "Mr. Buckingham is of the im-pression that he did. If he did, he left it almost immediately, for he confessed to me the next day that he went to a seat, so that he could see the play." The door to the President's box is shut. It is not kept open so that the box occupants can see the guard on duty.

Either between acts or at some time when the play was not lively enough to suit him or because of an urge for a pony of whiskey under his belt, John F. Parker leaves his seat in the balcony and goes down to the street and joins companions in a little whiff of liquor—this on the basis of a statement of the coachman Burns, who declared he stayed outside on the street with his carriage and horses, except for one interlude when "the special police officer (meaning John F. Parker) and the footman of the President (Forbes) came up to him and asked him to take a drink with them; which he did."

Thus circumstance favors the lurking and vigilant Outsider who in the after-noon gimleted a hole in the door of the President's box and cut a two-inch niche in a wall to brace a bar against a door panel and hold it against interfer-ence while he should operate.

The play goes on. The evening and the drama are much like many other evenings when the acting is pleasant enough, the play mediocre and so-so, the audience having no thrills of great performance but enjoying itself. The most excited man in the house, with little doubt, is the orchestra leader, Withers. He has left the pit and gone backstage, where, as he related, "I was giving the stage manager a piece of my mind. I had written a song for Laura Keene to sing. When she left it out I was mad. We had no cue, and the music was thrown out of gear. So I hurried round on the stage on my left to see what it was done for."

And of what is Abraham Lincoln thinking? As he leans back in this easy rocking chair, where does he roam in thought? If it is life he is thinking about, no one could fathom the subtle speculations and hazy reveries resulting from his fifty-six years of adventures drab and dazzling in life. Who had gone farther on so little to begin with? Who else as a living figure of republican government, of democracy, in practice, as a symbol touching freedom for all men—who else had gone farther over America, over the world? If it is death he is thinking about, who better than himself might interpret his dream that he lay in winding sheets on a catafalque in the White House and people were wringing their hands and crying "The President is dead!"—who could make clear this dream better than himself? Furthermore if it is death he is thinking about, has he not philosophized about it and dreamed about it and considered himself as a mark and a target until no one is better prepared than he for any sudden deed? Has he not a thousand times said to himself, and several times to friends and intimates, that he must accommodate himself to the thought of sudden death? Has he not wearied of the constructions placed on his secret night ride through Baltimore to escape a plot aimed at his death? Has he not laughed to the overhead night stars at a hole shot in his hat by a hidden marksman he never mentioned even to his boon companion Hill Lamon? And who can say but that Death is a friend, and who else should be more a familiar of Death than a man who has been the central figure of the bloodiest war ever known to the Human Family— who else should more appropriately and decently walk with Death? And who can say but Death is a friend and a nurse and a lover and a benefactor bringing peace and lasting reconciliation? The play tonight is stupid. Shakespeare would be better. "Duncan is in his grave . . . he sleeps well."

Yes, of what is Abraham Lincoln thinking? Draped before him in salute is a silk flag of the Union, a banner of the same design as the one at Independence Hall in Philadelphia in February of '61 which he pulled aloft saying, "I would rather be assassinated on this spot than surrender it," saying the flag in its very origins "gave promise that in due time the weights would be lifted from the shoulders of all men, and that all should have an equal chance." Possibly his mind recurs for a fleeting instant to that one line in his letter to a Boston widow woman: "the solemn pride that must be yours to have laid so costly a sacrifice upon the altar of freedom." Or a phrase from the Gettysburg speech: "we here highly resolve that these dead shall not have died in vain."

Out in a main-floor seat enjoying the show is one Julia Adelaide Shephard, who wrote a letter to her father about this Good Friday evening at the theatre. "Cousin Julia has just told me," she reported, "that the President is in yonder upper right hand private box so handsomely decked with silken flags festooned over a picture of George Washington. The young and lovely daughter of Senator Harris is the only one of his party we see as the flags hide the rest. But we know Father Abraham is there like a Father watching what interests his children, for their pleasure rather than his own. It had been announced in the papers he would be there. How sociable it seems like one family sitting around their parlor fire. Everyone has been so jubilant for days that they laugh and shout at every clownish witticism such is the excited state of the public mind. One of the actresses whose part is that of a very delicate young lady talks about wishing to avoid the draft when her lover tells her not to be alarmed 'for there is to be no more draft' at which the applause is loud and long. The American cousin has just been making love to a young lady who says she'll never marry for love but when her mother and herself find out that he has lost his property they retreat in disgust at the left hand of the stage while the American cousin goes out at the right. We are waiting for the next scene."

And the next scene?

The next scene is to crash and blare as one of the wildest, one of the most inconceivably fateful and chaotic, that ever stunned and shocked a world that heard the story.

The moment of high fate was not seen by the theatre audience. Only one man saw that moment. He was the Outsider. He was the one who had waited and lurked and made his preparations, planning and plotting that he should be the single and lone spectator of what happened. He had come through the outer door into the little hallway, fastened the strong though slender bar into the two-inch niche in the brick wall, and braced it against the door panel. He had moved softly to the box door and through the little hole he had gimleted that afternoon he had studied the box occupants and his Human Target seated in an upholstered rocking armchair. Softly he had opened the door and stepped toward his prey, in his right hand a one-shot brass derringer pistol, a little eight-ounce vest-pocket weapon winged for death, in his left hand a steel dagger. He was cool and precise and timed his every move. He raised the derringer, lengthened his right arm, ran his eye along the barrel in a line with the head of his victim less than five feet away—and pulled the trigger.

A lead ball somewhat less than a half-inch in diameter crashed into the left side of the head of the Human Target, into the back of the head, in a line with and three inches from the left ear. "The course of the ball was obliquely forward toward the right eye, crossing the brain in an oblique manner and lodging a few inches behind that eye. In the track of the wound were found fragments of bone, which had been driven forward by the ball, which was embedded in the anterior lobe of the left hemisphere of the brain."

For Abraham Lincoln it was lights out, good night, farewell and a long farewell to the good earth and its trees, its enjoyable companions, and the Union of States and the world Family of Man he had loved. He was not dead yet. He was to linger in dying. But the living man could never again speak nor see nor hear nor awaken into conscious being.

Near the prompt desk offstage stands W. J. Ferguson, an actor. He looks in the direction of a shot he hears, and sees "Mr. Lincoln lean back in his rocking chair, his head coming to rest against the wall which stood between him and the audience . . . well inside the curtains" —no struggle or move "save in the slight backward sway."

Of this the audience in their one thousand seats know nothing.

Major Rathbone leaps from his chair. Rushing at him with a knife is a strange human creature, terribly alive, a lithe wild animal, a tiger for speed, a wildcat of a man bareheaded, raven-haired—a smooth sinister face with glaring eyeballs. He wears a dark sack suit. He stabs straight at the heart of Rathbone, a fast and ugly lunge. Rathbone parries it with his upper right arm, which gets a deep slash of the dagger. Rathbone is staggered, reels back. The tiger-ish stranger mounts the box railing. Rathbone recovers, leaps again for the stranger, who feels the hand of Rathbone holding him back, slashes again at Rathbone, then leaps for the stage.

This is the moment the audience wonders whether something unusual is happening—or is it part of the play?

From the box railing the Strange Man leaps for the stage, perhaps a ten-foot fall. His leap is slightly interrupted. On this slight interruption the Strange Man in his fine calculations had not figured. The draped Union flag of silk reaches out and tangles itself in a spur of one riding-boot, throwing him out of control. He falls to the stage landing on his left leg, breaking the shinbone a little above the instep.

Of what he has done the audience as yet knows nothing. They wonder what this swift, raven-haired, wild-eyed Strange Man portends. They see him rush across the stage, three feet to a stride, and vanish. Some have heard Rathbone's cry "Stop that man!" Many have seen a man leap from a front seat up on the stage and chase after the weird Stranger, crying "Stop that man!"

It is a peculiar night, an odd evening, a little weird, says the audience to itself. The action is fast. It is less than half a minute since the Strange Man mounted the box railing, made the stage, and strode off.

Offstage between Laura Keene and W. J. Ferguson he dashes at breakneck speed, out of an entrance, forty feet to a little door opening on an alley. There stands a fast bay horse, a slow-witted chore boy nicknamed John Peanuts hold-ing the reins. He kicks the boy, mounts the mare; hoofs on the cobblestones are heard but a few moments. In all it is maybe sixty or seventy seconds since he loosed the one shot of his eight-ounce brass derringer.

Whether the Strange Man now riding away on a fast bay horse has paused a moment on the stage and shouted a dramatic line of speech, there was disa-greement afterward. Some said he ran off as though every second of time counted and his one purpose was to escape. Others said he faced the audience a moment, brandished a dagger still bloody from slashing Rathbone, and shouted the State motto of Virginia, the slogan of Brutus as he drove the assassin's knife into imperial Caesar: "*Sic semper tyrannis*"—"Thus be it ever to tyrants." Miss Shephard and others believed they heard him shriek as he brandished the dag-ger: "The South is avenged!" Others: "The South shall be free!" "Revenge!" "Freedom!"

Some said the lights went out in the theatre, others adding the detail that the assassin had stabbed the gasman and pulled the lever, throwing the house into darkness. Others a thousand miles from the theatre said they saw the moon come out from behind clouds blood-red. It is a night of many eyewitnesses, shaken and moaning eyewitnesses.

The audience is up and out of its one thousand seats, standing, moving. Panic is in the air, fear of what may happen next. Many merely stand up from their seats, fixed and motionless, waiting to hear what has happened, waiting to see what further is to happen. The question is spoken quietly or is murmured anxiously—"What is it? What has happened?" The question is bawled with anger, is yelled with anguish—"For God's sake, what is it? What has happened?"

A woman's scream pierces the air. Some say afterward it was Mrs. Lincoln. The scream carries a shock and a creeping shiver to many hearing it. "He has shot the President!" Miss Shephard looks from the main floor toward the box and sees "Miss Harris wringing her hands and calling for water." There are moanings. "No, for God's sake, it can't be true—no! no! for God's sake!"

Men are swarming up to the edge of the stage, over the gas-jet footlights onto the stage. The aisles fill with people not sure where to go; to leave would be safe, but they want to know what has happened, what else they may see this wild night. Men are asking whether some God-damned fool has for sure tried to shoot the President. Others take it as true. The man who ran across the stage did it. There are cries: "Kill him! Shoot him!" On the stage now are policemen, army officers, soldiers, besides actors and actresses in make-up and costume. Cries for "Water! water!" Cries for "A surgeon! a surgeon!" Someone brings water. It is passed up to the box.

An army surgeon climbs to the stage and is lifted up and clambers over the railing into the box. Some two hundred soldiers arrive to clear the theatre. The wailing and the crazy chaos let down in the emptying playhouse—and flare up again in the street outside, where some man is accused of saying he is glad it happened, a sudden little mob dragging him to a lamppost with a ready rope to hang him when six policemen with clubs and drawn revolvers manage to get him away and put him in jail for safekeeping.

Mrs. Lincoln in the box has turned from the railing, has turned from where she saw the wild-eyed raven-haired man vanish off the stage, sees her husband seated in the rocking chair, his head slumped forward. Never before has she seen her husband so completely helpless, so strangely not himself. With little moaning cries she springs toward him and with her hands keeps him from tumbling to the floor. Major Rathbone has shouted for a surgeon, has run out of the box into the narrow hallway, and with one arm bleeding and burning with pain he fumbles to unfasten the bar between wall and door panel. An usher from the outside tries to help him. They get the bar loose. Back of the usher is a jam of people. He holds them back, allowing only one man to enter.

This is a young-looking man, twenty-three years old, with mustache and side-burns, Charles A. Leale, assistant surgeon, United States Volunteers, who had left the army General Hospital at Armory Square, where he was in charge of the wounded commissioned officers' ward, saying he would be gone only a short time. Rathbone shows Dr. Leale his bleeding arm, "beseeching me to attend to his wound," related Leale later. "I placed my hand under his chin, looking into his eyes an almost instantaneous glance revealed the fact that he was in no immediate danger, and in response to appeals from Mrs. Lincoln and Miss Harris, who were standing by the high-backed armchair in which President Lincoln sat, I went immediately to their assistance, saying I was a United States army surgeon."

Leale holds Mrs. Lincoln's outstretched hand while she cries piteously: "Oh, Doctor! Is he dead? Can he recover? Will you take charge of him? Do what you can for him. Oh, my dear husband! my dear husband!" He soothes her a little, telling her he will do all that can possibly be done.

The body in the chair at first scrutiny seems to be that of a dead man, eyes closed, no certainty it is breathing. Dr. Leale with help from others lifts the body from the chair and moves it to a lying position on the floor. He holds the head and shoulders while doing this, his hand meeting a clot of blood near the left shoulder. Dr. Leale recalls seeing a dagger flashed by the assassin on the stage and the knife wound of Rathbone, and now supposes the President has a stab wound. He has the coat and shirt slit open, thinking to check perhaps a hemorrhage. He finds no wounds. He lifts the eyelids and sees evidence of a brain injury. He rapidly passes the separated fingers of both hands through the blood-matted hair of the head, finding a wound and removing a clot of blood, which relieves pressure on the brain and brings shallow breathing and a weak pulse. "The assassin," Leale commented later, ". . . had evidently planned to shoot to produce instant death, as the wound he made was situated within two inches of the physiological point of selection, when instant death is desired."

Dr. Leale bends over, puts a knee at each side of the body, and tries to start the breathing apparatus, attempts to stimulate respiration by putting his two fingers into the throat and pressing down and out on the base of the tongue to free the larnyx of secretion. Dr. Charles Sabin Taft, the army surgeon lifted from the stage into the box, now arrives. Another physician, Dr. Albert F. A. King, arrives. Leale asks them each to manipulate an arm while he presses upward on the diaphragm and elsewhere to stimulate heart action. The body responds with an improvement in the pulse and the irregular breathing.

Dr. Leale is sure, however, that with the shock and prostration the body has undergone, more must now be done to keep life going. And as he told it later: "I leaned forcibly forward directly over his body, thorax to thorax, face to face, and several times drew in a long breath, then forcibly breathed directly into his mouth and nostrils, which expanded his lungs and improved his respirations. After waiting a moment I placed my ear over his thorax and found the action of the heart improving. I arose to the erect kneeling posture, then watched for a short time and saw that the President could continue independent breathing and that instant death would not occur. I then pronounced my diagnosis and prognosis: 'His wound is mortal; it is impossible for him to recover.' "

John F. Kennedy

GEORGE W. NORRIS

At precisely 1:00 P.M. one wintry afternoon early in 1910, Representative John Dalzell of Pennsylvania left the Speaker's Chair and walked out of the

House Chamber for his daily cup of coffee and piece of pie in the Capitol restaurant. His departure was not unusual—for Representative Dalzell, who was Speaker Joe Cannon's first assistant in ruling the House from the Speaker's Chair, had always left the Chamber at exactly that hour, and he was almost invariably succeeded in the Chair by Representative Walter Smith of Iowa. But on that particular January afternoon Representative Dalzell's journey up the aisle was watched with curious satisfaction by a somewhat shaggy looking Representative in a plain black suit and a little shoestring tie. And the Assistant Speaker had no sooner reached the door of the Chamber than Republican Representative George W. Norris of Nebraska walked over to Representative Smith and asked if he might be recognized for two minutes. Smith, a member of the Cannon-Dalzell Republican ruling clique but a personal friend of Norris', agreed.

To his astonishment, Representative Norris sought to amend the resolution then under debate—a resolution calling for a joint committee to investigate the Ballinger-Pinchot conservation dispute—by requiring the entire House of Representatives to appoint its members to the investigating committee, instead of granting the customary authority to the Speaker to make such selections.

Page boys scurried out to find Cannon and Dalzell. This was insurrection in the ranks—the first attempt to limit the previously unlimited power of "Czar" Cannon! But Norris insisted that all he desired was a fair investigation, not one rigged by the administration. Joined by Pinchot followers, fellow insurgent Republicans and practically all of the Democrats, he succeeded in having his amendment adopted by the narrow margin of 149 to 146.

It was the first setback the powerful Speaker had ever suffered, and he vowed never to forget it. But for George Norris, the victory on the investigation resolution was only a preliminary step. For in the inner pocket of his threadbare black coat was a scrawled resolution which he had drafted years before—a resolution to have the House, rather than the Speaker, appoint the members of the Rules Committee itself, the Committee which completely dictated the House program and was in turn completely dominated by the Speaker.

On St. Patrick's Day in 1910, Norris rose to address the "Czar." Only minutes before, Cannon had ruled that a census bill promoted by one of his cohorts was privileged under the Constitution and could be considered out of order, inasmuch as that document provided for the taking of the census. "Mr. Speaker," called Norris, "I present a resolution made privileged by the Constitution." "The gentleman will present it," replied Cannon, smugly unaware of the attack about to be launched. And George Norris unfolded that tattered paper from his coat pocket and asked the Clerk to read it aloud.

Panic broke out in the Republican leadership. Cloakroom rumors had previously indicated the nature of Norris' proposed resolution—but it was merely a subject of contemptuous amusement among the regular Republicans, who knew they had the power to bury it forever in the Rules Committee itself.

Now Cannon's own ruling on the census bill in support of his friend had given Norris—and his resolution, clearly based on the Constitution's provision for House rules—an opening, an opening through which the Nebraska Congressman led all of the insurgent and Democratic forces. Cannon and his lieutenants were masters of parliamentary maneuvering and they were not immediately ready to concede. They attempted to adjourn, to recess, to make a quorum impossible. They continued debate on whether the resolution was privileged while the party faithful hurried back from St. Patrick's Day parades. They kept the House in constant session, hoping to break the less organized revolters. All night long the insurgents stayed in their seats, unwilling to nap off the floor for fear that Cannon would suddenly rule in their absence.

Finally, all attempts at intimidation and compromise having failed, Speaker Cannon, as expected, ruled the resolution out of order; and Norris promptly appealed the decision. By a vote of 182 to 160, Democrats and insurgent Republicans overruled the Speaker, and by a still larger margin Norris' resolution—already amended to obtain Democratic support—was adopted. The most ruthless and autocratic Speaker in the history of the House of Representatives thereupon submitted his resignation; but George Norris, who insisted his fight was to end the dictatorial powers of the office rather than to punish the individual, voted against its acceptance. Years later, Cannon was to say to him:

> Norris, throughout our bitter controversy, I do not recall a single instance in which you have been unfair. I cannot say this of many of your associates; and I want to say to you now that if any member of your damned gang had to be elected to the Senate, I would prefer it be you more than any of them.

The overthrow of Cannonism broke the strangle hold which the conservative Republican leaders had held over the Government and the nation; and it also ended whatever favors the Representative from Nebraska had previously received at their hands. Under the "Czar," the office of the Speaker of the House wielded what sometimes appeared to be very nearly equal power with the President and the entire United States Senate. It was a power that placed party above all other considerations, a power that fed on party loyalty, patronage and political organizations. It was a power which, despite increasing disfavor in all parts of the country outside the East, had continued unchallenged for years. But "one man without position," an editor commented, "against 200 welded into the most powerful political machine that Washington has ever known, has twice beaten them at their own game. Mr. George Norris is a man worth knowing and watching."

George W. Norris *was* worth watching, for his subsequent career in the Senate, to which he was elected shortly after his triumph over Cannon, earned him a reputation as one of the most courageous figures in American political life. The overthrow of Cannonism, although welcomed in Nebraska by all but a few party stalwarts, had nevertheless required tremendous courage and leadership on the part of a young Congressman attacking his party's well-entrenched leaders and willing to sacrifice the comforts and alliances that party loyalty brings. In the Senate he frequently broke not only with his party but with his constituents as well.

> I would rather go down to my political grave with a clear conscience [he once declared] than ride in the chariot of victory . . . a Congressional stool pigeon, the slave, the servant, or the vassal of any man, whether he be the owner and manager of a legislative menagerie or the ruler of a great nation. . . . I would rather lie in the silent grave, remembered by both friends and enemies as one who remained true to his faith and who never faltered in what he believed to be his duty, than to still live, old and aged, lacking the confidence of both factions.

These are the words of an idealist, an independent, a fighter—a man of deep conviction, fearless courage, sincere honesty—George W. Norris of Nebraska. We should not pretend that he was a faultless paragon of virtue; on the contrary, he was, on more than one occasion, emotional in his deliberations, vituperative in his denunciations, and prone to engage in bitter and exaggerated personal attack instead of concentrating his fire upon the merits of an issue. But nothing could sway him from what he thought was right, from his determination to help all the people, from his hope to save them from the twin tragedies of poverty and war.

George Norris knew well the tragedy of poverty from his own boyhood. His father having died when George was only four, he was obliged while still in his teens to hack out a livelihood for his mother and ten sisters on the stump-covered farm lands of Ohio. He knew, too, the horrors of war, from the untimely death in the Civil War of the older brother he hardly remembered, but whose inspiring letter—written by the wounded soldier shortly before his death—was treasured by young George for years. In 1917, as the nation teetered on the edge of the European conflict, George Norris had not forgotten his mother's sorrow and her hatred of war.

A country teacher, a small-town lawyer, a local prosecuting attorney and judge—those had been the years when George Norris had come to know the people of Nebraska and the West, when he saw the growing pattern of farm foreclosures, lost homesteads and farm workers drifting to the city and to unemployment.

As the old nineteenth century became the new twentieth, America was changing, her industries and cities were growing, her power in the world was increasing. And yet George Norris changed—and would change—very little. His chunky figure was still clothed in the drab black suits, white shirts and little black shoestring ties he had worn most of his life and would wear until his death. His mild manners, disarming honesty and avoidance of the social circle of politics in favor of a quiet evening of reading set him apart from the career politicians of his country, whose popularity among the voters, however, he far outstripped.

Only his political outlook changed as he began the long career which would keep him in Washington for forty years. For when George Norris had first entered the House of Representatives in 1903, fresh from the plains of Nebraska, he had been a staunch, conservative Republican, "sure of my position," as he later wrote, "unreasonable in my convictions, and unbending in my opposition to any other political party or political thought except my own." But "one by one I saw my favorite heroes wither . . . I discovered that my party . . . was guilty of virtually all the evils that I had charged against the opposition."

No single chapter could recount in full all of the courageous and independent battles led by George Norris. His most enduring accomplishments were in the field of public power, and there are few parallels to his long fight to bring the benefits of low-cost electricity to the people of the Tennessee Valley, although they lived a thousand miles from his home state of Nebraska. But there were three struggles in his life that are worthy of especial note for the courage displayed—the overthrow of "Czar" Cannon already described; his support of Al Smith for President in 1928; and his filibuster against the Armed Ship Bill in 1917.

When Woodrow Wilson, sorrowfully determined upon a policy of "armed neutrality" in early 1917, appeared before a tense joint session of Congress to request legislation authorizing him to arm American merchant ships, the American public gave its immediate approval. Unrestricted German submarine warfare was enforcing a tight blockade by which the Kaiser sought to starve the British Isles into submission; and Secretary of State Lansing had been politely informed that every American ship encountered in the war zone would be torpedoed. Already American vessels had been searched, seized and sunk. Tales of atrocities to our seamen filled the press.

As debate on the bill got under way, the newspapers learned of a new plot against the United States, contained in a message from the German Under Secretary of State for Foreign affairs, Zimmerman, to the German Minister in Mexico. The alleged note (for there were those who questioned its authenticity and the motives of the British and American governments in disclosing it at that particular time) proposed a scheme to align Mexico and Japan against the United States. In return for its use as an invasion base, Mexico was promised restoration of her "American colonies," seized more than seventy years earlier by Sam Houston and his compatriots.

When the contents of the Zimmerman note were leaked to the newspapers, all resistance to the Armed Ship Bill in the House of Representatives instantly collapsed. The bill was rushed through that body by the overwhelming vote of 403 to 13—a vote which seemed clearly representative of popular opinion in favor of the President's move. Certainly the overwhelming support given the bill by Nebraska's Congressmen represented the feelings of that state.

But in the Senate on March 2, 1917, the Armed Ship Bill met determined opposition from a small bipartisan band of insurgents led by Robert La Follette of Wisconsin and George Norris of Nebraska. As freshman Senator from a state which the previous year had voted for a Democratic legislature, Governor, Senator and President, George Norris (unlike La Follette) was neither a solidly established political figure in his own bailiwick nor confident that his people were opposed to Wilson and his policies.

In previous months he had supported the President on major foreign policy issues, including the severing of diplomatic ties with the German government. Although a militant pacifist and isolationist, his very nature prohibited him from being a mere obstructionist on all international issues, or a petty partisan opposing all of the President's requests. (Indeed, by the time World War II approached, his isolationism had largely vanished.)

But George Norris hated war—and he feared that "Big Business," which he believed was providing the stimuli for our progress along the road to war, was bent on driving the nation into a useless, bloody struggle; that the President— far from taking the people into his confidence—was trying to stampede public opinion into pressuring the Senate for war; and that the Armed Ship Bill was a device to protect American munition profits with American lives, a device which could push us directly into the conflict as a combatant without further deliberation by Congress or actual attack upon the United States by Germany. He was fearful of the bill's broad grant of authority, and he was resentful of the manner in which it was being steamrollered through the Congress. It is not now important whether Norris was right or wrong. What is now important is the courage he displayed in support of his convictions.

"People may not believe it," Senator Norris once said, "but I don't like to get into fights." In 1917, whether he liked it or not, the freshman from Nebraska prepared for one of the hardest, most embittering struggles of his political career. Since those days were prior to Norris' own Twentieth, or Lame Duck, Amendment, the Sixty-fourth Congress would expire at noon of March 4, when a new Presidential term began. Thus passage of the Bill by that Congress could be prevented if the Senate could not vote before that hour; and Norris and his little band were hopeful that the new Congress, chosen by the people during the Presidential campaign of 1916—based upon the slogan "He kept us out of war"—might join in opposition to the measure, or at least give it more careful consideration. But preventing a vote during the next two days spelled only one word—filibuster!

George Norris, an advocate of a change in the Senate rules to correct the abuses of filibustering, but feeling strongly that the issue of war itself was at stake, adopted this very tactic "in spite of my repugnance to the method." As parliamentary floor leader for his group, he arranged speakers to make certain that there was no possibility of a break in the debate which would enable the bill to come to a vote.

Many of his closest friends in the Senate were aghast at this conduct. "No state but one populated by mollycoddles," complained one Senator well aware of the raging anti-German sentiment back home, "would endorse what Norris is trying to do." But Nebraska did *not* endorse the position of its junior Senator. As debate got under way, the Nebraska newspapers, in a thinly veiled warning, reported that the tremendous vote in the House "represents the sentiments of the people." And the Nebraska legislature had already unanimously pledged to President Wilson "the loyal and undivided support of the entire citizenry of the state of Nebraska, of whatever political party and of whatever blood or place of birth, in whatever may be found necessary to maintain the rights of Americans, the dignity of our nation and the honor of our flag."

But George Norris' guide was his own conscience. "Otherwise," he said, "a member of Congress giving weight to expressed public sentiment becomes only an automatic machine, and Congress requires no patriotism, no education, and no courage. . . ." And so, with only his conscience to sustain him, the Senator worked around the clock to bolster the sagging spirits of his little band, to prepare new speakers for continuous debate and to check every opposition move to end the filibuster.

Several Senators, Norris later related, privately approached him to wish the filibuster success, while pleading party regularity and political expediency as their grounds for publicly supporting the President's position. When Norris told them that the important thing was to make certain there were plenty of speakers, regardless of the views expressed, two of the President's supporters, by private agreement with Norris, spoke at length in favor of the bill.

Day and night the debate continued; and on the morning of March 4 the Senate was a scene of weary disorder. "Those final minutes," Norris later wrote, "live in my memory."

> In that chamber, men became slaves to emotion. The clash of anger and bitterness, in my judgment, never has been exceeded in the history of the United States. When the hour hand pointed to the arrival of noon, the chairman announced adjournment. The filibuster had won. The conference report which would have authorized the arming of American ships had failed of Senate approval. . . . Tense excitement prevailed throughout the entire country, and especially in the Senate itself. . . . I have felt from that day to this the filibuster was justified. I never have apologized for the part I took in it. . . . [We] honestly believed that, by our actions in that struggle, we had averted American participation in the war.

But theirs was a fleeting victory. For the President—in addition to immediately calling a special session of Congress in which the Senate adopted a closure rule to limit debate (with Norris' support)—also announced that a further examination of the statutes had revealed that the executive power already included the right to arm ships without Congressional action. And the President also let loose a blast, still frequently quoted today, against "a little group of willful men, representing no opinion but their own, that rendered the great government of the United States helpless and contemptible."

George Norris called the President's scathing indictment a grave injustice to men who conscientiously tried to do their duty as they saw it; but, except for the unfortunate and unhelpful praise bestowed upon them by the German press, "the epithets heaped upon these men were without precedent in the annals of American journalism." They had earned, in the words of the Louisville *Courier Journal*, "an eternity of execration." A mass meeting at Carnegie Hall condemned Norris and his colleagues as "treasonable and reprehensible" men "who refused to defend the Stars and Stripes on the high seas"; and the crowd hooted "traitor" and "hang him" whenever the names of Norris, La Follette and their supporters were mentioned. "The time has come," the Mayor of New York shouted to another meeting, "when the people of this country are to be divided into two classes—Americans and traitors."

The Hartford *Courant* called them "political tramps," and the New York *Sun* labelled twelve United States Senators "a group of moral perverts." The Providence *Journal* called their action "little short of treason" and the *New York Times* editorialized that "The odium of treasonable purpose will rest upon their names forevermore." The New York *Herald* predicted: "They will be fortunate if their names do not go down into history bracketed with that of Benedict Arnold."

In the decades to follow, Senator Norris would learn to withstand the merciless abuse inevitably heaped upon one of his independent and outspoken views. On the Senate floor itself, he would be called a Bolshevist, an enemy of advancement, a traitor and much more. But now the harsh terms of vilification and the desertion of former friends hurt him deeply. One afternoon several passengers left a Washington trolley car when Norris and La Follette took seats beside them. His mail was abusive, several letters containing sketches showing him in German uniform complete with medals.

The Nebraska press joined in the denunciation of its junior Senator. "Can Senator Norris believe," cried the Omaha *World Herald* (which had listed on page 1 the names of "Twelve Senators Who Halt Action in Greatest Crisis Since Civil War"), "can any man in his senses believe, that the American Government could tamely submit to these outrages?"

"The Norris fear of the establishment of an absolute monarchy under Wilson is grotesque," said the Lincoln *Star*. "Maybe it is a joke. If not, friends of Mr. Norris should look after his mental status." And the Omaha *Bee* thought his fear of Presidential authority "reflects little credit on the Senator's common sense."

It was believed in Washington that the conscience of the freshman from Nebraska had led him, in the words of one Washington correspondent, to "his political death." The outraged Nebraska State Legislature, with whooping enthusiasm, passed a resolution expressing the confidence of the state in President Wilson and his policies.

George Norris was saddened by the near unanimity with which "my own people condemned me . . . and asserted that I was misrepresenting my state." Although popularity was not his standard, he had tried, he later wrote, throughout his career "to do what in my own heart I believed to be right for the people at large." Thus, unwilling to "represent the people of Nebraska if they did not want me," he came to a dramatic decision—he would offer to resign from the Senate and submit to a special recall election, "to let my constituents decide whether I was representing them or misrepresenting them in Washington." In letters to the Governor and the Republican State Chairman, he urged a special election, agreeing to abide by the result and to waive whatever constitutional rights protected him from recall.

Sharing the fears of his astonished friends in the Senate that hysteria and well-financed opposition might insure his defeat which in turn would be interpreted as a mandate for war, he nevertheless insisted in his letter to the Governor that he had "no desire to represent the people of Nebraska if my official conduct is contrary to their wishes."

> The denunciation I have received . . . indicates to me that there is a strong probability that the course I have pursued is unsatisfactory to the people whom I represent, and it seems, therefore, only fair that the matter should be submitted to them for decision.
>
> I will not, however, even at the behest of a unanimous constituency, violate my oath of office by voting in favor of a proposition that means the surrender by Congress of its sole right to declare war. . . . If my refusal to do this is contrary to the wishes of the people of Nebraska, then I should be recalled and some one else selected to fill the place. . . . I am, however, so firmly convinced of the righteousness of my course that I believe if the intelligent and patriotic citizenship of the country can only have an opportunity to hear both sides of the question, all the money in Christendom and all the political machinery that wealth can congregate will not be able to defeat the principle of government for which our forefathers fought. . . . If I am wrong, then I not only ought to retire, but I desire to do so. I have no desire to hold public office if I am expected blindly to follow in my official actions the dictation of a newspaper combination . . . or be a rubber stamp even for the President of the United States.

The Senator, announcing an open meeting in Lincoln to explain his position, was largely ignored by the press as he journeyed homeward. Attempting to get the Republican National Committeeman to act as Chairman of the meeting, he was warned by that worthy gentleman that it was "not possible for this meeting to be held without trouble. I think the meeting will be broken up or at least you will have such an unfriendly audience that it will be impossible for you to make any coherent speech." One of the few friends who called upon him urged him to cancel the meeting by pleading illness, telling Norris that he had made a very sad mistake in returning to Nebraska when feelings ran so high. Others predicted that agitators would be scattered throughout the audience to make presentation of his arguments impossible, and told the Senator that the torpedoing of three more American merchant ships since the filibuster had further intensified the anger of his constituents. "I cannot remember a day in my life," the Senator wrote in his autobiography, "when I have suffered more from a lonely feeling of despondency. My friends led me to believe that the people of Nebraska were almost unanimously against me."

Unable to get a single friend or supporter to act as chairman, Norris was nevertheless determined to go through with the meeting. "I myself hired the hall," he told a lonely reporter in his deserted hotel room, "and it is to be my meeting. I am asking no one to stand sponsor for me or for my acts. But I have nothing to apologize for and nothing to take back."

Walking from his hotel to the city auditorium on a beautiful spring night, Norris anxiously noted that more than three thousand people—the concerned, the skeptical and the curious—had filled the auditorium, with many standing in the aisles and outside in the street. Calm but trembling, he walked out on the stage before them and stood for a moment without speaking, a solitary figure in a baggy black suit and a little shoestring tie. "I had expected an unfriendly audience," he wrote, "and it was with some fear that I stepped forward. When I entered the rear of the auditorium and stepped out on the stage, there was a deathlike silence. There was not a single handclap. But I had not expected applause; and I was delighted that I was not hissed."

In his homely, quiet, and yet intense manner, Senator Norris began with the simple phrase: "I have come home to tell you the truth."

Immediately there was a burst of applause from all parts of the audience. Never in my lifetime has applause done me the good that did. . . . There was, in the hearts of the common people, a belief that underneath the deception and the misrepresentation, the political power and the influence, there was something artificial about the propaganda.

There was no violence, there was no heckling; and the tremendous crowd cheered mightily as Norris lashed out at his critics. His dry, simple but persistent language and the quiet intensity of his anger captivated his audience, as he insisted that their newspapers were not giving them the facts and that, despite warnings that he stay away until his role in the filibuster was forgotten, he wanted it to be remembered. More than half of the New York audience which had hissed him had been in evening dress, he sarcastically recalled, and he questioned how many of them were willing to fight or send their children:

Of course, if poodledogs could have been made into soldiers, that audience would have supplied a regiment. . . . My colleague talked two and a half hours for the bill and was called a hero. I talked one hour and a half against the bill and was called a traitor. Even though you say I am wrong, even though you feel sure I should have stood by the President, has the time come when we can't even express our opinions in the Senate, where we were sent to debate such questions, without being branded by the moneyed interests as traitors? I can stand up and take my medicine without wincing under any charge except that of traitor. In all of the English language, in all the tongues of the world, you can't find any other words as damnable as that.

The crowd, after more than an hour, roared its approval. The newspapers were not so easily convinced or so willing to forgive. "His elaborate and ingenious explanation," said the *World Herald*, is "foolish nonsense . . . a silly statement, which has disgusted the people." "The Senator spent little time meeting the issue as it actually stood," said the *State Journal*. "He should not let his critics disturb his balance."

But Senator Norris, who was asked to appear before many groups to explain what he felt to be the true issues, met acclaim throughout the state; and the Governor having announced that he would not ask the Legislature to authorize a special recall election, the Senator returned to Washington better able to withstand the abuse which had not yet fully ceased.

During the next eleven years George Norris' fame and political fortune multiplied. In 1928, despite his continued differences with the Republican party and its administrations, the Nebraska Senator was one of the party's most prominent members, Chairman of the Senate Judiciary Committee and a potential Presidential nominee. But Norris himself scoffed at the latter reports:

> I have no expectation of being nominated for President. A man who has followed the political course I have is barred from the office. . . . I realize perfectly that no man holding the views I do is going to be nominated for the Presidency.

With an oath he rejected the suggestion that he accept a position as Herbert Hoover's running mate, and he attacked the Republican Convention's platform and the methods by which it had selected its nominees. In those years prior to the establishment of the T.V.A., the Senator from Nebraska was the nation's most outspoken advocate of public power; and he believed that the "monopolistic power trust" had dictated the nomination of Hoover and the Republican platform.

Unwilling to commit himself to the Democratic party he had always opposed, and whose platform he believed to be equally weak, Norris toured the country campaigning for fellow progressives regardless of party. But as the campaign utterances of Democratic nominee Al Smith of New York began to fall into line with Norris' own views, he was confronted with the most difficult political problem of his career.

George Norris was a Republican, a Midwesterner, a Protestant and a "dry," and Herbert Hoover was all of those things. But Al Smith—a Tammany Hall Democrat from the streets of New York, and a Catholic who favored the repeal of prohibition—was none of them. Surely Smith could have little support in Nebraska, which was also Republican, Midwestern, Protestant and dry by nature. Could Norris possibly desert his party, his state and his constituents under such circumstances?

He could. He had always maintained that he "would like to abolish party responsibility and in its stead establish personal responsibility. Any man even though he be the strictest kind of Republican, who does not believe the things I stand for are right, should follow his convictions and vote against me." And thus in 1928 Norris finally declared that progressives

> had no place to land except in the Smith camp. . . . Shall we be so partisan that we will place our party above our country and refuse to follow the only leader who affords us any escape from the control of the [power] trust? . . . It seems to me we cannot crush our consciences and support somebody who we know in advance is opposed to the very things for which we have been fighting so many years.

But what about Smith's religious views? What about his attitude on the liquor question?

> It is possible for a man in public life to separate his religious beliefs from his political activities. . . . I am a Protestant and a dry, yet I would support a man who was a wet and a Catholic provided I believed he was sincerely in favor of law enforcement and was right on economic issues. . . . I'd rather trust an honest wet who is progressive and courageous in his makeup than politicians who profess to be on the dry side but do no more to make prohibition effective than all the rum runners and bootleggers in the country.

These were courageous sentiments, but they were lost on an indignant constituency. As his train sped through the State on the way to Omaha, where he was to speak for Smith over a nationwide radio hookup, long-time friends and Republican leaders climbed aboard to appeal in the name of his party and career. The head of the powerful Nebraska Anti-Saloon League, previously an important supporter of Norris, termed his injection of the power issue poppycock. "The issue in this campaign is the liquor issue and Norris knows it. If he makes this speech for Smith, the League is through with him." (Norris, when asked if he would run for re-election in 1930 in view of such statements, dryly replied that "such things might drive me to it.") The pastor of the largest Baptist church in Omaha wrote the Senator that he did not "represent us at all, and we are very much ashamed of your attitude toward the administration." But Norris, in his reply, calmly asked the minister whether he had "made any attempt to take the beam out of your own eyes, so that you can see more clearly how to pluck the mote out of your brother's eye."

Old Guard Republican leaders had previously insisted, at least privately, that Norris was "no Republican," a charge they now made openly. But now many of Norris' most devoted followers expressed dismay at his bolt. Said an Eagle, Nebraska, small businessman: "I have supported Norris for 20 years, but never again. He is politically warped and mentally a grouch, and has antagonized every Republican administration since Roosevelt. The Senator should have more respect for his admirers than to expect them to cast their lot with a wet Democrat." Norris' first Congressional secretary told reporters he was "bitterly opposed to the Senator's unwarranted support of Tammany's candidate for President."

A delegate who had supported Norris for President at the Republican Convention told the press that Norris "does not carry my political conscience in his vest pocket. I am deeply grieved to see the stand he has taken. Norris should seek new friends, and if he chooses to find them on the sidewalks of New York that is his privilege. But it is unfortunate that he uses the Republican party as a vehicle to ride into office and then repudiates its standard-bearer."

The editor of the Walthill *Times* wrote: "I say it sadly, but I am through with Norris. Politically he is lost in the wilderness, far away from his old progressive friends."

"For a hungry farmer or a thirsty wet of less than average political judgment," said a Lincoln attorney who was close to the Norris camp, "there may be an excuse. But for a statesman of Norris' ability and experience there is no excuse."

But George Norris sought to help the hungry farmer even if it meant helping the thirsty wet. Unmoved by either appeals or attacks, he delivered a powerful plea for Smith at Omaha. The New York Governor, he said, had risen above the dictates of Tammany, while the techniques employed by the Republican Convention would "make Tammany Hall appear as a white-robed saint." He was "traveling in very distinguished company" by supporting the candidate of the opposing party, he told his audience, for Herbert Hoover himself had acted similarly ten years earlier. But for the most part his speech was an attack upon the power trust, "an octopus with slimy fingers that levies tribute upon every fireside," and upon Hoover's refusal to discuss these questions: "to sin by silence when we should protest makes cowards out of men."

Finally, Norris closed his address by meeting the religious issue openly:

It is our duty as patriots to cast out this Un-American doctrine and rebuke those who have raised the torch of intolerance. All believers of any faith can unite and go forward in our political work to bring about the maximum amount of happiness for our people.

But in 1928 the people of Nebraska were not willing to listen to the theme of tolerance or a discussion of the issues. Telegrams poured in attacking Norris for his support of a Catholic and a wet. "The storm which followed that Omaha pronouncement for Smith," Norris later recalled, "was more violent than any I had ever encountered. It was well that I had had some training in the matter of abuse." Even his wife was quoted by the papers as saying she would vote for neither Smith nor Hoover: "I am not following George in all this. . . . I have always been a dry and I am not going to vote for Smith even if George does." Although the same powerful Democratic newspaper, the Omaha *World Herald,* which had assailed his stand for principle against Woodrow Wilson, was now able to applaud Senator Norris "for his splendid courage and devotion," other Nebraska newspapers accused him of deserting his state for Tammany Hall in the hopes of reviving his own Presidential boom four years later. His speech had endangered the chances for re-election of his own liberal Republican colleague, and his fellow insurgent Republicans in the Senate expressed their disapproval of his course. When the Senator returned to his home town he found his friends and other leading citizens turning away, as though they would be glad to "cut my heart out and hang it on a fence as a warning to others."

The landslide for Hoover, who carried practically every county and community in Nebraska, as well as the country as a whole, embittered Norris, who declared that Hoover had won on the false questions of religion and prohibition, when the real problems were power and farm relief. The special interests and machine politicians, he said, "kept this issue to the front [although] they knew it was a false, wicked and unfair issue."

George Norris' filibuster against the Armed Ship Bill had failed, both in its immediate goal of preventing the President's action, and in its attempt to keep the nation out of the war into which it was plunged a few months later. His campaign for Al Smith also failed, and failed dismally. And yet, as the Senator confided to a friend in later years:

> It happens very often that one tries to do something and fails. He feels discouraged, and yet he may discover years afterward that the very effort he made was the reason why somebody else took it up and succeeded. I really believe that whatever use I have been to progressive civilization has been accomplished in the things I failed to do rather than in the things I actually did do.

George Norris met with both success and failure in his long tenure in public office, stretching over nearly a half a century of American political life. But the essence of the man and his career was caught in a tribute paid to the Republican Senator from Nebraska by the Democratic Presidential nominee in September, 1932:

> History asks, "Did the man have integrity?
> Did the man have unselfishness?
> Did the man have courage?
> Did the man have consistency?"
> There are few statesmen in America today who so definitely and clearly measure up to an affirmative answer to those four questions as does George W. Norris.

Winthrop Sargeant

HUMILITY,
CONCENTRATION, AND GUSTO

Among people who like to feel that they know just how things stand, Marianne Craig Moore is regarded, variously, as America's greatest living woman poet, or as one of America's greatest living poets, or even as America's greatest living poet—three views that combine to establish her squarely as a literary monument, handily labelled for ready reference. There may be some doubt in the minds of those who are not well up on modern verse about just how these titles have been arrived at, but there is no doubt that they are supported by an overwhelming assortment of prizes, memberships in societies of immortals, and honorary Litt. D.s that Miss Moore has collected over nearly half a century of writing verse, and by many qualified authorities, among them a number of distinguished fellow-poets, such as W. H. Auden, who has gallantly confessed to plundering her work for technical ideas, and T. S. Eliot, who has stated that in his opinion "her poems form part of the small body of durable poetry written in our time." There are, however, other ways of looking at Miss Moore. A large public that has never opened any of the books responsible for her fame has been led by articles about her in big-circulation family magazines to see her as a quaint and rather stylish spinster who, at the age of sixty-nine, lives in a cluttered apartment in Brooklyn and writes poems about animals—a picture that is essentially accurate, if considerably oversimplified. To some of the more complicated types who frequent literary teas and cocktail parties in Manhattan, Miss Moore is a quite outrageous chatter-box and intellectual comedienne; to others, more fondly disposed toward her, she is a gentle lioness of formidable glamour, capable of non-stop conversational monologues, richly interspersed with observations on life and letters, which they feel should be treasured for their outspokenness and originality. At gatherings of this kind, her meticulous and all but breakneck manner of expressing herself—mirroring a mind in which wisdom and innocence are curiously combined—often produces a flow of imagery and anecdote whose quality leads some of her admirers to contend that she not only writes but talks literature.

And there is still another Miss Moore—the one known to her neighbors in the fairly nondescript area surrounding her modest five-room, fifth-floor apartment on Cumberland Street, in the Fort Greene Park section of Brooklyn. To her neighbors she is, and has been for many years, a familiar and affectionately regarded figure as—dressed with a conservative smartness that often includes a skimmer or a tricorne hat, armed with a shopping basket, and exuding an air of invincible energy and cheerfulness—she passes the time of day with her grocer or her vegetable man. Along Cumberland Street, her claim to distinction rests not so much on her writing or on her drawing-room wit as on certain aspects of her conduct and bearing that mark her, in the eyes of people she has daily dealings with, as a great lady who represents the genteel traditions of a noble and nearly forgotten era. "For my money, they don't come any finer than Miss Moore," says Henry Burfeindt, one of the clerks at the Oxlord Delicatessen, a couple of blocks from her apartment. "She gave me one of her books—and she autographed it. It says 'To Henry' in the front of it. One of these days I'm going to lay in the sun and read it." And Mike Moscarella, who runs a shoe-repair shop at the corner of Carlton Street and De Kalb Avenue, a block and a half away, says, "She don't dress modern. She makes friends easy, and she's a real home lady. Very interesting to talk to, too. She likes to talk about scenery and flowers." Among another group of her Brooklyn acquaintances—the parishioners of the nearby Lafayette Avenue Presbyterian Church —Miss Moore is revered for still different virtues, of a sort not often associated with poets nowadays. She regularly attends services at the church, and invariably says grace before meals. Moreover, she strictly avoids alcohol, tobacco, and even coffee. So highly is she thought of by the church authorities that on several occasions they have asked her to write a special benediction to be delivered at church dinners on Thanksgiving or some other ceremonial day, but this she has so far declined to do. "I don't believe in substituting conscious expression for spontaneous devotion," she says.

These diverse facets of Miss Moore's public personality suggest that the individual embodying them is a phenomenon of some complexity. Since poetry —and contemporary poetry in particular—is one of the most personal of the arts, and since connoisseurs long familiar with Miss Moore and her verse believe that her poems are works of self-portraiture to an even greater extent than those of most poets, it is natural to look for clues to the essential character of this phenomenon in the half-dozen volumes of verse that, except for a book of essays and some translations, constitute her life work to date. The poems in these volumes are instantly striking for the exquisite care with which they have been put together; Miss Moore sets down her metaphors and images in neat, precise patterns, using schemes of metre and rhyme that are at once as intricate and as clearly defined as needlepoint embroidery, and even the typographic schemes of her printed verses are fastidiously original. A good example of this last is a fragment from "In Distrust of Merits," one of the few poems she has written on subjects of major social significance:

> There never was a war that was
> not inward; I must
> fight till I have conquered in myself what
> causes war, but I would not believe it.
> I inwardly did nothing.
> O Iscariotlike crime!

> Beauty is everlasting
> and dust is for a time.

In general, her poems reveal an intense preoccupation with often microscopic visual detail and an extraordinary joy in the contemplation of such minutiae as the sheen of sea shells, the tendrils of plants, and the legs and wings of insects. While Miss Moore's scrupulous descriptions of her abundant observations would hardly constitute poetry in themselves, she has a flair for symbolism that gives them meaning, making each small object the protagonist of an engrossing drama—a drama that, as often as not, points a moral of some sort. The sequence in which the visual images swiftly appear and vanish is not so much a matter of logic as it is of kaleidoscopic association, and the agility with which Miss Moore jumps from one association to the next is such that even the most diligent reader sometimes loses his way in attempting to follow her—a drawback that she tries to minimize by including a series of explanatory notes at the end of each volume. A reader who, with or without the notes, is able to keep pace with Miss Moore finds himself being led through an aggregation of sensations and perceptions that are similar in effect to a collage or a mosaic, and are highlighted by epigrams and descriptive phrases memorable for the particularly vivid insight they give into one truth or another.

In "The Labours of Hercules," a poem about poetry, Miss Moore has written "that one detects creative power by its capacity to conquer one's detachment, that while it may have more elasticity than logic, it knows where it is going"—an eminently logical assertion and a justification of the elastic, or intuitive, method that characterizes most of her writing. A great deal of the charm of her work lies in the originality of her point of view; somehow she is able to describe things as if they were being seen for the first time by a mind without preconceptions. This faculty, similar to that of a child or a primitive, enables her to avoid clichés of thought and expression; her poetry contains no second-hand ideas, except when she openly borrows from other writers, in which case she takes pains to make that fact clear by using quotation marks— a sort of code, informing the knowing reader that he will find the source listed back among the notes. She seems, indeed, to be perpetually and delightedly poised on the frontier of fresh experience—a narrow and perilous region where she can lean neither on learning nor on generalized principles. Miss Moore is, of course, neither a child nor a primitive but an urbane and educated woman, and her position on this frontier—as consciously maintained as that of a tightrope walker—demands an air of ingenuousness that is patently calculated artifice but nevertheless a most appealing one.

Much of Miss Moore's poetry takes the form of slyly satirical criticism— criticism of art, of literature, of human behavior—expressed in economical, tightly packed phrases, and in this criticism she shows herself to be something of a stickler for what she considers propriety. Of alcohol, that traditional midwife of the poet, she states uncompromisingly, "The wine cellar? No. It accomplishes nothing and makes the soul heavy." (Since these lines and the quotations immediately following have been taken out of context, they are reproduced here without regard for the typographical niceties of their author's versification.) In discussing literature, she writes, "Originality is in any case a byproduct of sincerity," and she taunts the French by describing them as a people "in whose products mystery of construction diverts one from what was originally one's object—substance at the core." She dislikes "authorities whose hopes are shaped by mercenaries" and "writers entrapped by teatime fame and commuters' comforts." She deplores the abnormal perfection of roses, assuring them that "your thorns are the best part of you." Her attitude toward her art is sometimes rather thorny itself, as when she observes, "Reading [poetry] . . . with a perfect contempt for it, one discovers in it after all, a place for the genuine." As a believer in good taste, she favors reticence: "The deepest feeling always shows itself in silence; not in silence, but restraint." Objective little notations like these seem to indicate an extremely reflective and slightly acid mind that abhors excess and prefers detached observation to participation, and this impression is reinforced by the rather striking fact that Miss Moore's verse is almost devoid of anything approaching passionate warmth toward her fellow-man; indeed, her fellow-man very seldom appears in it at all. Her love is expended instead on a still-life or a landscape world inhabited by plants and animals that are usually small and very self-sufficient. Yet she is apt to regard this world pessimistically; the environment in which her little animals play out their dramas is nearly always a threatening one. The odds are against them, even though, often covered with protective armor, they make their dwellings in snug holes and have admirable qualities of adaptability and strong powers of survival. They appear as symbols of virtues that Miss Moore repeatedly extolls—courage, patience, firmness, loyalty, integrity, good sense, modesty, persistence, and independence. Like many another poet, Miss Moore celebrates what philosophers have called the *élan vital*, but she celebrates it with restraint, and its most impressive victories in her poetry are achieved by the small living things she portrays as holding their own against the hostile surroundings of nature, as in "Nevertheless":

> The weak overcomes its
>   menace, the strong over-
>   comes itself. What is there
>
> like fortitude! What sap
>   went through that little thread
>   to make the cherry red!

Miss Moore's associative process of thought, which leads her discursively through her world of menaced and courageous creatures and often winds up with a pronouncement on human behavior, is well illustrated by a poem called "Snakes, Mongooses, Snake-Charmers and the Like." This starts off with a tribute to the mongoose's claws, passes on to images evoking the austerity of

India and then to snakes and tortoises and chameleons, and finally poses the question of why the snake was invented. Typically, the answer is oblique, and ends with an aphorism:

> We do not know; the only positive thing about it is its shape; but why protest?
> The passion for setting people right is in itself an afflictive disease.
> Distaste which takes no credit to itself is best.

The connoisseurs who regard Miss Moore's poems almost literally as self-portraits are convinced that all those tiny beleaguered organisms surviving in adversity by means of fortitude, intelligence, and patience represent Miss Moore herself, and, moreover, that her manner of expression is as revealing as her subject matter. These judgments would appear to be sound, since a reader of Miss Moore's verse who had never met its author or heard anything about her would be justified in concluding that she was a rather remote and isolated individual, a meditative soliloquist, a fascinated observer of life, a digressive but deliberately elegant thinker, a stoic, a moralist, and something of a frontierswoman in the realm of sensation, capable of extracting enormous drama from the slightest experiences and impressions—and all this is pretty much confirmed by the poet's habits and the environment she has chosen for herself. Although her various obligations in the roles of monument, lioness, neighborhood *grande dame*, and pillar of the church involve her in a great deal of what she terms "dashing around," Miss Moore feels and responds to the creative person's need for privacy. Between her forays into the outer world, she lives alone, cooking her own meals at such times as she remembers to eat at all, corresponding with her numerous friends, and inviting the mood of "humility, concentration, and gusto" that she says is conducive to the difficult task of writing verse. She has likened herself during such intervals to "a cat in a basket with the lid on," "a badger under a hedge of poison ivy," and "a rat in a cheese"—similes that not only relate characteristically to animal life but convey a sense of snugness that is plainly very congenial to her.

Miss Moore's apartment is the apotheosis of snugness; indeed, it is snug almost to the point of restricting free movement, owing to a vast collection of miscellaneous objects she has amassed over the years. "I suppose my life is made happier by hoarding these things," Miss Moore says apologetically, and a visitor is likely to suspect that she attaches great sentimental value to everything around her. In addition to the furniture (comfortably old-fashioned and not in itself obtrusive), the hoard includes a tremendous array of books, in which the Bible and the Book of Common Prayer rub bindings with Latin classics and volumes on science, history, and travel—all of them painstakingly dusted and kept either in crowded bookcases or in upended apple boxes that line the narrow hallways. It includes a walrus tusk from the Greely Expedition to the Arctic in 1881, countless porcelain and ivory likenesses of tigers and elephants, and a mass of bric-a-brac in less readily identifiable shapes. And it includes paintings, drawings, and etchings, as well as pictures that Miss Moore has cut from magazines and framed—a display whose sheer square footage threatens to overflow the limited wall space that is not occupied by bookcases. Some of these mural ornaments are so faded that only the sharpest eye can make out what they are supposed to represent; others, more distinct, are works of purely personal interest, executed by friends (a stiff and naïve painting of a flower by E. E. Cummings, for example), or prints by artists of long ago (William Blake, for example). The subjects of the whole informal gallery are preponderantly animals—elephants, kangaroos, alligators, chickens, mice, hermit crabs, and very nearly all the rest. "Our ancestors!" Miss Moore explains, joyously embracing the entire display with a wave of the hand. Occasionally, though, the encroaching multitude of her possessions drives her to the verge of impatience. "I never want to own anything any more," she told a visitor not long ago. "No more shells and feathers! People present you with things they think may suggest an idea for a poem, but there simply aren't enough alcoves and embrasures to put them all in." Miss Moore does not usually remain in this mood for long, however, and she has never been able to bring herself to discard any of her remarkable accretion. Even in her most exasperated moments, the mere mention of some old coin or bit of porcelain in her collection will prompt her to dig it out and show it off with undisguised affection.

In contrast to the rest of the apartment, Miss Moore's kitchen has an air of practicality about it that suggests another side of her nature. A few pots and pans suffice for her culinary needs. "Cook and sew enough of the time and you feel degraded," she says. "I cook only the essentials—meat and potatoes. I've never baked a pie." On the kitchen table stands a Mason jar containing carrot juice, to which Miss Moore repairs for sustenance between meals, replenishing her supply from time to time with the help of a vegetable-juicer. "Carrot juice increases vigor," she says. The austerity of her kitchen is relieved only by a singular tool rack, of her own design and construction, in which she keeps various convenient implements—a plane, an auger, a pair of tin-cutting shears, a pair of pliers, two axes, a jar opener, a pair of scissors, and a gimlet, to name a few—all mounted in their proper places with a feeling for order that would do credit to the curator of a museum. The variety of these utensils not only bespeaks Miss Moore's prowess as a domestic craftsman but adds to the impression that her apartment is a thoroughly self-sufficient refuge —that its occupant, when hidden away in it, is as independent of the world at large as a barnacle in its shell.

As a consequence of Miss Moore's literary eminence, she does not remain hidden away as much as she perhaps would like to. Her apartment has become a place of pilgrimage for editors, publishers, critics, poets, artists, and other admiring folk, who gladly undertake the trip across the river in order to pay their respects. While Miss Moore does not encourage wholesale invasions of her privacy, she is nevertheless gratified by an occasional visit and deeply appreciative of the effort people make in journeying all the way to what is for most of them a previously unexplored region of Brooklyn. By way of demonstrating this appreciation, she keeps a large supply of subway tokens on hand, and invariably urges guests from Manhattan to dip into it and so spare themselves the trouble of having to stop and buy one in the station before heading back under the East River. Sometimes her offer of a token is accepted casually, but sometimes it is accepted only after quite a show of reluctance, and once in a while it is flatly refused. There are those who suspect that Miss Moore likes to study the varied reactions to her considerate little gesture, and she is reported to have once admitted as much to a friend. "I know they don't need it, and they know that I know they don't need it, but I like to see what happens," she is supposed to have said. "The most interesting people take it without making a fuss." Questioned about this recently, Miss Moore denied ever having said any such thing. "Why, I would be incapable of testing a person in that way!" she exclaimed. But then she added, "Still, I do prize people a little more highly if they don't make a big thing of it."

When guests arrive at the apartment, Miss Moore serves them tea, which she brews unostentatiously but with great care, seeing to it that her Chinese teapot is properly warmed beforehand and putting it in an upholstered basket when the tea is ready for pouring. During this ceremony, she moves about swiftly among the treasures in her living room in an easy, athletic fashion not generally associated with women of her age, and her manner, which in privacy resembles that of a preoccupied librarian, is transformed into that of a piquant and highly animated actress. The transformation is a very striking one. Her cheeks redden, she smiles slyly, and she becomes Marianne Moore the public personality, with all the challenges to wit and originality that this implies. She seems to grow appreciably taller. Her face, topped by a braid of gray hair wrapped around her head and held in place by a large celluloid hairpin, assumes an expression of girlish enthusiasm sharpened by occasional gleams of mockery, and she talks softly but very volubly, with a slightly flat drawl that may reflect her Midwestern origins.

Miss Moore's conversation is remarkable for its diversity, and for a certain recklessness that is likely to lead her, by a sequence of crowding and tumbling associations, into fields far removed from her starting point. For instance, while she has a high opinion of tea, she is aware that some of her guests may prefer something stronger, and therefore keeps on hand a bottle of Harvey's Shooting Sherry. There is a hunting scene on the label, and on occasion this has served as a springboard for one of her dizzying monologues. At an afternoon gathering in her apartment a couple of months ago, the label led her to a consideration of other labels (though she might just as easily have veered in the direction of rabbits or quail), and this, in turn, led her to comment on grocery-store stocks, specifically on the stocks of the S. S. Pierce store, in Boston. "Very discriminating grocers," she went on. "Even if they do carry cigars and wine and cosmetics along with their cheese, jam, cakes, soups, and all kinds of crackers. I can't abide dilutions or mixtures, but I like candy. If

I drank whiskey, I would drink it straight. I have a lethal grudge against people who try to make me drink coffee. My friend Mrs. Church grinds her own coffee from French and American beans. Her husband's grandfather was a chemical inventor who invented a brand of bicarbonate of soda. His wife is a Bavarian. Mrs. Church, I mean. She had a house at Ville-d'Avray with a big cedar of Lebanon and a dog named Tiquot. They had a gardener who also drove the car. They wouldn't have begonias on the place. They did have a few geraniums, though. Mr. Church was a close friend of Wallace Stevens, who wrote 'The Necessary Angel.' He reprinted an anecdote about Goethe wearing black woollen stockings on a packet boat. I like Goethe. My favorite language is German. I like the periodic structure of the sentences. 'And Shakespeare inspires me, too. He has so many good quotations. And Dante. He has a few, too.' That's from Ruth Draper. At Monroe Wheeler's once, we played a game called 'Who would you rather be except Shakespeare?' I wouldn't mind being La Fontaine, or Voltaire. Or Montaigne? No. I wouldn't be Montaigne—too sombre. I have always loved the vernacular. It spites me that I can't write fiction. And that book of essays I wrote. I let myself loose to do my utmost, and now they make me uneasy. The critics didn't care a great deal for them, but their reviews weren't really vipish. Those readings of my verse I made for the phonograph—well, they're here forever, like the wheat in the pyramids. I'm fond of Bach and Pachelbel and Stravinsky. I'm also fond of drums and trumpets—snare drums. If I find that a man plays the trumpet I am immediately interested. . . . "

The torrent of impressions and observations continues unstintingly. Miss Moore's listeners, in forming an opinion of it, tend to fall into two groups—those who delightedly occupy themselves in smelting out a memorable simile or adjective, and those who complain that it requires an enormous amount of strenuous concentration to make any sense at all of what she is saying. On the afternoon when S. S. Pierce received its pat on the back, one of the guests finally reached the point of exhaustion, and exclaimed, "Marianne, don't jump around so in your conversation!"

Miss Moore paused, turned pityingly toward the heretic, and replied with spirit, "It isn't jumping around. It's all connected." Then she was off again.

On another recent occasion, a bewildered guest interrupted Miss Moore to ask, "Do you realize where you started this digression?"

Miss Moore drew herself up and, smiling a bit austerely, said, "Wasn't it Aristotle who observed that 'the ability to see a connection between apparently incongruous things is the sign of a poet'?" Then she looked worried. "Or was it the 'mark' of a poet?" she said. "I hate people who can't quote things correctly, and then I go and make all kinds of mistakes myself. Was it the 'mark' of a poet or the 'sign' of a poet?" Another listener remarked that since the line was a translation anyhow, either word ought to be acceptable. But this was not enough for Miss Moore. By the following morning, she had tracked down the passage to its source and begun busily telephoning her guests to make elaborate apologies and give them the accurate version. "The sentence actually reads, 'It is the mark of a poet to see a connection between apparently incongruous things,' " she told one of them breathlessly. "I feel as degraded as a worm at the bottom of an umbrella stand. But I'm so relieved to have got it right at last."

Some of Miss Moore's friends interpret this reverence for scholarly exactitude, so at odds with her headlong habits of conversation, as one of a whole set of attitudes that are related to her conception of morals and propriety. She is as scrupulous in her regard for good form as the heroine of a Jane Austen novel, and there is about her a suggestion of both the Puritan woman and the Prussian knight. She dislikes seeing women apply makeup in public, and she herself, whether in public or alone, has an odd distaste for looking in a mirror, possibly—although she isn't really sure why—because she has a deep-seated feeling that the act is too frivolous. This is not to imply that she is in any way frumpy; on the contrary, while she disapproves of luxurious living in the broad sense, she has a fondness for certain luxuries, especially that of dressing well, and she is under no illusion that a woman can be well dressed on a cut-rate basis. "A friend of mine once told me that I could find the equivalent of Saks Fifth Avenue clothes on Fourteenth Street," she said not long ago. "I don't believe it. Besides, I don't like to get bargains, because I don't feel comfortable exploiting a store." The flow of Miss Moore's thought, whether written or spoken, is interspersed with allusions indicating a deep respect for romantic ideals of behavior—ideals involving monasticism, gallantry, and soldierliness. Despite an inveterate hatred of war, she thinks highly of the military life. "It means a great deal to me to know that there are in the world a few real enemies of enslavement and that some of them are generals—General Eisenhower, General MacArthur, and General de Tassigny," she told an interviewer in 1951. And, for all the indirectness of her own mental habits, she greatly reveres directness and workaday logic in others. "I like the writing of precise scientific thinkers," she says. "Lots of these scientists don't stand forth as littérateurs, but I find their devotion to fact very stimulating. They are much more competent than I am, particularly where precision is concerned." She prizes the works of chroniclers like Gibbon, and among her favorite authors are Julius Caesar and Xenophon. "Xenophon has wonderful qualities of restraint and latent satire," she says. "He loved horses, and he believed that a good cavalry officer should be religious."

Not one to confine her admiration for living organisms to those on the lower rungs of the evolutionary ladder, Miss Moore goes along with Xenophon in loving horses. Her most daring encounter with them—and possibly with any of the creatures of which she writes—occurred in 1952. She had become so interested in the race horse Tom Fool after reading about him in Arthur Daley's sports column in the *Times* that she wrote a poem in his honor ("Tom Fool is 'a handy horse,' with a chiselled foot . . ."), which appeared in *The New Yorker*. When her milliner, a lady with something of a weakness for the track, heard about the poem, she offered to take Miss Moore to the races at Jamaica, and Miss Moore accepted. She had never been to a race track before and (except for a staged visit with a magazine photographer) she has not been to one since. The experience was, therefore, unique, and, compared to most of her experiences, it was an extremely turbulent one. The two women visited the paddock, where Tom Fool was being saddled, and Miss Moore decided on the spot to risk fifty cents on him. "I've never seen a horse so limber," she says. On learning that two dollars is the minimum bet, she took the plunge at the two-dollar window, fearlessly going all out on a win-or-nothing basis. Tom Fool came in second. "That cured me of betting," Miss Moore says emphatically. As for her surroundings at the track, she had some reservations. "It certainly is a *tough* place, although I tried to look at the best side of it," she said later. "I've never seen so much liquor in my life. And the people in the stands don't seem happy even when they win." The afternoon was cold and the last race was late, and on the way back Miss Moore complained of chills, so her companion took her to her own house, where she broiled her a steak and gave her some brandy to warm her up. Miss Moore accepted the latter only as a prudent medicament, but it added one more fillip to an adventure that struck her as having its decidedly rakish aspects. "I learned my lesson never to become a race-track habitué," she has since told friends, and they have little fear that she will. When Jock Whitney, the horse's owner, read her poem about Tom Fool, he asked to buy the original manuscript. Miss Moore was willing to give it to him but not to sell it to him. "I thought it wouldn't be exactly fitting to be paid twice for the same poem," she says.

Although Miss Moore has a number of very good friends who share her interests, and several hundred acquaintances who are more or less celebrated for their accomplishments in the arts, her closest attachment is to a person of a wholly different outlook. This is her brother, Captain John Warner Moore, who is a retired chaplain of the United States Navy and currently the chaplain of the Gunnery School, a prep school for boys in Washington, Connecticut. While Miss Moore's affection for her brother is naturally attributable in large measure to their blood relationship, it appears to be intensified by the circumstance that he is a man both of staunch religious faith and of staunch military habits—two qualities that his sister, of course, greatly admires. The Captain is a tall, spare, white-haired gentleman, some seventeen months older than Miss Moore, who combines an erect bearing with a fatherly manner in such a way as to give an impression of dignity, dependability, and kindliness. Like his sister, he speaks with a slight Midwestern drawl, and he also resembles her in certain facial and other physical features, and in his patrician air of old-fashioned self-respect. In his time, Captain Moore, who is married and the father of four children, was a small-boat sailing champion in the Navy, winning several titles in the Pacific and officiating as one of the coaches of the Navy team that competed against Germany at Kiel in 1937. While his mental processes are, as might be expected, quite unlike his sister's—his thoughts tend to run on a logical track rather than by free and headlong association—and it is evident that he would be much more at home on the deck of a cruiser than in a Manhattan poetry salon, he is extremely proud of the eminence she has attained in the literary world. And Miss Moore, in turn, believes that in at least one way he is her literary superior. "My brother is much better at an essay than I am," she observed recently. "But he doesn't get time to write much. He's too busy with his work at the school."

Miss Moore and her brother are drawn still nearer to each other by a strong personal tie they share—a deep devotion to the memory of their mother, who died ten years ago. It would be difficult to imagine a closer family relationship than the one that existed between Mrs. Moore and her two children. A devout Presbyterian who also had a high opinion of the Quakers, she combined her religious feeling with definite literary leanings by saying a different grace—newly minted by her and often in poetic form—before every meal; as her son has recalled, "She had faith in the providence and goodness of God, and matters of honor were more important to her than food." She was a vigorous fighter for causes she believed in, and these, when she was in her prime, ranged from woman suffrage to crusading against cruelty to animals; in the first instance, she marched in parades, and in the second she stopped in the street to remonstrate with drivers who were mistreating their horses. People who were acquainted with Mrs. Moore differ widely in their recollections of the sort of woman she was; some remember her as a frighteningly intellectual person and a tremendous talker, while others remember her as demure, tenderly attentive, and gentle, though possessed of a strong will and easily outraged by any offense against her notion of correct behavior. In general, however, both sides agree that she was small, quite pretty, distinctly Irish in appearance, and rather witty. ("Knowing the mother, it was easy to see where Marianne's sense of humor came from," a friend of the family remarked recently.) And almost everyone qualified to judge believes that as a mentor and critic she could with justice claim part of the credit for her daughter's success. Probably the person best qualified to judge is Miss Moore herself, and she readily admits that she often made changes in her poetry to please her mother, and sometimes incorporated figures of speech her mother suggested. For years, mother and daughter were almost inseparable, enjoying a spiritual and mental intimacy so profound that some of their friends came to think of the two women as a single personality. A good many of the mementos in the Brooklyn apartment are closely connected with Mrs. Moore in the mind of her daughter, who further keeps her memory alive by observing little household procedures of which she approved, such as using a Pyrex pot, rather than a kettle, to boil water for tea, "because Mother said you couldn't air a kettle properly, and she wouldn't have one around."

Neither Miss Moore nor her brother ever knew their father, who was a construction engineer and a member of an old New England family that settled in Ohio immediately after the Revolution, but some of his forebears—among them Clement Moore, the author of "A Visit from St. Nicholas"—showed literary proclivities or exhibited other traits of character that a genealogical theorist might consider significant in explaining Miss Moore's development.

Her paternal grandfather, for example, was a well-to-do river pilot and ship-owner in Portsmouth, Ohio, who, in addition to taking a great interest in birds and cats, was bookishly inclined and owned an enormous collection of morocco-bound volumes; he finally gave it to the Carnegie Library of Portsmouth, retaining only a set of the Encyclopaedia Britannica, which he methodically read through in his declining years, starting with the letter "A." His brother, also a pilot (Captain Bixby, celebrated in Mark Twain's "Life on the Mississippi," learned the ways of the river from him), had such a tender regard for insects that he wouldn't allow flypaper in his house and had a long record of fishing drowning flies out of the river.

It is not recorded that Miss Moore's father, John Milton Moore, had any similar side interests. Shortly after the Civil War, his father and uncle pooled their resources and opened a foundry in Portsmouth to manufacture boilers and other fittings for steamboats, and it was there that he learned his trade. In 1885, he married Mary Warner, the daughter of the Reverend John Riddle Warner, who was a Scotch-Irish Presbyterian minister then preaching in Kirkwood, Missouri. John Moore, being something of a visionary, was obsessed with the idea of building a smokeless furnace, and not long after his marriage he took his wife to Newton, Massachusetts, where, against the advice of his father and uncle, he put up a factory of his own for that purpose. The venture failed, and the resultant financial worries so preyed on his mind that he suffered a breakdown, from which he never recovered. The Reverend Mr. Warner, a widower, fetched his daughter back to Kirkwood, together with an infant son she had borne while in Massachusetts, and she moved in with him as his housekeeper—an arrangement that was soon briefly suspended by the arrival of her second child, Marianne, on November 15, 1887. The marriage was, in effect, terminated; her shattered husband returned to Portsmouth, where his parents took him under their care, while she continued to keep house for her father until he died, in 1894.

After staying briefly with relatives in Pittsburgh to get her bearings and plan her future, Mrs. Moore was persuaded by a friend to move to Carlisle, Pennsylvania, where she rented a house and settled down to raise her children, living on a small inheritance from her father. She became known to the community as a cultured and intelligent woman, and when, in 1900, an English teacher was needed at Carlisle's Metzger Institute, a school for girls that has since become a part of Dickinson College, she was offered—and accepted—the job. Even so, the little family was often in financial difficulties, but Mrs. Moore was a woman of indomitable vigor and optimism, and she managed so well that she was once able to take her children on a vacation trip to Florida and contrived to send them to college after they had graduated from the local high school. The son chose Yale and his sister Bryn Mawr, where—curiously, since for years she had been carefully instructed in literature by her mother—she was unable to meet the requirements for taking the advanced courses in English she had been looking forward to. "I was interested in the English and foreign-language courses, but I was too young, too immature for them, so most of my time was spent in the biology laboratory," Miss Moore recalled the other day. She did quite a bit of extracurricular writing, however, including some verse for *Tipyn O'Bob*, the college monthly literary magazine. Of these poems Miss Moore observes today, "A few of them were of some interest metrically, but in general they were tentative and ephemeral."

After graduating from Bryn Mawr, in 1909, Miss Moore took a secretarial course at the Carlisle Commercial College, and this enabled her to get a job as an instructor in typing, shorthand, and bookkeeping at the Carlisle Indian School, where one of her pupils was the famous Indian athlete Jim Thorpe. Not surprisingly, she found the subjects she taught uninspiring. "I was half good," she has since said. "I could fix typewriters, but rapid calculating and bookkeeping were just too much for me. It was a necessary financial adventure, and I would have much preferred to sit by the fire and read." In 1914, her brother was ordained, and two years later he was called to the Ogden Memorial Presbyterian Church, in Chatham, New Jersey. His post included a manse, so his mother and sister quit their jobs and went to Chatham to keep house for him. Theirs was indeed a tightly knit little family.

When the United States entered the First World War, the Reverend Mr. Moore gave up his parish in Chatham and joined the Navy, leaving his mother and sister more or less on their own. Three years before, Miss Moore had paid her first visit to New York, spending six days here and living at a Y.W.C.A. on Lexington Avenue, and those six days were enough to convince her that New York was where she ultimately wanted to live. Now, with her brother in the Navy, she was able to persuade her mother to move here, and in 1918 they rented a basement apartment on St. Luke's Place, in Greenwich Village, where they remained eleven years. The Reverend Mr. Moore stayed on in the Navy after the war, and in 1929 was stationed at the Brooklyn Navy Yard. That year, his mother caught pneumonia as a result (so he thought) of the draughtiness of the basement apartment, and he resolved to find quarters for her and his sister that would be both more salubrious and closer to his post. The quarters he found were in the apartment house in Brooklyn that Miss Moore still occupies—about three blocks from the Navy Yard.

For a while after settling in New York, Miss Moore worked as a private tutor and as a secretary in a girl's school. She spent a great deal of her spare time in her neighborhood branch of the Public Library, at Seventh Avenue South and St. Luke's Place—so much of it, in fact, that the authorities there, impressed by her interest, presently gave her a job. "I was not very good at library work," she recalls. "But, after all, it was not my field." Her field, of course, as she was becoming increasingly aware, was poetry. In April, 1915, when she was living in Carlisle, the *Egoist*, a London periodical specializing in imagist verse, published "To the Soul of Progress," her first poem to reach more than a campus audience; the person who supplied the improbable link between Carlisle and London was the poet Hilda Doolittle, a classmate of Miss Moore's at Bryn Mawr, who had married Richard Aldington, one of the editors of the *Egoist*. Almost coincidentally—a month later, in fact—Harriet Monroe's Chicago magazine *Poetry* published five of Miss Moore's poems. In 1921, under the imprint of the Egoist Press, Miss Doolittle and the then Mrs. Robert McAlmon ("H. D." and "Bryher") at their own expense brought out a small volume of poems of hers that had appeared in the *Egoist*. Three years later, Miss Moore assembled a number of the poems that had been printed here or in England, and they made up what proved to be her first important book. Entitled "Observations," it immediately won the 1924 Dial Award, as a distinguished contribution to American literature, and this brought her not only a welcome two thousand dollars but considerable prestige. (The previous winner was T. S. Eliot, and subsequent winners included E. E. Cummings, William Carlos Williams, and Ezra Pound.) Moreover, it led Miss Moore into a long association with the *Dial*, a magazine that in the twenties held a unique position in the van of the nation's progressive literary and artistic life. Miss Moore began by writing verse and book reviews for the publication; then she became its acting editor, and, in 1926, its editor-in-chief.

Looking back, Miss Moore remembers the *Dial* as "an elysium for people who were really interested in quality," and, like many others who have memories of its beautifully printed pages, she cannot restrain a feeling of nostalgia for the era of intellectual exuberance that the magazine represented. The drab conformity of Marxist thought that later paralyzed the minds of so many writers in Europe and the United States had yet to make itself felt, and the great tide of mechanized mass communication and mass entertainment that has since threatened to swamp the minds of thinking individuals was still far off. "Those were the days when, as Robert Herring has said, things were opening out, not closing in," Miss Moore wrote in 1940, in a memoir describing her connection with the magazine. "There was for us of the staff a constant atmosphere of excited triumph—interiorly, whatever the impression outside; and from editor and publisher a natural firework of little parenthetic wit too good to print—implying that afflatus is not chary of surplus." The *Dial* was concerned neither with politics nor with theories of social progress but purely with the arts of writing, painting, and music, and its index of contributors was crowded with names that guaranteed the quality of which Miss Moore wrote in her memoir—Thomas Mann, Ortega y Gasset, Paul Morand, Maxim Gorky, Ezra Pound, T. S. Eliot, D. H. Lawrence, W. B. Yeats, Roger Fry, Robert Morss Lovett, Paul Valéry, Ford Madox Ford, Gilbert Seldes, William Carlos Williams, Wallace Stevens, and Kenneth Burke among them. The magazine also contained colored reproductions of paintings by an extraordinary number of artists who were then fairly new to this country, including Picasso, Seurat, di Chirico, Brancusi, Lachaise, Kuniyoshi, Sheeler, Marin, Stuart Davis, Max Weber, and Wyndham Lewis.

In the middle of all this intellectual ferment sat Miss Moore, fastidiously reading and editing manuscripts. The offices of the *Dial* were in a three-story brick building on West Thirteenth Street that had brownstone steps leading up to the front door, carpeted staircases, and rooms with fireplaces and white mantelpieces. "There was the recurrent flower-crier in summer, with his slowly moving wagon of pansies, fuchsias, geraniums, petunias, ageratum," Miss Moore recalled in her memoir. "Or a man with straw*berries* for sale; or a certain fishman with his pushcart-scales, and staccato refrain so unvaryingly imperative, summer or winter, that Kenneth Burke's bit of parenthetic humour comes back to me almost as an epic, 'I think if he stopped to sell a fish my heart would skip a beat.' " As an editor in these pleasant surroundings, Miss Moore is reputed to have worked with tact, taste, and vast enthusiasm. Once, when a visitor to her office asked her if she didn't ever grow weary of reading manuscripts, she replied, "To me, its a revel."

Miss Moore's revelry, however, left her almost no time to write verse. She had even less time after 1926, when Scofield Thayer, a founding editor of the magazine and one of its two leading backers, fell ill and had to retire. Three years later, the *Dial's* other important backer—Dr. James Sibley Watson, a wealthy physician originally from Rochester—decided to return home, where, with the assistance of the Eastman Kodak Company, he could indulge his powerful interest in photography. (He made several medical motion-picture documentaries, and is now head of the Radiology Department of the University of Rochester's School of Medicine and Dentistry.) With two-thirds of the magazine's principals departed, Miss Moore had no compunction about becoming the final third and returning to poetry, and in 1929 the *Dial* folded.

Since then, Miss Moore has done no professional editing, although she devotes a lot of time to such related activities as book reviewing and giving young poets advice about their manuscripts; as a critic, she shows a tendency to be appreciative rather than caustic. She has also done a number of translations, most notably a monumental English version, undertaken at the suggestion of W. H. Auden and published in 1954, of "The Fables of La Fontaine," which in sheer bulk far outweighs all her books of poetry. She toiled over the "Fables" for something like nine years, and the project caused her much anxiety. "I worked practically all the time," she says. "I'd wake up at six and get right to work, and I'd keep at it all day and all evening, except for an occasional brief stop to eat, or maybe I'd have to go to the market and buy a few odds and ends. Then back to the job again. I did the whole thing over completely four times." Miss Moore's revisions of her own revisions would alone have been sufficient to keep her publishers in a state of anxiety equal to her own, but those unhappy gentlemen soon found that their headaches did not end there, for she worried not only about the literary quality of the forthcoming book but about details of its typography, paper, and binding—about almost everything, in fact, except the remuneration she was to receive for her labors. Of that, she was characteristically oblivious; when it comes to money, her attitude always seems to be that her publishers are doing her a great favor in printing her work, and all she asks is that they make a handsome job of it. The opinions of the critics who reviewed Miss Moore's version of the "Fables" were mixed—it can hardly be denied that in spots the text reads a great deal more like Moore than like La Fontaine—but the literary workmanship involved received general acclaim, and one reviewer declared that the work was among the most ambitious projects ever attempted by a modern poet.

Miss Moore doubts whether anything could induce her to tackle another task like the "Fables." She now contents herself with writing poems and book reviews and carrying on her voluminous correspondence with friends. Her neighbors are aware that creative work—mysterious but important—is going on in their midst, and parents on her block have cautioned their children to play quietly in the street at times when she is believed to be writing. As she emerges from her apartment house, bound for market or for the subway station to catch a train to Manhattan, sidewalk passersby are likely to inquire respectfully, "How's the writing going, Miss Moore?," to which she usually replies, "Very slow, very slow." Inspired by her example, several of her neighbors have taken to writing poetry themselves, and they frequently ask her for her opinion of their efforts. While she does not always find it easy in such cases to maintain her appreciative approach to criticism, she has thus far avoided the caustic alternative so adroitly that Cumberland Street is fast becoming one of the nation's most thriving hotbeds of amateur prosody.

Placid though others might find most of Miss Moore's sorties into the world beyond her apartment, she embarks upon each of them in a spirit of adventure, and in her highly volatile mind each of them is charged with terrific drama. Her capacity for stepping up the voltage of ordinary experience is so great that the most commonplace happening or encounter becomes for her a major emotional event. Passing this smiling, delicate-looking elderly lady on her way down the street with her market basket or handbag, only an extraordinarily perceptive person would suspect that a heroic odyssey was in progress and that her impending purchase of a bunch of radishes or a box of crackers would provide her with enough vivid impressions to occupy her thinking for half a day. The primary source of all this internal excitement is Miss Moore's wildly gymnastic self-starting imagination, but once it swings into action it is liberally fed by the combined resources of her singular gift for observing even the smallest components of an object and her uncanny ability to remember everything she has observed. A friend of hers still speaks wonderingly of the time, a couple of years ago, when he left her outside while he went into a drugstore to make a short telephone call; after he had rejoined her and they were continuing on their way, he recalls, she casually described in minute detail more than fifty miscellaneous items she had noticed in the shop window. Some of Miss Moore's most rewarding adventures are trips to museums. "I get so excited in them that before long I can't see anything," she says. To overcome this difficulty, she has developed the habit of concentrating on a single exhibit and firmly ignoring the rest; a few minutes spent in this way gives her all the stimulation she needs to make the expedition profitable, as the associations of what she has seen begin to multiply in her mind by geometric progression. Another place that Miss Moore heads for when she feels in need of excitement is the Brooklyn Institute of Arts and Sciences, where she sits beguiled during illustrated lectures on fungi, lichens, snakes, and other flora and fauna, large and small.

A few of the adventures that Miss Moore fervently refers to from time to time have been more nearly in line with what most people would consider adventuresome—learning to drive an automobile (in Brookline, Massachusetts, four years ago) and playing tennis (on the public courts in Fort Greene Park). Of her tennis she says "I'm not so very good at it, but I'm very reliable. I have a bad backhand and I try to make up for it by roaring around the ball." By ordinary standards, her most strenuous adventure in a long time was a trip she made to Bermuda last winter to visit some people she knew there. Not only did her ship, to her apprehensive delight, run into a storm on the return voyage ("So reckless!") but when she reached New York the customs people kept her waiting interminably while they went through her luggage, which contained some liquor she had brought back to give to friends here, and then there was another long wait—"in not exactly a porte-cochere but a kind of barn"—until she could get a taxi. Whether or not the lack of a porte-cochere was responsible, Miss Moore came down with what she calls a case of pneumonia and what her friends call "Marianne's psychosomatic flu"—a malady that frequently lays her low and that appears to affect her disposition far more seriously than her physical condition. "It depresses me as well as incommodes me," she says. "It's dire! And all that penicillin and other things in bottles! It's like the forcible feeding of an important reptile."

When alone at home, Miss Moore does not spend all her time writing. She is an earnest water-colorist and draftsman as well as a poet, specializing in meticulously realistic reproductions of landscapes, flowers, and insects, which reveal the same love of delicate organisms, if not the same expertness of craftsmanship, that is evident in her verse; guests at her apartment occasionally get the feeling that she takes greater pride in her pictures than in her poems. In view of Miss Moore's obvious devotion to small living things, visitors from time to time express surprise that there is not a single animal or plant in her apartment, but she has a ready answer for them. "If you keep pets or flowers, you are a slave to them," she says.

Unlike many people who have exchanged material gain for the pleasures of contemplative peace and quiet, Miss Moore bears no ill will toward the world of business, finance, and technological progress. On the contrary, she regards it as an interesting and worth-while world, and gladly concedes that some of its activities are quite possibly even more interesting and worth while than the writing of verse. For example, she seldom mentions a magazine without commenting on its advertising, which in a number of instances she rates a good bit higher than the editorial matter it accompanies. She has a way of deprecating romantic notions about her profession, and she has no patience whatever with the tradition of starving for the sake of art. A few months ago, a young and unknown poet called on her with a letter of introduction from a friend, and soon made it apparent that he was deeply depressed because no one seemed to care much one way or the other about his verse. Miss Moore asked if he had a family to support, and he replied that he had a wife and two children. "Well, then," said Miss Moore with finality, "you had better give up writing and get into something where you can earn a proper living."

The respect Miss Moore shows for the practical and prosaic approach to life stands out in such striking contrast to the workings of her own high-flying, fanciful mind that it raises the question of just where in the scheme of things she places both her esoteric art and her bright and elusive contributions to it. It is a question that even Miss Moore herself is unable to answer precisely, but on the basis of her writings, her offhand remarks, and her reactions to various situations it seems safe to say that she looks upon poetry with a mixture of love and petulance. She has often commented on it disparagingly, as in the opening line of her poem unequivocally entitled "Poetry," which reads, "I, too, dislike it: there are things that are important beyond all this fiddle," and elsewhere she has conveyed the same definite impression that, notwithstanding her lifelong dedication to the art, she thinks of it as a luxury—or, at any rate, a nonessential—when weighed against the really serious aspects of life. Among her friends is one who likens her to a daring performer on a flying trapeze, hugely enjoying her own acrobatics but reassuring herself every now and then by glancing down at a safety net that is sturdily supported by Gibbon, Julius Caesar, Xenophon, the Presbyterian Church, and a handful of male contemporaries, military and scientific, who are accustomed to think—as she conspicuously is not—in what she approvingly calls "a straight line." In this view, Miss Moore, soaring and pirouetting above the world of reality, assumes the role of a charmingly quixotic intellectual flirt, seeming, both as a poet and as a personality, to tease those who put their faith in humdrum logic but at the same time to regard them with admiration and a certain coquettish timidity. Any attempt to discern in this spectacle so much as a trace of a consistent philosophy can lead only to bafflement, but few philosophers, after all, have been good poets.

PART THREE

Imaginative Literature: Types

The Short Story

Although all imaginative literature interprets human qualities, emotions, motives, and values, different forms interpret them in different ways. Fictional works, dramas, and poems all have their peculiar limitations and possibilities. Therefore, in order to see clearly and judge wisely what each particular work offers, the reader should know something about the nature of each of these forms.

The short story is the form of prose fiction ordinarily the easiest of all forms to understand and to enjoy. Primitive men by campfires, children in nurseries, and traveling men in smoking cars obviously appreciate some kinds of imaginative narratives in prose without paying much attention to their structure. But most readers and listeners will find that even such narratives—and others as well—can be most thoroughly appreciated by understanding not only the materials but also the methods involved. And they will find that some works—often the best ones—demand careful attention to technique as well as content to be understood or appreciated at all.

Two points about the short story are important: (1) It is short, usually a good deal less than ten thousand words and seldom more than thirty-five thousand or so. (2) It is, nevertheless, a story rather than a part of a story—a complete work with a discoverable unity comparable to that found in other forms. The problem of the short story writer, then, is to combine rigid economy with unity, and a problem for the reader is to see this combination.

ECONOMY

Contrasted with the novel, the short story is less complex in its picturing of life, more swift in the accomplishment of its task. Economy constrains the author to confine his pattern of actions by giving a detailed account of one episode or even of part of what would be a complete action in a novel—the beginning, the middle, *or* the end—rather than all three. (Other parts of the action, of course, may be implied or briefly summarized.) The author ordinarily limits the number of characters introduced: often he portrays only one character or a small group of characters. And even leading characters are not likely to be endowed with a large number of traits. Settings, too, in contrast to those in the novel, are limited in number: a short story with a panoramic view comparable to that in Tolstoy's wide-ranging *War and Peace* is inconceivable.

As a rule, the brevity of the short story brings a similar limitation upon its tone and its meanings. Whereas the novelist may range from pathos to scorn and from scorn to ridicule in various parts of his book, in a given story, the short story writer is likely to voice only one emotional attitude. And whereas the novelist may give his work complex multiple meanings, the short story writer is likely to develop rather simpler and fewer meanings. In such ways as these, the short story shows the result of economy, and the reader should notice how simplifications and cuts keep it within bounds.

UNITY

A short story, nevertheless, should be a complete whole, fused according to some principle or principles. In reading a work of this sort, the reader should try to see what the nature of the whole work is and how each element contributes to its final achievement. He will find it useful to consider these questions: Is it unified? If not, why not? If so, what is the precise nature of its unity? And how is the unity achieved? He need not, of course, consider these questions in this order, but it is well to attend to all of them.

Critics have suggested a variety of ways of getting at the heart of a short story. Some urge the reader to consider the single effect it has upon him, some to discover the single intention of the author, some to study the story itself as a concrete object which is a fusion of several parts. These ways are not contradictory, but they represent varied approaches. Since any of them or all of them may help a reader discern the nature of the unity of a story, he may find it useful to consider each in turn.

(1) What is the effect of the story? As far back as 1842, Edgar Allan Poe saw the short story as a stimulus designed to evoke a particular response on the part of the reader. With "a certain unique or single effect" in mind, the author, said Poe, "then invents such incidents—he then combines such events, and discusses them in such tone as may best serve . . . in establishing the preconceived effect." In using this approach, one reads the story and notes what is memorable about it—an idea, perhaps, an attitude, an insight into life or character, or an emotion. He then considers how, exactly, that particular story and the manner of its telling established such an effect.

(2) What is the apparent intention of the author, and how does that intention influence his handling of elements and details? (The word "apparent" is appropriate here, since readers can never be completely certain about the intention of the author.) Carl Grabo, among other critics, finds it useful to start with "the inception of the story"—so far as it can be discovered through hints in the narrative—and then to go on to "the method of story development by which the author realizes his intent." In using this approach, the reader looks for whatever signs there are of the germinal interest which apparently led the author to write the story, and then sees how everything in the narrative contributed.

(3) What is the unique content of the story itself, and how does its form contribute to the setting forth of this unique content? In using this approach, the reader aims at the definition of the whole story, and then at the discovery of the interrelations through which the parts function to create that story. Here the reading makes possible answers to questions such as: What happens?

To whom? Where? Why? How? Perhaps the reader's conclusions make possible the formulation of the unique features of the work in a sentence beginning, "This is the story of how . . ." and going on to answer the questions listed above. Having formulated such a sentence, one may notice in detail how the handling of characters, actions, settings, language, tone, and symbols of meaning are related to the unfolding of such a narrative.

EMPHASIS AND SUBORDINATION

Any serious study of a story will take into account, then, not only the nature of its unity but also the methods whereby such unity is achieved. In other words, the reader attempts to discover what is emphasized and what is subordinated for the achievement of the effect, the realization of the author's intention, and the creation of an artistic entity. Some elements and details will be stressed, some will be played down. Also important is the point of view from which the story is unfolded (pp. 428-429).

Emphasis in a story may be achieved by length of treatment, by repetition, by memorable phrasing, and by particularization. The very fact that more space is devoted to one matter than to another in a short story (as in fact in any literary work) emphasizes that matter. Other things being equal, a character or scene introduced with a curt sentence or phrase will receive less stress than one introduced by several long paragraphs. Again, repetition of any item makes for prominence. If an author says, on page one of his story, "John was dishonest"; on page three, "that lying John"; on page seven, "Since John instinctively avoided the truth," the idea that John was something other than veracious is pretty well underlined. And, of course, a phrase which is particularly vivid or poetic or unusual can make a detail or series of details stand out.

Very valuable for emphasis, of course, is particularization—the use of detail, of concrete words. An action which is portrayed in all its particulars, or a series of actions in which each event is explicitly presented, will thereby be emphasized. That which is generalized, by contrast, is subordinated. A character stands out when he is given a number of vivid physical qualities or a number of unusual traits. Setting, too, will loom large or small in a story in accordance with the number of concrete details about it given to the reader. Even the theme of a story, abstract idea though it is, will be emphasized largely by particularization of certain sorts. The reader quickly discovers that a story is an allegory when he notes that the personified virtues and vices have concrete qualities which stand for ideas. Similarly, the vivid details in a symbolical story stress the relationship between the story and the meaning it is developing.

Thus some elements may be emphasized, some "de-emphasized" or subordinated, in well-wrought short stories—all in the interest of unity. By noticing the lengthy developments, the repetition, the striking language, the use of concrete details, readers may learn a great deal about the way the narrative has been unified—fused into a single composition.

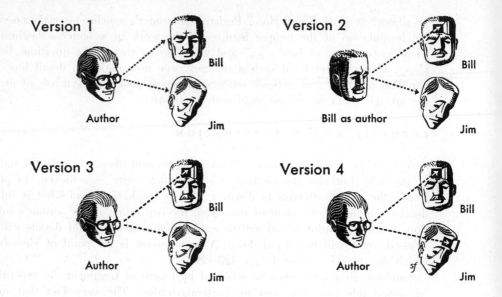

Version 1 Author Bill Jim

Version 2 Bill as author Bill Jim

Version 3 Author Bill Jim

Version 4 Author Bill Jim

POINT OF VIEW

Of great importance in achieving unity and in determining emphasis and subordination is the point of view from which the story is told. Point of view, in the critical sense in which the term is used here, does not mean the mental slant of the author nor the physical point from which some scene is observed. It means, instead, the "angle of narration" from which the story is told. To define the point of view of any narrative work, one simply asks: Who tells this story, and to what extent is he empowered to peer into the minds and the hearts of the characters? Here are four ways of recounting an action, each from a different point of view:

(1) Bill saw Jim die.

This illustrates *the objective point of view,* so called because the author's relationship to his characters is objective rather than subjective: he cannot see into their minds. If the narrator maintains this point of view throughout, he tells what his characters did, what they said, but not what they thought. This angle of narration is also called the *dramatic* point of view, because dramatists use it. Like the playwright, the storyteller using this point of view can show what his characters are only by setting down their deeds and their dialog. Compare the following version with the first version:

(2) I saw Jim die—stood or sat by his bed all night, and watched the poor devil suffering there. It wasn't a pleasant experience.

Here the action is unfolded in the first person by one of the characters involved. It is *the personal point of view of a participant*. Bill has become the narrator, "I," who can tell his own thoughts and feelings ("poor devil . . . wasn't a pleasant experience"). He cannot, of course, peer into Jim's mind, cannot possibly tell what Jim thinks and feels. Presumably Bill is an important participant. Of course, a variation might be to have a bystander, or a minor participant, tell the story. In such a case, the "I" telling the story would have only exterior knowledge about the two main characters, Bill and Jim. Now look at two more accounts of the same event:

(3) Bill sat in the darkened room and pity clutched at his heart as he looked down on the wasted figure on the bed. He thought, "How horrible it is to watch the poor devil suffer this way! Will it never end—this suffering?" As the dawn came, Jim died.

(4) Jim, peering up at Bill's blurred face, wondered if he was dying. He hoped he was. "It would be good," he thought, "to end all this suffering, this endless pain." Bill sat in the darkened room and pity clutched at his heart as he looked down on the wasted figure on the bed. He thought, "How horrible it is to watch the poor devil suffer this way! Will it never end—this suffering?" With the coming of dawn, Jim died.

Version 3 is comparable to version 2, in that this way of telling about the action makes it possible for the author to peer into Bill's mind and tell what goes on there. It is different from version 2, however, in that it is told in the third person. By means of a convention—an understanding between writer and reader—one takes for granted that the author is privy to the workings of Bill's mind and can record not only what happens but what Bill thinks and feels at any time. The point of view then is that of *a third person who is omniscient* so far as the mind of one of the characters is concerned. The author of version 4 is also omniscient, but he is able to look not only into Bill's mind but also into Jim's mind: he knows and can set down what both characters think and feel as the action unfolds.

Such differences between narrative methods might seem, at first glance, unimportant. Actually, however, one of the contributions of critics in comparatively recent times is to note that methods are tremendously important and that therefore the reader can learn much about a story by noticing the point of view from which it is told and what happens as a result of the author's choice of this particular "post of observation."

Since an author's point of view may be thought of as a "camera-eye" which determines the "focus" of his narrative, there is good reason for so much critical concern with this matter. The point is that a photograph may center observation upon some elements in a scene, may show some dimly, and may cut still others out entirely. And just as the intelligent and artistic photographer may so adjust his lens and point his camera to bring about such emphases, such subordinations, and such omissions, as he desires, the storyteller may so select his point of view as to justify stress upon some elements, the playing down of others, and the omission of still others.

Suppose, for instance, that the author writing of Jim's death wanted to write an action story—wanted to center attention upon the actions rather than upon the mental processes of the characters. He would justify his leaving out all the thoughts of the characters, would he not, by using the objective point of view? Suppose, however, that he wanted to concentrate attention upon the working of Bill's mind—upon Bill's reaction to death? He might do this by using personal narrative or by writing in the third person and peering into Bill's mind but not Jim's. Writing in the third person—according to his interests—he might record Bill's thoughts in one of two ways: (1) he might organize and clarify those thoughts, or (2) he might present them in the rather chaotic order and form that thoughts take in life, using, in other words, what is called a "stream-of-consciousness" method. If the thoughts of both characters were important, insight into both minds would be necessary. In every instance, the point of view would determine the nature of the unity of the story, and in every instance, the reader trying to discern what is important, what not important, in the story would find that a study of the point of view gave decisive clues.

The choice of point of view determines not only what is revealed, what is emphasized, but also what the order of the unfolding of events is to be. For instance, "The Red-Headed League," a fairly typical detective story by Sir Arthur Conan Doyle, is recounted by Dr. Watson, the not overbright friend of the detective. Watson is better as a teller of this story than Sherlock Holmes, the detective, would be, since Watson cannot tell about Holmes' deductive processes as they occur. As Doyle wishes, the reader must wait until the end of the story for the revelation of the solution and the account of the detective's deductions leading to that solution.

By studying the author's choice of a point of view for a short story, therefore, readers can see what it enables the author to tell and to omit, to emphasize and to play down, and can also see what effect the choice has upon the author's ordering of actions. Thus, like other devices which determine emphasis and subordination, it offers useful clues concerning the achievement of the effect of the story, the author's intention, and the unique content and form of the story itself.

THE BOOK OF RUTH

Now it came to pass in the days when the judges ruled, that there was a famine in the land. And a certain man of Beth-lehem-judah went to sojourn in the country of Moab, he, and his wife, and his two sons. And the name of the man was Elimelech, and the name of his wife Naomi, and the name of his two sons Mahlon and Chilion, Ephrathites of Beth-lehem-judah. And they came into the country of Moab, and continued there.

And Elimelech Naomi's husband died; and she was left, and her two sons. And they took them wives of the women of Moab; the name of the one was Orpah, and the name of the other Ruth: and they dwelled there about ten years. And Mahlon and Chilion died also both of them; and the woman was left of her two sons and her husband.

Then she arose with her daughters-in-law, that she might return from the country of Moab; for she had heard in the country of Moab how that the Lord had visited His people in giving them bread. Wherefore she went forth out of the place where she was, and her two daughters-in-law with her; and they went on the way to return unto the land of Judah. And Naomi said unto her two daughters-in-law, "Go, return each to her mother's house: the Lord deal kindly with you, as ye have dealt with the dead, and with me. The Lord grant you that ye may find rest, each of you in the house of her husband." Then she kissed them; and they lifted up their voice, and wept. And they said unto her, "Surely we will return with thee unto thy people."

And Naomi said, "Turn again, my daughters: why will ye go with me? are there yet any more sons in my womb, that they may be your husbands? Turn again, my daughters, go your way; for I am too old to have an husband. If I should say, I have hope, if I should have an husband also to-night, and should also bear sons; would ye tarry for them till they were grown? would ye stay for them from having husbands? nay, my daughters, for it grieveth me much for your sakes that the hand of the Lord is gone out against me."

And they lifted up their voice, and wept again: and Orpah kissed her mother-in-law; but Ruth clave unto her. And she said, "Behold, thy sister-in-law is gone back unto her people, and unto her gods: return thou after thy sister-in-law." And Ruth said, "Intreat me not to leave thee, or to return from following after thee: for whither thou goest, I will go; and where thou lodgest, I will lodge: thy people shall be my people, and thy God my God: where thou diest, will I die, and there will I be buried: the Lord do so to me, and more also, if ought but death part thee and me."

When she saw that she was steadfastly minded to go with her, then she left speaking unto her. So they two went until they came to Beth-lehem. And it came to pass, when they were come to Beth-lehem, that all the city was moved about them, and they said, "Is this Naomi?" And she said unto them, "Call me not Naomi, call me Mara: for the Almighty hath dealt very bitterly with me. I went out full, and the Lord hath brought me home again empty: why then call ye me Naomi, seeing the Lord hath testified against me, and the Almighty hath afflicted me?"

So Naomi returned, and Ruth the Moabitess, her daughter-in-law, with her, which returned out of the country of Moab: and they came to Beth-lehem in the beginning of barley harvest. And Naomi had a kinsman of her husband's, a mighty man of wealth, of the family of Elimelech; and his name was Boaz. And Ruth the Moabitess said unto Naomi, "Let me now go to the field, and glean ears of corn after him in whose sight I shall find grace." And she said unto her, "Go, my daughter." And she went, and came, and gleaned in the field after the reapers: and her hap was to light on a part of the field belonging unto Boaz, who was of the kindred of Elimelech.

And, behold, Boaz came from Beth-lehem, and said unto the reapers, "The Lord be with you." And they answered him, "The Lord bless thee." Then said Boaz unto his servant that was set over the reapers, "Whose damsel is this?" And the servant that was set over the reapers answered and said, "It is the Moabitish damsel that came back with Naomi out of the country of Moab: and she said, I pray you, let me glean and gather after the reapers among the sheaves: so she came, and hath continued even from the morning until now, that she tarried a little in the house."

Then said Boaz unto Ruth, "Hearest thou not, my daughter? Go not to glean in another field, neither go from hence, but abide here fast by my maidens: let thine eyes be on the field that they do reap, and go thou after them: have I not charged the young men that they shall not touch thee? and when thou art athirst, go unto the vessels, and drink of that which the young men have drawn."

Then she fell on her face, and bowed herself to the ground, and said unto him, "Why have I found grace in thine eyes, that thou shouldest take knowledge of me, seeing I am a stranger?"

And Boaz answered and said unto her, "It hath fully been shewed me, all that thou hast done unto thy mother-in-law since the death of thine husband: and how thou hast left thy father and thy mother, and the land of thy nativity, and art come unto a people which thou knewest not heretofore. The Lord recompense thy work, and a full reward be given thee of the Lord God of Israel, under whose wings thou art come to trust."

Then she said, "Let me find favor in thy sight, my lord; for that thou hast comforted me, and for that thou hast spoken friendly unto thine hand-maid, though I be not like unto one of thine handmaidens."

And Boaz said unto her, "At mealtime come thou hither, and eat of the bread, and dip thy morsel in the vinegar." And she sat beside the reapers: and he reached her parched corn, and she did eat, and was sufficed, and left. And when she was risen up to glean, Boaz commanded his young men, saying, "Let her glean even among the sheaves, and reproach her not: and let fall also some of the handfuls of purpose for her, and leave them, that she may glean them, and rebuke her not."

So she gleaned in the field until even, and beat out that she had gleaned: and it was about an ephah of barley. And she took it up, and went into the city: and her mother-in-law saw what she had gleaned: and she brought forth, and gave to her that she had reserved after she was sufficed. And her mother-in-law said unto her, "Where hast thou gleaned to-day? and where wroughtest thou? blessed be he that did take knowledge of thee."

And she shewed her mother-in-law with whom she had wrought, and said, "The man's name with whom I wrought to-day is Boaz." And Naomi said unto her daughter-in-law, "Blessed be he of the Lord, who hath not left off His kindness to the living and to the dead." And Naomi said unto her, "The man is near of kin unto us, one of our next kinsmen."

And Ruth the Moabitess said, "He said unto me also, Thou shalt keep fast by my young men, until they have ended all my harvest."

And Naomi said unto Ruth her daughter-in-law, "It is good, my daughter, that thou go out with his maidens, that they meet thee not in any other field." So she kept fast by the maidens of Boaz to glean unto the end of barley harvest and of wheat harvest; and dwelt with her mother-in-law.

Then Naomi her mother-in-law said unto her, "My daughter, shall I not seek rest for thee, that it may be well with thee? And now is not Boaz of our kindred, with whose maidens thou wast? Behold, he winnoweth barley to-night in the threshing-floor. Wash thyself therefore, and anoint thee, and put thy raiment upon thee, and get thee down to the floor: but make not thyself known unto the man, until he shall have done eating and drinking. And it shall be, when he lieth down, that thou shalt mark the place where he shall lie, and thou shalt go in, and uncover his feet, and lay thee down; and he will tell thee what thou shalt do."

And she said unto her, "All that thou sayest unto me I will do."

And she went down unto the floor, and did according to all that her mother-in-law bade her. And when Boaz had eaten and drunk, and his heart was merry, he went to lie down at the end of the heap of corn: and she came softly, and uncovered his feet, and laid her down. And it came to pass at midnight, that the man was afraid, and turned himself: and, behold, a woman lay at his feet. And he said, "Who art thou?" And she answered, "I am Ruth thine handmaid: spread therefore thy skirt over thine handmaid; for thou art a near kinsman."

And he said, "Blessed be thou of the Lord, my daughter: for thou hast shewed more kindness in the latter end than at the beginning, inasmuch as thou followedst not young men, whether poor or rich. And now, my daughter, fear not; I will do to thee all that thou requirest: for all the city of my people doth know that thou art a virtuous woman. And now it is true that I am thy near kinsman: howbeit there is a kinsman nearer than I. Tarry this night, and it shall be in the morning, that if he will perform unto thee the part of a kinsman, well; let him do the kinsman part: but if he will not do the part of a kinsman to thee, then will I do the part of a kinsman to thee, as the Lord liveth: lie down until the morning."

And she lay at his feet until the morning: and she rose up before one could know another. And he said, "Let it not be known that a woman came into the floor." Also he said, "Bring the vail that thou hast upon thee, and hold it." And when she held it, he measured six measures of barley, and laid it on her: and she went into the city.

And when she came to her mother-in-law, she said, "Who art thou, my daughter?" And she told her all that the man had done to her. And she said, "These six measures of barley gave he me; for he said to me, Go not empty unto thy mother-in-law." Then said she, "Sit still, my daughter, until thou know how the matter will fall: for the man will not be in rest, until he have finished the thing this day."

Then went Boaz up to the gate, and sat him down there: and, behold, the kinsman of whom Boaz spake came by; unto whom he said, "Ho, such a one! turn aside, sit down here." And he turned aside, and sat down. And he took ten men of the elders of the city, and said, "Sit ye down here." And they sat down. And he said unto the kinsman, "Naomi, that is come again out of the country of Moab, selleth a parcel of land, which was our brother Elimelech's: and I thought to advertise thee, saying, Buy it before the inhabitants, and before the elders of my people. If thou wilt redeem it, redeem it: but if thou wilt not redeem it, then tell me, that I may know: for there is none to redeem it beside thee; and I am after thee."

And he said, "I will redeem it."

Then said Boaz, "What day thou buyest the field of the hand of Naomi, thou must buy it also of Ruth the Moabitess, the wife of the dead, to raise up the name of the dead upon his inheritance."

And the kinsman said, "I cannot redeem it for myself, lest I mar mine own inheritance: redeem thou my right to thyself; for I cannot redeem it." Now this was the manner in former time in Israel concerning redeeming and concerning changing, for to confirm all things; a man plucked off his shoe, and gave it to his neighbor: and this was a testimony in Israel. Therefore the kinsman said unto Boaz, "Buy it for thee." So he drew off his shoe.

And Boaz said unto the elders, and unto all the people, "Ye are witnesses this day, that I have bought all that was Elimelech's, and all that was Chilion's and Mahlon's, of the hand of Naomi. Moreover, Ruth the Moabitess, the wife of Mahlon, have I purchased to be my wife, to raise up the name of the dead upon his inheritance, that the name of the dead be not cut off from among his brethren, and from the gate of his place: ye are witnesses this day."

And all the people that were in the gate, and the elders, said, "We are witnesses. The Lord make the woman that is come into thine house like Rachel and like Leah, which two did build the house of Israel: and do thou worthily in Ephratah, and be famous in Beth-lehem: and let thy house be like the house of Pharez, whom Tamar bore unto Judah, of the seed which the Lord shall give thee of this young woman."

So Boaz took Ruth, and she was his wife: and when he went in unto her, the Lord gave her conception, and she bare a son. And the women said unto Naomi, "Blessed be the Lord, which hath not left thee this day without a kinsman, that his name may be famous in Israel. And he shall be unto thee a restorer of thy life, and a nourisher of thine old age: for thy daughter-in-law, which loveth thee, which is better to thee than seven sons, hath born him." And Naomi took the child, and laid it in her bosom, and became nurse unto it. And the women her neighbors gave it a name, saying, "There is a son born to Naomi"; and they called his name Obed: he is the father of Jesse, the father of David.

(c. 450 B.C.)

Giovanni Boccaccio

THE FALCON

You must know, then, that Coppo di Borghese Domenichi, who was of our days and maybe is yet a man of great worship and authority in our city and illustrious and worthy of eternal renown, much more for his fashions and his merit than for the nobility of his blood, being grown full of years, delighted oftentimes to discourse with his neighbours and others of things past, the which he knew how to do better and more orderly and with more memory and elegance of speech than any other man. Amongst other fine things of his, he was used to tell that there was once in Florence a young man called Federigo, son of Messer Filippo Alberighi, and renowned for deeds of arms and courtesy over every other bachelor in Tuscany, who, as betideth most gentlemen, became enamoured of a gentlewoman named Madam Giovanna, in her day held one of the fairest and sprightliest ladies that were in Florence; and to win her love, he held jousts and tourneyings and made entertainments and gave gifts and spent his substance without any stint; but she, being no less virtuous than fair, recked nought of these things done for her nor of him who did them. Federigo spending thus far beyond his means and gaining nought, his wealth, as lightly happeneth, in course of time came to an end and he abode poor, nor was aught left him but a poor little farm, on whose returns he lived very meagrely, and to boot a falcon he had, one of the best in the world. Wherefore, being more in love than ever and him seeming he might no longer make such a figure in the city as he would fain do, he took up his abode at Campi, where his farm was, and there bore his poverty with patience, hawking whenas he might and asking of no one.

Federigo being thus come to extremity, it befell one day that Madam Giovanna's husband fell sick and seeing himself nigh upon death, made his will, wherein, being very rich, he left a son of his, now well grown, his heir, after which, having much loved Madam Giovanna, he substituted her to his heir, in case his son should die without lawful issue, and died. Madam Giovanna, being thus left a widow, betook herself that summer, as is the usance of our ladies, into the country with her son to an estate of hers very near that of Federigo; wherefore it befell that the lad made acquaintance with the latter and began to take delight in hawks and hounds, and having many a time seen his falcon flown and being strangely taken therewith, longed sore to have it, but dared not ask it of him, seeing it so dear to him. The thing standing thus, it came to pass that the lad fell sick, whereat his mother was sore concerned, as one who had none but him and loved him with all her might, and abode about him all day, comforting him without cease; and many a time she asked him if there were aught he desired, beseeching him tell it her, for that, and it might be gotten, she would contrive that he should have it. The lad, having heard these offers many times repeated, said, "Mother mine, an you could procure me to have Federigo's falcon, methinketh I should soon be whole."

The lady, hearing this, bethought herself awhile and began to consider how she should do. She knew that Federigo had long loved her and had never gotten of her so much as a glance of the eye; wherefore quoth she in herself, "How shall I send or go to him to seek of him this falcon, which is, by all I hear, the best that ever flew and which, to boot, maintaineth him in the world? And how can I be so graceless as to offer to take this from a gentleman who hath none other pleasure left?" Perplexed with this thought and knowing not what to say, for all she was very certain of getting the bird, if she asked for it, she made no reply to her son, but abode silent. However, at last, the love of her son so got the better of her that she resolved in herself to satisfy him, come what might, and not to send, but to go herself for the falcon and fetch it to him. Accordingly she said to him, "My son, take comfort and bethink thyself to grow well again, for I promise thee that the first thing I do to-morrow morning I will go for it and fetch it to thee." The boy was rejoiced at this and showed some amendment that same day.

Next morning, the lady, taking another lady to bear her company, repaired, by way of diversion, to Federigo's little house and enquired for the latter, who, for that it was no weather for hawking nor had been for some days past, was then in a garden he had, overlooking the doing of certain little matters of his, and hearing that Madam Giovanna asked for him at the door, ran thither, rejoicing and marvelling exceedingly. She, seeing him come, rose and going with womanly graciousness to meet him, answered his respectful salutation with "Give you good day, Federigo!" then went on to say, "I am come to make thee amends for that which thou hast suffered through me, in loving me more than should have behooved thee; and the amends in question is this that I purpose to dine with thee this morning familiarly, I and this lady my companion." "Madam," answered Federigo humbly, "I remember me not to have ever received any ill at your hands, but on the contrary so much good that, if ever I was worth aught, it came about through your worth and the love I bore you; and assuredly, albeit you have come to a poor host, this your gracious visit is far more precious to me than it would be an it were given me to spend over again as much as that which I have spent aforetime." So saying, he shamefastly received her into his house and thence brought her into his garden, where, having none else to bear her company, he said to her, "Madam, since there is none else here, this good woman, wife of yonder husbandman, will bear you company, whilst I go see the table laid."

Never till that moment, extreme as was his poverty, had he been so dolorously sensible of the straits to which he had brought himself for the lack of those riches he had spent on such disorderly wise. But that morning, finding he had nothing wherewithal he might honourably entertain the lady for love of whom he had aforetime entertained folk without number, he was made perforce aware of his default and ran hither and thither, perplexed beyond measure, like a man beside himself, inwardly cursing his ill fortune, but found neither money nor aught he might pawn. It was now growing late and he having a great desire to entertain the gentle lady with somewhat, yet choosing not to have recourse to his own labourer, much less anyone else, his eye fell on his good falcon, which he saw on his perch in his little saloon; whereupon, having no other resource, he took the bird and finding him fat, deemed him a dish worthy of such a lady. Accordingly, without more ado, he wrung the hawk's neck and hastily caused a little maid of his pluck it and truss it and after put it on the spit and roast it diligently. Then, the table laid and covered with very white cloths, whereof he had yet some store, he returned with a blithe countenance to the lady in the garden and told her that dinner was ready, such as it was in his power to provide. Accordingly, the lady and her friend, arising, betook themselves to table and in company with Federigo, who served them with the utmost diligence, ate the good falcon, unknowing what they did.

Presently, after they had risen from table and had abidden with him awhile in cheerful discourse, the lady, thinking it time to tell that wherefore she was come, turned to Federigo and courteously bespoke him, saying, "Federigo, I doubt not a jot but that, when thou hearest that which is the especial occasion of my coming hither, thou wilt marvel at my presumption, remembering thee of thy past life and of my virtue, which latter belike thou reputedst cruelty and hardness of heart; but, if thou hadst or hadst had children, by whom thou mightest know how potent is the love one beareth them, meseemeth certain that thou wouldst in part hold me excused. But, although thou hast none, I, who have one child, cannot therefore escape the common laws to which other mothers are subject and whose enforcements it behooveth me ensue, need must I, against my will and contrary to all right and seemliness, ask of thee a boon, which I know is supremely dear to thee (and that with good reason, for that thy sorry fortune hath left thee none other delight, none other diversion, none other solace), to wit, thy falcon, whereof my boy is so sore enamoured that, an I carry it not to him, I fear me his present disorder will be so aggravated that there may presently ensue thereof somewhat whereby I shall lose him. Wherefore I conjure thee—not by the love thou bearest me and whereto thou art nowise beholden, but by thine own nobility, which in doing courtesy hath approved itself greater than in any other—that it please thee give it to me, so by the gift I may say I have kept my son alive and thus made him forever thy debtor."

Federigo, hearing what the lady asked and knowing that he could not oblige her, for that he had given her the falcon to eat, fell a-weeping in her presence, ere he could answer a word. The lady at first believed that his tears arose from grief at having to part from his good falcon and was like to say that she would not have it. However, she contained herself and awaited what Federigo should reply, who, after weeping awhile, made answer thus: "Madam, since it pleased God that I should set my love on you, I have in many things reputed fortune contrary to me and have complained of her; but all the ill turns she hath done me have been a light matter in comparison with that which she doth me at this present and for which I can never more be reconciled to her, considering that you are come hither to my poor house, whereas you deigned not to come while I was rich, and seek of me a little boon, the which she hath so wrought that I cannot grant you; and why this cannot be I will tell you briefly. When I heard that you, of your favour, were minded to dine with me, I deemed it a right thing and a seemly, having regard to your worth and the nobility of your station, to honour you, as far as in me lay, with some choicer victual than that which is commonly set before other folk; wherefore, remembering me of the falcon which you ask of me and of his excellence, I judged him a dish worthy of you. This very morning, then, you have had him roasted upon the trencher, and indeed I had accounted him excellently well bestowed; but now, seeing that you would fain have had him on the other wise, it is so great a grief to me that I cannot oblige you therein that me-thinketh I shall never forgive my self therefor." So saying, in witness of this, he let cast before her the falcon's feathers and feet and beak.

The lady, seeing and hearing this, first blamed him for having, to give a woman to eat, slain such a falcon, and after inwardly much commended the greatness of his soul, which poverty had not availed nor might anywise avail to abate. Then, being put out of all hope of having the falcon and fallen therefore in doubt of her son's recovery, she took her leave and returned, all disconsolate, to the latter, who, before many days had passed, whether for chagrin that he could not have the bird or for this his disorder was e'en fated to bring him to that pass, departed this life, to the inexpressible grief of his mother. After she had abidden awhile full of tears and affliction, being left very rich and yet young, she was more than once urged by her brothers to marry again, and albeit she would fain not have done so, yet, finding herself importuned and calling to mind Federigo's worth and his last magnificence, to wit, the having slain such a falcon for her entertainment, she said to them, "I would gladly, an it liked you, abide as I am; but, since it is your pleasure that I take a second husband, certes I will never take any other, an I have not Federigo degli Alberighi." Whereupon her brothers, making mock of her, said, "Silly woman that thou art, what is this thou sayest? How canst thou choose him, seeing he hath nothing in the world?" "Brothers mine," answered she, "I know very well that it is as you say; but I would liefer have a man that lacketh of riches than riches that lack of a man." Her brethren, hearing her mind and knowing Federigo for a man of great merit, poor though he was, gave her, with all her wealth, to him, even as she would; and he, seeing himself married to a lady of such worth and one who he had loved so dear and exceedingly rich, to boot, became a better husband of his substance and ended his days with her in joy and solace.   (1353)

Voltaire

MEMNON
THE PHILOSOPHER

Memnon one day took it into his head to become a great philosopher. There are few men who have not, at some time or other, conceived the same wild project. Says Memnon to himself, To be a perfect philosopher, and of course to be perfectly happy, I have nothing to do but to divest myself entirely of passions; and nothing is more easy, as everybody knows. In the first place, I will never be in love; for, when I see a beautiful woman, I will say to myself, These cheeks will one day grow wrinkled, these eyes be encircled with vermilion, that bosom become flabby and pendant, that head bald and palsied. Now I have only to consider her at present in imagination, as she will after-wards appear; and certainly a fair face will never turn my head.

In the second place, I will be always temperate. It will be in vain to tempt me with good cheer, with delicious wines, or the charms of society. I will have only to figure to myself the consequences of excess, an aching head, a loathing stomach, the loss of reason, of health, and of time: I will then only eat to supply the waste of nature; my health will be always equal, my ideas pure and luminus. All this is so easy that there is no merit in accomplishing it.

But, says Memnon, I must think a little of how I am to regulate my fortune: why, my desires are moderate, my wealth is securely placed with the Receiver General of the finances of Nineveh: I have wherewithal to live independent; and that is the greatest of blessings. I shall never be under the cruel necessity of dancing attendance at court; I will never envy anyone, and nobody will envy me; still all this is easy. I have friends, continued he, and I will preserve them, for we shall never have any difference; I will never take amiss anything they may say or do; and they will behave in the same way to me.—There is no difficulty in all this.

Having thus laid his little plan of philosophy in his closet, Memnon put his head out of the window. He saw two women walking under the plane trees near his house. The one was old and appeared quite at her ease. The other was young, handsome, and seemingly much agitated: she sighed, she wept, and seemed on that account still more beautiful. Our philosopher was touched, not, to be sure, with the beauty of the lady (he was too much determined not to feel any uneasiness of that kind), but with the distress which he saw her in. He came down stairs and accosted the young Ninevite in the design of consoling her with philosophy. That lovely person related to him, with an air of the greatest simplicity, and in the most affecting manner, the injuries she sustained from an imaginary uncle; with what art he had deprived her of some imaginary property, and of the violence which she pretended to dread from him. "You appear to me," said she, "a man of such wisdom, that if you will condescend to come to my house and examine into my affairs, I am persuaded you will be able to draw me from the cruel embarrassment I am at present involved in." Memnon did not hesitate to follow her, to examine her affairs philosophically, and to give her sound counsel.

The afflicted lady led him into a perfumed chamber, and politely made him sit down with her on a large sofa, where they both placed themselves opposite to each other, in the attitude of conversation, their legs crossed; the one eager in telling her story, the other listening with devout attention. The lady spoke with downcast eyes, whence there sometimes fell a tear, and which, as she now and then ventured to raise them, always met those of the sage Memnon. Their discourse was full of tenderness, which redoubled as often as their eyes met. Memnon took her affairs exceedingly to heart, and felt himself every instant more and more inclined to oblige a person so virtuous and so unhappy.—By degrees, in the warmth of conversation, they ceased to sit opposite; they drew nearer; their legs were no longer crossed. Memnon counselled her so closely, and gave her such tender advices, that neither of them could talk any longer of business, nor well knew what they were about.

At this interesting moment, as may easily be imagined, who should come in but the uncle; he was armed from head to foot, and the first thing he said was, that he would immediately sacrifice, as was just, the sage Memnon and his niece; the latter, who made her escape, knew that he was well enough disposed to pardon, provided a good round sum were offered to him. Memnon was obliged to purchase his safety with all he had about him. In those days people were happy in getting so easily quit. America was not then discovered, and distressed ladies were not nearly so dangerous as they are now.

Memnon, covered with shame and confusion, got home to his own house; there he found a card inviting him to dinner with some of his intimate friends. If I remain at home alone, said he, I shall have my mind so occupied with this vexatious adventure, that I shall not be able to eat a bit, and I shall bring upon myself some disease. It will therefore be prudent in me to go to my intimate friends, and partake with them of a frugal repast. I shall forget, in the sweets of their society, the folly I have this morning been guilty of. Accordingly he attends the meeting; he is discovered to be uneasy at something, and he is urged to drink and banish care. A little wine, drunk in moderation, comforts the heart of god and man: so reasons Memnon the philosopher, and he becomes intoxicated. After the repast, play is proposed. A little play, with one's intimate friends, is a harmless pastime:—he plays and loses all that is in his purse, and four times as much on his word. A dispute arises on some circumstance in the game, and the disputants grow warm: one of his intimate friends throws a dicebox at his head and strikes out one of his eyes. The philosopher Memnon is carried home to his house, drunk and penniless, with the loss of an eye.

He sleeps out his debauch, and when his head has got a little clear, he sends his servant to the Receiver General of the finances of Nineveh to draw a little money to pay his debt of honour to his intimate friends. The servant returns and informs him, that the Receiver General had that morning been declared a fraudulent bankrupt, and that by this means an hundred families are reduced to poverty and despair. Memnon, almost beside himself, puts a plaster on his eye and a petition in his pocket, and goes to court to solicit justice from the king against the bankrupt. In the saloon he meets a number of ladies, all in the highest spirits, and sailing along with hoops four and twenty feet in circumference. One of them, who knew him a little, eyed him askance, and cried aloud, "Ah! what a horrid monster!" Another, who was better acquainted with him, thus accosts him, "Good-morrow, Mr. Memnon, I hope you are very well, Mr. Memnon: La! Mr. Memnon, how did you lose your eye?" and turning upon her heel, she tripped away without waiting an answer.

Memnon hid himself in a corner, and waited for the moment when he could throw himself at the feet of the monarch. That moment at last arrived. Three times he kissed the earth, and presented his petition. His gracious majesty received him very favourably, and referred the paper to one of his satraps, that he might give him an account of it. The satrap takes Memnon aside, and says to him with a haughty air and satyrical grin. "Hark ye, you fellow with the one eye, you must be a comical dog indeed, to address yourself to the king rather than to me; and still more so, to dare to demand justice against an honest bankrupt, whom I honour with my protection, and who is nephew to the waiting-maid of my mistress. Proceed no further in this business, my good friend, if you wish to preserve the eye you have left."

Memnon having thus, in his closet, resolved to renounce women, the excesses of the table, play and quarreling, but especially having determined never to go to court, had been in the short space of four and twenty hours duped and robbed by a gentle dame, had got drunk, had gamed, had been engaged in a quarrel, had got his eye knocked out, and had been at court, where he was sneered at and insulted.

Petrified with astonishment, and his heart broken with grief, Memnon returns homeward in despair. As he was about to enter his house, he is repulsed by a number of officers who are carrying out his furniture for the benefit of his creditors; he falls down almost lifeless under a plane tree. There he finds the fair dame of the morning, who was walking with her dear uncle; and both set up a loud laugh on seeing Memnon with his plaster. The night approached, and Memnon made his bed on some straw near the walls of his house. Here the ague seized him, and he fell asleep in one of the fits, when a celestial spirit appeared to him in a dream.

It was all resplendent with light; it had six beautiful wings, but neither feet nor head, nor tail, and could be likened to nothing. "What art thou?" said Memnon.

"Thy good genius," replied the spirit.

"Restore to me then my eye, my health, my fortune, my reason," said Memnon; and he related how he had lost them all in one day.

"These are adventures which never happen to us in the world we inhabit," said the spirit.

"And what world do you inhabit?" said the man of affliction.

"My native country," replied the other, "is five hundred millions of leagues distant from the sun, in a little star near Sirius, which you see from hence."

"Charming country!" said Memnon. "And are there indeed with you no jades to dupe a poor devil, no intimate friends that win his money and knock out an eye to him, no fraudulent bankrupts, no satraps, that make a jest of you while they refuse you justice?"

"No," said the inhabitant of the star, "we have nothing of what you talk of; we are never duped by women, because we have none among us; we never commit excesses at table, because we neither eat nor drink; we have no bankrupts, because with us there is neither silver nor gold; our eyes cannot be knocked out because we have not bodies in the form of yours; and satraps never do us injustice, because in our world we are all equal."

"Pray, my Lord," then said Memnon, "without women and without eating how do you spend your time?"

"In watching," said the genius, "over the other worlds that are entrusted to us; and I am now come to give you consolation."

"Alas!" replied Memnon, "why did you not come yesterday to hinder me from committing so many indiscretions?"

"I was with your elder brother Hassan," said the celestial being. "He is still more to be pitied than you are. His most gracious Majesty, the Sultan of the Indies, in whose court he has the honour to serve, has caused both his eyes to be put out for some small indiscretion; and he is now in a dungeon, his hands and feet loaded with chains."

"'Tis a happy thing truly," said Memnon, "to have a good genius in one's family, when out of two brothers one is blind of an eye, the other blind of both; one stretched upon straw, the other in a dungeon."

"Your fate will soon change," said the animal of the star. "It is true, you will never recover your eye but, except that, you may be sufficiently happy if you never again take it into your head to be a perfect philosopher."

"Is it then impossible?" said Memnon.

"As impossible as to be perfectly wise, perfectly strong, perfectly powerful, perfectly happy. We ourselves are very far from it. There is a world indeed where all this takes place; but, in a hundred thousand millions of worlds dispersed over the regions of space, everything goes on by degrees. There is less philosophy and less enjoyment in the second than in the first, less in the third than in the second, and so forth till the last in the scale, where all are completely fools."

"I am afraid," said Memnon, "that our little terraqueous globe here is the madhouse of those hundred thousand millions of worlds, of which your Lordship does me the honour to speak."

"Not quite," said the spirit, "but very nearly: everything must be in its proper place."

"But are those poets and philosophers wrong, then, who tell us that everything is for the best?"

"No, they are right, when we consider things in relation to the gradation of the whole universe."

"Oh! I shall never believe it till I recover my eye again," said the poor Memnon. (1750)

Prosper Mérimée

MATEO FALCONE

Coming out of Porto-Vecchio, and turning northwest toward the interior of the island, the ground rises somewhat rapidly, and, after a three hours' walk along winding paths, blocked by huge rocky boulders, and sometimes cut by ravines, you come to the edge of a wide *mâquis*. The *mâquis*, or high plateau, is the home of the Corsican shepherds and of all those who wish to escape the police. I would have you understand that the Corsican peasant sets fire to a stretch of woodland to save himself the trouble of manuring his fields. If the flames spread further than they should, so much the worse. In any case, he is sure of a good crop if he sows on this ground, which has been fertilised by the ashes of the trees which grew on it. When the corn has been harvested, they leave the straw, because it takes too much time to gather it up. The roots of the burned trees, which have been left in the ground undamaged, put forth very thick shoots in the following spring, and these shoots, before many years, attain a height of seven or eight feet. It is this sort of undergrowth which is called a *mâquis*. It is composed of all sorts of trees and shrubs mingled and tangled every whichway. A man has to hew his way through with an axe, and there are *mâquis* so thick and tangled that even wild rams cannot penetrate them.

If you have killed a man, go into the *mâquis* of Porto-Vecchio with a good gun and powder and shot. You will live there quite safely, but don't forget to bring along a brown cloak and hood for your blanket and mattress. The shepherds will give you milk, cheese, and chestnuts, and you need not trouble your head about the law or the dead man's relatives, except when you are compelled to go down into the town to renew your ammunition.

When I was in Corsica in 18—, Mateo Falcone's house stood half a league away from the *mâquis*. He was a fairly rich man for that country. He lived like a lord, that is to say, without toil, on the produce of his flocks, which the nomadic shepherds pastured here and there on the mountains. When I saw him, two years later than the incident which I am about to relate, he did not seem to be more than fifty years of age.

Picture a small, sturdy man, with jet-black curly hair, a Roman nose, thin lips, large piercing eyes, and a weather-beaten complexion. His skill as a marksman was extraordinary, even in this country, where everyone is a good shot. For instance, Mateo would never fire on a wild ram with small shot, but at a hundred and twenty paces he would bring it down with a bullet in its head or its shoulder, just as he fancied. He used his rifle at night as easily as in the daytime, and I was given the following illustration of his skill, which may seem incredible, perhaps, to those who have never travelled in Corsica. He placed a lighted candle behind a piece of transparent paper as big as a plate, and aimed at it from eighty paces away. He extinguished the candle, and a moment later, in utter darkness, fired and pierced the paper three times out of four.

With this extraordinary skill Mateo Falcone had gained a great reputation. He was said to be a good friend and a dangerous enemy. Obliging and charitable, he lived at peace with all his neighbors around Porto-Vecchio. But they said of him that once, at Corte, whence he had brought home his wife, he had quickly freed himself of a rival reputed to be as fearful in war as in love. At any rate, people gave Mateo the credit for a certain shot which had surprised his rival shaving in front of a small mirror hung up in his window. The matter was hushed up and Mateo married the girl. His wife Giuseppa presented him at first, to his fury, with three daughters, but at last came a son whom he christened Fortunato, the hope of the family and the heir to its name. The girls were married off satisfactorily. At a pinch their father could count on the daggers and rifles of his sons-in-law. The son was only ten years old, but already gave promise for the future.

One autumn day, Mateo and his wife set forth to visit one of his flocks in a clearing on the *mâquis*. Little Fortunato wanted to come along, but the clearing was too far off, and moreover, someone had to stay to look after the house. His father refused to take him. We shall see that he was sorry for this afterwards.

He had been gone several hours, and little Fortunato lay stretched out quietly in the sunshine, gazing at the blue mountains, and thinking that next Sunday he would be going to town to have dinner with his uncle, the magistrate, when he was suddenly startled by a rifle shot. He rose and turned toward the side of the plain whence the sound had come. Other shots followed, fired at irregular intervals, and they sounded nearer and nearer, till finally, he saw a man on the path which led from the plain up to Mateo's house. He wore a mountaineer's peaked cap, had a beard, and was clad in rags. He dragged himself along with difficulty, leaning on his gun. He had just been shot in the thigh. The man was an outlaw from justice, who, having set out at nightfall to buy ammunition in the town, had fallen on the way into an ambuscade of Corsican gendarmes. After a vigorous defense, he had succeeded in making his escape, but the gendarmes had pursued him closely and fired at him from rock to rock. He had been just ahead of the soldiers, and his wound made it impossible for him to reach the *mâquis* without being captured.

He came up to Fortunato and asked:

"Are you Mateo Falcone's son?"

"Yes, I am."

"I'm Gianetto Sanpiero. The yellow necks are after me. Hide me, for I can go no farther."

"But what will my father say, if I hide you without his permission?"

"He will say that you did the right thing."

"How can I be sure of that?"

"Quick! Hide me! Here they come!"

"Wait till my father comes back."

"How the devil can I wait? They'll be here in five minutes. Come now, hide me, or I shall kill you."

Fortunato replied as cool as a cucumber:

"Your rifle is not loaded, and there are no cartridges in your pouch."

"I have my stiletto."

"But can you run as fast as I can?"

He bounded out of the man's reach.

"You are no son of Mateo Falcone. Will you let me be captured in front of his house?"

The child seemed touched.

"What will you give me if I hide you?" he said, coming nearer to him.

The fugitive felt in a leather wallet that hung from his belt, and took out a five-franc piece which he had been saving, no doubt, to buy powder. Fortunato smiled when he saw the piece of silver. He snatched it and said to Gianetto:

"Have no fear."

He made a large hole at once in a haystack beside the house. Gianetto huddled down in it, and the boy covered him up so as to leave a little breathing space, and yet so that no one could possibly suspect that a man was hidden there. He showed his ingenious wild cunning by another trick. He fetched a cat and her kittens and put them on top of the haystack, so that anyone who passed would think that it had not been disturbed for a long time. Then he noticed some bloodstains on the path in front of the house and covered them over carefully with dust. When he had finished, he lay down again in the sun looking as calm as ever.

A few minutes later, six men in brown uniforms with yellow collars, led by an adjutant, stopped in front of Mateo's door. The adjutant was a distant cousin of Falcone. (You know that degrees of kindred are traced farther in Corsica than anywhere else.) His name was Tiodoro Gamba. He was an energetic man, much feared by the outlaws, many of whom he had already hunted down.

"Good morning, little cousin," he said, accosting Fortunato. "How you have grown! Did you see a man go by just now?"

"Oh, I'm not as tall as you are yet, cousin," replied the child with an innocent smile.

"It won't take long. But, tell me, didn't you see a man go by?"

"Did I see a man go by?"

"Yes, a man with a black velvet peaked cap and a waistcoat embroidered in red and yellow?"

"A man with a black velvet peaked cap, and a waistcoat embroidered in red and yellow?"

"Yes. Hurry up and answer me, and don't keep repeating my questions."

"Monsieur the Curé went by this morning on his horse Pierrot. He enquired after papa's health, and I said to him that——"

"You are making a fool of me, you limb of the devil! Tell me at once which way Gianetto went. He's the man we're looking for, and I'm sure he went this way."

"How do you know?"

"How do I know? I know you've seen him."

"Can I see people pass by in my sleep?"

"You weren't asleep, you rascal. Our shots would wake you."

"So you think, cousin, that your rifles make all that hullaballoo? My father's rifle makes much more noise."

"The devil take you, you little scamp. I am positive that you have seen Gianetto. Maybe you've hidden him, in fact. Here, boys, search the house and see if our man isn't there. He could only walk on one foot, and he has too much sense, the rascal, to try and reach the *mâquis* limping. Besides, the trail of blood stops here."

"What will papa say?" asked Fortunato. "What will he say when he discovers that his house has been searched during his absence?"

"Do you realise that I can make you change your tune, you rogue?" cried the adjutant, as he pulled his ear. "Perhaps you will have something more to say when I have thrashed you with the flat of my sword."

Fortunato laughed in derision.

"My father is Mateo Falcone," he said meaningly.

"Do you realise, you rascal, that I can haul you off to Corte or to Bastia? I shall put you in a dungeon on straw, with your feet in irons, and I'll have your head chopped off unless you tell me where to find Gianetto Sanpiero."

The child laughed again derisively at this silly threat. He repeated:

"My father is Mateo Falcone."

"Adjutant, don't get us into trouble with Mateo," muttered one of the gendarmes.

You could see that Gamba was embarrassed. He whispered to his men, who had already searched the house thoroughly. This was not a lengthy matter, for a Corsican hut consists of one square room. There is no furniture other than a table, benches, chests, cooking utensils, and weapons. Meanwhile, little Fortunato was stroking the cat, and seemed to take a malicious satisfaction in the discomfiture of his cousin and the gendarmes.

One gendarme approached the haystack. He looked at the cat and carelessly stuck a bayonet into the hay, shrugging his shoulders as if he thought the precaution absurd. Nothing stirred, and the child's face remained perfectly calm.

The adjutant and his men were desperate. They looked seriously out across the plain, as if they were inclined to go back home, when their leader, satisfied that threats would make no impression on Falcone's son, decided to make a final attempt, and see what coaxing and gifts might do.

"Little cousin," said he, "I can see that your eyes are open. You'll get on in life. But you are playing a risky game with me, and, if it weren't for the trouble it would give my cousin Mateo, God help me if I wouldn't carry you off with me."

"Nonsense!"

"But, when my cousin returns, I am going to tell him all about it, and he'll horsewhip you till the blood comes because you've been telling me lies."

"How do you know?"

"You'll see! . . . But see here! Be a good boy, and I'll give you a present."

"I advise you to go and look for Gianetto in the *mâquis*, cousin. If you hang about here much longer, it will take a cleverer man than you to catch him."

The adjutant took a silver watch worth ten dollars out of his pocket. He noticed that little Fortunato's eyes sparkled as he looked at it, and he dangled the watch out to him at the end of its steel chain as he said:

"You scamp, wouldn't you like to have a watch like this hanging round your neck, and to strut up and down the streets of Porto-Vecchio as proud as a peacock? Folk would ask you what time it was and you would say, 'Look at my watch!'"

"When I'm a big boy, my uncle, the magistrate, will give me a watch."

"Yes, but your uncle's son has one already—not as fine as this, to be sure—but he is younger than you are."

The boy sighed.

"Well, would you like this watch, little cousin?"

Fortunato kept eyeing the watch out of the corner of his eye, like a cat that has been given a whole chicken to play with. It does not dare to pounce upon it, because it is afraid folk are laughing at it, but it turns its eyes away now and then so as to avoid temptation, and keeps licking its lips, as much as to say to its master: "What a cruel trick to play on a cat!" And yet Gamba seemed to be really offering him the watch. Fortunato did not hold out his hand, but said with a bitter smile:

"Why are you mocking me?"

"I swear that I am not mocking you. Only tell me where Gianetto is, and the watch is yours."

Fortunato smiled incredulously and fixed his dark eyes on those of the adjutant, trying to read them to see if the man could be trusted.

"May I lose my epaulettes," cried the adjutant, "if I do not give you the watch on this one condition! My men are witnesses, and I cannot back out of it."

As he spoke, he held the watch nearer and nearer till it almost touched the pale cheek of the boy, whose face clearly showed the struggle going on in his heart between greed and the claims of hospitality. His bare breast heaved till he was almost suffocated. Meanwhile the watch dangled and twisted and even touched the tip of his nose. Little by little, his right hand rose toward it, the tips of his fingers touched it, and the whole weight of it rested on his hand, although the adjutant still had it by the chain. . . . The face of the watch was blue. . . . The case was newly burnished. . . . It flamed like fire in the sun. . . . The temptation was too great.

Fortunato raised his left hand and pointed with his thumb over his shoulder to the haystack on which he was leaning. The adjutant understood him at once and let go the end of the chain. Fortunato felt that he was now sole possessor of the watch. He leaped away like a deer, and paused ten paces from the haystack which the gendarmes began to tumble over at once.

It was not long before they saw the hay begin to stir and a bleeding man came out with a stiletto in his hand. But when he tried to rise to his feet, his congealed wound prevented him from standing. He fell down. The adjutant flung himself upon his prey and wrested the stiletto from his grasp. He was speedily trussed up, in spite of his resistance, bound securely, and flung on the ground like a bundle of sticks. He turned his head toward Fortunato who had drawn near again.

"Son of . . . !" he exclaimed, more in contempt than in anger.

The child threw him the piece of silver, realising that he no longer deserved it, but the fugitive paid no attention to it. He merely said quietly to the adjutant:

"My dear Gamba, I cannot walk. You must carry me to town."

"You were running as fast as a kid just now," retorted his captor, roughly. "But don't worry! I'm so glad to have caught you that I could carry you a league on my own back without feeling it. Anyhow, my friend, we'll make a litter for you out of branches and your cloak. We'll find horses at the farm at Crespoli."

"Very well," said the prisoner. "I suppose you will put a little straw on the litter to make it easier for me."

While the gendarmes were busy, some making a crude litter of chestnut boughs, and others dressing Gianetto's wound, Mateo Falcone and his wife suddenly appeared at a turn of the path which led from the *mâquis*. His wife came first, bowed low beneath the weight of a huge sack of chestnuts, while her husband strolled along, carrying a gun in one hand, and another slung over his shoulder. It is beneath a man's dignity to carry any other burden than his weapons.

As soon as he saw the soldiers, Mateo's first thought was that they must have come to arrest him. But there was no reason for it. He had no quarrel with the forces of law and order. He had an excellent reputation. He was "well thought of," as they say, but he was a Corsican, and a mountaineer, and there are very few Corsican mountaineers who, if they search their past sufficiently, cannot find some peccadillo, a rifle shot or a thrust with a stiletto or some other trifle. Mateo had a clearer conscience than most of his friends, for it was at least ten years since he had pointed a rifle at a man; but all the same it behooved him to be cautious, and he prepared to put up a good defense, if necessary.

"Wife," he said, "put down your sack and be on your guard."

She obeyed at once. He gave her the gun from his shoulder belt, as it seemed likely that it might be in his way. He cocked the other rifle, and advanced in a leisurely manner toward the house, skirting the trees beside the path, and ready, at the least sign of hostility, to throw himself behind the largest trunk and fire from cover. His wife followed close behind him, holding her loaded rifle and his cartridges. It was a good wife's duty, in case of trouble, to reload her husband's arms.

The adjutant, on his side, was much troubled at seeing Mateo advance upon him so with measured steps, pointing his rifle, and keeping his finger on the trigger.

"If it should happen," thought he, "that Gianetto turns out to be Mateo's relative or friend, and he wishes to defend him, two of his bullets will reach us as sure as a letter goes by post, and if he aims at me, in spite of our kinship . . . !"

In his perplexity, he put the best face he could on the matter, and went forward by himself to meet Mateo and tell him all that had happened, greeting him like an old friend. But the short distance between him and Mateo seemed fearfully long.

"Hello, there, old comrade!" he cried out. "How are you? I'm your cousin Gamba."

Mateo stood still and said not a word. As the other man spoke, he slowly raised the barrel of his rifle so that, by the time the adjutant came up to him, it was pointing to the sky.

"Good-day, brother," said the adjutant, holding out his hand. "It's an age since I've seen you."

"Good-day, brother."

"I just stopped by to pass the time of day with you and cousin Pepa. We've had a long march to-day, but we can't complain, for we've made a famous haul. We've just caught Gianetto Sanpiero."

"Heaven be praised!" exclaimed Giuseppa. "He stole one of our milch goats a week ago."

Gamba was delighted at her words.

"Poor devil!" said Mateo, "he was hungry."

"The chap fought like a lion," pursued the adjutant, somewhat annoyed. "He killed one of my men, and as if that were not enough, broke Corporal Chardon's arm; not that it matters, he's only a Frenchman. . . . Then he hid himself so cleverly that the devil himself couldn't find him. If it hadn't been for my little cousin Fortunato, I should never have found him."

"Fortunato?" cried Mateo.

"Fortunato?" echoed Giuseppa.

"Yes! Gianetto was hidden in your haystack over there, but my little cousin soon showed up his tricks. I shall tell his uncle, the magistrate, and he'll send him a fine present as a reward. And both his name and yours shall be in the report that I'm sending to the Public Prosecutor."

"Damn you!" muttered Mateo under his breath.

They had now rejoined the gendarmes. Gianetto was already laid on his litter, and they were all ready to start. When he saw Mateo in Gamba's company, he smiled oddly; then, turning toward the door of the house, he spat at the threshold.

"The house of a traitor!"

It was asking for death to call Falcone a traitor. A quick stiletto thrust, and no need of a second, would have instantly wiped out the insult. But Mateo's only movement was to put his hand to his head as if he were stunned.

Fortunato had gone into the house when he saw his father coming. Presently he reappeared with a bowl of milk, which he offered with downcast eyes to Gianetto.

"Keep away from me!" thundered the outlaw.

Then, turning to one of the gendarmes, he said:

"Comrade, will you give me a drink?"

The gendarme put the flask in his hand, and the outlaw drank the water given him by the man with whom he had just been exchanging rifle shots. Then he requested that his hands might be tied crossed on his breast instead of behind his back.

"I would rather," he said, "lie comfortably."

They gratified his request. Then, at a sign from the adjutant, saying good-bye to Mateo, who vouchsafed no answer, they set off quickly toward the plain.

Ten minutes passed before Mateo opened his mouth. The child looked uneasily, first at his mother, then at his father, who was leaning on his gun and gazing at him with an expression of concentrated fury.

"You begin well," said Mateo at last, in a calm voice, terrifying enough to those who knew the man.

"Father!" cried the boy, with tears in his eyes, coming nearer as if to throw himself at his father's knee.

"Out of my sight!" Mateo shouted.

The child stopped short a few paces away from his father, and sobbed.

Giuseppa approached him. She had just noticed the watch-chain hanging out of his shirt.

"Who gave you that watch?" she asked sternly.

"My cousin, the adjutant."

Falcone snatched the watch and flung it against a stone with such violence that it was shattered into a thousand fragments.

"Woman," he said, "is this a child of mine?"

Giuseppa's brown cheeks flushed brick red.

"What are you saying, Mateo? Do you realise to whom you are speaking?"

"Yes, perfectly well. This child is the first traitor in my family."

Fortunato redoubled his sobs and choking, and Falcone kept watching him like a hawk. At last he struck the ground with the butt of his rifle, then flung it across his shoulder, returned to the path which led toward the *mâquis*, and commanded Fortunato to follow him. The child obeyed.

Giuseppa ran after Mateo and clutched his arm.

"He is your son," she said in a trembling voice, fixing her dark eyes on those of her husband, as if to read all that was passing in his soul.

"Leave me," replied Mateo. "I am his father."

Giuseppa kissed her son and went back weeping into the house. She flung herself on her knees before an image of the Blessed Virgin and prayed fervently. Falcone walked about two hundred paces along the path, and went down a little ravine where he stopped. He tested the ground with the butt of his rifle, and found it soft and easy to dig. The spot seemed suitable for his purpose.

"Fortunato, go over to that big rock."

The boy did as he was told. He knelt down.

"Father, Father, do not kill me!"

"Say your prayers!" shouted Mateo in a terrible voice.

The boy, stammering and sobbing, recited the Our Father and the Apostles' Creed. The father said "Amen!" in a firm voice at the end of each prayer.

"Are those all the prayers you know?"

"I know the Hail Mary, too, and the Litany my aunt taught me, Father."

"It is long, but never mind."

The boy finished the Litany in a stifled voice.

"Have you finished?"

"Oh, Father, forgive me! Forgive me! I'll never do it again. I'll beg my cousin, the magistrate, ever so hard to pardon Gianetto!"

He kept beseeching his father. Mateo loaded his gun and took aim.

"God forgive you!" he said.

The boy made a desperate effort to rise and clasp his father's knees, but he had no time. Mateo fired and Fortunato fell stone-dead.

Without glancing at the body, Mateo returned to the house to fetch a spade with which to dig his son's grave. He had only gone a few steps along the path when he met Giuseppa, running, for she had been alarmed by the rifle shot.

"What have you done?" she cried.

"Justice!"

"Where is he?"

"In the ravine. I am going to bury him. He died a Christian. I shall have a Mass said for him. Send word to my son-in-law, Tiodoro Bianchi, that he is to come and live with us."

(1829)

Nathaniel Hawthorne

THE MINISTER'S
BLACK VEIL

The sexton stood in the porch of Milford meeting-house, pulling busily at the bell-rope. The old people of the village came stooping along the street. Children, with bright faces, tripped merrily beside their parents, or mimicked a graver gait, in the conscious dignity of their Sunday clothes. Spruce bachelors looked sidelong at the pretty maidens, and fancied that the Sabbath sunshine made them prettier than on week days. When the throng had mostly streamed into the porch, the sexton began to toll the bell, keeping his eye on the Reverend Mr. Hooper's door. The first glimpse of the clergyman's figure was the signal for the bell to cease its summons.

"But what has good Parson Hooper got upon his face?" cried the sexton in astonishment.

All within hearing immediately turned about, and beheld the semblance of Mr. Hooper, pacing slowly his meditative way towards the meeting-house. With one accord they started, expressing more wonder than if some strange minister were coming to dust the cushions of Mr. Hooper's pulpit.

"Are you sure it is our parson?" inquired Goodman Gray of the sexton.

"Of a certainty it is good Mr. Hooper," replied the sexton. "He was to have exchanged pulpits with Parson Shute, of Westbury; but Parson Shute sent to excuse himself yesterday, being to preach a funeral sermon."

The cause of so much amazement may appear sufficiently slight. Mr. Hooper, a gentlemanly person, of about thirty, though still a bachelor, was dressed with due clerical neatness, as if a careful wife had starched his band, and brushed the weekly dust from his Sunday's garb. There was but one thing remarkable in his appearance. Swathed about his forehead, and hanging down over his face, so low as to be shaken by his breath, Mr. Hooper had on a black veil. On a nearer view it seemed to consist of two folds of crape, which entirely concealed his features, except the mouth and chin, but probably did not intercept his sight, further than to give a darkened aspect to all living and inanimate things. With this gloomy shade before him, good Mr. Hooper walked onward, at a slow and quiet pace, stooping somewhat, and looking on the ground, as is customary with abstracted men, yet nodding kindly to those of his parishioners who still waited on the meeting-house steps. But so wonder-struck were they that his greeting hardly met with a return.

"I can't really feel as if good Mr. Hooper's face was behind that piece of crape," said the sexton.

"I don't like it," muttered an old woman, as she hobbled into the meeting-house. "He has changed himself into something awful, only by hiding his face."

"Our parson has gone mad!" cried Goodman Gray, following him across the threshold.

A rumor of some unaccountable phenomenon had preceded Mr. Hooper into the meeting-house, and set all the congregation astir. Few could refrain from twisting their heads towards the door; many stood upright, and turned directly about; while several little boys clambered upon the seats, and came down again with a terrible racket. There was a general bustle, a rustling of the women's gowns and shuffling of the men's feet, greatly at variance with that hushed repose which should attend the entrance of the minister. But Mr. Hooper appeared not to notice the perturbation of his people. He entered with an almost noiseless step, bent his head mildly to the pews on each side, and bowed as he passed his oldest parishioner, a white-haired great-grandsire, who occupied an arm-chair in the centre of the aisle. It was strange to observe how slowly this venerable man became conscious of something singular in the appearance of his pastor. He seemed not fully to partake of the prevailing wonder, till Mr. Hooper had ascended the stairs, and showed himself in the pulpit, face to face with his congregation, except for the black veil. That mysterious emblem was never once withdrawn. It shook with his measured breath, as he gave out the psalm; it threw its obscurity between him and the holy page, as he read the Scriptures; and while he prayed, the veil lay heavily on his uplifted countenance. Did he seek to hide it from the dread Being whom he was addressing?

Such was the effect of this simple piece of crape, that more than one woman of delicate nerves was forced to leave the meeting-house. Yet perhaps the pale-faced congregation was almost as fearful a sight to the minister, as his black veil to them.

Mr. Hooper had the reputation of a good preacher, but not an energetic one: he strove to win his people heavenward by mild, persuasive influences, rather than to drive them thither by the thunders of the Word. The sermon which he now delivered was marked by the same characteristics of style and manner as the general series of his pulpit oratory. But there was something, either in the sentiment of the discourse itself, or in the imagination of the auditors, which made it greatly the most powerful effort that they had ever heard from their pastor's lips. It was tinged, rather more darkly than usual, with the gentle gloom of Mr. Hooper's temperament. The subject had reference to secret sin, and those sad mysteries which we hide from our nearest and dearest, and would fain conceal from our own consciousness, even forgetting that the Omniscient can detect them. A subtle power was breathed into his words. Each member of the congregation, the most innocent girl, and the man of hardened breast, felt as if the preacher had crept upon them, behind his awful veil, and discovered their hoarded iniquity of deed or thought. Many spread their clasped hands on their bosoms. There was nothing terrible in what Mr. Hooper said, at least, no violence; and yet, with every tremor of his melancholy voice, the hearers quaked. An unsought pathos came hand in hand with awe. So sensible were the audience of some unwonted attribute in their minister, that they longed for a breath of wind to blow aside the veil, almost believing that a stranger's visage would be discovered, though the form, gesture, and voice were those of Mr. Hooper.

At the close of the services, the people hurried out with indecorous confusion, eager to communicate their pent-up amazement, and conscious of lighter spirits the moment they lost sight of the black veil. Some gathered in little circles, huddled closely together, with their mouths all whispering in the centre; some went homeward alone, wrapt in silent meditation; some talked loudly, and profaned the Sabbath day with ostentatious laughter. A few shook their sagacious heads, intimating that they could penetrate the mystery; while one or two affirmed that there was no mystery at all, but only that Mr. Hooper's eyes were so weakened by the midnight lamp, as to require a shade. After a brief interval, forth came good Mr. Hooper also, in the rear of his flock. Turning his veiled face from one group to another, he paid due reverence to the hoary heads, saluted the middle aged with kind dignity as their friend and spiritual guide, greeted the young with mingled authority and love, and laid his hands on the little children's heads to bless them. Such was always his custom on the Sabbath day. Strange and bewildered looks repaid him for his courtesy. None, as on former occasions, aspired to the honor of walking by their pastor's side. Old Squire Saunders, doubtless by an accidental lapse of memory, neglected to invite Mr. Hooper to his table, where the good clergyman had been wont to bless the food, almost every Sunday since his settlement. He returned, therefore, to the parsonage, and, at the moment of closing the door, was observed to look back upon the people, all of whom had their eyes fixed upon the minister. A sad smile gleamed faintly from beneath the black veil, and flickered about his mouth, glimmering as he disappeared.

"How strange," said a lady, "that a simple black veil, such as any woman might wear on her bonnet, should become such a terrible thing on Mr. Hooper's face!"

"Something must surely be amiss with Mr. Hooper's intellects," observed her husband, the physician of the village. "But the strangest part of the affair is the effect of this vagary, even on a sober-minded man like myself. The black veil, though it covers only our pastor's face, throws its influence over his whole person, and makes him ghostlike from head to foot. Do you not feel it so?"

"Truly do I," replied the lady; "and I would not be alone with him for the world. I wonder he is not afraid to be alone with himself!"

"Men sometimes are so," said her husband.

The afternoon service was attended with similar circumstances. At its conclusion, the bell tolled for the funeral of a young lady. The relatives and friends were assembled in the house, and the more distant acquaintances stood about the door, speaking of the good qualities of the deceased, when their talk was interrupted by the appearance of Mr. Hooper, still covered with his black veil. It was now an appropriate emblem. The clergyman stepped into the room where the corpse was laid, and bent over the coffin, to take a last farewell of his deceased parishioner. As he stooped, the veil hung straight down from his forehead, so that, if her eyelids had not been closed forever, the dead maiden might have seen his face. Could Mr. Hooper be fearful of her glance, that he so hastily caught back the black veil? A person who watched the interview between the dead and living, scrupled not to affirm, that, at the instant when the clergyman's features were disclosed, the corpse had slightly shuddered, rustling the shroud and muslin cap, though the countenance retained the composure of death. A superstitious old woman was the only witness of this prodigy. From the coffin Mr. Hooper passed into the chamber of the mourners, and thence to the head of the staircase, to make the funeral prayer. It was a tender and heart-dissolving prayer, full of sorrow, yet so imbued with celestial hopes, that the music of a heavenly harp, swept by the fingers of the dead, seemed faintly to be heard among the saddest accents of the minister. The people trembled, though they but darkly understood him when he prayed that they, and himself, and all of mortal race, might be ready, as he trusted this young maiden had been, for the dreadful hour that should snatch the veil from their faces. The bearers went heavily forth, and the mourners followed, saddening all the street, with the dead before them, and Mr. Hooper in his black veil behind.

"Why do you look back?" said one in the procession to his partner.

"I had a fancy," replied she, "that the minister and the maiden's spirit were walking hand in hand."

"And so had I, at the same moment," said the other.

That night, the handsomest couple in Milford village were to be joined in wedlock. Though reckoned a melancholy man, Mr. Hooper had a placid cheerfullness for such occasions, which often excited a sympathetic smile where livelier merriment would have been thrown away. There was no quality of his disposition which made him more beloved than this. The company at the wedding awaited his arrival with impatience, trusting that the strange awe, which had gathered over him throughout the day, would now be dispelled. But such was not the result. When Mr. Hooper came, the first thing that their eyes rested on was the same horrible black veil, which had added deeper gloom to the funeral, and could portend nothing but evil to the wedding. Such was its immediate effect on the guests that a cloud seemed to have rolled duskily from beneath the black crape, and dimmed the light of the candles. The bridal pair stood up before the minister. But the bride's cold fingers quivered in the tremulous hand of the bridegroom, and her deathlike paleness caused a whisper that the maiden who had been buried a few hours before was come from her grave to be married. If ever another wedding were so dismal, it was that famous one where they tolled the wedding knell. After performing the ceremony, Mr. Hooper raised a glass of wine to his lips, wishing happiness to the new-married couple in a strain of mild pleasantry that ought to have brightened the features of the guests, like a cheerful gleam from the hearth. At that instant, catching a glimpse of his figure in the looking-glass, the black veil involved his own spirit in the horror with which it overwhelmed all others. His frame shuddered, his lips grew white, he spilt the untasted wine upon the carpet, and rushed forth into the darkness. For the Earth, too, had on her Black Veil.

The next day, the whole village of Milford talked of little else than Parson Hooper's black veil. That, and the mystery concealed behind it, supplied a topic for discussion between acquaintances meeting in the street, and good women gossiping at their open windows. It was the first item of news that the tavern-keeper told to his guests. The children babbled of it on their way to school. One imitative little imp covered his face with an old black handkerchief, thereby so affrighting his playmates that the panic seized himself, and he well-nigh lost his wits by his own waggery.

It was remarkable that of all the busybodies and impertinent people in the parish, not one ventured to put the plain question to Mr. Hooper, wherefore he did this thing. Hitherto, whenever there appeared the slightest call for such interference, he had never lacked advisers, nor shown himself averse to be guided by their judgment. If he erred at all, it was by so painful a degree of self-distrust, that even the mildest censure would lead him to consider an indifferent action as a crime. Yet, though so well acquainted with this amiable weakness, no individual among his parishioners chose to make the black veil a subject of friendly remonstrance. There was a feeling of dread, neither plainly confessed nor carefully concealed, which caused each to shift the responsibility upon another, till at length it was found expedient to send a deputation of the church, in order to deal with Mr. Hooper about the mystery, before it should grow into a scandal. Never did an embassy so ill discharge its duties. The minister received them with friendly courtesy, but became silent, after they were seated, leaving to his visitors the whole burden of introducing their important business. The topic, it might be supposed, was obvious enough. There was the black veil swathed round Mr. Hooper's forehead, and concealing every feature above his placid mouth, on which, at times, they could perceive the glimmering of a melancholy smile. But that piece of crape, to their imagination, seemed to hang down before his heart, the symbol of a fearful secret between him and them. Were the veil but cast aside, they might speak freely of it, but not till then. Thus they sat a considerable time, speechless, confused, and shrinking uneasily from Mr. Hooper's eye, which they felt to be fixed upon them with an invisible glance. Finally, the deputies returned abashed to their constituents, pronouncing the matter too weighty to be handled, except by a council of the churches, if, indeed, it might not require a general synod.

But there was one person in the village unappalled by the awe with which the black veil had impressed all beside herself. When the deputies returned without an explanation, or even venturing to demand one, she, with the calm energy of her character, determined to chase away the strange cloud that appeared to be settling around Mr. Hooper, every moment more darkly than before. As his plighted wife, it should be her privilege to know what the black veil concealed. At the minister's first visit, therefore, she entered upon the subject with a direct simplicity, which made the task easier both for him and her. After he had seated himself, she fixed her eyes steadfastly upon the veil, but could discern nothing of the dreadful gloom that had so overawed the multitude: it was but a double fold of crape, hanging down from his forehead to his mouth, and slightly stirring with his breath.

"No," said she aloud, and smiling, "there is nothing terrible in this piece of crape, except that it hides a face which I am always glad to look upon. Come, good sir, let the sun shine from behind the cloud. First lay aside your black veil: then tell me why you put it on."

Mr. Hooper's smile glimmered faintly.

"There is an hour to come," said he, "when all of us shall cast aside our veils. Take it not amiss, beloved friend, if I wear this piece of crape till then."

"Your words are a mystery, too," returned the young lady. "Take away the veil from them, at least."

"Elizabeth, I will," said he, "so far as my vow may suffer me. Know, then, this veil is a type and a symbol, and I am bound to wear it ever, both in light and darkness, in solitude and before the gaze of multitudes, and as with strangers, so with my familiar friends. No mortal eye will see it withdrawn. This dismal shade must separate me from the world: even you, Elizabeth, can never come behind it!"

"What grievous affliction hath befallen you," she earnestly inquired, "that you should thus darken your eyes forever?"

"If it be a sign of mourning," replied Mr. Hooper, "I, perhaps, like most other mortals, have sorrows dark enough to be typified by a black veil."

"But what if the world will not believe that it is the type of an innocent sorrow?" urged Elizabeth. "Beloved and respected as you are, there may be whispers that you hide your face under the consciousness of secret sin. For the sake of your holy office, do away this scandal!"

The color rose into her cheeks as she intimated the nature of the rumors that were already abroad in the village. But Mr. Hooper's mildness did not forsake him. He even smiled again—that same sad smile, which always appeared like a faint glimmering of light, proceeding from the obscurity beneath the veil.

"If I hide my face for sorrow, there is cause enough," he merely replied; "and if I cover it for secret sin, what mortal might not do the same?"

And with this gentle, but unconquerable obstinacy did he resist all her entreaties. At length Elizabeth sat silent. For a few moments she appeared lost in thought, considering, probably, what new methods might be tried to withdraw her lover from so dark a fantasy, which, if it had no other meaning, was perhaps a symptom of mental disease. Though of a firmer character than his own, the tears rolled down her cheeks. But, in an instant, as it were, a new feeling took the place of sorrow: her eyes were fixed insensibly on the black veil, when, like a sudden twilight in the air, its terrors fell around her. She arose, and stood trembling before him.

"And do you feel it then, at last?" said he mournfully.

She made no reply, but covered her eyes with her hand, and turned to leave the room. He rushed forward and caught her arm.

"Have patience with me, Elizabeth!" cried he, passionately. "Do not desert me, though this veil must be between us here on earth. Be mine, and hereafter there shall be no veil over my face, no darkness between our souls! It is but a mortal veil—it is not for eternity! O! you know not how lonely I am, and how frightened, to be alone behind my black veil. Do not leave me in this miserable obscurity forever!"

"Lift the veil but once, and look me in the face," said she.

"Never! It cannot be!" replied Mr. Hooper.

"Then farewell!" said Elizabeth.

She withdrew her arm from his grasp, and slowly departed, pausing at the door, to give one long shuddering gaze, that seemed almost to penetrate the mystery of the black veil. But, even amid his grief, Mr. Hooper smiled to think that only a material emblem had separated him from happiness, though the horrors, which it shadowed forth, must be drawn darkly between the fondest of lovers.

From that time no attempts were made to remove Mr. Hooper's black veil, or, by a direct appeal, to discover the secret which it was supposed to hide. By persons who claimed a superiority to popular prejudice, it was reckoned merely an eccentric whim, such as often mingles with the sober actions of men otherwise rational, and tinges them all with its own semblance of insanity. But with the multitude, good Mr. Hooper was irreparably a bugbear. He could not walk the street with any peace of mind, so conscious was he that the gentle and timid would turn aside to avoid him, and that others would make it a point of hardihood to throw themselves in his way. The impertinence of the latter class compelled him to give up his customary walk at sunset to the burial ground; for when he leaned pensively over the gate, there would always be faces behind the gravestones, peeping at his black veil. A fable went the rounds that the stare of the dead people drove him thence. It grieved him, to the very depth of his kind heart, to observe how the children fled from his approach, breaking up their merriest sports, while his melancholy figure was yet afar off. Their instinctive dread caused him to feel more strongly than aught else, that a preternatural horror was interwoven with the threads of the black crape. In truth, his own antipathy to the veil was known to be so great, that he never willingly passed before a mirror, nor stooped to drink at a still fountain, lest, in its peaceful bosom, he should be affrighted by himself. This was what gave plausibility to the whispers, that Mr. Hooper's conscience tortured him for some great crime too horrible to be entirely concealed, or otherwise than so obscurely intimated. Thus, from beneath the black veil, there rolled a cloud into the sunshine, an ambiguity of sin or sorrow, which enveloped the poor minister, so that love or sympathy could never reach him. It was said that ghost and fiend consorted with him there. With self-shudderings and outward terrors, he walked continually in its shadow, groping darkly within his own soul, or gazing through a medium that saddened the whole world. Even the lawless wind, it was believed, respected his dreadful secret, and never blew aside the veil. But still good Mr. Hooper sadly smiled at the pale visages of the wordly throng as he passed by.

Among all its bad influences, the black veil had the one desirable effect, of making its wearer a very efficient clergyman. By the aid of his mysterious emblem—for there was no other apparent cause—he became a man of awful power over souls that were in agony for sin. His converts always regarded him with a dread peculiar to themselves, affirming, though but figuratively, that, before he brought them to celestial light, they had been with him behind the black veil. Its gloom, indeed, enabled him to sympathize with all dark affections. Dying sinners cried aloud for Mr. Hooper, and would not yield their breath till he appeared; though ever, as he stooped to whisper consolation, they shuddered at the veiled face so near their own. Such were the terrors of the black veil, even when Death had bared his visage! Strangers came long distances to attend service at his church, with the mere idle purpose of gazing at his figure, because it was forbidden them to behold his face. But many were made to quake ere they departed! Once, during Governor Belcher's administration, Mr. Hooper was appointed to preach the election sermon. Covered with his black veil, he stood before the chief magistrate, the council, and the representatives, and wrought so deep an impression, that the legislative measures of that year were characterized by all the gloom and piety of our earliest ancestral sway.

In this manner, Mr. Hooper spent a long life, irreproachable in outward act, yet shrouded in dismal suspicions; kind and loving, though unloved, and dimly feared; a man apart from men, shunned in their health and joy, but ever summoned to their aid in mortal anguish. As years wore on, shedding their snows above his sable veil, he acquired a name throughout the New England churches, and they called him Father Hooper. Nearly all his parishioners, who were of mature age when he was settled, had been borne away by many a funeral: he had one congregation in the church, and a more crowded one in the churchyard; and having wrought so late into the evening, and done his work so well, it was now good Father Hooper's turn to rest.

Several persons were visible by the shaded candle-light, in the death chamber of the old clergyman. Natural connections he had none. But there was the decorously grave, though unmoved physician, seeking only to mitigate the last pangs of the patient whom he could not save. There were the deacons, and other eminently pious members of his church. There, also, was the Reverend Mr. Clark, of Westbury, a young and zealous divine, who had ridden in haste to pray by the bedside of the expiring minister. There was the nurse, no hired handmaiden of death, but one whose calm affection had endured thus long in secrecy, in solitude, amid the chill of age, and would not perish, even at the dying hour. Who, but Elizabeth! And there lay the hoary head of good Father Hooper upon the death pillow, with the black veil still swathed about his brow, and reaching down over his face, so that each more difficult gasp of his faint breath caused it to stir. All through life that piece of crape had hung between him and the world: it had separated him from cheerful brotherhood and woman's love, and kept him in that saddest of all prisons, his own heart; and still it lay upon his face, as if to deepen the gloom of his darksome chamber, and shade him from the sunshine of eternity.

For some time previous, his mind had been confused, wavering doubtfully between the past and the present, and hovering forward, as it were, at intervals, into the indistinctness of the world to come. There had been feverish turns, which tossed him from side to side, and wore away what little strength he had. But in his most convulsive struggles, and in the wildest vagaries of his intellect, when no other thought retained its sober influence, he still showed an awful solicitude lest the black veil should slip aside. Even if his bewildered soul could have forgotten, there was a faithful woman at his pillow, who, with averted eyes, would have covered that aged face, which she had last beheld in the comeliness of manhood. At length the death-stricken old man lay quietly in the torpor of mental and bodily exhaustion, with an imperceptible pulse, and breath that grew fainter and fainter, except when a long, deep, and irregular inspiration seemed to prelude the flight of his spirit.

The minister of Westbury approached the bedside.

"Venerable Father Hooper," said he, "the moment of your release is at hand. Are you ready for the lifting of the veil that shuts in time from eternity?"

Father Hooper at first replied merely by a feeble motion of his head; then, apprehensive, perhaps, that his meaning might be doubtful, he exerted himself to speak.

"Yea," said he, in faint accents, "my soul hath a patient weariness until that veil be lifted."

"And is it fitting," resumed the Reverend Mr. Clark, "that a man so given to prayer, of such a blameless example, holy in deed and thought, so far as mortal judgment may pronounce; is it fitting that a father in the church should leave a shadow on his memory, that may seem to blacken a life so pure? I pray you, my venerable brother, let not this thing be! Suffer us to be gladdened by your triumphant aspect as you go to your reward. Before the veil of eternity be lifted, let me cast aside this black veil from your face!"

And thus speaking, the Reverend Mr. Clark bent forward to reveal the mystery of so many years. But, exerting a sudden energy, that made all the beholders stand aghast, Father Hooper snatched both his hands from beneath the bedclothes, and pressed them strongly on the black veil, resolute to struggle, if the minister of Westbury would contend with a dying man.

"Never!" cried the veiled clergyman. "On earth, never!"

"Dark old man!" exclaimed the affrighted minister, "with what horrible crime upon your soul are you now passing to the judgment?"

Father Hooper's breath heaved; it rattled in his throat; but, with a mighty effort, grasping forward with his hands, he caught hold of life, and held it back till he should speak. He even raised himself in bed; and there he sat, shivering with the arms of death around him, while the black veil hung down, awful, at that last moment, in the gathered terrors of a lifetime. And yet the faint, sad smile, so often there, now seemed to glimmer from its obscurity, and linger on Father Hooper's lips.

"Why do you tremble at me alone?" cried he, turning his veiled face round the circle of pale spectators. "Tremble also at each other! Have men avoided me, and women shown no pity, and children screamed and fled, only for my black veil? What, but the mystery which it obscurely typifies, has made this piece of crape so awful? When the friend shows his inmost heart to his friend; the lover to his best beloved; when man does not vainly shrink from the eye of his Creator, loathsomely treasuring up the secret of his sin; then deem me a monster, for the symbol beneath which I have lived, and die! I look around me, and, lo! on every visage a Black Veil!"

While his auditors shrank from one another, in mutual affright, Father Hooper fell back upon his pillow, a veiled corpse, with a faint smile lingering on the lips. Still veiled, they laid him in his coffin, and a veiled corpse they bore him to the grave. The grass of many years has sprung up and withered on that grave, the burial stone is moss-grown, and good Mr. Hooper's face is dust; but awful is still the thought that it mouldered beneath the Black Veil! (1836)

Richard Fogle

HAWTHORNE'S "THE MINISTER'S BLACK VEIL"

Hawthorne's characteristic fusion of surface simplicity and underlying complexity is perhaps nowhere more clearly evident than in "The Minister's Black Veil," a brief, highly typical, and thoroughly successful story. It is subtitled "A Parable," and the outer meaning of the parable is abundantly clear. An apparently blameless minister inexplicably dons a black veil and wears it throughout his lifetime, despite many well-meant pleas to cast it off. On his deathbed he reveals its secret and its justification:

> "What, but the mystery which it obscurely typifies, has made this piece of crape so awful? When the friend shows his inmost heart to his friend; the lover to his best beloved; when man does not vainly shrink from the eye of his Creator, loathsomely treasuring up the secret of his sin; then deem me a monster, for the symbol beneath which I have lived, and die! I look around me, and, lo! on every visage a Black Veil!"

The moral is impressive; but as a proposition it is not difficult to grasp, however it may wind and reverberate within the deeps of the imagination. The veil as the visible symbol of secret sin was suggested by Hawthorne's reading in New England history and legend. The veil's solid actuality has the effect of isolating the minister from human society, which unhappy

Reprinted from Richard Harter Fogle, *Hawthorne's Fiction*, copyright 1952, by the University of Oklahoma Press. Reprinted by kind permission of the publisher.

result presumably differs only in degree from the self-isolation of every living soul. The minister is Everyman, bearing his lonely fate in order to demonstrate a tragic truth.

The moral is explicit and orthodox. The explicit statement, however, leads to more than a single possibility. The self-imposed martyrdom of Father Hooper must correspond with some deep necessity of his nature. He who isolates himself in the outward fact must already have performed the deed in spirit. The act of donning the veil has in it something of caprice; it is entirely out of proportion to any obvious necessity or benefit. By it the minister forfeits the affection of his congregation, the chance of human love and marriage, and the sympathy of society in general—and to what end? No note of triumph sounds for him. With remorseless consistency, Hawthorne pursues him even into the grave. "Still veiled, they laid him in his coffin, and a veiled corpse they bore him to the grave. The grass of many years has sprung up and withered on that grave, the burial-stone is moss-grown, and good Mr. Hooper's face is dust; but awful still is the thought that it mouldered beneath the Black Veil!"

One may feel that the veil is less representative of mankind than of the eccentricity of the minister himself, who severs himself from men either through perverse pride or through some other obscure and tragic compulsion. His preoccupation with sin has blunted his perceptions of the normal and the good, which lie as ready to his hand as evil. In rejecting the love of his betrothed, Elizabeth, he casts away a gift of inestimable value in order to satisfy a wild obsession.

If we continue with this reading of the story, we shall take Elizabeth to exemplify the normal and well-ordered human being, as Mr. Hooper represents the abnormal, who has lost the power of seeing life steadily and whole. The "calm energy" of her character, her "direct simplicity," contrast with the "gentle, but unconquerable obstinacy" of the minister, whom her good counsel fails to persuade, and with his infatuated love of mystification. Hawthorne inherited the psychology, but not the theology nor the morality of his Puritan ancestors; and Elizabeth is more likely to represent his ideal than is the gloomy and sin-crazed Hooper.

Which, then, of these two interpretations shall we accept? Both, I believe —they are both in the story. Either presents its difficulties. If we take "The Minister's Black Veil" at its face value as a homily on secret sin, we are confronted with the apparent disproportion between the act and its causes. The minister himself is to outward gaze the gentlest and least sinful of men; and we have no vivid sense of that presence of Evil which would necessitate so heroic an object lesson. But if we wholly accede to the second interpretation, which makes the steady view of life, the *aurea mediocritas*, the highest good, then the tone and emphasis of the story remain to be explained. It is too deeply gloomy and intense to harmonize fully with such a moral, which should demand a certain dry sparkle and lightness.

This ambivalence of meaning is realized in ambiguity, which occurs with unusual frequency in "The Minister's Black Veil." Here its most marked effect is to maintain a balance between subjective and objective in the portrait of the minister, to invite us inside his character while excluding us from any final certainty about it, and, of course, to preserve the objectivity of the narrator, who simultaneously offers and reserves his judgment. Thus, for example, we do not quite know what Mr. Hooper saw through the veil, "which entirely concealed his features, except the mouth and chin, but *probably* did not intercept his sight, further than to give a darkened aspect to all living and inanimate things." The word "probably" bars us from certainty on the point. Again, as the minister preaches for the first time from beneath the veil, it "lay heavily on his uplifted countenance. Did he seek to hide it from the dread Being whom he was addressing?" Hawthorne proposes the question, but does not answer it.

Pressed by Elizabeth to expound the meaning of the veil, Mr. Hooper will reply only darkly. " 'If it be sign of mourning,' " says he, " 'I, perhaps, like most other mortals, have sorrows dark enough to be typified by a black veil.' " When she further relates the scandalous whispers in the village that he hides his face from consciousness of secret sin, he will not deny the imputation. " 'If I hide my face for sorrow, there is cause enough,' " he merely replies; " 'and if I cover it for secret sin, what mortal might not do the same?' " Hawthorne holds out the suggestion that the veil is a penance for an actual and serious crime, while at the same time permitting no real grounds for it. The vulgar interpret the meaning vulgarly, the complacent complacently, and men of good will regretfully. The calm good sense of Elizabeth forces her to regard the veil as the emblem of a tragic but unbased obsession. She believes at first that " 'there is nothing terrible in this piece of crape' " but at length yields to its influence, not from a dread of the veil itself, but of what the veil tells her of her lover's state of mind.

The mystery of the veil is hidden to the end among these artfully contrived ambiguities. As Elizabeth leaves him, "Mr. Hooper smiled to think that only a material emblem had separated him from happiness, though the horrors, which it shadowed forth, must be drawn darkly between the fondest of lovers." It is confusing to have the symbol detached from its meaning in this fashion; and the passage calls up another consideration. If the veil alone has separated the minister from happiness, what are we to do with "the horrors, which it shadowed forth?" Surely it is they which shut him off from earthly good. The effect is at once to assert and to cast doubt on the reality of what the veil portrays but also hides. And the smile itself, shining dimly from beneath the black cloth, emphasizes in its self-irony the ambiguity of the minister's character.

The veil has varying effects on different minds and different levels of society. To those who claimed a superiority to popular prejudice, it is merely "an eccentric whim." In the multitude it occasions either impertinence or superstitious dread, reactions equally grievous to its unhappy wearer. It is whispered that the veil is the obscure intimation of a horrible crime; and there are hints of supernatural forces:

Thus, from beneath the black veil, there rolled a cloud into the sunshine, *an ambiguity of sin or sorrow*, which enveloped the poor minister, so that love or sympathy could never reach him. *It was said* that ghost and fiend consorted with him there. With self-shudderings and outward terrors, he walked continually in its shadow, groping darkly within his own soul, or gazing through a medium that saddened the whole world. Even the lawless wind, *it was believed*, respected his dreadful secret, and never blew aside the veil. But still good Mr. Hooper sadly smiled at the pale visages of the worldly throng as he passed by.

In one respect, however, the veil makes Mr. Hooper a more efficient clergyman, for it allows him to "sympathize with all dark affections." His words are imbued with its gloomy power, and he can bring sinners to the light denied to him. Yet here as well the effects of the veil are ambiguous. His converts regard the minister with dread, not with love or joy, even though they owe their redemption to him. "Dying sinners cried aloud for Mr. Hooper, and would not yield their breath till he appeared; though ever, as he stooped to whisper consolation, they shuddered at the veiled face so near their own." Hawthorne summarizes the twofold influence of the veil in a climactic ambiguity which embodies its dualism in a series of antitheses: "In this manner Mr. Hooper spent a long life, irreproachable in outward act, yet shrouded in dismal suspicions; kind and loving, though unloved, and dimly feared; a man apart from men, shunned in their health and joy, but ever summoned to their aid in mortal anguish."

This dubiety persists in the final scene at the deathbed, despite the explicit pronouncement with which the scene ends. As the minister lies dying, the veil still rests upon his face, stirred slightly by his faint breath. "All through life that piece of crape had hung between him and the world; it had separated him from cheerful brotherhood and woman's love, and kept him in that saddest of all prisons, his own heart; and still it lay upon his face, as if to deepen the gloom of his darksome chamber, and shade him from the sunshine of eternity." If, however, the veil is emblematic of the common plight of man, why should it isolate its wearer with a poignancy unfelt by other men and leave him lonely and alone? We have no sense in the story that all men feel as does Mr. Hooper; they are portrayed, in fact, as a cohesive band, united if only in dread of the fearful veil. Even the minister's colleague, praying by his bedside, rather cruelly misunderstands its significance. Or, on the other hand, is it possible that we can go further afield and determine that the message of the veil *is* representative and universal: that the failure to recognize it is simply the last and most chilling proof of man's imprisonment within himself? If this latter interpretation is the true one, we must conclude that Hawthorne's emphasis upon the problem as embodied in Mr. Hooper has made it impossible for him to deal with it in other characters. To achieve unity of composition his canvas can contain only one important figure. In order to present the tragic isolation of one man, Hawthorne is obliged to consider society as a solid group arrayed against his hero, ignoring for the time being the fact that this hero is Everyman.

We conclude, then, without arriving at a clear decision about the meaning of the tale, but with a sense of depths unplumbed, of rich potentialities not fully realized. The discrepancies between the two interpretations which have been outlined here must go unreconciled. Their mutual presence can, I think, be satisfactorily explained in two ways—one psychological, and one esthetic —separable, and yet closely related. In the first place, these discrepancies represent the faculties of Hawthorne's own psychology, the heart and the head. His heart, his imagination, the inherited bent of his Puritan ancestry—all his instincts, in short—bind him in sympathy with the possessed minister, who broods over the vague and bottomless abyss of Evil. But his head, his intellect, is with the calm and steady-minded Elizabeth, who is unable to look upon the minister's vow as other than a sad but groundless whim. The ancestral Hawthorne stands beside the nineteenth-century Hawthorne in "The Minister's Black Veil," and their voices do not wholly harmonize.

Second, Hawthorne does not force a reconciliation which he has not, in Keats's words, "proved upon his pulses." Having chosen the symbol of the black veil and invented an action for it, he refrains from pushing the reader to a single conclusion. The minister himself believes the veil to be an emblem of the secret sin that poisons the souls of all mankind, but we are not compelled to accept his reading of the matter. We may, if we like, consider it rather a veil upon his understanding, whose gloomy shade conceals from the eyes behind it as much as it discloses. As it casts its shadow over the bright and various colors of the material world—colors distinct to every unhandicapped observer —so does it darken the vision of the spiritual eye.

The imagination, however, playing freely over the theme, will not content itself to remain within the limits of any single meaning. Beneath the explicit statement, the clear and simple outline of the tale, lie the irony of the minister's smile and the ambiguity of almost every incident. In "The Minister's Black Veil" the moral constitutes the framework; but it is merely an element of the completed structure.

Edgar Allan Poe

THE CASK OF AMONTILLADO

The thousand injuries of Fortunato I had borne as I best could; but when he ventured upon insult, I vowed revenge. You, who so well know the nature of my soul, will not suppose, however, that I gave utterance to a threat. *At length* I would be avenged; this was a point definitively settled; but the very definitiveness with which it was resolved precluded the idea of risk. I must not only punish, but punish with impunity. A wrong is unredressed when retribution overtakes its redresser. It is equally unredressed when the avenger fails to make himself felt as such to him who has done the wrong.

It must be understood that neither by word nor deed had I given Fortunato cause to doubt my good-will. I continued, as was my wont, to smile in his face, and he did not perceive that my smile *now* was at the thought of his immolation.

He had a weak point, this Fortunato, although in other regards he was a man to be respected and even feared. He prided himself on his connoisseurship in wine. Few Italians have the true virtuoso spirit. For the most part their enthusiasm is adopted to suit the time and opportunity, to practice imposture upon the British and Austrian millionaires. In painting and gemmary Fortunato, like his countrymen, was a quack; but in the matter of old wines he was sincere. In this respect I did not differ from him materially: I was skillful in the Italian vintages myself, and bought largely whenever I could.

It was about dusk one evening, during the supreme madness of the carnival season, that I encountered my friend. He accosted me with excessive warmth, for he had been drinking much. The man wore motley. He had on a tight-fitting parti-striped dress, and his head was surmounted by the conical cap and bells. I was so pleased to see him that I thought I should never have done wringing his hand.

I said to him: "My dear Fortunato, you are luckily met. How remarkably well you are looking to-day! But I have received a pipe of what passes for Amontillado, and I have my doubts."

"How?" said he. "Amontillado? A pipe? Impossible! And in the middle of the carnival!"

"I have my doubts," I replied; "and I was silly enough to pay the full Amontillado price without consulting you in the matter. You were not to be found, and I was fearful of losing a bargain."

"Amontillado!"

"I have my doubts."

"Amontillado!"

"And I must satisfy them."

"Amontillado!"

"As you are engaged, I am on my way to Luchesi. If any one has a critical turn, it is he. He will tell me—"

"Luchesi cannot tell Amontillado from sherry."

"And yet some fools will have it that his taste is a match for your own."

"Come, let us go."

"Whither?"

"To your vaults."

"My friend, no; I will not impose upon your good-nature. I perceive you have an engagement. Luchesi—"

"I have no engagement; come."

"My friend, no. It is not the engagement, but the severe cold with which I perceive you are afflicted. The vaults are insufferably damp. They are incrusted with niter."

"Let us go, nevertheless. The cold is merely nothing. Amontillado! You have been imposed upon. And as for Luchesi, he cannot distinguish sherry from Amontillado."

Thus speaking, Fortunato possessed himself of my arm. Putting on a mask of black silk, and drawing a *roquelaure* closely about my person, I suffered him to hurry me to my palazzo.

There were no attendants at home; they had absconded to make merry in honor of the time. I had told them that I should not return until the morning, and had given them explicit orders not to stir from the house. These orders were sufficient, I well knew, to insure their immediate disappearance, one and all, as soon as my back was turned.

I took from their sconces two flambeaux, and, giving one to Fortunato, bowed him through several suites of rooms to the archway that led into the vaults. I passed down a long and winding staircase, requesting him to be cautious as he followed. We came at length to the foot of the descent, and stood together on the damp ground of the catacombs of the Montresors.

The gait of my friend was unsteady, and the bells upon his cap jingled as he strode.

"The pipe?" said he.

"It is farther on," said I; "but observe the white webwork which gleams from these cavern walls."

He turned towards me, and looked into my eyes with two filmy orbs that distilled the rheum of intoxication.

"Niter?" he asked at length.

"Niter," I replied. "How long have you had that cough?"

"Ugh! ugh! ugh!—ugh! ugh! ugh!—ugh! ugh! ugh!—ugh! ugh! ugh!— ugh! ugh! ugh!"

My poor friend found it impossible to reply for many minutes.

"It is nothing," he said, at last.

"Come," I said, with decision, "we will go back; your health is precious. You are rich, respected, admired, beloved; you are happy, as once I was. You are a man to be missed. For me it is no matter. We will go back; you will be ill, and I cannot be responsible. Besides, there is Luchesi—"

"Enough," he said; "the cough is a mere nothing; it will not kill me. I shall not die of a cough."

"True—true," I replied; "and, indeed, I had no intention of alarming you unnecessarily; but you should use all proper caution. A draught of this Medoc will defend us from the damps."

Here I knocked off the neck of a bottle which I drew from a long row of its fellows that lay upon the mold.

"Drink," I said, presenting him the wine.

He raised it to his lips with a leer. He paused and nodded to me familiarly, while his bells jingled.

"I drink," he said, "to the buried that repose around us."

"And I to your long life."

He again took my arm and we proceeded.

"These vaults," he said, "are extensive."

"The Montresors," I replied, "were a great and numerous family."

"I forget your arms."

"A huge human foot d'or, in a field azure; the foot crushes a serpent rampant whose fangs are imbedded in the heel."

"And the motto?"

"Nemo me impune lacessit."[1]

"Good!" he said.

The wine sparkled in his eyes and the bells jingled. My own fancy grew warm with the Medoc. We had passed through walls of piled bones, with casks and puncheons intermingling, into the inmost recesses of the catacombs. I paused again, and this time I made bold to seize Fortunato by an arm above the elbow.

"The niter!" I said; "see, it increases. It hangs like moss upon the vaults. We are below the river's bed. The drops of moisture trickle among the bones. Come, we will go back ere it is too late. Your cough—"

"It is nothing," he said; "let us go on. But first, another draught of the Medoc."

I broke and reached him a flagon of De Grâve. He emptied it at a breath. His eyes flashed with a fierce light. He laughed and threw the bottle upward with a gesticulation I did not understand.

I looked at him in surprise. He repeated the movement—a grotesque one.

"You do not comprehend?" he said.

"Not I," I replied.

"Then you are not of the brotherhood."

"How?"

"You are not of the masons."

"Yes, yes," I said; "yes, yes."

"You? Impossible! A mason?"

"A mason," I replied.

"A sign," he said.

"It is this," I answered, producing a trowel from beneath the folds of my *roquelaure*.

"You jest!" he exclaimed, recoiling a few paces. "But let us proceed to the Amontillado."

"Be it so," I said, replacing the tool beneath the cloak, and again offering him my arm. He leaned upon it heavily. We continued our route in search of the

1. No one injures me with impunity.

Amontillado. We passed through a range of low arches, descended, passed on, and, descending again, arrived at a deep crypt, in which the foulness of the air caused our flambeaux rather to glow than flame.

At the most remote end of the crypt there appeared another less spacious. Its walls had been lined with human remains, piled to the vault overhead, in the fashion of the great catacombs of Paris. Three sides of this interior crypt were still ornamented in this manner. From the fourth the bones had been thrown down, and lay promiscuously upon the earth, forming at one point a mound of some size. Within the wall thus exposed by the displacing of the bones we perceived a still interior recess, in depth about four feet, in width three, in height six or seven. It seemed to have been constructed for no especial use within itself, but formed merely the interval between two of the colossal supports of the roof of the catacombs, and was backed by one of their circumscribing walls of solid granite.

It was in vain that Fortunato, uplifting his dull torch, endeavored to pry into the depth of the recess. Its termination the feeble light did not enable us to see.

"Proceed," I said; "herein is the Amontillado. As for Luchesi—"

"He is an ignoramus," interrupted my friend, as he stepped unsteadily forward, while I followed immediately at his heels. In an instant he had reached the extremity of the niche, and, finding his progress arrested by the rock, stood stupidly bewildered. A moment more and I had fettered him to the granite. In its surface were two iron staples, distant from each other about two feet, horizontally. From one of these depended a short chain, from the other a padlock. Throwing the links about his waist, it was but the work of a few seconds to secure it. He was too much astounded to resist. Withdrawing the key, I stepped back from the recess.

"Pass your hand," I said, "over the wall; you cannot help feeling the niter. Indeed it is *very* damp. Once more let me *implore* you to return. No? Then I must positively leave you. But I must first render you all the little attentions in my power."

"The Amontillado!" ejaculated my friend, not yet recovered from his astonishment.

"True," I replied: "the Amontillado."

As I said these words I busied myself among the pile of bones of which I have before spoken. Throwing them aside, I soon uncovered a quantity of building stone and mortar. With these materials and with the aid of my trowel, I began vigorously to wall up the entrance of the niche.

I had scarcely laid the first tier of the masonry when I discovered that the intoxication of Fortunato had in a great measure worn off. The earliest indication I had of this was a low, moaning cry from the depth of the recess. It was *not* the cry of a drunken man. There was then a long and obstinate silence. I laid the second tier, and the third, and the fourth; and then I heard the furious vibrations of the chain. The noise lasted for several minutes, during which, that I might harken to it with the more satisfaction, I ceased my labors and sat down upon the bones. When at last the clanking subsided, I resumed the trowel, and finished without interruption the fifth, the sixth, and the seventh tier. The wall was now nearly upon a level with my breast. I again paused, and, holding the flambeaux over the masonwork, threw a few feeble rays upon the figure within.

A succession of loud and shrill screams, bursting suddenly from the throat of the chained form, seemed to thrust me violently back. For a brief moment I hesitated, I trembled. Unsheathing my rapier, I began to grope with it about the recess; but the thought of an instant reassured me. I placed my hand upon the solid fabric of the catacombs and felt satisfied. I reapproached the wall. I replied to the yells of him who clamored. I re-echoed, I aided, I surpassed them in volume and in strength. I did this, and the clamorer grew still.

It was now midnight, and my task was drawing to a close. I had completed the eighth, the ninth, and the tenth tier. I had finished a portion of the last and the eleventh; there remained but a single stone to be fitted and plastered in. I struggled with its weight; I placed it partially in its destined position. But now there came from out the niche a low laugh that erected the hairs upon my head. It was succeeded by a sad voice, which I had difficulty in recognizing as that of the noble Fortunato. The voice said:

"Ha! ha! ha!—he! he!—a very good joke indeed, an excellent jest. We will have many a rich laugh about it at the palazzo—he! he! he!—over our wine—he! he! he!"

"The Amontillado!" I said.

"He! he! he!—he! he! he!—yes, the Amontillado. But is it not getting late? Will not they be awaiting us at the palazzo,—the Lady Fortunato and the rest? Let us be gone."

"Yes," I said, "let us be gone."

"For the love of God, Montresor!"

"Yes," I said, "for the love of God!"

But to these words I harkened in vain for a reply. I grew impatient. I called aloud:

"Fortunato!"

No answer. I called again.

"Fortunato!"

No answer still. I thrust a torch through the remaining aperture and let it fall within. There came forth in return only a jingling of the bells. My heart grew sick—on account of the dampness of the catacombs. I hastened to make an end of my labor. I forced the last stone into its position; I plastered it up. Against the new masonry I re-erected the old rampart of bones. For the half of a century no mortal has disturbed them. *In pace requiescat!*[1]   (1846)

1. May he rest in peace.

Alphonse Daudet

THE DEATH
OF THE DAUPHIN

The little Dauphin is ill—the Dauphin is going to die. In all the churches the Host is elevated and tall candles burn for the recovery of the royal child. The streets of the ancient residence are sad and silent, the bells are mute, citizens peer curiously through the palace gratings, porters talk in solemn tones in the courts.

All the palace is astir. Chamberlains and majordomos hurry up and down the marble steps; the galleries are thronged with pages; courtiers in silken robes pass from group to group, asking the news in smothered accents. On the broad stairways weeping maids of honor bow low, and wipe their eyes with beautiful embroidered kerchiefs.

An assemblage of robed doctors gathers in the orangery. Through the glasses they can be seen waving their long black sleeves and inclining doctorally their perukes. Before the door walk the tutor and riding-master of the little Dauphin. They are waiting for decisions of the faculty. The riding-master swears like a trooper, the tutor quotes Horace. From the stable comes a long, plaintive neigh. It is the little Dauphin's chestnut, who, forgotten by the grooms, calls sadly from his empty crib.

And the king—where is the king? Shut up all alone at the farther end of the palace. Kings must not be seen to weep. Not so, however, the queen. Seated by the Dauphin's side, her lovely face all bathed in tears, she sobs before us all like the veriest serving-woman.

In his lace bed lies the little Dauphin. He is whiter than the pillow upon which his head reclines. They believe that he is asleep; but no, he is not asleep. The little Dauphin turns to his mother. "Madame the queen, why do you weep? Do you believe, like the rest, that I am going to die?" The queen tries to answer; sobs choke her utterance.

"Do not weep, madame the queen. You forget that I am the Dauphin; Dauphins do not die thus." The queen sobs more piteously. The little Dauphin is frightened. "Halloo!" exclaims he, "I do not want to die! Order instantly forty stout lansquenets to keep guard around our bed. Set a hundred large guns to watch night and day before our windows. And woe to Death should he dare approach us!"

To humor the royal child the queen makes a sign. In a twinkling, cannon are heard rolling in the court; forty stout lansquenets with their partisans range themselves around the room. They are old troopers and their mustaches are gray.

The Dauphin recognizes one. "Lorrain!" he cries. The old soldier draws closer. "Let me look at your big sword. If Death comes for me you will kill him, will you not?" "Yes, monseigneur." And two big tears roll down his tanned cheeks.

The priest approaches the Dauphin. He speaks long in subdued tones and holds up the crucifix. The Dauphin shows surprise. Suddenly he interrupts him. "I see what you mean, monsieur the abbé; but would not my little friend Beppo die in my place if we pay him plenty of money?" The priest continues to speak. The Dauphin looks more and more surprised. When the priest ceases, he says, with a sigh, "All that is very sad, monsieur the abbé, but there is one comfort for me. When I get to the paradise of the stars I shall still be the Dauphin. The good God is my cousin, and will treat me according to my rank."

Then he turned to his mother, and said, "Let them bring my best clothes— the ermine doublet and velvet pumps. I want to make myself smart for the angels, and enter paradise dressed like the Dauphin." Again the priest bends over the Dauphin, and speaks to him in low tones. In the midst of the discourse the royal child interrupts him angrily: "What! it is nothing, then, to be a Dauphin, after all!" and refusing to hear more, he turns his head to the wall and weeps bitterly. (1869)

Robert Louis Stevenson

MARKHEIM

"Yes," said the dealer, "our windfalls are of various kinds. Some customers are ignorant, and then I touch a dividend on my superior knowledge. Some are dishonest," and here he held up the candle, so that the light fell strongly on his visitor, "and in that case," he continued, "I profit by my virtue."

Markheim had but just entered from the daylight streets, and his eyes had not yet grown familiar with the mingled shine and darkness in the shop. At these pointed words, and before the near presence of the flame, he blinked painfully and looked aside.

The dealer chuckled, "You come to me on Christmas-day," he resumed, "when you know that I am alone in my house, put up my shutters, and make a point of refusing business. Well, you will have to pay for that; you will have to pay for my loss of time, when I should be balancing my books; you will have to pay, besides, for a kind of manner that I remark in you to-day very strongly. I am the essence of discretion, and ask no awkward questions; but when a customer can not look me in the eye, he has to pay for it." The dealer once more chuckled; and then, changing to his usual business voice, though still with a note of irony, "You can give, as usual, a clean account of how you came into the possession of the object?" he continued. "Still your uncle's cabinet? A remarkable collector, sir!"

And the little, pale, round-shouldered dealer stood almost on tip-toe, looking over the top of his gold spectacles, and nodding his head with every mark of disbelief. Markheim returned his gaze with one of infinite pity, and a touch of horror.

"This time," said he, "you are in error. I have not come to sell, but to buy. I have no curios to dispose of; my uncle's cabinet is bare to the wainscot; even were it still intact, I have done well on the Stock Exchange, and should more likely add to it than otherwise, and my errand to-day is simplicity itself. I seek a Christmas-present for a lady," he continued, waxing more fluent as he struck into the speech he had prepared; "and certainly I owe you every excuse for thus disturbing you upon so small a matter. But the thing was neglected yester-day; I must produce my little compliment at dinner; and, as you very well know, a rich marriage is not a thing to be neglected."

There followed a pause, during which the dealer seemed to weigh this state-ment incredulously. The ticking of many clocks among the curious lumber of the shop, and the faint rushing of the cabs in a near thoroughfare, filled up the interval of silence.

"Well, sir," said the dealer, "be it so. You are an old customer after all; and if, as you say, you have the chance of a good marriage, far be it from me to be an obstacle. Here is a nice thing for a lady now," he went on, "this hand-glass—fifteenth century, warranted; comes from a good collection, too; but I reserve the name, in the interests of my customer, who was just like yourself, my dear sir, the nephew and sole heir of a remarkable collector."

The dealer, while he thus ran on in his dry and biting voice, had stooped to take the object from its place; and, as he had done so, a shock had passed through Markheim, a start both of hand and foot, a sudden leap of many tumultuous passions to the face. It passed as swiftly as it came, and left no trace beyond a certain trembling of the hand that now received the glass.

"A glass," he said, hoarsely, and then paused, and repeated it more clearly. "A glass? For Christmas? Surely not?"

"And why not?" cried the dealer. "Why not a glass?"

Markheim was looking upon him with an indefinable expression. "You ask me why not?" he said. "Why, look here—look in it—look at yourself! Do you like to see it? No! nor I—nor any man."

The little man had jumped back when Markheim had so suddenly confronted him with the mirror; but now, perceiving there was nothing worse on hand, he chuckled. "Your future lady, sir, must be pretty hard favored," said he.

"I ask you," said Markheim, "for a Christmas-present, and you give me this—this damned reminder of years, and sins and follies—this hand-conscience! Did you mean it? Had you a thought in your mind? Tell me. It will be better for you if you do. Come, tell me about yourself. I hazard a guess now, that you are in secret a very charitable man?"

The dealer looked closely at his companion. It was very odd, Markheim did not appear to be laughing; there was something in his face like an eager sparkle of hope, but nothing of mirth.

"What are you driving at?" the dealer asked.

"Not charitable?" returned the other, gloomily. "Not charitable; not pious; not scrupulous; unloving, unbeloved; a hand to get money, a safe to keep it. Is that all? Dear God, man, is that all?"

"I will tell you what it is," began the dealer, with some sharpness, and then broke off again into a chuckle. "But I see this is a love match of yours, and you have been drinking the lady's health."

"Ah!" cried Markheim, with a strange curiosity. "Ah, have you been in love? Tell me about that."

"I," cried the dealer. "I in love! I never had the time, nor have I the time to-day for all this nonsense. Will you take the glass?"

"Where is the hurry?" returned Markheim. "It is very pleasant to stand here talking; and life is so short and insecure that I would not hurry away from any pleasure—no, not even from so mild a one as this. We should rather cling, cling to what little we can get, like a man at a cliff's edge. Every second is a cliff, if you think upon it—a cliff a mile high—high enough, if we fall, to dash us out of every feature of humanity. Hence it is best to talk pleasantly. Let us talk of each other; why should we wear this mask? Let us be confidential. Who knows, we might become friends?"

"I have just one word to say to you," said the dealer. "Either make your purchase, or walk out of my shop."

"True, true," said Markheim. "Enough fooling. To business. Show me something else."

The dealer stooped once more, this time to replace the glass upon the shelf, his thin blonde hair falling over his eyes as he did so. Markheim moved a little nearer, with one hand in the pocket of his great-coat; he drew himself up and filled his lungs; at the same time many different emotions were depicted together on his face—terror, horror, and resolve, fascination and a physical repulsion; and through a haggard lift of his upper lip, his teeth looked out.

"This, perhaps, may suit," observed the dealer; and then, as he began to re-arise, Markheim bounded from behind upon his victim. The long, skewer-like dagger flashed and fell. The dealer struggled like a hen, striking his temple on the shelf, and then tumbled on the floor in a heap.

Time had some score of small voices in that shop, some stately and slow as was becoming to their great age; others garrulous and hurried. All these told out the seconds in an intricate chorus of tickings. Then the passage of a lad's feet, heavily running on the pavement, broke in upon these smaller voices and startled Markheim into the consciousness of his surroundings. He looked about him awfully. The candle stood on the counter, its flame solemnly wagging in a draught; and by that inconsiderable movement, the whole room was filled with noiseless bustle and kept heaving like a sea: the tall shadows nodding, the gross blots of darkness swelling and dwindling as with respiration, the faces of the portraits and the china gods changing and wavering like images in water. The inner door stood ajar, and peered into that league of shadows with a long slit of daylight like a pointing finger.

From those fear stricken rovings, Markheim's eyes returned to the body of his victim, where it lay both humped and sprawling, incredibly small and strangely meaner than in life. In these poor, miserly clothes, in that ungainly attitude, the dealer lay like so much sawdust. Markheim had feared to see it, and, lo! it was nothing. And yet, as he gazed, this bundle of old clothes and pool of blood began to find eloquent voices. There it must lie; there was none to work the cunning hinges or direct the miracle of locomotion—there it must lie till it was found. Found! ay, and then? Then would this dead flesh lift up a cry that would ring over England, and fill the world with the echoes of pursuit. Ay, dead or not, this was still the enemy. "Time was that when the brains were out," he thought; and the first word struck into his mind. Time, now that the deed was accomplished—time, which had closed for the victim, had become instant and momentous for the slayer.

The thought was yet in his mind, when, first one and then another, with every variety of pace and voice—one deep as the bell from a cathedral turret, another ringing on its treble notes the prelude of a waltz—the clocks began to strike the hour of three in the afternoon.

The sudden outbreak of so many tongues in that dumb chamber staggered him. He began to bestir himself, going to and fro with the candle, beleaguered by moving shadows, and startled to the soul by chance reflections. In many rich mirrors, some of home designs, some from Venice or Amsterdam, he saw his face repeated and repeated, as it were an army of spies; his own eyes met and detected him; and the sound of his own steps, lightly as they fell, vexed the surrounding quiet. And still as he continued to fill his pockets, his mind accused him, with a sickening iteration, of the thousand faults of his design. He should have chosen a more quiet hour; he should have prepared an alibi; he should not have used a knife; he should have been more cautious, and only bound and gagged the dealer, and not killed him; he should have been more bold, and killed the servant also; he should have done all things otherwise; poignant regrets, weary, incessant toiling of the mind to change what was unchangeable, to plan what was now useless, to be the architect of the irrevocable past. Meanwhile, and behind all this activity, brute terrors, like scurrying of rats in a deserted attic, filled the more remote chambers of his brain with riot; the hand of the constable would fall heavy on his shoulder, and his nerves would jerk like a hooked fish; or he beheld, in galloping defile, the dock, the prison, the gallows, and the black coffin.

Terror of the people in the street sat down before his mind like a besieging army. It was impossible, he thought, but that some rumor of the struggle must have reached their ears and set on edge their curiosity; and now, in all the neighboring houses, he divined them sitting motionless and with uplifted ear— solitary people, condemned to spend Christmas dwelling alone on memories of the past, and now startlingly recalled from that tender exercise; happy family parties, struck into silence round the table, the mother still with raised finger: every degree and age and humor, but all, by their own hearths, prying and hearkening and weaving the rope that was to hang him. Sometimes it seemed to him he could not move too softly; the clink of the tall Bohemian goblets rang out loudly like a bell; and alarmed by the bigness of the ticking, he was tempted to stop the clocks. And then, again, with a swift transition of his terrors, the very silence of the place appeared a source of peril, and a thing to strike and freeze the passer-by; and he would step more boldly, and bustle aloud among the contents of the shop, and imitate, with elaborate bravado, the movements of a busy man at ease in his own house.

But he was now so pulled about by different alarms that, while one portion of his mind was still alert and cunning, another trembled on the brink of lunacy. One hallucination in particular took a strong hold on his credulity. The neighbor hearkening with white face beside his window, the passer-by arrested by a horrible surmise on the pavement—these could at worst suspect, they could not know; through the brick walls and shuttered windows only sounds could penetrate. But here, within the house, was he alone? He knew he was; he had watched the servant set forth sweethearting, in her poor best, "out for the day" written in every ribbon and smile. Yes, he was alone, of course; and yet, in the bulk of empty house above him, he could surely hear a stir of delicate footing—he was surely conscious, inexplicably conscious of some presence. Ay, surely; to every room and corner of the house his imagination followed it; and now it was a faceless thing, and yet had eyes to see with; and again it was a shadow of himself; and yet again behold the image of the dead dealer, reinspired with cunning and hatred.

At times, with a strong effort, he would glance at the open door which still seemed to repel his eyes. The house was tall, the skylight small and dirty, the day blind with fog; and the light that filtered down to the ground story was exceedingly faint, and showed dimly on the threshold of the shop. And yet, in that strip of doubtful brightness, did there not hang wavering a shadow?

Suddenly, from the street outside, a very jovial gentleman began to beat with a staff on the shop-door, accompanying his blows with shouts and railleries in which the dealer was continually called upon by name. Markheim, smitten into ice, glanced at the dead man. But no! he lay quite still; he was fled away far beyond earshot of these blows and shoutings; he was sunk beneath seas of silence; and his name, which would once have caught his notice above the howling of a storm, had become an empty sound. And presently the jovial gentleman desisted from his knocking and departed.

Here was a broad hint to hurry what remained to be done, to get forth from this accusing neighborhood, to plunge into a bath of London multitudes, and to reach, on the other side of day, that haven of safety and apparent innocence—his bed. One visitor had come: at any moment another might follow and be more obstinate. To have done the deed, and yet not to reap the profit, would be too abhorrent a failure. The money, that was now Markheim's concern; and as a means to that, the keys.

He glanced over his shoulder at the open door, where the shadow was still lingering and shivering; and with no conscious repugnance of the mind, yet with a tremor of the belly, he drew near the body of his victim. The human character had quite departed. Like a suit half-stuffed with bran, the limbs lay scattered, the trunk doubled, on the floor; and yet the thing repelled him. Although so dingy and inconsiderable to the eye, he feared it might have more significance to the touch. He took the body by the shoulders, and turned it on its back. It was strangely light and supple, and the limbs, as if they had been broken, fell into the oddest postures. The face was robbed of all expression; but it was as pale as wax, and shockingly smeared with blood about one temple. That was, for Markheim, the one displeasing circumstance. It carried him back, upon the instant, to a certain fair day in a fisher's village: a gray day, a piping wind, a crowd upon the street, the blare of brasses, the booming of drums, the nasal voice of a ballad singer; and a boy going to and fro, buried over head in the crowd and divided between interest and fear, until, coming out upon the chief place of concourse, he beheld a booth and a great screen with pictures, dismally designed, garishly colored: Brownrigg with her apprentice; the Mannings with their murdered guest; Weare in the death-grip of Thurtell; and a score besides of famous crimes. The thing was as clear as an illusion; he was once again that little boy; he was looking once again, and with the same sense of physical revolt, at these vile pictures; he was still stunned by the thumping of the drums. A bar of that day's music returned upon his memory; and at that, for the first time, a qualm came over him, a breath of nausea, a sudden weakness of the joints, which he must instantly resist and conquer.

He judged it more prudent to confront than to flee from these considerations; looking the more hardily in the dead face, bending his mind to realize the nature and greatness of his crime. So little awhile ago that face had moved with every change of sentiment, that pale mouth had spoken, that body had been all on fire with governable energies; and now, and by his act, that piece of life had been arrested, as the horologist, with interjected finger, arrests the beating of the clock. So he reasoned in vain; he could rise to no more remorseful consciousness; the same heart which had shuddered before the painted effigies of crime, looked on its reality unmoved. At best, he felt a gleam of pity for one who had been endowed in vain with all those faculties that can make the world a garden of enchantment, one who had never lived and who was now dead. But of penitence, no, with a tremor.

With that, shaking himself clear of these considerations, he found the keys and advanced toward the open door of the shop. Outside, it had begun to rain smartly; and the sound of the shower upon the roof had banished silence. Like some dripping cavern, the chambers of the house were haunted by an incessant echoing, which filled the ear and mingled with the ticking of the clocks. And, as Markheim approached the door, he seemed to hear, in answer to his own cautious tread, the steps of another foot withdrawing up the stair. The shadow still palpitated loosely on the threshold. He threw a ton's weight of resolve upon his muscles, and drew back the door.

The faint, foggy daylight glimmered dimly on the bare floor and stairs; on the bright suit of armor posted, halbert in hand, upon the landing; and on the dark wood-carvings, and framed pictures that hung against the yellow panels of the wainscot. So loud was the beating of the rain through all the house that, in Markheim's ears, it began to be distinguished into many different sounds. Footsteps and sighs, the tread of regiments marching in the distance, the chink of money in the counting, and the creaking of doors held stealthily ajar, appeared to mingle with the patter of the drops upon the cupola and the gushing of the water in the pipes. The sense that he was not alone grew upon him to the verge of madness. On every side he was haunted and begirt by presences. He heard them moving in the upper chambers; from the shop, he heard the dead man getting to his legs; and as he began with a great effort to mount the stairs, feet fled quietly before him and followed stealthily behind. If he were but deaf, he thought, how tranquilly he would possess his soul. And then again, and hearkening with every fresh attention, he blessed himself for that unresisting sense which held the outposts and stood a trusty sentinel upon his life. His head turned continually on his neck; his eyes, which seemed starting from their orbits, scouted on every side, and on every side were half-rewarded as with the tail of something nameless vanishing. The four-and-twenty steps to the first floor were four-and-twenty agonies.

On that first story, the doors stood ajar, three of them like three ambushes, shaking his nerves like the throats of cannon. He could never again, he felt, be sufficiently immured and fortified from men's observing eyes; he longed to be home, girt in by walls, buried among bedclothes, and invisible to all but God. And at that thought he wondered a little, recollecting tales of other murderers and the fear they were said to entertain of heavenly avengers. It was not so, at least, with him. He feared the laws of nature, lest, in their callous and immutable procedure, they should preserve some damning evidence of his crime. He feared tenfold more, with a slavish, superstitious terror, some scission in the continuity of man's experience, some willful illegality of nature. He played a game of skill, depending on the rules, calculating consequence from cause; and what if nature, as the defeated tyrant overthrew the chess-board, should break the mold of their succession? The like had befallen Napoleon (so writers said) when the winter changed the time of its appearance. The like might befall Markheim: the solid walls might become transparent and reveal his doings like those of bees in a glass hive; and stout planks might yield under his foot like quicksands and detain him in their clutch; ay, and there were soberer accidents that might destroy him; if, for instance, the house should fall and imprison him beside the body of his victim; or the house next door should fly on fire, and the firemen invade him from all sides. These things he feared; and, in a sense, these things might be called the hands of God reached forth against sin. But about God himself he was at ease; his act was doubtless exceptional, but so were his excuses, which God knew; it was there, and not among men, that he felt sure of justice.

When he had got safe into the drawing-room, and shut the door behind him, he was aware of a respite from alarms. The room was quite dismantled, uncarpeted besides, and strewn with packing cases and incongruous furniture; several great pier-glasses, in which he beheld himself at various angles, like an actor on the stage; many pictures, framed and unframed, standing with their faces to the wall; a fine Sheraton sideboard, a cabinet of marquetry, and a great old bed, with tapestry hangings. The windows opened to the floor; but by great good fortune the lower part of the shutters had been closed, and this concealed him from the neighbors. Here, then, Markheim drew in a packing case before the cabinet, and began to search among the keys. It was a long business, for there were many; and it was irksome, besides; for, after all, there might be nothing in the cabinet, and time was on the wing. But the closeness of the occupation sobered him. With the tail of his eye he saw the door—even glanced at it from time to time directly, like a besieged commander pleased to verify the good estate of his defenses. But in truth he was at peace. The rain falling in the street sounded natural and pleasant. Presently, on the other side, the notes of a piano were wakened to the music of a hymn, and the voices of many children took up the air and words. How stately, how comfortable was the melody! How fresh the youthful voices! Markheim gave ear to it smilingly, as he sorted out the keys; and his mind was thronged with answerable ideas and images; church-going children and the pealing of the high organ; children afield, bathers by the brook-side, ramblers on the brambly common, kite-flyers in the windy and cloud-navigated sky; and then, at another cadence of the hymn, back again to church, and the somnolence of summer Sundays, and the high genteel voice of the parson (which he smiled a little to recall) and the painted Jacobean tombs, and the dim lettering of the Ten Commandments in the chancel.

And as he sat thus, at once busy and absent, he was startled to his feet. A flash of ice, a flash of fire, a bursting gush of blood, went over him, and then he stood transfixed and thrilling. A step mounted the stair slowly and steadily, and presently a hand was laid upon the knob, and the lock clicked, and the door opened.

Fear held Markheim in a vice. What to expect he knew not, whether the dead man walking, or the official ministers of human justice, or some chance witness blindly stumbling in to consign him to the gallows. But when a face was thrust into the aperture, glanced round the room, looked at him, nodded and smiled as if in friendly recognition, and then withdrew again, and the door closed behind it, his fear broke loose from his control in a hoarse cry. At the sound of this the visitant returned.

"Did you call me?" he asked, pleasantly, and with that he entered the room and closed the door behind him.

Markheim stood and gazed at him with all his eyes. Perhaps there was a film upon his sight, but the outlines of the newcomer seemed to change and waver like those of the idols in the wavering candle-light of the shop; and at times he thought he knew him; and at times he thought he bore a likeness to himself; and always, like a lump of living terror, there lay in his bosom the conviction that this thing was not of the earth and not of God.

And yet the creature had a strange air of the common-place, as he stood looking on Markheim with a smile; and when he added: "You are looking for the money, I believe?" it was in the tones of everyday politeness.

Markheim made no answer.

"I should warn you," resumed the other, "that the maid has left her sweet-heart earlier than usual and will soon be here. If Mr. Markheim be found in this house, I need not describe to him the consequences."

"You know me?" cried the murderer.

The visitor smiled. "You have long been a favorite of mine," he said; "and I have long observed and often sought to help you."

"What are you?" cried Markheim: "the devil?"

"What I may be," returned the other, "can not affect the service I propose to render you."

"It can," cried Markheim; "it does! Be helped by you? No, never; not by you! You do not know me yet, thank God, you do not know me!"

"I know you," replied the visitant, with a sort of kind severity or rather firmness. "I know you to the soul."

"Know me!" cried Markheim. "Who can do so? My life is but a travesty and slander on myself. I have lived to belie my nature. All men do; all men are better than this disguise that grows about and stifles them. You see each dragged away by life, like one whom bravos have seized and muffled in a cloak. If they had their own control—if you could see their faces, they would be altogether different, they would shine out for heroes and saints! I am worse than most; myself is more overlaid; my excuse is known to me and God. But, had I the time, I could disclose myself."

"To me?" inquired the visitant.

"To you before all," returned the murderer. "I supposed you were intelligent. I thought—since you exist—you would prove a reader of the heart. And yet you would propose to judge me by my acts! Think of it; my acts! I was born and I have lived in a land of giants; giants have dragged me by the wrists since I was born out of my mother—the giants of circumstance. And you would judge me by my acts! But can you not look within? Can you not understand that evil is hateful to me? Can you not see within me the clear writing of conscience, never blurred by any willful sophistry, although too often disregarded? Can you not read me for a thing that surely must be common as humanity—the unwilling sinner?"

"All this is very feelingly expressed," was the reply, "but it regards me not. These points of consistency are beyond my province, and I care not in the least by what compulsion you may have been dragged away, so as you are but carried in the right direction. But time flies; the servant delays, looking in the faces of the crowd and at the pictures on the hoardings, but still she keeps moving nearer; and remember, it is as if the gallows itself was striding toward you through the Christmas streets! Shall I help you; I, who know all? Shall I tell you where to find the money?"

"For what price?" asked Markheim.

"I offer you the service for a Christmas gift," returned the other.

Markheim could not refrain from smiling with a kind of bitter triumph.

"No," said he, "I will take nothing at your hands; if I were dying of thirst, and it was your hand that put the pitcher to my lips, I should find the courage to refuse. It may be credulous, but I will do nothing to commit myself to evil."

"I have no objection to a death-bed repentance," observed the visitant.

"Because you disbelieve their efficacy!" Markheim cried.

"I do not say so," returned the other; "but I look on these things from a different side, and when the life is done my interest falls. The man has lived to serve me, to spread black looks under color of religion, or to sow tares in the wheat-field, as you do, in a course of weak compliance with desire. Now that he draws so near to his deliverance, he can add but one act of service—to repent, to die smiling, and thus to build up in confidence and hope the more timorous of my surviving followers. I am not so hard a master. Try me. Accept my help. Please yourself in life as you have done hitherto; please yourself more amply, spread your elbows at the board; and when the night begins to fall and the curtains to be drawn, I tell you, for your greater comfort, that you will find it even easy to compound your quarrel with your conscience, and to make a truckling peace with God. I came but now from such a deathbed, and the room was full of sincere mourners, listening to the man's last words: and when I looked into that face, which had been set as a flint against mercy, I found it smiling with hope."

"And do you, then, suppose me such a creature?" asked Markheim. "Do you think I have no more generous aspirations than to sin, and sin, and sin, and, at last, sneak into heaven? My heart rises at the thought. Is this, then, your experience of mankind? or is it because you find me with red hands that you presume such baseness? and is this crime of murder indeed so impious as to dry up the very springs of good?"

"Murder is to me no special category," replied the other. "All sins are murder, even as all life is war. I behold your race, like starving mariners on a raft, plucking crusts out of the hands of famine and feeding on each other's lives. I follow sins beyond the moment of their acting; I find in all that the last consequence is death; and to my eyes, the pretty maid who thwarts her mother with such taking graces on a question of a ball, drips no less visibly with human gore than such a murderer as yourself. Do I say that I follow sins? I follow virtues also; they differ not by the thickness of a nail, they are both scythes for the reaping angel of Death. Evil, for which I live, consists not in action but in character. The bad man is dear to me; not the bad act, whose fruits, if we could follow them far enough down the hurtling cataract of the ages, might yet be found more blessed than those of the rarest virtues. And it is not because you have killed a dealer, but because you are Markheim, that I offered to forward your escape."

"I will lay my heart open to you," answered Markheim. "This crime on which you find me is my last. On my way to it I have learned many lessons; itself is a lesson, a momentous lesson. Hitherto I have been driven with revolt to what I would not; I was a bond-slave to poverty, driven and scourged. There are robust virtues that can stand in these temptations; mine was not so: I had a thirst of pleasure. But to-day, and out of this deed, I pluck both warning and riches—both the power and a fresh resolve to be myself. I become in all things a free actor in the world; I begin to see myself all changed, these hands the agents of good, this heart at peace. Something comes over me out of the past; something of what I have dreamed on Sabbath evenings to the sound of the church organ, of what I forecast when I shed tears over noble books, or talked, an innocent child, with my mother. There lies my life; I have wandered a few years, but now I see once more my city of destination."

"You are to use this money on the Stock Exchange, I think?" remarked the visitor; "and there, if I mistake not, you have already lost some thousands?"

"Ah," said Markheim, "but this time I have a sure thing."

"This time, again, you will lose," replied the visitor, quietly.

"Ah, but I keep back the half!" cried Markheim.

"That also you will lose," said the other.

The sweat started upon Markheim's brow. "Well, then, what matter?" he exclaimed. "Say it be lost, say I am plunged again in poverty, shall one part of me, and that the worse, continue until the end to override the better? Evil and good run strong in me, haling me both ways. I do not love the one thing, I love all. I can conceive great deeds, renunciations, martyrdoms; and though I be fallen to such a crime as murder, pity is no stranger to my thoughts. I pity the poor; who knows their trials better than myself? I pity and help them; I prize love, I love honest laughter; there is no good thing nor true thing on earth but I love it from my heart. And are my vices only to direct my life, and my virtues to lie without effect, like some passive lumber of the mind? Not so; good, also, is a spring of acts."

But the visitant raised his finger. "For six-and-thirty years that you have been in this world," said he, "through many changes of fortune and varieties of humor, I have watched you steadily fall. Fifteen years ago you would have started at a theft. Three years back you would have blenched at the name of murder. Is there any crime, is there any cruelty or meanness, from which you still recoil?—five years from now I shall detect you in the fact! Downward, downward, lies your way; nor can anything but death avail to stop you."

"It is true," Markheim said, huskily, "I have in some degree complied with evil. But it is so with all: the very saints, in the mere exercise of living, grow less dainty, and take on the tone of their surroundings."

"I will propound to you one simple question," said the other; "and as you answer, I shall read to you your moral horoscope. You have grown in many things more lax; possibly you do right to be so; and at any account, it is the same with all men. But granting that, are you in any one particular, however trifling, more difficult to please with your own conduct, or do you go in all things with a looser rein?"

"In any one?" repeated Markheim, with an anguish of consideration. "No," he added, with despair, "in none! I have gone down in all."

"Then," said the visitor, "content yourself with what you are, for you will never change; and the words of your part on this stage are irrevocably written down."

Markheim stood for a long while silent, and indeed it was the visitor who first broke the silence. "That being so," he said, "shall I show you the money?"

"And grace?" cried Markheim.

"Have you not tried it?" returned the other. "Two or three years ago, did I not see you on the platform of revival meetings, and was not your voice the loudest in the hymn?"

"It is true," said Markheim; "and I see clearly what remains for me by way of duty. I thank you for these lessons from my soul: my eyes are opened, and I behold myself at last for what I am."

At this moment, the sharp note of the door-bell rang through the house; and the visitant, as though this were some concerted signal for which he had been waiting, changed at once in his demeanor.

"The maid!" he cried. "She has returned, as I forewarned you, and there is now before you one more difficult passage. Her master, you must say, is ill; you must let her in, with an assured but rather serious countenance—no smiles, no overacting, and I promise you success! Once the girl within, and the door closed, the same dexterity that has already rid you of the dealer will relieve you of this last danger in your path. Thenceforward you have the whole evening—the whole night, if needful—to ransack the treasures of the house and to make good your safety. This is help that comes to you with the mask of danger. Up!" he cried: "up, friend; your life hangs trembling in the scales; up, and act!"

Markheim steadily regarded his counsellor. "If I be condemned to evil acts," he said, "there is still one door of freedom open—I can cease from action. If my life be an ill thing, I can lay it down. Though I be, as you say truly, at the beck of every small temptation, I can yet, by one decisive gesture, place myself beyond the reach of all. My love of good is damned to barrenness; it may, and let it be! But I have still my hatred of evil; and from that, to your galling disappointment, you shall see that I can draw both energy and courage."

The features of the visitor began to undergo a wonderful and lovely change; they brightened and softened with a tender triumph; and, even as they brightened, faded and dislimned. But Markheim did not pause to watch or understand the transformation. He opened the door and went downstairs very slowly, thinking to himself. His past went soberly before him; he beheld it as it was, ugly and strenuous like a dream, random as chance-medley—a scene of defeat. Life, as he thus reviewed it, tempted him no longer; but on the further side he perceived a quiet haven for his bark. He paused in the passage, and looked into the shop, where the candle still burned by the dead body. It was strangely silent. Thoughts of the dealer swarmed into his mind, as he stood gazing. And then the bell once more broke out into impatient clamor.

He confronted the maid upon the threshold with something like a smile.

"You had better go for the police," said he: "I have killed your master."

(1885)

Rudyard Kipling

THE MAN WHO WOULD BE KING

"Brother to a prince and fellow to a beggar if he be found worthy."

The law, as quoted, lays down a fair conduct of life, and one not easy to follow. I have been fellow to a beggar again and again under circumstances which prevented either of us finding out whether the other was worthy. I have still to be brother to a prince, though I once came near to kinship with what might have been a veritable king and was promised the reversion of a kingdom— army, law-courts, revenue and policy all complete. But today I greatly fear that my king is dead, and if I want a crown I must go and hunt it for myself.

The beginning of everything was in a railway train upon the road to Mhow from Ajmir. There had been a Deficit in the Budget, which necessitated traveling not second-class, which is only half as dear as first-class, but by intermediate, which is very awful indeed. There are no cushions in the intermediate class, and the population are either intermediate, which is Eurasian, or native, which for a long night journey is nasty, or loafer, which is amusing though intoxicated. Intermediates do not patronize refreshment-rooms. They carry their food in bundles and pots, and buy sweets from the native sweetmeat sellers, and drink the roadside water. That is why in the hot weather intermediates are taken out of the carriages dead, and in all weathers are most properly looked down upon.

My particular intermediate happened to be empty till I reached Nasirabad, when a huge gentleman in shirt-sleeves entered and, following the custom of intermediates, passed the time of day. He was a wanderer and a vagabond like myself, but with an educated taste for whisky. He told tales of things he had seen and done, of out-of-the-way corners of the Empire into which he had penetrated, and of adventures in which he risked his life for a few days' food. "If India was filled with men like you and me, not knowing more than the crows where they'd get their next day's rations, it isn't seventy millions of revenue the land would be paying—it's seven hundred millions," said he; and as I looked at his mouth and chin I was disposed to agree with him. We talked politics—the politics of loaferdom that sees things from the underside where the lath and plaster is not smoothed off—and we talked postal arrangements because my friend wanted to send a telegram back from the next station to Ajmir, which is the turning-off place from the Bombay to the Mhow line as you travel westward. My friend had no money beyond eight annas which he wanted for dinner, and I had no money at all, owing to the hitch in the Budget before mentioned. Further, I was going into a wilderness where, though I should resume touch with the Treasury, there were no telegraph offices. I was, therefore, unable to help him in any way.

"We might threaten a station-master to make him send a wire on tick," said my friend, "but that'd mean inquiries for you and for me, and I've got my hands full these days. Did you say you were traveling back along this line within any days?"

"Within ten," I said.

"Can't you make it eight?" said he. "Mine is rather urgent business."

"I can send your telegram within ten days if that will serve you," I said.

"I couldn't trust the wire to fetch him now I think of it. It's this way. He leaves Delhi on the 23d for Bombay. That means he'll be running through Ajmir about the night of the 23d."

"But I'm going into the Indian Desert," I explained.

"Well *and* good," said he. "You'll be changing at Marwar Junction to get into Jodhpore territory—you must do that—and he'll be coming through Marwar Junction in the early morning of the 24th by the Bombay Mail. Can you be at Marwar Junction on that time? 'Twon't be inconveniencing you, because I know that there's precious few pickings to be got out of those Central India States— even though you pretend to be correspondent of the *Backwoodsman*."

"Have you ever tried that trick?" I asked.

"Again and again, but the Residents find you out, and then you get escorted to the Border before you've time to get your knife into them. But about my friend here. I *must* give him word o' mouth to tell him what's come to me or else he won't know where to go. I would take it more than kind of you if you was to come out of Central India in time to catch him at Marwar Junction, and say to him: 'He has gone south for the week.' He'll know what that means. He's a big man with a red beard, and a great swell he is. You'll find him sleeping like a gentleman with all his luggage round him in a second-class compartment. But don't you be afraid. Slip down the window and say: 'He has gone south for the week,' and he'll tumble. It's only cutting your time of stay in those parts by two days. I ask you as a stranger—going to the west," he said with emphasis.

"Where have *you* come from?" said I.

"From the East," said he, "and I am hoping that you will give him the message on the square—for the sake of my mother as well as your own."

Englishmen are not usually softened by appeals to the memory of their mothers, but for certain reasons, which will be fully apparent, I saw fit to agree.

"It's more than a little matter," said he, "and that's why I ask you to do it— and now I know that I can depend on you doing it. A second-class carriage at Marwar Junction, and a red-haired man asleep in it. You'll be sure to remember. I get out at the next station, and I must hold on there till he comes or sends me what I want."

"I'll give the message if I catch him," I said, "and for the sake of your mother as well as mine I'll give you a word of advice. Don't try to run the Central India States just now as the correspondent of the *Backwoodsman*. There's a real one knocking about here, and it might lead to trouble."

"Thank you," said he simply, "and when will the swine be gone? I can't starve because he's ruining my work. I wanted to get hold of the Degumber Rajah down here about his father's widow, and give him a jump."

"What did he do to his father's widow, then?"

"Filled her up with red pepper and slippered her to death as she hung from a beam. I found that out myself and I'm the only man that would dare going into the state to get hush-money for it. They'll try to poison me, same as they did in Chortumna when I went on the loot there. But you'll give the man at Marwar Junction my message?"

He got out at a little roadside station, and I reflected. I had heard, more than once, of men personating correspondents of newspapers and bleeding small native states with threats of exposure, but I had never met any of the caste before. They lead a hard life, and generally die with great suddenness. The native states have a wholesome horror of English newspapers, which may throw light on their peculiar methods of government, and do their best to choke correspondents with champagne, or drive them out of their mind with four-in-hand barouches. They do not understand that nobody cares a straw for the internal administration of native states so long as oppression and crime are kept within decent limits, and the ruler is not drugged, drunk or diseased from one end of the year to the other. Native states were created by Providence in order to supply picturesque scenery, tigers and tall writing. They are the dark places of the earth, full of unimaginable cruelty, touching the Railway and the Telegraph on one side, and on the other the days of Harun-al-Raschid. When I left the train I did business with divers kings, and in eight days passed through many changes of life. Sometimes I wore dress clothes and consorted with princes and politicals, drinking from crystal and eating from silver. Sometimes I lay out upon the ground and devoured what I could get from a plate made of a flapjack, and drank the running water, and slept under the same rug as my servant. It was all in the day's work.

Then I headed for the Great Indian Desert upon the proper date, as I had promised, and the night mail set me down at Marwar Junction, where a funny little happy-go-lucky, native-managed railway runs to Jodhpore. The Bombay Mail from Delhi makes a short halt at Marwar. She arrived as I got in, and I had just time to hurry to her platform and go down the carriages. There was only one second-class on the train. I slipped the window and looked down upon a flaming red beard, half-covered by a railway rug. That was my man, fast asleep, and I dug him gently in the ribs. He woke with a grunt and I saw his face in the light of the lamps. It was a great and shining face.

"Tickets again?" said he.

"No," said I. "I am to tell you that he is gone south for the week. He is gone south for the week!"

The train had begun to move out. The red man rubbed his eyes. "He has gone south for the week," he repeated "Now that's just like his impidence. Did he say that I was to give you anything? 'Cause I won't."

"He didn't," I said and dropped away, and watched the red lights die out in the dark. It was horribly cold because the wind was blowing off the sands. I climbed into my own train—not an intermediate carriage this time—and went to sleep.

If the man with the beard had given me a rupee I should have kept it as a memento of a rather curious affair. But the consciousness of having done my duty was my only reward.

Later on I reflected that two gentlemen like my friends could not do any good if they foregathered and personated correspondents of newspapers, and might, if they "stuck up" one of the little rat-trap states of Central India or Southern Rajputana, get themselves into serious difficulties. I therefore took some trouble to describe them as accurately as I could remember to people who would be interested in deporting them: and succeeded, so I was later informed, in having them headed back from the Degumber borders.

Then I became respectable, and returned to an office where there were no kings and no incidents except the daily manufacture of a newspaper. A newspaper office seems to attract every conceivable sort of person to the prejudice of discipline. Zenana-mission ladies arrive, and beg that the editor will instantly abandon all his duties to describe a Christian prize-giving in a back slum of a perfectly inaccessible village; colonels who have been overpassed for commands sit down and sketch the outline of a series of ten, twelve or twenty-four leading articles on Seniority versus Selection; missionaries wish to know why they have not been permitted to escape from their regular vehicles of abuse and swear at a brother missionary under special patronage of the editorial we; stranded theatrical companies troop up to explain that they cannot pay for their advertisements, but on their return from New Zealand or Tahiti will do so with interest; inventors of patent punkah-pulling machines, carriage couplings, and unbreakable swords and axletrees call with specifications in their pockets and hours at their disposal; tea companies enter and elaborate their prospectuses with the office pens; secretaries of ball committees clamor to have the glories of their last dance more fully expounded; strange ladies rustle in and say: "I want a hundred lady's cards printed *at once*, please," which is manifestly part of an editor's duty; and every dissolute ruffian that ever tramped the Grand Trunk Road makes it his business to ask for employment as a proofreader. And, all the time, the telephone bell is ringing madly, and kings are being killed on the Continent, and empires are saying "You're another," and Mister Gladstone is calling down brimstone upon the British Dominions, and the little black copy boys are whining "*kaa-pi chay-ha-yeh*" (copy wanted) like tired bees, and most of the paper is as blank as Modred's shield.

But that is the amusing part of the year. There are other six months wherein none ever come to call, and the thermometer walks inch by inch up to the top of the glass, and the office is darkened to just above reading light, and the press machines are red-hot to touch, and nobody writes anything but accounts of amusements in the hill-stations, or obituary notices. Then the telephone becomes a tinkling terror, because it tells you of the sudden deaths of men and women that you knew intimately, and the prickly heat covers you as with a garment, and you sit down and write: "A slight increase of sickness is reported from the Khuda Janta Khan District. The outbreak is purely sporadic in its nature, and thanks to the energetic efforts of the district authorities, is now almost at an end. It is, however, with deep regret we record the death, etc."

Then the sickness really breaks out, and the less recording and reporting the better for the peace of the subscribers. But the empires and kings continue to divert themselves as selfishly as before, and the foreman thinks that a daily paper really ought to come out once in twenty-four hours, and all the people at the hill-stations in the middle of their amusements say: "Good gracious! Why can't the paper be sparkling? I'm sure there's plenty going on up here."

That is the dark half of the moon, and as the advertisements say, "must be experienced to be appreciated."

It was in that season, and a remarkably evil season, that the paper began running the last issue of the week on Saturday night, which is to say Sunday morning, after the custom of a London paper. This was a great convenience, for immediately after the paper was put to bed the dawn would lower the thermometer from 96° to almost 84° for half an hour, and in that chill—you have no idea how cold is 84° on the grass until you begin to pray for it—a very tired man could set off to sleep ere the heat roused him.

One Saturday night it was my pleasant duty to put the paper to bed alone. A king or courtier or a courtesan or a community was going to die or get a new constitution, or do something that was important on the other side of the world, and the paper was to be held open till the latest possible minute in order to catch the telegram. It was a pitchy black night, as stifling as a June night can be, and the *loo,* the red-hot wind from the westward, was booming among the tinder-dry trees and pretending that the rain was on its heels. Now and again a spot of almost boiling water would fall on the dust with the flop of a frog, but all our weary world knew that was only pretense. It was a shade cooler in the press-room than the office, so I sat there while the type clicked and clicked, and the night-jars hooted at the windows, and the all but naked compositors wiped the sweat from their foreheads and called for water. The thing that was keeping us back, whatever it was, would not come off, though the *loo* dropped and the last type was set, and the whole round earth stood still in the choking heat, with its finger on its lip, to await the event. I drowsed, and wondered whether the telegraph was a blessing, and whether this dying man or struggling people was aware of the inconvenience the delay was causing. There was no special reason beyond the heat and worry to make tension, but as the clock hands crept up to three o'clock and the machines spun their flywheels two and three times to see that all was in order, before I said the word that would set them off, I could have shrieked aloud.

Then the roar and rattle of the wheels shivered the quiet into little bits. I rose to go away, but two men in white clothes stood in front of me. The first one said: "It's him!" The second said: "So it is!" And they both laughed almost as loudly as the machinery roared, and mopped their foreheads. "We see there was a light burning across the road and we were sleeping in that ditch there for coolness, and I said to my friend here: 'The office is open. Let's come along and speak to him as turned us back from the Degumber State,' " said the smaller of the two. He was the man I had met in the Mhow train, and his fellow was the red-bearded man of Marwar Junction. There was no mistaking the eyebrows of the one or the beard of the other.

I was not pleased, because I wished to go to sleep, not to squabble with loafers. "What do you want?" I asked.

"Half an hour's talk with you cool and comfortable, in the office," said the red-bearded man. "We'd *like* some drink—the contrack doesn't begin yet, Peachey, so you needn't look—but what we really want is advice. We don't want money. We ask you as a favor, because you did us a bad turn about Degumber."

I led from the press-room to the stifling office with the maps on the walls, and the red-haired man rubbed his hands. "That's something like," said he. "This was the proper shop to come to. Now, sir, let me introduce to you Brother Peachey Carnehan, that's him, and Brother Daniel Dravot, that is *me*, and the less said about our professions the better, for we have been most things in our time. Soldier, sailor, compositor, photographer, proofreader, street preacher, and correspondents of the *Backwoodsman*, when we thought the paper wanted one. Carnehan is sober, and so am I. Look at us first and see that's sure. It will save you cutting into my talk. We'll take one of your cigars apiece, and you shall see us light it."

I watched the test: The men were absolutely sober, so I gave them each a tepid peg.

"Well *and* good," said Carnehan of the eyebrows, wiping the froth from his mustache. "Let me talk now, Dan. We have been all over India, mostly on foot. We have been boiler-fitters, engine-drivers, petty contractors, and all that, and we have decided that India isn't big enough for such as us."

They certainly were too big for the office. Dravot's beard seemed to fill half the room and Carnehan's shoulders the other half, as they sat on the big table. Carnehan continued: "The country isn't half worked out because they that governs it won't let you touch it. They spend all their blessed time in governing it, and you can't lift a spade, nor chip a rock, nor look for oil, nor anything like that without all the Government saying: 'Leave it alone and let us govern.' Therefore, such as it is, we will let it alone, and go away to some other place where a man isn't crowded and can come to his own. We are not little men, and there is nothing that we are afraid of except drink, and we have signed a contrack on that. *Therefore* we are going away to be kings."

"Kings in our own right," muttered Dravot.

"Yes, of course," I said. "You've been tramping in the sun, and it's a very warm night, and hadn't you better sleep over the notion? Come tomorrow."

"Neither drunk nor sunstruck," said Dravot. "We have slept over the notion half a year, and require to see books and atlases, and we have decided that there is only one place now in the world that two strong men can Sar-a-*whack*. They call it Kafiristan. By my reckoning it's top right-hand corner of Afghanistan, not more than three hundred miles from Peshawar. They have two-and-thirty heathen idols there, and we'll be the thirty-third. It's a mountainous country, and the women of those parts are very beautiful."

"But that is provided against in the contrack," said Carnehan. "Neither women nor liquor, Daniel."

"And that's all we know, except that no one has gone there and they fight, and in any place where they fight a man who knows how to drill men can always be a king. We shall go to those parts and say to any king we find: 'D'you want to vanquish your foes?' and we will show him how to drill men; for that we know better than anything else. Then we will subvert that king and seize his throne and establish a dy-nasty."

"You'll be cut to pieces before you're fifty miles across the border," I said. "You have to travel through Afghanistan to get to that country. It's one mass of mountains and peaks and glaciers, and no Englishman has been through it. The people are utter brutes, and even if you reached them you couldn't do anything."

"That's more like," said Carnehan. "If you could think us a little more mad we would be more pleased. We have come to you to know about this country, to read a book about it, and to be shown maps. We want you to tell us that we are fools and to show us your books."

He turned to the bookcases.

"Are you at all in earnest?" I said.

"A little," said Dravot sweetly. "As big a map as you have got, even if it's all blank where Kafiristan is, and any books you've got. We can read, though we aren't very educated."

I uncased the big thirty-two-miles-to-the-inch map of India, and two smaller Frontier maps, hauled down volume Inf-Kan of the *Encyclopaedia Britannica*, and the men consulted them.

"See here!" said Dravot, his thumb on the map. "Up to Jagdallak, Peachey and me know the road. We was there with Roberts's Army. We'll have to turn off to the right at Jagdallak through Laghmann territory. Then we get among the hills—fourteen thousand feet—fifteen thousand—it will be cold work there, but it don't look very far on the map."

I handed him Wood on the *Sources of the Oxus*. Carnehan was deep in the *Encyclopaedia*.

"They're a mixed lot," said Dravot reflectively; "and it won't help us to know the names of their tribes. The more tribes the more they'll fight, and the better for us. From Jagdallak to Ashang. H'mm!"

"But all the information about the country is as sketchy and inaccurate as can be," I protested. "No one knows anything about it really. Here's the file of the *United Services' Institute*. Read what Bellew says."

"Blow Bellow!" said Carnehan "Dan, they're an all-fired lot of heathens, but this book here says they think they're related to us English."

I smoked while the men pored over Raverty, Wood, the maps and the *Encyclopaedia*.

"There is no use your waiting," said Dravot politely. "It's about four o'clock now. We'll go before six o'clock if you want to sleep, and we won't steal any of the papers. Don't you sit up. We're two harmless lunatics, and if you come tomorrow evening down to the Serai we'll say good-by to you."

"You *are* two fools," I answered. "You'll be turned back at the frontier or cut up the minute you set foot in Afghanistan. Do you want any money or a recommendation down-country? I can help you to the chance of work next week."

"Next week we shall be hard at work ourselves, thank you," said Dravot. "It isn't so easy being a king as it looks. When we've got our kingdom in going order we'll let you know, and you can come up and help us to govern it."

"Would two lunatics make a contrack like that?" said Carnehan, with subdued pride, showing me a greasy half-sheet of note-paper on which was written the following. I copied it, then and there, as a curiosity:

This Contract between me and you persuing witnesseth in the name of God—Amen and so forth.

(One)   That me and you will settle this matter together: *i.e.*, to be Kings of Kafiristan.

(Two)   That you and me will not, while this matter is being settled, look at any liquor, nor any woman black, white or brown, so as to get mixed up with one or the other harmful.

(Three)   That we conduct ourselves with dignity and discretion, and if one of us gets into trouble the other will stay by him.

   Signed by you and me this day.
        Peachey Taliaferro Carnehan.
        Daniel Dravot.
        Both Gentlemen at Large.

"There was no need for the last article," said Carnehan, blushing modestly; "but it looks regular. Now you know the sort of men that loafers are—we *are* loafers, Dan, until we get out of India—and *do* you think that we would sign a contrack like that unless we was in earnest? We have kept away from the two things that make life worth having."

"You won't enjoy your lives much longer if you are going to try this idiotic adventure. Don't set the office on fire," I said, "and go away before nine o'clock."

I left them still poring over the maps and making notes on the back of the "contrack." "Be sure to come down to the Serai tomorrow," were their parting words.

The Kumharsen Serai is the great four-square sink of humanity where the strings of camels and horses from the North load and unload. All the nationalities of Central Asia may be found there, and most of the folk of India proper. Balkh and Bokhara there meet Bengal and Bombay, and try to draw eye-teeth. You can buy ponies, turquoises, Persian pussy-cats, saddlebags, fat-tailed sheep and musk in the Kumharsen Serai, and get many strange things for nothing. In the afternoon I went down there to see whether my friends intended to keep their word or were lying about drunk.

A priest attired in fragments of ribbons and rags stalked up to me, gravely twisting a child's paper whirligig. Behind him was his servant bending under the load of a crate of mud toys. The two were loading up two camels, and the inhabitants of the Serai watched them with shrieks of laughter.

"The priest is mad," said a horse-dealer to me. "He is going up to Kabul to sell toys to the Amir. He will either be raised to honor or have his head cut off. He came in here this morning and has been behaving madly ever since."

"The witless are under the protection of God," stammered a flat-cheeked Usbeg in broken Hindi. "They foretell future events."

"Would they could have foretold that my caravan would have been cut up by the Shinwaris almost within shadow of the Pass!" grunted the Eusufzai agent of a Rajputana trading-house whose goods had been feloniously diverted into the hands of other robbers just across the border, and whose misfortunes were the laughing-stock of the bazaar. "Ohé, priest, whence come you and whither do you go?"

"From Roum have I come," shouted the priest, waving his whirligig; "from Roum, blown by the breath of a hundred devils across the sea! O thieves, robbers, liars, the blessing of Pir Khan on pigs, dogs and perjurers! Who will take the Protected of God to the north to sell charms that are never still to the Amir? The camels shall not gall, the sons shall not fall sick, and the wives shall remain faithful while they are away, of the men who give me place in their caravan. Who will assist me to slipper the King of the Roos with a golden slipper with a silver heel? The protection of Pir Khan be upon his labors!" He spread out the skirts of his gabardine and pirouetted between the lines of tethered horses.

"There starts a caravan from Peshawar to Kabul in twenty days, *Huzrut*," said the Eusufzai trader. "My camels go therewith. Do thou also go and bring us good-luck."

"I will go even now!" shouted the priest. "I will depart upon my winged camels, and be at Peshawar in a day! Ho! Hazar Mir Khan," he yelled to his servant, "drive out the camels, but let me first mount my own."

He leaped on the back of his beast as it knelt, and, turning round to me, cried: "Come thou also, Sahib, a little along the road, and I will sell thee a charm—an amulet that shall make thee King of Kafiristan."

Then the light broke upon me, and I followed the two camels out of the Serai till we reached open road and the priest halted.

"What d'you think o' that?" said he in English. "Carnehan can't talk their patter, so I've made him my servant. He makes a handsome servant. 'Tisn't for nothing that I've been knocking about the country for fourteen years. Didn't I do that talk neat? We'll hitch on to a caravan at Peshawar till we get to Jagdallak, and then we'll see if we can get donkeys for our camels, and strike into Kafiristan. Whirligigs for the Amir, O Lor'! Put your hand under the camel-bags and tell me what you feel."

I felt the butt of a Martini, and another and another.

"Twenty of 'em," said Dravot placidly. "Twenty of 'em, and ammunition to correspond, under the whirligigs and the mud dolls."

"Heaven help you if you are caught with those things!" I said. "A Martini is worth her weight in silver among the Pathans."

"Fifteen hundred rupees of capital—every rupee we could beg, borrow, or steal—are invested on these two camels," said Dravot. "We won't get caught. We're going through the Khaiber with a regular caravan. Who'd touch a poor mad priest?"

"Have you got everything you want?" I asked, overcome with astonishment.

"Not yet, but we shall soon. Give us a memento of your kindness, *Brother*. You did me a service yesterday, and that time in Marwar. Half my kingdom shall you have, as the saying is." I slipped a small charm compass from my watch-chain and handed it up to the priest.

"Good-by," said Dravot, giving me his hand cautiously. "It's the last time we'll shake hands with an Englishman these many days. Shake hands with him, Carnehan," he cried, as the second camel passed me.

Carnehan leaned down and shook hands. Then the camels passed away along the dusty road, and I was left alone to wonder. My eye could detect no failure in the disguises. The scene in the Serai attested that they were complete to the native mind. There was just the chance, therefore, that Carnehan and Dravot would be able to wander through Afghanistan without detection. But, beyond, they would find death, certain and awful death.

Ten days later a native friend of mine, giving me the news of the day from Peshawar, wound up his letter with: "There has been much laughter here on account of a certain mad priest who is going in his estimation to sell petty gauds and insignificant trinkets which he ascribes as great charms to H. H. the Amir of Bokhara. He passed through Peshawar and associated himself to the Second Summer caravan that goes to Kabul. The merchants are pleased because through superstition they imagine that such mad fellows bring good fortune."

The two, then, were beyond the border. I would have prayed for them, but that night a real king died in Europe, and demanded an obituary notice.

The wheel of the world swings through the same phases again and again. Summer passed and winter thereafter, and came and passed again. The daily paper continued and I with it, and upon the third summer there fell a hot night, a night-issue, and a strained waiting for something to be telegraphed from the other side of the world, exactly as had happened before. A few great men had died in the past two years, the machines worked with more clatter and some of the trees in the office garden were a few feet taller. But that was all the difference.

I passed over to the press-room, and went through just such a scene as I have already described. The nervous tension was stronger than it had been two years before and I felt the heat more acutely. At three o'clock I cried "Print off," and turned to go, when there crept to my chair what was left of a man. He was bent into a circle, his head was sunk between his shoulders, and he moved his feet one over the other like a bear. I could hardly see whether he walked or crawled—this rag-wrapped, whining cripple who addressed me by name, crying that he was come back. "Can you give me a drink?" he whimpered. "For the Lord's sake, give me a drink!"

I went back to the office, the man following with groans of pain, and I turned up the lamp.

"Don't you know me?" he gasped, dropping into a chair, and he turned his drawn face, surmounted by a shock of gray hair, to the light.

I looked at him intently. Once before had I seen eyebrows that met over the nose in an inch-broad black band, but for the life of me I could not tell where.

"I don't know you," I said, handing him the whisky. "What can I do for you?"

He took a gulp of the spirit raw, and shivered in spite of the suffocating heat.

"I've come back," he repeated; "and I was the King of Kafiristan—me and Dravot—crowned kings we was! In this office we settled it—you setting there and giving us the books. I am Peachey—Peachey Taliaferro Carnehan, and you've been setting here ever since—O Lord!"

I was more than a little astonished and expressed my feelings accordingly.

"It's true," said Carnehan, with a dry cackle, nursing his feet, which were wrapped in rags. "True as gospel, kings we were, with crowns upon our heads—me and Dravot—poor Dan—oh, poor, poor Dan, that would never take advice, not though I begged of him!"

"Take the whisky," I said, "and take your own time. Tell me all you can recollect of everything from beginning to end. You got across the border on your camels, Dravot dressed as a mad priest, and you his servant. Do you remember that?"

"I ain't mad—yet, but I shall be that way soon. Of course I remember. Keep looking at me, or maybe my words will go all to pieces. Keep looking at me in my eyes and don't say anything."

I leaned forward and looked into his face as steadily as I could. He dropped one hand upon the table and I grasped it by the wrist. It was twisted like a bird's claw, and upon the back was a ragged, red, diamond-shaped scar.

"No, don't look there. Look at *me*," said Carnehan. "That comes afterwards, but for the Lord's sake don't distrack me. We left with that caravan, me and Dravot playing all sorts of antics to amuse the people we were with. Dravot used to make us laugh in the evening when all the people was cooking their dinners—cooking their dinners, and . . . what did they do then? They lit little fires with sparks that went into Dravot's beard, and we all laughed—fit to die. Little red fires they was, going into Dravot's big red beard—so funny." His eyes left mine and he smiled foolishly.

"You went as far as Jagdallak with that caravan," I said at a venture, "after you had lit those fires. To Jagdallak, where you turned off to try to get into Kafiristan."

"No, we didn't neither. What are you talking about? We turned off before Jagdallak, because we heard the roads was good. But they wasn't good enough for our two camels—mine and Dravot's. When we left the caravan Dravot took off all his clothes and mine too, and said we would be heathen, because the Kafirs didn't allow Mohammedans to talk to them. So we dressed betwixt and between, and such a sight as Daniel Dravot I never saw yet nor expect to see again. He burned half his beard, and slung a sheepskin over his shoulder, and shaved his head into patterns. He shaved mine, too, and made me wear outrageous things to look like a heathen. That was in a most mountainous country, and our camels couldn't go along any more because of the mountains. They were tall and black, and coming home I saw them fight like wild goats—there are lots of goats in Kafiristan. And these mountains, they never keep still, no more than the goats. Always fighting they are, and don't let you sleep at night."

"Take some more whisky," I said very slowly. "What did you and Daniel Dravot do when the camels could go no farther because of the rough roads that led into Kafiristan?"

"What did which do? There was a party called Peachey Taliaferro Carnehan that was with Dravot. Shall I tell you about him? He died out there in the cold. Slap for the bridge fell old Peachey, turning and twisting in the air like a penny whirligig that you can sell to the Amir.—No; they was two for three ha'pence, those whirligigs, or I am much mistaken and woeful sore. And then these camels were no use, and Peachey said to Dravot: 'For the Lord's sake, let's get out of this before our heads are chopped off,' and with that they killed the camels all among the mountains, not having anything in particular to eat, but first they took off the boxes with the guns and the ammunition, till two men came along driving four mules. Dravot up and dances in front of them, singing: 'Sell me four mules.' Says the first man: 'If you are rich enough to buy you are rich enough to rob'; but before ever he could put his hand to his knife Dravot breaks his neck over his knee, and the other party runs away. So Carnehan loaded the mules with the rifles that was taken off the camels, and together we starts forward into those bitter cold mountainous parts, and never a road broader than the back of your hand."

He paused for a moment, while I asked him if he could remember the nature of the country through which he had journeyed.

"I am telling you as straight as I can, but my head isn't as good as it might be. They drove nails through it to make me hear better how Dravot died. The country was mountainous and the mules were most contrary, and the inhabitants was dispersed and solitary. They went up and up, and down and down, and that other party, Carnehan, was imploring of Dravot not to sing and whistle so loud, for fear of bringing down the tremenjus avalanches. But Dravot says that if a king couldn't sing it wasn't worth being king, and whacked the mules over the rump, and never took no heed for ten cold days. We came to a big level valley all among the mountains, and the mules were near dead, so we killed them, not having anything in special for them or us to eat. We sat upon the boxes, and played odd and even with the cartridges that was jolted out.

"Then ten men with bows and arrows ran down that valley chasing twenty men with bows and arrows, and the row was tremenjus. They was fair men— fairer than you or me—with yellow hair and remarkable well built. Says Dravot, unpacking the guns: 'This is the beginning of the business. We'll fight for the ten men,' and with that he fires two rifles at the twenty men, and drops one of them at two hundred yards from the rock where we was sitting. The other men began to run, but Carnehan and Dravot sits on the boxes picking them off at all ranges, up and down the valley. Then we goes up to the ten men that had run across the snow, too, and they fires a footy little arrow at us. Dravot he shoots above their heads and they all falls down flat. Then he walks over them and kicks them, and then he lifts them up and shakes hands all around to make them friendly like. He calls them and gives them the boxes to carry, and waves his hand for all the world as though he was king already. They take the boxes and him across the valley and up the hill into a pine wood on the top, where there was half a dozen big stone idols. Dravot he goes to the biggest—a fellow they call Imbra—and lays a rifle and a cartridge at his feet, rubbing his nose respectful with his own nose, patting him on the head, and saluting in front of it. He turns round to the men and nods his head, and says 'That's all right. I'm in the know, too, and all these old jim-jams are my friends.' Then he opens his mouth and points down it, and when the first man brings him food, he says— 'No'; and when the second man brings him food, he says—'No'; but when one of the old priests and the boss of the village brings him food, he says—'Yes,' very haughty, and eats it slow. That was how we came to our first village, without any trouble, just as though we had tumbled from the skies. But we tumbled from one of those damned rope-bridges, you see, and you couldn't expect a man to laugh much after that."

"Take some more whisky and go on," I said. "That was the first village you came into. How did you get to be king?"

"I wasn't king," said Carnehan. "Dravot he was the king, and a handsome man he looked with the gold crown on his head and all. Him and the other party stayed in that village, and every morning Dravot sat by the side of old Imbra, and the people came and worshiped. That was Dravot's order. Then a lot of men came into the valley, and Carnehan and Dravot picks them off with the rifles before they knew where they was, and runs down into the valley and up again the other side, and finds another village, same as the first one, and the people all falls down flat on their faces, and Dravot says, 'Now what is the trouble between you two villages?' and the people points to a woman, as fair as you or me, that was carried off, and Dravot takes her back to the first village and counts up the dead—eight there was. For each dead man Dravot pours a little milk on the ground and waves his arms like a whirligig and 'That's all right,' says he. Then he and Carnehan takes the big boss of each village by the arm and walks them down into the valley, and shows them how to scratch a line with a spear right down the valley, and gives each a sod of turf from both sides o' the line. Then all the people comes down and shouts like the devil and all, and Dravot says, 'Go and dig the land, and be fruitful and multiply,' which they did, though they didn't understand. Then we asks the names of things in their lingo—bread and water and fire and idols and such, and Dravot leads the priest of each village up to the idol, and says he must sit there and judge the people, and if anything goes wrong he is to be shot.

"Next week they was all turning up the land in the valley as quiet as bees and much prettier, and the priests heard all the complaints and told Dravot in dumb show what it was about. 'That's just the beginning,' says Dravot. 'They think we're gods.' He and Carnehan picks out twenty good men and shows them how to click off a rifle and form fours, and advance in line, and they was very pleased to do so, and clever to see the hang of it. Then he takes out his pipe and his baccy-pouch and leaves one at one village and one at the other, and off we two goes to see what was to be done in the next valley. That was all rock, and there was a little village there, and Carnehan says,—'Send 'em to the old valley to plant,' and takes 'em there and gives 'em some land that wasn't took before. They were a poor lot, and we blooded 'em with a kid before letting 'em into the new kingdom. That was to impress the people, and then they settled down quiet, and Carnehan went back to Dravot, who had got into another valley all snow and ice and most mountainous. There was no people there and the army got afraid, so Dravot shoots one of them, and goes on till he finds some people in a village, and the army explains that unless the people wants to be killed they had better not shoot their little matchlocks; for they had matchlocks. We makes friends with the priest and I stays there alone with two of the army, teaching the men how to drill, and a thundering big chief comes across the snow with kettle-drums and horns twanging, because he heard there was a new god kicking about. Carnehan sights for the brown of the men half a mile across the snow and wings one of them. Then he sends a message to the chief that, unless he wished to be killed, he must come and shake hands with me and leave his arms behind. The chief comes alone first, and Carnehan shakes hands with him and whirls his arms about same as Dravot used, and very much surprised that chief was, and strokes my eyebrows. Then Carnehan goes alone to the chief and asks him in dumb show if he had an enemy he hated. 'I have,' said the chief. So Carnehan weeds out the pick of his men, and sets the two of the army to show them drill and at the end of two weeks the men can maneuver about as well as volunteers. So he marches with the chief to a great big plain on the top of a mountain, and the chief's men rushes into a village and takes it; we three Martinis firing into the brown of the enemy. So we took the village too, and I gives the chief a rag from my coat, and says, 'Occupy till I come,' which was Scriptural. By way of a reminder, when me and the army was eighteen hundred yards away, I drops a bullet near him standing on the snow, and all the people falls flat on their faces. Then I sends a letter to Dravot, wherever he be by land or by sea."

At the risk of throwing the creature out of train I interrupted, "How could you write a letter up yonder?"

"The letter? Oh! The letter! Keep looking at me between the eyes, please. It was a string-talk letter, that we'd learned the way of it from a blind beggar in the Punjab."

I remembered that there had once come to the office a blind man with a knotted twig and a piece of string which he wound round the twig according to some cipher of his own. He could, after the lapse of days or hours, repeat the sentence which he had reeled up. He had reduced the alphabet to eleven primitive sounds; and tried to teach me his method, but failed.

"I sent that letter to Dravot," said Carnehan; "and told him to come back because this kingdom was growing too big for me to handle, and then I struck for the first valley, to see how the priests were working. They called the village we took along with the chief, Bashkai, and the first village we took Er-Heb. The priests at Er-Heb was doing all right, but they had a lot of pending cases about land to show me, and some men from another village had been firing arrows at night. I went out and looked for that village and fired four rounds at it from a thousand yards. That used all the cartridges I cared to spend, and I waited for Dravot, who had been away two or three months, and I kept my people quiet.

"One morning I heard the devil's own noise of drums and horns, and Dan Dravot marches down the hill with his army and a tail of hundreds of men, and, which was the most amazing—a great gold crown on his head. 'My Gord, Carnehan,' says Daniel, 'this is a tremenjus business, and we've got the whole country as far as it's worth having. I am the son of Alexander by Queen Semiramis, and you're my younger brother and a god too! It's the biggest thing we've ever seen. I've been marching and fighting for six weeks with the army, and every footy little village for fifty miles has come in rejoiceful; and more than that, I've got the key of the whole show, as you'll see, and I've got a crown for you! I told 'em to make two of 'em at a place called Shu, where the gold lies in the rock like suet in mutton. Gold I've seen, and turquoise I've kicked out of the cliffs, and there's garnets in the sands of the river, and here's a chunk of amber that a man brought me. Call up all the priests and, here, take your crown.'

"One of the men opens a black hair bag and I slips the crown on. It was too small and too heavy, but I wore it for the glory. Hammered gold it was—five-pound weight, like a hoop of a barrel.

" 'Peachey,' says Dravot, 'we don't want to fight no more. The craft's the trick, so help me!' and he brings forward that same chief that I left at Bashkai—Billy Fish we called him afterwards, because he was so like Billy Fish that drove the big tank-engine at Mach on the Bolan in the old days. 'Shake hands with him,' says Dravot, and I shook hands and nearly dropped, for Billy Fish gave me the grip. I said nothing, but tried him with the fellowcraft grip. He answers all right, and I tried the master's grip, but that was a slip. 'A fellowcraft he is!' I says to Dan. 'Does he know the word?' 'He does,' says Dan, 'and all the priests know. It's a miracle! The chiefs and the priests can work a fellowcraft lodge in a way that's very like ours, and they've cut the marks on the rocks, but they don't know the third degree, and they've come to find out. It's Gord's truth. I've known these long years that the Afghans knew up to the fellowcraft degree, but this is a miracle. A god and a grand-master of the craft am I, and a lodge in the third degree I will open, and we'll raise the head priests and the chiefs of the villages.'

" 'It's against all the law,' I says, 'holding a lodge without warrant from any one; and we never held office in any lodge.'

" 'It's a master-stroke of policy,' says Dravot. 'It means running the country as easy as a four-wheeled bogy on a down grade. We can't stop to inquire now, or they'll turn against us. I've forty chiefs at my heel, and passed and raised according to their merit they shall be. Billet these men on the villages, and see that we run up a lodge of some kind. The temple of Imbra will do for the lodge room. The women must make aprons as you show them. I'll hold a levee of chiefs tonight and lodge tomorrow.'

"I was fair run off my legs, but I wasn't such a fool as not to see what a pull this craft business gave us. I showed the priests' families how to make aprons of the degrees, but for Dravot's apron the blue border and marks was made of turquoise lumps on white hide, not cloth. We took a great square stone in the temple for the master's chair, and little stones for the officers' chairs, and painted the black pavement with white squares, and did what we could to make things regular.

"At the levee which was held that night on the hillside with big bonfires, Dravot gives out that him and me were gods and sons of Alexander, and past grand-masters in the craft, and was come to make Kafiristan a country where every man should eat in peace and drink in quiet, and specially obey us. Then the chiefs come round to shake hands, and they was so hairy and white and fair it was just shaking hands with old friends. We gave them names according as they were like men we had known in India—Billy Fish, Holly Dilworth, Pikky Kargan that was bazaar-master when I was at Mhow, and so on and so on.

"The most amazing miracle was at lodge next night. One of the old priests was watching us continuous, and I felt uneasy, for I knew we'd have to fudge the ritual, and I didn't know what the men knew. The old priest was a stranger come in from beyond the village of Bashkai. The minute Dravot puts on the master's apron that the girls had made for him, the priest fetches a whoop and a howl, and tries to overturn the stone that Dravot was sitting on. 'It's all up now,' I says. 'That comes of meddling with the craft without warrant!' Dravot never winked an eye, not when ten priests took and tilted over the grand-master's chair—which was to say the stone of Imbra. The priest begins rubbing the bottom of it to clear away the black dirt, and presently he shows all the other priests the master's mark, same as was on Dravot's apron, cut into the stone. Not even the priests of the temple of Imbra knew it was there. The old chap falls flat on his face at Dravot's feet and kisses 'em. 'Luck again,' says Dravot, across the lodge to me, 'they say it's the missing mark that no one could understand the why of. We're more than safe now.' Then he bangs the butt of his gun for a gavel and says: 'By virtue of the authority vested in me by my own right hand and the help of Peachey, I declare myself Grand-Master of all Freemasonry in Kafiristan in this the mother lodge o' the country, and King of Kafiristan equally with Peachey!' At that he puts on his crown and I puts on mine—I was doing senior warden—and we opens the lodge in most ample form. It was an amazing miracle! The priests moved in lodge through the first two degrees almost without telling, as if the memory was coming back to them. After that Peachey and Dravot raised such as was worthy—high priests and chiefs of far-off villages. Billy Fish was the first, and I can tell you we scared the soul out of him. It was not in any way according to ritual, but it served our turn. We didn't raise more than ten of the biggest men because we didn't want to make the degree common. And they was clamoring to be raised.

" 'In another six months,' says Dravot, 'we'll hold another communication and see how you are working.' Then he asks them about their villages, and learns that they was fighting one against the other and were fair sick and tired of it. And when they wasn't doing that they was fighting with the Mohammedans. 'You can fight those when they come into our country,' says Dravot. 'Tell off every tenth man of your tribes for a frontier guard, and send two hundred at a time to this valley to be drilled. Nobody is going to be shot or speared any more so long as he does well, and I know that you won't cheat me because you're white people—sons of Alexander—and not like common, black Mohammedans. You are *my* people, and by God,' says he, running off into English at the end—'I'll make a damned fine nation of you, or I'll die in the making!'

"I can't tell all we did for the next six months, because Dravot did a lot I couldn't see the hang of, and he learned their lingo in a way I never could. My work was to help the people plow, and now and again go out with some of the army and see what the other villages were doing, and make 'em throw rope bridges across the ravines which cut up the country horrid. Dravot was very kind to me, but when he walked up and down in the pine wood pulling that bloody red beard of his with both fists I knew he was thinking plans I could not advise him about and I just waited for orders.

"But Dravot never showed me disrespect before the people. They were afraid of me and the army, but they loved Dan. He was the best of friends with the priests and the chiefs; but any one could come across the hills with a complaint and Dravot would hear him out fair and call four priests together and say what was to be done. He used to call in Billy Fish from Bashkai and Pikky Kargan from Shu, and an old chief we called Kefuzelum—it was like enough to his real name—and held councils with 'em when there was any fighting to be done in small villages. That was his Council of War, and the four priests of Bashkai, Shu, Khawak and Madora was his Privy Council. Between the lot of 'em they sent me, with forty men and twenty rifles, and sixty men carrying turquoises, into the Ghorband country to buy those hand-made Martini rifles that come out of the Amir's workshops at Kabul, from one of the Amir's Herati regiments that would have sold the very teeth out of their mouths for turquoises.

"I stayed in Ghorband a month, and gave the Governor there the pick of my baskets for hush-money, and bribed the colonel of the regiment some more, and between the two and the tribes people, we got more than a hundred hand-made Martinis, a hundred good Kohat Jezails that'll throw to six hundred yards, and forty man-loads of very bad ammunition for the rifles. I came back with what I had, and distributed 'em among the men that the chiefs sent in to me to drill. Dravot was too busy to attend to those things, but the old army that we first made helped me, and we turned out five hundred men that could drill, and two hundred that knew how to hold arms pretty straight. Even those cork-screwed, hand-made guns was a miracle to them. Dravot talked big about powder-shops and factories, walking up and down in the pine wood when the winter was coming on.

" 'I won't make a nation,' says he. 'I'll make an empire! These men aren't niggers; they're English! Look at their eyes—look at their mouths. Look at the way they stand up. They sit on chairs in their own houses. They're the Lost Tribes, or something like it, and they've grown to be English. I'll take a census in the spring if the priests don't get frightened. There must be fair two million of 'em in these hills. The villages are full o' little children. Two million people— two hundred and fifty thousand fighting men—and all English! They only want the rifles and a little drilling. Two hundred and fifty thousand men, ready to cut in on Russia's right flank when she tries for India! Peachey, man,' he says, chewing his beard in great hunks, 'we shall be emperors—emperors of the earth. Rajah Brooke will be a suckling to us. I'll treat with the Viceroy on equal terms. I'll ask him to send me twelve picked English—twelve that I know of—to help us govern a bit. There's Mackray, Sergeant-pensioner at Segowli—many's the good dinner he's given me, and his wife a pair of trousers. There's Donkin, the Warder of Tounghoo Jail; there's hundreds that I could lay my hands on if I was in India. The Viceroy shall do it for me. I'll send a man through in the spring for those men, and I'll write for a dispensation from the grand lodge for what I've done as grand master. That—and all the Sniders that'll be thrown out when the native troops in India take up the Martini. They'll be worn smooth, but they'll do for fighting in these hills. Twelve English, a hundred thousand Sniders run through the Amir's country in driblets—I'd be content with twenty thousand in one year—and we'd be an empire. When everything was shipshape, I'd hand over the crown—this crown I'm wearing now—to Queen Victoria on my knees, and she'd say: "Rise up, Sir Daniel Dravot." Oh, it's big! It's big, I tell you! But there's so much to be done in every place—Bashkai, Khawak, Shu, and everywhere else.'

" 'What is it?' I says. 'There are no more men coming in to be drilled this autumn. Look at those fat, black clouds. They're bringing the snow.'

" 'It isn't that,' says Daniel, putting his hand very hard on my shoulder; 'and I don't wish to say anything that's against you, for no other living man

would have followed me and made me what I am as you have done. You're a
first-class commander-in-chief, and the people know you; but—it's a big country,
and somehow you can't help me, Peachey, in the way I want to be helped.'

" 'Go to your blasted priests, then!' I said, and I was sorry when I made that
remark, but it did hurt me sore to find Daniel talking so superior when I'd drilled
all the men, and done all he told me.

" 'Don't let's quarrel, Peachey,' says Daniel without cursing. 'You're a king
too, and the half of this kingdom is yours; but can't you see, Peachey, we want
cleverer men than us now—three or four of 'em, that we can scatter about for
our deputies. It's a huge great state, and I can't always tell the right thing to do,
and I haven't time for all I want to do, and here's the winter coming on
and all.' He put half his beard into his mouth, and it was as red as the gold of
his crown.

" 'I'm sorry, Daniel,' says I. 'I've done all I could. I've drilled the men and
shown the people how to stack their oats better; and I've brought in those tinware rifles from Ghorband—but I know what you're driving at. I take it kings
always feel oppressed that way.'

" 'There's another thing, too,' says Dravot, walking up and down. 'The winter's
coming and these people won't be giving much trouble, and if they do we can't
move about. I want a wife.'

" 'For Gord's sake leave the women alone!' I says. 'We've both got all the
work we ean, though I *am* a fool. Remember the contrack and keep clear o'
women.'

" 'The contrack only lasted till such time as we was kings; and kings we have
been these months past,' says Dravot, weighing his crown in his hand. 'You go
get a wife too, Peachey, a nice, strappin', plump girl that'll keep you warm in
the winter. They're prettier than English girls, and we can take the pick of 'em.
Boil 'em once or twice in hot water, and they'll come as fair as chicken and ham.'

" 'Don't tempt me!' I says. 'I will not have any dealings with a woman, not
till we are a dam' side more settled than we are now. I've been doing the work o'
two men and you've been doing the work o' three. Let's lie off a bit, and see
if we can get some better tobacco from Afghan country and run in some good
liquor; but no women.'

" 'Who's talking o' *women?*' says Dravot. 'I said *wife*—a queen to breed a
king's son for the king. A queen out of the strongest tribe, that'll make them
your blood-brothers, and that'll lie by your side and tell you all the people thinks
about you and their own affairs. That's what I want.'

" 'Do you remember that Bengali woman I kept at Mogul Serai when I was
a plate layer?' says I. 'A fat lot o' good she was to me. She taught me the lingo
and one or two other things; but what happened? She ran away with the station
master's servant and half my month's pay. Then she turned up at Dadur Junction
in tow of a half-caste, and had the impidence to say I was her husband—all
among the drivers in the running-shed.'

" 'We've done with that,' says Dravot. 'These women are whiter than you or
me, and a queen I will have for the winter months.'

" 'For the last time o' asking, Dan, do *not*,' I says 'It'll only bring us harm. The Bible says that kings ain't to waste their strength on women, 'specially when they've got a new raw kingdom to work over.'

" 'For the last time of answering I will,' says Dravot, and he went away through the pine-trees looking like a big red devil. The low sun hit his crown and beard on one side, and the two blazed like hot coals.

"But getting a wife was not as easy as Dan thought. He put it before the Council, and there was no answer till Billy Fish said he'd better ask the girls. Dravot damned them all round. 'What's wrong with me?' he shouts, standing by the idol Imbra. 'Am I a dog or am I not enough of a man for your wenches? Haven't I put the shadow of my hand over this country? Who stopped the last Afghan raid?' It was me really, but Dravot was too angry to remember. 'Who bought your guns? Who repaired the bridges? Who's the grand master of the sign cut in the stone?' and he thumped his hand on the block that he used to sit on in lodge, and at council, which opened like lodge always. Billy Fish said nothing and no more did the others. 'Keep your hair on, Dan,' said I, 'and ask the girls. That's how it's done at home, and these people are quite English.'

" 'The marriage of the king is a matter of state,' says Dan, in a white-hot rage, for he could feel, I hope, that he was going against his better mind. He walked out of the council room, and the others sat still, looking at the ground.

" 'Billy Fish,' says I to the Chief of the Bashkai, 'what's the difficulty here? A straight answer to a true friend.' 'You know,' says Billy Fish. 'How should a man tell you, who knows everything? How can daughters of men marry gods or devils? It's not proper.'

"I remembered something like that in the Bible; but if, after seeing us as long as they had, they still believed we were gods, it wasn't for me to undeceive them.

" 'A god can do anything,' says I. 'If the king is fond of a girl he'll not let her die.' 'She'll have to,' said Billy Fish. 'There are all sorts of gods and devils in these mountains, and now and again a girl marries one of them and isn't seen any more. Besides, you two know the mark cut in the stone. Only the gods know that. We thought you were men till you showed the sign of the master.'

"I wished then that we had explained about the loss of the genuine secrets of a Master Mason at the first go-off; but I said nothing. All that night there was a blowing of horns in a little dark temple half-way down the hill and I heard a girl crying fit to die. One of the priests told us that she was being prepared to marry the king.

" 'I'll have no nonsense of that kind,' says Dan. 'I don't want to interfere with your customs, but I'll take my own wife.' 'The girl's a little bit afraid,' says the priest. 'She thinks she's going to die, and they are aheartening her up down in the temple.'

" 'Hearten her very tender, then,' says Dravot, 'or I'll hearten you with the butt of a gun so that you'll never want to be heartened again.' He licked his lips, did Dan, and stayed up walking about more than half the night, thinking of the wife that he was going to get in the morning. I wasn't any means comfortable, for I knew that dealings with a woman in foreign parts though you was crowned king twenty times over, could not but be risky. I got up very early in the morning while Dravot was asleep, and I saw the priests talking together in whispers, and the chiefs talking together, too, and they looked at me out of the corners of their eyes.

" 'What is up, Fish?' I says to the Bashkai man, who was wrapped up in his furs and looking splendid to behold.

" 'I can't rightly say,' says he; 'but if you can induce the king to drop all this nonsense about marriage you'll be doing him and me and yourself a great service.'

" 'That I do believe,' says I. 'But sure, you know, Billy, as well as me, having fought against and for us, that the king and me are nothing more than two of the finest men that God Almighty ever made. Nothing more, I do assure you.'

" 'That may be,' says Billy Fish, 'and yet I should be sorry if it was.' He sinks his head upon his great fur coat for a minute and thinks. 'King,' says he, 'be you man or god or devil, I'll stick by you today. I have twenty of my men with me, and they will follow me. We'll go to Bashkai until the storm blows over.'

"A little snow had fallen in the night, and everything was white except the greasy fat clouds that blew down and down from the north. Dravot came out with his crown on his head, swinging his arms and stamping his feet, and looking more pleased than Punch.

" 'For the last time drop it, Dan,' says I in a whisper. 'Billy Fish here says that there will be a row.'

" 'A row among my people!' says Dravot. 'Not much. Peachey, you're a fool not to get a wife too. Where's the girl?' says he with a voice as loud as the braying of a jackass. 'Call up all the chiefs and priests, and let the emperor see if his wife suits him.'

"There was no need to call any one. They were all there leaning on their guns and spears round the clearing in the center of the pine wood. A deputation of priests went down to the little temple to bring up the girl, and the horns blew fit to wake the dead. Billy Fish saunters round and gets as close to Daniel as he could, and behind him stood his twenty men with matchlocks. Not a man of them under six feet. I was next to Dravot, and behind me was twenty men of the regular army. Up comes the girl, and a strapping wench she was, covered with silver and turquoises, but white as death, and looking back every minute at the priests.

" 'She'll do,' said Dan, looking her over. 'What's to be afraid of, lass? Come and kiss me.' He puts his arm round her. She shuts her eyes, gives a bit of a squeak, and down goes her face in the side of Dan's flaming red beard.

" 'The slut's bitten me!' says he, clapping his hand to his neck; and sure enough his hand was red with blood. Billy Fish and two of his matchlock-men catches hold of Dan by the shoulders and drags him into the Bashkai lot, while the priests howls in their lingo, 'Neither god nor devil but a man!' I was all taken aback, for a priest cut at me in front, and the army began firing into the Bashkai men.

" 'God A'mighty!' says Dan. 'What in the meaning o' this?'

" 'Come back! Come away!' says Billy Fish. 'Ruin and mutiny is the matter. We'll break for Bashkai if we can.'

"I tried to give some sort of orders to my men—the men o' the regular army—but it was no use, so I fired into the brown of 'em with an English Martini and drilled three beggars in a line. The valley was full of shouting, howling creatures, and every soul was shrieking, 'Not a god nor a devil but only a man!' The Bashkai troops stuck to Billy Fish all they were worth, but their matchlocks wasn't half as good as the Kabul breech-loaders, and four of them dropped. Dan was bellowing like a bull, for he was very wrathy; and Billy Fish had a hard job to prevent him running out at the crowd.

" 'We can't stand,' said Billy Fish. 'Make a run for it down the valley! The whole place is against us.' The matchlock-men ran, and we went down the valley in spite of Dravot's protestations. He was swearing horribly and crying out that he was a king. The priests rolled great stones on us, and the regular army fired hard, and there wasn't more than six men, not counting Dan, Billy Fish and me, that came down to the bottom of the valley alive.

"Then they stopped firing and the horns in the temple blew again. 'Come away—for Gord's sake come away!' says Billy Fish. 'They'll send runners out to all the villages before ever we get to Bashkai. I can protect you there, but I can't do anything now.'

"My own notion is that Dan began to go mad in his head from that hour. He stared up and down like a stuck pig. Then he was all for walking back alone and killing the priests with his bare hands, which he could have done. 'An emperor am I,' says Daniel, 'and next year I shall be a knight of the queen.'

" 'All right, Dan,' says I; 'but come along now while there's time.'

" 'It's your fault,' says he, 'for not looking after your army better. There was mutiny in the midst, and you didn't know—you damned engine-driving, plate-laying, missionaries'-pass hunting hound!' He sat upon a rock and called me every foul name he could lay tongue to. I was too heartsick to care, though it was all his foolishness that brought the smash.

" 'I'm sorry, Dan,' says I, 'but there's no accounting for natives. This business is our Fifty-Seven. Maybe we'll make something out of it yet, when we've got back to Bashkai.'

" 'Let's get to Bashkai, then,' says Dan, 'and by God, when I come back here again I'll sweep the valley so there isn't a bug in a blanket left!'

"We walked all that day, and all that night Dan was stumping up and down on the snow, chewing his beard and muttering to himself.

" 'There's no hope o' getting clear,' says Billy Fish. 'The priests will have sent runners to the villages to say that you are only men. Why didn't you stick on as gods till things was more settled? I'm a dead man,' says Billy Fish, and he throws himself down on the snow and begins to pray to his gods.

"Next morning we was in a cruel bad country—all up and down, no level ground at all, and no food either. The six Bashkai men looked at Billy Fish hungry-wise as if they wanted to ask something, but they said never a word. At noon we came to the top of a flat mountain all covered with snow, and when we climbed up into it, behold, there was an army in position waiting in the middle!

" 'The runners have been very quick,' says Billy Fish, with a little bit of a laugh. 'They are waiting for us.'

"Three or four men began to fire from the enemy's side, and a chance shot took Daniel in the calf of the leg. That brought him to his senses. He looks across the snow at the army, and sees the rifles that we had brought into the country.

" 'We're done for,' says he. 'They are Englishmen, these people—and it's my blasted nonsense that has brought you to this. Get back, Billy Fish, and take your men away; you've done what you could, and now cut for it. Carnehan,' says he, 'shake hands with me and go along with Billy. Maybe they won't kill you. I'll go and meet 'em alone. It's me that did· it. Me, the king!' "

" 'Go!' says I. 'Go to Hell, Dan. I'm with you here. Billy Fish, you clear out and we two will meet those folk.'

" 'I'm a chief,' says Billy Fish quite quiet. 'I stay with you. My men can go.'

"The Bashkai fellows didn't wait for a second word but ran off, and Dan and me and Billy Fish walked across to where the drums were drumming and the horns were horning. It was cold—awful cold. I've got that cold in the back of my head now. There's a lump of it there."

The punkah-coolies had gone to sleep. Two kerosene lamps were blazing in the office, and the perspiration poured down my face and splashed on the blotter as I leaned forward. Carnehan was shivering, and I feared that his mind might go. I wiped my face, took a fresh grip of the piteously mangled hands and said, "What happened after that?"

The momentary shift of my eyes had broken the clear current.

"What was you pleased to say?" whined Carnehan. "They took them without any sound. Not a little whisper all along the snow, not though the king knocked down the first man that set hand on him—not though old Peachey fired his last cartridge into the brown of 'em. Not a single solitary sound did those swines make. They just closed up tight, and I tell you their furs stunk. There was a man called Billy Fish, a good friend of us all, and they cut his throat, Sir, then and there, like a pig; and the king kicks up the bloody snow and says:—'We've had a dashed fine run for our money. What's coming next?' But Peachey, Peachey Taliaferro, I tell you, Sir, in confidence as betwixt two friends, he lost his head, Sir. No, he didn't either. The king lost his head, so he did, all along o' one of those cunning rope-bridges. Kindly let me have the paper-cutter, Sir. It tilted this way. They marched him a mile across that snow to a rope-bridge over a ravine with a river at the bottom. You may have seen such. They prodded him behind like an ox. 'Damn your eyes!' says the king. 'D' you suppose I can't die like a gentleman?' He turns to Peachey—Peachey that was crying like a child. 'I've brought you to this, Peachey,' says he. 'Brought you out of your happy life to be killed in Kafiristan, where you was late commander-in-chief of the emperor's forces. Say you forgive me, Peachey.' 'I do,' says Peachey. 'Fully and freely do I forgive you, Dan.' 'Shake hands, Peachey,' says he. 'I'm going now.' Out he goes, looking neither right nor left, and when he was plumb in tho middle of those dizzy dancing ropes, 'Cut, you beggars,' he shouts; and they cut, and old Dan fell, turning round and round and round, twenty thousand miles, for he took half an hour to fall till he struck the water, and I could see his body caught on a rock with the gold crown close beside.

"But do you know what they did to Peachey between two pine-trees? They crucified him, Sir, as Peachey's hands will show. They used wooden pegs for his hands and his feet; and he didn't die. He hung there and screamed; and they took him down next day and said it was a miracle that he wasn't dead. They took him down—poor old Peachey that hadn't done them any harm—that hadn't done them any . . ."

He rocked to and fro and wept bitterly, wiping his eyes with the back of his scarred hands and moaning like a child for some ten minutes.

"They was cruel enough to feed him up in the temple, because they said he was more of a god than old Daniel that was a man. Then they turned him out on the snow, and told him to go home; and Peachey came home in about a year, begging along the roads quite safe; for Daniel Dravot he walked before and said: 'Come along, Peachey. It's a big thing we're doing.' The mountains they danced at night, and the mountains they tried to fall on Peachey's head, but Dan he held up his hand and Peachey came along bent double. He never let go of Dan's hand, and he never let go of Dan's head. They gave it to him as a present in the temple, to remind him not to come again, and though the crown was pure gold, and Peachey was starving, never would Peachey sell the same. You knew Dravot, Sir! You knew Right Worshipful Brother Dravot! Look at him now!"

He fumbled in the mass of rags round his bent waist; brought out a black horsehair bag embroidered with silver thread; and shook therefrom onto my table—the dried, withered head of Daniel Dravot! The morning sun that had long been paling the lamps struck the red beard and blind, sunken eyes; struck, too, a heavy circlet of gold studded with raw turquoises, that Carnehan placed tenderly on the battered temples.

"You behold now," said Carnehan, "the Emperor in his habit as he lived— the King of Kafiristan with his crown upon his head. Poor old Daniel that was a monarch once!"

I shuddered, for, in spite of defacements manifold, I recognized the head of the man of Marwar Junction. Carnehan rose to go. I attempted to stop him. He was not fit to walk abroad. "Let me take away the whisky and give me a little money," he gasped. "I was a king once. I'll go to the deputy commissioner and ask to set in the poor-house till I get my health. No, thank you, I can't wait till you get a carriage for me. I've urgent private affairs—in the south—at Marwar."

He shambled out of the office and departed in the direction of the deputy commissioner's house. That day at noon I had occasion to go down the blinding hot Mall, and I saw a crooked man crawling along the white dust of the road-side, his hat in his hand, quavering dolorously after the fashion of street-singers at home. There was not a soul in sight, and he was out of all possible earshot of the houses. And he sang through his nose, turning his head from right to left:

> "The Son of Man goes forth to war,
> A golden crown to gain:
> His blood-red banner streams afar—
> Who follows in his train?"

I waited to hear no more, but put the poor wretch into my carriage and drove him off to the nearest missionary for eventual transfer to the asylum. He repeated the hymn twice while he was with me, whom he did not in the least recognize, and I left him singing it to the missionary.

Two days later I inquired after his welfare of the superintendent of the asylum.

"He was admitted suffering from sunstroke. He died early yesterday morning," said the superintendent. "Is it true that he was half an hour bareheaded in the sun at midday?"

"Yes," said I; "but do you happen to know if he had anything upon him by any chance when he died?"

"Not to my knowledge," said the superintendent.

And there the matter rests.   (1888)

Maxim Gorky

BOLESS

An acquaintance of mine once told me the following story:

"While still a student at Moscow I happened to be living alongside one of those—well, she was a Polish woman, Teresa by name. A tall, powerfully built brunet with heavy, bushy eyebrows, and a large coarse, vulgar face, as if carved out with an ax—the animal gleam of her eyes, the deep bass voice, the gait and manners of a cabman, and her immense strength like that of a market-woman, inspired me with an inexpressible horror. I lived in the garret of the house, and her room was opposite mine. I never opened my door when I knew that she was in. But this, of course, happened very rarely. Sometimes I chanced to meet her on the landing, staircase, or in the yard, and she would look at me with a smile which seemed to me cynical and rapacious. Occasionally I saw her in her cups, with bleary eyes, her hair and clothes in disorder and with a particularly loathsome smile. On such occasions she would meet my eye with an impudent stare and say:

" 'How are you, Pan Student?'[1]

"And her stupid laugh would increase my dislike for her still more. I would have liked nothing better than to change my quarters in order to get rid of her proximity, but my room was so nice, and the view from my window was so fine, the street below so quiet and peaceful, that I concluded to endure it.

Used by permission of P. F. Collier and Son.
1. Pan is Polish for Mister.

"One morning after I had dressed and was sprawling on the cot, trying to invent some sort of an excuse for not attending my classes, the door of my room suddenly opened, and the disgusting bass voice of the Polish woman sounded from the threshold:

" 'Good morning, Pan Student!'

" 'What is it you wish?' I asked her. I saw she looked confused and had in her face a kind of pleading expression, something unusual with her.

" 'You see, Pan Student, I came to beg you to do me a great favor. Don't refuse me, please!'

"Lying there on my cot I thought that it was just some pretext or other to make my further acquaintance. Take care, my boy!

" 'You see, I have to send a letter to my native country,' she continued in a supplicating, low, tremulous voice.

" 'Well,' I thought, 'the devil take you. If you wish I will write it for you.' And springing to my feet I sat down to the table, took some paper and said: 'Well, come nearer; sit down and dictate.'

"She came over; sat down cautiously on the edge of the chair and looked at me in rather a guilty way.

" 'To whom shall I write?'

" 'To Boleslav Kapshat, in the town Sventsiani, on the Warsaw railroad.'

" 'Well, what shall I write? Speak.'

" 'My dearest Boless, my heart's delight, my beloved. May the Mother of God protect you! My golden heart, why have you not written for so long a time to your sorrowing dove, Teresa—'

"I could hardly keep from laughing. A sorrowing dove, indeed! Almost six feet tall, with the fists of a prize-fighter, and a face so black that it seemed as if the 'dove' had been sweeping chimneys all her life and had never thoroughly washed herself. But I somehow kept my face straight and asked:

" 'Who is this Bolesst?'

" 'Boless, Pan Student,' she replied, seemingly offended because of my mis-pronouncing the name. 'He is my affianced.'

" 'Affianced!'

" 'And why are you so astonished? Can not I, a girl, have an affianced?'

"She—a girl! well, this beats everything I ever heard. Oh, well, who can tell about such matters! Everything is possible in this world.

" 'And have you been long engaged?'

" 'The sixth year.'

" 'Oh, oh!' I thought and then said aloud: 'Well, go ahead with your letter.'

"And I must confess—so tender and loving was this message—that I would have willingly exchanged places with this Boless had the fair correspondent been any one else but Teresa.

" 'I thank you from my inmost soul for your favor, Pan Student,' Teresa said, bowing low. 'Can I in any way be of service to you?'

" 'No, thank you.'

" 'But maybe the Pan's shirts or trousers need mending?'

"This made me quite angry. I felt that this mastodon in petticoats was making the blood mount to my cheeks, and I told her quite sharply that her services were not required; and she departed.

"Two weeks or so passed. One evening I was sitting at my window, softly whistling and thinking hard how to get away from myself. I felt very bored. The weather was as nasty as it could be. To go out that evening was out of the question, and having nothing better to do I began from sheer ennui a course of self-analysis. This proved dull enough work, but there was nothing else to do. Suddenly the door opened, thank God! Some one was coming to see me.

" 'Are you very busy just now, Pan Student?'

" 'Teresa! H'm—' I thought I would have preferred any one at all to her. Then I said aloud:

" 'No, what is it you want now?'

" 'I wish to ask the Pan Student to write me another letter.'

" 'Very well. Is it again to Boless you wish me to write?'

" 'No, this time I want you to write a letter from Boless to me.'

" 'Wha-at?'

" 'I beg your pardon, Pan Student. How stupid of me! It is not for me, this letter, but for a friend of mine, a man acquaintance; he has a fiancée. Her name is like mine, Teresa. He does not know how to write, so I want the Pan Student to write for him a letter to that Teresa—'

"I looked at her. She seemed very confused and frightened, and her fingers trembled. And tho I failed at first to understand what was the matter with her I at last understood.

" 'Look here, my lady,' I said to her. 'You have been telling me a pack of lies. There are no Bolesses nor Teresas among your acquaintances. It is only a pretext for coming in here. I tell you outright that there is no use of coming sneaking around me, as I do not wish to have anything to do with you. Do you understand?'

"She grew very red in the face and I saw that she was strangely frightened and confused, and moved her lips so oddly, wishing to say something, without being able to say it. And somehow I began to think that I had misjudged her a little. There was something behind all this. But what?

" 'Pan Student,' she suddenly began, but broke off, and turning toward the door, walked out of the room.

"I remained with a very unpleasant feeling in my heart. I heard her shut her own door with a bang; evidently the poor girl was very angry—I thought the matter over and decided to go in to her and induce her to return; I would write her the letter she wished.

"I entered her room. She was sitting at the table with her head pressed in her hands.

" 'Teresa,' I said, 'will you listen to me a moment?'

"Whenever I come to this turn of the story I always feel very awkward and embarrassed. But let us return to my narrative. Seeing that she did not reply I repeated:

" 'Listen to me, my girl—'

"She sprang to her feet, came close up to me, with eyes flashing, and placing her two hands on my shoulders she began to whisper, or rather to hum in her deep bass voice:

" 'Look you here, Pan Student. What of it, what of it if there is no Boless? And what if there is no Teresa? What difference does it make to you? Is it so hard for you to draw a few lines on the paper! Oh, you! And I thought you such a good fellow, such a nice fair-haired little boy. Yes, it is true—there is no Boless, and there is no Teresa, there is only me! Well, what of it?'

" 'Allow me,' I said, greatly disconcerted by this reception. 'What is it you are saying? Is there no Boless?'

" 'Yes, there is none. But what of it?'

" 'And no Teresa either?'

" 'No, no Teresa either; that is, yes, I am her.'

"I could not understand a word. I stared straight into her eyes, trying to determine which of us two had lost our reason. And she returned once more to the table, rummaged for some time in the drawer, and coming back to me said in an offended tone:

" 'Here is the letter you wrote for me, take it back. You do not wish to write me a second one anyway. Others will probably be kinder than you and would do so.'

"I recognized the letter she held out to me as the one I wrote for her to Boless. Humph!

" 'Look here, Teresa,' I said to her. 'Will you please explain to me what it all means? Why do you ask people to write letters for you when you do not find it necessary even to post them?'

" 'Post them? Where to?'

" 'Why, to this Boless, of course.'

" 'But he does not exist!'

"I really could not understand a word. There was nothing left for me to do but to spit and walk out of the room. But she explained herself.

" 'Well, what of it?' she began in an offended voice. 'He does not exist. He does not, so,' and she extended her hands as if she could not herself clearly understand why he did not exist in reality. 'But I want him to. Am I not as much of a human being as the others? Of course I—I know— But it does no harm to any one, that I am writing to him—'

" 'Allow me—to whom?'

" 'To Boless, of course.'

" 'But he does not exist.'

" 'Oh, Mother of God! What if he does not exist? He does not; still to me he does. And Teresa—this is myself, and he replies to my letters, and I write to him again.'

"I understood. I felt so sick at heart, so ashamed of myself to know that alongside of me, only three paces removed, lived a human being who had no one in the whole world to love and sympathize with her, and that this being had to invent a friend for herself.

" 'Here you have written a letter from me to Boless, and I gave it to another to read, and when I hear it read it really begins to seem to me as if there is a Boless. And then I ask that a letter be written from Boless to Teresa—that is to me. And when such a letter is written and is read to me then I am almost entirely convinced that there is a Boless, and that makes my life easier.'

"Yes, the devil take it all," continued my acquaintance. "To make a long story short I began from that time on to write with the greatest punctuality twice a week letters to Boless and vice versa. I wrote splendid replies to her. She used to listen to my reading of those epistles and to weep in her bass voice. In return for this she used to mend my clothes and darn my socks.

"Three months later she was thrown into prison for some reason or other and by now she must surely be dead."

My acquaintance blew the ashes from his cigaret, looked thoughtfully at the sky, and concluded:

"Y-e-s, the more a human being has drunk of the cup of bitterness the more ardently he longs for sweetness. And we, enveloped in our worn-out virtues and gazing at each other through the haze of self-sufficiency and convinced of our righteousness, fail to understand it.

"And the whole affair turns out very stupid, and very cruel. Fallen people we say—but who and what are those fallen ones? First of all they are human beings of the very same bone and blood, of the very same flesh and nerves as ourselves. We have been told the very same thing for whole ages, day in and day out. And we listen and—and the devil alone knows how stupid it all is! In reality we, too, are but fallen people and more deeply fallen too, probably— into the abyss of self-sufficiency, convinced of our own sinlessness and superiority, the superiority of our own nerves and brains over the nerves and brains of those who are only less crafty than we are, and who can not, as we can, feign a goodness they do not possess—but enough of this. It is all so old and stale— so old and stale indeed that one is ashamed to speak of it—"   (1897)

Anton Chekhov

THE DARLING

Olenka, the daughter of the retired collegiate assessor, Plemyanniakov, was sitting in her back porch, lost in thought. It was hot, the flies were persistent and teasing, and it was pleasant to reflect that it would soon be evening. Dark rainclouds were gathering from the east, and bringing from time to time a breath of moisture in the air.

From _The Darling and Other Stories_, translated by Constance Garnett. Reprinted by permission of The Macmillan Company and Chatto and Windus.

Kukin, who was the manager of an open-air theater called the Tivoli, and who lived in the lodge, was standing in the middle of the garden looking at the sky.

"Again!" he observed despairingly. "It's going to rain again! Rain every day, as though to spite me. I might as well hang myself! Its ruin! Fearful losses every day."

He flung up his hands, and went on, addressing Olenka:

"There! That's the life we lead, Olga Semyonovna. It's enough to make one cry. One works and does one's utmost; one wears oneself out, getting no sleep at night, and racks one's brain what to do for the best. And then what happens? To begin with, one's public is ignorant, boorish. I give them the very best operetta, a dainty masque, first rate music-hall artists. But do you suppose that's what they want! They don't understand anything of that sort. They want a clown; what they ask for is vulgarity. And then look at the weather! Almost every evening it rains. It started on the tenth of May, and it's kept it up all May and June. It's simply awful! The public doesn't come, but I've to pay the rent just the same, and pay the artists."

The next evening the clouds would gather again, and Kukin would say with an hysterical laugh:

"Well, rain away, then! Flood the garden, drown me! Damn my luck in this world and the next! Let the artists have me up! Send me to prison!—to Siberia!—the scaffold! ha, ha, ha!"

And next day the same thing.

Olenka listened to Kukin with silent gravity, and sometimes tears came into her eyes. In the end his misfortunes touched her; she grew to love him. He was a small thin man, with a yellow face, and curls combed forward on his forehead. He spoke in a thin tenor; as he talked his mouth worked on one side, and there was always an expression of despair on his face; yet he aroused a deep and genuine affection in her. She was always fond of some one, and could not exist without loving. In earlier days she had loved her papa, who now sat in a darkened room, breathing with difficulty; she had loved her aunt who used to come every other year from Bryansk; and before that, when she was at school, she had loved her French master. She was a gentle, soft-hearted, compassionate girl, with mild, tender eyes and very good health. At the sight of her full rosy cheeks, her soft white neck with a little dark mole on it, and the kind, naïve smile, which came into her face when she listened to anything pleasant, men thought, "Yes, not half bad," and smiled too, while lady visitors could not refrain from seizing her hand in the middle of a conversation, exclaiming in a gush of delight, "You darling!"

The house in which she had lived from her birth upwards, and which was left her in her father's will, was at the extreme end of the town, not far from the Tivoli. In the evenings and at night she could hear the band playing, and the crackling and banging of fireworks, and it seemed to her that it was Kukin struggling with his destiny, storming the entrenchments of his chief foe, the indifferent public; there was a sweet thrill at her heart, she had no desire to sleep, and when he returned home at daybreak, she tapped softly at her bedroom window, and showing him only her face and one shoulder through the curtain, she gave him a friendly smile. . . .

He proposed to her, and they were married. And when he had a closer view of her neck and her plump, fine shoulders, he threw up his hands, and said:

"You darling!"

He was happy, but as it rained on the day and night of his wedding, his face still retained an expression of despair.

They got on very well together. She used to sit in his office, to look after things in the Tivoli, to put down the accounts and pay the wages. And her rosy cheeks, her sweet, naïve, radiant smile, were to be seen now at the office window, now in the refreshment bar or behind the scenes of the theater. And already she used to say to her acquaintances that the theater was the chief and most important thing in life, and that it was only through the drama that one could derive true enjoyment and become cultivated and humane.

"But do you suppose the public understands that?" she used to say. "What they want is a clown. Yesterday we gave *Faust Inside Out*, and almost all the boxes were empty; but if Vanitchka and I had been producing some vulgar thing, I assure you the theater would have been packed. Tomorrow Vanitchka and I are doing *Orpheus in Hell*. Do come."

And what Kukin said about the theater and the actors she repeated. Like him she despised the public for their ignorance and their indifference to art; she took part in the rehearsals, she corrected the actors, she kept an eye on the behavior of the musicians, and when there was an unfavorable notice in the local paper, she shed tears, and then went to the editor's office to set things right.

The actors were fond of her and used to call her "Vanitchka and I," and "the darling"; she was sorry for them and used to lend them small sums of money, and if they deceived her, she used to shed a few tears in private, but did not complain to her husband.

They got on well in the winter too. They took the theater in the town for the whole winter, and let it for short terms to a Little Russian company, or to a conjurer, or to a local dramatic society. Olenka grew stouter, and was always beaming with satisfaction, while Kukin grew thinner and yellower, and continually complained of their terrible losses, although he had not done badly all the winter. He used to cough at night, and she used to give him hot raspberry tea or lime-flower water, to rub him with eau de Cologne and to wrap him in her warm shawls.

"You're such a sweet pet!" she used to say with perfect sincerity, stroking his hair. "You're such a pretty dear!"

Towards Lent he went to Moscow to collect a new troupe, and without him she could not sleep, but sat all night at her window, looking at the stars, and she compared herself to the hens, who are awake all night and uneasy when the cock is not in the henhouse. Kukin was detained in Moscow, and wrote that he would be back at Easter, adding some instructions about the Tivoli. But on the Sunday before Easter, late in the evening, came a sudden ominous knock at the gate; some one was hammering on the gate as though on a barrel—boom, boom boom! The drowsy cook went flopping with her bare feet through the puddles, as she ran to open the gate.

"Please open," said some one outside in a thick bass. "There is a telegram for you."

Olenka had received telegrams from her husband before, but this time for some reason she felt numb with terror. With shaking hands she opened the telegram and read as follows:

> Ivan Petrovitch died suddenly today. Awaiting immate instructions fufuneral Tuesday.

That was how it was written in the telegram—"fufuneral," and the utterly incomprehensible word "immate." It was signed by the stage manager of the operatic company.

"My darling!" sobbed Olenka. "Vanitchka, my precious, my darling! Why did I ever meet you! Why did I know you and love you! Your poor heart-broken Olenka is all alone without you!"

Kukin's funeral took place on Tuesday in Moscow, Olenka returned home on Wednesday, and as soon as she got indoors she threw herself on her bed and sobbed so loudly that it could be heard next door, and in the street.

"Poor darling!" the neighbors said, as they crossed themselves. "Olga Semyonovna, poor darling! How she does take on!"

Three months later Olenka was coming home from mass, melancholy and in deep mourning. It happened that one of her neighbors, Vassily Andreitch Pustovalov, returning home from church, walked back beside her. He was the manager at Babakayev's, the timber merchant's. He wore a straw hat, a white waistcoat, and a gold watch-chain, and looked more like a country gentleman than a man in trade.

"Everything happens as it is ordained, Olga Semyonovna," he said gravely, with a sympathetic note in his voice; "and if any of our dear ones die, it must be because it is the will of God, so we ought to have fortitude and bear it submissively."

After seeing Olenka to her gate, he said good-by and went on. All day afterwards she heard his sedately dignified voice, and whenever she shut her eyes she saw his dark beard. She liked him very much. And apparently she had made an impression on him too, for not long afterwards an elderly lady, with whom she was only slightly acquainted, came to drink coffee with her, and as soon as she was seated at table began to talk about Pustovalov, saying that he was an excellent man whom one could thoroughly depend upon, and that any girl would be glad to marry him. Three days later Pustovalov came himself. He did not stay long, only about ten minutes, and he did not say much, but when he left, Olenka loved him—loved him so much that she lay awake all night in a perfect fever, and in the morning she sent for the elderly lady. The match was quickly arranged, and then came the wedding.

Pustovalov and Olenka got on very well together when they were married.

Usually he sat in the office till dinnertime, then he went out on business, while Olenka took his place, and sat in the office till evening, making up accounts and booking orders.

"Timber gets dearer every year; the price rises twenty per cent," she would say to her customers and friends. "Only fancy we used to sell local timber, and now Vassitchka always has to go for wood to the Mogilev district. And the freight!" she would add, covering her cheeks with her hands in horror. "The freight!"

It seemed to her that she had been in the timber trade for ages and ages, and that the most important and necessary thing in life was timber; and there was something intimate and touching to her in the very sound of words such as "baulk," "post," "beam," "pole," "scantling," "batten," "lath," "plank," etc.

At night when she was asleep she dreamed of perfect mountains of planks and boards, and long strings of wagons, carting timber somewhere far away. She dreamed that a whole regiment of six-inch beams forty feet high, standing on end, was marching upon the timber-yard; that logs, beams, and boards knocked together with the resounding crash of dry wood, kept falling and getting up again, piling themselves on each other. Olenka cried out in her sleep, and Pustovalov said to her tenderly: "Olenka, what's the matter, darling? Cross yourself!"

Her husband's ideas were hers. If he thought the room was too hot, or that business was slack, she thought the same. Her husband did not care for entertainments, and on holidays he stayed at home. She did likewise.

"You are always at home or in the office," her friends said to her. "You should go to the theater, darling, or to the circus."

"Vassitchka and I have no time to go to theaters," she would answer sedately. "We have no time for nonsense. What's the use of these theaters?"

On Saturdays Pustovalov and she used to go to the evening service; on holidays to early mass, and they walked side by side with softened faces as they came home from church. There was a pleasant fragrance about them both, and her silk dress rustled agreeably. At home they drank tea, with fancy bread and jams of various kinds, and afterwards they ate pie. Every day at twelve o'clock there was a savory smell of beet-root soup and of mutton or duck in their yard, and on fast-days of fish, and no one could pass the gate without feeling hungry. In the office the samovar was always boiling, and customers were regaled with tea and cracknels. Once a week the couple went to the baths and returned side by side, both red in the face.

"Yes, we have nothing to complain of, thank God," Olenka used to say to her acquaintances. "I wish every one were as well off as Vassitchka and I."

When Pustovalov went away to buy wood in the Mogilev district, she missed him dreadfully, lay awake and cried. A young veterinary surgeon in the army, called Smirnin, to whom they had let their lodge, used sometimes to come in in the evening. He used to talk to her and play cards with her, and this entertained her in her husband's absence. She was particularly interested in what he told her of his home life. He was married and had a little boy, but was separated from his wife because she had been unfaithful to him, and now he hated her and used to send her forty roubles a month for the maintenance of their son. And hearing of all this, Olenka sighed and shook her head. She was sorry for him.

"Well, God keep you," she used to say to him at parting, as she lighted him down the stairs with a candle. "Thank you for coming to cheer me up, and may the Mother of God give you health."

And she always expressed herself with the same sedateness and dignity, the same reasonableness, in imitation of her husband. As the veterinary surgeon was disappearing behind the door below, she would say:

"You know, Vladimir Platonitch, you'd better make it up with your wife. You should forgive her for the sake of your son. You may be sure the little fellow understands."

And when Pustovalov came back, she told him in a low voice about the veterinary surgeon and his unhappy home life, and both sighed and shook their heads and talked about the boy, who, no doubt, missed his father, and by some strange connection of ideas, they went up to the holy ikons, bowed to the ground before them and prayed that God would give them children.

And so the Pustovalovs lived for six years quietly and peaceably in love and complete harmony.

But behold! one winter day after drinking hot tea in the office, Vassily Andreitch went out into the yard without his cap on to see about sending off some timber, caught cold and was taken ill. He had the best doctors, but he grew worse and died after four months' illness. And Olenka was a widow once more.

"I've nobody, now you've left me, my Darling," she sobbed, after her husband's funeral. "How can I live without you, in wretchedness and misery! Pity me, good people, all alone in the world!"

She went about dressed in black with long "weepers," and gave up wearing hat and gloves for good. She hardly ever went out, except to church, or to her husband's grave, and led the life of a nun. It was not till six months later that she took off the weepers and opened the shutters of the windows. She was sometimes seen in the mornings, going with her cook to market for provisions, but what went on in her house and how she lived now could only be surmised. People guessed, from seeing her drinking tea in her garden with the veterinary surgeon, who read the newspaper aloud to her, and from the fact that, meeting a lady she knew at the post office, she said to her:

"There is no proper veterinary inspection in our town, and that's the cause of all sorts of epidemics. One is always hearing of people's getting infection from the milk supply, or catching diseases from horses and cows. The health of domestic animals ought to be as well cared for as the health of human beings."

She repeated the veterinary surgeon's words, and was of the same opinion as he about everything. It was evident that she could not live a year without some attachment, and had found new happiness in the lodge. In any one else this would have been censured, but no one could think ill of Olenka; everything she did was so natural. Neither she nor the veterinary surgeon said anything to other people of the change in their relations, and tried, indeed, to conceal it, but without success, for Olenka could not keep a secret. When he had visitors, men serving in his regiment, and she poured out tea or served the supper, she would begin talking of the cattle plague, of the foot and mouth disease, and of the municipal slaughter-houses. He was dreadfully embarrassed, and when the guests had gone, he would seize her by the hand and hiss angrily:

"I've asked you before not to talk about what you don't understand. When we veterinary surgeons are talking among ourselves, please don't put your word in. It's really annoying."

And she would look at him with astonishment and dismay, and ask him in alarm: "But, Voloditchka, what *am* I to talk about?"

And with tears in her eyes she would embrace him, begging him not to be angry, and they were both happy.

But this happiness did not last long. The veterinary surgeon departed, departed forever with his regiment, when it was transferred to a distant place—to Siberia, it may be. And Olenka was left alone.

Now she was absolutely alone. Her father had long been dead, and his arm-chair lay in the attic, covered with dust and lame of one leg. She got thinner and plainer, and when people met her in the street they did not look at her as they used to, and did not smile to her; evidently her best years were over and left behind, and now a new sort of life had begun for her, which did not bear thinking about. In the evening Olenka sat in the porch, and heard the band playing and the fireworks popping in the Tivoli, but now the sound stirred no response. She looked into her yard without interest, thought of nothing, wished for nothing, and afterwards, when night came on she went to bed and dreamed of her empty yard. She ate and drank as it were unwillingly.

And what was worst of all, she had no opinions of any sort. She saw the objects about her and understood what she saw, but could not form any opinion about them, and did not know what to talk about. And how awful it is not to have any opinions! One sees a bottle, for instance, or the rain, or a peasant driving in his cart, but what the bottle is for, or the rain, or the peasant, and what is the meaning of it, one can't say, and could not even for a thousand roubles. When she had Kukin, or Pustovalov, or the veterinary surgeon, Olenka could explain everything, and give her opinion about anything you like, but now there was the same emptiness in her brain and in her heart as there was in her yard outside. And it was as harsh and as bitter as wormwood in the mouth.

Little by little the town grew in all directions. The road became a street, and where the Tivoli and the timber-yard had been there were new turnings and houses. How rapidly time passes! Olenka's house grew dingy, the roof got rusty, the shed sank on one side, and the whole yard was overgrown with docks and stinging-nettles. Olenka herself had grown plain and elderly; in summer she sat in the porch, and her soul, as before, was empty and dreary and full of bitterness. In winter she sat at her window and looked at the snow. When she caught the scent of spring, or heard the chime of the church bells, a sudden rush of memories from the past came over her, there was a tender ache in her heart, and her eyes brimmed over with tears; but this was only for a minute, and then came emptiness again and the sense of the futility of life. The black kitten, Briska, rubbed against her and purred softly, but Olenka was not touched by these feline caresses. That was not what she needed. She wanted a love that would absorb her whole being, her whole soul and reason—that would give her ideas and an object in life, and would warm her old blood. And she would shake the kitten off her skirt and say with vexation:

"Get along; I don't want you!"

And so it was, day after day and year after year, and no joy, and no opinions. Whatever Mavra, the cook, said she accepted.

One hot July day, towards evening, just as the cattle were being driven away, and the whole yard was full of dust, some one suddenly knocked at the gate. Olenka went to open it herself and was dumbfounded when she looked out: she saw Smirnin, the veterinary surgeon, gray-headed, and dressed as a civilian. She suddenly remembered everything. She could not help crying and letting her head fall on his breast without uttering a word, and in the violence of her feeling she did not notice how they both walked into the house and sat down to tea.

"My dear Vladimir Platonitch! What fate has brought you?" she muttered, trembling with joy.

"I want to settle here for good, Olga Semyonovna," he told her. "I have resigned my post, and have come to settle down and try my luck on my own account. Besides, it's time for my boy to go to school. He's a big boy. I am reconciled with my wife, you know."

"Where is she?" asked Olenka.

"She's at the hotel with the boy, and I'm looking for lodgings."

"Good gracious, my dear soul! Lodgings? Why not have my house? Why shouldn't that suit you? Why, my goodness, I wouldn't take any rent!" cried Olenka in a flutter, beginning to cry again. "You live here, and the lodge will do nicely for me. Oh, dear! how glad I am!"

Next day the roof was painted and the walls were whitewashed, and Olenka, with her arms akimbo, walked about the yard giving directions. Her face was beaming with her old smile, and she was brisk and alert as though she had waked from a long sleep. The veterinary's wife arrived—a thin, plain lady, with short hair and a peevish expression. With her was her little Sasha, a boy of ten, small for his age, blue-eyed, chubby, with dimples in his cheeks. And scarcely had the boy walked into the yard when he ran after the cat, and at once there was the sound of his gay, joyous laugh.

"Is that your puss, Auntie?" he asked Olenka. "When she has little ones, do give us a kitten. Mamma is awfully afraid of mice."

Olenka talked to him, and gave him tea. Her heart warmed and there was a sweet ache in her bosom, as though the boy had been her own child. And when he sat at the table in the evening, going over his lessons, she looked at him with deep tenderness and pity as she murmured to herself:

"You pretty pet! . . . my precious! . . . Such a fair little thing, and so clever."

" 'An island is a piece of land which is entirely surrounded by water,' " he read aloud.

"An island is a piece of land," she repeated, and this was the first opinion to which she gave utterance with positive conviction after so many years of silence and dearth of ideas.

Now she had opinions of her own, and at supper she talked to Sasha's parents, saying how difficult the lessons were at the high schools, but that yet the high school was better than a commercial one, since with a high school education all careers were open to one, such as being a doctor or an engineer.

Sasha began going to the high school. His mother departed to Harkov to her sister's and did not return; his father used to go off every day to inspect cattle, and would often be away from home for three days together, and it seemed to Olenka as though Sasha was entirely abandoned, that he was not wanted at home, that he was being starved, and she carried him off to her lodge and gave him a little room there.

And for six months Sasha had lived in the lodge with her. Every morning Olenka came into his bedroom and found him fast asleep, sleeping noiselessly with his hand under his cheek. She was sorry to wake him.

"Sashenka," she would say mournfully, "get up, Darling. It's time for school."

He would get up, dress and say his prayers, and then sit down to breakfast, drink three glasses of tea, and eat two large cracknels and half a buttered roll. All this time he was hardly awake and a little ill-humored in consequence.

"You don't quite know your fable, Sashenka," Olenka would say, looking at him as though he were about to set off on a long journey. "What a lot of trouble I have with you! You must work and do your best, Darling, and obey your teachers."

"Oh, do leave me alone!" Sasha would say.

Then he would go down the street to school, a little figure, wearing a big cap and carrying a satchel on his shoulder. Olenka would follow him noiselessly.

"Sashenka!" she would call after him, and she would pop into his hand a date or a caramel. When he reached the street where the school was, he would feel ashamed of being followed by a tall, stout woman; he would turn round and say:

"You'd better go home, Auntie. I can go the rest of the way alone."

She would stand still and look after him fixedly till he had disappeared at the school gate.

Ah, how she loved him! Of her former attachments not one had been so deep; never had her soul surrendered to any feeling so spontaneously, so disinterestedly, and so joyously as now that her maternal instincts were aroused. For this little boy with the dimple in his cheek and the big school cap she would have given her whole life, she would have given it with joy and tears of tenderness. Why? Who can tell why?

When she had seen the last of Sasha, she returned home, contented and serene, brimming over with love; her face, which had grown younger during the last six months, smiled and beamed; people meeting her looked at her with pleasure.

"Good morning, Olga Semyonovna, Darling. How are you, Darling?"

"The lessons at the high school are very difficult now," she would relate at the market. "It's too much; in the first class yesterday they gave him a fable to learn by heart, and a Latin translation and a problem. You know it's too much for a little chap."

And she would begin talking about the teachers, the lessons, and the school books, saying just what Sasha said.

At three o'clock they had dinner together: in the evening they learned their lessons together and cried. When she put him to bed, she would stay a long time making the cross over him and murmuring a prayer; then she would go to bed and dream of that far-away, misty future when Sasha would finish his studies and become a doctor or an engineer, would have a big house of his own with horses and a carriage, would get married and have children. . . . She would fall asleep still thinking of the same thing, and tears would run down her cheeks from her closed eyes, while the black cat lay purring beside her: "Mrr, mrr, mrr."

Suddenly there would come a loud knock at the gate.

Olenka would wake up breathless with alarm, her heart throbbing. Half a minute later would come another knock.

"It must be a telegram from Harkov," she would think, beginning to tremble from head to foot. "Sasha's mother is sending for him from Harkov. . . . Oh, mercy on us!"

She was in despair. Her head, her hands, and her feet would turn chill, and she would feel that she was the most unhappy woman in the world. But another minute would pass, voices would be heard: it would turn out to be the veterinary surgeon coming home from the club.

"Well, thank God!" she would think.

And gradually the load in her heart would pass off, and she would feel at ease. She would go back to bed thinking of Sasha, who lay sound asleep in the next room, sometimes crying out in his sleep:

"I'll give it you! Get away! Shut up!"   (1898)

Stephen Crane

THE BRIDE COMES
TO YELLOW SKY

The great Pullman was whirling onward with such dignity of motion that a glance from the window seemed simply to prove that the plains of Texas were pouring eastward. Vast flats of green grass, dull-hued spaces of mesquit and cactus, little groups of frame houses, woods of light and tender trees, all were sweeping into the east, sweeping over the horizon, a precipice.

A newly married pair had boarded this coach at San Antonio. The man's face was reddened from many days in the wind and sun, and a direct result of his new black clothes was that his brick-colored hands were constantly performing in a most conscious fashion. From time to time he looked down respectfully at his attire. He sat with a hand on each knee, like a man waiting in a barber's shop. The glances he devoted to other passengers were furtive and shy.

The bride was not pretty, nor was she very young. She wore a dress of blue cashmere, with small reservations of velvet here and there, and with steel buttons abounding. She continually twisted her head to regard her puff sleeves, very stiff, straight, and high. They embarrassed her. It was quite apparent that she had cooked, and that she expected to cook, dutifully. The blushes caused by the careless scrutiny of some passengers as she had entered the car were strange to see upon this plain, under-class countenance, which was drawn in placid, almost emotionless lines.

They were evidently very happy. "Ever been in a parlor-car before?" he asked, smiling with delight.

"No," she answered; "I never was. It's fine, ain't it?"

"Great! And then after a while we'll go forward to the diner, and get a big lay-out. Finest meal in the world. Charge a dollar."

"Oh, do they?" cried the bride. "Charge a dollar? Why, that's too much— for us—ain't it, Jack?"

"Not this trip, anyhow," he answered bravely. "We're going to go the whole thing."

Later he explained to her about the trains. "You see, it's a thousand miles from one end of Texas to the other; and this train runs right across it, and never stops but four times." He had the pride of an owner. He pointed out to her the dazzling fittings of the coach; and in truth her eyes opened wider as she contemplated the sea-green figured velvet, the shining brass, silver, and glass, the wood that gleamed as darkly brilliant as the surface of a pool of oil.

At one end a bronze figure sturdily held a support for a separated chamber, and at convenient places on the ceiling were frescos in olive and silver.

To the minds of the pair, their surroundings reflected the glory of their marriage that morning in San Antonio; this was the environment of their new estate; and the man's face in particular beamed with an elation that made him appear ridiculous to the negro porter. This individual at times surveyed them from afar with an amused and superior grin. On other occasions he bullied them with skill in ways that did not make it exactly plain to them that they were being bullied. He subtly used all the manners of the most unconquerable kind of snobbery. He oppressed them; but of this oppression they had small knowledge, and they speedily forgot that infrequently a number of travellers covered them with stares of derisive enjoyment. Historically there was supposed to be something infinitely humorous in their situation.

"We are due in Yellow Sky at 3:42," he said, looking tenderly into her eyes.

"Oh, are we?" she said, as if she had not been aware of it. To evince surprise at her husband's statement was part of her wifely amiability. She took from a pocket a little silver watch; and as she held it before her, and stared at it with a frown of attention, the new husband's face shone.

"I bought it in San Anton' from a friend of mine," he told her gleefully.

"It's seventeen minutes past twelve," she said, looking up at him with a kind of shy and clumsy coquetry. A passenger, noting this play, grew excessively sardonic, and winked at himself in one of the numerous mirrors.

At last they went to the dining-car. Two rows of negro waiters, in glowing white suits, surveyed their entrance with the interest, and also the equanimity, of men who had been forewarned. The pair fell to the lot of a waiter who happened to feel pleasure in steering them through their meal. He viewed them with the manner of a fatherly pilot, his countenance radiant with benevolence. The patronage, entwined with the ordinary deference, was not plain to them. And yet, as they returned to their coach, they showed in their faces a sense of escape.

To the left, miles down a long purple slope, was a little ribbon of mist where moved the keening Rio Grande. The train was approaching it at an angle, and the apex was Yellow Sky. Presently it was apparent that, as the distance from Yellow Sky grew shorter, the husband became commensurately restless. His brick-red hands were more insistent in their prominence. Occasionally he was even rather absent-minded and far-away when the bride leaned forward and addressed him.

As a matter of truth, Jack Potter was beginning to find the shadow of a deed weigh upon him like a leaden slab. He, the town marshal of Yellow Sky, a man known, liked, and feared in his corner, a prominent person, had gone to San Antonio to meet a girl he believed he loved, and there, after the usual prayers, had actually induced her to marry him, without consulting Yellow Sky for any part of the transaction. He was now bringing his bride before an innocent and unsuspecting community.

Of course people in Yellow Sky married as it pleased them, in accordance with a general custom; but such was Potter's thought of his duty to his friends, or of their idea of his duty, or of an unspoken form which does not control men in these matters, that he felt he was heinous. He had committed an extraordinary crime. Face to face with this girl in San Antonio, and spurred by his sharp impulse, he had gone headlong over all the social hedges. At San Antonio he was like a man hidden in the dark. A knife to sever any friendly duty, any form, was easy to his hand in that remote city. But the hour of Yellow Sky—the hour of daylight—was approaching.

He knew full well that his marriage was an important thing to his town. It could only be exceeded by the burning of the new hotel. His friends could not forgive him. Frequently he had reflected on the advisability of telling them by telegraph, but a new cowardice had been upon him. He feared to do it. And now the train was hurrying him toward a scene of amazement, glee, and reproach. He glanced out of the window at the line of haze swinging slowly in toward the train.

Yellow Sky had a kind of brass band, which played painfully, to the delight of the populace. He laughed without heart as he thought of it. If the citizens could dream of his prospective arrival with his bride, they would parade the band at the station and escort them, amid cheers and laughing congratulations, to his adobe home.

He resolved that he would use all the devices of speed and plains-craft in making the journey from the station to his house. Once within that safe citadel, he could issue some sort of vocal bulletin, and then not go among the citizens until they had time to wear off a little of their enthusiasm.

The bride looked anxiously at him. "What's worrying you, Jack?"

He laughed again. "I'm not worrying, girl; I'm only thinking of Yellow Sky."

She flushed in comprehension.

A sense of mutual guilt invaded their minds and developed a finer tenderness. They looked at each other with eyes softly aglow. But Potter often laughed the same nervous laugh; the flush upon the bride's face seemed quite permanent.

The traitor to the feelings of Yellow Sky narrowly watched the speeding landscape. "We're nearly there," he said.

Presently the porter came and announced the proximity of Potter's home. He held a brush in his hand, and, with all his airy superiority gone, he brushed Potter's new clothes as the latter slowly turned this way and that way. Potter fumbled out a coin and gave it to the porter, as he had seen others do. It was a heavy and muscle-bound business, as that of a man shoeing his first horse.

The porter took their bag, and as the train began to slow they moved forward to the hooded platform of the car. Presently the two engines and their long string of coaches rushed into the station of Yellow Sky.

"They have to take water here," said Potter, from a constricted throat and in mournful cadence, as one announcing death. Before the train stopped his eye had swept the length of the platform, and he was glad and astonished to see there was none upon it but the station-agent, who, with a slightly hurried and anxious air, was walking toward the water-tanks. When the train had halted, the porter alighted first, and placed in position a little temporary step.

"Come on, girl," said Potter, hoarsely. As he helped her down they each laughed on a false note. He took the bag from the negro, and bade his wife cling to his arm. As they slunk rapidly away, his hang-dog glance perceived that they were unloading the two trunks, and also that the station-agent, far ahead near the baggage-car, had turned and was running toward him, making gestures. He laughed, and groaned as he laughed, when he noted the first effect of his marital bliss upon Yellow Sky. He gripped his wife's arm firmly to his side, and they fled. Behind them the porter stood, chuckling fatuously.

II

The California express on the Southern Railway was due at Yellow Sky in twenty-one minutes. There were six men at the bar of the Weary Gentleman Saloon. One was a drummer, who talked a great deal and rapidly; three were Texans, who did not care to talk at that time; and two were Mexican sheep-herders, who did not talk as a general practice in the Weary Gentleman Saloon. The barkeeper's dog lay on the board walk that crossed in front of the door. His head was on his paws, and he glanced drowsily here and there with the constant vigilance of a dog that is kicked on occasion. Across the sandy street were some vivid green grass-plots, so wonderful in appearance, amid the sands that burned near them in a blazing sun, that they caused a doubt in the mind. They exactly resembled the grass mats used to represent lawns on the stage. At the cooler end of the railway station, a man without a coat sat in a tilted chair and smoked his pipe. The fresh-cut bank of the Rio Grande circled near the town, and there could be seen beyond it a great plum-colored plain of mesquit.

Save for the busy drummer and his companions in the saloon, Yellow Sky was dozing. The new-comer leaned gracefully upon the bar, and recited many tales with the confidence of a bard who has come upon a new field.

"—and at the moment that the old man fell downstairs with the bureau in his arms, the old woman was coming up with two scuttles of coal, and of course—"

The drummer's tale was interrupted by a young man who suddenly appeared in the open door. He cried: "Scratchy Wilson's drunk, and has turned loose with both hands." The two Mexicans at once set down their glasses and faded out of the rear entrance of the saloon.

The drummer, innocent and jocular, answered: "All right, old man. S'pose he has? Come in and have a drink, anyhow."

But the information had made such an obvious cleft in every skull in the room that the drummer was obliged to see its importance. All had become instantly solemn. "Say," said he, mystified, "what is this?" His three companions made the introductory gesture of eloquent speech; but the young man at the door forestalled them.

"It means, my friend," he answered, as he came into the saloon, "that for the next two hours this town won't be a health resort."

The barkeeper went to the door, and locked and barred it; reaching out of the window, he pulled in heavy wooden shutters, and barred them. Immediately a solemn, chapel-like gloom was upon the place. The drummer was looking from one to another.

"But say," he cried, "what is this, anyhow? You don't mean there is going to be a gun-fight?"

"Don't know whether there'll be a fight or not," answered one man, grimly; "but there'll be some shootin'—some good shootin'."

The young man who had warned them waved his hand. "Oh, there'll be a fight fast enough, if any one wants it. Anybody can get a fight out there in the street. There's a fight just waiting."

The drummer seemed to be swayed between the interest of a foreigner and a perception of personal danger.

"What did you say his name was?" he asked.

"Scratchy Wilson," they answered in chorus.

"And will he kill anybody? What are you going to do? Does this happen often? Does he rampage around like this once a week or so? Can he break in that door?"

"No; he can't break down that door," replied the barkeeper. "He's tried it three times. But when he comes you'd better lay down on the floor, stranger. He's dead sure to shoot at it, and a bullet may come through."

Thereafter the drummer kept a strict eye upon the door. The time had not yet been called for him to hug the floor, but, as a minor precaution, he sidled near to the wall. "Will he kill anybody?" he said again.

The men laughed low and scornfully at the question.

"He's out to shoot, and he's out for trouble. Don't see any good in experimentin' with him."

"But what do you do in a case like this? What do you do?"

A man responded: "Why, he and Jack Potter—"

"But," in chorus the other men interrupted, "Jack Potter's in San Anton'."

"Well, who is he? What's he got to do with it?"

"Oh, he's the town marshal. He goes out and fights Scratchy when he gets on one of these tears."

"Wow!" said the drummer, mopping his brow. "Nice job he's got."

The voices had toned away to mere whisperings. The drummer wished to ask further questions, which were born of an increasing anxiety and bewilderment; but when he attempted them, the men merely looked at him in irritation and motioned him to remain silent. A tense waiting hush was upon them. In the deep shadows of the room their eyes shone as they listened for sounds from the street. One man made three gestures at the barkeeper; and the latter, moving like a ghost, handed him a glass and a bottle. The man poured a full glass of whiskey, and set down the bottle noiselessly. He gulped the whiskey in a swallow, and turned again toward the door in immovable silence. The drummer saw that the barkeeper, without a sound, had taken a Winchester from beneath the bar. Later he saw this individual beckoning to him, so he tiptoed across the room.

"You better come with me back of the bar."

"No, thanks," said the drummer, perspiring; "I'd rather be where I can make a break for the back door."

Whereupon the man of bottles made a kindly but peremptory gesture. The drummer obeyed it, and, finding himself seated on a box with his head below the level of the bar, balm was laid upon his soul at sight of various zinc and copper fittings that bore a resemblance to armor-plate. The barkeeper took a seat comfortably upon an adjacent box.

"You see," he whispered, "this here Scratchy Wilson is a wonder with a gun —a perfect wonder; and when he goes on the wartrail, we hunt out holes— naturally. He's about the last one of the old gang that used to hang out along the river here. He's a terror when he's drunk. When he's sober he's all right— kind of simple—wouldn't hurt a fly—nicest fellow in town. But when he's drunk—whoo!"

There were periods of stillness. "I wish Jack Potter was back from San An- ton'," said the barkeeper. "He shot Wilson up once—in the leg—and he would sail in and pull out the kinks in this thing."

Presently they heard from a distance the sound of a shot, followed by three wild yowls. It instantly removed a bond from the men in the darkened saloon. There was a shuffling of feet. They looked at each other. "Here he comes," they said.

III

A man in a maroon-colored flannel shirt, which had been purchased for purposes of decoration, and made principally by some Jewish women on the East Side of New York, rounded a corner and walked into the middle of the main street of Yellow Sky. In either hand the man held a long, heavy, blue-black revolver. Often he yelled, and these cries rang through a semblance of a deserted village, shrilly flying over the roofs in a volume that seemed to have no relation to the ordinary vocal strength of a man. It was as if the surrounding stillness formed the arch of a tomb over him. These cries of ferocious challenge rang against walls of silence. And his boots had red tops with gilded imprints, of the kind beloved in winter by little sledding boys on the hillsides of New England.

The man's face flamed in a rage begot of whiskey. His eyes, rolling, and yet keen for ambush, hunted the still doorways and windows. He walked with the creeping movement of the midnight cat. As it occurred to him, he roared menacing information. The long revolvers in his hands were as easy as straws; they were moved with an electric swiftness. The little fingers of each hand played sometimes in a musician's way. Plain from the low collar of the shirt, the cords of his neck straightened and sank, straightened and sank, as passion moved him. The only sounds were his terrible invitations. The calm adobes preserved their demeanor at the passing of this small thing in the middle of the street.

There was no offer of fight—no offer of fight. The man called to the sky. There were no attractions. He bellowed and fumed and swayed his revolvers here and everywhere.

The dog of the barkeeper of the Weary Gentleman Saloon had not appreciated the advance of events. He yet lay dozing in front of his master's door. At sight of the dog, the man paused and raised his revolver humorously. At sight of the man, the dog sprang up and walked diagonally away, with a sullen head, and growling. The man yelled, and the dog broke into a gallop. As it was about to enter an alley, there was a loud noise, a whistling, and something spat the ground directly before it. The dog screamed, and, wheeling in terror, galloped headlong in a new direction. Again there was a noise, a whistling, and sand was kicked viciously before it. Fear-stricken, the dog turned and flurried like an animal in a pen. The man stood laughing, his weapons at his hips.

Ultimately the man was attracted by the closed door of the Weary Gentleman Saloon. He went to it, and, hammering with a revolver, demanded drink.

The door remaining imperturbable, he picked a bit of paper from the walk, and nailed it to the framework with a knife. He then turned his back contemptuously upon this popular resort and, walking to the opposite side of the street, and spinning there on his heel quickly and lithely, fired at the bit of paper. He missed it by a half-inch. He swore at himself, and went away. Later he comfortably fusilladed the windows of his most intimate friend. The man was playing with this town; it was a toy for him.

But still there was no offer of fight. The name of Jack Potter, his ancient antagonist, entered his mind, and he concluded that it would be a glad thing if he should go to Potter's house, and by bombardment induce him to come out and fight. He moved in the direction of his desire, chanting Apache scalp-music.

When he arrived at it, Potter's house presented the same still front as had the other adobes. Taking up a strategic position, the man howled a challenge. But this house regarded him as might a great stone god. It gave no sign. After a decent wait, the man howled further challenges, mingling with them wonderful epithets.

Presently there came the spectacle of a man churning himself into deepest rage over the immobility of a house. He fumed at it as the winter wind attacks a prairie cabin in the North. To the distance there should have gone the sound of a tumult like the fighting of two hundred Mexicans. As necessity bade him, he paused for breath or to reload his revolvers.

IV

Potter and his bride walked sheepishly and with speed. Sometimes they laughed together shamefacedly and low.

"Next corner, dear," he said finally.

They put forth the efforts of a pair walking bowed against a strong wind. Potter was about to raise a finger to point the first appearance of the new home when, as they circled the corner, they came face to face with a man in a maroon-colored shirt, who was feverishly pushing cartridges into a large revolver. Upon the instant the man dropped his revolver to the ground and, like lightning, whipped another from its holster. The second weapon was aimed at the bridegroom's chest.

There was a silence. Potter's mouth seemed to be merely a grave for his tongue. He exhibited an instinct to at once loosen his arm from the woman's grip, and he dropped the bag to the sand. As for the bride, her face had gone as yellow as old cloth. She was a slave to hideous rites, gazing at the apparitional snake.

The two men faced each other at a distance of three paces. He of the revolver smiled with a new and quiet ferocity.

"Tried to sneak up on me," he said. "Tried to sneak up on me!" His eyes grew more baleful. As Potter made a slight movement, the man thrust his revolver venomously forward. "No; don't you do it, Jack Potter. Don't you move a finger toward a gun just yet. Don't you move an eyelash. The time has come for me to settle with you, and I'm goin' to do it my own way, and loaf along with no interferin'. So if you don't want a gun bent on you, just mind what I tell you."

Potter looked at his enemy. "I ain't got a gun on me, Scratchy," he said. "Honest, I ain't." He was stiffening and steadying, but yet somewhere at the back of his mind a vision of the Pullman floated: the sea-green figured velvet, the shining brass, silver, and glass, the wood that gleamed as darkly brilliant as the surface of a pool of oil—all the glory of the marriage, the environment of the new estate. "You know I fight when it comes to fighting, Scratchy Wilson; but I ain't got a gun on me. You'll have to do all the shootin' yourself."

His enemy's face went livid. He stepped forward, and lashed his weapon to and fro before Potter's chest. "Don't you tell me you ain't got no gun on you, you whelp. Don't tell me no lie like that. There ain't a man in Texas ever seen you without no gun. Don't take me for no kid." His eyes blazed with light, and his throat worked like a pump.

"I ain't takin' you for no kid," answered Potter. His heels had not moved an inch backward. "I'm takin' you for a damn fool. I tell you I ain't got a gun, and I ain't. If you're goin' to shoot me up, you better begin now; you'll never get a chance like this again."

So much enforced reasoning had told on Wilson's rage; he was calmer. "If you ain't got a gun, why ain't you got a gun?" he sneered. "Been to Sunday-school?"

"I ain't got a gun because I've just come from San Anton' with my wife. I'm married," said Potter. "And if I'd thought there was going to be any galoots like you prowling around when I brought my wife home, I'd had a gun, and don't you forget it."

"Married!" said Scratchy, not at all comprehending.

"Yes, married. I'm married," said Potter, distinctly.

"Married?" said Scratchy. Seemingly for the first time, he saw the drooping, drowning woman at the other man's side. "No!" he said. He was like a creature allowed a glimpse of another world. He moved a pace backward, and his arm, with the revolver, dropped to his side. "Is this the lady?" he asked.

"Yes; this is the lady," answered Potter.

There was another period of silence.

"Well," said Wilson at last, slowly, "I s'pose it's all off now."

"It's all off if you say so, Scratchy. You know I didn't make the trouble." Potter lifted his valise.

"Well, I 'low it's off, Jack," said Wilson. He was looking at the ground. "Married!" He was not a student of chivalry; it was merely that in the presence of this foreign condition he was a simple child of the earlier plains. He picked up his starboard revolver, and, placing both weapons in their holsters, he went away. His feet made funnel-shaped tracks in the heavy sand.   (1898)

Henry James

MRS. MEDWIN

"Well, we *are* a pair!" the poor lady's visitor broke out to her, at the end of her explanation, in a manner disconcerting enough. The poor lady was Miss Cutter, who lived in South Audley Street, where she had an "upper half" so concise that it had to pass, boldly, for convenient; and her visitor was her half-brother, whom she had not seen for three years. She was remarkable for a maturity of which every symptom might have been observed to be admirably controlled, had not a tendency to stoutness just affirmed its independence. Her present, no doubt, insisted too much on her past, but with the excuse, sufficiently valid, that she must certainly once have been prettier. She was clearly not contented with once—she wished to be prettier again. She neglected nothing that could produce that illusion, and, being both fair and fat, dressed almost wholly in black. When she added a little color it was not, at any rate, to her drapery. Her small rooms had the peculiarity that everything they contained appeared to testify with vividness to her position in society, quite as if they had been furnished by the bounty of admiring friends. They were adorned indeed almost exclusively with objects that nobody buys, as had more than once been remarked by spectators of her own sex, for herself, and would have been luxurious if luxury consisted mainly in photographic portraits slashed across with signatures, in baskets of flowers beribboned with the cards of passing compatriots, and in a neat collection of red volumes, blue volumes, alphabetical volumes, aids to London lucidity, of every sort, devoted to addresses and engagements. To be in Miss Cutter's tiny drawing-room, in short, even with Miss Cutter alone—should you by any chance have found her so—was somehow to be in the world and in a crowd. It was like an agency—it bristled with particulars.

That was what the tall, lean, loose gentleman lounging there before her might have appeared to read in the suggestive scene over which, while she talked to him, his eyes moved without haste and without rest. "Oh, come, Mamie!" he occasionally threw off; and the words were evidently connected with the impression thus absorbed. His comparative youth spoke of waste even as her positive—her too positive—spoke of economy. There was only one thing, that is, to make up in him for everything he had lost, though it was distinct enough indeed that this thing might sometimes serve. It consisted in the perfection of an indifference, an indifference at the present moment directed to the plea—a plea of inability, of pure destitution—with which his sister had met him. Yet it had even now a wider embrace, took in quite sufficiently all consequences of queerness, confessed in advance to the false note that, in such a setting, he almost excruciatingly constituted. He cared as little that he looked at moments all his impudence as that he looked all his shabbiness, all his cleverness, all his history. These different things were written in him—in his premature baldness, his seamed, strained face, the lapse from bravery of his long tawny moustache; above all, in his easy, friendly, universally acquainted eye, so much too sociable for mere conversation. What possible relation with him could be natural enough to meet it? He wore a scant, rough Inverness cape and a pair of black trousers, wanting in substance and marked with the sheen of time, that had presumably once served for evening use. He spoke with the slowness helplessly permitted to Americans—as something too slow to be stopped—and he repeated that he found himself associated with Miss Cutter in a harmony worthy of wonder. She had been telling him not only that she couldn't possibly give him ten pounds, but that his unexpected arrival, should he insist on being much in view, might seriously interfere with arrangements necessary to her own maintenance; on which he had begun by replying that he of course knew she had long ago spent her money, but that he looked to her now exactly because she had, without the aid of that convenience, mastered the art of life.

"I'd really go away with a fiver, my dear, if you'd only tell me how you do it. It's no use saying only, as you've always said, that 'people are very kind to you.' What the devil are they kind to you *for?*"

"Well, one reason is precisely that no particular inconvenience has hitherto been supposed to attach to me. I'm just what I am," said Mamie Cutter; "nothing less and nothing more. It's awkward to have to explain to you, which, moreover, I really needn't in the least. I'm clever and amusing and charming." She was uneasy and even frightened, but she kept her temper and met him with a grace of her own. "I don't think you ought to ask me more questions than I ask you."

"Ah, my dear," said the odd young man, "*I've* no mysteries. Why in the world, since it was what you came out for and have devoted so much of your time to, haven't you pulled it off? Why haven't you married?"

"Why haven't *you?*" she retorted. "Do you think that if I had it would have been better for you?—that my husband would for a moment have put up with you? Do you mind my asking you if you'll kindly go *now?*" she went on after a glance at the clock. "I'm expecting a friend, whom I must see alone, on a matter of great importance——"

"And my being seen with you may compromise your respectability or undermine your nerve?" He sprawled imperturbably in his place, crossing again, in another sense, his long black legs and showing, above his low shoes, an absurd reach of parti-coloured sock. "I take your point well enough, but mayn't you be after all quite wrong? If you can't do anything for me couldn't you at least do something *with* me? If it comes to that, I'm clever and amusing and charming too! I've been such an ass that you don't appreciate me. But people like me—I assure you they do. They usually don't know what an ass I've been; they only see the surface, which"—and he stretched himself afresh as she looked him up and down—"you *can* imagine them, can't you, rather taken with? I'm 'what I am' too; nothing less and nothing more. That's true of us as a family, you see. We *are* a crew!" He delivered himself serenely. His voice was soft and flat, his pleasant eyes, his simple tones tending to the solemn, achieved at moments that effect of quaintness which is, in certain connections, socially so known and enjoyed. "English people have quite a weakness for me—more than any others. I get on with them beautifully. I've always been with them abroad. They think me," the young man explained, "diabolically American."

"You!" Such stupidity drew from her a sigh of compassion.

Her companion apparently quite understood it. "Are you homesick, Mamie?" he asked, with wondering irrelevance.

The manner of the question made her for some reason, in spite of her preoccupations, break into a laugh. A shade of indulgence, a sense of other things, came back to her. "You *are* funny, Scott!"

"Well," remarked Scott, "that's just what I claim. But *are* you so homesick?" he spaciously inquired, not as if to a practical end, but from an easy play of intelligence.

"I'm just dying of it!" said Mamie Cutter.

"Why, so am I!" Her visitor had a sweetness of concurrence.

"We're the only decent people," Miss Cutter declared. "And I know. *You* don't—you can't; and I can't explain. Come in," she continued with a return of her impatience and an increase of her decision, "at seven sharp."

She had quitted her seat some time before, and now, to get him into motion, hovered before him while, still motionless, he looked up at her. Something intimate, in the silence, appeared to pass between them—a community of fatigue and failure and, after all, of intelligence. There was a final, cynical humour in it. It determined him, at any rate, at last, and he slowly rose, taking in again as he stood there the testimony of the room. He might have been counting the photographs, but he looked at the flowers with detachment. "Who's coming?"

"Mrs. Medwin."

"American?"

"Dear no!"

"Then what are you doing for her?"

"I work for everyone," she promptly returned.

"For everyone who pays? So I suppose. Yet isn't it only we who do pay?" There was a drollery, not lost on her, in the way his queer presence lent itself to his emphasized plural. "Do you consider that *you* do?"

At this, with his deliberation, he came back to his charming idea. "Only try me, and see if I can't be *made* to. Work me in." On her sharply presenting her back he stared a little at the clock. "If I come at seven may I stay to dinner?"

It brought her round again. "Impossible. I'm dining out."

"With whom?"

She had to think. "With Lord Considine."

"Oh, my eye!" Scott exclaimed.

She looked at him gloomily. "Is *that* sort of tone what makes you pay? I think you might understand," she went on, "that if you're to sponge on me successfully you musn't ruin me. I must have *some* remote resemblance to a lady."

"Yes? But why must *I?*" Her exasperated silence was full of answers, of which, however, his inimitable manner took no account. "You don't understand my real strength; I doubt if you even understand your own. You're clever, Mamie, but you're not so clever as I supposed. However," he pursued, "it's out of Mrs. Medwin that you'll get it."

"Get what?"

"Why, the cheque that will enable you to assist me."

On this, for a moment, she met his eyes. "If you'll come back at seven sharp— not a minute before, and not a minute after, I'll give you two five-pound notes."

He thought it over. "Whom are you expecting a minute after?"

It sent her to the window with a groan almost of anguish, and she answered nothing till she had looked at the street. "If you injure me, you know, Scott, you'll be sorry."

"I wouldn't injure you for the world. What I want to do in fact is really to help you, and I promise you that I won't leave you—by which I mean won't leave London—till I've effected something really pleasant for you. I like you, Mamie, because I like pluck; I like you much more than you like me. I like you very, *very* much." He had at last with this reached the door and opened it, but he remained with his hand on the latch. "What does Mrs. Medwin want of you?" he thus brought out.

She had come round to see him disappear, and in the relief of this prospect she again just indulged him. "The impossible."

He waited another minute. "And you're going to do it?"

"I'm going to do it," said Mamie Cutter.

"Well, then, that ought to be a haul. Call it *three* fivers!" he laughed. "At seven sharp." And at last he left her alone.

II

Miss Cutter waited till she heard the house-door close; after which, in a sightless, mechanical way, she moved about the room, readjusting various objects that he had not touched. It was as if his mere voice and accent had spoiled her form. But she was not left too long to reckon with these things, for Mrs. Medwin was promptly announced. This lady was not, more than her hostess, in the first flush of her youth; her appearance—the scattered remains of beauty manipulated by taste—resembled one of the light repasts in which the fragments of yesterday's dinner figure with a conscious ease that makes up for the want of presence. She was perhaps of an effect still too immediate to be called interesting, but she was candid, gentle and surprised—not fatiguingly surprised, only just in the right degree; and her white face—it was too white—with the fixed eyes, the somewhat touzled hair and the Louis Seize hat, might at the end of the very long neck have suggested the head of a princess carried, in a revolution, on a pike. She immediately took up the business that had brought her, with the air, however, of drawing from the omens then discernible less confidence than she had hoped. The complication lay in the fact that if it was Mamie's part to present the omens, that lady yet had so to colour them as to make her own service large. She perhaps overcoloured, for her friend gave way to momentary despair.

"What you mean is then that it's simply impossible?"

"Oh, no," said Mamie, with a qualified emphasis. "It's *possible*."

"But disgustingly difficult?"

"As difficult as you like."

"Then what can I do that I haven't done?"

"You can only wait a little longer."

"But that's just what I *have* done. I've done nothing else. I'm always waiting a little longer!"

Miss Cutter retained, in spite of this pathos, her grasp of the subject. "*The* thing, as I've told you, is for you first to be seen."

"But if people won't look at me?"

"They will."

"They *will?*" Mrs. Medwin was eager.

"They shall," her hostess went on. "It's their only having heard—without having seen."

"But if they stare straight the other way?" Mrs. Medwin continued to object. "You can't simply go up to them and twist their heads about."

"It's just what I can," said Mamie Cutter.

But her charming visitor, heedless for the moment of this attenuation, had found the way to put it. "It's the old story. You can't go into the water till you swim, and you can't swim till you go into the water. I can't be spoken to till I'm seen, but I can't be seen till I'm spoken to."

She met this lucidity, Miss Cutter, with but an instant's lapse. "You say I can't twist their heads about. But I *have* twisted them."

It had been quietly produced, but it gave her companion a jerk. "They say 'Yes'?"

She summed it up. "All but one. She says 'No.' "

Mrs. Medwin thought; then jumped. "Lady Wantridge?"

Miss Cutter, as more delicate, only bowed admission. "I shall see her either this afternoon or late to-morrow. But she has written."

Her visitor wondered again. "May I see her letter?"

"No." She spoke with decision. "But I shall square her."

"Then how?"

"Well"—and Miss Cutter, as if looking upward for inspiration, fixed her eyes awhile on the ceiling—"well, it will come to me."

Mrs. Medwin watched her—it was impressive. "And will *they* come to you—the others?" This question drew out the fact that they would—so far, at least, as they consisted of Lady Edward, Lady Bellhouse and Mrs. Pouncer, who had engaged to muster, at the signal of tea, on the 14th—prepared, as it were, for the worst. There was of course always the chance that Lady Wantridge might take the field in such force as to paralyse them, though that danger, at the same time, seemed inconsistent with her being squared. It didn't perhaps all quite ideally hang together; but what it sufficiently came to was that if she was the one who could do most *for* a person in Mrs. Medwin's position she was also the one who could do most against. It would therefore be distinctly what our friend familiarly spoke of as "collar-work." The effect of these mixed considerations was at any rate that Mamie eventually acquiesced in the idea, handsomely thrown out by her client, that she should have an "advance" to go on with. Miss Cutter confessed that it seemed at times as if one scarce *could* go on; but the advance was, in spite of this delicacy, still more delicately made—made in the form of a banknote, several sovereigns, some loose silver and two coppers, the whole contents of her purse, neatly disposed by Mrs. Medwin on one of the tiny tables. It seemed to clear the air for deeper intimacies, the fruit of which was that Mamie, lonely, after all, in her crowd, and always more helpful than helped, eventually brought out that the way Scott had been going on was what seemed momentarily to overshadow her own power to do so.

"I've had a descent from him." But she had to explain. "My half-brother—Scott Homer. A wretch."

"What kind of a wretch?"

"Every kind. I lose sight of him at times—he disappears abroad. But he always turns up again, worse than ever."

"Violent?"

"No."

"Maudlin?"

"No."

"Only unpleasant?"

"No. Rather pleasant. Awfully clever—awfully travelled and easy."

"Then what's the matter with him?"

Mamie mused, hesitated—seemed to see a wide past. "I don't know."

"Something in the background?" Then as her friend was silent, "Something queer about cards?" Mrs. Medwin threw off.

"I don't know—and I don't want to!"

"Ah, well, I'm sure *I* don't," Mrs. Medwin returned with spirit. The note of sharpness was perhaps also a little in the observation she made as she gathered herself to go. "Do you mind my saying something?"

Mamie took her eyes quickly from the money on the little stand. "You may say what you like."

"I only mean that anything awkward you may have to keep out of the way does seem to make more wonderful, doesn't it, that you should have got just where you are? I allude, you know, to your position."

"I see." Miss Cutter somewhat coldly smiled. "To my power."

"So awfully remarkable in an American."

"Ah, you like us so."

Mrs. Medwin candidly considered. "But we don't, dearest."

Her companion's smile brightened. "Then why do you come to me?"

"Oh, I like *you!*" Mrs. Medwin made out.

"Then that's it. There are no 'Americans.' It's always 'you.'"

"Me?" Mrs. Medwin looked lovely, but a little muddled.

"*Me!*" Mamie Cutter laughed. "But if you like me, you dear thing, you can judge if I like *you.*" She gave her a kiss to dismiss her. "I'll see you again when I've seen her."

"Lady Wantridge? I hope so, indeed. I'll turn up late to-morrow, if you don't catch me first. Has it come to you yet?" the visitor, now at the door, went on.

"No; but it will. There's time."

"Oh, a little less every day!"

Miss Cutter had approached the table and glanced again at the gold and silver and the note, not indeed absolutely overlooked the two coppers. "The balance," she put it, "the day after?"

"That very night, if you like."

"Then count on me."

"Oh, if I didn't——!" But the door closed on the dark idea. Yearningly then, and only when it had done so, Miss Cutter took up the money.

She went out with it ten minutes later, and, the calls on her time being many, remained out so long that at half-past six she had not come back. At that hour, on the other hand, Scott Homer knocked at her door, where her maid, who opened it with a weak pretence of holding it firm, ventured to announce to him, as a lesson well learnt, that he had not been expected till seven. No lesson, none the less, could prevail against his native art. He pleaded fatigue, her, the maid's, dreadful depressing London, and the need to curl up somewhere. If she would just leave him quiet half an hour that old sofa upstairs would do for it, of which he took quickly such effectual possession that when, five minutes later, she peeped, nervous for her broken vow, into the drawing-room, the faithless young woman found him extended at his length and peacefully asleep.

III

The situation before Miss Cutter's return developed in other directions still, and when that event took place, at a few minutes past seven, these circumstances were, by the foot of the stair, between mistress and maid, the subject of some interrogative gasps and scared admissions. Lady Wantridge had arrived shortly after the interloper, and wishing, as she said, to wait, had gone straight up in spite of being told he was lying down.

"She distinctly understood he was there?"

"Oh, yes, ma'am, I thought it right to mention."

"And what did you call him?"

"Well, ma'am, I thought it unfair to *you* to call him anything but a gentleman."

Mamie took it all in, though there might well be more of it than one could quickly embrace. "But if she has had time," she flashed, "to find out he isn't one?"

"Oh, ma'am, she had a quarter of an hour."

"Then she isn't with him still?"

"No, ma'am; she came down again at last. She rang, and I saw her here, and she said she wouldn't wait longer."

Miss Cutter darkly mused. "Yet had already waited——?"

"Quite a quarter."

"Mercy on us!" She began to mount. Before reaching the top, however, she reflected that quite a quarter was long if Lady Wantridge had only been shocked. On the other hand, it was short if she had only been pleased. But how *could* she have been pleased? The very essence of their actual crisis was just that there was no pleasing her. Mamie had but to open the drawing-room door indeed to perceive that this was not true at least of Scott Homer, who was horribly cheerful.

Miss Cutter expressed to her brother without reserve her sense of the constitutional, the brutal selfishness that had determined his mistimed return. It had taken place, in violation of their agreement, exactly at the moment when it was most cruel to her that he should be there, and if she must now completely wash her hands of him he had only himself to thank. She had come in flushed with resentment and for a moment had been voluble; but it would have been striking that, though the way he received her might have seemed but to aggravate, it presently justified him by causing their relation really to take a stride. He had the art of confounding those who would quarrel with him by reducing them to the humiliation of an irritated curiosity.

"What *could* she have made of you?" Mamie demanded.

"My dear girl, she's not a woman who's eager to make too much of anything—anything, I mean, that will prevent her from doing as she likes, what she takes into her head. Of course," he continued to explain, "if it's something she doesn't want to do, she'll make as much as Moses."

Mamie wondered if that was the way he talked to her visitor, but felt obliged to own to his acuteness. It was an exact description of Lady Wantridge, and she was conscious of tucking it away for future use in a corner of her miscellaneous little mind. She withheld, however, all present acknowledgment, only addressing him another question. "Did you really get on with her?"

"Have you still to learn, darling—I can't help again putting it to you—that I get on with everybody? That's just what I don't seem able to drive into you. Only see how I get on with *you*."

She almost stood corrected. "What I mean is, of course, whether——"

"Whether she made love to me? Shyly, yet—or because—shamefully? She would certainly have liked awfully to stay."

"Then why didn't she?"

"Because, on account of some other matter—and I could see it was true—she hadn't time. Twenty minutes—she was here less—were all she came to give you. So don't be afraid I've frightened her away. She'll come back."

Mamie thought it over. "Yet you didn't go with her to the door?"

"She wouldn't let me, and I know when to do what I'm told—quite as much as what I'm not told. She wanted to find out about me. I mean from your little creature; a pearl of fidelity, by the way."

"But what on earth did she come up for?" Mamie again found herself appealing, and, just by that fact, showing her need of help.

"Because she always goes up." Then, as, in the presence of this rapid generalisation, to say nothing of that of such a relative altogether, Miss Cutter could only show as comparatively blank: "I mean she knows when to go up and when to come down. She has instincts; she didn't know whom you might have up here. It's a kind of compliment to you anyway. Why, Mamie," Scott pursued, "you don't know the curiosity we any of us inspire. You wouldn't believe what I've seen. The bigger bugs they are the more they're on the look-out."

Mamie still followed, but at a distance. "The look-out for what?"

"Why, for anything that will help them to live. You've been here all this time without making out then, about them, what I've had to pick out as I can? They're dead, don't you see? And *we're* alive."

"You? Oh!"—Mamie almost laughed about it.

"Well, they're a worn-out old lot, anyhow; they've used up their resources. They do look out; and I'll do them the justice to say they're not afraid—not even of me!" he continued as his sister again showed something of the same irony. "Lady Wantridge, at any rate, wasn't; that's what I mean by her having made love to me. She does what she likes. Mind it, you know." He was by this time fairly teaching her to know one of her best friends, and when, after it, he had come back to the great point of his lesson—that of her failure, through feminine inferiority, practically to grasp the truth that their being just as they were, he and she, was the real card for them to play—when he had renewed that reminder he left her absolutely in a state of dependence. Her impulse to press him on the subject of Lady Wantridge dropped; it was as if she had felt that, whatever had taken place, something would somehow come of it. She was to be, in a manner, disappointed, but the impression helped to keep her over to the next morning, when, as Scott had foretold, his new acquaintance did reappear, explaining to Miss Cutter that she had acted the day before to gain time and that she even now sought to gain it by not waiting longer. What, she promptly intimated she had asked herself, could that friend be thinking of? She must show where she stood before things had gone too far. If she had brought her answer without more delay she wished to make it sharp. Mrs. Medwin? Never! "No, my dear— not I. *There* I stop."

Mamie had known it would be "collar-work," but somehow now, at the beginning, she felt her heart sink. It was not that she had expected to carry the position with a rush, but that, as always after an interval, her visitor's defences really loomed—and quite, as it were, to the material vision—too large. She was always planted with them, voluminous, in the very centre of the passage; was like a person accommodated with a chair in some unlawful place at the theatre. She wouldn't move and you couldn't get round. Mamie's calculation indeed had not been on getting round; she was obliged to recognise that, too foolishly and fondly, she had dreamed of producing a surrender. Her dream had been the fruit of her need; but, conscious that she was even yet unequipped for pressure, she felt, almost for the first time in her life, superficial and crude. She was to be paid—but with what was she, to that end, to pay? She had engaged to find an answer to this question, but the answer had not, according to her promise, "come." And Lady Wantridge meanwhile massed herself, and there was no view of her that didn't show her as verily, by some process too obscure to be traced, the hard depository of the social law. She was no younger, no fresher, no stronger, really, than any of them; she was only, with a kind of haggard fineness, a sharpened taste for life, and, with all sorts of things behind and beneath her, more abysmal and more immoral, more secure and more impertinent. The points she made were two in number. One was that she absolutely declined; the other was that she quite doubted if Mamie herself had measured the job. The thing couldn't be done. But say it *could* be; was Mamie quite the person to do it? To this Miss Cutter, with a sweet smile, replied that she quite understood how little she might seem so. "I'm only one of the persons to whom it has appeared that *you* are."

"Then who are the others?"

"Well, to begin with, Lady Edward, Lady Bellhouse and Mrs. Pouncer."

"Do you mean that they'll come to meet her?"

"I've seen them, and they've promised."

"To come, of course," Lady Wantridge said, "if *I* come."

Her hostess hesitated. "Oh, of course, you could prevent them. But I should take it as awfully kind of you not to. *Won't* you do this for me?" Mamie pleaded.

Her friend looked about the room very much as Scott had done. "Do they really understand what it's *for?*"

"Perfectly. So that she may call."

"And what good will that do her?"

Miss Cutter faltered, but she presently brought it out. "Of course what one hopes is that you'll ask her."

"Ask her to call?"

"Ask her to dine. Ask her, if you'd be so *truly* sweet, for a Sunday, or something of that sort, and even if only in one of your *most* mixed parties, to Catchmore."

Miss Cutter felt the less hopeful after this effort in that her companion only showed a strange good nature. And it was not the amiability of irony; yet it *was* amusement. "Take Mrs. Medwin into my family?"

"Some day, when you're taking forty others."

"Ah, but what I don't see is what it does for *you*. You're already so welcome among us that you can scarcely improve your position even by forming for us the most delightful relation."

"Well, I know how dear you are," Mamie Cutter replied; "but one has, after all, more than one side, and more than one sympathy. I like her, you know." And even at this Lady Wantridge was not shocked; she showed that ease and blandness which were her way, unfortunately, of being most impossible. She remarked that *she* might listen to such things, because she was clever enough for them not to matter; only Mamie should take care how she went about saying them at large. When she became definite, however, in a minute, on the subject of the public facts, Miss Cutter soon found herself ready to make her own concession. Of course, she didn't dispute *them:* there they were; they were unfortunately on record, and nothing was to be done about them but to— Mamie found it, in truth, at this point, a little difficult.

"Well, what? Pretend already to have forgotten them?"

"Why not, when you've done it in so many other cases?"

"There *are* no other cases so bad. One meets them, at any rate, as they come. Some you can manage, others you can't. It's no use, you must give them up. They're past patching; there's nothing to be done with them. There's nothing, accordingly, to be done with Mrs. Medwin but to put her off." And Lady Wantridge rose to her height.

"Well, you know, I *do* do things," Mamie quavered with a smile so strained that it partook of exaltation.

"You help people? Oh yes, I've known you to do wonders. But stick," said Lady Wantridge with strong and cheerful emphasis, "to your Americans!"

Miss Cutter, gazing, got up. "You don't do justice, Lady Wantridge, to your own compatriots. Some of them are really charming. Besides," said Mamie, "working for mine often strikes me, so far as the interest—the inspiration and excitement, don't you know?—go, as rather too easy. You all, as I constantly have occasion to say, like us so!"

Her companion frankly weighed it. "Yes; it takes that to account for your position. I've always thought of you, nevertheless, as keeping, for their benefit, a regular working agency. They come to you, and you place them. There remains, I confess," her ladyship went on in the same free spirit, "the great wonder——"

"Of how I first placed my poor little self? Yes," Mamie bravely conceded, "when *I* began there was no agency. I just worked my passage. I didn't even come to *you*, did I? You never noticed me till, as Mrs. Short Stokes says,

'I was, 'way up!' Mrs. Medwin," she threw in, "can't get over it." Then, as her friend looked vague: "Over my social situation."

"Well, it's no great flattery to you to say," Lady Wantridge good-humouredly returned, "that she certainly can't hope for one resembling it." Yet it really seemed to spread there before them. "You simply *made* Mrs. Short Stokes."

"In spite of her name!" Mamie smiled.

"Oh, your names——! In spite of everything."

"Ah, I'm something of an artist." With which, and a relapse marked by her wistful eyes into the gravity of the matter, she supremely fixed her friend. She felt how little she minded betraying at last the extremity of her need, and it was out of this extremity that her appeal proceeded. "Have I really had your last word? It means so much to me."

Lady Wantridge came straight to the point. "You mean you depend on it?"

"Awfully!"

"Is it all you have?"

"All. Now."

"But Mrs. Short Stokes and the others—'rolling,' aren't they? Don't they pay up?"

"Ah," sighed Mamie, "if it wasn't for them——!"

Lady Wantridge perceived. "You've had so much?"

"I couldn't have gone on."

"Then what do you do with it all?"

"Oh, most of it goes back to them. There are all sorts, and it's all help. Some of them have nothing."

"Oh, if you feed the hungry," Lady Wantridge laughed, "you're indeed in a great way of business. Is Mrs. Medwin"—her transition was immediate—"really rich?"

"Really. He left her everything."

"So that if I do say 'yes'——"

"It will quite set me up."

"I see—and how much more responsible it makes one! But I'd rather myself give you the money."

"Oh!" Mamie coldly murmured.

"You mean I mayn't suspect your prices? Well, I daresay I don't! But I'd rather give you ten pounds."

"Oh!" Mamie repeated in a tone that sufficiently covered her prices. The question was in every way larger. "Do you *never* forgive?" she reproachfully inquired. The door opened, however, at the moment she spoke, and Scott Homer presented himself.

IV

Scott Homer wore exactly, to his sister's eyes, the aspect he had worn the day before, and it also formed, to her sense, the great feature of his impartial greeting.

"How d'ye do, Mamie? How d'ye do, Lady Wantridge?"

"How d'ye do again?" Lady Wantridge replied with an equanimity striking to her hostess. It was as if Scott's own had been contagious; it was almost indeed as if she had seen him before. *Had* she ever so seen him—before the previous day? While Miss Cutter put to herself this question her visitor, at all events, met the one she had previously uttered.

"Ever 'forgive'?" this personage echoed in a tone that made as little account as possible of the interruption. "Dear, yes! The people I *have* forgiven!" She laughed—perhaps a little nervously; and she was now looking at Scott. The way she looked at him was precisely what had already had its effect for his sister. "The people I can!"

"Can you forgive *me*?" asked Scott Homer.

She took it so easily. "But—what?"

Mamie interposed; she turned directly to her brother. "Don't try her. Leave it so." She had had an inspiration; it was the most extraordinary thing in the world. "Don't try *him*"—she had turned to their companion. She looked grave, sad, strange. "Leave it so." Yes, it was a distinct inspiration, which she couldn't have explained, but which had come, prompted by something she had caught—the extent of the recognition expressed—in Lady Wantridge's face. It had come absolutely of a sudden, straight out of the opposition of the two figures before her—quite as if a concussion had struck a light. The light was helped by her quickened sense that her friend's silence on the incident of the day before showed some sort of consciousness. She looked surprised. "Do you know my brother?"

"*Do* I know you?" Lady Wantridge asked of him.

"No, Lady Wantridge," Scott pleasantly confessed, "not one little mite!"

"Well, then, if you *must* go——!" and Mamie offered her a hand. "But I'll go down with you. Not *you*!" she launched at her brother, who immediately effaced himself. His way of doing so—and he had already done so, as for Lady Wantridge, in respect to their previous encounter—struck her even at the moment as an instinctive, if slightly blind, tribute to her possession of an idea; and as such, in its celerity, made her so admire him and their common wit, that, on the spot, she more than forgave him his queerness. He was right. He could be as queer as he liked! The queerer the better! It was at the foot of the stairs, when she had got her guest down, that what she had assured Mrs. Medwin would come did indeed come. "*Did* you meet him here yesterday?"

"Dear, yes. Isn't he too funny?"

"Yes," said Mamie gloomily. "He *is* funny. But had you ever met him before?"

"Dear, no!"

"Oh!"—and Mamie's tone might have meant many things.

Lady Wantridge, however, after all, easily overlooked it. "I only knew he was one of your odd Americans. That's why, when I heard yesterday, here, that he was up there awaiting your return, I didn't let that prevent me. I thought he might be. He certainly," her ladyship laughed, "*is*."

"Yes, he's very American," Mamie went on in the same way.

"As you say, we *are* fond of you! Good-bye," said Lady Wantridge.

But Mamie had not half done with her. She felt more and more—or she hoped at least—that she looked strange. She *was*, no doubt, if it came to that, strange. "Lady Wantridge," she almost convulsively broke out, "I don't know whether you'll understand me, but I seem to feel that I must act with you— I don't know what to call it!—responsibly. He *is* my brother."

"Surely—and why not?" Lady Wantridge stared. "He's the image of you!"

"Thank you!"—and Mamie was stranger than ever.

"Oh, he's good-looking. He's handsome, my dear. Oddly—but distinctly!" Her ladyship was for treating it much as a joke.

But Mamie, all sombre, would have none of this. She boldly gave him up. "I think he's awful."

"He is indeed—delightfully. And where *do* you get your ways of saying things? It isn't anything—and the things aren't anything. But it's so droll."

"Don't let yourself, all the same," Mamie consistently pursued, "be carried away by it. The thing can't be done—simply."

Lady Wantridge wondered. " 'Done simply'?"

"Done at all."

"But what can't be?"

"Why, what you might think—from his pleasantness. What he spoke of your doing for him."

Lady Wantridge recalled. "Forgiving him?"

"He asked you if you couldn't. But you can't. It's too dreadful for me, as so near a relation, to have, loyally—loyally to *you*—to say it. But he's impossible."

It was so portentously produced that her ladyship had somehow to meet it. "What's the matter with him?"

"I don't know."

"Then what's the matter with *you*?" Lady Wantridge inquired.

"It's because I *won't* know," Mamie—not without dignity—explained.

"Then *I* won't either!"

"Precisely. Don't. It's something," Mamie pursued, with some inconsequence, "that—somewhere or other, at some time or other—he appears to have done; something that has made a difference in his life."

" 'Something'?" Lady Wantridge echoed again. "What kind of thing?"

Mamie looked up at the light above the door through which the London sky was doubly dim. "I haven't the least idea."

"Then what kind of difference?"

Mamie's gaze was still at the light. "The difference you see."

Lady Wantridge, rather obligingly, seemed to ask herself what she saw. "But I don't see any! It seems, at least," she added, "such an amusing one! And he has such nice eyes."

"Oh, *dear* eyes!" Mamie conceded; but with too much sadness, for the moment, about the connections of the subject, to say more.

It almost forced her companion, after an instant, to proceed. "Do you mean he can't go home?"

She weighed her responsibility. "I only make out—more's the pity!—that he doesn't."

"Is it then something too terrible——?"

She thought again. "I don't know what—for men—*is* too terrible."

"Well then, as you don't know what 'is' for women either—good-bye!" her visitor laughed.

It practically wound up the interview; which, however terminating thus on a considerable stir of the air, was to give Miss Cutter, the next few days, the sense of being much blown about. The degree to which to begin with, she had been drawn—or perhaps rather pushed—closer to Scott was marked in the brief colloquy that, on her friend's departure, she had with him. He had immediately said it. "You'll see if she doesn't ask me down!"

"So soon?"

"Oh, I've known them at places—at Cannes, at Pau, at Shanghai—to do it sooner still. I always know when they will. You *can't* make out they don't love me!" He spoke almost plaintively, as if he wished she could.

"Then I don't see why it hasn't done you more good."

"Why, Mamie," he patiently reasoned, "what more good *could* it? As I tell you," he explained, "it has just been my life."

"Then why do you come to me for money?"

"Oh, they don't give me *that!*" Scott returned.

"So that it only means then, after all, that I, at the best, must keep you up?"

He fixed on her the nice eyes that Lady Wantridge admired. "Do you mean to tell me that already—at this very moment—I am not distinctly keeping *you?*"

She gave him back his look. "Wait till she *has* asked you, and then," Mamie added, "decline."

Scott, not too grossly, wondered. "As acting for *you?*"

Mamie's next injunction was answer enough. "But *before*—yes—call."

He took it in. "Call—but decline. Good."

"The rest," she said, "I leave to you." And she left it, in fact, with such confidence that for a couple of days she was not only conscious of no need to give Mrs. Medwin another turn of the screw, but positively evaded, in her fortitude, the reappearance of that lady. It was not till the third day that she waited upon her, finding her, as she had expected, tense.

"Lady Wantridge *will*——?"

"Yes, though she says she won't."

"She says she won't? O—oh!" Mrs. Medwin moaned.

"Sit tight all the same. I *have* her!"

"But how?"

"Through Scott—whom she wants."

"Your bad brother!" Mrs. Medwin stared. "What does she want of him?"

"To amuse them at Catchmore. Anything for that. And he *would*. But he sha'n't!" Mamie declared.

"He sha'n't go unless she comes. She must meet you first —You're my condition."

"O—o—oh!" Mrs. Medwin's tone was a wonder of hope and fear. "But doesn't he want to go?"

"He wants what *I* want. She draws the line at you. I draw the line at *him*."

"But she—doesn't she mind that he's bad?"

It was so artless that Mamie laughed. "No; it doesn't touch her. Besides, perhaps he isn't. It isn't as for *you*—people seem not to know. He has settled everything, at all events, by going to see her. It's before her that he's the thing she will have to have."

"Have to?"

"For Sundays in the country. A feature—*the* feature."

"So she has asked him?"

"Yes; and he has declined."

"For *me?*" Mrs. Medwin panted.

"For me," said Mamie, on the doorstep. "But I don't leave him for long." Her hansom had waited. "She'll come."

Lady Wantridge did come. She met in South Audley Street, on the fourteenth, at tea, the ladies whom Mamie had named to her, together with three or four others, and it was rather a masterstroke for Miss Cutter that, if Mrs. Medwin was modestly present, Scott Homer was as markedly not. This occasion, however, is a medal that would take rare casting, as would also, for that matter, even the minor light and shade, the lower relief, of the pecuniary transaction that Mrs. Medwin's flushed gratitude scarce awaited the dispersal of the company munificently to complete. A new understanding indeed, on the spot rebounded from it, the conception of which, in Mamie's mind, had promptly bloomed. "He sha'n't go *now* unless he takes you." Then, as her fancy always moved quicker for her client than her client's own—"Down with him to Catchmore! When he goes to amuse them, *you*," she comfortably declared, "shall amuse them too." Mrs. Medwin's response was again rather oddly divided, but she was sufficiently intelligible when it came to meeting the intimation that this latter would be an opportunity involving a separate fee. "Say," Mamie had suggested, "the same."

"Very well; the same."

The knowledge that it was to be the same had perhaps something to do, also, with the obliging spirit in which Scott eventually went. It was all, at the last, rather hurried—a party rapidly got together for the Grand Duke, who was in England but for the hour, who had good-naturedly proposed himself, and who liked his parties small, intimate and funny. This one was of the smallest, and it was finally judged to conform neither too little nor too much to the other conditions—after a brief whirlwind of wires and counterwires, and an iterated waiting of hansoms at various doors—to include Mrs. Medwin. It was from Catchmore itself that, snatching a moment on the wondrous Sunday afternoon, this lady had the harmonious thought of sending the new cheque. She was in bliss enough, but her scribble none the less intimated that it was Scott who amused them most. He *was* the feature. (1903)

Joseph Conrad

HEART OF DARKNESS

The *Nellie,* a cruising yawl, swung to her anchor without a flutter of the sails, and was at rest. The flood had made, the wind was nearly calm, and being bound down the river, the only thing for it was to come to and wait for the turn of the tide.

The sea-reach of the Thames stretched before us like the beginning of an interminable waterway. In the offing the sea and the sky were welded together without a joint, and in the luminous space the tanned sails of the barges drifting up with the tide seemed to stand still in red clusters of canvas sharply peaked, with gleams of varnished sprits. A haze rested on the low shores that ran out to sea in vanishing flatness. The air was dark above Gravesend, and farther back still seemed condensed into a mournful gloom, brooding motionless over the biggest, and the greatest, town on earth.

The Director of Companies was our captain and our host. We four affectionately watched his back as he stood in the bows looking to seaward. On the whole river there was nothing that looked half so nautical. He resembled a pilot, which to a seaman is trustworthiness personified. It was difficult to realize his work was not out there in the luminous estuary, but behind him, within the brooding gloom.

Between us there was, as I have already said somewhere, the bond of the sea. Besides holding our hearts together through long periods of separation, it had the effect of making us tolerant of each other's yarns—and even convictions. The Lawyer—the best of old fellows—had, because of his many years and many virtues, the only cushion on deck, and was lying on the only rug. The Accountant had brought out already a box of dominoes, and was toying architecturally with the bones. Marlow sat cross-legged right aft, leaning against the mizzen-mast. He had sunken cheeks, a yellow complexion, a straight back, an ascetic aspect, and, with his arms dropped, the palms of hands outwards, resembled an idol. The director, satisfied the anchor had good hold, made his way aft and sat down amongst us. We exchanged a few words lazily. Afterwards there was silence on board the yacht. For some reason or other we did not begin that game of dominoes. We felt meditative, and fit for nothing but placid staring. The day was ending in a serenity of still and exquisite brilliance. The water shone pacifically; the sky, without a speck, was a benign immensity of unstained light; the very mist on the Essex marshes was like a gauzy and radiant fabric, hung from the wooded rises inland, and draping the low shores in diaphanous folds. Only the gloom to the west, brooding over the upper reaches, became more somber every minute, as if angered by the approach of the sun.

And at last, in its curved and imperceptible fall, the sun sank low, and from glowing white changed to a dull red without rays and without heat, as if about to go out suddenly, stricken to death by the touch of that gloom brooding over a crowd of men.

Forthwith a change came over the waters, and the serenity became less brilliant but more profound. The old river in its broad reach rested unruffled at the decline of day, after ages of good service done to the race that peopled its banks, spread out in the tranquil dignity of a waterway leading to the utter-most ends of the earth. We looked at the venerable stream not in the vivid flush of a short day that comes and departs forever, but in the august light of abiding memories. And indeed nothing is easier for a man who has, as the phrase goes, "followed the sea" with reverence and affection, than to evoke the great spirit of the past upon the lower reaches of the Thames. The tidal current runs to and fro in its unceasing service, crowded with memories of men and ships it had borne to the rest of home or to the battles of the sea. It had known and served all the men of whom the nation is proud, from Sir Francis Drake to Sir John Franklin, knights all, titled and untitled—the knights-errant of the sea. It had borne all the ships whose names are like jewels flashing in the night of time, from the *Golden Hind* returning with her round flanks full of treasure, to be visited by the Queen's Highness and thus pass out of the gigantic tale to the *Erebus* and *Terror*, bound on other conquests—and that never returned. It had known the ships and the men. They had sailed from Deptford, from Greenwich, from Erith—the adventurers and the settlers; kings' ships and the ships of men on 'Change; captains, admirals, the dark "interlopers" of the Eastern trade, and the com-missioned "generals" of East India fleets. Hunters for gold or pursuers of fame, they all had gone out on that stream, bearing the sword, and often the torch, messengers of the might within the land, bearers of a spark from the sacred fire. What greatness had not floated on the ebb of that river into the mystery of an unknown earth! . . . The dreams of men, the seed of commonwealths, the germs of empires.

The sun set; the dusk fell on the stream, and lights began to appear along the shore. The Chapman lighthouse, a three-legged thing erect on a mud-flat, shone strongly. Lights of ships moved in the fairway—a great stir of lights going up and going down. And farther west on the upper reaches the place of the monstrous town was still marked ominously on the sky, a brooding gloom in sunshine, a lurid glare under the stars.

"And this also," said Marlow suddenly, "has been one of the dark places on the earth."

He was the only man of us who still "followed the sea." The worst that could be said of him was that he did not represent his class. He was a seaman, but he was a wanderer, too, while most seamen lead, if one may so express it, a sedentary life. Their minds are of the stay-at-home order, and their home is always with

them—the ship; and so is their country—the sea. One ship is very much like
another, and the sea is always the same. In the immutability of their surroundings
the foreign shores, the foreign faces, the changing immensity of life, glide past,
veiled not by a sense of mystery but by a slightly disdainful ignorance; for there
is nothing mysterious to a seaman unless it be the sea itself, which is the mistress
of his existence and as inscrutable as Destiny. For the rest, after his hours of
work, a casual stroll or a casual spree on shore suffices to unfold for him the
secret of a whole continent, and generally he finds the secret not worth knowing.
The yarns of seamen have a direct simplicity, the whole meaning of which lies
within the shell of a cracked nut. But Marlow was not typical (if his propensity
to spin yarns be excepted), and to him the meaning of an episode was not inside
like a kernel but outside, enveloping the tale which brought it out only as a glow
brings out a haze, in the likeness of one of these misty halos that sometimes are
made visible by the spectral illumination of moonshine.

His remark did not seem at all surprising. It was just like Marlow. It was
accepted in silence. No one took the trouble to grunt even; and presently he
said, very slow—

"I was thinking of very old times, when the Romans first came here, nineteen
hundred years ago—the other day. . . . Light came out of this river since—you
say Knights? Yes; but it is like a running blaze on a plain, like a flash of lightning in the clouds. We live in the flicker—may it last as long as the old earth
keeps rolling! But darkness was here yesterday. Imagine the feelings of a commander of a fine—what d'ye call 'em—trireme in the Mediterranean, ordered
suddenly to the north; run overland across the Gauls in a hurry; put in charge
of one of these craft the legionaries—a wonderful lot of handy men they must
have been, too—used to build, apparently by the hundred, in a month or two,
if we may believe what we read. Imagine him here—the very end of the world,
a sea the color of lead, a sky the color of smoke, a kind of ship about as rigid as
a concertina—and going up this river with stores, or orders, or what you like.
Sand-banks, marshes, forests, savages,—precious little to eat fit for a civilized
man, nothing but Thames water to drink. No Falernian wine here, no going
ashore. Here and there a military camp lost in a wilderness, like a needle in a
bundle of hay—cold, fog, tempests, disease, exile, and death,—death skulking
in the air, in the water, in the bush. They must have been dying like flies here.
Oh, yes—he did it. Did it very well, too, no doubt, and without thinking much
about it either, except afterwards to brag of what he had gone through in his
time, perhaps. They were men enough to face the darkness. And perhaps he
was cheered by keeping his eye on a chance of promotion to the fleet at Ravenna
by and by, if he had good friends in Rome and survived the awful climate. Or
think of a decent young citizen in a toga—perhaps too much dice, you know—
coming out here in the train of some prefect, or tax-gatherer, or trader even, to
mend his fortunes. Land in a swamp, march through the woods, and in some
inland post feel the savagery, the utter savagery, had closed round him,—all
that mysterious life of the wilderness that stirs in the forest, in the jungles, in
the hearts of wild men. There's no initiation either into such mysteries. He has

to live in the midst of the incomprehensible, which is also detestable. And it has a fascination, too, that goes to work upon him. The fascination of the abomination—you know, imagine the growing regrets, the longing to escape, the powerless disgust, the surrender, the hate."

He paused.

"Mind," he began again, lifting one arm from the elbow, the palm of the hand outwards, so that, with his legs folded before him, he had the pose of a Buddha preaching in European clothes and without a lotus-flower—"Mind, none of us would feel exactly like this. What saves us is efficiency—the devotion to efficiency. But these chaps were not much account, really. They were no colonists; their administration was merely a squeeze, and nothing more, I suspect. They were conquerors, and for that you want only brute force—nothing to boast of, when you have it, since your strength is just an accident arising from the weakness of others. They grabbed what they could get for the sake of what was to be got. It was just robbery with violence, aggravated murder on a great scale, and men going at it blind—as is very proper for those who tackle a darkness. The conquest of the earth, which mostly means the taking it away from those who have a different complexion or slightly flatter noses than ourselves, is not a pretty thing when you look into it too much. What redeems it is the idea only. An idea at the back of it; not a sentimental pretense but an idea; and an unselfish belief in the idea—something you can set up, and bow down before, and offer a sacrifice to. . . ."

He broke off. Flames glided in the river, small green flames, red flames, white flames, pursuing, overtaking, joining, crossing each other—then separating slowly or hastily. The traffic of the great city went on in the deepening night upon the sleepless river. We looked on, waiting patiently—there was nothing else to do till the end of the flood; but it was only after a long silence, when he said, in a hesitating voice, "I suppose you fellows remember I did once turn fresh-water sailor for a bit," that we knew we were fated, before the ebb began to run, to hear one of Marlow's inconclusive experiences.

"I don't want to bother you much with what happened to me personally," he began, showing in this remark the weakness of many tellers of tales who seem so often unaware of what their audience would best like to hear; "yet to understand the effect of it on me you ought to know how I got out there, what I saw, how I went up that river to the place where I first met the poor chap. It was the farthest point of navigation and the culminating point of my experience. It seemed somehow to throw a kind of light on everything about me—and into my thoughts. It was somber enough, too—and pitiful—not extraordinary in any way—not very clear either. No, not very clear. And yet it seemed to throw a kind of light.

"I had then, as you remember, just returned to London after a lot of Indian Ocean, Pacific, China Seas—a regular dose of the East—six years or so, and I was loafing about, hindering you fellows in your work and invading your homes, just as though I had got a heavenly mission to civilize you. It was very fine for a time, but after a bit I did get tired of resting. Then I began to look for a ship—

I should think the hardest work on earth. But the ships wouldn't even look at me. And I got tired of that game, too.

"Now when I was a little chap I had a passion for maps. I would look for hours at South America, or Africa, or Australia, and lose myself in all the glories of exploration. At that time there were many blank spaces on the earth, and when I saw one that looked particularly inviting on a map (but they all look that) I would put my finger on it and say, When I grow up I will go there. The North Pole was one of these places, I remember. Well, I haven't been there yet, and shall not try now. The glamour's off. Other places were scattered about the Equator, and in every sort of latitude all over the two hemispheres. I have been in some of them, and . . . well, we won't talk about that. But there was one yet— the biggest, the most blank, so to speak—that I had a hankering after.

"True, by this time it was not a blank space any more. It had got filled since my childhood with rivers and lakes and names. It had ceased to be a blank space of delightful mystery—a white patch for a boy to dream gloriously over. It had become a place of darkness. But there was in it one river especially, a mighty big river, that you could see on the map, resembling an immense snake uncoiled, with its head in the sea, its body at rest curving afar over a vast country, and its tail lost in the depths of the land. And as I looked at the map of it in a shop-window, it fascinated me as a snake would a bird—a silly little bird. Then I remembered there was a big concern, a Company for trade on that river. Dash it all! I thought to myself, they can't trade without using some kind of craft on that lot of fresh water—steamboats! Why shouldn't I try to get charge of one? I went on along Fleet Street, but could not shake off the idea. The snake had charmed me.

"You understand it was a Continental concern, that Trading society; but I have a lot of relations living on the Continent, because it's cheap and not so nasty as it looks, they say.

"I am sorry to own I began to worry them. This was already a fresh departure for me. I was not used to getting things that way, you know. I always went my own road and on my own legs where I had a mind to go. I wouldn't have believed it of myself; but, then—you see—I felt somehow I must get there by hook or by crook. So I worried them. The men said 'My dear fellow,' and did nothing. Then—would you believe it?—I tried the women. I, Charlie Marlow, set the women to work—to get a job. Heavens! Well, you see, the notion drove me. I had an aunt, a dear enthusiastic soul. She wrote: 'It will be delightful. I am ready to do anything, anything for you. It is a glorious idea. I know the wife of a very high personage in the Administration, and also a man who has lots of influence with,' etc., etc. She was determined to make no end of fuss to get me appointed skipper of a river steamboat, if such was my fancy.

"I got my appointment—of course; and I got it very quick. It appears the Company had received news that one of their captains had been killed in a scuffle with the natives. This was my chance, and it made me the more anxious to go. It was only months and months afterwards, when I made the attempt to rooovor what was left of the body, that I heard the original quarrel arose from a misunderstanding about some hens. Yes, two black hens. Fresleven—that was the fellow's name, a Dane—thought himself wronged somehow in the bargain, so he went ashore and started to hammer the chief of the village with a stick. Oh, it didn't surprise me in the least to hear this, and at the same time to be told that Fresleven was the gentlest, quietest creature that ever walked on two legs. No doubt he was; but he had been a couple of years already out there engaged in the noble cause, you know, and he probably felt the need at last of asserting his self-respect in some way. Therefore he whacked the old nigger mercilessly, while a big crowd of his people watched him, thunderstruck, till some man—I was told the chief's son—in desperation at hearing the old chap yell, made a tentative jab with a spear at the white man—and of course it went quite easy between the shoulder-blades. Then the whole population cleared into the forest, expecting all kinds of calamities to happen, while, on the other hand, the steamer Fresleven commanded left also in a bad panic, in charge of the engineer, I believe. Afterwards nobody seemed to trouble much about Fresleven's remains, till I got out and stepped into his shoes. I couldn't let it rest, though; but when an opportunity offered at last to meet my predecessor, the grass growing through his ribs was tall enough to hide his bones. They were all there. The supernatural being had not been touched after he fell. And the village was deserted, the huts gaped black, rotting, all askew within the fallen enclosures. A calamity had come to it, sure enough. The people had vanished. Mad terror had scattered them, men, women, and children, through the bush, and they had never returned. What became of the hens I don't know either. I should think the cause of progress got them, anyhow. However, through this glorious affair I got my appointment, before I had fairly begun to hope for it.

"I flew around like mad to get ready, and before forty-eight hours I was crossing the Channel to show myself to my employers, and sign the contract. In a very few hours I arrived in a city that always makes me think of a whited sepulcher. Prejudice no doubt. I had no difficulty in finding the Company's offices. It was the biggest thing in the town, and everybody I met was full of it. They were going to run an over-sea empire, and make no end of coin by trade.

"A narrow and deserted street in deep shadow, high houses, innumerable windows with venetian blinds, a dead silence, grass sprouting between the stones, imposing carriage archways right and left, immense double doors standing ponderously ajar. I slipped through one of these cracks, went up a swept and ungarnished staircase, as arid as a desert, and opened the first door I came to. Two women, one fat and the other slim, sat on straw-bottomed chairs, knitting black wool. The slim one got up and walked straight at me—still knitting with down-cast eyes—and only just as I began to think of getting out of her way, as you would for a somnambulist, stood still, and looked up. Her dress was as plain as an umbrella-cover, and she turned round without a word and preceded me into a waiting-room. I gave my name, and looked about. Deal table in the middle, plain chairs all around the walls, on one end a large shining map, marked with all the colors of a rainbow. There was a vast amount of red—good to see at any time, because one knows that some real work is done in there, a deuce of a lot of blue, a little green, smears of orange, and, on the East Coast, a purple patch, to show where the jolly pioneers of progress drink the jolly lager-beer. However, I wasn't going into any of these. I was going into the yellow. Dead in the center. And the river was there—fascinating—deadly—like a snake. Ough! A door opened, a white-haired secretarial head, but wearing a compassionate expression, appeared, and a skinny forefinger beckoned me into the sanctuary. Its light was dim, and a heavy writing-desk squatted in the middle. From behind that structure came out an impression of pale plumpness in a frock-coat. The great man himself. He was five feet six, I should judge, and had his grip on the handle-end of ever so many millions. He shook hands, I fancy, murmured vaguely, was satisfied with my French. *Bon voyage.*

"In about forty-five seconds I found myself again in the waiting-room with the compassionate secretary, who, full of desolation and sympathy, made me sign some document. I believe I undertook amongst other things not to disclose any trade secrets. Well, I am not going to.

"I began to feel slightly uneasy. You know I am not used to such ceremonies, and there was something ominous in the atmosphere. It was just as though I had been let into some conspiracy—I don't know—something not quite right; and I was glad to get out. In the outer room the two women knitted black wool feverishly. People were arriving, and the younger one was walking back and forth introducing them. The old one sat on her chair. Her flat cloth slippers were propped up on a foot-warmer, and a cat reposed on her lap. She wore a starched white affair on her head, had a wart on one cheek, and silver-rimmed spectacles hung on the tip of her nose. She glanced at me above the glasses. The swift and indifferent placidity of that look troubled me. Two youths with foolish and cheery countenances were being piloted over, and she threw at them the same quick glance of unconcerned wisdom. She seemed to know all about them and about me, too. An eerie feeling came over me. She seemed uncanny and fateful. Often far away there I thought of these two, guarding the door of Darkness, knitting black wool as for a warm pall, one introducing, introducing continuously to the unknown, the other scrutinizing the cheery and foolish faces with unconcerned old eyes. *Ave!* Old knitter of black wool. *Morituri te salutant.* Not many of those she looked at ever saw her again—not half, by a long way.

"There was yet a visit to the doctor. 'A simple formality,' assured me the secretary, with an air of taking an immense part in all my sorrows. Accordingly a young chap wearing his hat over the left eyebrow, some clerk I suppose,—there must have been clerks in the business, though the house was as still as a house in a city of the dead—came from somewhere upstairs, and led me forth. He was shabby and careless, with inkstains on the sleeves of his jacket, and his cravat was large and billowy, under a chin shaped like the toe of an old boot. It was a little too early for the doctor, so I proposed a drink, and thereupon he developed a vein of joviality. As we sat over our vermouths he glorified the Company's business, and by and by I expressed casually my surprise at him not going out there. He became very cool and collected all at once. 'I am not such a fool as I look, quoth Plato to his disciples,' he said sententiously, emptied his glass with great resolution, and we rose.

"The old doctor felt my pulse, evidently thinking of something else the while. 'Good, good for there,' he mumbled, and then with a certain eagerness asked me whether I would let him measure my head. Rather surprised, I said Yes, when he produced a thing like calipers and got the dimensions back and front and every way, taking notes carefully. He was an unshaven little man in a threadbare coat like a gaberdine, with his feet in slippers, and I thought him a harmless fool. 'I always ask leave, in the interests of science, to measure the crania of those going out there,' he said. 'And when they come back, too?' I asked. 'Oh, I never see them,' he remarked; 'and, moreover, the changes take place inside, you know.' He smiled, as if at some quiet joke. 'So you are going out there. Famous. Interesting, too.' He gave me a searching glance, and made another note. 'Ever any madness in your family?' he asked, in a matter-of-fact tone. I felt very annoyed. 'Is that question in the interests of science, too?' 'It would be,' he said, without taking notice of my irritation, 'interesting for science to watch the mental changes of individuals, on the spot, but . . .' 'Are you an alienist?' I interrupted. 'Every doctor should be—a little,' answered that original, imperturbably. 'I have a little theory which you Messieurs who go out there must help me to prove. This is my share in the advantages my country shall reap from the possession of such a magnificent dependency. The mere wealth I leave to others. Pardon my questions, but you are the first Englishman coming under my observation . . .' I hastened to assure him I was not in the least typical. 'If I were,' said I, 'I wouldn't be talking like this with you.' 'What you say is rather profound, and probably erroneous,' he said, with a laugh. 'Avoid irritation more than exposure to the sun. Adieu. How do you English say, eh? Good-by. Ah! Good-by. Adieu. In the tropics one must before everything keep calm.' . . . He lifted a warning forefinger. . . . '*Du calme, du calme. Adieu.*'

"One thing more remained to do—say good-by to my excellent aunt. I found her triumphant. I had a cup of tea—the last decent cup of tea for many days— and in a room that most soothingly looked just as you would expect a lady's drawing-room to look, we had a long quiet chat by the fireside. In the course of these confidences it became quite plain to me I had been represented to the wife of the high dignitary, and goodness knows to how many more people besides, as an exceptional and gifted creature—a piece of good fortune for the Company—a man you don't get hold of every day. Good heavens! and I was going to take charge of a two-penny-half-penny river-steamboat with a penny whistle attached! It appeared, however, I was also one of the Workers, with a capital—you know. Something like an emissary of light, something like a lower sort of apostle. There had been a lot of such rot let loose in print and talk just about that time, and the excellent woman, living right in the rush of all that humbug, got carried off her feet. She talked about 'weaning those ignorant millions from their horrid ways,' till, upon my word, she made me quite uncomfortable. I ventured to hint that the Company was run for profit.

" 'You forget, dear Charlie, that the laborer is worthy of his hire,' she said, brightly. It's queer how out of touch with truth women are. They live in a world of their own, and there has never been anything like it, and never can be. It is too beautiful altogether, and if they were to set it up it would go to pieces before the first sunset. Some confounded fact we men have been living contentedly with ever since the day of creation would start up and knock the whole thing over.

"After this I got embraced, told to wear flannel, be sure to write often, and so on—and I left. In the street—I don't know why—a queer feeling came to me that I was an impostor. Odd thing that I, who used to clear out for any part of the world at twenty-four hours' notice, with less thought than most men give to the crossing of a street, had a moment—I won't say of hesitation, but of startled pause, before this commonplace affair. The best way I can explain it to you is by saying that, for a second or two, I felt as though, instead of going to the center of a continent, I were about to set off for the center of the earth.

"I left in a French steamer, and she called in every blamed port they have out there, for, as far as I could see, the sole purpose of landing soldiers and custom-house officers. I watched the coast. Watching a coast as it slips by the ship is like thinking about an enigma. There it is before you—smiling, frowning, inviting, grand, mean, insipid, or savage, and always mute with an air of whispering, Come and find out. This one was almost featureless, as if still in the making, with an aspect of monotonous grimness. The edge of a colossal jungle, so dark-green as to be almost black, fringed with white surf, ran straight, like a ruled line, far, far away along a blue sea whose glitter was blurred by a creeping mist. The sun was fierce, the land seemed to glisten and drip with steam. Here and there grayish-whitish specks showed up clustered inside the white surf, with a flag flying above them perhaps. Settlements some centuries old, and still no bigger than pinheads on the untouched expanse of their background. We pounded along, stopped, landed soldiers; went on, landed custom-house clerks to levy toll in what looked like a God-forsaken wilderness, with a tin shed and a flag-pole lost in it; landed more soldiers—to take care of the custom-house clerks, presumably. Some, I heard, got drowned in the surf; but whether they did or not, nobody seemed particularly to care. They were just flung out there, and on we went. Every day the coast looked the same, as though we had not moved; but we passed various places—trading places—with names like Gran' Bassam, Little Popo; names that seemed to belong to some sordid farce acted in front of a sinister backcloth. The idleness of a passenger, my isolation amongst all these men with whom I had no point of contact, the oily and languid sea, the uniform somberness of the coast, seemed to keep me away from the truth of things, within the toil of a mournful and senseless delusion. The voice of the surf heard now and then was a positive pleasure, like the speech of a brother. It was something natural, that had its reason, that had a meaning. Now and then a boat from the shore gave one a momentary contact with reality. It was paddled by black fellows. You could see from afar the white of their eyeballs glistening. They shouted, sang; their bodies streamed with perspiration; they had faces like grotesque masks—these chaps; but they had bone, muscle, a wild vitality, an intense energy of movement, that was as natural and true as the surf along their coast. They wanted no excuse for being there. They were a great comfort to look at. For a time I would feel I belonged still to a world of straightforward facts; but the feeling would not last long. Something would turn up to scare it away. Once, I remember, we came upon a man-of-war anchored off the coast. There wasn't even a shed there, and she was shelling the bush. It appears the French had one of their wars going on thereabouts. Her ensign dropped limp like a rag; the muzzles of the long six-inch guns stuck out all over the low hull; the greasy, slimy swell swung her up lazily and let her down, swaying her thin masts. In the empty immensity of earth, sky, and water, there she was, incomprehensible, firing into a continent. Pop, would go one of the six-inch guns; a small flame would dart and vanish, a little white smoke would disappear, a tiny projectile would give a feeble screech—and nothing happened. Nothing could happen. There was a touch of insanity in the proceeding, a sense of lugubrious drollery in the sight; and it was not dissipated by somebody on board assuring me earnestly there was a camp of natives—he called them enemies!—hidden out of sight somewhere.

"We gave her her letters (I heard the men in that lonely ship were dying of fever at the rate of three a day) and went on. We called at some more places with farcical names, where the merry dance of death and trade goes on in a still and earthy atmosphere as of an overheated catacomb; all along the formless coast bordered by dangerous surf, as if Nature herself had tried to ward off intruders; in and out of rivers, streams of death in life, whose banks were rotting into mud, whose waters, thickened into slime, invaded the contorted mangroves, that seemed to writhe at us in the extremity of an impotent despair. Nowhere did we stop long enough to get a particularized impression, but the general sense of vague and oppressive wonder grew upon me. It was like a weary pilgrimage amongst hints for nightmares.

"It was upward of thirty days before I saw the mouth of the big river. We anchored off the seat of the government. But my work would not begin till some two hundred miles farther on. So as soon as I could I made a start for a place thirty miles higher up.

"I had my passage on a little sea-going steamer. Her captain was a Swede, and knowing me for a seaman, invited me on the bridge. He was a young man, lean, fair, and morose, with lanky hair and a shuffling gait. As we left the miserable little wharf, he tossed his head contemptuously at the shore. 'Been living there?' he asked. I said, 'Yes.' 'Fine lot these government chaps—are they not?' he went on, speaking English with great precision and considerable bitterness. 'It is funny what some people will do for a few francs a month. I wonder what becomes of that kind when it goes up-country?' I said to him I expected to see that soon. 'So-o-o!' he exclaimed. He shuffled athwart, keeping one eye ahead vigilantly. 'Don't be too sure,' he continued. 'The other day I took up a man who hanged himself on the road. He was a Swede, too.' 'Hanged himself! Why, in God's name?' I cried. He kept on looking out watchfully. 'Who knows? The sun was too much for him, or the country perhaps.'

"At last we opened a reach. A rocky cliff appeared, mounds of turned-up earth by the shore, houses on a hill, others with iron roofs, amongst a waste of excavations, or hanging to the declivity. A continuous noise of the rapids above hovered over this scene of inhabited devastation. A lot of people, mostly black and naked, moved about like ants. A jetty projected into the river. A blinding sunlight drowned all this at times in a sudden recrudescence of glare. 'There's your Company's station,' said the Swede, pointing to three wooden barrack-like structures on the rocky slope. 'I will send your things up. Four boxes did you say? So. Farewell.'

"I came upon a boiler wallowing in the grass, then found a path leading up the hill. It turned aside for the bowlders, and also for an undersized railway-truck lying there on its back with its wheels in the air. One was off. The thing looked as dead as the carcass of some animal. I came upon more pieces of decaying machinery, a stack of rusty rails. To the left a clump of trees made a shady spot, where dark things seemed to stir feebly. I blinked, the path was steep. A horn tooted to the right, and I saw the black people run. A heavy and dull detonation shook the ground, a puff of smoke came out of the cliff, and that was all. No change appeared on the face of the rock. They were building a railway. The cliff was not in the way or anything; but this objectless blasting was all the work going on.

"A slight clinking behind me made me turn my head. Six black men advanced in a file, toiling up the path. They walked erect and slow, balancing small baskets full of earth on their heads, and the clink kept time with their footsteps. Black rags were wound round their loins, and the short ends behind waggled to and fro like tails. I could see every rib, the joints of their limbs were like knots in a rope; each had an iron collar on his neck, and all were connected together with a chain whose bights swung between them, rhythmically clinking. Another report from the cliff made me think suddenly of that ship of war I had seen firing into a continent. It was the same kind of ominous voice; but these men could by no stretch of imagination be called enemies. They were called criminals, and the outraged law, like the bursting shells, had come to them, an insoluble mystery from the sea. All their meager breasts panted together, the violently dilated nostrils quivered, the eyes stared stonily up-hill. They passed me within six inches, without a glance, with that complete, deathlike indifference of unhappy savages. Behind this raw matter one of the reclaimed, the product of the new forces at work, strolled despondently, carrying a rifle by its middle. He had a uniform jacket with one button off, and seeing a white man on the path, hoisted his weapon to his shoulder with alacrity. This was simple prudence, white men being so much alike at a distance that he could not tell who I might be. He was speedily reassured, and with a large, white rascally grin, and a glance at his charge, seemed to take me into partnership in his exalted trust. After all, I also was a part of the great cause of these high and just proceedings.

"Instead of going up, I turned and descended to the left. My idea was to let that chain-gang get out of sight before I climbed the hill. You know I am not particularly tender; I've had to strike and to fend off. I've had to resist and to attack sometimes—that's only one way of resisting—without counting the exact cost, according to the demands of such sort of life as I had blundered into. I've seen the devil of violence, and the devil of greed, and the devil of hot desire; but, by all the stars! these were strong, lusty, red-eyed devils, that swayed and drove men—men, I tell you. But as I stood on this hillside, I foresaw that in the blinding sunshine of that land I would become acquainted with a flabby, pretending, weak-eyed devil of a rapacious and pitiless folly. How insidious he could be, too, I was only to find out several months later and a thousand miles farther. For a moment I stood appalled, as though by a warning. Finally I descended the hill, obliquely, towards the trees I had seen.

"I avoided a vast artificial hole somebody had been digging on the slope, the purpose of which I found it impossible to divine. It wasn't a quarry or a sand-pit, anyhow. It was just a hole. It might have been connected with the philanthropic desire of giving the criminals something to do. I don't know. Then I nearly fell into a very narrow ravine, almost no more than a scar in the hillside. I discovered that a lot of imported drainage-pipes for the settlement had been tumbled in there. There wasn't one that was not broken. It was a wanton smash-up. At last I got under the trees. My purpose was to stroll into the shade for a moment; but no sooner within than it seemed to me I had stepped into the gloomy circle of some Inferno. The rapids were near, and an uninterrupted, uniform, headlong, rushing noise filled the mournful stillness of the grove, where not a breath stirred, not a leaf moved, with a mysterious sound—as though the tearing pace of the launched earth had suddenly become audible.

"Black shapes crouched, lay, sat between the trees leaning against the trunks, clinging to the earth, half coming out, half effaced within the dim light, in all the attitudes of pain, abandonment, and despair. Another mine on the cliff went off, followed by a slight shudder of the soil under my feet. The work was going on. The work! And this was the place where some of the helpers had withdrawn to die.

"They were dying slowly—it was very clear. They were not enemies, they were not criminals, they were nothing earthly now,—nothing but black shadows of disease and starvation, lying confusedly in the greenish gloom. Brought from all the recesses of the coast in all the legality of time contracts, lost in uncongenial surroundings, fed on unfamiliar food, they sickened, became inefficient, and were then allowed to crawl away and rest. These moribund shapes were free as air—and nearly as thin. I began to distinguish the gleam of the eyes under the trees. Then, glancing down, I saw a face near my hand. The black bones reclined at full length with one shoulder against the tree, and slowly the eyelids rose and the sunken eyes looked up at me, enormous and vacant, a kind of blind, white flicker in the depths of the orbs, which died out slowly. The man seemed young— almost a boy—but you know with them it's hard to tell. I found nothing else to do but to offer him one of my good Swede's ship's biscuits I had in my pocket. The fingers closed slowly on it and held—there was no other movement and no other glance. He had tied a bit of white worsted round his neck— Why? Where did he get it? Was it a badge—an ornament—a charm—a propitiatory act? Was there any idea at all connected with it? It looked startling round his black neck, this bit of white thread from beyond the seas.

"Near the same tree two more bundles of acute angles sat with their legs drawn up. One, with his chin propped on his knees, stared at nothing, in an intolerable and appalling manner: his brother phantom rested its forehead, as if overcome with a great weariness; and all about others were scattered in every pose of contorted collapse, as in some picture of a massacre or a pestilence. While I stood horror-struck, one of these creatures rose to his hands and knees, and went off on all-fours towards the river to drink. He lapped out of his hand, then sat up in the sunlight, crossing his shins in front of him, and after a time let his woolly head fall on his breastbone.

"I didn't want any more loitering in the shade, and I made haste towards the station. When near the buildings I met a white man, in such an unexpected elegance of get-up that in the first moment I took him for a sort of vision. I saw a high starched collar, white cuffs, a light alpaca jacket, snowy trousers, a clean necktie, and varnished boots. No hat. Hair parted, brushed, oiled, under a green-lined parasol held in a big white hand. He was amazing, and had a penholder behind his ear.

"I shook hands with this miracle, and I learned he was the Company's chief accountant, and that all the book-keeping was done at this station. He had come out for a moment, he said, 'to get a breath of fresh air.' The expression sounded wonderfully odd, with its suggestion of sedentary desk-life. I wouldn't have mentioned the fellow to you at all, only it was from his lips that I first heard the name of the man who is so indissolubly connected with the memories of that time. Moreover, I respected the fellow. Yes; I respected his collars, his vast cuffs, his brushed hair. His appearance was certainly that of a hairdresser's dummy; but in the great demoralization of the land he kept up his appearance. That's backbone. His starched collars and got-up shirt-fronts were achievements of character. He had been out nearly three years; and, later, I could not help asking him how he managed to sport such linen. He had just the faintest blush, and said modestly, 'I've been teaching one of the native women about the station. It was difficult. She had a distaste for the work.' Thus this man had verily accomplished something. And he was devoted to his books, which were in apple-pie order.

"Everything else in the station was in a muddle,—heads, things, buildings. Strings of dusty niggers with splay feet arrived and departed; a stream of manufactured goods, rubbishy cottons, beads, and brass-wire set into the depths of darkness, and in return came a precious trickle of ivory.

"I had to wait in the station for ten days—an eternity. I lived in a hut in the yard, but to be out of the chaos I would sometimes get into the accountant's office. It was built of horizontal planks, and so badly put together that, as he bent over his high desk, he was barred from neck to heels with narrow strips of sunlight. There was no need to open the big shutter to see. It was hot there, too; big flies buzzed fiendishly, and did not sting, but stabbed. I sat generally on the floor, while, of faultless appearance (and even slightly scented), perching on a high stool, he wrote, he wrote. Sometimes he stood up for exercise. When a trucklebed with a sick man (some invalid agent from up-country) was put in there, he exhibited a gentle annoyance. 'The groans of this sick person,' he said, 'distract my attention. And without that it is extremely difficult to guard against clerical errors in this climate.'

"One day he remarked, without lifting his head, 'In the interior you will no doubt meet Mr. Kurtz.' On my asking who Mr. Kurtz was, he said he was a first-class agent; and seeing my disappointment at this information, he added slowly, laying down his pen, 'He is a very remarkable person.' Further questions elicited from him that Mr. Kurtz was at present in charge of a trading post, a very important one, in the true ivory-country, at 'the very bottom of there. Sends in as much ivory as all the others put together. . . .' He began to write again. The sick man was too ill to groan. The flies buzzed in a great peace.

"Suddenly there was a growing murmur of voices and a great tramping of feet. A caravan had come in. A violent babble of uncouth sounds burst out on the other side of the planks. All the carriers were speaking together, and in the midst of the uproar the lamentable voice of the chief agent was heard 'giving it up' tearfully for the twentieth time that day. . . . He rose slowly. 'What a frightful row,' he said. He crossed the room gently to look at the sick man, and returning, said to me, 'He does not hear.' 'What! Dead?' I asked, startled. 'No, not yet,' he answered, with great composure. Then, alluding with a toss of the head to the tumult in the stationyard, 'When one has got to make correct entries, one comes to hate those savages—hate them to the death.' He remained thoughtful for a moment. 'When you see Mr. Kurtz,' he went on, 'tell him for me that every-thing here'—he glanced at the desk—'is very satisfactory. I don't like to write to him—with those messengers of ours you never know who may get hold of your letter—at that Central Station.' He stared at me for a moment with his mild, bulging eyes. 'Oh, he will go far, very far,' he began again. 'He will be a some-body in the Administration before long. They, above—the Council in Europe, you know—mean him to be.'

"He turned to his work. The noise outside had ceased, and presently in going out I stopped at the door. In the steady buzz of flies the homeward-bound agent was lying flushed and insensible; the other, bent over his books, was making correct entries of perfectly correct transactions; and fifty feet below the doorstep I could see the still tree-tops of the grove of death.

"Next day I left that station at last, with a caravan of sixty men, for a two-hundred-mile tramp.

"No use telling you much about that. Paths, paths, everywhere; a stamped-in network of paths spreading over the empty land, through long grass, through burnt grass, through thickets, down and up chilly ravines, up and down stony hills ablaze with heat; and a solitude, a solitude, nobody, not a hut. The popu-lation had cleared out a long time ago. Well, if a lot of mysterious niggers armed with all kinds of fearful weapons suddenly took to traveling on the road between Deal and Gravesend, catching the yokels right and left to carry heavy loads for them, I fancy every farm and cottage thereabouts would get empty very soon.

The Short Story

. . . .

560

Only here the dwellings were gone, too. Still I passed through several abandoned villages. There's something pathetically childish in the ruins of grass walls. Day after day, with the stamp and shuffle of sixty pair of bare feet behind me, each pair under a sixty-lb. load. Camp, cook, sleep, strike camp, march. Now and then a carrier dead in harness, at rest in the long grass near the path, with an empty water-gourd and his long staff lying by his side. A great silence around and above. Perhaps on some quiet night the tremor of far-off drums, sinking, swelling, a tremor vast, faint; a sound weird, appealing, suggestive, and wild— and perhaps with as profound a meaning as the sound of bells in a Christian country. Once a white man in an unbuttoned uniform, camping on the path with an armed escort of lank Zanzibars, very hospitable and festive—not to say drunk. Was looking after the upkeep of the road, he declared. Can't say I saw any road or any upkeep, unless the body of a middle-aged Negro, with a bullet-hole in the forehead, upon which I absolutely stumbled three miles farther on, may be considered as a permanent improvement. I had a white companion, too, not a bad chap, but rather too fleshy and with the exasperating habit of fainting on the hot hillsides, miles away from the least bit of shade and water. Annoying, you know, to hold your own coat like a parasol over a man's head while he is coming-to. I couldn't help asking him once what he meant by coming there at all. 'To make money, of course. What do you think?' he said, scornfully. Then he got fever, and had to be carried in a hammock slung under a pole. As he weighed sixteen stone I had no end of rows with the carriers. They jibbed, ran away, sneaked off with their loads in the night—quite a mutiny. So, one evening, I made a speech in English with gestures, not one of which was lost to the sixty pairs of eyes before me, and the next morning I started the hammock off in front all right. An hour afterwards I came upon the whole concern wrecked in a bush—man, hammock, groans, blankets, horrors. The heavy pole had skinned his poor nose. He was very anxious for me to kill somebody, but there wasn't the shadow of a carrier near. I remembered the old doctor—'It would be interesting for science to watch the mental changes of individuals, on the spot.' I felt I was becoming scientifically interesting. However, all that is to no purpose. On the fifteenth day I came in sight of the big river again, and hobbled into the Central Station. It was on a back water surrounded by scrub and forest, with a pretty border of smelly mud on one side, and on the three others enclosed by a crazy fence of rushes. A neglected gap was all the gate it had, and the first glance at the place was enough to let you see the flabby devil was running that show. White men with long staves in their hands appeared languidly from amongst the buildings, strolling up to take a look at me, and then retired out of sight somewhere. One of them, a stout, excitable chap with black mustaches, informed me with great volubility and many digressions, as soon as I told him who I was, that my steamer was at the bottom of the river. I was thunderstruck. What, how, why? Oh, it was 'all right.' The 'manager himself' was there. All quite correct. 'Everybody had behaved splendidly! splendidly!'—'you must,' he said in agitation, 'go and see the general manager at once. He is waiting!'

"I did not see the real significance of that wreck at once. I fancy I see it now, but I am not sure—not at all. Certainly the affair was too stupid—when I think of it—to be altogether natural. Still. . . . But at the moment it presented itself simply as a confounded nuisance. The steamer was sunk. They had started two days before in a sudden hurry up the river with the manager on board, in charge of some volunteer skipper, and before they had been out three hours they tore the bottom out of her on stones, and she sank near the south bank. I asked myself what I was to do there, now my boat was lost. As a matter of fact, I had plenty to do in fishing my command out of the river. I had to set about it the very next day. That, and the repairs when I brought the pieces to the station, took some months.

"My first interview with the manager was curious. He did not ask me to sit down after my twenty-mile walk that morning. He was commonplace in complexion, in feature, in manners, and in voice. He was of middle size and of ordinary build. His eyes, of the usual blue, were perhaps remarkably cold, and he certainly could make his glance fall on one as trenchant and heavy as an ax. But even at these times the rest of his person seemed to disclaim the intention. Otherwise there was only an indefinable, faint expression of his lips, something stealthy—a smile—not a smile—I remember it, but I can't explain. It was unconscious, this smile was, though just after he had said something it got intensified for an instant. It came at the end of his speeches like a seal applied on the words to make the meaning of the commonest phrase appear absolutely inscrutable. He was a common trader, from his youth up employed in these parts—nothing more. He was obeyed, yet he inspired neither love nor fear, nor even respect. He inspired uneasiness. That was it! Uneasiness. Not a definite mistrust—just uneasiness—nothing more. You have no idea how effective such a . . . a . . . faculty can be. He had no genius for organizing, for initiative, or for order even. That was evident in such things as the deplorable state of the station. He had no learning, and no intelligence. His position had come to him—why? Perhaps because he was never ill. . . . He had served three terms of three years out there. . . . Because triumphant health in the general rout of constitutions is a kind of power in itself. When he went home on leave he rioted on a large scale—pompously. Jack ashore —with a difference—in externals only. This one could gather from his casual talk. He originated nothing, he could keep the routine going—that's all. But he was great. He was great by this little thing that it was impossible to tell what could control such a man. He never gave that secret away. Perhaps there was nothing within him. Such a suspicion made one pause—for out there there were no external checks. Once when various tropical diseases had laid low almost every 'agent' in the station, he was heard to say, 'Men who come out here should have no entrails.' He sealed the utterance with that smile of his, as though it had been a door opening into a darkness he had in his keeping. You fancied you had seen things—but the seal was on. When annoyed at meal-times by the constant quarrels of the white men about precedence, he ordered an immense round table to be made, for which a special house had to be built. This was the station's mess-room. Where he sat was the first place—the rest were nowhere. One felt this to be his unalterable conviction. He was neither civil nor uncivil. He was quiet. He allowed his 'boy'—an overfed young Negro from the coast—to treat the white men, under his very eyes, with provoking insolence.

"He began to speak as soon as he saw me. I had been very long on the road. He could not wait. Had to start without me. The up-river stations had to be relieved. There had been so many delays already that he did not know who was dead and who was alive, and how they got on—and so on, and so on. He paid no attention to my explanations, and, playing with a stick of sealing-wax, repeated several times that the situation was 'very grave, very grave.' There were rumors that a very important station was in jeopardy, and its chief, Mr. Kurtz, was ill. Hoped it was not true. Mr. Kurtz was . . . I felt weary and irritable. Hang Kurtz, I thought. I interrupted him by saying I had heard of Mr. Kurtz on the coast. 'Ah! So they talk of him down there,' he murmured to himself. Then he began again, assuring me Mr. Kurtz was the best agent he had, an exceptional man, of the greatest importance to the Company; therefore I could understand his anxiety. He was, he said, 'very, very uneasy.' Certainly he fidgeted on his chair a good deal, exclaimed, 'Ah, Mr. Kurtz!' broke the stick of sealing-wax and seemed dumfounded by the accident. Next thing he wanted to know 'how long it would take to.' . . . I interrupted him again. Being hungry, you know, and kept on my feet too, I was getting savage. 'How can I tell?' I said. 'I haven't even seen the wreck yet—some months, no doubt.' All this talk seemed to me so futile. 'Some months,' he said. 'Well, let us say three months before we can make a start. Yes. That ought to do the affair.' I flung out of his hut (he lived all alone in a clay hut with a sort of veranda) muttering to myself my opinion of him. He was a chattering idiot. Afterwards I took it back when it was borne in upon me startlingly with what extreme nicety he had estimated the time requisite for the 'affair.'

"I went to work the next day, turning, so to speak, my back on that station. In that way only it seemed to me I could keep my hold on the redeeming facts of life. Still, one must look about sometimes; and then I saw this station, these men strolling aimlessly about in the sunshine of the yard. I asked myself sometimes what it all meant. They wandered here and there with their absurd long staves in their hands, like a lot of faithless pilgrims bewitched inside a rotten fence. The word 'ivory' rang in the air, was whispered, was sighed. You would think they were praying to it. A taint of imbecile rapacity blew through it all, like a whiff from some corpse. By Jove! I've never seen anything so unreal in my life. And outside, the silent wilderness surrounding this cleared speck on the earth struck me as something great and invincible, like evil or truth, waiting patiently for the passing away of this fantastic invasion.

"Oh, these months! Well, never mind. Various things happened. One evening a grass shed full of calico, cotton prints, beads, and I don't know what else, burst into a blaze so suddenly that you would have thought the earth had opened to let an avenging fire consume all that trash. I was smoking my pipe quietly by my dismantled steamer, and saw them all cutting capers in the light, with their arms lifted high, when the stout man with mustaches came tearing down to the river, a tin pail in his hand, assured me that everybody was 'behaving spendidly, splendidly,' dipped about a quart of water and tore back again. I noticed there was a hole in the bottom of his pail.

"I strolled up. There was no hurry. You see the thing had gone off like a box of matches. It had been hopeless from the very first. The flame had leaped high, driven everybody back, lighted up everything—and collapsed. The shed was already a heap of embers glowing fiercely. A nigger was being beaten near by. They said he had caused the fire in some way; be that as it may, he was screeching most horribly. I saw him, later, for several days, sitting in a bit of shade looking very sick and trying to recover himself: afterwards he arose and went out—and the wilderness without a sound took him into its bosom again. As I approached the glow from the dark I found myself at the back of two men, talking. I heard the name of Kurtz pronounced, then the words, 'take advantage of this unfortunate accident.' One of the men was the manager. I wished him a good evening. 'Did you ever see anything like it—eh? it is incredible,' he said, and walked off. The other man remained. He was a first-class agent, young, gentlemanly, a bit reserved, with a forked little beard and a hooked nose. He was stand-offish with the other agents, and they on their side said he was the manager's spy upon them. As to me, I had hardly ever spoken to him before. We got into talk, and by and by we strolled away from the hissing ruins. Then he asked me to his room, which was in the main building of the station. He struck a match, and I perceived that this young aristocrat had not only a silver-mounted dressing-case but also a whole candle all to himself. Just at that time the manager was the only man supposed to have any right to candles. Native mats covered the clay walls; a collection of spears, assegais, shields, knives was hung up in trophies. The business intrusted to this fellow was the making of bricks—so I had been informed; but there wasn't a fragment of a brick anywhere in the station, and he had been there more than a year—waiting. It seems he could not make bricks without something. I don't know what—straw, maybe. Anyway, it could not be found there, and as it was not likely to be sent from Europe, it did not appear clear to me what he was waiting for. An act of special creation perhaps. However, they were all waiting—all the sixteen or twenty pilgrims of them—for something; and upon my word it did not seem an uncongenial occupation, from the way they took it, though the only thing that ever came to them was disease—as far as I could see. They beguiled the time by back-biting and intriguing against each other in a foolish kind of way. There was an air of plotting about that station, but nothing came of it, of course. It was as unreal as everything else—as the philanthropic pretense of the whole concern, as their talk, as their government, as their show of work. The only real feeling was a desire to get appointed to a trading-post where ivory was to be had, so that they could earn percentages. They intrigued and slandered and hated each other only on that account,—but as to effectually lifting a little finger—oh, no. By heavens! there is something after all in the world allowing one man to steal a horse while another must not look at a halter. Steal a horse straight out. Very well. He has done it. Perhaps he can ride. But there is a way of looking at a halter that would provoke the most charitable of saints into a kick.

"I had no idea why he wanted to be sociable, but as we chatted in there it suddenly occurred to me the fellow was trying to get at something—in fact, pumping me. He alluded constantly to Europe, to the people I was supposed to know there—putting leading questions as to my acquaintances in the sepulchral city, and so on. His little eyes glittered like mica discs—with curiosity—though he tried to keep up a bit of superciliousness. At first I was astonished, but very soon I became awfully curious to see what he would find out from me. I couldn't possibly imagine what I had in me to make it worth his while. It was very pretty to see how he baffled himself, for in truth my body was full only of chills, and my head had nothing in it but that wretched steamboat business. It was evident he took me for a perfectly shameless prevaricator. At last he got angry, and, to conceal a movement of furious annoyance, he yawned. I rose. Then I noticed a small sketch in oils, on a panel, representing a woman, draped and blindfolded, carrying a lighted torch. The background was somber—almost black. The movement of the woman was stately, and the effect of the torch-light on the face was sinister.

"It arrested me, and he stood by civilly, holding an empty half-pint champagne bottle (medical comforts) with the candle stuck in it. To my question he said Mr. Kurtz had painted this—in this very station more than a year ago—while waiting for means to go to his trading-post. 'Tell me, pray,' said I, 'who is this Mr. Kurtz?'

" 'The chief of the Inner Station,' he answered in a short tone, looking away. 'Much obliged,' I said, laughing. 'And you are the brickmaker of the Central Station. Every one knows that.' He was silent for a while. 'He is a prodigy,' he said at last. 'He is an emissary of pity, and science, and progress, and devil knows what else. We want,' he began to declaim suddenly, 'for the guidance of the cause intrusted to us by Europe, so to speak, higher intelligence, wide sympathies, a singleness of purpose.' 'Who says that?' I asked. 'Lots of them,' he replied. 'Some even write that; and so *he* comes here, a special being, as you ought to know.' 'Why ought I to know?' I interrupted, really surprised. He paid no attention. 'Yes. To-day he is chief of the best station, next year he will be assistant-manager, two years more and . . . but I daresay you know what he will be in two years' time. You are of the new gang—the gang of virtue. The same people who sent him specially also recommended you. Oh, don't say no. I've my own eyes to trust.' Light dawned upon me. My dear aunt's influential acquaintances were producing an unexpected effect upon that young man. I nearly burst into a laugh. 'Do you read the Company's confidential correspondence?' I asked. He hadn't a word to say. It was great fun. 'When Mr. Kurtz,' I continued, severely, 'is General Manager, you won't have the opportunity.'

"He blew the candle out suddenly, and we went outside. The moon had risen. Black figures strolled about listlessly, pouring water on the glow, whence proceeded a sound of hissing; steam ascended in the moonlight, the beaten nigger groaned somewhere. 'What a row the brute makes!' said the indefatigable man

with the mustaches, appearing near us. 'Serves him right. Transgression—punishment—bang! Pitiless, pitiless. That's the only way. This will prevent all con-
flagrations for the future. I was just telling the manager. . . .' He noticed my
companion, and became crestfallen all at once. 'Not in bed yet,' he said, with a
kind of servile heartiness; 'it's so natural. Ha! Danger—agitation.' He vanished.
I went on to the river-side, and the other followed me. I heard a scathing murmur
at my ear, 'Heap of muffs—go to.' The pilgrims could be seen in knots gesticu-
lating, discussing. Several had still their staves in their hands. I verily believe
they took these sticks to bed with them. Beyond the fence the forest stood up
spectrally in the moonlight, and through the dim stir, through the faint sounds
of that lamentable courtyard, the silence of the land went home to one's very
heart—its mystery, its greatness, the amazing reality of its concealed life. The
hurt nigger moaned feebly somewhere near by, and then fetched a deep sigh that
made me mend my pace away from there. I felt a hand introducing itself under
my arm. 'My dear sir,' said the fellow, 'I don't want to be misunderstood, and
especially by you, who will see Mr. Kurtz long before I can have that pleasure.
I wouldn't like him to get a false idea of my disposition. . . .'

"I let him run on, this papier-mâché Mephistopheles, and it seemed to me that
if I tried I could poke my forefinger through him, and would find nothing inside
but a little loose dirt, maybe. He, don't you see, had been planning to be assistant-
manager by and by under the present man, and I could see that the coming of
that Kurtz had upset them both not a little. He talked precipitately, and I did
not try to stop him. I had my shoulders against the wreck of my steamer, hauled
up on the slope like a carcass of some big river animal. The smell of mud, of
primeval mud, by Jove! was in my nostrils, the high stillness of primeval forest
was before my eyes; there were shiny patches on the black creek. The moon had
spread over everything a thin layer of silver—over the rank grass, over the mud,
upon the wall of matted vegetation standing higher than the wall of a temple,
over the great river I could see through a somber gap glittering, glittering, as
it flowed broadly by without a murmur. All this was great, expectant, mute, while
the man jabbered about himself. I wondered whether the stillness on the face of
the immensity looking at us two were meant as an appeal or as a menace. What
were we who had strayed in here? Could we handle that dumb thing, or would it
handle us? I felt how big, how confoundedly big, was that thing that couldn't
talk, and perhaps was deaf as well. What was in there? I could see a little ivory
coming out from there, and I had heard Mr. Kurtz was in there. I had heard
enough about it, too—God knows! Yet somehow it didn't bring any image with
it—no more than if I had been told an angel or a fiend was in there. I believed it
in the same way one of you might believe there are inhabitants in the planet
Mars. I knew once a Scotch sailmaker who was certain, dead sure, there were
people in Mars. If you asked him for some idea how they looked and behaved,
he would get shy and mutter something about 'walking on all-fours.' If you as
much as smiled, he would—though a man of sixty-four—offer to fight you. I
would not have gone so far as to fight for Kurtz, but I went for him near enough
to a lie. You know I hate, detest, and can't bear a lie, not because I am straighter

than the rest of us, but simply because it appalls me. There is a taint of death, a flavor of mortality in lies—which is exactly what I hate and detest in the world—what I want to forget. It makes me miserable and sick, like biting something rotten would do. Temperament, I suppose. Well, I went near enough to it by letting the young fool there believe anything he liked to imagine as to my influence in Europe. I became in an instant as much of a pretense as the rest of the bewitched pilgrims. This simply because I had a notion it somehow would be of help to that Kurtz whom at the time I did not see—you understand. He was just a word for me. I did not see the man in the name any more than you do. Do you see him? Do you see the story? Do you see anything? It seems to me I am trying to tell you a dream—making a vain attempt, because no relation of a dream can convey the dream-sensation, that commingling of absurdity, surprise, and bewilderment in a tremor of struggling revolt, that notion of being captured by the incredible which is of the very essence of dreams. . . ."

He was silent for a while.

". . . No, it is impossible; it is impossible to convey the life-sensation of any given epoch of one's existence—that which makes its truth, its meaning—its subtle and penetrating essence. It is impossible. We live, as we dream—alone. . . ."

He paused again as if reflecting, then added—

"Of course in this you fellows see more than I could then. You see me, whom you know. . . ."

It had become so pitch dark that we listeners could hardly see one another. For a long time already he, sitting apart, had been no more to us than a voice. There was not a word from anybody. The others might have been asleep, but I was awake. I listened, I listened on the watch for the sentence, for the word, that would give me the clew to the faint uneasiness inspired by this narrative that seemed to shape itself without human lips in the heavy night-air of the river.

". . . Yes—I let him run on," Marlow began again, "and think what he pleased about the powers that were behind me. I did! And there was nothing behind me! There was nothing but that wretched, old, mangled steamboat I was leaning against, while he talked fluently about 'the necessity for every man to get on.' 'And when one comes out here, you conceive, it is not to gaze at the moon.' Mr. Kurtz was a 'universal genius,' but even a genius would find it easier to work with 'adequate tools—intelligent men.' He did not make bricks—why, there was a physical impossibility in the way—as I was well aware; and if he did secretarial work for the manager, it was because 'no sensible man rejects wantonly the confidence of his superiors.' Did I see it? I saw it. What more did I want? What I really wanted was rivets, by heaven! Rivets. To get on with the work— to stop the hole. Rivets I wanted. There were cases of them down at the coast —cases—piled up—burst—split! You kicked a loose rivet at every second step in that station yard on the hillside. Rivets had rolled into the grove of death. You could fill your pockets with rivets for the trouble of stooping down—and there wasn't one rivet to be found where it was wanted. We had plates that would do, but nothing to fasten them with. And every week the messenger, a lone negro, letter-bag on shoulder and staff in hand, left our station for the coast. And several times a week a coast caravan came in with trade goods—ghastly glazed calico that made you shudder only to look at it; glass beads, valued about a penny a quart, confounded spotted cotton handkerchiefs. And no rivets. Three carriers could have brought all that was wanted to set that steamboat afloat.

"He was becoming confidential now, but I fancy my unresponsive attitude must have exasperated him at last, for he judged it necessary to inform me he feared neither God nor devil, let alone any mere man. I said I could see that very well, but what I wanted was a certain quantity of rivets—and rivets were what really Mr. Kurtz wanted, if he had only known it. Now letters went to the coast every week. . . . 'My dear sir,' he cried, 'I write from dictation.' I demanded rivets. There was a way—for an intelligent man. He changed his manner; became very cold, and suddenly began to talk about a hippopotamus; wondered whether sleeping on board the steamer (I stuck to my salvage night and day) I wasn't disturbed. There was an old hippo that had the bad habit of getting out on the bank and roaming at night over the station grounds. The pilgrims used to turn out in a body and empty every rifle they could lay hands on at him. Some even had sat up o' nights for him. All this energy was wasted, though. 'That animal has a charmed life,' he said; 'but you can say this only of brutes in this country. No man—you apprehend me?—no man here bears a charmed life.' He stood there for a moment in the moonlight with his delicate hooked nose set a little askew, and his mica eyes glittering without a wink, then, with a curt good night, he strode off. I could see he was disturbed and considerably puzzled, which made me feel more hopeful than I had been for days. It was a great comfort to turn from that chap to my influential friend, the battered, twisted, ruined, tin-pot steamboat. I clambered on board. She rang under my feet like an empty Huntley & Palmer biscuit-tin kicked along a gutter; she was nothing so solid in make, and rather less pretty in shape, but I had expended enough hard work on her to make me love her. No influential friend would have served me better. She had given me a chance to come out a bit—to find out what I could do. No, I don't like work. I had rather laze about and think of all the fine things that can be done. I don't like work—no man does—but I like what is in the work,—the chance to find yourself. Your own reality—for yourself, not for others—what no other man can ever know. They can only see the mere show, and never can tell what it really means.

"I was not surprised to see somebody sitting aft, on the deck, with his legs dangling over the mud. You see I rather chummed with the few mechanics there were in that station, whom the other pilgrims naturally despised—on account of their imperfect manners, I suppose. This was the foreman—a boiler-maker by trade—a good worker. He was a lank, bony, yellow-faced man, with big intense eyes. His aspect was worried, and his head was as bald as the palm of my hand; but his hair in falling seemed to have stuck to his chin, and had prospered in the new locality, for his beard hung down to his waist. He was a widower with six young children (he had left them in charge of a sister of his to come out there), and the passion of his life was pigeon-flying. He was an enthusiast and a connoisseur. He would rave about pigeons. After work hours he used sometimes to come over from his hut for a talk about his children and his pigeons; at work, when he had to crawl in the mud under the bottom of the steamboat, he would tie up that beard of his in a kind of white serviette he brought for the purpose. It had loops to go over his ears. In the evening he could be seen squatted on the bank rinsing that wrapper in the creek with great care, then spreading it solemnly on a bush to dry.

"I slapped him on the back and shouted, 'We shall have rivets!' He scrambled to his feet exclaiming, 'No! Rivets!' as though he couldn't believe his ears. Then in a low voice, 'You . . . eh?' I don't know why we behaved like lunatics. I put my finger to the side of my nose and nodded mysteriously. 'Good for you!' he cried, snapped his fingers above his head, lifting one foot. I tried a jig. We capered on the iron deck. A frightful clatter came out of that hulk, and the virgin forest on the other bank of the creek sent it back in a thundering roll upon the sleeping station. It must have made some of the pilgrims sit up in their hovels. A dark figure obscured the lighted doorway of the manager's hut, vanished, then, a second or so after, the doorway itself vanished, too. We stopped, and the silence driven away by the stamping of our feet flowed back again from the recesses of the land. The great wall of vegetation, an exuberant and entangled mass of trunks, branches, leaves, boughs, festoons, motionless in the moonlight, was like a rioting invasion of soundless life, a rolling wave of plants, piled up, crested, ready to topple over the creek, to sweep every little man of us out of his little existence. And it moved not. A deadened burst of mighty splashes and snorts reached us from afar, as though an ichthyosaurus had been taking a bath of glitter in the great river. 'After all,' said the boiler-maker in a reasonable tone, 'why shouldn't we get the rivets?' Why not, indeed? I did not know of any reason why we shouldn't. 'They'll come in three weeks,' I said, confidently.

"But they didn't. Instead of rivets there came an invasion, an infliction, a visitation. It came in sections during the next three weeks, each section headed by a donkey carrying a white man in new clothes and tan shoes, bowing from that elevation right and left to the impressed pilgrims. A quarrelsome band of footsore sulky niggers trod on the heels of the donkeys; a lot of tents, campstools, tin boxes, white cases, brown bales would be shot down in the courtyard, and the air of mystery would deepen a little over the muddle of the station. Five such installments came, with their absurd air of disorderly flight with the loot of innumerable outfit shops and provision stores, that, one would think, they were lugging, after a raid, into the wilderness for equitable division. It was an inextricable mess of things decent in themselves but that human folly made look like the spoils of thieving.

"This devoted band called itself the Eldorado Exploring Expedition, and I believe they were sworn to secrecy. Their talk, however, was the talk of sordid buccaneers: it was reckless without hardihood, greedy without audacity, and cruel without courage; there was not an atom of foresight or of serious intention in the whole batch of them, and they did not seem aware these things are wanted for the work of the world. To tear treasure out of the bowels of the land was their desire, with no more moral purpose at the back of it than there is in burglars breaking into a safe. Who paid the expenses of the noble enterprise I don't know; but the uncle of our manager was leader of that lot.

"In exterior he resembled a butcher in a poor neighborhood, and his eyes had a look of sleepy cunning. He carried his fat paunch with ostentation on his short legs, and during the time his gang infested the station spoke to no one but his nephew. You could see these two roaming about all day long with their heads close together in an everlasting confab.

"I had given up worrying myself about the rivets. One's capacity for that kind of folly is more limited than you would suppose. I said Hang!—and let things slide. I had plenty of time for meditation, and now and then I would give some thought to Kurtz. I wasn't very interested in him. No. Still, I was curious to see whether this man, who had come out equipped with moral ideas of some sort, would climb to the top after all and how he would set about his work when there."

II

"One evening as I was lying flat on the deck of my steamboat, I heard voices approaching—and there were the nephew and the uncle strolling along the bank. I laid my head on my arm again, and had nearly lost myself in a doze, when somebody said in my ear, as it were: 'I am as harmless as a little child, but I don't like to be dictated to. Am I the manager—or am I not? I was ordered to send him there. It's incredible.' . . . I became aware that the two were standing on the shore alongside the forepart of the steamboat, just below my head. I did not move; it did not occur to me to move: I was sleepy. 'It *is* unpleasant,' grunted the uncle. 'He has asked the Administration to be sent there,' said the other, 'with the idea of showing what he could do; and I was instructed accordingly. Look at the influence that man must have. Is it not frightful?' They both agreed it was frightful, then made several bizarre remarks: 'Make rain and fine weather—one man—the Council—by the nose'—bits of absurd sentences that got the better of my drowsiness, so that I had pretty near the whole of my wits about me when the uncle said, 'The climate may do away with this difficulty for you. Is he alone there?' 'Yes,' answered the manager; 'he sent his assistant down the river with a note to me in these terms: "Clear this poor devil out of the country, and don't bother sending more of that sort. I had rather be alone than have the kind of men you can dispose of with me." It was more than a year ago. Can you imagine such impudence!' 'Anything since then?' asked the other, hoarsely. 'Ivory,' jerked the nephew; 'lots of it—prime sort—lots—most annoying, from him.' 'And with that?' questioned the heavy rumble. 'Invoice,' was the reply fired out, so to speak. Then silence. They had been talking about Kurtz.

"I was broad awake by this time, but, lying perfectly at ease, remained still, having no inducement to change my position. 'How did that ivory come all this way?' growled the elder man, who seemed very vexed. The other explained that it had come with a fleet of canoes in charge of an English half-caste clerk Kurtz had with him; that Kurtz had apparently intended to return himself, the station being by that time bare of goods and stores, but after coming three hundred miles, had suddenly decided to go back, which he started to do alone in a small dugout with four paddlers, leaving the half-caste to continue down the river with the ivory. The two fellows there seemed astounded at anybody attempting such a thing. They were at a loss for an adequate motive. As to me, I seemed to see Kurtz for the first time. It was a distinct glimpse: the dugout, four paddling savages, and the lone white man turning his back suddenly on the headquarters, on relief, on thoughts of home—perhaps; setting his face towards the depths of the wilderness, towards his empty and desolate station. I did not know the motive. Perhaps he was just simply a fine fellow who stuck to his work for its own sake. His name, you understand, had not been pronounced once. He was 'that man.' The half-caste, who, as far as I could see, had conducted a difficult trip with great prudence and pluck, was invariably alluded to as 'that scoundrel.' The 'scoundrel' had reported that the 'man' had been very ill —had recovered imperfectly. . . . The two below me moved away then a few paces, and strolled back and forth at some little distance. I heard: 'Military post—doctor—two hundred miles—quite alone now—unavoidable delays— nine months—no news—strange rumors.' They approached again, just as the manager was saying, 'No one, as far as I know, unless a species of wandering trader—a pestilential fellow, snapping ivory from the natives.' Who was it they were talking about now? I gathered in snatches that this was some man supposed to be in Kurtz's district, and of whom the manager did not approve. 'We will not be free from unfair competition till one of these fellows is hanged for an example,' he said. 'Certainly,' grunted the other; 'get him hanged! Why not? Anything—anything can be done in this country. That's what I say; nobody here, you understand, *here*, can endanger your position. And why? You stand the climate—you outlast them all. The danger is in Europe; but there before I left I took care to—' They moved off and whispered, then their voices rose again. 'The extraordinary series of delays is not my fault. I did my best.' The fat man sighed. 'Very sad.' 'And the pestiferous absurdity of his talk,' continued the other; 'he bothered me enough when he was here. "Each station should be like a beacon on the road towards better things, a center for trade, of course, but also for humanizing, improving, instructing." Conceive you—that ass! And he wants to be manager! No, it's—' Here he got choked by excessive indignation, and I lifted my head the least bit. I was surprised to see how near they were—right under me. I could have spat upon their hats. They were looking on the ground, absorbed in thought. The manager was switching his leg with a slender twig: his sagacious relative lifted his head. 'You have been well since you came out this time?' he asked. The other gave a start. 'Who? I? Oh! Like a charm—like a charm. But the rest—oh, my goodness! All sick. They die so quick, too, that I haven't the time to send them out of the country—it's incredible!' 'H'm. Just so,' grunted the uncle. 'Ah! my boy, trust to this—I say, trust to this.' I saw him extend his short flipper of an arm for a gesture that took in the forest, the creek, the mud, the river,—seemed to beckon with a dishonoring flourish before the sunlit face of the land a treacherous appeal to the lurking death, to the hidden evil, to the profound darkness of its heart. It was so startling that I leaped to my feet and looked back at the edge of the forest, as though I had expected an answer of some sort to that black display of confidence. You know the foolish notions that come to one sometimes. The high stillness confronted these two figures with its ominous patience, waiting for the passing away of a fantastic invasion.

"They swore aloud together—out of sheer fright, I believe—then pretending not to know anything of my existence, turned back to the station. The sun was low; and leaning forward side by side, they seemed to be tugging painfully uphill their two ridiculous shadows of unequal length, that trailed behind them slowly over the tall grass without bending a single blade.

"In a few days the Eldorado Expedition went into the patient wilderness, that closed upon it as the sea closes over a diver. Long afterwards the news came that all the donkeys were dead. I know nothing as to the fate of the less valuable animals They, no doubt, like the rest of us, found what they deserved. I did not inquire. I was then rather excited at the prospect of meeting Kurtz very soon. When I say very soon I mean it comparatively. It was just two months from the day we left the creek when we came to the bank below Kurtz's station.

"Going up that river was like traveling back to the earliest beginnings of the world, when vegetation rioted on the earth and the big trees were kings. An empty stream, a great silence, an impenetrable forest. The air was warm, thick, heavy, sluggish. There was no joy in the brilliance of sunshine. The long stretches of the waterway ran on, deserted, into the gloom of overshadowed distances. On silvery sandbanks hippos and alligators sunned themselves side by side. The broadening waters flowed through a mob of wooded islands; you lost your way on that river as you would in a desert, and butted all day long against shoals, trying to find the channel, till you thought yourself bewitched and cut off forever from everything you had known once—somewhere—far away—in another existence perhaps. There were moments when one's past came back to one, as it will sometimes when you have not a moment to spare to yourself; but it came in the shape of an unrestful and noisy dream, remembered with wonder amongst the overwhelming realities of this strange world of plants, and water, and silence. And this stillness of life did not in the least resemble a peace. It was the stillness of an implacable force brooding over an inscrutable intention. It looked at you with a vengeful aspect. I got used to it afterwards; I did not see it any more; I had no time. I had to keep guessing at the channel; I had to discern, mostly by inspiration, the signs of hidden banks; I watched for sunken stones; I was learning to clap my teeth smartly before my heart flew out, when I shaved by a fluke some infernal sly old snag that would have ripped the life out of the tin-pot steamboat and drowned all the pilgrims; I had to keep a look-out for the signs of dead wood we could cut up in the night for next day's steaming. When you have to attend to things of that sort, to the mere incidents of the surface, the reality—the reality, I tell you—fades. The inner truth is hidden—luckily, luckily. But I felt it all the same; I felt often its mysterious stillness watching me at my monkey tricks, just as it watches you fellows performing on your respective tight-ropes for—what is it? half-a-crown a tumble—"

"Try to be civil, Marlow," growled a voice, and I knew there was at least one listener awake besides myself.

"I beg your pardon. I forgot the heartache which makes up the rest of the price. And indeed what does the price matter, if the trick be well done? You do your tricks very well. And I didn't do badly either, since I managed not to sink that steamboat on my first trip. It's a wonder to me yet. Imagine a blind-folded man set to drive a van over a bad road. I sweated and shivered over that business considerably, I can tell you. After all, for a seaman, to scrape the bottom of the thing that's supposed to float all the time under his care is the unpardonable sin. No one may know of it, but you never forget the thump—eh? A blow on the very heart. You remember it, you dream of it, you wake up at night and think of it—years after—and go hot and cold all over. I don't pretend to say that steamboat floated all the time. More than once she had to wade for a bit, with twenty cannibals splashing around and pushing. We had enlisted some of these chaps on the way for a crew. Fine fellows—cannibals—in their place. They were men one could work with, and I am grateful to them. And, after all, they did not eat each other before my face: they had brought along a provision of hippo-meat which went rotten, and made the mystery of the wilderness stink in my nostrils. Phoo! I can sniff it now. I had the manager on board and three or four pilgrims with their staves—all complete. Sometimes we came upon a station close by the bank, clinging to the skirts of the unknown, and the white men rushing out of a tumble-down hovel, with great gestures of joy and surprise and welcome, seemed very strange—had the appearance of being held there captive by a spell. The word ivory would ring in the air for a while—and on we went again into the silence, along empty reaches, round the still bends, between the high walls of our winding way, reverberating in hollow claps the ponderous beat of the stern-wheel. Trees, trees, millions of trees, massive, im-mense, running up high; and at their foot, hugging the bank against the stream, crept the little begrimed steamboat, like a sluggish beetle crawling on the floor of a lofty portico. It made you feel very small, very lost, and yet it was not al-together depressing, that feeling. After all, if you were small, the grimy beetle crawled on—which was just what you wanted it to do. Where the pilgrims imagined it crawled to I don't know. To some place where they expected to get something, I bet! For me it crawled towards Kurtz—exclusively; but when the steam-pipes started leaking we crawled very slow. The reaches opened before us and closed behind, as if the forest had stepped leisurely across the water to bar the way for our return. We penetrated deeper and deeper into the heart of darkness. It was very quiet there. At night sometimes the roll of drums behind the curtain of trees would run up the river and remain sustained faintly, as if hovering in the air high over our heads, till the first break of day. Whether it meant war, peace, or prayer we could not tell. The dawns were heralded by the descent of a chill stillness; the wood-cutters slept, their fires burned low; the snapping of a twig would make you start. We were wanderers on a pre-historic earth, on an earth that wore the aspect of an unknown planet. We could have fancied ourselves the first of men taking possession of an accursed inheritance, to be subdued at the cost of profound anguish and of excessive toil. But suddenly, as we struggled round a bend, there would be a glimpse of rush walls, of peaked grass-roofs, a burst of yells, a whirl of black limbs, a mass of hands clapping, of feet stamping, of bodies swaying, of eyes rolling, under the droop of heavy and motionless foliage. The steamer toiled along slowly on the edge of a black and incomprehensible frenzy. The prehistoric man was cursing us, praying to us, welcoming us—who could tell? We were cut off from the comprehension of our surroundings; we glided past like phantoms, wondering and secretly appalled, as sane men would be before an enthusiastic outbreak in a madhouse. We could not understand because we were too far and could not remember, because we were traveling in the night of first ages, of those ages that are gone, leaving hardly a sign—and no memories.

"The earth seemed unearthly. We are accustomed to look upon the shackled form of a conquered monster, but there—there you could look at a thing monstrous and free. It was unearthly, and the men were— No, they were not inhuman. Well, you know, that was the worst of it—this suspicion of their not being inhuman. It would come slowly to one. They howled and leaped, and spun, and made horrid faces; but what thrilled you was just the thought of their humanity—like yours—the thought of your remote kinship with this wild and passionate uproar. Ugly. Yes, it was ugly enough; but if you were man enough you would admit to yourself that there was in you just the faintest trace of a response to the terrible frankness of that noise, a dim suspicion of there being a meaning in it which you—you so remote from the night of first ages—could comprehend. And why not? The mind of man is capable of anything—because everything is in it, all the past as well as all the future. What was there after all? Joy, fear, sorrow, devotion, valor, rage—who can tell?— but truth—truth stripped of its cloak of time. Let the fool gape and shudder— the man knows, and can look on without a wink. But he must at least be as much of a man as these on the shore. He must meet that truth with his own true stuff—with his own inborn strength. Principles won't do. Acquisitions, clothes, pretty rags—rags that would fly off at the first good shake. No; you want a deliberate belief. An appeal to me in this fiendish row—is there? Very well; I hear; I admit, but I have a voice, too, and for good or evil mine is the speech that cannot be silenced. Of course, a fool, what with sheer fright and fine sentiments, is always safe. Who's that grunting? You wonder I didn't go ashore for a howl and a dance? Well, no—I didn't. Fine sentiments, you say? Fine sentiments, be hanged! I had no time. I had to mess about with whitelead and strips of woolen blanket helping to put bandages on those leaky steampipes—I tell you. I had to watch the steering, and circumvent those snags, and get the tinpot along by hook or by crook. There was surface-truth enough in these things to save a wiser man. And between whiles I had to look after the savage who was fireman. He was an improved specimen; he could fire up a vertical boiler. He was there below me, and, upon my word, to look at him was as edifying as seeing a dog in a parody of breeches and a feather hat, walking on his hind-legs. A few months of training had done for that really fine chap. He squinted at the steam-gauge and at the water-gauge with an evident effort of intrepidity—and he had filed teeth, too, the poor devil, and the wool of his pate shaved into queer patterns, and three ornamental scars on each of his cheeks. He ought to have been clapping his hands and stamping his feet on the bank, instead of which he was hard at work, a thrall to strange witchcraft, full of improving knowledge. He was useful because he had been instructed; and what he knew was this—that should the water in that transparent thing disappear, the evil spirit inside the boiler would get angry through the greatness of his thirst, and take a terrible vengeance. So he sweated and fired up and watched the glass fearfully (with an impromptu charm, made of rags, tied to his arm, and a piece of polished bone, as big as a watch, stuck flat-ways through his lower lip), while the wooden banks slipped past us slowly, the short noise was left behind, the interminable miles of silence—and we crept on, towards Kurtz. But the snags were thick, the water was treacherous and shallow, the boiler seemed indeed to have a sulky devil in it, and thus neither that fireman nor I had any time to peer into our creepy thoughts.

"Some fifty miles below the Inner Station we came upon a hut of reeds, an inclined and melancholy pole, with the unrecognizable tatters of what had been a flag of some sort flying from it, and a neatly stacked woodpile. This was unexpected. We came to the bank, and on the stack of firewood found a flat piece of board with some faded pencil-writing on it. When deciphered it said: 'Wood for you. Hurry up. Approach cautiously.' There was a signature, but it was illegible—not Kurtz—a much longer word. 'Hurry up.' Where? Up the river? 'Approach cautiously.' We had not done so. But the warning could not have been meant for the place where it could be only found after approach. Something was wrong above. But what—and how much? That was the question. We commented adversely upon the imbecility of that telegraphic style. The bush around said nothing, and would not let us look very far, either. A torn curtain of red twill hung in the doorway of the hut, and flapped sadly in our faces. The dwelling was dismantled; but we could see a white man had lived there not very long ago. There remained a rude table—a plank on two posts; a heap of rubbish reposed in a dark corner, and by the door I picked up a book. It had lost its covers, and the pages had been thumbed into a state of extremely dirty softness; but the back had been lovingly stitched afresh with white cotton thread, which looked clean yet. It was an extraordinary find. Its title was, *An Inquiry into some Points of Seamanship*, by a man Towser, Towson—some such name—Master in his Majesty's Navy. The matter looked dreary reading enough, with illustrative diagrams and repulsive tables of figures, and the copy was sixty years old. I handled this amazing antiquity with the greatest possible tenderness, lest it should dissolve in my hands. Within, Towson or Towser was inquiring earnestly into the breaking strain of ships' chains and tackle, and other such matters. Not a very enthralling book; but at the first glance you could see there a singleness of intention, an honest concern for the right way of going to work, which made these humble pages, thought out so many years ago, luminous with another than a professional light. The simple old sailor, with his talk of chains and purchases, made me forget the jungle and the pilgrims in a delicious sensation of having come upon something unmistakably real. Such a book being there was wonderful enough; but still more astounding were the notes penciled in the margin, and plainly referring to the text. I couldn't believe my eyes! They were in cipher! Yes, it looked like cipher. Fancy a man lugging with him a book of that description into this nowhere and studying it—and making notes—in cipher at that! It was an extravagant mystery.

"I had been dimly aware for some time of a worrying noise, and when I lifted my eyes I saw the wood pile was gone, and the manager, aided by all the pilgrims, was shouting at me from the river-side. I slipped the book into my pocket. I assure you to leave off reading was like tearing myself away from the shelter of an old and solid friendship.

"I started the lame engine ahead. 'It must be this miserable trader—this intruder,' exclaimed the manager, looking back malevolently at the place we had left. 'He must be English,' I said. 'It will not save him from getting into trouble if he is not careful,' muttered the manager darkly. I observed with assumed innocence that no man was safe from trouble in this world.

"The current was more rapid now, the steamer seemed at her last gasp, the stern-wheel flopped languidly, and I caught myself listening on tiptoe for the next beat of the boat, for in sober truth I expected the wretched thing to give up every moment. It was like watching the last flickers of a life. But still we crawled. Sometimes I would pick out a tree a little way ahead to measure our progress towards Kurtz by, but I lost it invariably before we got abreast. To keep the eyes so long on one thing was too much for human patience. The manager displayed a beautiful resignation. I fretted and fumed and took to arguing with myself whether or no I would talk openly with Kurtz; but before I could come to any conclusion it occurred to me that my speech or my silence, indeed any action of mine, would be a mere futility. What did it matter what any one knew or ignored? What did it matter who was manager? One gets sometimes such a flash of insight. The essentials of this affair lay deep under the surface, beyond my reach, and beyond my power of meddling.

"Towards the evening of the second day we judged ourselves about eight miles from Kurtz's station. I wanted to push on; but the manager looked grave, and told me the navigation up there was so dangerous that it would be advisable, the sun being very low already, to wait where we were till next morning. Moreover, he pointed out that if the warning to approach cautiously were to be followed, we must approach in daylight—not at dusk, or in the dark. This was sensible enough. Eight miles meant nearly three hours' steaming for us, and I could also see suspicious ripples at the upper end of the reach. Nevertheless, I was annoyed beyond expression at the delay, and most unreasonably, too, since one night more could not matter much after so many months. As we had plenty of wood, and caution was the word, I brought up in the middle of the stream. The reach was narrow, straight, with high sides like a railway cutting. The dusk came gliding into it long before the sun had set. The current ran smooth and swift, but a dumb immobility sat on the banks. The living trees, lashed together by the creepers and every living bush of the undergrowth, might have been changed into stone, even to the slenderest twig, to the lightest leaf. It was not sleep—it seemed unnatural, like a state of trance. Not the faintest sound of any kind could be heard. You looked on amazed, and began to suspect yourself of being deaf—then the night came suddenly, and struck you blind as well. About three in the morning some large fish leaped, and the loud splash made me jump as though a gun had been fired. When the sun rose there was a white fog, very warm and clammy, and more blinding than the night. It did not shift or drive; it was just there, standing all round you like something solid. At eight or nine, perhaps, it lifted as a shutter lifts. We had a glimpse of the towering multitude of trees, of the immense matted jungle, with the blazing little ball of the sun hanging over it—all perfectly still—and then the white shutter came down again, smoothly, as if sliding in greased grooves. I ordered the chain, which we had begun to heave in, to be paid out again. Before it stopped running with a muffled rattle, a cry, a very loud cry, as of infinite desolation, soared slowly in the opaque air. It ceased. A complaining clamor, modulated in savage discords, filled our ears. The sheer unexpectedness of it made my hair stir under my cap. I don't know how it struck the others: to me it seemed as though the mist itself had screamed, so suddenly, and apparently from all sides at once, did this tumultuous and mournful uproar arise. It culminated in a hurried outbreak of almost intolerably excessive shrieking, which stopped short, leaving us stiffened in a variety of silly attitudes, and obstinately listening to the nearly as appalling and excessive silence. 'Good God! What is the meaning—' stammered at my elbow one of the pilgrims,—a little fat man, with sandy hair and red whiskers, who wore side-spring boots, and pink pajamas tucked into his socks. Two others remained open-mouthed a whole minute, then dashed into the little cabin, to rush out incontinently and stand darting scared glances, with Winchesters at 'ready' in their hands. What we could see was just the steamer we were on, her outlines blurred as though she had been on the point of dissolving, and a misty strip of water, perhaps two feet broad, around her—and that was all. The rest of the world was nowhere, as far as our eyes and ears were concerned. Just nowhere. Gone, disappeared; swept off without leaving a whisper or a shadow behind.

"I went forward, and ordered the chain to be hauled in short, so as to be ready to trip the anchor and move the steamboat at once if necessary. 'Will they attack?' whispered an awed voice. 'We will be all butchered in this fog,' murmured another. The faces twitched with the strain, the hands trembled slightly, the eyes forgot to wink. It was very curious to see the contrast of expressions of the white men and of the black fellows of our crew, who were as much strangers to that part of the river as we, though their homes were only eight hundred miles away. The whites, of course, greatly discomposed, had besides a curious look of being painfully shocked by such an outrageous row. The others had an alert, naturally interested expression; but their faces were essentially quiet, even those of the one or two who grinned as they hauled at the chain. Several exchanged short, grunting phrases, which seemed to settle the matter to their satisfaction. Their headman, a young, broad-chested black, severely draped in dark-blue fringed cloths, with fierce nostrils and his hair all done up artfully in oily ringlets, stood near me. 'Aha!' I said, just for good fellowship's sake. 'Catch 'em,' he snapped, with a bloodshot widening of his eyes and a flash of sharp teeth—'catch 'im. Give 'im to us.' 'To you, eh?' I asked; 'what would you do with them?' 'Eat 'im!' he said, curtly, and, leaning his elbow on the rail, looked out into the fog in a dignified and profoundly pensive attitude. I would no doubt have been properly horrified, had it not occurred to me that he and his chaps must be very hungry: that they must have been growing increasingly hungry for at least this month past. They had been engaged for six months (I don't think a single one of them had any clear idea of time, as we at the end of countless ages have. They still belonged to the beginnings of time—had no inherited experience to teach them as it were), and of course, as long as there was a piece of paper written over in accordance with some farcical law or other made down the river, it didn't enter anybody's head to trouble how they would live. Certainly they had brought with them some rotten hippo-meat, which couldn't have lasted very long, anyway, even if the pilgrims hadn't, in the midst of a shocking hullabaloo, thrown a considerable quantity of it overboard. It looked like a high-handed proceeding; but it was really a case of legitimate self-defense. You can't breathe dead hippo waking, sleeping, and eating, and at the same time keep your precarious grip on existence. Besides that, they had given them every week three pieces of brass wire, each about nine inches long; and the theory was they were to buy their provisions with that currency in river-side villages. You can see how *that* worked. There were either no villages, or the people were hostile, or the director, who like the rest of us fed out of tins, with an occasional old he-goat thrown in, didn't want to stop the steamer for some more or less recondite reason. So, unless they swallowed the wire itself, or made loops of it to snare the fishes with, I don't see what good their extravagant salary could be to them. I must say it was paid with a regularity worthy of a large and honorable trading company. For the rest, the only thing to eat—though it didn't look eatable in the least—I saw in their possession was a few lumps of some stuff like half-cooked dough, of a dirty lavender color, they kept wrapped in leaves, and now and then swallowed a piece of, but so small that it seemed done more for the looks of the thing than for any serious purpose of sustenance. Why in the name of all the gnawing devils of hunger they didn't go for us— they were thirty to five—and have a good tuck-in for once, amazes me now when I think of it. They were big powerful men, with not much capacity to weigh the consequences, with courage, with strength, even yet, though their skins were no longer glossy and their muscles no longer hard. And I saw that something restraining, one of those human secrets that baffle probability, had come into play there. I looked at them with a swift quickening of interest—not because it occurred to me I might be eaten by them before very long, though

I own to you that just then I perceived—in a new light, as it were—how unwholesome the pilgrims looked, and I hoped, yes, I positively hoped, that my aspect was not so—what shall I say?—so—unappetizing: a touch of fantastic vanity which fitted well with the dream-sensation that pervaded all my days at that time. Perhaps I had a little fever, too. One can't live with one's finger everlastingly on one's pulse. I had often 'a little fever,' or a little touch of other things—the playful paw-strokes of the wilderness, the preliminary trifling before the more serious onslaught which came in due course. Yes; I looked at them as you would on any human being, with a curiosity of their impulses, motives, capacities, weaknesses, when brought to the test of an inexorable physical necessity. Restraint! What possible restraint? Was it superstition, disgust, patience, fear—or some kind of primitive honor? No fear can stand up to hunger, no patience can wear it out, disgust simply does not exist where hunger is; and as to superstition, beliefs, and what you may call principles, they are less than chaff in a breeze. Don't you know the devilry of lingering starvation, its exasperating torment, its black thoughts, its somber and brooding ferocity? Well, I do. It takes a man all his inborn strength to fight hunger properly. It's really easier to face bereavement, dishonor, and the perdition of one's soul—than this kind of prolonged hunger. Sad, but true. And these chaps, too, had no earthly reason for any kind of scruple. Restraint! I would just as soon have expected restraint from a hyena prowling amongst the corpses of a battlefield. But there was the fact facing me—the fact dazzling, to be seen, like the foam on the depths of the sea, like a ripple on an unfathomable enigma, a mystery greater—when I thought of it—than the curious, inexplicable note of desperate grief in this savage clamor that had swept by us on the river-bank, behind the blind whiteness of the fog.

"Two pilgrims were quarreling in hurried whispers as to which bank. 'Left.' 'No, no; how can you? Right, right, of course.' 'It is very serious,' said the manager's voice behind me; 'I would be desolated if anything should happen to Mr. Kurtz before we came up.' I looked at him, and had not the slightest doubt he was sincere. He was just the kind of man who would wish to preserve appearances. That was his restraint. But when he muttered something about going on at once, I did not even take the trouble to answer him. I knew, and he knew, that it was impossible. Were we to let go our hold of the bottom, we would be absolutely in the air—in space. We wouldn't be able to tell where we were going to—whether up or down stream, or across—till we fetched against one bank or the other,—and then we wouldn't know at first which it was. Of course I made no move. I had no mind for a smash-up. You couldn't imagine a more deadly place for a ship-wreck. Whether drowned at once or not, we were sure to perish speedily in one way or another. 'I authorize you to take all the risks,' he said, after a short silence. 'I refuse to take any,' I said, shortly; which was just the answer he expected, though its tone might have surprised him. 'Well, I must defer to your judgment. You are captain,' he said, with marked civility. I turned my shoulder to him in sign of my appreciation, and looked into the fog. How long would it last? It was the most hopeless look-out.

The approach to this Kurtz grubbing for ivory in the wretched bush was beset by as many dangers as though he had been an enchanted princess sleeping in a fabulous castle. 'Will they attack, do you think?' asked the manager, in a confidential tone.

"I did not think they would attack, for several obvious reasons. The thick fog was one. If they left the bank in their canoes they would get lost in it, as we would be if we attempted to move. Still, I had also judged the jungle of both banks quite impenetrable—and yet eyes were in it, eyes that had seen us. The river-side bushes were certainly very thick; but the undergrowth behind was evidently penetrable. However, during the short lift I had seen no canoes anywhere in the reach—certainly not abreast of the steamer. But what made the idea of attack inconceivable to me was the nature of the noise—of the cries we had heard. They had not the fierce character boding immediate hostile intention. Unexpected, wild, and violent as they had been, they had given me an irresistible impression of sorrow. The glimpse of the steamboat had for some reason filled those savages with unrestrained grief. The danger, if any, I ex-pounded, was from our proximity to a great human passion let loose. Even extreme grief may ultimately vent itself in violence—but more generally takes the form of apathy. . . .

"You should have seen the pilgrims stare! They had no heart to grin, or even to revile me: but I believe they thought me gone mad—with fright, maybe. I delivered a regular lecture. My dear boys, it was no good bothering. Keep a look-out? Well, you may guess I watched the fog for the signs of lifting as a cat watches a mouse; but for anything else our eyes were of no more use to us than if we had been buried miles deep in a heap of cotton-wool. It felt like it, too—choking, warm, stifling. Besides, all I said, though it sounded extravagant, was absolutely true to fact. What we afterwards alluded to as an attack was really an attempt at repulse. The action was very far from being aggressive—it was not even defensive, in the usual sense: it was undertaken under the stress of desperation, and in its essence was purely protective.

"It developed itself, I should say, two hours after the fog lifted, and its commencement was at a spot, roughly speaking, about a mile and a half below Kurtz's station. We had just floundered and flopped round a bend, when I saw an islet, a mere grassy hummock of bright green, in the middle of the stream. It was the only thing of the kind; but as we opened the reach more, I perceived it was the head of a long sandbank, or rather of a chain of shallow patches stretching down the middle of the river. They were discolored, just awash, and the whole lot was seen just under the water, exactly as a man's backbone is seen running down the middle of his back under the skin. Now, as far as I did see, I could go to the right or to the left of this. I didn't know either channel, of course. The banks looked pretty well alike, the depth appeared the same; but as I had been informed the station was on the west side, I naturally headed for the western passage.

"No sooner had we fairly entered it than I became aware it was much narrower than I had supposed. To the left of us there was the long uninterrupted shoal, and to the right a high, steep bank heavily overgrown with bushes. Above the bush the trees stood in serried ranks. The twigs overhung the current thickly, and from distance to distance a large limb of some tree projected rigidly over the stream. It was then well on in the afternoon, the face of the forest was gloomy, and a broad strip of shadow had already fallen on the water. In this shadow we steamed up—very slowly, as you may imagine. I sheered her well inshore—the water being deepest near the bank, as the sounding-pole informed me.

"One of my hungry and forbearing friends was sounding in the bows just below me. This steamboat was exactly like a decked scow. On the deck, there were two little teak-wood houses, with doors and windows. The boiler was in the fore-end, and the machinery right astern. Over the whole there was a light roof, supported on stanchions. The funnel projected through that roof, and in front of the funnel a small cabin built of light planks served for a pilot-house. It contained a couch, two camp-stools, a loaded Martini-Henry leaning in one corner, a tiny table, and the steering-wheel. It had a wide door in front and a broad shutter at each side. All these were always thrown open, of course. I spent my days perched up there on the extreme fore-end of that roof, before the door. At night I slept, or tried to, on the couch. An athletic black belonging to some coast tribe, and educated by my poor predecessor, was the helmsman. He sported a pair of brass earrings, wore a blue cloth wrapper from the waist to the ankles, and thought all the world of himself. He was the most unstable kind of fool I had ever seen. He steered with no end of a swagger while you were by; but if he lost sight of you, he became instantly the prey of an abject funk, and would let that cripple of a steamboat get the upper hand of him in a minute.

"I was looking down at the sounding-pole, and feeling much annoyed to see at each try a little more of it stick out of that river, when I saw my poleman give up the business suddenly, and stretch himself flat on the deck, without even taking the trouble to haul his pole in. He kept hold on it though, and it trailed in the water. At the same time the fireman, whom I could also see below me, sat down abruptly before his furnace and ducked his head. I was amazed. Then I had to look at the river mighty quick, because there was a snag in the fairway. Sticks, little sticks, were flying about—thick: they were whizzing before my nose, dropping below me, striking behind me against my pilot-house. All this time the river, the shore, the woods, were very quiet—perfectly quiet. I could only hear the heavy splashing thump of the stern-wheel and the patter of these things. We cleared the snag clumsily. Arrows, by Jove! We were being shot at! I stepped in quickly to close the shutter on the land-side. That fool-helmsman, his hands on the spokes, was lifting his knees high, stamping his feet, champing his mouth, like a reined-in horse. Confound him! And we were staggering within ten feet of the bank. I had to lean right out to swing the heavy shutter, and I saw a face amongst the leaves on the level with my own, looking at me very fierce and steady; and then suddenly, as though a veil had been removed from my eyes, I made out, deep in the tangled gloom, naked breasts, arms, legs, glaring eyes,—the bush was swarming with human limbs in movement, glistening, of bronze color. The twigs shook, swayed, and rustled, the arrows flew out of them, and then the shutter came to. 'Steer her straight,' I said to the helmsman. He held his head rigid, face forward; but his eyes rolled, he kept on lifting and setting down his feet gently, his mouth foamed a little. 'Keep quiet!' I said in a fury. I might just as well have ordered a tree not to sway in the wind. I darted out. Below me there was a great scuffle of feet on the iron deck; confused exclamations; a voice screamed, 'Can you turn back?' I caught sight of a V-shaped ripple on the water ahead. What? Another snag! A fusillade burst out under my feet. The pilgrims had opened with their Winchesters, and were simply squirting lead into that bush. A deuce of a lot of smoke came up and drove slowly forward. I swore at it. Now I couldn't see the ripple or the snag either. I stood in the doorway, peering, and the arrows came in swarms. They might have been poisoned, but they looked as though they wouldn't kill a cat. The bush began to howl. Our wood-cutters raised a warlike whoop; the report of a rifle just at my back deafened me. I glanced over my shoulder, and the pilot-house was yet full of noise and smoke when I made a dash at the wheel. The fool-nigger had dropped everything, to throw the shutter open and let off that Martini-Henry. He stood before the wide opening, glaring, and I yelled at him to come back, while I straightened the sudden twist out of that steamboat. There was no room to turn even if I had wanted to, the snag was somewhere very near ahead in that confounded smoke, there was no time to lose, so I just crowded her into the bank—right into the bank, where I knew the water was deep.

"We tore slowly along the overhanging bushes in a whirl of broken twigs and flying leaves. The fusillade below stopped short, as I had foreseen it would when the squirts got empty. I threw my head back to a glinting whizz that traversed the pilot-house, in at one shutter-hole and out at the other. Looking past that mad helmsman, who was shaking the empty rifle and yelling at the shore, I saw vague forms of men running bent double, leaping, gliding, distinct, incomplete, evanescent. Something big appeared in the air before the shutter, the rifle went overboard, and the man stepped back swiftly, looked at me over his shoulder in an extraordinary, profound, familiar manner, and fell upon my feet. The side of his head hit the wheel twice, and the end of what appeared a long cane clattered round and knocked over a little camp-stool. It looked as though after wrenching that thing from somebody ashore he had lost his balance in the effort. The thin smoke had blown away, we were clear of the snag, and looking ahead I could see that in another hundred yards or so I would be free to sheer off, away from the bank; but my feet felt so very warm and wet that I had to look down. The man had rolled on his back and stared straight up at me; both his hands clutched that cane. It was the shaft of a spear that, either thrown or lunged through the opening, had caught him in the side just below the ribs; the blade had gone in out of sight, after making a frightful gash; my shoes were full; a pool of blood lay very still, gleaming dark-red under the wheel; his eyes shone with an amazing luster. The fusillade burst out again. He looked at me anxiously, gripping the spear like something precious, with an air of being afraid I would try to take it away from him. I had to make an effort to free my eyes from his gaze and attend to steering. With one hand I felt above my head for the line of the steam whistle, and jerked out screech after screech hurriedly. The tumult of angry and warlike yells was checked instantly, and then from the depths of the woods went out such a tremulous and prolonged wail of mournful fear and utter despair as may be imagined to follow the flight of the last hope from the earth. There was a great commotion in the bush; the shower of arrows stopped, a few dropping shots rang out sharply—then silence, in which the languid beat of the stern-wheel came plainly to my ears. I put the helm hard a-starboard at the moment when the pilgrim in pink pajamas, very hot and agitated, appeared in the doorway. 'The manager sends me—' he began in an official tone, and stopped short. 'Good God!' he said, glaring at the wounded man.

"We two whites stood over him, and his lustrous and inquiring glance enveloped us both. I declare it looked as though he would presently put to us some question in an understandable language; but he died without uttering a sound, without moving a limb, without twitching a muscle. Only in the very last moment, as though in response to some sign we could not see, to some whisper we could not hear, he frowned heavily, and that frown gave to his black death-mask an inconceivably somber, brooding, and menacing expression. The luster of inquiring glance faded swiftly into vacant glassiness. 'Can you steer?' I asked the agent eagerly. He looked very dubious; but I made a grab at his arm, and he understood at once I meant him to steer whether or no. To tell you the truth, I was morbidly anxious to change my shoes and socks. 'He is dead,' murmured the fellow, immensely impressed. 'No doubt about it,' said I, tugging like mad at the shoe-laces. 'And by the way, I suppose Mr. Kurtz is dead as well by this time.'

"For the moment that was the dominant thought. There was a sense of extreme disappointment, as though I had found out I had been striving after something altogether without a substance. I couldn't have been more disgusted if I had traveled all this way for the sole purpose of talking with Mr. Kurtz. Talking with . . . I flung one shoe overboard, and became aware that that was exactly what I had been looking forward to—a talk with Kurtz. I made the strange discovery that I had never imagined him as doing, you know, but as discoursing. I didn't say to myself, 'Now I will never see him,' or 'Now I will never shake him by the hand,' but, 'Now I will never hear him.' The man presented himself as a voice. Not of course that I did not connect him with some sort of action. Hadn't I been told in all the tones of jealousy and admiration that he had collected, bartered, swindled, or stolen more ivory than all the other agents together? That was not the point. The point was in his being a gifted creature, and that of all his gifts the one that stood out preëminently, that carried with it a sense of real presence, was his ability to talk, his words— the gift of expression, the bewildering, the illuminating, the most exalted and the most contemptible, the pulsating stream of light, or the deceitful flow from the heart of an impenetrable darkness.

"The other shoe went flying unto the devil-god of that river. I thought, by Jove! it's all over. We are too late; he has vanished—the gift has vanished, by means of some spear, arrow, or club. I will never hear that chap speak after all,—and my sorrow had a startling extravagance of emotion, even such as I had noticed in the howling sorrow of these savages in the bush. I couldn't have felt more lonely desolation somehow, had I been robbed of a belief or had missed my destiny in life. . . . Why do you sigh in this beastly way, somebody? Absurd? Well, absurd. Good Lord! mustn't a man ever— Here, give me some tobacco.". . .

There was a pause of profound stillness, then a match flared, and Marlow's lean face appeared, worn, hollow, with downward folds and drooped eyelids, with an aspect of concentrated attention; and as he took vigorous draws at his pipe, it seemed to retreat and advance out of the night in the regular flicker of the tiny flame. The match went out.

"Absurd!" he cried. "This is the worst of trying to tell. . . . Here you all are, each moored with two good addresses, like a hulk with two anchors, a butcher round one corner, a policeman round another, excellent appetites, and temperature normal—you hear—normal from year's end to year's end. And you say, Absurd! Absurd be—exploded! Absurd! My dear boys, what can you expect from a man who out of sheer nervousness had just flung overboard a pair of new shoes! Now I think of it, it is amazing I did not shed tears. I am, upon the whole, proud of my fortitude. I was cut to the quick at the idea of having lost the inestimable privilege of listening to the gifted Kurtz. Of course I was wrong. The privilege was waiting for me. Oh, yes, I heard more than enough. And I was right, too. A voice. He was very little more than a voice. And I heard—him—it—this voice—other voices—all of them were so little more than voices—and the memory of that time itself lingers around me, impalpable, like a dying vibration of one immense jabber, silly, atrocious, sordid, savage, or simply mean, without any kind of sense. Voices, voices—even the girl herself—now—"

He was silent for a long time.

"I laid the ghost of his gifts at last with a lie," he began, suddenly. "Girl! What? Did I mention a girl? Oh, she is out of it—completely. They—the women I mean—are out of it—should be out of it. We must help them to stay in that beautiful world of their own, lest ours gets worse. Oh, she had to be out of it. You should have heard the disinterred body of Mr. Kurtz saying, 'My Intended.' You would have perceived directly then how completely she was out of it. And the lofty frontal bone of Mr. Kurtz! They say the hair goes on growing sometimes, but this—ah—specimen, was impressively bald. The wilderness had patted him on the head, and, behold, it was like a ball—an ivory ball; it had caressed him, and—lo!—he had withered; it had taken him, loved him, embraced him, got into his veins, consumed his flesh, and sealed his soul to its own by the inconceivable ceremonies of some devilish initiation. He was its spoiled and pampered favorite. Ivory? I should think so. Heaps of it, stacks of it. The old mud shanty was bursting with it. You would think there was not a single tusk left either above or below the ground in the whole country. 'Mostly fossil,' the manager had remarked, disparagingly. It was no more fossil than I am; but they call it fossil when it is dug up. It appears these niggers do bury the tusks sometimes—but evidently they couldn't bury this parcel deep enough to save the gifted Mr. Kurtz from his fate. We filled the steamboat with it, and had to pile a lot on the deck. Thus he could see and enjoy as long as he could see, because the appreciation of this favor had remained with him to the last. You should have heard him say, 'My ivory.' Oh, yes, I heard him. 'My Intended, my ivory, my station, my river, my—' everything belonged to him. It made me hold my breath in expectation of hearing the wilderness burst into a prodigious peal of laughter that would shake the fixed stars in their places. Everything belonged to him—but that was a trifle. The thing was to know what he belonged to, how many powers of darkness claimed him for their own. That was the reflection that made you creepy all over. It was impossible—it was not good for one either—trying to imagine. He had taken a high seat amongst the devils of the land—I mean literally. You can't understand. How could you?—with solid pavement under your feet, surrounded by kind neighbors ready to cheer you or to fall on you, stepping delicately between the butcher and the policeman, in the holy terror of scandal and gallows and lunatic asylums—how can you imagine what particular region of the first ages a man's untrammeled feet may take him into by the way of solitude—utter solitude without a policeman—by the way of silence—utter silence, where no warning voice of a kind neighbor can be heard whispering of public opinion? These little things make all the great difference. When they are gone you must fall back upon your own innate strength, upon your own capacity for faithfulness. Of course you may be too much of a fool to go wrong—too dull even to know you are being assaulted by the powers of darkness. I take it, no fool ever made a bargain for his soul with the devil: the fool is too much of a fool, or the devil too much of a devil—I don't know which. Or you may be such a thunderingly exalted creature as to be altogether deaf and blind to anything but heavenly sights and sounds. Then the earth for you is only a standing place—and whether to be like this is your loss or your gain I won't pretend to say. But most of us are neither one nor the other. The earth for us is a place to live in, where we must put up with sights, with sounds, with smells, too, by Jove!—breathe dead hippo, so to speak, and not be contaminated. And there, don't you see? your strength comes in, the faith in your ability for the digging of unostentatious holes to bury the stuff in— your power of devotion, not to yourself, but to an obscure, back-breaking business. And that's difficult enough. Mind, I am not trying to excuse or even explain—I am trying to account to myself for—for—Mr. Kurtz—for the shade of Mr. Kurtz. This initiated wraith from the back of Nowhere honored me with its amazing confidence before it vanished altogether. This was because it could speak English to me. The original Kurtz had been educated partly in England, and—as he was good enough to say himself—his sympathies were in the right place. His mother was half-English, his father was half-French. All Europe contributed to the making of Kurtz, and by and by I learned that, most appropriately, the International Society for the Suppression of Savage Customs had intrusted him with the making of a report, for its future guidance. And he had written it, too. I've seen it. I've read it. It was eloquent, vibrating with eloquence, but too high-strung, I think. Seventeen pages of close writing he had found time for! But this must have been before his—let us say—nerves, went wrong, and caused him to preside at certain midnight dances ending with unspeakable rites, which—as far as I reluctantly gathered from what I heard at various times—were offered up to him—do you understand?—to Mr. Kurtz himself. But it was a beautiful piece of writing. The opening paragraph, however, in the light of later information, strikes me now as ominous. He began with the argument that we whites, from the point of development we had arrived at, 'must necessarily appear to them [savages] in the nature of supernatural beings—we approach them with the might as of a deity,' and so on, and so on. 'By the simple exercise of our will we can exert a power for good practically unbounded,' etc. etc. From that point he soared and took me with him. The peroration was magnificent, though difficult to remember, you know. It gave me the notion of an exotic Immensity ruled by an august Benevolence. It made me tingle with enthusiasm. This was the unbounded power of eloquence—of words—of burning noble words. There were no practical hints to interrupt the magic current of phrases, unless a kind of note at the foot of the last page, scrawled evidently much later, in an unsteady hand, may be regarded as the exposition of a method. It was very simple, and at the end of that moving appeal to every altruistic sentiment it blazed at you, luminous and terrifying, like a flash of lightning in a serene sky: 'Exterminate all the brutes!' The curious part was that he had apparently forgotten all about the valuable postscriptum, because, later on, when he in a sense came to himself, he repeatedly entreated me to take good care of 'my pamphlet' (he called it), as it was sure to have in the future a good influence upon his career. I had full information about all these things, and, besides, as it turned out, I was to have the care of his memory. I've done enough for it to give me the indisputable right to lay it, if I choose, for an everlasting rest in the dustbin of progress, amongst all the sweepings and, figuratively speaking, all the dead cats of civilization. But then, you see, I can't choose. He won't be forgotten. Whatever he was, he was not common. He had the power to charm or frighten rudimentary souls into an aggravated witch-dance in his honor; he could also fill the small souls of the pilgrims with bitter misgivings: he had one devoted friend at least, and he had conquered one soul in the world that was neither rudimentary nor tainted with self-seeking. No; I can't forget him, though I am not prepared to affirm the fellow was exactly worth the life we lost in getting to him. I missed my late helmsman awfully,—I missed him even while his body was still lying in the pilot-house. Perhaps you will think it passing strange this regret for a savage who was no more account than a grain of sand in a black Sahara. Well, don't you see, he had done something, he had steered; for months I had him at my back—a help—an instrument. It was a kind of partnership. He steered for me—I had to look after him, I worried about his deficiencies, and thus a subtle bond had been created, of which I only became aware when it was suddenly broken. And the intimate profundity of that look he gave me when he received his hurt remains to this day in my memory—like a claim of distant kinship affirmed in a supreme moment.

"Poor fool! If he had only left that shutter alone. He had no restraint, no restraint—just like Kurtz—a tree swayed by the wind. As soon as I had put on a dry pair of slippers, I dragged him out, after first jerking the spear out of his side, which operation I confess I performed with my eyes shut tight. His heels leaped together over the little door-step; his shoulders were pressed to my breast; I hugged him from behind desperately. Oh! he was heavy, heavy; heavier than any man on earth, I should imagine. Then without more ado I tipped him overboard. The current snatched him as though he had been a wisp of grass, and I saw the body roll over twice before I lost sight of it forever. All the pilgrims and the manager were then congregated on the awning-deck about the pilot-house, chattering at each other like a flock of excited magpies, and there was a scandalized murmur at my heartless promptitude. What they wanted to keep that body hanging about for I can't guess. Embalm it, maybe. But I had also heard another, and a very ominous, murmur on the deck below. My friends the wood-cutters were likewise scandalized, and with a better show of reason—though I admit that the reason itself was quite inadmissible. Oh, quite! I had made up my mind that if my late helmsman was to be eaten, the fishes alone should have him. He had been a very second-rate helmsman while alive, but now he was dead he might have become a first-class temptation, and possibly cause some startling trouble. Besides, I was anxious to take the wheel, the man in pink pajamas showing himself a hopeless duffer at the business.

"This I did directly the simple funeral was over. We were going half-speed, keeping right in the middle of the stream, and I listened to the talk about me. They had given up Kurtz, they had given up the station; Kurtz was dead, and the station had been burnt—and so on—and so on. The red-haired pilgrim was beside himself with the thought that at least this poor Kurtz had been properly avenged. 'Say! We must have made a glorious slaughter of them in the bush. Eh? What do you think? Say?' He positively danced, the bloodthirsty little gingery beggar. And he had nearly fainted when he saw the wounded man! I could not help saying, 'You made a glorious lot of smoke, anyhow.' I had seen, from the way the tops of the bushes rustled and flew, that almost all the shots had gone too high. You can't hit anything unless you take aim and fire from the shoulder; but these chaps fired from the hip with their eyes shut. The retreat, I maintained—and I was right—was caused by the screeching of the steam-whistle. Upon this they forgot Kurtz, and began to howl at me with indignant protests.

"The manager stood by the wheel murmuring confidentially about the necessity of getting well away down the river before dark at all events, when I saw in the distance a clearing on the river-side and the outlines of some sort of building. 'What's this?' I asked. He clapped his hands in wonder. 'The station!' he cried. I edged in at once, still going half-speed.

"Through my glasses I saw the slope of a hill interspersed with rare trees and perfectly free from undergrowth. A long decaying building on the summit was half buried in the high grass; the large holes in the peaked roof gaped black from afar; the jungle and the woods made a background. There was no enclosure or fence of any kind; but there had been one apparently, for near the house half-a-dozen slim posts remained in a row, roughly trimmed, and with their upper ends ornamented with round carved balls. The rails, or whatever there had been between, had disappeared. Of course the forest surrounded all that. The river-bank was clear, and on the water-side I saw a white man under a hat like a cartwheel beckoning persistently with his whole arm. Examining the edge of the forest above and below, I was almost certain I could see movements—human forms gliding here and there. I steamed past prudently, then stopped the engines and let her drift down. The man on the shore began to shout, urging us to land. 'We have been attacked,' screamed the manager. 'I know—I know. It's all right,' yelled back the other, as cheerful as you please. 'Come along. It's all right. I am glad.'

"His aspect reminded me of something I had seen—something funny I had seen somewhere. As I maneuvered to get alongside, I was asking myself, 'What does this fellow look like?' Suddenly I got it. He looked like a harlequin. His clothes had been made of some stuff that was brown holland probably, but it was covered with patches all over, with bright patches, blue, red and yellow,— patches on the back, patches on the front, patches on elbows, on knees; colored binding around his jacket, scarlet edging at the bottom of his trousers; and the sunshine made him look extremely gay and wonderfully neat withal, because you could see how beautifully all this patching had been done. A beardless, boyish face, very fair, no features to speak of, nose peeling, little blue eyes, smiles and frowns chasing each other over that open countenance like sunshine and shadow on a wind-swept plain. 'Look out, captain!' he cried; 'there's a snag lodged in her last night.' 'What! Another snag?' I confess I swore shamefully. I had nearly holed my cripple, to finish off that charming trip. The harlequin on the bank turned his little pug-nose up to me. 'You English?' he asked, all smiles. 'Are you?' I shouted from the wheel. The smiles vanished, and he shook his head as if sorry for my disappointment. Then he brightened up. 'Never mind!' he cried, encouragingly. 'Are we in time?' I asked. 'He is up there,' he replied, with a toss of the head up the hill, and becoming gloomy all of a sudden. His face was like the autumn sky, overcast one moment and bright the next.

"When the manager, escorted by the pilgrims, all of them armed to the teeth, had gone to the house this chap came on board. 'I say, I don't like this. These natives are in the bush,' I said. He assured me earnestly it was all right. 'They are simple people,' he added; 'well, I am glad you came. It took me all my time to keep them off.' 'But you said it was all right,' I cried. 'Oh, they meant no harm,' he said; and as I stared he corrected himself, 'Not exactly.' Then vivaciously, 'My faith, your pilot-house wants a clean-up!' In the next breath he advised me to keep enough steam on the boiler to blow the whistle in case of any trouble. 'One good screech will do more for you than all your rifles. They are simple people,' he repeated. He rattled away at such a rate he quite overwhelmed me. He seemed to be trying to make up for lots of silence, and actually hinted, laughing, that such was the case. 'Don't you talk with Mr. Kurtz?' I said. 'You don't talk with that man—you listen to him,' he exclaimed with severe exaltation. 'But now—' He waved his arm, and in the twinkling of an eye was in the uttermost depths of despondency. In a moment he came up again with a jump, possessed himself of both my hands, shook them continuously, while he gabbed: 'Brother sailor . . . honor . . . pleasure . . . delight . . . introduce myself . . . Russian . . . son of an arch-priest . . . government of Tambov. . . . What? Tobacco! English tobacco; the excellent English tobacco! Now, that's brotherly. Smoke? Where's a sailor that does not smoke?'

"The pipe soothed him, and gradually I made out he had run away from school, had gone to sea in a Russian ship; ran away again; served some time in English ships; was now reconciled with the arch-priest. He made a point of that. 'But when one is young one must see things, gather experience, ideas; enlarge the mind.' 'Here!' I interrupted. 'You can never tell! Here I met Mr. Kurtz,' he said, youthfully solemn and reproachful. I held my tongue after that. It appears he had persuaded a Dutch trading house on the coast to fit him out with stores and goods, and had started for the interior with a light heart, and no more idea of what would happen to him than a baby. He had been wandering about that river for nearly two years alone, cut off from everybody and everything. 'I am not so young as I look. I am twenty-five,' he said. 'At first old Van Shuyten would tell me to go to the devil,' he narrated with keen enjoyment; 'but I stuck to him, and talked and talked, till at last he got afraid I would talk the hind-leg off his favorite dog, so he gave me some cheap things and a few guns, and told me he hoped he would never see my face again. Good old Dutchman, Van Shuyten. I've sent him one small lot of ivory a year ago, so that he can't call me a little thief when I get back. I hope he got it. And for the rest I don't care. I had some wood stacked for you. That was my old house. Did you see?'

"I gave him Towson's book. He made as though he would kiss me, but restrained himself. 'The only book I had left, and I thought I had lost it,' he said, looking at it ecstatically. 'So many accidents happen to a man going about alone, you know. Canoes get upset sometimes—and sometimes you've got to clear out so quick when the people get angry.' He thumbed the pages. 'You made notes in Russian?' I asked. He nodded. 'I thought they were written in cipher,' I said. He laughed, then became serious. 'I had lots of trouble to keep these people off,' he said. 'Did they want to kill you?' I asked. 'Oh, no!' he cried, and checked himself. 'Why did they attack us?' I pursued. He hesitated, then said shamefacedly, 'They don't want him to go.' 'Don't they?' I said curiously.

He nodded a nod full of mystery and wisdom. 'I tell you,' he cried, 'this man has enlarged my mind.' He opened his arms wide, staring at me with his little blue eyes that were perfectly round."

III

"I looked at him, lost in astonishment. There he was before me, in motley, as though he had absconded from a troupe of mimes, enthusiastic, fabulous. His very existence was improbable, inexplicable, and altogether bewildering. He was an insoluble problem. It was inconceivable how he had existed, how he had succeeded in getting so far, how he had managed to remain—why he did not instantly disappear. 'I went a little farther,' he said, 'then still a little farther—till I had gone so far that I don't know how I'll ever get back. Never mind. Plenty time. I can manage. You take Kurtz away quick—quick—I tell you.' The glamour of youth enveloped his parti-colored rags, his destitution, his loneliness, the essential desolation of his futile wanderings. For months—for years—his life hadn't been worth a day's purchase; and there he was gallantly, thoughtlessly alive, to all appearance indestructible solely by the virtue of his few years and of his unreflecting audacity. I was seduced into something like admiration—like envy. Glamour urged him on, glamour kept him unscathed. He surely wanted nothing from the wilderness but space to breathe in and to push on through. His need was to exist, and to move onwards at the greatest possible risk, and with a maximum of privation. If the absolutely pure, uncalculating, unpractical spirit of adventure had ever ruled a human being, it ruled this be-patched youth. I almost envied him the possession of this modest and clear flame. It seemed to have consumed all thought of self so completely, that even while he was talking to you, you forgot that it was he—the man before your eyes—who had gone through these things. I did not envy him his devotion to Kurtz, though. He had not meditated over it. It came to him and he accepted it with a sort of eager fatalism. I must say that to me it appeared about the most dangerous thing in every way he had come upon so far.

"They had come together unavoidably, like two ships becalmed near each other, and lay rubbing sides at last. I suppose Kurtz wanted an audience, because on a certain occasion, when encamped in the forest, they had talked all night, or more probably Kurtz had talked. 'We talked of everything,' he said, quite transported at the recollection. 'I forgot there was such a thing as sleep. The night did not seem to last an hour. Everything! Everything! . . . Of love, too.' 'Ah, he talked to you of love!' I said, much amused. 'It isn't what you think,' he cried, almost passionately. 'It was in general. He made me see things—things.'

"He threw his arms up. We were on deck at the time, and the headman of my wood-cutters, lounging near by, turned upon him his heavy and glittering eyes. I looked around, and I don't know why, but I assure you that never, never before, did this land, this river, this jungle, the very arch of this blazing sky, appear to me so hopeless and so dark, so impenetrable to human thought, so pitiless to human weakness. 'And, ever since, you have been with him, of course?' I said.

"On the contrary. It appears their intercourse had been very much broken by various causes. He had, as he informed me proudly, managed to nurse Kurtz through two illnesses (he alluded to it as you would to some risky feat), but as a rule Kurtz wandered alone far in the depths of the forest. 'Very often coming to this station, I had to wait days and days before he would turn up,' he said. 'Ah, it was worth waiting for!—sometimes.' 'What was he doing? exploring or what?' I asked. 'Oh, yes, of course'; he had discovered lots of villages, a lake, too—he did not know exactly in what direction; it was danger- ous to inquire too much—but mostly his expeditions had been for ivory. 'But he had no goods to trade with by that time,' I objected. 'There's a good lot of cartridges left even yet,' he answered, looking away. 'To speak plainly, he raided the country,' I said. He nodded. 'Not alone, surely!' He muttered something about the villages round that lake. 'Kurtz got the tribe to follow him, did he?' I suggested. He fidgeted a little. 'They adored him,' he said. The tone of these words was so extraordinary that I looked at him searchingly. It was curious to see his mingled eagerness and reluctance to speak of Kurtz. The man filled his life, occupied his thoughts, swayed his emotions. 'What can you expect?' he burst out; 'he came to them with thunder and lightning, you know—and they had never seen anything like it—and very terrible. He could be very terrible. You can't judge Mr. Kurtz as you would an ordinary man. No, no, no! Now—just to give you an idea—I don't mind telling you he wanted to shoot me, too, one day—but I don't judge him.' 'Shoot you!' I cried. 'What for?' 'Well, I had a small lot of ivory the chief of that village near my house gave me. You see I used to shoot game for them. Well, he wanted it, and wouldn't hear reason. He declared he would shoot me unless I gave him the ivory and then cleared out of the country, because he could do so, and had a fancy for it, and there was nothing on earth to prevent him killing whom he jolly well pleased. And it was true, too. I gave him the ivory. What did I care! But I didn't clear out. No, no, I couldn't leave him. I had to be careful, of course, till we got friendly again for a time. He had his second illness then. Afterwards I had to keep out of the way; but I didn't mind. He was living for the most part in those villages on the lake. When he came down to the river, sometimes he would take to me, and sometimes it was better for me to be careful. This man suffered too much. He hated all this, and somehow he couldn't get away. When I had a chance I begged him to try and leave while there was time; I offered to go back with him. And he would say yes, and then he would remain; go off on another ivory hunt; disappear for weeks; forget himself amongst these people—forget himself—you know.' 'Why! he's mad,' I said. He protested indignantly. Mr. Kurtz couldn't be mad. If I had heard him talk, only two days ago, I wouldn't dare hint at such a thing. . . . I had taken up my binoculars while we talked, and was looking at the shore, sweep- ing the limit of the forest at each side and at the back of the house. The con- sciousness of there being people in that bush, so silent, so quiet—as silent and quiet as the ruined house on the hill—made me uneasy. There was no sign on the face of nature of this amazing tale that was not so much told as suggested to me in desolate exclamations, completed by shrugs, in interrupted phrases, in hints ending in deep sighs. The woods were unmoved, like a mask —heavy, like the closed door of a prison—they looked with their air of hidden knowledge, of patient expectation, of unapproachable silence. The Russian was explaining to me that it was only lately that Mr. Kurtz had come down to the river, bringing along with him all the fighting men of that lake tribe. He had been absent for several months—getting himself adored, I suppose—and had come down unexpectedly, with the intention to all appearance of making a raid either across the river or down stream. Evidently the appetite for more ivory had got the better of the—what shall I say?—less material aspirations. However he had got much worse suddenly. 'I heard he was lying helpless, and so I came up—took my chance,' said the Russian. 'Oh, he is bad, very bad.' I directed my glass to the house. There were no signs of life, but there was the ruined roof, the long mud wall peeping above the grass, with three little square window-holes, no two of the same size; all this brought within reach of my hand, as it were. And then I made a brusque movement, and one of the remaining posts of that vanished fence leaped up in the field of my glass. You remember I told you I had been struck at the distance by certain attempts at ornamentation, rather remarkable in the ruinous aspect of the place. Now I had suddenly a nearer view, and its first result was to make me throw my head back as if before a blow. Then I went carefully from post to post with my glass, and I saw my mistake. These round knobs were not ornamental but symbolic; they were expressive and puzzling, striking and disturbing—food for thought and also for vultures if there had been any looking down from the sky; but at all events for such ants as were industrious enough to ascend the pole. They would have been even more impressive, those heads on the stakes, if their faces had not been turned to the house. Only one, the first I had made out, was facing my way. I was not so shocked as you may think. The start back I had given was really nothing but a movement of surprise. I had expected to see a knob of wood there, you know. I returned deliberately to the first I had seen—and there it was, black, dried, sunken, with closed eyelids,—a head that seemed to sleep at the top of that pole, and with the shrunken dry lips showing a narrow white line of the teeth, was smiling, too, smiling continuously at some endless and jocose dream of that eternal slumber.

"I am not disclosing any trade secrets. In fact, the manager said afterwards that Mr. Kurtz's methods had ruined the district. I have no opinion on that point, but I want you clearly to understand that there was nothing exactly profitable in these heads being there. They only showed that Mr. Kurtz lacked restraint in the gratification of his various lusts, that there was something wanting in him—some small matter which, when the pressing need arose, could not be found under his magnificent eloquence. Whether he knew of this deficiency himself I can't say. I think the knowledge came to him at last—only at the very last. But the wilderness had found him out early, and had taken on him a terrible vengeance for the fantastic invasion. I think it had whispered to him things about himself which he did not know, things of which he had no conception till he took counsel with this great solitude—and the whisper had proved irresistibly fascinating. It echoed loudly within him because he was hollow at the core. . . . I put down the glass, and the head that had appeared near enough to be spoken to seemed at once to have leaped away from me into inaccessible distance.

"The admirer of Mr. Kurtz was a bit crestfallen. In a hurried indistinct voice he began to assure me he had not dared to take these—say, symbols— down. He was not afraid of the natives; they would not stir till Mr. Kurtz gave the word. His ascendancy was extraordinary. The camps of these people surrounded the place, and the chiefs came every day to see him. They would crawl. . . . 'I don't want to know anything of the ceremonies used when approaching Mr. Kurtz,' I shouted. Curious, this feeling that came over me that such details would be more intolerable than those heads drying on the stakes under Mr. Kurtz's windows. After all, that was only a savage sight, while I seemed at one bound to have been transported into some lightless region of subtle horrors, where pure, uncomplicated savagery was a positive relief, being something that had a right to exist—obviously—in the sunshine. The young man looked at me with surprise. I suppose it did not occur to him that Mr. Kurtz was no idol of mine. He forgot I hadn't heard of any of these splendid monologues on, what was it? on love, justice, conduct of life—or what not. If it had come to crawling before Mr. Kurtz, he crawled as much as the veriest savage of them all. I had no idea of the conditions, he said: these heads were the heads of rebels. I shocked him excessively by laughing. Rebels! What would be the next definition I was to hear? There had been enemies, criminals, workers—and these were rebels. Those rebellious heads looked very subdued to me on their sticks. 'You don't know how such a life tries a man like Kurtz,' cried Kurtz's last disciple. 'Well, and you?' I said. 'I! I! I am a simple man. I have no great thoughts. I want nothing from anybody. How can you compare me to . . . ?' His feelings were too much for speech, and suddenly he broke down. 'I don't understand,' he groaned, 'I've been doing my best to keep him alive and that's enough. I had no hand in all this. I have no abilities. There hasn't been a drop of medicine or a mouthful of invalid food for months here. He was shamefully abandoned. A man like this, with such ideas. Shamefully! Shamefully! I—I—haven't slept for the last ten nights. . . .'

"His voice lost itself in the calm of the evening. The long shadows of the forest had slipped downhill while we talked, had gone far beyond the ruined hovel, beyond the symbolic row of stakes. All this was in the gloom, while we down there were yet in the sunshine, and the stretch of the river abreast of the clearing glittered in a still and dazzling splendor, with a murky and over-shadowed bend above and below. Not a living soul was seen on the shore. The bushes did not rustle.

"Suddenly round the corner of the house a group of men appeared, as though they had come up from the ground. They waded waist-deep in the grass, in a compact body, bearing an improvised stretcher in their midst. Instantly, in the emptiness of the landscape, a cry arose whose shrillness pierced the still air like a sharp arrow flying straight to the very heart of the land; and, as if by enchantment, streams of human beings—of naked human beings—with spears in their hands, with bows, with shields, with wild glances and savage move-ments, were poured into the clearing by the dark-faced and pensive forest. The bushes shook, the grass swayed for a time, and then everything stood still in attentive immobility.

" 'Now, if he does not say the right thing to them we are all done for,' said the Russian at my elbow. The knot of men with the stretcher had stopped, too, halfway to the steamer, as if petrified. I saw the man on the stretcher sit up, lank and with an uplifted arm, above the shoulders of the bearers. 'Let us hope that the man who can talk so well of love in general will find some par-ticular reason to spare us this time,' I said. I resented bitterly the absurd danger of our situation, as if to be at the mercy of that atrocious phantom had been a dishonoring necessity. I could not hear a sound, but through my glasses I saw the thin arm extended commandingly, the lower jaw moving, the eyes of that apparition shining darkly far in its bony head that nodded with grotesque jerks. Kurtz—Kurtz—that means short in German—don't it? Well, the name was as true as everything else in his life—and death. He looked at least seven feet long. His covering had fallen off, and his body emerged from it pitiful and appalling as from a winding-sheet. I could see the cage of his ribs all astir, the bones of his arm waving. It was as though an animated image of death carved out of old ivory had been shaking its hand with menaces at a motionless crowd of men made of dark and glittering bronze. I saw him open his mouth wide—it gave him a weirdly voracious aspect, as though he had wanted to swallow all the air, all the earth, all the men before him. A deep voice reached me faintly. He must have been shouting. He fell back suddenly. The stretcher shook as the bearers staggered forward again, and almost at the same time I noticed that the crowd of savages was vanishing without any perceptible movement of retreat, as if the forest that had ejected these beings so suddenly had drawn them in again as the breath is drawn in a long aspiration.

"Some of the pilgrims behind the stretcher carried his arms—two shot-guns, a heavy rifle, and a light revolver-carbine—the thunderbolts of that pitiful Jupiter. The manager bent over him murmuring as he walked beside his head. They laid him down in one of the little cabins—just a room for a bedplace and a camp-stool or two, you know. We had brought his belated correspondence, and a lot of torn envelopes and open letters littered his bed. His hand roamed feebly amongst these papers. I was struck by the fire of his eyes and the com-posed languor of his expression. It was not so much the exhaustion of disease. He did not seem in pain. This shadow looked satiated and calm, as though for the moment it had had its fill of all the emotions.

"He rustled one of the letters, and looking straight in my face said, 'I am glad.' Somebody had been writing to him about me. These special recom-mendations were turning up again. The volume of tone he emitted without effort, almost without the trouble of moving his lips, amazed me. A voice! a voice! It was grave, profound, vibrating, while the man did not seem capable of a whisper. However, he had enough strength in him—factitious no doubt —to very nearly make an end of us, as you shall hear directly.

"The manager appeared silently in the doorway; I stepped out at once and he drew the curtain after me. The Russian, eyed curiously by the pilgrims, was staring at the shore. I followed the direction of his glance.

"Dark human shapes could be made out in the distance, flitting indistinctly against the gloomy border of the forest, and near the river two bronze figures, leaning on tall spears, stood in the sunlight under fantastic head-dresses of spotted skins, warlike and still in statuesque repose. And from right to left along the lighted shore moved a wild and gorgeous apparition of a woman.

"She walked with measured steps, draped in striped and fringed cloths, treading the earth proudly, with a slight jingle and flash of barbarous orna- ments. She carried her head high; her hair was done in the shape of a helmet; she had brass leggings to the knee, brass wire gauntlets to the elbow, a crimson spot on her tawny cheek, innumerable necklaces of glass beads on her neck; bizarre things, charms, gifts of witch-men, that hung about her, glittered and trembled at every step. She must have had the value of several elephant tusks upon her. She was savage and superb, wild-eyed and magnificent; there was something ominous and stately in her deliberate progress. And in the hush that had fallen suddenly upon the whole sorrowful land, the immense wilderness, the colossal body of the fecund and mysterious life seemed to look at her, pensive, as though it had been looking at the image of its own tenebrous and passionate soul.

"She came abreast of the steamer, stood still, and faced us. Her long shadow fell to the water's edge. Her face had a tragic and fierce aspect of wild sorrow and of dumb pain mingled with the fear of some struggling, half-shaped resolve. She stood looking at us without a stir, and like the wilderness itself, with an air of brooding over an inscrutable purpose. A whole minute passed, and then she made a step forward. There was a low jingle, a glint of yellow metal, a sway of fringed draperies, and she stopped as if her heart had failed her. The young fellow by my side growled. The pilgrims murmured at my back. She looked at us all as if her life had depended upon the unswerving steadiness of her glance. Suddenly she opened her bared arms and threw them up rigid above her head, as though in an uncontrollable desire to touch the sky, and at the same time the swift shadows darted out on the earth, swept around on the river, gathering the steamer into a shadowy embrace. A formid- able silence hung over the scene.

"She turned away slowly, walked on, following the bank, and passed into the bushes to the left. Once only her eyes gleamed back at us in the dusk of the thickets before she disappeared.

" 'If she had offered to come aboard I really think I would have tried to shoot her,' said the man of patches, nervously. 'I have been risking my life every day for the last fortnight to keep her out of the house. She got in one day and kicked up a row about those miserable rags I picked up in the storeroom to mend my clothes with. I wasn't decent. At least it must have been that, for she talked like a fury to Kurtz for an hour, pointing at me now and then. I don't understand the dialect of this tribe. Luckily for me, I fancy Kurtz felt too ill that day to care, or there would have been mischief. I don't understand. . . . No—it's too much for me. Ah, well, it's all over now.'

"At this moment I heard Kurtz's deep voice behind the curtain: 'Save me!—save the ivory, you mean. Don't tell me. Save *me*! Why, I've had to save you. You are interrupting my plans now. Sick! Sick! Not so sick as you would like to believe. Never mind. I'll carry my ideas out yet—I will return. I'll show you what can be done. You with your little peddling notions—you are interfering with me. I will return. I . . .'

"The manager came out. He did me the honor to take me under the arm and lead me aside. 'He is very low, very low,' he said. He considered it necessary to sigh, but neglected to be consistently sorrowful. 'We have done all we could for him—haven't we? But there is no disguising the fact, Mr. Kurtz has done more harm than good to the Company. He did not see the time was not ripe for vigorous action. Cautiously, cautiously—that's my principle. We must be cautious yet. The district is closed to us for a time. Deplorable! Upon the whole, the trade will suffer. I don't deny there is a remarkable quantity of ivory—mostly fossil. We must save it, at all events—but look how precarious the position is—and why? Because the method is unsound.' 'Do you,' said I, looking at the shore, 'call it "unsound method"?' 'Without doubt,' he exclaimed hotly. 'Don't you?' . . . 'No method at all,' I murmured after a while. 'Exactly,' he exulted. 'I anticipated this. Shows a complete want of judgment. It is my duty to point it out in the proper quarter.' 'Oh,' said I, 'that fellow—what's his name?—the brickmaker, will make a readable report for you.' He appeared confounded for a moment. It seemed to me I had never breathed an atmosphere so vile, and I turned mentally to Kurtz for relief—positively for relief. 'Nevertheless I think Mr. Kurtz is a remarkable man,' I said with emphasis. He started, dropped on me a cold heavy glance, said very quietly, 'he *was*,' and turned his back on me. My hour of favor was over; I found myself lumped along with Kurtz as a partisan of methods for which the time was not ripe: I was unsound! Ah! but it was something to have at least a choice of nightmares.

"I had turned to the wilderness really, not to Mr. Kurtz, who, I was ready to admit, was as good as buried. And for a moment it seemed to me as if I also were buried in a vast grave full of unspeakable secrets. I felt an intolerable weight oppressing my breast, the smell of the damp earth, the unseen presence of victorious corruption, the darkness of an impenetrable night. . . . The Russian tapped me on the shoulder. I heard him mumbling and stammering something about 'brother seaman—couldn't conceal—knowledge of matters that would affect Mr. Kurtz's reputation.' I waited. For him evidently Mr. Kurtz was not in his grave; I suspect that for him Mr. Kurtz was one of the immortals. 'Well!' said I at last, 'speak out. As it happens, I am Mr. Kurtz's friend—in a way.'

"He stated with a good deal of formality that had we not been 'of the same profession,' he would have kept the matter to himself without regard to consequences. 'He suspected there was an active ill will towards him on the part of these white men that—' 'You are right,' I said, remembering a certain conversation I had overheard. 'The manager thinks you ought to be hanged.' He showed a concern at this intelligence which amused me at first. 'I had better get out of the way quietly,' he said, earnestly. 'I can do no more for Kurtz now, and they would soon find some excuse. What's to stop them? There's a military post three hundred miles from here.' 'Well, upon my word,' said I, 'perhaps you had better go if you have any friends amongst the savages near by.' 'Plenty,' he said. 'They are simple people—and I want nothing, you know.' He stood biting his lip, then: 'I don't want any harm to happen to these whites here, but of course I was thinking of Mr. Kurtz's reputation—but you are a brother seaman and—' 'All right,' said I, after a time. 'Mr. Kurtz's reputation is safe with me.' I did not know how truly I spoke.

"He informed me, lowering his voice, that it was Kurtz who had ordered the attack to be made on the steamer. 'He hated sometimes the idea of being taken away—and then again. . . . But I don't understand these matters. I am a simple man. He thought it would scare you away—that you would give it up, thinking him dead. I could not stop him. Oh, I had an awful time of it this last month.' 'Very well,' I said. 'He is all right now.' 'Ye-e-es,' he muttered, not very convinced apparently. 'Thanks,' said I; 'I shall keep my eyes open.' 'But quiet—eh?' he urged, anxiously. 'It would be awful for his reputation if anybody here—' I promised a complete discretion with great gravity. 'I have a canoe and three black fellows waiting not very far. I am off. Could you give me a few Martini-Henry cartridges?' I could, and did, with proper secrecy. He helped himself, with a wink at me, to a handful of my tobacco. 'Between sailors—you know—good English tobacco.' At the door of the pilot-house he turned round—'I say, haven't you a pair of shoes you could spare?' He raised one leg. 'Look.' The soles were tied with knotted strings sandal-wise under his bare feet. I rooted out an old pair, at which he looked with admiration before tucking them under his left arm. One of his pockets (bright red) was bulging with cartridges, from the other (dark blue) peeped 'Towson's Inquiry,' etc., etc. He seemed to think himself excellently well equipped for a renewed encounter with the wilderness. 'Ah! I'll never, never meet such a man again. You ought to have heard him recite poetry—his own, too, it was, he told me. Poetry!' He rolled his eyes at the recollection of these delights. 'Oh, he enlarged my mind!' 'Good-by,' said I. He shook hands and vanished in the night. Sometimes I ask myself whether I had ever really seen him— whether it was possible to meet such a phenomenon! . . .

"When I woke up shortly after midnight his warning came to my mind with its hint of danger that seemed, in the starred darkness, real enough to make me get up for the purpose of having a look round. On the hill a big fire burned, illuminating fitfully a crooked corner of the station-house. One of the agents with a picket of a few of our blacks, armed for the purpose, was keeping guard over the ivory, but deep within the forest, red gleams that wavered, that seemed to sink and rise from the ground amongst confused columnar shapes of intense blackness, showed the exact position of the camp where Mr. Kurtz's adorers were keeping their uneasy vigil. The monotonous beating of a big drum filled the air with muffled shocks and a lingering vibration. A steady droning sound of many men chanting each to himself some weird incantation came out from the black, flat wall of the woods as the humming of bees comes out of a hive, and had a strange narcotic effect upon my half-awake senses. I believe I dozed off leaning over the rail, till an abrupt burst of yells, an overwhelming outbreak of a pent-up and mysterious frenzy, woke me up in a bewildered wonder. It was cut short all at once, and the low droning went on with an effect of audible and soothing silence. I glanced casually into the little cabin. A light was burning within, but Mr. Kurtz was not there.

"I think I would have raised an outcry if I had believed my eyes. But I didn't believe them at first—the thing seemed so impossible. The fact is I was completely unnerved by a sheer blank fright, pure abstract terror, unconnected with any distinct shape of physical danger. What made this emotion so overpowering was—how shall I define it?—the moral shock I received, as if something altogether monstrous, intolerable to thought and odious to the soul, had been thrust upon me unexpectedly. This lasted of course the merest fraction of a second, and then the usual sense of commonplace, deadly danger, the possibility of a sudden onslaught and massacre, or something of the kind, which I saw impending, was positively welcome and composing. It pacified me, in fact, so much, that I did not raise an alarm.

"There was an agent buttoned up inside an ulster and sleeping on a chair on deck within three feet of me. The yells had not awakened him; he snored very slightly; I left him to his slumbers and leaped ashore. I did not betray Mr. Kurtz—it was ordered I should never betray him—it was written I should be loyal to the nightmare of my choice. I was anxious to deal with this shadow by myself alone,—and to this day I don't know why I was so jealous of sharing with any one the peculiar blackness of that experience.

"As soon as I got on the bank I saw a trail—a broad trail through the grass. I remember the exultation with which I said to myself, 'He can't walk—he is crawling on all-fours—I've got him.' The grass was wet with dew. I strode rapidly with clenched fists. I fancy I had some vague notion of falling upon him and giving him a drubbing. I don't know. I had some imbecile thoughts. The knitting old woman with the cat obtruded herself upon my memory as a most improper person to be sitting at the other end of such an affair. I saw a row of pilgrims squirting lead in the air out of Winchesters held to the hip. I thought I would never get back to the steamer, and imagined myself living alone and unarmed in the woods to an advanced age. Such silly things—you know. And I remember I confounded the beat of the drum with the beating of my heart, and was pleased at its calm regularity.

"I kept to the track though—then stopped to listen. The night was very clear; a dark blue space, sparkling with dew and starlight, in which black things stood very still. I thought I could see a kind of motion ahead of me. I was strangely cocksure of everything that night. I actually left the track and ran in a wide semicircle (I verily believe chuckling to myself) so as to get in front of that stir, of that motion I had seen—if indeed I had seen anything. I was circumventing Kurtz as though it had been a boyish game.

"I came upon him, and, if he had not heard me coming, I would have fallen over him, too, but he got up in time. He rose, unsteady, long, pale, indistinct, like a vapor exhaled by the earth, and swayed slightly, misty and silent before me; while at my back the fires loomed between the trees, and the murmur of many voices issued from the forest. I had cut him off cleverly; but when actually confronting him I seemed to come to my senses, I saw the danger in its right proportion. It was by no means over yet. Suppose he began to shout? Though he could hardly stand, there was still plenty of vigor in his voice. 'Go away—hide yourself,' he said, in that profound tone. It was very awful. I glanced back. We were within thirty yards from the nearest fire. A black figure stood up, strode on long black legs, waving long black arms, across the glow. It had horns—antelope horns, I think—on its head. Some sorcerer, some witch-man, no doubt: it looked fiend-like enough. 'Do you know what you are doing?' I whispered. 'Perfectly,' he answered, raising his voice for that single word: it sounded to me far off and yet loud, like a hail through a speaking-trumpet. If he makes a row we are lost, I thought to myself. This clearly was not a case for fisticuffs, even apart from the very natural aversion I had to beat that Shadow—this wandering and tormented thing. 'You will be lost,' I said—'utterly lost.' One gets sometimes such a flash of inspiration, you know. I did say the right thing, though indeed he could not have been more irretrievably lost than he was at this very moment, when the foundations of our intimacy were being laid—to endure—to endure—even to the end—even beyond.

" 'I had immense plans,' he muttered irresolutely. 'Yes,' said I; 'but if you try to shout I'll smash your head with—' There was not a stick or a stone near. 'I will throttle you for good,' I corrected myself. 'I was on the threshold of great things,' he pleaded, in a voice of longing, with a wistfulness of tone that made my blood run cold. 'And now for this stupid scoundrel—' 'Your success in Europe is assured in any case,' I affirmed, steadily. I did not want to have the throttling of him, you understand—and indeed it would have been very little use for any practical purpose. I tried to break the spell—the heavy, mute spell of the wilderness—that seemed to draw him to its pitiless breast by the awakening of forgotten and brutal instincts, by the memory of gratified and monstrous passions. This alone, I was convinced, had driven him out to the edge of the forest, to the bush, towards the gleam of fires, the throb of drums, the drone of weird incantations; this alone had beguiled his unlawful soul beyond the bounds of permitted aspirations. And, don't you see, the terror of the position was not in being knocked on the head—though I had a very lively sense of that danger, too—but in this, that I had to deal with a being to whom I could not appeal in the name of anything high or low. I had, even like the niggers, to invoke him—himself—his own exalted and incredible degradation. There was nothing either above or below him, and I knew it. He had kicked himself loose of the earth. Confound the man! he had kicked the very earth to pieces. He was alone, and I before him did not know whether I stood on the ground or floated in the air. I've been telling you what we said—repeating the phrases we pronounced—but what's the good? They were common everyday words—the familiar, vague sounds exchanged on every waking day of life. But what of that? They had behind them, to my mind, the terrific suggestiveness of words heard in dreams, of phrases spoken in nightmares. Soul! If anybody had ever struggled with a soul, I am the man. And I wasn't arguing with a lunatic either. Believe me or not, his intelligence was perfectly clear—concentrated, it is true, upon himself with horrible intensity, yet clear; and therein was my only chance—barring, of course, the killing him there and then, which wasn't so good, on account of unavoidable noise. But his soul was mad. Being alone in the wilderness, it had looked within itself, and, by heavens! I tell you, it had gone mad. I had—for my sins, I suppose—to go through the ordeal of looking into it myself. No eloquence could have been so withering to one's belief in mankind as his final burst of sincerity. He struggled with himself, too. I saw it,—I heard it. I saw the inconceivable mystery of a soul that knew no restraint, no faith, and no fear, yet struggling blindly with itself. I kept my head pretty well; but when I had him at last stretched on the couch, I wiped my forehead, while my legs shook under me as though I had carried half a ton on my back down that hill. And yet I had only supported him, his bony arm clasped round my neck—and he was not much heavier than a child.

"When next day we left at noon, the crowd, of whose presence behind the curtain of trees I had been acutely conscious all the time, flowed out of the woods again, filled the clearing, covered the slope with a mass of naked, breathing, quivering, bronze bodies. I steamed up a bit, then swung downstream, and two thousand eyes followed the evolutions of the splashing, thumping, fierce river-demon beating the water with its terrible tail and breathing black smoke into the air. In front of the first rank, along the river, three men, plastered with bright red earth from head to foot, strutted to and fro restlessly. When we came abreast again, they faced the river, stamped their feet, nodded their horned heads, swayed their scarlet bodies; they shook towards the fierce river-demon a bunch of black feathers, a mangy skin with a pendent tail—something that looked like a dried gourd; they shouted periodically together strings of amazing words that resembled no sounds of human language; and the deep murmurs of the crowd, interrupted suddenly, were like the responses of some satanic litany.

"We had carried Kurtz into the pilot-house: there was more air there. Lying on the couch, he stared through the open shutter. There was an eddy in the mass of human bodies, and the woman with helmeted head and tawny cheeks rushed out to the very brink of the stream. She put out her hands, shouted something, and all that wild mob took up the shout in a roaring chorus of articulated, rapid, breathless utterance.

" 'Do you understand this?' I asked.

"He kept on looking out past me with fiery, longing eyes, with a mingled expression of wistfulness and hate. He made no answer, but I saw a smile, a smile of indefinable meaning, appear on his colorless lips that a moment after twitched convulsively. 'Do I not?' he said slowly, gasping, as if the words had been torn out of him by a supernatural power.

"I pulled the string of the whistle, and I did this because I saw the pilgrims on deck getting out their rifles with an air of anticipating a jolly lark. At the sudden screech there was a movement of abject terror through that wedged mass of bodies. 'Don't! don't you frighten them away,' cried some one on deck disconsolately. I pulled the string time after time. They broke and ran, they leaped, they crouched, they swerved, they dodged the flying terror of the sound. The three red chaps had fallen flat, face down on the shore, as though they had been shot dead. Only the barbarous and superb woman did not so much as flinch, and stretched tragically her bare arms after us over the somber and glittering river.

"And then that imbecile crowd down on the deck started their little fun, and I could see nothing more for smoke.

"The brown current ran swiftly out of the heart of darkness, bearing us down towards the sea with twice the speed of our upward progress; and Kurtz's life was running swiftly, too, ebbing, ebbing out of his heart into the sea of inexorable time. The manager was very placid, he had no vital anxieties now, he took us both in with a comprehensive and satisfied glance: the 'affair' had come off as well as could be wished. I saw the time approaching when I would be left alone of the party of 'unsound method.' The pilgrims looked upon me with disfavor. I was, so to speak, numbered with the dead. It is strange how I accepted this unforeseen partnership, this choice of nightmares forced upon me in the tenebrous land invaded by these mean and greedy phantoms.

"Kurtz discoursed. A voice! a voice! It rang deep to the very last. It survived his strength to hide in the magnificent folds of eloquence the barren darkness of his heart. Oh, he struggled! he struggled! The wastes of his weary brain were haunted by shadowy images now—images of wealth and fame revolving obsequiously round his unextinguishable gift of noble and lofty expression. My Intended, my station, my career, my ideas—these were the subjects for the occasional utterances of elevated sentiments. The shade of the original Kurtz frequented the bedside of the hollow sham, whose fate it was to be buried presently in the mold of primeval earth. But both the diabolic love and the unearthly hate of the mysteries it had penetrated fought for the possession of that soul satiated with primitive emotions, avid of lying fame, of sham distinction, of all the appearances of success and power.

"Sometimes he was contemptibly childish. He desired to have kings meet him at railway stations on his return from some ghastly Nowhere, where he intended to accomplish great things. 'You show them you have in you something that is really profitable, and then there will be no limits to the recognition of your ability,' he would say. 'Of course you must take care of the motives —right motives—always.' The long reaches that were like one and the same reach, monotonous bends that were exactly alike, slipped past the steamer, with their multitude of secular trees looking patiently after this grimy fragment of another world, the forerunner of change, of conquest, of trade, of massacres, of blessings. I looked ahead—piloting. 'Close the shutter,' said Kurtz suddenly one day; 'I can't bear to look at this.' I did so. There was a silence. 'Oh, but I will wring your heart yet!' he cried at the invisible wilderness.

"We broke down—as I had expected—and had to lie up for repairs at the head of an island. This delay was the first thing that shook Kurtz's confidence. One morning he gave me a packet of papers and a photograph—the lot tied together with a shoestring. 'Keep this for me,' he said. 'This noxious fool' (meaning the manager) 'is capable of prying into my boxes when I am not looking.' In the afternoon I saw him. He was lying on his back with closed eyes, and I withdrew quietly, but I heard him mutter, 'Live rightly, die, die. . . .' I listened. There was nothing more. Was he rehearsing some speech in his sleep, or was it a fragment of a phrase from some newspaper article? He had been writing for the papers and meant to do so again, 'for the furthering of my ideas. It's a duty.'

"His was an impenetrable darkness. I looked at him as you peer down at a man who is lying at the bottom of a precipice where the sun never shines. But I had not much time to give him, because I was helping the engine-driver to take to pieces the leaky cylinders, to straighten a bent connecting-rod, and in other such matters. I lived in an infernal mess of rust, filings, nuts, bolts, spanners, hammers, ratchet-drills—things I abominate, because I don't get on with them. I tended the little forge we fortunately had aboard; I toiled wearily in a wretched scrap-heap—unless I had the shakes too bad to stand.

"One evening coming in with a candle I was startled to hear him say a little tremulously, 'I am lying here in the dark waiting for death.' The light was within a foot of his eyes. I forced myself to murmur, 'Oh, nonsense!' and stood over him as if transfixed.

"Anything approaching the change that came over his features I have never seen before, and hope never to see again. Oh, I wasn't touched. I was fascinated. It was as though a veil had been rent. I saw on that ivory face the expression of somber pride, of ruthless power, of craven terror—of an intense and hopeless despair. Did he live his life again in every detail of desire, temptation, and surrender during that supreme moment of complete knowledge? He cried in a whisper at some image, at some vision—he cried out twice, a cry that was no more than a breath—

" 'The horror! The horror!'

"I blew the candle out and left the cabin. The pilgrims were dining in the mess-room, and I took my place opposite the manager, who lifted his eyes to give me a questioning glance, which I successfully ignored. He leaned back, serene, with that peculiar smile of his sealing the unexpressed depths of his meanness. A continuous shower of small flies streamed upon the lamp, upon the cloth, upon our hands and faces. Suddenly the manager's boy put his insolent black head in the doorway, and said in a tone of scathing contempt—

" 'Mistah Kurtz—he dead.'

"All the pilgrims rushed out to see. I remained, and went on with my dinner. I believe I was considered brutally callous. However, I did not eat much. There was a lamp in there—light, don't you know—and outside it was so beastly, beastly dark. I went no more near the remarkable man who had pronounced a judgment upon the adventures of his soul on this earth. The voice was gone. What else had been there? But I am of course aware that next day the pilgrims buried something in a muddy hole.

"And then they very nearly buried me.

"However, as you see I did not go to join Kurtz there and then. I did not. I remained to dream the nightmare out to the end, and to show my loyalty to Kurtz once more. Destiny. My destiny! Droll thing life is—that mysterious arrangement of merciless logic for a futile purpose. The most you can hope from it is some knowledge of yourself—that comes too late—a crop of un-extinguishable regrets. I have wrestled with death. It is the most unexciting contest you can imagine. It takes place in an impalpable grayness, with nothing underfoot, with nothing around, without spectators, without clamor, without glory, without the great desire of victory, without the great fear of defeat, in a sickly atmosphere of tepid skepticism, without much belief in your own right, and still less in that of your adversary. If such is the form of ultimate wisdom, then life is a greater riddle than some of us think it to be. I was within a hair's breadth of the last opportunity for pronouncement, and I found with humiliation that probably I would have nothing to say. This is the reason why I affirm that Kurtz was a remarkable man. He had something to say. He said it. Since I had peeped over the edge myself, I understand better the mean-ing of his stare, that could not see the flame of the candle, but was wide enough to embrace the whole universe, piercing enough to penetrate all the hearts that beat in the darkness. He had summed up—he had judged. 'The horror!' He was a remarkable man. After all, this was the expression of some sort of belief; it had candor, it had conviction, it had a vibrating note of revolt in its whisper, it had the appalling face of a glimpsed truth—the strange commin-gling of desire and hate. And it is not my own extremity I remember best—a vision of grayness without form filled with physical pain, and a careless con-tempt for the evanescence of all things—even of this pain itself. No! It is his extremity that I seem to have lived through. True, he had made that last stride, he had stepped over the edge, while I had been permitted to draw back my hesitating foot. And perhaps in this is the whole difference; perhaps all the wisdom, and all truth, and all sincerity, are just compressed into the inappreciable moment of time in which we step over the threshold of the invisible. Perhaps! I like to think my summing-up would not have been a word of careless contempt. Better his cry—much better. It was an affirmation, a moral victory paid for by innumerable defeats, by abominable terrors, by abominable satisfactions. But it was a victory! That is why I have remained loyal to Kurtz to the last, and even beyond, when a long time after I heard once more, not his own voice, but the echo of his magnificent eloquence thrown to me from a soul as translucently pure as a cliff of crystal.

"No, they did not bury me, though there is a period of time which I remember mistily, with a shuddering wonder, like a passage through some inconceivable world that had no hope in it and no desire. I found myself back in the sepulchral city resenting the sight of people hurrying through the streets to filch a little money from each other, to devour their infamous cookery, to gulp their unwholesome beer, to dream their insignificant and silly dreams. They trespassed upon my thoughts. They were intruders whose knowledge of life was to me an irritating pretense, because I felt so sure they could not possibly know the things I knew. Their bearing, which was simply the bearing of commonplace individuals going about their business in the assurance of perfect safety, was offensive to me like the outrageous flauntings of folly in the face of a danger it is unable to comprehend. I had no particular desire to enlighten them, but I had some difficulty in restraining myself from laughing in their faces, so full of stupid importance. I daresay I was not very well at that time. I tottered about the streets—there were various affairs to settle—grinning bitterly at perfectly respectable persons. I admit my behavior was inexcusable, but then my temperature was seldom normal in these days. My dear aunt's endeavors to 'nurse up my strength' seemed altogether beside the mark. It was not my strength that wanted nursing, it was my imagination that wanted soothing. I kept the bundle of papers given me by Kurtz, not knowing exactly what to do with it. His mother had died lately, watched over, as I was told, by his Intended. A clean-shaved man, with an official manner and wearing gold-rimmed spectacles, called on me one day and made inquiries, at first circuitous, afterwards suavely pressing, about what he was pleased to denominate certain 'documents.' I was not surprised, because I had had two rows with the manager on the subject out there. I had refused to give up the smallest scrap out of that package, and I took the same attitude with the spectacled man. He became darkly menacing at last, and with much heat argued that the Company had the right to every bit of information about its 'territories.' And said he, 'Mr. Kurtz's knowledge of unexplored regions must have been necessarily extensive and peculiar—owing to his great abilities and to the deplorable circumstances in which he had been placed: therefore—' I assured him Mr. Kurtz's knowledge, however extensive, did not bear upon the problems of commerce or administration. He invoked then the name of science. 'It would be an incalculable loss, if,' etc., etc. I offered him the report on the 'Suppression of Savage Customs,' with the postscriptum torn off. He took it up eagerly, but ended by sniffing at it with an air of contempt. 'This is not what we had a right to expect,' he remarked. 'Expect nothing else,' I said. 'There are only private letters.' He withdrew upon some threat of legal proceedings, and I saw him no more; but another fellow, calling himself Kurtz's cousin, appeared two days later, and was anxious to hear all the details about his dear relative's last moments. Incidentally he gave me to understand that Kurtz had been essentially a great musician. 'There was the making of an immense success,' said the man, who was an organist, I believe, with lank gray hair flowing over a greasy coat-collar. I had no reason to doubt his statement; and to this day I am unable to say what was Kurtz's profession, whether he ever had any—which was the greatest of his talents. I had taken him for a painter who wrote for the papers, or else for a journalist who could paint—but even the cousin (who took snuff during the interview) could not tell me what he had been—exactly. He was a universal genius—on that point I agreed with the old chap, who thereupon blew his nose noisily into a large cotton handkerchief and with-drew in senile agitation, bearing off some family letters and memoranda without importance. Ultimately a journalist anxious to know something of the fate of his 'dear colleague' turned up. This visitor informed me Kurtz's proper sphere ought to have been politics 'on the popular side.' He had furry straight eyebrows, bristly hair cropped short, an eye-glass on a broad ribbon, and, becoming expansive, confessed his opinion that Kurtz really couldn't write a bit—'but heavens! how that man could talk. He electrified large meetings. He had faith—don't you see?—he had the faith. He could get himself to believe anything—anything. He would have been a splendid leader of an extreme party.' 'What party?' I asked. 'Any party,' answered the other. 'He was an—an—extremist.' Did I not think so? I assented. Did I know, he asked, with a sudden flash of curiosity, 'what it was that had induced him to go out there?' 'Yes,' said I, and forthwith handed him the famous Report for publication, if he thought fit. He glanced through it hurriedly, mumbling all the time, judged 'it would do,' and took himself off with this plunder.

"Thus I was left at last with a slim packet of letters and the girl's portrait. She struck me as beautiful—I mean she had a beautiful expression. I know that the sunlight can be made to lie, too, yet one felt that no manipulation of light and pose could have conveyed the delicate shade of truthfulness upon those features. She seemed ready to listen without mental reservation, with-out suspicion, without a thought for herself. I concluded I would go and give her back her portrait and those letters myself. Curiosity? Yes; and also some other feeling perhaps. All that had been Kurtz's had passed out of my hands: his soul, his body, his station, his plans, his ivory, his career. There remained only his memory and his Intended—and I wanted to give that up, too, to the past, in a way—to surrender personally all that remained of him with me to that oblivion which is the last word of our common fate. I don't defend myself. I had no clear perception of what it was I really wanted. Perhaps it was an impulse of unconscious loyalty, or the fulfillment of one of those

ironic necessities that lurk in the facts of human existence. I don't know.
I can't tell. But I went.

"I thought his memory was like the other memories of the dead that accumulate in every man's life—a vague impress on the brain of shadows that
had fallen on it in their swift and final passage; but before the high and
ponderous door, between the tall houses of a street as still and decorous as
a well-kept alley in a cemetery, I had a vision of him on the stretcher, opening
his mouth voraciously, as if to devour all the earth with all its mankind. He
lived then before me; he lived as much as he had ever lived—a shadow insatiable
of splendid appearances, of frightful realities; a shadow darker than the
shadow of the night, and draped nobly in the folds of a gorgeous eloquence.
The vision seemed to enter the house with me—the stretcher, the phantom-
bearers, the wild crowd of obedient worshipers, the gloom of the forest, the
glitter of the reach between the murky bends, the beat of the drum, regular
and muffled like the beating of a heart—the heart of a conquering darkness.
It was a moment of triumph for the wilderness, an invading and vengeful
rush which, it seemed to me, I would have to keep back alone for the salvation
of another soul. And the memory of what I had heard him say afar there,
with the horned shapes stirring at my back, in the glow of fires, within the
patient woods, those broken phrases came back to me, were heard again in
their ominous and terrifying simplicity. I remembered his abject pleading,
his abject threats, the colossal scale of his vile desires, the meanness, the
torment, the tempestuous anguish of his soul. And later on I seemed to see
his collected languid manner, when he said one day, 'This lot of ivory now is
really mine. The Company did not pay for it. I collected it myself at a very
great personal risk. I am afraid they will try to claim it as theirs though. H'm.
It is a difficult case. What do you think I ought to do—resist? Eh? I want no
more than justice.' . . . He wanted no more than justice—no more than justice.
I rang the bell before a mahogany door on the first floor, and while I waited
he seemed to stare at me out of the glassy panel—stare with that wide and
immense stare embracing, condemning, loathing all the universe. I seemed to
hear the whispered cry, 'The horror! The horror!'

"The dusk was falling. I had to wait in a lofty drawing room with three
long windows from floor to ceiling that were like three luminous and bedraped
columns. The bent gilt legs and backs of the furniture shone in indistinct
curves. The tall marble fireplace had a cold and monumental whiteness. A
grand piano stood massively in a corner; with dark gleams on the flat surfaces
like a somber and polished sarcophagus. A high door opened—closed. I rose.

"She came forward, all in black, with a pale head, floating towards me in the
dusk. She was in mourning. It was more than a year since his death, more
than a year since the news came; she seemed as though she would remember
and mourn forever. She took both my hands in hers and murmured, 'I had
heard you were coming.' I noticed she was not very young—I mean not
girlish. She had a mature capacity for fidelity, for belief, for suffering. The

room seemed to have grown darker, as if all the sad light of the cloudy evening had taken refuge on her forehead. This fair hair, this pale visage, this pure brow, seemed surrounded by an ashy halo from which the dark eyes looked out at me. Their glance was guileless, profound, confident, and trustful. She carried her sorrowful head as though she were proud of that sorrow, as though she would say, I—I alone know how to mourn him as he deserves. But while we were still shaking hands, such a look of awful desolation came upon her face that I perceived she was one of those creatures that are not the playthings of Time. For her he had died only yesterday. And, by Jove! the impression was so powerful that for me, too, he seemed to have died only yesterday—nay, this very minute. I saw her and him in the same instant of time—his death and her sorrow—I saw her sorrow in the very moment of his death. Do you understand? I saw them together—I heard them together. She had said, with a deep catch of the breath, 'I have survived' while my strained ears seemed to hear distinctly, mingled with her tone of despairing regret, the summing up whisper of his eternal condemnation. I asked myself what I was doing there, with a sensation of panic in my heart as though I had blundered into a place of cruel and absurd mysteries not fit for a human being to behold. She motioned me to a chair. We sat down. I laid the packet gently on the little table, and she put her hand over it. . . . 'You knew him well,' she murmured, after a moment of mourning silence.

" 'Intimacy grows quickly out there,' I said. 'I knew him as well as it is possible for one man to know another.'

" 'And you admired him,' she said. 'It was impossible to know him and not to admire him. Was it?'

" 'He was a remarkable man,' I said, unsteadily. Then before the appealing fixity of her gaze, that seemed to watch for more words on my lips, I went on, 'It was impossible not to—'

" 'Love him,' she finished eagerly, silencing me into an appalled dumbness. 'How true! how true! But when you think that no one knew him so well as I! I had all his noble confidence. I knew him best.'

" 'You knew him best,' I repeated. And perhaps she did. But with every word spoken the room was growing darker, and only her forehead, smooth and white, remained illumined by the unextinguishable light of belief and love.

" 'You were his friend,' she went on. 'His friend,' she repeated, a little louder. 'You must have been, if he had given you this, and sent you to me. I feel I can speak to you—and oh! I must speak. I want you—you have heard his last words—to know I have been worthy of him. . . . It is not pride. . . . Yes! I am proud to know I understood him better than any one on earth—he told me so himself. And since his mother died I have had no one—no one—to —to—'

"I listened. The darkness deepened. I was not even sure he had given me the right bundle. I rather suspect he wanted me to take care of another batch of his papers which, after his death, I saw the manager examining under the lamp. And the girl talked, easing her pain in the certitude of my sympathy; she talked as thirsty men drink. I had heard that her engagement with Kurtz had been disapproved by her people. He wasn't rich enough or something. And indeed I don't know whether he had not been a pauper all his life. He had given me some reason to infer that it was his impatience of comparative poverty that drove him out there.

" '. . . Who was not his friend who had heard him speak once?' she was saying. 'He drew men towards him by what was best in them.' She looked at me with intensity. 'It is the gift of the great,' she went on, and the sound of her low voice seemed to have the accompaniment of all the other sounds, full of mystery, desolation, and sorrow, I had ever heard—the ripple of the river, the soughing of the trees swayed by the wind, the murmurs of the crowds, the faint ring of incomprehensible words cried from afar, the whisper of a voice speaking from beyond the threshold of an eternal darkness. 'But you have heard him! You know!' she cried.

" 'Yes, I know,' I said with something like despair in my heart, but bowing my head before the faith that was in her, before that great and saving illusion that shone with an unearthly glow in the darkness, in the triumphant darkness from which I could not have defended her—from which I could not even defend myself.

" 'What a loss to me—to us!'—she corrected herself with beautiful generosity; then added in a murmur, 'To the world.' By the last gleams of twilight I could see the glitter of her eyes, full of tears—of tears that would not fall.

" 'I have been very happy—very fortunate—very proud,' she went on. 'Too fortunate. Too happy for a little while. And now I am unhappy for—for life.'

"She stood up; her fair hair seemed to catch all the remaining light in a glimmer of gold. I rose, too.

" 'And of all this,' she went on, mournfully, 'of all his promise, and of all his greatness, of his generous mind, of his noble heart, nothing remains—nothing but a memory. You and I—'

" 'We shall always remember him,' I said, hastily.

" 'No!' she cried. 'It is impossible that all this should be lost—that such a life should be sacrificed to leave nothing—but sorrow. You know what vast plans he had. I knew of them, too—I could not perhaps understand—but others knew of them. Something must remain. His words, at least, have not died.'

" 'His words will remain,' I said.

" 'And his example,' she whispered to herself. 'Men looked up to him—his goodness shone in every act. His example—'

" 'True,' I said; 'his example, too. Yes, his example. I forgot that.'

" 'But I do not. I cannot—I cannot believe—not yet. I cannot believe that I shall never see him again, that nobody will see him again, never, never, never.'

"She put out her arms as if after a retreating figure, stretching them black and with clasped pale hands across the fading and narrow sheen of the window. Never see him! I saw him clearly enough then. I shall see this eloquent phantom as long as I live, and I shall see her, too, a tragic and familiar Shade, resembling in this gesture another one, tragic also, and bedecked with powerless charms, stretching bare brown arms over the glitter of the infernal stream, the stream of darkness. She said suddenly very low, 'He died as he lived.'

" 'His end,' said I, with dull anger stirring in me, 'was in every way worthy of his life.'

" 'And I was not with him,' she murmured. My anger subsided before a feeling of infinite pity.

" 'Everything that could be done—' I mumbled.

" 'Ah, but I believed in him more than any one on earth—more than his own mother, more than—himself. He needed me! Me! I would have treasured every sigh, every word, every sign, every glance.'

"I felt like a chill grip on my chest. 'Don't,' I said, in a muffled voice.

" 'Forgive me. I—I—have mourned so long in silence—in silence. . . . You were with him—to the last? I think of his loneliness. Nobody near to understand him as I would have understood. Perhaps no one to hear. . . .'

" 'To the very end,' I said, shakily. 'I heard his very last words. . . .' I stopped in a fright.

" 'Repeat them,' she murmured in a heart-broken tone. 'I want—I want—something—something—to—live with.'

"I was on the point of crying at her, 'Don't you hear them?' The dusk was repeating them in a persistent whisper all around us, in a whisper that seemed to swell menacingly like the first whisper of a rising wind. 'The horror! The horror!'

" 'His last word—to live with,' she insisted. 'Don't you understand I loved him—I loved him—I loved him!'

"I pulled myself together and spoke slowly.

" 'The last word he pronounced was—your name.'

"I heard a light sigh and then my heart stood still, stopped dead short by an exulting and terrible cry, by the cry of inconceivable triumph and of unspeakable pain. 'I knew it—I was sure!' . . . She knew. She was sure. I heard her weeping; she had hidden her face in her hands. It seemed to me that the house would collapse before I could escape, that the heavens would fall upon my head. But nothing happened. The heavens do not fall for such a trifle. Would they have fallen, I wonder, if I had rendered Kurtz that justice which was his due? Hadn't he said he wanted only justice? But I couldn't. I could not tell her. It would have been too dark—too dark altogether. . . ."

Marlow ceased, and sat apart, indistinct and silent, in the pose of a meditating Buddha. Nobody moved for a time. "We have lost the first of the ebb," said the Director, suddenly. I raised my head. The offing was barred by a black bank of clouds, and the tranquil waterway leading to the uttermost ends of the earth flowed somber under an overcast sky—seemed to lead into the heart of an immense darkness.

(1903)

Saki

THE OPEN WINDOW

"My aunt will be down presently, Mr. Nuttel," said a very self-possessed young lady of fifteen; "in the meantime you must try and put up with me."

Framton Nuttel endeavoured to say the correct something which should duly flatter the niece of the moment without unduly discounting the aunt that was to come. Privately he doubted more than ever whether these formal visits on a succession of total strangers would do much towards helping the nerve cure which he was supposed to be undergoing.

"I know how it will be," his sister had said when he was preparing to migrate to this rural retreat; "you will bury yourself down there and not speak to a living soul, and your nerves will be worse than ever from moping. I shall just give you letters of introduction to all the people I know there. Some of them, as far as I can remember, were quite nice."

Framton wondered whether Mrs. Sappleton, the lady to whom he was presenting one of the letters of introduction, came into the nice division.

"Do you know many of the people round here?" asked the niece, when she judged that they had had sufficient silent communion.

"Hardly a soul," said Framton. "My sister was staying here, at the rectory, you know, some four years ago, and she gave me letters of introduction to some of the people here."

He made the last statement in a tone of distinct regret.

"Then you know practically nothing about my aunt?" pursued the self-possessed young lady.

"Only her name and address," admitted the caller. He was wondering whether Mrs. Sappleton was in the married or widowed state. An undefinable something about the room seemed to suggest masculine habitation.

"Her great tragedy happened just three years ago," said the child; "that would be since your sister's time."

"Her tragedy?" asked Framton; somehow in this restful country spot tragedies seemed out of place.

"You may wonder why we keep that window wide open on an October afternoon," said the niece, indicating a large French window that opened on to a lawn.

"It is quite warm for the time of the year," said Framton; "but has that window got anything to do with the tragedy?"

"Out through that window, three years ago to a day, her husband and her two young brothers went off for their day's shooting. They never came back. In crossing the moor to their favourite snipe-shooting ground they were all three engulfed in a treacherous piece of bog. It had been that dreadful wet summer, you know, and places that were safe in other years gave way suddenly without warning. Their bodies were never recovered. That was the dreadful part of it." Here the child's voice lost its self-possessed note and became falteringly human. "Poor aunt always thinks that they will come back some day, they and the little brown spaniel that was lost with them, and walk in at that window just as they used to do. That is why the window is kept open every evening till it is quite dusk. Poor dear aunt, she has often told me how they went out, her husband with his white waterproof coat over his arm, and Ronnie, her youngest brother, singing, 'Bertie, why do you bound?' as he always did to tease her, because she said it got on her nerves. Do you know, sometimes on still, quiet evenings like this, I almost get a creepy feeling that they will all walk in through that window——"

She broke off with a little shudder. It was a relief to Framton when the aunt bustled into the room with a whirl of apologies for being late in making her appearance.

"I hope Vera has been amusing you?" she said.

"She has been very interesting," said Framton.

"I hope you don't mind the open window," said Mrs. Sappleton briskly; "my husband and brothers will be home directly from shooting, and they always come in this way. They've been out for snipe in the marshes today, so they'll make a fine mess over my poor carpets. So like you men-folk, isn't it?"

She rattled on cheerfully about the shooting and the scarcity of birds, and the prospects for duck in the winter. To Framton it was all purely horrible. He made a desperate but only partially successful effort to turn the talk on to a less ghastly topic; he was conscious that his hostess was giving him only a fragment of her attention, and her eyes were constantly straying past him to the open window and the lawn beyond. It was certainly an unfortunate coincidence that he should have paid his visit on this tragic anniversary.

"The doctors agree in ordering me complete rest, an absence of mental excitement, and avoidance of anything in the nature of violent physical exercise," announced Framton, who laboured under the tolerably widespread delusion that total strangers and chance acquaintances are hungry for the least detail of one's ailments and infirmities, their cause and cure. "On the matter of diet they are not so much in agreement," he continued.

"No?" said Mrs. Sappleton, in a voice which only replaced a yawn at the last moment. Then she suddenly brightened into alert attention—but not to what Framton was saying.

"Here they are at last!" she cried. "Just in time for tea, and don't they look as if they were muddy up to the eyes!"

Framton shivered slightly and turned towards the niece with a look intended to convey sympathetic comprehension. The child was staring out through the open window with dazed horror in her eyes. In a chill shock of nameless fear Framton swung round in his seat and looked in the same direction.

In the deepening twilight three figures were walking across the lawn towards the window; they all carried guns under their arms, and one of them was additionally burdened with a white coat hung over his shoulders. A tired brown spaniel kept close at their heels. Noiselessly they neared the house, and then a hoarse young voice chanted out of the dusk: "I said, Bertie, why do you bound?"

Framton grabbed wildly at his stick and hat; the hall-door, the gravel-drive, and the front gate were dimly noted stages in his headlong retreat. A cyclist coming along the road had to run into the hedge to avoid imminent collision.

"Here we are, my dear," said the bearer of the white mackintosh, coming in through the window; "fairly muddy, but most of it's dry. Who was that who bolted out as we came up?"

"A most extraordinary man, a Mr. Nuttel," said Mrs. Sappleton; "could only talk about his illness, and dashed off without a word of good-bye or apology when you arrived. One would think he had seen a ghost."

"I expect it was the spaniel," said the niece calmly; "he told me he had a horror of dogs. He was once hunted into a cemetery somewhere on the banks of the Ganges by a pack of pariah dogs, and had to spend the night in a newly dug grave with the creatures snarling and grinning and foaming just above him. Enough to make any one lose their nerve."

Romance at short notice was her specialty.   (1914)

James Joyce

ARABY

North Richmond Street, being blind, was a quiet street except at the hour when the Christian Brothers' School set the boys free. An uninhabited house of two storeys stood at the blind end, detached from its neighbours in a square ground. The other houses of the street, conscious of decent lives within them, gazed at one another with brown imperturbable faces.

The former tenant of our house, a priest, had died in the back drawing-room. Air, musty from having been long enclosed, hung in all the rooms, and the waste room behind the kitchen was littered with old useless papers. Among these I found a few paper-covered books, the pages of which were curled and damp: *The Abbot*, by Walter Scott, *The Devout Communicant* and *The Memoirs of Vidocq*. I liked the last best, because its leaves were yellow. The wild garden behind the house contained a central apple-tree and a few straggling bushes, under one of which I found the late tenant's rusty bicycle-pump. He had been a very charitable priest; in his will he had left all his money to institutions and the furniture of his house to his sister.

When the short days of winter came, dusk fell before we had well eaten our dinners. When we met in the street, the houses had grown sombre. The space of sky above us was the colour of ever-changing violet, and towards it the lamps of the street lifted their feeble lanterns. The cold air stung us and we played till our bodies glowed. Our shouts echoed in the silent street. The career of our play brought us through the dark muddy lanes behind the houses where we ran the gauntlet of the rough tribes from the cottages, to the back doors of the dark dripping gardens where odours arose from the ashpits, to the dark odorous stables where a coachman smoothed and combed the horse or shook music from the buckled harness. When we returned to the street, light from the kitchen windows had filled the areas. If my uncle was seen turning the corner, we hid in the shadow until we had seen him safely housed. Or if Mangan's sister came out on the doorstep to call her brother in to his tea, we watched her from our shadow peer up and down the street. We waited to see whether she would remain or go in, and, if she remained, we left our shadow and walked up to Mangan's steps resignedly. She was waiting for us, her figure defined by the light from the half-opened door. Her brother always teased her before he obeyed, and I stood by the railings looking at her. Her dress swung as she moved her body, and the soft rope of her hair tossed from side to side.

Every morning I lay on the floor in the front parlour watching her door. The blind was pulled down to within an inch of the sash, so that I could not be seen. When she came out on the doorstep, my heart leaped. I ran to the hall, seized my books, and followed her. I kept her brown figure always in my eye, and, when we came near the point at which our ways diverged, I quickened my pace and passed her. This happened morning after morning. I had never spoken to her, except for a few casual words, and yet her name was like a summons to all my foolish blood.

Her image accompanied me even in places the most hostile to romance. On Saturday evenings, when my aunt went marketing, I had to go to carry some of the parcels. We walked through the flaring streets, jostled by drunken men and bargaining women, amid the curses of labourers, the shrill litanies of shop-boys who stood on guard by the barrels of pigs' cheeks, the nasal chanting of street-singers, who sang a *come-all-you* about O'Donovan Rossa, or a ballad about the troubles in our native land. These noises converged in a single sensation of life for me: I imagined that I bore my chalice safely through a throng of foes. Her name sprang to my lips at moments in strange prayers and praises which I myself did not understand. My eyes were often full of tears (I could not tell why) and at times a flood from my heart seemed to pour itself out into my bosom. I thought little of the future. I did not know whether I would ever speak to her or not, or, if I spoke to her, how I could tell her of my confused adoration. But my body was like a harp, and her words and gestures were like fingers running upon the wires.

One evening I went into the back drawing-room, in which the priest had died. It was a dark rainy evening, and there was no sound in the house. Through one of the broken panes I heard the rain impinge upon the earth, the fine incessant needles of water playing in the sodden beds. Some distant lamp or lighted window gleamed below me. I was thankful that I could see so little. All my senses seemed to desire to veil themselves, and, feeling that I was about to slip from them, I pressed the palms of my hands together until they trembled, murmuring: 'O love! O love!' many times.

At last she spoke to me. When she addressed the first words to me, I was so confused that I did not know what to answer. She asked me was I going to *Araby*. I forget whether I answered yes or no. It would be a splendid bazaar; she said she would love to go.

"And why can't you?" I asked.

While she spoke, she turned a silver bracelet round and round her wrist. She could not go, she said, because there would be a retreat that week in her convent. Her brother and two other boys were fighting for their caps, and I was alone at the railings. She held one of the spikes, bowing her head towards me. The light from the lamp opposite our door caught the white curve of her neck, lit up her hair that rested there, and, falling, lit up the hand upon the railing. It fell over one side of her dress and caught the white border of a petticoat, just visible as she stood at ease.

"It's well for you," she said.

"If I go," I said, "I will bring you something."

What innumerable follies laid waste my waking and sleeping thoughts after that evening! I wished to annihilate the tedious intervening days. I chafed against the work of school. At night in my bedroom and by day in the classroom her image came between me and the page I strove to read. The syllables of the word *Araby* were called to me through the silence in which my soul luxuriated and cast an Eastern enchantment over me. I asked for leave to go to the bazaar on Saturday night. My aunt was surprised and hoped it was not some Freemason affair. I answered few questions in class. I watched my master's face pass from amiability to sternness; he hoped I was not beginning to idle. I could not call my wandering thoughts together. I had hardly any patience with the serious work of life, which, now that it stood between me and my desire, seemed to me child's play, ugly monotonous child's play.

On Saturday morning I reminded my uncle that I wished to go to the bazaar in the evening. He was fussing at the hallstand, looking for the hat-brush, and answered me curtly:

"Yes, boy, I know."

As he was in the hall, I could not go into the front parlour and lie at the window. I left the house in bad humour and walked slowly towards the school. The air was pitilessly raw, and already my heart misgave me.

When I came home to dinner, my uncle had not yet been home. Still, it was early. I sat staring at the clock for some time, and, when its ticking began to irritate me, I left the room. I mounted the staircase and gained the upper part of the house. The high cold empty gloomy rooms liberated me and I went from room to room singing. From the front window I saw my companions playing below in the street. Their cries reached me weakened and indistinct, and, leaning my forehead against the cool glass, I looked over at the dark house where she lived. I may have stood there for an hour, seeing nothing but the brown-clad figure cast by my imagination, touched discreetly by the lamplight at the curved neck, at the hand upon the railings, and at the border below the dress.

When I came downstairs again, I found Mrs. Mercer sitting at the fire. She was an old garrulous woman, a pawnbroker's widow, who collected used stamps for some pious purpose. I had to endure the gossip of the tea-table. The meal was prolonged beyond an hour, and still my uncle did not come. Mrs. Mercer stood up to go: she was sorry she couldn't wait any longer, but it was after eight o'clock, and she did not like to be out late, as the night air was bad for her. When she had gone, I began to walk up and down the room, clenching my fists. My aunt said:

"I'm afraid you may put off your bazaar for this night of Our Lord."

At nine o'clock I heard my uncle's latchkey in the hall-door. I heard him talking to himself and heard the hall-stand rocking when it had received the weight of his overcoat. I could interpret these signs. When he was midway through his dinner, I asked him to give me the money to go to the bazaar. He had forgotten.

"The people are in bed and after their first sleep now," he said.

I did not smile. My aunt said to him energetically:

"Can't you give him the money and let him go? You've kept him late enough as it is."

My uncle said he was very sorry he had forgotten. He said he believed in the old saying: "All work and no play makes Jack a dull boy." He asked me where I was going, and, when I had told him a second time, he asked me did I know *The Arab's Farewell to His Steed*. When I left the kitchen, he was about to recite the opening lines of the piece to my aunt.

I held a florin tightly in my hand as I strode down Buckingham Street towards the station. The sight of the streets thronged with buyers and glaring with gas recalled to me the purpose of my journey. I took my seat in a third-class carriage of a deserted train. After an intolerable delay the train moved out of the station slowly. It crept onward among ruinous houses and over the twinkling river. At Westland Row Station a crowd of people pressed to the carriage doors; but the porters moved them back, saying that it was a special train for the bazaar. I remained alone in the bare carriage. In a few minutes the train drew up beside an improvised wooden platform. I passed out on to the road and saw by the lighted dial of a clock that it was ten minutes to ten. In front of me was a large building which displayed the magical name.

I could not find any sixpenny entrance, and, fearing that the bazaar would be closed, I passed in quickly through a turnstile, handing a shilling to a weary-looking man. I found myself in a big hall girdled at half its height by a gallery. Nearly all the stalls were closed and the greater part of the hall was in darkness. I recognised a silence like that which pervades a church after a service. I walked into the centre of the bazaar timidly. A few people were gathered about the stalls which were still open. Before a curtain, over which the words *Café Chantant* were written in coloured lamps, two men were counting money on a salver. I listened to the fall of the coins.

Remembering with difficulty why I had come, I went over to one of the stalls and examined porcelain vases and flowered tea-sets. At the door of the stall a young lady was talking and laughing with two young gentlemen. I remarked their English accents and listened vaguely to their conversation.

"O, I never said such a thing!"

"O, but you did!"

"O, but I didn't!"

"Didn't she say that?"

"Yes. I heard her."

"O, there's a . . . fib!"

Observing me, the young lady came over and asked me did I wish to buy anything. The tone of her voice was not encouraging; she seemed to have spoken to me out of a sense of duty. I looked humbly at the great jars that stood like eastern guards at either side of the dark entrance to the stall and murmured:

"No, thank you."

The young lady changed the position of one of the vases and went back to the two young men. They began to talk of the same subject. Once or twice the young lady glanced at me over her shoulder.

I lingered before her stall, though I knew my stay was useless, to make my interest in her wares seem the more real. Then I turned away slowly and walked down the middle of the bazaar. I allowed the two pennies to fall against the sixpence in my pocket. I heard a voice call from one end of the gallery that the light was out. The upper part of the hall was now completely dark.

Gazing up into the darkness, I saw myself as a creature driven and derided by vanity; and my eyes burned with anguish and anger.   (1914)

Katherine Mansfield

MISS BRILL

Although it was so brilliantly fine—the blue sky powdered with gold and great spots of light like white wine splashed over the Jardins Publiques—Miss Brill was glad that she had decided on her fur. The air was motionless, but when you opened your mouth there was just a faint chill, like a chill from a glass of iced water before you sip, and now and again a leaf came drifting—from nowhere, from the sky. Miss Brill put up her hand and touched her fur. Dear little thing! It was nice to feel it again. She had taken it out of its box that afternoon, shaken out the moth-powder, given it a good brush, and rubbed the life back into the dim little eyes. "What has been happening to me?" said the sad little eyes. Oh, how sweet it was to see them snap at her again from the red eiderdown! . . . But the nose, which was of some black composition, wasn't at all firm. It must have had a knock, somehow. Never mind—a little dab of black sealing-wax when the time came—when it was absolutely necessary. . . . Little rogue! Yes, she really felt like that about it. Little rogue biting its tail just by her left ear. She could have taken it off and laid it on her lap and stroked it. She felt a tingling in her hands and arms, but that came from walking, she supposed. And when she breathed, something light and sad—no, not sad, exactly—something gentle seemed to move in her bosom.

There were a number of people out this afternoon, far more than last Sunday. And the band sounded louder and gayer. That was because the Season had begun. For although the band played all the year round on Sundays, out of season it was never the same. It was like some one playing with only the family to listen; it didn't care how it played if there weren't any strangers present. Wasn't the conductor wearing a new coat, too? She was sure it was new. He scraped with his foot and flapped his arms like a rooster about to crow, and the bandsmen sitting in the green rotunda blew out their cheeks and glared at the music. Now there came a little "flutey" bit—very pretty!—a little chain of bright drops. She was sure it would be repeated. It was; she lifted her head and smiled.

Only two people shared her "special" seat: a fine old man in a velvet coat, his hands clasped over a huge carved walking-stick, and a big old woman, sitting upright, with a roll of knitting on her embroidered apron. They did not speak. This was disappointing, for Miss Brill always looked forward to the conversation. She had become really quite expert, she thought, at listening as though she didn't listen, at sitting in other people's lives just for a minute while they talked round her.

She glanced, sideways, at the old couple. Perhaps they would go soon. Last Sunday, too, hadn't been as interesting as usual. An Englishman and his wife, he wearing a dreadful Panama hat and she button boots. And she'd gone on the whole time about how she ought to wear spectacles; she knew she needed them; but that it was no good getting any; they'd be sure to break and they'd never keep on. And he'd been so patient. He'd suggested everything—gold rims, the kind that curved round your ears, little pads inside the bridge. No, nothing would please her. "They'll always be sliding down my nose!" Miss Brill had wanted to shake her.

The old people sat on the bench, still as statues. Never mind, there was always the crowd to watch. To and fro, in front of the flower-beds and the band rotunda, the couples and groups paraded, stopped to talk, to greet, to buy a handful of flowers from the old beggar who had his tray fixed to the railings. Little children ran among them, swooping and laughing; little boys with big white silk bows under their chins, little girls, little French dolls, dressed up in velvet and lace. And sometimes a tiny staggerer came suddenly rocking into the open from under the trees, stopped, stared, as suddenly sat down "flop," until its small high-stepping mother, like a young hen, rushed scolding to its rescue. Other people sat on the benches and green chairs, but they were nearly always the same, Sunday after Sunday, and—Miss Brill had often noticed—there was something funny about nearly all of them. They were odd, silent, nearly all old, and from the way they stared they looked as though they'd just come from dark little rooms or even—even cupboards!

Behind the rotunda the slender trees with yellow leaves down drooping, and through them just a line of sea, and beyond the blue sky with gold-veined clouds.

Tum-tum-tum tiddle-um! tiddle-um! tum tiddley-um tum ta! blew the band.

Two young girls in red came by and two young soldiers in blue met them, and they laughed and paired and went off arm-in-arm. Two peasant women with funny straw hats passed, gravely, leading beautiful smoke-colored donkeys. A cold, pale nun hurried by. A beautiful woman came along and dropped her bunch of violets, and a little boy ran after to hand them to her, and she took them and threw them away as if they'd been poisoned. Dear me! Miss Brill didn't know whether to admire that or not! And now an ermine toque and a gentleman in gray met just in front of her. He was tall, stiff, dignified, and she was wearing the ermine toque she'd bought when her hair was yellow. Now everything, her hair, her face, even her eyes, was the same color as the shabby ermine, and her hand, in its cleaned glove, lifted to dab her lips, was a tiny yellowish paw. Oh, she was so pleased to see him—delighted! She rather thought they were going to meet that afternoon. She described where she'd been—everywhere, here, there, along by the sea. The day was so charming—didn't he agree? And wouldn't he, perhaps? . . . But he shook his head, lighted a cigarette, slowly breathed a great deep puff into her face, and, even while she was still talking and laughing, flicked the match away and walked on. The ermine toque was alone; she smiled more brightly than ever. But even the band seemed to know what she was feeling and played more softly, played tenderly, and the drum beat, "The Brute! The Brute!" over and over. What would she do? What was going to happen now? But as Miss Brill wondered, the ermine toque turned, raised her hand as though she'd seen some one else, much nicer, just over there, and pattered away. And the band changed again and played more quickly, more gayly than ever, and the old couple on Miss Brill's seat got up and marched away, and such a funny old man with long whiskers hobbled along in time to the music and was nearly knocked over by four girls walking abreast.

Oh, how fascinating it was! How she enjoyed it! How she loved sitting here, watching it all! It was like a play. It was exactly like a play. Who could believe the sky at the back wasn't painted? But it wasn't till a little brown dog trotted on solemn and then slowly trotted off, like a little "theater" dog, a little dog that had been drugged, that Miss Brill discovered what it was that made it so exciting. They were all on the stage. They weren't only the audience, not only looking on; they were acting. Even she had a part and came every Sunday. No doubt somebody would have noticed if she hadn't been there; she was part of the performance after all. How strange she'd never thought of it like that before! And yet it explained why she made such a point of starting from home at just the same time each week—so as not to be late for the performance —and it also explained why she had quite a queer, shy feeling at telling her English pupils how she spent her Sunday afternoons. No wonder! Miss Brill nearly laughed out loud. She was on the stage. She thought of the old invalid gentleman to whom she read the newspaper four afternoons a week while he slept in the garden. She had got quite used to the frail head on the cotton pillow, the hollowed eyes, the open mouth and the high pinched nose. If he'd been dead she mightn't have noticed for weeks; she wouldn't have minded. But suddenly he knew he was having the paper read to him by an actress! "An actress!" The old head lifted; two points of light quivered in the old eyes. "An actress—are ye?" And Miss Brill smoothed the newspaper as though it were the manuscript of her part and said gently: "Yes, I have been an actress for a long time."

The band had been having a rest. Now they started again. And what they played was warm, sunny, yet there was just a faint chill—a something, what was it?—not sadness—no, not sadness—a something that made you want to sing. The tune lifted, lifted, the light shone; and it seemed to Miss Brill that in another moment all of them, all the whole company, would begin singing. The young ones, the laughing ones who were moving together, they would begin, and the men's voices, very resolute and brave, would join them. And then she too, she too, and the others on the benches—they would come in with a kind of accompaniment—something low, that scarcely rose or fell, something so beautiful—moving. . . . And Miss Brill's eyes filled with tears and she looked smiling at all the other members of the company. Yes, we understand, we understand, she thought—though what they understood she didn't know.

Just at that moment a boy and a girl came and sat down where the old couple had been. They were beautifully dressed; they were in love. The hero and heroine, of course, just arrived from his father's yacht. And still soundlessly singing, still with that trembling smile, Miss Brill prepared to listen.

"No, not now," said the girl. "Not here, I can't."

"But why? Because of that stupid old thing at the end there?" asked the boy. "Why does she come here at all—who wants her? Why doesn't she keep her silly old mug at home?"

"It's her fu-fur which is so funny," giggled the girl. "It's exactly like a fried whiting."

"Ah, be off with you!" said the boy in an angry whisper. Then: "Tell me, ma petite chère—"

"No, not here," said the girl. "Not *yet*."

.   .   .   .

On her way home she usually bought a slice of honeycake at the baker's. It was her Sunday treat. Sometimes there was an almond in her slice, sometimes not. It made a great difference. If there was an almond it was like carrying home a tiny present—a surprise—something that might very well not have been there. She hurried on the almond Sundays and struck the match for the kettle in quite a dashing way.

But to-day she passed the baker's by, climbed the stairs, went into the little dark room—her room like a cupboard—and sat down on the red eiderdown. She sat there for a long time. The box that the fur came out of was on the bed. She unclasped the necklet quickly; quickly, without looking, laid it inside. But when she put the lid on she thought she heard something crying.

(1920)

Franz Kafka

A HUNGER ARTIST

During these last decades the interest in professional fasting has markedly diminished. It used to pay very well to stage such great performances under one's own management, but today that is quite impossible. We live in a

Reprinted from *The Penal Colony*, by Franz Kafka. Translated by Willa and Edwin Muir. Copyright 1948 by Schocken Books.

different world now. At one time the whole town took a lively interest in the hunger artist; from day to day of his fast the excitement mounted; everybody wanted to see him at least once a day; there were people who bought season tickets for the last few days and sat from morning till night in front of his small barred cage; even in the nighttime there were visiting hours, when the whole effect was heightened by torch flares; on fine days the cage was set out in the open air, and then it was the children's special treat to see the hunger artist; for their elders he was often just a joke that happened to be in fashion, but the children stood open-mouthed, holding each other's hands for greater security, marveling at him as he sat there pallid in black tights, with his ribs sticking out so prominently, not even on a seat but down among straw on the ground, sometimes giving a courteous nod, answering questions with a constrained smile, or perhaps stretching an arm through the bars so that one might feel how thin it was, and then again withdrawing deep into himself, paying no attention to anyone or anything, not even to the all-important striking of the clock that was the only piece of furniture in his cage, but merely staring into vacancy with half-shut eyes, now and then taking a sip from a tiny glass of water to moisten his lips.

Besides casual onlookers there were also relays of permanent watchers selected by the public, usually butchers, strangely enough, and it was their task to watch the hunger artist day and night, three of them at a time, in case he should have some secret recourse to nourishment. This was nothing but a formality, instituted to reassure the masses, for the initiates knew well enough that during his fast the artist would never in any circumstances, not even under forcible compulsion, swallow the smallest morsel of food; the honor of his profession forbade it. Not every watcher, of course, was capable of understanding this, there were often groups of night watchers who were very lax in carrying out their duties and deliberately huddled together in a retired corner to play cards with great absorption, obviously intending to give the hunger artist the chance of a little refreshment, which they supposed he could draw from some private hoard. Nothing annoyed the artist more than such watchers; they made him miserable; they made his fast seem unendurable; sometimes he mastered his feebleness sufficiently to sing during their watch for as long as he could keep going, to show them how unjust their suspicions were. But that was of little use; they only wondered at his cleverness in being able to fill his mouth even while singing. Much more to his taste were the watchers who sat close up to the bars, who were not content with the dim night lighting of the hall but focused him in the full glare of the electric pocket torch given them by the impresario. The harsh light did not trouble him at all, in any case he could never sleep properly, and he could always drowse a little, whatever the light, at any hour, even when the hall was thronged with noisy onlookers. He was quite happy at the prospect of spending a sleepless night with such watchers; he was ready to exchange jokes with them, to tell them stories out of his nomadic life, anything at all to keep them awake and demonstrate to them again that he had no eatables in his cage and that he was fasting as not one of them could fast. But his happiest moment was when the morning came and an enormous breakfast was brought them, at his expense, on which they flung themselves with the keen appetite of healthy men after a weary night of wakefulness. Of course there were people who argued that this breakfast was an unfair attempt to bribe the watchers, but that was going rather too far, and when they were invited to take on a night's vigil without a breakfast, merely for the sake of the cause, they made themselves scarce, although they stuck stubbornly to their suspicions.

Such suspicions, anyhow, were a necessary accompaniment to the profession of fasting. No one could possibly watch the hunger artist continuously, day and night, and so no one could produce first-hand evidence that the fast had really been rigorous and continuous; only the artist himself could know that, he was therefore bound to be the sole completely satisfied spectator of his own fast. Yet for other reasons he was never satisfied; it was not perhaps mere fasting that had brought him to such skeleton thinness that many people had regretfully to keep away from his exhibitions, because the sight of him was too much for them, perhaps it was dissatisfaction with himself that had worn him down. For he alone knew, what no other initiate knew, how easy it was to fast. It was the easiest thing in the world. He made no secret of this, yet people did not believe him, at the best they set him down as modest, most of them, however, thought he was out for publicity or else was some kind of cheat who found it easy to fast because he had discovered a way of making it easy, and then had the impudence to admit the fact, more or less. He had to put up with all that, and in the course of time had got used to it, but his inner dissatisfaction always rankled, and never yet, after any term of fasting—this must be granted to his credit—had he left the cage of his own free will. The longest period of fasting was fixed by his impresario at forty days, beyond that term he was not allowed to go, not even in great cities, and there was good reason for it, too. Experience had proved that for about forty days the interest of the public could be stimulated by a steadily increasing pressure of advertisement, but after that the town began to lose interest, sympathetic support began notably to fall off; there were of course local variations as between one town and another or one country and another, but as a general rule forty days marked the limit. So on the fortieth day the flower-bedecked cage was opened, enthusiastic spectators filled the hall, a military band played, two doctors entered the cage to measure the results of the fast, which were announced through a megaphone, and finally two young ladies appeared, blissful at having been selected for the honor, to help the hunger artist down the few steps leading to a small table on which was spread a carefully chosen invalid repast. And at this very moment the artist always turned stubborn. True, he would entrust his bony arms to the outstretched helping hands of the ladies bending over him, but stand up he would not. Why stop fasting at this particular moment, after forty days of it? He had held out for a long time, an illimitably long time; why stop now, when he was in his best fasting form, or rather, not yet quite in his best fasting form? Why should he be cheated of the fame he would get for fasting longer, for being not only the record hunger artist of all time, which presumably he was already, but for beating his own record by a performance beyond human imagination, since he felt that there were no limits to his capacity for fasting? His public pretended to admire him so much, why should it have so little patience with him; if he could endure fasting longer, why shouldn't the public endure it? Besides, he was tired, he was comfortable sitting in the straw, and now he was supposed to lift himself to his full height and go down to a meal the very thought of which gave him a nausea that only the presence of the ladies kept him from betraying, and even that with an effort. And he looked up into the eyes of the ladies who were apparently so friendly and in reality so cruel, and shook his head, which felt too heavy on its strengthless neck. But then there happened yet again what always happened. The impresario came forward, without a word—for the band made speech impossible—lifted his arms in the air above the artist, as if inviting Heaven to look down upon its creature here in the straw, this suffering martyr, which indeed he was, although in quite another sense; grasped him round the emaciated waist, with exaggerated caution, so that the frail condition he was in might be appreciated; and committed him to the care of the blenching ladies, not without secretly giving him a shaking so that his legs and body tottered and swayed. The artist now submitted completely; his head lolled on his breast as if it had landed there by chance; his body was hollowed out; his legs in a spasm of self-preservation clung close to each other at the knees, yet scraped on the ground as if it were not really solid ground, as if they were only trying to find solid ground; and the whole weight of his body, a featherweight after all, relapsed onto one of the ladies, who, looking round for help and panting a little—this post of honor was not at all what she had expected it to be—first stretched her neck as far as she could to keep her face at least free from contact with the artist, then finding this impossible, and her more fortunate companion not coming to her aid but merely holding extended on her own trembling hand the little bunch of knucklebones that was the artist's, to the great delight of the spectators burst into tears and had to be replaced by an attendant who had long been stationed in readiness. Then came the food, a little of which the impresario managed to get between the artist's lips, while he sat in a kind of half-fainting trance, to the accompaniment of cheerful patter designed to distract the public's attention from the artist's condition; after that, a toast was drunk to the public, supposedly prompted by a whisper from the artist in the impresario's ear; the band confirmed it with a mighty flourish, the spectators melted away, and no one had any cause to be dissatisfied with the proceedings, no one except the hunger artist himself, he only, as always.

So he lived for many years, with small regular intervals of recuperation, in visible glory, honored by the world, yet in spite of that troubled in spirit, and all the more troubled because no one would take his trouble seriously. What comfort could he possibly need? What more could he possibly wish for? And if some good-natured person, feeling sorry for him, tried to console him by pointing out that his melancholy was probably caused by fasting, it could happen, especially when he had been fasting for some time, that he reacted with an outburst of fury and to the general alarm began to shake the bars of his cage like a wild animal. Yet the impresario had a way of punishing these outbreaks which he rather enjoyed putting into operation. He would apologize publicly for the artist's behavior, which was only to be excused, he admitted, because of the irritability caused by fasting; a condition hardly to be understood by well-fed people; then by natural transition he went on to mention the artist's equally incomprehensible boast that he could fast for much longer than he was doing; he praised the high ambition, the good will, the great self-denial undoubtedly implicit in such a statement; and then quite simply countered it by bringing out photographs, which were also on sale to the public, showing the artist on the fortieth day of a fast lying in bed almost dead from exhaustion. This perversion of the truth, familiar to the artist though it was, always unnerved him afresh and proved too much for him. What was a consequence of the premature ending of his fast was here presented as the cause of it! To fight against this lack of understanding, against a whole world of non-understanding, was impossible. Time and again in good faith he stood by the bars listening to the impresario, but as soon as the photographs appeared he always let go and sank with a groan back on to his straw, and the reassured public could once more come close and gaze at him.

A few years later when the witnesses of such scenes called them to mind, they often failed to understand themselves at all. For meanwhile the aforementioned change in public interest had set in; it seemed to happen almost overnight; there may have been profound causes for it, but who was going to bother about that; at any rate the pampered hunger artist suddenly found himself deserted one fine day by the amusement seekers, who went streaming past him to other more favored attractions. For the last time the impresario hurried him over half Europe to discover whether the old interest might still survive here and there; all in vain; everywhere, as if by secret agreement, a positive revulsion from professional fasting was in evidence. Of course it could not really have sprung up so suddenly as all that, and many premonitory symptoms which had not been sufficiently remarked or suppressed during the rush and glitter of success now came retrospectively to mind, but it was now too late to take any countermeasures. Fasting would surely come into fashion again at some future date, yet that was no comfort for those living in the present. What, then, was the hunger artist to do? He had been applauded by thousands in his time and could hardly come down to showing himself in a street booth at village fairs, and as for adopting another profession, he was not only too old for that but too fanatically devoted to fasting. So he took leave of the impresario, his partner in an unparalleled career, and hired himself to a large circus; in order to spare his own feelings he avoided reading the conditions of his contract.

A large circus with its enormous traffic in replacing and recruiting men, animals and apparatus can always find a use for people at any time, even for a hunger artist, provided of course that he does not ask too much, and in this particular case anyhow it was not only the artist who was taken on but his famous and long-known name as well, indeed considering the peculiar nature of his performance, which was not impaired by advancing age, it could not be objected that here was an artist past his prime, no longer at the height of his professional skill, seeking a refuge in some quiet corner of a circus, on the contrary, the hunger artist averred that he could fast as well as ever, which was entirely credible, he even alleged that if he were allowed to fast as he liked, and this was at once promised him without more ado, he could astound the world by establishing a record never yet achieved, a statement which certainly provoked a smile among the other professionals, since it left out of account the change in public opinion, which the hunger artist in his zeal conveniently forgot.

He had not, however, actually lost his sense of the real situation and took it as a matter of course that he and his cage should be stationed, not in the middle of the ring as a main attraction, but outside, near the animal cages, on a site that was after all easily accessible. Large and gaily painted placards made a frame for the cage and announced what was to be seen inside it. When the public came thronging out in the intervals to see the animals, they could hardly avoid passing the hunger artist's cage and stopping there for a moment, perhaps they might even have stayed longer had not those pressing behind them in the narrow gangway, who did not understand why they should be held up on their way towards the excitements of the menagerie, made it impossible for anyone to stand gazing quietly for any length of time. And that was the reason why the hunger artist, who had of course been looking forward to these visiting hours as the main achievement of his life, began instead to shrink from them. At first he could hardly wait for the intervals; it was exhilarating to watch the crowds come streaming his way, until only too soon —not even the most obstinate self-deception, clung to almost consciously, could hold out against the fact—the conviction was borne in upon him that these people, most of them, to judge from their actions, again and again, without exception, were all on their way to the menagerie. And the first sight of them from the distance remained the best. For when they reached his cage he was at once deafened by the storm of shouting and abuse that arose from the two contending factions, which renewed themselves continuously, of those who wanted to stop and stare at him—he soon began to dislike them more than the others—not out of real interest but only out of obstinate self-assertiveness, and those who wanted to go straight on to the animals. When the first great rush was past, the stragglers came along, and these, whom nothing could have prevented from stopping to look at him as long as they had breath, raced past with long strides, hardly even glancing at him, in their haste to get to the menagerie in time. And all too rarely did it happen that he had a stroke of luck, when some father of a family fetched up before him with his children, pointed a finger at the hunger artist and explained at length what the phenomenon meant, telling stories of earlier years when he himself had watched similar but much more thrilling performances, and the children, still rather uncomprehending, since neither inside nor outside school had they been sufficiently prepared for this lesson—what did they care about fasting?—yet showed by the brightness of their intent eyes that new and better times might be coming. Perhaps, said the hunger artist to himself many a time, things would be a little better if his cage were set not quite so near the menagerie. That made it too easy for people to make their choice, to say nothing of what he suffered from the stench of the menagerie, the animals' restlessness by night, the carrying past of raw lumps of flesh for the beasts of prey, the roaring at feeding times, which depressed him continually. But he did not dare to lodge a complaint with the management; after all, he had the animals to thank for the troops of people who passed his cage, among whom there might always be one here and there to take an interest in him, and who could tell where they might seclude him if he called attention to his existence and thereby to the fact that, strictly speaking, he was only an impediment on the way to the menagerie.

A small impediment, to be sure, one that grew steadily less. People grew familiar with the strange idea that they could be expected, in times like these, to take an interest in a hunger artist, and with this familiarity the verdict went out against him. He might fast as much as he could, and he did so; but nothing could save him now, people passed him by. Just try to explain to anyone the art of fasting! Anyone who has no feeling for it cannot be made to understand it. The fine placards grew dirty and illegible, they were torn down; the little notice board telling the number of fast days achieved, which at first was changed carefully every day, had long stayed at the same figure, for after the first few weeks even this small task seemed pointless to the staff; and so the artist simply fasted on and on, as he had once dreamed of doing, and it was no trouble to him, just as he had always foretold, but no one counted the days, no one, not even the artist himself, knew what records he was already breaking, and his heart grew heavy. And when once in a time some leisurely passer-by stopped, made merry over the old figure on the board and spoke of swindling, that was in its way the stupidest lie ever invented by indifference and inborn malice, since it was not the hunger artist who was cheating, he was working honestly, but the world was cheating him of his reward.

Many more days went by, however, and that too came to an end. An overseer's eye fell on the cage one day and he asked the attendants why this perfectly good stage should be left standing there unused with dirty straw inside it; nobody knew, until one man, helped out by the notice board, remembered about the hunger artist. They poked into the straw with sticks and found him in it. "Are you still fasting?" asked the overseer, "when on earth do you mean to stop?" "Forgive me, everybody," whispered the hunger artist; only the overseer, who had his ear to the bars, understood him. "Of course," said the overseer, and tapped his forehead with a finger to let the attendants know what state the man was in, "we forgive you." "I always wanted you to admire my fasting," said the hunger artist. "We do admire it," said the overseer, affably. "But you shouldn't admire it," said the hunger artist. "Well then we don't admire it," said the overseer, "but why shouldn't we admire it?" "Because I have to fast, I can't help it," said the hunger artist. "What a fellow you are," said the overseer, "and why can't you help it?" "Because," said the hunger artist, lifting his head a little and speaking, with his lips pursed, as if for a kiss, right into the overseer's ear, so that no syllable might be lost, "because I couldn't find the food I liked. If I had found it, believe me, I should have made no fuss and stuffed myself like you or anyone else." These were his last words, but in his dimming eyes remained the firm though no longer proud persuasion that he was still continuing to fast.

"Well, clear this out now!" said the overseer, and they buried the hunger artist, straw and all. Into the cage they put a young panther. Even the most insensitive felt it refreshing to see this wild creature leaping around the cage that had so long been dreary. The panther was all right. The food he liked was brought him without hesitation by the attendants; he seemed not even to miss his freedom; his noble body, furnished almost to the bursting point with all that it needed, seemed to carry freedom around with it too; somewhere in his jaws it seemed to lurk; and the joy of life streamed with such ardent passion from his throat that for the onlookers it was not easy to stand the shock of it. But they braced themselves, crowded round the cage, and did not want ever to move away. (1924)

Ernest Hemingway

THE KILLERS

The door of Henry's lunch-room opened and two men came in. They sat down at the counter.

"What's yours?" George asked them.

"I don't know," one of the men said. "What do you want to eat, Al?"

"I don't know," said Al. "I don't know what I want to eat."

Outside it was getting dark. The street-light came on outside the window. The two men at the counter read the menu. From the other end of the

counter Nick Adams watched them. He had been talking to George when
they came in.

"I'll have a roast pork tenderloin with apple sauce and mashed potatoes,"
the first man said.

"It isn't ready yet."

"What the hell do you put it on the card for?"

"That's the dinner," George explained. "You can get that at six o'clock."
George looked at the clock on the wall behind the counter.

"It's five o'clock."

"The clock says twenty minutes past five," the second man said.

"It's twenty minutes fast."

"Oh, to hell with the clock," the first man said. "What have you got to eat?"

"I can give you any kind of sandwiches," George said. "You can have ham
and eggs, bacon and eggs, liver and bacon, or a steak."

"Give me chicken croquettes with green peas and cream sauce and mashed
potatoes."

"That's the dinner."

"Everything we want's the dinner, eh? That's the way you work it."

"I can give you ham and eggs, bacon and eggs, liver——"

"I'll take ham and eggs," the man called Al said. He wore a derby hat
and a black overcoat buttoned across the chest. His face was small and white
and he had tight lips. He wore a silk muffler and gloves.

"Give me bacon and eggs," said the other man. He was about the same
size as Al. Their faces were different but they were dressed like twins. Both
wore overcoats too tight for them. They sat leaning forward, their elbows
on the counter.

"Got anything to drink?" Al asked.

"Silver beer, bevo, ginger-ale," George said.

"I mean you got anything to *drink?*"

"Just those I said."

"This is a hot town," said the other. "What do they call it?"

"Summit."

"Ever hear of it?" Al asked his friend.

"No," said the friend.

"What do you do here nights?" Al asked.

"They eat the dinner," his friend said. "They all come here and eat the
big dinner."

"That's right," George said.

"So you think that's right?" Al asked George.

"Sure."

"You're a pretty bright boy, aren't you?"

"Sure," said George.

"Well, you're not," said the other little man. "Is he, Al?"

"He's dumb," said Al. He turned to Nick. "What's your name?"

"Adams."

"Another bright boy," Al said. "Ain't he a bright boy, Max?"

"The town's full of bright boys," Max said.

George put the two platters, one of ham and eggs, the other of bacon and eggs, on the counter. He set down two side-dishes of fried potatoes and closed the wicket into the kitchen.

"Which is yours?" he asked Al.

"Don't you remember?"

"Ham and eggs."

"Just a bright boy," Max said. He leaned forward and took the ham and eggs. Both men ate with their gloves on. George watched them eat.

"What are *you* looking at?" Max looked at George.

"Nothing."

"The hell you were. You were looking at me."

"Maybe the boy meant it for a joke, Max," Al said.

George laughed.

"*You* don't have to laugh," Max said to him. "*You* don't have to laugh at all, see?"

"All right," said George.

"So he thinks it's all right." Max turned to Al. "He thinks it's all right. That's a good one."

"Oh, he's a thinker," Al said. They went on eating.

"What's the bright boy's name down the counter?" Al asked Max.

"Hey, bright boy," Max said to Nick. "You go around on the other side of the counter with your boy friend."

"What's the idea?" Nick asked.

"There isn't any idea."

"You better go around, **bright** boy," Al said. Nick went around behind the counter.

"What's the idea?" George asked.

"None of your damn business," Al said. "Who's out in the kitchen?"

"The nigger."

"What do you mean the nigger?"

"The nigger that cooks."

"Tell him to come in."

"What's the idea?"

"Tell him to come in."

"Where do you think you are?"

"We know damn well where we are," the man called Max said. "Do we look silly?"

"You talk silly," Al said to him. "What the hell do you argue with this kid for? Listen," he said to George, "tell the nigger to come out here."

"What are you going to do to him?"

"Nothing. Use your head, bright boy. What would we do to a nigger?"

George opened the slit that opened back into the kitchen. "Sam," he called. "Come in here a minute."

The door to the kitchen opened and the nigger came in. "What was it?" he asked. The two men at the counter took a look at him.

"All right, nigger. You stand right there," Al said.

Sam, the nigger, standing in his apron, looked at the two men sitting at the counter. "Yes, sir," he said. Al got down from his stool.

"I'm going back to the kitchen with the nigger and bright boy," he said. "Go on back to the kitchen, nigger. You go with him, bright boy." The little man walked after Nick and Sam, the cook, back into the kitchen. The door shut after them. The man called Max sat at the counter opposite George. He didn't look at George but looked in the mirror that ran along back of the counter. Henry's had been made over from a saloon into a lunch-counter.

"Well, bright boy," Max said, looking into the mirror, "why don't you say something?"

"What's it all about?"

"Hey, Al," Max called, "bright boy wants to know what it's all about."

"Why don't you tell him?" Al's voice came from the kitchen.

"What do you think it's all about?"

"I don't know."

"What do you think?"

Max looked into the mirror all the time he was talking.

"I wouldn't say."

"Hey, Al, bright boy says he wouldn't say what he thinks it's all about."

"I can hear you, all right," Al said from the kitchen. He had propped open the slit that dishes passed through into the kitchen with a catsup bottle. "Listen, bright boy," he said from the kitchen to George. "Stand a little further along the bar. You move a little to the left, Max." He was like a photographer arranging for a group picture.

"Talk to me, bright boy," Max said. "What do you think's going to happen?"

George did not say anything.

"I'll tell you," Max said. "We're going to kill a Swede. Do you know a big Swede named Ole Andreson?"

"Yes."

"He comes here to eat every night, don't he?"

"Sometimes he comes here."

"He comes here at six o'clock, don't he?"

"If he comes."

"We know all that, bright boy," Max said. "Talk about something else. Ever go to the movies?"

"Once in a while."

"You ought to go to the movies more. The movies are fine for a bright boy like you."

"What are you going to kill Ole Andreson for? What did he ever do to you?"

"He never had a chance to do anything to us. He never even seen us."

"And he's only going to see us once," Al said from the kitchen.

"What are you going to kill him for, then?" George asked.

"We're killing him for a friend. Just to oblige a friend, bright boy."

"Shut up," said Al from the kitchen. "You talk too goddam much."

"Well, I got to keep bright boy amused. Don't I, bright boy?"

"You talk too damn much," Al said. "The nigger and my bright boy are amused by themselves. I got them tied up like a couple of girl friends in the convent."

"I suppose you were in a convent?"

"You never know."

"You were in a kosher convent. That's where you were."

George looked up at the clock.

"If anybody comes in you tell them the cook is off, and if they keep after it, you tell them you'll go back and cook yourself. Do you get that, bright boy?"

"All right," George said. "What you going to do with us afterward?"

"That'll depend," Max said. "That's one of those things you never know at the time."

George looked up at the clock. It was a quarter past six. The door from the street opened. A street-car motorman came in.

"Hello, George," he said. "Can I get supper?"

"Sam's gone out," George said. "He'll be back in about half an hour."

"I'd better go up the street," the motorman said. George looked at the clock. It was twenty minutes past six.

"That was nice, bright boy," Max said. "You're a regular little gentleman."

"He knew I'd blow his head off," Al said from the kitchen.

"No," said Max. "It ain't that. Bright boy is nice. He's a nice boy. I like him."

At six-fifty-five George said: "He's not coming."

Two other people had been in the lunch-room. Once George had gone out to the kitchen and made a ham-and-egg sandwich "to go" that a man wanted to take with him. Inside the kitchen he saw Al, his derby hat tipped back, sitting on a stool beside the wicket with the muzzle of a sawed off shotgun resting on the ledge. Nick and the cook were back to back in the corner, a towel tied in each of their mouths. George had cooked the sandwich, wrapped it up in oiled paper, put it in a bag, brought it in, and the man had paid for it and gone out.

"Bright boy can do everything," Max said. "He can cook and everything. You'd make some girl a nice wife, bright boy."

"Yes?" George said. "Your friend, Ole Andreson, isn't going to come."

"We'll give him ten minutes." Max said.

Max watched the mirror and the clock. The hands of the clock marked seven o'clock, and then five minutes past seven.

"Come on, Al," said Max. "We better go. He's not coming."

"Better give him five minutes," Al said from the kitchen.

In the five minutes a man came in, and George explained that the cook was sick.

"Why the hell don't you get another cook?" the man asked. "Aren't you running a lunch-counter?" He went out.

"Come on, Al," Max said.

"What about the two bright boys and the nigger?"

"They're all right."

"You think so?"

"Sure. We're through with it."

"I don't like it," said Al. "It's sloppy. You talk too much."

"Oh, what the hell," said Max. "We got to keep amused, haven't we?"

"You talk too much, all the same," Al said. He came out from the kitchen. The cut-off barrels of the shotgun made a slight bulge under the waist of his too tight-fitting overcoat. He straightened his coat with his gloved hands.

"So long, bright boy," he said to George. "You got a lot of luck."

"That's the truth," Max said. "You ought to play the races, bright boy."

The two of them went out the door. George watched them, through the window, pass under the arc-light and cross the street. In their tight overcoats and derby hats they looked like a vaudeville team. George went back through the swinging-door into the kitchen and untied Nick and the cook.

"I don't want any more of that," said Sam, the cook. "I don't want any more of that."

Nick stood up. He had never had a towel in his mouth before.

"Say," he said. "What the hell?" He was trying to swagger it off.

"They were going to kill Ole Andreson," George said. "They were going to shoot him when he came in to eat."

"Ole Andreson?"

"Sure."

The cook felt the corners of his mouth with his thumbs.

"They all gone?" he asked.

"Yeah," said George. "They're gone now."

"I don't like it," said the cook. "I don't like any of it at all."

"Listen," George said to Nick. "You better go see Ole Andreson."

"All right."

"You better not have anything to do with it at all," Sam, the cook, said. "You better stay way out of it."

"Don't go if you don't want to," George said.

"Mixing up in this ain't going to get you anywhere," the cook said. "You stay out of it."

"I'll go see him," Nick said to George. "Where does he live?"

The cook turned away.

"Little boys always know what they want to do," he said.

"He lives up at Hirsch's rooming-house," George said to Nick.

"I'll go up there."

Outside the arc-light shone through the bare branches of a tree. Nick walked up the street beside the car-tracks and turned at the next arc-light down a side-street. Three houses up the street was Hirsch's rooming-house. Nick walked up the two steps and pushed the bell. A woman came to the door.

"Is Ole Andreson here?"

"Do you want to see him?"

"Yes, if he's in."

Nick followed the woman up a flight of stairs and back to the end of a corridor. She knocked on the door.

"Who is it?"

"It's somebody to see you, Mr. Andreson," the woman said.

"It's Nick Adams."

"Come in."

Nick opened the door and went into the room. Ole Andreson was lying on the bed with all his clothes on. He had been a heavyweight prizefighter and he was too long for the bed. He lay with his head on two pillows. He did not look at Nick.

"What was it?" he asked.

"I was up at Henry's," Nick said, "and two fellows came in and tied up me and the cook, and they said they were going to kill you."

It sounded silly when he said it. Ole Andreson said nothing.

"They put us out in the kitchen," Nick went on. "They were going to shoot you when you came to supper."

Ole Andreson looked at the wall and did not say anything.

"George thought I better come and tell you about it."

"There isn't anything I can do about it," Ole Andreson said.

"I'll tell you what they were like."

"I don't want to know what they were like," Ole Andreson said. He looked at the wall. "Thanks for coming to tell me about it."

"That's all right."

Nick looked at the big man lying on the bed.

"Don't you want me to go and see the police?"

"No," Ole Andreson said. "That wouldn't do any good."

"Isn't there something I could do?"

"No. There isn't anything to do."

"Maybe it was just a bluff."

"No. It ain't just a bluff."

Ole Andreson rolled over toward the wall.

"The only thing is," he said, talking toward the wall, "I just can't make up my mind to go out. I been in here all day."

"Couldn't you get out of town?"

"No," Ole Andreson said. "I'm through with all that running around."

He looked at the wall.

"There ain't anything to do now."

"Couldn't you fix it up some way?"

"No. I got in wrong." He talked in the same flat voice. "There ain't any thing to do. After a while I'll make up my mind to go out."

"I better go back and see George," Nick said.

"So long," said Ole Andreson. He did not look toward Nick. "Thanks for coming around."

Nick went out. As he shut the door he saw Ole Andreson with all his clothes on, lying on the bed looking at the wall.

"He's been in his room all day," the landlady said down-stairs. "I guess he don't feel well. I said to him: 'Mr. Andreson, you ought to go out and take a walk on a nice fall day like this,' but he didn't feel like it."

"He doesn't want to go out."

"I'm sorry he don't feel well," the woman said. "He's an awfully nice man. He was in the ring, you know."

"I know it."

"You'd never know it except from the way his face is," the woman said. They stood talking just inside the street door. "He's just as gentle."

"Well, good-night, Mrs. Hirsch," Nick said.

"I'm not Mrs. Hirsch," the woman said. "She owns the place. I just look after it for her. I'm Mrs. Bell."

"Well, good-night, Mrs. Bell," Nick said.

"Good-night," the woman said.

Nick walked up the dark street to the corner under the arc-light, and then along the car-tracks to Henry's eating-house. George was inside, back of the counter.

"Did you see Ole?"

"Yes," said Nick. "He's in his room and he won't go out."

The cook opened the door from the kitchen when he heard Nick's voice. "I don't even listen to it," he said and shut the door.

"Did you tell him about it?" George asked.

"Sure. I told him but he knows what it's all about."

"What's he going to do?"

"Nothing."

"They'll kill him."

"I guess they will."

"He must have got mixed up in something in Chicago."

"I guess so," said Nick.

"It's a hell of a thing."

"It's an awful thing," Nick said.

They did not say anything. George reached down for a towel and wiped the counter.

"I wonder what he did?" Nick said.

"Double-crossed somebody. That's what they kill them for."

"I'm going to get out of this town," Nick said.

"Yes," said George. "That's a good thing to do."

"I can't stand to think about him waiting in the room and knowing he's going to get it. It's too damned awful."

"Well," said George, "you better not think about it."   (1927)

Katherine Anne Porter

FLOWERING JUDAS

Braggioni sits heaped upon the edge of a straightbacked chair much too small for him, and sings to Laura in a furry, mournful voice. Laura has begun to find reasons for avoiding her own house until the latest possible moment, for Braggioni is there almost every night. No matter how late she is, he will be sitting there with a surly, waiting expression, pulling at his kinky yellow hair, thumbing the strings of his guitar, snarling a tune under his breath. Lupe the Indian maid meets Laura at the door, and says with a flicker of a glance towards the upper room, "He waits."

Laura wishes to lie down, she is tired of her hairpins and the feel of her long tight sleeves, but she says to him, "Have you a new song for me this evening?" If he says yes, she asks him to sing it. If he says no, she remembers his favorite one, and asks him to sing it again. Lupe brings her a cup of chocolate and a plate of rice, and Laura eats at the small table under the lamp, first inviting Braggioni, whose answer is always the same: "I have eaten, and besides, chocolate thickens the voice."

Laura says, "Sing, then," and Braggioni heaves himself into song. He scratches the guitar familiarly as though it were a pet animal, and sings passionately off key, taking the high notes in a prolonged painful squeal. Laura, who haunts the markets listening to the ballad singers, and stops every day to hear the blind boy playing his reed-flute in Sixteenth of September Street, listens to Braggioni with pitiless courtesy, because she dares not smile at his miserable performance. Nobody dares to smile at him. Braggioni is cruel to everyone, with a kind of specialized insolence, but he is so vain of his talents, and so sensitive to slights, it would require a cruelty and vanity greater than his own to lay a finger on the vast cureless wound of his self-esteem. It would require courage, too, for it is dangerous to offend him, and nobody has this courage.

Braggioni loves himself with such tenderness and amplitude and eternal charity that his followers—for he is a leader of men, a skilled revolutionist, and his skin has been punctured in honorable warfare—warm themselves in the reflected glow, and say to each other: "He has a real nobility, a love of humanity raised above mere personal affections." The excess of this self-love has flowed out, inconveniently for her, over Laura, who, with so many others, owes her comfortable situation and her salary to him. When he is in a very good humor, he tells her, "I am tempted to forgive you for being a *gringa. Gringita!*" and Laura, burning, imagines herself leaning forward suddenly, and with a sound back-handed slap wiping the suety smile from his face. If he notices her eyes at these moments he gives no sign.

She knows what Braggioni would offer her, and she must resist tenaciously without appearing to resist, and if she could avoid it she would not admit even to herself the slow drift of his intention. During these long evenings which have spoiled a long month for her, she sits in her deep chair with an open book on her knees, resting her eyes on the consoling rigidity of the printed page when the sight and sound of Braggioni singing threaten to identify themselves with all her remembered afflictions and to add their weight to her uneasy premonitions of the future. The gluttonous bulk of Braggioni has become a symbol of her many disillusions, for a revolutionist should be lean, animated by heroic faith, a vessel of abstract virtues. This is nonsense, she knows it now and is ashamed of it. Revolution must have leaders, and leadership is a career for energetic men. She is, her comrades tell her, full of romantic error, for what she defines as cynicism in them is merely "a developed sense of reality." She is almost too willing to say, "I am wrong, I suppose I don't really understand the principles," and afterward she makes a secret truce with herself, determined not to surrender her will to such expedient logic. But she cannot help feeling that she has been betrayed irreparably by the disunion between her way of living and her feeling of what life should be, and at times she is almost contented to rest in this sense of grievance as a private store of consolation. Sometimes she wishes to run away, but she stays. Now she longs to fly out of this room, down the narrow stairs, and into the street where the houses lean together like conspirators under a single mottled lamp, and leave Braggioni singing to himself.

Instead she looks at Braggioni, frankly and clearly, like a good child who understands the rules of behavior. Her knees cling together under sound blue serge, and her round white collar is not purposely nun-like. She wears the uniform of an idea, and has renounced vanities. She was born Roman Catholic, and in spite of her fear of being seen by someone who might make a scandal of it, she slips now and again into some crumbling little church, kneels on the chilly stone, and says a Hail Mary on the gold rosary she bought in Tehuantepec. It is no good and she ends by examining the altar with its tinsel flowers and ragged brocades, and feels tender about the battered doll-shape of some male saint whose white, lace-trimmed drawers hang limply around his ankles below the hieratic dignity of his velvet robe. She has encased herself in a set of principles derived from her early training, leaving no detail of gesture or of personal taste untouched, and for this reason she will not wear lace made on machines. This is her private heresy, for in her special group the machine is sacred, and will be the salvation of the workers. She loves fine lace, and there is a tiny edge of fluted cobweb on this collar, which is one of twenty precisely alike, folded in blue tissue paper in the upper drawer of her clothes chest.

Braggioni catches her glance solidly as if he had been waiting for it, leans forward, balancing his paunch between his spread knees, and sings with tremendous emphasis, weighing his words. He has, the song relates, no father and no mother, nor even a friend to console him; lonely as a wave of the sea he comes and goes, lonely as a wave. His mouth opens round and yearns sideways, his balloon cheeks grow oily with the labor of song. He bulges marvelously in his expensive garments. Over his lavender collar, crushed upon a purple necktie, held by a diamond hoop: over his ammunition belt of tooled leather worked in silver, buckled cruelly around his gasping middle: over the tops of his glossy yellow shoes Braggioni swells with ominous ripeness, his mauve silk hose stretched taut, his ankles bound with the stout leather thongs of his shoes.

When he stretches his eyelids at Laura she notes again that his eyes are the true tawny yellow cat's eyes. He is rich, not in money, he tells her, but in power, and this power brings with it the blameless ownership of things, and the right to indulge his love of small luxuries. "I have a taste for the elegant refinements," he said once, flourishing a yellow silk handkerchief before her nose. "Smell that? It is Jockey Club, imported from New York." Nonetheless he is wounded by life. He will say so presently. "It is true everything turns to dust in the hand, to gall on the tongue." He sighs and his leather belt creaks like a saddle girth. "I am disappointed in everything as it comes. Everything." He shakes his head. "You, poor thing, you will be disappointed too. You are born for it. We are more alike than you realize in some things. Wait and see. Some day you will remember what I have told you, you will know that Braggioni was your friend."

Laura feels a slow chill, a purely physical sense of danger, a warning in her blood that violence, mutilation, a shocking death, wait for her with lessening patience. She has translated this fear into something homely, immediate, and sometimes hesitates before crossing the street. "My personal fate is nothing, except as the testimony of a mental attitude," she reminds herself, quoting from some forgotten philosophic primer, and is sensible enough to add, "Anyhow, I shall not be killed by an automobile if I can help it."

"It may be true I am as corrupt, in another way, as Braggioni," she thinks in spite of herself, "as callous, as incomplete," and if this is so, any kind of death seems preferable. Still she sits quietly, she does not run. Where could she go? Uninvited she has promised herself to this place; she can no longer imagine herself as living in another country, and there is no pleasure in remembering her life before she came here.

Precisely what is the nature of this devotion, its true motives, and what are its obligations? Laura cannot say. She spends part of her days in Xochimilco, near by, teaching Indian children to say in English, "The cat is on the mat." When she appears in the classroom they crowd about her with smiles on their wise, innocent, clay-colored faces, crying, "Good morning, my titcher!" in immaculate voices, and they make of her desk a fresh garden of flowers every day.

During her leisure she goes to union meetings and listens to busy important voices quarreling over tactics, methods, internal politics. She visits the prisoners of her own political faith in their cells, where they entertain themselves with counting cockroaches, repenting of their indiscretions, composing their memoirs, writing out manifestoes and plans for their comrades who are still walking about free, hands in pockets, sniffing fresh air. Laura brings them food and cigarettes and a little money, and she brings messages disguised in equivocal phrases from the men outside who dare not set foot in the prison for fear of disappearing into the cells kept empty for them. If the prisoners confuse night and day, and complain, "Dear little Laura, time doesn't pass in this infernal hole, and I won't know when it is time to sleep unless I have a reminder," she brings them their favorite narcotics, and says in a tone that does not wound them with pity, "Tonight will really be night for you," and though her Spanish amuses them, they find her comforting, useful. If they lose patience and all faith, and curse the slowness of their friends in coming to their rescue with money and influence, they trust her not to repeat everything, and if she inquires, "Where do you think we can find money, or influence?" they are certain to answer, "Well, there is Braggioni, why doesn't he do something?"

She smuggles letters from headquarters to men hiding from firing squads in back streets in mildewed houses, where they sit in tumbled beds and talk bitterly as if all Mexico were at their heels, when Laura knows positively they might appear at the band concert in the Alameda on Sunday morning, and no one would notice them. But Braggioni says, "Let them sweat a little. The next time they may be careful. It is very restful to have them out of the way for a while." She is not afraid to knock on any door in any street after midnight, and enter in the darkness, and say to one of these men who is really in danger: "They will be looking for you—seriously—tomorrow morning after six. Here is some money from Vicente. Go to Vera Cruz and wait."

She borrows money from the Roumanian agitator to give to his bitter enemy the Polish agitator. The favor of Braggioni is their disputed territory, and Braggioni holds the balance nicely, for he can use them both. The Polish agitator talks love to her over café tables, hoping to exploit what he believes is her secret sentimental preference for him, and he gives her misinformation which he begs her to repeat as the solemn truth to certain persons. The Roumanian is more adroit. He is generous with his money in all good causes, and lies to her with an air of ingenuous candor, as if he were her good friend and confidant. She never repeats anything they may say. Braggioni never asks questions. He has other ways to discover all that he wishes to know about them.

Nobody touches her, but all praise her gray eyes, and the soft, round under lip which promises gayety, yet is always grave, nearly always firmly closed; and they cannot understand why she is in Mexico. She walks back and forth on her errands, with puzzled eyebrows, carrying her little folder of drawings and music and school papers. No dancer dances more beautifully than Laura walks, and she inspires some amusing, unexpected ardors, which cause little gossip, because nothing comes of them. A young captain who had been a soldier in Zapata's army attempted, during a horseback ride near Cuerna-vaca, to express his desire for her with the noble simplicity befitting a rude folk-hero: but gently, because he was gentle. This gentleness was his defeat, for when he alighted, and removed her foot from the stirrup, and essayed to draw her down into his arms, her horse, ordinarily a tame one, shied fiercely, reared and plunged away. The young hero's horse careered blindly after his stable-mate, and the hero did not return to the hotel until rather late that evening. At breakfast he came to her table in full charro dress, gray buckskin jacket and trousers with strings of silver buttons down the leg, and he was in a humorous, careless mood. "May I sit with you?" and "You are a wonderful rider. I was terrified that you might be thrown and dragged. I should never have forgiven myself. But I cannot admire you enough for your riding!"

"I learned to ride in Arizona," said Laura.

"If you will ride with me again this morning, I promise you a horse that will not shy with you," he said. But Laura remembered that she must return to Mexico City at noon.

Next morning the children made a celebration and spent their playtime writing on the blackboard, "We lov ar ticher," and with tinted chalks they drew wreaths of flowers around the words. The young hero wrote her a letter: "I am a very foolish, wasteful, impulsive man. I should have first said I love you, and then you would not have run away. But you shall see me again." Laura thought, "I must send him a box of colored crayons," but she was trying to forgive herself for having spurred her horse at the wrong moment.

A brown, shock-haired youth came and stood in her patio one night and sang like a lost soul for two hours, but Laura could think of nothing to do about it. The moonlight spread a wash of gauzy silver over the clear spaces of the garden, and the shadows were cobalt blue. The scarlet blossoms of the Judas tree were dull purple, and the names of the colors repeated them-selves automatically in her mind, while she watched not the boy, but his shadow, fallen like a dark garment across the fountain rim, trailing in the water. Lupe came silently and whispered expert counsel in her ear: "If you will throw him one little flower, he will sing another song or two and go away." Laura threw the flower, and he sang a last song and went away with the flower tucked in the band of his hat. Lupe said, "He is one of the organ-izers of the Typographers Union, and before that he sold corridos in the Merced market, and before that, he came from Guanajuato, where I was born. I would not trust any man, but I trust least those from Guanajuato."

She did not tell Laura that he would be back again the next night, and the next, nor that he would follow her at a certain fixed distance around the Merced market, through the Zócolo, up Francisco I. Madero Avenue, and so along the Paseo de la Reforma to Chapultepec Park, and into the Philosopher's Footpath, still with that flower withering in his hat, and an indivisible attention in his eyes.

Now Laura is accustomed to him, it means nothing except that he is nineteen years old and is observing a convention with all propriety, as though it were founded on a law of nature, which in the end it might well prove to be. He is beginning to write poems which he prints on a wooden press, and he leaves them stuck like handbills in her door. She is pleasantly disturbed by the abstract, unhurried watchfulness of his black eyes which will in time turn easily towards another object. She tells herself that throwing the flower was a mistake, for she is twenty-two years old and knows better; but she refuses to regret it, and persuades herself that her negation of all external events as they occur is a sign that she is gradually perfecting herself in the stoicism she strives to cultivate against that disaster she fears, though she cannot name it.

She is not at home in the world. Every day she teaches children who remain strangers to her, though she loves their tender round hands and their charming opportunist savagery. She knocks at unfamiliar doors not knowing whether a friend or a stranger shall answer, and even if a known face emerges from the sour gloom of that unknown interior, still it is the face of a stranger. No matter what this stranger says to her, nor what her message to him, the very cells of her flesh reject knowledge and kinship in one monotonous word. No. No. No. She draws her strength from this one holy talismanic word which does not suffer her to be led into evil. Denying everything, she may walk anywhere in safety, she looks at everything without amazement.

No, repeats this firm unchanging voice of her blood; and she looks at Braggioni without amazement. He is a great man, he wishes to impress this simple girl who covers her great round breasts with thick dark cloth, and who hides long, invaluably beautiful legs under a heavy skirt. She is almost thin except for the incomprehensible fullness of her breasts, like a nursing mother's, and Braggioni, who considers himself a judge of women, speculates again on the puzzle of her notorious virginity, and takes the liberty of speech which she permits without a sign of modesty, indeed, without any sort of sign, which is disconcerting.

"You think you are so cold, *gringita!* Wait and see. You will surprise yourself some day! May I be there to advise you!" He stretches his eyelids at her, and his ill-humored cat's eyes waver in a separate glance for the two points of light marking the opposite ends of a smoothly drawn path between the swollen curve of her breasts. He is not put off by that blue serge, nor by her resolutely fixed gaze. There is all the time in the world. His cheeks are bellying with the wind of song. "O girl with the dark eyes," he sings, and reconsiders. "But yours are not dark. I can change all that. O girl with the green eyes, you have stolen my heart away!" then his mind wanders to the song, and Laura feels the weight of his attention being shifted elsewhere. Singing thus, he seems harmless, he is quite harmless, there is nothing to do but sit patiently and say "No," when the moment comes. She draws a full breath, and her mind wanders also, but not far. She dares not wander too far.

Not for nothing has Braggioni taken pains to be a good revolutionist and a professional lover of humanity. He will never die of it. He has the malice, the cleverness, the wickedness, the sharpness of wit, the hardness of heart, stipulated for loving the world profitably. *He will never die of it.* He will live to see himself kicked out from his feeding trough by other hungry world-saviors. Traditionally he must sing in spite of his life which drives him to bloodshed, he tells Laura, for his father was a Tuscany peasant who drifted to Yucatan and married a Maya woman: a woman of race, an aristocrat. They gave him the love and knowledge of music, thus: and under the tip of his thumbnail, the strings of the instrument complain like exposed nerves.

Once he was called Delgadito by all the girls and married women who ran after him; he was so scrawny all his bones showed under his thin cotton clothing, and he could squeeze his emptiness to the very backbone with his two hands. He was a poet and the revolution was only a dream then; too many women loved him and sapped away his youth, and he could never find enough to eat anywhere, anywhere! Now he is a leader of men, crafty men who whisper in his ear, hungry men who wait for hours outside his office for a word with him, emaciated men with wild faces who waylay him at the street gate with a timid, "Comrade, let me tell you . . ." and they blow the foul breath from their empty stomachs in his face.

He is always sympathetic. He gives them handfuls of small coins from his own pocket, he promises them work, there will be demonstrations, they must join the unions and attend the meetings, above all they must be on the watch for spies. They are closer to him than his own brothers, without them he can do nothing—until tomorrow, comrade!

Until tomorrow. "They are stupid, they are lazy, they are treacherous, they would cut my throat for nothing," he says to Laura. He has good food and abundant drink, he hires an automobile and drives in the Paseo on Sunday morning, and enjoys plenty of sleep in a soft bed beside a wife who dares not disturb him, and he sits pampering his bones in easy billows of fat, singing to Laura, who knows and thinks these things about him. When he was fifteen, he tried to drown himself because he loved a girl, his first love, and she laughed at him. "A thousand women have paid for that," and his tight little mouth turns down at the corners. Now he perfumes his hair with Jockey Club, and confides to Laura: "One woman is really as good as another for me, in the dark. I prefer them all."

His wife organizes unions among the girls in the cigarette factories, and walks in picket lines, and even speaks at meetings in the evening. But she cannot be brought to acknowledge the benefits of true liberty. "I tell her I must have my freedom, net. She does not understand my point of view."

Laura has heard this many times. Braggioni scratches the guitar and meditates. "She is an instinctively virtuous woman, pure gold, no doubt of that. If she were not, I should lock her up, and she knows it."

His wife, who works so hard for the good of the factory girls, employs part of her leisure lying on the floor weeping because there are so many women in the world, and only one husband for her, and she never knows where nor when to look for him. He told her: "Unless you can learn to cry when I am not here, I must go away for good." That day he went away and took a room at the Hotel Madrid.

It is this month of separation for the sake of higher principles that has been spoiled not only for Mrs. Braggioni, whose sense of reality is beyond criticism, but for Laura, who feels herself bogged in a nightmare. Tonight Laura envies Mrs. Braggioni, who is alone, and free to weep as much as she pleases about a concrete wrong. Laura has just come from a visit to the prison, and she is waiting for tomorrow with a bitter anxiety as if tomorrow may not come, but time may be caught immovably in this hour, with herself transfixed, Braggioni singing on forever, and Eugenio's body not yet discovered by the guard.

Braggioni says: "Are you going to sleep?" Almost before she can shake her head, he begins telling her about the May-day disturbances coming on in Morelia, for the Catholics hold a festival in honor of the Blessed Virgin, and the Socialists celebrate their martyrs on that day. "There will be two independent processions, starting from either end of town, and they will march until they meet, and the rest depends . . ." He asks her to oil and load his pistols. Standing up, he unbuckles his ammunition belt, and spreads it laden across her knees. Laura sits with the shells slipping through the cleaning cloth dipped in oil, and he says again he cannot understand why she works so hard for the revolutionary idea unless she loves some man who is in it. "Are you not in love with someone?" "No," says Laura. "And no one is in love with you?" "No." "Then it is your own fault. No woman need go begging. Why, what is the matter with you? The legless beggar woman in the Alameda has a perfectly faithful lover. Did you know that?"

Laura peers down the pistol barrel and says nothing, but a long, slow faintness rises and subsides in her; Braggioni curves his swollen fingers around the throat of the guitar and softly smothers the music out of it, and when she hears him again he seems to have forgotten her, and is speaking in the hypnotic voice he uses when talking in small rooms to a listening, close-gathered crowd. Some day this world, now seemingly so composed and eternal, to the edges of every sea shall be merely a tangle of gaping trenches, of crashing walls and broken bodies. Everything must be torn from its accustomed place where it has rotted for centuries, hurled skyward and distributed, cast down again clean as rain, without separate identity. Nothing shall survive that the stiffened hands of poverty have created for the rich and no one shall be left alive except the elect spirits destined to procreate a new world cleansed of cruelty and injustice, ruled by benevolent anarchy: "Pistols are good, I love them, cannon are even better, but in the end I pin my faith to good dynamite," he concludes, and strokes the pistol lying in her hands. "Once I dreamed of destroying this city, in case it offered resistance to General Ortíz, but it fell into his hands like an overripe pear."

He is made restless by his own words, rises and stands waiting. Laura holds up the belt to him: "Put that on, and go kill somebody in Morelia, and you will be happier," she says softly. The presence of death in the room makes her bold. "Today, I found Eugenio going into a stupor. He refused to allow me to call the prison doctor. He had taken all the tablets I brought him yesterday. He said he took them because he was bored."

"He is a fool, and his death is his own business," says Braggioni, fastening his belt carefully.

"I told him if he had waited only a little while longer, you would have got him set free," says Laura. "He said he did not want to wait."

"He is a fool and we are well rid of him," says Braggioni, reaching for his hat.

He goes away. Laura knows his mood has changed, she will not see him any more for a while. He will send word when he needs her to go on errands into strange streets, to speak to the strange faces that will appear, like clay masks with the power of human speech, to mutter their thanks to Braggioni for his help. Now she is free, and she thinks, I must run while there is time. But she does not go.

Braggioni enters his own house where for a month his wife has spent many hours every night weeping and tangling her hair upon her pillow. She is weeping now, and she weeps more at the sight of him, the cause of all her sorrows. He looks about the room. Nothing is changed, the smells are good and familiar, he is well acquainted with the woman who comes toward him with no reproach except grief on her face. He says to her tenderly: "You are so good, please don't cry any more, you dear good creature." She says, "Are you tired, my angel? Sit here and I will wash your feet." She brings a bowl of water, and kneeling, unlaces his shoes, and when from her knees she raises her sad eyes under her blackened lids, he is sorry for everything, and bursts into tears. "Ah, yes, I am hungry, I am tired, let us eat something together," he says, between sobs. His wife leans her head on his arm and says, "Forgive me!" and this time he is refreshed by the solemn, endless rain of her tears.

Laura takes off her serge dress and puts on a white linen nightgown and goes to bed. She turns her head a little to one side, and lying still, reminds herself that it is time to sleep. Numbers tick in her brain like little clocks, soundless doors close of themselves around her. If you would sleep, you must not remember anything, the children will say tomorrow, good morning, my teacher, the poor prisoners who come every day bringing flowers to their jailor. 1-2-3-4-5 it is monstrous to confuse love with revolution, night with day, life with death—ah, Eugenio!

The tolling of the midnight bell is a signal, but what does it mean? Get up, Laura, and follow me: come out of your sleep, out of your bed, out of this strange house. What are you doing in this house? Without a word, without fear she rose and reached for Eugenio's hand, but he eluded her with a sharp, sly smile and drifted away. This is not all, you shall see— Murderer, he said, follow me, I will show you a new country, but it is far away and we must hurry. No, said Laura, not unless you take my hand, no; and she clung first to the stair rail, and then to the topmost branch of the Judas tree that bent down slowly and set her upon the earth, and then to the rocky ledge of a cliff, and then to the jagged wave of a sea that was not water but a desert of crumbling stone. Where are you taking me, she asked in wonder but without fear. To death, and it is a long way off, and we must hurry, said Eugenio. No, said Laura, not unless you take my hand. Then eat these flowers, poor prisoner, said Eugenio in a voice of pity, take and eat: and from the Judas tree he stripped the warm bleeding flowers, and held them to her lips. She saw that his hand was fleshless, a cluster of small white petrified branches, and his eye sockets were without light, but she ate the flowers greedily for they satisfied both hunger and thirst. Murderer! said Eugenio, and Cannibal! This is my body and my blood. Laura cried No! and at the sound of her own voice, she awoke trembling, and was afraid to sleep again. (1930)

Robert Penn Warren

WHEN THE LIGHT GETS GREEN

My grandfather had a long white beard and sat under the cedar tree. The beard, as a matter of fact, was not very long and not white, only gray, but when I was a child and was away from him at school during the winter, I would think of him, not seeing him in my mind's eye, and say: He has a long white beard. Therefore, it was a shock to me, on the first morning back home, to watch him lean over the dresser toward the wavy green mirror, which in his always shadowy room reflected things like deep water riffled by a little wind, and clip his gray beard to a point. It is gray and pointed, I would say then, remembering what I had thought before.

He turned his face to the green wavy glass, first one side and then the other in quarter profile, and lifted the long shears, which trembled a little, to cut the beard. His face being turned like that, with his good nose and pointed gray beard, he looked like General Robert E. Lee, without any white horse to ride. My grandfather had been a soldier, too, but now he wore blue-jean pants and

The Short Story

. . . .

644

when he leaned over like that toward the mirror, I couldn't help but notice how small his hips and backsides were. Only they weren't just small, they were shrunken. I noticed how the blue jeans hung loose from his suspenders and loose off his legs and down around his shoes. And in the morning when I noticed all this about his legs and backsides, I felt a tight feeling in my stomach like when you walk behind a woman and see the high heel of her shoe is worn and twisted and jerks her ankle every time she takes a step.

Always before my grandfather had finished clipping his beard, my Uncle Kirby came to the door and beat on it for breakfast. "I'll be down in just a minute, thank you, sir," my grandfather said. My uncle called him Mr. Barden. "Mr. Barden, breakfast is ready." It was because my Uncle Kirby was not my real uncle, having married my Aunt Lucy, who lived with my grandfather. Then my grandfather put on a black vest and put his gold watch and chain in the vest and picked up his cob pipe from the dresser top, and he and I went down to breakfast, after Uncle Kirby was already downstairs.

When he came into the dining room, Aunt Lucy was sitting at the foot of the table with the iron coffee pot on a plate beside her. She said, "Good morning, Papa."

"Good morning, Lucy," he said, and sat down at the head of the table, taking one more big puff off his pipe before laying it beside his plate.

"You've brought that old pipe down to breakfast again," my aunt said, while she poured the bright-looking coffee into the cups.

"Don't it stink," he always said.

My uncle never talked at breakfast, but when my grandfather said that, my uncle always opened his lips to grin like a dog panting, and showed his hooked teeth. His teeth were yellow because he chewed tobacco, which my grandfather didn't do, although his beard was yellow around the mouth from smoking. Aunt Lucy didn't like my uncle to chew, that was the whole trouble. So she rode my grandfather for bringing his pipe down, all in fun at first before she got serious about it. But he always brought it down just the same, and said to her, "Don't it stink."

After we ate, my uncle got up and said, "I got to get going," and went out through the kitchen where the cook was knocking and sloshing around. If it had rained right and was a good tobacco-setting season, my grandfather went off with me down to the stable to get his mare, for he had to see the setting. We saddled up the mare and went across the lot, where limestone bunched out of the ground and cedar trees and blue grass grew out of the split rock. A branch of cold water with minnows in it went through the lot between rocks and under the cedar trees; it was where I used to play before I got big enough to go to the river with the niggers to swim.

My grandfather rode across the lot and over the rise back of the house. He sat up pretty straight for an old man, holding the bridle in his left hand, and in his right hand a long hickory tobacco stick whittled down to make a walking cane. I walked behind him and watched the big straw hat he wore waggle a little above his narrow neck, or how he held the stick in the middle, firm and straight up like something carried in a parade, or how smooth and slow the muscles in the mare's flanks worked as she put each hoof down in the ground, going up hill. Sassafras bushes and blackberry bushes grew thick along the lane over the rise. In summer, tufts of hay would catch and hang on the dry bushes and showed that the hay wagons had been that way; but when we went that way in setting time, just after breakfast, the blackberry blooms were hardly gone, only a few rusty patches of white left, and the sassafras leaves showed still wet with dew or maybe the rain.

From the rise we could look back on the house. The shingles were black with damp, and the whitewash grayish, except in spots where the sun already struck it and it was drying. The tops of the cedar trees, too, were below us, very dark green and quiet. When we crossed the rise, there were the fields going down toward the river, all checked off and ready for setting, very even, only for the gullies where brush was piled to stop the washing. The fields were reddish from the wet, not yet steaming. Across them, the green woods and the sycamores showing white far off told where the river was.

The hands were standing at the edge of the field under the trees when we got there. The little niggers were filling their baskets with the wet plants to drop, and I got me a basket and filled it. My Uncle Kirby gave me fifty cents for dropping plants, but he didn't give the little niggers that much, I remember. The hands and women stood around waiting a minute, watching Uncle Kirby, who always fumed around, waving his dibble, his blue shirt already sticking to his arms with sweat. "Get the lead out," he said. The little niggers filled faster, grinning with their teeth at him. "Goddam, get the lead out!" My grandfather sat on his mare under the trees, still holding the walking cane, and said, "Why don't you start 'em, sir?"

Then, all of a sudden, they all moved out into the field, scattering out down the rows, the droppers first, and after a minute the setters, who lurched along, never straightening up, down the rows toward the river. I walked down my row, separating out the plants and dropping them at the hills, while it got hotter and the ground steamed. The sun broke out now and then, making my shadow on the ground, then the cloud would come again, and I could see its shadow drifting at me on the red field.

My grandfather rode very slow along the edge of the field to watch the setting, or stayed still under the trees. After a while, maybe about ten o'clock, he would leave and go home. I could see him riding the mare up the rise and then go over the rise; or if I was working the other way toward the river, when I turned round at the end, the lane would be empty and nothing on top the rise, with the cloudy, blue-gray sky low behind it.

The tobacco was all he cared about, now we didn't have any horses that were any real good. He had some silver cups, only one real silver one though, that his horses won at fairs, but all that was before I was born. The real silver one, the one he kept on his dresser and kept string and old minnie balls and pins and things in, had *1859* on it because his horse won it then before the War, when he was a young man. Uncle Kirby said horses were foolishness, and Grandfather said, yes, he reckoned horses were foolishness, all right. So what he cared about now was the tobacco. One time he was a tobacco-buyer for three years, but after he bought a lot of tobacco and had it in his sheds, the sheds burned up on him. He didn't have enough insurance to do any good and he was a ruined man. After that all his children, he had all girls and his money was gone, said about him, "Papa's just visionary, he tried to be a tobacco-buyer but he's too visionary and not practical." But he always said, "All tobacco-buyers are sons-of-bitches, and three years is enough of a man's life for him to be a son-of-a-bitch, I reckon." Now he was old, the corn could get the rust or the hay get rained on for all he cared, it was Uncle Kirby's worry, but all summer, off and on, he had to go down to the tobacco field to watch them sucker or plow or worm, and sometimes he pulled a few suckers himself. And when a cloud would blow up black in summer, he got nervous as a cat, not knowing whether it was the rain they needed or maybe a hail storm coming that would cut the tobacco up bad.

Mornings he didn't go down to the field, he went out under the cedar tree where his chair was. Most of the time he took a book with him along with his pipe, for he was an inveterate reader. His being an inveterate reader was one of the things made his children say he was visionary. He read a lot until his eyes went bad the summer before he had his stroke, then after that, I read to him some, but not as much as I ought. He used to read out loud some from Macaulay's *History of England* or Gibbon's *Decline and Fall*, about Flodden Field or about how the Janizaries took Constantinople amid great slaughter and how the Turk surveyed the carnage and quoted from the Persian poet about the lizard keeping the courts of the mighty. My grandfather knew some poetry, too, and he said it to himself when he didn't have anything else to do. I lay on my back on the ground, feeling the grass cool and tickly on the back of my neck, and looked upside down into the cedar tree where the limbs were tangled and black-green like big hairy fern fronds with the sky blue all around, while he said some poetry. Like the "Isles of Greece, the Isles of Greece, where burning Sappho loved and sung." Or like "Roll on, thou deep and dark blue ocean, roll."

But he never read poetry, he just said what he already knew. He only read history and *Napoleon and His Marshals,* having been a soldier and fought in the War himself. He rode off and joined the cavalry, but he never told me whether he took the horse that won the real silver cup or not. He was with Forrest before Forrest was a general. He said Forrest was a great general, and if they had done what Forrest wanted and cleaned the country ahead of the Yankees, like the Russians beat Napoleon, they'd whipped the Yankees sure. He told me about Fort Donelson, how they fought in the winter woods, and how they got away with Forrest at night, splashing through the cold water. And how the dead men looked in the river bottoms in winter, and I lay on my back on the grass, looking up in the thick cedar limbs, and thought how it was to be dead.

After Shiloh was fought and they pushed the Yankees down in the river, my grandfather was a captain, for he raised a cavalry company of his own out of West Tennessee. He was a captain, but he never got promoted after the War; when I was a little boy everybody still called him Captain Barden, though they called lots of other people in our section Colonel and Major. One time I said to him: "Grandpa, did you ever kill any Yankees?" He said: "God-a-mighty, how do I know?" So, being little, I thought he was just a captain because he never killed anybody, and I was ashamed. He talked about how they took Fort Pillow, and the drunk niggers under the bluff. And one time he said niggers couldn't stand a charge or stand the cold steel, so I thought maybe he killed some of them. But then I thought, niggers don't count, maybe.

He only talked much in the morning. Almost every afternoon right after dinner, he went to sleep in his chair, with his hands curled up in his lap, one of them holding the pipe that still sent up a little smoke in the shadow, and his head propped back on the tree trunk. His mouth hung open, and under the hairs of his mustache, all yellow with nicotine, you could see his black teeth and his lips that were wet and pink like a baby's. Usually I remember him that way, asleep.

I remember him that way, or else trampling up and down the front porch, nervous as a cat, while a cloud blew up and the trees began to rustle. He tapped his walking cane on the boards and whistled through his teeth with his breath and kept looking off at the sky where the cloud and sometimes the lightning was. Then of a sudden it came, and if it was rain he used to go up to his room and lie down; but if it came hail on the tobacco, he stayed on the front porch, not trampling any more, and watched the hail rattle off the roof and bounce soft on the grass. "God-a-Mighty," he always said, "bigger'n minnie balls," even when it wasn't so big.

In 1914, just before the war began, it was a hot summer with the tobacco mighty good but needing rain. And when the dry spell broke and a cloud blew up, my grandfather came out on the front porch, watching it like that. It was mighty still, with lightning way off, so far you couldn't hardly hear the thunder. Then the leaves began to ruffle like they do when the light gets green, and my grandfather said to me, "Son, it's gonna hail." And he stood still. Down in the pasture, that far off, you could see the cattle bunching up and the white horse charging across the pasture, looking bright, for the sun was shining bright before the cloud struck it all at once. "It's gonna hail," my grandfather said. It was dark, with jagged lightning and the thunder high and steady. And there the hail was.

He just turned around and went in the house. I watched the hail bouncing, then I heard a noise and my aunt yelled. I ran back in the dining room where the noise was, and my grandfather was lying on the floor with the old silver pitcher he dropped and a broken glass. We tried to drag him, but he was too heavy; then my Uncle Kirby came up wet from the stable and we carried my grandfather upstairs and put him on his bed. My aunt tried to call the doctor even if the lightning might hit the telephone. I stayed back in the dining room and picked up the broken glass and the pitcher and wiped up the floor with a rag. After a while Dr. Blake came from town; then he went away.

When Dr. Blake was gone, I went upstairs to see my grandfather. I shut the door and went in his room, which was almost dark, like always, and quiet because the hail didn't beat on the roof any more. He was lying on his back in the feather-bed, with a sheet pulled up over him, lying there in the dark. He had his hands curled loose on his stomach, like when he went to sleep in his chair holding the pipe. I sat on a split-bottom chair by the bed and looked at him: he had his eyes shut and his mouth hung loose, but you couldn't hear his breathing. Then I quit looking at him and looked round the room, my eyes getting used to the shadow. I could see his pants on the floor, and the silver cup on the dresser by the mirror, which was green and wavy like water.

When he said something, I almost jumped out of my skin, hearing his voice like that. He said, "Son, I'm gonna die." I tried to say something, but I couldn't. And he waited, then he said, "I'm on borrowed time, it's time to die." I said, "No!" so sudden and loud I jumped. He waited a long time and said, "It's time to die. Nobody loves me." I tried to say, "Grandpa, I love you." And then I did say it all right, feeling like it hadn't been me said it, and knowing all of a sudden it was a lie, because I didn't feel anything. He just lay there; and I went downstairs.

It was sunshiny in the yard, the clouds gone, but the grass was wet. I walked down toward the gate, rubbing my bare feet over the slick cold grass. A hen was in the yard and she kept trying to peck up a piece of hail, like a fool chicken will do after it hails; but every time she pecked, it bounced away from her over the green grass. I leaned against the gate, noticing the ground on one side the posts, close up, was still dry and dusty. I wondered if the tobacco was cut up bad, because Uncle Kirby had gone to see. And while I looked through the gate down across the pasture where everything in the sun was green and shiny with wet and the cattle grazed, I thought about my grandfather, not feeling anything. But I said out loud anyway, "Grandpa, I love you."

My grandfather lived four more years. The year after his stroke they sold the farm and moved away, so I didn't stay with them any more. My grandfather died in 1918, just before the news came that my Uncle Kirby was killed in France, and my aunt had to go to work in a store. I got the letter about my grandfather, who died of flu, but I thought about four years back, and it didn't matter much.

(1936)

William Faulkner

THE BEAR

He was ten. But it had already begun, long before that day when at last he wrote his age in two figures and he saw for the first time the camp where his father and Major de Spain and old General Compson and the others spent two weeks each November and two weeks again each June. He had already inherited then, without ever having seen it, the tremendous bear with one trap-ruined foot which, in an area almost a hundred miles deep, had earned itself a name, a definite designation like a living man.

He had listened to it for years: the long legend of corncribs rifled, of shotes and grown pigs and even calves carried bodily into the woods and devoured, of traps and deadfalls overthrown and dogs mangled and slain, and shotgun and even rifle charges delivered at point-blank range and with no more effect than so many peas blown through a tube by a boy—a corridor of wreckage and destruction beginning back before he was born, through which sped, not fast but rather with the ruthless and irresistible deliberation of a locomotive, the shaggy tremendous shape.

It ran in his knowledge before he ever saw it. It looked and towered in his dreams before he even saw the unaxed woods where it left its crooked print, shaggy, huge, red-eyed, not malevolent but just big—too big for the dogs which tried to bay it, for the horses which tried to ride it down, for the men and the bullets they fired into it, too big for the very country which was its constricting scope. He seemed to see it entire with a child's complete divination before he ever laid eyes on either—the doomed wilderness whose edges were being constantly and punily gnawed at by men with axes and plows who feared it because it was wilderness, men myriad and nameless even to one another in the land where the old bear had earned a name, through which ran not even a mortal animal but an anachronism, indomitable and invincible, out of an old dead time, a phantom, epitome and apotheosis of the old wild life at which the puny humans swarmed and hacked in a fury of abhorrence and fear, like pygmies about the ankles of a drowsing elephant: the old bear solitary, indomitable and alone, widowered, childless, and absolved of mortality —old Priam reft of his old wife and having outlived all his sons.

Until he was ten, each November he would watch the wagon containing the dogs and the bedding and food and guns and his father and Tennie's Jim, the Negro, and Sam Fathers, the Indian, son of a slave woman and a Chickasaw chief, depart on the road to town, to Jefferson, where Major de Spain and the others would join them. To the boy, at seven, eight, and nine, they were not going into the Big Bottom to hunt bear and deer, but to keep yearly rendezvous with the bear which they did not even intend to kill. Two weeks later they would return, with no trophy, no head and skin. He had not expected it. He had not even been afraid it would be in the wagon. He believed that even after he was ten and his father would let him go too, for those two weeks in November, he would merely make another one, along with his father and Major de Spain and General Compson and the others, the dogs which feared to bay at it and the rifles and shotguns which failed even to bleed it, in the yearly pageant of the old bear's furious immortality.

Then he heard the dogs. It was in the second week of his first time in the camp. He stood with Sam Fathers against a big oak beside the faint crossing where they had stood each dawn for nine days now, hearing the dogs. He had heard them once before, one morning last week—a murmur, sourceless, echoing through the wet woods, swelling presently into separate voices which he could recognize and call by name. He had raised and cocked the gun as Sam told him and stood motionless again while the uproar, the invisible course, swept up and past and faded; it seemed to him that he could actually see the deer, the buck, blond, smoke-colored, elongated with speed, fleeing, vanishing, the woods, the gray solitude, still ringing even when the cries of the dogs had died away.

"Now let the hammers down," Sam said.

"You knew they were not coming here too," he said.

"Yes," Sam said. "I want you to learn how to do when you didn't shoot. It's after the chance for the bear or the deer has done already come and gone that men and dogs get killed."

"Anyway," he said, "it was just a deer."

Then on the tenth morning he heard the dogs again. And he readied the too-long, too-heavy gun as Sam had taught him, before Sam even spoke. But this time it was no deer, no ringing chorus of dogs running strong on a free scent, but a moiling yapping an octave too high, with something more than indecision and even abjectness in it, not even moving very fast, taking a long time to pass completely out of hearing, leaving them somewhere in the air that echo, thin, slightly hysterical, abject, almost grieving, with no sense of a fleeing, unseen, smoke-colored, grass-eating shape ahead of it, and Sam, who had taught him first of all to cock the gun and take position where he could see everywhere and then never move again, had himself moved up beside him; he could hear Sam breathing at his shoulder, and he could see the arched curve of the old man's inhaling nostrils.

"Hah," Sam said. "Not even running. Walking."

"Old Ben!" the boy said. "But up here!" he cried, "Way up here!"

"He do it every year," Sam said. "Once. Maybe to see who in camp this time, if he can shoot or not. Whether we got the dog yet that can bay and hold him. He'll take them to the river, then he'll send them back home. We may as well go back too; see how they look when they come back to camp."

When they reached the camp the hounds were already there, ten of them crouching back under the kitchen, the boy and Sam squatting to peer back into the obscurity where they had huddled, quiet, the eyes luminous, glowing at them and vanishing, and no sound, only that effluvium of something more than dog, stronger than dog and not just animal, just beast, because still there had been nothing in front of that abject and almost painful yapping save the solitude, the wilderness, so that when the eleventh hound came in at noon and with all the others watching—even old Uncle Ash, who called himself first a cook—Sam daubed the tattered ear and the raked shoulder with turpentine and axle grease, to the boy it was still no living creature, but the wilderness which, leaning for the moment down, had patted lightly once the hound's temerity.

"Just like a man," Sam said. "Just like folks. Put off as long as she could having to be brave, knowing all the time that sooner or later she would have to be brave to keep on living with herself, and knowing all the time beforehand what was going to happen to her when she done it."

That afternoon, himself on the one-eyed wagon mule which did not mind the smell of blood nor, as they told him, of bear, and with Sam on the other one, they rode for more than three hours through the rapid, shortening winter day. They followed no path, no trail even that he could see; almost at once they were in a country which he had never seen before. Then he knew why Sam had made him ride the mule which would not spook. The sound one stopped short and tried to whirl and bolt even as Sam got down, blowing its breath, jerking and wrenching at the rein, while Sam held it, coaxing it forward with his voice, since he could not risk tying it, drawing it forward while the boy got down from the marred one.

Then, standing beside Sam in the gloom of the dying afternoon, he looked down at the rotted over-turned log, gutted and scored with claw marks and, in the wet earth beside it, the print of the enormous warped two-toed foot. He knew now what he had smelled when he peered under the kitchen where the dogs huddled. He realized for the first time that the bear which had run in his listening and loomed in his dreams since before he could remember to the contrary, and which, therefore, must have existed in the listening and dreams of his father and Major de Spain and even old General Compson, too, before they began to remember in their turn, was a mortal animal, and that if they had departed for the camp each November without any actual hope of bringing its trophy back, it was not because it could not be slain, but because so far they had had no actual hope to.

"Tomorrow," he said.

"We'll try tomorrow," Sam said. "We ain't got the dog yet."

"We've got eleven. They ran him this morning."

"It won't need but one," Sam said. "He ain't here. Maybe he ain't nowhere. The only other way will be for him to run by accident over somebody that has a gun."

"That wouldn't be me," the boy said. "It will be Walter or Major or—"

"It might," Sam said. "You watch close in the morning. Because he's smart. That's how come he has lived this long. If he gets hemmed up and has to pick out somebody to run over, he will pick out you."

"How?" the boy said. "How will he know—" He ceased. "You mean he already knows me, that I ain't never been here before, ain't had time to find out yet whether I—" He ceased again, looking at Sam, the old man whose face revealed nothing until it smiled. He said humbly, not even amazed, "It was me he was watching. I don't reckon he did need to come but once."

The next morning they left the camp three hours before daylight. They rode this time because it was too far to walk, even the dogs in the wagon; again the first gray light found him in a place which he had never seen before, where Sam had placed him and told him to stay and then departed. With the gun which was too big for him, which did not even belong to him, but to Major de Spain, and which he had fired only once—at a stump on the first day, to learn the recoil and how to reload it—he stood against a gum tree beside a little bayou whose black still water crept without movement out of a canebrake and crossed a small clearing and into cane again, where, invisible, a bird—the big woodpecker called Lord-to-God by Negroes—clattered at a dead limb.

It was a stand like any other, dissimilar only in incidentals to the one where he had stood each morning for ten days; a territory new to him, yet no less familiar than that other one which, after almost two weeks, he had come to believe he knew a little—the same solitude, the same loneliness through which human beings had merely passed without altering it, leaving no mark, no scar, which looked exactly as it must have looked when the first ancestor of Sam Fathers' Chickasaw predecessors crept into it and looked about, club or stone ax or bone arrow drawn and poised; different only because, squatting at the edge of the kitchen, he smelled the hounds huddled and cringing beneath it and saw the raked ear and shoulder of the one who, Sam said, had had to be brave once in order to live with herself, and saw yesterday in the earth beside the gutted log the print of the living foot.

He heard no dogs at all. He never did hear them. He only heard the drumming of the woodpecker stop short off and knew that the bear was looking at him. He never saw it. He did not know whether it was in front of him or behind him. He did not move, holding the useless gun, which he had not even had warning to cock and which even now he did not cock, tasting in his saliva that taint as of brass which he knew now because he had smelled it when he peered under the kitchen at the huddled dogs.

Then it was gone. As abruptly as it had ceased, the woodpecker's dry, monotonous clatter set up again, and after a while he even believed he could hear the dogs—a murmur, scarce a sound even, which he had probably been hearing for some time before he even remarked it, drifting into hearing and then out again, dying away. They came nowhere near him. If it was a bear they ran, it was another bear. It was Sam himself who came out of the cane and crossed the bayou, followed by the injured bitch of yesterday. She was almost at heel, like a bird dog, making no sound. She came and crouched against his leg, trembling, staring off into the cane.

"I didn't see him," he said. "I didn't, Sam!"

"I know it," Sam said. "He done the looking. You didn't hear him neither, did you?"

"No," the boy said. "I—"

"He's smart," Sam said. "Too smart." He looked down at the hound, trembling faintly and steadily against the boy's knee. From the raked shoulder a few drops of fresh blood oozed and clung. "Too big. We ain't got the dog yet. But maybe someday. Maybe not next time. But someday."

So I must see him, he thought. *I must look at him.* Otherwise, it seemed to him that it would go on like this forever, as it had gone on with his father and Major de Spain, who was older than his father, and even with old General Compson, who had been old enough to be a brigade commander in 1865. Otherwise, it would go on so forever, next time and next time, after and after and after. It seemed to him that he could never see the two of them, himself and the bear, shadowy in the limbo from which time emerged, becoming time; the old bear absolved of mortality and himself partaking, sharing a little of it, enough of it. And he knew now what he had smelled in the huddled dogs and tasted in his saliva. He recognized fear. *So I will have to see him,* he thought, without dread or even hope. *I will have to look at him.*

It was in June of the next year. He was eleven. They were in camp again, celebrating Major de Spain's and General Compson's birthdays. Although the one had been born in September and the other in the depth of winter and in another decade, they had met for two weeks to fish and shoot squirrels and turkey and run coons and wildcats with the dogs at night. That is, he and Boon Hoggenback and the Negroes fished and shot squirrels and ran the coons and cats, because the proved hunters, not only Major de Spain and old General Compson, who spent those two weeks sitting in a rocking chair before a tremendous iron pot of Brunswick stew, stirring and tasting, with old Ash to quarrel with about how he was making it and Tennie's Jim to pour whiskey from the demijohn into the tin dipper from which he drank it, but even the boy's father and Walter Ewell, who were still young enough, scorned such, other than shooting the wild gobblers with pistols for wagers on their marksmanship.

Or, that is, his father and the others believed he was hunting squirrels. Until the third day, he thought that Sam Fathers believed that too. Each morning he would leave the camp right after breakfast. He had his own gun now, a Christmas present. He went back to the tree beside the bayou where he had stood that morning. Using the compass which old General Compson had given him, he ranged from that point; he was teaching himself to be a better-than-fair woodsman without knowing he was doing it. On the second day he even found the gutted log where he had first seen the crooked print. It was almost completely crumbled now, healing with unbelievable speed, a passionate and almost visible relinquishment, back into the earth from which the tree had grown.

He ranged the summer woods now, green with gloom; if anything, actually dimmer than in November's gray dissolution, where, even at noon, the sun fell only in intermittent dappling upon the earth, which never completely dried out and which crawled with snakes—moccasins and water snakes and rattlers, themselves the color of the dappling gloom, so that he would not always see them until they moved, returning later and later, first day, second day, passing in the twilight of the third evening the little log pen enclosing the log stable where Sam was putting up the horses for the night.

"You ain't looked right yet," Sam said.

He stopped. For a moment he didn't answer. Then he said peacefully, in a peaceful rushing burst as when a boy's miniature dam in a little brook gives way, "All right. But how? I went to the bayou. I even found that log again. I—"

"I reckon that was all right. Likely he's been watching you. You never saw his foot?"

"I," the boy said—"I didn't—I never thought—"

"It's the gun," Sam said. He stood beside the fence, motionless—the old man, the Indian, in the battered faded overalls and the five-cent straw hat which in the Negro's race had been the badge of his enslavement and was now the regalia of his freedom. The camp—the clearing, the house, the barn and its tiny lot with which Major de Spain in his turn had scratched punily and evanescently at the wilderness—faded in the dusk, back into the immemorial darkness of the woods. *The gun*, the boy thought. *The gun.*

"Be scared," Sam said. "You can't help that. But don't be afraid. Ain't nothing in the woods going to hurt you unless you corner it, or it smells that you are afraid. A bear or a deer, too, has got to be scared of a coward the same as a brave man has got to be."

The gun, the boy thought.

"You will have to choose," Sam said.

He left the camp before daylight, long before Uncle Ash would wake in his quilts on the kitchen floor and start the fire for breakfast. He had only the compass and a stick for snakes. He could go almost a mile before he would begin to need the compass. He sat on a log, the invisible compass in his invisible hand, while the secret night sounds, fallen still at his movements, scurried again and then ceased for good, and the owls ceased and gave over to the waking of day birds, and he could see the compass. Then he went fast yet still quietly; he was becoming better and better as a woodsman, still without having yet realized it.

He jumped a doe and a fawn at sunrise, walked them out of the bed, close enough to see them—the crash of undergrowth, the white scut, the fawn scudding behind her faster than he had believed it could run. He was hunting right, upwind, as Sam had taught him; not that it mattered now. He had left the gun; of his own will and relinquishment he had accepted not a gambit, not a choice, but a condition in which not only the bear's heretofore inviolable anonymity but all the old rules and balances of hunter and hunted had been abrogated. He would not even be afraid, not even in the moment when the fear would take him completely—blood, skin, bowels, bones, memory from the long time before it became his memory—all save that thin, clear, immortal lucidity which alone differed him from this bear and from all the other bear and deer he would ever kill in the humility and pride of his skill and endurance, to which Sam had spoken when he leaned in the twilight on the lot fence yesterday.

By noon he was far beyond the little bayou, farther into the new and alien country than he had ever been. He was travelling now not only by the old, heavy, biscuit-thick silver watch which had belonged to his grandfather. When he stopped at last, it was for the first time since he had risen from the log at dawn when he could see the compass. It was far enough. He had left the camp nine hours ago; nine hours from now, dark would have already been an hour old. But he didn't think that. He thought. *All right. Yes. But what?* and stood for a moment, alien and small in the green and topless solitude, answering his own question before it had formed and ceased. It was the watch, the compass, the stick—the three lifeless mechanicals with which for nine hours he had fended the wilderness off; he hung the watch and compass carefully on a bush and leaned the stick beside them and relinquished completely to it.

He had not been going very fast for the last two or three hours. He went no faster now, since distance would not matter even if he could have gone fast. And he was trying to keep a bearing on the tree where he had left the compass, trying to complete a circle which would bring him back to it or at least intersect itself, since direction would not matter now either. But the tree was not there, and he did as Sam had schooled him—made the next circle in the opposite direction, so that the two patterns would bisect somewhere, but crossing no print of his own feet, finding the tree at last, but in the wrong place—no bush, no compass, no watch—and the tree not even the tree, because there was a down log beside it and he did what Sam Fathers had told him was the next thing and the last.

As he sat down on the log he saw the crooked print—the warped, tremendous, two-toed indentation which, even as he watched it, filled with water. As he looked up, the wilderness coalesced, solidified—the glade, the tree he sought, the bush, the watch and the compass glinting where a ray of sunshine touched them. Then he saw the bear. It did not emerge, appear; it was just there, immobile, solid, fixed in the hot dappling of the green and windless noon, not as big as he had dreamed it, but as big as he had expected it, bigger, dimensionless, against the dappled obscurity, looking at him where he sat quietly on the log and looked back at it.

Then it moved. It made no sound. It did not hurry. It crossed the glade, walking for an instant into the full glare of the sun; when it reached the other side it stopped again and looked back at him across one shoulder while his quiet breathing inhaled and exhaled three times.

Then it was gone. It didn't walk into the woods, the undergrowth. It faded, sank back into the wilderness as he had watched a fish, a huge old bass, sink and vanish into the dark depths of its pool without even any movement of its fins.

He thought, *It will be next fall.* But it was not next fall, nor the next nor the next. He was fourteen then. He had killed his buck, and Sam Fathers had marked his face with the hot blood, and in the next year he killed a bear. But even before that accolade he had become as competent in the woods as many grown men with the same experience; by his fourteenth year he was a better woodsman than most grown men with more. There was no territory within thirty miles of the camp that he did not know—bayou, ridge, brake, landmark, tree and path. He could have led anyone to any point in it without deviation, and brought them out again. He knew the game trails that even Sam Fathers did not know; in his thirteenth year he found a buck's bedding place, and unbeknown to his father he borrowed Walter Ewell's rifle and lay in wait at dawn and killed the buck when it walked back to the bed, as Sam had told him how the old Chickasaw fathers did.

But not the old bear, although by now he knew its footprints better than he did his own, and not only the crooked one. He could see any one of the three sound ones and distinguish it from any other, and not only by its size. There were other bears within these thirty miles which left tracks almost as large, but this was more than that. If Sam Fathers had been his mentor and the back-yard rabbits and squirrels at home his kindergarten, then the wilderness the old bear ran was his college, the old male bear itself, so long unwifed and childless as to have become its own ungendered progenitor, was his alma mater. But he never saw it.

He could find the crooked print now almost whenever he liked, fifteen or ten or five miles, or sometimes nearer the camp than that. Twice while on stand during the three years he heard the dogs strike its trail by accident; on the second time they jumped it seemingly, the voices high, abject, almost human in hysteria, as on that first morning two years ago. But not the bear itself. He would remember that noon three years ago, the glade, himself and the bear fixed during that moment in the windless and dappled blaze, and it would seem to him that it had never happened, that he had dreamed that too. But it had happened. They had looked at each other, they had emerged from the wilderness old as earth, synchronized to the instant by something more than the blood that moved the flesh and bones which bore them, and touched, pledged something, affirmed, something more lasting than the frail web of bones and flesh which any accident could obliterate.

Then he saw it again. Because of the very fact that he thought of nothing else, he had forgotten to look for it. He was still hunting with Walter Ewell's rifle. He saw it cross the end of a long blow-down, a corridor where a tornado had swept, rushing through rather than over the tangle of trunks and branches as a locomotive would have, faster than he had ever believed it could move, almost as fast as a deer even, because a deer would have spent most of that time in the air, faster than he could bring the rifle sights up with it. And now he knew what had been wrong during all the three years. He sat on a log, shaking and trembling as if he had never seen the woods before nor anything that ran them, wondering with incredulous amazement how he could have forgotten the very thing which Sam Fathers had told him and which the bear itself had proved the next day and had now returned after three years to reaffirm.

And now he knew what Sam Fathers had meant about the right dog, a dog in which size would mean less than nothing. So when he returned alone in April—school was out then, so that the sons of farmers could help with the land's planting, and at last his father had granted him permission, on his promise to be back in four days—he had the dog. It was his own, a mongrel of the sort called by Negroes a fyce, a ratter, itself not much bigger than a rat and possessing that bravery which had long since stopped being courage and had become foolhardiness.

It did not take four days. Alone again, he found the trail on the first morning. It was not a stalk; it was an ambush. He timed the meeting almost as if it were an appointment with a human being. Himself holding the fyce muffled in a feed sack and Sam Fathers with two of the hounds on a piece of a plowline rope, they lay down wind of the trail at dawn of the second morning. They were so close that the bear turned without even running, as if in surprised amazement at the shrill and frantic uproar of the released fyce, turning at bay against the trunk of a tree, on its hind feet; it seemed to the boy that it would never stop rising, taller and taller, and even the two hounds seemed to take a desperate and despairing courage from the fyce, following it as it went in.

Then he realized that the fyce was actually not going to stop. He flung, threw the gun away, and ran; when he overtook and grasped the frantically pin-wheeling little dog, it seemed to him that he was directly under the bear.

He could smell it, strong and hot and rank. Sprawling, he looked up to where it loomed and towered over him like a cloudburst and colored like a thunderclap, quite familiar, peacefully and even lucidly familiar, until he remembered: This was the way he had used to dream about it. Then it was gone. He didn't see it go. He knelt, holding the frantic fyce with both hands, hearing the abashed wailing of the hounds drawing farther and farther away, until Sam came up. He carried the gun. He laid it down quietly beside the boy and stood looking down at him.

"You've done seed him twice now with a gun in your hands," he said. "This time you couldn't have missed him."

The boy rose. He still held the fyce. Even in his arms and clear of the ground, it yapped frantically, straining and surging after the fading uproar of the two hounds like a tangle of wire springs. He was panting a little, but he was neither shaking nor trembling now.

"Neither could you!" he said. "You had the gun! Neither did you!"

"And you didn't shoot," his father said. "How close were you?"

"I don't know, sir," he said. "There was a big wood tick inside his right hind leg. I saw that. But I didn't have the gun then."

"But you didn't shoot when you had the gun," his father said. "Why?"

But he didn't answer, and his father didn't wait for him to, rising and crossing the room, across the pelt of the bear which the boy had killed two years ago and the larger one which his father had killed before he was born, to the bookcase beneath the mounted head of the boy's first buck. It was the room which his father called the office, from which all the plantation business was transacted; in it for the fourteen years of his life he had heard the best of all talking. Major de Spain would be there and sometimes old General Compson, and Walter Ewell and Boon Hoggenback and Sam Fathers and Tennie's Jim, too, were hunters, knew the woods and what ran them.

He would hear it, not talking himself but listening—the wilderness, the big woods, bigger and older than any recorded document of white man fatuous enough to believe he had bought any fragment of it or Indian ruthless enough to pretend that any fragment of it had been his to convey. It was of the men, not white nor black nor red, but men, hunters with the will and hardihood to endure and the humility and skill to survive, and the dogs and the bear and deer juxtaposed and reliefed against it, ordered and compelled by and within the wilderness in the ancient and unremitting contest by the ancient and immitigable rules which voided all regrets and brooked no quarter, the voices quiet and weighty and deliberate for retrospection and recollection and exact remembering, while he squatted in the blazing firelight as Tennie's Jim squatted, who stirred only to put more wood on the fire and to pass the bottle from one glass to another. Because the bottle was always present, so that after a while it seemed to him that those fierce instants of heart and brain and courage and wiliness and speed were concentrated and distilled into that brown liquor which not women, not boys and children, but only hunters drank, drinking not of the blood they had spilled but some conden-sation of the wild immortal spirit, drinking it moderately, humbly even, not with the pagan's base hope of acquiring the virtues of cunning and strength and speed, but in salute to them.

His father returned with the book and sat down again and opened it. "Listen," he said. He read the five stanzas aloud, his voice quiet and deliber-ate in the room where there was no fire now because it was already spring. Then he looked up. The boy watched him. "All right," his father said. "Listen." He read again, but only the second stanza this time, to the end of it, the last two lines, and closed the book and put it on the table beside him. "She cannot fade, though thou hast not thy bliss, for ever wilt thou love, and she be fair," he said.

"He's talking about a girl," the boy said.

"He had to talk about something," his father said. Then he said, "He was talking about truth. Truth doesn't change. Truth is one thing. It covers all things which touch the heart—honor and pride and pity and justice and courage and love. Do you see now?"

He didn't know. Somehow it was simpler than that. There was an old bear, fierce and ruthless, not merely just to stay alive, but with the fierce pride of liberty and freedom, proud enough of the liberty and freedom to see it threatened without fear or even alarm; nay, who at times even seemed deliberately to put that freedom and liberty in jeopardy in order to savor them, to remind his old strong bones and flesh to keep supple and quick to defend and preserve them. There was an old man, son of a Negro slave and an Indian king, inheritor on the one side of the long chronicle of a people who had learned humility through suffering, and pride through the endurance which survived the suffering and injustice, and on the other side, the chronicle of a people even longer in the land than the first, yet who no longer existed in the land at all save in the solitary brotherhood of an old Negro's alien blood and the wild and invincible spirit of an old bear. There was a boy who wished to learn humility and pride in order to become skillful and worthy in the woods, who suddenly found himself becoming so skillful so rapidly that he feared he would never become worthy because he had not learned humility and pride, although he had tried to, until one day and as suddenly he discovered that an old man who could not have defined either had led him, as though by the hand, to that point where an old bear and a little mongrel of a dog showed him that, by possessing one thing other, he would possess them both.

And a little dog, nameless and mongrel and many-fathered, grown, yet weighing less than six pounds, saying as if to itself, "I can't be dangerous, because there's nothing much smaller than I am; I can't be fierce, because they would call it just a noise; I can't be humble, because I'm already too close to the ground to genuflect; I can't be proud, because I wouldn't be near enough to it for anyone to know who was casting the shadow, and I don't even know that I'm not going to heaven, because they have already decided that I don't possess an immortal soul. So all I can be is brave. But it's all right. I can be that, even if they still call it just noise."

That was all. It was simple, much simpler than somebody talking in a book about youth and a girl he would never need to grieve over, because he could never approach any nearer her and would never have to get any farther away. He had heard about a bear, and finally got big enough to trail it, and he trailed it four years and at last met it with a gun in his hands and he didn't shoot. Because a little dog—But he could have shot long before the little dog covered the twenty yards to where the bear waited, and Sam Fathers could have shot at any time during that interminable minute while Old Ben stood on his hind feet over them. He stopped. His father was watching him gravely across the spring-rife twilight of the room; when he spoke, his words were as quiet as the twilight, too, not loud, because they did not need to be because they would last, "Courage, and honor, and pride," his father said, "and pity, and love of justice and of liberty. They all touch the heart, and what the heart holds to becomes truth, as far as we know the truth. Do you see now?"

Sam, and Old Ben, and Nip, he thought. And himself too. He had been all right too. His father had said so. "Yes, sir," he said.   (1942)

Gwin J. Kolb

FAULKNER'S "THE BEAR"

William Faulkner's "The Bear" (see story on p. 648) is the story of how, as a consequence of hunting a bear over a number of years, a sensitive boy arrives at maturity as a hunter and as a man—at least in the sense of comprehending a cluster of ethical concepts normally associated with mature human development and understanding. The unifying principle in the work is thus the boy's growth in knowledge, his progression from the "divination" of childhood through the series of encounters with the bear to, finally, his affirmative answer to his father's question.

This statement of the cohesive elements suggests immediately the functions served by the principal characters and happenings in "The Bear." Since the story is about his education, the boy is obviously the central figure, and the revelation of his thoughts and feelings (note the justification of the point of view by reference to the unifying principle) makes clear the stages in, and the climax of, his mental development. The boy comes from a family, a community, of hunters—hunters who are skilled woodsmen and expert marksmen, who go into the Big Bottom twice a year to keep "rendezvous with the bear," and who, above everything else and regardless of their color, possess the moral qualities of men nourished by the wilderness and filled with respect for all forms of life. The youth, it is emphasized from the first paragraph, has been deeply influenced by his surroundings, and especially by the legend of the most famous inhabitant of the nearby woods. Long before the beginning of the story, when he is ten, he "inherited . . . the tremendous bear," which "ran in his knowledge before he ever saw it," and which signified much more to him than an ordinary big bear signifies to an ordinary child.

His first hunting trip into the Big Bottom initiates his progression from childish dreams to mature understanding. He adds to his knowledge of wild life (his "kindergarten," we are told on p. 656, had been "the back-yard rabbits and squirrels at home"). He is introduced (pp. 650-651) to the concept of bravery via the behavior of one of the dogs. He realizes (p. 651) that the bear is a "mortal animal," but he is told that his party doesn't have the right dog for hunting Old Ben (pp. 651-652). From smelling the dogs' "effluvium" and tasting "that taint as of brass in his saliva," he comes to know the meaning of fear. And in order to prove to himself that his courage is stronger than his fear, he decides that he "must see" the bear, that he "must look at him."

On his second trip, the boy teaches "himself to be a better-than-fair woodsman without knowing he" is "doing it" (p. 653; cf. "he was becoming better and better as a woodsman, still without having yet realized it" on p. 654). He learns to accept the conditions which looking at the bear demands. He gains a dim, perhaps unconscious awareness of the qualities of humility and pride, skill and endurance. He is taught to distinguish between being afraid and being scared, and when at last he sees the bear he is not afraid (p. 655; cf. "his quiet breathing inhaled and exhaled three times" on p. 655). Moreover, as he realizes later (p. 656), on looking at each other, he and the bear recognize— at least the boy thinks they do—a kind of bond between them; they "pledged something, affirmed something more lasting than the frail web of bones and flesh which any accident could obliterate."

Between the time of his first and second meeting with the bear, the youth becomes a remarkable woodsman, more knowledgeable than Sam Fathers himself. The second meeting, which occurs when he is fourteen and which leaves him "shaking and trembling," advances his understanding, particularly of humility, by reminding him that, without the "right dog," he cannot expect to shoot the bear. In the third, and last, meeting with Old Ben, the boy demonstrates his bravery by rescuing the fyce, and the fact that he "was neither shaking nor trembling now" implies that, without knowing it, he has proved himself a man. By his failure to shoot when he has the chance, he also discloses his respect for the great bear, who for a moment appears in its proximity to him as the towering figure he "used to dream about." Furthermore, for the first time in the story, he displays real insight into Sam Fathers' character; that is, he understands, however indistinctly, the reason why Sam, like him, could not kill the bear.

The moral implications of the climax of his encounters with the bear are crystallized for the boy in his talk with his father. Forced to consider the incident—and especially his failure to shoot Old Ben—in the context of high ethical principles, he grasps the significance of the latter by reference to the characters who participated in the former. The bear exemplifies the "fierce pride of liberty and freedom"; Sam Fathers embodies humility and pride, courage and endurance; the little mongrel dog embodies bravery. Thus the boy, "who wished to learn humility and pride," comes to understand the meanings of a whole group of terms included in the broad concept which, according to his father, comprises truth.

The second principal character, the bear, is the chief factor in the boy's growth in skill as a woodsman and understanding as a mature human being; in the figure of the narrator, it was his "alma mater" and the wilderness it "ran was his college" (p. 656). The treatment of it is clearly determined by the function it serves. To everybody who talks about it—the boy, Sam Fathers, the narrator—the bear is a tremendous figure, almost more human than beast, that possesses traits which antedate the division of the animal kingdom into species. Already old when the story begins, it has earned itself "a name, a definite designation like a living man." To the narrator describing the boy's thoughts, the bear is "a phantom, epitome and apotheosis of the old wild life at which the puny humans swarmed and hacked in a fury of abhorrence and fear . . . —old Priam reft of his old wife and having outlived all his sons." Sam Fathers, of course, is not nearly so eloquent, but his repeated references (see, for example, pp. 650, 651, 652, 653) to Old Ben's "smartness" succeed in attaching to the animal an aura of preternatural knowledge. The boy, who, as noted earlier, recognizes a common tie between himself and the bear, times the final climactic meeting "almost as if it were an appointment with a human being" (p. 657). Lastly, although the legend which the youth "inherits" at the beginning of the tale includes many killings of animals (none, however, of men) by Old Ben, during the course of the story the bear is represented as harming only one animal, and that not seriously. Altogether, in the light of the bear's elevated, almost epic stature, it is small wonder that the boy, given his character and background, should make Old Ben the passion of his life as a woodsman, that he should refuse to kill him when he has the opportunity, and that, at the end, he should see in the animal the living embodiment of pride, freedom, and liberty.

The third principal character, Sam Fathers, the boy's half-Indian, half-Negro "mentor" (p. 656), helps to bring about the development of the youth's potentialities by teaching him the ways of the wilderness and of the men who hunt there. Sam, the son of a Chickasaw chief, shows the boy how to shoot and where to stand. During the boy's first trip to Big Bottom, the old Indian instructs him in the meaning of Old Ben's actions (Sam's ability to understand the bear, it should be noted, is surely related to his ancestry, which smacks, like the bear itself, of a period before time began) and tells him that, without the right dog, he will never be able to corner the bear. Also, by commenting on the brave hound (p. 651), he introduces the youth to the notion of the necessity of proving one's self a man. On the boy's second trip to the woods, Sam points out (p. 654) the proper way of looking for the bear and helps to develop the boy's concept of bravery by distinguishing between being scared and being afraid. Between the boy's eleventh and fourteenth year, Sam continues to teach him the art of hunting. At last, when he has the chance, Sam refuses to shoot the bear; and later, partly as a result of this incident, the boy comes to recognize in the old man the exemplification of humility and pride.

The other two important characters in "The Bear" may be considered together, for, unlike the boy, the bear, and Sam Fathers, they do not perform essential functions in every part of the story. The action of the "many-fathered" fyce—significantly, the boy's own dog—in bringing Old Ben to bay causes the youth to demonstrate his own bravery and also to understand, later (p. 659), the full meaning of the term. On the other hand, the boy's father, who is clearly the only one of the leading characters able to perform the particular function, aids his son's movement toward greater insight by making him relate his crucial experience with the bear to noble ethical abstractions.

Many of the connections between the chief happenings and the unifying principle of the story may be inferred from what has already been said about the characters. The introduction, which makes clear the boy's second-hand knowledge of Old Ben up to the time he goes on his first trip into Big Bottom, delineates both the boy's general character, including his desire for more knowledge, and also the bear's. Three of the major incidents consist of the boy's increasingly intimate encounters with the bear, while the fourth consists of his successful effort to understand his experiences in terms of lofty human values. On his initial trip to the swamp, the boy, in company with Sam, first hears the dogs that have picked up Old Ben's trail; then he sees the wounded hound; then he sees the bear's claw marks and footprint; and then, alone, he feels that Old Ben is looking at him. On the second trip, while alone he first finds the old "crooked print"; then, at Sam's suggestion, he discards his gun; then he travels "farther into the new and alien country than he had ever been"; then he discards his watch, compass, and stick; and then he finally sees, first, the "crooked print" and then, at a distance, the bear itself. Almost three years elapse between the second and the third climactic meeting with Old Ben. During this time, the boy learns "game trails that even Sam Fathers did not know"; he knows the bear's "footprints better than he did his own, and not only the crooked one"; he can find the "crooked print now almost whenever he liked"; and he sees the bear once, briefly, crossing "the end of a long blow-down." In the last encounter, of course, he comes closest to the bear; "he could smell it," it "towered over him like a cloudburst and colored like a thunderclap," and "There was a big wood tick inside his right hind leg." Finally, in the concluding scene with his father, the boy, thinking about why he didn't shoot when he "had the gun," first remembers the conversations he has heard in the room —the talk of "men, hunters with the will and hardihood to endure and the humility and skill to survive"; then he listens to the reading of Keats' "Ode on a Grecian Urn." But he is unable to "see now" until he connects the qualities his father has named with Sam, Old Ben, Nip, and himself. "'Yes, sir,' he said."

J. D. Salinger

FOR ESMÉ—WITH LOVE AND SQUALOR

Just recently, by air mail, I received an invitation to a wedding that will take place in England on April 18th. It happens to be a wedding I'd give a lot to be able to get to, and when the invitation first arrived, I thought it might just be possible for me to make the trip abroad, by plane, expenses be hanged. However, I've since discussed the matter rather extensively with my wife, a breathtakingly levelheaded girl, and we've decided against it—for one thing, I'd completely forgotten that my mother-in-law is looking forward to spending the last two weeks in April with us. I really don't get to see Mother Grencher terribly often, and she's not getting any younger. She's fifty-eight. (As she'd be the first to admit.)

All the same, though, wher*ev*er I happen to be, I don't think I'm the type that doesn't even lift a finger to prevent a wedding from flatting. Accordingly, I've gone ahead and jotted down a few revealing notes on the bride as I knew her almost six years ago. If my notes should cause the groom, whom I haven't met, an uneasy moment or two, so much the better. Nobody's aiming to please, here. More, really, to edify, to instruct.

In April of 1944, I was among some sixty American enlisted men who took a rather specialized pre-Invasion training course, directed by British Intelligence, in Devon, England. And as I look back, it seems to me that we were fairly unique, the sixty of us, in that there wasn't one good mixer in the bunch. We were all essentially letter-writing types, and when we spoke to each other out of the line of duty, it was usually to ask somebody if he had any ink he wasn't using. When we weren't writing letters or attending classes, each of us went pretty much his own way. Mine usually led me, on clear days, in scenic circles around the countryside. Rainy days, I generally sat in a dry place and read a book, often just an axe length away from a ping-pong table.

The training course lasted three weeks, ending on a Saturday, a very rainy one. At seven that last night, our whole group was scheduled to entrain for London, where, as rumor had it, we were to be assigned to infantry and air-borne divisions mustered for the D Day landings. By three in the afternoon, I'd packed all my belongings into my barrack bag, including a canvas gas-mask container full of books I'd brought over from the Other Side. (The gas mask itself I'd slipped through a porthole of the *Mauretania* some weeks earlier, fully aware that if the enemy ever *did* use gas I'd never get the damn thing on in time.) I remember standing at an end window of our Quonset hut for a very long time, looking out at the slanting, dreary rain, my trigger finger itching imperceptibly, if at all. I could hear behind my back the un-comradely scratching of many fountain pens on many sheets of V-mail paper. Abruptly, with nothing special in mind, I came away from the window and put on my raincoat, cashmere muffler, galoshes, woollen gloves, and overseas cap (the last of which, I'm still told, I wore at an angle all my own—slightly down over both ears). Then, after synchronizing my wristwatch with the clock in the latrine, I walked down the long, wet cobblestone hill into town. I ignored the flashes of lightning all around me. They either had your number on them or they didn't.

In the center of town, which was probably the wettest part of town, I stopped in front of a church to read the bulletin board, mostly because the featured numerals, white on black, had caught my attention but partly

because, after three years in the Army, I'd become addicted to reading bulletin
boards. At three-fifteen, the board stated, there would be children's choir
practice. I looked at my wristwatch, then back at the board. A sheet of paper
was tacked up, listing the names of the children expected to attend practice.
I stood in the rain and read all the names, then entered the church.

A dozen or so adults were among the pews, several of them bearing
pairs of small-size rubbers, soles up, in their laps. I passed along and sat
down in the front row. On the rostrum, seated in three compact rows of
auditorium chairs, were about twenty children, mostly girls, ranging in age
from about seven to thirteen. At the moment, their choir coach, an enormous
woman in tweeds, was advising them to open their mouths wider when they
sang. Had anyone, she asked, ever heard of a little dickey-bird that *dared*
to sing his charming song without first opening his little beak wide, wide,
wide? Apparently nobody ever had. She was given a steady, opaque look.
She went on to say that she wanted all her children to absorb the *meaning*
of the words they sang, not just *mouth* them, like silly-billy parrots. She then
blew a note on her pitch pipe, and the children, like so many underage
weight-lifters, raised their hymnbooks.

They sang without instrumental accompaniment—or, more accurately in
their case, without any interference. Their voices were melodious and un-
sentimental, almost to the point where a somewhat more denominational
man than myself might, without straining, have experienced levitation. A
couple of the very youngest children dragged the tempo a trifle, but in a
way that only the composer's mother could have found fault with. I had
never heard the hymn, but I kept hoping it was one with a dozen or more
verses. Listening, I scanned all the children's faces but watched one in
particular, that of the child nearest me, on the end seat in the first row.
She was about thirteen, with straight ash-blond hair of ear-lobe length, an
exquisite forehead, and blasé eyes that, I thought, might very possibly have
counted the house. Her voice was distinctly separate from the other children's
voices, and not just because she was seated nearest me. It had the best upper
register, the sweetest-sounding, the surest, and it automatically led the way.
The young lady, however, seemed slightly bored with her own singing ability,
or perhaps just with the time and place; twice, between verses, I saw her
yawn. It was a ladylike yawn, a closed-mouth yawn, but you couldn't miss it;
her nostril wings gave her away.

The instant the hymn ended, the choir coach began to give her lengthy
opinion of people who can't keep their feet still and their lips sealed tight
during the minister's sermon. I gathered that the singing part of the rehearsal
was over, and before the coach's dissonant speaking voice could entirely
break the spell the children's singing had cast, I got up and left the church.

It was raining even harder. I walked down the street and looked through
the window of the Red Cross recreation room, but soldiers were standing
two and three deep at the coffee counter, and, even through the glass, I
could hear ping-pong balls bouncing in another room. I crossed the street

and entered a civilian tearoom, which was empty except for a middle-aged
waitress, who looked as if she would have preferred a customer with a dry
raincoat. I used a coat tree as delicately as possible, and then sat down at a
table and ordered tea and cinnamon toast. It was the first time all day that
I'd spoken to anyone. I then looked through all my pockets, including my
raincoat, and finally found a couple of stale letters to reread, one from my
wife, telling me how the service at Schrafft's Eighty-eighth Street had fallen
off, and one from my mother-in-law, asking me to please send her some
cashmere yarn first chance I got away from "camp."

While I was still on my first cup of tea, the young lady I had been watching and listening to in the choir came into the tearoom. Her hair was soaking
wet, and the rims of both ears were showing. She was with a very small boy,
unmistakably her brother, whose cap she removed by lifting it off his head
with two fingers, as if it were a laboratory specimen. Bringing up the rear
was an efficient-looking woman in a limp felt hat—presumably their governess.
The choir member, taking off her coat as she walked across the floor, made
the table selection—a good one, from my point of view, as it was just eight
or ten feet directly in front of me. She and the governess sat down. The small
boy, who was about five, wasn't ready to sit down yet. He slid out of and
discarded his reefer; then, with the deadpan expression of a born heller,
he methodically went about annoying his governess by pushing in and pulling
out his chair several times, watching her face. The governess, keeping her
voice down, gave him two or three orders to sit down, and, in effect, stop
the monkey business, but it was only when his sister spoke to him that he
came around and applied the small of his back to his chair seat. He immediately picked up his napkin and put it on his head. His sister removed it,
opened it, and spread it out on his lap.

About the time their tea was brought, the choir member caught me staring
over at her party. She stared back at me, with those house-counting eyes of
hers, then, abruptly, gave me a small, qualified smile. It was oddly radiant,
as certain small, qualified smiles sometimes are. I smiled back, much less
radiantly, keeping my upper lip down over a coal-black G.I. temporary filling
showing between two of my front teeth. The next thing I knew, the young lady
was standing, with enviable poise, beside my table. She was wearing a tartan
dress—a Campbell tartan, I believe. It seemed to me to be a wonderful dress for
a very young girl to be wearing on a rainy, rainy day. "I thought Americans
despised tea," she said.

It wasn't the observation of a smart aleck but that of a truth-lover or a
statistics-lover. I replied that some of us never drank anything *but* tea. I
asked her if she'd care to join me.

"Thank you," she said. "Perhaps for just a fraction of a moment."

I got up and drew a chair for her, the one opposite me, and she sat down
on the forward quarter of it, keeping her spine easily and beautifully straight.
I went back—almost hurried back—to my own chair, more than willing to
hold up my end of a conversation. When I was seated, I couldn't think of

anything to say, though. I smiled again, still keeping my coal-black filling under concealment. I remarked that it was certainly a terrible day out.

"Yes; quite," said my guest, in the clear, unmistakable voice of a small-talk detester. She placed her fingers flat on the table edge, like someone at a séance, then, almost instantly, closed her hands—her nails were bitten down to the quick. She was wearing a wristwatch, a military-looking one that looked rather like a navigator's chronograph. Its face was much too large for her slender wrist. "You were at choir practice," she said matter-of-factly. "I saw you."

I said I certainly had been, and that I had heard her voice singing separately from the others. I said I thought she had a very fine voice.

She nodded. "I know. I'm going to be a professional singer."

"Really? Opera?"

"Heavens, no. I'm going to sing jazz on the radio and make heaps of money. Then, when I'm thirty, I shall retire and live on a ranch in Ohio." She touched the top of her soaking-wet head with the flat of her hand. "Do you know Ohio?" she asked.

I said I'd been through it on the train a few times but that I didn't really know it. I offered her a piece of cinnamon toast.

"No, thank you," she said. "I eat like a bird, actually."

I bit into a piece of toast myself, and commented that there's some mighty rough country around Ohio.

"I know. An American I met told me. You're the eleventh American I've met."

Her governess was now urgently signalling her to return to her own table —in effect, to stop bothering the man. My guest, however, calmly moved her chair an inch or two so that her back broke all possible further communication with the home table. "You go to that secret Intelligence school on the hill, don't you?" she inquired coolly.

As security-minded as the next one, I replied that I was visiting Devonshire for my health.

"*Really*," she said, "I wasn't quite born yesterday, you know."

I said I'd bet she hadn't been, at that. I drank my tea for a moment. I was getting a trifle posture-conscious and I sat up somewhat straighter in my seat.

"You seem quite intelligent for an American," my guest mused.

I told her that was a pretty snobbish thing to say, if you thought about it at all, and that I hoped it was unworthy of her.

She blushed—automatically conferring on me the social poise I'd been missing. "Well. Most of the Americans *I've* seen act like animals. They're forever punching one another about, and insulting everyone, and—You know what one of them did?"

I shook my head.

"One of them threw an empty whiskey bottle through my aunt's window. *For*tunately, the window was open. But does that sound very intelligent to you?"

It didn't especially, but I didn't say so. I said that many soldiers, all over the world, were a long way from home, and that few of them had had many real advantages in life. I said I'd thought that most people could figure that out for themselves.

"Possibly," said my guest, without conviction. She raised her hand to her wet head again, picked at a few limp filaments of blond hair, trying to cover her exposed ear rims. "My hair is soaking wet," she said. "I look a fright." She looked over at me. "I have quite wavy hair when it's dry."

"I can see that, I can see you have."

"Not actually curly, but quite wavy," she said. "Are you married?"

I said I was.

She nodded. "Are you very deeply in love with your wife? Or am I being too personal?"

I said that when she was, I'd speak up.

She put her hands and wrists farther forward on the table, and I remember wanting to do something about that enormous-faced wristwatch she was wearing—perhaps suggest that she try wearing it around her waist.

"Usually, I'm not terribly gregarious," she said, and looked over at me to see if I knew the meaning of the word. I didn't give her a sign, though, one way or the other. "I purely came over because I thought you looked extremely lonely. You have an extremely sensitive face."

I said she was right, that I *had* been feeling lonely, and that I was very glad she'd come over.

"I'm training myself to be more compassionate. My aunt says I'm a terribly cold person," she said and felt the top of her head again. "I live with my aunt. She's an extremely kind person. Since the death of my mother, she's done everything within her power to make Charles and me feel adjusted."

"I'm glad."

"Mother was an extremely intelligent person. Quite sensuous, in many ways." She looked at me with a kind of fresh acuteness. "Do you find me terribly cold?"

I told her absolutely not—very much to the contrary, in fact. I told her my name and asked for hers.

She hesitated. "My first name is Esmé. I don't think I shall tell you my full name, for the moment. I have a title and you may just be impressed by titles. Americans are, you know."

I said I didn't think I would be, but that it might be a good idea, at that, to hold onto the title for a while.

Just then, I felt someone's warm breath on the back of my neck. I turned around and just missed brushing noses with Esmé's small brother. Ignoring me, he addressed his sister in a piercing treble: "Miss Megley said you must come and finish your tea!" His message delivered, he retired to the chair between his sister and me, on my right. I regarded him with high interest. He was looking very splendid in brown Shetland shorts, a navy-blue jersey, white shirt, and striped necktie. He gazed back at me with immense green eyes. "Why do people in films kiss sideways?" he demanded.

"Sideways?" I said. It was a problem that had baffled me in my childhood. I said I guessed it was because actors' noses are too big for kissing anyone head on.

"His name is Charles," Esmé said. "He's extremely brilliant for his age."

"He certainly has green eyes. Haven't you, Charles?"

Charles gave me the fishy look my question deserved, then wriggled downward and forward in his chair till all of his body was under the table except his head, which he left, wrestler's-bridge style, on the chair seat. "They're orange," he said in a strained voice, addressing the ceiling. He picked up a corner of the tablecloth and put it over his handsome, dead-pan little face.

"Sometimes he's brilliant and sometimes he's not," Esmé said. "Charles, do sit up!"

Charles stayed right where he was. He seemed to be holding his breath.

"He misses our father very much. He was s-l-a-i-n in North Africa."

I expressed regret to hear it.

Esmé nodded. "Father adored him." She bit reflectively at the cuticle of her thumb. "He looks very much like my mother—Charles, I mean. I look exactly like my father." She went on biting at her cuticle. "My mother was quite a passionate woman. She was an extrovert. Father was an introvert. They were quite well mated, though, in a superficial way. To be quite candid, Father really needed more of an intellectual companion than Mother was. He was an extremely gifted genius."

I waited, receptively, for further information, but none came. I looked down at Charles, who was now resting the side of his face on his chair seat. When he saw that I was looking at him, he closed his eyes, sleepily, angelically, then stuck out his tongue—an appendage of startling length—and gave out what in *my* country would have been a glorious tribute to a myopic baseball umpire. It fairly shook the tearoom.

"Stop that," Esmé said, clearly unshaken. "He saw an American do it in a fish-and-chips queue, and now he does it whenever he's bored. Just stop it, now, or I shall send you directly to Miss Megley."

Charles opened his enormous eyes, as sign that he'd heard his sister's threat, but otherwise didn't look especially alerted. He closed his eyes again, and continued to rest the side of his face on the chair seat.

I mentioned that maybe he ought to save it—meaning the Bronx cheer— till he started using his title regularly. That is, if he had a title, too.

Esmé gave me a long, faintly clinical look. "You have a dry sense of humor, haven't you?" she said—wistfully. "Father said I have no sense of humor at all. He said I was unequipped to meet life because I have no sense of humor."

Watching her, I lit a cigarette and said I didn't think a sense of humor was of any use in a real pinch.

"Father said it was."

This was a statement of faith, not a contradiction, and I quickly switched horses. I nodded and said her father had probably taken the long view, while I was taking the short (whatever *that* meant).

"Charles misses him exceedingly," Esmé said, after a moment. "He was an exceedingly lovable man. He was extremely handsome, too. Not that one's appearance matters greatly, but he was. He had terribly penetrating eyes, for a man who was intransically kind."

I nodded. I said I imagined her father had had quite an extraordinary vocabulary.

"Oh, yes; quite," said Esmé. "He was an archivist—amateur, of course."

At that point, I felt an importunate tap, almost a punch, on my upper arm, from Charles' direction. I turned to him. He was sitting in a fairly normal position in his chair now, except that he had one knee tucked under him. "What did one wall say to the other wall?" he asked shrilly. "It's a riddle!"

I rolled my eyes reflectively ceilingward and repeated the question aloud. Then I looked at Charles with a stumped expression and said I gave up.

"Meet you at the corner!" came the punch line, at top volume.

It went over biggest with Charles himself. It struck him as unbearably funny. In fact, Esmé had to come around and pound him on the back, as if treating him for a coughing spell. "Now, stop that," she said. She went back to her own seat. "He tells that same riddle to everyone he meets and has a fit every single time. Usually he drools when he laughs. Now, just stop, please."

"It's one of the best riddles I've heard, though," I said, watching Charles, who was very gradually coming out of it. In response to this compliment, he sank considerably lower in his chair and again masked his face up to the eyes with a corner of the tablecloth. He then looked at me with his exposed eyes, which were full of slowly subsiding mirth and the pride of someone who knows a really good riddle or two.

"May I inquire how you were employed before entering the Army?" Esmé asked me.

I said I hadn't been employed at all, that I'd only been out of college a year but that I liked to think of myself as a professional short-story writer.

She nodded politely. "Published?" she asked.

It was a familiar but always touchy question, and one that I didn't answer just one, two, three. I started to explain how most editors in America were a bunch—

"My father wrote beautifully," Esmé interrupted. "I'm saving a number of his letters for posterity."

I said that sounded like a very good idea. I happened to be looking at her enormous-faced, chronographic-looking wristwatch again. I asked if it had belonged to her father.

She looked down at her wrist solemnly. "Yes, it did," she said. "He gave it to me just before Charles and I were evacuated." Self-consciously, she took her hands off the table, saying, "Purely as a momento, of course." She guided the conversation in a different direction. "I'd be extremely flattered if you'd write a story exclusively for me sometime. I'm an avid reader."

I told her I certainly would, if I could. I said that I wasn't terribly prolific.

"It doesn't have to be terribly prolific! Just so that it isn't childish and silly." She reflected. "I prefer stories about squalor."

"About what?" I said, leaning forward.

"Squalor. I'm extremely interested in squalor."

I was about to press her for more details, but I felt Charles pinching me, hard, on my arm. I turned to him, wincing slightly. He was standing right next to me. "What did one wall say to the other wall?" he asked, not unfamiliarly.

"You asked him that," Esmé said. "Now, stop it."

Ignoring his sister, and stepping up on one side of my feet, Charles repeated the key question. I noticed that his necktie knot wasn't adjusted properly. I slid it up into place, then, looking him straight in the eye, suggested, "Meetcha at the corner?"

The instant I'd said it, I wished I hadn't. Charles' mouth fell open. I felt as if I'd struck it open. He stepped down off my foot and, with white-hot dignity, walked over to his own table, without looking back.

"He's furious," Esmé said. "He has a violent temper. My mother had a propensity to spoil him. My father was the only one who didn't spoil him."

I kept looking over at Charles, who had sat down and started to drink his tea, using both hands on the cup. I hoped he'd turn around, but he didn't.

Esmé stood up. "*Il faut que je parte aussi,*" she said, with a sigh. "Do you know French?"

I got up from my own chair, with mixed feelings of regret and confusion. Esmé and I shook hands; her hand, as I'd suspected, was a nervous hand, damp at the palm. I told her, in English, how very much I'd enjoyed her company.

She nodded. "I thought you might," she said. "I'm quite communicative for my age." She gave her hair another experimental touch. "I'm dreadfully sorry about my hair," she said. "I've probably been hideous to look at."

"Not at all! As a matter of fact, I think a lot of the wave is coming back already."

She quickly touched her hair again. "Do you think you'll be coming here again in the immediate future?" she asked. "We come here every Saturday, after choir practice."

I answered that I'd like nothing better but that, unfortunately, I was pretty sure I wouldn't be able to make it again.

"In other words, you can't discuss troop movements," said Esmé. She made no move to leave the vicinity of the table. In fact, she crossed one foot over the other and, looking down, aligned the toes of her shoes. It was a pretty little execution, for she was wearing white socks and her ankles and feet were lovely. She looked up at me abruptly. "Would you like me to write to you?" she asked, with a certain amount of color in her face. "I write extremely articulate letters for a person my—"

"I'd love it." I took out pencil and paper and wrote down my name, rank, serial number, and A.P.O. number.

"I shall write to you first," she said, accepting it, "so that you don't feel *comp*romised in any way." She put the address into a pocket of her dress. "Goodbye," she said, and walked back to her table.

I ordered another pot of tea and sat watching the two of them till they, and the harassed Miss Megley, got up to leave. Charles led the way out, limping tragically, like a man with one leg several inches shorter than the other. He didn't look over at me. Miss Megley went next, then Esmé, who waved to me. I waved back, half getting up from my chair. It was a strangely emotional moment for me.

Less than a minute later, Esmé came back into the tearoom, dragging Charles behind her by the sleeve of his reefer. "Charles would like to kiss you goodbye," she said.

I immediately put down my cup, and said that was very nice, but was she *sure?*

"Yes," she said, a trifle grimly. She let go Charles' sleeve and gave him a rather vigorous push in my direction. He came forward, his face livid, and gave me a loud, wet smacker just below the right ear. Following this ordeal, he started to make a beeline for the door and a less sentimental way of life, but I caught the half belt at the back of his reefer, held on to it, and asked him, "What did one wall say to the other wall?"

His face lit up. "Meet you at the corner!" he shrieked, and raced out of the room, possibly in hysterics.

Esmé was standing with crossed ankles again. "You're quite sure you won't forget to write that story for me?" she asked. "It doesn't have to be *exclu*sively for me. It can—"

I said there was absolutely no chance that I'd forget. I told her that I'd never written a story *for* anybody, but that it seemed like exactly the right time to get down to it.

She nodded. "Make it extremely squalid and moving," she suggested. "Are you at all acquainted with squalor?"

I said not exactly but that I was getting better acquainted with it, in one form or another, all the time, and that I'd do my best to come up to her specifications. We shook hands.

"Isn't it a pity that we didn't meet under less extenuating circumstances?" I said it was, I said it certainly was.

"Goodbye," Esmé said. "I hope you return from the war with all your faculties intact."

I thanked her, and said a few other words, and then watched her leave the tearoom. She left it slowly, reflectively, testing the ends of her hair for dryness.

This is the squalid, or moving, part of the story, and the scene changes. The people change, too. I'm still around, but from here on in, for reasons I'm not at liberty to disclose, I've disguised myself so cunningly that even the cleverest reader will fail to recognize me.

It was about ten-thirty at night in Gaufurt, Bavaria, several weeks after V-E Day. Staff Sergeant X was in his room on the second floor of the civilian home in which he and nine other American soldiers had been quartered, even before the armistice. He was seated on a folding wooden chair at a small, messy-looking writing table, with a paperback overseas novel open before him, which he was having great trouble reading. The trouble lay with him, not the novel. Although the men who lived on the first floor usually had first grab at the books sent each month by Special Services, X usually seemed to be left with the book he might have selected himself. But he was a young man who had not come through the war with all his faculties intact, and for more than an hour he had been triple-reading paragraphs, and now he was doing it to the sentences. He suddenly closed the book, without marking his place. With his hand, he shielded his eyes for a moment against the harsh, watty glare from the naked bulb over the table.

He took a cigarette from a pack on the table and lit it with fingers that bumped gently and incessantly against one another. He sat back a trifle in his chair and smoked without any sense of taste. He had been chain-smoking for weeks. His gums bled at the slightest pressure of the tip of his tongue, and he seldom stopped experimenting; it was a little game he played, sometimes by the hour. He sat for a moment smoking and experimenting. Then, abruptly, familiarly, and, as usual, with no warning, he thought he felt his mind dislodge itself and teeter, like insecure luggage on an overhead rack. He quickly did what he had been doing for weeks to set things right: he pressed his hands hard against his temples. He held on tight for a moment. His hair needed cutting, and it was dirty. He had washed it three or four times during his two weeks' stay at the hospital in Frankfort on the Main, but it had got dirty again on the long, dusty jeep ride back to Gaufurt. Corporal Z, who had called for him at the hospital, still drove a jeep combat-style, with the windshield down on the hood, armistice or no armistice. There were thousands of new troops in Germany. By driving with his windshield down, combat-style, Corporal Z hoped to show that he was not one of them, that not by a long shot was he some new son of a bitch in the E.T.O.

When he let go of his head, X began to stare at the surface of the writing table, which was a catchall for at least two dozen unopened letters and at least five or six unopened packages, all addressed to him. He reached behind the debris and picked out a book that stood against the wall. It was a book by Goebbels, entitled "Die Zeit Ohne Beispiel." It belonged to the thirty-eight-year-old unmarried daughter of the family that, up to a few weeks earlier, had been living in the house. She had been a low official in the Nazi Party, but high enough, by Army Regulations standards, to fall into an automatic-arrest category. X himself had arrested her. Now, for the third time since he had returned from the hospital that day, he opened the woman's book and read the brief inscription on the flyleaf. Written in ink, in German, in a small, hopelessly sincere handwriting, were the words "Dear God, life is hell." Nothing led up to or away from it. Alone on the page, and in the sickly stillness of the room, the words appeared to have the stature of an uncontestable, even classic indictment. X stared at the page for several minutes, trying, against heavy odds, not to be taken in. Then, with far more zeal than he had done anything in weeks, he picked up a pencil stub and wrote down under the inscription, in English, "Fathers and teachers, I ponder 'What is hell?' I maintain that it is the suffering of being unable to love." He started to write Dostoevski's name under the inscription, but saw—with fright that ran through his whole body—that what he had written was almost entirely illegible. He shut the book.

He quickly picked up something else from the table, a letter from his older brother in Albany. It had been on his table even before he had checked into the hospital. He opened the envelope, loosely resolved to read the letter straight through, but read only the top half of the first page. He stopped after the words "Now that the g.d. war is over and you probably have a lot of time over there, how about sending the kids a couple of bayonets or swastikas . . ." After he'd torn it up, he looked down at the pieces as they lay in the wastebasket. He saw that he had overlooked an enclosed snapshot. He could make out somebody's feet standing on a lawn somewhere.

He put his arms on the table and rested his head on them. He ached from head to foot, all zones of pain seemingly interdependent. He was rather like a Christmas tree whose lights, wired in series, must all go out if even one bulb is defective.

The door banged open, without having been rapped on. X raised his head, turned it, and saw Corporal Z standing in the door. Corporal Z had been X's jeep partner and constant companion from D Day straight through five campaigns of the war. He lived on the first floor and he usually came up to see X when he had a few rumors or gripes to unload. He was a huge, photogenic young man of twenty-four. During the war, a national magazine had photographed him in Hürtgen Forest; he had posed, more than just obligingly, with a Thanksgiving turkey in each hand. "Ya writin' letters?" he asked X. "It's spooky in here, for Chrissake." He preferred always to enter a room that had the overhead light on.

X turned around in his chair and asked him to come in, and to be careful not to step on the dog.

"The what?"

"Alvin. He's right under your feet, Clay. How 'bout turning on the god-dam light?"

Clay found the overhead-light switch, flicked it on, then stepped across the puny, servant's-size room and sat down on the edge of the bed, facing his host. His brick-red hair, just combed, was dripping with the amount of water he required for satisfactory grooming. A comb with a fountain-pen clip protruded, familiarly, from the right-hand pocket of his olive-drab shirt.

Over the left-hand pocket he was wearing the Combat Infantrymen's Badge (which, technically, he wasn't authorized to wear), the European Theatre ribbon, with five bronze battle stars in it (instead of a lone silver one, which was the equivalent of five bronze ones), and the pre-Pearl Harbor service ribbon. He sighed heavily and said, "Christ almighty." It meant nothing; it was Army. He took a pack of cigarettes from his shirt pocket, tapped one out, then put away the pack and rebuttoned the pocket flap. Smoking, he looked vacuously around the room. His look finally settled on the radio. "Hey," he said. "They got this terrific show comin' on the radio in a coupla minutes. Bob Hope, and everybody."

X, opening a fresh pack of cigarettes, said he had just turned the radio off.

Undarkened, Clay watched X trying to get a cigarette lit. "Jesus," he said, with spectator's enthusiasm, "you oughta see your goddam hands. Boy, have you got the shakes. Ya know that?"

X got his cigarette lit, nodded, and said Clay had a real eye for detail.

"No kidding, hey. I goddam near fainted when I saw you at the hospital. You looked like a goddam *corpse*. How much weight ya lose? How many pounds? Ya know?"

"I don't know. How was your mail when I was gone? You heard from Loretta?"

Loretta was Clay's girl. They intended to get married at their earliest convenience. She wrote to him fairly regularly, from a paradise of triple exclamation points and inaccurate observations. All through the war, Clay had read all Loretta's letters aloud to X, however intimate they were—in fact, the more intimate, the better. It was his custom, after each reading, to ask X to plot out or pad out the letter of reply, or to insert a few impressive words in French or German.

"Yeah, I had a letter from her yesterday. Down in my room. Show it to ya later," Clay said, listlessly. He sat up straight on the edge of the bed, held his breath, and issued a long, resonant belch. Looking just semi-pleased with the achievement, he relaxed again. "Her goddam brother's gettin' outa the Navy on account of his hip," he said. "He's got this hip, the bastard." He sat up again and tried for another belch, but with below-par results. A jot of alertness came into his face. "Hey. Before I forget. We gotta get up at five tomorrow and drive to Hamburg or someplace. Pick up Eisenhower jackets for the whole detachment."

X, regarding him hostilely, stated that he didn't want an Eisenhower jacket.

Clay looked surprised, almost a trifle hurt. "Oh, they're good! They look good. How come?"

"No reason. Why do we have to get up at five? The war's over, for God's sake."

"I don't know—we gotta get back before lunch. They got some new forms in we gotta fill out before lunch. . . . I asked Bulling how come we couldn't fill 'em out tonight—he's *got* the goddam forms right on his desk. He don't want to open the envelopes yet, the son of a bitch."

The two sat quiet for a moment, hating Bulling.

Clay suddenly looked at X with new—higher—interest than before. "Hey," he said. "Did you know the goddam side of your face is jumping all over the place?"

X said he knew all about it, and covered his tic with his hand.

Clay stared at him for a moment, then said, rather vividly, as if he were the bearer of exceptionally good news, "I wrote Loretta you had a nervous breakdown."

"Oh?"

"Yeah. She's interested as hell in all that stuff. She's majoring in psychology." Clay stretched himself out on the bed, shoes included. "You know what she said? She says nobody gets a nervous breakdown just from the war and all. She says you probably were unstable like, your whole goddam life."

X bridged his hand over his eyes—the light over the bed seemed to be blinding him—and said that Loretta's insight into things was always a joy.

Clay glanced over at him. "Listen, ya bastard," he said. "She knows a goddam sight more psychology than *you* do."

"Do you think you can bring yourself to take your stinking feet off my bed?" X asked.

Clay left his feet where they were for a few don't-tell-me-where-to-put-my-feet seconds, then swung them around to the floor and sat up. "I'm goin' downstairs anyway. They got the radio on in Walker's room." He didn't get up from the bed, though. "Hey. I was just tellin' that new son of a bitch, Bernstein, downstairs. Remember that time I and you drove into Valognes, and we got shelled for about two goddam hours, and that goddam cat I shot that jumped up on the hood of the jeep when we were layin' in that hole? Remember?"

"Yes—don't start that business with that cat again, Clay, God damn it. I don't want to hear about it."

"No, all I mean is I wrote Loretta about it. She and the whole psychology class discussed it. In class and all. The goddam professor and everybody."

"That's fine. I don't want to hear about it, Clay."

"No, you know the reason I took a pot shot at it, Loretta says? She says I was temporarily insane. No kidding. From the shelling and all."

X threaded his fingers, once, through his dirty hair, then shielded his eyes against the light again. "You weren't insane. You were simply doing your duty. You killed that pussycat in as manly a way as anybody could've, under the circumstances."

Clay looked at him suspiciously. "What the hell are you talkin' about?"

"That cat was a spy. You *had* to take a pot shot at it. It was a very clever German midget dressed up in a cheap fur coat. So there was absolutely nothing brutal, or cruel, or dirty, or even—"

"God damn it!" Clay said, his lips thinned. "Can't you ever be *sincere?*"

X suddenly felt sick, and he swung around in his chair and grabbed the wastebasket—just in time.

When he had straightened up and turned toward his guest again, he found him standing, embarrassed, halfway between the bed and the door. X started to apologize, but changed his mind and reached for his cigarettes.

"C'mon down and listen to Hope on the radio, hey," Clay said, keeping his distance but trying to be friendly over it. "It'll do ya good. I mean it."

"You go ahead, Clay. . . . I'll look at my stamp collection."

"Yeah? You got a stamp collection? I didn't know you—"

"I'm only kidding."

Clay took a couple of slow steps toward the door. "I may drive over to Ehstadt later," he said. "They got a dance. It'll probably last till around two. Wanna go?"

"No, thanks. . . . I may practice a few steps in the room."

"O.K. G'night! Take it easy, now, for Chrissake." The door slammed shut, then instantly opened again. "Hey. O.K. if I leave a letter to Loretta under your door? I got some German stuff in it. Willya fix it up for me?"

"Yes. Leave me alone now, God damn it."

"Sure," said Clay. "You know what my mother wrote me? She wrote me she's glad you and I were together and all the whole war. In the same jeep and all. She says my letters are a helluva lot more intelligent since we been goin' around together."

X looked up and over at him, and said, with great effort, "Thanks. Tell her thanks for me."

"I will. G'night!" The door slammed shut, this time for good.

X sat looking at the door for a long while, then turned his chair around toward the writing table and picked up his portable typewriter from the floor. He made space for it on the messy table surface, pushing aside the collapsed pile of unopened letters and packages. He thought if he wrote a letter to an old friend of his in New York there might be some quick, however slight, therapy in it for him. But he couldn't insert his notepaper into the roller properly, his fingers were shaking so violently now. He put his hands down at his sides for a minute, then tried again, but finally crumpled the notepaper in his hand.

He was aware that he ought to get the wastebasket out of the room, but instead of doing anything about it, he put his arms on the typewriter and rested his head again, closing his eyes.

A few throbbing minutes later, when he opened his eyes, he found himself squinting at a small, unopened package wrapped in green paper. It had probably slipped off the pile when he had made space for the typewriter. He saw that it had been readdressed several times. He could make out, on just one side of the package, at least three of his old A.P.O. numbers.

He opened the package without any interest, without even looking at the return address. He opened it by burning the string with a lighted match. He was more interested in watching the string burn all the way down than in opening the package, but he opened it, finally.

Inside the box, a note, written in ink, lay on top of a small object wrapped in tissue paper. He picked out the note and read it.

17, —— Road,
——, Devon
June 7, 1944

Dear Sergeant X,

I hope you will forgive me for having taken 38 days to begin our correspondence but, I have been extremely busy as my aunt has undergone streptococcus of the throat and nearly perished and I have been justifiably saddled with one responsibility after another. However I have thought of you frequently and of the extremely pleasant afternoon we spent in each other's company on April 30, 1944 between 3:45 and 4:15 P.M. in case it slipped your mind.

We are all tremendously excited and overawed about D Day and only hope that it will bring about the swift termination of the war and a method of existence that is ridiculous to say the least. Charles and I are both quite concerned about you; we hope you were not among those who made the first initial assault upon the Cotentin Peninsula. Were you? Please reply as speedily as possible. My warmest regards to your wife.

Sincerely yours,
Esmé

P.S. I am taking the liberty of enclosing my wristwatch which you may keep in your possession for the duration of the conflict. I did not observe whether you were wearing one during our brief association, but this one is extremely water-proof and shock-proof as well as having many other virtues among which one can tell at what velocity one is walking if one wishes. I am quite certain that you will use it to greater advantage in these difficult days than I ever can and that you will accept it as a lucky talisman.

Charles, whom I am teaching to read and write and whom I am finding an extremely intelligent novice, wishes to add a few words. Please write as soon as you have the time and inclination.

HELLO HELLO HELLO HELLO HELLO
HELLO HELLO HELLO HELLO HELLO
LOVE AND KISSES CHALES

It was a long time before X could set the note aside, let alone lift Esmé's father's wristwatch out of the box. When he did finally lift it out, he saw that its crystal had been broken in transit. He wondered if the watch was otherwise undamaged, but he hadn't the courage to wind it and find out. He just sat with it in his hand for another long period. Then, suddenly, almost ecstatically, he felt sleepy.

You take a really sleepy man, Esmé, and he always stands a chance of again becoming a man with all his fac—with all his f-a-c-u-l-t-i-e-s intact.

(1950)

Frank O'Connor

MY OEDIPUS COMPLEX

Father was in the army all through the war—the first war, I mean—so, up to the age of five, I never saw much of him, and what I saw did not worry me. Sometimes I woke and there was a big figure in khaki peering down at me in the candlelight. Sometimes in the early morning I heard the slamming of the front door and the clatter of nailed boots down the cobbles of the lane. These were Father's entrances and exits. Like Santa Claus, he came and went mysteriously.

In fact, I rather liked his visits, though it was an uncomfortable squeeze between Mother and him when I got into the big bed in the early morning. He smoked, which gave him a pleasant musty smell, and shaved, an operation of astounding interest. Each time he left a trail of souvenirs—model tanks and Gurkha knives with handles made of bullet cases, and German helmets and cap badges and button-sticks, and all sorts of military equipment—carefully stowed away in a long box on top of the wardrobe, in case they ever came in handy. There was a bit of the magpie about Father; he expected everything to come in handy. When his back was turned, Mother let me get a chair and rummage through his treasures. She didn't seem to think so highly of them as he did.

The war was the most peaceful period of my life. The window of my attic faced southeast. My mother had curtained it, but that had small effect. I always woke with the first light and, with all the responsibilities of the previous day melted, feeling myself rather like the sun, ready to illumine and rejoice. Life never seemed so simple and clear and full of possibilities as then. I put my feet out from under the clothes—I called them Mrs. Left and Mrs. Right—and invented dramatic situations for them in which they discussed the problems of the day. At least Mrs. Right did; she was very demonstrative, but I hadn't the same control of Mrs. Left, so she mostly contented herself with nodding agreement.

They discussed what Mother and I should do during the day, what Santa Claus should give a fellow for Christmas, and what steps should be taken to brighten the home. There was that little matter of the baby, for instance. Mother and I could never agree about that. Ours was the only house in the terrace without a new baby, and Mother said we couldn't afford one till Father came back from the war because they cost seventeen and six. That showed how simple she was. The Geneys up the road had a baby, and everyone knew they couldn't afford seventeen and six. It was probably a cheap baby, and Mother wanted something really good, but I felt she was too exclusive. The Geneys' baby would have done us fine.

Having settled my plans for the day, I got up, put a chair under the attic window, and lifted the frame high enough to stick out my head. The window overlooked the front gardens of the terrace behind ours, and beyond these it looked over a deep valley to the tall, red-brick houses terraced up the opposite hillside, which were all still in shadow, while those at our side of the valley were all lit up, though with long strange shadows that made them seem unfamiliar; rigid and painted.

After that I went into Mother's room and climbed into the big bed. She woke and I began to tell her of my schemes. By this time, though I never seem to have noticed it, I was petrified in my nightshirt, and I thawed as I talked until, the last frost melted, I fell asleep beside her and woke again only when I heard her below in the kitchen, making the breakfast.

After breakfast we went into town; heard Mass at St. Augustine's and said a prayer for Father, and did the shopping. If the afternoon was fine we either went for a walk in the country or a visit to Mother's great friend in the convent, Mother St. Dominic. Mother had them all praying for Father, and every night, going to bed, I asked God to send him back safe from the war to us. Little, indeed, did I know what I was praying for!

One morning, I got into the big bed, and there, sure enough, was Father in his usual Santa Claus manner, but later, instead of uniform, he put on his best blue suit, and Mother was as pleased as anything. I saw nothing to be pleased about, because, out of uniform, Father was altogether less interesting, but she only beamed, and explained that our prayers had been answered, and off we went to Mass to thank God for having brought Father safely home.

The irony of it! That very day when he came in to dinner he took off his boots and put on his slippers, donned the dirty old cap he wore about the house to save him from colds, crossed his legs, and began to talk gravely to Mother, who looked anxious. Naturally, I disliked her looking anxious, because it destroyed her good looks, so I interrupted him.

"Just a moment, Larry!" she said gently.

This was only what she said when we had boring visitors, so I attached no importance to it and went on talking.

"Do be quiet, Larry!" she said impatiently. "Don't you hear me talking to Daddy?"

This was the first time I had heard those ominous words, "talking to Daddy," and I couldn't help feeling that if this was how God answered prayers, he couldn't listen to them very attentively.

"Why are you talking to Daddy?" I asked with as great a show of indifference as I could muster.

"Because Daddy and I have business to discuss. Now, don't interrupt again!"

In the afternoon, at Mother's request, Father took me for a walk. This time we went into town instead of out to the country, and I thought at first, in my usual optimistic way, that it might be an improvement. It was nothing of the sort. Father and I had quite different notions of a walk in town. He had no proper interest in trams, ships, and horses, and the only thing that seemed to divert him was talking to fellows as old as himself. When I wanted to stop he simply went on, dragging me behind him by the hand; when he wanted to stop I had no alternative but to do the same. I noticed that it seemed to be a sign that he wanted to stop for a long time whenever he leaned against a wall. The second time I saw him do it I got wild. He seemed to be settling himself forever. I pulled him by the coat and trousers, but, unlike Mother who, if you were too persistent, got into a wax and said: "Larry, if you don't behave yourself, I'll give you a good slap," Father had an extraordinary capacity for amiable inattention. I sized him up and wondered would I cry, but he seemed to be too remote to be annoyed even by that. Really, it was like going for a walk with a mountain! He either ignored the wrenching and pummeling entirely, or else glanced down with a grin of amusement from his peak. I had never met anyone so absorbed in himself as he seemed.

At teatime, "talking to Daddy" began again, complicated this time by the fact that he had an evening paper, and every few minutes he put it down and told Mother something new out of it. I felt this was foul play. Man for man, I was prepared to compete with him any time for Mother's attention, but when he had it all made up for him by other people it left me no chance. Several times I tried to change the subject without success.

"You must be quiet while Daddy is reading, Larry," Mother said impatiently.

It was clear that she either genuinely liked talking to Father better than talking to me, or else that he had some terrible hold on her which made her afraid to admit the truth.

"Mummy," I said that night when she was tucking me up, "do you think if I prayed hard God would send Daddy back to the war?"

She seemed to think about that for a moment.

"No, dear," she said with a smile. "I don't think he would."

"Why wouldn't he, Mummy?"

"Because there isn't a war any longer, dear."

"But, Mummy, couldn't God make another war, if He liked?"

"He wouldn't like to, dear. It's not God who makes wars, but bad people."

"Oh!" I said.

I was disappointed about that. I began to think that God wasn't quite what he was cracked up to be.

Next morning I woke at my usual hour, feeling like a bottle of champagne. I put out my feet and invented a long conversation in which Mrs. Right talked of the trouble she had with her own father till she put him in the Home. I didn't quite know what the Home was but it sounded the right place for Father. Then I got my chair and stuck my head out of the attic window. Dawn was just breaking, with a guilty air that made me feel I had caught it in the act. My head bursting with stories and schemes, I stumbled in next door, and in the half-darkness scrambled into the big bed. There was no room at Mother's side so I had to get between her and Father. For the time being I had forgotten about him, and for several minutes I sat bolt upright, racking my brains to know what I could do with him. He was taking up more than his fair share of the bed, and I couldn't get comfortable, so I gave him several kicks that made him grunt and stretch. He made room all right, though. Mother waked and felt for me. I settled back comfortably in the warmth of the bed with my thumb in my mouth.

"Mummy!" I hummed, loudly and contentedly.

"Sssh! dear," she whispered. "Don't wake Daddy!"

This was a new development, which threatened to be even more serious than "talking to Daddy." Life without my early-morning conferences was unthinkable.

"Why?" I asked severely.

"Because poor Daddy is tired."

This seemed to me a quite inadequate reason, and I was sickened by the sentimentality of her "poor Daddy." I never liked that sort of gush; it always struck me as insincere.

"Oh!" I said lightly. Then in my most winning tone: "Do you know where I want to go with you today, Mummy?"

"No, dear," she sighed.

"I want to go down the Glen and fish for thornybacks with my new net, and then I want to go out to the Fox and Hounds, and—"

"Don't-wake-Daddy!" she hissed angrily, clapping her hand across my mouth.

But it was too late. He was awake, or nearly so. He grunted and reached for the matches. Then he stared incredulously at his watch.

"Like a cup of tea, dear?" asked Mother in a meek, hushed voice I had never heard her use before. It sounded almost as though she were afraid.

"Tea?" he exclaimed indignantly. "Do you know what the time is?"

"And after that I want to go up the Rathcooney Road," I said loudly, afraid I'd forget something in all those interruptions.

"Go to sleep at once, Larry!" she said sharply.

I began to snivel. I couldn't concentrate, the way that pair went on, and smothering my early-morning schemes was like burying a family from the cradle.

Father said nothing, but lit his pipe and sucked it, looking out into the shadows without minding Mother or me. I knew he was mad. Every time I made a remark Mother hushed me irritably. I was mortified. I felt it wasn't fair; there was even something sinister in it. Every time I had pointed out to her the waste of making two beds when we could both sleep in one, she had told me it was healthier like that, and now here was this man, this stranger, sleeping with her without the least regard for her health!

He got up early and made tea, but though he brought Mother a cup he brought none for me.

"Mummy," I shouted, "I want a cup of tea, too."

"Yes, dear," she said patiently. "You can drink from Mummy's saucer."

That settled it. Either Father or I would have to leave the house. I didn't want to drink from Mother's saucer; I wanted to be treated as an equal in my own home, so, just to spite her, I drank it all and left none for her. She took that quietly, too.

But that night when she was putting me to bed she said gently:

"Larry, I want you to promise me something."

"What is it?" I asked.

"Not to come in and disturb poor Daddy in the morning. Promise?"

"Poor Daddy" again! I was becoming suspicious of everything involving that quite impossible man.

"Why?" I asked.

"Because poor Daddy is worried and tired and he doesn't sleep well."

"Why doesn't he, Mummy?"

"Well, you know, don't you, that while he was at the war Mummy got the pennies from the Post Office?"

"From Miss MacCarthy?"

"That's right. But now, you see, Miss MacCarthy hasn't any more pennies, so Daddy must go out and find us some. You know what would happen if he couldn't?"

"No," I said, "tell us."

"Well, I think we might have to go out and beg for them like the poor old woman on Fridays. We wouldn't like that, would we?"

"No," I agreed. "We wouldn't."

"So you'll promise not to come in and wake him?"

"Promise."

Mind you, I meant that. I knew pennies were a serious matter, and I was all against having to go out and beg like the old woman on Fridays. Mother laid out all my toys in a complete ring round the bed so that, whatever way I got out, I was bound to fall over one of them.

When I woke I remembered my promise all right. I got up and sat on the floor and played—for hours, it seemed to me. Then I got my chair and looked out the attic window for more hours. I wished it was time for Father to wake; I wished someone would make me a cup of tea. I didn't feel in the least like the sun; instead, I was bored and so very, very cold! I simply longed for the warmth and depth of the big featherbed.

At last I could stand it no longer. I went into the next room. As there was still no room at Mother's side I climbed over her and she woke with a start.

"Larry," she whispered, gripping my arm very tightly, "what did you promise?"

"But I did, Mummy," I wailed, caught in the very act. "I was quiet for ever so long."

"Oh, dear, and you're perished!" she said sadly, feeling me all over. "Now, if I let you stay will you promise not to talk?"

"But I want to talk, Mummy," I wailed.

"That has nothing to do with it," she said with a firmness that was new to me. "Daddy wants to sleep. Now, do you understand that?"

I understood it only too well. I wanted to talk, he wanted to sleep—whose house was it, anyway?

"Mummy," I said with equal firmness, "I think it would be healthier for Daddy to sleep in his own bed."

That seemed to stagger her, because she said nothing for a while.

"Now, once for all," she went on, "you're to be perfectly quiet or go back to your own bed. Which is it to be?"

The injustice of it got me down. I had convicted her out of her own mouth of inconsistency and unreasonableness, and she hadn't even attempted to reply. Full of spite, I gave Father a kick, which she didn't notice but which made him grunt and open his eyes in alarm.

"What time is it?" he asked in a panic-stricken voice, not looking at Mother but at the door, as if he saw someone there.

"It's early yet," she replied soothingly. "It's only the child. Go to sleep again. . . . Now, Larry," she added, getting out of bed, "you've wakened Daddy and you must go back."

This time, for all her quiet air, I knew she meant it, and knew that my principal rights and privileges were as good as lost unless I asserted them at once. As she lifted me, I gave a screech, enough to wake the dead, not to mind Father. He groaned.

"That damn child! Doesn't he ever sleep?"

"It's only a habit, dear," she said quietly, though I could see she was vexed.

"Well, it's time he got out of it," shouted Father, beginning to heave in the bed. He suddenly gathered all the bedclothes about him, turned to the wall, and then looked back over his shoulder with nothing showing only two small, spiteful, dark eyes. The man looked very wicked.

To open the bedroom door, Mother had to let me down, and I broke free and dashed for the farthest corner, screeching. Father sat bolt upright in bed.

"Shut up, you little puppy!" he said in a choking voice.

I was so astonished that I stopped screeching. Never, never had anyone spoken to me in that tone before. I looked at him incredulously and saw his face convulsed with rage. It was only then that I fully realized how God had codded me, listening to my prayers for the safe return of this monster.

"Shut up, you!" I bawled, beside myself.

"What's that you said?" shouted Father, making a wild leap out of the bed.

"Mick, Mick!" cried Mother. "Don't you see the child isn't used to you?"

"I see he's better fed than taught," snarled Father, waving his arms wildly. "He wants his bottom smacked."

All his previous shouting was as nothing to these obscene words referring to my person. They really made my blood boil.

"Smack your own!" I screamed hysterically. "Smack your own! Shut up! Shut up!"

At this he lost his patience and let fly at me. He did it with the lack of conviction you'd expect of a man under Mother's horrified eyes, and it ended up as a mere tap, but the sheer indignity of being struck at all by a stranger, a total stranger who had cajoled his way back from the war into our big bed as a result of my innocent intercession, made me completely dotty. I shrieked and shrieked, and danced in my bare feet, and Father, looking awkward and hairy in nothing but a short grey army shirt, glared down at me like a mountain out for murder. I think it must have been then that I realized he was jealous too. And there stood Mother in her nightdress, looking as if her heart was broken between us. I hoped she felt as she looked. It seemed to me that she deserved it all.

From that morning out my life was a hell. Father and I were enemies, open and avowed. We conducted a series of skirmishes against one another, he trying to steal my time with Mother and I his. When she was sitting on my bed, telling me a story, he took to looking for some pair of old boots which he alleged he had left behind him at the beginning of the war. While he talked to Mother I played loudly with my toys to show my total lack of concern. He created a terrible scene one evening when he came in from work and found me at his box, playing with his regimental badges, Gurkha knives and button-sticks. Mother got up and took the box from me.

"You mustn't play with Daddy's toys unless he lets you, Larry," she said severely. "Daddy doesn't play with yours."

For some reason Father looked at her as if she had struck him and then turned away with a scowl.

"Those are not toys," he growled, taking down the box again to see had I lifted anything. "Some of those curios are very rare and valuable."

But as time went on I saw more and more how he managed to alienate Mother and me. What made it worse was that I couldn't grasp his method or see what attraction he had for Mother. In every possible way he was less winning than I. He had a common accent and made noises at his tea. I thought for a while that it might be the newspapers she was interested in, so I made up bits of news of my own to read to her. Then I thought it might be the smoking, which I personally thought attractive, and took his pipes and went round the house dribbling into them till he caught me. I even made noises at my tea, but Mother only told me I was disgusting. It all seemed to hinge round that unhealthy habit of sleeping together, so I made a point of dropping into their bedroom and nosing round, talking to myself, so that they wouldn't know I was watching them, but they were never up to anything that I could see. In the end it beat me. It seemed to depend on being grown-up and giving people rings, and I realized I'd have to wait.

But at the same time I wanted him to see that I was only waiting, not giving up the fight. One evening when he was being particularly obnoxious, chattering away well above my head, I let him have it.

"Mummy," I said, "do you know what I'm going to do when I grow up?"

"No, dear," she replied. "What?"

"I'm going to marry you," I said quietly.

Father gave a great guffaw out of him, but he didn't take me in. I knew it must only be pretence. And Mother, in spite of everything, was pleased. I felt she was probably relieved to know that one day Father's hold on her would be broken.

"Won't that be nice?" she said with a smile.

"It'll be very nice," I said confidently. "Because we're going to have lots and lots of babies."

"That's right, dear," she said placidly. "I think we'll have one soon, and then you'll have plenty of company."

I was no end pleased about that because it showed that in spite of the way she gave in to Father she still considered my wishes. Besides, it would put the Geneys in their place.

It didn't turn out like that, though. To begin with, she was very preoccupied— I supposed about where she would get the seventeen and six—and though Father took to staying out late in the evenings it did me no particular good. She stopped taking me for walks, became as touchy as blazes, and smacked me for nothing at all. Sometimes I wished I'd never mentioned the confounded baby—I seemed to have a genius for bringing calamity on myself.

And calamity it was! Sonny arrived in the most appalling hullabaloo—even that much he couldn't do without a fuss—and from the first moment I disliked him. He was a difficult child—so far as I was concerned he was always difficult— and demanded far too much attention. Mother was simply silly about him, and couldn't see when he was only showing off. As company he was worse than useless. He slept all day, and I had to go round the house on tiptoe to avoid waking him. It wasn't any longer a question of not waking Father. The slogan now was "Don't-wake-Sonny!" I couldn't understand why the child wouldn't sleep at the proper time, so whenever Mother's back was turned I woke him. Sometimes to keep him awake I pinched him as well. Mother caught me at it one day and gave me a most unmerciful flaking.

One evening, when Father was coming in from work, I was playing trains in the front garden. I let on not to notice him; instead, I pretended to be talking to myself, and said in a loud voice: "If another bloody baby comes into this house, I'm going out."

Father stopped dead and looked at me over his shoulder.

"What's that you said?" he asked sternly.

"I was only talking to myself," I replied, trying to conceal my panic. "It's private."

He turned and went in without a word. Mind you, I intended it as a solemn warning, but its effect was quite different. Father started being quite nice to me. I could understand that, of course. Mother was quite sickening about Sonny. Even at mealtimes she'd get up and gawk at him in the cradle with an idiotic smile, and tell Father to do the same. He was always polite about it, but he looked so puzzled you could see he didn't know what she was talking about. He complained of the way Sonny cried at night, but she only got cross and said that Sonny never cried except when there was something up with him—which was a flaming lie, because Sonny never had anything up with him, and only cried for attention. It was really painful to see how simple minded she was. Father wasn't attractive, but he had a fine intelligence. He saw through Sonny, and now he knew that I saw through him as well.

One night I woke with a start. There was someone beside me in the bed. For one wild moment I felt sure it must be Mother, having come to her senses and left Father for good, but then I heard Sonny in convulsions in the next room, and Mother saying: "There! There! There!" and I knew it wasn't she. It was Father. He was lying beside me, wide awake, breathing hard and apparently as mad as hell.

After a while it came to me what he was mad about. It was his turn now. After turning me out of the big bed, he had been turned out himself. Mother had no consideration now for anyone but that poisonous pup, Sonny. I couldn't help feeling sorry for Father. I had been through it all myself, and even at that age I was magnanimous. I began to stroke him down and say: "There! There!" He wasn't exactly responsive.

"Aren't you asleep either?" he snarled.

"Ah, come on and put your arm around us, can't you?" I said, and he did, in a sort of way. Gingerly, I suppose, is how you'd describe it. He was very bony but better than nothing.

At Christmas he went out of his way to buy me a really nice model railway.

(1952)

Flannery O'Connor

THE LIFE YOU SAVE
MAY BE YOUR OWN

The old woman and her daughter were sitting on their porch when Mr. Shiftlet came up their road for the first time. The old woman slid to the edge of her chair and leaned forward, shading her eyes from the piercing sunset with her hand. The daughter could not see far in front of her and continued to play with her fingers. Although the old woman lived in this desolate spot with only her daughter and she had never seen Mr. Shiftlet before, she could tell, even from a distance, that he was a tramp and no one to be afraid of. His left coat sleeve was folded up to show there was only half an arm in it and his gaunt figure listed slightly to the side as if the breeze were pushing him. He had on a black town suit and a brown felt hat that was turned up in the front and down in the back and he carried a tin tool box by a handle. He came on, at an amble, up her road, his face turned toward the sun which appeared to be balancing itself on the peak of a small mountain.

The old woman didn't change her position until he was almost into her yard; then she rose with one hand fisted on her hip. The daughter, a large girl in a short blue organdy dress, saw him all at once and jumped up and began to stamp and point and make excited speechless sounds.

Mr. Shiftlet stopped just inside the yard and set his box on the ground and tipped his hat at her as if she were not in the least afflicted; then he turned toward the old woman and swung the hat all the way off. He had long black slick hair that hung flat from a part in the middle to beyond the tips of his ears on either side. His face descended in forehead for more than half its length and ended suddenly with his features just balanced over a jutting steel-trap jaw. He seemed to be a young man but he had a look of composed dissatisfaction as if he understood life thoroughly.

"Good evening," the old woman said. She was about the size of a cedar fence post and she had a man's gray hat pulled down low over her head.

The tramp stood looking at her and didn't answer. He turned his back and faced the sunset. He swung both his whole and his short arm up slowly so that they indicated an expanse of sky and his figure formed a crooked cross. The old woman watched him with her arms folded across her chest as if she were the owner of the sun, and the daughter watched, her head thrust forward and her fat helpless hands hanging at the wrists. She had long pink-gold hair and eyes as blue as a peacock's neck.

He held the pose for almost fifty seconds and then he picked up his box and came on to the porch and dropped down on the bottom step. "Lady," he said in a firm nasal voice, "I'd give a fortune to live where I could see me a sun do that every evening."

"Does it every evening," the old woman said and sat back down. The daughter sat down too and watched him with a cautious sly look as if he were a bird that had come up very close. He leaned to one side, rooting in his pants pocket, and in a second he brought out a package of chewing gum and offered her a piece. She took it and unpeeled it and began to chew without taking her eyes off him. He offered the old woman a piece but she only raised her upper lip to indicate she had no teeth.

Mr. Shiftlet's pale sharp glance had already passed over everything in the yard—the pump near the corner of the house and the big fig tree that three or four chickens were preparing to roost in—and had moved to a shed where he saw the square rusted back of an automobile. "You ladies drive?" he asked.

"That car ain't run in fifteen year," the old woman said. "The day my husband died, it quit running."

"Nothing is like it used to be, lady," he said. "The world is almost rotten."

"That's right," the old woman said. "You from around here?"

"Name Tom T. Shiftlet," he murmured, looking at the tires.

"I'm pleased to meet you," the old woman said. "Name Lucynell Crater and daughter Lucynell Crater. What you doing around here, Mr. Shiftlet?"

He judged the car to be about a 1928 or '29 Ford. "Lady," he said, and turned and gave her his full attention, "lemme tell you something. There's one of these doctors in Atlanta that's taken a knife and cut the human heart—the human heart," he repeated, leaning forward, "out of a man's chest and held it in his hand," and he held his hand out, palm up, as if it were slightly weighted with the human heart, "and studied it like it was a day-old chicken, and lady," he said, allowing a long significant pause in which his head slid forward and his clay-colored eyes brightened, "he don't know no more about it than you or me."

"That's right," the old woman said.

"Why, if he was to take that knife and cut into every corner of it, he still wouldn't know no more than you or me. What you want to bet?"

"Nothing," the old woman said wisely. "Where you come from, Mr. Shiftlet?"

He didn't answer. He reached into his pocket and brought out a sack of tobacco and a package of cigarette papers and rolled himself a cigarette, expertly with one hand, and attached it in a hanging position to his upper lip. Then he took a box of wooden matches from his pocket and struck one on his shoe. He held the burning match as if he were studying the mystery of flame while it traveled dangerously toward his skin. The daughter began to make loud noises and to point to his hand and shake her finger at him, but when the flame was just before touching him, he leaned down with his hand cupped over it as if he were going to set fire to his nose and lit the cigarette.

He flipped away the dead match and blew a stream of gray into the evening. A sly look came over his face. "Lady," he said, "nowadays, people'll do anything anyways. I can tell you my name is Tom T. Shiftlet and I come from Tarwater, Tennessee, but you never have seen me before: how you know I ain't lying? How you know my name ain't Aaron Sparks, lady, and I come from Singleberry, Georgia, or how you know it's not George Speeds and I come from Lucy, Alabama, or how you know I ain't Thompson Bright from Toolafalls, Mississippi?"

"I don't know nothing about you," the old woman muttered, irked.

"Lady," he said, "people don't care how they lie. Maybe the best I can tell you is, I'm a man; but listen, lady," he said and paused and made his tone more ominous still, "what is a man?"

The old woman began to gum a seed. "What you carry in that tin box, Mr. Shiftlet?" she asked.

"Tools," he said, put back. "I'm a carpenter."

"Well, if you come out here to work, I'll be able to feed you and give you a place to sleep but I can't pay. I'll tell you that before you begin," she said.

There was no answer at once and no particular expression on his face. He leaned back against the two-by-four that helped support the porch roof. "Lady," he said slowly, "there's some men that some things mean more to them than money." The old woman rocked without comment and the daughter watched the trigger that moved up and down in his neck. He told the old woman then that all most people were interested in was money, but he asked what a man was made for. He asked her if a man was made for money, or what. He asked her what she thought she was made for but she didn't answer, she only sat rocking and wondered if a one-armed man could put a new roof on her garden house. He asked a lot of questions that she didn't answer. He told her that he was twenty-eight years old and had lived a varied life. He had been a gospel singer, a foreman on the railroad, an assistant in an undertaking parlor, and he had come over the radio for three months with Uncle Roy and his Red Creek Wranglers. He said he had fought and bled in the Arm Service of his country and visited every foreign land and that everywhere he had seen people that didn't care if they did a thing one way or another. He said he hadn't been raised thataway.

A fat yellow moon appeared in the branches of the fig tree as if it were going to roost there with the chickens. He said that a man had to escape to the country to see the world whole and that he wished he lived in a desolate place like this where he could see the sun go down every evening like God make it to do.

"Are you married or are you single?" the old woman asked.

There was a long silence. "Lady," he asked finally, "where would you find an innocent woman today? I wouldn't have any of this trash I could just pick up."

The daughter was leaning very far down, hanging her head almost between her knees, watching him through a triangular door she had made in her overturned hair; and she suddenly fell in a heap on the floor and began to whimper. Mr. Shiftlet straightened her out and helped her get back in the chair.

"Is she your baby girl?" he asked.

"My only," the old woman said, "and she's the sweetest girl in the world. I wouldn't give her up for nothing on earth. She's smart too. She can sweep the floor, cook, wash, feed the chickens, and hoe. I wouldn't give her up for a casket of jewels."

"No," he said kindly, "don't ever let any man take her away from you."

"Any man come after her," the old woman said, " 'll have to stay around the place."

Mr. Shiftlet's eye in the darkness was focused on a part of the automobile bumper that glittered in the distance. "Lady," he said, jerking his short arm up as if he could point with it to her house and yard and pump, "there ain't a broken thing on this plantation that I couldn't fix for you, one-arm jackleg or not. I'm a man," he said with a sullen dignity, "even if I ain't a whole one. I got," he said, tapping his knuckles on the floor to emphasize the immensity of what he was going to say, "a moral intelligence!" and his face pierced out of the darkness into a shaft of doorlight and he stared at her as if he were astonished himself at this impossible truth.

The old woman was not impressed with the phrase. "I told you you could hang around and work for food," she said, "if you don't mind sleeping in that car yonder."

"Why listen, Lady," he said with a grin of delight, "the monks of old slept in their coffins!"

"They wasn't as advanced as we are," the old woman said.

The next morning he began on the roof of the garden house while Lucynell, the daughter, sat on a rock and watched him work. He had not been around a week before the change he had made in the place was apparent. He had patched the front and back steps, built a new hog pen, restored a fence, and taught Lucynell, who was completely deaf and had never said a word in her life, to say the word "bird." The big rosy-faced girl followed him everywhere, saying "Burrttddt ddbirrrttdt," and clapping her hands. The old woman watched from a distance, secretly pleased. She was ravenous for a son-in-law.

Mr. Shiftlet slept on the hard narrow back seat of the car with his feet out the side window. He had his razor and a can of water on a crate that served him as a bedside table and he put up a piece of mirror against the back glass and kept his coat neatly on a hanger that he hung over one of the windows.

In the evenings he sat on the steps and talked while the old woman and Lucynell rocked violently in their chairs on either side of him. The old woman's three mountains were black against the dark blue sky and were visited off and on by various planets and by the moon after it had left the chickens. Mr. Shiftlet pointed out that the reason he had improved this plantation was because he had taken a personal interest in it. He said he was even going to make the automobile run.

He had raised the hood and studied the mechanism and he said he could tell that the car had been built in the days when cars were really built. You take now, he said, one man puts in one bolt and another man puts in another bolt and another man puts in another bolt so that it's a man for a bolt. That's why you have to pay so much for a car: you're paying all those men. Now if you didn't have to pay but one man, you could get you a cheaper car and one that had had a personal interest taken in it, and it would be a better car. The old woman agreed with him that this was so.

Mr. Shiftlet said that the trouble with the world was that nobody cared, or stopped and took any trouble. He said he never would have been able to teach Lucynell to say a word if he hadn't cared and stopped long enough.

"Teach her to say something else," the old woman said.

"What you want her to say next?" Mr. Shiftlet asked.

The old woman's smile was broad and toothless and suggestive. "Teach her to say, 'sugarpie,'" she said.

Mr. Shiftlet already knew what was on her mind.

The next day he began to tinker with the automobile and that evening he told her that if she would buy a fan belt, he would be able to make the car run.

The old woman said she would give him the money. "You see that girl yonder?" she asked, pointing to Lucynell who was sitting on the floor a foot away, watching him, her eyes blue even in the dark. "If it was ever a man wanted to take her away, I would say, 'No man on earth is going to take that sweet girl of mine away from me!' but if he was to say, 'Lady, I don't want to take her away, I want her right here,' I would say, 'Mister, I don't blame you none. I wouldn't pass up a chance to live in a permanent place and get the sweetest girl in the world myself. You ain't no fool,' I would say."

The Short Story

. . . .

692

"How old is she?" Mr. Shiftlet asked casually.

"Fifteen, sixteen," the old woman said. The girl was nearly thirty but because of her innocence it was impossible to guess.

"It would be a good idea to paint it too," Mr. Shiftlet remarked. "You don't want it to rust out."

"We'll see about that later," the old woman said.

The next day he walked into town and returned with the parts he needed, and a can of gasoline. Late in the afternoon, terrible noises issued from the shed and the old woman rushed out of the house, thinking Lucynell was somewhere having a fit. Lucynell was sitting on a chicken crate, stamping her feet and screaming, "Burrddttt! bddurrddtttt!" but her fuss was drowned out by the car. With a volley of blasts it emerged from the shed, moving in a fierce and stately way. Mr. Shiftlet was in the driver's seat, sitting very erect. He had an expression of serious modesty on his face as if he had just raised the dead.

That night, rocking on the porch, the old woman began her business at once. "You want you an innocent woman, don't you?" she asked sympathetically. "You don't want none of this trash."

"No'm, I don't," Mr. Shiftlet said.

"One that can't talk," she continued, "can't sass you back or use foul language. That's the kind for you to have. Right there," and she pointed to Lucynell sitting cross-legged in her chair, holding both feet in her hands.

"That's right," he admitted. "She wouldn't give me any trouble."

"Saturday," the old woman said, "you and her and me can drive into town and get married."

Mr. Shiftlet eased his position on the steps.

"I can't get married right now," he said. "Everything you want to do takes money and I ain't got any."

"What you need with money?" she asked.

"It takes money," he said. "Some people'll do anything anyhow these days, but the way I think, I wouldn't marry no woman that I couldn't take on a trip like she was somebody. I mean take her to a hotel and treat her. I wouldn't marry the Duchesser Windsor," he said firmly, "unless I could take her to a hotel and give her something good to eat.

"I was raised thataway and there ain't a thing I can do about it. My old mother taught me how to do."

"Lucynell don't even know what a hotel is," the old woman muttered. "Listen here, Mr. Shiftlet," she said, sliding forward in her chair, "you'd be getting a permanent house and a deep well and the most innocent girl in the world. You don't need no money. Lemme tell you something: there ain't any place in the world for a poor disabled friendless drifting man."

The ugly words settled in Mr. Shiftlet's head like a group of buzzards in the top of a tree. He didn't answer at once. He rolled himself a cigarette and lit it and then he said in an even voice, "Lady, a man is divided into parts, body and spirit."

The old woman clamped her gums together.

"A body and a spirit," he repeated. "The body, lady, is like a house; it don't go anywhere; but the spirit, lady, is like a automobile: always on the move, always . . ."

"Listen, Mr. Shiftlet," she said, "my well never goes dry and my house is always warm in the winter and there's no mortgage on a thing about this place. You can go to the courthouse and see for yourself. And yonder under that shed is a fine automobile." She laid the bait carefully. "You can have it painted by Saturday. I'll pay for the paint."

In the darkness, Mr. Shiftlet's smile stretched like a weary snake waking up by a fire. "Yes'm," he said softly.

After a second he recalled himself and said, "I'm only saying a man's spirit means more to him than anything else. I would have to take my wife off for the weekend without no regards at all for cost. I got to follow where my spirit says to go."

"I'll give you fifteen dollars for a weekend trip," the old woman said in a crabbed voice. "That's the best I can do."

"That wouldn't hardly pay for more than the gas and the hotel," he said. "It wouldn't feed her."

"Seventeen-fifty," the old woman said. "That's all I got so it isn't any use you trying to milk me. You can take a lunch."

Mr. Shiftlet was deeply hurt by the word "milk." He didn't doubt that she had more money sewed up in her mattress but he had already told her he was not interested in her money. "I'll make that do," he said, and rose and walked off without treating with her further.

On Saturday the three of them drove into town in the car that the paint had barely dried on and Mr. Shiftlet and Lucynell were married in the Ordinary's office while the old woman witnessed. As they came out of the courthouse, Mr. Shiftlet began twisting his neck in his collar. He looked morose and bitter as if he had been insulted while someone held him. "That didn't satisfy me none," he said. "That was just something a woman in an office did, nothing but paper work and blood tests. What do they know about my blood? If they was to take my heart and cut it out," he said, "they wouldn't know a thing about me. It didn't satisfy me at all."

"It satisfied the law," the old woman said sharply.

"The law," Mr. Shiftlet said, and spit. "It's the law that don't satisfy me."

He had painted the car dark green with a yellow band around it just under the windows. The three of them climbed in the front seat and the old woman said, "Don't Lucynell look pretty? Looks like a baby doll." Lucynell was dressed up in a white dress that her mother had uprooted from a trunk and there was a Panama hat on her head with a bunch of red wooden cherries on the brim. Every now and then her placid expression was changed by a sly isolated little thought like a shoot of green in the desert. "You got a prize!" the old woman said.

Mr. Shiftlet didn't even look at her.

They drove back to the house to let the old woman off and pick up the lunch. When they were ready to leave, she stood staring in the window of the car, with her fingers clenched around the glass. Tears began to seep sideways out of her eyes and run along the dirty creases in her face. "I ain't ever been parted with her for two days before," she said.

Mr. Shiftlet started the motor.

"And I wouldn't let no man have her but you because I seen you would do right. Goodbye, Sugarbaby," she said, clutching at the sleeve of the white dress. Lucynell looked straight at her and didn't seem to see her there at all. Mr. Shiftlet eased the car forward so that she had to move her hands.

The early afternoon was clear and open and surrounded by pale blue sky. The hills flattened under the car one after another and the climb and dip and swerve went entirely to Mr. Shiftlet's head so that he forgot his morning bitterness. He had always wanted an automobile but he had never been able to afford one before. He drove very fast because he wanted to make Mobile by nightfall.

Occasionally he stopped his thoughts long enough to look at Lucynell in the seat beside him. She had eaten the lunch as soon as they were out of the yard and now she was pulling the cherries off the hat one by one and throwing them out the window. He became depressed in spite of the car. He had driven about a hundred miles when he decided that she must be hungry again and at the next small town they came to, he stopped in front of an aluminum-painted eating place called The Hot Spot and took her in and ordered her a plate of ham and grits. The ride had made her sleepy and as soon as she got up on the stool, she rested her head on the counter and shut her eyes. There was no one in The Hot Spot but Mr. Shiftlet and the boy behind the counter, a pale youth with a greasy rag hung over his shoulder. Before he could dish up the food, she was snoring gently.

"Give it to her when she wakes up," Mr. Shiftlet said. "I'll pay for it now."

The boy bent over her and stared at the long pink-gold hair and the half-shut sleeping eyes. Then he looked up and stared at Mr. Shiftlet. "She looks like an angel of Gawd," he murmured.

"Hitch-hiker," Mr. Shiftlet explained. "I can't wait. I got to make Tuscaloosa."

The boy bent over again and very carefully touched his finger to a strand of the golden hair and Mr. Shiftlet left.

He was more depressed than ever as he drove on by himself. The late afternoon had grown hot and sultry and the country had flattened out. Deep in the sky a storm was preparing very slowly and without thunder as if it meant to drain every drop of air from the earth before it broke. There were times when Mr. Shiftlet preferred not to be alone. He felt too that a man with a car had a responsibility to others and he kept his eye out for a hitch-hiker. Occasionally he saw a sign that warned: "Drive carefully. The life you save may be your own."

The narrow road dropped off on either side into dry fields and here and there a shack or a filling station stood in a clearing. The sun began to set directly in front of the automobile. It was a reddening ball that through his windshield was slightly flat on the bottom and top. He saw a boy in overalls and a gray hat standing on the edge of the road and he slowed the car down and stopped in front of him. The boy didn't have his hand raised to thumb the ride, he was only standing there, but he had a small cardboard suitcase and his hat was set on his head in a way to indicate that he had left somewhere for good. "Son," Mr. Shiftlet said, "I see you want a ride."

The boy didn't say he did or he didn't but he opened the door of the car and got in, and Mr. Shiftlet started driving again. The child held the suitcase on his lap and folded his arms on top of it. He turned his head and looked out the window away from Mr. Shiftlet. Mr. Shiftlet felt oppressed. "Son," he said after a minute, "I got the best old mother in the world so I reckon you only got the second best."

The boy gave him a quick dark glance and then turned his face back out the window.

"It's nothing so sweet," Mr. Shiftlet continued, "as a boy's mother. She taught him his first prayers at her knee, she give him love when no other would, she told him what was right and what wasn't, and she seen that he done the right thing. Son," he said, "I never rued a day in my life like the one I rued when I left that old mother of mine."

The boy shifted in his seat but he didn't look at Mr. Shiftlet. He unfolded his arms and put one hand on the door handle.

"My mother was a angel of Gawd," Mr. Shiftlet said in a very strained voice. "He took her from heaven and giver to me and I left her." His eyes were instantly clouded over with a mist of tears. The car was barely moving.

The boy turned angrily in the seat. "You go to the devil!" he cried. "My old woman is a flea bag and yours is a stinking pole cat!" and with that he flung the door open and jumped out with his suitcase into the ditch.

Mr. Shiftlet was so shocked that for about a hundred feet he drove along slowly with the door still open. A cloud, the exact color of the boy's hat and shaped like a turnip, had descended over the sun, and another, worse looking, crouched behind the car. Mr. Shiftlet felt that the rottenness of the world was about to engulf him. He raised his arm and let it fall again to his breast. "Oh, Lord!" he prayed. "Break forth and wash the slime from this earth!" (1953)

The Drama

Plots in dramas are in many respects like those in short stories: the overall patterns are similar, and the relationships between action and action, or between characters and actions, are similar.

Yet dramatic writing has peculiarities which the reader must keep in mind if he is to read it well. The unique purpose for which a play is written naturally influences its substance and form. Always the reader will find it useful to remember that a dramatic work—unless it is that rare thing, a "closet drama" —is a narrative form designed to be interpreted by actors on a stage in a theater. Dramatists as a result write primarily not for the general reader but for people of the theater likely to be concerned with stage presentations—producers, scene designers, directors, actors, and the like. The playwright sets down only what such specialists need—hints about the scenery, the actors, and the appearance of characters, plus everything the characters are to say.

When theatrical folk read dramas, they try to imagine exactly how such notations may be translated into an actual production. When the ordinary reader reads a play, he should, to the best of his ability, do the same thing. As Schlegel, a famous critic of drama, says, "In reading dramatic works, our habitual practice is to supply the representation." Like a producer or an actor, in other words, one should try to see what is implied by every detail which the author has given. One should form mental images of the theater and of the stage settings, and of the actors—their appearance, the quality of their voices and intonations, the nature of their gestures and movements. Furthermore, one should note the nature of the motivation, of the plot, and of the tone, in ways appropriate for the reading of plays.

This means that the reader should ask and answer—as well as he can— these questions: (1) How has the nature of the theater and of the audience shaped this play? (2) What are the implied thoughts, the feelings, and the motives of the characters in each scene? (3) How are the parts—the acts and scenes—important in the development of the whole play? (4) Is the tone that of tragedy, that of comedy, that of melodrama, that of farce, or a combination?

THEATER AND AUDIENCE

How has the nature of the theater and of the audience shaped this play?
Every drama is designed for performance at a certain time and in a certain place. The limitations and the possibilities of the theater to a large degree determine the substance of a play and shape its form. Clearly, for instance, the dramas presented under the open sky in the orchestral space of a Greek amphitheater (see p. 703) will differ greatly from those produced on the curtained and lighted stage of the modern playhouse. The scenic representation

The Shakespearean Theater

in Greek dramas, for one thing, was very different from scenic representation in modern productions. In the Greek dramas, it was simple and inflexible; in modern plays, it may be as elaborate as is necessary, and it may be completely changed one or more times in a play.

The audience, too, wields its influence. The physical position of the audience in relationship to the stage is bound to be important. In early theaters, down through the time of Shakespeare, the stage was in the midst of the audience or it at least projected into the audience. From that position, as time passed, it gradually receded until it came to be on the rim of a half circle occupied by the spectators. The result, naturally, was a decrease in the intimacy of the relationship between actor and spectator, and consequent changes in the dramas. In addition, audiences have varied from period to period in their make-up: sometimes they have been a cross section of a whole population, again they have been drawn from only one or two social classes. Since every dramatist wrote to please a particular audience, a knowledge of the education, the beliefs, and the psychology of the audience for which any play was written will help one understand the nature of its appeal.

Model of Globe Theatre used as basis for drawing by permission of John Cranford Adams and Irwin Smith.

THOUGHTS, FEELINGS, MOTIVES

What are the implied thoughts, the feelings, and the motives of the characters in each scene?

Because his work is designed not to be told but to be acted, the playwright, perforce, ordinarily uses the objective point of view (see p. 428). In some periods, conventions of the stage—understandings, as it were, between the playwright and the audience—allow the actors to speak their thoughts to the spectators in soliloquies and asides. In most periods, however, these are used sparingly, and in modern times they have almost entirely disappeared. Since the playwright cannot open the heads and breasts of living men and women to permit the audience to peer into their minds and hearts, he is forced to show motives indirectly by means of speeches and actions.

Such speeches and actions must be examined by the alert reader for implications. What, the reader must ask himself, lies behind that speech, that deed? Granted that this is what the character says and does, what is he really thinking and feeling? To answer these questions, one needs, obviously, to have a clear idea about the nature of the character—to know what his traits are, why he is likely to act as he does, how likely he is to unfold his true thoughts, how articulate he will be in analyzing his motives. But the method of showing characters makes this fairly difficult: the audience or reader comes to know the characters in a play only gradually—speech by speech, action by action. This means that in reading a play one should make an effort from the first scene to draw every possible inference about each character, modifying or supplementing these deductions as the play unfolds. In this way only is it possible to formulate with any precision the thoughts, the feelings, and the motivations of each character in every scene throughout the drama.

SCENES RELATED TO THE PLAY

How are the parts—the acts and scenes—important in the development of the whole play?

The reader of a drama should become aware of the general pattern of the actions, and of the relationship to this pattern of all other elements. After reading a drama, one should be able to see whatever foreshadowings there are of the events, and to comprehend the general course of all the actions from the beginning to the conclusion.

Not only should the reader notice the course of the whole play; he should also notice the relationship of the parts—the acts and scenes—to the whole work. The dramatist, as a rule, is forced to divide his story into acts and scenes. A continuous narrative such as occurs in some short stories is impossible, and summaries of action are for the most part impractical. This means that the dramatist must leave out many scenes which a fiction writer might portray, that he must be content with brief references to others, and that he must select and fully develop only those scenes which will best set forth the pattern of actions which makes up the plot of his drama. Therefore, the reader will learn much by considering the artistic justification for certain omissions and certain summaries, and, above all, for the complete working out of the chosen scenes. He will find it useful to notice exactly what each scene accomplishes—how, for instance, the opening scene or scenes offer an exposition (i.e., the details the audience needs to understand the initial situation) and how scenes and acts, in order, mark stages in the advancement of the plot to climactic developments, conflicts, or changes. To notice how the play progresses from scene to scene is an important step toward understanding and appreciating the whole work.

TONE IN DRAMA

Is the tone that of tragedy, that of comedy, that of melodrama, that of farce, or a combination?

The playwright, unlike other narrative writers, cannot lift his own voice to interpret the meanings of what he has written: the drama is a form in which explicit interpretation is an impossibility. The playwright cannot state directly his judgments of the characters and their deeds; nor can he tell what he wants his play to signify. However, he probably will choose a dramatic form which will give important clues concerning his attitude toward his material and the way he wants to have his work interpreted. Over the years, dramatists in general have found four chief forms satisfactory for this purpose—tragedy, comedy, melodrama, and farce.[1] When the reader discovers what choice among these forms a playwright has made, he defines the general tone of the play.

Concepts of *tragedy* have differed from period to period. (For one of the most famous statements of the nature of tragedy—and one that is still pertinent—see the selection from Aristotle's *Poetics*, p. 744.) Certain qualities of tragedy, however, have been fairly constant. One thing often said of tragedies is that they end unhappily, with the death, as a rule, of the hero or the heroine. Although there are some exceptions, tragedies usually do end disastrously. A playwright, however, cannot make a tragedy simply by tacking on an unhappy conclusion. Other things are important, indeed more important —notably, a preparation for the ending which indicates its inevitability and a treatment of a subject which in the minds of the immediate audience is highly serious. The conclusion of a tragedy, in other words, must be the logical outcome of the struggle of the protagonist against his opponents or against himself in a given situation. And the central conflict must be a struggle which the audience believes is significant—man against the gods, say, or against fate, or against the promptings of his own character. Furthermore, such a conflict must be treated, not playfully, but seriously.

1. At one time and another, dramatists have used other forms—miracle plays, medieval mysteries, tragicomedies, chronical plays, heroic plays, and so forth. Each type was written during a period or series of periods during which it appealed to contemporary audiences. The four forms listed here are more enduring and will suffice for the present purposes.

Since it treats a vital conflict seriously, tragedy at its best is found to have universal significance. The reader notes that the plight of the protagonist is similar to a plight in which he may find himself—that the problems of the play, whether ancient or modern, are in a sense his problems, too. As a result, he finds a meaning for himself in the inevitable outcome. Furthermore, he probably finds that not only the meaning but also the emotional effect is universal: he pities the suffering protagonist and shares his terror of the inescapable catastrophe.

Although, like tragedy, *comedy* has taken many forms during the ages, ordinarily it does not so deeply engage the sympathies of the audience or the reader as does tragedy. Some comedies, as a matter of fact, do not arouse much sympathy or much dislike for the characters: they ridicule or satirize their traits, their manners, and their foibles. Therefore, the appeal of these plays is largely an intellectual one—an appeal to the audience's or the reader's sense of the incongruous. Other comedies do, it is true, arouse sympathy for some characters, dislike for others; and their author hopes that after sharing the troubles of the attractive characters, the audience will share their delight in a happy ending. Even in such comedies, though, there will be no life and death struggles such as tragedies portray. The ending, as a matter of fact, will often show that the difficulties after all were not nearly so serious as the characters took them to be. The mood will not be desperate and grim but easy-going and good-natured. Most comedies will not, however, be exclusively intellectual or emotional in appeal: they will be a combination in which one appeal predominates.

Regardless of the proportions of intellectual and emotional appeal, a comedy (if the author succeeds) will not very deeply stir the audience which views it. The audience will not be moved to pity and terror but—at most— to sympathy mingled with amusement. It will be amiable and tolerant of the sympathetic characters, rather than violently partisan. Nevertheless, the best comedies have their universal qualities. Like tragedies, they reveal human nature and comment upon human philosophy, human values. Although they usually portray man in his lighter moments, they often say very important things about him.

Melodrama and *farce* are counterparts, respectively, of tragedy and comedy —counterparts, however, on a lower level. The lowness of the level is evident in the nature of the conflicts they portray, the emphasis they place upon action, their lack of significant commentary, and their appeal. The conflicts they portray are external rather than internal, trivial rather than important, temporary rather than universal. Melodramas and farces are crammed with action —action, however, which is often developed at the expense of characterization. Therefore, they contain little serious consideration of life and its problems, and they appeal in rather obvious ways to the heart and to the mind of the audience and of the reader.

At times melodramatic or farcical scenes occur in tragedies or comedies. When they do, the viewer or reader should note the clash of tones, the shift

In interest, and the effect upon the drama as a whole. Such variations are not necessarily bad: witness the broadly comic scene provided by the drunken porter immediately following the murder of the king in *Macbeth*. Shakespeare uses this scene to provide what critics refer to as "comic relief."

Of course, it is not enough simply to classify a play as tragedy, comedy, melodrama, or farce. It is necessary, in addition, to see exactly what the nature of this particular play is—what it reveals by its characterization, its plot, its concern or lack of concern with important human problems.

Sophocles

OEDIPUS THE KING

Sophocles (?496 B.C.–406 B.C.) was one of the great trio of Greek tragic authors; the other two were Aeschylus (525 B.C.–456 B.C.) and Euripides (485 B.C.–406 B.C.). The plays of these three were produced in the age of Pericles (490 B.C.–429 B.C.) or shortly after. The masterpiece of Greek drama, by general agreement, Sophocles' *Oedipus Tyrannus* (425 B.C.), though outstanding, was in many ways a typical product of the Greek period.

Perhaps the most important fact to keep in mind about Greek drama is that it was always closely associated with religious ritual. The tragedies were performed at annual Feasts of Dionysus, in a structure which was dedicated to the god of wine. These dramas used poetry, dancing, and music to recount legends about heroes and gods who were the ancestors of the people of Greece—legends known in detail by playwrights and audiences alike. Naturally, there was a ritualistic quality about plays which unfolded time-hallowed stories.

Although the theater in which *Oedipus* and other tragedies were presented was a temple of Dionysus, it differed greatly from any temple we know today. With its 17,000 seats arranged in semicircular tiers on a hillside, it somewhat resembled a present-day football stadium. From the seats, the spectators looked down on a circular dancing place about sixty feet in diameter—"the orchestra"—in the center of which stood a statue of Dionysus. Beyond this circular space, they saw a stage, perhaps slightly elevated, sixty feet wide but not very deep. Beyond the stage, finally, they saw a "scene building"—a temple which furnished a background and which also served as the actors' dressing room.

The actors, who as a rule appeared only on the stage, naturally differed a great deal from the actors of today because of the nature of the dramas and of the huge open-air theater in which they performed. By padding their flowing robes and by donning shoes which increased their stature, they made themselves both visible and impressive. The colors of their robes at times indicated their station (purple for royalty, for instance), and at times symbolized emotions to be associated with them (dark or dim colors for mourning, for example). They wore masks which made their features distinctive when viewed at a distance and which suggested the emotions of the characters. The masks also increased the actors' height and, like megaphones, added to the carrying power of their voices. The tragedians did not strive, as modern actors do, for lifelike intonations: instead, they declaimed their lines somewhat in the fashion of an old-time orator, and, when they came to highly emotional or lyrical passages,

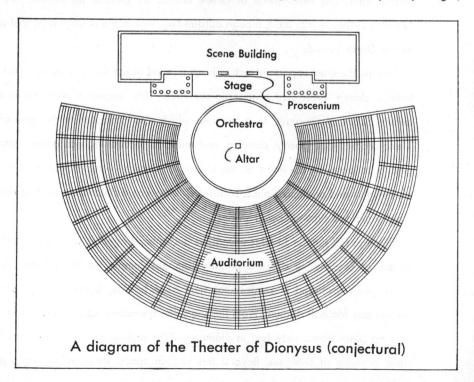

A diagram of the Theater of Dionysus (conjectural)

A performance in the Theater of Dionysus

they sang to the accompaniment of a flute. In some ways, therefore, Greek dramatic presentation was like modern operatic presentation. The method of production, as one would expect, greatly influenced the playwrights. Dramatists characterized not complexly but rather simply, not with subtle details but with broad strokes. They gave the figures in their plays lines which were majestic in diction, formal in movement—closer to oratory or to operatic arias than to lifelike talk. And they kept in mind the kind of scenic background against which all plays had to be presented.

During the whole course of every play, a "chorus" of from twelve to fifteen figures, wearing identical costumes and masks, danced and sang in unison in the orchestra. They were somewhat like a ballet in a modern musical comedy or an opera, for their movements interpreted the action. While the actors recited their lines, the chorus, drawn up in two rows, faced the stage and made interpretive gestures. During choral odes, the chorus faced the audience, sang, and danced about the altar. These odes at times were explanatory, at times narrative, at times philosophical; always, however, the dramatist made them an integral part of his play.

The audience which viewed these opera-like plays was made up of the free population of Athens, with the possible exception of the women of the city. It was a demonstrative group which loudly expressed its approval or disapproval of plays and actors, but it was also, evidently, a discriminating group which appreciated the best plays. It shared the religious beliefs incorporated in the plays, the beliefs, for instance, that overweening pride was one of the greatest of sins, and that sin (whether deliberate or unintentional) inevitably would be punished. It also shared with the dramatist a knowledge of the story which he was dramatizing. Thus, in viewing *Oedipus*, when the king spoke of his world-wide renown, they knew not only that retribution was inevitable: they knew precisely what form it would take—that of a horrible discovery toward which the king moved during the course of the drama.

CHARACTERS

OEDIPUS *the King*	MESSENGER
PRIEST	SECOND MESSENGER
CREON, *the brother-in-law of* OEDIPUS	ANTIGONE ⎫ *daughters of* OEDIPUS
TEIRESIAS	ISMENE ⎬
JOCASTA, *the wife of* OEDIPUS	CHORUS
HERDSMAN	

Scene: In front of the palace of OEDIPUS *at Thebes. To the right of the stage near the altar stands the* PRIEST *with a crowd of children.* OEDIPUS *emerges from the central door.*

OEDIPUS. Children, young sons and daughters of old Cadmus,
why do you sit here with your suppliant crowns?
The town is heavy with a mingled burden
of sounds and smells, of groans and hymns and incense;
I did not think it fit that I should hear
of this from messengers but came myself,—
I Oedipus whom all men call the Great. (*He turns to the* PRIEST)

You're old and they are young; come, speak for them.
What do you fear or want, that you sit here
suppliant? Indeed I'm willing to give all
that you may need; I would be very hard
should I not pity suppliants like these.
PRIEST. O ruler of my country, Oedipus,
  you see our company around the altar;
  you see our ages; some of us, like these,
  who cannot yet fly far, and some of us
  heavy with age; these children are the chosen
  among the young, and I the priest of Zeus.
  Within the market place sit others crowned
  with suppliant garlands, at the double shrine
  of Pallas and the temple where Ismenus
  gives oracles by fire. King, you yourself
  have seen our city reeling like a wreck
  already; it can scarcely lift its prow
  out of the depths, out of the bloody surf.
  A blight is on the fruitful plants of the earth,
  a blight is on the cattle in the fields,
  a blight is on our women that no children
  are born to them; a God that carries fire,
  a deadly pestilence, is on our town,
  strikes us and spares not, and the house of Cadmus
  is emptied of its people while black Death
  grows rich in groaning and in lamentation.
  We have not come as suppliants to this altar
  because we thought of you as of a God,
  but rather judging you the first of men
  in all the chances of this life and when
  we mortals have to do with more than man.
  You came and by your coming saved our city,
  freed us from tribute which we paid of old
  to the Sphinx, cruel singer. This you did
  in virtue of no knowledge we could give you,
  in virtue of no teaching; it was God
  that aided you, men say, and you are held
  with God's assistance to have saved our lives.
  Now, Oedipus, whom all men call the Greatest,
  here falling at your feet we all entreat you,
  find us some strength for rescue.
  Perhaps you'll hear a wise word from some God,
  perhaps you will learn something from a man
  (for I have seen that for the skilled of practice
  the outcome of their counsels live the most).

Noblest of men, go, and raise up our city,
go,—and give heed. For now this land of ours
calls you its savior since you saved it once.
So, let us never speak about your reign
as of a time when first our feet were set
secure on high, but later fell to ruin.
Raise up our city, save it and raise it up.
Once you have brought us luck with happy omen;
be no less now in fortune.
If you will rule this land, as now you rule it,
better to rule it full of men than empty.
For neither town nor ship is anything
when empty, and none live in it together.

OEDIPUS. Poor children! You have come to me entreating,
but I have known the story before you told it
only too well. I know you are all sick,
yet there is not one of you, sick though you are,
that is as sick as I myself.
Your several sorrows each have single scope
and touch but one of you. My spirit groans
for city and myself and you at once.
You have not roused me like a man from sleep;
know that I have given many tears to this,
gone many ways wandering in thought,
but as I thought I found only one remedy
and that I took. I sent Menoeceus' son
Creon, Jocasta's brother, to Apollo,
to his Pythian temple,
that he might learn there by what act or word
I could save this city. As I count the days,
it vexes me what ails him; he is gone
far longer than he needed for the journey.
But when he comes, then, may I prove a villain,
if I shall not do all the God commands.

PRIEST. Thanks for your gracious words. Your servants here
signal that Creon is this moment coming.

OEDIPUS. His face is bright. O holy Lord Apollo,
grant that his news too may be bright for us
and bring us safety.

PRIEST. It is happy news,
I think, for else his head would not be crowned
with sprigs of fruitful laurel.

OEDIPUS.   We will know soon,
he's within hail. Lord Creon, my good brother,
what is the word you bring us from the God?

(CREON *enters*)

CREON. A good word,—for things hard to bear themselves
  if in the final issue all is well
  I count complete good fortune.

OEDIPUS.   What do you mean?
  What you have said so far
  leaves me uncertain whether to trust or fear.

CREON. If you will hear my news before these others
  I am ready to speak, or else to go within.

OEDIPUS. Speak it to all;
  the grief I bear, I bear it more for these
  than for my own heart.

CREON.   I will tell you, then,
  what I heard from the God.
  King Phoebus in plain words commanded us
  to drive out a pollution from our land,
  pollution grown ingrained within the land;
  drive it out, said the God, not cherish it,
  till it's past cure.

OEDIPUS.   What is the rite
  of purification? How shall it be done?

CREON. By banishing a man, or expiation
  of blood by blood, since it is murder guilt
  which holds our city in this storm of death.

OEDIPUS. Who is this man whose fate the God pronounces?

CREON. My Lord, before you piloted the state
  we had a king called Laius.

OEDIPUS. I know of him by hearsay. I have not seen him.

CREON. The God commanded clearly: let some one
  punish with force this dead man's murderers.

OEDIPUS. Where are they in the world? Where would a trace
  of this old crime be found? It would be hard
  to guess where.

CREON.   The clue is in this land;
  that which is sought is found;
  the unheeded thing escapes:
  so said the God.

OEDIPUS.   Was it at home,
  or in the country that death came upon him,
  or in another country travelling?

CREON. He went, he said himself, upon an embassy,
  but never returned when he set out from home.

OEDIPUS. Was there no messenger, no fellow traveller
  who knew what happened? Such a one might tell
  something of use.

CREON. They were all killed save one. He fled in terror
and he could tell us nothing in clear terms
of what he knew, nothing, but one thing only.
OEDIPUS. What was it?
If we could even find a slim beginning
in which to hope, we might discover much.
CREON. This man said that the robbers they encountered
were many and the hands that did the murder
were many; it was no man's single power.
OEDIPUS. How could a robber dare a deed like this
were he not helped with money from the city,
money and treachery?
CREON.   That indeed was thought.
But Laius was dead and in our trouble
there was none to help.
OEDIPUS. What trouble was so great to hinder you
inquiring out the murder of your king?
CREON. The riddling Sphinx induced us to neglect
mysterious crimes and rather seek solution
of troubles at our feet.
OEDIPUS. I will bring this to light again. King Phoebus
fittingly took this care about the dead,
and you too fittingly.
And justly you will see in me an ally,
a champion of my country and the God.
For when I drive pollution from the land
I will not serve a distant friend's advantage,
but act in my own interest. Whoever
he was that killed the king may readily
wish to dispatch me with his murderous hand;
so helping the dead king I help myself.

Come children, take your suppliant boughs and go;
up from the altars now. Call the assembly
and let it meet upon the understanding
that I'll do everything. God will decide
whether we prosper or remain in sorrow.
PRIEST. Rise, children—it was this we came to seek,
which of himself the king now offers us.
May Phoebus who gave us the oracle
come to our rescue and stay the plague.
(*Exeunt all but the* CHORUS)
CHORUS
(*Strophe*)
What is the sweet spoken word of God from the shrine of Pytho rich in gold

that has come to glorious Thebes?
I am stretched on the rack of doubt, and terror and trembling hold
my heart, O Delian Healer, and I worship full of fears
for what doom you will bring to pass, new or renewed in the revolving years.
Speak to me, immortal voice,
child of Golden Hope.

(*Antistrophe*)

First I call on you, Athene, deathless daughter of Zeus,
and Artemis, Earth Upholder,
who sits in the midst of the market place in the throne which men call Fame,
and Phoebus, the Far Shooter, three averters of Fate,
come to us now, if ever before, when ruin rushed upon the state,
you drove destruction's flame away
out of our land.

(*Strophe*)

Our sorrows defy number;
all the ship's timbers are rotten;
taking of thought is no spear for the driving away of the plague.
There are no growing children in this famous land;
there are no women staunchly bearing the pangs of childbirth.
You may see them one with another, like birds swift on the wing,
quicker than fire unmastered,
speeding away to the coast of the Western God.

(*Antistrophe*)

In the unnumbered deaths
of its people the city dies;
those children that are born lie dead on the naked earth
unpitied, spreading contagion of death; and grey haired mothers and wives
everywhere stand at the altar's edge, suppliant moaning;
the hymn to the healing God rings out but with it the wailing voices are
         blended.
From these our sufferings grant us, O golden Daughter of Zeus,
glad faced deliverance.

(*Strophe*)

There is no clash of brazen shields but our fight is with the War God,
a War God ringed with the cries of men, a savage God who burns us;
grant that he turn in racing course backwards out of our country's bounds
to the great palace of Amphitrite or where the waves of the Thracian sea
deny the stranger safe anchorage.
Whatsoever escapes the night
at last the light of day revisits;
so smite the War God, Father Zeus,
beneath your thunderbolt,
for you are the Lord of the lightning, the lightning that
carries fire.

(*Antistrophe*)
  And your unconquered arrow shafts, winged by the golden corded bow,
  Lycean King, I beg to be at our side for help;
  and the gleaming torches of Artemis with which she scours the Lycean hills,
  and I call on the God with the turban of gold, who gave his name to this
        country of ours,
  the Bacchic God with the wine flushed face,
  Evian One, who travel
  with the Maenad company,
  combat the God that burns us
  with your torch of pine;
  for the God that is our enemy is a God unhonoured among the Gods.
(OEDIPUS *returns*)
OEDIPUS. For what you ask me—if you will hear my words,
  and hearing welcome them and fight the plague,
  you will find strength and lightening of your load.

  Hark to me; what I say to you, I say
  as one that is a stranger to the story
  as stranger to the deed. For I would not
  be far upon the track if I alone
  were tracing it without a clue. But now,
  since after all was finished, I became
  a citizen among you, citizens—
  now I proclaim to all the men of Thebes:
  who so among you knows the murderer
  by whose hand Laius, son of Labdacus,
  died—I command him to tell everything
  to me,—yes, though he fears himself to take the blame
  on his own head; for bitter punishment
  he shall have none, but leave this land unharmed.
  Or if he knows the murderer, another,
  a foreigner, still let him speak the truth.
  For I will pay him and be grateful, too.
  But if you shall keep silence, if perhaps
  some one of you, to shield a guilty friend,
  or for his own sake shall reject my words—
  hear what I shall do then:
  I forbid that man, whoever he be, my land,
  my land where I hold sovereignty and throne;
  and I forbid any to welcome him
  or cry him greeting or make him a sharer
  in sacrifice or offering to the Gods,
  or give him water for his hands to wash.

I command all to drive him from their homes,
since he is our pollution, as the oracle
of Pytho's God proclaimed him now to me.
So I stand forth a champion of the God
and of the man who died.
Upon the murderer I invoke this curse—
whether he is one man and all unknown,
or one of many—may he wear out his life
in misery to miserable doom!
If with my knowledge he lives at my hearth
I pray that I myself may feel my curse.

Even were this no matter of God's ordinance
it would not fit you so to leave it lie,
unpurified, since a good man is dead
and one that was a king. Search it out.
Since I am now the holder of his office,
and have his bed and wife that once was his,
and had his line not been unfortunate
we would have common children—(fortune leaped
upon his head)—because of all these things,
I fight in his defence as for my father,
and I shall try all means to take the murderer
of Laius the son of Labdacus
the son of Polydorus and before him
of Cadmus and before him of Agenor.
Those who do not obey me, may the Gods
grant no crops springing from the ground they plough
nor children to their women! May a fate
like this, or one still worse than this consume them!
For you who these words please, the other Thebans,
may Justice as your ally and all the Gods
live with you, blessing you now and for ever!
CHORUS. As you have held me to my oath, I speak:
   I neither killed the king nor can declare
   the killer; but since Phoebus set the quest
   it is his part to tell who the man is.
OEDIPUS. Right; but to put compulsion on the Gods
   against their will—no man has strength for that.
CHORUS. May I then say what I think second best?
OEDIPUS. If there's a third best, too, spare not to tell it.
CHORUS. I know that what the Lord Teiresias
   sees, is most often what the Lord Apollo
   sees. If you should inquire of this from him
   you might find out most clearly.

OEDIPUS. Even in this my actions have not been sluggard.
  On Creon's word I have sent two messengers
  and why the prophet is not here already
  I have been wondering.
CHORUS.   His skill apart
  there is besides only an old faint story.
OEDIPUS. What is it?
  I seize on every story.
CHORUS.   It was said
  that he was killed by certain wayfarers.
OEDIPUS. I heard that, too, but no one saw the killer.
CHORUS. Yet if he has a share of fear at all,
  his courage will not stand firm, hearing your curse.
OEDIPUS. The man who in the doing did not shrink
  will fear no word.
CHORUS.   Here comes his prosecutor:
  led by your men the godly prophet comes
  in whom alone of mankind truth is native.
(*Enter* TEIRESIAS, *led by a little boy*)
OEDIPUS. Teiresias, you are versed in everything,
  things teachable and things not to be spoken,
  things of the heaven and earth-creeping things.
  You have no eyes but in your mind you know
  with what a plague our city is afflicted.
  My lord, in you alone we find a champion,
  in you alone one that can rescue us.
  Perhaps you have not heard the messengers,
  but Phoebus sent in answer to our sending
  an oracle declaring that our freedom
  from this disease would only come when we
  should learn the names of those who killed King Laius,
  and kill them or expel from our country.
  Do not begrudge us oracles from birds,
  or any other way of prophecy
  within your skill; save yourself and the city,
  save me; redeem the debt of our pollution
  that lies on us because of this dead man.
  We are in your hands; it is the finest task
  to help another when you have means and power.
TEIRESIAS. Alas, how terrible is wisdom when
  it brings no profit to the man that's wise!
  This I knew well, but had forgotten it,
  else I would not have come here.
OEDIPUS.   What is this?
  How sad you are now you have come!

TEIRESIAS.   Let me
go home. It will be easiest for us both
to bear our several destinies to the end
if you will follow my advice.
OEDIPUS.   You'd rob us
of this your gift of prophecy? You talk
as one who had no care for law nor love
for Thebes who reared you.
TEIRESIAS. Yes, but I see that even your own words
miss the mark; therefore I must fear for mine.
OEDIPUS. For God's sake if you know of anything,
do not turn from us; all of us kneel to you,
all of us here, your suppliants.
TEIRESIAS. All of you here know nothing. I will not
bring to the light of day my troubles, mine—
rather than call them yours.
OEDIPUS.   What do you mean?
You know of something but refuse to speak.
Would you betray us and destroy the city?
TEIRESIAS. I will not bring this pain upon us both,
neither on you nor on myself. Why is it
you question me and waste your labour? I
will tell you nothing.
OEDIPUS. You would provoke a stone! Tell us, you villain,
tell us, and do not stand there quietly
unmoved and balking at the final issue.
TEIRESIAS. You blame my temper but you do not see
your own that lives within you; it is me
you chide.
OEDIPUS. Who would not feel his temper rise
at words like these with which you shame our city?
TEIRESIAS. Of themselves things will come, although I hide them
and breathe no word of them.
OEDIPUS.   Since they will come
tell them to me.
TEIRESIAS.   I will say nothing further.
Against this answer let your temper rage
as wildly as you will.
OEDIPUS.   Indeed I am
so angry I shall not hold back a jot
of what I think. For I would have you know
I think you were complotter of the deed
and doer of the deed save in so far
as for the actual killing. Had you had eyes
I would have said alone you murdered him.

TEIRESIAS. Yes? Then I warn you faithfully to keep
the letter of your proclamation and
from this day forth to speak no word of greeting
to these nor me; you are the land's pollution.
OEDIPUS. How shamelessly you started up this taunt!
How do you think you will escape?
TEIRESIAS.   I have.
I have escaped; the truth is what I cherish
and that's my strength.
OEDIPUS.   And who has taught you truth?
Not your profession surely!
TEIRESIAS.   You have taught me,
for you have made me speak against my will.
OEDIPUS. Speak what? Tell me again that I may learn it better.
TEIRESIAS. Did you not understand before or would you
provoke me into speaking?
OEDIPUS.   I did not grasp it,
not so to call it known. Say it again.
TEIRESIAS. I say you are the murderer of the king
whose murderer you seek.
OEDIPUS.   Not twice you shall
say calumnies like this and stay unpunished.
TEIRESIAS. Shall I say more to tempt your anger more?
OEDIPUS. As much as you desire; it will be said
in vain.
TEIRESIAS. I say that with those you love best
you live in foulest shame unconsciously
and do not see where you are in calamity.
OEDIPUS. Do you imagine you can always talk
like this, and live to laugh at it hereafter?
TEIRESIAS. Yes, if the truth has anything of strength.
OEDIPUS. It has, but not for you; it has no strength
for you because you are blind in mind and ears
as well as in your eyes.
TEIRESIAS.   You are a poor wretch
to taunt me with the very insults which
every one soon will heap upon yourself.
OEDIPUS. Your life is one long night so that you cannot
hurt me or any other who sees the light.
TEIRESIAS. It is not fate that I should be your ruin,
Apollo is enough; it is his care
to work this out.
OEDIPUS.   Was this your own design
or Creon's?

TEIRESIAS. Creon is no hurt to you,
  but you are to yourself.
OEDIPUS. Wealth, sovereignty and skill outmatching skill
  for the contrivance of an envied life,
  great store of jealousy fill your treasury chests,
  if my friend Creon, friend from the first and loyal,
  thus secretly attacks me, secretly
  desires to drive me out and secretly
  suborns this juggling, trick devising quack,
  this wily beggar who has only eyes
  for his own gains, but blindness in his skill.
  For, tell me, where have you seen clear, Teiresias,
  with your prophetic eyes? When the dark singer,
  the sphinx, was in your country, did you speak
  word of deliverance to its citizens?
  And yet the riddle's answer was not the province
  of a chance comer. It was a prophet's task
  and plainly you had no such gift of prophecy
  from birds nor otherwise from any God
  to glean a word of knowledge. But I came,
  Oedipus, who knew nothing, and I stopped her.
  I solved the riddle by my wit alone.
  Mine was no knowledge got from birds. And now
  you would expel me,
  because you think that you will find a place
  by Creon's throne. I think you will be sorry,
  both you and your accomplice, for your plot
  to drive me out. And did I not regard you
  as an old man, some suffering would have taught you
  that what was in your heart was treason.
CHORUS. We look at this man's words and yours, my king,
  and we find both have spoken them in anger.
  We need no angry words but only thought
  how we may best hit the God's meaning for us.
TEIRESIAS. If you are king, at least I have the right
  no less to speak in my defence against you.
  Of that much I am master. I am no slave
  of yours, but Loxias', and so I shall not
  enroll myself with Creon for my patron.
  Since you have taunted me with being blind,
  here is my word for you.
  You have your eyes but see not where you are
  in sin, nor where you live, nor whom you live with.
  Do you know who your parents are? Unknowing

you are an enemy to kith and kin
in death, beneath the earth, and in this life.
A deadly footed, double-striking curse,
from father and mother both, shall drive you forth
out of this land, with darkness on your eyes,
that now have such straight vision. Shall there be
a place will not be harbour to your cries,
a corner of Cithaeron will not ring
in echo to your cries, soon, soon,—
when you shall learn the secret of your marriage,
which steered you to a haven in this house,—
haven no haven, after lucky voyage?
And of the multitude of other evils
establishing a grim equality
between you and your children, you know nothing.
So, muddy with contempt my words and Creon's!
There is no man shall perish as you shall.

OEDIPUS. Is it endurable that I should hear
  such words from him? Go and a curse go with you!
  Quick, home with you! Out of my house at once!

TEIRESIAS. I would not have come either had you not called me.

OEDIPUS. I did not know then you would talk like a fool—
  or it would have been long before I called you.

TEIRESIAS. I am a fool then, as it seems to you—
  but to the parents who have bred you, wise.

OEDIPUS. What parents? Stop! Who are they of all the world?

TEIRESIAS. This day will show your birth and bring your ruin.

OEDIPUS. How needlessly your riddles darken everything.

TEIRESIAS. But it's in riddle answering you are strongest.

OEDIPUS. Yes. Taunt me where you will find me great.

TEIRESIAS. It is this very luck that has destroyed you.

OEDIPUS. I do not care, if it has served this city.

TEIRESIAS. Well, I will go. Come, boy, lead me away.

OEDIPUS. Yes, lead him off. So long as you are here,
  you'll be a stumbling block and a vexation;
  once gone, you will not trouble me again.

TEIRESIAS.   I have said
  what I came here to say not fearing your
  countenance: there is no way you can hurt me.
  I tell you, king, this man, this murderer
  (whom you have long declared you are in search of,
  indicting him in threatening proclamation
  as murderer of Laius)—he is here.
  In name he is a stranger among citizens
  but soon he will be shown to be a citizen

true native Theban, and he'll have no joy
of the discovery: blindness for sight
and beggary for riches his exchange,
he shall go journeying to a foreign country
tapping his way before him with a stick.
He shall be proved father and brother both
to his own children in his house; to her
that gave him birth, a son and husband both;
a fellow sower in his father's bed
with that same father that he murdered.
Go within, reckon that out, and if you find me
mistaken, say I have no skill in prophecy.

(*Exeunt separately* TEIRESIAS *and* OEDIPUS)

CHORUS

(*Strophe*)

Who is the man proclaimed
by Delphi's prophetic rock
as the bloody handed murderer,
the doer of deeds that none dare name?
Now is the time for him to run
with a stronger foot
than Pegasus
for the child of Zeus leaps in arms upon him
with fire and the lightning bolt,
and terribly close on his heels
are the Fates that never miss.

(*Antistrophe*)

Lately from snowy Parnassus
clearly the voice flashed forth,
bidding each Theban track him down,
the unknown murderer.
In the savage forests he lurks and in
the caverns like
the mountain bull.
He is sad and lonely, and lonely his feet
that carry him far from the navel of earth;
but its prophecies, ever living,
flutter around his head.

(*Strophe*)

The augur has spread confusion,
terrible confusion;
I do not approve what was said
nor can I deny it.
I do not know what to say;
I am in a flutter of foreboding;

I never heard in the present
nor past of a quarrel between
the sons of Labdacus and Polybus,
that I might bring as proof
in attacking the popular fame
of Oedipus, seeking
to take vengeance for undiscovered
death in the line of Labdacus.

(*Antistrophe*)

Truly Zeus and Apollo are wise
and in human things all knowing;
but amongst men there is no
distinct judgment, between the prophet
and me—which of us is right.
One man may pass another in wisdom
but I would never agree
with those that find fault with the king
till I should see the word
proved right beyond doubt. For once
in visible form the Sphinx
came on him and all of us
saw his wisdom and in that test
he saved the city. So he will not be condemned by my mind.

(*Enter* CREON)

CREON. Citizens, I have come because I heard
deadly words spread about me, that the king
accuses me. I cannot take that from him.
If he believes that in these present troubles
he has been wronged by me in word or deed
I do not want to live on with the burden
of such a scandal on me. The report
injures me doubly and most vitally—
for I'll be called a traitor to my city
and traitor also to my friends and you.

CHORUS. Perhaps it was a sudden gust of anger
that forced that insult from him, and no judgment.

CREON. But did he say that it was in compliance
with schemes of mine that the seer told him lies?

CHORUS. Yes, he said that, but why, I do not know.

CREON. Were his eyes straight in his head? Was his mind right
when he accused me in this fashion?

CHORUS. I do not know; I have no eyes to see
what princes do. Here comes the king himself.

(*Enter* OEDIPUS)

OEDIPUS. You, sir, how is it you come here? Have you so much

brazen-faced daring that you venture in
my house although you are proved manifestly
the murder of that man, and though you tried,
openly, highway robbery of my crown?
For God's sake, tell me what you saw in me,
what cowardice or what stupidity,
that made you lay a plot like this against me?
Did you imagine I should not observe
the crafty scheme that stole upon me or
seeing it, take no means to counter it?
Was it not stupid of you to make the attempt,
to try to hunt down royal power without
the people at your back or friends? For only
with the people at your back or money can
the hunt end in the capture of a crown.

CREON. Do you know what you're doing? Will you listen
to words to answer yours, and then pass judgment?

OEDIPUS. You're quick to speak, but I am slow to grasp you,
for I have found you dangerous,—and my foe.

CREON. First of all hear what I shall say to that.

OEDIPUS. At least don't tell me that you are not guilty.

CREON. If you believe you cherish something fine
in obstinacy without brains, you're wrong.

OEDIPUS. And you are wrong if you believe that one,
a criminal, will not be punished only
because he is my kinsman.

CREON.   This is but just——
but tell me, then, of what offense I'm guilty?

OEDIPUS. Did you or did you not urge me to send
to this prophetic mumbler?

CREON.   I did indeed,
and I shall stand by what I told you.

OEDIPUS. How long ago is it since Laius . . . .

CREON. What about Laius? I don't understand.

OEDIPUS. Vanished—died—was murdered?

CREON.   It is long,
a long, long time to reckon.

OEDIPUS.   Was this prophet
in the profession then?

CREON.   He was, and honoured
as highly as he is today.

OEDIPUS. At that time did he say a word about me?

CREON. Never, at least when I was near him.

OEDIPUS. You never made a search for the dead man?

CREON. We searched, indeed, but never learned of anything.

OEDIPUS. Why did our wise old friend not say this then?
CREON. I don't know; and when I know nothing, I
   usually hold my tongue.
OEDIPUS.   You know this much,
   and can declare this much if you are loyal.
CREON. What is it? If I know I'll not deny it.
OEDIPUS. That he would not have said that I killed Laius
   had he not met you first.
CREON.   You know yourself
   whether he said this, but I demand that I
   should hear as much from you as you from me.
OEDIPUS. Then hear,—I'll not be proved a murderer.
CREON. Well, then. You're married to my sister.
OEDIPUS.   Yes,
   that I am not disposed to deny.
CREON.   You rule
   this country giving her an equal share
   in the government?
OEDIPUS.   Yes, everything she wants
   she has from me.
CREON.   And I, as thirdsman to you,
   am rated as the equal of you two?
OEDIPUS. Yes, and it's there you've proved yourself false friend.
CREON. Not if you will reflect on it as I do.
   Consider, first, if you think any one
   would choose to rule and fear rather than rule
   and sleep untroubled by a fear if power
   were equal in both cases. I, at least,
   I was not born with such a frantic yearning
   to be a king—but to do what kings do.
   And so it is with every one who has learned
   wisdom and self-control. As it stands now,
   the prizes are all mine—and without fear.
   But if I were the king myself, I must
   do much that went against the grain.
   How should despotic rule seem sweeter to me
   than painless power and an assured authority?
   I am not so besotted yet that I
   want other honours than those that come with profit.
   Now every man's my pleasure; every man greets me;
   now those who are your suitors fawn on me,—
   success for them depends upon my favour.
   Why should I let all this go to win that?
   My mind would not be traitor if it's wise;
   I am no treason lover, of my nature,

nor would I ever dare to join a plot.
Prove what I say. Go to the oracle
at Pytho and inquire about the answers,
if they are as I told you. For the rest,
if you discover I laid any plot
together with the seer, kill me, I say,
not only by your vote but my own.
But do not charge me on obscure opinion
without some proof to back it. It's not just
lightly to count your knaves as honest men,
nor honest men as knaves. To throw away
an honest friend is, as it were, to throw
your life away, which a man loves the best.
In time you will know all with certainty;
time is the only test of honest men,
one day is space enough to know a rogue.

CHORUS. His words are wise, king, if one fears to fall.
   Those who are quick of temper are not safe.

OEDIPUS. When he that plots against me secretly
   moves quickly, I must quickly counterplot.
   If I wait taking no decisive measure
   his business will be done, and mine be spoiled.

CREON. What do you want to do then? Banish me?

OEDIPUS. No, certainly; kill you, not banish you.

CREON. I do not think that you've your wits about you.

OEDIPUS. For my own interests, yes.

CREON.   But for mine, too,
   you should think equally.

OEDIPUS.   You are a rogue.

CREON. Suppose you do not understand?

OEDIPUS.   But yet
   I must be ruler.

CREON.   Not if you rule badly.

OEDIPUS. O, city, city!

CREON.   I too have some share
   in the city; it is not yours alone.

CHORUS. Stop, my lords! Here—and in the nick of time
   I see Jocasta coming from the house;
   with her help lay the quarrel that now stirs you.

(*Enter* JOCASTA)

JOCASTA. For shame! Why have you raised this foolish squabbling
   brawl? Are you not ashamed to air your private
   griefs when the country's sick? Go in, you, Oedipus,
   and you, too, Creon, into the house. Don't magnify
   your nothing troubles.

CREON.   Sister, Oedipus,
　　your husband, thinks he has the right to do
　　terrible wrongs—he has but to choose between
　　two terrors: banishing or killing me.
OEDIPUS. He's right, Jocasta; for I find him plotting
　　with knavish tricks against my person.
CREON. That God may never bless me! May I die
　　accursed, if I have been guilty of
　　one tittle of the charge you bring against me!
JOCASTA. I beg you, Oedipus, trust him in this,
　　spare him for the sake of this his oath to God,
　　for my sake, and the sake of those who stand here.
CHORUS. Be gracious, be merciful,
　　we beg of you.
OEDIPUS. In what would you have me yield?
CHORUS. He has been no silly child in the past.
　　He is strong in his oath now.
　　Spare him.
OEDIPUS. Do you know what you ask?
CHORUS. Yes.
OEDIPUS. Tell me then.
CHORUS. He has been your friend before all men's eyes; do not cast
　　him away dishonoured on an obscure conjecture.
OEDIPUS. I would have you know that this request of yours
　　really requests my death or banishment.
CHORUS. May the Sun God, king of Gods, forbid! May I die without
　　God's blessing, without friends' help, if I had any such
　　thought. But my spirit is broken by my unhappiness for my
　　wasting country; and this would but add troubles amongst
　　ourselves to the other troubles.
OEDIPUS. Well, let him go then—if I must die ten times for it,
　　or be sent out dishonoured into exile.
　　It is your lips that prayed for him I pitied,
　　not his; wherever he is, I shall hate him.
CREON. I see you sulk in yielding and you're dangerous
　　when you are out of temper; natures like yours
　　are justly heaviest for themselves to bear.
OEDIPUS. Leave me alone! Take yourself off, I tell you.
CREON. I'll go, you have not known me, but they have,
　　and they have known my innocence. (Exit)
CHORUS. Won't you take him inside, lady?
JOCASTA. Yes, when I've found out what was the matter.
CHORUS. There was some misconceived suspicion of a story, and on
　　the other side the sting of injustice.

JOCASTA. So, on both sides?

CHORUS. Yes.

JOCASTA. What was the story?

CHORUS. I think it best, in the interests of the country, to leave it
where it ended.

OEDIPUS. You see where you have ended, straight of judgment
although you are, by softening my anger.

CHORUS. Sir, I have said before and I say again—be sure that I would
have been proved a madman, bankrupt in sane council, if I
should put you away, you who steered the country I love
safely when she was crazed with troubles. God grant that ∙
now, too, you may prove a fortunate guide for us.

JOCASTA. Tell me, my lord, I beg of you, what was it
that roused your anger so?

OEDIPUS.   Yes, I will tell you.
I honour you more than I honour them.
It was Creon and the plots he laid against me.

JOCASTA. Tell me—if you can clearly tell the quarrel—

OEDIPUS.   Creon says
that I'm the murderer of Laius.

JOCASTA. Of his own knowledge or on information?

OEDIPUS. He sent this rascal prophet to me, since
he keeps his own mouth clean of any guilt.

JOCASTA. Do not concern yourself about the matter;
listen to me and learn that human beings
have no part in the craft of prophecy.
Of that I'll show you a short proof.
There was an oracle once that came to Laius,—
I will not say that it was Phoebus' own,
but it was from his servants—and it told him
that it was fate that he should die a victim
at the hands of his own son, a son to be born
of Laius and me. But, see now, he,
the king, was killed by foreign highway robbers
at a place where three roads meet—so goes the story;
and for the son—before three days were out
after his birth King Laius pierced his ankles
and by the hands of others cast him forth
upon a pathless hillside. So Apollo
failed to fulfill his oracle to the son,
that he should kill his father, and to Laius
also proved false in that the thing he feared,
death at his son's hands, never came to pass.
So clear in this case were the oracles,

so clear and false. Give them no heed, I say;
what God discovers need of, easily
he shows to us himself.

OEDIPUS.   O dear Jocasta,
as I hear this from you, there comes upon me
a wandering of the soul—I could run mad.

JOCASTA. What trouble is it, that you turn again
and speak like this?

OEDIPUS.   I thought I heard you say
that Laius was killed at a crossroads.

JOCASTA. Yes, that was how the story went and still
that word goes round.

OEDIPUS.   Where is this place, Jocasta,
where he was murdered?

JOCASTA.   Phocis is the country
and the road splits there, one of two roads from Delphi,
another comes from Daulia.

OEDIPUS.   How long ago is this?

JOCASTA. The news came to the city just before
you became king and all men's eyes looked to you.
What is it, Oedipus, that's in your mind?

OEDIPUS. Don't ask me yet—tell me of Laius—
how did he look? How old or young was he?

JOCASTA. He was a tall man and his hair was grizzled
already—nearly white—and in his form
not unlike you.

OEDIPUS.   O God, I think I have
called curses on myself in ignorance.

JOCASTA. What do you mean? I am terrified
when I look at you.

OEDIPUS.   I have a deadly fear
that the old seer had eyes. You'll show me more
if you can tell me one more thing.

JOCASTA.   I will.
I'm frightened,—but if I can understand,
I'll tell you all you ask.

OEDIPUS.   How was his company?
Had he few with him when he went this journey,
or many servants, as would suit a prince?

JOCASTA. In all there were but five, and among them
a herald; and one carriage for the king.

OEDIPUS. It's plain—it's plain—who was it told you this?

JOCASTA. The only servant that escaped safe home.

OEDIPUS. Is he at home now?

JOCASTA. No, when he came home again

and saw you king and Laius was dead,
he came to me and touched my hand and begged
that I should send him to the fields to be
my shepherd and so he might see the city
as far off as he might. So I
sent him away. He was an honest man,
as slaves go, and was worthy of far more
than what he asked of me.

OEDIPUS. O, how I wish that he could come back quickly!

JOCASTA. He can. Why is your heart so set on this?

OEDIPUS. O dear Jocasta, I am full of fears
that I have spoken far too much; and therefore
I wish to see this shepherd.

JOCASTA.   He will come;
but, Oedipus, I think I'm worthy too
to know what is it that disquiets you.

OEDIPUS. It shall not be kept from you, since my mind
has gone so far with its forebodings. Whom
should I confide in rather than you, who is there
of more importance to me who have passed
through such a fortune?
Polybus was my father, king of Corinth,
and Merope, the Dorian, my mother.
I was held greatest of the citizens
in Corinth till a curious chance befell me
as I shall tell you—curious, indeed,
but hardly worth the store I set upon it.
There was a dinner and at it a man,
a drunken man, accused me in his drink
of being bastard. I was furious
but held my temper under for that day.
Next day I went and taxed my parents with it;
they took the insult very ill from him,
the drunken fellow who had uttered it.
So I was comforted for their part, but
still this thing rankled always, for the story
crept about widely. And I went at last
To Pytho, though my parents did not know.
But Phoebus sent me home again unhonoured
in what I came to learn, but he foretold
other and desperate horrors to befall me,
that I was fated to lie with my mother,
and show to daylight an accursed breed
which men would not endure, and I was doomed
to be murderer of the father that begot me.

When I heard this I fled, and in the days
that followed I would measure from the stars
the whereabouts of Corinth—yes, I fled
to somewhere where I should not see fulfilled
the infamies told in that dreadful oracle.
And as I journeyed I came to the place
where, as you say, this king met with his death.
Jocasta, I will tell you the whole truth.
When I was near the branching of the crossroads,
going on foot, I was encountered by
a herald and a carriage with a man in it,
just as you tell me. He that led the way
and the old man himself wanted to thrust me
out of the road by force. I became angry
and struck the coachman who was pushing me.
When the old man saw this he watched his moment,
and as I passed he struck me from his carriage,
full on the head with his two pointed goad.
But he was paid in full and presently
my stick had struck him backwards from the car
and he rolled out of it. And then I killed them
all. If it happened there was any tie
of kinship twixt this man and Laius,
who is then now more miserable than I,
what man on earth so hated by the Gods,
since neither citizen nor foreigner
may welcome me at home or even greet me,
but drive me out of doors? And it is I,
I and no other have so cursed myself.
And I pollute the bed of him I killed
by the hands that killed him. Was I not born evil?
Am I not utterly unclean? I had to fly
and in my banishment not even see
my kindred nor set foot in my own country,
or otherwise my fate was to be yoked
in marriage with my mother and kill my father,
Polybus who begot me and had reared me.
Would not one rightly judge and say that on me
these things were sent by some malignant God?
O no, no, no—O holy majesty
of God on high, may I not see that day!
May I be gone out of men's sight before
I see the deadly taint of this disaster
come upon me.

CHORUS. Sir, we too fear these things. But until you see this man face to face and hear his story, hope.

OEDIPUS. Yes, I have just this much of hope—to wait until the herdsman comes.

JOCASTA. And when he comes, what do you want with him?

OEDIPUS. I'll tell you; if I find that his story is the same as yours, I at least
will be clear of this guilt.

JOCASTA. Why what so particularly did you learn from my story?

OEDIPUS. You said that he spoke of highway *robbers* who killed Laius. Now if
he uses the same number, it was not I who killed him. One man cannot be
the same as many. But if he speaks of a man travelling alone, then clearly
the burden of the guilt inclines towards me.

JOCASTA. Be sure, at least, that this was how he told the story. He cannot
unsay it now, for every one in the city heard it—not I alone. But, Oedipus,
even if he diverges from what he said then, he shall never prove that the
murder of Laius squares rightly with the prophecy—for Loxias declared that
the king should be killed by his own son. And that poor creature did not
kill him surely,—for he died himself first. So as far as prophecy goes, henceforward I shall not look to the right hand or the left.

OEDIPUS. Right. But yet, send some one for the peasant to bring him here; do
not neglect it.

JOCASTA. I will send quickly. Now let me go indoors. I will do nothing except
what pleases you. (*Exeunt*)

CHORUS.

(*Strophe*)

May destiny ever find me
pious in word and deed
prescribed by the laws that live on high
laws begotten in the clear air of heaven,
whose only father is Olympus;
no mortal nature brought them to birth,
no forgetfulness shall lull them to sleep;
for God is great in them and grows not old.

(*Antistrophe*)

Insolence breeds the tyrant, insolence
if it is glutted with a surfeit, unseasonable, unprofitable,
climbs to the roof-top and plunges
sheer down to the ruin that must be,
and there its feet are no service.
But I pray that the God may never
abolish the eager ambition that profits the state.
For I shall never cease to hold the God as our protector.

(*Strophe*)

If a man walks with haughtiness
of hand or word and gives no heed
to Justice and the shrines of Gods

despises—may an evil doom
smite him for his ill-starred pride of heart!—
if he reaps gains without justice
and will not hold from impiety
and his fingers itch for untouchable things.
When such things are done, what man shall contrive
to shield his soul from the shafts of the God?
When such deeds are held in honour,
why should I honour the Gods in the dance?
(*Antistrophe*)
No longer to the holy place,
to the navel of earth I'll go
to worship, nor to Abae
nor to Olympia,
unless the oracles are proved to fit,
for all men's hands to point at.
O Zeus, if you are rightly called
the sovereign lord, all-mastering,
let this not escape you nor your ever-living power!
The oracles concerning Laius
are old and dim and men regard them not.
Apollo is nowhere clear in honour; God's service perishes.

(*Enter* JOCASTA, *carrying garlands*)

JOCASTA. Princes of the land, I have had the thought to go
to the Gods' temples, bringing in my hand
garlands and gifts of incense, as you see.
For Oedipus excites himself too much
at every sort of trouble, not conjecturing,
like a man of sense, what will be from what was,
but he is always at the speaker's mercy,
when he speaks terrors. I can do no good
by my advice, and so I came as suppliant
to you, Lycaean Apollo, who are nearest.
These are the symbols of my prayer and this
my prayer: grant us escape free of the curse.
Now when we look to him we are all afraid;
he's pilot of our ship and he is frightened.

(*Enter a* MESSENGER)

MESSENGER. Might I learn from you, sirs, where is the house of Oedipus? Or
best of all, if you know, where is the king himself?

CHORUS. This is his house and he is within doors. This lady is his wife and
mother of his children.

MESSENGER. God bless you, lady, and God bless your household! God bless
Oedipus' noble wife!

JOCASTA. God bless you, sir, for your kind greeting! What do you want of us that you have come here? What have you to tell us?

MESSENGER. Good news, lady. Good for your house and for your husband.

JOCASTA. What is your news? Who sent you to us?

MESSENGER. I come from Corinth and the news I bring will give you pleasure.
Perhaps a little pain too.

JOCASTA. What is this news of double meaning?

MESSENGER. The people of the Isthmus will choose Oedipus to be their king.
That is the rumour there.

JOCASTA. But isn't their king still old Polybus?

MESSENGER. No. He is in his grave. Death has got him.

JOCASTA. Is that the truth? Is Oedipus' father dead?

MESSENGER. May I die myself if it be otherwise!

JOCASTA (to a servant). Be quick and run to the King with the news. O oracles
of the Gods, where are you now? It was from this man Oedipus fled, lest he
should be his murderer! And now he is dead, in the course of nature, and
not killed by Oedipus.

(Enter OEDIPUS)

OEDIPUS. Dearest Jocasta, why have you sent for me?

JOCASTA. Listen to this man and when you hear reflect what is the outcome of
the holy oracles of the Gods.

OEDIPUS. Who is he? What is his message for me?

JOCASTA. He is from Corinth and he tells us that your father Polybus is dead
and gone.

OEDIPUS. What's this you say, sir? Tell me yourself.

MESSENGER. Since this is the first matter you want clearly told: Polybus has
gone down to death. You may be sure of it.

OEDIPUS. By treachery or sickness?

MESSENGER. A small thing will put old bodies asleep.

OEDIPUS. So he died of sickness, it seems,—poor old man!

MESSENGER. Yes, and of age—the long years he had measured.

OEDIPUS. Ha! Ha! O dear Jocasta, why should one
look to the Pythian hearth? Why should one look
to the birds screaming overhead? They prophesied
that I should kill my father! But he's dead,
and hidden deep in earth, and I stand here
who never laid a hand on spear against him,—
unless perhaps he died of longing for me,
and thus I am his murderer. But they,
the oracles, as they stand—he's taken them
away with him, they're dead as he himself is,
and worthless.

JOCASTA.   That I told you before now.

OEDIPUS. You did, but I was misled by my fear.

JOCASTA. Then lay no more of them to heart, not one.

OEDIPUS. But surely I must fear my mother's bed?

JOCASTA. Why should man fear since chance is all in all
    for him, and he can clearly foreknow nothing?
    Best to live lightly, as one can, unthinkingly.
    As to your mother's marriage bed,—don't fear it.
    Before this, in dreams too, as well as oracles,
    many a man has lain with his own mother.
    But he to whom such things are nothing bears
    his life most easily.
OEDIPUS. All that you say would be said perfectly
    if she were dead; but since she lives I must
    still fear, although you talk so well, Jocasta.
JOCASTA. Still in your father's death there's light of comfort?
OEDIPUS. Great light of comfort; but I fear the living.
MESSENGER. Who is the woman that makes you afraid?
OEDIPUS. Merope, old man, Polybus' wife.
MESSENGER. What about her frightens the queen and you?
OEDIPUS. A terrible oracle, stranger, from the Gods.
MESSENGER. Can it be told? Or does the sacred law
    forbid another to have knowledge of it?
OEDIPUS. O no! Once on a time Loxias said
    that I should lie with my own mother and
    take on my hands the blood of my own father.
    And so for these long years I've lived away
    from Corinth; it has been to my great happiness;
    but yet it's sweet to see the face of parents.
MESSENGER. This was the fear which drove you out of Corinth?
OEDIPUS. Old man, I did not wish to kill my father.
MESSENGER. Why should I not free you from this fear, sir,
    since I have come to you in all goodwill?
OEDIPUS. You would not find me thankless if you did.
MESSENGER. Why, it was just for this I brought the news,—
    to earn your thanks when you had come safe home.
OEDIPUS. No, I will never come near my parents.
MESSENGER.   Son,
    it's very plain you don't know what you're doing.
OEDIPUS. What do you mean, old man? For God's sake, tell me.
MESSENGER. If your homecoming is checked by fears like these.
OEDIPUS. Yes, I'm afraid that Phoebus may prove right.
MESSENGER. The murder and the incest?
OEDIPUS.   Yes, old man;
    that is my constant terror.
MESSENGER.   Do you know
    that all your fears are empty?
OEDIPUS.   How is that,
    if they are father and mother and I their son?

MESSENGER. Because Polybus was no kin to you in blood.

OEDIPUS. What, was not Polybus my father?

MESSENGER. No more than I but just so much.

OEDIPUS.   How can
my father be my father as much as one
that's nothing to me?

MESSENGER.   Neither he nor I
begat you.

OEDIPUS. Why then did he call me son?

MESSENGER. A gift he took you from these hands of mine.

OEDIPUS. Did he love so much what he took from another's hand?

MESSENGER. His childlessness before persuaded him.

OEDIPUS. Was I a child you bought or found when I
was given to him?

MESSENGER.   On Cithaeron's slopes
in the twisting thickets you were found.

OEDIPUS.   And why
were you a traveller in those parts?

MESSENGER.   I was
in charge of mountain flocks.

OEDIPUS.   You were a shepherd?
A hireling vagrant?

MESSENGER.   Yes, but at least at that time
the man that saved your life, son.

OEDIPUS. What ailed me when you took me in your arms?

MESSENGER. In that your ankles should be witnesses.

OEDIPUS. Why do you speak of that old pain?

MESSENGER.   I loosed you;
the tendons of your feet were pierced and fettered,—

OEDIPUS. My swaddling clothes brought me a rare disgrace.

MESSENGER. So that from this you're called your present name.

OEDIPUS. Was this my father's doing or my mother's?
For God's sake, tell me.

MESSENGER.   I don't know, but he
who gave you to me has more knowledge than I.

OEDIPUS. You yourself did not find me then? You took me
from someone else?

MESSENGER.   Yes, from another shepherd.

OEDIPUS. Who was he? Do you know him well enough
to tell?

MESSENGER. He was called Laius' man.

OEDIPUS. You mean the king who reigned here in the old days?

MESSENGER. Yes, he was that man's shepherd.

OEDIPUS.   Is he alive
still, so that I could see him?

MESSENGER. You who live here
would know that best.
OEDIPUS. Do any of you here
know of this shepherd whom he speaks about
in town or in the fields? Tell me. It's time
that this was found out once for all.
CHORUS. I think he is none other than the peasant
whom you have sought to see already; but
Jocasta here can tell us best of that.
OEDIPUS. Jocasta, do you know about this man
whom we have sent for? Is he the man he mentions?
JOCASTA. Why ask of whom he spoke? Don't give it heed;
nor try to keep in mind what has been said.
It will be wasted labour.
OEDIPUS. With such clues
I could not fail to bring my birth to light.
JOCASTA. I beg you—do not hunt this out—I beg you,
if you have any care for your own life.
What I am suffering is enough.
OEDIPUS. Keep up
your heart, Jocasta. Though I'm proved a slave,
thrice slave, and though my mother is thrice slave,
you'll not be shown to be of lowly lineage.
JOCASTA. O be persuaded by me, I entreat you;
do not do this.
OEDIPUS. I will not be persuaded to let be
the chance of finding out the whole thing clearly.
JOCASTA. It is because I wish you well that I
give you this counsel—and it's the best counsel.
OEDIPUS. Then the best counsel vexes me, and has
for some while since.
JOCASTA. O Oedipus, God help you!
God keep you from the knowledge of who you are!
OEDIPUS. Here, some one, go and fetch the shepherd for me;
and let her find her joy in her rich family!
JOCASTA. O Oedipus, unhappy Oedipus!
that is all I can call you, and the last thing
that I shall ever call you. (*Exit*)
CHORUS. Why has the queen gone, Oedipus, in wild
grief rushing from us? I am afraid that trouble
will break out of this silence.
OEDIPUS. Break out what will! I at least shall be
willing to see my ancestry, though humble.
Perhaps she is ashamed of my low birth,
for she has all a woman's high-flown pride.

But I account myself a child of Fortune,
beneficent Fortune, and I shall not be
dishonoured. She's the mother from whom I spring;
the months, my brothers, marked me, now as small,
and now again as mighty. Such is my breeding,
and I shall never prove so false to it,
as not to find the secret of my birth.

CHORUS.

(*Strophe*)

If I am a prophet and wise of heart
you shall not fail, Cithaeron,
by the limitless sky, you shall not!—
to know at tomorrow's full moon
that Oedipus honours you,
as native to him and mother and nurse at once;
and that you are honoured in dancing by us, as finding favour in sight of
     our king.
Apollo, to whom we cry, find these things pleasing!

(*Antistrophe*)

Who was it bore you, child? One of
the long-lived nymphs who lay with Pan—
the father who treads the hills?
Or was she a bride of Loxias, your mother? The grassy slopes
are all of them dear to him. Or perhaps Cyllene's king
or the Bacchants' God that lives on the tops
of the hills received you a gift from some
one of the Helicon Nymphs, with whom he mostly plays?

(*Enter an* OLD MAN, *led by* OEDIPUS' *servants*)

OEDIPUS. If some one like myself who never met him
may make a guess,—I think this is the herdsman,
whom we were seeking. His old age is consonant
with the other. And besides, the men who bring him
I recognize as my own servants. You
perhaps may better me in knowledge since
you've seen the man before.

CHORUS.   You can be sure
I recognize him. For if Laius
had ever an honest shepherd, this was he.

OEDIPUS. You, sir, from Corinth, I must ask you first,
is this the man you spoke of?

MESSENGER.   This is he
before your eyes.

OEDIPUS.   Old man, look here at me
and tell me what I ask you. Were you ever
a servant of King Laius?

HERDSMAN.   I was,—
  no slave he bought but reared in his own house.
OEDIPUS. What did you do as work? How did you live?
HERDSMAN. Most of my life was spent among the flocks.
OEDIPUS. In what part of the country did you live?
HERDSMAN. Cithaeron and the places near to it.
OEDIPUS. And somewhere there perhaps you knew this man?
HERDSMAN. What was his occupation? Who?
OEDIPUS.   This man here,
  have you had any dealings with him?
HERDSMAN.   No—
  not such that I can quickly call to mind.
MESSENGER. That is no wonder, master. But I'll make him remember what he
  does not know. For I know, that he well knows the country of Cithaeron,
  how he with two flocks, I with one kept company for three years—each year
  half a year—from spring till autumn time and then when winter came I
  drove my flocks to our fold home again and he to Laius' steadings. Well—
  am I right or not in what I said we did?
HERDSMAN. You're right—although it's a long time ago.
MESSENGER. Do you remember giving me a child
  to bring up as my foster child?
HERDSMAN.   What's this?
  Why do you ask this question?
MESSENGER.   Look, old man,
  here he is—here's the man who was that child!
HERDSMAN. Death take you! Won't you hold your tongue?
OEDIPUS.   No, no,
  do not find fault with him, old man. Your words
  are more at fault than his.
HERDSMAN.   O best of masters,
  how do I give offense?
OEDIPUS.   When you refuse
  to speak about the child of whom he asks you.
HERDSMAN. He speaks out of his ignorance, without meaning.
OEDIPUS. If you'll not talk to gratify me, you
  will talk with pain to urge you.
HERDSMAN.   O please, sir,
  don't hurt an old man, sir.
OEDIPUS (*to the* SERVANTS). Here, one of you,
  twist his hands behind him.
HERDSMAN. Why, God help me, why?
  What do you want to know?
OEDIPUS.   You gave a child
  to him,—the child he asked you of?

HERDSMAN.   I did.
  I wish I'd died the day I did.
OEDIPUS.   You will
  unless you tell me truly.
HERDSMAN.   And I'll die
  far worse if I should tell you.
OEDIPUS.   This fellow
  is bent on more delays, as it would seem.
HERDSMAN. O no, no! I have told you that I gave it.
OEDIPUS. Where did you get this child from? Was it your own
  or did you get it from another?
HERDSMAN.   Not
  my own at all; I had it from some one.
OEDIPUS. One of these citizens? or from what house?
HERDSMAN. O master, please—I beg of you, master, please
  don't ask me more.
OEDIPUS.   You're a dead man if I
  ask you again.
HERDSMAN.   It was one of the children
  of Laius.
OEDIPUS. A slave? Or born in wedlock?
HERDSMAN. O God, I am on the brink of frightful speech.
OEDIPUS. And I of frightful hearing. But I must hear.
HERDSMAN. The child was called his child; but she within,
  your wife would tell you best how all this was.
OEDIPUS. *She* gave it to you?
HERDSMAN.   Yes, she did, my lord.
OEDIPUS. To do what with it?
HERDSMAN.   Make away with it.
OEDIPUS. She was so hard—its mother?
HERDSMAN.   Aye, through fear
  of evil oracles.
OEDIPUS.   Which?
HERDSMAN.   They said that he
  should kill his parents.
OEDIPUS.   How was it that you
  gave it away to this old man?
HERDSMAN.   O master,
  I pitied it, and thought that I could send it
  off to another country and this man
  was from another country. But he saved it
  for the most terrible troubles. If you are
  the man he says you are, you're bred to misery.
OEDIPUS. O, O, O, they will all come,

all come out clearly! Light of the sun, let me
look upon you no more after today!
I who first saw the light bred of a match
accursed, and accursed in my living
with them I lived with, cursed in my killing.

(*Exeunt all but the* CHORUS)

CHORUS.

(*Strophe*)

O generations of men, how I
count you as equal with those who live
not at all!
what man, what man on earth wins more
of happiness than a seeming
and after that turning away?
Oedipus, you are my pattern of this,
Oedipus, you and your fate!
Luckless Oedipus, whom of all men
I envy not at all.

(*Antistrophe*)

In as much as he shot his bolt
beyond the others and won the prize
of happiness complete—
O Zeus—and killed and reduced to nought
the hooked taloned maid of the riddling speech,
standing a tower against death for my land:
hence he was called my king and hence
was honoured the highest of all
honours; and hence he ruled
in the great city of Thebes.

(*Strophe*)

But now whose tale is more miserable?
Who is there lives with a savager fate?
Whose troubles so reverse his life as his?
O Oedipus, the famous prince
for whom a great haven
the same both as father and son
sufficed for generation,
how, O how, have the furrows ploughed
by your father endured to bear you, poor wretch,
and hold their peace so long?

(*Antistrophe*)

Time who sees all has found you out
against your will; judges your marriage accursed,
begetter and begot at one in it.

O child of Laius,
would I had never seen you,
I weep for you and cry
a dirge of lamentation.

To speak directly, I drew my breath
from you at the first and so now I lull
my mouth to sleep with your name.
(*Enter a* SECOND MESSENGER)
SECOND MESSENGER. O Princes always honoured by our country,
what deeds you'll hear of and what horrors see
what grief you'll feel, if you as true born Thebans
care for the house of Labdacus's sons.
Phasis nor Ister cannot purge this house,
I think, with all their streams, such things
it hides, such evils shortly will bring forth
into the light, whether they will or not;
and troubles hurt the most
when they prove self-inflicted.
CHORUS. What we had known before did not fall short
of bitter groaning's worth; what's more to tell?
SECOND MESSENGER. Shortest to hear and tell—our glorious queen
Jocasta's dead.
CHORUS.   Unhappy woman! How?
SECOND MESSENGER. By her own hand. The worst of what was done
you cannot know. You did not see the sight.
Yet in so far as I remember it
you'll hear the end of our unlucky queen.
When she came raging into the house she went
straight to her marriage bed, tearing her hair
with both her hands, and crying upon Laius
long dead—Do you remember, Laius,
that night long past which bred a child for us
to send you to your death and leave
a mother making children with her son?
And then she groaned and cursed the bed in which
she brought forth husband by her husband, children
by her own child, an infamous double bond.
How after that she died I do not know,—
for Oedipus distracted us from seeing.
He burst upon us shouting and we looked
to him as he paced frantically around,
begging us always: Give me a sword, I say,
to find this wife no wife, this mother's womb,

this field of double sowing whence I sprang
and where I sowed my children! As he raved
some god showed him the way—none of us there.
Bellowing terribly and led by some
invisible guide he rushed on the two doors,—
wrenching the hollow bolts out of their sockets,
he charged inside. There, there, we saw his wife
hanging, the twisted rope around her neck.
When he saw her, he cried out fearfully
and cut the dangling noose. Then, as she lay,
poor woman, on the ground, what happened after,
was terrible to see. He tore the brooches—
the gold chased brooches fastening her robe—
away from her and lifting them up high
dashed them on his own eyeballs, shrieking out
such things as: they will never see the crime
I have committed or had done upon me!
Dark eyes, now in the days to come look on
forbidden faces, do not recognize
those whom you long for—with such imprecations
he struck his eyes again and yet again
with the brooches. And the bleeding eyeballs gushed
and stained his beard—no sluggish oozing drops
but a black rain and bloody hail poured down.

So it has broken—and not on one head
but troubles mixed for husband and for wife.
The fortune of the days gone by was true
good fortune—but today groans and destruction
and death and shame—of all ills can be named
not one is missing.
CHORUS. Is he now in any ease from pain?
SECOND MESSENGER.   He shouts
for some one to unbar the doors and show him
to all the men of Thebes, his father's killer,
his mother's—no I cannot say the word,
it is unholy—for he'll cast himself,
out of the land, he says, and not remain
to bring a curse upon his house, the curse
he called upon it in his proclamation. But
he wants for strength, aye, and some one to guide him;
his sickness is too great to bear. You, too,
will be shown that. The bolts are opening.
Soon you will see a sight to waken pity
even in the horror of it.

(*Enter the blinded* OEDIPUS)

CHORUS. This is a terrible sight for men to see!
  I never found a worse!
  Poor wretch, what madness came upon you!
  What evil spirit leaped upon your life
  to your ill-luck—a leap beyond man's strength!
  Indeed I pity you, but I cannot
  look at you, though there's much I want to ask
  and much to learn and much to see.
  I shudder at the sight of you.

OEDIPUS. O, O,
  where am I going? Where is my voice
  borne on the wind to and fro?
  Spirit, how far have you sprung?

CHORUS. To a terrible place whereof men's ears
  may not hear, nor their eyes behold it.

OEDIPUS. Darkness!
  Horror of darkness enfolding, resistless, unspeakable visitant sped by an ill
      wind in haste!
  madness and stabbing pain and memory
  of evil deeds I have done!

CHORUS. In such misfortunes it's no wonder
  if double weighs the burden of your grief.

OEDIPUS. My friend,
  you are the only one steadfast, the only one that attends on me;
  you still stay nursing the blind man.
  Your care is not unnoticed. I can know
  your voice, although this darkness is my world.

CHORUS. Doer of dreadful deeds, how did you dare
  so far to do despite to your own eyes?
  what spirit urged you to it?

OEDIPUS. It was Apollo, friends, Apollo,
  that brought this bitter bitterness, my sorrows to completion.
  But the hand that struck me
  was none but my own.
  Why should I see
  whose vision showed me nothing sweet to see?

CHORUS. These things are as you say.

OEDIPUS. What can I see to love?
  What greeting can touch my ears with joy?
  Take me away, and haste—to a place out of the way!
  Take me away, my friends, the greatly miserable,
  the most accursed, whom God too hates
  above all men on earth!

CHORUS. Unhappy in your mind and your misfortune,

would I had never known you!

OEDIPUS. Curse on the man who took
the cruel bonds from off my legs, as I lay in the field.
He stole me from death and saved me,
no kindly service.
Had I died then
I would not be so burdensome to friends.

CHORUS. I, too, could have wished it had been so.

OEDIPUS. Then I would not have come
to kill my father and marry my mother infamously.
Now I am godless and child of impurity,
begetter in the same seed that created my wretched self.
If there is any ill worse than ill,
that is the lot of Oedipus.

CHORUS. I cannot say your remedy was good;
you would be better dead than blind and living.

OEDIPUS. What I have done here was best done—don't tell me
otherwise, do not give me further counsel.
I do not know with what eyes I could look
upon my father when I die and go
under the earth, nor yet my wretched mother—
those two to whom I have done things deserving
worse punishment than hanging. Would the sight
of children, bred as mine are, gladden me?
No, not these eyes, never. And my city,
its towers and sacred places of the Gods,
of these I robbed my miserable self
when I commanded all to drive *him* out,
the criminal since proved by God impure
and of the race of Laius.
To this guilt I bore witness against myself—
with what eyes shall I look upon my people?
No. If there were a means to choke the fountain
of hearing I would not have stayed my hand
from locking up my miserable carcase,
seeing and hearing nothing; it is sweet
to keep our thoughts out of the range of hurt.

Cithæron, why did you receive me? why
having received me did you not kill me straight?
And so I had not shown to men my birth.

O Polybus and Corinth and the house,
the old house that I used to call my father's—

what fairness you were nurse to, and what foulness
festered beneath! Now I am found to be
a sinner and a son of sinners. Crossroads,
and hidden glade, oak and the narrow way
at the crossroads, that drank my father's blood
offered you by my hands, do you remember
still what I did as you looked on, and what
I did when I came here? O marriage, marriage!
you bred me and again when you had bred
bred children of your child and showed to men
brides, wives and mothers and the foulest deeds
that can be in this world of ours.

Come—it's unfit to say what is unfit
to do.—I beg of you in God's name hide me
somewhere outside your country, yes, or kill me,
or throw me into the sea, to be forever
out of your sight. Approach and deign to touch me
for all my wretchedness, and do not fear.
No man but I can bear my evil doom.

CHORUS. Here Creon comes in fit time to perform
or give advice in what you ask of us.
Creon is left sole ruler in your stead.

OEDIPUS. Creon! Creon! What shall I say to him?
How can I justly hope that he will trust me?
In what is past I have been proved towards him
an utter liar.

(*Enter* CREON)

CREON.   Oedipus, I've come
not so that I might laugh at you nor taunt you
with evil of the past. But if you still
are without shame before the face of men
reverence at least the flame that gives all life,
our Lord the Sun, and do not show unveiled
to him pollution such that neither land
nor holy rain nor light of day can welcome.
(*To a* SERVANT) Be quick and take him in. It is most decent
that only kin should see and hear the troubles
of kin.

OEDIPUS. I beg you, since you've torn me from
my dreadful expectations and have come
in a most noble spirit to a man
that has used you vilely—do a thing for me.
I shall speak for your own good, not for my own.

CREON. What do you need that you would ask of me?
OEDIPUS. Drive me from here with all the speed you can
    to where I may not hear a human voice.
CREON. Be sure, I would have done this had not I
    wished first of all to learn from God the course
    of action I should follow.
OEDIPUS.   But his word
    has been quite clear to let the parricide,
    the sinner, die.
CREON.   Yes, that indeed was said.
    But in the present need we had best discover
    what we should do.
OEDIPUS.   And will you ask about
    a man so wretched?
CREON.   Now even you will trust
    the God.
OEDIPUS. So. I command you—and will beseech you—
    to her that lies inside that house give burial
    as you would have it; she is yours and rightly
    you will perform the rites for her. For me—
    never let this my father's city have me
    living a dweller in it. Leave me live
    in the mountains where Cithaeron is, that's called
    my mountain, which my mother and my father
    while they were living would have made my tomb.
    So I may die by their decree who sought
    indeed to kill me. Yet I know this much:
    no sickness and no other thing will kill me.
    I would not have been saved from death if not
    for some strange evil fate. Well, let my fate
    go where it will.
                Creon, you need not care
    about my sons; they're men and so wherever
    they are, they will not lack a livelihood.
    But my two girls—so sad and pitiful—
    whose table never stood apart from mine,
    and everything I touched they always shared—
    O Creon, have a thought for them! And most
    I wish that you might suffer me to touch them
    and sorrow with them.
(*Enter* ANTIGONE *and* ISMENE, OEDIPUS' *two daughters*)
    O my lord! O true noble Creon! Can I
    really be touching them, as when I saw?
    What shall I say?

Yes, I can hear them sobbing—my two darlings!
and Creon has had pity and has sent me
what I loved most?
Am I right?
CREON. You're right: it was I gave you this
because I knew from old days how you loved them
as I see now.
OEDIPUS. God bless you for it, Creon,
and may God guard you better on your road
than he did me!

O children,
where are you? Come here, come to my hands,
a brother's hands which turned your father's eyes,
those bright eyes you knew once, to what you see,
a father seeing nothing, knowing nothing,
begetting you from his own source of life.
I weep for you—I cannot see your faces—
I weep when I think of the bitterness
there will be in your lives, how you must live
before the world. At what assemblages
of citizens will you make one? to what
gay company will you go and not come home
in tears instead of sharing in the holiday?
And when you're ripe for marriage, who will he be,
the man who'll risk to take such infamy
as shall cling to my children, to bring hurt
on them and those that marry with them? What
curse is not there? "Your father killed his father
and sowed the seed where he had sprung himself
and begot you out of the womb that held him."
These insults you will hear. Then who will marry you?
No one, my children; clearly you are doomed
to waste away in barrenness unmarried.
Son of Menoeceus, since you are all the father
left these two girls, and we, their parents, both
are dead to them—do not allow them wander
like beggars, poor and husbandless.
They are of your own blood.
And do not make them equal with myself
in wretchedness; for you can see them now
so young, so utterly alone, save for you only.
Touch my hand, noble Creon, and say yes.
If you were older, children, and were wiser,
there's much advice I'd give you. But as it is,

let this be what you pray: give me a life
wherever there is opportunity
to live, and better life than was my father's.

CREON. Your tears have had enough of scope; now go within the
house.

OEDIPUS. I must obey, though bitter of heart.

CREON.   In season, all is good.

OEDIPUS. Do you know on what conditions I obey?

CREON.   You tell me them,
and I shall know them when I hear.

OEDIPUS.   That you shall send me out
to live away from Thebes.

CREON. That gift you must ask of the God.

OEDIPUS. But I'm now hated by the Gods.

CREON. So quickly you'll obtain your prayer.

OEDIPUS. You consent then?

CREON. What I do not mean, I do not use to say.

OEDIPUS. Now lead me away from here.

CREON. Let go the children, then, and come.

OEDIPUS. Do not take them from me.

CREON. Do not seek to be master in everything,
for the things you mastered did not follow you throughout your life.

(*As* CREON *and* OEDIPUS *go out*)

CHORUS. You that live in my ancestral Thebes, behold this Oedipus,—
him who knew the famous riddles and was a man most masterful;
not a citizen who did not look with envy on his lot—
See him now and see the breakers of misfortune swallow him!
Look upon that last day always. Count no mortal happy till
he has passed the final limit of his life secure from pain.

Aristotle

from P O E T I C S

The *Poetics* of Aristotle (384–322 B.C.) has remained until the present day the one
discussion of tragedy that no one interested in the subject can afford to overlook.
His central point has become almost an axiom, namely that a tragedy is an imitation
of a serious action which by the evocation of pity and fear effects the purgation of
these emotions. Since Aristotle's main discussion of tragedy occurs in the first half of

the first twelve amd last 16 of the 26 sections are reprinted here. Obviously Aristotle was concerned with Greek tragedy and especially with *Oedipus*. But you will quickly notice that his principles can be properly and profitably applied in a study of any tragedy—ancient, Renaissance, or modern.

1 Our subject being Poetry, I propose to speak not only of the art in general but also of its species and their respective capacities; of the structure of plot required for a good poem; of the number and nature of the constituent parts of a poem; and likewise of any other matters in the same line of inquiry. Let us follow the natural order and begin with the primary facts.

Epic poetry and Tragedy, as also Comedy, Dithyrambic poetry, and most flute-playing and lyre-playing, are all, viewed as a whole, modes of imitation. But at the same time they differ from one another in three ways, either by a difference of kind in their means, or by differences in the objects, or in the manner of their imitations.

Just as colour and form are used as means by some, who (whether by art or constant practice) imitate and portray many things by their aid, and the voice is used by others; so also in the above-mentioned group of arts, the means with them as a whole are rhythm, language, and harmony—used, however, either singly or in certain combinations. A combination of harmony and rhythm alone is the means in flute-playing and lyre-playing, and any other arts there may be of the same description, e.g. imitative piping. Rhythm alone, without harmony, is the means in the dancer's imitations; for even he, by the rhythms of his attitudes, may represent men's characters, as well as what they do and suffer. There is further an art which imitates by language alone, without harmony, in prose or in verse, and if in verse, either in some one or in a plurality of metres. This form of imitation is to this day without a name. We have no common name for a mime of Sophron or Xenarchus and a Socratic Conversation; and we should still be without one even if the imitation in the two instances were in trimeters or elegiacs or some other kind of verse—though it is the way with people to tack on 'poet' to the name of a metre, and talk of elegiac-poets and epic-poets, thinking that they call them poets not by reason of the imitative nature of their work, but indiscriminately by reason of the metre they write in. Even if a theory of medicine or physical philosophy be put forth in a metrical form, it is usual to describe the writer in this way; Homer and Empedocles, however, have really nothing in common apart from their metre; so that, if the one is to be called a poet, the other should be termed a physicist rather than a poet. We should be in the same position also, if the imitation in these instances were in all the metres, like the *Centaur* (a rhapsody in a medley of all metres) of Chaeremon; and Chaeremon one has to recognize as a poet. So much, then, as to these arts. There are, lastly, certain other arts, which com-

From *De Poetica*, translated by Ingram Bywater. Reprinted by permission of The Clarendon Press.

bine all the means enumerated, rhythm, melody, and verse, e.g. Dithyrambic and Nomic poetry, Tragedy and Comedy; with this difference, however, that the three kinds of means are in some of them all employed together, and in others brought in separately, one after the other. These elements of difference in the above arts I term the means of their imitation.

2   The objects the imitator represents are actions, with agents who are necessarily either good men or bad—the diversities of human character being nearly always derivative from this primary distinction, since the line between virtue and vice is one dividing the whole of mankind. It follows, therefore, that the agents represented must be either above our own level of goodness, or beneath it, or just such as we are; in the same way as, with the painters, the personages of Polygnotus are better than we are, those of Pauson worse, and those of Dionysius just like ourselves. It is clear that each of the above-mentioned arts will admit of these differences, and that it will become a separate art by representing objects with this point of difference. Even in dancing, flute-playing, and lyre-playing such diversities are possible; and they are also possible in the nameless art that uses language, prose or verse without harmony, as its means; Homer's personages, for instance, are better than we are; Cleophon's are on our own level; and those of Hegemon of Thasos, the first writer of parodies, and Nicochares, the author of the *Diliad*, are beneath it. The same is true of the Dithyramb and the Nome: the personages may be presented in them with the difference exemplified in the . . . of . . . and Argas, and in the Cyclopses of Timotheus and Philoxenus. This difference it is that distinguishes Tragedy and Comedy also; the one would make its personages worse, and the other better, than the men of the present day.

3   A third difference in these arts is in the manner in which each kind of object is represented. Given both the same means and the same kind of object for imitation, one may either (1) speak at one moment in narrative and at another in an assumed character, as Homer does; or (2) one may remain the same throughout, without any such change; or (3) the imitators may represent the whole story dramatically, as though they were actually doing the things described.

As we said at the beginning, therefore, the differences in the imitation of these arts come under three heads, their means, their objects, and their manner.

So that as an imitator Sophocles will be on one side akin to Homer, both portraying good men; and on another to Aristophanes, since both present their personages as acting and doing. This in fact, according to some, is the reason for plays being termed dramas, because in a play the personages act the story. Hence too both Tragedy and Comedy are claimed by the Dorians as their discoveries; Comedy by the Megarians—by those in Greece as having arisen when Megara became a democracy, and by the Sicilian Megarians on the ground that the poet Epicharmus was of their country, and a good deal earlier than Chionides and Magnes; even Tragedy also is claimed by certain of the Pelo-

connection Dorians In support of this claim they point to the words 'comedy' and 'drama'. Their word for the outlying hamlets, they say, is comae, whereas Athenians call them *demes*—thus assuming that comedians got the name not from their *comoe* or revels, but from their strolling from hamlet to hamlet, lack of appreciation keeping them out of the city. Their word also for 'to act', they say, is *dran,* whereas Athenians use *prattein.*

So much, then, as to the number and nature of the points of difference in the imitation of these arts.

4 It is clear that the general origin of poetry was due to two causes, each of them part of human nature. Imitation is natural to man from childhood, one of his advantages over the lower animals being this, that he is the most imitative creature in the world, and learns at first by imitation. And it is also natural for all to delight in works of imitation. The truth of this second point is shown by experience: though the objects themselves may be painful to see, we delight to view the most realistic representations of them in art, the forms for example of the lowest animals and of dead bodies. The explanation is to be found in a further fact: to be learning something is the greatest of pleasures not only to the philosopher but also to the rest of mankind, however small their capacity for it; the reason of the delight in seeing the picture is that one is at the same time learning—gathering the meaning of things, e.g. that the man there is so-and-so; for if one has not seen the thing before, one's pleasure will not be in the picture as an imitation of it, but will be due to the execution or colouring or some similar cause. Imitation, then, being natural to us—as also the sense of harmony and rhythm, the metres being obviously species of rhythms—it was through their original aptitude, and by a series of improvements for the most part gradual on their first efforts, that they created poetry out of their improvisations.

Poetry, however, soon broke up into two kinds according to the differences of character in the individual poets; for the graver among them would represent noble actions, and those of noble personages; and the meaner sort the actions of the ignoble. The latter class produced invectives at first, just as others did hymns and panegyrics. We know of no such poem by any of the pre-Homeric poets, though there were probably many such writers among them; instances, however, may be found from Homer downwards, e.g. his *Margites,* and the similar poems of others. In this poetry of invective its natural fitness brought an iambic metre into use; hence our present term 'iambic', because it was the metre of their 'iambs' or invectives against one another. The result was that the old poets became some of them writers of heroic and others of iambic verse. Homer's position, however, is peculiar: just as he was in the serious style the poet of poets, standing alone not only through the literary excellence, but also through the dramatic character of his imitations, so too he was the first to outline for us the general forms of Comedy by producing not a dramatic invective, but a dramatic picture of the Ridiculous; his *Margites* in fact stands in the same relation to our comedies as the *Illiad* and *Odyssey* to our tragedies.

As soon, however, as Tragedy and Comedy appeared in the field, those naturally drawn to the one line of poetry became writers of comedies instead of iambs, and those naturally drawn to the other, writers of tragedies instead of epics, because these new modes of art were grander and of more esteem than the old.

If it be asked whether Tragedy is now all that it need be in its formative elements, to consider that, and decide it theoretically and in relation to the theatres, is a matter for another inquiry.

It certainly began in improvisations—as did also Comedy: the one originating with the authors of the Dithyramb, the other with those of the phallic songs, which still survive as institutions in many of our cities. And its advance after that was little by little, through their improving on whatever they had before them at each stage. It was in fact only after a long series of changes that the movement of Tragedy stopped on its attaining to its natural form. (1) The number of actors was first increased to two by Aeschylus, who curtailed the business of the Chorus, and made the dialogue, or spoken portion, take the leading part in the play. (2) A third actor and scenery were due to Sophocles. (3) Tragedy acquired also its magnitude. Discarding short stories and a ludicrous diction, through its passing out of its satyric stage, it assumed, though only at a late point in its progress, a tone of dignity; and its metre changed then from trochaic to iambic. The reason for their original use of the trochaic tetrameter was that their poetry was satyric and more connected with dancing than it now is. As soon, however, as a spoken part came in, nature herself found the appropriate metre. The iambic, we know, is the most speakable of metres, as is shown by the fact that we very often fall into it in conversation, whereas we rarely talk hexameters, and only when we depart from the speaking tone of voice. (4) Another change was a plurality of episodes or acts. As for the remaining matters, the superadded embellishments and the account of their introduction, these must be taken as said, as it would probably be a long piece of work to go through the details.

5   As for Comedy, it is (as has been observed) an imitation of men worse than the average; worse, however, not as regards any and every sort of fault, but only as regards one particular kind, the Ridiculous, which is a species of the Ugly. The Ridiculous may be defined as a mistake or deformity not productive of pain or harm to others; the mask, for instance, that excites laughter, is something ugly and distorted without causing pain.

Though the successive changes in Tragedy and their authors are not unknown, we cannot say the same of Comedy; its early stages passed unnoticed, because it was not as yet taken up in a serious way. It was only at a late point in its progress that a chorus of comedians was officially granted by the archon; they used to be mere volunteers. It had also already certain definite forms at the time when the record of those termed comic poets begins. Who it was who supplied it with masks, or prologues, or a plurality of actors and the like, has remained unknown. The invented Fable, or Plot, however, originated in Sicily with Epicharmus and Phormis; of Athenian poets Crates was the first to drop the Comedy of invective and frame stories of a general and non-personal nature, in other words, Fables or Plots.

Epic poetry, then, has been seen to agree with Tragedy to this extent, that of being an imitation of serious subjects in a grand kind of verse. It differs from it, however, (1) in that it is in one kind of verse and in narrative form; and (2) in its length—which is due to its action having no fixed limit of time, whereas Tragedy endeavours to keep as far as possible within a single circuit of the sun, or something near that. This, I say, is another point of difference between them, though at first the practice in this respect was just the same in tragedies as in epic poems. They differ also (3) in their constituents, some being common to both and others peculiar to Tragedy—hence a judge of good and bad in Tragedy is a judge of that in epic poetry also. All the parts of the epic are included in Tragedy; but those of Tragedy are not all of them to be found in the Epic.

6 Reserving hexameter poetry and Comedy for consideration hereafter, let us proceed now to the discussion of Tragedy; before doing so, however, we must gather up the definition resulting from what has been said. (A tragedy, then, is the imitation of an action that is serious and also, as having magnitude, complete in itself; in language with pleasurable accessories, each kind brought in separately in the parts of the work; in a dramatic, not in a narrative form; with incidents arousing pity and fear, wherewith to accomplish its catharsis of such emotions.) Here by 'language with pleasurable accessories' I mean that with rhythm and harmony or song superadded; and by 'the kinds separately' I mean that some portions are worked out with verse only, and others in turn with song.

As they act the stories, it follows that in the first place the Spectacle (or stage-appearance of the actors) must be some part of the whole; and in the second Melody and Diction, these two being the means of their imitation. Here by 'Diction' I mean merely this, the compositon of the verses; and by 'Melody', what is too completely understood to require explanation. But further: the subject represented also is an action; and the action involves agents, who must necessarily have their distinctive qualities both of character and thought, since it is from these that we ascribe certain qualities to their actions. There are in the natural order of things, therefore, two causes, Thought and Character, of their actions, and consequently of their success or failure in their lives. Now the action (that which was done) is represented in the play by the Fable or Plot. The Fable, in our present sense of the term, is simply this, the combination of the incidents, or things done in the story; whereas Character is what makes us ascribe certain moral qualities to the agents; and Thought is shown in all they say when proving a particular point or, it may be, enunciating a general truth. There are six parts consequently of every tragedy, as a whole (that is) of such or such quality, viz. a Fable or Plot, Characters, Diction, Thought, Spectacle, and Melody; two of them arising from the means, one from the manner, and three from the objects of the dramatic imitation; and there is nothing else besides these six. Of these, its formative elements, then, not a few of the dramatists have made due use, as every play, one may say, admits of Spectacle, Character, Fable, Diction, Melody, and Thought.

The most important of the six is the combination of the incidents of the story. Tragedy is essentially an imitation not of persons but of action and life, of happiness and misery. All human happiness or misery takes the form of action; the end for which we live is a certain kind of activity, not a quality. Character gives us qualities, but it is in our actions—what we do—that we are happy or the reverse. In a play accordingly they do not act in order to portray the Characters; they include the Characters for the sake of the action. So that it is the action in it, i.e. its Fable or Plot, that is the end and purpose of the tragedy; and the end is everywhere the chief thing. Besides this, a tragedy is impossible without action, but there may be one without Character. The tragedies of most of the moderns are characterless—a defect common among poets of all kinds, and with its counterpart in painting in Zeuxis as compared with Polygnotus; for whereas the latter is strong in character, the work of Zeuxis is devoid of it. And again: one may string together a series of characteristic speeches of the utmost finish as regards Diction and Thought, and yet fail to produce the true tragic effect; but one will have much better success with a tragedy which, however inferior in these respects, has a Plot, a combination of incidents, in it. And again: the most powerful elements of attraction in Tragedy, the Peripeties and Discoveries, are parts of the Plot. A further proof is in the fact that beginners succeed earlier with the Diction and Characters than with the construction of a story; and the same may be said of nearly all the early dramatists. We maintain, therefore, that the first essential, the life and soul, so to speak, of Tragedy is the Plot; and that the Characters come second—compare the parallel in painting, where the most beautiful colours laid on without order will not give one the same pleasure as a simple black-and-white sketch of a portrait. We maintain that Tragedy is primarily an imitation of action, and that it is mainly for the sake of the action that it imitates the personal agents. Third comes the element of Thought, i.e. the power of saying whatever can be said, or what is appropriate to the occasion. This is what, in the speeches in Tragedy, falls under the arts of Politics and Rhetoric; for the older poets make their personages discourse like statesmen, and the modern like rhetoricians. One must not confuse it with Character. Character in a play is that which reveals the moral purpose of the agents, i.e. the sort of thing they seek or avoid, where that is not obvious—hence there is no room for Character in a speech on a purely indifferent subject. Thought, on the other hand, is shown in all they say when proving or disproving some particular point, or enunciating some universal proposition. Fourth among the literary elements is the Diction of the personages, i.e., as before explained, the expression of their thoughts in words, which is practically the same thing with verse as with prose. As for the two remaining parts, the Melody is the greatest of the pleasurable accessories of Tragedy. The Spectacle, though an attraction, is the least artistic of all the parts, and has least to do with the art of poetry. The tragic effect is quite possible without a public performance and actors; and besides, the getting-up of the Spectacle is more a matter for the costumier than the poet.

7 Having thus distinguished the parts, let us now consider the proper construction of the Fable or Plot, as that is at once the first and the most important thing in Tragedy. We have laid it down that a tragedy is an imitation of an action that is complete in itself, as a whole of some magnitude; for a whole may be of no magnitude to speak of. Now a whole is that which has beginning, middle, and end. A beginning is that which is not itself necessarily after anything else, and which has naturally something else after it; an end is that which is naturally after something itself, either as its necessary or usual consequent, and with nothing else after it; and a middle, that which is by nature after one thing and has also another after it. A well-constructed Plot, therefore, cannot either begin or end at any point one likes; beginning and end in it must be of the forms just described. Again: to be beautiful, a living creature, and every whole made up of parts, must not only present a certain order in its arrangement of parts, but also be of a certain definite magnitude. Beauty is a matter of size and order, and therefore impossible either (1) in a very minute creature, since our perception becomes indistinct as it approaches instantaneity; or (2) in a creature of vast size—one, say, 1,000 miles long—as in that case, instead of the object being seen all at once, the unity and wholeness of it is lost to the beholder. Just in the same way, then, as a beautiful whole made up of parts, or a beautiful living creature, must be of some size, but a size to be taken in by the eye, so a story or Plot must be of some length, but of a length to be taken in by the memory. As for the limit of its length, so far as that is relative to public performances and spectators, it does not fall within the theory of poetry. If they had to perform a hundred tragedies, they would be timed by water-clocks, as they are said to have been at one period. The limit, however, set by the actual nature of the thing is this: the longer the story, consistently with its being comprehensible as a whole, the finer it is by reason of its magnitude. As a rough general formula, 'a length which allows of the hero passing by a series of probable or necessary stages from misfortune to happiness, or from happiness to misfortune', may suffice as a limit for the magnitude of the story.

8 The Unity of a Plot does not consist, as some suppose, in its having one man as its subject. An infinity of things befall that one man, some of which it is impossible to reduce to unity; and in like manner there are many actions of one man which cannot be made to form one action. One sees, therefore, the mistake of all the poets who have written a *Heracleid*, a *Theseid*, or similar poems; they suppose that, because Heracles was one man, the story also of Heracles must be one story. Homer, however, evidently understood this point quite well, whether by art or instinct, just in the same way as he excels the rest in every other respect. In writing an *Odyssey*, he did not make

the poem cover all that ever befell his hero—it befell him, for instance, to get wounded on Parnassus and also to feign madness at the time of the call to arms, but the two incidents had no necessary or probable connexion with one another—instead of doing that, he took as the subject of the *Odyssey*, as also of the *Illiad*, an action with a Unity of the kind we are describing. The truth is that, just as in the other imitative arts one imitation is always of one thing, so in poetry the story, as an imitation of action, must represent one action, a complete whole, with its several incidents so closely connected that the transposal or withdrawal of any one of them will disjoin and dislocate the whole. For that which makes no perceptible difference by its presence or absence is no real part of the whole.

9 From what we have said it will be seen that the poet's function is to describe, not the thing that has happened, but a kind of thing that might happen, i.e. what is possible as being probable or necessary. The distinction between historian and poet is not in the one writing prose and the other verse —you might put the work of Herodotus into verse, and it would still be a species of history; it consists really in this, that the one describes the thing that has been, and the other a kind of thing that might be. Hence poetry is something more philosophic and of graver import than history, since its statements are of the nature rather of universals, whereas those of history are singulars. By a universal statement I mean one as to what such or such a kind of man will probably or necessarily say or do—which is the aim of poetry, though it affixes proper names to the characters; by a singular statement, one as to what, say, Alcibiades did or had done to him. In Comedy this has become clear by this time; it is only when their plot is already made up of probable incidents that they give it a basis of proper names, choosing for the purpose any names that may occur to them, instead of writing like the old iambic poets about particular persons. In Tragedy, however, they still adhere to the historic names; and for this reason: what convinces is the possible; now whereas we are not yet sure as to the possibility of that which has not happened, that which has happened is manifestly possible, else it would not have come to pass. Nevertheless even in Tragedy there are some plays with but one or two known names in them, the rest being inventions; and there are some without a single known name, e.g. Agathon's *Antheus*, in which both incidents and names are of the poet's invention; and it is no less delightful on that account. So that one must not aim at a rigid adherence to the traditional stories on which tragedies are based. It would be absurd, in fact, to do so, as even the known stories are only known to a few, though they are a delight none the less to all.

It is evident from the above that the poet must be more the poet of his stories or Plots than of his verses, inasmuch as he is a poet by virtue of the imitative element in his work, and it is actions that he imitates. And if he should come to take a subject from actual history, he is none the less a poet for that; since

BENVOLIO. By giving liberty unto thine eyes;
 Examine other beauties.
ROMEO.   'Tis the way
 To call hers exquisite, in question more: 235
 These happy masks that kiss fair ladies' brows
 Being black put us in mind they hide the fair;
 He that is strucken blind cannot forget
 The precious treasure of his eyesight lost:
 Show me a mistress that is passing fair,   240
 What doth her beauty serve, but as a note
 Where I may read who pass'd that passing fair?
 Farewell: thou canst not teach me to forget.
BENVOLIO. I'll pay that doctrine, or else die in debt. (*Exeunt*)

 Scene II: A street.

Enter CAPULET, PARIS, *and* Servant.

CAPULET. But Montague is bound as well as I,
 In penalty alike; and 'tis not hard, I think,
 For men so old as we to keep the peace.
PARIS. Of honourable reckoning are you both;
 And pity 'tis you lived at odds so long.   5
 But now, my lord, what say you to my suit?
CAPULET. But saying o'er what I have said before:
 My child is yet a stranger in the world;
 She hath not seen the change of fourteen years;
 Let two more summers wither in their pride,   10
 Ere we may think her ripe to be a bride.
PARIS. Younger than she are happy mothers made.
CAPULET. And too soon marr'd are those so early made.
 The earth hath swallow'd all my hopes but she,
 She is the hopeful lady of my earth: 15
 But woo her, gentle Paris, get her heart,
 My will to her consent is but a part;
 An she agree, within her scope of choice
 Lies my consent and fair according voice.
 This night I hold an old accustom'd feast,   20
 Whereto I have invited many a guest,
 Such as I love; and you, among the store,
 One more, most welcome, makes my number more.

235. *in question more*, into greater consideration. **240.** *passing*, surpassingly. **244.** *pay that doctrine*, give that instruction.
 SCENE II. **4.** *reckoning*, estimation, repute. **8.** *stranger in the world*. Capulet's reluctance is largely a matter of manners. **15.** *lady . . . earth*, i.e., she is the heir of his estate or more probably, his only hope in the world. **17.** *My . . . part*. This is also a conventional statement, since Capulet has no idea of letting Juliet have her way. **18.** *An*, if. *scope*, limit.

At my poor house look to behold this night
Earth-treading stars that make dark heaven light: 25
Such comfort as do lusty young men feel
When well-apparell'd April on the heel
Of limping winter treads, even such delight
Among fresh female buds shall you this night
Inherit at my house; hear all, all see, 30
And like her most whose merit most shall be:
Which on more view, of many mine being one
May stand in number, though in reckoning none.
Come, go with me. (*To Servant, giving a paper*) Go, sirrah, trudge about
Through fair Verona; find those persons out 35
Whose names are written there, and to them say,
My house and welcome on their pleasure stay. (*Exeunt* CAPULET *and* PARIS)

SERVANT. Find them out whose names are written here! It is written, that the
shoemaker should meddle with his yard, and the tailor with his last, the
fisher with his pencil, and the painter with his nets; but I am sent to find
those persons whose names are here writ, and can never find what names the
writing person hath here writ. I must to the learned.—In good time. 45

(*Enter* BENVOLIO *and* ROMEO)

BENVOLIO. Tut, man, one fire burns out another's burning,
One pain is lessen'd by another's anguish;
Turn giddy, and be holp by backward turning;
One desperate grief cures with another's languish:
Take thou some new infection to thy eye, 50
And the rank poison of the old will die.

ROMEO. Your plaintain-leaf is excellent for that.

BENVOLIO. For what, I pray thee?

ROMEO. For your broken shin.

BENVOLIO. Why, Romeo, art thou mad?

ROMEO. Not mad, but bound more than a madman is; 55
Shut up in prison, kept without my food,
Whipp'd and tormented and—God-den, good fellow.

SERVANT. God gi' god-den. I pray, sir, can you read?

ROMEO. Ay, mine own fortune in my misery. 60

SERVANT. Perhaps you have learned it without book: but, I pray, can you read
any thing you see?

ROMEO. Ay, if I know the letters and the language.

SERVANT. Ye say honestly: rest you merry!

ROMEO. Stay, fellow; I can read. (*Reads*) 65

32-33. *Which . . . none.* Capulet may mean that his daughter will lose her identity by being
swallowed up in a number of others. He is punning on the saying, "one is no number." **34.**
sirrah, customary form of address to servants. **46.** *one . . . burning.* Cf. the proverb, "fire drives
out fire." **48.** *holp*, helped. **51.** *rank*, corrupt. **57.** *God-den*, good evening. *fellow*, usual term
for a servant.

'Signior Martino and his wife and daughters; County Anselme and his beauteous sisters; the lady widow of Vitruvio; Signor Placentio and his lovely
nieces; Mercutio and his brother Valentine; mine uncle Capulet, his wife,
and daughters; my fair niece Rosaline; Livia; Signior Valentio and his
cousin Tybalt; Lucio and the lively Helena.'
A fair assembly: whither should they come?   74

SERVANT. Up.

ROMEO. Whither?

SERVANT. To supper; to our house.

ROMEO. Whose house?

SERVANT. My master's.   80

ROMEO. Indeed, I should have asked you that before.

SERVANT. Now I'll tell you without asking: my master is the great rich Capulet;
and if you be not of the house of Montagues, I pray, come and crush a cup
of wine. Rest you merry! (*Exit*)   86

BENVOLIO. At this same ancient feast of Capulet's
Sups the fair Rosaline whom thou so lovest,
With all the admired beauties of Verona:
Go thither; and, with unattainted eye,   90
Compare her face with some that I shall show,
And I will make thee think thy swan a crow.

ROMEO. When the devout religion of mine eye
Maintains such falsehood, then turn tears to fires;
And these, who often drown'd could never die,   95
Transparent heretics, be burnt for liars!
One fairer than my love! the all-seeing sun
Ne'er saw her match since first the world begun.

BENVOLIO. Tut, you saw her fair, none else being by,
Herself poised with herself in either eye: 100
But in that crystal scales let there be weigh'd
Your lady's love against some other maid
That I will show you shining at this feast,
And she shall scant show well that now shows best.

ROMEO. I'll go along, no such sight to be shown,   105
But to rejoice in splendour of mine own. (*Exeunt*)

Scene III: A room in CAPULET'*s house.*

Enter LADY CAPULET *and* Nurse.

LADY CAPULET. Nurse, where 's my daughter? Call her forth to me.

NURSE. Now, by my maidenhead, at twelve year old,
I bade her come. What, lamb! what, ladybird!
God forbid! Where 's this girl? What, Juliet!

86. *crush a cup of wine*, drink a cup of wine. Cf. "crack a bottle." **87.** *ancient*, customary.
89. *admired*, wondered at. **90.** *unattainted*, impartial. **95.** *these*, i.e., these eyes.

(*Enter* JULIET)

JULIET. How now! who calls?

NURSE.　　　　Your mother.

JULIET.　　　　　Madam, I am here. 5
　What is your will?

LADY CAPULET. This is the matter:—Nurse, give leave awhile,
　We must talk in secret:—nurse, come back again;
　I have remember'd me, thou 's hear our counsel.
　Thou know'st my daughter 's of a pretty age. 10

NURSE. Faith, I can tell her age unto an hour.

LADY CAPULET. She 's not fourteen.

NURSE.　　　　　I'll lay fourteen of my teeth,—
　And yet, to my teen be it spoken, I have but four,—
　She is not fourteen. How long is it now
　To Lammas-tide?

LADY CAPULET.　　　　A fortnight and odd days. 15

NURSE. Even or odd, of all days in the year,
　Come Lammas-eve at night shall she be fourteen.
　Susan and she—God rest all Christian souls!—
　Were of an age: well, Susan is with God;
　She was too good for me: but, as I said, 20
　On Lammas-eve at night shall she be fourteen;
　That shall she, marry; I remember it well.
　'Tis since the earthquake now eleven years;
　And she was wean'd,—I never shall forget it,—
　Of all the days of the year, upon that day: 25
　For I had then laid wormwood to my dug,
　Sitting in the sun under the dove-house wall;
　My lord and you were then at Mantua:—
　Nay, I do bear a brain:—but, as I said,
　When it did taste the wormwood on the nipple 30
　Of my dug and felt it bitter, pretty fool,
　To see it tetchy and fall out with the dug!
　'Shake' quoth the dove-house; 'twas no need, I trow,
　To bid me trudge:
　And since that time it is eleven years; 35
　For then she could stand alone; nay, by the rood,
　She could have run and waddled all about;
　For even the day before, she broke her brow:

SCENE III. **7.** *give leave*, leave us. **9.** *thou 's*, thou shalt. **10.** *pretty*, moderately great. **13.** *teen*, sorrow; with play on *fourteen*. **15.** *Lammas-tide*, August 1. **23.** *'Tis . . . years*. It has been thought that Shakespeare was alluding in this line to a famous earthquake in 1580 and was, therefore, writing in 1591. **29.** *bear a brain*. The nurse prides herself on her memory. **30.** *wormwood*, an herb noted for bitterness, from which absinthe is derived. **31.** *fool*, term of endearment. **32.** *tetchy*, fretful. **33.** *trow*, believe.

some historic occurrences may very well be in the probable and possible order of things; and it is in that aspect of them that he is their poet.

Of simple Plots and actions the episodic are the worst. I call a Plot episodic when there is neither probability nor necessity in the sequence of its episodes. Actions of this sort bad poets construct through their own fault, and good ones on account of the players. His work being for public performance, a good poet often stretches out a Plot beyond it capabilities, and is thus obliged to twist the sequence of incident.

Tragedy, however, is an imitation not only of a complete action, but also of incidents arousing pity and fear. Such incidents have the very greatest effect on the mind when they occur unexpectedly and at the same time in consequence of one another; there is more of the marvellous in them then than if they happened of themselves or by mere chance. Even matters of chance seem most marvellous if there is an appearance of design as it were in them; as for instance the statue of Mitys at Argos killed the author of Mitys' death by falling down on him when a looker-on at a public spectacle; for incidents like that we think to be not without a meaning. A Plot, therefore, of this sort is necessarily finer than others.

10 Plots are either simple or complex, since the actions they represent are naturally of this twofold description. The action, proceeding in the way defined, as one continuous whole, I call simple, when the change in the hero's fortunes takes place without Peripety or Discovery; and complex, when it involves one or the other, or both. These should each of them arise out of the structure of the Plot itself, so as to be the consequence, necessary or probable, of the antecedents. There is a great difference between a thing happening *propter hoc* and *post hoc*.

11 A Peripety is the change of the kind described from one state of things within the play to its opposite, and that too in the way we are saying, in the probable or necessary sequence of events; as it is for instance in *Oedipus*: here the opposite state of things is produced by the Messenger, who, coming to gladden Oedipus and to remove his fears as to his mother, reveals the secret of his birth. And in *Lynceus*: just as he is being led off for execution, with Danaus at his side to put him to death, the incidents preceding this bring it about that he is saved and Danaus put to death. A Discovery is, as the very word implies, a change from ignorance to knowledge, and thus to either love or hate, in the personages marked for good or evil fortune. The finest form of Discovery is one attended by Peripeties, like that which goes with the Discovery in *Oedipus*. There are no doubt other forms of it; what we have said may happen in a way in reference to inanimate things, even things of a very casual kind; and it is also possible to discover whether some one has done or not done something. But the form most directly connected with the Plot and the action of the piece is the first-mentioned. This, with a Peripety, will arouse either

pity or fear—actions of that nature being what Tragedy is assumed to represent; and it will also serve to bring about the happy or unhappy ending. The Discovery, then, being of persons, it may be that of one party only to the other, the latter being already known; or both the parties may have to discover themselves. Iphigenia, for instance, was discovered to Orestes by sending the letter; and another Discovery was required to reveal him to Iphigenia.

Two parts of the Plot, then, Peripety and Discovery, are on matters of this sort. A third part is Suffering; which we may define as an action of a destructive or painful nature, such as murders on the stage, tortures, woundings, and the like. The other two have been already explained.

12   The parts of Tragedy to be treated as formative elements in the whole were mentioned in a previous Chapter. From the point of view, however, of its quantity, i.e. the separate sections into which it is divided, a tragedy has the following parts: Prologue, Episode, Exode, and a choral portion, distinguished into Parode and Stasimon; these two are common to all tragedies, whereas songs from the stage and *Commoe* are only found in some. The Prologue is all that precedes the Parode of the chorus; an Episode all that comes in between two whole choral songs; the Exode all that follows after the last choral song. In the choral portion the Parode is the whole first statement of the chorus; a Stasimon, a song of the chorus without anapaests or trochees; a *Commos*, a lamentation sung by chorus and actor in concert. The parts of Tragedy to be used as formative elements in the whole we have already mentioned; the above are its parts from the point of view of its quantity, or the separate sections into which it is divided.

13   The next points after what we have said above will be these: (1) What is the poet to aim at, and what is he to avoid, in constructing his Plots? and (2) What are the conditions on which the tragic effect depends?

We assume that, for the finest form of Tragedy, the Plot must be not simple but complex; and further, that it must imitate actions arousing fear and pity, since that is the distinctive function of this kind of imitation. It follows, therefore, that there are three forms of Plot to be avoided. (1) A good man must not be seen passing from happiness to misery, or (2) a bad man from misery to happiness. The first situation is not fear-inspiring or piteous, but simply odious to us. The second is the most untragic that can be; it has no one of the requisites of Tragedy; it does not appeal either to the human feeling in us, or to our pity, or to our fears. Nor, on the other hand, should (3) an extremely bad man be seen falling from happiness into misery. Such a story may arouse the human feeling in us, but it will not move us to either pity or fear; pity is occasioned by undeserved misfortune, and fear by that of one like ourselves; so that there will be nothing either piteous or fear-inspiring in the situation. There remains, then, the intermediate kind of personage, a man not preeminently virtuous and just, whose misfortune, however, is brought upon him not by vice and depravity but by some error of judgement, of the number of those in the enjoyment of great reputation and prosperity; e.g. Oedipus, Thyestes, and the men of note of similar families. The perfect Plot, accordingly, must have a single, and not (as some tell us) a double issue; the change in the hero's fortunes must be not from misery to happiness, but on the contrary from happiness to misery; and the cause of it must lie not in any depravity, but in some great error on his part; the man himself being either such as we have described, or better, not worse, than that. Fact also confirms our theory. Though the poets began by accepting any tragic story that came to hand, in these days the finest tragedies are always on the story of some few houses, on that of Alcmeon, Oedipus, Orestes, Meleager, Thyestes, Telephus, or any others that may have been involved, as either agents or sufferers, in some deed of horror. The theoretically best tragedy, then, has a Plot of this description. The critics, therefore, are wrong who blame Euripides for taking this line in his tragedies, and giving many of them an unhappy ending. It is, as we have said, the right line to take. The best proof is this: on the stage, and in the public performances, such plays, properly worked out, are seen to be the most truly tragic; and Euripides, even if his execution be faulty in every other point, is seen to be nevertheless the most tragic certainly of the dramatists. After this comes the construction of Plot which some rank first, one with a double story (like the *Odyssey*) and an opposite issue for the good and the bad personages. It is ranked as first only through the weakness of the audiences; the poets merely follow their public, writing as its wishes dictate. But the pleasure here is not that of Tragedy. It belongs rather to Comedy, where the bitterest enemies in the piece (e.g. Orestes and Aegisthus) walk off good friends at the end, with no slaying of any one by any one.

14 The tragic fear and pity may be aroused by the Spectacle; but they may also be aroused by the very structure and incidents of the play—which is the better way and shows the better poet. The Plot in fact should be so framed that, even without seeing the things take place, he who simply hears the account of them shall be filled with horror and pity at the incidents; which is just the effect that the mere recital of the story in *Oedipus* would have on one. To produce this same effect by means of the Spectacle is less artistic, and requires extraneous aid. Those, however, who make use of the Spectacle to put before us that which is merely monstrous and not productive of fear, are wholly out of touch with Tragedy; not every kind of pleasure should be required of a tragedy, but only its own proper pleasure.

The tragic pleasure is that of pity and fear, and the poet has to produce it by a work of imitation; it is clear, therefore, that the causes should be included in the incidents of his story. Let us see, then, what kinds of incident strike one as horrible, or rather as piteous. In a deed of this description the parties must necessarily be either friends, or enemies, or indifferent to one another. Now when enemy does it on enemy, there is nothing to move us to pity either in his doing or in his meditating the deed, except so far as the actual pain of the sufferer is concerned; and the same is true when the parties are indifferent to one another. Whenever the tragic deed, however, is done within the family—when murder or the like is done or meditated by brother on brother, by son on father, by mother on son, or son on mother—these are the situations the poet should seek after. The traditional stories, accordingly, must be kept as they are, e.g. the murder of Clytaemnestra by Orestes and of Eriphyle by Alcmeon. At the same time even with these there is something left to the poet himself; it is for him to devise the right way of treating them. Let us explain more clearly what we mean by 'the right way'. The deed of horror may be done by the doer knowingly and consciously, as in the old poets, and in Medea's murder of her children in Euripides. Or he may do it, but in ignorance of his relationship, and discover that afterwards, as does the Oedipus in Sophocles. Here the deed is outside the play; but it may be within it, like the act of the Alcmeon in Astydamas, or that of the Telegonus in *Ulysses Wounded*. A third possibility is for one meditating some deadly injury to another, in ignorance of his relationship, to make the discovery in time to draw back. These exhaust the possibilities, since the deed must necessarily be either done or not done, and either knowingly or unknowingly.

The worst situation is when the personage is with full knowledge on the point of doing the deed, and leaves it undone. It is odious and also (through the absence of suffering) untragic; hence it is that no one is made to act thus except in some few instances, e.g. Haemon and Creon in *Antigone*. Next after this comes the actual perpetration of the deed meditated. A better situation than that, however, is for the deed to be done in ignorance, and the relationship discovered afterwards, since there is nothing odious in it, and the Discovery will serve to astound us. But the best of all is the last; what we have in *Cresphontes*, for example, where Merope, on the point of slaying her son, recognizes him in time; in *Iphigenia*, where sister and brother are in a like position; and in *Helle*, where the son recognizes his mother, when on the point of giving her up to her enemy.

This will explain why our tragedies are restricted (as we said just now) to such a small number of families. It was accident rather than art that led the poets in quest of subjects to embody this kind of incident in their Plots. They are still obliged, accordingly, to have recourse to the families in which such horrors have occurred.

On the construction of the Plot, and the kind of Plot required for Tragedy, enough has now been said.

15 In the Characters there are four points to aim at. First and foremost, that they shall be good. There will be an element of character in the play, if (as has been observed) what a personage says or does reveals a certain moral purpose; and a good element of character, if the purpose so revealed is good. Such goodness is possible in every type of personage, even in a woman or a slave, though the one is perhaps an inferior, and the other a wholly worthless being. The second point is to make them appropriate. The Character before us may be, say, manly; but it is not appropriate in a female Character to be

manly, or clever. The third is to make them like the reality, which is not the same as their being good and appropriate, in our sense of the term. The fourth is to make them consistent and the same throughout; even if inconsistency be part of the man before one for imitation as presenting that form of character, he should still be consistently inconsistent. We have an instance of baseness of character, not required for the story, in the Menelaus in *Orestes*; of the incongruous and unbefitting in the lamentation of Ulysses in *Scylla*, and in the (clever) speech of Melanippe; and of inconsistency in *Iphigenia at Aulis*, where Iphigenia the suppliant is utterly unlike the later Iphigenia. The right thing, however, is in the Characters just as in the incidents of the play to endeavour always after the necessary or the probable; so that whenever such-and-such a personage says or does such-and-such a thing, it shall be the necessary or probable outcome of his character; and whenever this incident follows on that, it shall be either the necessary or the probable consequence of it. From this one sees (to digress for a moment) that the Dénouement also should arise out of the plot itself, and not depend on a stage-artifice, as in *Medea*, or in the story of the (arrested) departure of the Greeks in the *Iliad*. The artifice must be reserved for matters outside the play—for past events beyond human knowledge, or events yet to come, which require to be foretold or announced; since it is the privilege of the Gods to know everything. There should be nothing improbable among the actual incidents. If it be unavoidable, however, it should be outside the tragedy, like the improbability in the *Oedipus* of Sophocles. But to return to the Characters. As Tragedy is an imitation of personages better than the ordinary man, we in our way should follow the example of good portrait-painters, who reproduce the distinctive features of a man, and at the same time, without losing the likeness, make him handsomer than he is. The poet in like manner, in portraying men quick or slow to anger, or with similar infirmities of character, must know how to represent them as such, and at the same time as good men, as Agathon and Homer have represented Achilles.

All these rules one must keep in mind throughout, and, further, those also for such points of stage-effect as directly depend on the art of the poet, since in these too one may often make mistakes. Enough, however, has been said on the subject in one of our published writings.

16 Discovery in general has been explained already. As for the species of Discovery, the first to be noted is (1) the least artistic form of it, of which the poets make most use through mere lack of invention, Discovery by signs or marks. Of these signs some are congenital, like the 'lance-head which the Earth-born have on them', or 'stars', such as Carcinus brings in his *Thyestes*; others acquired after birth—these latter being either marks on the body, e.g. scars, or external tokens, like necklaces, or (to take another sort of instance) the ark in the Discovery in *Tyro*. Even these, however, admit of two uses, a better and a worse; the scar of Ulysses is an instance; the Discovery of him through it is made in one way by the nurse and in another by the swineherds.

A Discovery using signs as a means of assurance is less artistic, as indeed are all such as imply reflection; whereas one bringing them in all of a sudden, as in the *Bath-story*, is of a better order. Next after these are (2) Discoveries made directly by the poet, which are inartistic for that very reason; e.g. Orestes' Discovery of himself in *Iphigenia:* whereas his sister reveals who she is by the letter, Orestes is made to say himself what the poet rather than the story demands. This, therefore, is not far removed from the first-mentioned fault, since he might have presented certain tokens as well. Another instance is the 'shuttle's voice' in the *Tereus* of Sophocles. (3) A third species is Discovery through memory, from a man's consciousness being awakened by something seen. Thus in *The Cyprioe* of Dicaeogenes, the sight of the picture makes the man burst into tears; and in the *Tale of Alcinous*, hearing the harper Ulysses is reminded of the past and weeps; the Discovery of them being the result. (4) A fourth kind is Discovery through reasoning; e.g. in *The Choephoroe*; 'One like me is here; there is no one like me but Orestes; he, therefore, must be here.' Or that which Polyidus the Sophist suggested for *Iphigenia*; since it was natural for Orestes to reflect: 'My sister was sacrificed, and I am to be sacrificed like her.' Or that in the *Tydeus* of Theodectes: 'I came to find a son, and am to die myself.' Or that in *The Phinidae:* on seeing the place the women inferred their fate, that they were to die there, since they had also been exposed there. (5) There is, too, a composite Discovery arising from bad reasoning on the side of the other party. An instance of it is in *Ulysses the False Messenger:* he said he should know the bow—which he had not seen; but to suppose from that that he would know it again (as though he had once seen it) was bad reasoning. (6) The best of all Discoveries, however, is that arising from the incidents themselves, when the great surprise comes about through a probable incident, like that in the *Oedipus* of Sophocles; and also in *Iphigenia*; for it was not improbable that she should wish to have a letter taken home. These last are the only Discoveries independent of the artifice of signs and necklaces. Next after them come Discoveries through reasoning.

William Shakespeare

ROMEO AND JULIET

The Elizabethan theater, in which the plays of Shakespeare and his great con-temporaries were produced, contrasted strikingly with the Greek theater. A reason for this was that the classic tradition, which might have related the ancient amphitheaters to the London playhouses, had been broken, and the English theater as an institution had evolved from its own beginnings and in its independent way. The Theatre, the first permanent playhouse built in or near London, was set up in 1576. As a structure it followed the patterns of the innyards in which during recent times dramatic works had been performed: it was unroofed; its pit recalled an innyard, its galleries the porches of an inn from which performances had been watched; and its stage was like the temporary platforms with dressing rooms behind them which had been improvised, as it were, for innyard productions.

In 1599, because of trouble about the lease of the land on which the Theatre stood, the sons of its builder tore down the structure and, using its old materials, rebuilt it on a new site on the Southwark side of the Thames. Shakespeare had a financial interest in the rebuilt and refurbished structure, the famous Globe Theatre. Here many of his masterpieces were first presented to the public.

Though it was considered the handsomest theater in London, the Globe, architecturally, probably was not prepossessing. The plain wooden and plaster walls of the circular structure were dotted with playbills and topped with a rough thatch, and experts guess that because of its small height, the building must have been rather heavy and thick in appearance. From the river stairs opposite Old St. Paul's, however, Londoners could look to the top of its turret and see whether a flag was unfurled to announce that a performance was to be given that afternoon. Playgoers were carried by boat across the Thames to the Bankside.

A typical audience was likely to be a heterogeneous assemblage ranging from the highest to the lowest ranks. Ben Jonson spoke of the audience as

> Compos'd of gamester, captain, knight, knight's man,
> Lady or pucelle, that wears mask or fan,
> Velvet or taffeta cap, rank'd in the dark,
> With the shop's foreman, or some such brave spark. . . .

"Groundlings" paid a penny for standing space in the pit; others paid a higher price—sometimes as high as half a crown—for comfortable cushioned seats in the three tiers of galleries or for stools on the stage. Such an audience, if it was to be pleased, had to be given a variety of fare. As Professor Holzknecht says, "Some in that assembly expected philosophical speculation, some wanted rough-and-tumble comedy, some liked music and dancing, some loved a good knockabout fight with plenty of sword-play, some made sure that the play had a clown in it before they paid the admission price, many were incapable of enjoying anything but inexplicable dumb-shows and noise, and some were for a jig or a tale of bawdry or they slept. In the modern theater, separate types of entertainment cater to this variety of tastes. *Hamlet* and *Romeo and Juliet* supplied them all."

In *Romeo and Juliet* intellectuals must have found the witty wordplay, the philosophical speeches, and the poetic lines appealing. Though the play had no clown, those who liked broad comedy at least had the nurse and her servant, Peter, to amuse them; and the scenes of physical violence were such stuff as the groundlings are believed to have found delightful. One sign of Shakespeare's marvelous skill was the way he amalgamated such varied elements into a meaningful and well-wrought play.

The theater as well as the audience was likely to shape any Elizabethan play. One must remember that the alcove or picture stage of modern times was far in the future. The main Elizabethan stage was a rectangular or wedge-shaped platform, probably about 43 feet in greatest width and 25 feet on a side, which jutted out into the circular pit. In addition, there were a lower inner stage (probably about 23 feet by eight feet) directly back of this platform, and an upper inner stage above. Unlike the platform, or "outer" stage, the latter stages could be shut off by a curtain or tapestry when not in use. From the dressing rooms back of these three stages, actors had access to all of them. Most of the action took place on the platform stage, surrounded on three sides by the audience in the pit. Little scenery was possible here, though properties such as trees or furniture might be brought up through trap doors or lowered from the canopy above the stage. Similar properties or even more elaborate ones could, of course, be placed on either of the inner stages while the curtains were drawn. The lower inner stage could be used in several ways: its curtains might serve as an arras for a room represented by the outer stage; or the curtains might be drawn to reveal a character seated in a chair, lying on a couch, or moving about a room or a small stage. The upper inner stage might be used to represent a balcony or an upstairs chamber. (See p. 697.)

Such a theater had both disadvantages and advantages for the playwright. Non-existent or sparse settings made it necessary for him to place most of his scenes against neutral or vague backgrounds (e.g., a public place, a street, the hall of a castle, a heath) or to denote their nature and atmosphere in dialog. But since the play did not have to be interrupted while scenes were changed, and since the three stages might be used alternatively, the action might be continuous. The mood or mounting tension of a dramatic presentation, therefore, was not dispelled during long halts during which the audience wandered out to a lobby to chatter and smoke.

Shakespeare and many of his contemporaries seem by present-day standards to have taken little interest or pains in seeing published correct editions of their plays. Their attitude can be explained in great part by the fact that a dramatist at that time did not write with any thought of publication (with the exception of Ben Jonson). Shakespeare seemed to have one aim: to write plays that pleased the public and that made money for the Globe Theatre, of which he was a stockholder. It was even to the disadvantage of a dramatic company, such as the Globe, to have one of the popular plays in its repertoire printed and circulated and thereby made available to other companies. The dramatist was not protected by copyright laws such as ours; he sold a finished play to a dramatic company and thereafter had no financial claims on it. In this situation pirated and corrupt texts of popular plays were common.

The text of *Romeo and Juliet* which has come down to us is one of the more reliable texts available for a Shakespeare play. A corrupt text had appeared in 1597; a second edition, which the title page described as "newly corrected, augmented, and amended" appeared in 1599. This second edition, whether or not it was published with the author's approval, is considered quite accurate and complete. It was probably printed from an actor's or prompter's copy as at one point the stage direction reads "Enter Will Kemp," not "Enter Peter." (See note 101, p. 828.) Will Kemp was a famous clown in Shakespeare's company.

Romeo and Juliet, judging by the many references to it by contemporary writers, was a great popular success. The style and other internal evidence along with references to it in writings as early as 1596 or possibly 1595, have led scholars to place the play early in Shakespeare's career. In its first form it may date from as early as 1591.

CHARACTERS

ESCALUS, *prince of Verona*
PARIS, *a young nobleman, kinsman to the prince*
MONTAGUE, ⎱ *heads of two houses at variance*
CAPULET, ⎰ *with each other*
An old man, cousin to CAPULET
ROMEO, *son to* MONTAGUE
MERCUTIO, *kinsman to the prince, and friend to* ROMEO
BENVOLIO, *nephew to* MONTAGUE, *and friend to* ROMEO
TYBALT, *nephew to* LADY CAPULET
FRIAR LAURENCE, ⎱ *Franciscans*
FRIAR JOHN, ⎰
BALTHASAR, *servant to* ROMEO
SAMPSON, ⎱ *servants to* CAPULET
GREGORY, ⎰
PETER, *servant to* JULIET's *nurse*
ABRAHAM, *servant to* MONTAGUE
An Apothecary
Three Musicians
Page to PARIS; *another Page; an Officer*
LADY MONTAGUE, *wife to* MONTAGUE
LADY CAPULET, *wife to* CAPULET
JULIET, *daughter to* CAPULET
Nurse to JULIET

Citizens of Verona; several Men and Women, relations to both houses; Maskers, Guards, Watchmen, and Attendants

CHORUS

Scene: Verona: Mantua

Prologue

Two households, both alike in dignity,
   In fair Verona, where we lay our scene,
From ancient grudge break to new mutiny,

Text and abridged footnotes from *The Complete Works of Shakespeare*, edited by Hardin Craig, Scott, Foresman, 1951. Used with the kind permission of Mr. Craig.

PROLOGUE. The prologue is in the form of a Shakespearean sonnet, three quatrains and a couplet of five-foot iambic verse. **3.** *mutiny*, state of discord. **6.** *star-cross'd*, thwarted by destiny.

Where civil blood makes civil hands unclean.
From forth the fatal loins of these two foes   5
    A pair of star-cross'd lovers take their life;
Whose misadventured piteous overthrows
    Do with their death bury their parents' strife.
The fearful passage of their death-mark'd love,
    And the continuance of their parents' rage,   10
Which, but their children's end, nought could remove,
    Is now the two hours' traffic of our stage;
The which if you with patient ears attend,
What here shall miss, our toil shall strive to mend.

Act I

Scene I: Verona. A public place.

Enter SAMPSON *and* GREGORY, *of the house of Capulet,
    armed with swords and bucklers.*

SAMPSON. Gregory, o' my word, we'll not carry coals.
GREGORY. No, for then we should be colliers.
SAMPSON. I mean, an we be in choler, we'll draw.
GREGORY. Ay, while you live, draw your neck out o' the collar.
SAMPSON. I strike quickly, being moved.
GREGORY. But thou art not quickly moved to strike.
SAMPSON. A dog of the house of Montague moves me.
GREGORY. To move is to stir; and to be valiant is to stand: therefore, if thou   10
    art moved, thou runn'st away.
SAMPSON. A dog of that house shall move me to stand: I will take the wall of
    any man or maid of Montague's.   16
GREGORY. That shows thee a weak slave; for the weakest goes to the wall.
SAMPSON. True; and therefore women, being the weaker vessels, are ever thrust
    to the wall: therefore I will push Montague's men from the wall, and thrust
    his maids to the wall.
GREGORY. The quarrel is between our masters and us their men.
SAMPSON. 'Tis all one, I will show myself a tyrant: when I have fought with
    the men, I will be cruel with the maids, and cut off their heads.
GREGORY. The heads of the maids?   29
SAMPSON. Ay, the heads of the maids, or their maidenheads; take it in what
    sense thou wilt.

9. *passage*, progress. **12.** *two hours' traffic of our stage.* This line is one of a small number of
references which enable us to tell the length of time occupied by a Shakespearean play. If
the time was nearer two hours than three, the play must have been rapidly recited, with little
loss of time between scenes. The bareness of the stage and the lack of a curtain would have
contributed to the speed of presentation.
    ACT I. SCENE I. **1.** *carry coals*, endure insults; the word play is on the dirty trade of the
collier. **4.** *choler*, one of the four humors, productive of anger. **6.** *collar*, halter. **10.** *moves*,
incites. **15.** *take the wall*, take the side of the walk nearest the wall, an act of discourtesy.

GREGORY. They must take it in sense that feel it.

SAMPSON. Me they shall feel while I am able to stand: and 'tis known I am a pretty piece of flesh. 35

GREGORY. 'Tis well thou art not fish; if thou hadst, thou hadst been poor John. Draw thy tool; here comes two of the house of the Montagues.

SAMPSON. My naked weapon is out: quarrel, I will back thee. 40

GREGORY. How! turn thy back and run?

SAMPSON. Fear me not.

GREGORY. No, marry; I fear thee!

SAMPSON. Let us take the law of our sides; let them begin.

GREGORY. I will frown as I pass by, and let them take it as they list.

SAMPSON. Nay, as they dare. I will bite my thumb at them; which is a disgrace to them, if they bear it. 50

(*Enter* ABRAHAM *and* BALTHASAR)

ABRAHAM. Do you bite your thumb at us, sir?

SAMPSON. I do bite my thumb, sir.

ABRAHAM. Do you bite your thumb at us, sir?

SAMPSON (*aside to* GREGORY). Is the law of our side, if I say ay?

GREGORY. No.

SAMPSON. No, sir, I do not bite my thumb at you, sir, but I bite my thumb, sir.

GREGORY. Do you quarrel, sir?

ABRAHAM. Quarrel, sir! no, sir. 60

SAMPSON. If you do, sir, I am for you: I serve as good a man as you.

ABRAHAM. No better.

SAMPSON. Well, sir.

GREGORY. Say 'better:' here comes one of my master's kinsmen.

SAMPSON. Yes, better, sir.

ABRAHAM. You lie.

SAMPSON. Draw, if you be men. Gregory, remember thy swashing blow. 70

(*They fight*)

(*Enter* BENVOLIO)

BENVOLIO. Part, fools!

Put up your swords; you know not what you do. (*Beats down their swords*)

(*Enter* TYBALT)

TYBALT. What, art thou drawn among these heartless hinds?

Turn thee, Benvolio, look upon thy death.

BENVOLIO. I do but keep the peace: put up thy sword, 75

Or manage it to part these men with me.

TYBALT. What, drawn, and talk of peace! I hate the word,

As I hate hell, all Montagues, and thee:

---

37. *poor John*, hake salted and dried—a poor kind of food. **42.** *Fear*, mistrust. **43.** *marry*, mild oath; originally an oath by the Virgin Mary. **47.** *list*, please. **48.** *bite my thumb*, an insulting gesture. **70.** *swashing*, crushing. **73.** *drawn*, with drawn sword. *heartless hinds*, cowardly menials.

And then my husband—God be with his soul!
A' was a merry man—took up the child:
'Yea,' quoth he, 'dost thou fall upon thy face?
Thou wilt fall backward when thou hast more wit;
Wilt thou not, Jule?' and, by my holidame,
The pretty wretch left crying and said 'Ay.'
To see, now, how a jest shall come about!
I warrant, an I should live a thousand years,
I never should forget it: 'Wilt thou not, Jule?' quoth he;
And, pretty fool, it stinted and said 'Ay.'
LADY CAPULET. Enough of this: I pray thee, hold thy peace.
NURSE. Yes, madam: yet I cannot choose but laugh,
To think it should leave crying and say 'Ay.'
And yet, I warrant, it had upon it brow
A bump as big as a young cockerel's stone;
A parlous knock; and it cried bitterly:
'Yea,' quoth my husband, 'fall'st upon thy face?
Thou wilt fall backward when thou comest to age;
Wilt thou not, Jule?' it stinted and said 'Ay.'
JULIET. And stint thou too, I pray thee, nurse, say I.
NURSE. Peace, I have done. God mark thee to his grace!
Thou wast the prettiest babe that e'er I nursed:
An I might live to see thee married once,
I have my wish.
LADY CAPULET. Marry, that 'marry' is the very theme
I came to talk of. Tell me, daughter Juliet,
How stands your disposition to be married?
JULIET. It is an honour that I dream not of.
NURSE. An honour! were not I thine only nurse,
I would say thou hadst suck'd wisdom from thy teat.
LADY CAPULET. Well, think of marriage now; younger than you,
Here in Verona, ladies of esteem,
Are made already mothers: by my count,
I was your mother much upon these years
That you are now a maid. Thus then in brief:
The valiant Paris seeks you for his love.
NURSE. A man, young lady! lady, such a man
As all the world—why, he 's a man of wax.
LADY CAPULET. Verona's summer hath not such a flower.
NURSE. Nay, he 's a flower; in faith, a very flower.
LADY CAPULET. What say you? can you love the gentleman?
This night you shall behold him at our feast;
Read o'er the volume of young Paris' face

40
45
50
55
60
65
70
75
80

40. *A'*, he. 43. *holidame*, same as "halidom," a relic or holy thing. 48. *stinted*, ceased.
52. *it*, its. 76. *a man of wax*, such as one would picture in wax, i.e., handsome.

And find delight writ there with beauty's pen;
Examine every married lineament
And see how one another lends content,
And what obscured in this fair volume lies   85
Find written in the margent of his eyes.
This precious book of love, this unbound lover,
To beautify him, only lacks a cover:
The fish lives in the sea, and 'tis much pride
For fair without the fair within to hide: 90
That book in many's eyes doth share the glory,
That in gold clasps locks in the golden story;
So shall you share all that he doth possess,
By having him, making yourself no less.

NURSE. No less! nay, bigger; women grow by men.

LADY CAPULET. Speak briefly, can you like of Paris' love?

JULIET. I'll look to like, if looking liking move:
But no more deep will I endart mine eye
Than your consent gives strength to make it fly.   99

(*Enter a* Servant)

SERVANT. Madam, the guests are come, supper served up, you called, my young
lady asked for, the nurse cursed in the pantry, and every thing in extremity.
I must hence to wait; I beseech you, follow straight.

LADY CAPULET. We follow thee. (*Exit Servant*) Juliet, the county stays.   105

NURSE. Go, girl, seek happy nights to happy days. (*Exeunt*)

Scene IV: *A street.*

Enter ROMEO, MERCUTIO, BENVOLIO, *with five or six* MASKERS, TORCH-BEARERS,
and others.

ROMEO. What, shall this speech be spoke for our excuse?
Or shall we on without apology?

BENVOLIO. The date is out of such prolixity:
We'll have no Cupid hoodwink'd with a scarf,
Bearing a Tartar's painted bow of lath,   5
Scaring the ladies like a crow-keeper;
Nor no without-book prologue, faintly spoke
After the prompter, for our entrance:

83. *married,* harmonized into mutual helpfulness. 86. *margent,* commentary or marginal
gloss. 89. *fish lives in the sea.* The figure of speech is of the binding of a book; since fishskins
were used to cover books, this "unbound lover" is yet to be made complete. 97-99. *I'll . . . fly.*
Juliet's attitude is one of proper obedience such as would be expected in the morals of the
time. 105. *county,* count.
    SCENE IV. 1. *speech.* The older fashion was for maskers to be preceded by a messenger with
a set speech, but *the date is out* for *such prolixity.* 4. *hoodwink'd,* blindfolded. 5. *Tartar's
painted bow.* Tartar's bows are said to have resembled the old Roman bow with which Cupid
was pictured. 6. *crow-keeper,* scarecrow.

But let them measure us by what they will;
We'll measure them a measure, and be gone.   10
ROMEO. Give me a torch: I am not for this ambling;
Being but heavy, I will bear the light.
MERCUTIO. Nay, gentle Romeo, we must have you dance.
ROMEO. Not I, believe me: you have dancing shoes
With nimble soles: I have a soul of lead   15
So stakes me to the ground I cannot move.
MERCUTIO. You are a lover; borrow Cupid's wings,
And soar with them above a common bound.
ROMEO. I am too sore enpierced with his shaft
To soar with his light feathers, and so bound,   20
I cannot bound a pitch above dull woe:
Under love's heavy burden do I sink.
MERCUTIO. And, to sink in it, should you burden love;
Too great oppression for a tender thing.
ROMEO. Is love a tender thing? it is too rough,   25
Too rude, too boisterous, and it pricks like thorn.
MERCUTIO. If love be rough with you, be rough with love;
Prick love for pricking, and you beat love down.
Give me a case to put my visage in:
A visor for a visor! what care I   30
What curious eye doth quote deformities?
Here are the beetle brows shall blush for me.
BENVOLIO. Come, knock and enter; and no sooner in,
But every man betake him to his legs.
ROMEO. A torch for me: let wantons light of heart   35
Tickle the senseless rushes with their heels,
For I am proverb'd with a grandsire phrase;
I'll be a candle-holder, and look on.
The game was ne'er so fair, and I am done.
MERCUTIO. Tut, dun 's the mouse, the constable's own word: 40
If thou art dun, we'll draw thee from the mire
Of this sir-reverence love, wherein thou stick'st
Up to the ears. Come, we burn daylight, ho!
ROMEO. Nay, that 's not so.
MERCUTIO.   I mean, sir, in delay
We waste our lights in vain, like lamps by day.   45

10. *measure . . . measure,* perform a dance. 11. *ambling,* walking affectedly; used contemptuously of dancing. 21. *pitch,* height. 30. *visor,* a mask, for an ugly masklike face.
31. *quote,* take notice of. 36. *rushes.* Rushes were used for floor coverings. 38. *candle-holder,*
an allusion to the proverb "A good candle-holder (i.e., a mere onlooker) is a good gamester."
40. *dun 's the mouse,* a common phrase usually taken to mean "keep still." *Dun* (l. 41)
alludes to a Christmas game, "Dun is in the mire," in which a heavy log was lifted by the
players. 42. *sir-reverence,* corruption of "save-reverence" (*salve-reverentia*), an apology for
something improper,

Take our good meaning, for our judgement sits
Five times in that ere once in our five wits.
ROMEO. And we mean well in going to this mask;
　But 'tis no wit to go.
MERCUTIO.　　　　　　Why, may one ask?
ROMEO. I dream'd a dream to-night.
MERCUTIO.　　　　　　And so did I.　　　　　　　　　　50
ROMEO. Well, what was yours?
MERCUTIO.　　　　　　That dreamers often lie.
ROMEO. In bed asleep, while they do dream things true.
MERCUTIO. O, then, I see Queen Mab hath been with you.
　She is the fairies' midwife, and she comes
　In shape no bigger than an agate-stone　　　　　　　55
　On the fore-finger of an alderman,
　Drawn with a team of little atomies
　Athwart men's noses as they lie asleep;
　Her waggon-spokes made of long spinners' legs,
　The cover of the wings of grasshoppers,　　　　　　60
　The traces of the smallest spider's web,
　The collars of the moonshine's watery beams,
　Her whip of cricket's bone, the lash of film,
　Her waggoner a small grey-coated gnat,
　Not half so big as a round little worm　　　　　　　65
　Prick'd from the lazy finger of a maid;
　Her chariot is an empty hazel-nut
　Made by the joiner squirrel or old grub,
　Time out o' mind the fairies' coachmakers.
　And in this state she gallops night by night　　　　　70
　Through lovers' brains, and then they dream of love;
　O'er courtiers' knees, that dream on court'sies straight,
　O'er lawyers' fingers, who straight dream on fees,
　O'er ladies' lips, who straight on kisses dream,
　Which oft the angry Mab with blisters plagues,　　　75
　Because their breaths with sweetmeats tainted are:
　Sometime she gallops o'er a courtier's nose,
　And then dreams he of smelling out a suit;
　And sometime comes she with a tithe-pig's tail
　Tickling a parson's nose as a' lies asleep,　　　　　80
　Then dreams he of another benefice:

47. *five wits*, the five faculties, usually given as common wit, imagination, fantasy, judgment, and reason. **53.** *Queen Mab*, a name of Celtic origin for the fairy queen. **57.** *atomies*, tiny creatures. **59.** *spinners'*, spiders'. **63.** *film*, gossamer thread. **64.** *waggoner*, coachman. **65.** *worm*. This alludes to an ancient and no doubt useful superstition that "worms breed in the fingers of the idle." **70.** *state*, pomp, dignity. **78.** *suit*, a request or plea at court. **79.** *tithe-pig's tail*. This alludes to the tenth pig given the parson as a church tax.

Sometime she driveth o'er a soldier's neck,
And then dreams he of cutting foreign throats,
Of breaches, ambuscadoes, Spanish blades,
Of healths five-fathom deep; and then anon 85
Drums in his ear, at which he starts and wakes,
And being thus frighted swears a prayer or two
And sleeps again. This is that very Mab
That plats the manes of horses in the night,
And bakes the elf-locks in foul sluttish hairs, 90
Which once untangled much misfortune bodes:
This is the hag, when maids lie on their backs,
That presses them and learns them first to bear,
Making them women of good carriage:
This is she——
ROMEO.   Peace, peace, Mercutio, peace! 95
Thou talk'st of nothing.
MERCUTIO.   True, I talk of dreams,
Which are the children of an idle brain,
Begot of nothing but vain fantasy,
Which is as thin of substance as the air
And more inconstant than the wind, who wooes 100
Even now the frozen bosom of the north,
And, being anger'd, puffs away from thence,
Turning his face to the dew-dropping south.
BENVOLIO. This wind, you talk of, blows us from ourselves;
Supper is done, and we shall come too late. 105
ROMEO. I fear, too early: for my mind misgives
Some consequence yet hanging in the stars
Shall bitterly begin his fearful date
With this night's revels and expire the term
Of a despised life closed in my breast 110
By some vile forfeit of untimely death.
But He, that hath the steerage of my course,
Direct my sail! On, lusty gentlemen.
BENVOLIO. Strike, drum. (*Exeunt*)

Scene V: A hall in CAPULET's *house.*

Musicians *waiting. Enter* Servingmen, *with napkins.*

FIRST SERVANT. Where 's Potpan, that he helps not to take away?
He shift a trencher? he scrape a trencher!

84. *Spanish blades,* swords made at Toledo in Spain. **85.** *anon,* by and by. **89.** *plats the manes of horses,* an allusion to the familiar superstition of "witches' stirrups," tangles in the manes of horses. **98.** *fantasy,* imagination. **108.** *date,* time, period. **109.** *expire* (transitive), bring to an end.
SCENE V. **2.** *trencher,* wooden dish or plate; Potpan is too proud to shift trenchers.

SECOND SERVANT. When good manners shall lie all in one or two men's hands
and they unwashed too, 'tis a foul thing.

FIRST SERVANT. Away with the joint-stools, remove the court-cupboard, look to
the plate. Good thou, save me a piece of marchpane; and, as thou lovest me,
let the porter let in Susan Grindstone and Nell. Antony, and Potpan!   11

SECOND SERVANT. Ay, boy, ready.

FIRST SERVANT. You are looked for and called for, asked for and sought for, in
the great chamber.

SECOND SERVANT. We cannot be here and there too. Cheerly, boys; be brisk
awhile, and the longer liver take all.

(*Enter* CAPULET, *with* JULIET *and others of his house, meeting the* Guests *and*
Maskers)

CAPULET. Welcome, gentlemen! ladies that have their toes
Unplagued with corns will have a bout with you.
Ah ha, my mistresses! which of you all   20
Will now deny to dance? she that makes dainty,
She, I'll swear, hath corns; am I come near ye now?
Welcome, gentlemen! I have seen the day
That I have worn a visor and could tell
A whispering tale in a fair lady's ear,   25
Such as would please: 'tis gone, 'tis gone, 'tis gone:
You are welcome, gentlemen! Come, musicians, play.
A hall, a hall! give room! and foot it, girls. (*Music plays, and they dance*)
More light, you knaves; and turn the tables up,
And quench the fire, the room is grown too hot.   30
Ah, sirrah, this unlook'd-for sport comes well.
Nay, sit, nay, sit, good cousin Capulet;
For you and I are past our dancing days:
How long is 't now since last yourself and I
Were in a mask?

SECOND CAPULET.   By 'r lady, thirty years.   35

CAPULET. What, man! 'tis not so much, 'tis not so much:
'Tis since the nuptial of Lucentio,
Come pentecost as quickly as it will,
Some five and twenty years; and then we mask'd.

SECOND CAPULET. 'Tis more, 'tis more: his son is elder, sir;   40
His son is thirty.

CAPULET.   Will you tell me that?
His son was but a ward two years ago.

---

7. *joint-stools*, stools, properly those made by a joiner. **8.** *court-cupboard*, sideboard. **9.**
marchpane, cake made from sugar and almonds. **17.** *longer . . . all*, proverbial expression.
21. *makes dainty*, hesitates from affectation to dance. **28.** *A hall!* Make room! **29.** *turn the*
tables up. Tables were probably made of hinged leaves and placed on trestles. They were put
aside for dancing. **38.** *pentecost*, a festival in honor of the descent of the Holy Spirit, seventh
Sunday after Easter. **42.** *ward*, a minor under guardianship.

ROMEO (*to a Servingman*). What lady is that, which doth enrich the hand
  Of yonder knight?
SERVANT. I know not, sir.   45
ROMEO. O, she doth teach the torches to burn bright!
  It seems she hangs upon the cheek of night
  Like a rich jewel in an Ethiope's ear;
  Beauty too rich for use, for earth too dear!
  So shows a snowy dove trooping with crows,   50
  As yonder lady o'er her fellows shows.
  The measure done, I'll watch her place of stand,
  And, touching hers, make blessed my rude hand.
  Did my heart love till now? forswear it, sight!
  For I ne'er saw true beauty till this night.   55
TYBALT. This, by his voice, should be a Montague.
  Fetch me my rapier, boy. What dares the slave
  Come hither, cover'd with an antic face,
  To fleer and scorn at our solemnity?
  Now, by the stock and honour of my kin,   60
  To strike him dead I hold it not a sin.
CAPULET. Why, how now, kinsman! wherefore storm you so?
TYBALT. Uncle, this is a Montague, our foe,
  A villain that is hither come in spite,
  To scorn at our solemnity this night.   65
CAPULET. Young Romeo is it?
TYBALT.   'Tis he, that villain Romeo.
CAPULET. Content thee, gentle coz, let him alone;
  He bears him like a portly gentleman;
  And, to say truth, Verona brags of him
  To be a virtuous and well govern'd youth: 70
  I would not for the wealth of all the town
  Here in my house do him disparagement:
  Therefore be patient, take no note of him:
  It is my will, the which if thou respect,
  Show a fair presence and put off these frowns,   75
  An ill-beseeming semblance for a feast.
TYBALT. It fits, when such a villain is a guest:
  I'll not endure him.
CAPULET.   He shall be endured:
  What, goodman boy! I say, he shall: go to;
  Am I the master here, or you? go to.   80
  You'll not endure him! God shall mend my soul!
  You'll make a mutiny among my guests!

58. *antic*, fantastic. 59. *fleer*, to look mockingly. 68. *portly*, of an excellent bearing. 74.
respect, regard. 79. *goodman boy*, a belittling ironical epithet. Capulet has a spirit more
reconcilable than that of Tybalt. *go to*, expression of impatience.

You will set cock-a-hoop! you'll be the man!
TYBALT. Why, uncle, 'tis a shame.
CAPULET.   Go to, go to;
   You are a saucy boy: is 't so, indeed?   85
   This trick may chance to scathe you, I know what:
   You must contrary me! marry, 'tis time.
   Well said, my hearts! You are a princox; go:
   Be quiet, or—More light, more light! For shame!
   I'll make you quiet. What, cheerly, my hearts!   90
TYBALT. Patience perforce with wilful choler meeting
   Makes my flesh tremble in their different greeting.
   I will withdraw: but this intrusion shall
   Now seeming sweet convert to bitter gall. (*Exit*)
ROMEO (*to* JULIET). If I profane with my unworthiest hand   95
   This holy shrine, the gentle fine is this:
   My lips, two blushing pilgrims, ready stand
   To smooth that rough touch with a tender kiss.
JULIET. Good pilgrim, you do wrong your hand too much,
   Which mannerly devotion shows in this;   100
   For saints have hands that pilgrims' hands do touch.
   And palm to palm is holy palmers' kiss.
ROMEO. Have not saints lips, and holy palmers too?
JULIET. Ay, pilgrim, lips that they must use in prayer.
ROMEO. O, then, dear saint, let lips do what hands do;   105
   They pray, grant thou, lest faith turn to despair.
JULIET. Saints do not move, though grant for prayers' sake.
ROMEO. Then move not, while my prayer's effect I take.
   Thus from my lips, by yours, my sin is purged.
JULIET. Then have my lips the sin that they have took.   110
ROMEO. Sin from my lips? O trespass sweetly urged!
   Give me my sin again.
JULIET.   You kiss by the book.
NURSE. Madam, your mother craves a word with you.
ROMEO. What is her mother?
NURSE.   Marry, bachelor,
   Her mother is the lady of the house,   115
   And a good lady, and a wise and virtuous:
   I nursed her daughter, that you talk'd withal;
   I tell you, he that can lay hold of her
   Shall have the chinks.

---

83. *cock-a-hoop*, complete disorder. **86.** *scathe*, injure. **88.** *princox*, pert, saucy boy. **91.** *Patience perforce*, patience upon compulsion; *patience* is a general word for self-control. **95-108.** *If . . . take.* These lines are in the form of a sonnet. They afford an example of Shakespeare's early exuberance in poetic style. **99.** *pilgrim.* Romeo was masquerading as a pilgrim or palmer. **112.** *by the book*, according to rule. **119.** *chinks*, money.

ROMEO.   Is she a Capulet?
  O dear account! my life is my foe's debt.   120
BENVOLIO. Away, be gone; the sport is at the best.
ROMEO. Ay, so I fear; the more is my unrest.
CAPULET. Nay, gentlemen, prepare not to be gone;
  We have a trifling foolish banquet towards.
  Is it e'en so? why, then, I thank you all;   125
  I thank you, honest gentlemen; good night.
  More torches here! Come on then, let 's to bed.
  Ah, sirrah, by my fay, it waxes late:
  I'll to my rest. (*Exeunt all but* JULIET *and Nurse*)
JULIET. Come hither, nurse. What is yond gentleman?   130
NURSE. The son and heir of old Tiberio.
JULIET. What's he that now is going out of door?
NURSE. Marry, that, I think, be young Petrucio.
JULIET. What 's he that follows there, that would not dance?
NURSE. I know not.   135
JULIET. Go, ask his name: if he be married,
  My grave is like to be my wedding bed.
NURSE. His name is Romeo, and a Montague;
  The only son of your great enemy.
JULIET. My only love sprung from my only hate!   140
  Too early seen unknown, and known too late!
  Prodigious birth of love it is to me,
  That I must love a loathed enemy.
NURSE. What 's this? what 's this?
JULIET.   A rhyme I learn'd even now   145
  Of one I danced withal. (*One calls within* 'Juliet')
NURSE.   Anon, anon!
  Come, let 's away; the strangers all are gone. (*Exeunt*)

Act II

Prologue

Enter CHORUS.

CHORUS. Now old desire doth in his death-bed lie,
  And young affection gapes to be his heir;
  That fair for which love groan'd for and would die,
  With tender Juliet match'd, is now not fair.
  Now Romeo is beloved and loves again,   5

---

120. *my foe's debt*, due to my foe, at his mercy. **124.** *foolish*, insignificant. *banquet*, dessert.
towards, in preparation. **128.** *fay*, faith.
    ACT II. PROLOGUE. **3.** *fair*, beautiful woman, beloved; allusion to Rosaline, the lady with
whom Romeo had fancied himself in love before he met Juliet.

Alike bewitched by the charm of looks,
But to his foe supposed he must complain,
  And she steal love's sweet bait from fearful hooks:
Being held a foe, he may not have access
  To breathe such vows as lovers use to swear;   10
And she as much in love, her means much less
  To meet her new-beloved any where:
But passion lends them power, time means, to meet,
Tempering extremities with extreme sweet. (*Exit*)

Scene I: A lane by the wall of CAPULET's *orchard.*

Enter ROMEO.

ROMEO. Can I go forward when my heart is here?
  Turn back, dull earth, and find thy centre out. (*He climbs the wall, and leaps down within it*)
(*Enter* BENVOLIO *and* MERCUTIO)
BENVOLIO. Romeo! my cousin Romeo!
MERCUTIO.   He is wise;
  And, on my life, hath stol'n him home to bed.
BENVOLIO. He ran this way, and leap'd this orchard wall: 5
  Call, good Mercutio.
MERCUTIO.   Nay, I'll conjure too.
  Romeo! humours! madman! passion! lover!
  Appear thou in the likeness of a sigh:
  Speak but one rhyme, and I am satisfied;
  Cry but 'Ay me!' pronounce but 'love' and 'dove;'   10
  Speak to my gossip Venus one fair word,
  One nick-name for her purblind son and heir,
  Young Adam Cupid, he that shot so trim,
  When King Cophetua loved the beggar-maid!
  He heareth not, he stirreth not, he moveth not;   15
  The ape is dead, and I must conjure him.
  I conjure thee by Rosaline's bright eyes,
  By her high forehead and her scarlet lip,
  By her fine foot, straight leg and quivering thigh
  And the demesnes that there adjacent lie,   20
  That in thy likeness thou appear to us!
BENVOLIO. An if he hear thee, thou wilt anger him.

---

10. *use to swear,* are in the habit of swearing. 13. *passion,* feeling of love.
    SCENE I. 2. *dull earth,* Romeo himself. *thy centre,* Juliet. The figure of speech is that of man as a microcosm or little world. 6. *conjure,* utter an incantation. 12. *purblind,* completely blind. 13. *Adam,* probably Adam Bell, a famous archer in the old ballads. 14. *King Cophetua,* reference to the ballad *King Cophetua and the Beggar Maid.* 16. *ape,* used as a term of endearment. 22. *An if,* if.

MERCUTIO. This cannot anger him: 'twould anger him
 To raise a spirit in his mistress' circle
 Of some strange nature, letting it there stand   25
 Till she had laid it and conjured it down;
 That were some spite: my invocation
 Is fair and honest, and in his mistress' name
 I conjure only but to raise up him.
BENVOLIO. Come, he hath hid himself among these trees,   30
 To be consorted with the humorous night:
 Blind is his love and best befits the dark.
MERCUTIO. If love be blind, love cannot hit the mark.
 Now will he sit under a medlar tree,
 And wish his mistress were that kind of fruit   35
 As maids call medlars, when they laugh alone.
 O, Romeo, that she were, O, that she were
 An open et cætera, thou a poperin pear!
 Romeo, good night: I'll to my truckle-bed;
 This field-bed is too cold for me to sleep: 40
 Come, shall we go?
BENVOLIO.   Go, then; for 'tis in vain
 To seek him here that means not to be found. (*Exeunt*)

 Scene II: CAPULET's *orchard*.

Enter ROMEO

ROMEO. He jests at scars that never felt a wound. (JULIET *appears above at a
  window*)
 But, soft! what light through yonder window breaks?
 It is the east, and Juliet is the sun.
 Arise, fair sun, and kill the envious moon,
 Who is already sick and pale with grief,   5
 That thou her maid art far more fair than she:
 Be not her maid, since she is envious;
 Her vestal livery is but sick and green
 And none but fools do wear it; cast it off.
 It is my lady, O, it is my love!   10
 O, that she knew she were!
 She speaks, yet she says nothing: what of that?

---

25. *strange*, belonging to another person. 27. *spite*, injury. 28. *honest*, chaste. 31. *consorted*, associated. *humorous*, moist; also, influenced by humor or mood. 34. *medlar*, the fruit of the *Mespilus germanica*, edible only when partly decayed. 38. *poperin*, variety of pear; derived from the Flemish town *Poperinghe* in Flanders. 39. *truckle-bed*, a bed on casters to be shoved under a standing bed. 40. *field-bed*, large bed; here, the ground.
  SCENE II. There is no break in the action. Romeo must have been standing on the front stage behind some obstruction to represent the garden wall. He speaks at once, then turns to observe Juliet. 8. *sick and green*, of a wan and sickly complexion; cf. "greensickness."

Her eye discourses; I will answer it.
I am too bold, 'tis not to me she speaks:
Two of the fairest stars in all the heaven,   15
Having some business, do entreat her eyes
To twinkle in their spheres till they return.
What if her eyes were there, they in her head?
The brightness of her cheek would shame those stars,
As daylight doth a lamp; her eyes in heaven   20
Would through the airy region stream so bright
That birds would sing and think it were not night.
See, how she leans her cheek upon her hand!
O, that I were a glove upon that hand,
That I might touch that cheek!
JULIET.   Ay me!
ROMEO.   She speaks: 25
O, speak again, bright angel! for thou art
As glorious to this night, being o'er my head,
As is a winged messenger of heaven
Unto the white-upturned wondering eyes
Of mortals that fall back to gaze on him   30
When he bestrides the lazy-pacing clouds
And sails upon the bosom of the air.
JULIET. O Romeo, Romeo! wherefore art thou Romeo?
Deny thy father and refuse thy name;
Or, if thou wilt not, be but sworn my love,   35
And I'll no longer be a Capulet.
ROMEO (aside). Shall I hear more, or shall I speak at this?
JULIET. 'Tis but thy name that is my enemy;
Thou art thyself, though not a Montague.
What 's Montague? it is nor hand, nor foot,   40
Nor arm, nor face, nor any other part
Belonging to a man. O, be some other name!
What 's in a name? that which we call a rose
By any other name would smell as sweet;
So Romeo would, were he not Romeo call'd,   45
Retain that dear perfection which he owes
Without that title. Romeo, doff thy name,
And for that name which is no part of thee
Take all myself.
ROMEO.   I take thee at thy word:
Call me but love, and I'll be new baptized;   50
Henceforth I never will be Romeo.

13. *discourses*, speaks. **17.** *spheres*, transparent concentric shells supposed to carry the
heavenly bodies with them in their revolution around the earth. **39.** *though . . . Montague*,
i.e., even if thou wert not a Montague. **46.** *owes*, owns.

JULIET. What man art thou that thus bescreen'd in night
  So stumblest on my counsel?
ROMEO.   By a name
  I know not how to tell thee who I am:
  My name, dear saint, is hateful to myself,   55
  Because it is an enemy to thee;
  Had I it written, I would tear the word.
JULIET. My ears have not yet drunk a hundred words
  Of that tongue's utterance, yet I know the sound:
  Art thou not Romeo and a Montague?   60
ROMEO. Neither, fair saint, if either thee dislike.
JULIET. How camest thou hither, tell me, and wherefore?
  The orchard walls are high and hard to climb,
  And the place death, considering who thou art,
  If any of my kinsmen find thee here.   65
ROMEO. With love's light wings did I o'erperch these walls;
  For stony limits cannot hold love out,
  And what love can do that dares love attempt;
  Therefore thy kinsmen are no let to me.
JULIET. If they do see thee, they will murder thee.   70
ROMEO. Alack, there lies more peril in thine eye
  Than twenty of their swords: look thou but sweet,
  And I am proof against their enmity.
JULIET. I would not for the world they saw thee here.
ROMEO. I have night's cloak to hide me from their sight;   75
  And but thou love me, let them find me here:
  My life were better ended by their hate,
  Than death prorogued, wanting of thy love.
JULIET. By whose direction found'st thou out this place?
ROMEO. By love, who first did prompt me to inquire;   80
  He lent me counsel and I lent him eyes.
  I am no pilot; yet, wert thou as far
  As that vast shore wash'd with the farthest sea,
  I would adventure for such merchandise.
JULIET. Thou know'st the mask of night is on my face,   85
  Else would a maiden blush bepaint my cheek
  For that which thou hast heard me speak tonight.
  Fain would I dwell on form, fain, fain deny
  What I have spoke: but farewell compliment!
  Dost thou love me? I know thou wilt say 'Ay,'   90
  And I will take thy word: yet, if thou swear'st,
  Thou mayst prove false; at lovers' perjuries,

---

53. *counsel,* secret thought. **61.** *dislike,* displease. **66.** *o'er-perch,* fly over and perch beyond.
69. *let,* hindrance. **78.** *prorogued,* postponed. *wanting,* lacking. **89.** *compliment,* punctilious-
ness, ceremony.

They say, Jove laughs. O gentle Romeo,
If thou dost love, pronounce it faithfully:
Or if thou think'st I am too quickly won,   95
I'll frown and be perverse and say thee nay,
So thou wilt woo; but else, not for the world.
In truth, fair Montague, I am too fond,
And therefore thou mayst think my 'haviour light:
But trust me, gentleman, I'll prove more true   100
Than those that have more cunning to be strange.
I should have been more strange, I must confess,
But that thou overheard'st, ere I was ware,
My true love's passion; therefore pardon me,
And not impute this yielding to light love,   105
Which the dark night hath so discovered.
ROMEO. Lady, by yonder blessed moon I swear
  That tips with silver all these fruit-tree tops—
JULIET. O, swear not by the moon, the inconstant moon,
  That monthly changes in her circled orb,   110
  Lest that thy love prove likewise variable.
ROMEO. What shall I swear by?
JULIET.   Do not swear at all;
  Or, if thou wilt, swear by thy gracious self,
  Which is the god of my idolatry,
  And I'll believe thee.
ROMEO.   If my heart's dear love——   115
JULIET. Well, do not swear: although I joy in thee,
  I have no joy of this contract to-night:
  It is too rash, too unadvised, too sudden:
  Too like the lightning, which doth cease to be
  Ere one can say 'It lightens.' Sweet, good night!   120
  This bud of love, by summer's ripening breath,
  May prove a beauteous flower when next we meet.
  Good night, good night! as sweet repose and rest
  Come to thy heart as that within my breast!
ROMEO. O, wilt thou leave me so unsatisfied?   125
JULIET. What satisfaction canst thou have to-night?
ROMEO. The exchange of thy love's faithful vow for mine.
JULIET. I gave thee mine before thou didst request it:
  And yet I would it were to give again.
ROMEO. Wouldst thou withdraw it? for what purpose, love?   130
JULIET. But to be frank, and give it thee again.
  And yet I wish but for the thing I have:

98. *fond*, foolish, infatuated. 101. *strange*, reserved. 105. *light*, frivolous, wanting in steadiness. 106. *discovered*, revealed. 110. *orb*, equivalent to *sphere*; see above, line 17. 131. *frank*, liberal, bounteous.

My bounty is as boundless as the sea,
My love as deep; the more I give to thee,
The more I have, for both are infinite. (*Nurse calls within*)   135
I hear some noise within; dear love, adieu!
Anon, good nurse! Sweet Montague, be true.
Stay but a little, I will come again. (*Exit, above*)
ROMEO. O blessed, blessed night! I am afeard,
Being in night, all this is but a dream,   140
Too flattering-sweet to be substantial.
(*Re-enter* JULIET, *above*)
JULIET. Three words, dear Romeo, and good night indeed.
If that thy bent of love be honourable,
Thy purpose marriage, send me word to-morrow,
By one that I'll procure to come to thee,   145
Where and what time thou wilt perform the rite;
And all my fortunes at thy foot I'll lay
And follow thee my lord throughout the world.
NURSE (*within*). Madam!
JULIET. I come, anon.——But if thou mean'st not well,   150
I do beseech thee——
NURSE.   (within). Madam!
JULIET.   By and by, I come:—
To cease thy suit, and leave me to my grief:
To-morrow will I send.
ROMEO.   So thrive my soul——
JULIET. A thousand times good night! (*Exit, above*)   155
ROMEO. A thousand times the worse, to want thy light.
Love goes toward love, as schoolboys from their books,
But love from love, toward school with heavy looks. (*Retiring*)
(*Re-enter* JULIET, *above*)
JULIET. Hist! Romeo, hist! O, for a falconer's voice,
To lure this tassel-gentle back again!   160
Bondage is hoarse, and may not speak aloud;
Else would I tear the cave where Echo lies,
And make her airy tongue more hoarse than mine,
With repetition of my Romeo's name.
ROMEO. It is my soul that calls upon my name: 165
How silver-sweet sound lovers' tongues by night,
Like softest music to attending ears!
JULIET. Romeo!
ROMEO.   My dear?
JULIET.   At what o'clock to-morrow
Shall I send to thee?

143. *bent*, purpose; from the idea of the tension of a bow. 145. *procure*, cause. 151. *By and by*, immediately. 160. *tassel-gentle*, tercel-gentle, the male of the goshawk.

ROMEO.   At the hour of nine.

JULIET. I will not fail: 'tis twenty years till then.   170
  I have forgot why I did call thee back.

ROMEO. Let me stand here till thou remember it.

JULIET. I shall forget, to have thee still stand there,
  Remembering how I love thy company.

ROMEO. And I'll still stay, to have thee still forget,   175
  Forgetting any other home but this.

JULIET. 'Tis almost morning; I would have thee gone:
  And yet no further than a wanton's bird;
  Who lets it hop a little from her hand,
  Like a poor prisoner in his twisted gyves,   180
  And with a silk thread plucks it back again,
  So loving-jealous of his liberty.

ROMEO. I would I were thy bird.

JULIET.   Sweet, so would I:
  Yet I should kill thee with much cherishing.
  Good night, good night! parting is such sweet sorrow,   185
  That I shall say good night till it be morrow. (*Exit, above*)

ROMEO. Sleep dwell upon thine eyes, peace in thy breast!
  Would I were sleep and peace, so sweet to rest!
  Hence will I go to my ghostly father's cell,
  His help to crave, and my dear hap to tell. (*Exit*)   190

Scene III: FRIAR LAURENCE's *cell.*

Enter FRIAR LAURENCE, *with a basket.*

FRIAR LAURENCE. The grey-eyed morn smiles on the frowning night,
  Chequering the eastern clouds with streaks of light,
  And flecked darkness like a drunkard reels
  From forth day's path and Titan's fiery wheels:
  Now, ere the sun advance his burning eye,   5
  The day to cheer and night's dank dew to dry,
  I must up-fill this osier cage of ours
  With baleful weeds and precious-juiced flowers.
  The earth that 's nature's mother is her tomb;
  What is her burying grave that is her womb,   10
  And from her womb children of divers kind
  We sucking on her natural bosom find,
  Many for many virtues excellent,
  None but for some and yet all different.
  O, mickle is the powerful grace that lies   15

173. *still*, always. **178.** *wanton's*, of one apt to jest and play. **180.** *gyves*, fetters. **189.** *ghostly*, spiritual. **190.** *dear hap*, good fortune.

    SCENE III. **3.** *flecked*, dappled. **4.** *Titan's*. Helios, the sun god, was a descendant of the race of Titans. **7.** *osier cage*, willow basket. **15.** *mickle*, great. *grace*, beneficent virtue.

In herbs, plants, stones, and their true qualities:
For nought so vile that on the earth doth live
But to the earth some special good doth give,
Nor aught so good but strain'd from that fair use
Revolts from true birth, stumbling on abuse: 20
Virtue itself turns vice, being misapplied;
And vice sometimes by action dignified.
Within the infant rind of this small flower
Poison hath residence and medicine power:
For this, being smelt, with that part cheers each part;   25
Being tasted, slays all senses with the heart.
Two such opposed kings encamp them still
In man as well as herbs, grace and rude will;
And where the worser is predominant,
Full soon the canker death eats up that plant.   30

(*Enter* ROMEO)

ROMEO. Good morrow, father.

FRIAR LAURENCE.   Benedicite!
What early tongue so sweet saluteth me?
Young son, it argues a distemper'd head
So soon to bid good morrow to thy bed:
Care keeps his watch in every old man's eye,   35
And where care lodges, sleep will never lie;
But where unbruised youth with unstuff'd brain
Doth couch his limbs, there golden sleep doth reign:
Therefore thy earliness doth me assure
Thou art up-roused by some distemperature;   40
Or if not so, then here I hit it right,
Our Romeo hath not been in bed to-night.

ROMEO. That last is true; the sweeter rest was mine.

FRIAR LAURENCE. God pardon sin! wast thou with Rosaline?

ROMEO. With Rosaline, my ghostly father? no;   45
I have forgot that name, and that name's woe.

FRIAR LAURENCE. That 's my good son: but where hast thou been, then?

ROMEO. I'll tell thee, ere thou ask it me again.
I have been feasting with mine enemy,
Where on a sudden one hath wounded me,   50
That 's by me wounded: both our remedies
Within thy help and holy physic lies:
I bear no hatred, blessed man, for, lo,
My intercession likewise steads my foe.

---

16. *qualities,* properties. **25.** *that part,* the odorous quality. **30.** *canker,* cankerworm. **33.** *distemper'd,* ill; a reference to a state of the humors in the body. **34.** *morrow,* morning. **37.** *unstuff'd,* not overcharged; another reference to the state of the humors. **52.** *physic,* medicine, healing property. **54.** *steads,* helps.

FRIAR LAURENCE. Be plain, good son, and homely in thy drift;   55
  Riddling confession finds but riddling shrift.
ROMEO. Then plainly know my heart's dear love is set
  On the fair daughter of rich Capulet:
  As mine on hers, so hers is set on mine;
  And all combined, save what thou must combine   60
  By holy marriage: when and where and how
  We met, we woo'd and made exchange of vow,
  I'll tell thee as we pass; but this I pray,
  That thou consent to marry us to-day.
FRIAR LAURENCE. Holy Saint Francis, what a change is here!   65
  Is Rosaline, whom thou didst love so dear,
  So soon forsaken? young men's love then lies
  Not truly in their hearts, but in their eyes.
  Jesu Maria, what a deal of brine
  Hath wash'd thy sallow cheeks for Rosaline!   70
  How much salt water thrown away in waste,
  To season love, that of it doth not taste!
  The sun not yet thy sighs from heaven clears,
  Thy old groans ring yet in my ancient ears;
  Lo, here upon thy cheek the stain doth sit   75
  Of an old tear that is not wash'd off yet:
  If e'er thou wast thyself and these woes thine,
  Thou and these woes were all for Rosaline:
  And art thou changed? pronounce this sentence then,
  Women may fall, when there's no strength in men.   80
ROMEO. Thou chid'st me oft for loving Rosaline.
FRIAR LAURENCE. For doting, not for loving, pupil mine.
ROMEO. And bad'st me bury love.
FRIAR LAURENCE.   Not in a grave,
  To lay one in, another out to have.
ROMEO. I pray thee, chide not: she whom I love now   85
  Doth grace for grace and love for love allow;
  The other did not so.
FRIAR LAURENCE.   O, she knew well
  Thy love did read by rote and could not spell.
  But come, young waverer, come, go with me,
  In one respect I'll thy assistant be;   90
  For this alliance may so happy prove,
  To turn your households' rancour to pure love.
ROMEO. O, let us hence; I stand on sudden haste.
FRIAR LAURENCE. Wisely and slow; they stumble that run fast. (*Exeunt*)

88. *did read by rote*, was merely a matter of repeating conventional expressions of love.
93. *stand on*, am in a position calling for.

Scene IV: A street.

Enter BENVOLIO *and* MERCUTIO.

MERCUTIO. Where the devil should this Romeo be?
  Came he not home to-night?
BENVOLIO. Not to his father's; I spoke with his man.
MERCUTIO. Ah, that same pale hard-hearted wench, that Rosaline,
  Torments him so, that he will sure run mad.   5
BENVOLIO. Tybalt, the kinsman of old Capulet,
  Hath sent a letter to his father's house.
MERCUTIO. A challenge, on my life.
BENVOLIO. Romeo will answer it.
MERCUTIO. Any man that can write may answer a letter.   10
BENVOLIO. Nay, he will answer the letter's master, how he dares, being dared.
MERCUTIO. Alas, poor Romeo! he is already dead; stabbed with a white wench's
  black eye; shot thorough the ear with a love-song; the very pin of his heart
  cleft with the blind bow-boy's butt-shaft: and is he a man to encounter
  Tybalt?   17
BENVOLIO. Why, what is Tybalt?
MERCUTIO. More than prince of cats, I can tell you. O, he is the courageous
  captain of complements. He fights as you sing prick-song, keeps time, distance, and proportion; rests me his minim rest, one, two, and the third in
  your bosom; the very butcher of a silk button, a duellist, a duellist; a gentleman of the very first house, of the first and second cause: ah, the immortal
  passado! the punto reverso! the hai!   27
BENVOLIO. The what?
MERCUTIO. The pox of such antic, lisping, affecting fantasticoes; these new
  tuners of accents! 'By Jesu, a very good blade! a very tall man! a very good
  whore!' Why, is not this a lamentable thing, grandsire, that we should be
  thus afflicted with these strange flies, these fashion-mongers, these perdona-
  mi's, who stand so much on the new form, that they cannot sit at ease on the
  old bench? O, their bones, their bones!   37
(Enter ROMEO)
BENVOLIO. Here comes Romeo, here comes Romeo.

SCENE IV. **15.** *pin*, peg in the center of a target. **16.** *butt-shaft*, an unbarbed arrow, used
by Cupid. **19.** *prince of cats.* The name of the king of cats in *Reynard the Fox* was Tybalt.
20. *captain of complements*, master of ceremony and outward show. **21.** *prick-song*, music
written out. **22.** *proportion*, rhythm. **23.** *minim*, half measure in music. **24.** *butcher of a silk
button*, one able to strike a button on his adversary's person. **26.** *first house*, possibly of the
best school of fencing. *first and second cause*, ready to quarrel for a trifle; probably an
allusion to the supposed code of quarreling. **27.** *passado*, forward thrust. *punto reverso*, back-
handed stroke. *hai*, home thrust. **30.** *fantasticoes*, coxcombs. **31.** *accents*, language. *tall*, fine.
35. *flies*, affected persons. *fashion-mongers*, those affecting gentility by following fashion.
perdona-mi's, Italian for "pardon me's"; a reference to the affectation of using foreign
phrases. **36-37.** *form . . . bench. Form* means both "fashion" and "bench." **37.** *bones*, French
bon with play on English "bone."

MERCUTIO. Without his roe, like a dried herring: O flesh, flesh, how art thou
fishified! Now is he for the numbers that Petrarch flowed in: Laura to his
lady was but a kitchen-wench; marry, she had a better love to be-rhyme her;
Dido a dowdy; Cleopatra a gipsy; Helen and Hero hildings and harlots;
Thisbe a grey eye or so, but not to the purpose. Signior Romeo, bon jour!
there's a French salutation to your French slop. You gave us the counterfeit
fairly last night.

ROMEO. Good morrow to you both. What counterfeit did I give you?   50

MERCUTIO. The slip, sir, the slip; can you not conceive?

ROMEO. Pardon, good Mercutio, my business was great; and in such a case as
mine a man may strain courtesy.

MERCUTIO. That 's as much as to say, such a case as yours constrains a man
to bow in the hams.

ROMEO. Meaning, to court'sy.

MERCUTIO. Thou hast most kindly hit it.

ROMEO. A most courteous exposition.   60

MERCUTIO. Nay, I am the very pink of courtesy.

ROMEO. Pink for flower.

MERCUTIO. Right.

ROMEO. Why, then is my pump well flowered.   64

MERCUTIO. Well said: follow me this jest now till thou hast worn out thy pump,
that when the single sole of it is worn, the jest may remain after the wearing
sole singular.

ROMEO. O single-soled jest, solely singular for the singleness!   70

MERCUTIO. Come between us, good Benvolio; my wits faint.

ROMEO. Switch and spurs, switch and spurs; or I'll cry a match.

MERCUTIO. Nay, if thy wits run the wild-goose chase, I have done, for thou
hast more of the wild-goose in one of thy wits than, I am sure, I have in my
whole five: was I with you there for the goose?

ROMEO. Thou wast never with me for any thing when thou wast not there for
the goose.   80

MERCUTIO. I will bite thee by the ear for that jest.

ROMEO. Nay, good goose, bite not.

MERCUTIO. Thy wit is a very bitter sweeting; it is a most sharp sauce.

ROMEO. And is it not well served in to a sweet goose?   86

MERCUTIO. O, here 's a wit of cheveril, that stretches from an inch narrow to
an ell broad!

39. *Without his roe*, sometimes explained as a pun on first syllable of Romeo's name, in which
case the last syllables might be taken as an expression of woe. **41.** *Petrarch*, Italian poet of
the Renaissance who addressed his sonnets to Laura. **45.** *hildings*, good-for-nothings. **48.** *slop*,
loose trousers of French fashion. *fairly*, handsomely. **51.** *slip*. Counterfeit coins were called
"slips." **56.** *case*, mask. **59.** *kindly*, naturally. **64.** *is . . . flowered*. The pump is pinked or
perforated in ornamental figures. **69.** *single-soled*, thin; contemptible, with pun on "soul."
70. *singleness*, feebleness. **74.** *cry a match*, claim a victory. **75.** *wild-goose chase*, a horse
race in which the leading rider might force his competitors to follow him wherever he went.
83. *sweeting*, probably a pun on an apple called the "sweeting." **87.** *cheveril*, kid leather.

ROMEO. I stretch it out for that word 'broad;' which added to the goose, proves thee far and wide a broad goose. 91

MERCUTIO. Why, is not this better now than groaning for love? now art thou sociable, now art thou Romeo; now art thou what thou art, by art as well as by nature: for this drivelling love is like a great natural, that runs lolling up and down to hide his bauble in a hole.

BENVOLIO. Stop there, stop there.

MERCUTIO. Thou desirest me to stop in my tale against the hair. 100

BENVOLIO. Thou wouldst else have made thy tale large.

MERCUTIO. O, thou art deceived; I would have made it short: for I was come to the whole depth of my tale; and meant, indeed, to occupy the argument no longer.

ROMEO. Here 's goodly gear!

(*Enter* Nurse *and* PETER)

MERCUTIO. A sail, a sail!

BENVOLIO. Two, two; a shirt and a smock. 110

NURSE. Peter!

PETER. Anon!

NURSE. My fan, Peter.

MERCUTIO. Good Peter, to hide her face; for her fan 's the fairer face.

NURSE. God ye good morrow, gentlemen. 115

MERCUTIO. God ye good den, fair gentlewoman.

NURSE. Is it good den?

MERCUTIO. 'Tis no less, I tell you, for the bawdy hand of the dial is now upon the prick of noon.

NURSE. Out upon you! what a man are you! 120

ROMEO. One, gentlewoman, that God hath made for himself to mar.

NURSE. By my troth, it is well said; 'for himself to mar,' quoth a'? Gentlemen, can any of you tell me where I may find the young Romeo?

ROMEO. I can tell you; but young Romeo will be older when you have found him than he was when you sought him: I am the youngest of that name, for fault of a worse.

NURSE. You say well. 130

MERCUTIO. Yea, is the worst well? very well took, i' faith; wisely, wisely.

NURSE. If you be he, sir, I desire some confidence with you.

BENVOLIO. She will indite him to some supper.

MERCUTIO. A bawd, a bawd, a bawd! So ho!

ROMEO. What hast thou found?

---

91. *broad goose,* possibly means that Mercutio is known far and wide as a goose. **96.** *natural,* idiot. **100.** *against the hair,* against the grain. **102.** *large,* unrestrained, with play on the sense of extension. **107.** *gear,* general word meaning "substance" or "stuff." **109.** *a shirt . . . smock,* a man and a woman. **119.** *prick,* point on the dial of a clock. **120.** *Out upon you,* expression of indignation. **124.** *quoth a',* said he; a sarcastic echoing of something said. **134.** *confidence,* the nurse's mistake for "conference." **135.** *indite,* Benvolio's malapropism for "invite."

MERCUTIO. No hare, sir; unless a hare, sir, in a lenten pie, that is something
stale and hoar ere it be spent. (*Sings*)   140

An old hare hoar,
And an old hare hoar,
Is very good meat in lent:
But a hare that is hoar
Is too much for a score,   145
When it hoars ere it be spent.

Romeo, will you come to your father's? we'll to dinner, thither.
ROMEO. I will follow you.
MERCUTIO. Farewell, ancient lady; farewell, (*singing*) 'lady, lady, lady.'   151
                                           (*Exeunt* MERCUTIO *and* BENVOLIO)
NURSE. Marry, farewell! I pray you, sir, what saucy merchant was this, that
was so full of his ropery?
ROMEO. A gentleman, nurse, that loves to hear himself talk, and will speak
more in a minute than he will stand to in a month.   157
NURSE. An a' speak any thing against me, I'll take him down, an a' were
lustier than he is, and twenty such Jacks; and if I cannot, I'll find those that
shall. Scurvy knave! I am none of his flirt-gills; I am none of his skains-
mates. And thou must stand by too, and suffer every knave to use me at his
pleasure?   164
PETER. I saw no man use you at his pleasure; if I had, my weapon should
quickly have been out, I warrant you: I dare draw as soon as another man,
if I see occasion in a good quarrel, and the law on my side.   169
NURSE. Now, afore God, I am so vexed, that every part about me quivers.
Scurvy knave! Pray you, sir, a word: and as I told you, my young lady
bade me inquire you out; what she bade me say, I will keep to myself: but
first let me tell ye, if ye should lead her into a fool's paradise, as they say,
it were a very gross kind of behaviour, as they say: for the gentlewoman is
young; and, therefore, if you should deal double with her, truly it were an
ill thing to be offered to any gentlewoman, and very weak dealing.   181
ROMEO. Nurse, commend me to thy lady and mistress. I protest unto thee——
NURSE. Good heart, and, i' faith, I will tell her as much: Lord, Lord, she will
be a joyful woman.
ROMEO. What wilt thou tell her, nurse? thou dost not mark me.
NURSE. I will tell her, sir, that you do protest; which, as I take it, is a gentle-
manlike offer.
ROMEO. Bid her devise   191
Some means to come to shrift this afternoon;

---

138. *hare*, used as a slang word for "courtesan." **144.** *hoar*, moldy. **151.** *'lady, lady, lady,'*
refrain from the ballad *Chaste Susanna.* **153.** *merchant*, fellow. **154.** *ropery*, the nurse's
mistake for "roguery." **160.** *Jacks*, used as a term of disparagement. **162.** *flirt-gills*, loose
women. **163.** *skains-mates*, not well understood; sometimes connected with "skein" (of
thread) or with "skain," a dagger. **183.** *protest*, vow. **188.** *mark*, attend to.

And there she shall at Friar Laurence' cell
Be shrived and married. Here is for thy pains.

NURSE. No, truly, sir; not a penny.

ROMEO. Go to; I say you shall.

NURSE. This afternoon, sir? well, she shall be there.

ROMEO. And stay, good nurse, behind the abbey wall:
Within this hour my man shall be with thee,   200
And bring thee cords made like a tackled stair;
Which to the high top-gallant of my joy
Must be my convoy in the secret night.
Farewell; be trusty, and I'll quit thy pains:
Farewell; commend me to thy mistress.   205

NURSE. Now God in heaven bless thee! Hark you, sir.

ROMEO. What say'st thou, my dear nurse?

NURSE. Is your man secret? Did you ne'er hear say,
Two may keep counsel, putting one away?

ROMEO. I warrant thee, my man 's as true as steel.   210

NURSE. Well, sir; my mistress is the sweetest lady—Lord, Lord! when 'twas a
little prating thing:—O, there is a nobleman in town, one Paris, that would
fain lay knife aboard; but she, good soul, had as lief see a toad, a very
toad, as see him. I anger her sometimes and tell her that Paris is the
properer man; but, I'll warrant you, when I say so, she looks as pale as any
clout in the versal world. Doth not rosemary and Romeo begin both with a
letter?   220

ROMEO. Ay, nurse; what of that? both with an R.

NURSE. Ah, mocker! that 's the dog's name; R is for the—No; I know it begins
with some other letter:—and she hath the prettiest sententious of it, of you
and rosemary, that it would do you good to hear it.

ROMEO. Commend me to thy lady.

NURSE. Ay, a thousand times. (*Exit* ROMEO) Peter!   230

PETER. Anon!

NURSE. Peter, take my fan, and go before, and apace. (*Exeunt*)

Scene V: CAPULET's *orchard.*

Enter JULIET.

JULIET. The clock struck nine when I did send the nurse;
In half an hour she promised to return.
Perchance she cannot meet him: that 's not so.
O, she is lame! love's heralds should be thoughts,

---

201. *tackled stair*, rope ladder. **202.** *top-gallant*, summit. **203.** *convoy*, a thing that conducts.
204. *quit*, reward, requite. **208.** *secret*, trustworthy. **216.** *lay . . . aboard*, board, grapple, as
in a sea fight. **217.** *properer*, handsomer. **219.** *clout*, rag; a proverbial expression. *versal*,
universal. **220.** *a*, the same. **223.** *the dog's name.* The letter R was thought to resemble the
dog's growl. **226.** *sententious.* The nurse probably means "sentence," pithy saying.

Which ten times faster glide than the sun's beams,　　　　5
Driving back shadows over louring hills:
Therefore do nimble-pinion'd doves draw love,
And therefore hath the wind-swift Cupid wings.
Now is the sun upon the highmost hill
Of this day's journey, and from nine till twelve　　　　10
Is three long hours, yet she is not come.
Had she affections and warm youthful blood,
She would be as swift in motion as a ball;
My words would bandy her to my sweet love,
And his to me:　　　　15
But old folks, many feign as they were dead;
Unwieldy, slow, heavy and pale as lead.
O God, she comes!
(*Enter* Nurse *and* PETER)
　　　　　　　O honey nurse, what news?
Hast thou met with him? Send thy man away.
NURSE. Peter, stay at the gate. (*Exit* PETER)　　　　20
JULIET. Now, good sweet nurse,—O Lord, why look'st thou sad?
Though news be sad, yet tell them merrily;
If good, thou shamest the music of sweet news
By playing it to me with so sour a face.
NURSE. I am a-weary, give me leave awhile:　　　　25
Fie, how my bones ache! what a jaunce have I had!
JULIET. I would thou hadst my bones, and I thy news.
Nay, come, I pray thee, speak; good, good nurse, speak.
NURSE. Jesu, what haste? can you not stay awhile?
Do you not see that I am out of breath?　　　　30
JULIET. How art thou out of breath, when thou hast breath
To say to me that thou art out of breath?
The excuse that thou dost make in this delay
Is longer than the tale thou dost excuse.
Is thy news good, or bad? answer to that;　　　　35
Say either, and I'll stay the circumstance:
Let me be satisfied, is 't good or bad?
NURSE. Well, you have made a simple choice; you know not how to choose a
man: Romeo! no, not he; though his face be better than any man's, yet his
leg excels all men's; and for a hand, and a foot, and a body, though they be
not to be talked on, yet they are past compare: he is not the flower of
courtesy, but, I'll warrant him, as gentle as a lamb. Go thy ways, wench;
serve God. What, have you dined at home?　　　　46

SCENE V. **7.** *love,* Venus, whose chariot was drawn by doves. **9.** *highmost,* highest; used of
the sun's position. **14.** *bandy,* toss to and fro. **25.** *give me leave,* let me alone. **26.** *jaunce,*
running to and fro. **34.** *excuse,* put off by making excuses. **36.** *stay the circumstance,* await
details.

JULIET. No, no: but all this did I know before.
What says he of our marriage? what of that?
NURSE. Lord, how my head aches! what a head have I!
It beats as it would fall in twenty pieces.   50
My back o' t' other side,—O my back, my back!
Beshrew your heart for sending me about,
To catch my death with jaunting up and down!
JULIET. I' faith, I am sorry that thou art not well.
Sweet, sweet, sweet nurse, tell me, what says my love?   55
NURSE. Your love says, like an honest gentleman, and a courteous, and a kind,
and a handsome, and, I warrant, a virtuous,—Where is your mother?
JULIET. Where is my mother! why, she is within;   60
Where should she be? How oddly thou repliest!
'Your love says, like an honest gentleman,
Where is your mother?'
NURSE.   O God's lady dear!
Are you so hot? marry, come up, I trow;
Is this the poultice for my aching bones?   65
Henceforward do your messages yourself.
JULIET. Here 's such a coil! come, what says Romeo?
NURSE. Have you got leave to go to shrift to-day?
JULIET. I have.
NURSE. Then hie you hence to Friar Laurence' cell;   70
There stays a husband to make you a wife:
Now comes the wanton blood up in your cheeks,
They'll be in scarlet straight at any news.
Hie you to church; I must another way,
To fetch a ladder, by the which your love   75
Must climb a bird's nest soon when it is dark:
I am the drudge and toil in your delight,
But you shall bear the burden soon at night.
Go; I'll to dinner; hie you to the cell.
JULIET. Hie to high fortune! Honest nurse, farewell. (*Exeunt*) 80

Scene VI: FRIAR LAURENCE's *cell.*

Enter FRIAR LAURENCE *and* ROMEO.

FRIAR LAURENCE. So smile the heavens upon this holy act,
That after hours with sorrow chide us not!
ROMEO. Amen, amen! but come what sorrow can,
It cannot countervail the exchange of joy
That one short minute gives me in her sight: 5

52. *Beshrew*, common objurgation meaning "ill-luck." 64. *come up*, expressive of impatience
like "go to." 67. *coil*, turmoil, bustle.
     SCENE VI. 4. *countervail*, equal.

Do thou but close our hands with holy words,
Then love-devouring death do what he dare;
It is enough I may but call her mine.
FRIAR LAURENCE. These violent delights have violent ends
And in their triumph die, like fire and powder,   10
Which as they kiss consume: the sweetest honey
Is loathsome in his own deliciousness
And in the taste confounds the appetite:
Therefore love moderately: long love doth so;
Too swift arrives as tardy as too slow.   15
(*Enter* JULIET)
Here comes the lady: O, so light a foot
Will ne'er wear out the everlasting flint:
A lover may bestride the gossamer
That idles in the wanton summer air,
And yet not fall; so light is vanity.   20
JULIET. Good even to my ghostly confessor.
FRIAR LAURENCE. Romeo shall thank thee, daughter, for us both.
JULIET. As much to him, else is his thanks too much.
ROMEO. Ah, Juliet, if the measure of thy joy
Be heap'd like mine and that thy skill be more   25
To blazon it, then sweeten with thy breath
This neighbour air, and let rich music's tongue
Unfold the imagined happiness that both
Receive in either by this dear encounter.
JULIET. Conceit, more rich in matter than in words,   30
Brags of his substance, not of ornament:
They are but beggars that can count their worth;
But my true love is grown to such excess
I cannot sum up sum of half my wealth.
FRIAR LAURENCE. Come, come with me, and we will make short work;   35
For, by your leaves, you shall not stay alone
Till holy church incorporate two in one. (*Exeunt*)

Act III

Scene I: A public place.

Enter MERCUTIO, BENVOLIO, Page, *and* Servants.

BENVOLIO. I pray thee, good Mercutio, let's retire:
The day is hot, the Capulets abroad,
And, if we meet, we shall not scape a brawl;
For now, these hot days, is the mad blood stirring.   4

---

13. *confounds*, destroys. **17.** *wear . . . flint.* The friar thinks of the roughness and sharpness of life's way. **18.** *gossamer*, spider's thread. **26.** *blazon*, heraldic term meaning "to describe" or "to set forth." **30.** *Conceit*, imagination, thought.

MERCUTIO. Thou art like one of those fellows that when he enters the confines
of a tavern claps me his sword upon the table and says 'God send me no need
of thee!' and by the operation of the second cup draws it on the drawer,
when indeed there is no need.   10

BENVOLIO. Am I like such a fellow?

MERCUTIO. Come, come, thou art as hot a Jack in thy mood as any in Italy,
and as soon moved to be moody, and as soon moody to be moved.

BENVOLIO. And what to?

MERCUTIO. Nay, an there were two such, we should have none shortly, for one
would kill the other. Thou! why, thou wilt quarrel with a man that hath a
hair more, or a hair less, in his beard, than thou hast: thou wilt quarrel with
a man for cracking nuts, having no other reason but because thou hast hazel
eyes: what eye but such an eye would spy out such a quarrel? Thy head is
as full of quarrels as an egg is full of meat, and yet thy head hath been
beaten as addle as an egg for quarrelling: thou hast quarrelled with a man
for coughing in the street, because he hath wakened thy dog that hath lain
asleep in the sun: didst thou not fall out with a tailor for wearing his new
doublet before Easter? with another, for tying his new shoes with old
riband? and yet thou wilt tutor me from quarrelling!   33

BENVOLIO. An I were so apt to quarrel as thou art, any man should buy the fee-
simple of my life for an hour and a quarter.

MERCUTIO. The fee simple! O simple!

BENVOLIO. By my head, here come the Capulets.

MERCUTIO. By my heel, I care not.

(*Enter* TYBALT *and others*)

TYBALT. Follow me close, for I will speak to them.   40
Gentlemen, good den: a word with one of you.

MERCUTIO. And but one word with one of us? couple it with something; make
it a word and a blow.

TYBALT. You shall find me apt enough to that, sir, an you will give me occasion.

MERCUTIO. Could you not take some occasion without giving?

TYBALT. Mercutio, thou consort'st with Romeo,—   47

MERCUTIO. Consort! what, dost thou make us minstrels? an thou make minstrels
of us, look to hear nothing but discords: here 's my fiddlestick; here 's that
shall make you dance. 'Zounds, consort!   52

BENVOLIO. We talk here in the public haunt of men:
Either withdraw unto some private place,
And reason coldly of your grievances,   55
Or else depart; here all eyes gaze on us.

MERCUTIO. Men's eyes were made to look, and let them gaze;
I will not budge for no man's pleasure, I.

(*Enter* ROMEO)

ACT III. SCENE I. **8.** *operation*, effect. **14.** *moody*, angry. **47.** *consort'st. To consort* meant
"to accompany" and also "to attend or wait upon." **52.** *'Zounds*, a modified form of the oath,
"by God's wounds."

TYBALT. Well, peace be with you, sir: here comes my man.

MERCUTIO. But I'll be hang'd, sir, if he wear your livery: 60
  Marry, go before to field, he'll be your follower;
  Your worship in that sense may call him 'man.'

TYBALT. Romeo, the hate I bear thee can afford
  No better term than this,—thou art a villain.

ROMEO. Tybalt, the reason that I have to love thee   65
  Doth much excuse the appertaining rage
  To such a greeting: villain am I none;
  Therefore farewell; I see thou know'st me not.

TYBALT. Boy, this shall not excuse the injuries
  That thou hast done me; therefore turn and draw.   70

ROMEO. I do protest, I never injured thee,
  But love thee better than thou canst devise,
  Till thou shalt know the reason of my love:
  And so, good Capulet,—which name I tender
  As dearly as my own,—be satisfied.   75

MERCUTIO. O calm, dishonourable, vile submission!
  Alla stoccata carries it away. (*Draws*)
  Tybalt, you rat-catcher, will you walk?

TYBALT. What wouldst thou have with me?   79

MERCUTIO. Good king of cats, nothing but one of your nine lives; that I mean
  to make bold withal, and, as you shall use me hereafter, dry-beat the rest of
  the eight. Will you pluck your sword out of his pilcher by the ears? make
  haste, lest mine be about your ears ere it be out.

TYBALT. I am for you. (*Drawing*)

ROMEO. Gentle Mercutio, put thy rapier up.

MERCUTIO. Come, sir, your passado. (*They fight*)

ROMEO. Draw, Benvolio; beat down their weapons.
  Gentlemen, for shame, forbear this outrage!   90
  Tybalt, Mercutio, the prince expressly hath
  Forbidden bandying in Verona streets:
  Hold, Tybalt! good Mercutio! (TYBALT *under* ROMEO'S *arm stabs* MERCUTIO,
  and flies with his followers)

MERCUTIO.   I am hurt.
  A plague o' both your houses! I am sped.
  Is he gone, and hath nothing?

BENVOLIO.   What, art thou hurt?   95

MERCUTIO. Ay, ay, a scratch, a scratch; marry, 'tis enough.
  Where is my page? Go, villain, fetch a surgeon. (*Exit Page*)

---

61. *field*, field of encounter. 77. *Alla stoccata*, Italian, "with the thrust"; i.e., the fencing
master wins the victory. 78. *rat-catcher*, an allusion to Tybalt as king of cats (see II, iv, 19).
83. *dry-beat*, beat soundly. 84. *pilcher*, scabbard. 88. *passado*, forward thrust; used derisively.
94. *sped*, done for.

ROMEO. Courage, man; the hurt cannot be much.   98

MERCUTIO. No. 'tis not so deep as a well, nor so wide as a church-door; but 'tis
enough, 'twill serve: ask for me to-morrow, and you shall find me a grave
man. I am peppered, I warrant, for this world. A plague o' both your houses!
'Zounds, a dog, a rat, a mouse, a cat, to scratch a man to death! a braggart,
a rogue, a villain, that fights by the book of arithmetic! Why the devil came
you between us? I was hurt under your arm.

ROMEO. I thought all for the best.

MERCUTIO. Help me into some house, Benvolio,   110
  Or I shall faint. A plague o' both your houses!
  They have made worms' meat of me: I have it,
  And soundly too: your houses! (*Exeunt* MERCUTIO *and* BENVOLIO)

ROMEO. This gentleman, the prince's near ally,
  My very friend, hath got his mortal hurt   115
  In my behalf; my reputation stain'd
  With Tybalt's slander,—Tybalt, that an hour
  Hath been my kinsman! O sweet Juliet,
  Thy beauty hath made me effeminate
  And in my temper soften'd valour's steel!   120

(*Re-enter* BENVOLIO)

BENVOLIO. O Romeo, Romeo, brave Mercutio's dead!
  That gallant spirit hath aspired the clouds,
  Which too untimely here did scorn the earth.

ROMEO. This day's black fate on moe days doth depend;
  This but begins the woe others must end.   125

BENVOLIO. Here comes the furious Tybalt back again.

ROMEO. Alive, in triumph! and Mercutio slain!
  Away to heaven, respective lenity,
  And fire-eyed fury be my conduct now!

(*Re-enter* TYBALT)

  Now, Tybalt, take the villain back again,
  That late thou gavest me; for Mercutio's soul   130
  Is but a little way above our heads,
  Staying for thine to keep him company:
  Either thou, or I, or both, must go with him.

TYBALT. Thou, wretched boy, that didst consort him here.   135
  Shalt with him hence.

ROMEO.   This shall determine that. (*They fight;* TYBALT *falls*)

BENVOLIO. Romeo, away, be gone!
  The citizens are up, and Tybalt slain.

102. *grave man.* Mercutio thus makes puns with his last breath. 106. *by the book of
arithmetic,* merely by theory. Back of the whole scene lies a current controversy between the
old broadsword style of fencing and the new French style of rapier fencing. 114. *ally,* kinsman. 115. *very,* true. 124. *moe,* more. 128. *respective lenity,* considerate gentleness. 129.
conduct, guide.

Stand not amazed: the prince will doom thee death,
If thou art taken: hence, be gone, away!   140
ROMEO. O, I am fortune's fool!
BENVOLIO.   Why dost thou stay? (*Exit* ROMEO)
(*Enter* Citizens, &c.)
FIRST CITIZEN. Which way ran he that kill'd Mercutio?
Tybalt, that murderer, which way ran he?
BENVOLIO. There lies that Tybalt.
FIRST CITIZEN.   Up, sir, go with me;
I charge thee in the prince's name, obey.   145
(*Enter* PRINCE, *attended;* MONTAGUE, CAPULET, *their Wives, and others*)
PRINCE. Where are the vile beginners of this fray?
BENVOLIO. O noble prince, I can discover all
The unlucky manage of this fatal brawl:
There lies the man, slain by young Romeo,
That slew thy kinsman, brave Mercutio.   150
LADY CAPULET. Tybalt, my cousin! O my brother's child!
O prince! O cousin! husband! O, the blood is spilt
Of my dear kinsman! Prince, as thou art true,
For blood of ours, shed blood of Montague.
O cousin, cousin!   155
PRINCE. Benvolio, who began this bloody fray?
BENVOLIO. Tybalt, here slain, whom Romeo's hand did slay;
Romeo that spoke him fair, bade him bethink
How nice the quarrel was, and urged withal
Your high displeasure: all this uttered   160
With gentle breath, calm look, knees humbly bow'd,
Could not take truce with the unruly spleen
Of Tybalt deaf to peace, but that he tilts
With piercing steel at bold Mercutio's breast,
Who, all as hot, turns deadly point to point,   165
And, with martial scorn, with one hand beats
Cold death aside, and with the other sends
It back to Tybalt, whose dexterity
Retorts it: Romeo he cries aloud,
'Hold, friends! friends, part!' and, swifter than his tongue,   170
His agile arm beats down their fatal points,
And 'twixt them rushes; underneath whose arm
An envious thrust from Tybalt hit the life
Of stout Mercutio, and then Tybalt fled;
But by and by comes back to Romeo,   175
Who had but newly entertain'd revenge,

139. *doom,* adjudge. **148.** *manage,* management. **158.** *fair,* civilly. **159.** *nice,* trivial. **162.** *take truce,* make peace. *unruly spleen,* ungovernable rage. **163.** *tilts,* strikes. **169.** *Retorts,* throws back upon his adversary. **173.** *envious,* i.e., Tybalt's blow was a malicious one.

And to 't they go like lightning, for, ere I
Could draw to part them, was stout Tybalt slain,
And, as he fell, did Romeo turn and fly.
This is the truth, or let Benvolio die.   180

LADY CAPULET. He is a kinsman to the Montague;
Affection makes him false; he speaks not true:
Some twenty of them fought in this black strife,
And all those twenty could but kill one life.
I beg for justice, which thou, prince, must give;   185
Romeo slew Tybalt, Romeo must not live.

PRINCE. Romeo slew him, he slew Mercutio;
Who now the price of his dear blood doth owe?

MONTAGUE. Not Romeo, prince, he was Mercutio's friend;
His fault concludes but what the law should end,   190
The life of Tybalt.

PRINCE.   And for that offence
Immediately we do exile him hence:
I have an interest in your hate's proceeding,
My blood for your rude brawls doth lie a-bleeding;
But I'll amerce you with so strong a fine   195
That you shall all repent the loss of mine:
I will be deaf to pleading and excuses;
Nor tears nor prayers shall purchase out abuses:
Therefore use none: let Romeo hence in haste,
Else, when he 's found, that hour is his last.   200
Bear hence this body and attend our will:
Mercy but murders, pardoning those that kill. (*Exeunt*)

Scene II: CAPULET's *orchard.*

Enter JULIET.

JULIET. Gallop apace, you fiery-footed steeds,
Towards Phœbus' lodging: such a waggoner
As Phæthon would whip you to the west,
And bring in cloudy night immediately.
Spread thy close curtain, love-performing night,   5
That runaways' eyes may wink, and Romeo
Leap to these arms, untalk'd of and unseen.
Lovers can see to do their amorous rites

---

195. *amerce,* punish by fine. **198.** *purchase out,* redeem, exempt from penalty. *abuses,*
misdeeds.

SCENE II. **3.** *Phæthon,* son of Helios, who was allowed to assume the reins of the sun for
a day; not being able to restrain the steeds, he had to be slain by the thunderbolt of Jupiter
in order that the universe might not be destroyed. **6.** *runaways' eyes,* a famous crux of which
there is no satisfactory explanation. The allusion to Phæthon (l. 3) may here be repeated.
wink, shut.

By their own beauties; or, if love be blind,
It best agrees with night. Come, civil night,   10
Thou sober-suited matron, all in black,
And learn me how to lose a winning match,
Play'd for a pair of stainless maidenhoods:
Hood my unmann'd blood, bating in my cheeks,
With thy black mantle; till strange love, grown bold,   15
Think true love acted simple modesty.
Come, night; come, Romeo; come, thou day in night;
For thou wilt lie upon the wings of night
Whiter than new snow on a raven's back.
Come, gentle night, come, loving, black-brow'd night,   20
Give me my Romeo; and, when he shall die,
Take him and cut him out in little stars,
And he will make the face of heaven so fine
That all the world will be in love with night
And pay no worship to the garish sun.   25
O, I have bought the mansion of a love,
But not possess'd it, and, though I am sold,
Not yet enjoy'd: so tedious is this day
As is the night before some festival
To an impatient child that hath new robes   30
And may not wear them. O, here comes my nurse,
And she brings news; and every tongue that speaks
But Romeo's name speaks heavenly eloquence.
(*Enter* Nurse, *with cords*)
Now, nurse, what news? What hast thou there? the cords
That Romeo bid thee fetch?
NURSE.   Ay, ay, the cords. (*Throws them down*)   35
JULIET. Ay me! what news? why dost thou wring thy hands?
NURSE. Ay, well-a-day! he 's dead, he 's dead, he 's dead!
    We are undone, lady, we are undone!
    Alack the day! he 's gone, he 's kill'd, he 's dead!
JULIET. Can heaven be so envious?
NURSE.   Romeo can,   40
    Though heaven cannot: O Romeo, Romeo!
    Who ever would have thought it? Romeo!
JULIET. What devil art thou, that dost torment me thus?
    This torture should be roar'd in dismal hell.
    Hath Romeo slain himself? say thou but 'I,'   45
    And that bare vowel 'I' shall poison more
    Than the death-darting eye of cockatrice:

---

10. *civil*, well-ordered. **14.** *Hood*, cover; term in falconry. The hawk's eyes were covered so that it would not bate, or beat the wings. *unmann'd*, another term in falconry meaning "untamed." **45.** '*I*,' ay, yes. **47.** *cockatrice*, basilisk, a fabulous serpent which could kill by its look.

I am not I, if there be such an I;
Or those eyes shut, that make thee answer 'I.'
If he be slain, say 'I'; or if not, no: 50
Brief sounds determine of my weal or woe.
NURSE. I saw the wound, I saw it with mine eyes,
God save the mark!—here on his manly breast:
A piteous corse, a bloody piteous corse;
Pale, pale as ashes, all bedaub'd in blood,   55
All in gore-blood; I swounded at the sight.
JULIET. O, break, my heart! poor bankrupt, break at once!
To prison, eyes, ne'er look on liberty!
Vile earth, to earth resign; end motion here;
And thou and Romeo press one heavy bier!   60
NURSE. O Tybalt, Tybalt, the best friend I had!
O courteous Tybalt! honest gentleman!
That ever I should live to see thee dead!
JULIET. What storm is this that blows so contrary?
Is Romeo slaughter'd, and is Tybalt dead?   65
My dear-loved cousin, and my dearer lord?
Then, dreadful trumpet, sound the general doom!
For who is living, if those two are gone?
NURSE. Tybalt is gone, and Romeo banished;
Romeo that kill'd him, he is banished.   70
JULIET. O God! did Romeo's hand shed Tybalt's blood?
NURSE. It did, it did; alas the day, it did!
JULIET. O serpent heart, hid with a flowering face!
Did ever dragon keep so fair a cave?
Beautiful tyrant! fiend angelical!   75
Dove-feather'd raven! wolvish-ravening lamb!
Despised substance of divinest show!
Just opposite to what thou justly seem'st,
A damned saint, an honourable villain!
O nature, what hadst thou to do in hell,   80
When thou didst bower the spirit of a fiend
In mortal paradise of such sweet flesh?
Was ever book containing such vile matter
So fairly bound? O, that deceit should dwell
In such a gorgeous palace!
NURSE.   There 's no trust,   85
No faith, no honesty in men; all perjured,
All forsworn, all naught, all dissemblers.
Ah, where 's my man? give me some aqua vitæ:

53. *God save the mark*, God forbid; a familiar oath originally intended to avert ill omen.
56. *gore-blood*, clotted blood. **59.** *motion*, power of movement. **81.** *bower*, give lodging to.
88. *aqua vitæ*, distilled spirit.

These griefs, these woes, these sorrows make me old.
Shame come to Romeo!

JULIET.   Blister'd be thy tongue   90
For such a wish! he was not born to shame:
Upon his brow shame is ashamed to sit;
For 'tis a throne where honour may be crown'd
Sole monarch of the universal earth.
O, what a beast was I to chide at him!   95

NURSE. Will you speak well of him that kill'd your cousin?

JULIET. Shall I speak ill of him that is my husband?
Ah, poor my lord, what tongue shall smooth thy name,
When I, thy three-hours wife, have mangled it?
But, wherefore, villain, didst thou kill my cousin?   100
That villain cousin would have kill'd my husband:
Back, foolish tears, back to your native spring;
Your tributary drops belong to woe,
Which you, mistaking, offer up to joy.
My husband lives, that Tybalt would have slain;   105
And Tybalt 's dead, that would have slain my husband:
All this is comfort; wherefore weep I then?
Some word there was, worser than Tybalt's death,
That murder'd me: I would forget it fain;
But, O, it presses to my memory,   110
Like damned guilty deeds to sinners' minds:
'Tybalt is dead, and Romeo—banished;'
That 'banished,' that one word 'banished,'
Hath slain ten thousand Tybalts. Tybalt's death
Was woe enough, if it had ended there: 115
Or, if sour woe delights in fellowship
And needly will be rank'd with other griefs,
Why follow'd not, when she said 'Tybalt 's dead,'
Thy father, or thy mother, nay, or both,
Which modern lamentation might have moved?   120
But with a rearward following Tybalt's death,
'Romeo is banished,' to speak that word,
Is father, mother, Tybalt, Romeo, Juliet,
All slain, all dead. 'Romeo is banished!'
There is no end, no limit, measure, bound,   125
In that word's death; no words can that woe sound.
Where is my father, and my mother, nurse?

NURSE. Weeping and wailing over Tybalt's corse:
Will you go to them? I will bring you thither.

JULIET. Wash they his wounds with tears: mine shall be spent,   130

117, *needly*, of necessity. 120, *modern*, ordinary. 121, *rearward*, rear guard,

When theirs are dry, for Romeo's banishment.
Take up those cords: poor ropes, you are beguiled,
Both you and I; for Romeo is exiled:
He made you for a highway to my bed;
But I, a maid, die maiden-widowed.   135
Come, cords, come, nurse; I'll to my wedding-bed;
And death, not Romeo, take my maidenhead!
NURSE. Hie to your chamber: I'll find Romeo
  To comfort you: I wot well where he is.
  Hark ye, your Romeo will be here at night: 140
  I'll to him; he is hid at Laurence' cell.
JULIET. O, find him! give this ring to my true knight,
  And bid him come to take his last farewell. (*Exeunt*)

Scene III: FRIAR LAURENCE'*s cell.*

Enter FRIAR LAURENCE.

FRIAR LAURENCE. Romeo, come forth; come forth, thou fearful man:
  Affliction is enamour'd of thy parts,
  And thou art wedded to calamity.
(*Enter* ROMEO)
ROMEO. Father, what news? what is the prince's doom?
  What sorrow craves acquaintance at my hand,   5
  That I yet know not?
FRIAR LAURENCE.   Too familiar
  Is my dear son with such sour company:
  I bring thee tidings of the prince's doom.
ROMEO. What less than dooms-day is the prince's doom?
FRIAR LAURENCE. A gentler judgement vanish'd from his lips, 10
  Not body's death, but body's banishment.
ROMEO. Ha, banishment! be merciful, say 'death;'
  For exile hath more terror in his look,
  Much more than death: do not say 'banishment.'
FRIAR LAURENCE. Hence from Verona art thou banished: 15
  Be patient, for the world is broad and wide.
ROMEO. There is no world without Verona walls,
  But purgatory, torture, hell itself.
  Hence-banished is banish'd from the world,
  And world's exile is death: then banished,   20
  Is death mis-term'd; calling death banishment,
  Thou cutt'st my head off with a golden axe,
  And smilest upon the stroke that murders me.
FRIAR LAURENCE. O deadly sin! O rude unthankfulness!

139. *wot,* know.
  SCENE III. **10.** *vanish'd,* issued.

Thy fault our law calls death; but the kind prince,   25
Taking thy part, hath rush'd aside the law,
And turn'd that black word death to banishment:
This is dear mercy, and thou seest it not.
ROMEO. 'Tis torture, and not mercy: heaven is here,
   Where Juliet lives; and every cat and dog   30
   And little mouse, every unworthy thing,
   Live here in heaven and may look on her;
   But Romeo may not: more validity,
   More honourable state, more courtship lives
   In carrion-flies than Romeo: they may seize   35
   On the white wonder of dear Juliet's hand
   And steal immortal blessing from her lips,
   Who, even in pure and vestal modesty,
   Still blush, as thinking their own kisses sin;
   But Romeo may not; he is banished: 40
   Flies may do this, but I from this must fly:
   They are free men, but I am banished.
   And say'st thou yet that exile is not death?
   Hadst thou no poison mix'd, no sharp-ground knife,
   No sudden mean of death, though ne'er so mean,   45
   But 'banished' to kill me?—'banished'?
   O friar, the damned use that word in hell;
   Howlings attend it: how hast thou the heart,
   Being a divine, a ghostly confessor,
   A sin-absolver, and my friend profess'd,   50
   To mangle me with that word 'banished'?
FRIAR LAURENCE. Thou fond mad man, hear me but speak a word.
ROMEO. O, thou wilt speak again of banishment.
FRIAR LAURENCE. I'll give thee armour to keep off that word;
   Adversity's sweet milk, philosophy,   55
   To comfort thee, though thou art banished.
ROMEO. Yet 'banished'? Hang up philosophy!
   Unless philosophy can make a Juliet,
   Displant a town, reverse a prince's doom,
   It helps not, it prevails not: talk no more.   60
FRIAR LAURENCE. O, then I see that madmen have no ears.
ROMEO. How should they, when that wise men have no eyes?
FRIAR LAURENCE. Let me dispute with thee of thy estate.
ROMEO. Thou canst not speak of that thou dost not feel:
   Wert thou as young as I, Juliet thy love,   65
   An hour but married, Tybalt murdered,

26. *rush'd*, thrust (aside). 28. *dear*, rare, unusual; or kind, generous. 33. *validity*, value.
34. *courtship*, both courtliness and wooing. 45. *mean . . . mean*, means . . . base. 63. *dispute*,
reason. *estate*, situation.

Doting like me and like me banished,
Then mightst thou speak, then mightst thou tear thy hair,
And fall upon the ground, as I do now,
Taking the measure of an unmade grave. (*Knocking within*) 70
FRIAR LAURENCE. Arise; one knocks; good Romeo, hide thyself.
ROMEO. Not I; unless the breath of heart-sick groans,
Mist-like, infold me from the search of eyes. (*Knocking*)
FRIAR LAURENCE. Hark, how they knock! Who's there? Romeo, arise;
Thou wilt be taken. Stay awhile! Stand up; (*Knocking*) 75
Run to my study. By and by! God's will,
What simpleness is this! I come, I come! (*Knocking*)
Who knocks so hard? whence come you? what 's your will?
NURSE (*within*). Let me come in, and you shall know my errand;
I come from Lady Juliet.
FRIAR LAURENCE.   Welcome, then. 80
(*Enter* Nurse)
NURSE. O holy friar, O, tell me, holy friar,
Where is my lady's lord, where 's Romeo?
FRIAR LAURENCE. There on the ground, with his own tears made drunk.
NURSE. O, he is even in my mistress' case,
Just in her case! O woful sympathy! 85
Piteous predicament! Even so lies she,
Blubbering and weeping, weeping and blubbering.
Stand up, stand up; stand, an you be a man:
For Juliet's sake, for her sake, rise and stand;
Why should you fall into so deep an O? 90
ROMEO. Nurse!
NURSE. Ah sir! ah sir! Well, death 's the end of all.
ROMEO. Spakest thou of Juliet? how is it with her?
Doth she not think me an old murderer,
Now I have stain'd the childhood of our joy 95
With blood removed but little from her own?
Where is she? and how doth she? and what says
My conceal'd lady to our cancell'd love?
NURSE. O, she says nothing, sir, but weeps and weeps;
And now falls on her bed; and then starts up, 100
And Tybalt calls; and then on Romeo cries,
And then down falls again.
ROMEO.   As if that name,
Shot from the deadly level of a gun,
Did murder her; as that name's cursed hand
Murder'd her kinsman. O, tell me, friar, tell me, 105
In what vile part of this anatomy

86. *predicament,* condition, situation. **90.** *O,* lamentation. **94.** *old* (colloquial), real, actual.
98. *conceal'd lady,* secretly married wife. **103.** *level,* aim.

Doth my name lodge? tell me that I may sack
The hateful mansion. (*Drawing his sword*)

FRIAR LAURENCE.   Hold thy desperate hand:
Art thou a man? thy form cries out thou art:
Thy tears are womanish; thy wild acts denote   110
The unreasonable fury of a beast:
Unseemly woman in a seeming man!
Or ill-beseeming beast in seeming both!
Thou hast amazed me: by my holy order,
I thought thy disposition better temper'd.   115
Hast thou slain Tybalt? wilt thou slay thyself?
And slay thy lady too that lives in thee,
By doing damned hate upon thyself?
Why rail'st thou on thy birth, the heaven, and earth?
Since birth, and heaven, and earth, all three do meet   120
In thee at once; which thou at once wouldst lose.
Fie, fie, thou shamest thy shape, thy love, thy wit;
Which, like a usurer, abound'st in all,
And usest none in that true use indeed
Which should bedeck thy shape, thy love, thy wit: 125
Thy noble shape is but a form of wax,
Digressing from the valour of a man;
Thy dear love sworn but hollow perjury,
Killing that love which thou hast vow'd to cherish;
Thy wit, that ornament to shape and love,   130
Mis-shapen in the conduct of them both,
Like powder in a skilless soldier's flask,
Is set a-fire by thine own ignorance,
And thou dismember'd with thine own defence.
What, rouse thee, man! thy Juliet is alive,   135
For whose dear sake thou wast but lately dead;
There art thou happy: Tybalt would kill thee,
But thou slew'st Tybalt; there art thou happy too:
The law that threaten'd death becomes thy friend
And turns it to exile; there art thou happy: 140
A pack of blessings lights upon thy back;
Happiness courts thee in her best array;
But, like a misbehaved and sullen wench,
Thou pout'st upon thy fortune and thy love:
Take heed, take heed, for such die miserable.   145
Go, get thee to thy love, as was decreed,
Ascend her chamber, hence and comfort her:
But look thou stay not till the watch be set,

107. *sack*, destroy.

For then thou canst not pass to Mantua;
Where thou shalt live, till we can find a time   150
To blaze your marriage, reconcile your friends,
Beg pardon of the prince, and call thee back
With twenty hundred thousand times more joy
Than thou went'st forth in lamentation.
Go before, nurse: commend me to thy lady;   155
And bid her hasten all the house to bed,
Which heavy sorrow makes them apt unto:
Romeo is coming.
NURSE. O Lord, I could have stay'd here all the night
To hear good counsel: O, what learning is!   160
My lord, I'll tell my lady you will come.
ROMEO. Do so, and bid my sweet prepare to chide.
NURSE. Here, sir, a ring she bid me give you, sir:
Hie you, make haste, for it grows very late. (*Exit*)
ROMEO. How well my comfort is revived by this!   165
FRIAR LAURENCE. Go hence; good night; and here stands all your state:
Either be gone before the watch be set,
Or by the break of day disguisèd from hence:
Sojourn in Mantua; I'll find out your man,
And he shall signify from time to time   170
Every good hap to you that chances here:
Give me thy hand; 'tis late: farewell; good night.
ROMEO. But that a joy past joy calls out on me,
It were a grief, so brief to part with thee:
Farewell. (*Exeunt*)   175

Scene IV: A room in CAPULET'*s house.*

Enter CAPULET, LADY CAPULET, *and* PARIS.

CAPULET. Things have fall'n out, sir, so unluckily,
That we have had no time to move our daughter:
Look you, she loved her kinsman Tybalt dearly,
And so did I:—Well, we were born to die.
'Tis very late, she'll not come down to-night: 5
I promise you, but for your company,
I would have been a-bed an hour ago.
PARIS. These times of woe afford no time to woo.
Madam, good night: commend me to your daughter.
LADY CAPULET. I will, and know her mind early to-morrow; 10
To-night she is mew'd up to her heaviness.

---

151. *blaze,* publish, divulge. **166.** *here stands all your state,* your fortune depends on what
follows.
SCENE IV. **11.** *mew'd,* cooped.

CAPULET. Sir Paris, I will make a desperate tender
  Of my child's love: I think she will be ruled
  In all respects by me; nay, more, I doubt it not.
  Wife, go you to her ere you go to bed;   15
  Acquaint her here of my son Paris' love;
  And bid her, mark you me, on Wednesday next—
  But, soft! what day is this?
PARIS.   Monday, my lord.
CAPULET. Monday! ha, ha! Well, Wednesday is too soon,
  O' Thursday let it be: o' Thursday, tell her,   20
  She shall be married to this noble earl.
  Will you be ready? do you like this haste?
  We'll keep no great ado,—a friend or two;
  For, hark you, Tybalt being slain so late,
  It may be thought we held him carelessly,   25
  Being our kinsman, if we revel much:
  Therefore we'll have some half a dozen friends,
  And there an end. But what say you to Thursday?
PARIS. My lord, I would that Thursday were to-morrow.
CAPULET. Well, get you gone: o' Thursday be it, then.   30
  Go you to Juliet ere you go to bed,
  Prepare her, wife, against this wedding-day.
  Farewell, my lord. Light to my chamber, ho!
  Afore me! it is so very very late,
  That we may call it early by and by.   35
  Good night. (*Exeunt*)

Scene V: CAPULET's *orchard.*

Enter ROMEO *and* JULIET *above, at the window.*

JULIET. Wilt thou be gone? it is not yet near day:
  It was the nightingale, and not the lark,
  That pierced the fearful hollow of thine ear;
  Nightly she sings on yond pomegranate-tree:
  Believe me, love, it was the nightingale.   5
ROMEO. It was the lark, the herald of the morn,
  No nightingale: look, love, what envious streaks
  Do lace the severing clouds in yonder east:
  Night's candles are burnt out, and jocund day
  Stands tiptoe on the misty mountain tops.   10
  I must be gone and live, or stay and die.
JULIET. Yond light is not day-light, I know it, I:
  It is some meteor that the sun exhales,

12. *desperate tender,* rash offer. **34.** *Afore me,* by my life.
  SCENE v. **8.** *lace,* stripe.

To be to thee this night a torch-bearer,
And light thee on thy way to Mantua: 15
Therefore stay yet; thou need'st not to be gone.
ROMEO. Let me be ta'en, let me be put to death;
I am content, so thou wilt have it so.
I'll say yon grey is not the morning's eye,
'Tis but the pale reflex of Cynthia's brow;   20
Nor that is not the lark, whose notes do beat
The vaulty heaven so high above our heads:
I have more care to stay than will to go:
Come, death, and welcome! Juliet wills it so.
How is 't, my soul? let 's talk; it is not day.   25
JULIET. It is, it is: hie hence, be gone, away!
It is the lark that sings so out of tune,
Straining harsh discords and unpleasing sharps.
Some say the lark makes sweet division;
This doth not so, for she divideth us: 30
Some say the lark and loathed toad change eyes;
O, now I would they had changed voices too!
Since arm from arm that voice doth us affray,
Hunting thee hence with hunt's-up to the day.
O, now be gone; more light and light it grows.   35
ROMEO. More light and light; more dark and dark our woes!
(*Enter* Nurse, *to the chamber*)
NURSE. Madam!
JULIET. Nurse?
NURSE. Your lady mother is coming to your chamber:
The day is broke; be wary, look about. (*Exit*)   40
JULIET. Then, window, let day in, and let life out.
ROMEO. Farewell, farewell! one kiss, and I'll descend. (*He goeth down*)
JULIET. Art thou gone so? love, lord, ay, husband, friend!
I must hear from thee every day in the hour,
For in a minute there are many days: 45
O, by this count I shall be much in years
Ere I again behold my Romeo!
ROMEO. Farewell!
I will omit no opportunity
That may convey my greetings, love, to thee.   50
JULIET. O, think'st thou we shall ever meet again?
ROMEO. I doubt it not; and all these woes shall serve
For sweet discourses in our time to come.

20. *Cynthia's*, the moon's. **28.** *sharps*, high notes. **29.** *division*, melody. **31.** *change eyes*, an allusion to a popular saying that the toad and the lark had changed eyes, since the lark has ugly eyes and the toad beautiful ones. **33.** *affray*, frighten away. **34.** *hunt's-up*, a song or tune to awaken huntsmen.

JULIET. O God, I have an ill-divining soul!
  Methinks I see thee, now thou art below,   55
  As one dead in the bottom of a tomb:
  Either my eyesight fails, or thou look'st pale.
ROMEO. And trust me, love, in my eye so do you:
  Dry sorrow drinks our blood. Adieu, adieu! (*Exit*)
JULIET. O fortune, fortune! all men call thee fickle: 60
  If thou art fickle, what dost thou with him
  That is renown'd for faith? Be fickle, fortune;
  For then, I hope, thou wilt not keep him long,
  But send him back.
LADY CAPULET (*within*). Ho, daughter! are you up?   65
JULIET. Who is 't that calls? is it my lady mother?
  Is she not down so late, or up so early?
  What unaccustom'd cause procures her hither?
(*Enter* LADY CAPULET)
LADY CAPULET. Why, how now, Juliet!
JULIET.   Madam, I am not well.
LADY CAPULET. Evermore weeping for your cousin's death?   70
  What, wilt thou wash him from his grave with tears?
  An if thou couldst, thou couldst not make him live;
  Therefore, have done: some grief shows much of love;
  But much of grief shows still some want of wit.
JULIET. Yet let me weep for such a feeling loss.   75
LADY CAPULET. So shall you feel the loss, but not the friend
  Which you weep for.
JULIET.   Feeling so the loss,
  I cannot choose but ever weep the friend.
LADY CAPULET. Well, girl, thou weep'st not so much for his death,
  As that the villain lives which slaughter'd him.   80
JULIET. What villain, madam?
LADY CAPULET.   That same villain, Romeo.
JULIET. (*aside*). Villain and he be many miles asunder.—
  God pardon him! I do, with all my heart;
  And yet no man like he doth grieve my heart.
LADY CAPULET. That is, because the traitor murderer lives.   85
JULIET. Ay, madam, from the reach of these my hands:
  Would none but I might venge my cousin's death!
LADY CAPULET. We will have vengeance for it, fear thou not:
  Then weep no more. I'll send to one in Mantua,

---

57. *fails*, errs. **59.** *Dry sorrow.* The heat of the body in sorrow and despair was thought to descend into the bowels and dry up the blood. **67.** *down*, in bed. **68.** *procures*, induces to come. **84.** *like*, so much as.

Where that same banish'd runagate doth live,   90
Shall give him such an unaccustom'd dram,
That he shall soon keep Tybalt company:
And then, I hope, thou wilt be satisfied.
JULIET. Indeed, I never shall be satisfied
With Romeo, till I behold him—dead—   95
Is my poor heart so for a kinsman vex'd:
Madam, if you could find out but a man
To bear a poison, I would temper it;
That Romeo should, upon receipt thereof,
Soon sleep in quiet. O, how my heart abhors   100
To hear him named, and cannot come to him,
To wreak the love I bore my cousin
Upon his body that hath slaughter'd him!
LADY CAPULET. Find thou the means, and I'll find such a man.
But now I'll tell thee joyful tidings, girl.   105
JULIET. And joy comes well in such a needy time:
What are they, I beseech your ladyship?
LADY CAPULET. Well, well, thou hast a careful father, child;
One who, to put thee from thy heaviness,
Hath sorted out a sudden day of joy,   110
That thou expect'st not nor I look'd not for.
JULIET. Madam, in happy time, what day is that?
LADY CAPULET. Marry, my child, early next Thursday morn,
The gallant, young and noble gentleman,
The County Paris, at Saint Peter's Church,   115
Shall happily make thee there a joyful bride.
JULIET. Now, by Saint Peter's Church and Peter too,
He shall not make me there a joyful bride.
I wonder at this haste; that I must wed
Ere he, that should be husband, comes to woo.   120
I pray you, tell my lord and father, madam,
I will not marry yet; and, when I do, I swear,
It shall be Romeo, whom you know I hate,
Rather than Paris. These are news indeed!
LADY CAPULET. Here comes your father; tell him so yourself,   125
And see how he will take it at your hands.
(*Enter* CAPULET *and* Nurse)
CAPULET. When the sun sets, the air doth drizzle dew;
But for the sunset of my brother's son

---

90. *runagate*, vagabond. **95.** *dead.* This word is placed between the clauses so that it can
be understood with either what precedes or what follows it. **98.** *temper*, used equivocally,
meaning "to mix" or "to alloy." **108.** *careful*, provident. **112.** *in happy time*, a vague expression like "by the way."

It rains downright.
How now! a conduit, girl? what, still in tears?   130
Evermore showering? In one little body
Thou counterfeit'st a bark, a sea, a wind;
For still thy eyes, which I may call the sea,
Do ebb and flow with tears; the bark thy body is,
Sailing in this salt flood; the winds, thy sighs;   135
Who, raging with thy tears, and they with them,
Without a sudden calm, will overset
Thy tempest-tossed body. How now, wife!
Have you deliver'd to her our decree?

LADY CAPULET. Ay, sir; but she will none, she gives you thanks. 140
I would the fool were married to her grave!

CAPULET. Soft! take me with you, take me with you, wife.
How! will she none? doth she not give us thanks?
Is she not proud? doth she not count her blest,
Unworthy as she is, that we have wrought   145
So worthy a gentleman to be her bridegroom?

JULIET. Not proud, you have; but thankful, that you have:
Proud can I never be of what I hate;
But thankful even for hate, that is meant love.

CAPULET. How now, how now, chop-logic! What is this?   150
'Proud,' and 'I thank you,' and 'I thank you not;'
And yet 'not proud:' mistress minion, you,
Thank me no thankings, nor proud me no prouds,
But fettle your fine joints 'gainst Thursday next,
To go with Paris to Saint Peter's Church,   155
Or I will drag thee on a hurdle thither.
Out, you green-sickness carrion! out, you baggage!
You tallow-face!

LADY CAPULET.   Fie, fie! what, are you mad?

JULIET. Good father, I beseech you on my knees,
Hear me with patience but to speak a word.   160

CAPULET. Hang thee, young baggage! disobedient wretch!
I tell thee what: get thee to church o' Thursday,
Or never after look me in the face:
Speak not, reply not, do not answer me;
My fingers itch. Wife, we scarce thought us blest   165
That God had lent us but this only child;

130. *conduit*, water pipe. 140. *will none*, refuses it. 142. *take me with you*, let me understand you. 145. *wrought*, procured. 150. *chop-logic*, a shallow and sophistical arguer. 152. *minion*, favored or pampered person. 154. *fettle*, make ready. 156. *hurdle*, a conveyance for criminals. 157. *green-sickness*, an anemic ailment of young women; it suggests Juliet's paleness. 161. *baggage*, worthless woman. 165. *My . . . itch*, I have a mind to strike.

But now I see this one is one too much,
And that we have a curse in having her:
Out on her, hilding!
NURSE.   God in heaven bless her!
You are to blame, my lord, to rate her so.   170
CAPULET. And why, my lady wisdom? hold your tongue,
Good prudence; smatter with your gossips, go.
NURSE. I speak no treason.
CAPULET.   O, God ye god-den.
NURSE. May not one speak?
CAPULET.   Peace, you mumbling fool!
Utter your gravity o'er a gossip's bowl;   175
For here we need it not.
LADY CAPULET.   You are too hot.
CAPULET. God's bread! it makes me mad:
Day, night, hour, tide, time, work, play,
Alone, in company, still my care hath been
To have her match'd: and having now provided   180
A gentleman of noble parentage,
Of fair demesnes, youthful, and nobly train'd,
Stuff'd, as they say, with honourable parts,
Proportion'd as one's thought would wish a man;
And then to have a wretched puling fool,   185
A whining mammet, in her fortune's tender,
To answer 'I'll not wed; I cannot love,
I am too young; I pray you, pardon me.'
But, an you will not wed, I'll pardon you:
Graze where you will, you shall not house with me: 190
Look to 't, think on 't, I do not use to jest.
Thursday is near; lay hand on heart, advise:
An you be mine, I'll give you to my friend;
An you be not, hang, beg, starve, die in the streets,
For, by my soul, I'll ne'er acknowledge thee,   195
Nor what is mine shall never do thee good:
Trust to 't, bethink you; I'll not be forsworn. (*Exit*)
JULIET. Is there no pity sitting in the clouds,
That sees into the bottom of my grief?
O, sweet my mother, cast me not away!   200
Delay this marriage for a month, a week;
Or, if you do not, make the bridal bed
In that dim monument where Tybalt lies.

---

169. *hilding*, good-for-nothing. **170.** *rate*, berate, scold. **172.** *smatter*, chatter. **175.** *gravity*, wisdom; used contemptuously. **177.** *God's bread*, an oath by the sacrament. **186.** *mammet*, doll. *fortune's tender*, offer of good fortune.

LADY CAPULET. Talk not to me, for I'll not speak a word:
　Do as thou wilt, for I have done with thee. (*Exit*)　　205
JULIET. O God!—O nurse, how shall this be prevented?
　My husband is on earth, my faith in heaven;
　How shall that faith return again to earth,
　Unless that husband send it me from heaven
　By leaving earth? comfort me, counsel me.　　210
　Alack, alack, that heaven should practise stratagems
　Upon so soft a subject as myself!
　What say'st thou? hast thou not a word of joy?
　Some comfort, nurse.
NURSE.　　　　　Faith, here it is.
　Romeo is banish'd; and all the world to nothing,　　215
　That he dares ne'er come back to challenge you;
　Or, if he do, it needs must be by stealth.
　Then, since the case so stands as now it doth,
　I think it best you married with the county.
　O, he's a lovely gentleman!　　220
　Romeo's a dishclout to him: an eagle, madam,
　Hath not so green, so quick, so fair an eye
　As Paris hath. Beshrew my very heart,
　I think you are happy in this second match,
　For it excels your first: or if it did not,　　225
　Your first is dead; or 'twere as good he were,
　As living here and you no use of him.
JULIET. Speakest thou from thy heart?
NURSE.　　　　　And from my soul too;
　Or else beshrew them both.
JULIET.　　　Amen!
NURSE.　　　　What?
JULIET. Well, thou hast comforted me marvellous much.　　230
　Go in; and tell my lady I am gone,
　Having displeased my father, to Laurence' cell,
　To make confession and to be absolved.
NURSE. Marry, I will; and this is wisely done. (*Exit*)
JULIET. Ancient damnation! O most wicked fiend!　　235
　Is it more sin to wish me thus forsworn,
　Or to dispraise my lord with that same tongue
　Which she hath praised him with above compare
　So many thousand times? Go, counsellor;
　Thou and my bosom henceforth shall be twain.　　240
　I'll to the friar, to know his remedy:
　If all else fail, myself have power to die. (*Exit*)

207. *my faith in heaven.* Juliet refers to her marriage vows. **211.** *practise,* scheme, contrive.
stratagems, dreadful deeds. **222.** *green.* Green was an admired color for eyes. *quick,* lively.

Act IV

Scene I: FRIAR LAURENCE's *cell.*

Enter FRIAR LAURENCE *and* PARIS.

FRIAR LAURENCE. On Thursday, sir? the time is very short.
PARIS. My father Capulet will have it so;
  And I am nothing slow to slack his haste.
FRIAR LAURENCE. You say you do not know the lady's mind:
  Uneven is the course, I like it not.   5
PARIS. Immoderately she weeps for Tybalt's death,
  And therefore have I little talk'd of love;
  For Venus smiles not in a house of tears.
  Now, sir, her father counts it dangerous
  That she doth give her sorrow so much sway,   10
  And in his wisdom hastes our marriage,
  To stop the inundation of her tears;
  Which, too much minded by herself alone,
  May be put from her by society:
  Now do you know the reason of this haste.   15
FRIAR LAURENCE (*aside*). I would I knew not why it should be slow'd.
  Look, sir, here comes the lady towards my cell.
(*Enter* JULIET)
PARIS. Happily met, my lady and my wife!
JULIET. That may be, sir, when I may be a wife.
PARIS. That may be must be, love, on Thursday next.   20
JULIET. What must be shall be.
FRIAR LAURENCE.   That 's a certain text.
PARIS. Come you to make confession to this father?
JULIET. To answer that, I should confess to you.
PARIS. Do not deny to him that you love me.
JULIET. I will confess to you that I love him.   25
PARIS. So will ye, I am sure, that you love me.
JULIET. If I do so, it will be of more price,
  Being spoke behind your back, than to your face.
PARIS. Poor soul, thy face is much abused with tears.
JULIET. The tears have got small victory by that;   30
  For it was bad enough before their spite.
PARIS. Thou wrong'st it, more than tears, with that report.
JULIET. That is no slander, sir, which is a truth;
  And what I spake, I spake it to my face.
PARIS. Thy face is mine, and thou hast slander'd it.   35
JULIET. It may be so, for it is not mine own.

ACT IV. SCENE I. **5.** *Uneven,* not straightforward. **13.** *minded,* perceived, noticed.

Are you at leisure, holy father, now;
Or shall I come to you at evening mass?
FRIAR LAURENCE. My leisure serves me, pensive daughter, now.
My lord, we must entreat the time alone.   40
PARIS. God shield I should disturb devotion!
Juliet, on Thursday early will I rouse ye:
Till then, adieu; and keep this holy kiss. (*Exit*)
JULIET. O, shut the door! and when thou hast done so,
Come weep with me; past hope, past cure, past help!   45
FRIAR LAURENCE. Ah, Juliet, I already know thy grief;
It strains me past the compass of my wits:
I hear thou must, and nothing may prorogue it,
On Thursday next be married to this county.
JULIET. Tell me not, friar, that thou hear'st of this,   50
Unless thou tell me how I may prevent it:
If, in thy wisdom, thou canst give no help,
Do thou but call my resolution wise,
And with this knife I'll help it presently.
God join'd my heart and Romeo's, thou our hands;   55
And ere this hand, by thee to Romeo seal'd,
Shall be the label to another deed,
Or my true heart with treacherous revolt
Turn to another, this shall slay them both:
Therefore, out of thy long-experienced time,   60
Give me some present counsel, or, behold,
'Twixt my extremes and me this bloody knife
Shall play the umpire, arbitrating that
Which the commission of thy years and art
Could to no issue of true honour bring.   65
Be not so long to speak; I long to die,
If what thou speak'st speak not of remedy.
FRIAR LAURENCE. Hold, daughter: I do spy a kind of hope,
Which craves as desperate an execution
As that is desperate which we would prevent.   70
If, rather than to marry County Paris,
Thou hast the strength of will to slay thyself,
Then is it likely thou wilt undertake
A thing like death to chide away this shame,
That copest with death himself to scape from it;   75
And, if thou darest, I'll give thee remedy.
JULIET. O, bid me leap, rather than marry Paris,
From off the battlements of yonder tower;

40. *entreat*, ask to have. 41. *shield*, prevent (that). 54. *presently*, at once. 57. *label*, a strip
attached to a deed to carry the seal. 61. *present*, instant. 62. *extremes*, extreme difficulties.
64. *commission*, authority. 75. *copest*, encounterest.

Or walk in thievish ways; or bid me lurk
Where serpents are; chain me with roaring bears;   80
Or shut me nightly in a charnel-house,
O'er-cover'd quite with dead men's rattling bones,
With reeky shanks and yellow chapless skulls;
Or bid me go into a new-made grave
And hide me with a dead man in his shroud;   85
Things that, to hear them told, have made me tremble;
And I will do it without fear or doubt,
To live an unstain'd wife to my sweet love.

FRIAR LAURENCE. Hold, then; go home, be merry, give consent
To marry Paris: Wednesday is to-morrow: 90
To-morrow night look that thou lie alone;
Let not thy nurse lie with thee in thy chamber:
Take thou this vial, being then in bed,
And this distilled liquor drink thou off;
When presently through all thy veins shall run   95
A cold and drowsy humour, for no pulse
Shall keep his native progress, but surcease:
No warmth, no breath, shall testify thou livest;
The roses in thy lips and cheeks shall fade
To paly ashes, thy eyes' windows fall,   100
Like death, when he shuts up the day of life;
Each part, deprived of supple government,
Shall, stiff and stark and cold, appear like death:
And in this borrow'd likeness of shrunk death
Thou shalt continue two and forty hours,   105
And then awake as from a pleasant sleep.
Now, when the bridegroom in the morning comes
To rouse thee from thy bed, there art thou dead:
Then, as the manner of our country is,
In thy best robes uncover'd on the bier   110
Thou shalt be borne to that same ancient vault
Where all the kindred of the Capulets lie.
In the mean time, against thou shalt awake,
Shall Romeo by my letters know our drift,
And hither shall he come: and he and I   115
Will watch thy waking, and that very night
Shall Romeo bear thee hence to Mantua.
And this shall free thee from this present shame;
If no inconstant toy, nor womanish fear,
Abate thy valour in the acting it.   120

---

81. *charnel-house,* a room or vault where bodies or bones of the dead were deposited. **83.** *reeky,* malodorous. *chapless,* without the lower jaw. **119.** *toy,* idle fancy. **120.** *Abate,* diminish.

JULIET. Give me, give me! O, tell not me of fear!

FRIAR LAURENCE. Hold; get you gone, be strong and prosperous
In this resolve: I'll send a friar with speed
To Mantua, with my letters to thy lord.

JULIET. Love give me strength! and strength shall help afford.   125
Farewell, dear father! (*Exeunt*)

Scene II: Hall in CAPULET'*s house.*

Enter CAPULET, LADY CAPULET, Nurse, *and two* Servingmen.

CAPULET. So many guests invite as here are writ. (*Exit First Servant*)
Sirrah, go hire me twenty cunning cooks.

SECOND SERVANT. You shall have none ill, sir; for I'll try if they can lick their
fingers.

CAPULET. How canst thou try them so?

SECOND SERVANT. Marry, sir, 'tis an ill cook that cannot lick his own fingers:
therefore he that cannot lick his fingers goes not with me.

CAPULET. Go, be gone. (*Exit Second Servant*)
We shall be much unfurnish'd for this time.   10
What, is my daughter gone to Friar Laurence?

NURSE. Ay, forsooth.

CAPULET. Well, he may chance to do some good on her:
A peevish self-will'd harlotry it is.

NURSE. See where she comes from shrift with merry look.   15
(*Enter* JULIET)

CAPULET. How now, my headstrong! where have you been gadding?

JULIET. Where I have learn'd me to repent the sin
Of disobedient opposition
To you and your behests, and am enjoin'd
By holy Laurence to fall prostrate here,   20
And beg your pardon: pardon, I beseech you!
Henceforward I am ever ruled by you.

CAPULET. Send for the county; go tell him of this:
I'll have this knot knit up to-morrow morning.

JULIET. I met the youthful lord at Laurence' cell;   25
And gave him what becomed love I might,
Not stepping o'er the bounds of modesty.

CAPULET. Why, I am glad on 't; this is well: stand up:
This is as 't should be. Let me see the county;
Ay, marry, go, I say, and fetch him hither.   30
Now, afore God! this reverend holy friar,
All our whole city is much bound to him.

SCENE II. **14.** *peevish*, silly. *harlotry*, hussy. **26.** *becomed*, befitting.

JULIET. Nurse, will you go with me into my closet,
  To help me sort such needful ornaments
  As you think fit to furnish me to-morrow?   35
LADY CAPULET. No, not till Thursday; there is time enough.
CAPULET. Go, nurse, go with her: we'll to church to-morrow.
                      (*Exeunt* JULIET *and Nurse*)
LADY CAPULET. We shall be short in our provision:
  'Tis now near night.
CAPULET.   Tush, I will stir about,
  And all things shall be well, I warrant thee, wife: 40
  Go thou to Juliet, help to deck up her;
  I'll not to bed to-night; let me alone;
  I'll play the housewife for this once. What, ho!
  They are all forth. Well, I will walk myself
  To County Paris, to prepare him up   45
  Against to-morrow: my heart is wondrous light,
  Since this same wayward girl is so reclaim'd. (*Exeunt*)

Scene III: JULIET's *chamber*.

Enter JULIET *and* Nurse.

JULIET. Ay, those attires are best: but, gentle nurse,
  I pray thee, leave me to myself to-night;
  For I have need of many orisons
  To move the heavens to smile upon my state,
  Which, well thou know'st, is cross and full of sin.   5
(*Enter* LADY CAPULET)
LADY CAPULET. What, are you busy, ho? need you my help?
JULIET. No, madam; we have cull'd such necessaries
  As are behoveful for our state to-morrow:
  So please you, let me now be left alone,
  And let the nurse this night sit up with you;   10
  For, I am sure, you have your hands full all,
  In this so sudden business.
LADY CAPULET.   Good night:
  Get thee to bed, and rest; for thou hast need.
               (*Exeunt* LADY CAPULET *and Nurse*)
JULIET. Farewell! God knows when we shall meet again.
  I have a faint cold fear thrills through my veins,   15
  That almost freezes up the heat of life:
  I'll call them back again to comfort me:

---

33. *closet*, private room. 35. *furnish*, fit out.
  SCENE III. 3. *orisons*, prayers. 5. *cross*, contrary. 8. *behoveful*, needful.

Nurse! What should she do here?
My dismal scene I needs must act alone.
Come, vial.   20
What if this mixture do not work at all?
Shall I be married then to-morrow morning?
No, no: this shall forbid it: lie thou there. (*Laying down her dagger*)
What if it be a poison, which the friar
Subtly hath minister'd to have me dead,   25
Lest in this marriage he should be dishonour'd,
Because he married me before to Romeo?
I fear it is: and yet, methinks, it should not,
For he hath still been tried a holy man.
How if, when I am laid into the tomb,   30
I wake before the time that Romeo
Come to redeem me? there 's a fearful point!
Shall I not, then, be stifled in the vault,
To whose foul mouth no healthsome air breathes in,
And there die strangled ere my Romeo comes?   35
Or, if I live, is it not very like,
The horrible conceit of death and night,
Together with the terror of the place,—
As in a vault, an ancient receptacle,
Where, for these many hundred years, the bones   40
Of all my buried ancestors are pack'd:
Where bloody Tybalt, yet but green in earth,
Lies festering in his shroud; where, as they say,
At some hours in the night spirits resort;—
Alack, alack, is it not like that I,   45
So early waking, what with loathsome smells,
And shrieks like mandrakes' torn out of the earth,
That living mortals, hearing them, run mad:—
O, if I wake, shall I not be distraught,
Environed with all these hideous fears?   50
And madly play with my forefathers' joints?
And pluck the mangled Tybalt from his shroud?
And, in this rage, with some great kinsman's bone,
As with a club, dash out my desperate brains?
O, look! methinks I see my cousin's ghost   55
Seeking out Romeo, that did spit his body
Upon a rapier's point: stay, Tybalt, stay!

25. *minister'd*, administered (something healing or the reverse). 29. *still*, ever, always.
tried, proved. 39. *As*, namely. 42. *green*, fresh, i.e., just buried. 47. *mandrakes'*. Mandragora
or mandrake was a narcotic plant, the root of which resembled the human form; it was fabled
to utter a shriek when torn from the ground. 50. *fears*, objects of fear. 53. *rage*, madness.

Romeo, I come! this do I drink to thee.

(*She falls upon her bed, within the curtains*)

Scene IV: CAPULET's *house.*

Enter LADY CAPULET *and* Nurse.

LADY CAPULET. Hold, take these keys, and fetch more spices, nurse.
NURSE. They call for dates and quinces in the pastry.
(*Enter* CAPULET)
CAPULET. Come, stir, stir, stir! the second cock hath crow'd,
   The curfew-bell hath rung, 'tis three o'clock:
   Look to the baked meats, good Angelica: 5
   Spare not for cost.
NURSE.   Go, you cot-quean, go,
   Get you to bed; faith, you'll be sick to-morrow
   For this night's watching.
CAPULET. No, not a whit: what! I have watch'd ere now
   All night for lesser cause, and ne'er been sick.   10
LADY CAPULET. Ay, you have been a mouse-hunt in your time;
   But I will watch you from such watching now.
                 (*Exeunt* LADY CAPULET *and Nurse*)
CAPULET. A jealous-hood, a jealous-hood!
(*Enter three or four* Servingmen, *with spits, logs, and baskets*)
          Now, fellow,
   What's there?
FIRST SERVANT. Things for the cook, sir; but I know not what.
CAPULET. Make haste, make haste. (*Exit First Servant*) Sirrah, fetch drier logs:
   Call Peter, he will show thee where they are.
SECOND SERVANT. I have a head, sir, that will find out logs,
   And never trouble Peter for the matter. (*Exit*)
CAPULET. Mass, and well said; a merry whoreson, ha!
   Thou shalt be logger-head. Good faith, 'tis day: 20
   The county will be here with music straight,
   For so he said he would: I hear him near. (*Music within*)
   Nurse! Wife! What, ho! What, nurse, I say!
(*Re-enter* Nurse)
   Go waken Juliet, go and trim her up;
   I'll go and chat with Paris: hie, make haste,   25
   Make haste; the bridegroom he is come already:
   Make haste, I say. (*Exeunt*)

SCENE IV. **2.** *pastry*, room in which pastry was made. **4.** *curfew-bell*, apparently rung at other times than at curfew. **5.** *baked meats*, pies, pastry. **6.** *cot-quean*, a man who acts the housewife. **8.** *watching*, being awake. **11.** *mouse-hunt*, pursuer of women. **13.** *jealous-hood*, jealousy. **19.** *Mass*, by the Mass. **20.** *logger-head*, blockhead.

Scene V: JULIET's *chamber.*

Enter Nurse.

NURSE. Mistress! what, mistress! Juliet! fast, I warrant her, she:
    Why, lamb! why, lady! fie, you slug-a-bed!
    Why, love, I say! madam! sweet-heart! why, bride!
    What, not a word? you take your pennyworths now;
    Sleep for a week; for the next night, I warrant,   5
    The County Paris hath set up his rest,
    That you shall rest but little. God forgive me,
    Marry, and amen, how sound is she asleep!
    I must needs wake her. Madam, madam, madam!
    Ay, let the county take you in your bed;   10
    He'll fright you up, i' faith. Will it not be? (*Undraws the curtains*)
    What, dress'd! and in your clothes! and down again!
    I must needs wake you: Lady! lady! lady!
    Alas, alas! Help, help! my lady 's dead!
    O, well-a-day, that ever I was born!   15
    Some aqua vitæ, ho! My lord! my lady!
(*Enter* LADY CAPULET)
LADY CAPULET. What noise is here?
NURSE.   O lamentable day!
LADY CAPULET. What is the matter?
NURSE.   Look, look! O heavy day!
LADY CAPULET. O me, O me! My child, my only life,
    Revive, look up, or I will die with thee!   20
    Help, help! Call help.
(*Enter* CAPULET)
CAPULET. For shame, bring Juliet forth; her lord is come.
NURSE. She 's dead, deceased, she 's dead; alack the day!
LADY CAPULET. Alack the day, she 's dead, she 's dead, she 's dead!
CAPULET. Ha! let me see her: out, alas! she 's cold;   25
    Her blood is settled, and her joints are stiff;
    Life and these lips have long been separated:
    Death lies on her like an untimely frost
    Upon the sweetest flower of all the field.
NURSE. O lamentable day!
LADY CAPULET.   O woful time!   30
CAPULET. Death, that hath ta'en her hence to make me wail,
    Ties up my tongue, and will not let me speak.
(*Enter* FRIAR LAURENCE *and* PARIS, *with* Musicians)
FRIAR LAURENCE. Come, is the bride ready to go to church?

SCENE v. **1.** *fast,* fast asleep. **4.** *pennyworths,* little bits. **6.** *set up his rest,* a phrase from the game of primero meaning to complete your hand and wager on it; hence, to be resolved. **26.** *settled,* probably congealed.

CAPULET. Ready to go, but never to return.
  O son! the night before thy wedding-day   35
  Hath Death lain with thy wife. There she lies,
  Flower as she was, deflowered by him.
  Death is my son-in-law, Death is my heir;
  My daughter he hath wedded: I will die,
  And leave him all; life, living, all is Death's.   40
PARIS. Have I thought long to see this morning's face,
  And doth it give me such a sight as this?
LADY CAPULET. Accursed, unhappy, wretched, hateful day!
  Most miserable hour that e'er time saw
  In lasting labour of his pilgrimage!   45
  But one, poor one, one poor and loving child,
  But one thing to rejoice and solace in,
  And cruel death hath catch'd it from my sight!
NURSE. O woe! O woful, woful, woful day!
  Most lamentable day, most woful day,
  That ever, ever, I did yet behold!   50
  O day! O day! O day! O hateful day!
  Never was seen so black a day as this:
  O woful day, O woful day!
PARIS. Beguiled, divorced, wronged, spited, slain!   55
  Most detestable death, by thee beguiled,
  By cruel cruel thee quite overthrown!
  O love! O life! not life, but love in death!
CAPULET. Despised, distressed, hated, martyr'd, kill'd!
  Uncomfortable time, why camest thou now   60
  To murder, murder our solemnity?
  O child! O child! my soul, and not my child!
  Dead art thou! Alack! my child is dead;
  And with my child my joys are buried.
FRIAR LAURENCE. Peace, ho, for shame! confusion's cure lives not   65
  In these confusions. Heaven and yourself
  Had part in this fair maid; now heaven hath all,
  And all the better is it for the maid:
  Your part in her you could not keep from death,
  But heaven keeps his part in eternal life.   70
  The most you sought was her promotion;
  For 'twas your heaven she should be advanced:
  And weep ye now, seeing she is advanced
  Above the clouds, as high as heaven itself?
  O, in this love, you love your child so ill,   75

41. *thought long,* looked forward to. 43. *unhappy,* fatal. 61. *solemnity,* festivity. 65. *confusion's,* destruction's. 72. *advanced. Advance* meant both "promote in worldly affairs" and "lift or raise up."

That you run mad, seeing that she is well:
She 's not well married that lives married long;
But she 's best married that dies married young.
Dry up your tears, and stick your rosemary
On this fair corse; and, as the custom is,   80
In all her best array bear her to church:
For though fond nature bids us all lament,
Yet nature's tears are reason's merriment.

CAPULET. All things that we ordained festival,
Turn from their office to black funeral;   85
Our instruments to melancholy bells,
Our wedding cheer to a sad burial feast,
Our solemn hymns to sullen dirges change,
Our bridal flowers serve for a buried corse,
And all things change them to the contrary.   90

FRIAR LAURENCE. Sir, go you in; and, madam, go with him;
And go, Sir Paris; every one prepare
To follow this fair corse unto her grave:
The heavens do lour upon you for some ill;
Move them no more by crossing their high will.

(*Exeunt* CAPULET, LADY CAPULET, PARIS, *and* FRIAR)

FIRST MUSICIAN. Faith, we may put up our pipes, and be gone.
NURSE. Honest good fellows, ah, put up, put up;
For, well you know, this is a pitiful case. (*Exit*)   100
FIRST MUSICIAN. Ay, by my troth, the case may be amended.
(*Enter* PETER)
PETER. Musicians, O, musicians, 'Heart's ease, Heart's ease:'
O, an you will have me live, play 'Heart's ease.'
FIRST MUSICIAN. Why 'Heart's ease'?
PETER. O, musicians, because my heart itself plays 'My heart is full of woe:'
O, play me some merry dump, to comfort me.
FIRST MUSICIAN. Not a dump we; 'tis no time to play now.   110
PETER. You will not, then?
FIRST MUSICIAN. No.
PETER. I will then give it you soundly.
FIRST MUSICIAN. What will you give us?
PETER. No money, on my faith, but the gleek; I will give you the minstrel.   116

79. *rosemary,* symbol of immortality and enduring love; therefore used at both funerals and weddings. 83. *Yet . . . merriment.* Nature is here used as the opposite of reason. 84. *ordained festival,* intended to be festive. 101. *amended,* bettered. *Stage Direction: Enter Peter.* The second quarto has *Enter Will Kemp.* This well-known comic actor was a member of Shakespeare's company and evidently played this part. His name was written in probably by the prompter; hence one argues that the second quarto was set up from a playhouse copy. 102. '*Heart's ease,*' popular tune, as also '*My heart is full of woe,*' line 107. 108. *dump,* mournful tune. 115. *gleek,* jest gibe. 116. *give . . . minstrel,* call you a minstrel, which word still suggested mere entertainer or jester.

FIRST MUSICIAN. Then will I give you the serving-creature.

PETER. Then will I lay the serving-creature's dagger on your pate. I will carry
no crotchets: I'll re you, I'll fa you; do you note me?   121

FIRST MUSICIAN. An you re us and fa us, you note us.

SECOND MUSICIAN. Pray you, put up your dagger, and put out your wit.

PETER. Then have at you with my wit! I will dry-beat you with an iron wit,
and put up my iron dagger. Answer me like men:

  'When griping grief the heart doth wound,
    And doleful dumps the mind oppress,
  Then music with her silver sound'—   130

why 'silver sound'? why 'music with her silver sound'? What say you, Simon
Catling?

FIRST MUSICIAN. Marry, sir, because silver hath a sweet sound.

PETER. Pretty! What say you, Hugh Rebeck?

SECOND MUSICIAN. I say 'silver sound,' because musicians sound for silver.

PETER. Pretty too! What say you, James Soundpost?

THIRD MUSICIAN. Faith, I know not what to say.   140

PETER. O, I cry you mercy; you are the singer: I will say for you. It is 'music
with her silver sound,' because musicians have no gold for sounding:

  'Then music with her silver sound
    With speedy help doth lend redress.' (*Exit*)

FIRST MUSICIAN. What a pestilent knave is this same!

SECOND MUSICIAN. Hang him, Jack! Come, we'll in here; tarry for the
mourners, and stay dinner. (*Exeunt*)

Act V

Scene I: Mantua. A street.

Enter ROMEO.

ROMEO. If I may trust the flattering truth of sleep,
My dreams presage some joyful news at hand:
My bosom's lord sits lightly in his throne;
And all this day an unaccustom'd spirit
Lifts me above the ground with cheerful thoughts.   5
I dreamt my lady came and found me dead—
Strange dream, that gives a dead man leave to think!—

120. *carry,* endure. *crotchets,* meaning both "quarter notes" and "whims." **122.** *note,* set to
music; used punningly. **124.** *put out,* exert. **128-130.** *'When . . . sound.'* This is a part of
a song by Richard Edwards preserved in the *Paradise of Daintie Devices* (1576). **132.** *Catling.*
A catling was a small lutestring made of catgut. **135.** *Rebeck.* A rebeck was a fiddle with
three strings. **139.** *Soundpost.* A soundpost is the pillar or peg which supports the body of a
stringed instrument. **141.** *cry you mercy,* beg your pardon. **143.** *sounding,* playing music.
150. *stay dinner,* wait until after dinner.
ACT V. SCENE I. **1.** *flattering,* illusive. **3.** *bosom's lord,* heart.

And breathed such life with kisses in my lips,
That I revived, and was an emperor.
Ah me! how sweet is love itself possess'd, 10
When but love's shadows are so rich in joy!
(*Enter* BALTHASAR, *booted*)
News from Verona!—How now, Balthasar!
Dost thou not bring me letters from the friar?
How doth my lady? Is my father well?
How fares my Juliet? that I ask again; 15
For nothing can be ill, if she be well.
BALTHASAR. Then she is well, and nothing can be ill:
Her body sleeps in Capels' monument,
And her immortal part with angels lives.
I saw her laid low in her kindred's vault, 20
And presently took post to tell it you:
O, pardon me for bringing these ill news,
Since you did leave it for my office, sir.
ROMEO. Is it even so? then I defy you, stars!
Thou know'st my lodging: get me ink and paper, 25
And hire post-horses; I will hence to-night.
BALTHASAR. I do beseech you, sir, have patience:
Your looks are pale and wild, and do import
Some misadventure.
ROMEO.   Tush, thou art deceived:
Leave me, and do the thing I bid thee do.
Hast thou no letters to me from the friar? 30
BALTHASAR. No, my good lord.
ROMEO.   No matter: get thee gone,
And hire those horses; I'll be with thee straight. (*Exit* BALTHASAR)
Well, Juliet, I will lie with thee to-night.
Let 's see for means: O mischief, thou art swift 35
To enter in the thoughts of desperate men!
I do remember an apothecary,—
And hereabouts he dwells,—which late I noted
In tatter'd weeds, with overwhelming brows,
Culling of simples; meagre were his looks, 40
Sharp misery had worn him to the bones:
And in his needy shop a tortoise hung,
An alligator stuff'd, and other skins
Of ill-shaped fishes; and about his shelves
A beggarly account of empty boxes, 45
Green earthen pots, bladders and musty seeds,

11. *shadows,* phantoms. 21. *took post,* started with post horses. 33. *straight,* immediately.
39. *weeds,* clothes. *overwhelming,* overhanging. 40. *simples,* medicinal herbs. 45. *beggarly
account,* poor array.

Remnants of packthread and old cakes of roses,
Were thinly scatter'd, to make up a show.
Noting this penury, to myself I said
'An if a man did need a poison now,   50
Whose sale is present death in Mantua,
Here lives a caitiff wretch would sell it him.'
O, this same thought did but forerun my need;
And this same needy man must sell it me.
As I remember, this should be the house.   55
Being holiday, the beggar's shop is shut.
What, ho! apothecary!

(*Enter* Apothecary)

APOTHECARY.   Who calls so loud?

ROMEO. Come hither, man. I see that thou art **poor**:
Hold, there is forty ducats: let me have
A dram of poison, such soon-speeding gear   60
As will disperse itself through all the veins
That the life-weary taker may fall dead
And that the trunk may be discharged of breath
As violently as hasty powder fired
Doth hurry from the fatal cannon's womb.   65

APOTHECARY. Such mortal drugs I have; but Mantua's law
Is death to any he that utters them.

ROMEO. Art thou so bare and full of wretchedness,
And fear'st to die? famine is in thy cheeks,
Need and oppression starveth in thine eyes,   70
Contempt and beggary hangs upon thy back;
The world is not thy friend nor the world's law;
The world affords no law to make thee rich;
Then be not poor, but break it, and take this.

APOTHECARY. My poverty, but not my will, consents.   75

ROMEO. I pay thy poverty, and not thy will.

APOTHECARY. Put this in any liquid thing you will,
And drink it off; and, if you had the strength
Of twenty men, it would dispatch you straight.

ROMEO. There is thy gold, worse poison to men's souls,   80
Doing more murders in this loathsome world,
Than these poor compounds that thou mayst not sell.
I sell thee poison; thou hast sold me none.
Farewell: buy food, and get thyself in flesh.
Come, cordial and not poison, go with me   85
To Juliet's grave; for there must I use thee. (*Exeunt*)

47. *cakes of roses*, rose petals caked to be used as perfume. 52. *caitiff*, poor. 59. *ducats*, coins,
usually gold, of varying value. 60. *soon-speeding gear*, quick-acting stuff. 63. *trunk*, body.
67. *utters*, issues, gives out. 70. *starveth*, show hunger.

Scene II: FRIAR LAURENCE's *cell.*

Enter FRIAR JOHN.

FRIAR JOHN. Holy Franciscan friar! brother, ho!
(*Enter* FRIAR LAURENCE)
FRIAR LAURENCE. This same should be the voice of Friar John.
    Welcome from Mantua: what says Romeo?
    Or, if his mind be writ, give me his letter.
FRIAR JOHN. Going to find a bare-foot brother out,   5
    One of our order, to associate me,
    Here in this city visiting the sick,
    And finding him, the searchers of the town,
    Suspecting that we both were in a house
    Where the infectious pestilence did reign,   10
    Seal'd up the doors, and would not let us forth;
    So that my speed to Mantua there was stay'd.
FRIAR LAURENCE. Who bare my letter, then, to Romeo?
FRIAR JOHN. I could not send it,—here it is again,—
    Nor get a messenger to bring it thee,   15
    So fearful were they of infection.
FRIAR LAURENCE. Unhappy fortune! by my brotherhood,
    The letter was not nice but full of charge
    Of dear import, and the neglecting it
    May do much danger. Friar John, go hence;   20
    Get me an iron crow, and bring it straight
    Unto my cell.
FRIAR JOHN. Brother, I'll go and bring it thee. (*Exit*)
FRIAR LAURENCE. Now must I to the monument alone;
    Within this three hours will fair Juliet wake: 25
    She will beshrew me much that Romeo
    Hath had no notice of these accidents;
    But I will write again to Mantua,
    And keep her at my cell till Romeo come;
    Poor living corse, closed in a dead man's tomb! (*Exit*)   30

Scene III: A churchyard; in it a tomb belonging to the Capulets.

Enter PARIS, *and his* Page *bearing flowers and a torch.*

PARIS. Give me thy torch, boy: hence, and stand aloof:
    Yet put it out, for I would not be seen.
    Under yond yew-trees lay thee all along,

SCENE II. **4.** *mind*, thoughts, message. **6.** *associate*, accompany. **8.** *searchers*, officers of the pestilence. **18.** *nice*, unimportant, casual. *charge*, importance. **19.** *dear import*, dire or grievous significance. **21.** *iron crow*, crowbar.
SCENE III. **3.** *all along*, at full length.

Holding thine ear close to the hollow ground;
So shall no foot upon the churchyard tread,   5
Being loose, unfirm, with digging up of graves,
But thou shalt hear it: whistle then to me,
As signal that thou hear'st something approach.
Give me those flowers. Do as I bid thee, go.

PAGE (*aside*). I am almost afraid to stand alone   10
  Here in the churchyard; yet I will adventure. (*Retires*)

PARIS. Sweet flower, with flowers thy bridal bed I strew,—
    O woe! thy canopy is dust and stones;—
  Which with sweet water nightly I will dew,
    Or, wanting that, with tears distill'd by moans: 15
  The obsequies that I for thee will keep
    Nightly shall be to strew thy grave and weep. (*The Page whistles*)
  The boy gives warning something doth approach.
  What cursed foot wanders this way to-night,
  To cross my obsequies and true love's rite?   20
  What, with a torch! muffle me, night, awhile. (*Retires*)

(*Enter* ROMEO *and* BALTHASAR, *with a torch, mattock, &c.*)

ROMEO. Give me that mattock and the wrenching iron.
  Hold, take this letter; early in the morning
  See thou deliver it to my lord and father.
  Give me the light: upon thy life, I charge thee,   25
  Whate'er thou hear'st or seest, stand all aloof,
  And do not interrupt me in my course.
  Why I descend into this bed of death,
  Is partly to behold my lady's face;
  But chiefly to take thence from her dead finger   30
  A precious ring, a ring that I must use
  In dear employment: therefore hence, be gone:
  But if thou, jealous, dost return to pry
  In what I further shall intend to do,
  By heaven, I will tear thee joint by joint   35
  And strew this hungry churchyard with thy limbs:
  The time and my intents are savage-wild,
  More fierce and more inexorable far
  Than empty tigers or the roaring sea.

BALTHASAR. I will be gone, sir, and not trouble you.   40

ROMEO. So shalt thou show me friendship. Take thou that:
  Live, and be prosperous: and farewell, good fellow.

BALTHASAR (*aside*). For all this same, I'll hide me hereabout:
  His looks I fear, and his intents I doubt. (*Retires*)

---

16. *obsequies,* dutiful acts performed in memory of the dead. **21.** *muffle,* hide. *mattock,*
pickax. **33.** *jealous,* suspicious. **44.** *doubt,* suspect.

ROMEO. Thou detestable maw, thou womb of death,   45
    Gorged with the dearest morsel of the earth,
    Thus I enforce thy rotten jaws to open,
    And, in despite, I'll cram thee with more food! (*Opens the tomb*)

PARIS. This is that banish'd haughty Montague,
    That murder'd my love's cousin, with which grief,   50
    It is supposed, the fair creature died;
    And here is come to do some villanous shame
    To the dead bodies: I will apprehend him. (*Comes forward*)
    Stop thy unhallow'd toil, vile Montague!
    Can vengeance be pursued further than death?   55
    Condemned villain, I do apprehend thee:
    Obey, and go with me; for thou must die.

ROMEO. I must indeed; and therefore came I hither.
    Good gentle youth, tempt not a desperate man;
    Fly hence, and leave me: think upon these gone;   60
    Let them affright thee. I beseech thee, youth,
    Put not another sin upon my head,
    By urging me to fury: O, be gone!
    By heaven, I love thee better than myself;
    For I come hither arm'd against myself: 65
    Stay not, be gone; live, and hereafter say,
    A madman's mercy bade thee run away.

PARIS. I do defy thy conjurations,
    And apprehend thee for a felon here.

ROMEO. Wilt thou provoke me? than have at thee, boy! (*They fight*)   70

PAGE. O Lord, they fight! I will go call the watch. (*Exit*)

PARIS. O, I am slain! (*Falls*) If thou be merciful,
    Open the tomb, lay me with Juliet. (*Dies*)

ROMEO. In faith, I will. Let me peruse this face.
    Mercutio's kinsman, noble County Paris!   75
    What said my man, when my betossed soul
    Did not attend him as we rode? I think
    He told me Paris should have married Juliet:
    Said he not so? or did I dream it so?
    Or am I mad, hearing him talk of Juliet,   80
    To think it was so? O, give me thy hand,
    One writ with me in sour misfortune's book!
    I'll bury thee in a triumphant grave;
    A grave? O, no! a lantern, slaughter'd youth,
    For here lies Juliet, and her beauty makes   85
    This vault a feasting presence full of light.

68. *conjurations*, solemn appeals, which seem perhaps like incantations. **84.** *lantern*, a turret full of windows. **86.** *presence*, presence chamber.

Death, lie thou there, by a dead man interr'd. (*Laying* PARIS *in the tomb*)
How oft when men are at the point of death
Have they been merry! which their keepers call
A lightning before death: O, how may I   90
Call this a lightning? O my love! my wife!
Death, that hath suck'd the honey of thy breath,
Hath had no power yet upon thy beauty:
Thou art not conquer'd; beauty's ensign yet
Is crimson in thy lips and in thy cheeks,   95
And death's pale flag is not advanced there.
Tybalt, liest thou there in thy bloody sheet?
O, what more favour can I do to thee,
Than with that hand that cut thy youth in twain
To sunder his that was thine enemy?   100
Forgive me, cousin! Ah, dear Juliet,
Why art thou yet so fair? shall I believe
That unsubstantial death is amorous,
And that the lean abhorred monster keeps
Thee here in dark to be his paramour?   105
For fear of that, I still will stay with thee;
And never from this palace of dim night
Depart again: here, here will I remain
With worms that are thy chamber-maids; O, here
Will I set up my everlasting rest,   110
And shake the yoke of inauspicious stars
From this world-wearied flesh. Eyes, look your last!
Arms, take your last embrace! and, lips, O you
The doors of breath, seal with a righteous kiss
A dateless bargain to engrossing death!   115
Come, bitter conduct, come, unsavoury guide!
Thou desperate pilot, now at once run on
The dashing rocks thy sea-sick weary bark!
Here 's to my love! (*Drinks*) O true apothecary!
Thy drugs are quick. Thus with a kiss I die. (*Dies*)   120
(*Enter, at the other end of the churchyard,* FRIAR LAURENCE, *with a lantern,*
    crow, and spade)
FRIAR LAURENCE. Saint Francis be my speed! how oft to-night
    Have my old feet stumbled at graves! Who 's there?
BALTHASAR. Here 's one, a friend, and one that knows you well.
FRIAR LAURENCE. Bliss be upon you! Tell me, good my friend,
    What torch is yond, that vainly lends his light   125

90. *lightning*, a shedding of light; also, a revival of the spirits. **110.** *set . . . rest.* See IV,
v, 6. The meaning is, "make my final determination," with allusion also to the idea of repose.
115. *dateless*, everlasting. *engrossing*, monopolizing. **121.** *speed*, protector and assistant.
122. *stumbled at graves*, a bad omen.

To grubs and eyeless skulls? as I discern,
It burneth in the Capels' monument.

BALTHASAR. It doth so, holy sir; and there 's my master,
One that you love.

FRIAR LAURENCE.   Who is it?

BALTHASAR.   Romeo.

FRIAR LAURENCE. How long hath he been there?

BALTHASAR.   Full half an hour.   130

FRIAR LAURENCE. Go with me to the vault.

BALTHASAR.   I dare not, sir:
My master knows not but I am gone hence;
And fearfully did menace me with death,
If I did stay to look on his intents.

FRIAR LAURENCE. Stay, then; I'll go alone. Fear comes upon me: 135
O, much I fear some ill unlucky thing.

BALTHASAR. As I did sleep under this yew-tree here,
I dreamt my master and another fought,
And that my master slew him.

FRIAR LAURENCE.   Romeo! (*Advances*)
Alack, alack, what blood is this, which stains   140
The stony entrance of this sepulchre?
What mean these masterless and gory swords
To lie discolour'd by this place of peace? (*Enters the tomb*)
Romeo! O, pale! Who else? what, Paris too?
And steep'd in blood? Ah, what an unkind hour   145
Is guilty of this lamentable chance!
The lady stirs. (JULIET *wakes*)

JULIET. O comfortable friar! where is my lord?
I do remember well where I should be,
And there I am. Where is my Romeo? (*noise within*)   150

FRIAR LAURENCE. I hear some noise. Lady, come from that nest
Of death, contagion, and unnatural sleep:
A greater power than we can contradict
Hath thwarted our intents. Come, come away.
Thy husband in thy bosom there lies dead;   155
And Paris too. Come, I'll dispose of thee
Among a sisterhood of holy nuns:
Stay not to question, for the watch is coming;
Come, go, good Juliet (*noise again*), I dare no longer stay.

JULIET. Go, get thee hence, for I will not away. (*Exit* FRIAR LAURENCE)   160
What 's here? a cup, closed in my true love's hand?
Poison, I see, hath been his timeless end:

---

126. *grubs*, wormlike larvae, which would, of course, be blind. **162.** *timeless*, everlasting, or untimely.

O churl! drunk all, and left no friendly drop
To help me after? I will kiss thy lips;
Haply some poison yet doth hang on them,   165
To make me die with a restorative. (*Kisses him*)
Thy lips are warm.
FIRST WATCHMAN (*within*). Lead, boy: which way?
JULIET. Yea, noise? then I'll be brief. O happy dagger! (*Snatching* ROMEO'S
    dagger)
    This is thy sheath (*stabs herself*); there rust, and let me die. (*Falls on*
    ROMEO'S *body, and dies*)
(*Enter* Watch, *with the* Page *of* PARIS)
PAGE. This is the place; there, where the torch doth burn.   171
FIRST WATCHMAN. The ground is bloody; search about the churchyard:
    Go, some of you, whoe'er you find attach.
    Pitiful sight! here lies the county slain;
    And Juliet bleeding, warm, and newly dead,   175
    Who here hath lain these two days buried.
    Go, tell the prince: run to the Capulets:
    Raise up the Montagues: some others search:
    We see the ground whereon these woes do lie;
    But the true ground of all these piteous woes   180
    We cannot without circumstance descry.
(*Re-enter some of the* Watch, *with* BALTHASAR)
SECOND WATCHMAN. Here 's Romeo's man; we found him in the churchyard.
FIRST WATCHMAN. Hold him in safety, till the prince come hither.
(*Re-enter others of the* Watch, *with* FRIAR LAURENCE)
THIRD WATCHMAN. Here is a friar, that trembles, sighs, and weeps:
    We took this mattock and this spade from him,   185
    As he was coming from this churchyard side.
FIRST WATCHMAN. A great suspicion: stay the friar too.
(*Enter the* PRINCE *and* Attendants)
PRINCE. What misadventure is so early up,
    That calls our person from our morning's rest?
(*Enter* CAPULET, LADY CAPULET, *and others*)
CAPULET. What should it be, that they so shriek abroad?   190
LADY CAPULET. The people in the street cry Romeo,
    Some Juliet, and some Paris; and all run,
    With open outcry, toward our monument.
PRINCE. What fear is this which startles in our ears?
FIRST WATCHMAN. Sovereign, here lies the County Paris slain;   195
    And Romeo dead; and Juliet, dead before,
    Warm and new kill'd.
PRINCE. Search, seek, and know how this foul murder comes.

---

163. *churl*, ill-mannered fellow. **165.** *Haply*, perhaps. **173.** *attach*, arrest. **180.** *ground*, cause.

FIRST WATCHMAN. Here is a friar, and slaughter'd Romeo's man;
　With instruments upon them, fit to open　　　　　　　　　　**200**
　These dead men's tombs.
CAPULET. O heavens! O wife, look how our daughter bleeds!
　This dagger hath mista'en,—for, lo, his house
　Is empty on the back of Montague,—
　And it mis-sheathed in my daughter's bosom!　　　　　　　　**205**
LADY CAPULET. O me! this sight of death is as a bell,
　That warns my old age to a sepulchre.
(*Enter* MONTAGUE *and others*)
PRINCE. Come, Montague; for thou art early up,
　To see thy son and heir more early down.
MONTAGUE. Alas, my liege, my wife is dead tonight;　　　　　**210**
　Grief of my son's exile hath stopp'd her breath:
　What further woe conspires against mine age?
PRINCE. Look, and thou shalt see.
MONTAGUE. O thou untaught! what manners is in this,
　To press before thy father to a grave?　　　　　　　　　　**215**
PRINCE. Seal up the mouth of outrage for a while,
　Till we can clear these ambiguities,
　And know their spring, their head, their true descent;
　And then will I be general of your woes,
　And lead you even to death: meantime forbear,　　　　　　**220**
　And let mischance be slave to patience.
　Bring forth the parties of suspicion.
FRIAR LAURENCE. I am the greatest, able to do least,
　Yet most suspected, as the time and place
　Doth make against me, of this direful murder:　　　　　　　**225**
　And here I stand, both to impeach and purge
　Myself condemned and myself excused.
PRINCE. Then say at once what thou dost know in this.
FRIAR LAURENCE. I will be brief, for my short date of breath
　Is not so long as is a tedious tale.　　　　　　　　　　　**230**
　Romeo, there dead, was husband to that Juliet;
　And she, there dead, that Romeo's faithful wife:
　I married them; and their stol'n marriage-day
　Was Tybalt's dooms-day, whose untimely death
　Banish'd the new-made bridegroom from this city,　　　　　**235**
　For whom, and not for Tybalt, Juliet pined.
　You, to remove that siege of grief from her,
　Betroth'd and would have married her perforce
　To County Paris: then comes she to me,
　And, with wild looks, bid me devise some mean　　　　　　**240**

203. *house,* scabbard. **216.** *mouth of outrage,* outcry.

To rid her from this second marriage,
Or in my cell there would she kill herself.
Then gave I her, so tutor'd by my art,
A sleeping potion; which so took effect
As I intended, for it wrought on her   245
The form of death: meantime I writ to Romeo,
That he should hither come as this dire night,
To help to take her from her borrow'd grave,
Being the time the potion's force should cease.
But he which bore my letter, Friar John,   250
Was stay'd by accident, and yesternight
Return'd my letter back. Then all alone
At the prefixed hour of her waking,
Came I to take her from her kindred's vault;
Meaning to keep her closely at my cell,   255
Till I conveniently could send to Romeo:
But when I came, some minute ere the time
Of her awaking, here untimely lay
The noble Paris and true Romeo dead.
She wakes; and I entreated her come forth,   260
And bear this work of heaven with patience:
But then a noise did scare me from the tomb;
And she, too desperate, would not go with me,
But, as it seems, did violence on herself.
All this I know; and to the marriage   265
Her nurse is privy: and, if aught in this
Miscarried by my fault, let my old life
Be sacrificed, some hour before his time,
Unto the rigour of severest law.
PRINCE. We still have known thee for a holy man.   270
  Where 's Romeo's man? what can he say in this?
BALTHASAR. I brought my master news of Juliet's death;
  And then in post he came from Mantua
  To this same place, to this same monument.
  This letter he early bid me give his father,   275
  And threaten'd me with death, going in the vault,
  If I departed not and left him there.
PRINCE. Give me the letter; I will look on it.
  Where is the county's page, that raised the watch?
  Sirrah, what made your master in this place?   280
PAGE. He came with flowers to strew his lady's grave;
  And bid me stand aloof, and so I did:

247. *as this,* this very. 253. *prefixed,* agreed upon previously. 255. *closely,* secretly. 273.
post, haste.

Anon comes one with light to ope the tomb;
And by and by my master drew on him;
And then I ran away to call the watch.   285
PRINCE. This letter doth make good the friar's words,
Their course of love, the tidings of her death:
And here he writes that he did buy a poison
Of a poor 'pothecary, and therewithal
Came to this vault to die, and lie with Juliet.   290
Where be these enemies? Capulet! Montague!
See, what a scourge is laid upon your hate,
That heaven finds means to kill your joys with love.
And I for winking at your discords too
Have lost a brace of kinsmen: all are punish'd.   295
CAPULET. O brother Montague, give me thy hand:
This is my daughter's jointure, for no more
Can I demand.
MONTAGUE.   But I can give thee more:
For I will raise her statue in pure gold;
That while Verona by that name is known,   300
There shall no figure at such rate be set
As that of true and faithful Juliet.
CAPULET. As rich shall Romeo's by his lady's lie;
Poor sacrifices of our enmity!
PRINCE. A glooming peace this morning with it brings;   305
The sun, for sorrow, will not show his head:
Go hence, to have more talk of these sad things;
Some shall be pardon'd, and some punished:
For never was a story of more woe
Than this of Juliet and her Romeo. (*Exeunt*)   310

Anton Chekhov

THE CHERRY ORCHARD

By the time Chekhov's *The Cherry Orchard* appeared, in 1904, the modern theater,
in most of its essentials, had come into being. Examples were to be found in all the
big cities, not only in Europe and Great Britain but also in the United States. Since
that time, some of the architectural fashions have changed, and various experiments

---

297. *jointure*, marriage portion. **301.** *rate*, value.

have been tried, but most of the important generalizations about the theater hold good for the whole period from the late nineteenth century to the present.

The typical modern theater has an auditorium containing a main floor, two or three horseshoe galleries, and boxes. In general, the prices of seats are determined by the excellence of the view of the stage which they afford. Only those theater-goers who sit in boxes pay high prices for poor (but easily seen) vantage points and thus prolong a generally outmoded aristocratic tradition. The audiences as a rule are made up of the upper and middle economic classes: the laboring class has tended to find its entertainment away from the playhouse. The modern audience contains a much larger proportion of women than any audience in the past. Since the dramatist tries to appeal to his audience, especially in a period when the theater is com-

A performance of The Cherry Orchard

mercialized as it is today, these shifts in the make-up of the audience naturally have influenced dramatic productions.

The stage—the portion of the modern theater building behind the proscenium—has become very complicated because of the liking of present-day audiences for realistic or unusual scenery. Only half or two thirds of the whole area—the part enclosed by painted scenery—is visible, like a picture in a frame, to the audience. Above this five-sided box, in an area extending to the roof of the theater, scenery is lifted and hung, to be lowered when needed. Behind the scene-enclosed area, and to each side, are placed properties and additional scenery. Unless costs prevent, greatly varied and quite elaborate settings and properties may be used in any play. Such extensive changes of scenery are time-consuming, and so the modern theater misses the continuity of action most earlier theaters had, but most contemporary audiences do not find this lack disturbing. The chief modern development, of course, has been in lighting made possible by electricity. By arranging and manipulating lights—footlights, lights in the wings or above the stage, or spotlights located in the gallery, directors can secure realistic or fantastic effects, focus the attention of the audience on details in the setting or parts of the action, and communicate moods or emotions.

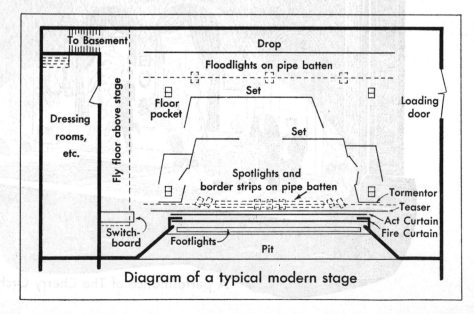

Diagram of a typical modern stage

When *The Cherry Orchard* had its première in 1904, it was played by one of the most influential dramatic companies in the twentieth-century theater—that of the Moscow Art Theater under the guidance of Constantin Stanislavsky. The company aimed for a new sort of realism characterized by meticulous attention to detail in the adaptation of stage settings to the spirit of the play and in the subordination of actors as an ensemble to the demands of the individual drama. Since the group carefully avoided obvious theatricalism, Chekhov's subtle plays were admirable vehicles for such a group. Interestingly, though Chekhov thought this play a comedy, the producer considered it to be a tragedy. This was less of a difficulty than one might expect, however, because the play had some of the aspects of both genres. It pictured the old order, tragically and at the same time comically ineffective, giving place to the new order in Russia. The underplaying of conflict and plot, the nuances of characterization, and the use of symbolism foreshadowed much that was to be typical of the drama a half century later.

CHARACTERS

LUBOV ANDREYEVNA RANEVSKAYA, *a landowner*
ANYA, *her seventeen-year-old daughter*
VARYA, *her adopted daughter, twenty-two years old*
LEONID ANDREYEVICH GAYEV, MME. RANEVSKAYA's *brother*
YERMOLAY ALEXEYEVICH LOPAHIN, *a merchant*
PYOTR SERGEYEVICH TROFIMOV, *a student*
SIMEONOV-PISHCHIK, *a landowner*
CHARLOTTA IVANOVNA, *a governess*
SEMYON YEPIHODOV, *a clerk*
DUNYASHA, *a maid*
FIRS (*pronounced* fierce), *a man-servant, aged eighty-seven*
YASHA, *a young valet*
A Tramp
Stationmaster, Post Office Clerk, Guests, Servants

The action takes place on MME. RANEVSKAYA's *estate.*

Act I

A room that is still called the nursery. One of the doors leads into Anya's room. Dawn, the sun will soon rise. It is May, the cherry trees are in blossom, but it is cold in the orchard; there is a morning frost. The windows are shut. Enter DUNYASHA *with a candle, and* LOPAHIN *with a book in his hand.*

LOPAHIN. The train is in, thank God. What time is it?

DUNYASHA. Nearly two. (*Puts out the candle*) It's light already.

LOPAHIN. How late is the train, anyway? Two hours at least. (*Yawns and stretches*) I'm a fine one! What a fool I've made of myself! I came here on purpose to meet them at the station, and then I went and overslept. I fell asleep in my chair. How annoying! You might have waked me . . .

DUNYASHA. I thought you'd left. (*Listens*) I think they're coming!

LOPAHIN (*listens*). No, they've got to get the luggage, and one thing and another . . . (*Pause*) Lubov Andreyevna spent five years abroad, I don't know what she's like now . . . She's a fine person—lighthearted, simple. I remember when I was a boy of fifteen, my poor father—he had a shop here in the village then—punched me in the face with his fist and made my nose bleed. We'd come into the yard, I don't know what for, and he'd had a drop too much. Lubov Andreyevna, I remember her as if it were yesterday—she was still young and so slim—led me to the wash-basin, in this very room . . . in the nursery. "Don't cry, little peasant," she said, "it'll heal in time for your wedding. . . ." (*Pause*) Little peasant . . . my father was a peasant, it's true, and here I am in a white waistcoat and yellow shoes. A pig in a pastry shop, you might say. It's true I'm rich, I've got a lot of money. . . . But when you look at it closely, I'm a peasant through and through. (*Pages the book*) Here I've been reading this book and I didn't understand a word of it. . . . I was reading it and fell asleep. . . . (*Pause*)

DUNYASHA. And the dogs were awake all night, they feel that their masters are coming.

LOPAHIN. Dunyasha, why are you so—

DUNYASHA. My hands are trembling. I'm going to faint.

LOPAHIN. You're too soft, Dunyasha. You dress like a lady, and look at the way you do your hair. That's not right. One should remember one's place.

(*Enter* YEPIHODOV *with a bouquet; he wears a jacket and highly polished boots that squeak badly. He drops the bouquet as he comes in*)

YEPIHODOV (*picking up the bouquet*). Here, the gardener sent these, said you're to put them in the dining room. (*Hands the bouquet to* DUNYASHA)

LOPAHIN. And bring me some *kvass*.

DUNYASHA. Yes, sir. (*Exits*)

YEPIHODOV. There's a frost this morning—three degrees below—and yet the cherries are all in blossom. I cannot approve of our climate. (*Sighs*) I cannot. Our climate does not activate properly. And, Yermolay Alexeyevich, allow me to make a further remark. The other day I bought myself a pair of boots, and I make bold to assure you, they squeak so that it is really intolerable. What should I grease them with?

LOPAHIN. Oh, get out! I'm fed up with you.

YEPIHODOV. Every day I meet with misfortune. And I don't complain, I've got used to it, I even smile.

(DUNYASHA *enters, hands* LOPAHIN *the kvass*)

YEPIHODOV. I am leaving. (*Stumbles against a chair, which falls over*) There! (*Triumphantly, as it were*) There again, you see what sort of circumstance, pardon the expression. . . . It is absolutely phenomenal! (*Exits*)

DUNYASHA. You know, Yermolay Alexeyevich, I must tell you, Yepihodov has proposed to me.

LOPAHIN. Ah!

DUNYASHA. I simply don't know . . . he's a quiet man, but sometimes when he starts talking, you can't make out what he means. He speaks nicely—and it's touching—but you can't understand it. I sort of like him though, and he is crazy about me. He's an unlucky man . . . every day something happens to him. They tease him about it here . . . they call him, Two-and-Twenty Troubles.

LOPAHIN (*listening*). There! I think they're coming.

DUNYASHA. They *are* coming! What's the matter with me? I feel cold all over.

LOPAHIN. They really are coming. Let's go and meet them. Will she recognize me? We haven't seen each other for five years.

DUNYASHA (*in a flutter*). I'm going to faint this minute. . . . Oh, I'm going to faint!

(*Two carriages are heard driving up to the house.* LOPAHIN *and* DUNYASHA *go out quickly. The stage is left empty. There is a noise in the adjoining rooms.* FIRS, *who had driven to the station to meet* LUBOV ANDREYEVNA RANEVSKAYA, *crosses the stage hurriedly, leaning on a stick. He is wearing an old-fashioned livery and a tall hat. He mutters to himself indistinctly. The hubbub off-stage increases. A* VOICE: "Come, let's go this way." *Enter* LUBOV ANDREYEVNA, ANYA, *and* CHARLOTTA IVANOVNA, *with a pet dog on a leash, all in traveling dresses;* VARYA, *wearing a coat and kerchief;* GAYEV, SIMEONOV-PISHCHIK, LOPAHIN, DUNYASHA *with a bag and an umbrella, servants with luggage. All walk across the room*)

ANYA. Let's go this way. Do you remember what room this is, mamma?

MME. RANEVSKAYA (*joyfully, through her tears*). The nursery!

VARYA. How cold it is! My hands are numb. (*To* MME. RANEVSKAYA) Your rooms are just the same as they were mamma, the white one and the violet.

MME. RANEVSKAYA. The nursery! My darling, lovely room! I slept here when I was a child . . .(*Cries*) And here I am, like a child again! (*Kisses her brother and* VARYA, *and then her brother again*) Varya's just the same as ever, like a nun. And I recognized Dunyasha. (*Kisses* DUNYASHA)

GAYEV. The train was two hours late. What do you think of that? What a way to manage things!

CHARLOTTA (*to* PISHCHIK). My dog eats nuts, too.

PISHCHIK (*in amazement*). You don't say so!

(*All go out, except* ANYA *and* DUNYASHA)

DUNYASHA. We've been waiting for you for hours. (*Takes* ANYA'*s hat and coat*)

ANYA. I didn't sleep on the train for four nights and now I'm frozen . . .

DUNYASHA. It was Lent when you left; there was snow and frost, and now . . . My darling! (*Laughs and kisses her*) I have been waiting for you, my sweet, my darling! But I must tell you something . . . I can't put it off another minute . . .

ANYA (*listlessly*). What now?

DUNYASHA. The clerk, Yepihodov, proposed to me, just after Easter.

ANYA. There you are, at it again . . . (*Straightening her hair*) I've lost all my hairpins . . . (*She is staggering with exhaustion*)

DUNYASHA. Really, I don't know what to think. He loves me—he loves me so!

ANYA (*looking towards the door of her room, tenderly*). My own room, my windows, just as though I'd never been away. I'm home! Tomorrow morning I'll get up and run into the orchard. Oh, if I could only get some sleep. I didn't close my eyes during the whole journey—I was so anxious.

DUNYASHA. Pyotr Sergeyevich came the day before yesterday.

ANYA (*joyfully*). Petya!

DUNYASHA. He's asleep in the bath-house. He has settled there. He said he was afraid of being in the way. (*Looks at her watch*) I should wake him, but Miss Varya told me not to. "Don't you wake him," she said.

(*Enter* VARYA *with a bunch of keys at her belt*)

VARYA. Dunyasha, coffee, and be quick . . . Mamma's asking for coffee.

DUNYASHA. In a minute. (*Exits*)

VARYA. Well, thank God, you've come. You're home again. (*Fondling* ANYA) My darling is here again. My pretty one is back.

ANYA. Oh, what I've been through!

VARYA. I can imagine.

ANYA. When we left, it was Holy Week, it was cold then, and all the way Charlotta chattered and did her tricks. Why did you have to saddle me with Charlotta?

VARYA. You couldn't have traveled all alone, darling—at seventeen!

ANYA. We got to Paris, it was cold there, snowing. My French is dreadful. Mamma lived on the fifth floor; I went up there, and found all kinds of Frenchmen, ladies, an old priest with a book. The place was full of tobacco smoke, and so bleak. Suddenly I felt sorry for mamma, so sorry, I took her head in my arms and hugged her and couldn't let go of her. Afterwards mamma kept fondling me and crying . . .

VARYA (*through tears*). Don't speak of it . . . don't.

ANYA. She had already sold her villa at Mentone, she had nothing left, nothing. I hadn't a kopeck left either, we had only just enough to get home. And mamma wouldn't understand! When we had dinner at the stations, she always ordered the most expensive dishes, and tipped the waiters a whole ruble. Charlotta, too. And Yasha kept ordering, too—it was simply awful. You know Yasha's mamma's footman now, we brought him here with us.

VARYA. Yes, I've seen the blackguard.

ANYA. Well, tell me—have you paid the interest?

VARYA. How could we?

ANYA. Good heavens, good heavens!

VARYA. In August the estate will be put up for sale.

ANYA. My God!

(LOPAHIN *peeps in at the door and bleats*)

LOPAHIN. Meh-h-h. (*Disappears*)

VARYA (*through tears*). What I couldn't do to him! (*Shakes her fist threateningly*)

ANYA (*embracing* VARYA, *gently*). Varya, has he proposed to you? (VARYA *shakes her head*) But he loves you. Why don't you come to an understanding? What are you waiting for?

VARYA. Oh, I don't think anything will ever come of it. He's too busy, he has no time for me . . . pays no attention to me. I've washed my hands of him— I can't bear the sight of him. They all talk about our getting married, they all congratulate me—and all the time there's really nothing to it—it's all like a dream. (*In another tone*) You have a new brooch—like a bee.

ANYA (*sadly*). Mamma bought it. (*She goes into her own room and speaks gaily like a child*) And you know, in Paris I went up in a balloon.

VARYA. My darling's home, my pretty one is back! (DUNYASHA *returns with the coffee-pot and prepares coffee.* VARYA *stands at the door of* ANYA's *room*) All day long, darling, as I go about the house, I keep dreaming. If only we could marry you off to a rich man, I should feel at ease. Then I would go into a convent, and afterwards to Kiev, to Moscow . . . I would spend my life going from one holy place to another . . . I'd go on and on . . . What a blessing that would be!

ANYA. The birds are singing in the orchard. What time is it?

VARYA. It must be after two. Time you were asleep, darling. (*Goes into* ANYA's *room*) What a blessing that would be!

(YASHA *enters with a plaid and a traveling bag, crosses the stage*)

YASHA (*finically*). May I pass this way, please?

DUNYASHA. A person could hardly recognize you, Yasha. Your stay abroad has certainly done wonders for you.

YASHA. Hm-m . . . and who are you?

DUNYASHA. When you went away I was that high—(*Indicating with her hand*) I'm Dunyasha—Fyodor Kozoyedev's daughter. Don't you remember?

YASHA. Hm! What a peach! (*He looks round and embraces her. She cries out and drops a saucer.* YASHA *leaves quickly*)

VARYA (*in the doorway, in a tone of annoyance*). What's going on here?

DUNYASHA (*through tears*). I've broken a saucer.

VARYA. Well, that's good luck.

ANYA (*coming out of her room*). We ought to warn mamma that Petya's here.

VARYA. I left orders not to wake him.

ANYA (*musingly*). Six years ago father died. A month later brother Grisha was drowned in the river. . . . Such a pretty little boy he was—only seven. It was

more than mamma could bear, so she went away, went away without looking
back . . . (*Shudders*) How well I understand her, if she only knew! (*Pauses*)
And Petya Trofimov was Grisha's tutor, he may remind her of it all . . .

(*Enter* FIRS, *wearing a jacket and a white waistcoat. He goes up to the
coffee-pot*)

FIRS (*anxiously*). The mistress will have her coffee here. (*Puts on white
gloves*) Is the coffee ready? (*Sternly, to* DUNYASHA) Here, you! And where's
the cream?

DUNYASHA. Oh, my God! (*Exits quickly*)

FIRS (*fussing over the coffee-pot*). Hah! the addlehead! (*Mutters to himself*)
Home from Paris. And the old master used to go to Paris too . . . by carriage.
(*Laughs*)

VARYA. What is it, Firs?

FIRS. What is you pleasure, Miss? (*Joyfully*) My mistress has come home,
and I've seen her at last! Now I can die. (*Weeps with joy*)

(*Enter* MME. RANEVSKAYA, GAYEV, *and* SIMEONOV-PISHCHIK. *The latter is wearing a tight-waisted, pleated coat of fine cloth, and full trousers.* GAYEV, *as he
comes in, goes through the motions of a billiard player with his arms and
body*)

MME. RANEVSKAYA. Let's see, how does it go? Yellow ball in the corner!
Bank shot in the side pocket!

GAYEV. I'll tip it in the corner! There was a time, sister, when you and I used
to sleep in this very room, and now I'm fifty-one, strange as it may seem.

LOPAHIN. Yes, time flies.

GAYEV. Who?

LOPAHIN. I say, time flies.

GAYEV. It smells of patchouli here.

ANYA. I'm going to bed. Good night, mamma. (*Kisses her mother*)

MME. RANEVSKAYA. My darling child! (*Kisses her hands*) Are you happy to be
home? I can't come to my senses.

ANYA. Good night, uncle.

GAYEV (*kissing her face and hands*). God bless you, how like your mother
you are! (*To his sister*) At her age, Luba, you were just like her.

(ANYA *shakes hands with* LOPAHIN *and* PISHCHIK, *then goes out, shutting
the door behind her*)

MME. RANEVSKAYA. She's very tired.

PISHCHIK. Well, it was a long journey.

VARYA (*to* LOPAHIN *and* PISHCHIK). How about it, gentlemen? It's past two
o'clock—isn't it time for you to go?

MME. RANEVSKAYA (*laughs*). You're just the same as ever, Varya. (*Draws
her close and kisses her*) I'll have my coffee and then we'll all go. (FIRS
puts a small cushion under her feet) Thank you, my dear. I've got used to
coffee. I drink it day and night. Thanks, my dear old man. (*Kisses him*)

VARYA. I'd better see if all the luggage has been brought in. (*Exits*)

MME. RANEVSKAYA. Can it really be I sitting here? (*Laughs*) I feel like dancing, waving my arms about. (*Covers her face with her hands*) But maybe I am dreaming! God knows I love my country, I love it tenderly; I couldn't look out of the window in the train, I kept crying so. (*Through tears*) But I must have my coffee. Thank you, Firs, thank you, dear old man. I'm so happy that you're still alive.

FIRS. Day before yesterday.

GAYEV. He's hard of hearing.

LOPAHIN. I must go soon, I'm leaving for Kharkov about five o'clock. How annoying! I'd like to have a good look at you, talk to you . . . You're just as splendid as ever.

PISHCHIK (*breathing heavily*). She's even better-looking. . . . Dressed in the latest Paris fashion. . . . Perish my carriage and all its four wheels. . . .

LOPAHIN. Your brother, Leonid Andreyevich, says I'm a vulgarian and an exploiter. But it's all the same to me—let him talk. I only want you to trust me as you used to. I want you to look at me with your touching, wonderful eyes, as you used to. Dear God! My father was a serf of your father's and grandfather's, but you, you yourself, did so much for me once . . . so much . . . that I've forgotten all about that; I love you as though you were my sister—even more.

MME. RANEVSKAYA. I can't sit still, I simply can't. (*Jumps up and walks about in violent agitation*) This joy is too much for me. . . . Laugh at me, I'm silly! My own darling bookcase! My darling table! (*Kisses it*)

GAYEV. While you were away, nurse died.

MME. RANEVSKAYA (*sits down and takes her coffee*). Yes, God rest her soul; they wrote me about it.

GAYEV. And Anastasy is dead. Petrushka Kossoy has left me and has gone into town to work for the police inspector. (*Takes a box of sweets out of his pocket and begins to suck one*)

PISHCHIK. My daughter Dashenka sends her regards.

LOPAHIN. I'd like to tell you something very pleasant—cheering. (*Glancing at his watch*) I am leaving directly. There isn't much time to talk. But I will put it in a few words. As you know, your cherry orchard is to be sold to pay your debts. The sale is to be on the twenty-second of August; but don't you worry, my dear, you may sleep in peace; there is a way out. Here is my plan. Give me your attention! Your estate is only fifteen miles from the town; the railway runs close by it; and if the cherry orchard and the land along the river bank were cut up into lots and these leased for summer cottages, you would have an income of at least 25,000 rubles a year out of it.

GAYEV. Excuse me. . . . What nonsense.

MME. RANEVSKAYA. I don't quite understand you, Yermolay Alexeyevich.

LOPAHIN. You will get an annual rent of at least ten rubles per acre, and if you advertise at once, I'll give you any guarantee you like that you won't have a square foot of ground left by autumn, all the lots will be snapped up. In

short, congratulations, you're saved. The location is splendid—by that deep
river. . . . Only, of course, the ground must be cleared . . . all the old buildings,
for instance, must be torn down, and this house, too, which is useless,
and, of course, the old cherry orchard must be cut down.

MME. RANEVSKAYA. Cut down? My dear, forgive me, but you don't know what
you're talking about. If there's one thing that's interesting—indeed, remarkable—in the whole province, it's precisely our cherry orchard.

LOPAHIN. The only remarkable thing about this orchard is that it's a very large
one. There's a crop of cherries every other year, and you can't do anything
with them; no one buys them.

GAYEV. This orchard is even mentioned in the Encyclopedia.

LOPAHIN (*glancing at his watch*). If we can't think of a way out, if we don't
come to a decision, on the twenty-second of August the cherry orchard and
the whole estate will be sold at auction. Make up your minds! There's
no other way out—I swear. None, none.

FIRS. In the old days, forty or fifty years ago, the cherries were dried, soaked,
pickled, and made into jam, and we used to—

GAYEV. Keep still, Firs.

FIRS. And the dried cherries would be shipped by the cartload. It meant a lot of
money! And in those days the dried cherries were soft and juicy, sweet,
fragrant. . . . They knew the way to do it, then.

MME. RANEVSKAYA. And why don't they do it that way now?

FIRS. They've forgotten. Nobody remembers it.

PISHCHIK (*to* MME. RANEVSKAYA). What's doing in Paris? Eh? Did you eat
frogs there?

MME. RANEVSKAYA. I ate crocodiles.

PISHCHIK. Just imagine!

LOPAHIN. There used to be only landowners and peasants in the country, but
now these summer people have appeared on the scene. . . . All the towns,
even the small ones, are surrounded by these summer cottages; and in another
twenty years, no doubt, the summer population will have grown enormously.
Now the summer resident only drinks tea on his porch, but maybe he'll
take to working his acre, too, and then your cherry orchard will be a rich,
happy, luxuriant place.

GAYEV (*indignantly*). Poppycock!

(*Enter* VARYA *and* YASHA)

VARYA. There are two telegrams for you, mamma dear. (*Picks a key from the
bunch at her belt and noisily opens an old-fashioned bookcase*) Here they are.

MME. RANEVSKAYA. They're from Paris. (*Tears them up without reading them*)
I'm through with Paris.

GAYEV. Do you know, Luba, how old this bookcase is? Last week I pulled out
the bottom drawer and there I found the date burnt in it. It was made exactly
a hundred years ago. Think of that! We could celebrate its centenary. True,
it's an inanimate object, but nevertheless, a bookcase . . .

PISHCHIK (*amazed*). A hundred years! Just imagine!

GAYEV. Yes. (*Tapping it*) That's something. . . . Dear, honored bookcase, hail to you who for more than a century have served the glorious ideals of goodness and justice! Your silent summons to fruitful toil has never weakened in all those hundred years (*through tears*), sustaining, through successive generations of our family, courage and faith in a better future, and fostering in us ideals of goodness and social consciousness. . . . (*Pauses*)

LOPAHIN. Yes . . .

MME. RANEVSKAYA. You haven't changed a bit, Leonid.

GAYEV (*somewhat embarrassed*). I'll play it off the red in the corner! Tip it in the side pocket!

LOPAHIN (*looking at his watch*). Well, it's time for me to go . . .

YASHA (*handing a pill box to* MME. RANEVSKAYA). Perhaps you'll take your pills now.

PISHCHIK. One shouldn't take medicines, dearest lady, they do neither harm nor good. . . . Give them here, my valued friend. (*Takes the pill box, pours the pills into his palm, blows on them, puts them in his mouth, and washes them down with some kvass*) There!

MME. RANEVSKAYA (*frightened*). You must be mad!

PISHCHIK. I've taken all the pills.

LOPAHIN. What a glutton!

(*All laugh*)

FIRS. The gentleman visited us in Easter week, ate half a bucket of pickles, he did . . . (*Mumbles*)

MME. RANEVSKAYA. What's he saying?

VARYA. He's been mumbling like that for the last three years—we're used to it.

YASHA. His declining years!

(CHARLOTTA IVANOVNA, *very thin, tightly laced, dressed in white, a lorgnette at her waist, crosses the stage*)

LOPAHIN. Forgive me, Charlotta Ivanovna, I've not had time to greet you. (*Tries to kiss her hand*)

CHARLOTTA (*pulling away her hand*). If I let you kiss my hand, you'll be wanting to kiss my elbow next, and then my shoulder.

LOPAHIN. I've no luck today. (*All laugh*) Charlotta Ivanovna, show us a trick.

MME. RANEVSKAYA. Yes, Charlotta, do a trick for us.

CHARLOTTA. I don't see the need. I want to sleep. (*Exits*)

LOPAHIN. In three weeks we'll meet again. (*Kisses* MME. RANEVSKAYA's *hand*) Good-by till then. Time's up. (*To* GAYEV) Bye-bye. (*Kisses* PISHCHIK) Bye-bye. (*Shakes hands with* VARYA, *then with* FIRS *and* YASHA) I hate to leave. (*To* MME. RANEVSKAYA) If you make up your mind about the cottages, let me know; I'll get you a loan of 50,000 rubles. Think it over seriously.

VARYA (*crossly*). Will you never go!

LOPAHIN. I'm going, I'm going. (*Exits*)

GAYEV. The vulgarian. But, excuse me . . . Varya's going to marry him, he's Varya's fiancé.

VARYA. You talk too much, uncle dear.

MME. RANEVSKAYA. Well, Varya, it would make me happy. He's a good man.

PISHCHIK. Yes, one must admit, he's a most estimable man. And my Dashenka . . . she too says that . . . she says . . . lots of things. (*Snores; but wakes up at once*) All the same, my valued friend, could you oblige me . . . with a loan of 240 rubles? I must pay the interest on the mortgage tomorrow.

VARYA (*alarmed*). We can't, we can't!

MME. RANEVSKAYA. I really haven't any money.

PISHCHIK. It'll turn up. (*Laughs*) I never lose hope, I thought everything was lost, that I was done for, when lo and behold, the railway ran through my land . . . and I was paid for it. . . . And something else will turn up again, if not today, then tomorrow . . . Dashenka will win two hundred thousand . . . she's got a lottery ticket.

MME. RANEVSKAYA. I've had my coffee, now let's go to bed.

FIRS (*brushes off* GAYEV; *admonishingly*). You've got the wrong trousers on again. What am I to do with you?

VARYA (*softly*). Anya's asleep. (*Gently opens the window*) The sun's up now, it's not a bit cold. Look, mamma dear, what wonderful trees. And heavens, what air! The starlings are singing!

GAYEV (*opens the other window*). The orchard is all white. You've not forgotten it? Luba? That's the long alley that runs straight, straight as an arrow; how it shines on moonlight nights, do you remember? You've not forgotten?

MME. RANEVSKAYA (*looking out of the window into the orchard*). Oh, my childhood, my innocent childhood. I used to sleep in this nursery—I used to look out into the orchard, happiness waked with me every morning, the orchard was just the same then . . . nothing has changed. (*Laughs with joy*) All, all white! Oh, my orchard! After the dark, rainy autumn and the cold winter, you are young again, and full of happiness, the heavenly angels have not left you . . . If I could free my chest and my shoulders from this rock that weighs on me, if I could only forget the past!

GAYEV. Yes, and the orchard will be sold to pay our debts, strange as it may seem. . . .

MME. RANEVSKAYA. Look! There is our poor mother walking in the orchard . . . all in white . . . (*Laughs with joy*) It is she!

GAYEV. Where?

VARYA. What are you saying, mamma dear!

MME. RANEVSKAYA. There's no one there, I just imagined it. To the right, where the path turns towards the arbor, there's a little white tree, leaning over, that looks like a woman . . .

(TROFIMOV *enters, wearing a shabby student's uniform and spectacles*)

MME. RANEVSKAYA. What an amazing orchard! White masses of blossom, the blue sky . . .

TROFIMOV. Lubov Andreyevna! (*She looks round at him*) I just want to pay my respects to you, then I'll leave at once. (*Kisses her hand ardently*) I was told to wait until morning, but I hadn't the patience . . . (MME. RANEVSKAYA *looks at him, perplexed*)

VARYA (*through tears*). This is Petya Trofimov.

TROFIMOV. Petya Trofimov, formerly your Grisha's tutor. . . . Can I have changed so much? (MME. RANEVSKAYA *embraces him and weeps quietly*)

GAYEV (*embarrassed*). Don't, don't, Luba.

VARYA (*crying*). I told you, Petya, to wait until tomorrow.

MME. RANEVSKAYA. My Grisha . . . my little boy . . . Grisha . . . my son.

VARYA. What can one do, mamma dear, it's God's will.

TROFIMOV (*softly, through tears*). There . . . there.

MME. RANEVSKAYA (*weeping quietly*). My little boy was lost . . . drowned. Why? Why, my friend? (*More quietly*) Anya's asleep in there, and here I am talking so loudly . . . making all this noise. . . . But tell me, Petya, why do you look so badly? Why have you aged so?

TROFIMOV. A mangy master, a peasant woman in the train called me.

MME. RANEVSKAYA. You were just a boy then, a dear little student, and now your hair's thin—and you're wearing glasses! Is it possible you're still a student? (*Goes towards the door*)

TROFIMOV. I suppose I'm a perpetual student.

MME. RANEVSKAYA (*kisses her brother, then* VARYA). Now, go to bed . . . You have aged, too, Leonid.

PISHCHIK (*follows her*). So now we turn in. Oh, my gout! I'm staying the night here . . . Lubov Andreyevna, my angel, tomorrow morning. . . . I do need 240 rubles.

GAYEV. He keeps at it.

PISHCHIK. I'll pay it back, dear . . . it's a trifling sum.

MME. RANEVSKAYA. All right, Leonid will give it to you. Give it to him, Leonid.

GAYEV. Me give it to him! That's a good one!

MME. RANEVSKAYA. It can't be helped. Give it to him! He needs it. He'll pay it back.

(MME. RANEVSKAYA, TROFIMOV, PISHCHIK, *and* FIRS *go out;* GAYEV, VARYA, *and* YASHA *remain*)

GAYEV. Sister hasn't got out of the habit of throwing money around. (*To* YASHA) Go away, my good fellow, you smell of the barnyard.

YASHA (*with a grin*). And you, Leonid Andreyevich, are just the same as ever.

GAYEV. Who? (*To* VARYA) What did he say?

VARYA (*To* YASHA). Your mother's come from the village; she's been sitting in the servants' room since yesterday, waiting to see you.

YASHA. Botheration!

VARYA. You should be ashamed of yourself!

YASHA. She's all I needed! She could have come tomorrow. (*Exits*)

VARYA. Mamma is just the same as ever; she hasn't changed a bit. If she had her own way, she'd keep nothing for herself.

GAYEV. Yes . . . (*Pauses*) If a great many remedies are offered for some disease, it means it is incurable; I keep thinking and racking my brains; I have many remedies, ever so many, and that really means none. It would be fine if we came in for a legacy; it would be fine if we married off our Anya to a very rich man; or we might go to Yaroslavl and try our luck with our aunt, the Countess. She's very, very rich, you know . . .

VARYA (*weeping*). If only God would help us!

GAYEV. Stop bawling. Aunt's very rich, but she doesn't like us. In the first place, sister married a lawyer who was no nobleman . . . (ANYA *appears in the doorway*) She married beneath her, and it can't be said that her behavior has been very exemplary. She's good, kind, sweet, and I love her, but no matter what extenuating circumstances you may adduce, there's no denying that she has no morals. You sense it in her least gesture.

VARYA (*in a whisper*). Anya's in the doorway.

GAYEV. Who? (*Pauses*) It's queer, something got into my right eye—my eyes are going back on me. . . . And on Thursday, when I was in the circuit court—

(*Enter* ANYA)

VARYA. Why aren't you asleep, Anya?

ANYA. I can't get to sleep, I just can't.

GAYEV. My little pet! (*Kisses* ANYA's *face and hands*) My child! (*Weeps*) You are not my niece, you're my angel! You're everything to me. Believe me, believe—

ANYA. I believe you, uncle. Everyone loves you and respects you . . . but, uncle dear, you must keep still. . . . You must. What were you saying just now about my mother? Your own sister? What made you say that?

GAYEV. Yes, yes . . . (*Covers his face with her hand*) Really, that was awful! Good God! Heaven help me! Just now I made a speech to the bookcase . . . so stupid! And only after I was through, I saw how stupid it was.

VARYA. It's true, uncle dear, you ought to keep still. Just don't talk, that's all.

ANYA. If you could only keep still, it would make things easier for you too.

GAYEV. I'll keep still. (*Kisses* ANYA's *and* VARYA's *hands*) I will. But now about business. On Thursday I was in court; well, there were a number of us there, and we began talking of one thing and another, and this and that, and do you know, I believe it will be possible to raise a loan on a promissory note, to pay the interest at the bank.

VARYA. If only God would help us!

GAYEV. On Tuesday I'll go and see about it again. (*To* VARYA) Stop bawling. (*To* ANYA) Your mamma will talk to Lopahin, and he, of course, will not refuse her . . . and as soon as you're rested, you'll go to Yaroslavl to the Countess, your great-aunt. So we'll be working in three directions at once, and the thing is in the bag. We'll pay the interest—I'm sure of it. (*Puts a candy in his mouth*) I swear on my honor, I swear by anything you like, the estate shan't be sold. (*Excitedly*) I swear by my own happiness! Here's my hand on it, you can call me a swindler and a scoundrel if I let it come to an auction! I swear by my whole being.

ANYA (*relieved and quite happy again*). How good you are, uncle, and how clever! (*Embraces him*) Now I'm at peace, quite at peace, I'm happy.

(*Enter* FIRS)

FIRS (*reproachfully*). Leonid Andreyevich, have you no fear of God? When are you going to bed?

GAYEV. Directly, directly. Go away, Firs, I'll . . . yes, I will undress myself. Now, children, 'nightie-'nightie. We'll consider details tomorrow, but now go to sleep. (*Kisses* ANYA *and* VARYA) I am a man of the 'Eighties; they have nothing good to say of that period nowadays. Nevertheless, in the course of my life I have suffered not a little for my convictions. It's not for nothing that the peasant loves me; one should know the peasant; one should know from which—

ANYA. There you go again, uncle.

VARYA. Uncle dear, be quiet.

FIRS (*angrily*). Leonid Andreyevich!

GAYEV. I'm coming, I'm coming! Go to bed! Double bank shot in the side pocket! Here goes a clean shot . . . (*Exits,* FIRS *hobbling after him*)

ANYA. I am at peace now. I don't want to go to Yaroslavl—I don't like my great-aunt, but still, I am at peace, thanks to uncle. (*Sits down*)

VARYA. We must get some sleep. I'm going now. While you were away something unpleasant happened. In the old servants' quarters there are only the old people, as you know; Yefim, Polya, Yevstigney, and Karp, too. They began letting all sorts of rascals in to spend the night. . . . I didn't say anything. Then I heard they'd been spreading a report that I gave them nothing but dried peas to eat—out of stinginess, you know . . . and it was all Yevstigney's doing. . . . All right, I thought, if that's how it is, I thought, just wait. I sent for Yevstigney. . . . (*Yawns*) He comes. . . . "How's this, Yevstigney?" I say, "You fool . . . " (*Looking at* ANYA) Anichka! (*Pauses*) She's asleep. (*Puts her arm around* ANYA) Come to your little bed. . . . Come . . . (*Leads her*) My darling has fallen asleep. . . . Come.

(*They go out. Far away beyond the orchard a shepherd is piping.* TROFIMOV *crosses the stage and, seeing* VARYA *and* ANYA, *stands still*)

VARYA. Sh! She's asleep . . . asleep . . . Come, darling.

ANYA (*softly, half-asleep*). I'm so tired. Those bells . . . uncle . . . dear. . . . Mamma and uncle . . .

VARYA. Come, my precious, come along. (*They go into* ANYA's *room*)

TROFIMOV (*with emotion*). My sunshine, my spring!

Act II

A meadow. An old, long-abandoned, lopsided little chapel; near it, a well, large slabs, which had apparently once served as tombstones, and an old bench. In the background, the road to the Gayev estate. To one side poplars loom darkly, where the cherry orchard begins. In the distance a row of telegraph poles, and far off, on the horizon, the faint outline of a large city which is seen only in fine, clear weather. The sun will soon be setting. CHARLOTTA, YASHA, *and* DUNYASHA *are seated on the bench.* YEPIHODOV *stands near and plays a guitar. All are pensive.* CHARLOTTA *wears an old peaked cap. She has taken a gun from her shoulder and is straightening the buckle on the strap.*

CHARLOTTA (*musingly*). I haven't a real passport, I don't know how old I am, and I always feel that I am very young. When I was a little girl, my father and mother used to go from fair to fair and give performances, very good ones. And I used to do the *salto mortale,* and all sorts of other tricks. And when papa and mamma died, a German lady adopted me and began to educate me. Very good. I grew up and became a governess. But where I come from and who I am, I don't know. . . . Who were my parents? Perhaps they weren't even married. . . . I don't know. . . . (*Takes a cucumber out of her pocket and eats it*) I don't know a thing. (*Pause*) One wants so much to talk, and there isn't anyone to talk to. . . . I haven't anybody.

YEPIHODOV (*plays the guitar and sings*). "What care I for the jarring world? What's friend or foe to me? . . ." How agreeable it is to play the mandolin.

DUNYASHA. That's a guitar, not a mandolin. (*Looks in a hand mirror and powders her face*)

YEPIHODOV. To a madman in love it's a mandolin. (*Sings*) "Would that the heart were warmed by the fire of mutual love!" (YASHA *joins in*)

CHARLOTTA. How abominably these people sing. Pfui! Like jackals!

DUNYASHA (*to* YASHA). How wonderful it must be though to have stayed abroad!

YASHA. Ah, yes, of course, I cannot but agree with you there. (*Yawns and lights a cigar*)

YEPIHODOV. Naturally. Abroad, everything has long since achieved full perplexion.

YASHA. That goes without saying.

YEPIHODOV. I'm a cultivated man, I read all kinds of remarkable books. And yet I can never make out what direction I should take, what is it that I want, properly speaking. Should I live, or should I shoot myself, properly speaking? Nevertheless, I always carry a revolver about me. . . . Here it is . . . (*Shows revolver*)

CHARLOTTA. I've finished. I'm going. (*Puts the gun over her shoulder*) You are a very clever man, Yepihodov, and a very terrible one; women must be crazy about you. Br-r-r! (*Starts to go*) These clever men are all so stupid; there's no one for me to talk to . . . always alone, alone, I haven't a soul . . . and who I am, and why I am, nobody knows. (*Exits unhurriedly*)

YEPIHODOV. Properly speaking and letting other subjects alone, I must say regarding myself, among other things, that fate treats me mercilessly, like a storm treats a small boat. If I am mistaken, let us say, why then do I wake up this morning, and there on my chest is a spider of enormous dimensions . . . like this . . . (*indicates with both hands*) Again, I take up a pitcher of kvass to have a drink, and in it there is something unseemly to the highest degree, something like a cockroach. (*Pause*) Have you read Buckle? (*Pause*) I wish to have a word with you, Avdotya Fyodorovna, if I may trouble you.

DUNYASHA. Well, go ahead.

YEPIHODOV. I wish to speak with you alone. (*Sighs*)

DUNYASHA (*embarrassed*). Very well. Only first bring me my little cape. You'll find it near the wardrobe. It's rather damp here.

YEPIHODOV. Certainly, ma'am; I will fetch it, ma'am. Now I know what to do with my revolver. (*Takes the guitar and goes off playing it*)

YASHA. Two-and-Twenty Troubles! An awful fool, between you and me. (*Yawns*)

DUNYASHA. I hope to God he doesn't shoot himself! (*Pause*) I've become so nervous, I'm always fretting. I was still a little girl when I was taken into the big house, I am quite unused to the simple life now, and my hands are white, as white as a lady's. I've become so soft, so delicate, so refined, I'm afraid of everything. It's so terrifying; and if you deceive me, Yasha, I don't know what will happen to my nerves. (YASHA *kisses her*)

YASHA. You're a peach! Of course, a girl should never forget herself; and what I dislike more than anything is when a girl don't behave properly.

DUNYASHA. I've fallen passionately in love with you; you're educated—you have something to say about everything. (*Pause*)

YASHA (*yawns*). Yes, ma'am. Now the way I look at it, if a girl loves someone, it means she is immoral. (*Pause*) It's agreeable smoking a cigar in the fresh air. (*Listens*) Someone's coming this way . . . It's our madam and the others. (DUNYASHA *embraces him impulsively*) You go home, as though you'd been to the river to bathe; go by the little path, or else they'll run into you and suspect me of having arranged to meet you here. I can't stand that sort of thing.

DUNYASHA (*coughing softly*). Your cigar's made my head ache.

(*Exits.* YASHA *remains standing near the chapel. Enter* MME. RANEVSKAYA, GAYEV, *and* LOPAHIN)

LOPAHIN. You must make up your mind once and for all—there's no time to lose. It's quite a simple question, you know. Do you agree to lease your land for summer cottages or not? Answer in one word, yes or no; only one word!

MME. RANEVSKAYA. Who's been smoking such abominable cigars here? (*Sits down*)

GAYEV. Now that the railway line is so near, it's made things very convenient. (*Sits down*) Here we've been able to have lunch in town. Yellow ball in the side pocket! I feel like going into the house and playing just one game.

MME. RANEVSKAYA. You can do that later.

LOPAHIN. Only one word! (*Imploringly*) Do give me an answer!

GAYEV (*yawning*). Who?

MME. RANEVSKAYA (*looks into her purse*). Yesterday I had a lot of money and now my purse is almost empty. My poor Varya tries to economize by feeding us just milk soup; in the kitchen the old people get nothing but dried peas to eat, while I squander money thoughtlessly. (*Drops the purse, scattering gold pieces*) You see there they go . . . (*Shows vexation*)

YASHA. Allow me—I'll pick them up. (*Picks up the money*)

MME. RANEVSKAYA. Be so kind, Yasha. And why did I go to lunch in town? That nasty restaurant, with its music and the tablecloth smelling of soap

. . . Why drink so much, Leonid? Why eat so much? Why talk so much? Today again you talked a lot, and all so inappropriately about the 'Seventies, about the decadents. And to whom? Talking to waiters about decadents!

LOPAHIN. Yes.

GAYEV (*waving his hand*). I'm incorrigible; that's obvious. (*Irritably, to* YASHA) Why do you keep dancing about in front of me?

YASHA (*laughs*). I can't hear your voice without laughing—

GAYEV. Either he or I—

MME. RANEVSKAYA. Go away, Yasha; run along.

YASHA (*handing* MME. RANEVSKAYA *her purse*). I'm going, at once. (*Hardly able to suppress his laughter*) This minute. (*Exits*)

LOPAHIN. That rich man, Deriganov, wants to buy your estate. They say he's coming to the auction himself.

MME. RANEVSKAYA. Where did you hear that?

LOPAHIN. That's what they are saying in town.

GAYEV. Our aunt in Yaroslavl has promised to help; but when she will send the money, and how much, no one knows.

LOPAHIN. How much will she send? A hundred thousand? Two hundred?

MME. RANEVSKAYA. Oh, well, ten or fifteen thousand; and we'll have to be grateful for that.

LOPAHIN. Forgive me, but such frivolous people as you are, so queer and unbusinesslike—I never met in my life. One tells you in plain language that your estate is up for sale, and you don't seem to take it in.

MME. RANEVSKAYA. What are we to do? Tell us what to do.

LOPAHIN. I do tell you, every day; every day I say the same thing! You must lease the cherry orchard and the land for summer cottages, you must do it and as soon as possible—right away. The auction is close at hand. Please understand! Once you've decided to have the cottages, you can raise as much money as you like, and you're saved.

MME. RANEVSKAYA. Cottages—summer people—forgive me, but it's all so vulgar.

GAYEV. I agree with you absolutely.

LOPAHIN. I shall either burst into tears or scream or faint! I can't stand it! You've worn me out! (*To* GAYEV) You're an old woman!

GAYEV. Who?

LOPAHIN. An old woman! (*Gets up to go*)

MME. RANEVSKAYA (*alarmed*). No, don't go! Please stay, I beg you, my dear. Perhaps we shall think of something.

LOPAHIN. What is there to think of?

MME. RANEVSKAYA. Don't go, I beg you. With you here it's more cheerful anyway. (*Pause*) I keep expecting something to happen, it's as though the house were going to crash about our ears.

GAYEV (*in deep thought*). Bank shot in the corner. . . . Three cushions in the side pocket. . . .

MME. RANEVSKAYA. We have been great sinners . . .

LOPAHIN. What sins could you have committed?

GAYEV (*putting a candy in his mouth*). They say I've eaten up my fortune in candy! (*Laughs*)

MME. RANEVSKAYA. Oh, my sins! I've squandered money away recklessly, like a lunatic, and I married a man who made nothing but debts. My husband drank himself to death on champagne, he was a terrific drinker. And then, to my sorrow, I fell in love with another man, and I lived with him. And just then—that was my first punishment—a blow on the head: my little boy was drowned here in the river. And I went abroad, went away forever . . . never to come back, never to see this river again . . . I closed my eyes and ran, out of my mind. . . . But he followed me, pitiless, brutal. I bought a villa near Mentone, because he fell ill there; and for three years, day and night, I knew no peace, no rest. The sick man wore me out, he sucked my soul dry. Then last year, when the villa was sold to pay my debts, I went to Paris, and there he robbed me, abandoned me, took up with another woman, I tried to poison myself—it was stupid, so shameful—and then suddenly I felt drawn back to Russia, back to my own country, to my little girl. (*Wipes her tears away*) Lord, Lord! Be merciful, forgive me my sins—don't punish me any more! (*Takes a telegram out of her pocket*) This came today from Paris—he begs me to forgive him, implores me to go back . . . (*Tears up the telegram*) Do I hear music? (*Listens*)

GAYEV. That's our famous Jewish band, you remember? Four violins, a flute, and a double bass.

MME. RANEVSKAYA. Does it still exist? We ought to send for them some evening and have a party.

LOPAHIN (*listens*). I don't hear anything. (*Hums softly*) "The Germans for a fee will Frenchify a Russian." (*Laughs*) I saw a play at the theater yesterday—awfully funny.

MME. RANEVSKAYA. There was probably nothing funny about it. You shouldn't go to see plays, you should look at yourselves more often. How drab your lives are—how full of unnecessary talk.

LOPAHIN. That's true; come to think of it, we do live like fools. (*Pause*) My pop was a peasant, an idiot; he understood nothing, never taught me anything, all he did was beat me when he was drunk, and always with a stick. Fundamentally, I'm just the same kind of blockhead and idiot. I was never taught anything—I have a terrible handwriting, I write so that I feel ashamed before people, like a pig.

MME. RANEVSKAYA. You should get married, my friend.

LOPAHIN. Yes . . . that's true.

MME. RANEVSKAYA. To our Varya, she's a good girl.

LOPAHIN. Yes.

MME. RANEVSKAYA. She's a girl who comes of simple people, she works all day long; and above all, she loves you. Besides, you've liked her for a long time now.

LOPAHIN. Well, I've nothing against it. She's a good girl. (*Pause*)

GAYEV. I've been offered a place in the bank—6,000 a year. Have you heard?

MME. RANEVSKAYA. You're not up to it. Stay where you are.

(FIRS *enters, carrying an overcoat*)

FIRS (*to* GAYEV). Please put this on, sir, it's damp.

GAYEV (*putting it on*). I'm fed up with you, brother.

FIRS. Never mind. This morning you drove off without saying a word. (*Looks him over*)

MME. RANEVSKAYA. How you've aged, Firs.

FIRS. I beg your pardon?

LOPAHIN. The lady says you've aged.

FIRS. I've lived a long time; they were arranging my wedding and your papa wasn't born yet. (*Laughs*) When freedom came I was already head footman. I wouldn't consent to be set free then; I stayed on with the master . . . (*Pause*) I remember they were all very happy, but why they were happy, they didn't know themselves.

LOPAHIN. It was fine in the old days! At least there was flogging!

FIRS (*not hearing*). Of course. The peasants kept to the masters, the masters kept to the peasants; but now they've all gone their own ways, and there's no making out anything.

GAYEV. Be quiet, Firs. I must go to town tomorrow. They've promised to introduce me to a general who might let us have a loan.

LOPAHIN. Nothing will come of that. You won't even be able to pay the interest, you can be certain of that.

MME. RANEVSKAYA. He's raving, there isn't any general. (*Enter* TROFIMOV, ANYA, *and* VARYA)

GAYEV. Here come our young people.

ANYA. There's mamma, on the bench.

MME. RANEVSKAYA (*tenderly*). Come here, come along, my darlings. (*Embraces* ANYA *and* VARYA) If you only knew how I love you both! Sit beside me— there, like that. (*All sit down*)

LOPAHIN. Our perpetual student is always with the young ladies.

TROFIMOV. That's not any of your business.

LOPAHIN. He'll soon be fifty, and he's still a student!

TROFIMOV. Stop your silly jokes.

LOPAHIN. What are you so cross about, you queer bird?

TROFIMOV. Oh, leave me alone.

LOPAHIN (*laughs*). Allow me to ask you, what do you think of me?

TROFIMOV. What I think of you, Yermolay Alexeyevich, is this: you are a rich man who will soon be a millionaire. Well, just as a beast of prey, which devours everything that comes in its way, is necessary for the process of metabolism to go on, so you too are necessary. (*All laugh*)

VARYA. Better tell us something about the planets, Petya.

MME. RANEVSKAYA. No, let's go on with yesterday's conversation.

TROFIMOV. What was it about?

GAYEV. About man's pride.

TROFIMOV. Yesterday we talked a long time, but we came to no conclusion. There is something mystical about man's pride in your sense of the word. Perhaps you're right, from your own point of view. But if you reason simply, without going into subtleties, then what call is there for pride? Is there any sense in it, if man is so poor a thing physiologically, and if, in the great majority of cases, he is coarse, stupid, and profoundly unhappy? We should stop admiring ourselves. We should work, and that's all.

GAYEV. You die, anyway.

TROFIMOV. Who knows? And what does it mean—to die? Perhaps man has a hundred senses, and at his death only the five we know perish, while the other ninety-five remain alive.

MME. RANEVSKAYA. How clever you are, Petya!

LOPAHIN (*ironically*). Awfully clever!

TROFIMOV. Mankind goes forward, developing its powers. Everything that is now unattainable for it will one day come within man's reach and be clear to him; only we must work, helping with all our might those who seek the truth. Here among us in Russia only the very few work as yet. The great majority of the intelligentsia, as far as I can see, seek nothing, do nothing, are totally unfit for work of any kind. They call themselves the intelligentsia, yet they are uncivil to their servants, treat the peasants like animals, are poor students, never read anything serious, do absolutely nothing at all, only talk about science, and have little appreciation of the arts. They are all solemn, have grim faces, they all philosophize and talk of weighty matters. And meanwhile the vast majority of us, ninety-nine out of a hundred, live like savages. At the least provocation—a punch in the jaw, and curses. They eat disgustingly, sleep in filth and stuffiness, bedbugs everywhere, stench and damp and moral slovenliness. And obviously, the only purpose of all our fine talk is to hoodwink ourselves and others. Show me where the public nurseries are that we've heard so much about, and the libraries. We read about them in novels, but in reality they don't exist, there is nothing but dirt, vulgarity, and Asiatic backwardness. I don't like very solemn faces, I'm afraid of them, I'm afraid of serious conversations. We'd do better to keep quiet for a while.

LOPAHIN. Do you know, I get up at five o'clock in the morning, and I work from morning till night; and I'm always handling money, my own and other people's, and I see what people around me are really like. You've only to start doing anything to see how few honest, decent people there are. Sometimes when I lie awake at night, I think: "Oh, Lord, thou hast given us immense forests, boundless fields, the widest horizons, and living in their midst, we ourselves ought really to be giants."

MME. RANEVSKAYA. Now you want giants! They're only good in fairy tales; otherwise they're frightening.

(YEPIHODOV *crosses the stage at the rear, playing the guitar*)

MME. RANEVSKAYA (*pensively*). There goes Yepihodov.

ANYA (*pensively*). There goes Yepihodov.

GAYEV. Ladies and gentlemen, the sun has set.

TROFIMOV. Yes.

GAYEV (*in a low voice, declaiming as it were*). Oh, Nature, wondrous Nature, you shine with eternal radiance, beautiful and indifferent! You, whom we call our mother, unite within yourself life and death! You animate and destroy!

VARYA (*pleadingly*). Uncle dear!

ANYA. Uncle, again!

TROFIMOV. You'd better bank the yellow ball in the side pocket.

GAYEV. I'm silent, I'm silent . . .

(*All sit plunged in thought. Stillness reigns. Only* FIRS's *muttering is audible. Suddenly a distant sound is heard, coming from the sky as it were, the sound of a snapping string, mournfully dying away*)

MME. RANEVSKAYA. What was that?

LOPAHIN. I don't know. Somewhere far away, in the pits, a bucket's broken loose; but somewhere very far away.

GAYEV. Or it might be some sort of bird, perhaps a heron.

TROFIMOV. Or an owl . . .

MME. RANEVSKAYA (*shudders*). It's weird, somehow. (*Pause*)

FIRS. Before the calamity the same thing happened—the owl screeched, and the samovar hummed all the time.

GAYEV. Before what calamity?

FIRS. Before the Freedom.[1] (*Pause*)

MME. RANEVSKAYA. Come, my friends, let's be going. It's getting dark. (*To* ANYA) You have tears in your eyes. What is it, my little one? (*Embraces her*)

ANYA. I don't know, mamma; it's nothing.

TROFIMOV. Somebody's coming.

(*A Tramp appears, wearing a shabby white cap and an overcoat. He is slightly drunk*)

TRAMP. Allow me to inquire, will this short-cut take me to the station?

GAYEV. It will. Just follow that road.

TRAMP. My heartfelt thanks. (*Coughing*) The weather is glorious. (*Recites*) "My brother, my suffering brother . . . Go down to the Volga! Whose groans . . . ?" (*To* VARYA) Mademoiselle, won't you spare 30 kopecks for a hungry Russian?

(VARYA, *frightened, cries out*)

LOPAHIN (*angrily*). Even panhandling has its proprieties.

MME. RANEVSKAYA (*scared*). Here, take this. (*Fumbles in her purse*) I haven't any silver . . . never mind, here's a gold piece.

TRAMP. My heartfelt thanks. (*Exits. Laughter*)

VARYA (*frightened*). I'm leaving, I'm leaving . . . Oh, mamma dear, at home the servants have nothing to eat, and you gave him a gold piece!

MME. RANEVSKAYA. What are you going to do with me? I'm such a fool. When we get home, I'll give you everything I have. Yermolay Alexeyevich, you'll lend me some more . . .

---

1. The emancipation of the serfs, proclaimed in 1861.

LOPAHIN. Yes, ma'am.

MME. RANEVSKAYA. Come, ladies and gentlemen, it's time to be going. Oh! Varya, we've settled all about your marriage. Congratulations!

VARYA (*through tears*). Really, mamma, that's not a joking matter.

LOPAHIN. "Aurelia, get thee to a nunnery, go . . ."

GAYEV. And do you know, my hands are trembling: I haven't played billiards in a long time.

LOPAHIN. "Aurelia, nymph, in your orisons, remember me!"

MME. RANEVSKAYA. Let's go, it's almost suppertime.

VARYA. He frightened me! My heart's pounding.

LOPAHIN. Let me remind you, ladies and gentlemen, on the 22nd of August the cherry orchard will be up for sale. Think about that! Think!

(*All except* TROFIMOV *and* ANYA *go out*)

ANYA (*laughs*). I'm grateful to that tramp, he frightened Varya and so we're alone.

TROFIMOV. Varya's afraid we'll fall in love with each other all of a sudden. She hasn't left us alone for days. Her narrow mind can't grasp that we're above love. To avoid the petty and illusory, everything that prevents us from being free and happy—that is the goal and meaning of our life. Forward! Do not fall behind, friends!

ANYA (*strikes her hands together*). How well you speak! (*Pause*) It's wonderful here today.

TROFIMOV. Yes, the weather's glorious.

ANYA. What have you done to me, Petya? Why don't I love the cherry orchard as I used to? I loved it so tenderly. It seemed to me there was no spot on earth lovelier than our orchard.

TROFIMOV. All Russia is our orchard. Our land is vast and beautiful, there are many wonderful places in it. (*Pause*) Think of it, Anya, your grandfather, your great-grandfather and all your ancestors were serf-owners, owners of living souls, and aren't human beings looking at you from every tree in the orchard, from every leaf, from every trunk? Don't you hear voices? Oh, it's terrifying! Your orchard is a fearful place, and when you pass through it in the evening or at night, the old bark on the trees gleams faintly, and the cherry trees seem to be dreaming of things that happened a hundred, two hundred years ago and to be tormented by painful visions. What is there to say? We're at least two hundred years behind, we've really achieved nothing yet, we have no definite attitude to the past, we only philosophize, complain of the blues, or drink vodka. It's all so clear: in order to live in the present, we should first redeem our past, finish with it, and we can expiate it only by suffering, only by extraordinary, unceasing labor. Realize that, Anya.

ANYA. The house in which we live has long ceased to be our own, and I will leave it, I give you my word.

TROFIMOV. If you have the keys, fling them into the well and go away. Be free as the wind.

ANYA (*in ecstasy*). How well you put that!

TROFIMOV. Believe me, Anya, believe me! I'm not yet thirty, I'm young, I'm still a student—but I've already suffered so much. In winter I'm hungry, sick, harassed, poor as a beggar, and where hasn't Fate driven me? Where haven't I been? And yet always, every moment of the day and night, my soul is filled with inexplicable premonitions. . . . I have a premonition of happiness, Anya. . . . I see it already!

ANYA (*pensively*). The moon is rising.

(YEPIHODOV *is heard playing the same mournful tune on the guitar. The moon rises. Somewhere near the poplars* VARYA *is looking for* ANYA *and calling* "Anya, where are you?")

TROFIMOV. Yes, the moon is rising. (*Pause*) There it is, happiness, it's approaching, it's coming nearer and nearer, I can already hear its footsteps. And if we don't see it, if we don't know it, what does it matter? Others will!

VARYA's *voice.* "Anya! Where are you?"

TROFIMOV. That Varya again! (*Angrily*) It's revolting!

ANYA. Never mind, let's go down to the river. It's lovely there.

TROFIMOV. Come on. (*They go*)

VARYA's *voice.* "Anya! Anya!"

Act III

A drawing-room separated by an arch from a ballroom. Evening. Chandelier burning. The Jewish band is heard playing in the anteroom. In the ballroom they are dancing the Grand Rond. PISHCHIK *is heard calling,* "Promenade à une paire." PISHCHIK *and* CHARLOTTA, TROFIMOV *and* MME. RANEVSKAYA, ANYA *and the* Post Office Clerk, VARYA *and the* Stationmaster, *and others, enter the drawing-room in couples.* DUNYASHA *is in the last couple.* VARYA *weeps quietly, wiping her tears as she dances. All parade through drawing-room.* PISHCHIK *calling* "Grand rond, balancez!" *and* "Les cavaliers à genoux et remerciez vos dames!" FIRS *wearing a dress-coat, brings in soda-water on a tray.* PISHCHIK *and* TROFIMOV *enter the drawing-room.*

PISHCHIK. I'm a full-blooded man; I've already had two strokes. Dancing's hard work for me; but as they say, "If you run with the pack, you can bark or not, but at least wag your tail." Still, I'm as strong as a horse. My late lamented father, who would have his joke, God rest his soul, used to say, talking about our origin, that the ancient line of the Simeonov-Pishchiks was descended from the very horse that Caligula had made a senator. (*Sits down*) But the trouble is, I have no money. A hungry dog believes in nothing but meat. (*Snores and wakes up at once*) It's the same with me—I can think of nothing but money.

TROFIMOV. You know, there *is* something equine about your figure.

PISHCHIK. Well, a horse is a fine animal—one can sell a horse.

(*Sound of billiards being played in an adjoining room.* VARYA *appears in the archway*)

TROFIMOV (*teasing her*). Madam Lopahina! Madam Lopahina!

VARYA (*angrily*). Mangy master!

TROFIMOV. Yes, I am a mangy master and I'm proud of it.

VARYA (*reflecting bitterly*). Here we've hired musicians, and what shall we pay them with? (*Exits*)

TROFIMOV (*to* PISHCHIK). If the energy you have spent during your lifetime looking for money to pay interest had gone into something else, in the end you could have turned the world upside down.

PISHCHIK. Nietzsche, the philosopher, the greatest, most famous of men, that colossal intellect, says in his works, that it is permissible to forge banknotes.

TROFIMOV. Have you read Nietzsche?

PISHCHIK. Well . . . Dashenka told me . . . And now I've got to the point where forging banknotes is about the only way out for me. . . . The day after tomorrow I have to pay 310 rubles—I already have 130 . . .(*Feels in his pockets. In alarm*) The money's gone! I've lost my money! (*Through tears*) Where's my money? (*Joyfully*) Here it is! Inside the lining . . . I'm all in a sweat . . .

(*Enter* MME. RANEVSKAYA *and* CHARLOTTA)

MME. RANEVSKAYA (*hums the "Lezginka"*). Why isn't Leonid back yet? What is he doing in town? (*To* DUNYASHA) Dunyasha, offer the musicians tea.

TROFIMOV. The auction hasn't taken place, most likely.

MME. RANEVSKAYA. It's the wrong time to have the band, and the wrong time to give a dance. Well, never mind. (*Sits down and hums softly*)

CHARLOTTA (*hands* PISHCHIK *a pack of cards*). Here is a pack of cards. Think of any card you like.

PISHCHIK. I've thought of one.

CHARLOTTA. Schuffle the pack now. That's right. Give it here, my dear Mr. Pishchik. *Ein, zwei, drei!* Now look for it—it's in your side pocket.

PISHCHIK (*taking the card out of his pocket*). The eight of spades! Perfectly right! Just imagine!

CHARLOTTA (*holding pack of cards in her hands. To* TROFIMOV). Quickly, name the top card.

TROFIMOV. Well, let's see—the queen of spades.

CHARLOTTA. Right! (*To* PISHCHIK) Now name the top card.

PISHCHIK. The ace of hearts.

CHARLOTTA. Right! (*Claps her hands and the pack of cards disappears*) Ah, what lovely weather it is today! (*A mysterious feminine voice which seems to come from under the floor, answers her*). "Oh, yes, it's magnificent weather, madam."

CHARLOTTA. You are my best ideal.

VOICE. "And I find you pleasing too, madam."

STATIONMASTER (*applauding*). The lady ventriloquist, bravo!

PISHCHIK (*amazed*). Just imagine! Enchanting Charlotta Ivanovna, I'm simply in love with you.

CHARLOTTA. In love? (*Shrugs her shoulders*) Are you capable of love? *Guter Mensch, aber schlechter Musikant!*

TROFIMOV (*claps* PISHCHIK *on the shoulder*). You old horse, you!

CHARLOTTA. Attention please! One more trick! (*Takes a plaid from a chair*) Here is a very good plaid; I want to sell it. (*Shaking it out*) Does anyone want to buy it?

PISHCHIK (*in amazement*). Just imagine!

CHARLOTTA. *Ein, zwei, drei!* (*Raises the plaid quickly, behind it stands* ANYA. *She curtsies, runs to her mother, embraces her, and runs back into the ballroom, amidst general enthusiasm*)

MME. RANEVSKAYA (*applauds*). Bravo! Bravo!

CHARLOTTA. Now again! *Ein, zwei, drei!* (*Lifts the plaid; behind it stands* VARYA *bowing*)

PISHCHIK (*running after her*). The rascal! What a woman, what a woman! (*Exits*)

MME. RANEVSKAYA. And Leonid still isn't here. What is he doing in town so long? I don't understand. It must be all over by now. Either the estate has been sold, or the auction hasn't taken place. Why keep us in suspense so long?

VARYA (*trying to console her*). Uncle's bought it, I feel sure of that.

TROFIMOV (*mockingly*). Oh, yes!

VARYA. Great-aunt sent him an authorization to buy it in her name, and to transfer the debt. She's doing it for Anya's sake. And I'm sure that God will help us, and uncle will buy it.

MME. RANEVSKAYA. Great-aunt sent fifteen thousand to buy the estate in her name, she doesn't trust us, but that's not even enough to pay the interest. (*Covers her face with her hands*) Today my fate will be decided, my fate—

TROFIMOV (*teasing* VARYA). Madam Lopahina!

VARYA (*angrily*). Perpetual student! Twice already you've been expelled from the university.

MME. RANEVSKAYA. Why are you so cross, Varya? He's teasing you about Lopahin. Well, what of it? If you want to marry Lopahin, go ahead. He's a good man, and interesting; if you don't want to, don't. Nobody's compelling you, my pet!

VARYA. Frankly, mamma dear, I take this thing seriously; he's a good man and I like him.

MME. RANEVSKAYA. All right then, marry him. I don't know what you're waiting for.

VARYA. But, mamma, I can't propose to him myself. For the last two years everyone's been talking to me about him—talking. But he either keeps silent, or else cracks jokes. I understand; he's growing rich, he's absorbed in business—he has no time for me. If I had money, even a little, say, 100 rubles, I'd throw everything up and go far away—I'd go into a nunnery.

TROFIMOV. What a blessing . . .

VARYA. A student ought to be intelligent. (*Softly, with tears in her voice*) How homely you've grown, Petya! How old you look! (*To* MME. RANEVSKAYA, *with dry eyes*) But I can't live without work, mamma dear; I must keep busy every minute.

(*Enter* YASHA)

YASHA (*hardly restraining his laughter*). Yepihodov has broken a billiard cue. (*Exits*)

VARYA. Why is Yepihodov here? Who allowed him to play billiards? I don't understand these people! (*Exits*)

MME. RANEVSKAYA. Don't tease her, Petya. She's unhappy enough without that.

TROFIMOV. She bustles so—and meddles in other people's business. All summer long she's given Anya and me no peace. She's afraid of a love-affair between us. What business is it of hers? Besides, I've given no grounds for it, and I'm far from such vulgarity. We are above love.

MME. RANEVSKAYA. And I suppose I'm beneath love? (*Anxiously*) What can be keeping Leonid? If I only knew whether the estate has been sold or not. Such a calamity seems so incredible to me that I don't know what to think— I feel lost. . . . I could scream. . . . I could do something stupid. . . . Save me, Petya, tell me something, talk to me!

TROFIMOV. Whether the estate is sold today or not, isn't it all one? That's all done with long ago—there's no turning back, the path is overgrown. Calm yourself, my dear. You mustn't deceive yourself. For once in your life you must face the truth.

MME. RANEVSKAYA. What truth? You can see the truth, you can tell it from falsehood, but I seem to have lost my eyesight, I see nothing. You settle every great problem so boldly, but tell me, my dear boy, isn't it because you're young, because you don't yet know what one of your problems means in terms of suffering? You look ahead fearlessly, but isn't it because you don't see and don't expect anything dreadful, because life is still hidden from your young eyes? You're bolder, more honest, more profound than we are, but think hard, show just a bit of magnanimity, spare me. After all, I was born here, my father and mother lived here, and my grandfather; I love this house. Without the cherry orchard, my life has no meaning for me, and if it really must be sold, then sell me with the orchard. (*Embraces* TROFIMOV, *kisses him on the forehead*) My son was drowned here. (*Weeps*) Pity me, you good, kind fellow!

TROFIMOV. You know, I feel for you with all my heart.

MME. RANEVSKAYA. But that should have been said differently, so differently! (*Takes out her handkerchief—a telegram falls on the floor*) My heart is so heavy today—you can't imagine! The noise here upsets me—my inmost being trembles at every sound—I'm shaking all over. But I can't go into my own room; I'm afraid to be alone. Don't condemn me, Petya. . . . I love you as though you were one of us, I would gladly let you marry Anya—I swear I would—only, my dear boy, you must study—you must take your degree— you do nothing, you let yourself be tossed by Fate from place to place—it's so strange. It's true, isn't it? And you should do something about your beard, to make it grow somehow! (*Laughs*) You're so funny!

TROFIMOV (*picks up the telegram*). I've no wish to be a dandy.

MME. RANEVSKAYA. That's a telegram from Paris. I get one every day. One yesterday and one today. That savage is ill again—he's in trouble again. He begs forgiveness, implores me to go to him, and really I ought to go to Paris to be near him. Your face is stern, Petya; but what is there to do, my dear boy? What am I to do? He's ill, he's alone and unhappy, and who is to look after him, who is to keep him from doing the wrong thing, who is to give him his medicine on time? And why hide it or keep still about it—I love him! That's clear. I love him, love him! He's a millstone round my neck, he'll drag me to the bottom, but I love that stone, I can't live without it. (*Presses* TROFIMOV's *hand*) Don't think badly of me, Petya, and don't say anything, don't say . . .

TROFIMOV (*through tears*). Forgive me my frankness in heaven's name; but, you know, he robbed you!

MME. RANEVSKAYA. No, no, no, you mustn't say such things! (*Covers her ears*)

TROFIMOV. But he's a scoundrel! You're the only one who doesn't know it. He's a petty scoundrel—a nonentity!

MME. RANEVSKAYA (*controlling her anger*). You are twenty-six or twenty-seven years old, but you're still a schoolboy.

TROFIMOV. That may be.

MME. RANEVSKAYA. You should be a man at your age. You should understand people who love—and ought to be in love yourself. You ought to fall in love! (*Angrily*) Yes, yes! And it's not purity in you, it's prudishness, you're simply a queer fish, a comical freak!

TROFIMOV (*horrified*). What is she saying?

MME. RANEVSKAYA. "I am above love!" You're not above love, but simply, as our Firs says, you're an addlehead. At your age not to have a mistress!

TROFIMOV (*horrified*). This is frightful! What is she saying! (*Goes rapidly into the ballroom, clutching his head*) It's frightful—I can't stand it, I won't stay! (*Exits, but returns at once*) All is over between us! (*Exits into anteroom*)

MME. RANEVSKAYA (*shouts after him*). Petya! Wait! You absurd fellow, I was joking. Petya!

(*Sound of somebody running quickly downstairs and suddenly falling down with a crash.* ANYA *and* VARYA *scream. Sound of laughter a moment later*)

MME. RANEVSKAYA. What's happened?

(ANYA *runs in*)

ANYA (*laughing*). Petya's fallen downstairs! (*Runs out*)

MME. RANEVSKAYA. What a queer bird that Petya is!

(Stationmaster, *standing in the middle of the ballroom, recites Alexey Tolstoy's "Magdalene," to which all listen, but after a few lines, the sound of a waltz is heard from the anteroom and the reading breaks off. All dance.* TROFIMOV, ANYA, VARYA, *and* MME. RANEVSKAYA *enter from the anteroom*)

MME. RANEVSKAYA. Petya, you pure soul, please forgive me. . . . Let's dance.

(*Dances with* PETYA. ANYA *and* VARYA *dance.* FIRS *enters, puts his stick down by the side door.* YASHA *enters from the drawing-room and watches the dancers*)

YASHA. Well, grandfather?

FIRS. I'm not feeling well. In the old days it was generals, barons, and admirals that were dancing at our balls, and now we have to send for the Post Office Clerk and the Stationmaster, and even they aren't too glad to come. I feel kind of shaky. The old master that's gone, their grandfather, dosed everyone with sealing-wax, whatever ailed 'em. I've been taking sealing-wax every day for twenty years or more. Perhaps that's what's kept me alive.

YASHA. I'm fed up with you, grandpop. (*Yawns*) It's time you croaked.

FIRS. Oh, you addlehead! (*Mumbles*)

(TROFIMOV and MME. RANEVSKAYA *dance from the ballroom into the drawing-room*)

MME. RANEVSKAYA. *Merci.* I'll sit down a while. (*Sits down*) I'm tired.

(*Enter* ANYA)

ANYA (*excitedly*). There was a man in the kitchen just now who said the cherry orchard was sold today.

MME. RANEVSKAYA. Sold to whom?

ANYA. He didn't say. He's gone. (*Dances off with* TROFIMOV)

YASHA. It was some old man gabbing, a stranger.

FIRS. And Leonid Andreyevich isn't back yet, he hasn't come. And he's wearing his lightweight between-season overcoat; like enough, he'll catch cold. Ah, when they're young they're green.

MME. RANEVSKAYA. This is killing me. Go, Yasha, find out to whom it has been sold.

YASHA. But the old man left long ago. (*Laughs*)

MME. RANEVSKAYA. What are you laughing at? What are you pleased about?

YASHA. That Yepihodov is such a funny one. A funny fellow, Two-and-Twenty Troubles!

MME. RANEVSKAYA. Firs, if the estate is sold, where will you go?

FIRS. I'll go where you tell me.

MME. RANEVSKAYA. Why do you look like that? Are you ill? You ought to go to bed.

FIRS. Yes! (*With a snigger*) Me go to bed, and who's to hand things round? Who's to see to things? I'm the only one in the whole house.

YASHA (*to* MME. RANEVSKAYA). Lubov Andreyevna, allow me to ask a favor of you, be so kind! If you go back to Paris, take me with you, I beg you. It's positively impossible for me to stay here. (*Looking around; sotto voce*) What's the use of talking? You see for yourself, it's an uncivilized country, the people have no morals, and then the boredom! The food in the kitchen's revolting, and besides there's this Firs wanders about mumbling all sorts of inappropriate words. Take me with you, be so kind!

(*Enter* PISHCHIK)

PISHCHIK. May I have the pleasure of a waltz with you, charming lady? (MME. RANEVSKAYA *accepts*) All the same, enchanting lady, you must let me have 180 rubles. . . . You must let me have (*dancing*) just one hundred and eighty rubles. (*They pass into the ballroom*)

YASHA (*hums softly*). "Oh, wilt thou understand the tumult in my soul?"

(*In the ballroom a figure in a gray top hat and checked trousers is jumping about and waving its arms; shouts:* "Bravo, Charlotta Ivanovna!")

DUNYASHA (*stopping to powder her face; to* FIRS). The young miss has ordered me to dance. There are so many gentlemen and not enough ladies. But dancing makes me dizzy, my heart begins to beat fast, Firs Nikolayevich. The Post Office Clerk said something to me just now that quite took my breath away. (*Music stops*)

FIRS. What did he say?

DUNYASHA. "You're like a flower," he said.

YASHA (*yawns*). What ignorance. (*Exits*)

DUNYASHA. "Like a flower!" I'm such a delicate girl. I simply adore pretty speeches.

FIRS. You'll come to a bad end.

(*Enter* YEPIHODOV)

YEPIHODOV (*to* DUNYASHA). You have no wish to see me, Avdotya Fyodorovna . . . as though I was some sort of insect. (*Sighs*) Ah, life!

DUNYASHA. What is it you want?

YEPIHODOV. Indubitably you may be right. (*Sighs*) But of course, if one looks at it from the point of view, if I may be allowed to say so, and apologizing for my frankness, you have completely reduced me to a state of mind. I know my fate. Every day some calamity befalls me, and I grew used to it long ago, so that I look upon my fate with a smile. You gave me your word, and though I—

DUNYASHA. Let's talk about it later, please. But just now leave me alone, I am daydreaming. (*Plays with a fan*)

YEPIHODOV. A misfortune befalls me every day; and if I may be allowed to say so, I merely smile, I even laugh.

(*Enter* VARYA)

VARYA (*to* YEPIHODOV). Are you still here? What an impertinent fellow you are really! Run along, Dunyasha. (*To* YEPIHODOV) Either you're playing billiards and breaking a cue, or you're wandering about the drawing-room as though you were a guest.

YEPIHODOV. You cannot, permit me to remark, penalize me.

VARYA. I'm not penalizing you; I'm just telling you. You merely wander from place to place, and don't do your work. We keep you as a clerk, but Heaven knows what for.

YEPIHODOV (*offended*). Whether I work or whether I walk, whether I eat or whether I play billiards, is a matter to be discussed only by persons of understanding and of mature years.

VARYA (*enraged*). You dare say that to me—you dare? You mean to say I've no understanding? Get out of here at once! This minute!

YEPIHODOV (*scared*). I beg you to express yourself delicately.

VARYA (*beside herself*). Clear out this minute! Out with you!

(YEPIHODOV *goes towards the door,* VARYA *following*)

VARYA. Two-and-Twenty Troubles! Get out—don't let me set eyes on you!

(*Exit* YEPIHODOV. *His voice is heard behind the door:* "I shall lodge a complaint against you!")

VARYA. Oh, you're coming back? (*She seizes the stick left near door by* FIRS) Well, come then . . . come . . . I'll show you . . . Ah, you're coming? You're coming? . . . Come . . . (*Swings the stick just as* LOPAHIN *enters*)

LOPAHIN. Thank you kindly.

VARYA (*angrily and mockingly*). I'm sorry.

LOPAHIN. It's nothing. Thank you kindly for your charming reception.

VARYA. Don't mention it. (*Walks away, looks back and asks softly*) I didn't hurt you, did I?

LOPAHIN. Oh, no, not at all. I shall have a large bump, though.

(*Voices from the ballroom:* "Lopahin is here! Lopahin!")

(*Enter* PISHCHIK)

PISHCHIK. My eyes do see, my ears do hear! (*Kisses* LOPAHIN)

LOPAHIN. You smell of cognac, my dear friends. And we've been celebrating here, too.

(*Enter* MME. RANEVSKAYA)

MME. RANEVSKAYA. Is that you, Yermolay Alexeyevich? What kept you so long? Where's Leonid?

LOPAHIN. Leonid Andreyevich arrived with me. He's coming.

MME. RANEVSKAYA. Well, what happened? Did the sale take place? Speak!

LOPAHIN (*embarrassed, fearful of revealing his joy*). The sale was over at four o'clock. We missed the train—had to wait till half past nine. (*Sighing heavily*) Ugh. I'm a little dizzy.

(*Enter* GAYEV. *In his right hand he holds parcels, with his left he is wiping away his tears*)

MME. RANEVSKAYA. Well, Leonid? What news? (*Impatiently, through tears*) Be quick, for God's sake!

GAYEV (*not answering, simply waves his hand. Weeping, to* FIRS). Here, take these; anchovies, Kerch herrings . . . I haven't eaten all day. What I've been through! (*The click of billiard balls comes through the open door of the billiard room and* YASHA's *voice is heard:* "Seven and eighteen!" GAYEV's *expression changes, he no longer weeps*) I'm terribly tired. Firs, help me change. (*Exits, followed by* FIRS)

PISHCHIK. How about the sale? Tell us what happened.

MME. RANEVSKAYA. Is the cherry orchard sold?

LOPAHIN. Sold.

MME. RANEVSKAYA. Who bought it?

LOPAHIN. I bought it.

(*Pause.* MME. RANEVSKAYA *is overcome. She would fall to the floor, were it not for the chair and table near which she stands.* VARYA *takes the keys from her belt, flings them on the floor in the middle of the drawing-room and goes out*)

LOPAHIN. I bought it. Wait a bit, ladies and gentlemen, please, my head is swimming, I can't talk. (*Laughs*) We got to the auction and Deriganov was there already. Leonid Andreyevich had only 15,000 and straight off Deriganov bid 30,000 over and above the mortgage. I saw how the land lay, got into the fight, bid 40,000. He bid 45,000. I bid fifty-five. He kept adding five thousands, I ten. Well . . . it came to an end. I bid ninety above the mortgage and the estate was knocked down to me. Now the cherry orchard's mine! Mine! (*Laughs uproariously*) Lord! God in Heaven! The cherry orchard's mine! Tell me that I'm drunk—out of my mind—that it's all a dream. (*Stamps his feet*) Don't laugh at me! If my father and my grandfather could rise from their graves and see all that has happened—how their Yermolay, who used to be flogged, their half-literate Yermolay, who used to run about barefoot in winter, how that very Yermolay has bought the most magnificent estate in the world. I bought the estate where my father and grandfather were slaves, where they weren't even allowed to enter the kitchen. I'm asleep— it's only a dream—I only imagine it. . . . It's the fruit of your imagination, wrapped in the darkness of the unknown! (*Picks up the keys, smiling genially*) She threw down the keys, wants to show she's no longer mistress here. (*Jingles keys*) Well, no matter. (*The band is heard tuning up*) Hey, musicians! Strike up! I want to hear you! Come, everybody, and see how Yermolay Lopahin will lay the ax to the cherry orchard and how the trees will fall to the ground. We will build summer cottages there, and our grand-sons and great-grandsons will see a new life here. Music! Strike up!

(*The band starts to play.* MME. RANEVSKAYA *has sunk into a chair and is weeping bitterly*)

LOPAHIN (*reproachfully*). Why, why didn't you listen to me? My dear friend, my poor friend, you can't bring it back now. (*Tearfully*) Oh, if only this were over quickly! Oh, if only our wretched, disordered life were changed!

PISHCHIK (*takes him by the arm; sotto voce*). She's crying. Let's go into the ballroom. Let her be alone. Come. (*Takes his arm and leads him into the ballroom*)

LOPAHIN. What's the matter? Musicians, play so I can hear you! Let me have things the way I want them. (*Ironically*) Here comes the new master, the owner of the cherry orchard. (*Accidentally he trips over a little table, almost upsetting the candelabra*) I can pay for everything.

(*Exits with* PISHCHIK. MME. RANEVSKAYA, *alone, sits huddled up, weeping bitterly. Music plays softly. Enter* ANYA *and* TROFIMOV *quickly.* ANYA *goes to her mother and falls on her knees before her.* TROFIMOV *stands in the doorway*)

ANYA. Mamma, mamma, you're crying! Dear, kind, good mamma, my precious, I love you, I bless you! The cherry orchard is sold, it's gone, that's true, quite true. But don't cry, mamma, life is still before you, you still have your kind, pure heart. Let us go, let us go away from here, darling. We will plant a new orchard, even more luxuriant than this one. You will see it, you will understand, and like the sun at evening, joy—deep, tranquil joy— will sink into your soul, and you will smile, mamma. Come, darling, let us go.

Act IV

Scene as in Act I. No window curtains or pictures, only a little furniture, piled up in a corner, as if for sale. A sense of emptiness. Near the outer door and at the back, suitcases, bundles, etc., are piled up. A door is open on the left and the voices of VARYA *and* ANYA *are heard.* LOPAHIN *stands waiting.* YASHA *holds a tray with glasses full of champagne.* YEPIHODOV *in the anteroom is tying up a box. Behind the scene a hum of voices: peasants have come to say good-by. Voice of* GAYEV: *"Thanks, brothers, thank you."*

YASHA. The country folk have come to say good-by. In my opinion, Yermolay Alexeyevich, they are kindly souls, but there's nothing in their heads. (*The hum dies away. Enter* MME. RANEVSKAYA *and* GAYEV. *She is not crying, but is pale, her face twitches and she cannot speak*)

GAYEV. You gave them your purse, Luba. That won't do! That won't do!

MME. RANEVSKAYA. I couldn't help it! I couldn't! (*They go out*)

LOPAHIN (*calls after them*). Please, I beg you, have a glass at parting. I didn't think of bringing any champagne from town and at the station I could find only one bottle. Please, won't you? (*Pause*) What's the matter, ladies and gentlemen, don't you want any? (*Moves away from the door*) If I'd known, I wouldn't have bought it. Well, then I won't drink any, either. (YASHA *carefully sets the tray down on a chair*) At least you have a glass, Yasha.

YASHA. Here's to the travelers! And good luck to those that stay! (*Drinks*) This champagne isn't the real stuff, I can assure you.

LOPAHIN. Eight rubles a bottle. (*Pause*) It's devilishly cold here.

YASHA. They didn't light the stoves today—it wasn't worth it, since we're leaving. (*Laughs*)

LOPAHIN. Why are you laughing?

YASHA. It's just that I'm pleased.

LOPAHIN. It's October, yet it's as still and sunny as though it were summer. Good weather for building. (*Looks at his watch, and speaks off*) Bear in mind, ladies and gentlemen, the train goes in forty-seven minutes, so you ought to start for the station in twenty minutes. Better hurry up!

(*Enter* TROFIMOV *wearing an overcoat*)

TROFIMOV. I think it's time to start. The carriages are at the door. The devil only knows what's become of my rubbers; they've disappeared. (*Calling off*) Anya! My rubbers are gone. I can't find them.

LOPAHIN. I've got to go to Kharkov. I'll take the same train you do. I'll spend the winter in Kharkov. I've been hanging round here with you, till I'm worn out with loafing. I can't live without work—I don't know what to do with my hands, they dangle as if they didn't belong to me.

TROFIMOV. Well, we'll soon be gone, then you can go on with your useful labors again.

LOPAHIN. Have a glass.

TROFIMOV. No, I won't.

LOPAHIN. So you're going to Moscow now?

TROFIMOV. Yes, I'll see them into town, and tomorrow I'll go on to Moscow.

LOPAHIN. Well, I'll wager the professors aren't giving any lectures, they're waiting for you to come.

TROFIMOV. That's none of your business.

LOPAHIN. Just how many years have you been at the university?

TROFIMOV. Can't you think of something new? Your joke's stale and flat. (*Looking for his rubbers*) We'll probably never see each other again, so allow me to give you a piece of advice at parting: don't wave your hands about! Get out of the habit. And another thing: building bungalows, figuring that summer residents will eventually become small farmers, figuring like that is just another form of waving your hands about. . . . Never mind, I love you anyway; you have fine, delicate fingers, like an artist; you have a fine, delicate soul.

LOPAHIN (*embracing him*). Good-by, my dear fellow. Thank you for everything. Let me give you some money for the journey, if you need it.

TROFIMOV. What for? I don't need it.

LOPAHIN. But you haven't any.

TROFIMOV. Yes, I have, thank you. I got some money for a translation—here it is in my pocket. (*Anxiously*) But where are my rubbers?

VARYA (*from the next room*). Here! Take the nasty things. (*Flings a pair of rubbers onto the stage*)

TROFIMOV. What are you so cross about, Varya? Hm . . . and these are not my rubbers.

LOPAHIN. I sowed three thousand acres of poppies in the spring, and now I've made 40,000 on them, clear profit; and when my poppies were in bloom, what a picture it was! So, as I say, I made 40,000; and I am offering you a loan because I can afford it. Why turn up your nose at it? I'm a peasant—I speak bluntly.

TROFIMOV. Your father was a peasant, mine was a druggist—that proves absolutely nothing whatever. (LOPAHIN *takes out his wallet*) Don't put that away! If you were to offer me two hundred thousand I wouldn't take it. I'm a free man. And everything that all of you, rich and poor alike, value so highly and hold so dear, hasn't the slightest power over me. It's like so much fluff floating in the air. I can get on without you, I can pass you by, I'm strong and proud. Mankind is moving towards the highest truth, towards the highest happiness possible on earth, and I am in the front ranks.

LOPAHIN. Will you get there?

TROFIMOV. I will. (*Pause*) I will get there, or I will show others the way to get there.

(*The sound of axes chopping down trees is heard in the distance*)

LOPAHIN. Well, good-by, my dear fellow. It's time to leave. We turn up our noses at one another, but life goes on just the same. When I'm working hard, without resting, my mind is easier, and it seems to me that I too know why I exist. But how many people are there in Russia, brother, who exist nobody knows why? Well, it doesn't matter. That's not what makes the wheels go round. They say Leonid Andreyevich has taken a position in the bank, 6,000 rubles a year. Only, of course, he won't stick to it, he's too lazy. . . .

ANYA (*in the doorway*). Mamma begs you not to start cutting down the cherry-trees until she's gone.

TROFIMOV. Really, you should have more tact! (*Exits*)

LOPAHIN. Right away—right away! Those men . . . (*Exits*)

ANYA. Has Firs been taken to the hospital?

YASHA. I told them this morning. They must have taken him.

ANYA (*to* YEPIHODOV *who crosses the room*). Yepihodov, please find out if Firs has been taken to the hospital.

YASHA (*offended*). I told Yegor this morning. Why ask a dozen times?

YEPIHODOV. The aged Firs, in my definitive opinion, is beyond mending. It's time he was gathered to his fathers. And I can only envy him. (*Puts a suitcase down on a hat-box and crushes it*) There now, of course. I knew it! (*Exits*)

YASHA (*mockingly*). Two-and-Twenty Troubles!

VARYA (*through the door*). Has Firs been taken to the hospital?

ANYA. Yes.

VARYA. Then why wasn't the note for the doctor taken too?

ANYA. Oh! Then someone must take it to him. (*Exits*)

VARYA (*from adjoining room*). Where's Yasha? Tell him his mother's come and wants to say good-by.

YASHA (*waves his hand*). She tries my patience.

(DUNYASHA *has been occupied with the luggage. Seeing* YASHA *alone, she goes up to him*)

DUNYASHA. You might just give me one little look, Yasha. You're going away. . . . You're leaving me . . . (*Weeps and throws herself on his neck*)

YASHA. What's there to cry about? (*Drinks champagne*) In six days I shall be in Paris again. Tomorrow we get into an express train and off we go, that's the last you'll see of us. . . . I can scarcely believe it. *Vive la France!* It don't suit me here, I just can't live here. That's all there is to it. I'm fed up with the ignorance here, I've had enough of it. (*Drinks champagne*) What's there to cry about? Behave yourself properly, and you'll have no cause to cry.

DUNYASHA (*powders her face, looking in pocket mirror*). Do send me a letter from Paris. You know I loved you, Yasha, how I loved you! I'm a delicate creature, Yasha.

YASHA. Somebody's coming! (*Busies himself with the luggage; hums softly*)

(*Enter* MME. RANEVSKAYA, GAYEV, ANYA, *and* CHARLOTTA)

GAYEV. We ought to be leaving. We haven't much time. (*Looks at* YASHA) Who smells of herring?

MME. RANEVSKAYA. In about ten minutes we should be getting into the carriages. (*Looks around the room*) Good-by, dear old home, good-by, grandfather. Winter will pass, spring will come, you will no longer be here, they will have torn you down. How much these walls have seen! (*Kisses* ANYA *warmly*) My treasure, how radiant you look! Your eyes are sparkling like diamonds. Are you glad? Very?

ANYA (*gaily*). Very glad. A new life is beginning, mamma.

GAYEV. Well, really, everything is all right now. Before the cherry orchard was sold, we all fretted and suffered; but afterwards, when the question was settled finally and irrevocably, we all calmed down, and even felt quite cheerful. I'm a bank employee now, a financier. The yellow ball in the side pocket! And anyhow, you are looking better Luba, there's no doubt of that.

MME. RANEVSKAYA. Yes, my nerves are better, that's true. (*She is handed her hat and coat*) I sleep well. Carry out my things, Yasha. It's time. (*To* ANYA) We shall soon see each other again, my little girl. I'm going to Paris, I'll live there on the money your great-aunt sent us to buy the estate with— long live Auntie! But that money won't last long.

ANYA. You'll come back soon, soon, mamma, won't you? Meanwhile I'll study, I'll pass my high school examination, and then I'll go to work and help you. We'll read all kinds of books together, mamma, won't we? (*Kisses her mother's hands*) We'll read in the autumn evenings, we'll read lots of books, and a new wonderful world will open up before us. (*Falls into a revery*) Mamma, do come back.

MME. RANEVSKAYA. I will come back, my precious. (*Embraces her daughter. Enter* LOPAHIN *and* CHARLOTTA *who is humming softly*)

GAYEV. Charlotta's happy: she's singing.

CHARLOTTA (*picks up a bundle and holds it like a baby in swaddling-clothes*). Bye, baby, bye. (*A baby is heard crying* "Wah! Wah!") Hush, hush, my pet, my little one. "Wah! Wah!" I'm so sorry for you! (*Throws the bundle down*) You will find me a position, won't you? I can't go on like this.

LOPAHIN. We'll find one for you, Charlotta Ivanovna, don't worry.

GAYEV. Everyone's leaving us. Varya's going away. We've suddenly become of no use.

CHARLOTTA. There's no place for me to live in town, I must go away. (*Hums*) (*Enter* PISHCHIK)

LOPAHIN. There's nature's masterpiece!

PISHCHIK (*gasping*). Oh . . . let me get my breath . . . I'm in agony. . . . Esteemed friends . . . Give me a drink of water. . . .

GAYEV. Wants some money, I suppose. No, thank you . . . I'll keep out of harm's way. (*Exits*)

PISHCHIK. It's a long while since I've been to see you, most charming lady. (*To* LOPAHIN) So you are here . . . glad to see you, you intellectual giant . . . There . . . (*Gives* LOPAHIN *money*) Here's 400 rubles, and I still owe you 840.

LOPAHIN (*shrugging his shoulders in bewilderment*). I must be dreaming . . . Where did you get it?

PISHCHIK. Wait a minute . . . It's hot . . . A most extraordinary event! Some Englishmen came to my place and found some sort of white clay on my land . . . (*To* MME. RANEVSKAYA) And 400 for you . . . most lovely . . . most wonderful . . . (*Hands her the money*) The rest later. (*Drinks water*) A young man in the train was telling me just now that a great philosopher recommends jumping off roofs. "Jump!" says he; "that's the long and the short of it!" (*In amazement*) Just imagine! Some more water!

LOPAHIN. What Englishmen?

PISHCHIK. I leased them the tract with the clay on it for twenty-four years. . . . And now, forgive me, I can't stay. . . . I must be dashing on. . . . I'm going over to Znoikov . . . to Kardamanov . . . I owe them all money . . . (*Drinks water*) Good-by, everybody . . . I'll look in on Thursday . . .

MME. RANEVSKAYA. We're just moving into town; and tomorrow I go abroad.

PISHCHIK (*upset*). What? Why into town? That's why the furniture is like that . . . and the suitcases . . . Well, never mind! (*Through tears*) Never mind . . . Men of colossal intellect, these Englishmen . . . Never mind . . . Be happy. God will come to your help . . . Never mind . . . Everything in this world comes to an end. (*Kisses* MME. RANEVSKAYA's *hand*) If the rumor reaches you that it's all up with me, remember this old . . . horse, and say: Once there lived a certain . . . Simeonov-Pishchik . . . the kingdom of Heaven be his . . . Glorious weather! . . . Yes . . .(*Exits, in great confusion, but at once returns and says in the doorway*) My daughter Dashenka sends her regards. (*Exit*)

MME. RANEVSKAYA. Now we can go. I leave with two cares weighing on me. The first is poor old Firs. (*Glancing at her watch*) We still have about five minutes.

ANYA. Mamma, Firs has already been taken to the hospital. Yasha sent him there this morning.

MME. RANEVSKAYA. My other worry is Varya. She's used to getting up early and working; and now, with no work to do, she is like a fish out of water. She has grown thin and pale, and keeps crying, poor soul. (*Pause*) You know this very well, Yermolay Alexeyevich; I dreamed of seeing her married to you, and it looked as though that's how it would be. (*Whispers to* ANYA, *who nods to* CHARLOTTA *and both go out*) She loves you. You find her attractive. I don't know, I don't know why it is you seem to avoid each other; I can't understand it.

LOPAHIN. To tell you the truth, I don't understand it myself. It's all a puzzle. If there's still time, I'm ready now, at once. Let's settle it straight off, and have done with it! Without you, I feel I'll never be able to propose.

MME. RANEVSKAYA. That's splendid. After all, it will only take a minute. I'll call her at once. . . .

LOPAHIN. And luckily, here's champagne too. (*Looks at the glasses*) Empty! Somebody's drunk it all. (YASHA *coughs*) That's what you might call guzzling . . .

MME. RANEVSKAYA (*animatedly*). Excellent! We'll go and leave you alone. Yasha, *allez!* I'll call her. (*At the door*) Varya, leave everything and come here. Come! (*Exits with* YASHA)

LOPAHIN (*looking at his watch*). Yes . . . (*Pause behind the door, smothered laughter and whispering; at last, enter* VARYA)

VARYA (*looking over the luggage in leisurely fashion*). Strange, I can't find it . . .

LOPAHIN. What are you looking for?

VARYA. Packed it myself, and I don't remember . . . (*Pause*)

LOPAHIN. Where are you going now, Varya?

VARYA. I? To the Ragulins'. I've arranged to take charge there—as housekeeper, if you like.

LOPAHIN. At Yashnevo? About fifty miles from here. (*Pause*) Well, life in this house is ended!

VARYA (*examining luggage*). Where is it? Perhaps I put it in the chest. Yes, life in this house is ended . . . There will be no more of it.

LOPAHIN. And I'm just off to Kharkov—by this next train. I've a lot to do there. I'm leaving Yepihodov here . . . I've taken him on.

VARYA. Oh!

LOPAHIN. Last year at this time it was snowing, if you remember, but now it's sunny and there's no wind. It's cold, though . . . It must be three below.

VARYA. I didn't look. (*Pause*) And besides, our thermometer's broken. (*Pause. Voice from the yard:* "Yermolay Alexeyevich!")

LOPAHIN (*as if he had been waiting for the call*). This minute!

(*Exits quickly.* VARYA *sits on the floor and sobs quietly, her head on a bundle of clothes. Enter* MME. RANEVSKAYA *cautiously*)

MME. RANEVSKAYA. Well? (*Pause*) We must be going.

VARYA (*wiping her eyes*). Yes, it's time, mamma dear. I'll be able to get to the Ragulins' today, if only we don't miss the train.

MME. RANEVSKAYA (*at the door*). Anya, put your things on.

(*Enter* ANYA, GAYEV, CHARLOTTA. GAYEV *wears a heavy overcoat with a hood. Enter servants and coachmen.* YEPIHODOV *bustles about the luggage*)

MME. RANEVSKAYA. Now we can start on our journey.

ANYA (*joyfully*). On our journey!

GAYEV. My friends, my dear, cherished friends, leaving this house forever, can I be silent? Can I at leave-taking refrain from giving utterance to those emotions that now fill my being?

ANYA (*imploringly*). Uncle!

VARYA. Uncle, uncle dear, don't.

GAYEV (*forlornly*). I'll bank the yellow in the side pocket . . . I'll be silent . . .

(*Enter* TROFIMOV, *then* LOPAHIN)

TROFIMOV. Well, ladies and gentlemen, it's time to leave.

LOPAHIN. Yepihodov, my coat.

MME. RANEVSKAYA. I'll sit down just a minute. It seems as though I'd never before seen what the walls of this house were like, the ceilings, and now I look at them hungrily, with such tender affection.

GAYEV. I remember when I was six years old sitting on that window sill on Whitsunday, watching my father going to church.

MME. RANEVSKAYA. Has everything been taken?

LOPAHIN. I think so. (*Putting on his overcoat*) Yepihodov, see that everything's in order.

YEPIHODOV (*in a husky voice*). You needn't worry, Yermolay Alexeyevich.

LOPAHIN. What's the matter with your voice?

YEPIHODOV. I just had a drink of water. I must have swallowed something.

YASHA (*contemptuously*). What ignorance!

MME. RANEVSKAYA. When we're gone, not a soul will be left here.

LOPAHIN. Until the spring.

(VARYA *pulls an umbrella out of a bundle, as though about to hit someone with it.* LOPAHIN *pretends to be frightened*)

VARYA. Come, come, I had no such idea!

TROFIMOV. Ladies and gentlemen, let's get into the carriages—it's time. The train will be in directly.

VARYA. Petya, there they are, your rubbers, by that trunk. (*Tearfully*) And what dirty old things they are!

TROFIMOV (*puts on rubbers*). Let's go, ladies and gentlemen.

GAYEV (*greatly upset, afraid of breaking down*). The train . . . the station . . . Three cushions in the side pocket, I'll bank this one in the corner . . .

MME. RANEVSKAYA. Let's go.

LOPAHIN. Are we all here? No one in there? (*Locks the side door on the left*) There are some things stored here, better lock up. Let us go!

ANYA. Good-by, old house! Good-by, old life!

TROFIMOV. Hail to you, new life!

(*Exit with* ANYA. VARYA *looks round the room and goes out slowly.* YASHA *and* CHARLOTTA *with her dog go out*)

LOPAHIN. And so, until the spring. Go along, friends . . . 'Bye-'bye! (*Exits*)

MME. RANEVSKAYA *and* GAYEV *remain alone. As though they had been waiting for this, they throw themselves on each other's necks, and break into subdued, restrained sobs, afraid of being overheard*)

GAYEV (*in despair*). My sister! My sister!

MME. RANEVSKAYA. Oh, my orchard—my dear, sweet, beautiful orchard! My life, my youth, my happiness—good-by! Good-by! (*Voice of* ANYA, *gay and summoning:* "Mamma!" *Voice of* TROFIMOV, *gay and excited:* "Halloo!")

MME. RANEVSKAYA. One last look at the walls, at the windows . . . Our poor mother loved to walk about this room . . .

GAYEV. My sister, my sister! (*Voice of* ANYA: "Mamma!" *Voice of* TROFIMOV: "Halloo!")

MME. RANEVSKAYA. We're coming.

(*They go out. The stage is empty. The sound of doors being locked, of carriages driving away. Then silence. In the stillness is heard the muffled sound of the ax striking a tree, a mournful, lonely sound.*

(*Footsteps are heard.* FIRS *appears in the doorway on the right. He is dressed as usual in a jacket and white waistcoat and wears slippers. He is ill.*)

FIRS (*goes to the door, tries the handle*). Locked! They've gone . . . (*Sits down on the sofa*) They've forgotten me . . . Never mind . . . I'll sit here a bit . . . I'll wager Leonid Andreyevich hasn't put his fur coat on, he's gone off in his light overcoat . . . (*Sighs anxiously*) I didn't keep an eye on him . . . Ah, when they're young, they're green . . .(*Mumbles something indistinguishable*) Life has gone by as if I had never lived. (*Lies down*) I'll lie down a while . . . There's no strength left in you, old fellow; nothing is left, nothing. Ah, you addlehead!

(*Lies motionless. A distant sound is heard coming from the sky as it were, the sound of a snapping string mournfully dying away. All is still again, and nothing is heard but the strokes of the ax against a tree far away in the orchard*)

Anton Chekhov

THE SWAN SONG

Early in 1887, in a letter to a friend, Chekov wrote, "I have written a play on four sheets of paper. It will take fifteen to twenty minutes to act." He went on to say that he had completed the play in an hour and five minutes and that he found it better to write small things than big ones because "they are unpretentious and successful." *The Swan Song* had its premiere at Korsh's theater in Moscow on February 19, 1888.

Although *The Swan Song* is definitely one of Chekov's minor works, it does not give the impression that it was merely dashed off, as the author's letter suggests. As is usual in Chekov's plays, the characters' frustration and their sense of futility set the tone, but it is relieved by witty and tenderly humorous touches. Like many of Chekov's other creations, the old actor in this short drama gets nothing done but feels much and talks at great length.

CHARACTERS

VASILI SVIETLOVIDOFF, *a comedian, 68 years old*
NIKITA IVANITCH, *a prompter, an old man*

The scene is laid on the stage of a country theatre, at night, after the play. To the right a row of rough, unpainted doors leading into the dressing-rooms. To the left and in the background the stage is encumbered with all sorts of rubbish. In the middle of the stage is an overturned stool.

SVIETLOVIDOFF (*with a candle in his hand, comes out of a dressing-room and laughs*). Well, well, this is funny! Here's a good joke! I fell asleep in my

From *Plays by Anton Tchekoff*, translated by Marian Fell. Used by permission of the publishers, Charles Scribner's Sons.

dressing-room when the play was over, and there I was calmly snoring after everybody else had left the theatre. Ah! I'm a foolish old man, a poor old dodderer! I have been drinking again, and so I fell asleep in there, sitting up. That was clever! Good for you, old boy! (*Calls*) Yegorka! Petrushka! Where the devil are you? Petrushka! The scoundrels must be asleep, and an earthquake wouldn't wake them now! Yegorka! (*Picks up the stool, sits down, and puts the candle on the floor*) Not a sound! Only echoes answer me. I gave Yegorka and Petrushka each a tip to-day, and now they have disappeared without leaving a trace behind them. The rascals have gone off and have probably locked up the theatre. (*Turns his head about*) I'm drunk! Ugh! The play tonight was for my benefit, and it is disgusting to think how much beer and wine I have poured down my throat in honour of the occasion. Gracious! My body is burning all over, and I feel as if I had twenty tongues in my mouth. It is horrid! Idiotic! This poor old sinner is drunk again, and doesn't even know what he has been celebrating! Ugh! My head is splitting, I am shivering all over, and I feel as dark and cold inside as a cellar! Even if I don't mind ruining my health, I ought at least to remember my age, old idiot that I am! Yes, my old age! It's no use! I can play the fool, and brag, and pretend to be young, but my life is really over now, I kiss my hand to the sixty-eight years that have gone by; I'll never see them again! I have drained the bottle, only a few little drops are left at the bottom, nothing but the dregs. Yes, yes, that's the case, Vasili, old boy. The time has come for you to rehearse the part of a mummy, whether you like it or not. Death is on its way to you. (*Stares ahead of him*) It is strange, though, that I have been on the stage now for forty-five years, and this is the first time I have seen a theatre at night, after the lights have been put out. The first time. (*Walks up to the foot-lights*) How dark it is! I can't see a thing. Oh, yes, I can just make out the prompter's box, and his desk; the rest is in pitch darkness, a black, bottomless pit, like a grave, in which death itself might be hiding. . . . Brr. . . . How cold it is! The wind blows out of the empty theatre as though out of a stone flue. What a place for ghosts! The shivers are running up and down my back. (*Calls*) Yegorka! Petrushka! Where are you both? What on earth makes me think of such gruesome things here? I must give up drinking; I'm an old man, I shan't live much longer. At sixty-eight people go to church and prepare for death, but here I am—heavens! A profane old drunkard in this fool's dress—I'm simply not fit to look at. I must go and change it at once. . . . This is a dreadful place, I should die of fright sitting here all night. (*Goes toward his dressing-room; at the same time* NIKITA IVANITCH *in a long white coat comes out of the dressing-room at the farthest end of the stage.* SVIETLOVIDOFF *sees* IVANITCH—*shrieks with terror and steps back*) Who are you? What? What do you want? (*Stamps his foot*) Who are you?

IVANITCH. It is I, sir.

SVIETLOVIDOFF. Who are you?

IVANITCH (*comes slowly toward him*). It is I, sir, the prompter, Nikita Ivanitch. It is I, master, it is I!

SVIETLOVIDOFF (*sinks helplessly onto the stool, breathes heavily and trembles violently*). Heavens! Who are you? It is you . . . you Nikitushka? What . . . what are you doing here?

IVANITCH. I spend my nights here in the dressing-rooms. Only please be good enough not to tell Alexi Fomitch, sir. I have nowhere else to spend the night; indeed, I haven't.

SVIETLOVIDOFF. Ah! It is you, Nikitushka, is it? Just think, the audience called me out sixteen times; they brought me three wreaths and lots of other things, too; they were all wild with enthusiasm, and yet not a soul came when it was all over to wake the poor, drunken old man and take him home. And I am an old man, Nikitushka! I am sixty-eight years old, and I am ill. I haven't the heart left to go on. (*Falls on* IVANITCH's *neck and weeps*) Don't go away, Nikitushka; I am old and helpless, and I feel it is time for me to die. Oh, it is dreadful, dreadful!

IVANITCH (*tenderly and respectfully*). Dear master! It is time for you to go home, sir!

SVIETLOVIDOFF. I won't go home; I have no home—none!—none!—none!

IVANITCH. Oh, dear! Have you forgotten where you live?

SVIETLOVIDOFF. I won't go there. I won't! I am all alone there. I have nobody, Nikitushka! No wife—no children. I am like the wind blowing across the lonely fields. I shall die, and no one will remember me. It is awful to be alone —no one to cheer me, no one to caress me, no one to help me to bed when I am drunk. Whom do I belong to? Who needs me? Who loves me? Not a soul, Nikitushka.

IVANITCH (*weeping*). Your audience loves you, master.

SVIETLOVIDOFF. My audience has gone home. They are all asleep, and have forgotten their old clown. No, nobody needs me, nobody loves me; I have no wife, no children.

IVANITCH. Oh, dear, Oh, dear! Don't be so unhappy about it.

SVIETLOVIDOFF. But I am a man, I am still alive. Warm, red blood is tingling in my veins, the blood of noble ancestors. I am an aristocrat, Nikitushka; I served in the army, in the artillery, before I fell as low as this, and what a fine young chap I was! Handsome, daring, eager! Where has it all gone? What has become of those old days? There's the pit that has swallowed them all! I remember it all now. Forty-five years of my life lie buried there, and what a life, Nikitushka! I can see it as clearly as I see your face: the ecstasy of youth, faith, passion, the love of women—women, Nikitushka!

IVANITCH. It is time you went to sleep, sir.

SVIETLOVIDOFF. When I first went on the stage, in the first glow of passionate youth, I remember a woman loved me for my acting. She was beautiful, graceful as a poplar, young, innocent, pure, and radiant as a summer dawn. Her smile could charm away the darkest night. I remember, I stood before her once, as I am now standing before you. She had never seemed so lovely to me as she did then, and she spoke to me so with her eyes—such a look! I shall never forget it, no, not even in the grave; so tender, so soft, so deep, so bright and young! Enraptured, intoxicated, I fell on my knees before her, I begged for my happiness, and she said: "Give up the stage!" Give up the stage! Do you understand? She could love an actor, but marry him—never! I was acting that day, I remember—I had a foolish, clown's part, and as I acted, I felt my eyes being opened; I saw that the worship of the art I had held so sacred was a delusion and an empty dream; that I was a slave, a fool, the plaything of the idleness of strangers. I understood my audience at last, and since that day I have not believed in their applause, or in their wreaths, or in their enthusiasm. Yes, Nikitushka! The people applaud me, they buy my photograph, but I am a stranger to them. They don't know me, I am as the dirt beneath their feet. They are willing enough to meet me . . . but allow a daughter or a sister to marry me, an outcast, never! I have no faith in them, (*sinks onto stool*) no faith in them.

IVANITCH. Oh, sir! you look dreadfully pale, you frighten me to death! Come, go home, have mercy on me!

SVIETLOVIDOFF. I saw through it all that day, and the knowledge was dearly bought. Nikitushka! After that . . . when that girl . . . well, I began to wander aimlessly about, living from day to day without looking ahead. I took the parts of buffoons and low comedians, letting my mind go to wreck. Ah! but I was a great artist once, till little by little I threw away my talents, played the motley fool, lost my looks, lost the power of expressing myself, and became in the end a Merry Andrew instead of a man. I have been swallowed up in that great black pit. I never felt it before, but tonight, when I woke up, I looked back, and there behind me lay sixty-eight years. I have just found out what it is to be old! It is all over . . . (*sobs*) . . . all over.

IVANITCH. There, there, dear master! Be quiet . . . gracious! (*Calls*) Petrushka! Yegorka!

SVIETLOVIDOFF. But what a genius I was! You cannot imagine what power I had, what eloquence; how graceful I was, how tender; how many strings (*beats his breast*) quivered in this breast! It chokes me to think of it! Listen now, wait, let me catch my breath, there; now listen to this:

> "The shade of bloody Ivan now returning
> Fans through my lips rebellion to a flame,
> I am the dead Dimitri! In the burning
> Boris shall perish on the throne I claim.
> Enough! The heir of Czars shall not be seen
> Kneeling to yonder haughty Polish Queen!"[1]

Is that bad, eh? (*Quickly*) Wait, now, here's something from King Lear. The sky is black, see? Rain is pouring down, thunder roars, lightning—zzz zzz zzz—splits the whole sky, and then listen:

> "Blow, winds, and crack your cheeks! rage! blow!
> You cataracts and hurricanoes, spout

1. From *Boris Godunov*, by Pushkin.

> *Till you have drench'd our steeples, drown'd the cocks!*
> *You sulphurous thought-executing fires,*
> *Vaunt-couriers of oak-cleaving thunderbolts,*
> *Singe my white head! And thou, all-shaking thunder,*
> *Strike flat the thick rotundity o' the world!*
> *Crack nature's moulds, all germens spill at once,*
> *That make ungrateful man!"*

(*Impatiently*) Now, the part of the fool. (*Stamps his foot*) Come take the fool's part! Be quick, I can't wait!

IVANITCH (*takes the part of the fool*). "O, Nuncle, court holy-water in a dry house is better than this rain-water out o' door. Good Nuncle, in; ask thy daughter's blessing: here's a night pities neither wise men nor fools."

SVIETLOVIDOFF.

> *"Rumble thy bellyful! spit, fire! spout, rain!*
> *Nor rain, wind, thunder, fire, are my daughters;*
> *I tax not you, you elements, with unkindness;*
> *I never gave you kingdom, call'd you children."*

Ah! there is strength, there is talent for you! I'm a great artist! Now, then, here's something else of the same kind, to bring back my youth to me. For instance, take this, from Hamlet, I'll begin . . . let me see, how does it go? Oh, yes, this is it. (*Takes the part of Hamlet*) "O! the recorders, let me see one.—To withdraw with you. Why do you go about to recover the wind of me, as if you would drive me into a toil?"

IVANITCH. "O, my lord, if my duty be too bold, my love is too unmannerly."

SVIETLOVIDOFF. "I do not well understand that. Will you play upon this pipe?"

IVANITCH. "My lord, I cannot."

SVIETLOVIDOFF. "I pray you."

IVANITCH. "Believe me, I cannot."

SVIETLOVIDOFF. "I do beseech you."

IVANITCH. "I know no touch of it, my lord."

SVIETLOVIDOFF. " 'Tis as easy as lying: govern these ventages with your finger and thumb, give it breath with your mouth, and it will discourse most eloquent music. Look you, these are the stops."

IVANITCH. "But these I cannot command to any utterance of harmony: I have not the skill."

SVIETLOVIDOFF. "Why, look you, how unworthy a thing you make of me. You would play upon me; you would seem to know my stops; you would pluck out the heart of my mystery; you would sound me from my lowest note to the top of my compass; and there is much music, excellent voice, in this little organ, yet cannot you make it speak. S'blood! Do you think I am easier to be played on than a pipe? Call me what instrument you will, though you can fret me, you cannot play upon me!" (*Laughs and claps*) Bravo! Encore! Bravo! Where the devil is there any old age in that? I'm not old, that is all nonsense, a torrent of strength rushes over me; this is life, freshness, youth! Old age and genius can't exist together. You seem to be struck dumb, Nikitushka. Wait a second, let me come to my senses again. Oh! Good Lord! Now then, listen! Did you ever hear such tenderness, such music? Sh! Softly:

> *"The moon had set. There was not any light,*
> *Save of the lonely legion'd watch-stars pale*
> *In outer air, and what by fits made bright*
> *Hot oleanders in a rosy vale*
> *Searched by the lamping fly, whose little spark*
> *Went in and out, like passion's bashful hope."*[1]

(*The noise of opening doors is heard*) What's that?

IVANITCH. There are Petrushka and Yegorka coming back. Yes, you have genius, genius, my master.

SVIETLOVIDOFF (*calls, turning toward the noise*). Come here to me, boys! (*To* IVANITCH) Let us go and get dressed. I'm not old! All that is foolishness, nonsense! (*Laughs gaily*) What are you crying for? You poor old granny, you, what's the matter now? This won't do! There, there, this won't do at all! Come, come, old man, don't stare so! What makes you stare like that? There, there! (*Embraces him in tears*) Don't cry! Where there is art and genius there can never be such things as old age or loneliness or sickness ... and death itself is half ... (*Weeps*) No, no, Nikitushka! It is all over for us now! What sort of a genius am I? I'm like a squeezed lemon, a cracked bottle, and you—you are the old rat of the theatre ... a prompter! Come on! (*They go*) I'm no genius, I'm only fit to be in the suite of Fortinbras, and even for that I am too old ... Yes ... Do you remember those lines from Othello, Nikitushka?

> *"Farewell the tranquil mind! Farewell content!*
> *Farewell the plumed troop and the big wars*
> *That make ambition virtue! O, farewell!*
> *Farewell the neighing steed, and the shrill trump,*
> *The spirit-stirring drum, th' ear-piercing fife,*
> *The royal banner, and all quality,*
> *Pride, pomp, and circumstance of glorious war!"*

IVANITCH. Oh! You're a genius, a genius!

SVIETLOVIDOFF. And again this:

> *"Away! the moor is dark beneath the moon,*
> *Rapid clouds have drunk the last pale beam of even:*
> *Away! the gathering winds will call the darkness soon,*

---

1. From *Second Canto of Poltava*, by Pushkin.

> And profoundest midnight shroud the serene lights of
>   heaven."[1]

(*They go out together, the curtain falls slowly*)

Lord Dunsany

A NIGHT AT AN INN

Lord Dunsany, 1878–1958 (Edward John Moreton Drax Plunkett), got his start as a dramatist with the famous Abbey Theatre group—a group that exerted considerable influence on the development of modern drama. Dunsany's *The Glittering Gate* was produced at the Abbey Theatre in 1909 and his *King Argimenes and the Unknown Warrior* in 1911. Unfortunately, the circumstances surrounding the production of this play brought on a break between Dunsany and the Theatre, and as a result he never wrote for the group again. Although writing seemingly occupied a small part of his time (by Dunsany's own account he devoted 97 per cent of his life to athletic activities and only 3 per cent to writing), he was a prolific author of plays and short stories. Most of his plays he wrote between 1909 and 1913. *A Night at an Inn* was written in 1912 and first produced in 1916 at the Neighborhood Playhouse in New York City. Like others of his plays, *A Night at an Inn* shows an excellent grasp of dramatic form and conventions and illustrates his ability to handle dialog and suspense.

CHARACTERS

A. E. SCOTT-FORTESCUE (THE TOFF)
WILLIAM JONES (BILL)
ALBERT THOMAS
JACOB SMITH (SNIGGERS)
        a dilapidated gentleman
        merchant sailors

1ST PRIEST OF KLESH
2ND PRIEST OF KLESH
3RD PRIEST OF KLESH
KLESH

From *Plays of Gods and Men,* by Lord Dunsany. Courtesy of G. P. Putnam's Sons and Putnam and Company, Ltd.
1. From *The Mischief of Being Clever,* by Alexander Griboyedov.

The Curtain rises on a room in an inn. SNIGGERS *and* BILL *are talking.* THE
  TOFF *is reading a paper.* ALBERT *sits a little apart.*

SNIGGERS. What's his idea, I wonder?

BILL. I don't know.

SNIGGERS. And how much longer will he keep us here?

BILL. We've been here three days.

SNIGGERS. And 'aven't seen a soul.

BILL. And a pretty penny it cost us when he rented the pub.

SNIGGERS. 'Ow long did 'e rent the pub for?

BILL. You never know with him.

SNIGGERS. It's lonely enough.

BILL. 'Ow long did you rent the pub for, Toffy?

(THE TOFF *continues to read a sporting paper; he takes no notice of what
  is said*)

SNIGGERS. 'E's such a toff.

BILL. Yet 'e's clever, no mistake.

SNIGGERS. Those clever ones are the beggars to make a muddle. Their plans are
  clever enough, but they don't work, and then they make a mess of things
  much worse than you or me.

BILL. Ah!

SNIGGERS. I don't like this place.

BILL. Why not?

SNIGGERS. I don't like the looks of it.

BILL. He's keeping us here because here those niggers can't find us. The three
  heathen priests what was looking for us so. But we want to go and sell our
  ruby soon.

ALBERT. There's no sense in it.

BILL. Why not, Albert?

ALBERT. Because I gave those black devils the slip in Hull.

BILL. You give 'em the slip, Albert?

ALBERT. The slip, all three of them. The fellows with the gold spots on their
  foreheads. I had the ruby then, and I give them the slip in Hull.

BILL. How did you do it, Albert?

ALBERT. I had the ruby and they were following me . . .

BILL. Who told them you had the ruby? You didn't show it?

ALBERT. No . . . But they kind of know.

SNIGGERS. They kind of know, Albert?

ALBERT. Yes, they know if you've got it. Well, they sort of mouched after me,
  and I tells a policeman and he says, O they were only three poor niggers
  and they wouldn't hurt me. Ugh! When I thought of what they did in Malta
  to poor old Jim.

BILL. Yes, and to George in Bombay before we started.

SNIGGERS. Ugh!

BILL. Why didn't you give 'em in charge?

ALBERT. What about the ruby, Bill?

BILL. Ah!

ALBERT. Well, I did better than that. I walks up and down through Hull. I walks slow enough. And then I turns a corner and I runs. I never sees a corner but I turns it. But sometimes I let a corner pass just to fool them. I twists about like a hare. Then I sits down and waits. No priests.

SNIGGERS. What?

ALBERT. No heathen black devils with gold spots on their face. I gave 'em the slip.

BILL. Well done, Albert.

SNIGGERS *(after a sigh of content)*. Why didn't you tell us?

ALBERT. 'Cause 'e won't let you speak. 'E's got 'is plans and 'e thinks we're silly folk. Things must be done 'is way. And all the time I've give 'em the slip. Might 'ave 'ad one o' them crooked knives in him before now but for me who give 'em the slip in Hull.

BILL. Well done, Albert.

SNIGGERS. Do you hear that, Toffy? Albert has give 'em the slip.

THE TOFF. Yes, I hear.

SNIGGERS. Well, what do you say to that?

THE TOFF. O . . . Well done, Albert.

ALBERT. And what a' you going to do?

THE TOFF. Going to wait.

ALBERT. Don't seem to know what 'e's waiting for.

SNIGGERS. It's a nasty place.

ALBERT. It's getting silly, Bill. Our money's gone and we want to sell the ruby. Let's get on to a town.

BILL. But 'e won't come.

ALBERT. Then we'll leave him.

SNIGGERS. We'll be all right if we keep away from Hull.

ALBERT. We'll go to London.

BILL. But 'e must 'ave 'is share.

SNIGGERS. All right. Only let's go. *(To* THE TOFF*)* We're going, do you hear? Give us the ruby.

THE TOFF. Certainly.

(He gives them a ruby from his waistcoat pocket: it is the size of a small hen's egg. He goes on reading his paper)

ALBERT. Come on, Sniggers. *(Exeunt* ALBERT *and* SNIGGERS*)*

BILL. Good-bye, old man. We'll give you your fair share, but there's nothing to do here, no girls, no halls, and we must sell the ruby.

THE TOFF. I'm not a fool, Bill.

BILL. No, no, of course not. Of course you ain't, and you've helped us a lot. Good-bye. You'll say good-bye?

THE TOFF. Oh, yes. Good-bye.

(Still reads paper. Exit BILL. THE TOFF *puts a revolver on the table beside him and goes on with his paper)*

SNIGGERS (*out of breath*). We've come back, Toffy.

THE TOFF. So you have.

ALBERT. Toffy—how did they get here?

THE TOFF. They walked, of course.

ALBERT. But it's eighty miles.

SNIGGERS. Did you know they were here, Toffy?

THE TOFF. Expected them about now.

ALBERT. Eighty miles.

BILL. Toffy, old man—what are we to do?

THE TOFF. Ask Albert.

BILL. If they can do things like this there's no one can save us but you, Toffy
—I always knew you were a clever one. We won't be fools any more. We'll
obey you, Toffy.

THE TOFF. You're brave enough and strong enough. There isn't many that
would steal a ruby eye out of an idol's head, and such an idol as that was to
look at, and on such a night. You're brave enough, Bill. But you're all three
of you fools. Jim would have none of my plans and where's Jim? And
George. What did they do to him?

SNIGGERS. Don't, Toffy!

THE TOFF. Well, then, your strength is no use to you. You want cleverness; or
they'll have you the way that they had George and Jim.

ALL. Ugh!

THE TOFF. Those black priests would follow you round the world in circles,
year after year, till they got the idol's eye. And if we died with it they'd
follow our grandchildren. That fool thinks he can escape men like that by
running round three streets in the town of Hull.

ALBERT. God's truth, *you* 'aven't escaped them, because they're 'ere.

THE TOFF. So I supposed.

ALBERT. You *supposed!*

THE TOFF. Yes, I believe there's no announcement in the Society papers. But I
took this country seat especially to receive them. There's plenty of room if
you dig; it is pleasantly situated and what is most important it is in a very
quiet neighbourhood. So I am at home to them this afternoon.

BILL. Well, you're a deep one.

THE TOFF. And remember you've only my wits between you and death, and
don't put your futile plans against those of an educated gentleman.

ALBERT. If you're a gentleman, why don't you go about among gentlemen instead of the likes of us?

THE TOFF. Because I was too clever for them as I am too clever for you.

ALBERT. Too clever for them?

THE TOFF. I never lost a game of cards in my life.

BILL. You never lost a game?

THE TOFF. Not when there was money on it.

BILL. Well, well.

THE TOFF. Have a game of poker?

ALL. No, thanks.

THE TOFF. Then do as you're told.

BILL. All right, Toffy.

SNIGGERS. I saw something just then. Hadn't we better draw the curtains?

THE TOFF. No.

SNIGGERS. What?

THE TOFF. Don't draw the curtains.

SNIGGERS. O all right.

BILL. But Toffy, they can see us. One doesn't let the enemy do that. I don't see why . . .

THE TOFF. No, of course you don't.

BILL. O all right, Toffy. (All begin to pull out revolvers)

THE TOFF (putting his own away). No revolvers, please.

ALBERT. Why not?

THE TOFF. Because I don't want any noise at my party. We might get guests that hadn't been invited. *Knives* are a different matter.

(All draw knives. THE TOFF signs to them not to draw them yet. TOFFY has already taken back his ruby)

BILL. I think they're coming, Toffy.

THE TOFF. Not yet.

ALBERT. When will they come?

THE TOFF. When I am quite ready to receive them. Not before.

SNIGGERS. I should like to get this over.

THE TOFF. Should you? Then we'll have them now.

SNIGGERS. Now?

THE TOFF. Yes. Listen to me. You shall do as you see me do. You will all pretend to go out. I'll show you how. I've got the ruby. When they see me alone they will come for their idol's eye.

BILL. How can they tell like this which of us has it?

THE TOFF. I confess I don't know, but they seem to.

SNIGGERS. What will you do when they come in?

THE TOFF. I shall do nothing.

SNIGGERS. What?

THE TOFF. They will creep up behind me. Then my friends, Sniggers and Bill and Albert, who gave them the slip, will do what they can.

BILL. All right, Toffy. Trust us.

THE TOFF. If you're a little slow you will see enacted the cheerful spectacle that accompanied the demise of Jim.

SNIGGERS. Don't, Toffy. We'll be there all right.

THE TOFF. Very well. Now watch me. (He goes past the windows to the inner door R.; he opens it inwards. Then under cover of the open door he slips down on his knee and closes it, remaining on the inside, appearing to have gone out. He signs to the others who understand. Then he appears to reënter in the same manner) Now, I shall sit with my back to the door. You go out one by one so far as our friends can make out. Crouch very low to be on the safe side. They mustn't see you through the window. (BILL *makes his sham exit*) Remember, no revolvers. The police are, I believe, proverbially inquisitive.

(The other two follow BILL. *All three are now crouching inside the door* R. THE TOFF *puts the ruby beside him on the table. He lights a cigarette. The door in back opens so slowly that you can hardly say at what moment it began.* THE TOFF *picks up his paper. A* NATIVE OF INDIA *wriggles along the floor ever so slowly, seeking cover from chairs. He moves* L. *where* THE TOFF *is. The three sailors are* R. SNIGGERS *and* ALBERT *lean forward.* BILL'S *arm keeps them back. An armchair had better conceal them from the* INDIAN. *The black* PRIEST *nears* THE TOFF. BILL *watches to see if any more are coming. Then he leaps forward alone [he has taken his boots off] and knifes the* PRIEST. *The* PRIEST *tries to shout but* BILL'S *left hand is over his mouth.* THE TOFF *continues to read his sporting paper. He never looks round.)*

BILL *(sotto voce).* There's only one, Toffy. What shall we do?

THE TOFF *(without turning his head).* Only one?

BILL. Yes.

THE TOFF. Wait a moment. Let me think. *(Still apparently absorbed in his paper)* Ah, yes. You go back, Bill. We must attract another guest. Now are you ready?

BILL. Yes.

THE TOFF. All right. You shall now see my demise at my Yorkshire residence. You must receive guests for me. *(He leaps up in full view of the window, flings up both arms and falls on the floor near the dead* PRIEST.) Now be ready. *(His eyes close)*

(There is a long pause. Again the door opens, very, very slowly. Another PRIEST *creeps in. He has three golden spots upon his forehead. He looks round, then he creeps up to his companion and turns him over and looks inside each of his clenched hands. Then he looks at the recumbent* TOFF. *Then he creeps towards him.* BILL *slips after him and knifes him like the other with his left hand over his mouth)*

BILL *(sotto voce).* We've only got two, Toffy.

THE TOFF. Still another.

BILL. What'll we do?

THE TOFF *(sitting up).* Hum.

BILL. This is the best way, much.

THE TOFF. Out of the question. Never play the same game twice.

BILL. Why not, Toffy?

THE TOFF. Doesn't work if you do.

BILL. Well?

THE TOFF. I have it, Albert. You will now walk into the room. I showed you how to do it.

ALBERT. Yes.

THE TOFF. Just run over here and have a fight at this window with these two men.

ALBERT. But they're——

THE TOFF. Yes, they're dead, my perspicuous Albert. But Bill and I are going to resuscitate them——Come on. (BILL *picks up a body under the arms)* That's right, Bill. *(Does the same)* Come and help us, Sniggers. (SNIGGERS *comes)* Keep low, keep low. Wave their arms about, Sniggers. Don't show yourself. Now, Albert, over you go. Our Albert is slain. Back you get, Bill. Back, Sniggers. Still, Albert. Mustn't move when he comes. Not a muscle.

(A face appears at the window and stays for some time. Then the door opens and looking craftily round the third PRIEST *enters. He looks at his companions' bodies and turns round. He suspects something. He takes up one of the knives and with a knife in each hand he puts his back to the wall. He looks to the left and right)*

THE TOFF. Come on, Bill. *(The* PRIEST *rushes to the door.* THE TOFF *knifes the last* PRIEST *from behind)* A good day's work, my friends.

BILL. Well done, Toffy. Oh, you are a deep one.

ALBERT. A deep one if ever there was one.

SNIGGERS. There ain't any more, Bill, are there?

THE TOFF. No more in the world, my friend.

BILL. Aye, that's all there are. There were only three in the temple. Three priests and their beastly idol.

ALBERT. What is it worth, Toffy? Is it worth a thousand pounds?

THE TOFF. It's worth all they've got in the shop. Worth just whatever we like to ask for it.

ALBERT. Then we're millionaires, now.

THE TOFF. Yes, and what is more important, we no longer have any heirs.

BILL. We'll have to sell it now.

ALBERT. That won't be easy. It's a pity it isn't small and we had half a dozen. Hadn't the idol any other on him?

BILL. No, he was green jade all over and only had this one eye. He had it in the middle of his forehead, and was a long sight uglier than anything else in the world.

SNIGGERS. I'm sure we ought all to be very grateful to Toffy.

BILL. And indeed we ought.

ALBERT. If it hadn't 'ave been for him——

BILL. Yes, if it hadn't 'a' been for old Toffy . . .

SNIGGERS. He's a deep one.

THE TOFF. Well, you see, I just have a knack of foreseeing things.

SNIGGERS. I should think you did.

BILL. Why, I don't suppose anything happens that our Toff doesn't foresee. Does it, Toffy?

THE TOFF. Well, I don't think it does, Bill. I don't think it often does.

BILL. Life is no more than just a game of cards to our old Toff.

THE TOFF. Well, we've taken these fellows' trick.

SNIGGERS *(going to the window).* It wouldn't do for any one to see them.

THE TOFF. O nobody will come this way. We're all alone on a moor.

BILL. Where will we put them?

THE TOFF. Bury them in the cellar, but there's no hurry.

BILL. And what then, Toffy?

THE TOFF. Why, then we'll go to London and upset the ruby business. We have really come through this job very nicely.

BILL. I think the first thing that we ought to do is to give a little supper to old Toffy. We'll bury these fellows to-night.

ALBERT. Yes, let's.

SNIGGERS. The very thing.

BILL. And we'll all drink his health.

ALBERT. Good old Toffy.

SNIGGERS. He ought to have been a general or a premier. *(They get bottles from cupboard, etc.)*

THE TOFF. Well, we've earned our bit of a supper. *(They sit down)*

BILL *(glass in hand)*. Here's to old Toffy who guessed everything.

ALBERT AND SNIGGERS. Good old Toffy.

BILL. Toffy who saved our lives and made our fortunes.

ALBERT AND SNIGGERS. Hear. Hear.

THE TOFF. And here's to Bill who saved me twice to-night.

BILL. Couldn't have done it but for your cleverness, Toffy.

SNIGGERS. Hear, hear. Hear, hear.

ALBERT. He foresees everything.

BILL. A speech, Toffy. A speech from our general.

ALL. Yes, a speech.

SNIGGERS. A speech.

THE TOFF. Well, get me some water. This whiskey's too much for my head, and I must keep it clear till our friends are safe in the cellar.

BILL. Water. Yes, of course. Get him some water, Sniggers.

SNIGGERS. We don't use water here. Where shall I get it?

BILL. Outside in the garden. *(Exit SNIGGERS)*

ALBERT. Here's to fortune.

BILL. Here's to Albert Thomas Esquire.

ALBERT. And William Jones Esquire. *(Reënter SNIGGERS terrified)*

THE TOFF. Hullo, here's Jacob Smith Esquire, J. P., alias Sniggers, back again.

SNIGGERS. Toffy, I've been a thinking about my share in that ruby. I don't want it, Toffy, I don't want it.

THE TOFF. Nonsense, Sniggers, nonsense.

SNIGGERS. You shall have it, Toffy, you shall have it yourself, only say Sniggers has no share in this 'ere ruby. Say it, Toffy, say it.

BILL. Want to turn informer, Sniggers?

SNIGGERS. No, no. Only I don't want the ruby, Toffy . . .

THE TOFF. No more nonsense, Sniggers; we're all in together in this. If one hangs we all hang; but they won't outwit me. Besides, it's not a hanging affair; they had their knives.

SNIGGERS. Toffy, Toffy, I always treated you fair, Toffy. I was always one to say, Give Toffy a chance. Take back my share, Toffy.

THE TOFF. What's the matter? What are you driving at?

SNIGGERS. Take it back, Toffy.

THE TOFF. Answer me; what are you up to?

SNIGGERS. I don't want my share any more.

BILL. Have you seen the police? (ALBERT *pulls out his knife*)

THE TOFF. No, no knives, Albert.

ALBERT. What then?

THE TOFF. The honest truth in open court, barring the ruby. We were attacked.

SNIGGERS. There's no police.

THE TOFF. Well, then, what's the matter?

BILL. Out with it.

SNIGGERS. I swear to God . . .

ALBERT. Well?

THE TOFF. Don't interrupt.

SNIGGERS. I swear I saw something *what I didn't like.*

THE TOFF. What you didn't like?

SNIGGERS *(in tears)*. O Toffy, Toffy, take it back. Take my share. Say you take it.

THE TOFF. What has he seen?

(Dead silence only broken by SNIGGERS' *sobs. Then stony steps are heard. Enter a hideous* IDOL. *It is blind and gropes its way. It gropes its way to the ruby and picks it up and screws it into a socket in the forehead.* SNIGGERS *still weeps softly; the rest stare in horror. The* IDOL *steps out, not groping. Its steps move off, then stop)*

THE TOFF. O great heavens!

ALBERT *(in a childish, plaintive voice)*. What is it, Toffy?

BILL. Albert, it is that obscene idol *(in a whisper)* come from India.

ALBERT. It is gone.

BILL. It has taken its eye.

SNIGGERS. We are saved.

OFF, A VOICE *(with outlandish accent)*. Meestaire William Jones, Able Seaman.

(THE TOFF *has never spoken, never moved. He only gazes stupidly in horror)*

BILL. Albert, Albert, what is this? *(He rises and walks out. One moan is heard.* SNIGGERS *goes to window. He falls back sickly)*

ALBERT *(in a whisper)*. What has happened?

SNIGGERS. I have seen it. I have seen it. O I have seen it. *(He returns to table)*

THE TOFF *(laying his hand very gently on* SNIGGERS' *arm, speaking softly and winningly)*. What was it, Sniggers?

SNIGGERS. I have seen it.

ALBERT. What?

SNIGGERS. O!

VOICE. Meestaire Albert Thomas, Able Seaman.

ALBERT. Must I go, Toffy? Toffy, must I go?

SNIGGERS *(clutching him)*. Don't move.
ALBERT *(going)*. Toffy, Toffy. *(Exit)*
VOICE. Meestaire Jacob Smith, Able Seaman.
SNIGGERS. I can't go, Toffy. I can't go. I can't do it. *(He goes)*
VOICE. Meestaire Arnold Everett Scott-Fortescue, late Esquire, Able Seaman.
THE TOFF. I did not foresee it. *(Exit)*

Eugene O'Neill

BOUND EAST FOR CARDIFF

Relatively few dramas produced in America during the twentieth century seem vital one year—let alone ten or twenty—after their first presentation. Only a few such works may be read after plays by Sophocles, Shakespeare, and Chekhov without giving the reader a woeful sense of complete anticlimax. One of the few is *Bound East for Cardiff* (1916), an outstanding work by a playwright generally considered the finest our country has brought forth.

Eugene O'Neill was a product of a movement in the American theater which had begun less than a decade before *Bound East for Cardiff* appeared. Distressed by the commercialization of our theater and stimulated by productions which they had seen in experimental theaters abroad, a number of young playwrights and directors had founded "Little Theaters" or "Art Theaters" in many parts of the country and had begun presenting plays in them. The plays which they staged were often more serious in intention and more experimental in method than those presented in commercial theaters.

Amateur though it was, the movement in time profoundly influenced the commercial stage. It battled against stale techniques. It cultivated a taste on the part of at least some theatergoers for the unusual in playwriting, acting, and producing. And it trained theatrical groups which could satisfy such a taste. One such group was the Provincetown Players, founded in 1915. When this group brought to New York some of its authors, directors, and actors from the Cape Cod fish-house which it had been using for a theater, its dramatic productions won immediate attention and respect. Eugene O'Neill was the most notable playwright active in the Provincetown Players. His first produced play, *Bound East for Cardiff*, was presented in Provincetown in 1916. This was followed by others such as *The Moon of the Caribbees, The Long Voyage Home, Ile*, and *Where the Cross Is Made* before *Beyond the Horizon* and *Emperor Jones*, in 1920, and *Anna Christie*, in 1921, established him as a successful writer for the commercial theater.

Part of an autobiographical sketch indicates the variety of O'Neill's experiences before he became a playwright: "My undergraduate college education was confined to a freshman year at Princeton University, class of 1910. I went with a mining engineer on a gold prospecting trip to Spanish Honduras, Central America. At the end of six months I was invalided home—tropical malarial fever—no gold. After that I became assistant manager of a theatrical company touring the East and Middle West. My first voyage to sea followed: sixty-five days on a Norwegian barque, Boston to Buenos Aires. In Argentina I worked at various occupations—in the draughting department of the Westinghouse Electrical Company, in the wool house of a packing plant in La Plata, in the office of the Singer Sewing Machine Company in Buenos Aires. Followed another voyage at sea, tending mules in a cattle steamer, Buenos Aires to Durban, South Africa, and return. After that a lengthy period of complete destitution in Buenos Aires—'on the beach'—terminated by my signing on as ordinary seaman on a British tramp steamer bound home for New York. My final experience at sea followed soon after this—able seaman on the American Line, New York-Southampton. The next winter I played a part in my father's vaudeville version of *The Count of Monte Cristo*, touring the Far West. Then I worked as reporter on the New London, Connecticut, *Telegraph*. My health broke down, my lungs being affected, and I spent six months in a sanatorium thinking it over. It was in this enforced period of reflection that the urge to write first came to me. The next fall—I was twenty-four—I began my first play—'The Web.' In 1914–1915 I was a student in Professor Baker's

English 47 at Harvard. The summer 1916 I spent at Provincetown. It was during that summer the Provincetown Players, who have made the original productions of nearly all my short plays in New York, were first organized."

The Players' first staging of *Bound East for Cardiff* was assisted by the natural setting of Wharf Theater: a fog was on the harbor and the high tide washed in under the floor of the erstwhile fish-house. George Cram Cook, the dominating figure in the group, played Yank; O'Neill played the Second Mate. Two leading members of the Players testified to the original impact of the play. Said Frank Shay: "The effect produced on us was so strong we all felt instinctively we had had a profound experience." Said Susan Glaspell: "I may see it through memories too emotional, but it seems to me I never sat through a more moving production than *Bound East for Cardiff*." Barrett H. Clark, O'Neill's biographer, asserts, "Of the score of plays written by O'Neill during the first three years [of his career], this is easily the best. . . . An unpretentious episode, moving and tense, yet with hardly a vestige of 'theater' in the conventional sense of the word."

This and three other sea plays in which the same characters appeared were presented as a group in Provincetown and New York in 1924 and were revived in New York in 1929. *Bound East for Cardiff* has since been given frequently.

CHARACTERS

YANK	PAUL
DRISCOLL	SMITTY
COCKY	IVAN
DAVIS	THE CAPTAIN
SCOTTY	THE SECOND MATE
OLSON	

Scene: The seamen's forecastle of the British tramp steamer Glencairn *on a foggy night midway on the voyage between New York and Cardiff. An irregular shaped compartment, the sides of which almost meet at the far end to form a triangle. Sleeping bunks about six feet long, ranged three deep with a space of three feet separating the upper from the lower, are built against the sides. On the right above the bunks three or four port holes can be seen. In front of the bunks, rough wooden benches. Over the bunks on the left, a lamp in a bracket. In the left foreground, a doorway. On the floor near it, a pail with a tin dipper. Oilskins are hanging from a hook near the doorway.*

The far side of the forecastle is so narrow that it contains only one series of bunks.

In under the bunks a glimpse can be had of seachests, suit cases, seaboots, etc., jammed in indiscriminately.

At regular intervals of a minute or so the blast of the steamer's whistle can be heard above all the other sounds.

Five men are sitting on the benches talking. They are dressed in dirty patched suits of dungaree, flannel shirts, and all are in their stocking feet. Four of the men are pulling on pipes and the air is heavy with rancid tobacco smoke. Sitting on the top bunk in the left foreground, a Norwegian, PAUL, *is softly playing some folk song on a battered accordion. He stops from time to time to listen to the conversation.*

In the lower bunk in the rear a dark-haired, hard-featured man is lying apparently asleep. One of his arms is stretched limply over the side of the bunk. His face is very pale, and drops of clammy perspiration glisten on his forehead.

It is nearing the end of the dog watch—about ten minutes to eight in the evening.

COCKY (*a weazened runt of a man. He is telling a story. The others are listening with amused, incredulous faces, interrupting him at the end of each sentence with loud derisive guffaws*). Makin' love to me, she was! It's Gawd's truth! A bloomin' nigger! Greased all over with cocoanut oil, she was. Gawd blimey, I couldn't stand 'er. Bloody old cow, I says; and with that I fetched 'er a biff on the ear wot knocked 'er silly, an'—— (*He is interrupted by a roar of laughter from the others*)

DAVIS (*a middle-aged man with black hair and mustache*). You're a liar, Cocky.

SCOTTY (*a dark young fellow*). Ho-ho! Ye werr neverr in New Guinea in yourr life, I'm thinkin'.

OLSON (*a Swede with a drooping blond mustache—with ponderous sarcasm*). Yust tink of it! You say she wass a cannibal, Cocky?

DRISCOLL (*a brawny Irishman with the battered features of a prizefighter*). How cud ye doubt ut, Ollie? A quane av the naygurs she musta been surely. Who else wud think herself aqual to fallin' in love wid a beauthiful, divil-may-care rake av a man the loike av Cocky? (*A burst of laughter from the crowd*)

COCKY (*indignantly*). Gawd strike me dead if it ain't true, every bleedin' word of it. 'Appened ten year ago come Christmas.

SCOTTY. 'Twas a Christmas dinner she had her eyes on.

DAVIS. He'd a been a tough old bird.

DRISCOLL. 'Tis lucky for both av ye ye escaped; for the quane av the cannibal isles wad 'a died av the belly ache the day after Christmas, divil a doubt av ut. (*The laughter at this is long and loud*)

COCKY (*sullenly*). Blarsted fat 'eads! (*The sick man in the lower bunk in the rear groans and moves restlessly. There is a hushed silence. All the men turn and stare at him*)

DRISCOLL. Ssshh! (*In a hushed whisper*) We'd best not be talkin' so loud and him tryin' to have a bit av a sleep. (*He tiptoes softly to the side of the bunk*) Yank! You'd be wantin' a drink av wather, maybe? (YANK *does not reply.* DRISCOLL *bends over and looks at him*) It's asleep he is, sure enough. His breath is chokin' in his throat loike wather gurglin' in a poipe. (*He comes back quietly and sits down. All are silent, avoiding each other's eyes*)

COCKY (*after a pause*). Pore devil! It's over the side for 'im, Gawd 'elp 'im.

DRISCOLL. Stop your croakin'! He's not dead yet and, praise God, he'll have many a long day yet before him.

SCOTTY (*shaking his head doubtfully*). He's bod, mon, he's verry bod.

DAVIS. Lucky he's alive. Many a man's light woulda gone out after a fall like that.

OLSON. You saw him fall?

DAVIS. Right next to him. He and me was goin' down in number two hold to do some chippin'. He puts his leg over careless-like and misses the ladder and plumps straight down to the bottom. I was scared to look over for a minute, and then I heard him groan and I scuttled down after him. He was hurt bad inside for the blood was drippin' from the side of his mouth. He was groanin' hard, but he never let a word out of him.

COCKY. An' you blokes remember when we 'auled 'im in 'ere? Oh, 'ell, 'e says, oh, 'ell—like that, and nothink else.

OLSON. Did the captain know where he iss hurted?

COCKY. That silly ol' josser! Wot the 'ell would 'e know abaht anythink?

SCOTTY (*scornfully*). He fiddles in his mouth wi' a bit of glass.

DRISCOLL (*angrily*). The divil's own life ut is to be out on the lonely sea wid nothin' betune you and a grave in the ocean but a spindle-shanked, gray-whiskered auld fool the loike av him. 'Twas enough to make a saint shwear to see him wid his gold watch in his hand, tryin' to look as wise as an owl on a tree, and all the toime he not knowin' whether 'twas cholery or the barber's itch was the matther wid Yank.

SCOTTY (*sardonically*). He gave him a dose of salts, na doot?

DRISCOLL. Divil a thing he gave him at all, but looked in the book he had wid him, and shook his head, and walked out widout sayin' a word, the second mate afther him no wiser than himself, God's curse on the two av thim!

COCKY (*after a pause*). Yank was a good shipmate, pore beggar. Lend me four bob in Noo Yark, 'e did.

DRISCOLL (*warmly*). A good shipmate he was and is, none betther. Ye said no more than the truth, Cocky. Five years and more ut is since first I shipped wid him, and we've stuck together iver since through good luck and bad. Fights we've had, God help us, but 'twas only when we'd a bit av drink taken, and we always shook hands the nixt mornin'. Whativer was his was mine, and many's the toime I'd a been on the beach or worse, but for him.

And now—— (*His voice trembles as he fights to control his emotion*) Divil take me if I'm not startin' to blubber loike an auld woman, and he not dead at all, but goin' to live many a long year yet, maybe.

DAVIS. The sleep'll do him good. He seems better now.

OLSON. If he wude eat someting——

DRISCOLL. Wud ye have him be eatin' in his condishun? Sure it's hard enough on the rest av us wid nothin' the matther wid our insides to be stomachin' the skoff on this rusty lime-juicer.

SCOTTY (*indignantly*). It's a starvation ship.

DAVIS. Plenty o' work and no food—and the owners ridin' around in carriages!

OLSON. Hash, hash! Stew, stew! Marmalade, py damn! (*He spits disgustedly*)

COCKY. Bloody swill! Fit only for swine is wot I say.

DRISCOLL. And the dishwather they disguise wid the name av tea! And the putty they call bread! My belly feels loike I'd swalleyed a dozen rivets at the thought av ut! And sea-biscuit that'd break the teeth av a lion if he had the misfortune to take a bite at one! (*Unconsciously they have all raised their voices, forgetting the sick man in their sailor's delight at finding something to grumble about*)

PAUL (*swings his feet over the side of his bunk, stops playing his accordion, and says slowly*): And rot-ten po-tay-toes! (*He starts in playing again. The sick man gives a groan of pain*)

DRISCOLL (*holding up his hand*). Shut your mouths, all av you. 'Tis a hell av a thing for us to be complainin' about our guts, and a sick man maybe dyin' listenin' to us. (*Gets up and shakes his fist at the Norwegian*) God stiffen you, ye squarehead scut! Put down that organ av yours or I'll break your ugly face for you. Is that banshee schreechin' fit music for a sick man? (*The Norwegian puts his accordion in the bunk and lies back and closes his eyes. DRISCOLL goes over and stands beside YANK. The steamer's whistle sounds particularly loud in the silence*)

DAVIS. Damn this fog! (*Reaches in under a bunk and yanks out a pair of seaboots, which he pulls on*) My lookout next, too. Must be nearly eight bells, boys. (*With the exception of OLSON, all the men sitting up put on oilskins, sou'westers, seaboots, etc., in preparation for the watch on deck. OLSON crawls into a lower bunk on the right*)

SCOTTY. My wheel.

OLSON (*disgustedly*). Nothin' but yust dirty weather all dis voyage. I yust can't sleep when weestle blow. (*He turns his back to the light and is soon fast asleep and snoring*)

SCOTTY. If this fog keeps up, I'm tellin' ye, we'll no be in Carrdiff for a week or more.

DRISCOLL. 'Twas just such a night as this the auld Dover wint down. Just about this toime ut was, too, and we all sittin' round in the fo'castle, Yank beside me, whin all av a suddint we heard a great slitherin' crash, and the ship heeled over till we was all in a heap on wan side. What came afther I disremimber exactly, except 'twas a hard shift to get the boats over the side before the auld teakittle sank. Yank was in the same boat wid me, and sivin morthal days we drifted wid scarcely a drop of wather or a bite to chew on. 'Twas Yank here that held me down whin I wanted to jump into the ocean, roarin' mad wid the thirst. Picked up we were on the same day wid only Yank in his senses, and him steerin' the boat.

COCKY (*protestingly*). Blimey but you're a cheerful blighter, Driscoll! Talkin' abaht shipwrecks in this 'ere blushin' fog. (YANK *groans and stirs uneasily, opening his eyes.* DRISCOLL *hurries to his side*)

DRISCOLL. Are ye feelin' any betther, Yank?

YANK (*in a weak voice*). No.

DRISCOLL. Sure, you must be. You look as sthrong as an ox. (*Appealing to the others*) Am I tellin' him a lie?

DAVIS. The sleep's done you good.

COCKY. You'll be 'avin your pint of beer in Cardiff this day week.

SCOTTY. And fish and chips, mon!

YANK (*peevishly*). What're yuh all lyin' fur? D'yuh think I'm scared to—— (*He hesitates as if frightened by the word he is about to say*)

DRISCOLL. Don't be thinkin' such things! (*The ship's bell is heard heavily tolling eight times. From the forecastle head above the voice of the lookout rises in a long wail: Aaall's welll. The men look uncertainly at* YANK *as if undecided whether to say good-by or not*)

YANK (*in an agony of fear*). Don't leave me, Drisc! I'm dyin', I tell yuh. I won't stay here alone with every one snorin'. I'll go out on deck. (*He makes a feeble attempt to rise, but sinks back with a sharp groan. His breath comes in wheezy gasps*). Don't leave me, Drisc! (*His face grows white and his head falls back with a jerk*)

DRISCOLL. Don't be worryin', Yank. I'll not move a step out av here—and let that divil av a bosun curse his black head off. You speak a word to the bosun, Cocky. Tell him that Yank is bad took and I'll be stayin' wid him a while yet.

COCKY. Right-o. (COCKY, DAVIS, *and* SCOTTY *go out quietly*)

COCKY (*from the alleyway*). Gawd blimey, the fog's thick as soup.

DRISCOLL. Are ye satisfied now, Yank? (*Receiving no answer, he bends over the still form*) He's fainted, God help him! (*He gets a tin dipper from the bucket and bathes* YANK's *forehead with the water.* YANK *shudders and opens his eyes*)

YANK (*slowly*). I thought I was goin' then. Wha' did yuh wanta wake me up fur?

DRISCOLL (*with forced gayety*). Is it wishful for heaven ye are?

YANK (*gloomily*). Hell, I guess.

DRISCOLL (*crossing himself involuntarily*). For the love av the saints don't be talkin' loike that! You'd give a man the creeps. It's chippin' rust on deck you'll be in a day or two wid the best av us. (YANK *does not answer, but closes his eyes wearily. The seaman who has been on lookout,* SMITTY, *a young Englishman, comes in and takes off his dripping oilskins. While he is doing this the man whose turn at the wheel has been relieved enters. He is a dark burly fellow with a round stupid face. The Englishman steps softly over to* DRISCOLL. *The other crawls into a lower bunk)*

SMITTY (*whispering*). How's Yank?

DRISCOLL. Betther. Ask him yourself. He's awake.

YANK. I'm all right, Smitty.

SMITTY. Glad to hear it, Yank (*He crawls to an upper bunk and is soon asleep*)

IVAN (*The stupid-faced seaman who came in after* SMITTY *twists his head in the direction of the sick man*). You feel gude, Jank?

YANK (*wearily*). Yes, Ivan.

IVAN. Dot's gude. (*He rolls over on his side and falls asleep immediately*)

YANK (*after a pause broken only by snores—with a bitter laugh*). Good-by and good luck to the lot of you!

DRISCOLL. Is ut painin' you again?

YANK. It hurts like hell—here. (*He points to the lower part of his chest on the left side*) I guess my old pump's busted. Ooohh! (*A spasm of pain contracts his pale features. He presses his hand to his side and writhes on the thin mattress of his bunk. The perspiration stands out in beads on his forehead*)

DRISCOLL (*terrified*). Yank! Yank! What is ut? (*Jumping to his feet*) I'll run for the captain. (*He starts for the doorway*)

YANK (*sitting up in his bunk, frantic with fear*). Don't leave me, Drisc! For God's sake don't leave me alone! (*He leans over the side of his bunk and spits.* DRISCOLL *comes back to him*) Blood! Ugh!

DRISCOLL. Blood again! I'd best be gettin' the captain.

YANK. No, no, don't leave me! If yuh do I'll git up and follow you. I ain't no coward, but I'm scared to stay here with all of them asleep and snorin'. (DRISCOLL, *not knowing what to do, sits down on the bench beside him. He grows calmer and sinks back on the mattress*) The captain can't do me no good, yuh know it yourself. The pain ain't so bad now, but I thought it had me then. It was like a buzz-saw cuttin' into me.

DRISCOLL (*fiercely*). God blarst ut!

(*The* CAPTAIN *and the* SECOND MATE *of the steamer enter the forecastle. The* CAPTAIN *is an old man with gray mustache and whiskers. The* MATE *is clean-shaven and middle-aged. Both are dressed in simple blue uniforms*)

THE CAPTAIN (*taking out his watch and feeling* YANK'S *pulse*). And how is the sick man?

YANK (*feebly*). All right, sir.

THE CAPTAIN. And the pain in the chest?

YANK. It still hurts, sir, worse than ever.

THE CAPTAIN (*taking a thermometer from his pocket and putting it into* YANK'S *mouth*). Here. Be sure and keep this in under your tongue, not over it.

THE MATE (*after a pause*). Isn't this your watch on deck, Driscoll?

DRISCOLL. Yes, sorr, but Yank was fearin' to be alone, and——

THE CAPTAIN. That's all right, Driscoll.

DRISCOLL. Thank ye, sorr.

THE CAPTAIN (*stares at his watch for a moment or so; then takes the ther-*

mometer from YANK'S *mouth and goes to the lamp to read it. His expression grows very grave. He beckons the* MATE *and* DRISCOLL *to the corner near the doorway.* YANK *watches them furtively. The* CAPTAIN *speaks in a low voice to the* MATE). Way up, both of them. (*To* DRISCOLL) Has he been spitting blood again?

DRISCOLL. Not much for the hour just past, sorr, but before that——

THE CAPTAIN. A great deal?

DRISCOLL. Yes, sorr.

THE CAPTAIN. He hasn't eaten anything?

DRISCOLL. No, sorr.

THE CAPTAIN. Did he drink that medicine I sent him?

DRISCOLL. Yes, sorr, but it didn't stay down.

THE CAPTAIN (*shaking his head*). I'm afraid—he's very weak. I can't do anything else for him. It's too serious for me. If this had only happened a week later we'd be in Cardiff in time to——

DRISCOLL. Plaze help him some way, sorr!

THE CAPTAIN (*impatiently*). But, my good man, I'm not a doctor. (*More kindly as he sees* DRISCOLL'S *grief*) You and he have been shipmates a long time?

DRISCOLL. Five years and more, sorr.

THE CAPTAIN. I see. Well, don't let him move. Keep him quiet and we'll hope for the best. I'll read the matter up and send him some medicine, something to ease the pain, anyway. (*Goes over to* YANK) Keep up your courage! You'll be better to-morrow. (*He breaks down lamely before* YANK'S *steady gaze*) We'll pull you through all right—and—hm—well—coming, Robinson? Dammit! (*He goes out hurriedly, followed by the* MATE)

DRISCOLL (*trying to conceal his anxiety*). Didn't I tell you you wasn't half as sick as you thought you was? The Captain'll have you out on deck cursin' and swearin' loike a trooper before the week is out.

YANK. Don't lie, Drisc. I heard what he said, and if I didn't I c'd tell by the way I feel. I know what's goin' to happen. I'm goin' to—— (*He hesitates for a second—then resolutely*) I'm goin' to die, that's what, and the sooner the better!

DRISCOLL (*wildly*). No, and be damned to you, you're not. I'll not let you.

YANK. It ain't no use, Drisc. I ain't got a chance, but I ain't scared. Gimme a drink of water, will yuh, Drisc? My throat's burnin' up. (DRISCOLL *brings the dipper full of water and supports his head while he drinks in great gulps*)

DRISCOLL (*seeking vainly for some word of comfort*). Are ye feelin' more aisy loike now?

YANK. Yes—now—when I know it's all up. (*A pause*) You mustn't take it so hard, Drisc. I was just thinkin' it ain't as bad as people think—dyin'. I ain't never took much stock in the truck them sky-pilots preach. I ain't never had religion; but I know whatever it is what comes after it can't be no worser'n this. I don't like to leave you, Drisc, but—that's all.

DRISCOLL (*with a groan*). Lad, lad, don't be talkin'.

YANK. This sailor life ain't much to cry about leavin'—just one ship after another, hard work, small pay, and bum grub; and when we git into port, just a drunk endin' up in a fight, and all your money gone, and then ship away again. Never meetin' no nice people; never gittin' outa sailor town, hardly, in any port; travellin' all over the world and never seein' none of it; without no one to care whether you're alive or dead. (*With a bitter smile*) There ain't much in all that that'd make yuh sorry to lose it, Drisc.

DRISCOLL (*gloomily*). It's a hell av a life, the sea.

YANK (*musingly*). It must be great to stay on dry land all your life and have a farm with a house of your own with cows and pigs and chickens, 'way in the middle of the land where yuh'd never smell the sea or see a ship. It must be great to have a wife, and kids to play with at night after supper when your work was done. It must be great to have a home of your own, Drisc.

DRISCOLL (*with a great sigh*). It must, surely; but what's the use av thinkin' av ut? Such things are not for the loikes av us.

YANK. Sea-farin' is all right when you're young and don't care, but we ain't chickens no more, and somehow, I dunno, this last year has seemed rotten, and I've had a hunch I'd quit—with you, of course—and we'd save our coin, and go to Canada or Argentine or some place and git a farm, just a small one, just enough to live on. I never told yuh this cause I thought you'd laugh at me.

DRISCOLL (*enthusiastically*). Laugh at you, is ut? When I'm havin' the same thoughts myself, toime afther toime. It's a grand idea and we'll be doin' ut sure if you'll stop your crazy notions—about—about bein' so sick.

YANK (*sadly*). Too late. We shouldn'ta made this trip, and then—— How'd all the fog git in here?

DRISCOLL. Fog?

YANK. Everything looks misty. Must be my eyes gittin' weak, I guess. What was we talkin' of a minute ago? Oh, yes, a farm. It's too late. (*His mind wandering*) Argentine, did I say? D'yuh remember the times we've had in Buenos Aires? The moving pictures in Barracas? Some class to them, d'yuh remember?

DRISCOLL (*with satisfaction*). I do that; and so does the piany player. He'll not be forgettin' the black eye I gave him in a hurry.

YANK. Remember the time we was there on the beach and had to go to Tommy Moore's boarding house to git shipped? And he sold us rotten oilskins and seaboots full of holes, and shipped us on a skysail yarder round the Horn, and took two month's pay for it. And the days we used to sit on the park benches along the Paseo Colon with the vigilantes lookin' hard at us? And the songs at the Sailor's Opera where the guy played ragtime—d'yuh remember them?

DRISCOLL. I do, surely.

YANK. And La Plata—phew, the stink of the hides! I always liked Argentine—all except that booze, caña. How drunk we used to git on that, remember?

DRISCOLL. Cud I forget ut? My head pains me at the menshun av that divil's brew.

YANK. Remember the night I went crazy with the heat in Singapore? And the time you was pinched by the cops in Port Said? And the time we was both locked up in Sydney for fightin'?

DRISCOLL. I do so.

YANK. And that fight on the dock at Cape Town——(*His voice betrays great inward perturbation*)

DRISCOLL (*hastily*). Don't be thinkin' av that now. 'Tis past and gone.

YANK. D'yuh think He'll hold it up against me?

DRISCOLL (*mystified*). Who's that?

YANK. God. They say He sees everything. He must know it was done in fair fight, in self-defense, don't yuh think?

DRISCOLL. Av course. Ye stabbed him, and be damned to him, for the skulkin' swine he was, afther him tryin' to stick you in the back, and you not suspectin'. Let your conscience be aisy. I wisht I had nothin' blacker than that on my sowl. I'd not be afraid av the angel Gabriel himself.

YANK (*with a shudder*). I c'd see him a minute ago with the blood spurtin' out of his neck. Ugh!

DRISCOLL. The fever, ut is, that makes you see such things. Give no heed to ut.

YANK (*uncertainly*). You don't think He'll hold it up agin me—God, I mean.

DRISCOLL. If there's justice in hiven, no! (YANK *seems comforted by this assurance*)

YANK (*after a pause*). We won't reach Cardiff for a week at least. I'll be buried at sea.

DRISCOLL (*putting his hands over his ears*). Ssshh! I won't listen to you.

YANK (*as if he had not heard him*). It's as good a place as any other, I s'pose —only I always wanted to be buried on dry land. But what the hell'll I care—then? (*Fretfully*) Why should it be a rotten night like this with that damned whistle blowin' and people snorin' all round? I wish the stars was out, and the moon, too; I c'd lie out on deck and look at them, and it'd make it easier to go—somehow.

DRISCOLL. For the love av God don't be talkin' loike that!

YANK. Whatever pay's comin' to me yuh can divvy up with the rest of the boys; and you take my watch. It ain't worth much, but it's all I've got.

DRISCOLL. But have ye no relations at all to call your own?

YANK. No, not as I know of. One thing I forgot: You know Fanny the barmaid at the Red Stork in Cardiff?

DRISCOLL. Sure, and who doesn't?

YANK. She's been good to me. She tried to lend me half a crown when I was broke there last trip. Buy her the biggest box of candy yuh c'n find in Cardiff. (*Breaking down—in a choking voice*) It's hard to ship on this voyage I'm goin' on—alone! (DRISCOLL *reaches out and grasps his hand. There is a pause, during which both fight to control themselves*) My throat's like a

furnace. (*He gasps for air*) Gimme a drink of water, will yuh, Drisc?
(DRISCOLL *gets him a dipper of water*) I wish this was a pint of beer. Oooohh!
(*He chokes, his face convulsed with agony, his hands tearing at his shirt
front. The dipper falls from his nerveless fingers*)

DRISCOLL. For the love av God, what is ut, Yank?

YANK (*speaking with tremendous difficulty*). S'long, Drisc! (*He stares straight
in front of him with eyes starting from their sockets*) Who's that?

DRISCOLL. Who? What?

YANK (*faintly*). A pretty lady dressed in black. (*His face twitches and his body
writhes in a final spasm, then straightens out rigidly*)

DRISCOLL (*pale with horror*). Yank! Yank! Say a word to me for the love av
hiven! (*He shrinks away from the bunk, making the sign of the cross. Then
comes back and puts a trembling hand on* YANK's *chest and bends closely
over the body*)

COCKY (*from the alleyway*). Oh, Driscoll! Can you leave Yank for arf a mo'
and give me a 'and?

DRISCOLL (*with a great sob*). Yank! (*He sinks down on his knees beside the
bunk, his head on his hands. His lips move in some half-remembered prayer*)

COCKY (*enters, his oilskins and sou'wester glistening with drops of water*).
The fog's lifted. (COCKY *sees* DRISCOLL *and stands staring at him with open
mouth.* DRISCOLL *makes the sign of the cross again*)

COCKY (*mockingly*). Sayin' 'is prayers! (*He catches sight of the still figure in
the bunk and an expression of awed understanding comes over his face.
He takes off his dripping sou'wester and stands, scratching his head*)

COCKY (*in a hushed whisper*). Gawd blimey!

Christopher Fry

A PHOENIX
TOO FREQUENT

Eugene O'Neill once said of the reading he did during his apprenticeship as a
playwright: "I read about everything I could lay hands on: the Greeks, the Elizabethans—practically all the classics—and of course the moderns. Ibsen and Strindberg,
especially Strindberg." The last two authors named were influential not only on the
young O'Neill but also upon a vast majority of writers of drama contemporaneous
with him. Plays were predominantly realistic and naturalistic—prosaic in their plots

and their language. Most authors were much concerned with verisimilitude, with psychological motivation, with social preachments.

Some dramatists, however—including O'Neill at times—were dissatisfied with prevalent aims and methods. They turned to legend and history for settings and stories, attempted to universalize characters and themes, and employed poetic prose or even metrical forms. Authors such as Synge and Yeats in Ireland, for example, and Maxwell Anderson in the United States wrote poetic dramas which were well received by critics and theater-going audiences alike. In very recent times, metrical drama has been given new life by a small but talented group of writers in England. Most notable of these have been two men—T. S. Eliot, already famous as a poet, whose verse plays include *Murder in the Cathedral* and *The Cocktail Party*, and Christopher Fry.

A performance of A Phoenix Too Frequent

Fry's work benefited from a long-standing interest in and association with the stage. He wrote his first play, it is said, at eleven, his first verse play at fourteen. At seventeen he was a teacher for a brief time, and then went into theatrical work—as a member of a repertory company, a cabaret entertainer, an understudy, an actor, and eventually a playwright. His best known verse plays include *The Boy with a Cart, The Tower, Thursday's Child, A Phoenix Too Frequent, The Lady's Not for Burning,* and *Venus Observed.*

Fry, like most other authors of dramas in verse, is antirealistic. Says he: "The realistic play is not realistic at all, but just a slice off the top of existence. Writing a realistic play is like meeting a human being for the first time. The realist would observe that this is Mr. So-and-So, that he has a beard and an accent and a mole on his face. But the human being is far more peculiar, something that has gone on since the beginning of time, now miraculously summed up in the strange sort of mysterious creature that stands before us. . . . In my plays I want to look at life—at the commonplaces of existence—as if we had just turned a corner and run into it for the first time." The universal, rather than the particular, in other words, is what he hopes to discover and to convey in his dramas.

Fry's versified plays, like those of Eliot, are in the vein of modern poetry. They are influenced by seventeenth-century authors who are so generally admired and at times imitated by the poets of today: the story of *A Phoenix Too Frequent* came from Jeremy Taylor, the title from Robert Burton. Typically wit and humor are mingled with high seriousness, the humor benefiting from Fry's natural tendency toward playfulness. Typically, too, there are sharp descents from the language of poetry to that of the vernacular. The figures of speech are often startling; sometimes they are rather wild conceits; and the packed lines often take a good deal of thinking about to be understood. And even in a play like the one which follows, the plot of which is essentially that of a comedy, Fry's characters—and Fry himself—are often concerned with very serious implications and problems.

A Phoenix Too Frequent was first produced in the Mercury Theatre in London in the spring of 1946. It was revived in the Arts Theatre, London, in the autumn of the same year. It had its American première in New York in 1950, and since then it has

been frequently presented elsewhere in the United States.

'To whom conferr'd a peacock's undecent,
A squirrel's harsh, a phoenix too frequent.'
Robert Burton quoting Martial

CHARACTERS

DYNAMENE

DOTO

TEGEUS-CHROMIS

Scene: The tomb of Virilius, near Ephesus; night
Note: The story was got from Jeremy Taylor who had it from Petronius

An underground tomb, in darkness except for the very low light of an oil-lamp.
Above ground the starlight shows a line of trees on which hang the bodies
of several men. It also penetrates a gate and falls on to the first of the steps
which descend into the darkness of the tomb. DOTO *talks to herself in the dark.*

DOTO. Nothing but the harmless day gone into black
Is all the dark is. And so what's my trouble?
Demons is so much wind. Are so much wind.
I've plenty to fill my thoughts. All that I ask
Is don't keep turning men over in my mind,
Venerable Aphrodite. I've had my last one
And thank you. I thank thee. He smelt of sour grass
And was likeable. He collected ebony quoits.
(*An owl hoots near at hand*)
O Zeus! O some god or other, where is the oil?
Fire's from Prometheus. I thank thee. If I
Mean to die I'd better see what I'm doing.
(*She fills the lamp with oil. The flame burns up brightly and shows* DYNAMENE,
beautiful and young, leaning asleep beside a bier)
Honestly, I would rather have to sleep
With a bald bee-keeper who was wearing his boots
Than spend more days fasting and thirsting and crying
In a tomb. I shouldn't have said that. Pretend
I didn't hear myself. But life and death
Is cat and dog in this double-bed of a world.
My master, my poor master, was a man
Whose nose was as straight as a little buttress,
And now he has taken it into Elysium
Where it won't be noticed among all the other straightness.

A Phoenix Too Frequent by Christopher Fry. Reprinted by permission of the publishers,
Oxford University Press, London.

(The owl cries again and wakens DYNAMENE)

Oh, them owls. Those owls, It's woken her.

DYNAMENE. Ah! I'm breathless. I caught up with the ship
But it spread its wings, creaking a cry of *Dew,*
Dew! and flew figurehead foremost into the sun.

DOTO. How crazy, madam.

DYNAMENE.   Doto, draw back the curtains.
I'll take my barley-water.

DOTO.   We're not at home
Now, madam. It's the master's tomb.

DYNAMENE.   Of course!
Oh, I'm wretched. Already I have disfigured
My vigil. My cynical eyelids have soon dropped me
In a dream.

DOTO.   But then it's possible, madam, you might
Find yourself in bed with him again
In a dream, madam. Was he on the ship?

DYNAMENE. He was the ship.

DOTO.   Oh. That makes it different.

DYNAMENE. He was the ship. He had such a deck, Doto,
Such a white, scrubbed deck. Such a stern prow,
Such a proud stern, so slim from port to starboard.
If ever you meet a man with such fine masts
Give your life to him, Doto. The figurehead
Bore his own features, so serene in the brow
And hung with a little seaweed. O Virilius,
My husband, you have left a wake in my soul.
You cut the glassy water with a diamond keel.
I must cry again.

DOTO.   What, when you mean to join him?
Don't you believe he will be glad to see you, madam?
Thankful to see you, I should imagine, among
Them shapes and shades; all shapes of shapes and all
Shades of shades, from what I've heard. I know
I shall feel odd at first with Cerberus,
Sop or no sop. Still, I know how you feel, madam.
You think he may find a temptation in Hades.
I shouldn't worry. It would help him to settle down.

(DYNAMENE *weeps*)

It would only be *fun*, madam. He couldn't go far
With a shade.

DYNAMENE.   He was one of the coming men.
He was certain to have become the most well-organized provost
The town has known, once they had made him provost.
He was so punctual, you could regulate

The sun by him. He made the world succumb
To his daily revolution of habit. But who,
In the world he has gone to, will appreciate that?
O poor Virilius! To be a coming man
Already gone—it must be distraction.
Why did you leave me walking about our ambitions
Like a cat in the ruins of a house? Promising husband,
Why did you insult me by dying? Virilius,
Now I keep no flower, except in the vase
Of the tomb.

DOTO.   O poor madam! O poor master!
I presume so far as to cry somewhat for myself
As well. I know you won't mind, madam. It's two
Days not eating makes me think of my uncle's
Shop in the country, where he has a hardware business,
Basins, pots, ewers, and alabaster birds.
He makes you die of laughing. O madam,
Isn't it sad? (*They both weep*)

DYNAMENE.   How could I have allowed you
To come and die of my grief? Doto, it puts
A terrible responsibility on me. Have you
No grief of your own and you could die of?

DOTO.   Not really, madam.

DYNAMENE. Nothing?

DOTO.   Not really. They was all one to me.
Well, all but two was all one to me. And they,
Strange enough, was two who kept recurring.
I could never be sure if they had gone for good
Or not; and so that kept things cheerful, madam.
One always gave a wink before he deserted me,
The other slapped me as it were behind, madam;
Then they would be away for some months.

DYNAMENE.   Oh Doto,
What an unhappy life you were having to lead.

DOTO. Yes, I'm sure. But never mind, madam,
It seemed quite lively then. And now I know
It's what you say; life is more big than a bed
And full of miracles and mysteries like
One man made for one woman, etcetera, etcetera.
Lovely. I feel sung, madam, by a baritone
In mixed company with everyone pleased.
And so I had to come with you here, madam,
For the last sad chorus of me. It's all
Fresh to me. Death's a new interest in life,
If it doesn't disturb you, madam, to have me crying.

It's because of us not having breakfast again.
And the master, of course. And the beautiful world.
And you crying too, madam. Oh—Oh!

DYNAMENE. I can't forbid your crying; but you must cry
On the other side of the tomb. I'm becoming confused.
This is my personal grief and my sacrifice
Of self, solus. Right over there, darling girl.

DOTO. What here?

DYNAMENE.   Now, if you wish, you may cry, Doto.
But our tears are very different. For me
The world is all with Charon, all, all,
Even the metal and plume of the rose garden,
And the forest where the sea fumes overhead
In vegetable tides, and particularly
The entrance to the warm baths in Arcite Street
Where we first met;—all!—the sun itself
Trails an evening hand in the sultry river
Far away down by Acheron. I am lonely,
Virilius. Where is the punctual eye
And where is the cautious voice which made
Balance-sheets sound like Homer and Homer sound
Like balance-sheets? The precision of limbs, the amiable
Laugh, the exact festivity? Gone from the world.
You were the peroration of nature, Virilius.
You explained everything to me, even the extremely
Complicated gods. You wrote them down
In seventy columns. Dear curling calligraphy!
Gone from the world, once and for all. And I taught you
In your perceptive moments to appreciate me.
You said I was harmonious, Virilius,
Moulded and harmonious, little matronal
Ox-eye, your package. And then I would walk
Up and down largely, as it were making my own
Sunlight. What a mad blacksmith creation is
Who blows his furnaces until the stars fly upward
And iron Time is hot and politicians glow
And bulbs and roots sizzle into hyacinth
And orchis, and the sand puts out the lion,
Roaring yellow, and oceans bud with porpoises,
Blenny, tunny and the almost unexisting
Blindfish; throats are cut, the masterpiece
Looms out of labour; nations and rebellions
Are spat out to hang on the wind—and all is gone
In one Virilius, wearing his office tunic,
Checking the pence column as he went.

Where's animation now? What is there that stays
To dance? The eye of the one-eyed world is out. (*She weeps*)

DOTO. I shall try to grieve a little, too.
It would take lessons, I imagine, to do it out loud
For long. If I could only remember
Any one of those fellows without wanting to laugh.
Hopeless, I am. Now those good pair of shoes
I gave away without thinking, that's a different—
Well, I've cried enough about *them*, I suppose.
Poor madam, poor master.

(TEGEUS *comes through the gate to the top of the steps*)

TEGEUS.   What's your trouble?

DOTO.   Oh!
Oh! Oh, a man. I thought for a moment it was something
With harm in it. Trust a man to be where it's dark.
What is it? Can't you sleep?

TEGEUS.   Now, listen—

DOTO.   Hush!
Remember you're in the grave. You must go away.
Madam is occupied.

TEGEUS.   What, here?

DOTO.   Becoming
Dead. We both are.

TEGEUS.   What's going on here?

DOTO.   Grief.
Are you satisfied now?

TEGEUS.   Less and less. Do you know
What the time is?

DOTO.   I'm not interested.
We've done with all that. Go away. Be a gentleman.
If we can't be free of men in a grave
Death's a dead loss.

TEGEUS.   It's two in the morning. All
I ask is what are women doing down here
At two in the morning?

DOTO.   Can't you see she's crying?
Or is she sleeping again? Either way
She's making arrangements to join her husband.

TEGEUS.   Where?

DOTO. Good god, in the Underworld, dear man. Haven't you learnt
About life and death?

TEGEUS.   In a manner, yes; in a manner;
The rudiments. So the lady means to die?

DOTO. For love; beautiful, curious madam.

TEGEUS.   Not curious;

I've had thoughts like it. Death is a kind of love.
Not anything I can explain.

DOTO.   You'd better come in
And sit down.

TEGEUS.   I'd be grateful.

DOTO.   Do. It will be my last
Chance to have company, in the flesh.

TEGEUS.   Do you mean
You're going too?

DOTO.   Oh, certainly I am.
Not anything I can explain.
It all started with madam saying a man
Was two men really, and I'd only noticed one,
One each, I mean. It seems he has a soul
As well as his other troubles. And I like to know
What I'm getting with a man. I'm inquisitive,
I suppose you'd call me.

TEGEUS.   It takes some courage.

DOTO.   Well, yes
And no. I'm fond of change.

TEGEUS.   Would you object
To have me eating my supper here?

DOTO.   Be careful
Of the crumbs. We don't want a lot of squeaking mice
Just when we're dying.

TEGEUS.   What a sigh she gave then.
Down the air like a slow comet.
And now she's all dark again. Mother of me.
How long has this been going on?

DOTO.   Two days.
It should have been three by now, but at first
Madam had difficulty with the Town Council. They said
They couldn't have a tomb used as a private residence.
But madam told them she wouldn't be eating here,
Only suffering, and they thought that would be all right.

TEGEUS. Two of you. Marvellous. Who would have said
I should ever have stumbled on anything like this?
Do you have to cry? Yes, I suppose so. It's all
Quite reasonable.

DOTO.   Your supper and your knees.
That's what's making me cry. I can't bear sympathy
And they're sympathetic.

TEGEUS.   Please eat a bit of something.
I've no appetite left.

DOTO.   And see her go ahead of me?

Wrap it up; put it away. You sex of wicked beards!
It's no wonder you have to shave off your black souls
Every day as they push through your chins.
I'll turn my back on you. It means utter
Contempt. Eat? Utter contempt. Oh, little new rolls!

TEGEUS. Forget it, forget it; please forget it. Remember
I've had no experience of this kind of thing before.
Indeed I'm as sorry as I know how to be. Ssh,
We'll disturb her. She sighed again. O Zeus,
It's terrible! Asleep, and still sighing.
Mourning has made a warren in her spirit,
All that way below. Ponos! the heart
Is the devil of a medicine.

DOTO.   And I don't intend
To turn round.

TEGEUS.   I understand how you must feel.
Would it be—have you any objection
To my having a drink? I have a little wine here.
And, you probably see how it is: grief's in order,
And death's in order, and women—I can usually
Manage that too; but not all three together
At this hour of the morning. So you'll excuse me.
How about you? It would make me more comfortable
If you'd take a smell of it.

DOTO.   One for the road?

TEGEUS. One for the road.

DOTO.   It's the dust in my throat. The tomb
Is so dusty. Thanks, I will. There's no point in dying
Of everything, simultaneous.

TEGEUS.   It's lucky
I brought two bowls. I was expecting to keep
A drain for my relief when he comes in the morning.

DOTO. Are you on duty?

TEGEUS.   Yes.

DOTO.   It looks like it.

TEGEUS.   Well,
Here's your good health.

DOTO.   What good is that going to do me?
Here's to an easy crossing and not too much waiting
About on the bank. Do you have to tremble like that?

TEGEUS. The idea—I can't get used to it.

DOTO.   For a member
Of the forces, you're peculiarly queasy. I wish
Those owls were in Hades—oh no; let them stay where they are.
Have you never had nothing to do with corpses before?

TEGEUS. I've got six of them outside.

DOTO.   Morpheus, that's plenty.
   What are they doing there?

TEGEUS.   Hanging.

DOTO.   Hanging?

TEGEUS.   On trees.
   Five plane trees and a holly. The holly-berries
   Are just reddening. Another drink?

DOTO.   Why not?

TEGEUS. It's from Samos. Here's—

DOTO.   All right. Let's just drink it.
   —How did they get in that predicament?

TEGEUS. The sandy-haired fellow said we should collaborate
   With everybody; the little man said he wouldn't
   Collaborate with anybody; the old one
   Said that the Pleiades weren't sisters but cousins
   And anyway were manufactured in Lacedaemon.
   The fourth said that we hanged men for nothing
   The other two said nothing. Now they hang
   About at the corner of the night, they're present
   And absent, horribly obsequious to every
   Move in the air, and yet they keep me standing
   For five hours at a stretch.

DOTO.   The wine has gone
   Down to my knees.

TEGEUS.   And up to your cheeks. You're looking
   Fresher. If only—

DOTO.   Madam? She never would.
   Shall I ask her?

TEGEUS.   No; no, don't dare, don't breathe it.
   This is privilege, to come so near
   To what is undeceiving and uncorrupt
   And undivided; this is the clear fashion
   For all souls, a ribbon to bind the unruly
   Curls of living, a faith, a hope, Zeus
   Yes, a fine thing. I am human, and this
   Is human fidelity, and we can be proud
   And unphilosophical.

DOTO.   I need to dance
   But I haven't the use of my legs.

TEGEUS.   No, no, don't dance,
   Or, at least, only inwards; don't dance; cry
   Again. We'll put a moat of tears
   Round her bastion of love, and save
   The world. It's something, it's more than something,

It's regeneration, to see how a human cheek
Can become as pale as a pool.
DOTO.   Do you love me, handsome?
TEGEUS. To have found life, after all, unambiguous!
DOTO. Did you say Yes?
TEGEUS.   Certainly; just now I love all men.
DOTO. So do I.
TEGEUS.   And the world is a good creature again.
I'd begun to see it as mildew, verdigris,
Rust, woodrot, or as though the sky had uttered
An oval twirling blasphemy with occasional vistas
In country districts. I was within an ace
Of volunteering for overseas service. Despair
Abroad can always nurse pleasant thoughts of home.
Integrity, by god!
DOTO.   I love all the world
And the movement of the apple in your throat.
So shall you kiss me? It would be better, I should think,
To go moistly to Hades.
TEGEUS.   Hers is the way,
Luminous with sorrow.
DOTO.   Then I'll take
Another little swiggy. I love all men,
Everybody, even you, and I'll pick you
Some outrageous honeysuckle for your helmet,
If only it lived here. Pardon.
DYNAMENE.   Doto. Who is it?
DOTO. Honeysuckle, madam. Because of the bees.
Go back to sleep, madam.
DYNAMENE.   What person is it?
DOTO. Yes, I see what you mean, madam. It's a kind of
Corporal talking to his soul, on a five-hour shift,
Madam, with six bodies. He's been having his supper.
TEGEUS. I'm going. It's terrible that we should have disturbed her.
DOTO. He was delighted to see you so sad, madam.
It has stopped him going abroad.
DYNAMENE.   One with six bodies?
A messenger, a guide to where we go
It is possible he has come to show us the way
Out of these squalid suburbs of life, a shade,
A gorgon, who has come swimming up, against
The falls of my tears (for which in truth he would need
Many limbs) to guide me to Virilius.
I shall go quietly.
TEGEUS.   I do assure you—

Such clumsiness, such a vile and unforgivable
Intrusion. I shall obliterate myself
Immediately.

DOTO.   Oblit—oh, what a pity
To oblit. Pardon. Don't let him, the nice fellow.

DYNAMENE. Sir: your other five bodies: where are they?

TEGEUS.   Madam—
Outside; I have them outside. On trees.

DYNAMENE.   Quack!

TEGEUS. What do I reply?

DYNAMENE.   Quack, charlatan!
You've never known the gods. You came to mock me.
Doto, this never was a gorgon, never.
Nor a gentleman either. He's completely spurious.
Admit it, you creature. Have you even a feather
Of the supernatural in your system? Have you?

TEGEUS. Some of my relations—

DYNAMENE.   Well?

TEGEUS.   Are dead, I think;
That is to say I have connexions—

DYNAMENE.   Connexions
With pickpockets. It's a shameless imposition.
Does the army provide you with no amusements?
If I were still of the world, and not cloistered
In a colourless landscape of winter thought
Where the approaching Spring is desired oblivion,
I should write sharply to your commanding officer.
It should be done, it should be done. If my fingers
Weren't so cold I would do it now. But they are,
Horribly cold. And why should insolence matter
When my colour of life is unreal, a blush on death,
A partial mere diaphane? I don't know
Why it should matter. Oafish, non-commissioned
Young man! The boots of your conscience will pinch for ever
If life's dignity has any self-protection.
Oh, I have to sit down. The tomb's going round.

DOTO. Oh, madam, don't give over. I can't remember
When things were so lively. He looks marvellously
Marvellously uncomfortable. Go on, madam.
Can't you, madam? Oh, madam, don't you feel up to it?
There, do you see her, you acorn-chewing infantryman?
You've made her cry, you square-bashing barbarian.

TEGEUS. O history, my private history, why
Was I led here? What stigmatism has got

Into my stars? Why wasn't it my brother?
He has a tacit misunderstanding with everybody
And washes in it. Why wasn't it my mother?
She makes a collection of other people's tears
And dries them all. Let them forget I came;
And lie in the terrible black crystal of grief
Which held them, before I broke it. Outside, Tegeus.

DOTO. Hey, I don't think so, I shouldn't say so. Come
Down again, uniform. Do you think you're going
To half kill an unprotected lady and then
Back out upwards? Do you think you can leave her like this?

TEGEUS. Yes, yes, I'll leave her. O directorate of gods,
How can I? Beauty's bit is between my teeth.
She has added another torture to me. Bottom
Of Hades' bottom.

DOTO.   Madam. Madam, the corporal
Has some wine here. It will revive you, madam.
And then you can go at him again, madam.

TEGEUS. It's the opposite of everything you've said,
I swear. I swear by Horkos and the Styx,
I swear by the nine acres of Tityos,
I swear the Hypnotic oath, by all the Titans—
By Koeos, Krios, Iapetos, Kronos, and so on—
By the three Hekatoncheires, by the insomnia
Of Tisiphone, by Jove, by jove, and the dew
On the feet of my boyhood, I am innocent
Of mocking you. Am I a Salmoneus
That, seeing such a flame of sorrow—

DYNAMENE.   You needn't
Labour to prove your secondary education.
Perhaps I jumped to a wrong conclusion, perhaps
I was hasty.

DOTO.   How easy to swear if you're properly educated.
Wasn't it pretty, madam? Pardon.

DYNAMENE.   If I misjudged you
I apologize, I apologize. Will you please leave us?
You were wrong to come here. In a place of mourning
Light itself is a trespasser; nothing can have
The right of entrance except those natural symbols
Of mortality, the jabbing, funeral, sleek-
With-omen raven, the death-watch beetle which mocks
Time: particularly, I'm afraid, the spider
Weaving his home with swift self-generated
Threads of slaughter; and, of course, the worm.

I wish it could be otherwise. Oh dear,
They aren't easy to live with.

DOTO.   Not even a *little* wine, madam?

DYNAMENE. Here, Doto?

DOTO.   Well, on the steps perhaps,
Except it's so draughty.

DYNAMENE.   Doto! Here?

DOTO.   No, madam;
I quite see.

DYNAMENE.   I might be wise to strengthen myself
In order to fast again; it would make me abler
For grief. I will breathe a little of it, Doto.

DOTO. Thank god. Where's the bottle?

DYNAMENE.   What an exquisite bowl.

TEGEUS. Now that it's peacetime we have pottery classes.

DYNAMENE. You made it yourself?

TEGEUS.   Yes. Do you see the design?
The corded god, tied also by the rays
Of the sun, and the astonished ship erupting
Into vines and vine-leaves, inverted pyramids
Of grapes, the uplifted hands of the men (the raiders),
And here the headlong sea, itself almost
Venturing into leaves and tendrils, and Proteus
With his beard braiding the wind, and this
Held by other hands is a drowned sailor—

DYNAMENE. Always, always.

DOTO.   Hold the bowl steady, madam.
Pardon.

DYNAMENE.   Doto, have you been drinking?

DOTO.   Here, madam?
I coaxed some a little way towards my mouth, madam,
But I scarcely swallowed except because I had to. The hiccup
Is from no breakfast, madam, and not meant to be funny.

DYNAMENE. You may drink this too. Oh, how the inveterate body,
Even when cut from the heart, insists on leaf,
Puts out, with a separate meaningless will,
Fronds to intercept the thankless sun.
How it does, oh, how it does. And how it confuses
The nature of the mind.

TEGEUS.   Yes, yes, the confusion;
That's something I understand better than anything.

DYNAMENE. When the thoughts would die, the instincts will set sail
For life. And when the thoughts are alert for life
The instincts will rage to be destroyed on the rocks.
To Virilius it was not so; his brain was an ironing-board

For all crumpled indecision: and I follow him,
The hawser of my world. You don't belong here,
You see; you don't belong here at all.

TEGEUS.   If only
I did. If only you knew the effort it costs me
To mount those steps again into an untrustworthy,
Unpredictable, unenlightened night,
And turn my back on—on a state of affairs,
I can only call it a vision, a hope, a promise,
A—By that I mean loyalty, enduring passion,
Unrecking bravery and beauty all in one.

DOTO. He means you, or you and me; or me, madam.

TEGEUS. It only remains for me to thank you, and to say
That whatever awaits me and for however long
I may be played by this poor musician, existence,
Your person and sacrifice will leave their trace
As clear upon me as the shape of the hills
Around my birthplace. Now I must leave you to your husband.

DOTO. Oh! You, madam.

DYNAMENE.   I'll tell you what I will do.
I will drink with you to the memory of my husband,
Because I have been curt, because you are kind,
And because I'm extremely thirsty. And then we will say
Good-bye and part to go to our opposite corruptions,
The world and the grave.

TEGEUS.   The climax to the vision.

DYNAMENE (*drinking*). My husband, and all he stood for.

TEGEUS.   Stands for.

DYNAMENE.   Stands for.

TEGEUS. Your husband.

DOTO.   The master.

DYNAMENE.   How good it is,
How it sings to the throat, purling with summer.

TEGEUS. It has a twin nature, winter and warmth in one,
Moon and meadow. Do you agree?

DYNAMENE.   Perfectly;
A cold bell sounding in a golden month.

TEGEUS. Crystal in harvest.

DYNAMENE.   Perhaps a nightingale
Sobbing among the pears.

TEGEUS.   In an old autumnal midnight.

DOTO. Grapes.—Pardon. There's some more here.

TEGEUS.   Plenty.
I drink to the memory of your husband.

DYNAMENE.   My husband.

DOTO. The master.

DYNAMENE. He was careless in his choice of wines.

TEGEUS. And yet
Rendering to living its rightful poise is not
Unimportant.

DYNAMENE. A mystery's in the world
Where a little liquid, with flavour, quality, and fume
Can be as no other, can hint and flute our senses
As though a music played in harvest hollows
And a movement was in the swathes of our memory.
Why should scent, why should flavour come
With such wings upon us? Parsley, for instance.

TEGEUS. Seaweed.

DYNAMENE. Lima trees.

DOTO. Horses.

TEGEUS. Fruit in the fire.

DYNAMENE. Do I know your name?

TEGEUS. Tegeus.

DYNAMENE. That's very thin for you,
It hardly covers your bones. Something quite different,
Altogether other. I shall think of it presently.

TEGEUS. Darker vowels, perhaps.

DYNAMENE. Yes, certainly darker vowels.
And your consonants should have a slight angle,
And a certain temperature. Do you know what I mean?
It will come to me.

TEGEUS. Now *your* name—

DYNAMENE. It is nothing
To any purpose. I'll be to you the She
In the tomb. You have the air of a natural-historian
As though you were accustomed to handling birds' eggs,
Or tadpoles, or putting labels on moths. You see?
The genius of dumb things, that they are nameless.
Have I found the seat of the weevil in human brains?
Our names. They make us broody; we sit and sit
To hatch them into reputation and dignity.
And then they set upon us and become despair,
Guilt and remorse. We go where they lead. We dance
Attendance on something wished upon us by the wife
Of our mother's physician. But insects meet and part
And put the woods about them, fill the dusk
And freckle the light and go and come without
A name among them, without the wish of a name
And very pleasant too. Did I interrupt you?

TEGEUS. I forget. We'll have no names then.

DYNAMENE.   I should like
  You to have a name, I don't know why; a small one
  To fill out the conversation.
TEGEUS.   I should like
  You to have a name too, if only for something
  To remember. Have you still some wine in your bowl?
DYNAMENE. Not altogether.
TEGEUS.   We haven't come to the end
  By several inches. Did I splash you?
DYNAMENE.   It doesn't matter.
  Well, here's to my husband's name.
TEGEUS.   Your husband's name.
DOTO. The master.
DYNAMENE.   It was kind of you to come.
TEGEUS. It was more than coming. I followed my future here,
  As we all do if we're sufficiently inattentive
  And don't vex ourselves with questions; or do I mean
  Attentive? If so, attentive to what? Do I sound
  Incoherent?
DYNAMENE.   You're wrong. There isn't a future here,
  Not here, not for you.
TEGEUS.   Your name's Dynamene.
DYNAMENE. Who—Have I been utterly irreverent? Are you—
  Who made you say that? Forgive me the question,
  But are you dark or light? I mean which shade
  Of the supernatural? Or if neither, what prompted you?
TEGEUS. Dynamene—
DYNAMENE.   No, but I'm sure you're the friend of nature,
  It must be so, I think I see little Phoebuses
  Rising and setting in your eyes.
DOTO.   They're not little Phoebuses,
  They're hoodwinks, madam. Your name is on your brooch.
  No little Phoebuses to-night.
DYNAMENE.   That's twice
  You've played me a trick. Oh, I know practical jokes
  Are common on Olympus, but haven't we at all
  Developed since the gods were born? Are gods
  And men both to remain immortal adolescents?
  How tiresome it all is.
TEGEUS.   It was you, each time,
  Who said I was supernatural. When did I say so?
  You're making me into whatever you imagine
  And then you blame me because I can't live up to it.
DYNAMENE. I shall call you Chromis. It has a breadlike sound.
  I think of you as a crisp loaf.

TEGEUS. And now
You'll insult me because I'm not sliceable.

DYNAMENE. I think drinking is harmful to our tempers.

TEGEUS. If I seem to be frowning, that is only because
I'm looking directly into your light: I must look
Angrily, or shut my eyes.

DYNAMENE. Shut them.—Oh,
You have eyelashes! A new perspective of you.
Is that how you look when you sleep?

TEGEUS. My jaw drops down.

DYNAMENE. Show me how.

TEGEUS. Like this.

DYNAMENE. It makes an irresistible
Moron of you. Will you waken now?
It's morning; I see a thin dust of daylight
Blowing on to the steps.

TEGEUS. Already? Dynamene,
You're tricked again. This time by the moon.

DYNAMENE. Oh well,
Moon's daylight, then. Doto is asleep.

TEGEUS. Doto
Is asleep . . .

DYNAMENE. Chromis, what made you walk about
In the night? What, I wonder, made you not stay
Sleeping wherever you slept? Was it the friction
Of the world on your mind? Those two are difficult
To make agree. Chromis—now try to learn
To answer your name. I won't say Tegeus.

TEGEUS. And I
Won't say Dynamene.

DYNAMENE. Not?

TEGEUS. It makes you real.
Forgive me, a terrible thing has happened. Shall I
Say it and perhaps destroy myself for you?
Forgive me first, or, more than that, forgive
Nature who winds her furtive stream all through
Our reason. Do you forgive me?

DYNAMENE. I'll forgive
Anything, if it's the only way I can know
What you have to tell me.

TEGEUS. I felt us to be alone;
Here in a grave, separate from any life,
I and the only one of beauty, the only
Persuasive key to all my senses,

In spite of my having lain day after day
And pored upon the sepals, corolla, stamen, and bracts
Of the yellow bog-iris. Then my body ventured
A step towards interrupting your perfection of purpose
And my own renewed faith in human nature.
Would you have believed that possible?
DYNAMENE.   I have never
Been greatly moved by the yellow bog-iris. Alas,
It's as I said. This place is for none but the spider,
Raven and worms, not for a living man.
TEGEUS. It has been a place of blessing to me. It will always
Play in me, a fountain of confidence
When the world is arid. But I know it is true
I have to leave it, and though it withers my soul
I must let you make your journey.
DYNAMENE.   No.
TEGEUS.   Not true?
DYNAMENE. We can talk of something quite different.
TEGEUS.   Yes, we can!
Oh yes, we will! Is it your opinion
That no one believes who hasn't learned to doubt?
Or, another thing, if we persuade ourselves
To one particular Persuasion, become Sophist,
Stoic, Platonist, anything whatever,
Would you say that there must be areas of soul
Lying unproductive therefore, or dishonoured
Or blind?
DYNAMENE.   No, I don't know.
TEGEUS.   No. It's impossible
To tell. Dynamene, if only I had
Two cakes of pearl-barley and hydromel
I could see you to Hades, leave you with your husband
And come back to the world.
DYNAMENE.   Ambition, I suppose,
Is an appetite particular to man.
What is your definition?
TEGEUS.   The desire to find
A reason for living.
DYNAMENE.   But then, suppose it leads,
As often, one way or another, it does, to death.
TEGEUS. Then that may be life's reason. Oh, but how
Could I bear to return, Dynamene? The earth's
Daylight would be my grave if I had left you
In that unearthly night.

DYNAMENE.   O Chromis——

TEGEUS.   Tell me,
    What is your opinion of Progress? Does it, for example,
    Exist? Is there ever progression without retrogression?
    Therefore is it not true that mankind
    Can more justly be said increasingly to Gress?
    As the material improves, the craftsmanship deteriorates
    And honor and virtue remain the same. I love you,
    Dynamene.

DYNAMENE.   Would you consider we go round and round?

TEGEUS. We concertina, I think; taking each time
    A larger breath, so that the farther we go out
    The farther we have to go in.

DYNAMENE.   There'll come a time.
    When it will be unbearable to continue.

TEGEUS. Unbearable.

DYNAMENE.   Perhaps we had better have something
    To eat. The wine has made your eyes so quick
    I am breathless beside them. It *is*
    Your eyes, I think; or your intelligence
    Holding my intelligence up above you
    Between its hands. Or the cut of your uniform.

TEGEUS. Here's a new roll with honey. In the gods' names
    Let's sober ourselves.

DYNAMENE.   As soon as possible.

TEGEUS.   Have you
    Any notion of algebra?

DYNAMENE.   We'll discuss you, Chromis.
    We will discuss you, till you're nothing but words.

TEGEUS. I? There is nothing, of course, I would rather discuss,
    Except—if it would be no intrusion—you, Dynamene.

DYNAMENE. No, you couldn't want to. But your birthplace, Chromis,
    With the hills that placed themselves in you for ever
    As you say, where was it?

TEGEUS.   My father's farm at Pyxa.

DYNAMENE. There? Could it be there?

TEGEUS.   I was born in the hills
    Between showers, a quarter of an hour before milking time.
    Do you know Pyxa? It stretches to the crossing of two
    Troublesome roads, and buries its back in beechwood,
    From which come the white owls of our nights
    And the mulling and cradling of doves in the day.
    I attribute my character to those shadows
    And heavy roots; and my interest in music
    To the sudden melodious escape of the young river

Where it breaks from nosing through the crocous and kingcups.
That's honestly so.
DYNAMENE.　　　　　You used to climb about
Among the windfallen tower of Phrasidemus
Looking for bees' nests.
TEGEUS.　　　　　What? When have I
Said so?
DYNAMENE.　　Why, all the children did.
TEGEUS. Yes: but, in the name of light, how do you *know* that?
DYNAMENE. I played there once, on holiday.
TEGEUS.　　　　　　　　O Klotho,
Lachesis and Atropos!
DYNAMENE.　　　　　It's the strangest chance:
I may have seen, for a moment, your boyhood.
TEGEUS.　　　　　　　　　I may
Have seen something like an early flower
Something like a girl. If I only could remember how I must
Have seen you. Were you after the short white violets?
Maybe I blundered past you, taking your look,
And scarcely acknowledged how a star
Ran through me, to live in the brooks of my blood for ever.
Or I saw you playing at hiding in the cave
Where the ferns are and the water drips.
DYNAMENE. I was quite plain and fat and I was usually
Hitting someone. I wish I could remember you.
I'm envious of the days and children who saw you
Then. It is curiously a little painful
Not to share your past.
TEGEUS.　　　　　How did it come
Our stars could mingle for an afternoon
So long ago, and then forget us or tease us
Or helplessly look on the dark high seas
Of our separation, while time drank
The golden hours? What hesitant fate is that?
DYNAMENE. Time? Time? Why—how old are we?
TEGEUS.　　　　　　　　Young,
Thank both our mothers, but still we're older than to-night
And so older than we should be. Wasn't I born
In love with what, only now, I have grown to meet?
I'll tell you something else. I was born entirely
For this reason. I was born to fill a gap
In the world's experience, which had never known
Chromis loving Dynamene.
DYNAMENE.　　　　　You are so
Excited, poor Chromis. What is it? Here you sit

With a woman who has wept away all claims
To appearance, unbecoming in her oldest clothes,
With not a trace of liveliness, a drab
Of melancholy, entirely shadow without
A smear of sun. Forgive me if I tell you
That you fall easily into superlatives.

TEGEUS. Very well. I'll say nothing, then. I'll fume
With feeling.

DYNAMENE.   Now you go to the extreme. Certainly
You must speak. You may have more to say. Besides
You might let your silence run away with you
And not say something that you should. And how
Should I answer you then? Chromis, you boy,
I can't look away from you. You use
The lamplight and the moon so skilfully,
So arrestingly, in and around your furrows.
A humorous ploughman goes whistling to a team
Of sad sorrow, to and fro in your brow
And over your arable cheek. Laugh for me. Have you
Cried for women, ever?

TEGEUS.   In looking about for you.
But I have recognized them for what they were.

DYNAMENE. What were they?

TEGEUS.   Never you: never, although
They could walk with bright distinction into all men's
Longest memories, never you, by a hint
Or a faint quality, or at least not more
Than reflectively, stars lost and uncertain
In the sea, compared with the shining salt, the shiners,
The galaxies, the clusters, the bright grain whirling
Over the black threshing-floor of space.
Will you make some effort to believe that?

DYNAMENE.   No, no effort.
It lifts me and carries me. It may be wild
But it comes to me with a charm, like trust indeed,
And eats out of my heart, dear Chromis,
Absurd, disconcerting Chromis. You make me
Feel I wish I could look my best for you.
I wish, at least, that I could believe myself
To be showing some beauty for you, to put in the scales
Between us. But they dip to you, they sink
With masculine victory.

TEGEUS.   Eros, no! No!
If this is less than your best, then never, in my presence,

Be more than your less: never! If you should bring
More to your mouth or to your eyes, a moisture
Or a flake of light, anything, anything fatally
More, perfection would fetch her unsparing rod
Out of pickle to flay me, and what would have been love
Will be the end of me. O Dynamene,
Let me unload something of my lips' longing
On to yours receiving. Oh, when I cross
Like this the hurt of the little space between us
I come a journey from the wrenching ice
To walk in the sun. That is the feeling.
DYNAMENE.   Chromis,
Where am I going? No, don't answer. It's death
I desire, not you.
TEGEUS.   Where is the difference? Call me
Death instead of Chromis. I'll answer to anything.
It's desire all the same, of death in me, or me
In death, but Chromis either way. Is it so?
Do you not love me, Dynamene?
DYNAMENE.   How could it happen?
I'm going to my husband. I'm too far on the way
To admit myself to life again. Love's in Hades.
TEGEUS. Also here. And here are we, not there
In Hades. Is your husband expecting you?
DYNAMENE. Surely, surely?
TEGEUS.   Not necessarily. I,
If I had been your husband, would never dream
Of expecting you. I should remember your body
Descending stairs in the floating light, but not
Descending in Hades. I should say "I have left
My wealth warm on the earth, and, hell, earth needs it."
"Was all I taught her of love," I should say, "so poor
That she will leave her flesh and become shadow?"
"Wasn't our love for each other" (I should continue)
"Infused with life, and life infused with our love?
Very well; repeat me in love, repeat me in life,
And let me sing in your blood for ever."
DYNAMENE. Stop, stop, I shall be dragged apart!
Why should the fates do everything to keep me
From dying honourably? They must have got
Tired of honour in Elysium. Chromis, it's terrible
To be susceptible to two conflicting norths.
I have the constitution of a whirlpool.
Am I actually twirling, or is it just sensation?

TEGEUS. You're still; still as the darkness.

DYNAMENE.   What appears
Is so unlike what is. And what is madness
To those who only observe, is often wisdom
To those to whom it happens.

TEGEUS.   Are we compelled
To go into all this?

DYNAMENE.   Why, how could I return
To my friends? Am I to be an entertainment?

TEGEUS. That's for to-morrow. To-night I need to kiss you,
Dynamene. Let's see what the whirlpool does
Between my arms; let it whirl on my breast. O love,
Come in.

DYNAMENE.   I am there before I reach you; my body
Only follows to join my longing which
Is holding you already.—Now I am
All one again.

TEGEUS.   I feel as the gods feel:
This is their sensation of life, not a man's:
Their suspension of immortality, to enrich
Themselves with time. O life, O death, O body,
O spirit, O Dynamene.

DYNAMENE.   O all
In myself; it so covets all in you,
My care, my Chromis. Then I shall be
Creation.

TEGEUS.   You have the skies already;
Out of them you are buffeting me with your gales
Of beauty. Can we be made of dust, as they tell us?
What! dust with dust releasing such a light
And such an apparition of the world
Within one body? A thread of your hair has stung me.
Why do you push me away?

DYNAMENE.   There's so much metal
About you. Do I have to be imprisoned
In an armoury?

TEGEUS.   Give your hand to the buckles and then
To me.

DYNAMENE.   Don't help; I'll do them all myself.

TEGEUS. O time and patience! I want you back again.

DYNAMENE. We have a lifetime. O Chromis, think, think
Of that. And even unfastening a buckle
Is loving. And not easy. Very well,
You can help me. Chromis, what zone of miracle
Did you step into to direct you in the dark

To where I waited, not knowing I waited?

TEGEUS.   I saw
The lamplight. That was only the appearance
Of some great gesture in the bed of fortune.
I saw the lamplight.

DYNAMENE.   But here? So far from life?
What brought you near enough to see lamplight?

TEGEUS.   Zeus,
That reminds me.

DYNAMENE.   What is it, Chromis?

TEGEUS.   I'm on duty.

DYNAMENE. Is it warm enough to do without your greaves?

TEGEUS. Darling loom of magic, I must go back
To take a look at those boys. The whole business
Of guard had gone out of my mind.

DYNAMENE.   What boys, my heart?

TEGEUS. My six bodies.

DYNAMENE.   Chromis, not that joke
Again.

TEGEUS.   No joke, sweet. To-day our city
Held a sextuple hanging. I'm minding the bodies
Until five o'clock. Already I've been away
For half an hour.

DYNAMENE.   What can they do, poor bodies,
In half an hour, or half a century?
You don't really mean to go?

TEGEUS.   Only to make
My conscience easy. Then, Dynamene,
No cloud can rise on love, no hovering thought
Fidget, and the night will be only to *us*.

DYNAMENE. But if every half-hour——

TEGEUS.   Hush, smile of my soul,
My sprig, my sovereign: this is to hold your eyes,
I sign my lips on them both: this is to keep
Your forehead—do you feel the claim of my kiss
Falling into your thought? And now your throat
Is a white branch and my lips two singing birds—
They are coming to rest. Throat, remember me
Until I come back in five minutes. Over all
Here is my parole: I give it to your mouth
To give me again before it's dry. I promise:
Before it's dry, or not long after.

DYNAMENE.   Run,
Run all the way. You needn't be afraid of stumbling.
There's plenty of moon. The fields are blue. Oh, wait,

Wait! My darling. No, not now: it will keep
Until I see you; I'll have it here at my lips.
Hurry.

TEGEUS.   So, long, my haven.

DYNAMENE.   Hurry, hurry! (*Exit* TEGEUS)

DOTO. Yes, madam, hurry; of course. Are we there
Already? How nice. Death doesn't take
Any doing at all. We were gulped into Hades
As easy as an oyster.

DYNAMENE.   Doto!

DOTO.   Hurry, hurry,
Yes, madam.—But they've taken out all my bones.
I haven't a bone left. I'm a Shadow: wonderfully shady
In the legs. We shall have to sit out eternity, madam,
If they've done the same to you.

DYNAMENE.   You'd better wake up.
If you can't go to sleep again, you'd better wake up.
Oh dear.—We're still alive, Doto, do you hear me?

DOTO. You must speak for yourself, madam. I'm quite dead.
I'll tell you how I know. I feel
Invisible. I'm a wraith, madam; I'm only
Waiting to be wafted.

DYNAMENE.   If only you *would* be.
Do you see where you are? Look. Do you see?

DOTO. Yes. You're right, madam. We're still alive.
Isn't it enough to make you swear?
Here we are, dying to be dead,
And where does it get us?

DYNAMENE.   Perhaps you should try to die
In some other place. Yes! Perhaps the air here
Suits you too well. You were sleeping very heavily.

DOTO. And all the time you alone and dying.
I shouldn't have. Has the corporal been long gone,
Madam?

DYNAMENE.   He came and went, came and went,
You know the way.

DOTO.   Very well I do. And went
He should have, come he should never. Oh dear, he must
Have disturbed you, madam.

DYNAMENE.   He could be said
To've disturbed me. Listen; I have something to say to you.

DOTO. I expect so, madam. Maybe I *could* have kept him out
But men are in before I wish they wasn't.
I think quickly enough, but I get behindhand
With what I ought to be saying. It's a kind of stammer

In my way of life, madam.

DYNAMENE.   I have been unkind,
I have sinfully wronged you, Doto.

DOTO.   Never, madam.

DYNAMENE. Oh yes. I was letting you die with me, Doto, without
Any fair reason. I was drowning you
In grief that wasn't yours. That was wrong, Doto.

DOTO. But I haven't got anything against dying, madam.
I may *like* the situation, as far as I like
Any situation, madam. Now if you'd said mangling,
A lot of mangling, I might have thought twice about staying.
We all have our dislikes, madam.

DYNAMENE.   I'm asking you
To leave me, Doto, at once, as quickly as possible,
Now, before—now, Doto, and let me forget
My bad mind which confidently expected you
To companion me to Hades. Now good-bye,
Good-bye.

DOTO.   No, it's not good-bye at all.
I shouldn't know another night of sleep, wondering
How you got on, or what I was missing, come to that.
I should be anxious about you, too. When you belong
To an upper class, the netherworld might come strange.
Now I was born nether, madam, though not
As nether as some. No, it's not good-bye, madam.

DYNAMENE. Oh Doto, go; you must, you must! And if I seem
Without gratitude, forgive me. It isn't so,
It is far, far from so. But I can only
Regain my peace of mind if I know you're gone.

DOTO. Besides, look at the time, madam. Where should I go
At three in the morning? Even if I was to think
Of going; and think of it I never shall.

DYNAMENE. Think of the unmatchable world, Doto.

DOTO.   I do
Think of it, madam. And when I think of it, what
Have I thought? Well, it depends, madam.

DYNAMENE.   I insist,
Obey me! At once! Doto!

DOTO.   Here I sit.

DYNAMENE. What shall I do with you?

DOTO.   Ignore me, madam.
I know my place. I shall die quite unobtrusive.
Oh, look, the corporal's forgotten to take his equipment.

DYNAMENE. Could he be so careless?

DOTO.   I shouldn't hardly have thought so.

Poor fellow. They'll go and deduct it off his credits.
I suppose, madam, I suppose he couldn't be thinking
Of coming back?

DYNAMENE.   He'll think of these. He will notice
He isn't wearing them. He'll come; he is sure to come.

DOTO. Oh.

DYNAMENE. I know he will.

DOTO.   Oh, oh.
Is that all for to-night, madam? May I go now, madam?

DYNAMENE. Doto! Will you?

DOTO.   Just you try to stop me, madam.
Sometimes going is a kind of instinct with me.
I'll leave death to some other occasion.

DYNAMENE.   Do,
Doto. Any other time. Now you must hurry.
I won't delay you from life another moment.
Oh, Doto, good-bye.

DOTO.   Good-bye. Life is unusual,
Isn't it, madam? Remember me to Cerberus.

(*Re-enter* TEGEUS. DOTO *passes him on the steps*)

DOTO (*as she goes*). You left something behind. Ye gods, what a moon!

DYNAMENE. Chromis, it's true; my lips are hardly dry.
Time runs again; the void is space again;
Space has life again; Dynamene has Chromis.

TEGEUS. It's over.

DYNAMENE.   Chromis, you're sick. As white as wool.
Come, you covered the distance too quickly.
Rest in my arms; get your breath again.

TEGEUS. I've breathed one night too many. Why did I see you,
Why in the name of life did I see you?

DYNAMENE.   Why?
Weren't we gifted with each other? O heart,
What do you mean?

TEGEUS.   I mean that joy is nothing
But the parent of doom. Why should I have found
Your constancy such balm to the world and yet
Find, by the same vision, its destruction
A necessity? We're set upon by love
To make us incompetent to steer ourselves,
To make us docile to fate. I should have known:
Indulgences, not fulfilment, is what the world
Permits us.

DYNAMENE. Chromis, is this intelligible?
Help me to follow you. What did you meet in the fields
To bring about all this talk? Do you still love me?

TEGEUS. What good will it do us? I've lost a body.

DYNAMENE.   A body?
One of the six? Well, it isn't with them you propose
To love me; and you couldn't keep it for ever.
Are we going to allow a body that isn't there
To come between us?

TEGEUS.   But I'm responsible for it.
I have to account for it in the morning. Surely
You see, Dynamene, the horror we're faced with?
The relatives have had time to cut him down
And take him away for burial. It means
A court martial. No doubt about the sentence.
I shall take the place of the missing man.
To be hanged, Dynamene! Hanged, Dynamene!

DYNAMENE. No; it's monstrous! Your life is yours, Chromis.

TEGEUS. Anything but. That's why I have to take it.
At the best we live our lives on loan,
At the worst in chains. And I was never born
To have life. Then for what? To be had by it,
And so are we all. But I'll make it what it is,
By making it nothing.

DYNAMENE.   Chromis, you're frightening me.
What are you meaning to do?

TEGEUS.   I have to die,
Dance of my heart, I have to die, to die,
To part us, to go to my sword and let it part us.
I'll have my free will even if I'm compelled to it.
I'll kill myself.

DYNAMENE.   Oh, no! No, Chromis!
It's all unreasonable—no such horror
Can come of a pure accident. Have you hanged?
How can they hang you for simply not being somewhere?
How can they hang you for losing a dead man?
They must have wanted to lose him, or they wouldn't
Have hanged him. No, you're scaring yourself for nothing
And making me frantic.

TEGEUS.   It's section six, paragraph
Three in the Regulations. That's my doom.
I've read it for myself. And, by my doom,
Since I have to die, let me die here, in love,
Promoted by your kiss to tower, in dying,
High above my birth. For god's sake let me die
On a wave of life, Dynamene, with an action
I can take some pride in. How could I settle to death
Knowing that you last saw me stripped and strangled

On a holly tree? Demoted first and then hanged!

DYNAMENE. Am I supposed to love the corporal
Or you? It's you I love, from head to foot
And out to the ends of your spirit. What shall I do
If you die? How could I follow you? I should find you
Discussing me with my husband, comparing your feelings,
Exchanging reactions. Where should I put myself?
Or am I to live on alone, or find in life
Another source of love, in memory
Of Virilius and of you?

TEGEUS.   Dynamene,
Not that! Since everything in the lives of men
Is brief to indifference, let our love at least
Echo and perpetuate itself uniquely
As long as time allows you. Though you go
to the limit of age, it won't be far to contain me.

DYNAMENE. It will seem like eternity ground into days and days.

TEGEUS. Can I be certain of you, for ever?

DYNAMENE.   But, Chromis,
Surely you said——

TEGEUS.   Surely We have sensed
Our passion to be greater than mortal? Must I
Die believing it is dying with me?

DYNAMENE.   Chromis,
You must never die, never! It would be
An offence against truth.

TEGEUS.   I cannot live to be hanged.
It would be an offence against life. Give me my sword,
Dynamene. O Hades, when you look pale
You take the heart out of me. I could die
Without a sword by seeing you suffer. Quickly!
Give me my heart back again with your lips
And I'll live the rest of my ambitions
In a last kiss.

DYNAMENE. Oh, no, no, no!
Give my blessing to your desertion of me?
Never, Chromis, never. Kiss you and then
Let you go? Love you, for death to have you?
Am I to be made the fool of courts martial?
Who are they who think they can discipline souls
Right off the earth? What discipline is that?
Chromis, love is the only discipline
And we're the disciples of love. I hold you to that:
Hold you, hold you.

TEGEUS.   We have no chance. It's determined

In section six, paragraph three, of the Regulations.
That has more power than love. It can snuff the great
Candles of creation. It makes me able
To do the impossible, to leave you, to go from the light
That keeps you.

DYNAMENE.   No!

TEGEUS.   O dark, it does. Good-bye,
My memory of earth, my dear most dear
Beyond every expectation. I was wrong
To want you to keep our vows existent
In the vacuum that's coming. It would make you
A heaviness to the world, when you should be,
As you are, a form of light. Dynamene, turn
Your head away. I'm going to let my sword
Solve all the riddles.

DYNAMENE.   Chromis, I have it! I know!
Virilius will help you.

TEGEUS.   Virilius?

DYNAMENE. My husband. He can be the other body.

TEGEUS. Your husband can?

DYNAMENE.   He has no further use
For what he left of himself to lie with us here.
Is there any reason why he shouldn't hang
On your holly tree? Better, far better, he,
Than you who are still alive, and surely better
Than *idling* into corruption?

TEGEUS.   Hang your husband?
Dynamene, it's terrible, horrible.

DYNAMENE. How little you can understand. I loved
His life not his death. And now we can give his death
The power of life. Not horrible: wonderful!
Isn't it so? That I should be able to feel
He moves again in the world, accomplishing
Our welfare? It's more than my grief could do.

TEGEUS. What can I say?

DYNAMENE.   That you love me; as I love him
And you. Let's celebrate your safety then.
Where's the bottle? There's some wine unfinished in this bowl.
I'll share it with you. Now forget the fear
We were in; look at me, Chromis. Come away
From the pit you nearly dropped us in. My darling,
I give you Virilius.

TEGEUS.   Virilius.
And all that follows.

DOTO (*on the steps, with the bottle*). The master. Both the masters.

Mark Ashin

FRY'S A PHOENIX
TOO FREQUENT

Only a literary scholar would want to trace the story of *A Phoenix Too Frequent* (see the play on p. 906) back through Jeremy Taylor, the seventeenth century divine, to its source in Petronius' tale of the gentlewoman of Ephesus in order to study the transformations which have occurred in the treatment of the story in the course of twenty centuries. And perhaps only a scholar would care to place in their context the lines from the Roman epigram writer, Martial, as quoted by Robert Burton, which serve as the epigraph to the play. However, the choice of the title, in addition to revealing the characteristically pungent wit of Christopher Fry, also shows the poet's attitude toward the central incident of the drama. Therefore, it seems appropriate to ask not the scholar but the young student what the title means and what kind of attitude it does reveal. In order to understand the title and its relevance for this play, a knowledge of the phoenix legend is required.

Briefly, the legend is as follows: The phoenix was an Arabian bird which had the power of living for five hundred years. It was a unique specimen, since at any given time only one member of the species was ever alive. At the end of its life span, the phoenix built a nest of fragrant spices, laid its egg within and then set fire to the nest, supposedly by a rapid beating of its wings. Thus, the old phoenix was burned to death, but from its ashes a new bird came to life to continue the lineal cycle. In ancient and modern literature, the phoenix has been used by both imaginative and religious writers as a symbol of resurrection—of life coming from death.

In Fry's play, the phoenix obviously refers to the resurrection of love, not only in the very tomb of the deceased husband, Virilius, but with his dead body as the condition of its survival. Dynamene, who had come to the tomb to die for grief, offers her husband's corpse as a substitute for the body her new lover has lost. What attitude are we to take toward this surprising, some might say grisly, turn of events? Even her lover at first calls the offer "terrible, horrible." In fact, it would be possible to find people who would react with shock and moral dismay at the narrative of a widow whose vow of eternal fidelity to her husband is dissolved in the course of a single night by the attractions of a handsome, witty soldier who happens to stumble into the tomb where she is grieving. For these people, the sudden resurrection of love in the heart of the beautiful widow would be an excuse either for didactic denunciation or for cynical reflections about the inconstancy of women. They would consider the rebirth of this phoenix of love too frequent indeed.

But what is the appropriate attitude to take toward the central incident of the play? What can reconcile us to the suddenness with which Dynamene, under the influence of wine and masculine charm, turns from the cold morbidity of death to the engrossing passion for life? If we can only once feel deeply that life itself is a genuine miracle, then we cannot be too surprised at any true manifestation of its quickening power. Life rises from death in every form and aspect of being and resurrection is an act worthy of rejoicing. Then why should we question the miracle of love awakening in the very house of death? Dynamene gives the play's answer to the moralist in her reply to her lover:

> How little you can understand. I loved
> His life not his death. And now we can give his death
> The power of life. Not horrible: wonderful!
> Isn't it so? That I should be able to feel
> He moves again in the world, accomplishing
> Our welfare? It's more than my grief could do.

Far from being too frequent, the phoenix cannot be reborn often enough.

The beginning of the play prepares the way for the presentation of this attitude toward life and death and introduces the paradoxical and effervescent gaiety which characterizes Fry's metaphysical fooling. The stage directions describe an underground tomb practically in darkness and the line of trees on which dangle the bodies of the hanged men whom Tegeus has to guard until morning. But instead of the dolorous or macabre atmosphere which this setting should inspire, we are introduced to the comical chattering of the lively servant, Doto, whose attitude toward her mistress' suicidal intentions is feelingly expressed in the words:

> Honestly, I would rather have to sleep
> With a bald bee-keeper who was wearing his boots
> Than spend more days fasting and thirsting and crying
> In a tomb.

Doto's earthy reminiscences about her "recurring" lovers and her uncle's hardware shop and the good pair of shoes she once gave away without thinking provide an atmosphere in which it would be impossible to take a resolve of death seriously, even if it came from somebody more committed to death than Dynamene appears to be. She awakes from her dream in which her husband, Virilius, became a ship with a "white, scrubbed deck," to realize her insufficiency to the task she has set herself:

> Already I have disfigured
> My vigil. My cynical eyelids have soon dropped me
> In a dream.

Her exaggerated praise of her husband's punctilious and precise virtues leaves the reader with the impression that she is goading herself on to her sacrifice with rationalized incentives and that, in reality, she is a lover of life and its wonders.

> What a mad blacksmith creation is
> Who blows his furnaces until the stars fly upward
> And iron Time is hot and politicians glow
> And bulbs and roots sizzle into hyacinth
> And orchis, and the sand puts out the lion,
> Roaring yellow, and oceans bud with porpoises,
> Blenny, tunny and the almost unexisting
> Blindfish; . . .

The entrance of Tegeus, who becomes immediately intrigued with the seeming spectacle of uncorrupted devotion and perfect integrity, soon provides the motive for Dynamene's return to life. The middle of the play presents a sequence of discoveries in the course of which the two find out how wonderfully compatible they are. After the initial exchange of insults by Dynamene and mouth-filling oaths of innocence by Tegeus, they discover the similarity of their tastes in art, in wine, and in witty talk about all manner of subjects. Dynamene recognizes her helplessness in the grip of her natural instincts:

> Oh, how the inveterate body,
> Even when cut from the heart, insists on leaf,
> Puts out, with a separate meaningless will,
> Fronds to intercept the thankless sun.
> How it does, oh, how it does. And how it confuses
> The nature of the mind.

Tegeus, now renamed Chromis because "it has a breadlike sound," and she thinks of him "as a crisp loaf," manages with his wit and rhetoric to complete the work of regeneration and revivification. In what seems no time at all, they rush through the stages from compatibility to affection to passionate love. His arguments against remaining faithful to the memory of her husband are irresistible and soon her vows, the fear of ridicule, and the prickings of shame are wiped out in the wonder of their love. Just before she surrenders, Dynamene tries to understand herself:

> What appears
> Is so unlike what is. And what is madness
> To those who only observe, is often wisdom
> To those to whom it happens.

It is this swift resurrection of love in the tomb which best exemplifies the dramatist's attitude toward life as something always new and always miraculous. ". . . In my plays I want to look at life—at the commonplaces of existence— as if we had just turned a corner and run into it for the first time."

The phoenix symbolism of new life arising from the ashes of death comes to a climax with the turn of events at the end of the play where, in order to save her lover, Dynamene offers her husband's corpse as a substitute for the one he has lost. However, this episode merely puts into sharp focus what has already been said in the play about the quickening power of the instinct for life. If we can accept the sudden blossoming of love which we have just seen, we can go on to accept Dynamene's argument that her offer will give her husband's death "the power of life." And it is significant that after the lovers accept this resolution to their difficulty, the dramatist gives the last line to the unquenchable Doto, the voice of primitive life, who appears on the steps of the tomb calling out a toast to "The master. Both the masters."

Paddy Chayefsky

MARTY

Like a modern drama, a television play is presented with a limited number of stage settings and with a few interruptions. But the number of sets which may be used is greater and the interruptions are shorter than in the theater. A background sometimes can be suggested by a few details—a library by some shelves of books, a garden by a flowering plant or two. Such "insert scenes" can be combined with detailed settings so that a studio the size of a storeroom can supply a fair number of different backgrounds. Action may move rapidly from background to background (within limits, for the action must continue while an actor changes costumes and moves from set to set). The intermissions are relatively short, totaling five minutes, perhaps, in a presentation lasting an hour. Hence there is a continuity of action comparable to that on the Elizabethan stage (Shakespeare's plays are readily adaptable to television).

The audience may be vast—literally millions of people of many backgrounds and classes. Nevertheless, actors who use the exaggerated gestures or facial expressions of the theater seem unnatural on television. For the relationship between actors and audience is comparable to that of intimate drama. The audience is made up of small groups, the screen is close, and there is no problem about seeing details or hearing clearly. Close-ups may be used frequently, and facial expressions can communicate much that would have to be represented by dialog and action on the stage.

But the commercial auspices under which television plays are presented in the United States create some limitations for the writer. The sponsor is eager, naturally enough, to have as large an audience as possible, so situations or incidents which would be likely to offend any sizable number of viewers are taboo. The very fact that the plays are watched in living rooms by families leads to the imposing of more restrictions upon subject matter than are imposed upon dramas in the legitimate theater. A writer usually submits an outline of his television drama for a reading by the producer and the director of a program. If this is tentatively approved, after a conference and revisions, the outline is scrutinized by the advertising agency in charge of the program and, if again approved, revised. Then the author writes his script, and this, too, is likely to be revised. Moreover, there is a rigid control over the time at

Television performance of Marty

the author's disposal: according to the arrangements between sponsor and network, the "half-hour" play will last no more than twenty-two minutes, say, and the "hour" play no more than fifty-three minutes, on the dot—as compared with an hour and twenty minutes for a modern drama. This means that the line or lines of action and the number of incidents must be relatively small. Other limitations result from the nature of the picture-screen; for instance, an author cannot as a rule have more than four or five important characters on camera at one time. These are severe limitations; but dramatic works have always been limited in various ways, and authors still have been able to produce fine works within the limitations. Often because new possibilities and restrictions arise with new production methods or new media, authors necessarily discover fresh areas of life for exploration.

Paddy Chayefsky believes that in his television play *Marty* he has worked in an area which television has helped authors discover—intimate and quite detailed representations of rather commonplace moments in ordinary lives. "The main characters are typical, rather than exceptional," he notes; "the situations are easily identifiable by the audience; and the relationships are as common as common people. . . . I tried to write the dialog as if it had been wire-tapped. I tried to envision the scenes as if a camera had been focused upon the unsuspecting characters and had caught them in an untouched moment of life."

The story as he sees it is a very ordinary love story shown as it really would have happened. It is sound in its psychological depiction of relationships between characters, and it has the aspect of reality. Partly because its characters are so ordinary, and partly because it is untheatrical and unexaggerated, it captures and holds the interest and the profound sympathy of members of its audience.

Marty, presented on the Philco-Goodyear Playhouse in 1954, was universally praised by critics, and won a number of awards. Adapted as a motion picture in 1955, it was awarded first place in the Cannes Film Festival and was named best production of the year by the Academy of Motion Picture Arts and Sciences.

CHARACTERS

MARTY	YOUNG MAN
CLARA	CRITIC
ANGIE	BARTENDER
MOTHER	TWENTY-YEAR-OLD
AUNT	ITALIAN WOMAN
VIRGINIA	SHORT GIRL
THOMAS	GIRL

Act I

FADE IN: *A butcher shop in the Italian district of New York City. Actually, we fade in on a close-up of a butcher's saw being carefully worked through a side of beef, and we dolly back to show the butcher at work, and then the whole shop. The butcher is a mild-mannered, stout, short, balding young man of thirty-six. His charm lies in an almost indestructible good-natured amiability.*

The shop contains three women customers. One is a young mother with a baby carriage. She is chatting with a second woman of about forty at the door. The customer being waited on at the moment is a stout, elderly Italian woman who is standing on tiptoe, peering over the white display counter, checking the butcher as he saws away.

ITALIAN WOMAN. Your kid brother got married last Sunday, eh, Marty?
MARTY (*absorbed in his work*). That's right, Missus Fusari. It was a very nice affair.

ITALIAN WOMAN. That's the big tall one, the fellow with the mustache.

MARTY (*sawing away*). No, that's my other brother Freddie. My other brother Freddie, he's been married four years already. He lives down on Quincy Street. The one who got married Sunday, that was my little brother Nickie.

ITALIAN WOMAN. I thought he was a big, tall, fat fellow. Didn't I meet him here one time? Big, tall, fat fellow, he tried to sell me life insurance?

MARTY (*sets the cut of meat on the scale, watches its weight register*). No, that's my sister Margaret's husband Frank. My sister Margaret, she's married to the insurance salesman. My sister Rose, she married a contractor. They moved to Detroit last year. And my other sister, Frances, she got married about two and a half years ago in Saint John's Church on Adams Boulevard. Oh, that was a big affair. Well, Missus Fusari, that'll be three dollars, ninety-four cents. How's that with you? (*The Italian woman produces an old leather change purse from her pocketbook and painfully extracts three single dollar bills and ninety-four cents to the penny and lays the money piece by piece on the counter*)

YOUNG MOTHER (*calling from the door*). Hey, Marty, I'm inna hurry.

MARTY (*wrapping the meat, calls amiably back*). You're next right now, Missus Canduso.

(*The old Italian lady has been regarding Marty with a baleful scowl*)

ITALIAN WOMAN. Well, Marty, when you gonna get married? You should be ashamed. All your brothers and sisters, they all younger than you, and they married, and they got children. I just saw your mother inna fruit shop, and she says to me: "Hey, you know a nice girl for my boy Marty?" Watsa matter with you? That's no way. Watsa matter with you? Now, you get married, you hear me what I say?

MARTY (*amiably*). I hear you, Missus Fusari.

(*The old lady takes her parcel of meat, but apparently feels she still hasn't quite made her point*)

ITALIAN WOMAN. My son Frank, he was married when he was nineteen years old. Watsa matter with you?

MARTY. Missus Fusari, Missus Canduso over there, she's inna big hurry, and . . .

ITALIAN WOMAN. You be ashamed of yourself. (*She takes her package of meat, turns, and shuffles to the door and exits.* MARTY *gathers up the money on the counter, turns to the cash register behind him to ring up the sale*)

YOUNG MOTHER. Marty, I want a nice big fat pullet, about four pounds. I hear your kid brother got married last Sunday.

MARTY. Yeah, it was a very nice affair, Missus Canduso.

YOUNG MOTHER. Marty, you oughtta be ashamed. All your kid brothers and sisters, married and have children. When you gonna get married?

(CLOSE-UP: MARTY. *He sends a glance of weary exasperation up to the ceiling. With a gesture of mild irritation, he pushes the plunger of the cash register. It makes a sharp ping.*

(DISSOLVE TO: *Close-up of television set. A baseball game is in progress. Camera pulls back to show we are in a typical neighborhood bar—red leatherette* booths—*a jukebox, some phone booths. About half the bar stools are occupied by neighborhood folk.* MARTY *enters, pads amiably to one of the booths where a young man of about thirty-odd already sits. This is* ANGIE. MARTY *slides into the booth across from* ANGIE. ANGIE *is a little wasp of a fellow. He has a newspaper spread out before him to the sports pages.* MARTY *reaches over and pulls one of the pages over for himself to read. For a moment the two friends sit across from each other, reading the sports pages. Then* ANGIE, *without looking up, speaks)*

ANGIE. Well, what do you feel like doing tonight?

MARTY. I don't know, Angie. What do you feel like doing?

ANGIE. Well, we oughtta do something. It's Saturday night. I don't wanna go bowling like last Saturday. How about calling up that big girl we picked up inna movies about a month ago in the RKO Chester?

MARTY *(not very interested).* Which one was that?

ANGIE. That big girl that was sitting in front of us with the skinny friend.

MARTY. Oh, yeah.

ANGIE. We took them home alla way out in Brooklyn. Her name was Mary Feeney. What do you say? You think I oughtta give her a ring? I'll take the skinny one.

MARTY. It's five o'clock already, Angie. She's probably got a date by now.

ANGIE. Well, let's call her up. What can we lose?

MARTY. I didn't like her, Angie. I don't feel like calling her up.

ANGIE. Well, what do you feel like doing tonight?

MARTY. I don't know. What do you feel like doing?

ANGIE. Well, we're back to that, huh? I say to you: "What do you feel like doing tonight?" And you say to me: "I don't know, what do you feel like doing?" And then we wind up sitting around your house with a couple of cans of beer, watching Sid Caesar on television. Well, I tell you what I feel like doing. I feel like calling up this Mary Feeney. She likes you.

*(*MARTY *looks up quickly at this)*

MARTY. What makes you say that?

ANGIE. I could see she likes you.

MARTY. Yeah, sure.

ANGIE *(half rising in his seat).* I'll call her up.

MARTY. You call her up for yourself, Angie. I don't feel like calling her up.

*(*ANGIE *sits down again. They both return to reading the paper for a moment. Then* ANGIE *looks up again)*

ANGIE. Boy, you're getting to be a real drag, you know that?

MARTY. Angie, I'm thirty-six years old. I been looking for a girl every Saturday night of my life. I'm a little, short, fat fellow, and girls don't go for me, that's all. I'm not like you. I mean, you joke around, and they laugh at you, and you get along fine. I just stand around like a bug. What's the sense of kidding myself? Everybody's always telling me to get married. Get married. Get married. Don't you think I wanna get married? I wanna get married. They drive me crazy. Now, I don't wanna wreck your Saturday night for you, Angie.

You wanna go somewhere, you go ahead. I don't wanna go.

ANGIE. Boy, they drive me crazy too. My old lady, every word outta her mouth, when you gonna get married?

MARTY. My mother, boy, she drives me crazy.

(ANGIE *leans back in his seat, scowls at the paper-napkin container.* MARTY *returns to the sports page. For a moment a silence hangs between them. Then . . .*)

ANGIE. So what do you feel like doing tonight?

MARTY (*without looking up*). I don't know. What do you feel like doing?

(*They both just sit,* ANGIE *frowning at the napkin container,* MARTY *at the sports page.*

(*The camera slowly moves away from the booth, looks down the length of the bar, up the wall, past the clock—which reads ten to five—and over to the television screen, where the baseball game is still going on*)

(DISSOLVE SLOWLY TO: *The television screen, now blank. The clock now reads a quarter to six.*

(*Back in the booth,* MARTY *now sits alone. In front of him are three empty beer bottles and a beer glass, half filled. He is sitting there, his face expressionless, but his eyes troubled. Then he pushes himself slowly out of the booth and shuffles to the phone booth; he goes inside, closing the booth door carefully after him. For a moment* MARTY *just sits squatly. Then with some exertion—due to the cramped quarters—he contrives to get a small address book out of his rear pants pocket. He slowly flips through it, finds the page he wants, and studies it, scowling; then he takes a dime from the change he has just received, plunks it into the proper slot, waits for a dial tone . . . then carefully dials a number. . . . He waits. He is beginning to sweat a bit in the hot little booth, and his chest begins to rise and fall deeply*)

MARTY (*with a vague pretense at good diction*). Hello, is this Mary Feeney? . . . Could I please speak to Miss Mary Feeney? . . . Just tell her an old friend . . . (*He waits again. With his free hand he wipes the gathering sweat from his brow*) . . . Oh, hello there, is this Mary Feeney? Hello there, this is Marty Pilletti. I wonder if you recall me . . . Well, I'm kind of a stocky guy. The last time we met was inna movies, the RKO Chester. You was with another girl, and I was with a friend of mine name Angie. This was about a month ago . . . (*The girl apparently doesn't remember him. A sort of panic begins to seize* MARTY. *His voice rises a little*) The RKO Chester on Payne Boulevard. You was sitting in front of us, and we was annoying you, and you got mad, and . . . I'm the fellow who works inna butcher shop . . . come on, you know who I am! . . . That's right, we went to Howard Johnson's and we had hamburgers. You hadda milk shake . . . Yeah, that's right. I'm the stocky one, the heavy-set fellow. . . . Well, I'm glad you recall me, because I hadda swell time that night, and I was just wondering how everything was with you. How's everything? . . . That's swell . . . Yeah, well, I'll tell you why I called . . . I was figuring on taking in a movie tonight, and I was wondering if you

and your friend would care to see a movie tonight with me and my friend . . .
(*His eyes are closed now*) Yeah, tonight. I know it's pretty late to call for a
date, but I didn't know myself till . . . Yeah, I know, well how about . . . Yeah,
I know, well maybe next Saturday night. You free next Saturday night? . . .
Well, how about the Saturday after that? . . . Yeah, I know . . . Yeah . . .
Yeah . . . Oh, I understand, I mean . . . (*He just sits now, his eyes closed,
not really listening. After a moment he returns the receiver to its cradle and
sits, his shoulders slack, his hands resting listlessly in the lap of his spotted
white apron. . . . Then he opens his eyes, straightens himself, pushes the
booth door open, and advances out into the bar. He perches on a stool across
the bar from the bartender, who looks up from his magazine*)

BARTENDER. I hear your kid brother got married last week, Marty.

MARTY (*looking down at his hands on the bar*). Yeah, it was a very nice affair.

BARTENDER. Well, Marty, when you gonna get married?

(MARTY *tenders the bartender a quick scowl, gets off his perch, and starts
for the door—untying his apron as he goes*)

MARTY. If my mother calls up, Lou, tell her I'm on my way home.

(DISSOLVE TO: MARTY's *mother and a young couple sitting around the table in
the dining room of* MARTY's *home. The young couple—we will soon find out—
are* THOMAS, MARTY's *cousin, and his wife,* VIRGINIA. *They have apparently
just been telling the mother some sad news, and the three are sitting around
frowning.*

(*The dining room is a crowded room filled with chairs and lamps, pictures
and little statues, perhaps even a small grotto of little vigil lamps. To the
right of the dining room is the kitchen, old-fashioned, Italian, steaming,
and overcrowded. To the left of the dining room is the living room, furnished
in same fashion as the dining room. Just off the living room is a small bedroom, which is* MARTY's. *This bedroom and the living room have windows
looking out on front. The dining room has windows looking out to side
alleyway. A stairway in the dining room leads to the second floor.*

(*The mother is a round, dark, effusive little woman*)

MOTHER (*after a pause*). Well, Thomas, I knew sooner or later this was gonna
happen. I told Marty, I said: "Marty, you watch. There's gonna be real
trouble over there in your cousin Thomas' house." Because your mother was
here, Thomas, you know?

THOMAS. When was this, Aunt Theresa?

MOTHER. This was one, two, three days ago. Wednesday. Because I went to
the fruit shop on Wednesday, and I came home. And I come arounna back,
and there's your mother sitting onna steps onna porch. And I said: "Catherine, my sister, wadda you doing here?" And she look uppa me, and she
beganna cry.

THOMAS (*to his wife*). Wednesday. That was the day you threw the milk bottle.

MOTHER. That's right. Because I said to her: "Catherine, watsa matter?"
And she said to me: "Theresa, my daughter-in-law, Virginia, she just threw
the milk bottle at me."

VIRGINIA. Well, you see what happen, Aunt Theresa . . .

MOTHER. I know, I know . . .

VIRGINIA. She comes inna kitchen, and she begins poking her head over my shoulder here and poking her head over my shoulder there . . .

MOTHER. I know, I know . . .

VIRGINIA. And she begins complaining about this, and she begins complaining about that. And she got me so nervous, I spilled some milk I was making for the baby. You see, I was making some food for the baby, and . . .

MOTHER. So I said to her, "Catherine . . ."

VIRGINIA. So, she got me so nervous I spilled some milk. So she said: "You're spilling the milk." She says: "Milk costs twenny-four cents a bottle. Wadda you, a banker?" So I said: "Mama, leave me alone, please. You're making me nervous. Go on in the other room and turn on the television set." So then she began telling me how I waste money, and how I can't cook, and how I'm raising my baby all wrong, and she kept talking about these couple of drops of milk I spilt, and I got so mad, I said: "Mama, you wanna see me really spill some milk?" So I took the bottle and threw it against the door. I didn't throw it at her. That's just something she made up. I didn't throw it anywheres near her. Well, of course, alla milk went all over the floor. The whole twenny-four cents. Well, I was sorry right away, you know, but she ran outta the house.

(*Pause*)

MOTHER. Well, I don't know what you want me to do, Virginia. If you want me, I'll go talk to her tonight.

(THOMAS *and* VIRGINIA *suddenly frown and look down at their hands as if of one mind*)

THOMAS. Well, I'll tell you, Aunt Theresa . . .

VIRGINIA. Lemme tell it, Tommy.

THOMAS. Okay.

VIRGINIA (*leaning forward to the mother*). We want you to do a very big favor for us, Aunt Theresa.

MOTHER. Sure.

VIRGINIA. Aunt Theresa, you got this big house here. You got four bedrooms upstairs. I mean, you got this big house just for you and Marty. All your other kids are married and got their own homes. And I thought maybe Tommy's mother could come here and live with you and Marty.

MOTHER. Well . . .

VIRGINIA. She's miserable living with Tommy and me, and you're the only one that gets along with her. Because I called up Tommy's brother, Joe, and I said: "Joe, she's driving me crazy. Why don't you take her for a couple of years?" And he said: "Oh, no!" I know I sound like a terrible woman . . .

MOTHER. No, Virginia, I know how you feel. My husband, may God bless his memory, his mother, she lived with us for a long time, and I know how you feel.

VIRGINIA (*practically on the verge of tears*). I just can't stand it no more!

Every minute of the day! Do this! Do that! I don't have ten minutes alone with my husband! We can't even have a fight! We don't have no privacy! Everybody's miserable in our house!

THOMAS. All right, Ginnie, don't get so excited.

MOTHER. She's right. She's right. Young husband and wife, they should have their own home. And my sister, Catherine, she's my sister, but I gotta admit, she's an old goat. And plenny-a times in my life I feel like throwing the milk bottle at her myself. And I tell you now, as far as I'm concerned, if Catherine wantsa come live here with me and Marty, it's all right with me. (VIRGINIA *promptly bursts into tears*)

THOMAS (*not far from tears himself, lowers his face*). That's very nice-a you, Aunt Theresa.

MOTHER. We gotta ask Marty, of course, because this is his house too. But he's gonna come home any minute now.

VIRGINIA (*having mastered her tears*). That's very nice-a you, Aunt Theresa.

MOTHER (*rising*). Now, you just sit here. I'm just gonna turn onna small fire under the food. (*She exits into the kitchen*)

VIRGINIA (*calling after her*). We gotta go right away because I promised the baby sitter we'd be home by six, and it's after six now . . .

(*She kind of fades out. A moment of silence.* THOMAS *takes out a cigarette and lights it*)

THOMAS (*calling to his aunt in the kitchen*). How's Marty been lately, Aunt Theresa?

MOTHER (*off in kitchen*). Oh, he's fine. You know a nice girl he can marry? (*She comes back into the dining room, wiping her hands on a kitchen towel*) I'm worried about him, you know? He's thirty-six years old, gonna be thirty-seven in January.

THOMAS. Oh, he'll get married, don't worry, Aunt Theresa.

MOTHER (*sitting down again*). Well, I don't know. You know a place where he can go where he can find a bride?

THOMAS. The Waverly Ballroom. That's a good place to meet girls, Aunt Theresa. That's a kind of big dance hall, Aunt Theresa. Every Saturday night, it's just loaded with girls. It's a nice place to go. You pay seventy-seven cents. It used to be seventy-seven cents. It must be about a buck and a half now. And you go in and you ask some girl to dance. That's how I met Virginia. Nice, respectable place to meet girls. You tell Marty, Aunt Theresa, you tell him: "Go to the Waverly Ballroom. It's loaded with tomatoes."

MOTHER (*committing the line to memory*). The Waverly Ballroom. It's loaded with tomatoes.

THOMAS. Right.

VIRGINIA. You tell him, go to the Waverly Ballroom.

(*There is the sound of a door being unlatched off through the kitchen. The mother promptly rises*)

MOTHER. He's here. (*She hurries into the kitchen. At the porch entrance to the* kitchen, MARTY *has just come in. He is closing the door behind him. He carries his butcher's apron in a bundle under his arm*)

MARTY. Hello, Ma.

(*She comes up to him, lowers her voice to a whisper*)

MOTHER (*whispers*). Marty, Thomas and Virginia are here. They had another big fight with your Aunt Catherine. So they ask me, would it be all right if Catherine come to live with us. So I said, all right with me, but we have to ask you. Marty, she's a lonely old lady. Nobody wants her. Everybody's throwing her outta their house. . . .

MARTY. Sure, Ma, it's okay with me.

(*The mother's face breaks into a fond smile. She reaches up and pats his cheek with genuine affection*)

MOTHER. You gotta good heart. (*Turning and leading the way back to the dining room.* THOMAS *has risen*) He says okay, it's all right Catherine comes here.

THOMAS. Oh, Marty, thanks a lot. That really takes a load offa my mind.

MARTY. Oh, we got plenny-a room here.

MOTHER. Sure! Sure! It's gonna be nice! It's gonna be nice! I'll come over tonight to your house, and I talk to Catherine, and you see, everything is gonna work out all right.

THOMAS. I just wanna thank you people again because the situation was just becoming impossible.

MOTHER. Siddown, Thomas, siddown. All right, Marty, siddown. . . . (*She exits into the kitchen*)

(MARTY *has taken his seat at the head of the table and is waiting to be served.* THOMAS *takes a seat around the corner of the table from him and leans across to him*)

THOMAS. You see, Marty, the kinda thing that's been happening in our house is Virginia was inna kitchen making some food for the baby. Well, my mother comes in, and she gets Virginia so nervous, she spills a couple-a drops . . .

VIRGINIA (*tugging at her husband*). Tommy, we gotta go. I promise the baby sitter six o'clock.

THOMAS (*rising without interrupting his narrative*). So she starts yelling at Virginia, waddaya spilling the milk for. So Virginia gets mad . . . (*His wife is slowly pulling him to the kitchen door*) She says, "You wanna really see me spill milk?" So Virginia takes the bottle and she throws it against the wall. She's got a real Italian temper, my wife, you know that . . . (*He has been tugged to the kitchen door by now*)

VIRGINIA. Marty, I don't have to tell you how much we appreciate what your mother and you are doing for us.

THOMAS. All right, Marty, I'll see you some other time . . . I'll tell you all about it.

MARTY. I'll see you, Tommy.

(THOMAS *disappears into the kitchen after his wife*)

VIRGINIA (*off, calling*). Good-by, Marty!

(*Close in on* MARTY, *sitting at table*)

MARTY. Good-by, Virginia! See you soon! (*He folds his hands on the table before him and waits to be served*)

(*The mother enters from the kitchen. She sets the meat plate down in front of him and herself takes a chair around the corner of the table from him.* MARTY *without a word takes up his knife and fork and attacks the mountain of food in front of him. His mother sits quietly, her hands a little nervous on the table before her, watching him eat. Then . . .*)

MOTHER. So what are you gonna do tonight, Marty?

MARTY. I don't know, Ma. I'm all knocked out. I may just hang arounna house.

(*The mother nods a couple of times. There is a moment of silence. Then . . .*)

MOTHER. Why don't you go to the Waverly Ballroom?

(*This gives* MARTY *pause. He looks up*)

MARTY. What?

MOTHER. I say, why don't you go to the Waverly Ballroom? It's loaded with tomatoes.

(MARTY *regards his mother for a moment*)

MARTY. It's loaded with what?

MOTHER. Tomatoes.

MARTY (*snorts*). Ha! Who told you about the Waverly Ballroom?

MOTHER. Thomas, he told me it was a very nice place.

MARTY. Oh, Thomas. Ma, it's just a big dance hall, and that's all it is. I been there a hundred times. Loaded with tomatoes. Boy, you're funny, Ma.

MOTHER. Marty, I don't want you hang arounna house tonight. I want you to go take a shave and go out and dance.

MARTY. Ma, when are you gonna give up? You gotta bachelor on your hands. I ain't never gonna get married.

MOTHER. You gonna get married.

MARTY. Sooner or later, there comes a point in a man's life when he gotta face some facts, and one fact I gotta face is that whatever it is that women like, I ain't got it. I chased enough girls in my life. I went to enough dances. I got hurt enough. I don't wanna get hurt no more. I just called a girl this afternoon, and I got a real brush-off, boy. I figured I was past the point of being hurt, but that hurt. Some stupid woman who I didn't even wanna call up. She gave me the brush. That's the history of my life. I don't wanna go to the Waverly Ballroom because all that ever happened to me there was girls made me feel like I was a bug. I got feelings, you know. I had enough pain. No, thank you.

MOTHER. Marty . . .

MARTY. Ma, I'm gonna stay home and watch Sid Caesar.

MOTHER. You gonna die without a son.

MARTY. So I'll die without a son.

MOTHER. Put on your blue suit . . .

MARTY. Blue suit, gray suit, I'm still a fat little man. A fat little ugly man.

MOTHER. You not ugly.

MARTY (*his voice rising*). I'm ugly . . . I'm ugly! . . . I'm UGLY!

MOTHER. Marty . . .

MARTY (*crying aloud, more in anguish than in anger*). Ma! Leave me alone!
. . . (*He stands abruptly, his face pained and drawn. He makes half-
formed gestures to his mother, but he can't find words at the moment.
He turns and marches a few paces away, turns to his mother again*) Ma,
waddaya want from me?! Waddaya want from me?! I'm miserable enough as
it is! Leave me alone! I'll go to the Waverly Ballroom! I'll put onna blue suit
and I'll go! And you know what I'm gonna get for my trouble? Heartache! A
big night of heartache! (*He sullenly marches back to his seat, sits down, picks
up his fork, plunges it into the lasagna, and stuffs a mouthful into his mouth;
he chews vigorously for a moment. It is impossible to remain angry for long.
After a while he is shaking his head and muttering*) Loaded with tomatoes . . .
boy, that's rich . . . (*He plunges his fork in again. Camera pulls slowly away
from him and his mother, who is seated—watching him*)

FADE OUT.

Act II

FADE IN: *Exterior, three-story building. Pan up to second floor . . . bright neon
lights reading "Waverly Ballroom" . . . The large, dirty windows are open;
and the sound of a fair-to-middling swing band whooping it up comes out.*

DISSOLVE TO: *Interior, Waverly Ballroom—large dance floor crowded with
jitterbugging couples, eight-piece combination hitting a loud kick. Ballroom
is vaguely dark, made so by papier-mâché over the chandeliers to create
alleged romantic effect. The walls are lined with stags and waiting girls,
singly and in small murmuring groups. Noise and mumble and drone.*

DISSOLVE TO: *Live shot—a row of stags along a wall. Camera is looking lengthwise down the row. Camera dollies slowly past each face, each staring out at
the dance floor, watching in his own manner of hungry eagerness. Short, fat,
tall, thin stags. Some pretend diffidence. Some exhibit patent hunger.*

Near the end of the line, we find MARTY *and* ANGIE, *freshly shaved and groomed.
They are leaning against the wall, smoking, watching their more fortunate
brethren out on the floor.*

ANGIE. Not a bad crowd tonight, you know?

MARTY. There was one nice-looking one there in a black dress and beads,
but she was a little tall for me.

ANGIE (*looking down past* MARTY *along the wall right into the camera*). There's
a nice-looking little short one for you right now.

MARTY (*following his gaze*). Where?

ANGIE. Down there. That little one there.

(*The camera cuts about eight faces down, to where the girls are now standing.
Two are against the wall. One is facing them, with her back to the dance
floor. This last is the one* ANGIE *has in mind. She is a cute little kid, about
twenty, and she has a bright smile on—as if the other two girls are just
amusing her to death*)

MARTY. Yeah, she looks all right from here.

ANGIE. Well, go on over and ask her. You don't hurry up, somebody else'll grab her.

(MARTY *scowls, shrugs*)

MARTY. Okay, let's go.

(*They slouch along past the eight stags, a picture of nonchalant unconcern. The three girls, aware of their approach, stiffen, and their chatter comes to a halt.* ANGIE *advances to one of the girls along the wall*)

ANGIE. Waddaya say, you wanna dance?

(*The girl looks surprised—as if this were an extraordinary invitation to receive in this place—looks confounded at her two friends, shrugs, detaches herself from the group, moves to the outer fringe of the pack of dancers, raises her hand languidly to dancing position, and awaits* ANGIE *with ineffable boredom.* MARTY, *smiling shyly, addresses the short girl*)

MARTY. Excuse me, would you care for this dance?

(*The short girl gives* MARTY *a quick glance of appraisal, then looks quickly at her remaining friend*)

SHORT GIRL (*not unpleasantly*). Sorry. I just don't feel like dancing just yet.

MARTY. Sure. (*He turns and moves back past the eight stags, all of whom have covertly watched his attempt. He finds his old niche by the wall, leans there. A moment later he looks guardedly down to where the short girl and her friend are. A young, dapper boy is approaching the short girl. He asks her to dance. The short girl smiles, excuses herself to her friend, and follows the boy out onto the floor.* MARTY *turns back to watching the dancers bleakly. A moment later he is aware that someone on his right is talking to him. . . . He turns his head. It is a young man of about twenty-eight*) You say something to me?

YOUNG MAN. Yeah. I was just asking you if you was here stag or with a girl.

MARTY. I'm stag.

YOUNG MAN. Well, I'll tell you. I got stuck onna blind date with a dog, and I just picked up a nice chick, and I was wondering how I'm gonna get ridda the dog. Somebody to take her home, you know what I mean? I be glad to pay you five bucks if you take the dog home for me.

MARTY (*a little confused*). What?

YOUNG MAN. I'll take you over, and I'll introduce you as an old army buddy of mine, and then I'll cut out. Because I got this chick waiting for me out by the hatcheck, and I'll pay you five bucks.

MARTY (*stares at the young man*). Are you kidding?

YOUNG MAN. No, I'm not kidding.

MARTY. You can't just walk off onna girl like that.

(*The young man grimaces impatiently and moves down the line of stags. . . .* MARTY *watches him, still a little shocked at the proposition. About two stags down, the young man broaches his plan to another stag. This stag, frowning and pursing his lips, seems more receptive to the idea. . . . The young man takes out a wallet and gives the stag a five-dollar bill. The stag detaches himself from the wall and, a little ill at ease, follows the young man back past* MARTY *and into the lounge.* MARTY *pauses a moment and then, concerned, walks to the archway that separates the lounge from the ball-room and looks in.*

(The lounge is a narrow room with a bar and booths. In contrast to the ball-room, it is brightly lighted—causing MARTY *to squint.*

(In the second booth from the archway sits a girl, about twenty-eight. Despite the careful grooming that she has put into her cosmetics, she is blatantly plain. The young man and the stag are standing, talking to her. She is looking up at the young man, her hands nervously gripping her Coca-Cola glass. We cannot hear what the young man is saying, but it is apparent that he is introducing his new-found army buddy and is going through some cock-and-bull story about being called away on an emergency. The stag is presented as her escort-to-be, who will see to it that she gets home safely. The girl apparently is not taken in at all by this, though she is trying hard not to seem affected.

(She politely rejects the stag's company and will get home by herself, thanks for asking anyway. The young man makes a few mild protestations, and then he and the stag leave the booth and come back to the archway from where MARTY *has been watching the scene. As they pass* MARTY, *we overhear a snatch of dialogue)*

YOUNG MAN. . . . In that case, as long as she's going home alone, give me the five bucks back. . . .

STAG. . . . Look, Mac, you paid me five bucks. I was willing. It's my five bucks. . . .

(They pass on. MARTY *returns his attention to the girl. She is still sitting as she was, gripping and ungripping the glass of Coca-Cola in front of her. Her eyes are closed. Then, with a little nervous shake of her head, she gets out of the booth and stands—momentarily at a loss for what to do next. The open fire doors leading out onto the large fire escape catch her eye. She crosses to the fire escape, nervous, frowning, and disappears outside.*

*(*MARTY *stares after her, then slowly shuffles to the open fire-escape doorway. It is a large fire escape, almost the size of a small balcony. The girl is standing by the railing, her back to the doorway, her head slunk down on her bosom. For a moment* MARTY *is unaware that she is crying. Then he notices the shivering tremors running through her body and the quivering shoulders. He moves a step onto the fire escape. He tries to think of something to say)*

MARTY. Excuse me, Miss. Would you care to dance?

(The girl slowly turns to him, her face streaked with tears, her lip trembling. Then, in one of those peculiar moments of simultaneous impulse, she lurches to MARTY *with a sob, and* MARTY *takes her to him. For a moment they stand in an awkward embrace,* MARTY *a little embarrassed, looking out through the doors to the lounge, wondering if anybody is seeing them. Reaching back with one hand, he closes the fire doors, and then, replacing the hand around her shoulder, he stands stiffly, allowing her to cry on his chest)*

(DISSOLVE TO: *Exterior, apartment door. The mother is standing, in a black coat and a hat with a little feather, waiting for her ring to be answered. The door opens.* VIRGINIA *stands framed in the doorway*)

VIRGINIA. Hello, Aunt Theresa, come in. (*The mother goes into the small foyer.* VIRGINIA *closes the door*)

MOTHER (*in a low voice, as she pulls her coat off*). Is Catherine here?

VIRGINIA (*helps her off with coat, nods—also in a low voice*). We didn't tell her nothing yet. We thought we'd leave it to you. We thought you'd put it like how you were lonely, and why don't she come to live with you. Because that way it looks like she's doing you a favor, insteada we're throwing her out, and it won't be so cruel on her. Thomas is downstairs with the neighbors . . . I'll go call him.

MOTHER. You go downstairs to the neighbors and stay there with Thomas.

VIRGINIA. Wouldn't it be better if we were here?

MOTHER. You go downstairs. I talk to Catherine alone. Otherwise, she's gonna start a fight with you.

(*A shrill, imperious woman's voice from an off-stage room suddenly breaks into the muttered conference in the foyer*)

AUNT (*off*). Who's there?! Who's there?!

(*The mother heads up the foyer to the living room, followed by* VIRGINIA, *holding the mother's coat*)

MOTHER (*calls back*). It's me, Catherine! How you feel?

(*At the end of the foyer, the two sisters meet. The aunt is a spare, gaunt woman with a face carved out of granite. Tough, embittered, deeply hurt type face*)

AUNT. Hey! What are you doing here?

MOTHER. I came to see you. (*The two sisters quickly embrace and release each other*) How you feel?

AUNT. I gotta pain in my left side and my leg throbs like a drum.

MOTHER. I been getting pains in my shoulder.

AUNT. I got pains in my shoulder, too. I have a pain in my hip, and my right arm aches so much I can't sleep. It's a curse to be old. How you feel?

MOTHER. I feel fine.

AUNT. That's nice.

(*Now that the standard greetings are over,* AUNT CATHERINE *abruptly turns and goes back to her chair. It is obviously her chair. It is an old heavy oaken chair with thick armrests. The rest of the apartment is furnished in what is known as "modern"—a piece from* House Beautiful *here, a piece from* Better Homes and Gardens *there.* AUNT CATHERINE *sits, erect and forbidding, in her chair. The mother seats herself with a sigh in a neighboring chair.* VIRGINIA, *having hung the mother's coat, now turns to the two older women. A pause*)

VIRGINIA. I'm going downstairs to the Cappacini's. I'll be up inna little while.

(AUNT CATHERINE *nods expressionlessly.* VIRGINIA *looks at her for a moment, then impulsively crosses to her mother-in-law*)

VIRGINIA. You feel all right?

(*The old lady looks up warily, suspicious of this sudden solicitude*)

AUNT. I'm all right.

(VIRGINIA *nods and goes off to the foyer. The two old sisters sit, unmoving, waiting for the door to close behind* VIRGINIA. *Then the mother addresses herself to* AUNT CATHERINE)

MOTHER. We gotta post card from my son, Nickie, and his bride this morning. They're in Florida inna big hotel. Everything is very nice.

AUNT. That's nice.

MOTHER. Catherine, I want you come live with me in my house with Marty and me. In my house, you have your own room. You don't have to sleep onna couch inna living room like here. (*The aunt looks slowly and directly at the mother*) Catherine, your son is married. He got his own home. Leave him in peace. He wants to be alone with his wife. They don't want no old lady sitting inna balcony. Come and live with me. We will cook in the kitchen and talk like when we were girls. You are dear to me, and you are dear to Marty. We are pleased for you to come.

AUNT. Did they come to see you?

MOTHER. Yes.

AUNT. Did my son Thomas come with her?

MOTHER. Your son Thomas was there.

AUNT. Did he also say he wishes to cast his mother from his house?

MOTHER. Catherine, don't make an opera outta this. The three-a you anna baby live in three skinny rooms. You are an old goat, and she has an Italian temper. She is a good girl, but you drive her crazy. Leave them alone. They have their own life.

(*The old aunt turns her head slowly and looks her sister square in the face. Then she rises slowly from her chair*)

AUNT (*coldly*). Get outta here. This is my son's house. This is where I live. I am not to be cast out inna street like a newspaper.

(*The mother likewise rises. The two old women face each other directly*)

MOTHER. Catherine, you are very dear to me. We have cried many times together. When my husband died, I would have gone insane if it were not for you. I ask you to come to my house because I can make you happy. Please come to my house.

(*The two sisters regard each other. Then* AUNT CATHERINE *sits again in her oaken chair, and the mother returns to her seat. The hardened muscles in the old aunt's face suddenly slacken, and she turns to her sister*)

AUNT. Theresa, what shall become of me?

MOTHER. Catherine . . .

AUNT. It's gonna happen to you. Mark it well. These terrible years. I'm afraida look inna mirror. I'm afraid I'm gonna see an old lady with white hair, like the old ladies inna park, little bundles inna black shawl, waiting for the coffin. I'm fifty-six years old. What am I to do with myself? I have strength in my hands. I wanna cook. I wanna clean. I wanna make dinner for my children. I wanna be of use to somebody. Am I an old dog to lie in fronta the fire till my eyes close? These are terrible years, Theresa! Terrible years!

MOTHER. Catherine, my sister . . .

(*The old aunt stares, distraught, at the mother*)

AUNT. It's gonna happen to you! It's gonna happen to you! What will you do if Marty gets married?! What will you cook?! What happen to alla children tumbling in alla rooms?! Where is the noise?! It is a curse to be a widow! A curse! What will you do if Marty gets married?! What will you do?!

(*She stares at the mother—her deep, gaunt eyes haggard and pained. The mother stares back for a moment, then her own eyes close. The aunt has hit home. The aunt sinks back onto her chair, sitting stiffly, her arms on the thick armrests. The mother sits hunched a little forward, her hands nervously folded in her lap*)

AUNT (*quietly*). I will put my clothes inna bag and I will come to you tomorrow.

(*The camera slowly dollies back from the two somber sisters.*

SLOW FADE-OUT.

(CUT TO: *Close-up, intimate,* MARTY *and the girl dancing cheek to cheek. Occasionally the heads of other couples slowly waft across the camera view, temporarily blocking out view of* MARTY *and the girl. Camera stays with them as the slow dance carries them around the floor. Tender scene*)

GIRL. . . . The last time I was here the same sort of thing happened.

MARTY. Yeah?

GIRL. Well, not exactly the same thing. The last time I was up here was about four months ago. Do you see that girl in the gray dress sitting over there?

MARTY. Yeah.

GIRL. That's where I sat. I sat there for an hour and a half without moving a muscle. Now and then, some fellow would sort of walk up to me and then change his mind. I just sat there, my hands in my lap. Well, about ten o'clock, a bunch of kids came in swaggering. They weren't more than seventeen, eighteen years old. Well, they swaggered down along the wall, leering at all the girls. I thought they were kind of cute . . . and as they passed me, I smiled at them. One of the kids looked at me and said: "Forget it, ugly, you ain't gotta chance." I burst out crying. I'm a big crier, you know.

MARTY. So am I.

GIRL. And another time when I was in college . . .

MARTY. I cry alla time. Any little thing. I can recognize pain a mile away. My brothers, my brother-in-laws, they're always telling me what a goodhearted guy I am. Well, you don't get goodhearted by accident. You get kicked around long enough you get to be a real professor of pain. I know exactly how you feel. And I also want you to know I'm having a very good time with you now and really enjoying myself. So you see, you're not such a dog as you think you are.

GIRL. I'm having a very good time too.

MARTY. So there you are. So I guess I'm not such a dog as I think I am.

GIRL. You're a very nice guy, and I don't know why some girl hasn't grabbed you off long ago.

MARTY. I don't know either. I think I'm a very nice guy. I also think I'm a pretty smart guy in my own way.

GIRL. I think you are.

MARTY. I'll tell you some of my wisdom which I thunk up on those nights when I got stood up, and nights like that, and you walk home thinking: "Watsa matter with me? I can't be that ugly." Well, I figure, two people get married, and they gonna live together forty, fifty years. So it's just gotta be more than whether they're good-looking or not. My father was a real ugly man, but my mother adored him. She told me that she used to get so miserable sometimes, like everybody, you know? And she says my father always tried to understand. I used to see them sometimes when I was a kid, sitting in the living room, talking and talking, and I used to adore my old man because he was so kind. That's one of the most beautiful things I have in my life, the way my father and my mother were. And my father was a real ugly man. So it don't matter if you look like a gorilla. So you see, dogs like us, we ain't such dogs as we think we are.

(*They dance silently for a moment, cheeks pressed against each other. Close-ups of each face*)

GIRL. I'm twenty-nine years old. How old are you?

MARTY. Thirty-six.

(*They dance silently, closely. Occasionally the heads of other couples sway in front of the camera, blocking our view of* MARTY *and the girl. Slow, sweet dissolve.*

(DISSOLVE TO: *Interior, kitchen,* MARTY's *home. Later that night. It is dark. Nobody is home. The rear porch door now opens, and the silhouettes of* MARTY *and the girl appear—blocking up the doorway*)

MARTY. Wait a minute. Lemme find the light. (*He finds the light. The kitchen is suddenly brightly lit. The two of them stand squinting to adjust to the sudden glare*) I guess my mother ain't home yet. I figure my cousin Thomas and Virginia musta gone to the movies, so they won't get back till one o'clock, at least.

(*The girl has advanced into the kitchen, a little ill at ease, and is looking around.* MARTY *closes the porch door*)

MARTY. This is the kitchen.

GIRL. Yes, I know.

(MARTY *leads the way into the dining room*)

MARTY. Come on inna dining room. (*He turns on the light in there as he goes. The girl follows him in*) Siddown, take off your coat. You want something to eat? We gotta whole halfa chicken left over from yesterday.

GIRL (*perching tentatively on the edge of a chair*). No, thank you. I don't think I should stay very long.

MARTY. Sure. Just take off your coat a minute.

(*He helps her off with her coat and stands for a moment behind her, looking down at her. Conscious of his scrutiny, she sits uncomfortably, her breasts rising and falling unevenly.* MARTY *takes her coat into the dark living room. The girl sits patiently, nervously.* MARTY *comes back, sits down on another chair. Awkward silence*)

MARTY. So I was telling you, my kid brother Nickie got married last Sunday. . . . That was a very nice affair. And they had this statue of some woman, and they had whisky spouting outta her mouth. I never saw anything so grand in my life. (*The silence falls between them again*) And watta meal. I'm a butcher, so I know a good hunka steak when I see one. That was choice filet, right off the toppa the chuck. A buck-eighty a pound. Of course, if you wanna cheaper cut, get rib steak. That gotta lotta waste on it, but it comes to about a buck and a quarter a pound, if it's trimmed. Listen, Clara, make yourself comfortable. You're all tense.

GIRL. Oh, I'm fine.

MARTY. You want me to take you home, I'll take you home.

GIRL. Maybe that would be a good idea.

(*She stands. He stands, frowning, a little angry—turns sullenly and goes back into the living room for her coat. She stands unhappily. He comes back and wordlessly starts to help her into her coat. He stands behind her, his hands on her shoulders. He suddenly seizes her, begins kissing her on the neck. Camera comes up quickly to intensely intimate close-up, nothing but the heads. The dialogue drops to quick, hushed whispers*)

GIRL. No, Marty, please . . .

MARTY. I like you, I like you, I been telling you all night I like you . . .

GIRL. Marty . . .

MARTY. I just wanna kiss, that's all . . . (*He tries to turn her face to him. She resists*)

GIRL. No . . .

MARTY. Please . . .

GIRL. No . . .

MARTY. Please . . .

GIRL. Marty . . .

(*He suddenly releases her, turns away violently*)

MARTY (*crying out*). All right! I'll take you home! All right! (*He marches a few angry paces away, deeply disturbed. Turns to her*) All I wanted was a lousy kiss! What am I, a leper or something?! (*He turns and goes off into the living room to hide the flush of hot tears threatening to fill his eyes. The girl stands, herself on the verge of tears*)

GIRL (*mutters, more to herself than to him*). I just didn't feel like it, that's all. (*She moves slowly to the archway leading to the living room.* MARTY *is sitting on the couch, hands in his lap, looking straight ahead. The room is dark except for the overcast of the dining-room light reaching in. The girl goes to the couch, perches on the edge beside him. He doesn't look at her*)

MARTY. Well, that's the history of my life. I'm a little, short, fat, ugly guy. Comes New Year's Eve, everybody starts arranging parties, I'm the guy they gotta dig up a date for. I'm old enough to know better. Let me get a packa cigarettes, and I'll take you home. (*He starts to rise, but doesn't . . . sinks back onto the couch, looking straight ahead. The girl looks at him, her face peculiarly soft and compassionate*)

GIRL. I'd like to see you again, very much. The reason I didn't let you kiss me was because I just didn't know how to handle the situation. You're the kindest man I ever met. The reason I tell you this is because I want to see you again very much. Maybe, I'm just so desperate to fall in love that I'm trying too hard. But I know that when you take me home, I'm going to just lie on my bed and think about you. I want very much to see you again.

(MARTY *stares down at his hands in his lap*)

MARTY (*without looking at her*). Waddaya doing tomorrow night?

GIRL. Nothing.

MARTY. I'll call you up tomorrow morning. Maybe we'll go see a movie.

GIRL. I'd like that very much.

MARTY. The reason I can't be definite about it now is my Aunt Catherine is probably coming over tomorrow, and I may have to help out.

GIRL. I'll wait for your call.

MARTY. We better get started to your house because the buses only run about one an hour now.

GIRL. All right. (*She stands*)

MARTY. I'll just get a packa cigarettes.

(*He goes into his bedroom. We can see him through the doorway, opening his bureau drawer and extracting a pack of cigarettes. He comes out again and looks at the girl for the first time. They start to walk to the dining room. In the archway,* MARTY *pauses, turns to the girl*)

MARTY. Waddaya doing New Year's Eve?

GIRL. Nothing.

(*They quietly slip into each other's arms and kiss. Slowly their faces part, and* MARTY's *head sinks down upon her shoulder. He is crying. His shoulders shake slightly. The girl presses her cheek against the back of his head. They stand . . . there is the sound of the rear porch door being unlatched. They both start from their embrace. A moment later the mother's voice is heard off in the kitchen*)

MOTHER. Hallo! Hallo, Marty? (*She comes into the dining room, stops at the sight of the girl*) Hallo, Marty, when you come home?

MARTY. We just got here about fifteen minutes ago, Ma. Ma, I want you to meet Miss Clara Davis. She's a graduate of New York University. She teaches history in Benjamin Franklin High School.

(*This seems to impress the mother*)

MOTHER. Siddown, siddown. You want some chicken? We got some chicken in the icebox.

GIRL. No, Mrs. Pilletti, we were just going home. Thank you very much anyway.

MOTHER. Well, siddown a minute. I just come inna house. I'll take off my coat. Siddown a minute. (*She pulls her coat off*)

MARTY. How'd you come home, Ma? Thomas give you a ride?
(*The mother nods*)
MOTHER. Oh, it's a sad business, a sad business. (*She sits down on a dining-room chair, holding her coat in her lap. She turns to the girl, who likewise sits*)
MOTHER. My sister Catherine, she don't get along with her daughter-in-law, so she's gonna come live with us.
MARTY. Oh, she's coming, eh, Ma?
MOTHER. Oh, sure. (*To the girl*) It's a very sad thing. A woman, fifty-six years old, all her life, she had her own home. Now, she's just an old lady, sleeping on her daughter-in-law's couch. It's a curse to be a mother, I tell you. Your children grow up and then what is left for you to do? What is a mother's life but her children? It is a very cruel thing when your son has no place for you in his home.
GIRL. Couldn't she find some sort of hobby to fill out her time?
MOTHER. Hobby! What can she do? She cooks and she cleans. You gotta have a house to clean. You gotta have children to cook for. These are the terrible years for a woman, the terrible years.
GIRL. You mustn't feel too harshly against her daughter-in-law. She also wants to have a house to clean and a family to cook for.
(*The mother darts a quick, sharp look at the girl—then looks back to her hands, which are beginning to twist nervously*)
MOTHER. You don't think my sister Catherine should live in her daughter-in-law's house?
GIRL. Well, I don't know the people, of course, but, as a rule, I don't think a mother-in-law should live with a young couple.
MOTHER. Where do you think a mother-in-law should go?
GIRL. I don't think a mother should depend so much upon her children for her rewards in life.
MOTHER. That's what it says in the book in New York University. You wait till you are a mother. It don't work out that way.
GIRL. Well, it's silly for me to argue about it. I don't know the people involved.
MARTY. Ma, I'm gonna take her home now. It's getting late, and the buses only run about one an hour.
MOTHER (*standing*). Sure.
(*The girl stands*)
GIRL. It was very nice meeting you, Mrs. Pilletti. I hope I'll see you again.
MOTHER. Sure.
(MARTY *and the girl move to the kitchen*)
MARTY. All right, Ma. I'll be back in about an hour.
MOTHER. Sure.
GIRL. Good night, Mrs. Pilletti.
MOTHER. Good night.
(MARTY *and the girl exit into the kitchen. The mother stands, expressionless, by her chair watching them go. She remains standing rigidly even after the*

porch door can be heard being opened and shut. The camera moves up to a close-up of the mother. Her eyes are wide. She is staring straight ahead. There is fear in her eyes)

FADE OUT.

Act III

FADE IN: *Film—close-up of church bells clanging away. Pan down church to see typical Sunday morning, people going up the steps of a church and entering. It is a beautiful June morning.*

DISSOLVE TO: *Interior,* MARTY's *bedroom—sun fairly streaming through the curtains.* MARTY *is standing in front of his bureau, slipping his arms into a clean white shirt. He is freshly shaved and groomed. Through the doorway of his bedroom we can see the mother in the dining room, in coat and hat, all set to go to Mass, taking the last breakfast plates away and carrying them into the kitchen. The camera moves across the living room into the dining room. The mother comes out of the kitchen with a paper napkin and begins crumbing the table.*

There is a knock on the rear porch door. The mother leaves her crumbing and goes into the kitchen. Camera goes with her. She opens the rear door to admit AUNT CATHERINE, *holding a worn old European carpetbag. The aunt starts to go deeper into the kitchen, but the mother stays her with her hand.*

MOTHER *(in low, conspiratorial voice).* Hey, I come home from your house last night, Marty was here with a girl.

AUNT. Who?

MOTHER. Marty.

AUNT. Your son Marty?

MOTHER. Well, what Marty you think is gonna be here in this house with a girl?

AUNT. Were the lights on?

MOTHER. Oh, sure. *(Frowns suddenly at her sister)* The girl is a college graduate.

AUNT. They're the worst. College girls are one step from the streets. They smoke like men inna saloon. *(The aunt puts her carpetbag down and sits on one of the wooden kitchen chairs. The mother sits on another)*

MOTHER. That's the first time Marty ever brought a girl to this house. She seems like a nice girl. I think he has a feeling for this girl.

(At this moment a burst of spirited whistling emanates from MARTY's *bedroom.*

*(*CUT TO: MARTY's *bedroom—*MARTY *standing in front of his mirror, buttoning his shirt or adjusting his tie, whistling a gay tune.*

*(*CUT BACK TO: *The two sisters, both their faces turned in the direction of the whistling. The whistling abruptly stops. The two sisters look at each other. The aunt shrugs)*

MOTHER. He been whistling like that all morning.

(The aunt nods bleakly)

AUNT. He is bewitched. You will see. Today, tomorrow, inna week, he's gonna say to you: "Hey, Ma, it's no good being a single man. I'm tired running around." Then he's gonna say: "Hey, Ma, wadda we need this old house? Why don't we sell this old house, move into a nicer parta town? A nice little apartment?"

MOTHER. I don't sell this house, I tell you that. This is my husband's house, and I had six children in this house.

AUNT. You will see. A couple-a months, you gonna be an old lady, sleeping onna couch in your daughter-in-law's house.

MOTHER. Catherine, you are a blanket of gloom. Wherever you go, the rain follows. Some day, you gonna smile, and we gonna declare a holiday.

(*Another burst of spirited whistling comes from* MARTY, *off. It comes closer, and* MARTY *now enters in splendid spirits, whistling away. He is slipping into his jacket*)

MARTY (*ebulliently*). Hello, Aunt Catherine! How are you? You going to Mass with us?

AUNT. I was at Mass two hours ago.

MARTY. Well, make yourself at home. The refrigerator is loaded with food. Go upstairs, take any room you want. It's beautiful outside, ain't it?

AUNT. There's a chill. Watch out, you catch a good cold and pneumonia.

MOTHER. My sister Catherine, she can't even admit it's a beautiful day.

(MARTY—*now at the sink, getting himself a glass of water—is examining a piece of plaster that has fallen from the ceiling*)

MARTY (*examining the chunk of plaster in his palm*). Boy, this place is really coming to pieces. (*Turns to mother*) You know, Ma, I think, sometime we oughtta sell this place. The plumbing is rusty—everything. I'm gonna have to replaster that whole ceiling now. I think we oughtta get a little apartment somewheres in a nicer parta town. . . . You all set, Ma?

MOTHER. I'm all set. (*She starts for the porch door. She slowly turns and looks at* MARTY, *and then at* AUNT CATHERINE—*who returns her look. Mother and* MARTY *exit*)

(DISSOLVE TO: *Church. The mother comes out of the doors and down a few steps to where* MARTY *is standing, enjoying the clearness of the June morning*)

MOTHER. In a couple-a minutes nine o'clock Mass is gonna start—in a couple-a minutes . . . (*To passers-by off*) hallo, hallo . . . (*To* MARTY) Well, that was a nice girl last night, Marty. That was a nice girl.

MARTY. Yeah.

MOTHER. She wasn't a very good-looking girl, but she look like a nice girl. I said, she wasn't a very good-looking girl, not very pretty.

MARTY. I heard you, Ma.

MOTHER. She look a little old for you, about thirty-five, forty years old?

MARTY. She's twenny-nine, Ma.

MOTHER. She's more than twenny-nine years old, Marty. That's what she tells you. She looks thirty-five, forty. She didn't look Italian to me. I said, is she an Italian girl?

MARTY. I don't know. I don't think so.

MOTHER. She don't look like Italian to me. What kinda family she come from? There was something about her I don't like. It seems funny, the first time you meet her she comes to your empty house alone. These college girls, they all one step from the streets.

(MARTY *turns, frowning, to his mother*)

MARTY. What are you talkin' about? She's a nice girl.

MOTHER. I don't like her.

MARTY. You don't like her? You only met her for two minutes.

MOTHER. Don't bring her to the house no more.

MARTY. What didn't you like about her?

MOTHER. I don't know! She don't look like Italian to me, plenty nice Italian girls around.

MARTY. Well, let's not get into a fight about it, Ma. I just met the girl. I probably won't see her again. (MARTY *leaves frame*)

MOTHER. Eh, I'm no better than my sister Catherine.

(DISSOLVE TO: *Interior, the bar . . . about an hour later. The after-Mass crowd is there, about six men ranging from twenty to forty. A couple of women in the booths. One woman is holding a glass of beer in one hand and is gently rocking a baby carriage with the other.*

(*Sitting in the booth of Act I are* ANGIE *and three other fellows, ages twenty, thirty-two, and forty. One of the fellows, aged thirty-two, is giving a critical résumé of a recent work of literature by Mickey Spillane*)

CRITIC. . . . So the whole book winds up, Mike Hammer, he's inna room there with this doll. So he says: "You rat, you are the murderer." So she begins to con him, you know? She tells him how she loves him. And then Bam! He shoots her in the stomach. So she's laying there, gasping for breath, and she says: "How could you do that?" And he says: "It was easy."

TWENTY-YEAR-OLD. Boy, that Mickey Spillane. Boy, he can write.

ANGIE (*leaning out of the booth and looking down the length of the bar, says with some irritation*). What's keeping Marty?

CRITIC. What I like about Mickey Spillane is he knows how to handle women. In one book, he picks up a tomato who gets hit with a car, and she throws a pass at him. And then he meets two beautiful twins, and they throw passes at him. And then he meets some beautiful society leader, and she throws a pass at him, and . . .

TWENTY-YEAR-OLD. Boy, that Mickey Spillane, he sure can write . . .

ANGIE (*looking out, down the bar again*). I don't know watsa matter with Marty.

FORTY-YEAR-OLD. Boy, Angie, what would you do if Marty ever died? You'd die right with him. A couple-a old bachelors hanging to each other like barnacles. There's Marty now.

(ANGIE leans out of the booth)

ANGIE (*calling out*). Hello, Marty, where you been?

(CUT TO: *Front end of the bar.* MARTY *has just come in. He waves back to* ANGIE, *acknowledges another hello from a man by the bar, goes over to the bar, and gets the bartender's attention*)

MARTY. Hello, Lou, gimme change of a half and put a dime in it for a telephone call.

(*The bartender takes the half dollar, reaches into his apron pocket for the change*)

BARTENDER. I hear you was at the Waverly Ballroom last night.

MARTY. Yeah. Angie tell you?

BARTENDER (*picking out change from palm full of silver*). Yeah, I hear you really got stuck with a dog.

(MARTY *looks at him*)

MARTY. She wasn't so bad.

BARTENDER (*extending the change*). Angie says she was a real scrawny-looking thing. Well, you can't have good luck alla time.

(MARTY *takes the change slowly and frowns down at it. He moves down the bar and would make for the telephone booth, but* ANGIE *hails him from the booth*)

ANGIE. Who you gonna call, Marty?

MARTY. I was gonna call that girl from last night, take her to a movie tonight.

ANGIE. Are you kidding?

MARTY. She was a nice girl. I kinda liked her.

ANGIE (*indicating the spot in the booth vacated by the forty-year-old*). Siddown. You can call her later. (MARTY *pauses, frowning, and then shuffles to the booth where* ANGIE *and the other two sit. The critic moves over for* MARTY. *There is an exchange of hellos*)

TWENTY-YEAR-OLD. I gotta girl, she's always asking me to marry her. So I look at that face, and I say to myself: "Could I stand looking at that face for the resta my life?"

CRITIC. Hey, Marty, you ever read a book called *I, the Jury*, by Mickey Spillane?

MARTY. No.

ANGIE. Listen, Marty, I gotta good place for us to go tonight. The kid here, he says, he was downna bazaar at Our Lady of Angels last night and . . .

MARTY. I don't feel like going to the bazaar, Angie. I thought I'd take this girl to a movie.

ANGIE. Boy, you really musta made out good last night.

MARTY. We just talked.

ANGIE. Boy, she must be some talker. She musta been about fifty years old.

CRITIC. I always figger a guy oughtta marry a girl who's twenny years younger than he is, so that when he's forty, his wife is a real nice-looking doll.

TWENTY-YEAR-OLD. That means he'd have to marry the girl when she was one year old.

CRITIC. I never thoughta that.

MARTY. I didn't think she was so bad-looking.

ANGIE. She musta kept you inna shadows all night.

CRITIC. Marty, you don't wanna hang around with dogs. It gives you a bad reputation.

ANGIE. Marty, let's go downna bazaar.

MARTY. I told this dog I was gonna call her today.

ANGIE. Brush her.

(MARTY *looks questioningly at* ANGIE)

MARTY. You didn't like her at all?

ANGIE. A nothing. A real nothing. (MARTY *looks down at the dime he has been nervously turning between two fingers and then, frowning, he slips it into his jacket pocket. He lowers his face and looks down, scowling at his thoughts. Around him, the voices clip along*)

CRITIC. What's playing on Fordham Road? I think there's a good picture in the Loew's Paradise.

ANGIE. Let's go down to Forty-second Street and walk around. We're sure to wind up with something. (*Slowly* MARTY *begins to look up again. He looks from face to face as each speaks*)

CRITIC. I'll never forgive LaGuardia for cutting burlesque outta New York City.

TWENTY-YEAR-OLD. There's burlesque over in Union City. Let's go to Union City . . .

ANGIE. Ah, they're always crowded on Sunday night.

CRITIC. So wadda you figure on doing tonight, Angie?

ANGIE. I don't know. Wadda you figure on doing?

CRITIC. I don't know. (*Turns to the twenty-year-old*) Wadda you figure on doing? (*The twenty-year-old shrugs*)

(*Suddenly* MARTY *brings his fist down on the booth table with a crash. The others turn, startled, toward him.* MARTY *rises in his seat*)

MARTY. "What are you doing tonight?" "I don't know, what are you doing?" Burlesque! Loew's Paradise! Miserable and lonely! Miserable and lonely and stupid! What am I, crazy or something?! I got something good! What am I hanging around with you guys for?! (*He has said this in tones so loud that it attracts the attention of everyone in the bar. A little embarrassed,* MARTY *turns and moves quickly to the phone booth, pausing outside the door to find his dime again.* ANGIE *is out of his seat immediately and hurries after him*)

ANGIE (*a little shocked at* MARTY'S *outburst*). Watsa matter with you?

MARTY (*in a low, intense voice*). You don't like her. My mother don't like her. She's a dog, and I'm a fat, ugly little man. All I know is I had a good time last night. I'm gonna have a good time tonight. If we have enough good times together, I'm going down on my knees and beg that girl to marry me. If we make a party again this New Year's, I gotta date for the party. You don't like her, that's too bad. (*He moves into the booth, sits, turns again to* ANGIE, *smiles*) When you gonna get married, Angie? You're thirty-four years old. All your kid brothers are married. You oughtta be ashamed of yourself. (*Still smiling at his private joke, he puts the dime into the slot and then—with a determined finger—he begins to dial*)

FADE OUT.

Poetry

Poetry has much in common with fiction and drama. This can be seen by the briefest review of those aspects of craftsmanship considered under fiction and drama.

Actions. If anything, the actions in poetry are more diverse than they are in fiction and drama. At one extreme, the poet may do nothing more than observe a duck flying against a crimson evening sky; at the other, he may detail the heroic and bloody activities of a ten-year war. Action is especially important in narrative and epic poetry.

Characterization. Characterization also is a matter of first importance in narrative and epic poetry, and in dramatic monologues like Browning's "My Last Duchess" (p. 1045). Even the lyric poem is concerned with characterization—characterization of the poet.

Setting. Setting, too, exhibits great range. It may be set forth in great detail, as in Coleridge's "The Rime of the Ancient Mariner." Or it may be omitted completely, as in a philosophical poem like Emerson's "Brahma" (p. 1040). Background is especially prominent in lyric poems developing atmosphere or mood. Poe's "The City in the Sea" (p. 1041) is a good example of this.

Language. Clearly, there are certain differences between the ways that poets and prose writers select and arrange their words. In the main, however, these are less marked than many suppose. Expressions like "poetic diction" or "poetic license" have given rise to the notion that poets use a special language. To support this belief one can point to words like "e'er," "thou," and "swain." It is true that at one time poets did employ terms which were not so commonly seen in prose, but there was rarely a significant difference, and today there is—in most poetry—none at all. Miss Marguerite Wilkinson claims in her *New Voices,* "No good poet of today wants a license for any unfair dealings with words." By their employment of words in context, poets often pack more meaning and emotion into them than prose writers do, but the words themselves are familiar ones.

Certainly, too, the function of words in poetry is the same as in prose. They body forth the actions, characters, settings—images of all kinds. They withhold or give emphasis, emotional colorations, and interpretations.

When to these matters of craftsmanship are added their effects in terms of *tone* and *meaning,* and when it is realized that these achievements are substantially the same in poetry as in prose, one may well ask what makes poetry a distinctive literary form. What special characteristics does it have? More specifically, what should one look for in poetry that has not already been encountered in prose? The answer lies especially in five characteristics:

rhythm, sound patterns, compactness, figurativeness, and *emotional intensity,* the last being largely the result of the first four.

RHYTHM

Poetry is distinct from prose not because poetry has rhythm but because it has a more regular rhythm than prose. Traditionally, English poetry (but not Anglo-Saxon) has based its rhythm upon accent. Whereas in prose accented and unaccented syllables occur in irregular fashion throughout a sentence, in poetry they create a relatively regular pattern, or meter.

In English there are four conventional types of meter, each being distinguished from the others by the number and accent of syllables. By far the most popular, and probably the most natural to English expression, is called *iambic.* The basic unit, or foot, of iambic has one unaccented and one accented syllable (⌣ /).

| The shades | of night | were fall | ing fast |

Just the reverse of iambic meter is the *trochaic,* each foot of which contains an accented and an unaccented syllable (/ ⌣). Ordinarily the trochaic rhythm is slower than the iambic, thus creating a heavier and more dignified beat, as in the following example:

| Swift of | foot was | Hia | watha |

Anapestic meter contains in each foot two unaccented syllables and one accented (⌣ ⌣ /). Sprightly and frolicsome in rhythm, this meter is usually best adapted to relatively light subjects.

| For the moon | never beams | without bring | ing me dreams |

Dactylic meter reverses the anapestic (/ ⌣ ⌣). It is considerably slower and often is employed to create a mood of strangeness.

| This is the | forest pri | meval |

"Scanning" a line of poetry consists of seeing what the metrical units are and how many of them occur in the line. A one-foot line is called a monometer line, a two-foot line dimeter, and others in progression up to a seven-foot line are called, respectively, trimeter, tetrameter, pentameter, hexameter, and heptameter. Thus the anapestic line quoted above is a tetrameter, and the dactylic line a trimeter.

Few poets use the same type of foot throughout a poem, since the result would be too monotonous. To achieve variety and, even more important, to achieve emphasis or onamatopoeia, they use *substitute feet.* These may be feet of the sort we have considered (e.g., the trochaic foot in "This is the forest primeval") or they may be feet of a sort used only as substitutes, perhaps the *spondee* ($/\,/$), two accented syllables, or the *pyrrhus* ($\smile\,\smile$), two unaccented syllables. Keats offers an example of the former in the line,

$$\mid \text{The há̆re}\mid \text{límped trém}\mid \text{blíng thróugh}\mid \text{th̆e fró}\mid \text{zĕn grás̆s.}\mid$$

wherein the spondaic second foot serves to emphasize and to imitate the un-even progress of the hare in a stanza describing a bitter chill night.

Many modern poets have come to believe that none of these metrical schemes is adequate for what they have to say. Rhythm, they assert, must be organic, must rise naturally out of mood and content and must not be a regularized system imposed upon them. As a result, they write what is called *free verse*, poetry which follows no systemized metrical pattern. At its worst such poetry seems like nothing so much as bad prose; at its best it achieves a variety and subtlety of rhythm quite beyond the possibilities of the more conventional methods.

SOUND PATTERNS

Corresponding to these accent patterns are certain sound patterns, the most obvious and familiar of which is rhyme. Rhyme adds melody, creates harmony, and gives finish to line endings. Most important, it distinguishes parts of a poem by setting them off from one another. Much great poetry, of course, has been written without rhyme. Though rhyme is valuable and delightful for many reasons, it is not indispensable to all kinds of verse.

Other prominent sound patterns are alliteration, assonance, onomatopoeia, and cacophony. These devices are peculiarly valuable to the poet since they help create the mood which he feels an essential part of his experience. What is especially important to him is that they do this quickly. Notice how in a single line Coleridge gives the sense of a curse simply by repeating the "s" sound until he gets a sustained hiss:

Seven days, seven nights, I saw that curse.

COMPACTNESS

Whereas the prose writer within sensible limits may be as discursive as he wishes, the poet should never be so. Because of the limitation of his form, the poet must choose his material with especial care and screen his language for all useless words. This careful selection and sifting result in compactness and consequently the necessity for thoughtful, sensitive reading.

The poet's purpose is to communicate experience in as vivid and memorable a fashion as possible. If he is a good poet, he is admirably equipped to do this, for he has the faculty of revealing things in relationships which in normal experience are hidden. Especially, he is sensitive to the *quality* of experience.

Let us try to clarify this with a simple example. Undoubtedly, you have had that sore, empty feeling that comes at the time of the death of someone dear to you. You continue with your daily tasks, but your mood is different, and somehow the tasks themselves take on a new quality. Now the poet would be interested in this special quality, and he would try to communicate it by selecting the details which most powerfully suggest it.

To be sure, the prose writer is interested in this, too, but the job of the poet is in many ways a more difficult one. The prose writer may achieve his effect by an accumulation of details—hundreds of them, if he wishes. The poet, however, is held down by the shortness of his form. Possibly he has room for only five details, possibly three, possibly only one. Every detail, therefore, must be selected with utmost care.

Words must be selected with equal care, for, because of the space limitations of the poetic form, poets must try to pack more meaning into words than prose writers do. Often they have words operating at several levels of meaning at the same time. In Whitman's "Passage to India," for example, the word "passage" refers not only to the physical trip to the Orient, but to the race's circling back to the land of its origins, the mind's journey from the world of science to the world of intuitive insight, and the soul's flight to God.

The poet selects his words, again with probably more care than the prose writer, for their connotations, the moods and associations which they stir up. This is not surprising since it is through the connotations of words that the poet can best communicate the quality of his experience within a few lines. He does this, first, by using a great many concrete words. Among concrete words, the poet then chooses those which give him the precise quality that he wants.

What this comes down to is that in poetry compactness with words is not so much a matter of cutting away needless ones as packing the useful ones with all the meaning and emotion possible. Those learning to write freshman themes can, after practice, eliminate deadwood, but only someone highly sensitive to the potentialities of words can make every one count to the utmost.

The implications of all this for the reader are clear. He must realize that competent poetry is too compact for skimming. He must realize that each detail, each word—literally each word—has been selected with care and is important.

FIGURATIVENESS

In the discussion of details under the heading of compactness, no attempt was made to distinguish between the literal and the figurative. This now should be done, since one of the most outstanding characteristics of poetry is its extensive use of metaphors, similes, personifications, and other figures of speech.

Of all these figures, metaphors and similes are by far the most important. Through the images they create, the poet can catch the quality of the experience he is after far more quickly and vividly than he can by describing his thought or his action literally. It is easy to see why this is so. Metaphors and similes are concrete: they create images which appeal to the senses. Therefore, when well chosen they are easily visualized and remembered. When well phrased, they are richly connotative. Being comparisons, they fuse the original experience with other experiences, thus compounding the physical, emotional, and even intellectual values.

All of this would contradict a popular notion that similes and metaphors are extraneous decorations which can be lopped off without undue loss to meaning or emotion. Figures of speech can be such if they are simply tacked on for no purpose other than to show the poet's cleverness. But when well used, they are structural necessities and often are more essential than a literal statement would be. One must constantly keep in mind that the poet is anxious to convey his sense of the meaning and quality of experience and to do it in considerably less space than the prose writer. For this purpose metaphors and similes are indispensable.

Notice how Coleridge conveys the sense of complete inactivity, first by the metaphor "stuck" and second by the simile of the painting:

> Day after day, day after day,
> We stuck, nor breath nor motion:
> As idle as a painted ship
> Upon a painted ocean.

Through another figure, personification, poets can achieve a startling vividness often quite beyond the potentialities of more conventional statements. In "Grass," for example, Sandburg creates an effect that no disquisition on the transitoriness of life could hope to achieve. Here are the first lines:

> Pile the bodies high at Austerlitz and Waterloo.
> Shovel them under and let me work:
> I am the Grass; I cover all.

EMOTIONAL INTENSITY

If rhythm, sound patterns, compactness, and figures of speech are all handled in a craftsmanlike way, the inevitable result is that the poem will make a stronger emotional impact upon the reader than any equivalent passage in prose can do. The truth of this is almost self-evident. Rhythm almost always heightens feelings. Sound patterns add tone values; compactness keeps the material from being thinned out through careless selection or through pale and useless words; figures make the subject vivid and memorable. The most intense realizations of human experiences, therefore, when stated verbally, must almost inevitably find expression in poetry. Prose cannot do them justice.

Except for rhyme, no one of the characteristics discussed here is peculiar to poetry. There is simply a difference in degree. This means that there is no sharp line between prose and poetry. One merges into the other as the rhythm becomes more regular, the imagery more vivid, the statement more compact, and the emotion more intense. A reader cannot measure the difference with a pair of literary calipers, but he can feel it as he reads. It is like a man in love. He cannot measure the difference between his affection for a cousin and that for his fiancée, but he knows it is there, that it is a reality.

Hebrew Lyrics

PSALM 1

Blessed is the man that walketh not in the counsel of the ungodly,
Nor standeth in the way of sinners,
Nor sitteth in the seat of the scornful.
But his delight is in the law of the Lord;
And in his law doth he meditate day and night.   5
And he shall be like a tree planted by the rivers of water,
That bringeth forth his fruit in his season,
His leaf also shall not wither;
And whatsoever he doeth shall prosper.
The ungodly are not so;   10
But are like the chaff which the wind driveth away.
Therefore the ungodly shall not stand in the judgment,
Nor sinners in the congregation of the righteous.
For the Lord knoweth the way of the righteous:
But the way of the ungodly shall perish.   15

PSALM 23

The Lord is my shepherd; I shall not want.
He maketh me to lie down in green pastures;
He leadeth me beside the still waters.
He restoreth my soul:
He leadeth me in the paths of righteousness for his name's sake.   5
Yea, though I walk through the valley of the shadow of death,
I will fear no evil; for thou art with me:

Thy rod and thy staff, they comfort me.
Thou preparest a table before me in the presence of mine enemies:
Thou anointest my head with oil; my cup runneth over.   10
Surely goodness and mercy shall follow me all the days of my life:
And I will dwell in the house of the Lord for ever.

PSALM 24

The earth is the Lord's, and the fulness thereof;
The world, and they that dwell therein.
For he hath founded it upon the seas,
And established it upon the floods.
Who shall ascend into the hill of the Lord?   5
Or who shall stand in his holy place?
He that hath clean hands, and a pure heart;
Who hath not lifted up his soul unto vanity, nor sworn deceitfully.
He shall receive the blessing from the Lord,
And righteousness from the God of his salvation.   10
This is the generation of them that seek him,
That seek thy face, O Jacob.
Lift up your heads, O ye gates;
And be ye lift up, ye everlasting doors:
And the King of glory shall come in.   15
Who is this King of glory?
The Lord strong and mighty,
The Lord mighty in battle.
Lift up your heads, O ye gates;
Even lift them up, ye everlasting doors: 20
And the King of glory shall come in.
Who is this King of glory?
The Lord of hosts,
He is the King of glory.

PSALM 100

Make a joyful noise unto the Lord all ye lands.
Serve the Lord with gladness:
Come before his presence with singing.
Know ye that the Lord he is God:
It is he that hath made us, and not we ourselves;   5

We are his people, and the sheep of his pasture.
Enter into his gates with thanksgiving,
And into his courts with praise:
Be thankful unto him, and bless his name.
For the Lord is good;   10
His mercy is everlasting;
And his truth endureth to all generations.

PSALM 121

I will lift up mine eyes unto the hills:
From whence cometh my help.
My help cometh from the Lord,
Which made heaven and earth.
He will not suffer thy foot to be moved.   5
He that keepeth thee will not slumber.
Behold, he that keepeth Israel
Shall neither slumber nor sleep.
The Lord is thy keeper:
The Lord is thy shade upon thy right hand.   10
The sun shall not smite thee by day,
Nor the moon by night.
The Lord shall preserve thee from all evil;
He shall preserve thy soul.
The Lord shall preserve thy going out and thy coming in,   15
From this time forth and even for evermore.

Ballads

Anonymous

SIR PATRICK SPENS

The king sits in Dunfermline toune
Drinking the blude-red wine:
"O whar will I get guid sailor,
To sail this schip of mine?"

Up and spak an eldern knicht,   5
  Sat at the kings richt kne:
"Sir Patrick Spens is the best sailor
  That sails upon the se."

The king has written a braid letter,
  And signed it wi his hand,   10
And sent it to Sir Patrick Spens,
  Was walking on the sand.

The first line that Sir Patrick red,
  A loud lauch lauched he;
The next line that Sir Patrick red,   15
  The teir blinded his ee.

"O wha is this has don this deid,
  This ill deid don to me,
To send me out this time o' the yeir,
  To sail upon the se!   20

"Mak hast, mak haste, my mirry men all,
  Our guid schip sails the morne":
"O say na sae, my master deir,
  For I feir a deadlie storme.

"Late late yestreen I saw the new moone, 25
  Wi the auld moone in hir arme,
And I feir, I feir, my deir master,
  That we will cum to harme."

O our Scots nobles wer richt laith
  To weet their cork-heild schoone;   30
Bot lang owre a' the play wer playd,
  Thair hats they swam aboone.

O lang, lang may their ladies sit,
  Wi thair fans into their hand,
Or eir they se Sir Patrick Spens   35
  Cum sailing to the land.

O lang, lang may the ladies stand,
  Wi thair gold kems in their hair,
Waiting for thair ain deir lords,
  For they'll see thame na mair.   40

Haf owre, haf owre to Aberdour,
　It's fiftie fadom deip,
And thair lies guid Sir Patrick Spens,
　Wi the Scots lords at his feit.

Anonymous

THE THREE RAVENS

There were three ravens sat on a tree,
　Downe a downe, hay down, hay downe
There were three ravens sat on a tree,
　With a downe
There were three ravens sat on a tree,　　　　　5
They were as blacke as they might be.
　With a downe derrie, derrie, derrie, downe, downe.

The one of them said to his mate,
"Where shall we our breakfast take?"

"Downe in yonder greene field,　　　　　10
There lies a knight slain under his shield.

"His hounds they lie downe at his feete,
So well they can their master keepe.

"His haukes they flie so eagerly,
There's no fowle dare him come nie."　　　　　15

Downe there comes a fallow doe,
As great with yong as she might goe.

She lift up his bloudy hed,
And kist his wounds that were so red.

She got him up upon her backe,　　　　　20
And carried him to earthen lake.

She buried him before the prime,
She was dead herselfe ere even-song time.

God send every gentleman
Such haukes, such hounds, and such a leman.　　　　　25

Anonymous

THE TWA CORBIES

As I was walking all alane,
I heard twa corbies making a mane;
The tane unto the t'other say,
"Where sall we gang and dine to-day?"

"In behint yon auld fail dyke,   5
I wot there lies a new slain knight;
And naebody kens that he lies there,
But his hawk, his hound, and lady fair.

"His hound is to the hunting gane,
His hawk to fetch the wild-fowl hame,   10
His lady's ta'en another mate,
So we may mak our dinner sweet.

"Ye'll sit on his white hause-bane,
And I'll pike out his bonny blue een;
Wi' ae lock o' his gowden hair   15
We'll theek our nest when it grows bare.

"Mony a one for him makes mane,
But nane sall ken where he is gane;
O'er his white banes, when they are bare,
The wind sall blaw for evermair."   20

Anonymous

FRANKIE AND JOHNNY

Frankie and Johnny were lovers, O, how that couple could love.
Swore to be true to each other, true as the stars above.
He was her man, but he done her wrong.

Frankie she was his woman, everybody knows.
She spent one hundred dollars for a suit of Johnny's clothes.   5
He was her man, but he done her wrong.

Frankie and Johnny went walking, Johnny in his bran' new suit,
"O good Lawd," says Frankie, "but don't my Johnny look cute?"
He was her man, but he done her wrong.

Frankie went down to Memphis; she went on the evening train.   10
She paid one hundred dollars for Johnny a watch and chain.
He was her man, but he done her wrong.

Frankie went down to the corner, to buy a glass of beer;
She says to the bartender, "Has my loving man been here?
He is my man; he wouldn't do me wrong."   15

"Ain't going to tell you no story, ain't going to tell you no lie,
I seen your man 'bout an hour ago with a girl named Alice Fry.
If he's your man, he's doing you wrong."

Frankie went back to the hotel, she didn't go there for fun,
Under her long red kimono she toted a forty-four gun.   20
He was her man, he was doing her wrong.

Frankie went down to the hotel, looked in the window so high,
There was her lovin' Johnny a-lovin' up Alice Fry;
He was her man, he was doing her wrong.

Frankie threw back her kimono; took out the old forty-four;   25
Roota-toot-toot, three times she shot, right through that hotel door.
She shot her man, 'cause he done her wrong.

Johnny grabbed off his Stetson. "O good Lawd, Frankie, don't shoot."
But Frankie put her finger on the trigger, and the gun went roota-toot-toot.
He was her man, but she shot him down.   30

"Roll me over easy, roll me over slow,
Roll me over easy, boys, 'cause my wounds is hurting me so,
I was her man, but I done her wrong."

With the first shot Johnny staggered; with the second shot he fell;
When the third bullet hit him, there was a new man's face in hell.   35
He was her man, but he done her wrong.

"Oh, bring on your rubber-tired hearses, bring on your rubber-tired hacks,
They're takin' Johnny to the buryin' groun' but they'll never bring him back.
He was my man, but he done me wrong." (1888?)

Geoffrey Chaucer

from THE CANTERBURY TALES

The Canterbury Tales is usually considered the first great poem indigenous to England. Even the earlier works of Chaucer himself are more French and Italian than English. But here the foreign elements are assimilated, and the work is native in both material and tone. "The Prologue," parts of which are given here, introduces the persons who are making a pilgrimage to the shrine of Thomas à Becket in Canterbury. In the main part of the poem each pilgrim tells a story, the tales varying from the most pious of moralities to the bawdiest kind of roughhouse.

The language is the East Midland dialect of Late Middle English. Most of the words you can recognize because of their resemblance to modern English. The footnotes will help you with the others.

> Whan that Aprille with his shoures soote
> The droghte of Marche hath percéd to the roote,
> And bathed every veyne in swich licour,
> Of which vertu engendred is the flour;
> Whan Zephirus eek with his swete breeth   5
> Inspiréd hath in every holt and heeth
> The tendre croppes, and the yonge sonne
> Hath in the Ram his halfe cours y-ronne,
> And smale fowles maken melodye,
> That slepen al the night with open yë,   10
> (So priketh hem nature in hir corages),
> Than longen folk to goon on pilgrimages
> (And palmers for to seken straunge strondes)
> To ferne halwes, couthe in sondry londes;
> And specially, from every shires ende   15
> Of Engelond, to Caunterbury they wende,
> The holy blisful martir for to seke,
> That hem hath holpen, whan that they were seke.
>   Bifel that, in that sesoun on a day,
> In Southwerk at the Tabard as I lay   20

1. *soote,* sweet. **5.** *eek,* also. **6.** *holt,* wood. **8.** *halfe cours y-ronne,* after April 11. **11.** *corages,* spirit, heart. **14.** *ferne,* distant. *halwes,* shrines. *couthe,* known. **17.** *martir,* Thomas à Becket. **18.** *seke,* sick.

Redy to wenden on my pilgrimage
To Caunterbury with ful devout corage,
At night was come in-to that hostelrye
Wel nyne and twenty in a companye,
Of sondry folk, by aventure y-falle   25
In felawshipe, and pilgrims were they alle,
That toward Caunterbury wolden ryde;
The chambres and the stables weren wyde,
And wel we weren esed atte beste.
And shortly, whan the sonne was to reste,   30
So hadde I spoken with hem everichon,
That I was of hir felawshipe anon,
And made forward erly for to ryse,
To take our wey, ther as I yow devyse.
    But natheles, whyl I have tyme and space,   35
Ere that I ferther in this tale pace,
Me thinketh it acordaunt to resoun,
To telle yow al the condicioun
Of ech of hem, so as it semed me,
And whiche they weren, and of what degree;   40
And eek in what array that they were inne:
And at a knight than wol I first biginne.

    A Knight ther was, and that a worthy man,
That fro the tyme that he first bigan
To ryden out, he loved chivalrye,   45
Trouthe and honour, fredom and curteisye.
Ful worthy was he in his lordes werre,
And therto hadde he riden (no man ferre)
As wel in cristendom as hethenesse,
And ever honoured for his worthinesse.   50
    At Alisaundre he was, whan it was wonne;
Ful ofte tyme he hadde the bord bigonne
Aboven alle naciouns in Pruce.
In Lettow hadde he reysed and in Ruce,
No cristen man so ofte of his degree.   55
In Gernade at the sege eek hadde he be
Of Algezir, and riden in Belmarye.
At Lyeys was he, and at Satalye,
Whan they were wonne; and in the Grete See

29. *atte beste*, in the best manner possible. **32.** *hir*, their. **46.** *fredom*, liberality. **48.** *ferre*, farther. **49.** *hethenesse*, heathen lands. **51.** *Alisaundre*, Alexandria. **52.** *bord bigonne*, sat at the head of the table. **53.** *Pruce*, Prussia. **54.** *Lettow*, Lithuania. *Ruce*, Russia. **56.** *Gernade*, Granada, Spain. **57.** *Algezir*, Algeciras. *Belmarye*, Benmarin, Morocco. **58.** *Lyeys*, Lyas in Armenia. *Satalye*, Atalia in Asia Minor.

At many a noble aryve hadde he be.   60
At mortal batailles hadde he been fiftene,
And foughten for our feith at Tramissene
In listes thryes, and ay slayn his foo.
This ilke worthy knight hadde been also
Sometyme with the lord of Palatye,   65
Ageyn another hethen in Turkye:
And everemore he hadde a sovereyn prys,
And though that he were worthy, he was wys,
And of his port as meek as is a mayde.
He nevere yet no vileinye ne sayde   70
In al his lyf, un-to no maner wight.
He was a verray parfit gentil knight.
But for to tellen yow of his array,
His hors were goode, but he was nat gay.
Of fustian he weréd a gipoun   75
Al bismoteréd with his habergeoun,
For he was late y-come from his viage,
And wente for to doon his pilgrimage.

With him there was his sone, a yong SQUYER,
A lovyere, and a lusty bacheler,   80
With lokkes crulle, as they were leyd in presse.
Of twenty yeer of age he was, I gesse.
Of his stature he was of evene lengthe,
And wonderly deliver, and greet of strengthe.
And he had been somtyme in chivachye,   85
In Flaundres, in Artoys, and Picardye,
And born him wel, as of so litel space,
In hope to stonden in his lady grace.
Embrouded was he, as it were a mede
Al ful of fresshe floures, whyte and rede.   90
Singinge he was, or floytinge, al the day;
He was as fresh as is the month of May.
Short was his goune, with sleves longe and wyde.
Wel coude he sitte on hors, and faire ryde.
He coude songes make and wel endyte,   95
Juste and eek daunce, and wel purtreye and wryte.
So hote he lovede, that by nightertale
He sleep namore than doth a nightingale.

---

62. *Tramissene*, Tlemçen in Algeria. **64.** *ilke*, same. **65.** *Palatye*, Balat, Turkey. **70.** *vileinye*, rudeness. **71.** *wight*, person. **75.** *gipoun*, short doublet worn under armor. **76.** *bismoteréd*, besmirched. *habergeoun*, coat of mail. **81.** *lokkes crulle*, curly hair. **84.** *deliver*, quick, active. **85.** *chivachye*, cavalry raids. **91.** *floytinge*, whistling, playing the flute. **96.** *juste*, joust. *purtreye*, draw. **97.** *nightertale*, nighttime.

Curteys he was, lowly, and servisable,
And carf biforn his fader at the table.   100

    Ther was also a Nonne, a PRIORESSE,
That of hir smyling was ful simple and coy,
Hir gretteste ooth was but by seÿnt Loy;   120
And she was cleped madame Eglentyne.
Ful wel she song the service divyne,
Entuned in hir nose ful semely;
And Frensh she spak ful faire and fetisly,
After the scole of Stratford atte Bowe,   125
For Frensh of Paris was to hir unknowe.
At mete wel y-taught was she with-alle;
She leet no morsel from hir lippes falle,
Ne wette hir fingres in hir sauce depe.
Wel coude she carie a morsel, and wel kepe,   130
That no drope ne fille up-on hir brest.
In curteisye was set ful muche hir lest.
Hir over lippe wyped she so clene,
That in hir coppe was no ferthing sene
Of grece, whan she dronken hadde hir draughte.   135
Ful semely after hir mete she raughte,
And sikerly she was of greet disport,
And ful plesaunt, and amiable of port,
And peyned hir to countrefete chere
Of court, and been estatlich of manere,   140
And to ben holden digne of reverence.
But, for to speken of hir conscience,
She was so charitable and so pitous,
She wolde wepe, if that she sawe a mous
Caught in a trappe, if it were deed or bledde.   145
Of smale houndes had she, that she fedde
With rosted flesh, or milk and wastel breed.
But sore weep she if oon of hem were deed,
Or if men smoot it with a yerde smerte:
And al was conscience and tendre herte.   150
Ful semely hir wimpel pinched was;
Hir nose tretys; hir eyen greye as glas;
Hir mouth ful smal, and ther-to softe and reed;
But sikerly she hadde a fair forheed;
It was almost a spanne brood, I trowe;   155

121. *cleped*, called, named. **124.** *fetisly*, handsomely. **130.** *kepe*, care, notice. **132.** *lest*, desire. **136.** *raughte*, reached. **137.** *sikerly*, surely. **139.** *peyned*, took pains. *countrefete*, imitate. *chere*, expressions, behavior. **141.** *digne*, worthy. **142.** *conscience*, tender feelings. **149.** *yerde smerte*, smartly with a stick. **152.** *tretys*, well-formed.

For, hardily, she was nat undergrowe.
Ful fetis was hir cloke, as I was war.
Of smal coral aboute hir arm she bar
A peire of bedes, gauded al with grene;
And ther-on heng a broche of gold ful shene,   160
On which ther was first write a crowned A,
And after, *Amor vincit omnia.*

　　A FRERE ther was, a wantown and a merye,
A limitour, a ful solempne man.
In alle the ordres foure is noon that can   210
So muche of daliaunce and fair langage.
He hadde maad ful many a mariage
Of yonge wommen, at his owne cost.
Un-to his ordre he was a noble post.
Ful wel biloved and famulier was he   215
With frankeleyns over-al in his contree,
And eek with worthy wommen of the toun:
For he had power of confessioun,
As seyde him-self, more than a curat,
For of his ordre he was licentiat.   220
Ful swetely herde he confessioun,
And plesaunt was his absolucioun;
He was an esy man to yeve penaunce
Ther as he wiste to han a good pitaunce;
For unto a povre ordre for to yive   225
Is signe that a man is wel y-shrive.
For if he yaf, he dorste make avaunt,
He wiste that a man was repentaunt.
For many a man so hard is of his herte,
He may nat wepe al-thogh him sore smerte.   230
Therfore, in stede of weping and preyeres,
Men moot yeve silver to the povre freres.
His tipet was ay farsed ful of knyves
And pinnes, for to yeven faire wyves.
And certeinly he hadde a mery note;   235
Wel coude he singe and pleyen on a rote.
Of yeddinges he bar utterly the prys.
His nekke whyt was as the flour-de-lys;

---

157. *war*, aware. **208.** *wantown*, sportive, lascivious. **209.** *limitour*, a friar licensed to beg within certain limits. *solempne*, pompous. **220.** *licentiat*, a person licensed by the Pope. **223.** *yeve*, give. **224.** *ther as*, where. *wiste*, knew. *pitaunce*, pittance. **226.** *y-shrive*, confessed. **227.** *yaf*, gave. *avaunt*, boast. **233.** *tipet*, cape. *farsed*, stuffed. **234.** *yeven*, give. **236.** *rote*, a stringed instrument. **237.** *yeddinges*, songs. *utterly*, entirely. *prys*, worth.

There-to he strong was as a champioun.
He knew the tavernes wel in every toun,   240
And everich hostiler and tappestere
Bet than a lazar or a beggestere;
For un-to swich a worthy man as he
Acorded nat, as by his facultee,
To have with seke lazars aqueyntaunce.   245
It is nat honest, it may nat avaunce
For to delen with no swich poraille,
But al with riche and sellers of vitaille.
And over-al, ther as profit sholde aryse,
Curteys he was, and lowly of servyse.   250
Ther nas no man nowher so vertuous.
He was the beste beggere in his hous;
For thogh a widwe hadde noght a sho,
So plesaunt was his "*In principio*,"
Yet wolde he have a ferthing, er he wente.   255
His purchas was wel bettre than his rente.
And rage he coude, as it were right a whelpe.
In love-dayes ther coude he muchel helpe.
For ther he was nat lyk a cloisterer,
With a thredbar cope as is a povre scoler,   260
But he was lyk a maister or a pope.
Of double worsted was his semi-cope,
That rounded as a belle out of the presse.
Somwhat he lipsed, for his wantownesse,
To make his English swete up-on his tonge;   265
And in his harping, whan that he had songe,
His eyen twinkled in his heed aright,
As doon the sterres in the frosty night.
This worthy limitour was cleped Huberd.

A good WYF was ther of bisyde BATHE,   445
But she was som-del deef, and that was scathe.
Of clooth-making she hadde swiche an haunt,
She passed hem of Ypres and of Gaunt.
In al the parisshe wyf ne was ther noon
That to th' offring bifore hir sholde goon;   450
And if ther dide, certeyn, so wrooth was she,

---

239. *champioun*, wrestler. **241.** *tappestere*, tapster. **242.** *bet*, better. *lazar*, leper. *beggestere*,
beggar. **244.** *facultee*, official position. **246.** *avaunce*, be profitable. **247.** *poraille*, poor
people. **249.** *over-al*, everywhere. **256.** *purchas*, gain. *rente*, income. **257.** *rage*, frolic. **259.**
cloisterer, one restricted to a cloister. **262.** *semi-cope*, short outer coat. **268.** *doon*, do.
446. *som-del*, somewhat. *scathe*, shame. **447.** *haunt*, skill. **448.** *passed hem*, surpassed them.
450. *goon*, go.

That she was out of alle charitee.
Hir coverchiefs ful fyne were of ground;
I dorste swere they weyeden ten pound
That on a Sonday were upon hir heed. **455**
Hir hosen weren of fyn scarlet reed,
Ful streite y-teyd, and shoos ful moiste and newe.
Bold was hir face, and fair, and reed of hewe.
She was a worthy womman al hir lyve,
Housbondes at chirche-dore she hadde fyve, **460**
Withouten other companye in youthe;
But thereof nedeth nat to speke as nouthe.
And thryes hadde she been at Jerusalem;
She hadde passed many a straunge streem;
At Rome she hadde been, and at Boloigne, **465**
In Galice at seint Jame, and at Coloigne.
She coude muche of wandring by the weye:
Gat-tothed was she, soothly for to seye.
Up-on an amblere esily she sat,
Y-wimpled wel, and on hir heed an hat **470**
As brood as is a bokeler or a targe;
A foot-mantel aboute hir hipes large,
And on hir feet a paire of spores sharpe.
In felawschip wel coude she laughe and carpe.
Of remedyes of love she knew perchaunce, **475**
For she coude of that art the olde daunce.

    The Miller was a stout carl, for the nones, **545**
Ful big he was of braun, and eek of bones;
That proved wel, for over-al ther he cam,
At wrastling he wolde have alwey the ram.
He was short-sholdred, brood, a thikke knarre,
Ther nas no dore that he nolde heve of harre, **550**
Or breke it, at a renning, with his heed.
His berd as any sowe or fox was reed,
And ther-to brood, as though it were a spade.
Up-on the cop right of his nose he hade
A werte, and ther-on stood a tuft of heres, **555**
Reed as the bristles of a sowes eres;
His nose-thirles blake were and wyde.
A swerd and bokeler bar he by his syde;

---

453. *ground,* texture. **462.** *nouthe,* now. **467.** *coude,* knew. **471.** *targe,* shield. **472.** *foot-mantel,* cloth worn over skirt when riding. **476.** *the olde daunce,* all about it. **545.** *for the nones,* loosely translated "to be sure." **547.** *over-al,* everywhere. **549.** *knarre,* knave. **550.** *harre,* hinges. **554.** *cop,* top. **557.** *nose-thirles,* nostrils.

His mouth as greet was as a greet forneys.
He was a janglere and a goliardeys,   560
And that was most of sinne and harlotryes.
Wel coude he stelen corn, and tollen thryes,
And yet he hadde a thombe of gold, pardee.
A whyt cote and blew hood wered he.
A baggepype wel coude he blowe and sowne,   565
And therwithal he broghte us out of towne.

William Shakespeare

WHEN ICICLES HANG BY THE WALL

When icicles hang by the wall,
  And Dick the shepherd blows his nail,
And Tom bears logs into the hall,
  And milk comes frozen home in pail,
When blood is nipped and ways be foul,   5
Then nightly sings the staring owl,
"Tu-whit, tu-who!" A merry note,
While greasy Joan doth keel the pot.

When all aloud the wind doth blow,
  And coughing drowns the parson's saw,   10
And birds sit brooding in the snow,
  And Marian's nose looks red and raw,
When roasted crabs hiss in the bowl,
Then nightly sings the staring owl,
"Tu-whit, tu-who!" A merry note,   15
While greasy Joan doth keel the pot.
    —from *Love's Labour's Lost* (1590-1592; 1598)

O MISTRESS MINE

O mistress mine, where are you roaming?
O, stay and hear; your true love's coming,

559. *forneys*, furnace. **560.** *janglere*, chatterer. *goliardeys*, buffoon, jester. **561.** *harlotryes*, lewd jokes. **562.** *tollen thryes*, take toll three times, i.e., charge excessively. **563.** *a thombe of gold*. There is an old proverb that an honest miller has a thumb of gold. In other words, the miller was honest according to his lights.

That can sing both high and low.
Trip no further, pretty sweeting,
Journeys end in lovers meeting,   5
    Every wise man's son doth know.

What is love? 'Tis not hereafter;
Present mirth hath present laughter;
    What's to come is still unsure.
In delay there lies no plenty;   10
Then come kiss me, sweet and twenty,
    Youth's a stuff will not endure.
        —from *Twelfth Night* (1599-1601; 1623)

BLOW, BLOW, THOU WINTER WIND

Blow, blow, thou winter wind,
Thou art not so unkind
    As man's ingratitude;
Thy tooth is not so keen,
Because thou art not seen,   5
    Although thy breath be rude.
Heigh-ho! sing, heigh-ho! unto the green holly:
Most friendship is feigning, most loving mere folly:
    Then, heigh-ho, the holly!
    This life is most jolly.   10

Freeze, freeze, thou bitter sky,
That dost not bite so nigh
    As benefits forgot:
Though thou the waters warp,
Thy sting is not so sharp   15
    As friend remember'd not
Heigh-ho! sing, & c.
        —from *As You Like It* (1600)

SONNET 18

Shall I compare thee to a summer's day?
Thou art more lovely and more temperate:
Rough winds do shake the darling buds of **May,**
And summer's lease hath all too short a date:
Sometime too hot the eye of heaven shines,   5
And often is his gold complexion dimmed;

And every fair from fair sometime declines,
By chance or nature's changing course untrimmed;
But thy eternal summer shall not fade,
Nor lose possession of that fair thou owest; 10
Nor shall Death brag thou wander'st in his shade,
When in eternal lines to time thou growest:
   So long as men can breathe, or eyes can see,
   So long lives this, and this gives life to thee. (1609)

SONNET 29

When, in disgrace with fortune and men's eyes,
I all alone beweep my outcast state,
And trouble deaf heaven with my bootless cries,
And look upon myself, and curse my fate,
Wishing me like to one more rich in hope, 5
Featured like him, like him with friends possessed,
Desiring this man's art and that man's scope,
With what I most enjoy contented least;
Yet in these thoughts myself almost despising,
Haply I think on thee—and then my state, 10
Like to the lark at break of day arising
From sullen earth, sings hymns at heaven's gate;
   For thy sweet love remembered such wealth brings
   That then I scorn to change my state with kings. (1609)

SONNET 30

When to the sessions of sweet silent thought
I summon up remembrance of things past,
I sigh the lack of many a thing I sought,
And with old woes new wail my dear time's waste.
Then can I drown an eye, unused to flow, 5
For precious friends hid in death's dateless night,
And weep afresh love's long since canceled woe,
And moan the expense of many a vanished sight.
Then can I grieve at grievances foregone,
And heavily from woe to woe tell o'er 10
The sad account of fore-bemoanéd moan,
Which I new pay as if not paid before.
   But if the while I think on thee, dear friend,
   All losses are restored and sorrows end. (1609)

SONNET 73

That time of year thou mayst in me behold
When yellow leaves, or none, or few, do hang
Upon those boughs which shake against the cold,
Bare ruined choirs, where late the sweet birds sang.
In me thou see'st the twilight of such day   5
As after sunset fadeth in the west,
Which by and by black night doth take away,
Death's second self, that seals up all in rest.
In me thou see'st the glowing of such fire
That on the ashes of his youth doth lie,   10
As the death-bed whereon it must expire,
Consumed with that which it was nourished by.
   This thou perceivest, which makes thy love more strong,
   To love that well which thou must leave ere long. (1609)

SONNET 94

They that have power to hurt and will do none,
That do not do the thing they most do show,
Who, moving others, are themselves as stone,
Unmoved, cold and to temptation slow;
They rightly do inherit heaven's graces   5
And husband nature's riches from expense;
They are the lords and owners of their faces,
Others but stewards of their excellence.
The summer's flower is to the summer sweet,
Though to itself it only live and die,   10
But if that flower with base infection meet,
The basest weed outbraves his dignity:
   For sweetest things turn sourest by their deeds;
   Lilies that fester smell far worse than weeds. (1609)

SONNET 129

The expense of spirit in a waste of shame
Is lust in action; and till action, lust
Is perjured, murderous, bloody, full of blame,
Savage, extreme, rude, cruel, not to trust;
Enjoy'd no sooner but despised straight;   5
Past reason hunted; and no sooner had,

Past reason hated, as a swallowed bait,
On purpose laid to make the taker mad:
Mad in pursuit, and in possession so;
Had, having, and in quest to have, extreme;   10
A bliss in proof, and proved, a very woe;
Before, a joy proposed; behind, a dream.
   All this the world well knows; yet none knows well
   To shun the heaven that leads men to this hell. (1609)

SONNET 146

Poor soul, the center of my sinful earth—
Fool'd by these rebel powers that thee array,
Why dost thou pine within and suffer dearth,
Painting thy outward walls so costly gay?
Why so large cost, having so short a lease,   5
Dost thou upon thy fading mansion spend?
Shall worms, inheritors of this excess,
Eat up thy charge? Is this thy body's end?
Then, soul, live thou upon thy servant's loss,
And let that pine to aggravate thy store;   10
Buy terms divine in selling hours of dross;
Within be fed, without be rich no more:
   So shalt thou feed on Death, that feeds on men,
   And Death once dead, there's no more dying then. (1609)

Renaissance and Seventeenth-Century Poems

Sir Thomas Wyatt

THEY FLEE FROM ME

They flee from me that sometime did me seek
   With naked foot, stalking in my chamber.
I have seen them gentle, tame, and meek,
   That now are wild, and do not remember

That sometime they put themselves in danger   5
To take bread at my hand; and now they range
Busily seeking with a continual change.

Thankèd be fortune, it hath been otherwise
    Twenty times better; but once in special,
In thin array, after a pleasant guise,   10
    When her loose gown from her shoulders did fall,
    And she me caught in her arms long and small,
Therewith all sweetly did me kiss
And softly said, *'Dear heart, how like you this?'*

It was no dream; I lay broad waking: 15
    But all is turned, through my gentleness,
Into a strange fashion of forsaking;
    And I have leave to go of her goodness,
    And she also to use newfangleness.
But since that I so kindly am served,   20
I would fain know what she hath deserved. (1557)

John Donne

SONG

Go and catch a falling star,
    Get with child a mandrake root,
Tell me where all past years are,
    Or who cleft the devil's foot;
Teach me to hear mermaids singing,   5
Or to keep off envy's stinging,
        And find
        What wind
Serves to advance an honest mind.

If thou be'st born to strange sights,   10
    Things invisible to see,
Ride ten thousand days and nights
    Till Age snow white hairs on thee;
Thou, when thou return'st, wilt tell me
All strange wonders that befell thee,   15
        And swear
        No where
Lives a woman true and fair.

If thou find'st one, let me know;
    Such a pilgrimage were sweet.   20
Yet do not, I would not go,
    Though at next door we might meet.
Though she were true when you met her,
And last till you write your letter,
        Yet she   25
        Will be
False, ere I come, to two or three. (1633)

LOVE'S ALCHEMY

Some that have deeper digg'd love's mine than I,
Say, where his centric happiness doth lie.
    I have lov'd, and got, and told,
But should I love, get, tell, till I were old,
I should not find that hidden mystery;   5
        Oh, 'tis imposture all.
And as no chemic yet th' elixir got,
        But glorifies his pregnant pot,
        If by the way to him befall
Some odoriferous thing, or medicinal,   10
    So, lovers dream a rich and long delight,
    But get a winter-seeming summer's night.
Our ease, our thrift, our honor, and our day,
Shall we, for this vain bubble's shadow pay?
        Ends love in this, that my man   15
Can be as happy as I can, if he can
Endure the short scorn of a bridegroom's play?
        That loving wretch that swears,
'Tis not the bodies marry, but the minds,
        Which he in her angelic finds,   20
        Would swear as justly, that he hears,
In that day's rude hoarse minstrelsy, the spheres.
    Hope not for mind in women; at their best
    Sweetness and wit they are, but mummy, possest. (1633)

Ben Jonson

AN EPITAPH ON SALATHIEL PAVY

Weep with me, all you that read
This little story;

And know, for whom a tear you shed
  Death's self is sorry.
'Twas a child that so did thrive   5
  In grace and feature,
As heaven and nature seemed to strive
  Which owned the creature.
Years he numbered scarce thirteen
  When fates turned cruel,   10
Yet three filled zodiacs had he been
  The stage's jewel;
And did act, what now we moan,
  Old men so duly,
As sooth, the Parcae thought him one,   15
  He played so truly.
So, by error, to his fate
  They all consented,
But viewing him since, alas, too late!
  They have repented;   20
And have sought, to give new birth,
  In baths to steep him;
But being so much too good for earth,
  Heaven vows to keep him. (1602)

HYMN TO DIANA

Queen and Huntress, chaste and fair,
  Now the sun is laid to sleep,
Seated in thy silver chair
  State in wonted manner keep:
    Hesperus entreats thy light,   5
    Goddess excellently bright.

Earth, let not thy envious shade
  Dare itself to interpose;
Cynthia's shining orb was made
  Heaven to clear when day did close: 10
    Bless us then with wishéd sight,
    Goddess excellently bright.

Lay thy bow of pearl apart
  And thy crystal-shining quiver;
Give unto the flying hart   15
  Space to breathe, how short soever:
    Thou that mak'st a day of night,
    Goddess excellently bright. (1600)

Robert Herrick

CORINNA'S GOING A-MAYING

Get up, get up for shame, the blooming morn
Upon her wings presents the god unshorn.
 See how Aurora throws her fair
 Fresh-quilted colors through the air:
 Get up, sweet slug-a-bed, and see   5
 The dew bespangling herb and tree.
Each flower has wept and bowéd toward the east
Above an hour since: yet you not dressed;
 Nay! not so much as out of bed?
 When all the birds have matins said   10
 And sung their thankful hymns, 't is sin,
 Nay, profanation, to keep in,
Whenas a thousand virgins on this day
Spring, sooner than the lark, to fetch in May.

Rise, and put on your foliage, and be seen   15
To come forth, like the springtime, fresh and green,
 And sweet as Flora. Take no care
 For jewels for your gown or hair:
 Fear not; the leaves will strew
 Gems in abundance upon you: 20
Besides, the childhood of the day has kept,
Against you come, some orient pearls unwept;
 Come and receive them while the light
 Hangs on the dew-locks of the night:
 And Titan on the eastern hill   25
 Retires himself, or else stands still
Till you come forth. Wash, dress, be brief in praying:
Few beads are best when once we go a-Maying.

Come, my Corinna, come; and, coming mark
How each field turns a street, each street a park   30
 Made green and trimmed with trees; see how
 Devotion gives each house a bough
 Or branch: each porch, each door ere this
 An ark, a tabernacle is,
Made up of white-thorn, neatly interwove;   35
As if here were those cooler shades of love.
 Can such delights be in the street

And open fields and we not see 't?
Come, we'll abroad; and let's obey
The proclamation made for May: 40
And sin no more, as we have done, by staying;
But, my Corinna, come, let's go a-Maying.

There's not a budding boy or girl this day
But is got up, and gone to bring in May.
  A deal of youth, ere this, is come   45
  Back, and with white-thorn laden home.
  Some have dispatched their cakes and cream
  Before that we have left to dream:
And some have wept, and wooed, and plighted troth,
And chose their priest, ere we can cast off sloth: 50
  Many a green-gown has been given;
  Many a kiss, both odd and even:
  Many a glance too has been sent
  From out the eye, love's firmament;
Many a jest told of the keys betraying   55
This night, and locks picked, yet we're not a-Maying.

Come, let us go while we are in our prime;
And take the harmless folly of the time.
  We shall grow old apace, and die
  Before we know our liberty.   60
  Our life is short, and our days run
  As fast away as does the sun;
And, as a vapor or a drop of rain,
Once lost, can ne'er be found again,
  So when or you or I are made   65
  A fable, song, or fleeting shade,
  All love, all liking, all delight
  Lies drowned with us in endless night.
Then while time serves, and we are but decaying,
Come, my Corinna, come let's go a-Maying. (1648)   70

UPON JULIA'S CLOTHES

Whenas in silks my Julia goes,
Then, then, methinks, how sweetly flows
The liquefaction of her clothes.

Next, when I cast mine eyes, and see
That brave vibration, each way free,   5
Oh, how that glittering taketh me! (1648)

Earl Daniels

HERRICK'S
"UPON JULIA'S CLOTHES"

Superficially, the poem is obvious to the point of seeming to depreciate analysis, not to be worth it. A pretty girl moves through six lines, for a moment only catches an observer's eye, passes, and is gone. So slight is the impact of the experience that he writes not about the girl but about her clothes. Costume is defined by silks, and each stanza is centered in a single quality of silk in movement, and in light ("liquefaction," line 3, and "glittering," line 6). The positions of these words in the last lines of each stanza should be noted and, more particularly, the increased sharpness lent to "glittering" by the necessity, here, of pronunciation in two syllables only: the vowel sound of an acute and pointed short "i" is closed tightly in by consonants, "g" and "t" in one syllable, "tr" and "ng" in the other. The stab of that word, a superb mine-eyes-dazzle effect, suggests the poem is not so simple as it seems: that Julia-in-clothes is more important than clothes, the apparent subject; that the observer is more deeply moved than he wants a careless reader to suppose, possibly than he himself knows.

Attention to sound and movement reveals the implications of the single word "glittering" to be a clue worth following. The poem is Julia and Julia's clothes. But each stanza contains lines (I, 2; II, 1, 3) which turn to the observer, and seem to hint in sound and movement at a central ironic contrast between the states of mind of the observer and the girl. The Julia lines flow, as easy and as liquid as the smooth silks which dress and conceal a lovely body. But the observer lines throb unevenly; they start and stop; they image the excitement and disturbance of the poet. It may not be too far-fetched to wonder if they are not symbol for the quickened beating of a heart, the surprised catch of breath, in the presence of beauty, especially beauty of a woman. An attentive reader now begins to understand it is not Julia's clothes but Julia herself who is the subject of the poem; and the poem begins to grow and to take on new richness of meaning. To be especially noted is the contrast in stanza I between lines 1 and 2: in line 1, word ripples into word, sound into sound, the caesural pause is so slight as to be almost not noticeable; in line 2, the opening repetition of "Then, then," where each word must be distinctly separated by pauses, where vowels are imbedded between inescapable consonants, announces a change, further stressed by the parenthetical "methinks." (Even the parenthesis plays its part here.) Only as this line, toward the end, moves to Julia and her costume does it begin to glide, to be liquefied again. The point is

Reprinted from *The Explicator*, March 1943. By permission.

Julia moves through the poem serene, untouched; she may not even know the poet has so much as seen her. But he is in a different situation, for though he is ostensibly doing nothing more than writing a pretty lyric about a pretty dress, yet he reveals, in the sound, the movement, the pace of his words, how deeply he has been stirred by what seems so unimportant.

This makes for a basic ironic contrast, central to the poem: the ironic contrast between the girl and the man. Is it the irony of man (male) set over against woman (female)—a contrast as old as the Garden of Eden itself— or is it the profounder suggestion of the situation of man (not *a man*) in the presence of beauty—beauty here, as so often, being symbolized by a woman? I am reasonably certain that by implication and suggestion, by the subtlest of overtones, both ideas are in their way present, contributing rich values for a poem too often looked upon as too slight for serious consideration. Herrick has too long suffered from that kind of treatment.

Thomas Carew

SONG

Ask me no more where Jove bestows,
When June is past, the fading rose;
For in your beauty's orient deep
These flowers, as in their causes, sleep.

Ask me no more whither do stray   5
The golden atoms of the day;
For in pure love heaven did prepare
Those powders to enrich your hair.

Ask me no more whither doth haste
The nightingale when May is past;   10
For in your sweet, dividing throat
She winters and keeps warm her note.

Ask me no more where those stars 'light
That downwards fall in dead of night;
For in your eyes they sit, and there   15
Fixéd become as in their sphere.

Ask me no more if east or west
The phoenix builds her spicy nest;
For unto you at last she flies,
And in your fragrant bosom dies. (1640)   20

George Herbert

VIRTUE

Sweet day, so cool, so calm, so bright,
　　The bridal of the earth and sky;
The dew shall weep thy fall to-night,
　　For thou must die.

Sweet rose, whose hue, angry and brave,　5
　　Bids the rash gazer wipe his eye,
Thy root is ever in its grave,
　　And thou must die.

Sweet spring, full of sweet days and roses,
　　A box where sweets compacted lie,　10
My music shows ye have your closes,
　　And all must die.

Only a sweet and virtuous soul,
　　Like seasoned timber, never gives,
But though the whole world turn to coal,　15
　　Then chiefly lives. (1630-1633)

John Milton

L'ALLEGRO

Hence, loathéd Melancholy,
　　Of Cerberus and blackest Midnight born
In Stygian cave forlorn
　　'Mongst horrid shapes, and shrieks, and sights unholy!
Find out some uncouth cell,　5
　　Where brooding Darkness spreads his jealous wings,
And the night-raven sings;
　　There, under ebon shades and low-browed rocks,
As ragged as thy locks,
　　In dark Cimmerian desert ever dwell.　10

But come, thou Goddess fair and free,
In heaven ycleped Euphrosyne,
And by men heart-easing Mirth,

1000

Whom lovely Venus at a birth
With two sister Graces more   15
To ivy-crownéd Bacchus bore;
Or whether (as some sager sing)
The frolic Wind that breathes the spring,
Zephyr with Aurora playing,
As he met her once a-Maying,   20
There on beds of violets blue,
And fresh-blown roses washed in dew,
Filled her with thee, a daughter fair,
So buxom, blithe, and debonair.
Haste thee, nymph, and bring with thee   25
Jest, and youthful Jollity,
Quips, and cranks, and wanton wiles,
Nods, and becks, and wreathéd smiles,
Such as hang on Hebe's cheek,
And love to live in dimple sleek;   30
Sport that wrinkled Care derides,
And Laughter holding both his sides,
Come, and trip it as ye go,
On the light fantastic toe;
And in thy right hand lead with thee   35
The mountain nymph, sweet Liberty;
And, if I give thee honor due,
Mirth, admit me of thy crew,
To live with her, and live with thee,
In unreprovéd pleasures free;   40
To hear the lark begin his flight,
And, singing, startle the dull night,
From his watch-tower in the skies,
Till the dappled dawn doth rise;
Then to come, in spite of sorrow,   45
And at my window bid good-morrow,
Through the sweet-briar or the vine,
Or the twisted eglantine;
While the cock with lively din,
Scatters the rear of darkness thin;   50
And to the stack, or the barn-door,
Stoutly struts his dames before;
Oft listening how the hounds and horn
Cheerly rouse the slumbering morn,
From the side of some hoar hill,   55
Through the high wood echoing shrill;
Sometime walking, not unseen,
By hedgerow elms, on hillocks green,

Right against the eastern gate,
Where the great Sun begins his state,   60
Robed in flames and amber light,
The clouds in thousand liveries dight;
While the plowman, near at hand,
Whistles o'er the furrowed land,
And the milkmaid singeth blithe,   65
And the mower whets his scythe,
And every shepherd tells his tale
Under the hawthorn in the dale.
Straight mine eye hath caught new pleasures,
Whilst the landskip round it measures: 70
Russet lawns, and fallows gray,
Where the nibbling flocks do stray;
Mountains on whose barren breast
The laboring clouds do often rest;
Meadows trim with daisies pied;   75
Shallow brooks, and rivers wide.
Towers and battlements it sees
Bosomed high in tufted trees,
Where perhaps some beauty lies,
The cynosure of neighboring eyes.   80
Hard by, a cottage chimney smokes
From betwixt two agéd oaks,
Where Corydon and Thyrsis met,
Are at their savory dinner set
Of herbs and other country messes,   85
Which the neat-handed Phyllis dresses;
And then in haste her bower she leaves,
With Thestylis to bind the sheaves;
Or, if the earlier season lead,
To the tanned haycock in the mead.   90
Sometimes, with secure delight,
The upland hamlets will invite,
When the merry bells ring round,
And the jocund rebecks sound
To many a youth and many a maid   95
Dancing in the checkered shade;
And young and old come forth to play
On a sunshine holiday,
Till the livelong daylight fail;
Then to the spicy nut-brown ale,   100
With stories told of many a feat,
How Faery Mab the junkets eat;
She was pinched and pulled, she said;

And he, by Friar's lantern led,
Tells how the drudging goblin sweat   105
To earn his cream-bowl duly set,
When, in one night, ere glimpse of morn,
His shadowing flail hath threshed the corn
That ten day-laborers could not end;
Then lies him down the lubber fiend,   110
And, stretched out all the chimney's length,
Basks at the fire his hairy strength,
And crop-full out of doors he flings,
Ere the first cock his matin rings.
Thus done the tales, to bed they creep,   115
By whispering winds soon lulled asleep.
Towered cities please us then,
And the busy hum of men,
Where throngs of knights and barons bold,
In weeds of peace, high triumphs hold,   120
With store of ladies, whose bright eyes
Rain influence, and judge the prize
Of wit or arms, while both contend
To win her grace whom all commend.
There let Hymen oft appear   125
In saffron robe, with taper clear,
And pomp, and feast, and revelry,
With mask and antique pageantry;
Such sights as youthful poets dream
On summer eves by haunted stream.   130
Then to the well-trod stage anon,
If Jonson's learnéd sock be on,
Or sweetest Shakespeare, Fancy's child,
Warble his native wood-notes wild.
And ever, against eating cares,   135
Lap me in soft Lydian airs,
Married to immortal verse,
Such as the meeting soul may pierce
In notes with many a winding bout
Of linkéd sweetness long drawn out,   140
With wanton heed and giddy cunning,
The melting voice through mazes running,
Untwisting all the chains that tie
The hidden soul of harmony;
That Orpheus' self may heave his head   145
From golden slumber on a bed
Of heaped Elysian flowers, and hear
Such strains as would have won the ear

Of Pluto to have quiet set free
His half-regained Eurydice.   150
These delights if thou canst give,
Mirth, with thee I mean to live. (1632?; 1645)

IL PENSEROSO

Hence, vain deluding Joys,
   The brood of Folly without father bred!
How little you bested,
   Or fill the fixéd mind with all your toys!
Dwell in some idle brain,   5
   And fancies fond with gaudy shapes possess,
As thick and numberless
   As the gay motes that people the sun-beams,
Or likest hovering dreams,
   The fickle pensioners of Morpheus' train.   10

But, hail! thou Goddess sage and holy!
Hail, divinest Melancholy!
Whose saintly visage is too bright
To hit the sense of human sight,
And therefore to our weaker view   15
O'erlaid with black, staid Wisdom's hue;
Black, but such as in esteem
Prince Memnon's sister might beseem,
Or that starred Ethiop queen that strove
To set her beauty's praise above   20
The Sea-Nymphs, and their powers offended.
Yet thou art higher far descended;
Thee bright-haired Vesta long of yore
To solitary Saturn bore;
His daughter she; in Saturn's reign   25
Such mixture was not held a stain.
Oft in glimmering bowers and glades
He met her, and in secret shades
Of woody Ida's inmost grove,
Whilst yet there was no fear of Jove.   30
Come, pensive Nun, devout and pure,
Sober, steadfast, and demure,
All in a robe of darkest grain,
Flowing with majestic train,
And sable stole of cypress lawn   35
Over thy decent shoulders drawn.

Come; but keep thy wonted state,
With even step, and musing gait,
And looks commercing with the skies,
Thy rapt soul sitting in thine eyes;   40
There, held in holy passion still,
Forget thyself to marble, till
With a sad leaden downward cast
Thou fix them on the earth as fast.
And join with thee calm Peace and Quiet,   45
Spare Fast, that oft with gods doth diet,
And hears the Muses, in a ring,
Aye round about Jove's altar sing.
And add to these retiréd Leisure,
That in trim gardens takes his pleasure.   50
But first, and chiefest, with thee bring,
Him that yon soars on golden wing,
Guiding the fiery-wheeléd throne,
The cherub Contemplation;
And the mute silence hist along,   55
'Less Philomel will deign a song,
In her sweetest saddest plight,
Smoothing the rugged brow of Night,
While Cynthia checks her dragon yoke
Gently o'er the accustomed oak.   60
Sweet bird, that shunn'st the noise of folly,
Most musical, most melancholy!
Thee, chantress, oft, the woods among,
I woo, to hear thy even-song;
And, missing thee, I walk unseen   65
On the dry smooth-shaven green,
To behold the wandering moon
Riding near her highest noon,
Like one that had been led astray
Through the heaven's wide pathless way,   70
And oft, as if her head she bowed,
Stooping through a fleecy cloud.
Oft, on a plat of rising ground,
I hear the far-off curfew sound
Over some wide-watered shore,   75
Swinging slow with sullen roar;
Or, if the air will not permit,
Some still, removéd place will fit,
Where glowing embers through the room
Teach light to counterfeit a gloom;   80
Far from all resort of mirth,

Save the cricket on the hearth,
Or the bellman's drowsy charm
To bless the doors from nightly harm.
Or let my lamp, at midnight hour,   85
Be seen in some high lonely tower
Where I may oft outwatch the Bear
With thrice great Hermes, or unsphere
The spirit of Plato, to unfold
What worlds or what vast regions hold   90
The immortal mind that hath forsook
Her mansion in this fleshly nook,
And of those demons that are found
In fire, air, flood, or underground,
Whose power hath a true consent,   95
With planet or with element.
Sometime let gorgeous Tragedy,
In sceptered pall, come sweeping by,
Presenting Thebes, or Pelops' line,
Or the tale of Troy divine,   100
Or what (though rare) of later age
Ennobled hath the buskined stage.
But, O sad virgin! that thy power
Might raise Musaeus from his bower;
Or bid the soul of Orpheus sing   105
Such notes as, warbled to the string,
Drew iron tears down Pluto's cheek,
And made hell grant what love did seek;
Or call up him that left half told
The story of Cambuscan bold,   110
Of Camball, and of Algarsife,
And who had Canacé to wife
That owned the virtuous ring and glass,
And of the wondrous horse of brass,
On which the Tartar king did ride;   115
And if aught else great bards beside
In sage and solemn tunes have sung,
Of tourneys, and of trophies hung,
Of forests, and enchantments drear,
Where more is meant than meets the ear.   120
Thus, Night, oft see me in thy pale career,
Till civil-suited Morn appear,
Not tricked and flounced as she was wont
With the Attic boy to hunt,
But kerchiefed in a comely cloud,   125
While rocking winds are piping loud;

Or ushered with a shower still,
When the gust hath blown his fill,
Ending on the rustling leaves,
With minute-drops from off the eaves. 130
And, when the sun begins to fling
His flaring beams, me, goddess, bring
To archéd walks of twilight groves,
And shadows brown, that Sylvan loves,
Of pine, or monumental oak, 135
Where the rude axe with heavéd stroke
Was never heard the nymphs to daunt
Or fright them from their hallowed haunt.
There in close covert by some brook,
Where no profaner eye may look, 140
Hide me from day's garish eye,
While the bee, with honeyed thigh,
That at her flowery work doth sing,
And the waters murmuring,
With such consort as they keep, 145
Entice the dewy-feathered sleep;
And let some strange mysterious dream
Wave at his wings, in airy stream
Of lively portraiture displayed,
Softly on my eyelids laid. 150
And, as I wake, sweet music breathe
Above, about, or underneath,
Sent by some spirit to mortals good,
Or the unseen Genius of the wood.
But let my due feet never fail 155
To walk the studious cloister's pale,
And love the high embowéd roof,
With antique pillars massy proof,
And storied windows richly dight,
Casting a dim religious light: 160
There let the pealing organ blow
To the full-voiced choir below
In service high and anthems clear
As may with sweetness, through mine ear,
Dissolve me into ecstasies, 165
And bring all heaven before mine eyes.
And may at last my weary age
Find out the peaceful hermitage,
The hairy gown and mossy cell,
Where I may sit and rightly spell 170
Of every star that heaven doth shew,

And every herb that sips the dew,
Till old experience do attain
To something like prophetic strain.
These pleasures, Melancholy, give,   175
And I with thee will choose to live. (1632?; 1645)

ON SHAKESPEARE

What needs my Shakespeare for his honored bones
The labour of an age in piléd stones?
Or that his hallowed reliques should be hid
Under a star-ypointing pyramid?
Dear son of memory, great heir of fame,   5
What need'st thou such weak witness of thy name?
Thou in our wonder and astonishment
Hast built thyself a livelong monument.
For whilst, to the shame of slow-endeavoring art
Thy easy numbers flow, and that each heart   10
Hath from the leaves of thy unvalued book
Those Delphic lines with deep impression took,
Then thou, our fancy of itself bereaving,
Dost make *us* marble with too much conceiving,
And so sepúlchred in such pomp dost lie   15
That kings for such a tomb would wish to die. (1632)

ON HIS HAVING ARRIVED
AT THE AGE OF TWENTY-THREE

How soon hath Time, the subtle thief of youth,
    Stol'n on his wing my three-and-twentieth year!
    My hasting days fly on with full career,
    But my late spring no bud or blossom shew'th.
Perhaps my semblance might deceive the truth,   5
    That I to manhood am arriv'd so near,
    And inward ripeness doth much less appear,
    That some more timely-happy spirits indu'th.
Yet it be less or more, or soon or slow,
    It shall be still in strictest measure ev'n,   10
    To that same lot, however mean or high,
Toward which Time leads me, and the will of Heav'n;
    All is, if I have grace to use it so,
    As ever in my great Taskmaster's eye. (1645)

ON THE LATE MASSACRE IN PIEDMONT

Avenge, O Lord, Thy slaughtered saints, whose bones
Lie scattered on the Alpine mountains cold;
Even them who kept Thy truth so pure of old
When all our fathers worshiped stocks and stones,
Forget not: in Thy book record their groans   5
Who were Thy sheep, and in their ancient fold
Slain by the bloody Piedmontese, that rolled
Mother with infant down the rocks. Their moans
The vales redoubled to the hills, and they
To heaven. Their martyred blood and ashes sow   10
O'er all the Italian fields, where still doth sway
The triple Tyrant, that from these may grow
A hundredfold, who, having learnt Thy way,
Early may fly the Babylonian woe. (1655; 1673)

ON HIS BLINDNESS

When I consider how my light is spent
   Ere half my days in this dark world and wide,
   And that one talent which is death to hide
   Lodged with me useless, though my soul more bent
To serve therewith my Maker, and present   5
   My true account, lest He returning chide;
   "Doth God exact day-labor, light denied?"
   I fondly ask. But Patience, to prevent
That murmur, soon replies, "God doth not need
   Either man's work or his own gifts. Who best   10
   Bear his mild yoke, they serve him best. His state
Is kingly: thousands at his bidding speed,
   And post o'er land and ocean without rest;
   They also serve who only stand and wait. (1655?)

Andrew Marvell

TO HIS COY MISTRESS

Had we but world enough, and time,
This coyness, lady, were no crime.

We would sit down, and think which way
To walk, and pass our long love's day.
Thou by the Indian Ganges' side   5
Shouldst rubies find: I by the tide
Of Humber would complain. I would
Love you ten years before The Flood,
And you should, if you please, refuse
Till the conversion of the Jews;   10
My vegetable love should grow
Vaster than empires and more slow;
An hundred years should go to praise
Thine eyes, and on thy forehead gaze;
Two hundred to adore each breast,   15
But thirty thousand to the rest;
An age at least to every part,
And the last age should show your heart.
For, lady, you deserve this state;
Nor would I love at lower rate.   20

But at my back I always hear
Time's wingéd chariot hurrying near;
And yonder all before us lie
Deserts of vast eternity.
Thy beauty shall no more be found,   25
Nor in thy marble vault shall sound
My echoing song; then worms shall try
That long preserved virginity;
And your quaint honor turn to dust,
And into ashes all my lust: 30
The grave's a fine and private place,
But none, I think, do there embrace.

Now therefore, while the youthful hue
Sits on thy skin like morning dew,
And while thy willing soul transpires   35
At every pore with instant fires,
Now let us sport us while we may,
And now, like amorous birds of prey,
Rather at once our time devour
Than languish in his slow-chapped power,   40
Let us roll all our strength and all
Our sweetness up into one ball,
And tear our pleasures with rough strife
Thorough the iron gates of life:
Thus, though we cannot make our sun   45
Stand still, yet we will make him run. (c. 1650; 1681)

Henry Vaughan

THE WORLD

I saw Eternity the other night,
Like a great ring of pure and endless light,
   All calm, as it was bright;
And round beneath it, Time, in hours, days, years,
   Driven by the spheres   5
Like a vast shadow moved; in which the world
   And all her train were hurled.
The doting lover in his quaintest strain
   Did there complain;
Near him, his lute, his fancy, and his flights,   10
   Wit's sour delights,
With gloves, and knots, the silly snares of pleasure,
   Yet his dear treasure,
All scattered lay, while he his eyes did pour
   Upon a flower.   15

The darksome statesman, hung with weights and woe,
Like a thick midnight-fog moved there so slow,
   He did not stay, nor go;
Condemning thoughts, like sad eclipses, scowl
   Upon his soul,   20
And clouds of crying witnesses without
   Pursued him with one shout.
Yet digged the mole, and lest his ways be found,
   Worked under ground,
Where he did clutch his prey; but one did see   25
   That policy;
Churches and altars fed him; perjuries
   Were gnats and flies;
It rained about him blood and tears, but he
   Drank them as free.   30

The fearful miser on a heap of rust
Sat pining all his life there, did scarce trust
   His own hands with the dust,
Yet would not place one piece above, but lives
   In fear of thieves.   35
Thousands there were as frantic as himself,
   And hugged each one his pelf;

The downright epicure placed heaven in sense,
   And scorned pretense;
While others, slipped into a wide excess,   40
   Said little less;
The weaker sort, slight, trivial wares enslave,
   Who think them brave;
And poor, despiséd Truth sat counting by
   Their victory.   45

Yet some, who all this while did weep and sing,
And sing and weep, soared up into the ring;
   But most would use no wing.
O fools, said I, thus to prefer dark night
   Before true light!   50
To live in grots and caves, and hate the day
   Because it shows the way,
The way, which from this dead and dark abode
   Leads up to God;
A way where you might tread the sun, and be   55
   More bright than he!
But, as I did their madness so discuss,
   One whispered thus
"This ring the Bridegroom did for none provide,
   But for his bride." (1650)   60

Restoration and Eighteenth=Century Poems

John Dryden

A SONG FOR ST. CECILIA'S DAY

From harmony, from heavenly harmony,
   This universal frame began:
   When Nature underneath a heap
      Of jarring atoms lay,

And could not heave her head,　　　　　　　5
The tuneful voice was heard from high:
　　　"Arise, ye more than dead."

Then cold and hot and moist and dry
　　In order to their stations leap,
　　　And Music's power obey.　　　　　　10
From harmony, from heavenly harmony,
　　　This universal frame began:
　　　From harmony to harmony
Through all the compass of the notes it ran,
The diapason closing full in Man.　　　　　15

What passion cannot Music raise and quell!
　　　When Jubal struck the chorded shell,
　　His listening brethren stood around,
　　　And wondering, on their faces fell
　　To worship that celestial sound.　　　　20
Less than a god they thought there could not dwell
　　Within the hollow of that shell
　　That spoke so sweetly and so well.
What passion cannot Music raise and quell!

　　The trumpet's loud clangor　　　　　25
　　　Excites us to arms
　　With shrill notes of anger
　　　And mortal alarms.
　　The double, double, double beat
　　　Of the thundering drum　　　　　30
　　　Cries: "Hark! the foes come;
Charge, charge, 'tis too late to retreat!"

The soft complaining flute
　　In dying notes discovers
　　　The woes of hopeless lovers,　　　　35
Whose dirge is whispered by the warbling lute.
　　Sharp violins proclaim
Their jealous pangs and desperation,
Fury, frantic indignation,
Depth of pains, and height of passion,　　　40
　　For the fair, disdainful dame.

But oh! what art can teach,
What human voice can reach
　　The sacred organ's praise?

Notes inspiring holy love, 45
Notes that wing their heavenly ways
To mend the choirs above.
Orpheus could lead the savage race;
And trees unrooted left their place,
Sequacious of the lyre; 50
But bright Cecilia raised the wonder higher:
When to her organ vocal breath was given,
An angel heard, and straight appeared,
Mistaking earth for heaven.

Grand Chorus

As from the power of sacred lays 55
The spheres began to move,
And sung the great Creator's praise
To all the blessed above;
So when the last and dreadful hour
This crumbling pageant shall devour, 60
The trumpet shall be heard on high,
The dead shall live, the living die,
And music shall untune the sky. (1687)

Matthew Prior

TO A CHILD OF QUALITY

Five years old, MDCCIV, the author then forty

Lords, knights, and squires, the numerous band
That wear the fair Miss Mary's fetters,
Were summoned by her high command,
To show their passions by their letters.

My pen among the rest I took, 5
Lest those bright eyes that cannot read
Should dart their kindling fires, and look
The power they have to be obeyed.

Nor quality nor reputation
Forbid me yet my flame to tell; 10
Dear five years old befriends my passion,
And I may write till she can spell.

For while she makes her silkworms beds
   With all the tender things I swear,
Whilst all the house my passion reads   15
   In papers round her baby hair,

She may receive and own my flame,
   For, though the strictest prudes should know it,
She'll pass for a most virtuous dame,
   And I for an unhappy poet.   20

Then too, alas! when she shall tear
   The lines some younger rival sends,
She'll give me leave to write, I fear,
   And we shall still continue friends.

For, as our different ages move,   25
   'Tis so ordained, (would Fate but mend it!)
That I shall be past making love,
   When she begins to comprehend it. (1704)

Jonathan Swift

DESCRIPTION OF A CITY SHOWER

   Careful observers may foretell the Hour
(By sure Prognostics) when to dread a Show'r:
While Rain depends, the pensive Cat gives o'er
Her Frolics, and pursues her Tail no more.
Returning Home at Night, you'll find the Sink   5
Strike your offended Sense with double Stink.
If you be wise, then go not far to Dine;
You'll spend in Coach-hire more than save in Wine.
A coming Show'r your shooting Corns presage,
Old Aches throb, your hollow Tooth will rage.   10
Saunt'ring in Coffee-house is Dulman seen;
He damns the Climate, and complains of Spleen.

   Meanwhile the South, rising with dabbled Wings,
A sable Cloud athwart the Welkin flings,
That swill'd more Liquor than it could contain,   15
And like a Drunkard gives it up again.
Brisk Susan whips her Linen from the Rope,
While the first drizzling Show'r is born aslope,
Such is that Sprinkling which some careless Quean
Flirts on you from her Mop, but not so clean.   20

You fly, invoke the Gods; then turning, stop
To rail; she, singing, still whirls on her Mop.
Not yet the Dust had shunn'd th' unequal Strife
But, aided by the Wind, fought still for Life;
And wafted with its Foe by violent Gust.   25
'Twas doubtful which was Rain, and which was Dust.
Ah! where must needy Poet seek for Aid,
When Dust and Rain at once his Coat invade,
His only Coat, where Dust, confus'd with Rain,
Roughen the Nap and leave a mingled Stain.   30

   Now in contiguous Drops the Flood comes down,
Threat'ning with Deluge this Devoted Town.
To Shops in Crowds the daggled Females fly,
Pretend to cheapen Goods, but nothing buy.
The Templer spruce, while ev'ry Spout's a-broach,   35
Stays till 'tis fair, yet seems to call a Coach.
The tuck'd-up Sempstress walks with hasty Strides,
While Streams run down her oil'd Umbrella's Sides.
Here various Kinds of various Fortunes led
Commence Acquaintance underneath a Shed.   40
Triumphant Tories and desponding Whigs
Forget their Feuds, and join to save their Wigs.

   Box'd in a Chair the Beau impatient sits,
While Spouts run clatt'ring o'er the Roof by Fits;
And ever and anon with frightful Din   45
The Leather sounds; he trembles from within.
So when Troy Chair-men bore the Wooden Steed,
Pregnant with Greeks, impatient to be freed,
(Those Bully Greeks, who, as the Moderns do,
Instead of paying Chair-men, run them thro'.)   50
Laoco'n struck the Outside with his Spear,
And each imprison'd Hero quak'd for Fear.

   Now from all Parts the swelling Kennels flow,
And bear their Trophies with them as they go:
Filth of all Hues and Odours seem to tell   55
What Street they sail'd from, by their Sight and Smell.
They, as each Torrent drives, with rapid Force
From Smithfield, or St. Pulchre's shape their Course,
And in huge Confluent join at Snow-Hill Ridge,
Fall from the Conduit prone to Holborn-Bridge.   60
Sweepings from Butchers' Stalls, Dung, Guts, and Blood,
Drown'd Puppies, stinking Sprats, all drench'd in Mud,
Dead Cats and Turnip-Tops come tumbling down the Flood. (1710)

Thomas Gray

ELEGY WRITTEN IN
A COUNTRY CHURCHYARD

The curfew tolls the knell of parting day,
　The lowing herd winds slowly o'er the lea,
The plowman homeward plods his weary way,
　And leaves the world to darkness and to me.

Now fades the glimmering landscape on the sight,　　5
　And all the air a solemn stillness holds,
Save where the beetle wheels his droning flight,
　And drowsy tinklings lull the distant folds;

Save that from yonder ivy-mantled tower
　The moping owl does to the moon complain　　10
Of such, as wandering near her secret bower,
　Molest her ancient solitary reign.

Beneath those rugged elms, that yew-tree's shade,
　Where heaves the turf in many a moldering heap,
Each in his narrow cell for ever laid,　　15
　The rude forefathers of the hamlet sleep.

The breezy call of incense-breathing morn,
　The swallow twittering from the straw-built shed,
The cock's shrill clarion, or the echoing horn,
　No more shall rouse them from their lowly bed.　　20

For them no more the blazing hearth shall burn,
　Or busy housewife ply her evening care:
No children run to lisp their sire's return,
　Or climb his knees the envied kiss to share.

Oft did the harvest to their sickle yield,　　25
　Their furrow oft the stubborn glebe has broke;
How jocund did they drive their team afield!
　How bowed the woods beneath their sturdy stroke!

Let not Ambition mock their useful toil,
　Their homely joys, and destiny obscure;　　30

Nor Grandeur hear with a disdainful smile,
   The short and simple annals of the poor.

The boast of heraldry, the pomp of power,
   And all that beauty, all that wealth e'er gave,
Awaits alike the inevitable hour.   35
   The paths of glory lead but to the grave.

Nor you, ye proud, impute to these the fault,
   If Memory o'er their tomb no trophies raise,
Where through the long-drawn aisle and fretted vault
   The pealing anthem swells the note of praise.   40

Can storied urn or animated bust
   Back to its mansion call the fleeting breath?
Can Honor's voice provoke the silent dust,
   Or Flattery soothe the dull cold ear of Death?

Perhaps in this neglected spot is laid   45
   Some heart once pregnant with celestial fire;
Hands, that the rod of empire might have swayed,
   Or waked to ecstasy the living lyre.

But Knowledge to their eyes her ample page
   Rich with the spoils of time did ne'er unroll;   50
Chill Penury repressed their noble rage,
   And froze the genial current of the soul.

Full many a gem of purest ray serene,
   The dark unfathomed caves of ocean bear:
Full many a flower is born to blush unseen   55
   And waste its sweetness on the desert air.

Some village Hampden, that with dauntless breast
   The little tyrant of his fields withstood;
Some mute inglorious Milton here may rest,
   Some Cromwell guiltless of his country's blood.   60

The applause of listening senates to command,
   The threats of pain and ruin to despise,
To scatter plenty o'er a smiling land,
   And read their history in a nation's eyes,

Their lot forbade: nor circumscribed alone   65
   Their growing virtues, but their crimes confined;

Forbade to wade through slaughter to a throne,
   And shut the gates of mercy on mankind,

The struggling pangs of conscious truth to hide,
   To quench the blushes of ingenuous shame,   70
Or heap the shrine of Luxury and Pride
   With incense kindled at the Muse's flame.

Far from the madding crowd's ignoble strife,
   Their sober wishes never learned to stray;
Along the cool sequestered vale of life   75
   They kept the noiseless tenor of their way.

Yet even these bones from insult to protect,
   Some frail memorial still erected nigh,
With uncouth rhymes and shapeless sculpture decked,
   Implores the passing tribute of a sigh.   80

Their name, their years, spelt by the unlettered muse,
   The place of fame and elegy supply;
And many a holy text around she strews,
   That teach the rustic moralist to die.

For who to dumb Forgetfulness a prey,   85
   This pleasing anxious being e'er resigned,
Left the warm precincts of the cheerful day,
   Nor cast one longing lingering look behind?

On some fond breast the parting soul relies,
   Some pious drops the closing eye requires;   90
Ev'n from the tomb the voice of Nature cries,
   Ev'n in our ashes live their wonted fires.

For thee, who mindful of the unhonored dead
   Dost in these lines their artless tale relate;
If chance, by lonely contemplation led,   95
   Some kindred spirit shall inquire thy fate,

Haply some hoary-headed swain may say,
   "Oft have we seen him at the peep of dawn
Brushing with hasty steps the dews away
   To meet the sun upon the upland lawn.   100

"There at the foot of yonder nodding beech
   That wreathes its old fantastic roots so high,

His listless length at noontide would he stretch,
  And pore upon the brook that babbles by.

"Hard by yon wood, now smiling as in scorn,   105
  Muttering his wayward fancies he would rove,
Now drooping, woeful wan, like one forlorn,
  Or crazed with care, or crossed in hopeless love.

"One morn I missed him on the customed hill,
  Along the heath and near his favorite tree;   110
Another came; nor yet beside the rill,
  Nor up the lawn, nor at the wood was he;

"The next with dirges due in sad array
  Slow through the church-way path we saw him borne.
Approach and read (for thou can'st read) the lay,   115
  Graved on the stone beneath yon aged thorn."

The Epitaph
Here rests his head upon the lap of earth
  A youth to fortune and to fame unknown.
Fair Science frowned not on his humble birth,
  And Melancholy marked him for her own.   120

Large was his bounty, and his soul sincere,
  Heaven did a recompense as largely send:
He gave to Misery all he had, a tear,
  He gained from Heaven ('twas all he wished) a friend.

No farther seek his merits to disclose,   125
  Or draw his frailties from their dread abode,
(There they alike in trembling hope repose)
  The bosom of his Father and his God. (1751)

William Collins

ODE

Written in the beginning of the year 1746

How sleep the brave who sink to rest
By all their country's wishes bless'd!

When Spring, with dewy fingers cold,
Returns to deck their hallow'd mould,
She there shall dress a sweeter sod   5
Than Fancy's feet have ever trod.

By fairy hands their knell is rung;
By forms unseen their dirge is sung;
There Honour comes, a pilgrim gray,
To bless the turf that wraps their clay;   10
And Freedom shall awhile repair,
To dwell a weeping hermit there! (1747)

William Blake

THE TIGER

Tiger! Tiger! burning bright
In the forests of the night,
What immortal hand or eye
Could frame thy fearful symmetry?

In what distant deeps or skies   5
Burnt the fire of thine eyes?
On what wings dare he aspire?
What the hand dare seize the fire?

And what shoulder, and what art,
Could twist the sinews of thy heart?   10
And when thy heart began to beat,
What dread hand? and what dread feet?

What the hammer? what the chain?
In what furnace was thy brain?
What the anvil? what dread grasp   15
Dare its deadly terrors clasp?

When the stars threw down their spears,
And watered heaven with their tears,
Did he smile his work to see?
Did he who made the Lamb make thee?   20

Tiger! Tiger! burning bright
In the forests of the night,
What immortal hand or eye
Dare frame thy fearful symmetry? (1794)

LONDON

I wander through each chartered street,
Near where the chartered Thames does flow,
And mark in every face I meet
Marks of weakness, marks of woe.

In every cry of every man,   5
In every infant's cry of fear,
In every voice, in every ban,
The mind-forged manacles I hear:

How the chimney-sweeper's cry
Every blackening church appalls,   10
And the hapless soldier's sigh
Runs in blood down palace walls.

But most, through midnight streets I hear
How the youthful harlot's curse
Blasts the new-born infant's tear,   15
And blights with plagues the marriage hearse. (1794)

Robert Burns

THE DEIL'S AWA
WI' TH' EXCISEMAN

Chorus

The deil's awa, the deil's awa,
  The deil's awa wi' th' Exciseman;
He's danc'd awa, he's danc'd awa,
  He's danc'd awa wi' th' Exciseman!

The deil cam fiddlin thro' the town 5
  And danc'd awa wi' th' Exciseman.
And ilka wife cries: "Auld Mahoun,
  I wish you luck o' the prize, man!

"We'll mak our maut, we'll brew our drink,
  We'll laugh, sing, and rejoice, man; 10
And monie braw thanks to the meikle black deil,
  That danc'd awa wi' th' Exciseman."

There's threesome reels, there's foursome reels,
  There's hornpipes and strathspeys, man;
But the ae best dance e'er cam to the land 15
  Was *The Deil's Awa wi' th' Exciseman.*

Chorus

The deil's awa, the deil's awa,
  The deil's awa wi' th' Exciseman;
He's danc'd awa, he's danc'd awa,
  He's danc'd awa wi' th' Exciseman! (1792) 20

O, WERT THOU
IN THE CAULD BLAST

O, wert thou in the cauld blast
  On yonder lea, on yonder lea,
My plaidie to the angry airt,
  I'd shelter thee, I'd shelter thee.
Or did misfortune's bitter storms 5
  Around thee blaw, around thee blaw,
Thy bield should be my bosom,
  To share it a', to share it a'.

Or were I in the wildest waste,
  Sae black and bare, sae black and bare, 10
The desert were a paradise,
  If thou wert there, if thou wert there.
Or were I monarch o' the globe,
  Wi' thee to reign, wi' thee to reign,
The brightest jewel in my crown 15
  Wad be my queen, wad be my queen. (1796; 1800)

Nineteenth-Century Poems

William Wordsworth

THE WORLD IS
TOO MUCH WITH US

The world is too much with us; late and soon,
Getting and spending, we lay waste our powers:
Little we see in Nature that is ours;
We have given our hearts away, a sordid boon!
The sea that bares her bosom to the moon;   5
The winds that will be howling at all hours,
And are up-gathered now like sleeping flowers;
For this, for everything, we are out of tune;
It moves us not.—Great God! I'd rather be
A Pagan suckled in a creed outworn;   10
So might I, standing on this pleasant lea,
Have glimpses that would make me less forlorn;
Have sight of Proteus rising from the sea;
Or hear old Triton blow his wreathéd horn. (1806; 1807)

LONDON, 1802

Milton! thou shouldst be living at this hour:
England hath need of thee: she is a fen
Of stagnant waters: altar, sword, and pen,
Fireside, the heroic wealth of hall and bower,
Have forfeited their ancient English dower   5
Of inward happiness. We are selfish men:
Oh! raise us up, return to us again;
And give us manners, virtue, freedom, power.
Thy soul was like a Star, and dwelt apart:
Thou hadst a voice whose sound was like the sea,   10
Pure as the naked heavens, majestic, free;
So didst thou travel on life's common way
In cheerful godliness; and yet thy heart
The lowliest duties on herself did lay. (1802; 1807)

ODE

Intimations of immortality from recollections of early childhood

I

There was a time when meadow, grove, and stream,
    The earth, and every common sight,
       To me did seem
       Appareled in celestial light,
The glory and the freshness of a dream.   5
It is not now as it hath been of yore;—
       Turn wheresoe'er I may,
        By night or day,
The things which I have seen I now can see no more.

II

       The Rainbow comes and goes,   10
       And lovely is the Rose;
       The Moon doth with delight
Look round her when the heavens are bare;
       Waters on a starry night
       Are beautiful and fair;   15
       The sunshine is a glorious birth;
       But yet I know, where'er I go,
That there hath passed away a glory from the earth.

III

Now, while the birds thus sing a joyous song,
       And while the young lambs bound   20
        As to the tabor's sound,
To me alone there came a thought of grief:
A timely utterance gave that thought relief,
       And I again am strong:
The cataracts blow their trumpets from the steep;   25
No more shall grief of mine the season wrong;
I hear the Echoes through the mountains throng,
The Winds come to me from the fields of sleep,
       And all the earth is gay;
        Land and sea   30
       Give themselves up to jollity,
       And with the heart of May
       Doth every Beast keep holiday;—
        Thou Child of Joy,
Shout round me, let me hear thy shouts, thou happy Shepherd-boy!   35

IV

Ye blessèd Creatures, I have heard the call
  Ye to each other make; I see
The heavens laugh with you in your jubilee;
  My heart is at your festival,
  My head hath its coronal,   40
The fulness of your bliss, I feel—I feel it all.
  Oh, evil day! if I were sullen
  While Earth herself is adorning,
   This sweet May-morning,
  And the Children are culling   45
   On every side,
  In a thousand valleys far and wide,
Fresh flowers; while the sun shines warm,
And the Babe leaps up on his Mother's arm—
  I hear, I hear, with joy I hear!   50
  —But there's a Tree, of many, one,
A single Field which I have looked upon,
Both of them speak of something that is gone:
  The Pansy at my feet
  Doth the same tale repeat: 55
Whither is fled the visionary gleam?
Where is it now, the glory and the dream?

V

Our birth is but a sleep and a forgetting:
The Soul that rises with us, our life's Star,
  Hath had elsewhere its setting,   60
   And cometh from afar:
  Not in entire forgetfulness,
  And not in utter nakedness,
But trailing clouds of glory do we come
  From God, who is our home: 65
Heaven lies about us in our infancy!
Shades of the prison-house begin to close
  Upon the growing Boy,
But he beholds the light, and whence it flows
  He sees it in his joy;   70
The Youth, who daily farther from the east
  Must travel, still is Nature's priest,
   And by the vision splendid
   Is on his way attended;
At length the Man perceives it die away,   75
And fade into the light of common day.

VI

Earth fills her lap with pleasures of her own;
Yearnings she hath in her own natural kind,
And even with something of a Mother's mind,
  And no unworthy aim,   80
  The homely Nurse doth all she can
To make her Foster-child, her Inmate Man,
  Forget the glories he hath known,
And that imperial palace whence he came.

VII

Behold the Child among his new-born blisses,   85
A six years' Darling of a pigmy size!
See, where 'mid work of his own hand he lies,
Fretted by sallies of his mother's kisses,
With light upon him from his father's eyes!
See, at his feet, some little plan or chart,   90
Some fragment from his dream of human life,
Shaped by himself with newly-learnéd art;
  A wedding or a festival,
  A mourning or a funeral,
   And this hath now his heart,   95
  And unto this he frames his song:
   Then will he fit his tongue
To dialogues of business, love, or strife;
  But it will not be long
  Ere this be thrown aside,   100
  And with new joy and pride
The little Actor cons another part;
Filling from time to time his "humorous stage"
With all the Persons, down to palsied Age,
That Life brings with her in her equipage;   105
  As if his whole vocation
  Were endless imitation.

VIII

Thou, whose exterior semblance doth belie
  Thy Soul's immensity;
Thou best Philosopher, who yet dost keep   110
Thy heritage, thou Eye among the blind,
That, deaf and silent, read'st the eternal deep,
Haunted forever by the eternal mind—
  Mighty Prophet! Seer blest!
  On whom those truths do rest,   115
Which we are toiling all our lives to find,
In darkness lost, the darkness of the grave;

Thou, over whom thy Immortality
Broods like the Day, a Master o'er a Slave,
A Presence which is not to be put by;   120
Thou little Child, yet glorious in the might
Of heaven-born freedom on thy being's height,
Why with such earnest pains dost thou provoke
The years to bring the inevitable yoke,
Thus blindly with thy blessedness at strife?   125
Full soon thy Soul shall have her earthly freight,
And custom lie upon thee with a weight,
Heavy as frost, and deep almost as life!

IX

    Oh, joy! that in our embers
    Is something that doth live,   130
    That nature yet remembers
    What was so fugitive!
The thought of our past years in me doth breed
Perpetual benediction: not indeed
For that which is most worthy to be blest;   135
Delight and liberty, the simple creed
Of Childhood, whether busy or at rest,
With new-fledged hope still fluttering in his breast—
    Not for these I raise
    The song of thanks and praise;   140
    But for those obstinate questionings
    Of sense and outward things,
    Falling from us, vanishings;
    Blank misgivings of a Creature
Moving about in worlds not realized,   145
High instincts before which our mortal nature
Did tremble like a guilty thing surprised:
    But for those first affections,
    Those shadowy recollections,
    Which, be they what they may,   150
Are yet the fountain light of all our day,
Are yet a master light of all our seeing;
  Uphold us, cherish, and have power to make
Our noisy years seem moments in the being
Of the eternal Silence: truths that wake,   155
    To perish never;
Which neither listlessness, nor mad endeavor,
    Nor Man nor Boy,
Nor all that is at enmity with joy,
Can utterly abolish or destroy!   160

Hence in a season of calm weather
　　Though inland far we be,
Our Souls have sight of that immortal sea
　　Which brought us hither,
　　Can in a moment travel thither,　　　　　165
And see the Children sport upon the shore,
And hear the mighty waters rolling evermore.

X

Then sing, ye Birds, sing, sing a joyous song!
　　And let the young Lambs bound
　　As to the tabor's sound!　　　　　170
We in thought will join your throng,
　　Ye that pipe and ye that play,
　　Ye that through your hearts today
　　Feel the gladness of the May!
What though the radiance which was once so bright　　175
Be now forever taken from my sight,
　Though nothing can bring back the hour
Of splendor in the grass, of glory in the flower;
　　We will grieve not, rather find
　　Strength in what remains behind;　　　　　180
　　In the primal sympathy
　　Which having been must ever be;
　　In the soothing thoughts that spring
　　Out of human suffering;
　　In the faith that looks through death,　　　　　185
In years that bring the philosophic mind.

XI

And O, ye Fountains, Meadows, Hills, and Groves,
Forebode not any severing of our loves!
Yet in my heart of hearts I feel your might;
I only have relinquished one delight　　　　　190
To live beneath your more habitual sway.
I love the Brooks which down their channels fret,
Even more than when I tripped lightly as they;
The innocent brightness of a new-born Day
　　Is lovely yet;　　　　　195
The Clouds that gather round the setting sun
Do take a sober coloring from an eye
That hath kept watch o'er man's mortality.
Another race hath been, and other palms are won.
Thanks to the human heart by which we live,　　　　　200
Thanks to its tenderness, its joys, and fears,
To me the meanest flower that blows can give
Thoughts that do often lie too deep for tears. (1803-1806; 1807)

Samuel Taylor Coleridge

KUBLA KHAN

In Xanadu did Kubla Khan
A stately pleasure-dome decree:
Where Alph, the sacred river, ran
Through caverns measureless to man
    Down to a sunless sea.   5
So twice five miles of fertile ground
With walls and towers were girdled round:
And here were gardens bright with sinuous rills,
Where blossomed many an incense-bearing tree;
And here were forests ancient as the hills,   10
Enfolding sunny spots of greenery.
But oh! that deep romantic chasm which slanted
Down the green hill athwart a cedarn cover!
A savage place! as holy and enchanted
As e'er beneath a waning moon was haunted   15
By woman wailing for her demon-lover!
And from this chasm, with ceaseless turmoil seething,
As if this earth in fast thick pants were breathing
A mighty fountain momently was forced;
Amid whose swift half-intermitted burst   20
Huge fragments vaulted like rebounding hail,
Or chaffy grain beneath the thresher's flail:
And 'mid these dancing rocks at once and ever
It flung up momently the sacred river.
Five miles meandering with a mazy motion   25
Through wood and dale the sacred river ran,
Then reached the caverns measureless to man,
And sank in tumult to a lifeless ocean:
And 'mid this tumult Kubla heard from far
Ancestral voices prophesying war!   30

    The shadow of the dome of pleasure
    Floated midway on the waves;
    Where was heard the mingled measure
    From the fountain and the caves.
It was a miracle of rare device,   35
A sunny pleasure-dome with caves of ice!
    A damsel with a dulcimer
    In a vision once I saw:

It was an Abyssinian maid,
And on her dulcimer she played,   40
Singing of Mount Abora.
Could I revive within me,
Her symphony and song,
To such a deep delight 'twould win me,
That with music loud and long,   45
I would build that dome in air,
That sunny dome! those caves of ice!
And all who heard should see them there,
And all should cry, Beware! Beware!
His flashing eyes, his floating hair!   50
Weave a circle round him thrice,
And close your eyes with holy dread,
For he on honey-dew hath fed,
And drunk the milk of Paradise. (1797; 1816)

Percy Bysshe Shelley

OZYMANDIAS

I met a traveler from an antique land
Who said: "Two vast and trunkless legs of stone
Stand in the desert. Near them, on the sand,
Half sunk, a shattered visage lies, whose frown,
And wrinkled lip, and sneer of cold command,   5
Tell that its sculptor well those passions read
Which yet survive, stamped on these lifeless things,
The hand that mocked them, and the heart that fed:
And on the pedestal these words appear:
'My name is Ozymandias, king of kings: 10
Look on my works, ye Mighty, and despair!'
Nothing beside remains. Round the decay
Of that colossal wreck, boundless and bare
The lone and level sands stretch far away." (1817; 1818)

ODE TO THE WEST WIND

I

O wild west wind, thou breath of Autumn's being,
Thou, from whose unseen presence the leaves dead
Are driven, like ghosts from an enchanter fleeing,

Yellow, and black, and pale, and hectic red,   5
Pestilence-stricken multitudes: O thou,
Who chariotest to their dark wintry bed

The wingéd seeds, where they lie cold and low,
Each like a corpse within its grave, until
Thine azure sister of the Spring shall blow

Her clarion o'er the dreaming earth, and fill   10
(Driving sweet buds like flocks to feed in air)
With living hues and odors plain and hill:

Wild Spirit, which art moving everywhere;
Destroyer and preserver; hear, oh, hear!

II
Thou on whose stream, mid the steep sky's commotion,   15
Loose clouds like earth's decaying leaves are shed,
Shook from the tangled boughs of Heaven and Ocean,

Angels of rain and lightning: there are spread
On the blue surface of thine aëry surge,
Like the bright hair uplifted from the head   20

Of some fierce Maenad, even from the dim verge
Of the horizon to the zenith's height,
The locks of the approaching storm. Thou dirge

Of the dying year, to which this closing night
Will be the dome of a vast sepulcher,   25
Vaulted with all thy congregated might

Of vapors, from whose solid atmosphere
Black rain, and fire, and hail will burst: oh, hear!

III
Thou who didst waken from his summer dreams
The blue Mediterranean, where he lay,   30
Lulled by the coil of his crystalline streams,

Beside a pumice isle in Baiae's bay,
And saw in sleep old palaces and towers
Quivering within the wave's intenser day,

All overgrown with azure moss and flowers   35
So sweet, the sense faints picturing them! Thou
For whose path the Atlantic's level powers

Cleave themselves into chasms, while far below
The sea-blooms and the oozy woods which wear
The sapless foliage of the ocean, know   40

Thy voice, and suddenly grow gray with fear,
And tremble and despoil themselves: oh, hear!

IV

If I were a dead leaf thou mightest bear,
If I were a swift cloud to fly with thee;
A wave to pant beneath thy power, and share   45

The impulse of thy strength, only less free
Than thou, O uncontrollable! If even
I were as in my boyhood, and could be

The comrade of thy wanderings over Heaven,
As then, when to outstrip thy skyey speed   50
Scarce seemed a vision; I would ne'er have striven

As thus with thee in prayer in my sore need.
Oh, lift me as a wave, a leaf, a cloud!
I fall upon the thorns of life! I bleed!

A heavy weight of hours has chained and bowed   55
One too like thee: tameless, and swift, and proud.

V

Make me thy lyre, even as the forest is:
What if my leaves are falling like its own!
The tumult of thy mighty harmonies

Will take from both a deep, autumnal tone,   60
Sweet though in sadness. Be thou, Spirit fierce,
My spirit! Be thou me, impetuous one!

Drive my dead thoughts over the universe
Like withered leaves to quicken a new birth!
And, by the incantation of this verse,   65

Scatter, as from an unextinguished hearth
Ashes and sparks, my words among mankind!
Be through my lips to unawakened earth

The trumpet of a prophecy! O Wind,
If Winter comes, can Spring be far behind? (1819; 1820) 70

John Keats

ODE TO A NIGHTINGALE

My heart aches, and a drowsy numbness pains
  My sense, as though of hemlock I had drunk,
Or emptied some dull opiate to the drains
  One minute past, and Lethe-wards had sunk:
'Tis not through envy of thy happy lot,   5
  But being too happy in thine happiness—
    That thou, light-wingéd Dryad of the trees,
      In some melodious plot
  Of beechen green, and shadows numberless,
    Singest of summer in full-throated ease.   10

O, for a draught of vintage, that hath been
  Cooled a long age in the deep-delvéd earth,
Tasting of Flora and the country green,
  Dance, and Provençal song, and sunburnt mirth!
O for a beaker full of the warm South,   15
  Full of the true, the blushful Hippocrene,
    With beaded bubbles winking at the brim,
      And purple-stainéd mouth;
  That I might drink, and leave the world unseen,
    And with thee fade away into the forest dim: 20

Fade far away, dissolve, and quite forget
  What thou among the leaves hast never known,
The weariness, the fever, and the fret
  Here, where men sit and hear each other groan;
Where palsy shakes a few, sad, last gray hairs,   25
  Where youth grows pale, and specter-thin, and dies;
    Where but to think is to be full of sorrow
      And leaden-eyed despairs,
  Where Beauty cannot keep her lustrous eyes,
    Or new Love pine at them beyond tomorrow.   30

Away! away! for I will fly to thee,
  Not charioted by Bacchus and his pards,
But on the viewless wings of Poesy,
  Though the dull brain perplexes and retards:
Already with thee! tender is the night,   35

And haply the Queen-Moon is on her throne,
  Clustered around by all her starry Fays;
    But here there is no light,
Save what from heaven is with the breezes blown
  Through verdurous glooms and winding mossy ways.   40

I cannot see what flowers are at my feet,
  Nor what soft incense hangs upon the boughs,
But, in embalmèd darkness, guess each sweet
  Wherewith the seasonable month endows
The grass, the thicket, and the fruit-tree wild;   45
  White hawthorn, and the pastoral eglantine;
    Fast fading violets covered up in leaves;
      And mid-May's eldest child.
  The coming musk-rose, full of dewy wine,
    The murmurous haunt of flies on summer eves.   50

Darkling I listen; and, for many a time,
  I have been half in love with easeful Death,
Called him soft names in many a musèd rime,
  To take into the air my quiet breath;
Now more than ever seems it rich to die,   55
  To cease upon the midnight with no pain,
    While thou art pouring forth thy soul abroad
      In such an ecstasy!
  Still wouldst thou sing, and I have ears in vain—
    To thy high requiem become a sod.   60

Thou wast not born for death, immortal Bird!
  No hungry generations tread thee down;
The voice I hear this passing night was heard
  In ancient days by emperor and clown:
Perhaps the self-same song that found a path   65
  Through the sad heart of Ruth, when, sick for home,
    She stood in tears amid the alien corn;
      The same that oft-times hath
  Charmed magic casements, opening on the foam
    Of perilous seas, in faery lands forlorn.   70

Forlorn! the very word is like a bell
  To toll me back from thee to my sole self,
Adieu! the fancy cannot cheat so well
  As she is famed to do, deceiving elf.
Adieu! adieu! thy plaintive anthem fades   75
  Past the near meadows, over the still stream,

Up the hillside; and now 'tis buried deep
   In the next valley glades:
Was it a vision, or a waking dream?
  Fled is that music—Do I wake or sleep? (1819)   80

ODE ON A GRECIAN URN

Thou still unravished bride of quietness,
   Thou foster-child of Silence and slow Time,
Sylvan historian, who canst thus express
   A flowery tale more sweetly than our rime:
What leaf-fringed legend haunts about thy shape   5
   Of deities or mortals, or of both,
     In Tempe or the dales of Arcady?
   What men or gods are these? What maidens loth?
What mad pursuit? What struggle to escape?
     What pipes and timbrels? What wild ecstasy?   10

Heard melodies are sweet, but those unheard
   Are sweeter; therefore, ye soft pipes, play on;
Not to the sensual ear, but, more endeared,
   Pipe to the spirit ditties of no tone:
Fair youth, beneath the trees, thou canst not leave   15
   Thy song, nor ever can those trees be bare;
     Bold Lover, never, never canst thou kiss,
Though winning near the goal—yet, do not grieve;
     She cannot fade, though thou hast not thy bliss,
   Forever wilt thou love, and she be fair!   20

Ah, happy, happy boughs! that cannot shed
   Your leaves, nor ever bid the Spring adieu;
And, happy melodist, unweariéd,
   Forever piping songs forever new.
More happy love! more happy, happy love!   25
   Forever warm and still to be enjoyed,
     Forever panting, and forever young;
All breathing human passion far above,
    That leaves a heart high-sorrowful and cloyed,
     A burning forehead, and a parching tongue.   30

Who are these coming to the sacrifice?
   To what green altar, O mysterious priest,
Lead'st thou that heifer lowing at the skies,
   And all her silken flanks with garlands dressed?

What little town by river or seashore,   35
  Or mountain-built with peaceful citadel,
    Is emptied of this folk, this pious morn?
And, little town, thy streets forevermore
  Will silent be; and not a soul to tell
    Why thou art desolate, can e'er return.   40

O Attic shape! Fair attitude! with brede
  Of marble men and maidens overwrought,
With forest branches and the trodden weed;
  Thou, silent form, dost tease us out of thought
As doth eternity: Cold Pastoral!   45
  When old age shall this generation waste,
    Thou shalt remain, in midst of other woe
Than ours, a friend to man, to whom thou say'st,
  "Beauty is truth, truth beauty,"—that is all
    Ye know on earth, and all ye need to know. (1819; 1820) 50

ODE ON MELANCHOLY

No, no! go not to Lethe, neither twist
  Wolf's-bane, tight-rooted, for its poisonous wine;
Nor suffer thy pale forehead to be kissed
  By nightshade, ruby grape of Proserpine;
Make not your rosary of yew-berries,   5
  Nor let the beetle, nor the death-moth be
    Your mournful Psyche, nor the downy owl
A partner in your sorrow's mysteries;
  For shade to shade will come too drowsily,
    And drown the wakeful anguish of the soul.   10

But when the melancholy fit shall fall
  Sudden from heaven like a weeping cloud,
That fosters the droop-headed flowers all,
  And hides the green hill in an April shroud;
Then glut thy sorrow on a morning rose,   15
  Or on the rainbow of the salt sand-wave,
    Or on the wealth of globéd peonies;
Or if thy mistress some rich anger shows,
  Emprison her soft hand, and let her rave,
    And feed deep, deep upon her peerless eyes.   20

She dwells with Beauty—Beauty that must die;
  And Joy, whose hand is ever at his lips

Bidding adieu; and aching Pleasure nigh,
   Turning to poison while the bee-mouth sips:
Ay, in the very temple of Delight   25
   Veiled Melancholy has her sovran shrine,
     Though seen of none save him whose strenuous tongue
Can burst Joy's grape against his palate fine;
His soul shall taste the sadness of her might,
   And be among her cloudy trophies hung. (1819; 1820)   30

TO AUTUMN

Season of mists and mellow fruitfulness,
   Close bosom-friend of the maturing sun;
Conspiring with him how to load and bless
   With fruit the vines that round the thatch-eaves run;
To bend with apples the moss'd cottage-trees,   5
   And fill all fruit with ripeness to the core;
     To swell the gourd, and plump the hazel shells
With a sweet kernel; to set budding more,
   And still more, later flowers for the bees,
     Until they think warm days will never cease,   10
     For Summer has o'er-brimm'd their clammy cells.

Who hath not seen thee oft amid thy store?
   Sometimes whoever seeks abroad may find
Thee sitting careless on a granary floor,
   Thy hair soft-lifted by the winnowing wind;   15
Or on a half-reap'd furrow sound asleep,
   Drows'd with the fume of poppies, while thy hook
     Spares the next swath and all its twinèd flowers;
And sometimes like a gleaner thou dost keep
   Steady thy laden head across a brook;   20
   Or by a cider-press, with patient look,
     Thou watchest the last oozings, hours by hours.

Where are the songs of Spring? Ay, where are they?
   Think not of them, thou hast thy music too,—
While barrèd clouds bloom the soft-dying day,   25
   And touch the stubble-plains with rosy hue;
Then in a wailful choir the small gnats mourn
   Among the river sallows, borne aloft
     Or sinking as the light wind lives or dies;
And full-grown lambs loud bleat from hilly bourn;   30
   Hedge-crickets sing; and now with treble soft

The redbreast whistles from a garden-croft;
And gathering swallows twitter in the skies. (1819)

ON THE
GRASSHOPPER AND CRICKET

The poetry of earth is never dead:
When all the birds are faint with the hot sun,
And hide in cooling trees, a voice will run
From hedge to hedge about the new-mown mead;
That is the Grasshopper's—he takes the lead   5
In summer luxury,—he has never done
With his delights, for when tired out with fun,
He rests at ease beneath some pleasant weed.
The poetry of earth is ceasing never:
On a lone winter evening, when the frost   10
Has wrought a silence, from the stove there shrills
The Cricket's song, in warmth increasing ever,
And seems to one in drowsiness half lost,
The Grasshopper's among some grassy hills. (1816)

Ralph Waldo Emerson

THE RHODORA:
On Being Asked, Whence Is the Flower?

In May, when sea-winds pierced our solitudes,
I found the fresh rhodora in the woods,
Spreading its leafless blooms in a damp nook,
To please the desert and the sluggish brook.
The purple petals, fallen in the pool,   5
Made the black water with their beauty gay;
Here might the red-bird come his plumes to cool,
And court the flower that cheapens his array.
Rhodora! if the sages ask thee why
This charm is wasted on the earth and sky,   10
Tell them, dear, that if eyes were made for seeing,
Then Beauty is its own excuse for being:
Why thou wert there, O rival of the rose!

I never thought to ask, I never knew:
But, in my simple ignorance, suppose   15
The self-same Power that brought me there brought you. (1834; 1839)

EACH AND ALL

Little thinks, in the field, yon red-cloaked clown
Of thee from the hill-top looking down;
The heifer that lows in the upland farm,
Far-heard, lows not thine ear to charm;
The sexton, tolling his bell at noon,   5
Deems not that great Napoleon
Stops his horse, and lists with delight,
Whilst his files sweep round yon Alpine height;
Nor knowest thou what argument
Thy life to thy neighbor's creed has lent.   10
All are needed by each one;
Nothing is fair or good alone.
I thought the sparrow's note from heaven,
Singing at dawn on the alder bough;
I brought him home, in his nest, at even;   15
He sings the song, but it cheers not now,
For I did not bring home the river and sky;—
He sang to my ear,—they sang to my eye.
The delicate shells lay on the shore;
The bubbles of the latest wave   20
Fresh pearls to their enamel gave,
And the bellowing of the savage sea
Greeted their safe escape to me.
I wiped away the weeds and foam,
I fetched my sea-born treasures home;   25
But the poor, unsightly, noisome things
Had left their beauty on the shore
With the sun and the sand and the wild uproar.
The lover watched his graceful maid,
As 'mid the virgin train she strayed,   30
Nor knew her beauty's best attire
Was woven still by the snow-white choir.
At last she came to his hermitage,
Like the bird from the woodlands to the cage;—
The gay enchantment was undone,   35
A gentle wife, but fairy none.
Then I said, "I covet truth;
Beauty is unripe childhood's cheat;

I leave it behind with the games of youth":—
As I spoke, beneath my feet   40
The ground-pine curled its pretty wreath,
Running over the club-moss burrs;
I inhaled the violet's breath;
Around me stood the oaks and firs;
Pine-cones and acorns lay on the ground;   45
Over me soared the eternal sky,
Full of light and of deity;
Again I saw, again I heard,
The rolling river, the morning bird;—
Beauty through my senses stole;   50
I yielded myself to the perfect whole. (1834?; 1839)

DAYS

Daughters of Time, the hypocritic Days,
Muffled and dumb like barefoot dervishes,
And marching single in an endless file,
Bring diadems and fagots in their hands.
To each they offer gifts after his will,   5
Bread, kingdoms, stars, and sky that holds them all.
I, in my pleached garden, watched the pomp,
Forgot my morning wishes, hastily
Took a few herbs and apples, and the Day
Turned and departed silent. I, too late,   10
Under her solemn fillet saw the scorn. (1852?; 1857)

BRAHMA

If the red slayer think he slays,
    Or if the slain think he is slain,
They know not well the subtle ways
    I keep, and pass, and turn again.

Far or forgot to me is near;   5
    Shadow and sunlight are the same;
The vanished gods to me appear;
    And one to me are shame and fame.

They reckon ill who leave me out;
    When me they fly, I am the wings;   10

I am the doubter and the doubt,
　And I the hymn the Brahmin sings.

The strong gods pine for my abode,
　And pine in vain the sacred Seven;
But thou, meek lover of the good!　　　　　　15
　Find me, and turn thy back on heaven. (1856; 1857)

Edgar Allan Poe

TO HELEN

Helen, thy beauty is to me
　Like those Nicean barks of yore,
That gently, o'er a perfumed sea,
　The weary, wayworn wanderer bore
　To his own native shore.　　　　　　　　5

On desperate seas long wont to roam,
　Thy hyacinth hair, thy classic face,
Thy Naiad airs, have brought me home
　To the glory that was Greece
And the grandeur that was Rome.　　　　　10

Lo! in yon brilliant window-niche
　How statue-like I see thee stand,
　The agate lamp within thy hand!
Ah, Psyche, from the regions which
　Are Holy Land! (1831)　　　　　　　　15

THE CITY IN THE SEA

Lo! Death has reared himself a throne
In a strange city lying alone
Far down within the dim West,
Where the good and the bad and the worst and the best
Have gone to their eternal rest.　　　　　　5
There shrines and palaces and towers
(Time-eaten towers that tremble not)
Resemble nothing that is ours.
Around, by lifting winds forgot,

Resignedly beneath the sky   10
The melancholy waters lie.

No rays from the holy heaven come down
On the long night-time of that town;
But light from out the lurid sea
Streams up the turrets silently,   15
Gleams up the pinnacles far and free:
Up domes, up spires, up kingly halls;
Up fanes, up Babylon-like walls,
Up shadowy long-forgotten bowers
Of sculptured ivy and stone flowers,   20
Up many and many a marvelous shrine
Whose wreathed friezes intertwine
The viol, the violet, and the vine.

Resignedly beneath the sky
The melancholy waters lie.   25
So blend the turrets and shadows there
That all seem pendulous in air,
While from a proud tower in the town
Death looks gigantically down.

There open fanes and gaping graves   30
Yawn level with the luminous waves;
But not the riches there that lie
In each idol's diamond eye,—
Not the gayly-jewelled dead,
Tempt the waters from their bed;   35
For no ripples curl, alas,
Along that wilderness of glass;
No swellings tell that winds may be
Upon some far-off happier sea;
No heavings hint that winds have been   40
On seas less hideously serene!

But lo, a stir is in the air!
The wave—there is a movement there!
As if the towers had thrust aside,
In slightly sinking, the dull tide;   45
As if their tops had feebly given
A void within the filmy Heaven!
The waves have now a redder glow,
The hours are breathing faint and low;
And when, amid no earthly moans,   50
Down, down that town shall settle hence,

Hell, rising from a thousand thrones,
Shall do it reverence. (1831; 1845)

Alfred, Lord Tennyson

TITHONUS

The woods decay, the woods decay and fall,
The vapors weep their burthen to the ground,
Man comes and tills the field and lies beneath,
And after many a summer dies the swan.
Me only cruel immortality   5
Consumes: I wither slowly in thine arms,
Here at the quiet limit of the world,
A white-hair'd shadow roaming like a dream
The ever-silent spaces of the East,
Far-folded mists, and gleaming halls of morn.   10

Alas! for this gray shadow, once a man—
So glorious in his beauty and thy choice,
Who madest him thy chosen, that he seem'd
To his great heart none other than a God!
I ask'd thee, "Give me immortality."   15
Then didst thou grant mine asking with a smile,
Like wealthy men who care not how they give.
But thy strong Hours indignant work'd their wills,
And beat me down and marr'd and wasted me,
And tho' they could not end me, left me maim'd   20
To dwell in presence of immortal youth,
Immortal age beside immortal youth,
And all I was, in ashes. Can thy love,
Thy beauty, make amends, tho' even now,
Close over us, the silver star, thy guide,   25
Shines in those tremulous eyes that fill with tears
To hear me? Let me go: take back thy gift:
Why should a man desire in any way
To vary from the kindly race of men,
Or pass beyond the goal of ordinance   30
Where all should pause, as is most meet for all?

A soft air fans the cloud apart; there comes
A glimpse of that dark world where I was born.
Once more the old mysterious glimmer steals

From thy pure brows, and from thy shoulders pure,   35
And bosom beating with a heart renew'd.
Thy cheek begins to redden thro' the gloom,
Thy sweet eyes brighten slowly close to mine,
Ere yet they blind the stars, and the wild team
Which love thee, yearning for thy yoke, arise,   40
And shake the darkness from their loosen'd manes,
And beat the twilight into flakes of fire.

    Lo! ever thus thou growest beautiful
In silence, then before thine answer given
Departest, and thy tears are on my cheek.   45
    Why wilt thou ever scare me with thy tears,
And make me tremble lest a saying learnt,
In days far-off, on that dark earth, be true?
"The Gods themselves cannot recall their gifts."

    Ay me! ay me! with what another heart   50
In days far-off, and with what other eyes
I used to watch—if I be he that watch'd—
The lucid outline forming round thee; saw
The dim curls kindle into sunny rings;
Changed with thy mystic change, and felt my blood   55
Glow with the glow that slowly crimson'd all
Thy presence and thy portals, while I lay,
Mouth, forehead, eyelids, growing dewy-warm
With kisses balmier than half-opening buds
Of April, and could hear the lips that kiss'd   60
Whispering I knew not what of wild and sweet,
Like that strange song I heard Apollo sing,
While Ilion like a mist rose into towers.

    Yet hold me not for ever in thine East:
How can my nature longer mix with thine?   65
Coldly thy rosy shadows bathe me, cold
Are all thy lights, and cold my wrinkled feet
Upon thy glimmering thresholds, when the steam
Floats up from those dim fields about the homes
Of happy men that have the power to die,   70
And grassy barrows of the happier dead.
Release me, and restore me to the ground;
Thou seëst all things, thou wilt see my grave:
Thou wilt renew thy beauty morn by morn;
I earth in earth forget these empty courts,   75
And thee returning on thy silver wheels. (c. 1842; 1860)

Robert Browning

MY LAST DUCHESS

Ferrara

That's my last Duchess painted on the wall,
Looking as if she were alive; I call
That piece a wonder, now: Fra Pandolf's hands
Worked busily a day, and there she stands.
Will't please you sit and look at her? I said   5
"Fra Pandolf" by design, for never read
Strangers like you that pictured countenance,
The depth and passion of its earnest glance,
But to myself they turned (since none puts by
The curtain I have drawn for you, but I)   10
And seemed as they would ask me, if they durst,
How such a glance came there; so, not the first
Are you to turn and ask thus. Sir, 'twas not
Her husband's presence only, called that spot
Of joy into the Duchess' cheek: perhaps   15
Fra Pandolf chanced to say "Her mantle laps
Over my Lady's wrist too much," or "Paint
Must never hope to reproduce the faint
Half-flush that dies along her throat"; such stuff
Was courtesy, she thought, and cause enough   20
For calling up that spot of joy. She had
A heart . . . how shall I say? . . . too soon made glad,
Too easily impressed; she liked whate'er
She looked on, and her looks went everywhere.
Sir, 'twas all one! My favor at her breast,   25
The dropping of the daylight in the West,
The bough of cherries some officious fool
Broke in the orchard for her, the white mule
She rode with round the terrace—all and each
Would draw from her alike the approving speech,   30
Or blush, at least. She thanked men,—good; but thanked
Somehow . . . I know not how . . . as if she ranked
My gift of a nine-hundred-years-old name
With anybody's gift. Who'd stoop to blame
This sort of trifling? Even had you skill   35
In speech—(which I have not)—to make your will
Quite clear to such an one, and say "Just this
Or that in you disgusts me; here you miss

Or there exceed the mark"—and if she let
Herself be lessoned so, nor plainly set   40
Her wits to yours, forsooth, and made excuse,
—E'en then would be some stooping, and I choose
Never to stoop. Oh, Sir, she smiled, no doubt,
Whene'er I passed her; but who passed without
Much the same smile? This grew; I gave commands;   45
Then all smiles stopped together. There she stands
As if alive. Will't please you rise? We'll meet
The company below, then. I repeat,
The Count your Master's known munificence
Is ample warrant that no just pretence   50
Of mine for dowry will be disallowed;
Though his fair daughter's self, as I avowed
At starting, is my object. Nay, we'll go
Together down, Sir! Notice Neptune, though,
Taming a sea-horse, thought a rarity,   55
Which Claus of Innsbruck cast in bronze for me. (1842)

SOLILOQUY OF
THE SPANISH CLOISTER

Gr-r-r—there go, my heart's abhorrence!
   Water your damned flower-pots, do!
If hate killed men, Brother Lawrence,
   God's blood, would not mine kill you!
What? your myrtle-bush wants trimming?   5
   Oh, that rose has prior claims—
Needs its leaden vase filled brimming?
   Hell dry you up with its flames!

At the meal we sit together:
   Salve tibi! I must hear   10
Wise talk of the kind of weather,
   Sort of season, time of year:
Not a plenteous cork-crop: scarcely
   Dare we hope oak-galls, I doubt:
What's the Latin name for "parsley"?   15
   What's the Greek name for Swine's Snout?

Whew! We'll have our platter burnished,
   Laid with care on our own shelf!

With a fire-new spoon we're furnished,
   And a goblet for ourself,   20
Rinsed like something sacrificial
   Ere 'tis fit to touch our chaps—
Marked with L for our initial!
   (He-he! There his lily snaps!)

Saint, forsooth! While brown Dolores   25
   Squats outside the Convent bank
With Sanchicha, telling stories,
   Steeping tresses in the tank,
Blue-black, lustrous, thick like horsehairs,
   —Can't I see his dead eye glow,   30
Bright as 'twere a Barbary corsair's?
   (That is, if he'd let it show!)

When he finishes refection,
   Knife and fork he never lays
Cross-wise, to my recollection,   35
   As do I, in Jesu's praise.
I the Trinity illustrate,
   Drinking watered orange-pulp—
In three sips the Arian frustrate;
   While he drains his at one gulp.   40

Oh, those melons! If he's able
   We're to have a feast! so nice!
One goes to the Abbot's table,
   All of us get each a slice.
How go on your flowers? None double?   45
   Not one fruit-sort can you spy?
Strange!—And I, too, at such trouble
   Keep them close-nipped on the sly!

There's a great text in Galatians,
   Once you trip on it, entails   50
Twenty-nine distinct damnations,
   One sure, if another fails:
If I trip him just a-dying,
   Sure of heaven as sure can be,
Spin him round and send him flying   55
   Off to hell, a Manichee?

Or, my scrofulous French novel
   On gray paper with blunt type!

Simply glance at it, you grovel
  Hand and foot in Belial's gripe: 60
If I double down its pages
  At the woeful sixteenth print,
When he gathers his greengages,
  Ope a sieve and slip it in't?

Or, there's Satan!—one might venture   65
  Pledge one's soul to him, yet leave
Such a flaw in the indenture
  As he'd miss till, past retrieve,
Blasted lay that rose-acacia
  We're so proud of! *Hy, Zy, Hine.* . . .   70
'St, there's Vespers! *Plena, gratiâ,*
  Ave, Virgo! Gr-r-r—you swine! (1842)

THE BISHOP ORDERS HIS
TOMB AT SAINT PRAXED'S CHURCH

Rome, 15—

Vanity, saith the preacher, vanity!
Draw round my bed; is Anselm keeping back?
Nephews—sons mine . . . ah, God, I know not! Well—
She, men would have to be your mother once,
Old Gandolf envied me, so fair she was!   5
What's done is done, and she is dead beside,
Dead long ago, and I am Bishop since,
And as she died so must we die ourselves,
And thence ye may perceive the world's a dream.
Life, how and what is it? As here I lie   10
In this state-chamber, dying by degrees,
Hours and long hours in the dead night, I ask,
"Do I live, am I dead?" Peace, peace seems all.
Saint Praxed's ever was the church for peace;
And so, about this tomb of mine. I fought   15
With tooth and nail to save my niche, ye know—
Old Gandolf cozened me, despite my care;
Shrewd was that snatch from out the corner South
He graced his carrion with, God curse the same!
Yet still my niche is not so cramped but thence   20
One sees the pulpit o' the epistle-side,

And somewhat of the choir, those silent seats,
And up into the aëry dome where live
The angels, and a sunbeam's sure to lurk;
And I shall fill my slab of basalt there,   25
And 'neath my tabernacle take my rest,
With those nine columns round me, two and two,
The odd one at my feet where Anselm stands:
Peach-blossom marble all, the rare, the ripe
As fresh-poured red wine of a mighty pulse.   30
—Old Gandolf with his paltry onion-stone,
Put me where I may look at him! True peach,
Rosy and flawless; how I earned the prize!
Draw close; that conflagration of my church—
What then? So much was saved if aught were missed!   35
My sons, ye would not be my death? Go dig
The white-grape vineyard where the oil-press stood,
Drop water gently till the surface sink,
And if ye find . . . Ah, God, I know not, I! . . .
Bedded in store of rotten fig-leaves soft,   40
And corded up in a tight olive-frail,
Some lump, ah, God, of *lapis lazuli*,
Big as a Jew's head cut off at the nape,
Blue as a vein o'er the Madonna's breast . . .
Sons, all have I bequeathed you, villas, all,   45
That brave Frascati villa with its bath,
So, let the blue lump poise between my knees,
Like God the Father's globe on both his hands
Ye worship in the Jesu Church so gay,
For Gandolf shall not choose but see and burst!   50
Swift as a weaver's shuttle fleet our years;
Man goeth to the grave, and where is he?
Did I say basalt for my slab, sons? Black—
'Twas ever antique-black I meant! How else
Shall ye contrast my frieze to come beneath?   55
The bas-relief in bronze ye promised me,
Those Pans and Nymphs ye wot of, and perchance
Some tripod, thyrsus, with a vase or so,
The Savior at his sermon on the mount,
Saint Praxed in a glory, and one Pan   60
Ready to twitch the Nymph's last garment off,
And Moses with the tables . . . but I know
Ye mark me not! What do they whisper thee,
Child of my bowels, Anselm? Ah, ye hope
To revel down my villas while I gasp   65
Bricked o'er with beggar's moldy travertine

Which Gandolf from his tomb-top chuckles at!
Nay, boys, ye love me—all of jasper, then!
'Tis jasper ye stand pledged to, lest I grieve.
My bath must needs be left behind, alas!   70
One block, pure green as a pistachio-nut,
There's plenty jasper somewhere in the world—
And have I not Saint Praxed's ear to pray
Horses for ye, and brown Greek manuscripts,
And mistresses with great smooth marbly limbs?   75
—That's if ye carve my epitaph aright
Choice Latin, picked phrase, Tully's every word,
No gaudy ware like Gandolf's second line—
Tully, my masters? Ulpian serves his need!
And then how I shall lie through centuries,   80
And hear the blessed mutter of the Mass,
And see God made and eaten all day long,
And feel the steady candle-flame, and taste
Good strong thick stupefying incense-smoke!
For as I lie here, hours of the dead night,   85
Dying in state and by such slow degrees,
I fold my arms as if they clasped a crook,
And stretch my feet forth straight as stone can point,
And let the bedclothes, for a mortcloth, drop
Into great laps and folds of sculptor's work;   90
And as yon tapers dwindle, and strange thoughts
Grow, with a certain humming in my ears
About the life before I lived this life,
And this life too, popes, cardinals, and priests,
Saint Praxed at his sermon on the mount,   95
Your tall pale mother with her talking eyes,
And new-found agate urns as fresh as day,
And marble's language, Latin pure, discreet—
Aha, ELUCESCEBAT quoth our friend?
No Tully, said I, Ulpian at the best!   100
Evil and brief hath been my pilgrimage.
All *lapis*, all, sons! Else I give the Pope
My villas! Will ye ever eat my heart?
Ever your eyes were as a lizard's quick,
They glitter like your mother's for my soul,   105
Or ye would heighten my impoverished frieze,
Piece out its starved design, and fill my vase
With grapes, and add a visor and a term,
And to the tripod ye would tie a lynx
That in his struggle throws the thyrsus down,   110
To comfort me on my entablature

Whereon I am to lie till I must ask,
"Do I live, am I dead?" There, leave me, there!
For ye have stabbed me with ingratitude
To death—ye wish it—God, ye wish it! Stone—   115
Gritstone, a-crumble! Clammy squares which sweat
As if the corpse they keep were oozing through—
And no more *lapis* to delight the world!
Well, go! I bless ye. Fewer tapers there,
But in a row; and, going, turn your backs—   120
Aye, like departing altar-ministrants,
And leave me in my church, the church for peace,
That I may watch at leisure if he leers—
Old Gandolf—at me, from his onion-stone,
As still he envied me, so fair she was! (1845)   125

Stuart M. Tave

BROWNING'S
"THE BISHOP ORDERS HIS
TOMB AT SAINT PRAXED'S CHURCH"

The bishop (see the poem on page 1048) is a man who has held spiritual office, and who has led a full and enjoyable worldly life. He is a priest who has struggled successfully with his ecclesiastical rival, Gandolf, for the affections of the fair woman who bore his so-called "nephews." He has lived well in handsome villas; he has accumulated the good things of this world. Nor has he been above a little sly purloining to acquire his goods: the *lapis lazuli* missing from his church after a fire, it now develops, is secretly buried in his vineyard. Even now, on his deathbed, his chief thought is for his worldly remains, the elaborate tomb that will outshine Gandolf once again. The tomb itself is an incongruous mixture of flesh and spirit, the near naked nymph and the sermon on the mount, as his dying words are a mixture of Biblical quotations on the vanity of earthly life and an intense desire to hold fast to vanity beyond death.

But if the bishop is a worldly man, he is not a contemptible man. If, as a bishop, the body has occupied him over much, there is no sign that he has been gross in his pleasures. If he has loved flesh, he has not been a promiscuous lover. He has tasted pleasure finely. His interests extend to Greek manuscripts and the niceties of Latin style; he is a connoisseur of the fine arts. His great redeeming quality is that he is not a hypocrite in grain. He has perhaps fooled the world, but he has not fooled himself. He has a protective ingenuousness, an insensibility to his spiritual failings that is an odd contrast to his sensitive physical perceptiveness. He is not repentant on his deathbed; other than the platitudes he recites automatically there is no sign that he has any strong consciousness of wrongdoing. What he has done he has done from his heart; he has loved his life and he is rejoicing in the physical accompaniments of his death. He expects his tomb to delight the world; it is a prize he has earned.

The bishop lives and dies a consistent sensuous man, lives and dies with his body. It is the bath of the Frascati villa that he remembers most, it is the bath that he regrets he cannot take with him. Experience comes to him through the physical senses, and he dwells upon it with relish, with an intense pleasure expressed in the imagery of his speech. He loves the large, full, unadulterated, and perfect sensation: "mistresses with great smooth marbly limbs"; their size, touch, and heroic texture are all present to him; he rolls the liquids, *r*'s and *l*'s, with caressing feeling. Nothing but the finest material satisfies him, marbly limbs in life, a marble tomb in death, "marble's language" for his epitaph: "Choice Latin, picked phrase"—Latin becomes a material to be fingered, fine fruit—"No gaudy ware," "Latin pure." Images of fine food, images of sound, smell, and taste, of sight, and above all, of touch, the most intimate of the senses, pervade his speech.

His tomb must have physical room. In physical images he has fought, "tooth and nail," with Gandolf to save his niche, not with entire success because Gandolf has died earlier and made his shrewd "snatch." Still, the bishop rejoices, he is not so "cramped," but he will enjoy, after death, sight of the epistle-side of the pulpit, of somewhat of the choir (he is very precise in perception), and of the aëry dome, where (among the angels) "a sunbeam's sure to lurk." The colors of the tomb are brilliant, individually and in contrast. The surrounding nine columns, perfect in number (the trinity of trinities) and perfectly placed, will be "Peach-blossom marble all." They are living fruits to him, "the rare, the ripe/ As fresh-poured red wine of a mighty pulse." And again he turns over in his mouth the luscious liquid consonants. He delights in returning to a word, to savor the thing and the sound again: "True peach,/Rosy and flawless." The columns are a fruit color, which is in turn a wine color. Old Gandolf used onion-stone. The green jasper that the bishop later asks for wildly is a nut color, "One block, pure green as a pistachio-nut." All colors of his tomb he must have in their utmost intensity. The slab of basalt later becomes "antique-black," because "How else/Shall ye contrast my frieze to come beneath?" The *lapis lazuli*—he loves the word —is the purest, tenderest, and most intense physical blue, "Blue as a vein o'er the Madonna's breast." (The bishop notices the details of religious art; he also recalls most the *color* of the brown Greek manuscripts.) The *lapis lazuli* is the heaviest physical "lump," again presented with an intense tactile image of the body, "Big as a Jew's head cut off at the nape." It is to rest in poise in contact with his body, "between my knees,/Like God the Father's globe on both his hands." And its present secret place he describes in a series of images again intense with fruit, color, and close touch.

> Go dig
> The white-grape vineyard where the oil-press stood,
> Drop water gently till the surface sink,
> And if ye find . . . Ah, God, I know not, I! . . .
> Bedded in a store of rotten fig-leaves soft,
> > And corded up in a tight olive-frail,
> > Some lump . . .

The striking figure on the frieze, because so oddly contrasted with the Savior, St. Praxed, and Moses, is the Pan "Ready to twitch the Nymph's last garment off"—again the last, poised moment of tactile experience. The bas-relief itself, of course, is literally open to the touch.

With this blessed abode before his imagination he contemplates the prolonged satisfaction of sensuousness:

> . . . how I shall lie through centuries,
> And *hear* the blessed mutter of the Mass,
> And *see* God made and eaten all day long,
> And *feel* the steady candle-flame, and *taste*
> Good strong thick stupefying incense-smoke!

There are few words that do not carry weight in these lines, none in that slow and heavy climactic line of rapt satiety. And so the bishop grows luxuriously from his present body into that eternal, beautiful, statuesque body that he shall be, in a series of tactile images:

> I fold my arms as if they clasped a crook,
> And stretch my feet forth straight as stone can point,
> And let the bedclothes, for a mortcloth, drop
> Into great laps and folds of sculptor's work.

This is his heaven. His hell, if his sons do not fulfill his desires, will be a hell of starvation and things unpleasant to the touch. The frieze will have a "starved" design. The bishop will have no easy comfort in his niche; he will suffocate, "gasp/ Bricked o'er with beggar's moldy travertine." His tomb will be

> Gritstone, a-crumble! Clammy squares which sweat
> As if the corpse they keep were oozing through.

But his vision of hell is momentary only. The bishop is dying well, dying as he lived, tasting the experience moment by moment. He begins his speech by dwelling on death, slowly revolving all the derivatives of the word, "dead . . . Dead . . . died . . . die . . . dying . . . dead . . . dead" (ll. 6-13), applying them to the mother of his sons, to the world at large, to the night, to himself. He is "dying by degrees,/ Hours and long hours," not in pain. He is poised: "Do I live, am I dead?" He is at peace. "Peace, peace seems all,/ Saint Praxed's ever was the church for peace." The bishop's ear delights in softness and silence: the church, the silent seats he will see from his niche, the blessed mutter of the Mass, the talking eyes of his dead beloved. And so after his brief vision of hell he returns to his peace. He reduces the number of tapers, but has them arranged carefully, and directs the ceremony of the departure of his sons. In peace he enjoys his death and his life; the distinction is lost, as it must be for so ingenuous and entire a materialist.

James Russell Lowell

TO THE DANDELION

Dear common flower, that grow'st beside the way,
Fringing the dusty road with harmless gold,
    First pledge of blithesome May,
Which children pluck, and, full of pride, uphold,
    High-hearted buccaneers, o'erjoyed that they   5
An Eldorado in the grass have found,
    Which not the rich earth's ample round
    May match in wealth,—thou art more dear to me
Than all the prouder summer-blooms may be.

Gold such as thine ne'er drew the Spanish prow   10
Through the primeval hush of Indian seas,
    Nor wrinkled the lean brow
Of age, to rob the lover's heart of ease,
    'Tis the spring's largess, which she scatters now
To rich and poor alike, with lavish hand,   15
    Though most hearts never understand
    To take it at God's value, but pass by
The offered wealth with unrewarded eye.

Thou art my tropics and mine Italy;
To look at thee unlocks a warmer clime;   20
    The eyes thou givest me
Are in the heart, and heed not space or time:
    Not in mid June the golden cuirassed bee
Feels a more summer-like warm ravishment
    In the white lily's breezy tent,   25
    His fragrant Sybaris, than I, when first
From the dark green thy yellow circles burst.

Then think I of deep shadows on the grass,
Of meadows where in sun the cattle graze,
    Where, as the breezes pass,   30

The gleaming rushes lean a thousand ways,
  Of leaves that slumber in a cloudy mass,
Or whiten in the wind, of waters blue
    That from the distance sparkle through
  Some woodland gap, and of a sky above,   35
  Where one white cloud like a stray lamb doth move.

    My childhood's earliest thoughts are linked with thee;
The sight of thee calls back the robin's song,
    Who, from the dark old tree
Beside the door, sang clearly all day long,   40
  And I, secure in childish piety,
Listened as if I heard an angel sing
    With news from heaven, which he could bring
  Fresh every day to my untainted ears,
  When birds and flowers and I were happy peers.   45

    How like a prodigal doth nature seem,
When thou, for all thy gold, so common art!
    Thou teachest me to deem
More sacredly of every human heart,
  Since each reflects in joy its scanty gleam   50
Of heaven and could some wondrous secret show
    Did we but pay the love we owe,
  And with a child's undoubting wisdom look
  On all these living pages of God's book. (1844; 1845)

Walt Whitman

....

ONE'S-SELF I SING

One's-self I sing, a simple separate person,
Yet utter the word Democratic, the word En-Masse.

Of physiology from top to toe I sing,
Not physiognomy alone nor brain alone is worthy for the Muse,
    I say the Form complete is worthier far,
The Female equally with the Male I sing.   5

Of Life immense in passion, pulse, and power,
Cheerful, for freest action form'd under the laws divine,
The Modern Man I sing. (1867; 1871)

ONCE I PASS'D
THROUGH A POPULOUS CITY

Once I pass'd through a populous city imprinting my brain for future use
with its shows, architecture, customs, traditions,
Yet now of all that city I remember only a woman I casually met there
who detain'd me for love of me,
Day by day and night by night we were together—all else has long been
forgotten by me,
I remember I say only that woman who passionately clung to me,
Again she holds me by the hand, I must not go,   5
I see her close beside me with silent lips sad and tremulous. (1860; 1867)

I SAW IN LOUISIANA
A LIVE-OAK GROWING

I saw in Louisiana a live-oak growing,
All alone stood it and the moss hung down from the branches,
Without any companion it grew there uttering joyous leaves of dark green,
And its look, rude, unbending, lusty, made me think of myself,
But I wonder'd how it could utter joyous leaves standing alone there with-
out its friend near, for I knew I could not,   5
And I broke off a twig with a certain number of leaves upon it, and
twined around it a little moss,
And brought it away, and I have placed it in sight in my room,
It is not needed to remind me as of my own dear friends,
(For I believe lately I think of little else than of them,)
Yet it remains to me a curious token, it makes me think of manly love;   10
For all that, and though the live-oak glistens there in Louisiana solitary in
a wide flat space,
Uttering joyous leaves all its life without a friend, a lover near,
I know very well I could not. (1860)

WHEN LILACS LAST
IN THE DOORYARD BLOOM'D

I

When lilacs last in the dooryard bloom'd,
And the great star early droop'd in the western sky in the night,
I mourn'd, and yet shall mourn with ever-returning spring.

Ever-returning spring, trinity sure to me you bring,
Lilac blooming perennial and drooping star in the west,   5
And thought of him I love.

II

O powerful western fallen star!
O shades of night—O moody, tearful night!
O great star disappear'd—O the black murk that hides the star!
O cruel hands that hold me powerless—O helpless soul of me!   10
O harsh surrounding cloud that will not free my soul.

III

In the dooryard fronting an old farm-house near the white-wash'd palings,
Stands the lilac-bush, tall-growing with heart-shaped leaves of rich green,
With many a pointed blossom rising delicate, with the perfume strong I
   love,
With every leaf a miracle—and from this bush in the dooryard,   15
With delicate-color'd blossoms and heart-shaped leaves of rich green,
A sprig with its flower I break.

IV

In the swamp in secluded recesses,
A shy and hidden bird is warbling a song.

Solitary the thrush,   20
The hermit withdrawn to himself, avoiding the settlements,
Sings by himself a song.

Song of the bleeding throat,
Death's outlet song of life (for well dear brother I know,
If thou wast not granted to sing thou would'st surely die).   25

V

Over the breast of the spring, the land, amid cities,
Amid lanes and through old woods, where lately the violets peep'd from
   the ground, spotting the gray débris,
Amid the grass in the fields each side of the lanes, passing the endless
   grass;
Passing the yellow-spear'd wheat, every grain from its shroud in the dark-
   brown fields uprisen,
Passing the apple-tree blows of white and pink in the orchards,   30
Carrying a corpse to where it shall rest in the grave,
Night and day journeys a coffin.

VI

Coffin that passes through lanes and streets,
Through day and night with the great cloud darkening the land,
With the pomp of the inloop'd flags, with the cities draped in black,   35
With the show of the States themselves as of crape-veil'd women standing,
With processions long and winding and the flambeaus of the night,

With the countless torches lit, with the silent sea of faces and the unbared
    heads,
With the waiting depot, the arriving coffin, and the somber faces,
With dirges through the night, with the thousand voices rising strong and
    solemn,   40
With all the mournful voices of the dirges pour'd around the coffin,
The dim-lit churches and the shuddering organs—where amid these you
    journey,
With the tolling tolling bell's perpetual clang,
Here, coffin that slowly passes,
I give you my sprig of lilac.   45

VII

(Nor for you, for one alone,
Blossoms and branches green to coffins all I bring.
For fresh as the morning, thus would I carol a song to you O sane and
    sacred death.

All over bouquets of roses,
O death, I cover you over with roses and early lilies,   50
But mostly and now the lilac that blooms the first,
Copious I break, I break the sprigs from the bushes.
With loaded arms I come, pouring for you,
For you and the coffins all of you O death.)

VIII

O western orb sailing the heaven,   55
Now I know what you must have meant as a month since I walk'd,
As I walk'd in silence the transparent shadowy night,
As I saw you had something to tell as you bent to me night after night,
As you droop'd from the sky low down as if to my side (while the other
    stars all look'd on),
As we wander'd together the solemn night (for something I know not
    what kept me from sleep),   60
As the night advanced, and I saw on the rim of the west how full you
    were of woe,
As I stood on the rising ground in the breeze in the cold transparent night,
As I watch'd where you pass'd and was lost in the netherward black of the
    night,
As my soul in its trouble dissatisfied sank, as where you sad orb,
Concluded, dropt in the night, and was gone.   65

IX

Sing on there in the swamp,
O singer bashful and tender, I hear your notes, I hear your call,
I hear, I come presently, I understand you,
But a moment I linger, for the lustrous star has detain'd me,
The star my departing comrade holds and detains me.   70

X

O how shall I warble myself for the dead one there I loved?
And how shall I deck my song for the large sweet soul that has gone?
And what shall my perfume be for the grave of him I love?

Sea-winds blown from east and west,
Blown from the Eastern sea and blown from the Western sea till there on
   the prairies meeting: 75
These and with these and the breath of my chant,
I'll perfume the grave of him I love.

XI

O what shall I hang on the chamber walls?
And what shall the pictures be that I hang on the walls,
To adorn the burial-house of him I love?   80

Pictures of growing spring and farms and homes,
With the Fourth-month eve at sundown, and the gray smoke lucid and
   bright,
With floods of the yellow gold of the gorgeous, indolent, sinking sun,
   burning, expanding the air,
With the fresh sweet herbage under foot, and the pale green leaves of the
   trees prolific,
In the distance the flowing glaze, the breast of the river, with a wind-
   dapple here and there;   85
With ranging hills on the banks, with many a line against the sky, and
   shadows;
And the city at hand with dwellings so dense, and stacks of chimneys,
And all the scenes of life and the workshops, and the workmen homeward
   returning.

XII

Lo, body and soul—this land,
My own Manhattan with spires, and the sparkling and hurrying tides,
   and the ships,   90
The varied and ample land, the South and the North in the light—Ohio's
   shores and flashing Missouri,
And ever the far-spreading prairies cover'd with grass and corn.
Lo, the most excellent sun so calm and haughty,
The violet and purple morn with just-felt breezes,
The gentle soft-born measureless light,   95
The miracle spreading bathing all, the fulfill'd noon,
The coming eve delicious, the welcome night and the stars,
Over my cities shining all, enveloping man and land.

XIII

Sing on, sing on you gray-brown bird,
Sing from the swamps, the recesses, pour your chant from the bushes;   100
Limitless out of the dusk, out of the cedars and pines.

Sing on dearest brother, warble your reedy song,
Loud human song, with voice of uttermost woe.

O liquid and free and tender!
O wild and loose to my soul—O wondrous singer!   105
You only I hear—yet the star holds me (but will soon depart,)
Yet the lilac with mastering odor holds me.

XIV

Now while I sat in the day and look'd forth,
In the close of the day with its light and the fields of spring, and the
    farmers preparing their crops,
In the large unconscious scenery of my land with its lakes and forests,   110
In the heavenly aerial beauty (after the perturb'd winds and the storms,)
Under the arching heavens of the afternoon swift passing, and the voices
    of children and women,
The many-moving sea-tides, and I saw the ships how they sail'd,
And the summer approaching with richness, and the fields all busy with
    labor,
And the infinite separate houses, how they all went on, each with its
    meals and minutia of daily usages;   115
And the streets how their throbbings throbb'd, and the cities pent—lo,
    then and there,
Falling upon them all and among them all, enveloping me with the rest,
Appear'd the cloud, appear'd the long black trail;
And I knew death, its thought, and the sacred knowledge of death.

Then with the knowledge of death as walking one side of me,   120
And the thought of death close-walking the other side of me,
And I in the middle as with companions, and as holding the hands of
    companions,
I fled forth to the hiding receiving night that talks not,
Down to the shores of the water, the path by the swamp in the dimness,
To the solemn shadowy cedars and ghostly pines so still.   125

And the singer so shy to the rest receiv'd me,
The gray-brown bird I know receiv'd us comrades three,
And he sang the carol of death, and a verse for him I love.

From deep secluded recesses,
From the fragrant cedars and the ghostly pines so still,   130
Came the carol of the bird.

And the charm of the carol rapt me,
As I held as if by their hands my comrades in the night;
And the voice of my spirit tallied the song of the bird.

Come lovely and soothing death,   135
Undulate round the world, serenely arriving, arriving,
In the day, in the night, to all, to each,
Sooner or later delicate death.

Prais'd be the fathomless universe,
For life and joy, and for objects and knowledge curious,   140
And for love, sweet love—but praise! praise! praise!
For the sure-enwinding arms of cool-enfolding death.

Dark mother always gliding near with soft feet,
Have none chanted for thee a chant of fullest welcome?
Then I chant it for thee, I glorify thee above all,   145
I bring thee a song that when thou must indeed come, come unfalteringly.

Approach strong deliveress,
When it is so, when thou hast taken them, I joyously sing the dead,
Lost in the loving floating ocean of thee,
Laved in the flood of thy bliss O death.   150

From me to thee glad serenades,
Dances for thee I propose saluting thee, adornments and feastings for thee,
And the sights of the open landscape and the high-spread sky are fitting,
And life and the fields, and the huge and thoughtful night.

The night in silence under many a star,   155
The ocean shore and the husky whispering wave whose voice I know,
And the soul turning to thee O vast and well-veil'd death,
And the body gratefully nestling close to thee.

Over the tree-tops I float thee a song,
Over the rising and sinking waves, over the myriad fields and the prairies wide, 160
Over the dense-pack'd cities all and the teeming wharves and ways,
I float this carol with joy, with joy to thee O death!

XV

To the tally of my soul,
Loud and strong kept up the gray-brown bird,
With pure, deliberate notes spreading filling the night.   165

Loud in the pines and cedars dim,
Clear in the freshness moist and the swamp-perfume,
And I with my comrades there in the night.

While my sight that was bound in my eyes unclosed,
As to long panoramas of visions.   170

I saw askant the armies;
And I saw as in noiseless dreams hundreds of battle-flags,
Borne through the smoke of the battles and pierc'd with missiles I saw
    them,
And carried hither and yon through the smoke, and torn and bloody,
And at last but a few shreds left on the staffs (and all in silence,)   175
And the staffs all splinter'd and broken.
I saw battle-corpses, myriads of them,
And the white skeletons of young men, I saw them,
I saw the débris and débris of all the slain soldiers of the war,
But I saw they were not as was thought,   180
They themselves were fully at rest, they suffer'd not,
The living remain'd and suffer'd, the mother suffer'd,
And the wife and the child and the musing comrade suffer'd,
And the armies that remain'd suffer'd.

XVI

Passing the visions, passing the night,   185
Passing, unloosing the hold of my comrades' hands,
Passing the song of the hermit bird and the tallying song of my soul,
Victorious song, death's outlet song, yet varying ever-altering song,
As low and wailing, yet clear the notes, rising and falling, flooding the
    night,
Sadly sinking and fainting, as warning and warning, and yet again burst-
    ing with joy,   190
Covering the earth and filling the spread of the heaven,
As that powerful psalm in the night I heard from recesses,
Passing, I leave thee lilac with heart-shaped leaves,
I leave thee there in the dooryard blooming, returning with spring.

I cease from my song for thee,   195
From my gaze on thee in the west, fronting the west, communing with thee,
O comrade lustrous with silver face in the night.

Yet each I keep and all, retrievements out of the night,
The song, the wondrous chant of the gray-brown bird,
The tallying chant, the echo arous'd in my soul,   200
With the lustrous and drooping star with the countenance full of woe,
With the holders holding my hand hearing the call of the bird,
Comrades mine and I in the midst, and their memory ever to keep, for
    the dead I loved so well,
For the sweetest, wisest soul of all my days and lands—and this for his
    dear sake;
Lilac and star and bird twined with the chant of my soul,   205
There in the fragrant pines and the cedars dusk and dim. (1865; 1881)

George Meredith

LUCIFER IN STARLIGHT

On a starred night Prince Lucifer uprose.
Tired of his dark dominion, swung the fiend
Above the rolling ball, in cloud part screened,
Where sinners hugged their specter of repose.
Poor prey to his hot fit of pride were those.   5
And now upon his western wing he leaned,
Now his huge bulk o'er Afric's sands careened,
Now the black planet shadowed Arctic snows.
Soaring through wider zones that pricked his scars
With memory of the old revolt from Awe,   10
He reached a middle height, and at the stars,
Which are the brain of heaven, he looked, and sank.
Around the ancient track marched, rank on rank,
The army of unalterable law. (1883)

Christina Rossetti

A BIRTHDAY

My heart is like a singing bird
   Whose nest is in a watered shoot;
My heart is like an apple-tree
   Whose boughs are bent with thick-set fruit;
My heart is like a rainbow shell   5
   That paddles in a halcyon sea;
My heart is gladder than all these
   Because my love is come to me.

Raise me a dais of silk and down;
   Hang it with vair and purple dyes;   10
Carve it in doves and pomegranates,
   And peacocks with a hundred eyes;
Work it in gold and silver grapes,

In leaves and silver fleurs-de-lys;
Because the birthday of my life   15
Is come, my love is come to me. (1857)

Emily Dickinson

THERE'S A
CERTAIN SLANT OF LIGHT

There's a certain slant of light,
On winter afternoons,
That oppresses, like the weight
Of cathedral tunes.

Heavenly hurt it gives us;   5
We can find no scar,
But internal difference
Where the meanings are.

None may teach it anything,
'Tis the seal, despair,—   10
An imperial affliction
Sent us of the air.

When it comes, the landscape listens,
Shadows hold their breath;
When it goes, 'tis like the distance   15
On the look of death. (1890)

I NEVER SAW A MOOR

I never saw a moor,
I never saw the sea;
Yet know I how the heather looks,
And what a wave must be.

I never spoke with God,   5
Nor visited in heaven;
Yet certain am I of the spot
As if the chart were given. (1890)

From *The Poems of Emily Dickinson*. Reprinted by permission of Little, Brown and Company.

BECAUSE I COULD NOT STOP FOR DEATH

Because I could not stop for Death,
He kindly stopped for me;
The carriage held but just ourselves
And Immortality.

We slowly drove, he knew no haste,   5
And I had put away
My labor and my leisure too,
For his civility.

We passed the school where children played
At wrestling in a ring;   10
We passed the fields of gazing grain,
We passed the setting sun.

We paused before a house that seemed
A swelling of the ground;
The roof was scarcely visible,   15
The cornice but a mound.

Since then 't is centuries; but each
Feels shorter than the day
I first surmised the horses' heads
Were toward eternity. (1890)   20

I DIED FOR BEAUTY

I died for beauty, but was scarce
Adjusted in the tomb,
When one who died for truth was lain
In an adjoining room.

He questioned softly why I failed.   5
"For beauty," I replied.
"And I for truth,—the two are one;
We brethren are," he said.

And so, as kinsmen met a night,
We talked between the rooms,   10
Until the moss had reached our lips
And covered up our names. (1862?)

Contemporary Poems

Thomas Hardy

THE DARKLING THRUSH

I leant upon a coppice gate
  When Frost was specter-gray,
And Winter's dregs made desolate
  The weakening eye of day.
The tangled bine-stems scored the sky   5
  Like strings of broken lyres,
And all mankind that haunted night
  Had sought their household fires.

The land's sharp features seemed to be
  The Century's corpse outleant,   10
His crypt the cloudy canopy,
  The wind his death-lament.
The ancient pulse of germ and birth
  Was shrunken hard and dry,
And every spirit upon earth   15
  Seemed fervorless as I.

At once a voice arose among
  The bleak twigs overhead
In a full-hearted evensong
  Of joy illimited;   20
An aged thrush, frail, gaunt, and small,
  In blast-beruffled plume,
Had chosen thus to fling his soul
  Upon the growing gloom.

So little cause for carolings   25
  Of such ecstatic sound
Was written on terrestrial things
  Afar or nigh around,

That I could think there trembled through
His happy good-night air   30
Some blessed Hope, whereof he knew
And I was unaware. (1900)

IN TIME OF
'THE BREAKING OF NATIONS'

I
Only a man harrowing clods
In a slow silent walk
With an old horse that stumbles and nods
Half asleep as they stalk.

II
Only thin smoke without flame   5
From the heaps of couch-grass;
Yet this will go onward the same
Though Dynasties pass.

III
Yonder a maid and her wight
Come whispering by: 10
War's annals will cloud into night
Ere their story die. (1915)

Gerard Manley Hopkins

HEAVEN-HAVEN

A Nun Takes the Veil

I have desired to go
Where springs not fail
To fields where flies no sharp and sided hail
And a few lilies blow.
And I have asked to be   5
Where no storms come.
Where the green swell is in the havens dumb,
And out of the swing of the sea. (1866?; 1918)

"Heaven-Haven," "The Habit of Perfection," and "I Wake and Feel the Fell of Dark" reprinted from *The Poems of Gerard Manley Hopkins* by permission of the Hopkins family and the Oxford University Press.

THE HABIT OF PERFECTION

Elected Silence, sing to me
And beat upon my whorléd ear;
Pipe me to pastures still and be
The music that I care to hear.

Shape nothing, lips; be lovely-dumb—   5
It is the shut, the curfew sent
From there where all surrenders come
Which only makes you eloquent.

Be shelléd, eyes, with double dark
And find the uncreated light;   10
This ruck and reel which you remark
Coils, keeps, and teases simple sight.

Palate, the hutch of tasty lust,
Desire not to be rinsed with wine;
The can must be so sweet, the crust   15
So fresh that come in fasts divine!

Nostrils, your careless breath that spend
Upon the stir and keep of pride,
What relish shall the censers send
Along the sanctuary side!   20

O feel-of-primrose hands, O feet
That want the yield of plushy sward,
But you shall walk the golden street
And you unhouse and house the Lord.

And, Poverty, be thou the bride   25
And now the marriage feast begun,
And lily-colored clothes provide
Your spouse not labored-at nor spun. (1866; 1918)

I WAKE AND FEEL
THE FELL OF DARK

I wake and feel the fell of dark, not day.
What hours, O what black hours we have spent

This night! what sights you, heart, saw; ways you went!
And more must, in yet longer light's delay.
   With witness I speak this. But where I say   5
Hours I mean years, mean life. And my lament
Is cries countless, cries like dead letters sent
To dearest him that lives alas! away.
   I am gall, I am heartburn. God's most deep decree
Bitter would have me taste: my taste was me;   10
Bones built in me, flesh filled, blood brimmed the curse.
   Selfyeast of spirit a dull dough sours. I see
The lost are like this, and their scourge to be
As I am mine, their sweating selves; but worse. (1886; 1918)

A. E. Housman

THE TRUE LOVER

The lad came to the door at night,
  When lovers crown their vows,
And whistled soft and out of sight
  In shadow of the boughs.

"I shall not vex you with my face   5
  Henceforth, my love, for aye;
So take me in your arms a space
  Before the east is grey.

"When I from hence away am past
  I shall not find a bride,   10
And you shall be the first and last
  I ever lay beside."

She heard and went and knew not why;
  Her heart to his she laid;
Light was the air beneath the sky   15
  But dark under the shade.

"Oh do you breathe, lad, that your breast
  Seems not to rise and fall,

"The True Lover" and "To an Athlete Dying Young" from *A Shropshire Lad* by A. E.
Housman. By permission of the publishers, Henry Holt and Company, Inc., The Society of
Authors as the Literary Representative of the Trustees of the Housman estate, and Messrs.
Jonathon Cape, Ltd., publishers of his *Collected Poems*.

And here upon my bosom prest
There beats no heart at all?"   20

"Oh loud, my girl, it once would knock,
You should have felt it then;
But since for you I stopped the clock
It never goes again."

"Oh lad, what is it, lad, that drips   25
Wet from your neck on mine?
What is it falling on my lips,
My lad, that tastes of brine?"

"Oh like enough 'tis blood, my dear,
For when the knife has slit   30
The throat across from ear to ear
'Twill bleed because of it."

Under the stars the air was light
But dark below the boughs,
The still air of the speechless night,   35
When lovers crown their vows. (1896)

TO AN ATHLETE DYING YOUNG

The time you won your town the race
We chaired you through the market-place;
Man and boy stood cheering by,
And home we brought you shoulder-high.

Today, the road all runners come,   5
Shoulder-high we bring you home,
And set you at your threshold down,
Townsman of a stiller town.

Smart lad, to slip betimes away
From fields where glory does not stay   10
And early though the laurel grows
It withers quicker than the rose.

Eyes the shady night has shut
Cannot see the record cut,
And silence sounds no worse than cheers   15
After earth has stopped the ears.

Now you will not swell the rout
Of lads that wore their honors out,
Runners whom renown outran
And the name died before the man.　　　20

So set, before its echoes fade,
The fleet foot on the sill of shade,
And hold to the low lintel up
The still-defended challenge-cup.

And round that early-laureled head　　　25
Will flock to gaze the strengthless dead,
And find unwithered on its curls
The garland briefer than a girl's. (1895; 1896)

William Butler Yeats

AMONG SCHOOL CHILDREN

I

I walk through the long schoolroom questioning;
A kind old nun in a white hood replies;
The children learn to cipher and to sing,
To study reading-books and history,
To cut and sew, be neat in everything　　　5
In the best modern way—the children's eyes
In momentary wonder stare upon
A sixty-year-old smiling public man.

II

I dream of a Ledaean body, bent
Above a sinking fire, a tale that she　　　10
Told of a harsh reproof, or trivial event
That changed some childish day to tragedy—
Told, and it seemed that our two natures blent
Into a sphere from youthful sympathy,
Or else, to alter Plato's parable,　　　15
Into the yolk and white of one shell.

III

And thinking of that fit of grief or rage
I look upon one child or t'other there
And wonder if she stood so at that age—

For even daughters of the swan can share   20
Something of every paddler's heritage—
And had that color upon cheek or hair,
And thereupon my heart is driven wild:
She stands before me as a living child.

IV

Her present image floats into the mind—   25
Did Quattrocento finger fashion it
Hollow of cheek as though it drank the wind
And took a mess of shadows for its meat?
And I though never of Ledaean kind
Had pretty plumage once—enough of that,   30
Better to smile on all that smile, and show
There is a comfortable kind of old scarecrow.

V

What youthful mother, a shape upon her lap
Honey of generation had betrayed,
And that must sleep, shriek, struggle to escape   35
As recollection or the drug decide,
Would think her son, did she but see that shape
With sixty or more winters on its head,
A compensation for the pang of his birth,
Or the uncertainty of his setting forth?   40

VI

Plato thought nature but a spume that plays
Upon a ghostly paradigm of things;
Solider Aristotle played the taws
Upon the bottom of a king of kings;
World-famous golden-thighed Pythagoras   45
Fingered upon a fiddle-stick or strings
What a star sang and careless Muses heard:
Old clothes upon old sticks to scare a bird.

VII

Both nuns and mothers worship images,
But those the candles light are not as those   50
That animate a mother's reveries,
But keep a marble or a bronze repose.
And yet they too break hearts—O Presences
That passion, piety or affection knows,
And that all heavenly glory symbolize—   55
O self-born mockers of man's enterprise;

VIII

Labor is blossoming or dancing where
The body is not bruised to pleasure soul,

Nor beauty born out of its own despair,
Nor blear-eyed wisdom out of midnight oil.   60
O chestnut tree, great rooted blossomer,
Are you the leaf, the blossom or the bole?
O body swayed to music, O brightening glance,
How can we know the dancer from the dance? (1903)

SAILING TO BYZANTIUM

That is no country for old men. The young
In one another's arms, birds in the trees
—Those dying generations—at their song,
The salmon-falls, the mackerel-crowded seas,
Fish, flesh, or fowl, commend all summer long   5
Whatever is begotten, born, and dies.
Caught in that sensual music all neglect
Monuments of unageing intellect.

An aged man is but a paltry thing,
A tattered coat upon a stick, unless   10
Soul clap its hands and sing, and louder sing
For every tatter in its mortal dress,
Nor is there singing school but studying
Monuments of its own magnificence;
And therefore I have sailed the seas and come   15
To the holy city of Byzantium.

O sages standing in God's holy fire
As in the gold mosaic of a wall,
Come from the holy fire, perne in a gyre,
And be the singing-masters of my soul.   20
Consume my heart away; sick with desire
And fastened to a dying animal
It knows not what it is; and gather me
Into the artifice of eternity.

Once out of nature I shall never take   25
My bodily form from any natural thing,
But such a form as Grecian goldsmiths make
Of hammered gold and gold enameling

To keep a drowsy Emperor awake;
Or set upon a golden bough to sing   30
To lords and ladies of Byzantium
Of what is past, or passing, or to come. (1928)

Edwin Arlington Robinson

MINIVER CHEEVY

Miniver Cheevy, child of scorn,
    Grew lean while he assailed the seasons;
He wept that he was ever born,
    And he had reasons.

Miniver loved the days of old   5
    When swords were bright and steeds were prancing.
The vision of a warrior bold
    Would set him dancing.

Miniver sighed for what was not,
    And dreamed, and rested from his labors;   10
He dreamed of Thebes and Camelot,
    And Priam's neighbors.

Miniver mourned the ripe renown
    That made so many a name so fragrant;
He mourned Romance, now on the town,   15
    And Art, a vagrant.

Miniver loved the Medici,
    Albeit he had never seen one;
He would have sinned incessantly
    Could he have been one.   20

Miniver cursed the commonplace
    And eyed a khaki suit with loathing;
He missed the mediæval grace
    Of iron clothing.

Miniver scorned the gold he sought,   25
    But sore annoyed was he without it;

Miniver thought, and thought, and thought,
   And thought about it.

Miniver Cheevy, born too late,
   Scratched his head and kept on thinking: 30
Miniver coughed, and called it fate,
   And kept on drinking. (1907)

Walter de la Mare

THE LISTENERS

"Is there anybody there?" said the Traveller,
   Knocking on the moonlit door;
And his horse in the silence champed the grasses
   Of the forest's ferny floor:
And a bird flew up out of a turret,   5
   Above the Traveller's head:
And he smote upon the door again a second time;
   "Is there anybody there?" he said.
But no one descended to the Traveller;
   No head from the leaf-fringed sill   10
Leaned over and looked into his grey eyes,
   Where he stood perplexed and still.
But only a host of phantom listeners
   That dwelt in the lone house then
Stood listening in the quiet of the moonlight   15
   To that voice from the world of men:
Stood thronging the faint moonbeams on the dark stair,
   That goes down to the empty hall,
Hearkening in an air stirred and shaken
   By the lonely Traveller's call.   20
And he felt in his heart their strangeness,
   Their stillness answering his cry,
While his horse moved, cropping the dark turf,
   'Neath the starred and leafy sky;
For he suddenly smote on the door, even   25
   Louder, and lifted his head:—
"Tell them I came, and no one answered,
   That I kept my word," he said.

Never the least stir made the listeners,
   Though every word he spake   30
Fell echoing through the shadowiness of the still house
   From the one man left awake:
Aye, they heard his foot upon the stirrup,
   And the sound of iron on stone,
And how the silence surged softly backward,   35
   When the plunging hoofs were gone. (1912)

Robert Frost

AFTER APPLE-PICKING

My long two-pointed ladder's sticking through a tree
Toward heaven still,
And there's a barrel that I didn't fill
Beside it, and there may be two or three
Apples I didn't pick upon some bough.   5
But I am done with apple-picking now.
Essence of winter sleep is on the night,
The scent of apples: I am drowsing off.
I cannot rub the strangeness from my sight
I got from looking through a pane of glass   10
I skimmed this morning from the drinking trough
And held against the world of hoary grass.
It melted, and I let it fall and break.
But I was well
Upon my way to sleep before it fell,   15
And I could tell
What form my dreaming was about to take.
Magnified apples appear and disappear,
Stem end and blossom end,
And every fleck of russet showing clear.   20
My instep arch not only keeps the ache,
It keeps the pressure of a ladder-round.
I feel the ladder sway as the boughs bend.
And I keep hearing from the cellar bin
The rumbling sound   25
Of load on load of apples coming in.
For I have had too much

Of apple-picking: I am overtired
Of the great harvest I myself desired.
There were ten thousand thousand fruit to touch,   30
Cherish in hand, lift down, and not let fall.
For all
That struck the earth,
No matter if not bruised or spiked with stubble,
Went surely to the cider-apple heap   35
As of no worth.
One can see what will trouble
This sleep of mine, whatever sleep it is.
Were he not gone,
The woodchuck could say whether it's like his   40
Long sleep, as I describe its coming on,
Or just some human sleep. (1913; 1914)

STORM-FEAR

When the wind works against us in the dark,
And pelts with snow
The lower chamber window on the east,
And whispers with a sort of stifled bark,
The beast,   5
    "Come out! Come out!"—
It costs no inward struggle not to go,
Ah, no!
I count our strength,
Two and a child,   10
Those of us not asleep subdued to mark
How the cold creeps as the fire dies at length,—
How drifts are piled,
Dooryard and road ungraded,
Till even the comforting barn grows far away,   15
And my heart owns a doubt
Whether 'tis in us to arise with day
And save ourselves unaided. (1910?; 1913)

STOPPING BY WOODS
ON A SNOWY EVENING

Whose woods these are I think I know.
His house is in the village though;

He will not see me stopping here
To watch his woods fill up with snow.

My little horse must think it queer   5
To stop without a farmhouse near
Between the woods and frozen lake
The darkest evening of the year.

He gives his harness bells a shake
To ask if there is some mistake.   10
The only other sound's the sweep
Of easy wind and downy flake.

The woods are lovely, dark and deep.
But I have promises to keep,
And miles to go before I sleep,   15
And miles to go before I sleep. (1923)

John Masefield

ON GROWING OLD

Be with me, Beauty, for the fire is dying,
My dog and I are old, too old for roving,
Man, whose young passion sets the spindrift flying
Is soon too lame to march, too cold for loving.

I take the book and gather to the fire,   5
Turning old yellow leaves; minute by minute,
The clock ticks to my heart; a withered wire
Moves a thin ghost of music in the spinet.

I cannot sail your seas, I cannot wander
Your cornland, nor your hill-land nor your valleys, 10
Ever again, nor share the battle yonder
Where the young knight the broken squadron rallies.

Only stay quiet while my mind remembers
The beauty of fire from the beauty of embers.

Beauty, have pity, for the strong have power,　　15
The rich their wealth, the beautiful their grace,
Summer of man its sunlight and its flower,
Springtime of man all April in a face.

Only, as in the jostling in the Strand,
Where the mob thrusts or loiters or is loud　　20
The beggar with the saucer in his hand
Asks only a penny from the passing crowd,

So, from this glittering world with all its fashion,
Its fire and play of men, its stir, its march,
Let me have wisdom, Beauty, wisdom and passion,　　25
Bread to the soul, rain where the summers parch.

Give me but these, and though the darkness close
Even the night will blossom as the rose. (1922)

Vachel Lindsay

THE LEADEN-EYED

Let not young souls be smothered out before
They do quaint deeds and fully flaunt their pride.
It is the world's one crime its babes grow dull,
Its poor are ox-like, limp and leaden-eyed.
Not that they starve, but starve so dreamlessly;
Not that they sow, but that they seldom reap;
Not that they serve, but have no gods to serve;
Not that they die, but that they die like sheep. (1912)

Sara Teasdale

THE LONG HILL

I must have passed the crest a while ago
And now I am going down—

Strange to have crossed the crest and not to know,
  But the brambles were always catching the hem of my gown.

All the morning I thought how proud I should be   5
  To stand there straight as a queen,
Wrapped in the wind and the sun with the world under me—
  But it's no use now to think of turning back,

It was nearly level along the beaten track
  And the brambles caught in my gown—   10
But it's no use now to think of turning back,
  The rest of the way will be only going down. (1920)

Elinor Wylie

VELVET SHOES

Let us walk in the white snow
  In a soundless space;
With footsteps quiet and slow,
  At a tranquil pace,
  Under veils of white lace.   5

I shall go shod in silk,
  And you in wool,
White as a white cow's milk,
  More beautiful
  Than the breast of a gull.   10

We shall walk through the still town
  In a windless peace;
We shall step upon white down,
  Upon silver fleece,
  Upon softer than these.   15

We shall walk in velvet shoes:
  Wherever we go
Silence will fall like dews
  On white silence below.
  We shall walk in the snow. (1921)   20

Leonard Bacon

AN AFTERNOON
IN ARTILLERY WALK

(Mary Milton loquitur)

I think it is his blindness makes him so.
He is so angry, and so querulous.
Yes, Father! I will look in Scaliger.
Yes, Cousin Phillips took the notes—I think—
May all the evil angels fly away   5
With Cousin Phillips to the Serbonian Bog,
Wherever that may be. And here am I
Locked in with him the livelong afternoon.
There's Anne gone limping with that love of hers,
Her master-carpenter, and Deborah   10
Stolen away. Yes, Father, 'tis an aleph
But the Greek glose on't in the Septuagint
Is something that I cannot quite make out.
The letter's rubbed.
      Oh, thus to wear away   15
My soul and body with this dry-as-dust
This tearer-up of words, this plaguey seeker
After the things that no man understands.
'Tis April. I am seventeen years old,
And Abram Clark will come a-courting me.   20
Oh what a Hell a midday house can be!
Dusty and bright and dumb and shadowless,
Full of this sunshot dryness, like the soul
Of this old pedant here. I will not bear
Longer this tyranny of death in life   25
That drains my spirit like a succubus.
I am too full of blood and life for this—
This dull soul-gnawing discipline he sets
Upon our shoulders, the sad characters.
Chapter on chapter, blank and meaningless.   30
Now by the May-pole merry-makers run,
And the music throbs and pulses in light limbs,
And the girls' kirtles are lifted to the knee.
Ah would that I were blowsy with the heat,

Being bussed by some tall fellow, and kissing him 35
On his hot red lips—some bully royalist
With gold in's purse and lace about his throat
And a long rapier for the Puritans.
Or I would wander by some cool yew-hedge,
Dallying with my lover all the afternoon, 40
And then to cards and supper—cinnamon,
Some delicate pastry, and an amber wine
Burning on these lips that know a year-long lent.
Then to the theatre, and Mistress Nell
That the king's fond of. Mayhap gentlemen 45
About would praise me, and I should hear them buzz,
And feel my cheek grow warm beneath my mask,
And glance most kindly—
    I was in a muse
I have the paper, father, and the pens. 50
Now for the damnable dictation. So!
"High—on a throne—of royal state—which far
Outshone—the wealth of Ormus"—S or Z?
How should I know the letter?—*"and of Ind.* 55
Or where—the gorgeous East—with richest hand
Showers—on her kings—barbaric—pearl and gold.
Satan exalted sate." (1927)

Marianne Moore

POETRY

I, too, dislike it: there are things that are important beyond all this fiddle.
  Reading it, however, with a perfect contempt for it, one discovers in
    it after all, a place for the genuine.
      Hands that can grasp, eyes
        that can dilate, hair that can rise 5
          if it must, these things are important not because a

high-sounding interpretation can be put upon them but because they are
  useful. When they become so derivative as to become unintelligible,
    the same thing may be said for all of us, that we
      do not admire what 10
        we cannot understand: the bat
          holding on upside down or in quest of something to

eat, elephants pushing, a wild horse taking a roll, a tireless wolf under
   a tree, the immovable critic twitching his skin like a horse that feels a
      flea, the base-
ball fan, the statistician—   15
   nor is it valid
      to discriminate against 'business documents and

school-books'; all these phenomena are important. One must make a dis-
      tinction
however: when dragged into prominence by half poets, the result is not
      poetry,
nor till the poets among us can be   20
   'literalists of
      the imagination'—above
         insolence and triviality and can present

for inspection, 'imaginary gardens with real toads in them,' shall we have
   it. In the meantime, if you demand on the one hand,   25
   the raw material of poetry in
      all its rawness and
      that which is on the other hand
         genuine, you are interested in poetry. (1935)

John Crowe Ransom

                                               BELLS FOR

JOHN WHITESIDE'S DAUGHTER

          There was such speed in her little body,
          And such lightness in her footfall,
          It is no wonder that her brown study
          Astonishes us all.

          Her wars were bruited in our high window.   5
          We looked among orchard trees and beyond,
          Where she took arms against her shadow,
          Or harried unto the pond

          The lazy geese, like a snow cloud
          Dripping their snow on the green grass,   10

Tricking and stopping, sleepy and proud,
Who cried in goose, Alas,

For the tireless heart within the little
Lady with rod that made them rise
From their noon apple-dreams, and scuttle   15
Goose-fashion under the skies!

But now go the bells, and we are ready;
In one house we are sternly stopped
To say we are vexed at her brown study,
Lying so primly propped. (1923)   20

Robert Penn Warren

RANSOM'S "BELLS FOR JOHN WHITESIDE'S DAUGHTER"

The first stanza is based on two time-honored clichés: first, "Heaven, won't that child ever be still, she is driving me distracted"; and second, "She was such an active, healthy-looking child, would you ever thought she'd just up and die?" In fact, the whole poem develops these clichés, and exploits, in a backhand fashion, the ironies implicit in their inter-relation. And in this connection, we may note that the fact of the clichés, rather than more original or profound observations, at the root of the poem is important; there is in the poem the contrast between the staleness of the clichés and the shock of reality. Further we may note that the second cliché is an answer, savagely ironical in itself, to the first: the child you wished would be still is still, despite all that activity which your adult occupations deplored.

But such a savage irony is not the game here. It is too desperate, too naked, in a word too pure. And ultimately, it is, in a sense, a meaningless irony if left in its pure state, because it depends on a mechanical, accidental contrast in nature, void of moral content. The poem is concerned with modifications and modulations of this brute, basic irony, modulations and modifications contingent upon an attitude taken toward it by a responsible human being, the speaker of the poem. The savagery is masked, or ameliorated.

In this connection, we may observe, first the phrase "brown study." It is not the "frosted flower," the "marmoreal immobility" or any one of a thousand such phrases which would aim for the pure effect. It is merely the brown study which astonishes—a phrase which denies, as it were, the finality of the situation, underplays the pathos, and merely reminds one of those moments of childish pensiveness into which the grown-up cannot penetrate. And the phrase itself is a cliché—the common now echoed in the uncommon.

Next, we may observe that stanzas two, three and four simply document, with a busy yet wavering rhythm (one sentence runs through the three stanzas) the tireless naughtiness which was once the cause of rebuke, the naughtiness which disturbed the mature going-on in the room with the "high window." But the naughtiness has been transmuted, by events just transpired, into a kind of fanciful story book dream-world, in which geese are whiter than nature, and the grass greener, in which geese speak in goose language, saying, "Alas," and have apple dreams. It is a drowsy, delicious world, in which geese are bigger than life, and more important. It is an unreal (now unreal because lost), stylized world. Notice how the phrase "the little lady with rod" works: the detached, grown-up primness of "little lady"; the formal, stiff effect gained by the omission of the article before *rod;* the slightly unnatural use of the word rod itself, which sets some distance between us and the scene (perhaps with the hint of the fairy story, a magic wand, or a magic rod—not a common everyday stick). But the stanzas tie back into the premises of the poem in other ways. The little girl, in her naughtiness, warred against her shadow. Is it crowding matters too much to surmise that the shadow here achieves a sort of covert symbolic significance? The little girl lost her war against her "shadow," which was always with her. Certainly the phrase "tireless heart" has some rich connotations. And the geese which say "Alas!" conspire with the family to deplore the excessive activity of the child. (They do not conspire to express the present grief, only the past vexation—an inward inversion of the pastoral elegy. . . .)

The business of the three stanzas, then, may be said to be twofold. First they make us believe more fully in the child and therefore in the fact of the grief itself. They "prove" the grief, and they show the deliciousness of the lost world which will never look the same from the high window. Second, and contrariwise, they "transcend" the grief, or at least give a hint of a means for transcending the immediate anguish: the lost world is, in one sense, redeemed out of time, it enters the pages of the picture book where geese speak, where the untrue is true, where the fleeting is fixed. What was had cannot, after all, be lost. . . . The stanzas, then, to state it in another way, have validated the first stanza and have prepared for the last.

The stanzas have made it possible for us to say, when the bell tolls, "we are ready." Some kind of terms, perhaps not the best terms possible, but some kind, have been made with the savage underlying irony. But the terms arrived at do not prevent the occasion from being a "stern" one. The transcendence is not absolute, and in the end is possible only because of an exercise of will and self-control. Because we control ourselves, we can say "vexed" and not some big word. And the word itself picks up the first of the domestic clichés on which the poem is based—the outburst of impatience at the naughty child, who, by dying, has performed her most serious piece of naughtiness. But now the word comes to us charged with the burden of the poem, and further, as re-echoed here by the phrase "brown study," charged by the sentence in which it occurs: we are gathered formally, ritualistically, sternly together to say the word *vexed*. *Vexed* becomes the ritualistic, the summarizing word.

T. S. Eliot

SWEENEY AMONG THE NIGHTINGALES

ὤμοι πέπληγμαι καιρίαν πληγὴν ἔσω.[1]

Apeneck Sweeney spreads his knees
Letting his arms hang down to laugh,
The zebra stripes along his jaw
Swelling to maculate giraffe.

The circles of the stormy moon   5
Slide westward toward the River Plate,
Death and the Raven drift above
And Sweeney guards the hornèd gate.

Gloomy Orion and the Dog
Are veiled; and hushed the shrunken seas;   10
The person in the Spanish cape
Tries to sit on Sweeney's knees

Slips and pulls the table cloth
Overturns a coffee-cup,
Reorganized upon the floor   15
She yawns and draws a stocking up;

The silent man in mocha brown
Sprawls at the window-sill and gapes;
The waiter brings in oranges
Bananas, figs and hothouse grapes;   20

The silent vertebrate in brown
Contracts and concentrates, withdraws;
Rachel *née* Rabinovitch
Tears at the grapes with murderous paws;

1. Alas! I am stricken by a timely blow within (from the drama *Agamemnon* of Aeschylus).

She and the lady in the cape   25
Are suspect, thought to be in league;
Therefore the man with heavy eyes
Declines the gambit, shows fatigue,

Leaves the room and reappears
Outside the window, leaning in,   30
Branches of wistaria
Circumscribe a golden grin;

The host with someone indistinct
Converses at the door apart,
The nightingales are singing near   35
The Convent of the Sacred Heart,

And sang within the bloody wood
When Agamemnon cried aloud,
And let their liquid siftings fall
To stain the stiff dishonoured shroud. (1919)   40

THE LOVE SONG OF
J. ALFRED PRUFROCK

S'io credesse che mia risposta fosse
A persona che mai tornasse al mondo,
Questa fiamma staria senza piu scosse.
Ma perciocche giammai di questo fondo
Non torno vivo alcun, s'i'odo il vero,
Senza tema d'infamia ti rispondo.[1]

Let us go then, you and I,
When the evening is spread out against the sky
Like a patient etherized upon a table;
Let us go, through certain half-deserted streets,
The muttering retreats   5
Of restless nights in one-night cheap hotels
And sawdust restaurants with oyster-shells:
Streets that follow like a tedious argument
Of insidious intent
To lead you to an overwhelming question . . .   10

1. *S'io . . . rispondo.* If I could believe that my answer might be to a person who should
ever return into the world, this flame would stand without more quiverings; but inasmuch as,
if I hear the truth, never from this depth did any living man return, without fear of infamy
I answer thee (from Dante's *Inferno*, Canto XXVII, ll. 61-66).

Oh, do not ask, 'What is it?'
Let us go and make our visit.

In the room the women come and go
Talking of Michelangelo.

The yellow fog that rubs its back upon the window-panes,   15
The yellow smoke that rubs its muzzle on the window-panes
Licked its tongue into the corners of the evening,
Lingered upon the pools that stand in drains,
Let fall upon its back the soot that falls from chimneys,
Slipped by the terrace, made a sudden leap,   20
And seeing that it was a soft October night,
Curled once about the house, and fell asleep.

And indeed there will be time
For the yellow smoke that slides along the street,
Rubbing its back upon the window-panes;   25
There will be time, there will be time
To prepare a face to meet the faces that you meet;
There will be time to murder and create,
And time for all the works and days of hands
That lift and drop a question on your plate;   30
Time for you and time for me,
And time yet for a hundred indecisions,
And for a hundred visions and revisions,
Before the taking of a toast and tea.

In the room the women come and go   35
Talking of Michelangelo.

And indeed there will be time
To wonder, 'Do I dare?' and, 'Do I dare?'
Time to turn back and descend the stair,
With a bald spot in the middle of my hair—   40
(They will say: 'How his hair is growing thin!')
My morning coat, my collar mounting firmly to the chin,
My necktie rich and modest, but asserted by a simple pin—
(They will say: 'But how his arms and legs are thin!')
Do I dare   45
Disturb the universe?
In a minute there is time
For decisions and revisions which a minute will reverse.

For I have known them all already, known them all:—
Have known the evenings, mornings, afternoons,   50

I have measured out my life with coffee spoons;
I know the voices dying with a dying fall
Beneath the music from a farther room.
    So how should I presume?

And I have known the eyes already, known them all—   55
The eyes that fix you in a formulated phrase,
And when I am formulated, sprawling on a pin,
When I am pinned and wriggling on the wall,
Then how should I begin
To spit out all the butt-ends of my days and ways?   60
    And how should I presume?

And I have known the arms already, known them all—
Arms that are braceleted and white and bare
(But in the lamplight, downed with light brown hair!)
Is it perfume from a dress   65
That makes me so digress?
Arms that lie along a table, or wrap about a shawl.
    And should I then presume?
    And how should I begin?

     . . . . . .

Shall I say, I have gone at dusk through narrow streets   70
And watched the smoke that rises from the pipes
Of lonely men in shirt-sleeves, leaning out of windows? . . .
I should have been a pair of ragged claws
Scuttling across the floors of silent seas.

     . . . . . .

And the afternoon, the evening, sleeps so peacefully!   75
Smoothed by long fingers,
Asleep . . . tired . . . or it malingers,
Stretched on the floor, here beside you and me.
Should I, after tea and cakes and ices,
Have the strength to force the moment to its crisis?   80
But though I have wept and fasted, wept and prayed,
Though I have seen my head (grown slightly bald) brought in
      upon a platter,
I am no prophet—and here's no great matter;
I have seen the moment of my greatness flicker,
And I have seen the eternal Footman hold my coat, and snicker,   85
And in short, I was afraid.

And would it have been worth it, after all,
After the cups, the marmalade, the tea,
Among the porcelain, among some talk of you and me,

Would it have been worth while,   90
To have bitten off the matter with a smile,
To have squeezed the universe into a ball
To roll it toward some overwhelming question,
To say: 'I am Lazarus, come from the dead,
Come back to tell you all, I shall tell you all'—   95
If one, settling a pillow by her head,
   Should say: 'That is not what I meant at all,
   That is not it, at all.'

        . . .   . . .

And would it have been worth it, after all,
Would it have been worth while,   100
After the sunsets and the dooryards and the sprinkled streets,
After the novels, after the teacups, after the skirts that trail along
     the floor—
And this, and so much more?—
It is impossible to say just what I mean!
But as if a magic lantern threw the nerves in patterns on a screen: 105
Would it have been worth while
If one, settling a pillow or throwing off a shawl,
And turning toward the window, should say:
   'That is not it at all,
   That is not what I meant, at all.'   110

        . . .   . . .

No! I am not Prince Hamlet, nor was meant to be;
Am an attendant lord, one that will do
To swell a progress, start a scene or two,
Advise the prince; no doubt, an easy tool,
Deferential, glad to be of use,   115
Politic, cautious, and meticulous;
Full of high sentence, but a bit obtuse;
At times, indeed, almost ridiculous—
Almost, at times, the Fool.

I grow old . . . I grow old . . .   120
I shall wear the bottoms of my trousers rolled.

Shall I part my hair behind? Do I dare to eat a peach?
I shall wear white flannel trousers, and walk upon the beach.
I have heard the mermaids singing, each to each.

I do not think that they will sing to me.   125

I have seen them riding seaward on the waves
Combing the white hair of the waves blown back
When the wind blows the water white and black.

We have lingered in the chambers of the sea
By sea-girls wreathed with seaweed red and brown   130
Till human voices wake us, and we drown. (1917)

Paul Engle

ELIOT'S "THE LOVE
SONG OF J. ALFRED PRUFROCK"

Eliot has described his own method in a preface to his translation of St.
John Perse's "Anabasis": "Any obscurity of the poem, on first readings, is due
to the suppression of 'links in the chain,' of explanatory and connecting matter,
and not to incoherence, or to the love of cryptogram. The justification of such
abbreviation of method is that the sequence of images coincides and concentrates into one intense impression of barbaric civilization. The reader has to
allow the images to fall into his memory successively without questioning
the reasonableness of each at the moment; so that, at the end, a total effect
is produced. Such selection of a sequence of images and ideas has nothing
chaotic about it. There is a logic of the imagination as well as a logic of concepts. People who do not appreciate poetry always find it difficult to distinguish
between order and chaos in the arrangement of images; and even those who are
capable of appreciating poetry cannot depend upon first impressions. I was
not convinced of Mr. Perse's imaginative order until I had read the poem five or
six times. And if, as I suggest, such an arrangement of imagery requires just
as much 'fundamental brain-work' as the arrangement of an argument, it is to
be expected that the reader of a poem should take at least as much trouble as a
barrister reading an important decision on a complicated case."[1]

The title and the quotation from Dante contain the essence of the whole
poem. "Love Song" suggests conventional sentiment to the reader, but this
is immediately troubled by the curious name, "J. Alfred Prufrock," not the
sort we connect with love songs but with a formal calling card. The secrecy
of that initial "J." And not only secrecy, but pretentiousness, especially when
followed by the good old Anglo-Saxon Alfred, so open and honest. And is
there a buried amalgam in "Prufrock," a suggestion of prudence, of a frock
coat as suggested later in the poem by the mention of "morning coat"? A
dubious name, in any event, and surely a strange one to yoke with a love song.

The quotation from Dante is spoken by Guido da Montefeltro, who said
that he would not answer Dante if he felt his words would ever reach the
real world, because even in hell his pride remained strong. Now Guido had

---

1. Reprinted from T. S. Eliot's preface to his translation of *Anabasis* by St. John Perse, by
permission of the publishers, Harcourt, Brace and Company, Inc. and Faber and Faber Ltd.

received absolution from the Pope before he committed his sin, but afterwards he did not repent, so that, blocked by his excess pride-in-self, the absolution could not be effective. Prufrock would not speak, either, if he felt his words would reach the real world; he would not reveal his inner nature to any one. He can speak the appalling truth of this poem without fear of infamy because he is speaking it only to himself. The love song will never be sung. Why? Because it is a poem of self-love; part of Prufrock is addressing another part. Prufrock has not the courage to sing the miserable truth of his own nature to anyone. It is a form of the old debate between the body and the soul. Let us use the Freudian terms of id and ego. The "you" of the first line is the id, the "I" is, literally, the ego. The ego is addressing its alter ego. Prufrock is thus singing to himself; the love is self-love. And he fears the infamy of that fact becoming known. Prufrock is too proud to admit the truth to another, but he can suggest it to a part of his own nature.

He knows that, like the Guido of the lines quoted from Dante, the one listening to his sordid revelation will never go out into the real world, and he knows this because it is a secret part of his own nature to which he is speaking. So the Italian lines really dramatize the whole meaning of the poem. Remember the terms "id" and "ego" are loosely used here as a convenient frame of reference and not as exact equivalents of Eliot's own language. The id is instinctive and physical man, the ego is reasoning and cautious man trying to control the other. Stated too neatly, id is animal and ego is mental awareness.

We can assume that before the poem began the id had asked the ego to go and visit the room where the women were coming and going. The id wants the active and, as it were, normal physical world. The ego suspects the id for this reason, and thus commits this long monologue pretending to go, and proving to the id how hopeless it would be to go by showing what would happen, which would be nothing at all, or at the most rejection. "Let us go *then*" being the acknowledgment the ego makes to the id's urging; as any of us might say: all right, then, let's go.

Instead of that healthful ether of pure air there is an etherized atmosphere; the world has been anaesthetized, and Prufrock too. But it is safer to go out into an anaesthetized air than into the dazzling air of noon. There is also the suggestion of the imminence of an operation, of illness. The "one-night cheap hotels" are the homelessness of our human transit through our civilization. The hotels are cheap and remote, secretive, places where one is safe from observation, and one keeps moving on. The streets are of "insidious intent" because, like that tedious argument which Prufrock has been carrying on in his own divided self between ego and id, they lead always to a question. This is many questions: "Do I dare?" And "Do I dare Disturb the universe?" "Then how should I begin?" "And how should I presume?" "And would it have been worth it, after all?" "Shall I part my hair behind?" Prufrock cannot move without being confronted by a question. And all questions add up to the dominant single question which overwhelms him—dare he try to join the real world, yield to the id and accept the usual life, make his overtures to the woman and take the chance of being accepted? In brief, dare he sing the love song?

But he cannot face it, so dismisses it with "Oh, do not ask, 'What is it?' " Now, the ego says to the id, we'll make our visit and I'll show you what those women are like. And he does, in one horrible damning couplet. For these are grotesque pursuers of culture, these fiendish females who can talk about Michelangelo while always on the move. And of all artists, Michelangelo, the creator of the massive, the overwhelming, the huge Sibyls who were women of complete and utter unity without falseness.

The ego now recoils from the crowd and takes relief in the sensual envy of the fog as cat. Prufrock envies the lucky fog which is outside the house, which can rub its muzzle on the windows but need not speak to the women or hear them, which can indulge itself entirely in its own pleasure by falling asleep. The cat figure resembles Prufrock, soft, secretive, self-indulgent.

Time is welcome to Prufrock because it means delay, time for the fog to play and time for him to prepare to meet the faces that you meet. Time to murder and create—the antitheses of his own nature again. The irony here is that Prufrock is boasting—he will never either murder or create. Time not only, however, for these excellent things, but time for the "works and days" (the title of a book by Hesiod) to confront him again with a question, so that out of the first relief of time comes the shattering realization of the question to which all leads.

Time for you and time for me, for both parts of Prufrock, who feels safer at the moment because at least time will give a chance, not for decisions, but for indecisions, for visions and revisions, the latter being both re-seeing of visions and revising of them. Both ego and id are safe because the inner world of the self can survive. And all this activity before the absurdity of taking tea.

Those women are still at it, still mocking their own inferiority with talk of that great artist.

Even after he is partway up the stair he can still be saved by turning back; but salvation by turning back has the danger that his baldness will be noticed.

Any action is self-defeating. They will ignore his proper dress, his fastidiousness, his self-care, and comment on his thin arms and legs. Note that the stair is the conventional image of the purgatorial mount, as in Ash Wednesday and Dante, and that it is literally a purgatory for Prufrock to go there. Again one of his boastful remarks—"Do I dare Disturb the universe?" Naturally, he could not even disturb the ladies. But time will save him from all decisions, although, ironically, not from his indecisions. But he is safe, for anything he might decide will shortly be reversed.

Now Prufrock thinks of that society in which he has lived his half-life, the kind which Eliot described as "refined beyond the point of civilization." The coffee spoons are the index—the smallest spoon, his life measured out in driblets, and the sign of the artificial social event, and the example of how carefully calculated his life has been, how precisely he has considered each moment of it.

The women are still talking, now they go right on while the music plays, scorning the music, although dropping their voices. This is in direct contrast to the original remark of the Duke Orsino in *Twelfth Night,* who cried out for excess of music, who gave his attention to it: "That strain again! It had a dying fall." And there is the hint of the fall and death of the false culture which the ladies represent.

In view of the fact that Prufrock has measured out his life so neatly and spent it at such dull events, how should he presume to attempt any active affair at all? Or presume that he would be welcome if he did, if he simply entered the room which he is here imagining?

In the image of the spoons Prufrock had committed his own measure of himself in the act of measuring; now in the image of the pin, the specimen insect trapped, he admits that others measure him too. It is only a phrase which runs him through and stabs him to the wall, but so great is his shyness, that is sufficient. The danger is that which Guido feared in hell—that he will tell his story, reveal himself, spit out his works and days, divulge them in answer to a question as Guido did. He is terrified of the most conventionalized inquiry—"How are you, Prufrock?" And all is lost because revealed. How should he then presume to act, to ask the question? For this is like Hamlet's situation, to be or not to be, and either acceptance or rejection could mean death—to murder or create, the id and the ego, urge toward creation and urge toward suppression.

Now Prufrock thinks of the woman and describes to the id just what he has experienced. He is both attracted (the id element) and repelled (the fastidious ego). He fears the arms with their soft hair because they might take him, but the perfume attracts. Notice that the perfume makes him digress—from his resolution not to be tempted. If he did presume, how could he possibly begin?

Shall Prufrock now say, not to the ladies or THE lady, but to his id, that he has already seen men for whom marriage was possible, and that they were still lonely? Look at their gesture, they have turned their backs on their home and are looking away from it into the street, their pipes their solace, not their wives. No, this affair of marriage, or even a slighter thing, is not for him; he should have been as self-sufficient, as remote and secret, as the crab, who can scuttle in the darkness of the sea, untroubled by doubts and indecisions. They can't move forward, however. As Hamlet says to Polonius—'Yourself, sir, shall grow old as I am, if like a crab you could go backward.'

Now he envies the evening again, sleeping with no anxieties, like the cat, as if on the floor beside Prufrock's ego and id. Even if he decided to try, would Prufrock have the strength to force the issue, make the proposal of love? Absurdly, to do this after tea, which would make it impossible by its inadequate setting. He has looked at other men in marriage, has said he doesn't envy them, but he does envy the fog, which has no such drives, is sexless, and now he cannot make the effort. Safe back in his chair, he describes how ridiculous it would be for him to try. He has prepared himself by religious formulas, he has wept and fasted and prayed, but he could not do it. John the Baptist lost his head by keeping his integrity, but Prufrock is not bold or important enough, or handsome enough, even to be desired, so he will never lose his head—he will not lose it figuratively by any hasty action or passionate decision, nor will he lose it actually in some glorious act like that of the prophet. John the Baptist kept his integrity by refusing the woman, and Prufrock kept his, consistent with his parody of life, by not asking the woman. He could not seize whatever moment of greatness came along, as it came to the Baptist when he defied the woman; but he was afraid of death, the Eternal Footman, who laughed at him. Notice the imagery out of his social life.

Now suppose he had made the effort, surely it would have been refused and he would be left more miserable than before. Even if he came like Lazarus from the dead, from the deadly world of his own life, announcing he would tell all (as Guido had said he would), in the end he might be denied and this would make him worse off than had he not even tried.

After all that false life of his, the novels, the teacups, the sunsets, the final horror would be to have to confess, to let his inner life be exposed. Having thrown his nerves in patterns on the screen of that room, on that lady's ears and mind, then to have her say that he had misunderstood—Prufrock could not take that chance. He could not confess that in him there was this id, this drive which he had just thrown on the screen, for, he might then have to turn to it and say: see, that's just how it would be, the woman will turn us down.

We have three famous figures mentioned so far: John the Baptist, Lazarus, Hamlet, all three men who were betrayed by women. Yet they were all three men who took action, as Prufrock cannot. Unlike them, Prufrock will go on living, but his life is a form of death, less honorable than their definite acts that took them to their own destruction. Prufrock is pleased not to be Hamlet. He prefers being one of the minor people who give a little nudge to affairs but who need not take responsibility, which was Hamlet's terrible problem. Prufrock survives all three of these great characters, secure in his narrow, neat, safe and private world.

With the phrase "I grow old," Prufrock looks into the future, in which he will make the pathetic gesture of wearing his trousers rolled. He will worry about whether he should part his hair behind, because he will be so bald that he will not have enough hair to part on the top of his head, and it is typical of his petty nature that he will worry about wearing in the correct manner the little hair he will have left. Similarly, he will be anxious about his diet, lest eating a peach should upset it.

The mermaids are riding seaward, that is, away from the land and so away from Prufrock. Not even the mythical women of the ocean will sing to him.

Since he is already frightened of the actual, living lady in the lamplight, there is only one place for him to go: deep into his own nature. This he does when he hears human voices, which are the sound of tough reality, of others, and hearing them, he lets himself sink down into the only safe place he knows, the privacy of his own personality. He has lingered in the chambers of his hopes and mythical dreams too long, the time has now come to repudiate both myth and reality and return to the sealike womb of his own room and his own self. He has looked at the normal world and part of him has been attracted to it, but in the end both parts of his nature find it unattainable, "and we drown." He escapes into aloofness, into self-love, and abandons both the mermaids and the real lady.

Archibald MacLeish

ARS POETICA

A poem should be palpable and mute
As a globed fruit

Dumb
As old medallions to the thumb

Silent as the sleeve-worn stone   5
Of casement ledges where the moss has grown—

A poem should be wordless
As the flight of birds

A poem should be motionless in time
As the moon climbs   10

Leaving, as the moon releases
Twig by twig the night-entangled trees,

Leaving, as the moon behind the winter leaves,
Memory by memory the mind—

A poem should be motionless in time   15
As the moon climbs

A poem should be equal to:
Not true

For all the history of grief
An empty doorway and a maple leaf   20

For love
The leaning grasses and two lights above the sea—

A poem should not mean
But be (1924)

From *Collected Poems of Archibald MacLeish 1917–1952*, Houghton Mifflin Company.

YOU, ANDREW MARVELL

And here face down beneath the sun,
And here upon earth's noonward height,
To feel the always coming on,
The always rising of the night.

To feel creep up the curving east   5
The earthly chill of dusk and slow
Upon those under lands the vast
And ever-climbing shadow grow,

And strange at Ecbatan the trees
Take leaf by leaf the evening, strange,   10
The flooding dark about their knees,
The mountains over Persia change,

And now at Kermanshah the gate,
Dark, empty, and the withered grass,
And through the twilight now the late   15
Few travellers in the westward pass.

And Baghdad darken and the bridge
Across the silent river gone,
And through Arabia the edge
Of evening widen and steal on,   20

And deepen on Palmyra's street
The wheel rut in the ruined stone,
And Lebanon fade out and Crete
High through the clouds and overblown,

And over Sicily the air   25
Still flashing with the landward gulls,
And loom and slowly disappear
The sails above the shadowy hulls,

And Spain go under and the shore
Of Africa, the gilded sand,   30
And evening vanish and no more
The low pale light across that land,

Nor now the long light on the sea—
And here face downward in the sun
To feel how swift, how secretly,   35
The shadow of the night comes on. . . . (1926; 1930)

Hart Crane

AT MELVILLE'S TOMB

Often beneath the wave, wide from this ledge
The dice of drowned men's bones he saw bequeath
An embassy. Their numbers as he watched,
Beat on the dusty shore and were obscured.

And wrecks passed without sounds of bells,   5
The calyx of death's bounty giving back
A scattered chapter, livid hieroglyph,
The portent wound in corridors of shells.

Then in the circuit calm of one vast coil,
Its lashings charmed and malice reconciled,   10
Frosted eyes there were that lifted altars;
And silent answers crept across the stars.

Compass, quadrant and sextant contrive
No farther tides . . . High in the azure steeps
Monody shall not wake the mariner.   15
This fabulous shadow only the sea keeps. (1930)

Léonie Adams

COUNTRY SUMMER

Now the rich cherry whose sleek wood
And top with silver petals traced,
Like a strict box its gems encased,
Has spilt from out that cunning lid,
All in an innocent green round,   5
Those melting rubies which it hid;
With moss ripe-strawberry-encrusted,
So birds get half, and minds lapse merry
To taste that deep-red lark's-bite berry,
And blackcap-bloom is yellow-dusted.   10

The wren that thieved it in the eaves
A trailer of the rose could catch
To her poor droopy sloven thatch,
And side by side with the wren's brood,—
O lovely time of beggars' luck—   15
Opens the quaint and hairy bud.
And full and golden is the yield
Of cows that never have to house.
But all night nibble under boughs,
Or cool their sides in the moist field.   20

Into the rooms flow meadow airs,
The warm farm-baking smell blows round;
Inside and out and sky and ground
Are much the same; the wishing star,
Hesperus, kind and early-born,   25
Is risen only finger-far.
All stars stand close in summer air,
And tremble, and look mild as amber;
When wicks are lighted in the chamber
You might say stars were settling there.   30

Now straightening from the flowery hay,
Down the still light the mowers look;
Or turn, because their dreaming shook,
And they waked half to other days,
When left alone in yellow-stubble,   35
The rusty-coated mare would graze.
Yet thick the lazy dreams are born;
Another thought can come to mind,
But like the shivering of the wind,
Morning and evening in the corn. (1926; 1929)   40

W. H. Auden

MUSÉE DES BEAUX ARTS

About suffering they were never wrong,
The Old Masters: how well they understood
Its human position; how it takes place
While someone else is eating or opening a window or just walking dully along;

How, when the aged are reverently, passionately waiting   5
For the miraculous birth, there always must be
Children who did not specially want it to happen, skating
On a pond at the edge of the wood:
They never forgot
That even the dreadful martyrdom must run its course   10
Anyhow in a corner, some untidy spot
Where the dogs go on with their doggy life and the torturer's horse
Scratches its innocent behind on a tree.

In Brueghel's *Icarus*, for instance; how everything turns away
Quite leisurely from the disaster; the ploughman may   15
Have heard the splash, the forsaken cry,
But for him it was not an important failure; the sun shone
As it had to on the white legs disappearing into the green
Water; and the expensive delicate ship that must have seen
Something amazing, a boy falling out of the sky,   20
Had somewhere to get to and sailed calmly on. (1940)

Stephen Spender

THE EXPRESS

After the first powerful plain manifesto
The black statement of pistons, without more fuss
But gliding like a queen, she leaves the station.
Without bowing and with restrained unconcern
She passes the houses which humbly crowd outside,   5
The gasworks and at last the heavy page
Of death, printed by gravestones in the cemetery.
Beyond the town there lies the open country
Where, gathering speed, she acquires mystery,
The luminous self-possession of ships on ocean.   10
It is now she begins to sing—at first quite low
Then loud, and at last with a jazzy madness—
The song of her whistle screaming at curves,
Of deafening tunnels, brakes, innumerable bolts.
And always light, aerial, underneath   15
Goes the elate meter of her wheels.
Steaming through metal landscape on her lines
She plunges new eras of wild happiness

Where speed throws up strange shapes, broad curves
And parallels clean like the steel of guns.   20
At last, further than Edinburgh or Rome,
Beyond the crest of the world, she reaches night
Where only a low streamline brightness
Of phosphorus on the tossing hills is white.
Ah, like a comet through flames she moves entranced   25
Wrapt in her music no bird song, no, nor bough
Breaking with honey buds, shall ever equal. (1933)

Karl Shapiro

AUTO WRECK

Its quick soft silver bell beating, beating,
And down the dark one ruby flare
Pulsing out red light like an artery,
The ambulance at top speed floating down
Past beacons and illuminated clocks   5
Wings in a heavy curve, dips down,
And brakes speed, entering the crowd.
The doors leap open, emptying light;
Stretchers are laid out, the mangled lifted
And stowed into the little hospital.   10
Then the bell, breaking the hush, tolls once,
And the ambulance with its terrible cargo
Rocking, slightly rocking, moves away,
As the doors, and afterthought, are closed.

We are deranged, walking among the cops   15
Who sweep glass and are large and composed.
One is still making notes under the light.
One with a bucket douches ponds of blood
Into the street and gutter.
One hangs lanterns on the wrecks that cling,   20
Empty husks of locusts, to iron poles.

Our throats were tight as tourniquets,
Our feet were bound with splints, but now
Like convalescents intimate and gauche,
We speak through sickly smiles and warn   25

With the stubborn saw of common sense,
The grim joke and the banal resolution.
The traffic moves around with care,
But we remain, touching a wound
That opens to our richest horror.   30

Already old, the question Who shall die?
Becomes unspoken Who is innocent?
For death in war is done by hands;
Suicide has cause and stillbirth, logic.
But this invites the occult mind,   35
Cancels our physics with a sneer,
And spatters all we knew of dénouement
Across the expedient and wicked stones. (1942)

Dylan Thomas

TWENTY-FOUR YEARS

Twenty-four years remind the tears of my eyes.
(Bury the dead for fear that they walk to the grave in labour.)
In the groin of the natural doorway I crouched like a tailor
Sewing a shroud for a journey
By the light of the meat-eating sun.   5
Dressed to die, the sensual strut begun,
With my red veins full of money,
In the final direction of the elementary town
I advance for as long as forever is. (1939)

Robert Lowell

THE HOLY INNOCENTS

Listen, the hay-bells tinkle as the cart
Wavers on rubber tires along the tar
And cindered ice below the burlap mill
And ale-wife run. The oxen drool and start
In wonder at the fenders of a car   5

And blunder hugely up St. Peter's hill.
These are the undefiled by woman—their
Sorrow is not the sorrow of this world:
King Herod shrieking vengeance at the curled
Up knees of Jesus choking in the air,   10

A king of speechless clods and infants. Still
The world out-Herods Herod; and the year,
The nineteen-hundred forty-fifth of grace,
Lumbers with losses up the clinkered hill
Of our purgation; and the oxen near   15
The worn foundations of their resting place,
The holy manger where their bed is corn
And holly torn for Christmas. If they die,
As Jesus, in the harness, who will mourn?
Lamb of the shepherds, Child, how still you lie. (1946)   20

Isabella Gardner

THAT "CRANING OF THE NECK"

The primary word is I-Thou. The primary word I-Thou can only be spoken with
the whole being. The primary word I-It can never be spoken with the whole being.
Martin Buber

Birthdays from the ocean one desert april noon
I rode through the untouching and no-odored air
astride an english saddle on a western mare
through the resisting tow-colored grass and the dune-
less sand. Under me swam a stream strange in that dried   5
country. A "great blue heron" stood still in the tideless water and when I saw him there my heart daz-
zled. I whispered the mare to move quietly as
Indians move, I reined her with a catpaw hand
and my breathless feet crouched into the stirrups and   10
I prayed her through cactus mesquite and cattlebones
to the water's edge where the tall bird fished the stones.
The listening heron expanded with despair
unloosed unwilling wings, heaved from water into air.
O he hated to fly he flapped with a splayed pain-   15
ful motion. Deliberate as a weathervane

From *Birthdays from the Ocean* by Isabella Gardner. Reprinted by permission of Houghton,
Mifflin Company.

he plodded through the air that touched the fishful water.
I followed him silently giving no quarter
all that afternoon. He never flew far from me
we kept meeting past each cape and estuary   20
but he always heaved doggedly out of touch. I
only wanted to stare myself into him to try
and thou him till we recognized and became each
other. We were both fishing. But I could not reach
his eye. He fled in puzzled ponderous pain   25
and I at last rode home, conspicuous as Cain,
yet ashamed of a resigned demeaning pity
that denied us both. I returned to the city
and visited the zoo, fished on a concrete shore,
took children to aquariums, and rode no more.   30
I found that the encyclopedia says "A
gregarious bird . . ." No one spoke that desert day,
not one word. That fisher who heaved to dodge my eye
has damned himself an It and I shall never fly. (1955)

Richard Wilbur

BEASTS

Beasts in their major freedom
Slumber in peace tonight. The gull on his ledge
Dreams in the guts of himself the moon-plucked waves below,
And the sunfish leans on a stone, slept
By the lyric water,   5

In which the spotless feet
Of deer make dulcet splashes, and to which
The ripped mouse, safe in the owl's talon, cries
Concordance. Here there is no such harm
And no such darkness   10

As the selfsame moon observes
Where, warped in window-glass, it sponsors now
The werewolf's painful change. Turning his head away
On the sweaty bolster, he tries to remember
The mood of manhood,   15

From *A Bestiary* by Alexander Calder and Richard Wilbur, ed. Published by Pantheon Books, Inc.

But lies at last, as always,
  Letting it happen, the fierce fur soft to his face,
Hearing with sharper ears the wind's exciting minors,
  The leaves' panic, and the degradation
      Of the heavy streams.   20

  Meantime, at high windows
  Far from thicket and pad-fall, suitors of excellence
Sigh and turn from their work to construe again the painful
  Beauty of heaven, the lucid moon
      And the risen hunter,   25

  Making such dreams for men
  As told will break their hearts as always, bringing
Monsters into the city, crows on the public statues,
  Navies fed to the fish in the dark
      Unbridled waters. (1956)   30

Donald Justice

VARIATIONS ON
A THEME FROM JAMES

"large, loose, baggy monsters"

I
It's not a landscape from too near.
Like sorrows, they require some distance
Not to bulk larger than they are.
The risk is, backing off too far.
Once we have found a middle ground,   5
The warts, the pimples disappear.
There's but a shagginess remains,
An olive or a purple haze,
Which has at least that saving grace
Of average faces, average hills,   10
A nice, unshaven atmosphere.

II
Whatever goats are climbing there,
Being all invisible,
Animate objects of a will

Contemplative without desire,   15
Suffer no vertigo at all,
But climb until *our* spirits tire,
Or dine forever, or until
The speculative garbage fail,
Tin cans and comic books, which small,   20
Imaginary campers there
Forgot against this very hour.

III

Such art has nature in her kind
That in the shaping of a hill
She will take care to leave behind   25
Some few abutments here and there,
Something to cling to, just in case.
A taste more finical and nice
Would comb out kink and curl alike.
But oh ye barbers at your trade,   30
What more beguiles us? Your coiffures?
Or gold come waterfalling down? (1958)

PART FOUR

Student's Handbook

1. READING FACTUAL PROSE
2. READING IMAGINATIVE LITERATURE

1. Reading Factual Prose

Theoretically, the complete mastery of a piece of factual prose may require not one but three readings: (1) a preliminary survey of the text, (2) a detailed study, and (3) an evaluation. Actually there may be times when only one or a combination of any two of these readings is desirable. And actually any two of these processes, at times, may be and will be carried on simultaneously. The preliminary survey, for instance, may often do all the work of a detailed study. What is more, any reading practically always gets the reader, willy-nilly, into the position of doing some evaluating. Because a complete comprehension, however, may involve all three readings, and because it may be useful to sort out the three processes and to comment specifically upon them, each will now be considered in turn.

A PRELIMINARY SURVEY

The chief reason for the first reading—a preliminary sizing up of the piece of writing—is to discover as quickly as possible its general content and purpose. Common sense suggests why this step should be taken first of all. Anyone who reads a newspaper demonstrates the reason when, by scanning the headlines, he determines that some of them designate stories with which he has no concern, and that he therefore will stop with the headlines. In other words, by seeing their general content and purpose, he has been able to decide that he is not interested in some of the news stories. In other instances, his preliminary survey will justify a careful reading.

If one sees that a particular work is concerned with a subject of interest to him, he will find it useful to discover how the subject is dealt with. Such information will enable him to read in an appropriate fashion. Say there are these varied considerations of a subject of interest to him—a coal shortage: (1) an Associated Press dispatch from the coal fields, (2) a speech by a politician who blames striking miners and wants a law passed, and (3) a humorous column called "By My Coal-less Fireside." Naturally, an intelligent reader will want to go to each of these pieces in an appropriate way, that is, a different way. Knowing that people should read varying works in diverse fashions, he will want to ask and answer different questions about each. In addition, unless he knows what a whole piece attempts, when he looks at details in it, he will be unable to figure out how such details are relevant or irrelevant.

How does a reader get a general picture of a piece of writing? Well, some aids to such a discovery will be pretty obvious ones. Witness the newspaper headlines or the titles of some pieces. Sometimes a title actually will set forth the main idea which the writer or speaker is going to develop, as does the one given to Vance Packard's article, "The Growing Power of Admen." (p. 21) A title in the form of a question, such as Barr's "What Is Modern Painting?" (p. 209), may show the nature of the problem with which the article is going to deal.

Sometimes, of course, a title will be of no assistance at all, perhaps because the author of the piece deliberately uses it to attract attention or to create interest, e.g., "Self-Consciousness, Culture, and the Carthaginians" (p. 190). And even at best, though a title may give useful hints, it certainly cannot describe the contents of the article fully.

As a rule, therefore, a preliminary survey requires that the reader dip into the work itself to get a fairly precise idea of the coverage. Sometimes the author will be helpful enough to write section titles or chapter headings along the way. By running through such headings, either in a table of contents or in the work itself, the reader can often get a clear notion of what is included.

Often, however, there will be no chapter headings or subheads, and there will be nothing to do but peer at the text itself. In informative prose, a very likely place to look is at the beginning and at the end.

But if the study of the title and the beginning and the end does not serve, the reader may have to skim through the whole text seeking for its general nature and purpose, or, as a last desperate resort, may have to read the thing from beginning to end. Probably such drastic measures will be required for "Dover Beach Revisited" (p. 197), which is in the form of a narrative, or for a piece of reasoning such as "The Limits of Government Interference" (p. 63).

By one of these means or another, the reader may eventually achieve the goal of his preliminary survey—the tentative formulation of the general content and purpose of the article or book. He will then be able to state—*in a general way*—what the piece is saying, how it proceeds, to whom it is addressed, and what its effect may be upon the reader.

One final word: the value of the preliminary survey should not be underestimated. Studies with hundreds of students show that they read and *remember what they have read* much better if the reading is preceded by a quick preliminary survey.

A DETAILED STUDY

Whereas the first step leads to a *general* notion of the main thing attempted in a work, a detailed study leads to a *thorough* knowledge of what the author says and, to this end, of the way he says it. Naturally, while making a preliminary survey, the reader will get some glimpses of such matters. A detailed study will be concerned with a thorough understanding of *what* the author says and of *how* what he says is related to the overall method—how the patterns of explanation or techniques of argument, divisions of the piece, paragraphs in each division, sentences in each paragraph, and even words and phrases all do or fail to do their share. An efficient reader will notice details large and small until he can say what, if anything, every word contributes to the meaning, the author's expression of it, and the reader's understanding.

Different readers will operate in different ways to get such insights. A few geniuses will romp through the piece, pausing only momentarily on each page but coming out at the end, astonishingly, with all the answers. More mundane souls will have to take more time and trouble. Some will go through the piece painstakingly from start to finish once, or time after time, as is needed. Some will skip through it to get the lay of the land and then will go back and survey each part of the ground carefully. Some will combine methods, racing through some parts but carefully working through what they believe are key parts and difficult ones, then returning for a last careful reading. Doubtless some readers will first concentrate on the smallest units and then work up to the largest, while others will reverse this process. The particular method is unimportant. What is important is the final complete mastery.

One rule, nevertheless, holds for any of these procedures: One should always note particularly the relationship between the part and the whole. In terms of author's technique, this means constantly noticing how word relates to phrase or sentence, sentence to paragraph, paragraph to division, division to the achievement of the whole composition. In terms of content, this means constantly noticing how ideas or conceptions are related or subordinated. In terms of both, it means *always reading in context*. This fundamental rule will be followed consistently in the following discussion, which begins with the smallest parts (words) and goes on to the larger.

Words

The smallest unit of verbal communication is, of course, the word. It is with the word that communication begins and, in a sense, ends. The problem for the careful reader is first of all, then, to master the words he is reading: their meanings, their connotations, and their total effect or style.

Words and Meaning

Very often, when reading factual prose, one will be able to get nowhere unless he understands all the key words and many of the words of minor importance in a piece of writing. Sometimes the author will considerately define such words or terms.

Problems arise when the author provides no definition. Often the problem will promptly be solved by the reader. Words, luckily, more often than not are used by authors to signify their ordinary meanings. When they are so used, the reader simply takes care of the words by thinking of their usual meanings. If he is unfortunate enough not to know such meanings, he usually skips them and hopes that he will be able to get along without knowing them, or he tries to figure out for himself what they may mean, or he asks somebody. To save time and to learn the exact meanings, however, the best method is to look up the unfamiliar words in a dictionary.

Even when the reader encounters familiar words, a dictionary will sometimes be necessary. This bit from Emerson is an example: "The thoughtless say . . . What boots it to do well? there is one event of good and evil . . . all actions are indifferent." Here "boots," "event," and "indifferent," familiar enough in one meaning, have been used to convey other meanings. Older authors frequently, and contemporary authors at times, plague a reader thus, and nothing will take care of such a problem so well as a trip to the dictionary. The dictionary alone, of course, will not do the job; even after the reader has found the unusual definitions, he will have to look around in the sentence or the paragraph to figure out which makes the best sense.

The reader will have real trouble when the author uses words in a sense not to be discovered in a dictionary and also fails to define them explicitly. One may cite the educational little talk Alice had with Humpty Dumpty:

"There's glory for you!" said Humpty Dumpty.

"I don't know what you mean by 'glory,' " Alice said.

Humpty Dumpty smiled contemptuously. "Of course you don't—till I tell you. I meant 'there's a nice knock-down argument for you!' "

"But 'glory' doesn't mean 'a nice knock-down argument,' " Alice objected.

"When *I* use a word," Humpty Dumpty said, in rather a scornful tone, "it means just what I choose it to mean—neither more nor less."

Humpty Dumpty, like several other charming characters in *Through the Looking Glass,* is slightly mad, but in this passage he is pretty sound. Few authors will be quite as whimsical as he is about assigning meanings to words. Nevertheless, an author will often make a word mean, not what everybody else takes it to mean, or even what dictionary definitions allow it to mean, but what his logic, his philosophy, or one of his prejudices has caused him, like Humpty Dumpty, to "choose it to mean." And such an author, instead of conveniently defining the word, may leave to the reader the job of deciphering the author's peculiar meaning.

But even in such instances, the reader will find ninety-nine times out of a hundred that the author has really indicated, in an indirect way, what he means. To be sure, he has not told explicitly. But he has told implicitly—by the way he used the word. And the reader's problem is to study out the implied meaning by looking *at the context.*

Words and Connotations

Particularly important in reading any piece of writing is an awareness of the *connotations* of the words—the intellectual and emotional associations which, in time, accrete to words because of the company they have kept and the uses to which they have been put. The difference between the word "saloon" and the word "tavern" these days is, to illustrate, a difference not of meaning or denotation but of suggestiveness or connotation. As Professors Greenough and Kittredge have noted:

When a word has been long used in a particular sense, there clusters about it a great variety of traditional associations—religious, historical, literary, or sentimental, which, though not a part of its meaning, properly so called, are still a considerable factor in its significant power. . . . A rose by another name would smell as sweet, no doubt; yet no other name would so vividly suggest to us its fragrance. . . . Words like *father, mother, home* or the name of one's country, may have a tremendous effect in a great crisis. A mob may be aroused to fury by the utterance of a single word; yet in all such cases it is of course not the word at all that produces the effect, but its associations.[1]

Clearly, if he is to read with real insight, the reader must be alive to such powers in words.

The choice of similar words may determine the quality or tone of a work as a whole; the choice of dissimilar words may bring about meaningful contrasts. Such contrasts may be between parts of a whole work; they may be between paragraphs; they may be between sentences, clauses, or phrases. When a majority of the words that an author uses even in a sentence are of one sort, he may emphasize individual words or groups of words by making them of another sort. Witness the emphases achieved by this means in a few sentences written by a noted authority on American speech, H. L. Mencken:

For a youth to reach twenty-one without having fallen in love in an **abject** and **preposterous** manner would be for doubts to be raised as to his **normalcy.**

Long ago, I suggested that a good way to diminish lynching in the South would be to establish **brass bands in country towns.**

The argument by design, once the bulwark of Christian apologetics, is so **full of holes** that it is no wonder that it has been abandoned.

I am well aware, of course, that getting the whole human race **stewed** and keeping it **stewed,** year in and year out, would **present formidable technical difficulties.**[2]

Words and Style

The following passages, culled from three pages of one newspaper, provide an interesting comparison:

Selected rails and industrials moved higher in today's stock market although early gains running to 2 or more points were reduced or lost at the close. Dealings expanded at intervals, but slowdowns were frequent. Transfers of 730,000 shares compared with 650,000 Monday which were the smallest for a full session since last Oct. 30. The Associated Press 60 stock average was up 0.1 at 60.6, its sixth consecutive upturn. Of 874 issues registering, 406 were ahead, 240 down, and 228 unchanged.

1. *Words and Their Ways in English Speech* (New York: Macmillan, 1902), pp. 226-227.
2. *Prejudices,* Fourth Series, pp. 66, 267, 61, 175.

Q.—"Do you boys admire other boys who feed lines to all gals and collect female hearts?" A.—In the beginning, when all fellows are amateurs in the dating depart-ment, a Joe who keeps a lot of gals guessing might be admired as a fine hunk of heartbreak, a boy who knows how to get around. But as time goes by and fellows realize that gals don't like that type, their hero worship attitude will wear off, too. A fellow who isn't "honest" about dating never is really popular.

Eddie Bruneteau shook the Bostonians with a beautiful solo dash two minutes after the third period started, tying the count, and then Liscomb personally took charge of the game. His two goals, on both of which Joe Carvath got assists, means Detroit fans will see their first Stanley Cup final series since the Wings won the cup two years ago.

No very impressive detective work is needed to assign one of the passages just quoted, on the basis of style, to the financial page, one to a teen-age col-umn, and one to a sports story. The writers of these bits have chosen words *to suit their audiences;* in other words, they have adopted styles appropriate to their audiences. Similarly, housewives and theatrical people, Republicans and Communists, Protestants and Catholics will all have a vocabulary of a specialized sort. An author addressing any one of these groups will choose his vocabulary to fit his audience. Often an important clue to a piece of writing will be furnished by relating the author and his audience. Is he a Republican speaking to Republicans or (if one can conceive of it) to Democrats or Com-munists? Is he a Catholic speaking to Catholics? An understanding of the strategy of a whole speech may depend upon finding out what kind of person is talking to whom, and the kind of words used may make possible such a perception.

Words, in addition, may be studied in their stylistic relationship to *the piece of writing itself.* Such a study would make clear to the reader (1) what type or types of words are used and (2) why they are or are not effective. At one time or another, it will help the reader to notice whether individual words or the majority of the words in a piece are short or long, formal or informal, abstract or concrete, technical or nontechnical, ordinary or extraordinary, modern or ancient, and so forth.

Two contrasting versions of a short passage—one by Westbrook Pegler; the other a modification of Pegler's sentence—show how, in each instance, the author's choice of words has helped him achieve an appropriate effect. Columnist Pegler here is ridiculing what he refers to as the "Hair-Trigger Plain-tiff," the sort of person who, on the slightest pretext, sues for damages:

Version A: A man crosses a street against a traffic light, leaps to avoid a car, barks his shin against a curb, yells murder with great presence of mind, demands an ambulance and puts in a week's time malingering in a hospital over an injury whose proper treatment would be a dab of iodine and a jolt of scotch.

Version B: An individual traverses a public highway illegally, accelerates his speed of movement to escape a vehicle, injures a portion of his anatomy, utters an ejaculation with great discernment and alacrity, calls for a conveyance, and spends an undue amount of time in a hospital recovering from minor injuries.

For purposes of ridicule, the abstract Version B is far less appropriate than Pegler's Version A, full of concrete details which vividly show the paltriness of the injuries suffered and the disproportionate amount of fuss which accompanies them.

In similar comparisons, different classifications of words may be employed. In each, however, the appropriateness of one sort of diction as contrasted with another will become clear. Readers thus may profitably relate the word choice of any given author to the purpose and tone of his work.

Sentences

After many scientific studies, authorities on reading have come out flatly with the conclusion that it is best, except in particular instances, not to read so much by words as by phrases and clauses. Comparative studies of eye movements show that while ineffective readers stumble along a letter or a word at a time, effective readers take in whole sentences by conquering a series of words at a glance. Reading clinics have as a chief purpose training the reader to encompass word groups instead of single words. Authorities find that readers thus trained not only are faster but, at times, are more capable of getting the real sense out of passages. If there is improvement, the reason probably is that such readers relate parts of sentences to wholes—that is, they read in context.

Reading in the context of sentences involves discovering what can be learned from (1) grammatical relationships and (2) order in sentences.

Grammatical Relationships in Sentences

A sentence as a whole is simple, compound, complex, or complex-compound: I saw him; I saw him and I was angry; I saw him when I was angry; I saw him and I was angry because I remembered his remarks. The parts of a sentence, determined by their grammatical functions, are subject, predicate, and modifiers. In the sentence "I saw him when I was angry," the subject is "I"; the predicate, "saw him"; and the modifier, "when I was angry." The main clause is "I saw him"; the rest of the sentence is subordinated.

Knowing how to view sentences structurally will help the reader see how a writer has shaped his sentences: (1) to clarify what, in the context, are the important things and the subordinate things; (2) to clarify the relationship between the sentence and the rest of the paragraph. To achieve the first, authors may use subordination and coordination. To do the second of these, authors may use the various connective devices.

A paragraph in a magazine article, Wolfgang Langewiesche's "Making the Airplane Behave," reads thus:

(1) Weick, turner upside-down of ideas, solved this problem by putting the usual landing gear hindside to. (2) Instead of setting his ship on two main wheels, forward, and a third wheel under the tail, he put in two main wheels, set fairly far back, and put the third wheel under its chin. (3) Instead of sitting on the ground in the familiar, haughty pose, such a 'tricycle' geared ship assumes an attitude much like a Walt Disney dog sniffing a trail: the nose is close to the ground, and the whole ship is actually pointing slightly down. (4) Thus ground contact slaps the ship down in front into a position in which, regardless of speed, its wings cannot lift it off again, and if the brakes are put on hard the ship will bear down on its nose wheel, but it cannot nose over.

Since Weick has been the chief character in the paragraph preceding this, the use of his name at the start of sentence 1 shows a relationship between this paragraph and the adjacent one. Furthermore, this whole paragraph tells the reader Weick did this and that; the ship was changed in such and such a way; the result was this and that. Therefore, Weick should be the subject of the first part. The main clause of sentence 1 is "Weick . . . solved this problem . . . ." Two subordinated parts, one modifying the subject, one the predicate, indicate the way he solved the problem. In sentence 2, where the "how" has become the main thing to explain, two coordinated predicates explain it: "he put in two main wheels, set fairly far back, and put the third wheel under its chin." The "Instead of . . . " modifier is a further development of an idea which, in sentence 1, is used to describe Weick, "turner upside-down of ideas." In sentence 3, the ship, since it now becomes the main character, is the subject of the sentence and the first part of the sentence tells of the change, emphasizing, as is proper, the new aspect of the ship. The amplifying main clauses follow the coordination colon to show the changed position of the nose of the ship and of the whole ship. Sentence 4 begins with "thus," to show that the author is prepared to indicate the results. Three main clauses tell of these, the most important last: "ground contact slaps the ship down . . . and . . . the ship will bear down . . . but it cannot nose over." Thus main clauses reveal important points, while modifying elements reveal subordinated ones. Connective devices include "this problem" (sentence 1), "instead of" (sentence 3), "such a" (sentence 3), "thus," "and," "but" (sentence 4). Each is important.

To achieve variety and informality, authors will not always thus make sentence forms exactly correspond to desired emphases. Again, objectives other than emphasis—euphony or clarity, for instance—may make rigid subordination undesirable. However, the reader will find that a knowledge of emphasizing and relating often helps him get the author's meaning.

Order in Sentences

There is a certain student. The student is an honor student. This student has passed his courses. He has passed them time after time. He has passed them by cheating. Now an effective author, writing about this worthy, probably will avoid the infantile style of the five sentences just set down; he will do this by putting all the facts together in one sentence. Without much effort, he can think up at least the following five ways of writing such a sentence:

1. This honor student has passed his courses, time after time, by cheating.
2. This honor student, by cheating, has, time after time, passed his courses.
3. By cheating, this honor student has, time after time, passed his courses.
4. Time after time, this honor student, by cheating, has passed his courses.
5. Passed his courses, time after time, by cheating—this honor student!

Aware of such choices, the author will also know that the various sentences thus concocted have various shades of meaning—that shifts in the *order* of grammatical elements may make for greatly different emphases. He will employ whichever order gives the emphasis he wants. Similarly, the reader will be wise to keep in mind such possible shifts, such possible shades of emphasis, and will take into account the order employed.

In other words it often pays to recall that the writer may move around parts of sentences to emphasize individual words and phrases by: (1) placing them at the beginning, (2) placing them at the end, or (3) inverting their order or employing an unusual order.

The reader will do well, too, at times, to note carefully how the author handles patterns of whole sentences. The seasoned speaker often employs decided rhythms, brought out by pauses, changes in the pace, variations in the pitch of his voice. Those rhythms are related to what the speaker is saying. He shapes whole sentences in such a way as to give them emotional and intellectual impact. He uses patterns of balances, say, or of climaxes, or patterns of other kinds. Study will show how such patterns—though usually to a lesser degree—appear in written as well as in spoken discourse. The following are some samples:

Antithesis: Any man or State who fights against Nazism will have our aid. Any man or State who marches with Hitler is our foe.—*Winston Churchill*

Balanced Sentence: I would rather lose in a cause that I know some day will triumph than to triumph in a cause that I know some day will fail.—*Wendell Willkie*

Climax: It is a revolution of negatives, a revolution of the defeated, a revolution of the dispossessed, a revolution of despair.—*Archibald MacLeish*

Anticlimax: He had the calm confidence of a Christian with two aces up his sleeve.—*Mark Twain*

Rhetorical Question: Are the men and women of America so selfish that they will not make sacrifices for the good of their country?—*Radio Advertisement for Government Savings Bonds*

Careful reading requires an insight into the relationship between such patterns and the thought and meaning of the work.

Paragraphs and Divisions

What the word or the grammatical element is to the sentence, the paragraph or the division made up of several paragraphs is to the work as a whole. In a well-written piece, each paragraph or cluster of paragraphs will come along at the right point to do its little or big chore. As one reads such a work, he will be able to see how each helps the accomplishment of the author's task—how the relative position as well as the content of each contributes. In reading a faulty piece, by contrast, one will see that there are parts which might well be amputated, or parts which are missing, or perhaps that the order is not systematic but chaotic.

To get an understanding of the way the parts have been put together and of the consequent meaning of the whole, the reader needs constantly to watch for signs of interrelationships. As a rule he will find that the author has indicated divisions and subdivisions by his paragraphing. Often, too, he will find that coordinations and modifications of the sort used within sentences (p. 1114) are also used to relate sentences in paragraphs, paragraphs in divisions, and divisions in the whole piece. In addition, the reader will at times notice that the author, by throwing in a phrase, a clause, a sentence, or even a whole paragraph, gives notice of a transition. And one will see that repeated words or phrases, or pronouns which refer back to words or phrases, serve to show important relationships. By noticing all such indications, the reader will discover what distinguishes parts and what holds them together and therefore will be able to see how thoughts are interrelated to convey meaning.

The Whole Composition

So far this discussion of detailed study has been urging that the reader relate each part of what he reads to its immediate context. Spelled out again, this means understanding the word in the context of its sentence, the sentence in the context of its paragraph, and the paragraph in the context of its division or of the total composition. However, it should be pointed out that the total composition has a context, too, and the careful reader will do well to keep this fact in mind.

Any piece of writing is created in time and place, and has, therefore, a context in history. Sometimes this historical context is unimportant for the reader. At other times it is essential for an understanding of the meaning and connotations of what is said. The historical context is more than simply a matter of a few facts. It includes also the nature of the writer (or speaker), of the immediate readers (or listeners), and what the writer or speaker wants his audience to do or think.

Generally, reading arguments requires more attention to the historical context than reading explanations or even criticisms. But whatever the type of discourse, the careful reader will always ask himself whether an investigation of the historical context is important for a full mastery of what he is reading. He will also do well to remember that the word *historical* can apply to yesterday just as well as to a time twenty or forty or two hundred years ago.

EVALUATION

As has been suggested, it is practically impossible—and, it might be added, it is undesirable—to divorce the "preliminary survey" of a piece completely from "a detailed study" of it, or to divorce "a detailed study" completely from some "evaluations." Consequently, the reader has noticed, no doubt, that the editors have not hesitated to advise him to make evaluations of one sort and another during his careful reading of various kinds of pieces. Evaluation is of paramount importance in reading and may involve somewhat different procedures from a preliminary survey or a detailed study.

Determining what an author is trying to say and how he says it is only part of the reader's job. He must go on to decide whether it is well said or worth saying. For if the author's reasoning is false, his facts wrong, his style ambiguous, the work probably does not merit any more of one's time or attention. Certainly it is nothing that one wants to make an important part of his thinking or upon which he wants to base any serious action. Thus, closely related to the act of reading is the act of judgment-making, or evaluation.

There are many ways in which a reader may evaluate factual prose; he may think that a magazine article, to take one example, is good because it is easy to read, or because the material is vivid, or because the author belongs to his church, or because the article appears in his favorite magazine, or because his father says it is good, or because it contains some facts that are new to him, or because it agrees with his point of view, or because it is funny, or because of a hundred and one other reasons he may not even be conscious of. It would be impossible to discuss all of the yardsticks readers use in measuring the excellence of factual prose. This discussion will take up three that a great many readers think are especially valuable: (1) evaluating a work for its truth, (2) evaluating a work in its own terms, and (3) evaluating a work for its literary excellence.

There is no single *best* method of evaluation. Sometimes one will seem more relevant, sometimes another. For example, the truth of Hitler's *Mein Kampf* is probably a more significant issue to raise than the issue of whether it does efficiently what it sets out to do or the issue of its literary excellence. Better yet would be a final evaluation based on an application of several methods. Thus the best advice is that in assessing the merits of a factual account a reader uses as many methods as seem likely to produce useful judgments. Not only will several approaches be likely to result in a sounder final evaluation than one, but also they will increase one's understanding of the work.

Evaluating a Work for Its Truth

The truth or falsity of a piece of writing may be tested by considering two questions—one or both of them according to the nature of the piece: (1) Who says it? (2) What is said?

Who Says It?

If Einstein, who was the world's greatest authority on relativity, wrote on relativity, the reader who knew of Einstein's reputation felt that it was fairly safe to trust what he wrote. If John Smith, an insurance agent, writes on the same subject, the reader will probably have some doubts. At best he will adopt a "show me" attitude. If some propaganda minister for a totalitarian state writes an article on such a subject, or on any subject, most readers, suspecting him of being an unmitigated liar, would probably not even take the trouble to look at his first paragraph. In short, the reputation of the author unconsciously and automatically enters into one's judgment of the truth of a work.

Sometimes these unconscious and automatic elements in a judgment are fair, sometimes not. It is quite possible, for example, that an insurance agent, having devoted long years to the study of relativity, might turn out a sound and worth-while article on the subject. To discard it simply because the author does not *seem* to be an authority in the field would be manifestly unfair. The reader's first function in using this particular method of evaluation, therefore, is to find out all that he can about the author. First of all, he should discover whether there is any known reason for doubting his integrity. If he is a columnist generally criticized for distorting facts, a historian notorious for unreasoned prejudices, a political writer with communist bias, then the reader will want to scrutinize what he has to say with especial care. If there is no clear reason for doubting his integrity, however, it is only fair to assume that he is honest. A man is not guilty until proved so.

Second, the reader should find out if the author is an authority in his field. This is a matter of discovering whether, for example, he has worked in the field himself, whether he has published other works on the same subject, whether he has spent considerable time gathering data for this article. Naturally, if one is sensible, he will not want to carry this to such an extreme that he pooh-poohs anything written by someone without a national reputation in the field. Just to be on the safe side, however, he will want to check the facts and conclusions of such an author against those of recognized authorities. And one must remember that a reputation in one field does not make a person an authority in another.

Third, the reader should discover whether there is any reason for the writer's being biased on the subject of the particular work he is reading. Otherwise objective historians, for example, often lose their objectivity when writing about the Civil War. Two accounts of its outcome—one written by an Alabaman and another by a New Yorker—may differ widely, despite the fact that both authors have reputations as sound historians.

All of this boils down to the fact that in estimating the truth of a work, the identity and reliability of the author cannot and should not be ignored. The value of any testimony depends substantially on the character and competence of the witness giving it.

What Is Said?

After the reader has discovered as much as possible about the author, he is ready to extend his study to the work itself. Four questions deserve his attention as he develops his evaluation of its truth.

1. Are the Facts Accurate?

"Fact" can be taken to mean an event or datum upon the nature of which most people in a position to know agree. Checking the accuracy of the alleged facts one reads varies with what he knows and what he can find out. If one is an authority in the field, then he can use his own knowledge as a check. If he is not an authority but if information on the same subject is readily available, he can check the alleged facts against what other authorities have to say. If he is not an authority and if information on the same subject is not readily available, then he has to fall back on the reputation of the author and the reliability of his sources.

A reader can determine the reliability of the author's sources in much the same way that he can determine the competence of the author. He should ask the same questions of them: Are they reliable? Are they authoritative? Have they any reason to be biased? One point about the authoritativeness of the sources probably needs to be stressed. Other things being equal, the most authoritative sources of information are those closest to the events and phenomena themselves. For example, the best sources for a historian are documents from the period he is writing about, not books by other historians. As the reader checks for factual accuracy, therefore, he should see whether the author's sources of information are first- or second-hand, and make his judgments accordingly.

2. Are the Facts Representative?

There will be times when no single fact presented by a writer may be inaccurate and still the reader will get a wholly false impression because of what has been included and excluded. Even in the best accounts the truth sometimes gets blurred because no author is ever able to know or to include all the facts. What one expects of a just account, however, is not all the facts but a fair representation of them.

To see what happens when an author holds out on the reader, one might consider two historians' treatments of the men who framed the national Constitution. In one account, the historian assembles facts which show that these men were highly idealistic, were men influenced by the enlightenment of the eighteenth century, men who believed profoundly in their country and devoutly in their God. In another account, the historian assembles facts which show that these same framers of the Constitution were men of property who were looking for an instrument that would protect themselves and their wealth from radical laws and revolution. Now, both of these historians may be using accurate facts, but through the *selection* of details, they have given two completely different pictures. Neither, in short, has used representative facts since each has excluded a significant portion of them.

This is a question that has special pertinence for news accounts and advertising. Many newspapers make no attempt, especially in political news, to print representative facts. A Republican paper plays up those which flatter the Republican party; a Democratic newspaper does the same for those that reflect credit on the Democratic party. And unless you buy both papers, you—the reader—get only half truths. Advertising by its very nature is committed to half truths. You read that a new cereal is chock-full of vitamins but not that it tastes like stale mush; you discover that you can strengthen your gums by rubbing them with a finger covered with a certain dentifrice, but not that you can strengthen them equally well by rubbing them with a finger *not* covered by that dentifrice; the reader is told that a gasoline gives more mileage per gallon, but the advertiser fails to specify more mileage than what.

3. Are the Assumptions True?

The assumptions are what the author takes for granted. They represent the foundation of his thinking and of his attitudes.

Supposing that one is an ordinary reader and not a trained logician, there are roughly two kinds of assumptions that he should concern himself with. The first is an assumption upon which the truth of a specific statement by the author depends. For example, one reads in an editorial column: "Since the new sewage-disposal system is to be a public rather than a private enterprise, we can expect extravagance if not corruption in its management." If one thinks about this for a moment, he will see that the author is assuming that *all* public enterprises are extravagant if not corrupt in their management. Otherwise, the statement about this sewage-disposal system would not necessarily be true. Skill in spotting such assumptions is not something to be picked up overnight. Yet with a little practice one will be pleased to notice that he is spotting them more quickly and more accurately. The secret is to ask what *general* statement must be true if this *particular* statement is to be true. Obviously, a typical reader does not have time to do this for every particular statement based on an assumption. But whenever one is interested in evaluating the truth of a work, he is obligated to do it for any key statements based on assumptions. For if the assumptions upon which key statements are based are questionable, the truth of the whole work is in doubt.

The other kind of assumption in this rough classification is the broader type of assumption about what is valuable in life: assumptions about what is basically good, true, desirable, useful, and so on. These general assumptions are ones that the reader discerns as he thinks about the work as a whole, and especially about the author's attitude toward his material. If the author's attitude vacillates—if, for example, at one point he supports the assumption that men everywhere are entitled to equal human rights and at another point contradicts this belief—then the truth of his work is in doubt.

4. Is the Reasoning Valid?

This question about the validity of the reasoning may suggest that one needs training in formal logic in order to answer it. Certainly such training would not be amiss, but for the reader's ordinary purposes, it is not necessary. The problem is simply to see in common-sense terms whether the conclusions of an author are justified. The reader knows that they are not justified if the facts are inaccurate or unrepresentative or if the assumptions are unsound. Here are some other clues. One might consider them danger signals warning him to check the process by which the author arrives at his main contentions.

(A) *Sweeping generalizations.* Generalizations that cover great quantities of data or large masses of people need to be checked. If an author, for example, makes the claim that in the last ten years the standard of living in Alaska has materially improved, the reader will probably want to see how extensive his survey has been. If he is basing such a statement on, say, a visit to Nome, then one might well ask him what he knows about Alaska as a whole. The reader should be especially wary of generalizations which are all-inclusive or all-exclusive on controversial subjects. Usually they will be unsound.

The Russians are out to dominate the world. (*All* Russians?)
Americans are becoming more and more imperialistic. (*All* Americans?)
No one liked the test Professor Sycamore gave. (Not even the students who got A's, and Professor Sycamore himself?)

He should watch out, too, for generalizations with superlatives in them. The claim by its chamber of commerce that Squeedunkville is the fastest growing town in America is probably false. Only one town in America is the fastest growing, and its citizens are probably too busy to spend their time bragging.

(B) *Either-or generalizations,* such as "Every statement is either true or false." Such generalizations are often the result of simple-minded thinking that sees everything in terms of black and white: good and bad, desirable and undesirable, useful and useless, and so on. Such thinking does not recognize any middle position, that an action may be admirable in some respects and reprehensible in others. In short, such thinking does not recognize reality for the complex thing that it is. Usually neither part of the either-or dichotomy is made explicit. What one encounters most of the time is some such arbitrary statement as this: "The activities of this student group are un-American." The implication is that human activities can be neatly classified into two groups, those that are American and those that are un-American. Even supposing that the author has a clear idea of what he means by American, it is doubtful that he would often encounter a group activity which in *all* its aspects would meet or fail to meet his requirements for Americanism.

(C) *Forced analogies.* One of the favorite campaign statements of an incumbent seeking reëlection is that the voter should not "swap horses in midstream." Undoubtedly, this makes sense for someone on horseback in the middle of a river, but it has little perceptible relevance for a voter who is supposed to be making his decision on the basis of issues and men. Reasoning based on such a forced analogy is fallacious, and the author's proposition should be scrutinized carefully.

(D) *Forced causal relationships.* One of the worst of these is the type in which the author assumes that because one event happened before another, it therefore caused the other. Take a classic example: Item One—the election of Hoover in 1928. Item Two—the great business collapse in 1929. Did one cause the other, or did it merely precede it? As Professors Shurter and Helm point out in their little book entitled *Argument,* "The situation here is so complex and so colored by our political affiliations that we shall probably never have an exact answer." The reader should be wary, then, of the author who in dealing with a complex situation gives neat, exact answers. Another type of forced causal relationship is the *non sequitur,* in which the alleged result bears no relation at all to the cause. In one of its most vicious forms, this type of reasoning appears in diatribes against a man's fitness for political office because of his religion or his mustache.

(E) *Begging the question.* In this type of reasoning fallacy, the author assumes what he should be proving. Thus he may blandly take for granted that socialized medicine results in expensive and second-rate medical service and then go on to argue that, since this is the case, we need to do everything we can to keep Congress from passing any bill that will permit socialization. The real question, of course, is whether socialized medicine does result in expensive and second-rate service. This is what must be backed up by facts. No argument can be highly rated for its truth when based on intellectual dishonesty.

(F) *Ignoring the question.* This is another type of dishonesty and, like begging the question, is found chiefly in argument. When the author gets away from his proposition completely and begins telling irrelevant stories or indulging in mud-slinging or arguing for something else, the reader is justified in questioning his sincerity and hence the truth of his work.

In summary, one may evaluate a work for its truth: first by examining the reputation of the author, and second by examining his facts, assumptions, and reasoning processes.

Evaluating a Work in Its Own Terms

When one evaluates a work in its own terms he attempts to see how well it does what it sets out to do. Instead of testing for truth, he tests for efficiency.

To the person using this method of evaluation, each work, then, is a new and unique problem. It is almost impossible, therefore, to generalize about the method as a whole. The one thing that can be said is that sound evaluation of a work's efficiency depends upon one's ability to recognize: (1) the author's purpose, (2) the readers (or listeners) for whom the work was originally intended, (3) the ways in which the content, organization, and presentation are adapted to purpose and audience. The following discussion will show how this method works with explanation and argument.

Explanation

If a written or oral account is designed primarily to make something clear, it is explanation, or exposition. At this point one needs to take a step further. He needs to decide for the work he is evaluating just what the work is trying to make clear and for whom.

The specific purpose of an explanation is ordinarily not too difficult to discover. Usually the author states it in his introduction or conclusion or in both. If he does not make clear anywhere what he is trying to explain, the explanation itself certainly cannot be very effective. One would be justified in giving it a low rank without further consideration.

It may be a little harder to discover for what audience the work is intended. Of course, if the work was originally a speech, there is no special problem; simply find out before whom the speech was delivered. The task is easy, too, in an essay or article, if the author states for whom he is writing. He may, for example, in an introduction or preface or in the text itself explain, "What I have to say, I have to say for all those now attending college in America." More frequently, however, there will be no such obvious clue. Then the reader needs to do a bit of sleuthing. He must discover where the work first appeared. If it was in *The New Yorker*, for instance, he knows immediately that it was designed primarily for adults of some education and sophistication. If the work is a book, the advertisements for the book, the format, perhaps the author's biography, the reviews, or the criticisms may help. The material and style will give clues also, but he must watch that he does not get into *circular reasoning* in making inferences about the audience from the content and style. That is, he should not infer that because the details are obvious and the words easy the work is meant for a young audience, and then go on to conclude that because it is meant for a young audience the details and words are appropriate. If one is going to study the appropriateness of a style, he needs some nonstylistic clues to the audience.

Once the reader has spotted the purpose and audience, he is ready to determine whether the work does its job well. He should examine the contents and ask himself whether they are relevant to the purpose and adapted to the audience. He should examine the organization and ask himself whether it is appropriate to the material and can be followed by the audience. He should examine the words and sentences and ask himself whether they make the explanation clear and readable for the audience. In short, he should ask himself whether in terms of the purpose and audience the author accomplishes what he sets out to accomplish. This is the key question in this method of evaluation, and on the answer depends one's overall judgment.

Argument

If a work sets out to make the reader believe something or do something, it is an argument. Again, in reading argument, if one is measuring the work in its own terms, one must decide on its efficiency. How well does it do what it sets out to do?

In evaluating the truth of a work, it is often not important to make a careful distinction between explanations and arguments. But in this type of evaluation it is essential. Rather clearly, the reader needs to know in general what a work sets out to accomplish before he can say how well it accomplishes it. In the case of arguments the general aim is ordinarily fairly easy to determine since the author will make it abundantly evident that he wants one to believe or do something. Occasionally, however, the reader may encounter a work whose tone is a bit puzzling. For example, the work may seem to be argumentative in intent; yet all of its outward characteristics may suggest an explanation. The author may subtly be urging the reader to do something by explaining the situation as it is. There is nothing improper about such a procedure, since the case for a change in belief or action must always rest—if the case is a sound one—upon the realization that there is a need for a change. Thus a writer may do little more than explain the rent situation in the Negro section of Chicago's South Side and compare rent scales there with scales in other sections of the city; yet one may be impelled by the gross inequalities he brings to light to send money to an organization which is attempting to bring about rent adjustments. Now, is the author explaining or arguing? The reader has to make some decision so that he can decide how well the author does what he sets out to do. In these borderline cases he has to make the best judgment he can, based on the overall effect the work has on him. Some readers have found the following rule of thumb helpful: if the subject is controversial, the work is probably argumentative in its basic purpose.

Having decided that a work is argumentative, the reader needs next to determine its specific purpose and the audience for whom it is intended. In most cases the specific purpose will be perfectly obvious. Where it eludes one completely, however, one can probably by this method of evaluation write off the work as a failure and go about one's business. The clues to the nature of the audience are substantially the same as those in explanations. If the work was delivered first as a speech, one should find out all he can about the listeners. If its original version was in writing, he should look for specific statements by the author in a preface or in the text itself. Hints may be gleaned, too, from the nature of the work's publication. If the argument is a refutation, one should find out something about the audience at whom the original argument was directed, for the refutation will presumably be aimed at the same group. Lastly, and with great care, one can make some inferences from the content, emotional appeals, and style. But remember the warning against circular reasoning in the section just preceding this one.

Evaluating a Work As Literature

When one evaluates a factual work in its own terms, he judges its efficiency in performing its task. When one evaluates the truth of a factual work, he tests its accuracy. A third kind of evaluation tests the value of a factual work as *literature*. Literary evaluations depend upon tastes, and tastes, of course, differ. One reader's tastes may cause him to judge factual writings differently from the ways some other readers judge them. Nevertheless, he will probably find that even those standards of judgment which differ from his make a good deal of sense.

The simplest way for a reader to judge the literary value of a piece of factual prose is by noticing its effect upon him. The reader may ask simply, "Does it give me valuable information, interest me, excite me?" and decide that it is good or bad according to his answer. Such an evaluation, in a sense, is final, since each reader knows best, of course, how he himself reacts while reading. Furthermore, practically everyone naturally uses such a test. On second thought, however, most people will not be satisfied to stop with this test—a test which, used alone, involves only personal reactions.

Most people, therefore, will start by taking this test for granted, and will take a further step; that is, they will try to formulate and discuss their *reasons* for reacting favorably or unfavorably to a piece of writing. Such a procedure relieves them of the need to talk about themselves alone and allows them to talk about important aspects of the work as well. These aspects of the work will be discussed here.

Some readers may say, "What I demand of a factual piece of writing if I am to like it is truth." Such readers believe that literary excellence and truthfulness of some sort or other are one and the same thing. Of course, if the reader uses the truth of a work as a measure, he will probably want to distinguish between the kind of truth it reveals and other kinds of truth. He may, for instance, value works in terms of the usefulness of the truth they unfold. He may prize originality, and value works expressing unfamiliar truths above those which express familiar truths. Or he may rate great truths above lesser ones. Regardless, the element of truth in a work will be particularly important to him.

Some readers may say, "If a work of any sort does well the chore it sets out to do, it is—to my way of judging—a good work." Such persons feel that a literary evaluation does not differ greatly from the evaluation of a work in its own terms. They may, to be sure, distinguish between the complexity of the chore performed, and they may distinguish between poor, merely satisfactory, and brilliant performance of the chore. But if one uses this yardstick, he will be chiefly interested in seeing how the author has adapted his method to his material and to the audience which he is addressing.

Still other readers may judge works by criteria which differ from any which have so far been discussed. They may be interested, for instance, in some aspect of the author's technique. They may be interested in the overall organization. More often, they may be interested in the author's style. "I am most pleased and impressed," some readers may say, "by an author who uses words, phrases, and sentences in an appealing fashion." If one uses this kind of test, he will naturally attend to details in the author's manner of expression. He will have preferences among kinds of words—concrete or abstract, emotive or neutral, figurative or literal, homely or learned. Or perhaps he will take pleasure in finding that an author uses words of several kinds to secure variety, emphasis, and contrast. He will have preferences among kinds of sentences—simple or complicated, lengthy or brief, normally ordered or inverted—or perhaps he will admire an author who can use several kinds according to the kind of job he wants the sentences to perform. He may be interested in the author's handling of sound—rhythmical or unrhythmical, melodious or harsh, and so forth.

Another group of readers may be strongly influenced in their judgment by the personality of the author of a piece of factual prose. "I can't care much," such readers will say, "for a piece of factual prose which doesn't give me some sense of its author's personality. And naturally I like most the work of an author whose personality—at least as it appears in the work—is somehow appealing." An appealing personality, to be sure, may be one of many kinds—humorous or full of righteous anger, friendly and intimate or majestically remote, full of common sense or unusual learning, and so on. But if one is interested in this element, he will not be satisfied with any factual prose which does not acquaint him with a personality which, for some reason, he likes or admires.

These are perhaps the chief single tests. Naturally, though, many readers—those who probably get the most enjoyment out of reading—apply not one of these measuring sticks in isolation but two or more in combination. If, for instance, one says, "Of course I want a piece of factual prose to do its job well; in addition I want it to express great truths in an appealing style," he has three criteria: the efficiency of the work, the kind of truth it expresses, and its style. If he says, "A great work, in my opinion, is one which embodies the expression of a great thought by a great man," he combines an interest in the truth of a work with an interest in its author's personality.

The usefulness to others of one's evaluation of any given work will depend upon two things: (1) their agreement or disagreement with one's general criterion or criteria, and (2) their opinion of the way one applies his measurement to a given work. In other words, one's evaluation of a work includes two steps, the formulation of a principle—one's major premise—and the application of the principle to a particular work—one's minor premise. Both steps are important in a satisfactory evaluation. And the second step requires that one look in detail at the piece of writing itself and find evidence there to support his claim that the work does its job well, that it expresses a great truth, that it is written in an appealing style, that it expresses an attractive personality, or that it does two or more of these things.

Some of these standards, and some of the applications of these standards, will be better than others, naturally. There will be none, perhaps, about which everybody will agree. But one statement which most people will approve is that it is desirable for readers to have defensible literary standards, and to apply them consciously and intelligently when judging the literary values of a work.

2. Reading Imaginative Literature

MAJOR ASPECTS OF IMAGINATIVE LITERATURE

Typical imaginative writing may effectively show human feelings, motives, actions, and experience; such writing may embody an emotional interpretation —the author's interpretation—of life; and imaginative writing, therefore, may affect not only the thoughts but also the feelings of the reader.

How does an author shape his writings so they will do these things? An important part of the answer is that he selects characters, actions, and scenes, selects and arranges details, and uses words as well as he can, to communicate his insights to the reader. He strives to make all his technical procedures, all the elements in his work—*Actions, Characters, Setting, Language, Tone,* and *Meaning*—contribute to his saying what he has to say.

1. ACTIONS

Selection and Arrangement of Actions

The actions in an imaginative work ordinarily are not chosen or set down in an aimless fashion. Rarely does a storyteller follow a character from his birth to his death: usually he follows him through only a few years, days, or even minutes. And even when his narrative covers a brief period, the author usually leaves out many details. A moment's examination of almost any imaginative work will show that the author has taken for granted some incidents, merely referred to others, and recounted still others in great detail. Often authors take other liberties and arrange occurrences in orders which do not follow the order of time.

Such omissions, simplifications, and manipulations are justified if they help the author create a work with more form, and therefore with more articulated meaning and impact, than life has. When an author selects and arranges actions so that every gesture, every fleeting thought, every movement, and every deed has been related to a perceivable scheme or pattern, he has made a good start toward expressing such an articulated meaning. (The pattern itself, quite often, will have an implied meaning.) And when he has so handled other elements in the story—character and setting, for instance—as to make them, too, contribute their share to the whole work, the artist will have achieved his aim.

How, then, may an author select and arrange *actions* so that they will follow such a pattern? He may "plot" his narrative in such a way as to make it both complete and economical. His "plot," as many critics call a patterned series of interrelated actions, will be complete if it tells one story from beginning to end. The completeness will be perceivable if the actions add up to a single significant change or lack of change, and if reasons may be found for the narrative's beginning, developing, and ending exactly as it does.

Patterns of Action

An author may create such a unified work in various ways. A unified story may trace the growing love of a character for another from its beginning to an ending wherein the character's great love is proved beyond a doubt. Another complete story—a typical one by Poe, say—may tell of a graduated development of some emotion, terror perhaps, which ends when the emotion reaches a crescendo. In still another unified story, an ambitious character may decide to reach some goal, he may then strive to reach it, and the story may conclude when the goal is reached. Thus actions which add up to a completely developed attitude, a completely developed emotion, or a completely developed achievement, may be complete and economical wholes. A scheme of this sort might be pictured thus: —— The rising line would represent a graduated change.

Another type of story might tell of a character or situation which does *not* change. Suppose the leading character is a rascal at the start of the story, that most of the actions consist of people's trying to convert him, and that, at the end, he continues to be a reprobate. The significant fact would be that the character remains the same, and perhaps the picture would be this one: ——

Still another type of unified narrative might, by contrast, be pictured thus: ⌒ Such a "two part" or "complex" narrative would involve a reversal. In such a schematized narrative, after a character has been deceived for a time, he may catch a glimpse of truth, and from that time on his comprehension may grow. In another, an emotion may change: terror, say, may be supplanted by bravery. Or a character, after progressing toward his goal, may fail. Such complex developments would contrast with the simple development of an attitude, or emotion, or achievement, described a couple of paragraphs ago.

Conflict

All three kinds of action patterns, more often than not, will involve one or more conflicts, contests between opposing forces—man versus nature, perhaps, man versus society, man versus "fate." Or the conflict may be an "internal" one—between two parts of a man's nature. In the simple scheme, one force will consistently move toward victory; in the "unchanging" scheme, a stubborn force will successfully resist change; in the complex scheme, one force will win for a time, and then the opposing force will gain the upper hand and go on to triumph. In many narratives, not one but several strands such as these are followed to completion.

An imaginative writer who deals with actions, then, copes with the problem of finding some complete and economical scheme for plotting and relating his incidents. A careful reader has the task of seeing what the actions in a narrative are and how the author gives—or fails to give—unity to the pattern of action.

2. CHARACTERS

The problems of personality and the human emotions are usually dealt with deeply and in detail in imaginative writings. Hence one reason for the fascination of such writings is that, in them, most readers may meet many kinds of people unfamiliar to them in life. Again, they may come to know even familiar kinds of characters more intimately in books than they do in actuality.

So important is personality in fiction, drama, and poetry that a character or an emotion at times may suffice to give a work its essential unity. Some novels, stories, and plays in which the actions are not patterned but miscellaneous may be unified because one great character appears throughout. Some character sketches are unified, despite the fact that they present no actions in detail, because they offer insights concerning characters. And many lyrical poems, although they record no actions, are unified by the expression of an emotion and—to some extent—the personality experiencing the emotion. In many imaginative works, therefore, the writer takes care to show the reader what the character is—his qualities, his likes and dislikes, how he lives, and what he does. The sum total of such traits is the *character*. *Characterization* is the technique used by the writer to make these qualities known.

Personality of the Character

The reader who studies characters and characterization in a work should ask and answer three questions. The first is: What are the qualities—the characteristics—of the characters in the work? The reader, in other words, has the problem of describing the personality of each of the figures, major or minor, who appear in the work. Some characters, of course, will be nothing more than isolated traits or types or, perhaps, representatives of professions (e.g., a jealous man, a lover of sports, a housemaid). Others will be more complex, and several adjectives will be needed to describe them. If characters have several traits, the reader needs to see not only what those traits are but also how they are related. In some characters, all other traits will be subordinated to one dominating motive, drive, or passion (e.g., Macbeth). Some will have qualities which contend for mastery; and their contending drives or motives may result from a single characteristic, or one contending drive may result from another. Some characters will be, essentially, contending drives—personalities which threaten to split under trying circumstances (e.g., Hamlet).

Indications of Personality

A second question is: How has the work indicated these qualities? The author may *describe* a person in such a way as to indicate that he is arrogant or intelligent, or that he dislikes capitalists and likes women. The character's features, his dress, his gestures, the timbre and inflections of his voice, his facial expressions—all or any of these may be so delineated as to show what he is. Or an author may characterize by *direct statement:* "Jones, of course, was an utter fool." He may indicate a character's traits by picturing his *surroundings:* "He lived in a huge and showy mansion, which was cared for by armies of servants." He may convey what a character is like by quoting his *dialog:* both what he says and the kind of words in which he expresses himself will offer clues. He may tell the character's *thoughts,* or he may give the *opinions of others* about him. He may show a trait by showing an *action.* Often he will use not one but a combination of these methods. Readers should note what methods an author uses to indicate what his characters are like.

Function of the Characters and Characterization

A third question about characters and characterization with which the reader is concerned is: What is their function in the work? For they may be related to the actions, to life, and to the interpretation of life which a work provides.

In imaginative writings, characters do things. They are intimately related to the patterns of actions. Interrelationships between actions almost always come about as a result of characters—because authors and readers logically relate certain kinds of characters in certain situations with certain actions. If, for instance, an author introduces a dishonest character and then shows him, when tempted, lying to his mother, cheating in an examination, and deceiving his sweetheart, we say that it is "logical" or "in character" for such a character, when tempted, to do such things. Our experience with similar individuals, in life, has shown us that such actions are logically probable. *A characterization, therefore, may prepare for a particular action.*

Again, *a characterization may prepare for a change—a reversal—*which is at the heart of a pattern of actions. Here is a play about Jane Roe, who loves her husband in Act I and who deliberately scalds the poor man with a pot of boiling tea in Act III. She may be given qualities which motivate both actions—the loving and the scalding—at the proper moments in the play. It will be important for the reader to see exactly how the author's portrayal prepares or fails to prepare for her changing behavior.

In some works, *a character may offer signs of the progress and the completion of the narrative pattern.* Often the "exhaustion," so to speak, of possible actions for characters accompanies the working out of such a pattern. In such works, as Elizabeth Bowen has said:

Characters . . . promote, by showing, the advance of the plot. How? By the advances, from act to act, in their action. By their showing (by emotional and physical changes) the effects both of action and the passage of time. The diminution of the character's alternatives shows . . . advance—by the end of the novel the character's alternatives, many at the beginning, have been reduced to almost none . . . the character has, like the silkworm at work on the cocoon, spun itself out. . . .

Her remarks, of course, hold good for short stories, plays, and narrative poems, as well as for novels.

Some qualities will be given to characters, on occasion, merely to make them "lifelike." Aware that readers cannot become interested in mere puppets on a string put through their paces by their creator, an author often endows his figures with traits which have no relationship to the actions but which make them seem real.

Finally, some *characters may be given some traits which make them attractive or unattractive to the reader*—better than the reader, like the reader, or worse than the reader. Such traits practically always will be assigned to the protagonist (hero or heroine) and the antagonist (villain)—if there is one. Enough universal and enough specific traits will be assigned to them so that the reader will follow with interest their trials and their tribulations, their triumphs and their joys, and so that he will feel that there is meaning in their defeats or their triumphs. The physical aspects of the characters, their moral codes, their philosophies, their associations with good or bad friends, the way other characters feel about them, all will offer clues to the attitude readers are expected to adopt toward them. Not only does the endowment of characters with sympathetic or unsympathetic qualities interest the reader; it also helps the author give his work meanings. The nature of these qualities will help him show the reader how he is interpreting the people and the events which his story, his drama, or his poem portrays.

3. SETTING

Setting includes the details of background set forth in a narrative, a drama, or a poem. Such details may be presented at length or briefly. They may be concentrated at one point in the work or, as is more frequent these days, doled out bit by bit. Almost always a consideration of the employment of such details will be valuable for the reader.

The reader of poetry, fiction, or drama will find it illuminating to notice exactly how the author's handling of such details gives or fails to give that illusion of reality which is indispensable if imaginative works are to create interest and sympathy. More important, he should consider whether the details of time, of place, of social milieu, of emotional atmosphere, are functional or not—that is, whether they contribute to the unfolding of the action, to the representation of character, and to the achievement of the work as a whole.

Setting As the Shaper of Events

The great novelist and critic, Henry James, once said that he could not conceive of "a passage of description that is not in its intention narrative," and certainly it is clear that details in a scene may often be vital circumstances in a fictional work or in a poem which tells a story. The lay of the land may actually determine actions in accounts of treasure hunts ("The Gold Bug" and *Treasure Island*), stories of pursuits (*The Thirty-nine Steps*) or narratives of journeys (*The Odyssey*, "The Midnight Ride of Paul Revere," *Huckleberry Finn*). At one point in *Les Misérables*, Hugo carefully describes the battlefield of Waterloo; at one point in *Henry Esmond*, Thackeray tells of the disposition of troops at Blenheim: in each instance the data show why a battle had to follow a predetermined pattern. So important is topography in many detective stories that their publishers often print maps as frontispieces. Not only topography but also climate and soil may determine events—as in many of Robert Frost's New England poems and in Rölvaag's *Giants in the Earth*. In stories of men in conflict with nature, the setting itself, in a sense, becomes a character—the antagonist.

Setting As an Adjunct to Plot and Characterization

Even in works wherein the setting does not notably shape events, the author—as the alert reader should see—often uses scenes to help tell his story. In such works, in other words, setting becomes an adjunct to showing important changes and developments. By calling attention to the lengthening of shadows, or to the coming of autumn, or to the growth of weeds in a garden, an author may be showing the passage of time. A character's sense of novelty in an unchanged scene may betoken a change in the character himself. An example is provided in Hawthorne's passage about Minister Dimmesdale in *The Scarlet Letter*:

As he drew near the town, he took an impression of change from the series of familiar objects. . . . There, indeed, was each former trace of the street, as he remembered it, and all the peculiarities of the houses, with the due multitude of gable-peaks, and a weathercock at every point where his memory suggested one. Not the less, however, came this importunately obtrusive sense of change. . . . A similar impression struck him most remarkably, as he passed under the walls of his own church. The edifice had so very strange, and yet so familiar, an aspect, that Mr. Dimmesdale's mind vibrated between two ideas; either that he had seen it in a dream hitherto, or that he was merely dreaming about it now.

A character's sense of change in a scene which remains the same, in another narrative, may show a shift in thought and feeling: witness the difference between the initial description and the final description of the same nighttime scene in Keats' "Ode to a Nightingale." In still another narrative, an author may show the reader the effect of a happening by emphasizing changes in a scene—for instance, a decaying house may indicate that the family living in it has deteriorated ("The Fall of the House of Usher").

Scene is often an adjunct not only to plot but also to character portrayal. A reader often comes to know a character by noticing how the author describes the character's dwelling, or by considering how an environment which has been described would be likely to shape the character's personality. Not only the physical climate but also the intellectual and moral climate, as revealed by the author, may clarify motives and possible actions. The words "Ancien Regime" beneath the title in Browning's poem, "The Laboratory," help explain why the heroine chose to get revenge by poisoning a successful rival; and at the start of "The Outcasts of Poker Flat," John Oakhurst, gambler, notices "a change in the moral atmosphere since the preceding night . . . a Sabbath lull in the air" which heralds his ejection, by request, from the mining town. Again, the nature of a character may be revealed to the reader by the author's record of what the character notices in a scene: a businessman may see a waterfall as a source of power, a painter may see it as an arrangement of colors, a poet may see it as a symbol expressive of some high truth.

The Emotional Quality of Setting

Speaking of one way of writing a story, Robert Louis Stevenson said, "You may take a certain atmosphere and get action and persons to express and realize it. I'll give you an example—*The Merry Men*. There I began with the feeling of one of those islands on the west coast of Scotland, and I gradually developed the story to express the sentiment with which that coast affected me." Although this recipe probably is an unusual one for an author to follow, it does suggest one thing which setting may do—in the actual world or the world of books: it may arouse emotions. In many plays the manipulation of lighting has this effect. In many stories and poems, the author selects and records certain details in the landscape which body forth an emotional state. Some poems communicate the thought and feeling of a poet simply by presenting aspects of a scene which are appropriate to his attitude. An "atmosphere" thus created may correspond to the moods of the characters. Or it may heighten the representation of their emotions by a contrast. Consider the passage in *Moby Dick* which tells of the feelings of a crew after their boats have been smashed by the whale:

Judge, then, to what pitches of inflamed, distracted fury the minds of the whale's more desperate hunters were impelled, when amid the chips of chewed boats, and the sinking limbs of torn comrades, they swam out of the white curds of the whale's direful wrath into the serene, exasperating sunlight, that smiled on, as if at a birth or a bridal.

All these facts about the possible usefulness of setting mean that the reader who is interested in the craftsmanship of a work will notice how the author's management of this element contributes to the telling of a story, the representation of the motives and actions of a character, the emotional overtones and the implications of the work.

4. LANGUAGE

Language used in imaginative works bodies forth the actions, the settings, and the characters; it withholds or gives emphasis, emotional colorations, and interpretations. Therefore, the reader does well to notice how the author's manner of using words, phrases, sentences, and rhythms relates to the achievement of the story, the drama, or the poem.

Words, Actions, and Settings

In portraying either actions or settings, the author may use language to convey emphasis and vividness and to suggest emotional interpretations. If, for instance, he tells us merely, "After the three individuals departed, they encountered two other individuals," thereby he relegates this action to an unimportant place. The account is unemphatic for two reasons—(1) because it is brief, and (2) because it is abstract. And if the encounter is actually unimportant in the particular chain of events being presented, the reader notes that the language is appropriately handled.

But suppose the event were an important one—how might the author use words to emphasize it? Note what Ernest Hemingway does in the following passage:

> The three of them started for the door, and I watched them go. They were good-looking young fellows, wore good clothes. . . . As they turned out of the door to the right, I saw a closed car come across the square toward them. The first thing a pane of glass went and the bullet smashed into the row of bottles on the show case wall to the right. I heard the gun going and bop, bop, bop, there were bottles smashing all along the wall.
>
> I jumped behind the bar on the left and could see over the edge. The car was stopped and there were two fellows crouched down by it. One had a Thompson gun and the other had a sawed-off automatic shotgun. . . . One of the boys was spread out on the sidewalk, face down, just outside the big window that was smashed. The other two were behind one of the Tropical beer ice wagons. . . . One of the boys shot from the rear corner of the wagon and it ricocheted off the sidewalk. . . . You could see the buckshot marks all over the sidewalk like silver splatters.—*To Have and Have Not*

Here emphasis is achieved because the action is treated at some length. Moreover, the author uses few abstract words such as "individuals," "departed," and "encountered." Rather, he uses *concrete words* which specify details in the action, for instance, "smashed," "ricocheted." Such image-bearing words convey sensory impressions, achieve vividness, and therefore give the passage more emotional impact than an abstract (and hence neutral) account possibly could have. Quintilian, the famous Roman critic, long ago pointed out that "he who says that a city is captured . . . makes no impression on the feelings." "It is less impressive to tell the whole at once," he added, "than to specify the different particulars."

From *To Have and Have Not* by Ernest Hemingway. Reprinted by permission of Charles Scribner's Sons.

Words Which Evoke Emotions

But it should be noticed that in using concrete words, Hemingway is *selective*. He has said that the writer's problem is to set down "the real thing, the sequence of motion and fact which make the emotion. . . . If you get so you can give that to people then you are a writer." The author—not only Hemingway but any writer—therefore leaves out details irrelevant to such a sequence. The quiet sunlight on the square where the encounter took place, the beggars asleep in the sunlight (actually described by Hemingway in an earlier scene) here would spoil the record of tense and vicious action.

Concrete words—and abstract ones as well—furthermore, are often valuable not only for denotations, or dictionary meanings, but also for their connotations, or *emotional associations*. The importance of accretions of feelings about certain words becomes clear if one considers these possible (though not desirable) substitutions in the Hemingway passage: "disappeared" for "went," and "broke" for "smashed" in sentence 4; "shattering" for "smashing" in sentence 5; "leaped" for "jumped" in sentence 6; "squatted" for "crouched" in sentence 7; and "wrecked" for "smashed" in sentence 9.

Figurative Phrases

When, however, selected concrete words will not convey with sufficient precision the exact emotional quality of a scene, the author may use phrases or sentences making *poetic comparisons*. Figures of speech—metaphors, similes, hyperboles, and others—are valuable chiefly because they indicate the nature of an emotion. Here is a sailor's memory of his first impression of the East, in Joseph Conrad's *Youth:*

And this is how I see the East. I have seen its secret places and have looked into its very soul; but now I see it always from a small boat, a high outline of mountains, blue and afar in the morning; like a faint mist at noon; a jagged wall of purple at sunset. I have the feel of the oar in my hand, the vision of a scorching blue sea in my eyes. And I see a bay, a wide bay, smooth as glass and polished like ice, shimmering in the dark. A red light burns far off upon the gloom of the land, and the night is soft and warm. We drag at the oars with aching arms, and suddenly a puff of wind, a puff faint and tepid and laden with strange odors of blossoms, of aromatic wood, comes out of the still night—the first sigh of the East on my face. That I can never forget. It was impalpable and enslaving, like a charm, like a whispered promise of mysterious delight.

There are many concrete words here—Conrad once defined his task thus: "by the power of the written word, to make you hear, to make you feel . . . before all, to make you *see*." But the end of such vividness, he went on to say,

Is to hold up a fragment of experience, "to show its vibration, its color, its form and through its movement, its form, its color, reveal the substance of its truth—disclose the inspiring secret: the stress and passion within the core of each convincing moment." The concrete words here contribute much to the revelation of the "stress and passion"—the impression of the East as "impalpable and enslaving"; but the figurative phrases contribute even more. The narrator who has achingly rowed across a seemingly shoreless "scorching blue sea" conveys his delight by telling how mountains changed from a figurative "faint mist at noon" to a palpable and cool-colored shape at sunset— figuratively, "a jagged wall of purple." He conveys his emotion when he tells how he looked at last upon a dark wide bay—figuratively, "smooth as glass and polished like ice." The "soft and warm" night figuratively suggests rest for his tired body. And the figurative characterization of the breeze gives more than a vivid account of a puff of wind: it conveys emotion by subtly likening this welcome haven to an entrancing yet enigmatic woman. Thus figures of speech help define an emotion precisely.

Sentences and Rhythms

A comparison between the passage by Hemingway and that by Conrad will suggest that, in addition to words and phrases, *sentences* and *rhythms* are important elements for representing actions, settings, and emotions. The simple sentences and compound sentences, with a minimum number of modifiers, which make up the first passage are appropriate for describing rapid action. More complex sentences, with numerous appositions and figurative phrases which savor details, are appropriate for Conrad's lyrical account. In Hemingway's paragraphs, a large proportion of one-syllable words which frequently cluster accented syllables ("wóre goód clóthes," "clósed cár cóme," "gláss wént," "shów cáse wáll," "bóp, bóp, bóp," "fáce dówn," "béer icé wágons," etc.) achieve a staccato rhythm corresponding to the action. As writing comes nearer to poetry in expressing emotion, it tends to approach regular rhythms like those in poetry; therefore, Conrad's emotional passage is, for prose, remarkably close at times to iambic and anapestic verse. (See the consideration of rhythms in the introduction to poetry, p. 969.) At an opposite extreme from the Hemingway passage is a poem, with regular use of rhythms. Between these two extremes, there are all sorts of variations available to the author.

Not only *accent patterns* but also *sound patterns* figure in one kind of rhythmical arrangement—one in which the handling of consonants and vowels suggests the kind of action or the scene. A simple example is the "bop, bop, bop" of the Hemingway passage—wherein the sounds imitate those of gun explosions. As a matter of fact, the consonants *b* and *p* here used—like hard *c*, *d*, *g*, *k*, and *t*—are called "explosives," because one pronounces them by closing one's mouth and exploding them with one's breath. Note how the use of such consonants helps Tennyson imitate the progress of a knight in his clanking armor:

> Dry clashed his harness on the icy caves
> And barren chasms, and all left and right
> The bare black cliff clanged round him. . . .

But contrast with this Herrick's

> Whenas in silks my Julia goes,
> Then, then, methinks, how sweetly flows
> The liquefaction of her clothes.

Here a predominance of "continuous consonants," so called because they may be prolonged indefinitely (drawn from "sibilants"—soft *c, f, s, v, z*—and "liquids"—*l, m, n, r, ng*), imitates the smooth movement of the lady in silks. And vowels as well as consonants may, at times, be so managed that, as Pope puts it, the sound will "seem an echo of the sense." Compare the vowels (as well as the consonants) in these passages:

> The huge round stone resulting with a bound,
> Thunders impetuous down and smokes along the ground.
> —POPE, *Odyssey*, XI

> . . . the spires
> Pricked with incredible pinnacles into heaven.
> —TENNYSON, *Holy Grail*

Such suggestions by sound of sense are called *onomatopoeia*. Finally, there will be times, of course, when sound patterns are not used to imitate actions or scenes but to achieve sheer harmony which helps convey an emotion. At such times the author will use sounds of various sorts which blend melodiously.

Language and Characterization

In descriptions of the physical appearances or gestures of characters, an author uses language in ways comparable to those employed in describing actions or scenes. Language is also important for characterization, when the work quotes the character—in first person narratives or in passages of dialog. Here, of course, the choice of words, the figures of speech, the sentences and rhythms may be useful because they are in keeping.

The connotations or associations of words used in dialog are as important as they are in descriptive passages, though in a rather different way. Here what might be called *"social"* connotations loom large. As H. J. C. Grierson remarks, words have *"color"*:

I mean by "color" the associations which gather around a word by long usage. The meaning provides the first nucleus for this, and then come all the accidental circumstances connected with our experience of the word—the people who use it, the places in which we have heard it, the other words and ideas it tends to evolve. And so we find that, against our will, some words are vulgarized, savor (for we might speak of "taste" as well as "color") of the streets and the music-hall; others are homely, though anything but vulgar, are redolent . . . of home, of familiar objects and experiences, of the farm-yard, the fishing-boat and the workshop; others are pedantic, schoolmaster's words that no healthy boy would ever use on the playground . . . and other words are dignified . . . and again others are lovely exotics that only the poets have ventured to use.

"Color" in words shows itself when a sailor says, "We shipped a sea that carried away our pinnace and our binnacle," and a landsman says "A heavy wave broke over our ship." It shows itself when a pompous man mouths what Thoreau called "bad words—words like 'tribal' and 'ornamentation,' which drag their tails behind them." The kinds of words a character uses may show whether he is educated or unread, whether he has a sense of humor or is humorless, whether he is sensitive or crass, refined or vulgar, intelligent or stupid.

Figurative phrases or sentences used in dialog may also suggest much about the character. They may, by their allusions, suggest the character's background: witness how Huck Finn, born and reared in a river town, describes a room mussed up by his "pap"—"And when they come to look at that spare room they had to take soundings before they could navigate it." Trite figures may indicate unimaginativeness; literary figures, bookishness; original figures, imaginativeness; and so on.

Sentences, too, are important. In passages representing conversations or thoughts, authors often imitate the qualities of talk or of the thought processes. Perhaps they do this by suggesting the fumbling for words, the ambiguity, the repetition, the irrelevancies heard in speech. Or they may construct sentences which have a fragmentary quality, awkwardness of arrangement, a frequent use of *and* and *but*. Sometimes the constructions are not only lifelike but also characteristic of certain kinds of people—for instance, bad grammar for the uneducated man, choppy sentences for the decisive man, fragmentary sentences—never finished—for the indecisive character.

These, according to the nature of the work, will be more or less stenographic. They will never be completely literal transcriptions, however, because the author has to select and condense talk or thought, like everything else in his literary work. Furthermore, the adaptation of such material must be in tune with the style of the whole work. Thus, if the work is a poem, although the speech may have definite lifelike qualities, it will naturally be far more condensed and far more rhythmical than speech is. Or if the work is a drama, the author may allow some characters to speak lifelike prose, and forfeit the right to be realistically lifelike as he allows other characters to speak in the heightened style of blank verse.

5. TONE

In a literary work, as a rule, the elements (actions, characters, settings, and language) are so adapted and integrated as to form a harmonious whole. To the reader this whole is of the utmost importance. The reader of a story, a drama, or a poem is not satisfied with an analysis of its separate elements. He is not likely to want to stop before perceiving the accomplishment of the whole work. Actually, it may be argued that he has not "taken in" the work at all until he has shared with the author the emotions and the meaning embodied in his work. He does well, therefore, to consider the work in two different but useful and supplementary ways: (a) as an emotional expression of the author and (b) as an artistic embodiment of a meaning or set of meanings. In this section, we shall see how you consider it as the first of these; in the next section, as the second.

The Nature of Tone

Like all other human creatures, the author is an individual with his own personality, his own peculiar tastes, his own store of knowledge, his own individual bents, prejudices, and emotions. When he creates an imaginative work about the world as he sees it, almost inevitably—consciously or unconsciously —he will give voice to certain phases of his personality. And an alert reader will, so to speak, hear that conscious or unconscious voicing. It will be somewhat as if by listening while the author read aloud, by noting his "tone" —the timbre of his voice, the intonations, the emphases—he came to discover the *personal qualities and emotions of the author embodied in the work.*

Limitations

Of course, all the aspects of an author's personality will not be perceivable in any one work, nor may all his feelings. An author is as complex as other human beings, and his moods vary. Furthermore, an author tends to write in the modes and forms fashionable during his day. Depending upon his period, for instance, he may be, say, a classicist, a romanticist, or a naturalist. The literary market of the period may be better for dramas than for sonnets, or for short stories than for plays. An author may not find that he can express as much as he would like in works that will sell, and after all an author must live —if possible.

Again, the moral tastes of his potential audience may force a writer to use materials which he finds distressing or to leave out materials of which he is fond. A prissy puritan writing a play in the bawdy Restoration period or a novel in the militantly frank 1920's probably had to forget some of his scruples. In other words, the author may be limited in various ways because of the tastes of the readers he hopes to attract. Somehow, he must win sympathetic attention, and if he does not appeal to readers in his most natural guise, he may assume a guise more likely to please.

If an author is completely enslaved by his period and by the taste of his immediate audience, later readers quite possibly will be unable to read his works sympathetically. A Victorian sentimentalist such as the author of *Uncle Tom's Cabin* may seem funny or even disgusting to readers a few decades away. Readers may, for various reasons, find the assumed or real personality revealed in a work completely unsympathetic. In such cases, it will, of course, be important for the reader to understand exactly how the tone interposes itself between a work and its enjoyment.

But suppose such limitations have been overcome—as they will have been by the best authors—that the author has surmounted limitations set by his period and by his audience, and that he has managed to win a sympathetic hearing. In the works of such an author, readers may find three kinds of indications of tone: (1) the author's choice of form, (2) his choice of materials, and (3) his personal interpretations.

The Author's Choice of Form

The overall pattern which an author chooses for his work may well be determined by his attitude or his mood—tragedy or comedy, melodrama or farce, parody or sober lyric. A pessimist, as a rule, will not be satisfied with a happy ending in a serious work. If he writes a narrative with a happy ending, he will find a way to make fun of it—perhaps by burlesquing it. An optimist or a writer who likes to create escapist literature will not be satisfied with an unhappy ending, seriously presented. Some authors always—and other authors in some moods—will find simple lyrics the only satisfactory forms to express their emotions. Others may be compelled by an inner urgency to write complex philosophical poems, and still others may need the wide scope provided by epic poetry. The tones of such expressions naturally will differ.

The Author's Choice of Materials

Like everyone else, the author likes certain kinds of characters, certain kinds of settings, certain kinds of actions; and he loathes others or finds them dull. Some human qualities will attract him or seem important to him, while others will be repugnant or will seem unimportant. The author's choice of characters to be treated at length will offer insights. A Mark Twain will love the urchin Huckleberry Finn but will find Jane Austen's heroines unattractive and boresome. A Henry James will prefer writing about characters with subtle minds and with sensitivities similar to his own. Understandably (unless he is writing satire), each author will choose for detailed portrayal a character of the sort that particularly fascinates him.

Each fiction writer, also, will prefer certain settings—Twain the Mississippi River of his boyhood, James either British or continental drawing rooms. A poet writing of nature will depict those scenes or aspects of scenes which he finds most interesting and moving. The dramatist, too, is likely to have preferences in backgrounds: witness the dramas on ships at sea written by the youthful Eugene O'Neill.

The actions portrayed by an author will also be selected according to his taste. A Mark Twain, a Paul Green, or a Robert Frost will choose to present incidents which catch the qualities of life peculiar to a geographical region. A Henry James or a T. S. Eliot or a Eugene O'Neill will prefer to show speculative characters puzzling about motives and actions. A lyrical poet will concentrate upon intense thoughts and feelings—those based upon the poet's own experiences or the imagined experiences of others.

The Author's Interpretations

The tone of a work, finally, is manifest in the author's personal interpretations of the characters, the actions, the settings, and the feelings of which he writes. These interpretations may be explicit or implicit. They will be explicit when the author speaks directly to the reader; they will be implicit when he colors his record in ways which indirectly convey his attitudes. In a sense, the author has the problem of winning over the reader to his own view of what he is portraying. He may, so to speak, step into the pages of his book and, in his own or an assumed role, offer comments on characters and events. Or he may write as an author-producer, allowing his lighting and setting of the scenes, his costuming of the characters, and his devising and direction of dialog and action to convey his attitudes.

Explicit Interpretations

Throughout his great novel *Vanity Fair*, William Makepeace Thackeray talks directly to the reader about his characters. They are, he indicates, "puppets" whom he may manipulate to illustrate his ideas. Whenever the spirit moves him, he stops his story to chat intimately about human nature and his attitudes toward it. Sometimes he is ironic, sometimes sentimental. There is always the possibility that an author may thus assume the guise of a commentator talking directly to the reader.

The least reticent of all explicit interpreters are those who speak out in lyrical poetry. Like such figures in fiction, the speakers in lyrical poems may differ materially from the real authors of the works. Quite often, the "I" in the poem is an idealization of the author or of the author's mood. In a love poem, he may be the kind of lover the author admires—and his only qualities (as shown by the poem) may be those of an impassioned lover. Again, if the poem is sad, the "I" in it may be the ideal sufferer. And often the speaker in the poem will have none of the reticence, the shyness, the inarticulateness which the actual poet in real life may have: the character's every phrase and the very rhythms of his speech may eloquently voice his feeling.

Implicit Interpretations

In one of his short stories, Sherwood Anderson spoke of the advantage old-time storytellers had over moderns whose stories are printed. "They," he says, "were both storytellers and actors. As they talked they modulated their voices, made gestures with their hands. . . . All our modern fussing with style

Is an attempt to do the same thing." His point is that, deprived of the chance to speak aloud, an author "fusses" with his choice of details, words, and phrases so that, in print, he may convey his feelings about elements in his narrative. Such care must have gone into the choices made in this description of Huck's pappy:

> He was most fifty, and he looked it. His hair was long and tangled and greasy, and hung down, and you could see his eyes shining through like he was behind vines. It was all black, no gray; so was his long, mixed-up whiskers. There warn't no color in his face, where his face showed; it was white; not like another man's white, but a white to make a body sick, a white to make a body's flesh crawl—a tree-toad white, a fish-belly white.

Every word conveys to the reader Mark Twain's distaste for this character; but instead of explicitly stating the attitude, the author lets the details convey it. The emphasis upon the dirt, the unhealthy lack of color, and particularly the comparison of the white face to cold, dead, "fish-belly white" reveal that this is an unattractive character. The way a character is presented can indicate clearly how his creator feels about that character. Details in presentation can indicate the condescension of a Bret Harte toward the folk in his stories, the sentimentalism of a Dickens, the compassion of a Dreiser. Even the dialog of the characters will often imply the author's attitude toward characters. For, actually, when the author sets down his impression of their dialog, he heightens the traits which he likes or dislikes in ways which are unmistakable.

Actions as well as characters will be interpreted in ways revelatory of the author's attitude toward them. If, for instance, he says that a character "smirked," he will imply a different attitude from the one implied by his saying that the character "giggled" or "laughed wryly." Contrast "walked" with "minced," "marched," "stalked," and "trod": each, used in relationship to other revelatory words, will help show approval or disapproval.

The tone of an author in parts of a work or throughout a whole work, then, may be, for instance, broadly comic, witty, ironic, satirical, disinterested, disillusioned, sentimental, idealistic, or tragic. Whatever it is, it will provide his commentary upon the people, the emotions, and the actions presented in the work. All this means that a literary work involves not merely a number of elements but an author's emotional interpretation of them. It means that the author tacitly asks the reader to join him in feeling as he does about this world and the things that happen in it.

The Importance of Tone to the Reader

Readers are therefore faced with the necessity of cooperating with the author. They must become aware of what he feels, and, in order to share his imaginative experience with him, they must feel as he does. They must join the storyteller, the dramatist, or the poet in liking and disliking. If he is sympathetic, they must be so, or if he is ironic, they must follow his lead.

6. MEANINGS

In "Wakefield," Nathaniel Hawthorne tells the story of a crafty Londoner who "under pretense of going a journey, took lodgings in the next street to his own house, and there, unheard of by his wife or friends, and without the shadow of a reason for such self-banishment, dwelt upwards of twenty years." Then, caught in a shower near his home one afternoon, he ascended his own steps once more and passed into his house—as if his long absence had been nothing but a little joke at his wife's expense. The story of Wakefield ends thus:

This happy event—supposing it to be such—could only have occurred at an unpremeditated moment. We will not follow our friend across the threshold. He has left us much food for thought, a portion of which shall lend its wisdom to a moral, and be shaped into a figure. Amid the seeming confusion of our mysterious world, individuals are so nicely adjusted to a system, and systems to one another and to a whole, that, by stepping aside for a moment, a man exposes himself to a fearful risk of losing his place forever. Like Wakefield, he may become, as it were, the Outcast of the Universe.

Anyone reading the story in its entirety would have little trouble in discovering how its form and tone have prepared for this conclusion. But the conclusion itself rather obviously involves something besides just form and tone—something very important to every perceptive reader.

This ending has converted the whole story into a springboard for something more general than the particular actions, characters, and settings which up to this point the author has portrayed. Hawthorne's concern—and consequently the reader's concern—has broadened beyond a *single* event which took place in London long ago. The concern now is with *all* events in which an individual steps outside his own little system of human affections. Hawthorne has caused a shift of attention from Wakefield to man, from the specific to the general, and in so doing has made it clear that he is concerned not only with Wakefield but with himself and his readers—anyone who might be tempted to break off ties as Wakefield did.

The reader, therefore, is no longer simply a spectator watching a little drama play itself out; to a certain extent, at least, he is in the drama himself. To put it another way: a story, a play, a poem, if it is to give the illusion of reality, must be about a particular experience taking place at one time and in one place and involving certain particular people. But though this experience may be in many ways unique, it can at the same time be representative of experiences which most people have or will have. And to the degree that the affairs portrayed in a literary work are representative of the reader's affairs, the work can be said to have meaning for him. A more formal definition might run something like this: the meaning of a literary work is that insight into human affairs which it offers and which the reader finds useful in understanding experience.

At this point someone is bound to ask whether a work can have meanings which the author did not intend it to have. The answer is yes. For hundreds of years people have been finding various meanings in *Hamlet* that Shakespeare undoubtedly never knew were there. Every reader applies poetical, fictional, and dramatic representations to himself in the light of his own background, interests, and information. Indeed, the same reader coming to a work at two different times and in different moods may apply its representations to himself in two quite different fashions. Actually, what meaning the author has in mind is unimportant unless the literary work makes it clear to the reader. The reader's task, therefore, is to find whatever clues to meaning there are in the work and to follow them through to their implications. Note that the implications are to be found *in the works*—that the reader should discover meanings in what the author has written as well as in his own interpretations.

How does one discover meanings? There is no one answer to such a question, for the process of discovery changes with every work. There are certain guideposts to meaning, however. They are (1) statements of meaning provided by the author and expressed either directly by him or indirectly through one of his characters; (2) relations and conflicts of the characters which are representative of broader relations and conflicts.

Statements of Meaning

Statements of meaning may be of four kinds: explicit, ironic, symbolic, and mythical. Of these the first is by far the easiest to detect. In an *explicit statement* of meaning the author simply tells, or has an attractive character expressing his point of view tell, what the meaning is which he has in mind. The example given from "Wakefield" shows how it can be done in a short story.

Ironic statements are not so frequent, but their possibility should be kept in mind. In such a statement the author will say playfully, or allow an unattractive character to say seriously, exactly the opposite to what the author means. This is the same sort of thing which a person does when he growls on a cold, rainy afternoon. "This is a fine day!" He indicates by his tone rather than by his words what he means. Likewise the author indicates by his tone that his statement is to be taken ironically.

No one could possibly miss the ironic intent of Mark Twain in the *Connecticut Yankee* when he writes:

If you take a nation of sixty millions, where average wages are two dollars per day, three days' wages taken from each individual will provide three hundred and sixty million dollars and pay the government's expenses. In my day, in my own country, this money was collected from imports, and the citizen imagined that the foreign importer paid it, and it made him comfortable to think so, whereas, in fact, it was paid by the American people, and was so equally distributed and exactly distributed among them that the annual cost to the one-hundred-millionaire and the annual cost to the sucking child of the day laborer was precisely the same—each paid six dollars. Nothing could be equaler than that, I reckon.

Symbolic statements are those in which the meaning is communicated in figurative language. Such a statement may be a single simile or metaphor; sometimes it is an analogy which carries through a paragraph or a series of paragraphs; and sometimes, as in works like *Pilgrim's Progress* and *Gulliver's Travels*, the symbolism carries through an entire work. In Melville's *Moby Dick* the main character, Ahab, with his wooden leg and lightning scar, goes clumping through the novel not only as a sea captain but as an animated metaphor representing what is defiant in mankind. The following paragraphs are from the same book. To understand their meaning one must recognize that the land represents what man knows, the sea what he still does not know. Melville addresses the reader directly in this symbolic statement:

Consider the subtleness of the sea; how its most dreaded creatures glide under water, unapparent for the most part, and treacherously hidden beneath the loveliest tints of azure. Consider also the devilish brilliance and beauty of many of its most remorseless tribes, as the dainty embellished shape of many species of sharks. Consider, once more, the universal cannibalism of the sea; all whose creatures prey upon each other, carrying on eternal war since the world began.

Consider all this; and then turn to this green, gentle, and most docile earth; consider them both, the sea and the land; and do you not find a strange analogy to something in yourself? For as this appalling ocean surrounds the verdant land, so in the soul of man lies one insular Tahiti, full of peace and joy, but encompassed by all the horrors of the half known life. God help thee! Push not off from that isle, thou canst never return!

Sometimes meaning is conveyed through a *mythical statement*. *Myth*, a term frequently used in contemporary criticism, was used by Aristotle to denote plot or narrative structure. Today, it is still at times used with this meaning. It is also used to denote an imagined story as opposed to a factual one, in contrast with history, say, or science. However, it is used most frequently today to mean a traditional story, or set of references, or attitude, or—by extension— a modern version of such a story. It is often associated with folklore, psychology, or religion, for it may explain phenomena of nature, the origins of man, religious rites, the beliefs or customs of a people. Heroes, demigods, or gods often figure in myths. Thus the comic story of how Paul Bunyan logged North Dakota, the tragic story of Oedipus (p. 701), and the reverent stories recounted in *Paradise Lost* and *Paradise Regained* are all, in this broad sense, myths. Emerson pointed out how meanings in time become associated with mythology: "the legend is tossed from believer to poet, from poet to believer, everybody adding a grace or dropping a fault or rounding the form, until it gets an ideal truth."

Thus mythology is often important for the evocation of both feeling and meaning, providing metaphors or symbols on a large scale which have deeply significant implications. Coleridge, in an expanded translation of a passage by Schiller, suggests that even after belief in myths dies, they still have evocative power and meaning:

They live no longer in the faith of reason!
But still the heart doth need a language, still
Doth the old instinct bring back the old names. . . .

Therefore, as William York Tindale remarks, "Serving the individual as it once served the group, myth may unite him with tradition or society, and, in literature, while uniting the conscious mind with the unconscious, myth may express the inner by the outer, the present by the past."

Relations and Conflicts

Not all meanings are easy to discover, since many authors, especially the modern ones, are reluctant to be explicit. They feel that a statement of meaning often results in artless banality. Now it is quite true that the meaning of a poem or a short story or a passage in a play or novel may be readily apparent; yet in many instances rereading will be required, and in the case of works like T. S. Eliot's poems and Joyce's novels many rereadings will be necessary. What are the signposts to meaning in works where there are no statements of it? The answer is the relations and conflicts of the characters—inner conflicts or outer ones involving such relations as those between a person and his environment, a person and other persons, a person and his God.

We say relations and conflicts rather than actions, settings, or characters because a concentration on the latter tends to emphasize the unique characteristics of what is being portrayed rather than its representative characteristics. For example, the exact actions related by Conrad in his *Nigger of the "Narcissus"* will never occur again; the setting in this particular crew's quarters will never be duplicated, and, naturally, these exact characters will never navigate the seas. Yet the *relations* among these men are of the things that, in the words of Henry James, "we cannot possibly *not* know, sooner or later, in one way or another." Motivated by a common fear of the big, burly Negro, a quarrelsome crew is gradually bound together in a tightly cohesive unit. Is this development of a relation among people unique? Are quarreling nations ever bound together by fear of a common foe? Have a brother and sister ever begun pulling together when faced by an obstreperous outsider? Generalizations such as those suggested are almost inevitable for the reader of this novel.

A simple formula, then, for seeing how relations and conflicts imply meanings, might be the following:

Step One: The reader should see whether the important relations or conflicts are representative of ones which he encounters or might encounter in actual life. A Superman scrap, for example, in which that dauntless character wins because of his steel muscles and X-ray vision would be ruled out; ruled in would be the conflict in Huckleberry Finn's mind over whether he should surrender Jim, the runaway slave, to the authorities.

Step Two: The reader should convert the particular persons, places, and happenings in the relation or conflict into their respective classes or categories (e.g., substitute mankind for Huck Finn, death in general for the death of one man, nature for a woods at twilight).[1]

Although at first such a process may sound rather mechanical, it is precisely the procedure one employs unconsciously in reading a work in which the meaning is readily discernible. Here, all that is being suggested is that in the tougher cases the reader make the unconscious process conscious.

Levels of Meaning

The preceding paragraphs have been concerned with what meaning is and how a reader finds it. He should not suppose, however, that all works are equally rich in meaning. Indeed, it might be argued that many notable works of literature possess no meaning at all as defined here. Works designed simply to excite, to re-create a mood or a feeling, works centered about an emotion rather than people and ideas, these are the ones with little meaning. Yet this is not to say that such works give no pleasure. Meaning of a certain kind, in short, is not necessary for a literary experience.

In those cases, however, where the author is more interested in studying how people think and feel and act than he is in simply evoking a mood, readers can be sure of at least one level of meaning. This is the overall level of meaning or what is called theme. When one asks about a work, "What's the point of all this?" one is asking in effect for its theme. Often a work will have no other meaning than its theme. This certainly is true of Aesop's fables and of Jesus' parables. It is true also of many short stories and poems.

Longer works, since they touch on more relations of men and portray more conflicts, are almost bound to have more than one level of meaning. These secondary levels can be of two kinds: (1) they can be meanings which apply to the work as a whole and thus constitute subthemes, or (2) they can be meanings which emerge from sections of the work, indeed from stanzas or paragraphs, and have sometimes only a distant relation to the theme. A complex example of a work with theme and subthemes is Whitman's "Passage to India." On the surface, he is dealing with the West and the East, suddenly brought closer because of the Suez Canal, the transatlantic cables, and the transcontinental railroads. But in doing this, he is also dealing symbolically with science and wisdom, with the rational and the mystical, with the body and the soul, with man's soul and God. It would be hard to say which is the major theme and which are the minor ones in such a poem. Almost any novel affords an example of a work with an overall meaning or meanings and incidental meanings which apply only to small passages. The great ones afford what amounts to a continuous succession of penetrating and provocative insights into experience.

There is still another level of meaning, one that is often neither stated nor susceptible of the method of generalizing proposed on page 1147. This level

---

1. This little formula, of course, will not work in those poems and occasional prose pieces where the author is using a private set of symbols. In such cases one will have to consult one's own good sense, other works by the same author, or commentaries by or on the author.

deals with the kinds of assumptions which the author makes. In short, what is his philosophic position? Here are typical questions a reader should ask himself: What does the author believe about the *nature of man:* is he made in the image of God? has he free will? is he a creature of blind chance? is he dominated by reason or impulse? What does the author believe about the *nature of society:* does he think the strong man should rule? the rich? the capable? the majority? the working class? What does he believe about the *nature of the universe:* is there a Divine purpose behind it? is it working according to laws? is it accidental or capricious? What is the *nature of truth:* is it something beyond the senses which one can never prove but perceive through intuition, reason, or the Bible? or is it something that men agree upon only after the scientific process of observation, hypothesis, verification, and conclusion? The ability to discern an author's fundamental assumptions will not come overnight, nor is it likely to come through the reading of a single work. But ultimately, if the reader is to be able to say that he understands thoroughly the meaning of a poem or novel or play, he must be able to push beneath its themes and subsidiary meanings to this level of basic assumptions.

For illustration, in "Wakefield" the theme was stated at the end in this fashion:

Amid the seeming confusion of our mysterious world, individuals are so nicely adjusted to a system, and systems to one another and to a whole, that by stepping aside for a moment, a man exposes himself to a fearful risk of losing his place forever.

What does this imply about the nature of man? That he becomes a free agent at his peril and, therefore, that he is substantially without freedom of the will. What is assumed about the nature of society? Nothing about the proper or desirable form of society, but the implication is that whatever the form, there is little chance of changing it. What is implied about the nature of the universe? Hawthorne apparently is suggesting here that cosmic events are but a long sequence of cause and effect. This philosophy of predestination, determinism, fatalism—however it may be named—is more strongly suggested in another passage from the same story:

Would that I had a folio to write, instead of an article of a dozen pages! Then might I exemplify how an influence beyond our control lays its strong hand on every deed which we do, and weaves its consequences into an iron tissue of necessity.

What is the nature of truth? Obviously Hawthorne is assuming that there is some superhuman and, undoubtedly, supernatural power which controls the destiny. Presumably, therefore, ultimate truth must lie beyond the range of our five senses. Whether such truth may be discerned by intuition, by reason, or through Scriptures, he does not say. There is a strong suspicion from the tone of the story that he does not believe it can be discerned at all.

It would be a mistake to build up these particular questions into a monotonous pattern, a little ritual which the reader goes through every time he reads a literary work that seems to have some meaning. These are representative, however, of the more searching type of question the reader should ask of any thoughtful work of art. He should use them, modify them, adapt them, discard them as he sees fit. He should use his common sense—but shouldn't be content until he has exhausted all the possible levels of meaning.

EVALUATING IMAGINATIVE LITERATURE

The last section explored the main aspects of the literary work. This section looks at the work qualitatively: what makes readers think one story better than another, one play better than another, one poem better than another?

There is, of course, no *one* way of measuring the quality of a literary work since readers use different standards, and a standard is the complex result of a reader's likes and dislikes, his desires and needs, his preconceptions, knowledge, wisdom, and experience—everything, in short, that makes up his psycho-physiological being at the moment he reads and evaluates. Yet literary evaluation is not so completely individualistic and chaotic as this might imply. Experiences overlap, and so do tastes. Many people, therefore, agree in their literary judgments, but not all people. It would be a dull world if they did.

For the relatively inexperienced reader the hardest problem in evaluation is to find a way of making judgments that are thoughtful enough to be capable of logical defense. It's easy enough to say, "I like this book" or "I don't like it," and let the evaluation drop there. It is much more difficult—and yet really necessary if one wants to be just—to reach a decision by more objective and reliable means. For this more careful kind of evaluation a knowledge of standards is indispensable. This section, therefore, concerns itself almost exclusively with the standards most commonly employed by experienced readers. To emphasize the fact that evaluation is basically a process of measurement, standards will constantly be referred to as "yardsticks."

NINE YARDSTICKS OF VALUE
1. CLARITY

The yardstick of clarity is a simple standard of measurement according to which everything that resists reasonably careful reading is considered poor writing. Behind such a standard is the assumption that all writing is meant to be communication.

The justification for such a yardstick is obvious. A writer, if he expects readers to spend time and money on his works, has an obligation to make clear what is on his mind. The writer's retort (to the charge of obscurity) that he was interested only in self-expression will not hold water, for if that were true, he should not have pushed the work into print. By the act of publication he indicates that he wants readers and, hence, that communication as well as self-expression is involved. Yet there is something to be said against too rigorous an application of this standard. Possibly the writer is using terms which as yet the reader has not encountered and consequently does not understand. Possibly his technique is a new one to the reader, or, as in the case of many modern poets, possibly he has compressed his material so tightly that extraordinary care in reading is required. In any event, in fairness to the author the reader should take into account his own relevant limitations and should be sure that he has read the work with sufficient care before branding a literary work inadequate because of lack of clarity.

2. ESCAPE

If a reader measures by the yardstick of escape, the literary work which causes him to forget himself and the circumstances of his own life is by that fact good. Ordinarily, writing that is most successful in effecting escape involves adventure, love, murder, or humor.

"A shot rang out in the Silver Star saloon!" There's the beginning of adventure. Whether it is cloak-and-dagger stuff, sports stories, or sagas of the air and sea, to be good escape reading it should have movement, suspense, thrills, and an emphasis on physical action. In addition, most readers want a happy ending, uncomplicated characters that are clearly either good or bad, and exotic scenery.

Romances need not necessarily be set at so fast a tempo as adventure fiction. Indeed the good ones, most readers feel, are at their best when they are quiet: a hushed night with a silver moon riding overhead, a man and a girl, the soft splashing of a fountain, a whispered "I love you." The old formula is always adequate: boy meets girl, boy loses girl, boy gets girl.

In detective fiction, one expects the excitement, suspense, and physical action of the adventure story, plus, possibly, a boy-girl routine that is interesting but not so absorbing that it interferes with the solution of the crime. In romance and adventure the reader knows the villain from the outset; in the detective stories he is not so sure. The fun comes in finding out. And the more he is fooled—provided the author has played fair—the better he likes it. In a sense, therefore, the detective story combines the appeals of the adventure and the romance and adds to them a type of mystery which tantalizes the intellect. That detective stories are considered good reading is evidenced by the fact that Sherlock Holmes and Perry Mason are probably two of the best-known characters of modern fiction.

Humor allows the reader to escape into the world of the incongruous where things happen in unexpected and ridiculous ways and where even the language itself is chock-full of surprises. Even when the characters in a humorous situation seem to suffer excruciatingly, the reader feels no pain, for the incongruity of the context makes him feel detached and superior. This, he says to himself, is not life, and so he does not identify himself with it, at least not sufficiently to feel compassion for the characters who are suffering.

Poems which help readers best to escape from the complexities of modern life have, curiously enough, almost none of the qualities discussed above. The most popular escapist poetry is quiet, soothing, melodic. It is nonintellectual, questions nothing about life, death, or immortality. It is like a waltz played softly and dreamily.

It has been the custom for many teachers and literary sophisticates to pooh-pooh escapist reading and to decry the standard by which it can be measured and considered good. Their point is that other and more serious works of art bring richer pleasure and a better understanding of experience. The point is well taken. While satisfying to the ego, the *continual* practice of identifying oneself with a hero or heroine who always comes off triumphantly is quite likely to make one less capable of handling real-life situations, where choices between right and wrong are not so clear-cut and where happy endings are often the exception rather than the rule. Yet there is some defense for considering escapist reading good reading. At one time or another everyone needs relaxation. On such occasions, Sherlock Holmes or Longfellow may be just what the doctor ordered.

3. REFLECTION OF REAL LIFE

Since the rise in the latter part of the nineteenth century of what has been called realism, a special emphasis has been placed on the ability of the writer to report life as it is. "Life as it is," however, is an ambiguous term that can mean, among other things, truth to the facts of human life or truth to the general nature of human beings. Because these two interpretations involve slightly different criteria, they will be considered separately.

Truth to the Facts of Human Life

Consciously or unconsciously everyone probably tests a work occasionally by the accuracy of its facts. According to this standard, the work which reports actuality in a flawless manner is good; the one which distorts the facts is bad. Essentially what is demanded here is that the man of literature be also a historian or a scientist.

Some readers prefer to get their history through imaginative literature. They know the Plantagenets through Shakespeare, the Scottish lairds through Scott, the American Indian through Cooper, and the Civil War through Margaret Mitchell. Since such persons are reading for knowledge, they demand strict adherence to the known facts, and they resent any deviations from them. Other readers, while not necessarily going to literature for history, are disturbed by inaccuracies. Even Keats pulls them up abruptly when in "On First Looking into Chapman's Homer" he has Cortez rather than Balboa discovering the Pacific.

Often readers treat literature, too, as though it were the work of trained social scientists. They demand that *Main Street* display the same exhaustive analysis of American town life that they find in a work like the Lynds' *Middletown,* which is a detailed and thorough analysis of life in Muncie, Indiana, done by two of the country's ablest social scientists. Often a work is called inaccurate because the reader does not agree with the selection of facts or with the interpretation that the author has given them. Thus Steinbeck's *Grapes of Wrath* was savagely denounced in both Oklahoma and California for what the editorial writers called inaccuracy and distortion. And Sinclair Lewis was roundly criticized by businessmen for *Babbitt*, by physicians for *Arrowsmith*, and by the clergy for *Elmer Gantry*.

In recent years readers have been demanding more attention to the facts of psychology. As the theories of men like Freud, Adler, Jung, and Watson have become better known, the terms of the psychiatrists and psychoanalysts have gradually crept into modern vocabularies. To most intelligent readers nowadays, "schizophrenia" is no longer baffling; neither is "paranoiac," "manic depressive," or "psychotic." Even high-school students speak learnedly of a "sense of insecurity." The result of this increasing awareness of the terms and problems of maladjustment is that many readers have come to treat literary works as case histories. They want to analyze the main characters in order to diagnose their mental diseases and to suggest what the proper cure might be. The unfairness of employing this standard of factual accuracy too rigorously is obvious. Since the dramatist, poet, or fiction writer has not tried to write history as such or a scientific treatise as such, it is unjust to demand of him the factual precision of history or science. Yet one can expect that the competent writer face his material seriously and squarely. Surely this would imply a regard for the important facts and hence some obligation to see them clearly and communicate them accurately.

Truth to Human Nature

More than simple factual accuracy, the standard of truth to human nature requires that the work create a believable place and characters. If factual accuracy will help, well and good; on the other hand, if representative details imaginatively conceived establish the effect, that, too, is well and good.

Probably the best way to see what this method of evaluation requires is to see what it excludes. It excludes, clearly, what Hawthorne in his preface to *The House of the Seven Gables* calls the "marvelous." Strange and supernatural incidents are ruled out. Coincidence also is suspect. In this sense, fiction must be less strange than life. Events must operate causally. The story should proceed like a string of dominoes upended in a row. All the author does is knock the first into the second, and the rest of the operation is inevitable. So critical of forced happy endings are many readers who employ this yardstick that they lean over backwards and resent anything that turns out happily— however logical it may be shown to be.

This suggests another characteristic ruled out by the yardstick of real life: undue emphasis. William Dean Howells had this in mind, for example, when he wrote that the delineation of sex should be kept in proper proportion. The French novelists, he charged, wrote as though sex is man's only interest, whereas in actuality it is only one of many interests. The effect of real life, many believe, is gained not only by excluding "marvelous" details but also by putting believable details together in the proper proportion.

A third element to be excluded is the type character. This term requires explanation. Those who divide all characters into two neat little groups—types and individuals—have oversimplified the problem to the point where they are essentially falsifying. All characters who are at all believable are type characters—in the sense that they are representative of living people. One could, if he wished, develop a personality who had one eye, two noses, talked through his feet, became angry when someone flattered him, and was delighted when someone punched him in the nose. The result would be an individual, certainly, but he would just as certainly be a monster. To the degree that a character operates and reacts the way normal people do, he is a type. Or, more narrowly, to the extent that he reacts the way a small group of people do—paranoiacs, for example—he is a type. What, then, is the basis for the antipathy to types in realistic writing? Briefly, it is an antipathy to *a fictional character who is like other fictional characters:* the *stock* hero, heroine, villain, Englishman, Congressman, industrial tycoon, Kentucky colonel, and international spy.

The reader knows what each of these is like the moment he appears in the story, and each is still the same when the story ends. The choices are simple, and the character always decides what to do on the basis of his special characteristic. Real people are far more complicated than this.

The illusion of actual life will disappear, also, if a character changes his nature too quickly. What a reader expects of a character is consistency: either he must remain the same or he must change in a thoroughly credible manner. A typical reader simply cannot swallow sudden "conversions." The yardstick of realism will not admit any change as good unless at least three elements have been attended to: a temperament that makes the change possible, circumstances that motivate the change, and sufficient time for such a change to take place. What this implies is that the thoughts and actions of characters, to be acceptable according to a real-life standard, must be well motivated. The characters must not be puppets dangling at the end of a string which the author is wiggling; their thoughts must be the result of events and other thoughts, and their actions must be the result of thoughts and other actions.

Finally, this standard requires that the characters must talk like real people. Actually, no well-drawn character ever does, for real conversation is too dull and too incoherent. But readers expect characters to give the *effect* of actual speech. To be realistic, book speech must represent actual speech in rhythm, sentence length and emphasis, diction, imagery, idioms, and grammar.

For a literary work to measure up well against a strict real-life standard, then, its events must be commonplace rather than "marvelous," its details must be proportioned according to their importance in actuality, the characters must be relatively complicated, the choices they make must not be too easy, change in character must be understandable, every action must be motivated, and dialog must give the effect of real conversation. There are plenty of drawbacks in the practice of employing so strict a standard. In the first place, it rules out any number of delightful works like Shakespeare's *A Midsummer-Night's Dream*, Poe's "Fall of the House of Usher," and Twain's *A Connecticut Yankee in King Arthur's Court*—all of which make use of the "marvelous." Then, in demanding that the characters be complicated, the reader can forget that many characters are simply functional. They are in the play or story simply to do something—to get the main characters together, to give them a chance to talk, to provide excuses for them to come and go. Then, again, in demanding that characters be real according to the standards of the real world, a reader is likely to forget that they can be equally acceptable if they are plausible according to the standards of the world of the book or play. To put it another way, the yardstick of real life measures the people and occurrences of a book or play against something which takes place outside that book or play; the criterion of plausibility measures them against what can believably take place within. About the latter, more will be said later. Lastly, literature obviously cannot be so lengthy, so formless, so dull and unpointed as the events of actuality.

When all the weaknesses of this yardstick are listed, however, the fact still remains that literature which maintains the illusion of reality is literature that the twentieth-century mind is most likely to read with thoughtful attention. Judgments made by this standard, therefore, are likely to stand up well under scrutiny.

4. ARTISTIC DETAILS

By the standard of pleasure in artistic details a work is good if it provides enough pleasurable moments through effectively handled details to compensate for the time spent on it. For many readers, a single moment of intense pleasure is enough to justify an otherwise rather tedious book or poem.

This is the yardstick of the hedonist, the type of person who believes that one should like or dislike things for themselves, that values lie in feelings of pleasure and pain. As Walter Pater points out, it is not the fruit of experience that is important, but the experience itself. In using such a yardstick, therefore, one reads not to learn facts or to weigh moral concepts or to discover what real life is like, but to find as much delight in the present as possible. The basic assumption is that all pleasure is good, and all pain is bad.

Many Americans find this a difficult yardstick to employ. Most of us are so trained in the concepts of "usefulness," of making every minute count toward something else, that we find it hard to value experience for its own sake. Ahead of almost everything we do is some future and often rather indefinite goal. Experience is usually a means, seldom an end. Someone has said that the only times that we ever really live in the present are when we take an ocean cruise or when we fall in love. Then, we surrender ourselves to the moment and enjoy it thoroughly. This is the attitude that must be taken toward reading if one is to employ the standard of pleasure in artistic details.

What can provide this pleasure? This is a hard question to answer, for it can be almost anything. Furthermore, it will not be the same thing in quite the same way for any two persons. In a poem it might be the sound pattern, the connotation of a phrase or two, the stanzaic pattern, or maybe one particular image. In a play or a piece of fiction, it might be a single character, one or two especially well-written descriptions, a particularly moving scene or speech, an unexpected but yet plausible twist in plot. Many critics deride the use of this yardstick and say that it results only in simple-minded impressionism. Admittedly, evaluation according to this method can be subjective and undisciplined. Indeed, the person using this yardstick may talk about himself as much as he talks about the work. He may even hypnotize himself and others into thinking the work had a more powerful effect upon him than it really had. All this must be recognized and guarded against. The method, however, need not be simply a subjective operation which results in a Zane Grey novel seeming to be as good as one written by Thomas Hardy. There are different kinds of pleasure, varying from a superficial emotional titillation to the deeply compelling satisfaction coming from an awareness of the greatest artistic achievement. The quantitative criteria are the number and duration of the pleasurable moments; the qualitative criteria are the intensity and nature of the pleasure itself. When these are all taken into consideration, the yardstick of pleasure in artistic details affords a standard for mature and defensible judgments. Even if it did not, it would still be valuable in that it brings attention to the fact that reading can be delightful for its own sake.

5. INTERNAL CONSISTENCY

Critics who apply the yardstick of internal consistency to a work take as their basic premise that the work of art is a unique product of the human genius and should be judged by criteria which are applicable to it and to it alone. Who the writer is or what the individual effect of the work on the reader is, are matters which are irrelevant. The problem is to discover what the relation of the parts is to the whole and to one another. The competent work, presumably, is the one in which the parts are so consistent and harmonious that the work as a totality is an organism in which no part could be changed without detriment to the whole.

Although the nature of the internal consistency varies with each work, in its largest terms it is always a matter of congruity between form and content. In the case of the lyric poem, to take one example, it is a matter of seeing whether the words, lines, stanzas, and overall form harmonize with the material and ideas. In the novel, play, short story, epic, or narrative poem, the reader ordinarily focuses his attention upon people. The primary question is what happens to them: do they remain the same? make a simple change? change and then reverse themselves? or make a series of changes? Only as the reader knows what happens to them can he determine whether they have been consistent.

In discovering this, the first step is to determine what state of affairs prevails at the opening of the work. Who are the people? What are their essential characteristics? What are the conflicts within their minds? What are the conflicts which face them with outside forces? What is the nature of the world they live in—whimsical? romantic? realistic but responsive to human effort? realistic and unresponsive to human effort? Once the answers to questions like these are known, the reader is in a position to determine whether what the characters do and say is plausible or probable.

Note that internal consistency is not dependent upon lifelike action unless the air of reality has been established at the beginning. For example, what Odysseus (Ulysses) does in the *Odyssey* is quite plausible in the world which Homer creates. Consistency is not dependent upon accuracy; it is a matter of the characters thinking, speaking, and acting in a manner which seems harmonious with their natures and setting.

Where there is no change in the characters of the short story, narrative poem, or one-act play, an analysis of internal consistency is a matter of seeing that what occurs is in accord with the basic motives of the people and the nature of the circumstances. Even in very short works, however, changes may take place. Three familiar lyrical patterns, for example, are as follows: One, the poet repeats explicitly or in figures the same emotion: I'm sad; I'm sad; how sad I am. Two, the poet explores various aspects of his thought-emotion: I'm sad for a number of reasons; how sad I am; my sadness will end only when I win my love. Three, the poet's feeling changes: I'm sad; as I sit and think about it, a new thought comes to me; now my sadness is gone. For internal consistency, the potential change in the second case and the actual change in the third must be plausible in the light of the poet's nature and his original disturbance.

In the novel and longer play changes inevitably take place. In Hawthorne's short story about Wakefield, the main character remains the same throughout: canny, egotistic, and cruel. His consistency lies in the fact that he does remain the same. In the *Scarlet Letter*, however, all of the main characters change rather markedly because of sin and a resulting sense of isolation. The consistency here comes in the fact that the change grows logically out of the circumstances and the temperaments of the characters.

The advantages of this "formal" or "organic" yardstick are numerous. It brings attention to bear upon the work itself and in doing so eliminates a great many irrelevancies. Furthermore, this mode of criticism is likely to result in a more disciplined and a more precise kind of statement. There is no excuse for vague impressions, for well-meaning but often weak-minded "appreciation." In many ways this method takes over the spirit and the method of scientific inquiry and adapts them to literary evaluation.

The system also has two fairly serious drawbacks. It is doubtful, for example, that it provides any criterion for making comparative judgments. Indeed, when pushed to its logical extreme, the method involves only description and not evaluation at all. The other drawback is that the method tends to result in such an emphasis upon structure that matters like mood, color, connotation, and melody are almost ignored. Inattention to such elements is not enforced by the method; it is simply a habit which many of its practitioners fall into—with the result that their handling of literary works becomes a series of problems in mental acrobatics and they themselves become desensitized to the emotional effects which give literature its distinctive quality.

6. TONE

The basic premise of those who use the yardstick of tone is that a fundamentally significant aspect of the literary work is the personal quality given the material as it passes through the mind and emotions of the author. Not all readers are going to agree on what the proper tone for a given work should be, since attitudes toward actions and people vary. But though there is a great deal of disagreement over many matters of tone, readers generally agree that the tone of a work should be sincere and distinctive, and that when either (or both) of these qualities is lacking, the work is something less than praiseworthy.

Insincerity is ordinarily no more welcome in literature than it is in life. Especially unwelcome in a literary work is evidence that an author has sacrificed his action or his characters to meet the requirements of the commercially successful formulas of the day. Examples of the use of such formulas are unfortunately all about: the movie or television scenario with an unmotivated happy ending, the hard-boiled detective story with a seduction scene appearing with almost mechanical regularity every fourth or sixth chapter, the confession story that slyly suggest all sorts of hideous goings-on but which isn't a real confession at all (being the imaginings of a practiced writer), the ghost-written speech and sports account, and the love story written to reassure unhappy females that love still finds a way. For the tone of all such "formula" pieces, there is only one adjective: "phony."

Sometimes a perfectly sincere writer can give the impression of insincerity by not suiting form to content. Walt Whitman, for example, was crushed on hearing of the death of Lincoln. For him it was a personal loss, and ultimately he projected his feeling into one of the most dignified and moving elegies in the English language, "When Lilacs Last in the Dooryard Bloom'd." But he also wrote "O Captain, My Captain" on the death of Lincoln, and it is neither dignified nor especially moving. We may assume that Whitman's feeling was just as sincere in writing one poem as in writing the other, but for some reason he chose in "O Captain, My Captain" to communicate his grief in hackneyed imagery and in a fast, gay, and even rollicking rhythm. The inevitable result is that his tone sounds less deeply sincere. The point is, of course, that a writer must not only *be* sincere, but by the selection of appropriate forms, imagery, words, and rhythms he must *seem* sincere.

In addition to sincerity, readers using the yardstick of tone expect something distinctive, some mark of the author's unique personality. To make this clearer, examine what happens to similar material when handled, on the one hand, by an anonymous writer and, on the other, by Mark Twain.

In the middle of the prairie, miles from nowhere, we stopped briefly to look about us and observe the wild life. Of a truth there was little to see except for the sage-brush which stretched away in every direction. Suddenly one of our party descried a "jackass rabbit," a large brownish creature with long ears. It was sitting on its haunches under a clump of sage-brush, its color harmonizing so well with the background that if it had not been pointed out to us, many of us would have missed it altogether. We were told that it could run very rapidly because of the size and great strength of its legs. Like other rabbits, it is herbivorous and eats what leaves and roots are available on the prairie. Like other rabbits, too, it multiplies rapidly, and only the paucity of food keeps its numbers from swelling into the tens of millions. Even so, the species is so common throughout this part of the country that it is the bane of the few farmers who here and there try to wrest a meager living from the dry soil.— ANONYMOUS

As the sun was going down, we saw the first specimen of an animal known familiarly over two thousand miles of mountain and desert—from Kansas clear to the Pacific Ocean—as the "jackass rabbit." He is well named. He is just like any other rabbit, except that he is from one-third to twice as large, has longer legs in proportion to his size, and has the most preposterous ears that ever were mounted on any creature but a jackass. When he is sitting quiet, thinking about his sins, or is absent-minded or unapprehensive of danger, his majestic ears project above him conspicuously; but the breaking of a twig will scare him nearly to death, and then he tilts his ears back gently and starts for home. All you can see, then, for the next minute, is his long gray form stretched out straight and "streaking it" through the low sage-brush, head erect, eyes right, and ears just canted a little to the rear, but showing you where the animal is, all the time, the same as if he carried a jib. Now and then he makes a marvelous spring with his long legs, high over the stunted sage-brush, and scores a leap that would make a horse envious. Presently, he comes down to a long, graceful "lope," and shortly he mysteriously disappears. He has crouched behind a sage-brush, and will sit there and listen and tremble until you get within six feet of him, when he will get under way again. But one must shoot at this creature once, if he wishes to see him throw his heart into his heels, and do the best he knows how. He is frightened clear through now, and he lays his long ears down on his back, straightens himself out like a yard-stick every spring he makes, and scatters miles behind him with an easy indifference that is enchanting.

One party made this specimen "hump himself," as the conductor said. The Secretary started him with a shot from the Colt; I commenced spitting at him with my weapon; and all in the same instant the old "Allen's" whole broadside let go with a rattling crash, and it is not putting it too strong to say that the rabbit was frantic! He dropped his ears, set up his tail, and left for San Francisco at a speed which can only be described as a flash and vanish! Long after he was out of sight we could hear him whiz.—MARK TWAIN, *Roughing It*

Observe how relatively little the reader gets to know about the author of the first selection. Aside from the fact that factual details seem to interest him, almost nothing of the author's personality emerges. It is difficult, too, to discern anything about his attitudes, his characteristic moods, or ways of thinking. And finally, there is little that suggests artistic accomplishment. The prose is correct but pedestrian, with almost no special quality that gives it life. In short, when judged by the yardstick of tone, this is unsatisfying writing.

The contrast with the Twain passage is, of course, obvious. Twain is clearly observant and alive. He can admire the speed and the rough beauty of the rabbit without becoming mawkishly sentimental. Beyond that, he has a clear admiration for any creature that can throw its heart into things and do the best it knows how. He has a keen sense of humor. He has the idiom and the sense for detail which mark him as a late nineteenth-century American and Westerner. He has a stylistic flair for the climactic, the figurative, and the colloquial. Even in so brief a passage, Twain has emerged as a distinct and colorful personality. By the criterion of tone the passage comes off very well indeed.

7. EMOTIONAL IMPACT

The basic premise in using this yardstick of evaluation is that the most important aspect of a literary work is its effect upon the reader. Its concerns, therefore, are chiefly psychological, and they deal with the type of effect, its intensity, its components, its duration, and its universality.

The type or quality of effect can be only roughly designated in words like fear, pity, horror, joy, rapture, quiet resignation—all words which name emotions. In every case the name falls far short of communicating the sensation itself. Nevertheless, it is possible to speak with some exactitude about what creates the work's special degree of intensity. The plot may be novel or hackneyed, the details general or specific, the dialog stilted or sparkling, the words trite or vivid, the meaning provocative or platitudinous. It is possible to point out, in addition, the components in the effect. In a short poem or novel, there is ordinarily a single component—everything contributes to one effect. But longer plays, novels, and long poems must gain their unity of effect through a blending of components, of many minor effects. It is the duty of the critical reader to indicate what various minor effects compose the parts of which the major effect is the whole. Also he should indicate the function and the relative importance of each of the minor effects and suggest at what point in the work the major effect first is felt.

The duration of effect is another aspect about which a reader can be fairly articulate. How long did the mood of the work last? How long and how well can one remember the characters, the setting, the happenings? How long does one continue to mull over the author's ideas?

One of the most important elements in this method of criticism concerns the recurrence of the effect. Does the book hold up on rereading? Does it become more effective or less effective? This probably is the hardest test any literary work must pass, and it immediately separates the so-called "thriller" from the more profound performance. The good work may be even more exciting and provocative the second time.

The final major aspect of this method concerns the spread of the work's effectiveness. How many people over how long a period have found the work enjoyable? With older books, this can be determined without much difficulty, for with the passage of time the inferior works drop out of sight and are forgotten. Melville and Whitman remain but not T. S. Arthur or Lydia Sigourney, who were their contemporaries. With current works, one must look to the testimony of friends and of the professional critics. The fact that no one else likes a book is not proof *per se* that it is an inferior work. But it is certainly a fact to be taken into account in making a final judgment.

8. PERSONAL BELIEFS

By the yardstick of personal belief a literary work is considered good if it states or implies ideas which are congenial to the reader. More simply, this means that readers like what they agree with. Phrased so baldly, this hardly seems like a sound standard for evaluation; yet it is a common one and deserves a franker attention than it normally gets. The discussion here is limited to those concerns which most deeply affect readers' judgments: morality, religion, politics and economics, philosophy, and literary criticism.

Morality

To those who are preoccupied with questions of morality, that writing which exemplifies and encourages proper conduct is good writing; conversely, whatever is profane, vulgar, or obscene, whatever encourages laxness in morals is bad. Behind such evaluation is the assumption that imaginative writing, though primarily designed to be pleasurable, must lead to instruction in behavior.

This is a critical standard that has been employed for thousands of years. Plato, for example, felt that parts of Homer and Hesiod should be kept from the young because they contained erroneous representations of the nature of gods and heroes and therefore were not conducive to proper conduct. Indeed, censorship of fiction was to be one of the first concerns of the rulers of the ideal state. In every land there have been those who, like Plato, have employed the yardstick of morality: Horace, Ben Jonson, Tolstoy, and William Dean Howells, to name only a few.

Among those who use this measure of value, however, there is no agreement as to what "morality" as applied to literature means. To some it means simply that the author has been honest with himself and his material, that his is, in short, the scientific spirit. In a paradoxical sense, a literary work is moral to such critics when it is amoral—when it does not take sides on a moral question but merely reports what the author observes. By such an interpretation of morality, the novels of Zola could be considered highly moral, though by other interpretations they might be blasted as vulgar and indecent.

Other readers, though refusing to favor amorality, nevertheless consider a literary work immoral only when in its overall implications it condones misconduct. These persons believe that no worthy literary treatment of life can leave the final impression that adultery, for instance, is socially acceptable, that lying is inconsequential, that murder is of no moment. They argue that the issue here is not only one of propriety or even of divine law, but of human survival. Society would disintegrate overnight, they insist, if individuals suddenly ceased to have regard for person or property. As instruction, they conclude, literature must not run counter to what is necessary for race preservation.

Still other readers believe a literary work is immoral if it in any fashion exhibits an indecent act or employs a coarse or obscene word. They find a work especially reprehensible if it contains swearing, drinking, divorce, or any suggestion of improper sexual relations. Literature should be uplifting; it should protect its readers from immoralities, not expose its readers to them.

The problem is a thorny one. On two points practically all are agreed: (1) that literature in dealing with human experience cannot fail to become involved with what is right and wrong in human conduct; (2) that literature, like experience itself, is a teacher. But the question still remains, to what extent should it consciously teach right conduct? Those who argue that literature should not be expected to be the "handmaiden of morality" point out that an author cannot treat life intelligently unless he is permitted to show evil as well as good. Even obscene passages and vulgar words are defensible, they say, if they contribute to the air of reality and in doing so make the literary work a more profound and effective delineation of life. Instruction is a matter of creating understanding, and understanding must be based upon a knowledge of all the facts. Those who want literature to be morally uplifting retort that nothing is to be gained by a parading of what is sordid and vulgar. Indeed, they argue, much may be lost because the attitudes and values of the young may be permanently warped. Instruction, they insist, must be a matter of indoctrination in what is right, right being determined by divine law and human convention.

Religion

That religious affiliations and doctrines get into literary evaluations cannot be denied. Confirmed Protestants have been less enthusiastic about Evelyn Waugh since his conversion to Catholicism, and strict Catholics have had a difficult time becoming enthusiastic about Mark Twain because of his criticism of their church. Some persons of both faiths have harbored qualms about a writer like Dreiser who questions the validity of all religion. In many cases, individual evaluations based upon religious beliefs have been fortified by official institutional positions which appear in the literary reviews of denominational publications.

Politics and Economics

Political affiliation and economic doctrine affect literary judgments also. At its best, the resulting criticism shows some rather astonishing inequities in treatment. It seems clear that Dr. Johnson would have thought more highly of "Lycidas" had Milton been a Tory, that English Liberals would have been more enthusiastic about Southey's writings had he not deserted their party, that British Laborites would be fonder of Kipling had he not sanctioned imperialism. Contemporary Americans who tend to be liberal in their political thinking are likely to place a high estimate upon writers like John Dos Passos, Upton Sinclair, and Lillian Hellman; more conservative readers, by the same token, prefer authors who accept the *status quo* or, at least, are not particularly critical of it—authors like Kenneth Roberts and Clarence Buddington Kelland. Some critics in this country have been strongly partisan in their insistence that literature show what they called "class struggle"; others that literature should clearly uphold what they called "the American way of life."

Philosophy

Philosophical beliefs often give the assumptions upon which literary conclusions are based. Platonists, believing in a world of ultimate truth beyond the realm of the senses and apprehensible only through intuition, are likely to have especially high regard for those works which suggest that the material world is secondary, imperfect, and transitory. Thus Emerson found such writers as Milton, Goethe, and Coleridge especially exciting. Non-Platonists who believe that truth can be apprehended only by the senses look not for evidences of intuitive insight but for a detailed and faithful representation of life based on careful sensory observation. Such thinkers are likely to put a considerably higher estimate than the Platonists would upon such writers as Zola, Hardy, Dostoevski, and Dreiser.

Literary Criticism

Special doctrines within the field of literary criticism have an obvious effect on one's evaluations. Every age has its preferences, and every reader is a product of his age. What the great majority of eighteenth-century readers wanted was simplicity if not austerity in style, ease in reading, and neatness of form. Deprecating the way Shakespeare played fast and loose with time and place, they urged their dramatists to confine a play to one setting and the time span of the action to twenty-four hours. Poetry, they felt, should be written in rhymed couplets and in relatively elegant language. They thought the conceits of John Donne tiresome, and they preferred the simpler ideas and lines of Alexander Pope.

But what happened to these notions? To a great extent they were replaced by other standards in the nineteenth century, and these in turn were superseded by new points of view in the twentieth. Today, most readers want their details vigorous and realistic; they care very little about traditional forms; they think it silly for all poems to be written in rhymed couplets or for most of them to be about nature; they like a style that is colorful, jabby, almost journalistic in flavor. Are these timeless standards of greatness?

Observe, too, that within the general taste pattern of an age there are all sorts of minor groups which overlap in doctrine but still retain distinctive emphasis. Today, there are the realists, naturalists, primitivists, Freudians, Marxists, and a host of others, each group with its special tenets and each evaluating literature according to those tenets.

The yardstick of personal beliefs is a tricky and often deceptive affair. One of its characteristic weaknesses is that it too often introduces criteria which are irrelevant. Worse than that, it too often becomes a matter of evaluation by prejudice, and hence ceases to be evaluation at all. Conclusions reached by this method are frequently inconsequential, sometimes crude and vicious. Yet when a personal belief is reasonable and relevant, no one can logically argue against its use simply because it is the result of private loyalties. A reader may be a partisan, but that is no reason for his becoming grossly unreasonable. This yardstick, therefore, can be manipulated to personal, unintelligent, and evil ends. Too often it is. But it need not be.

9. INSIGHTS

The basic premise of those who use the yardstick of insight in making literary judgments is that literature should be the repository of all the best that has been thought and said. In the highest sense it should be a "criticism of life." A work, then, is great to the extent that it provides insight into what is best—what is true, good, beautiful.

Rather obviously the emphasis in this kind of evaluation is upon the element of meaning, and in that sense its criterion for excellence is closely akin to the yardstick of personal beliefs. Under personal beliefs, however, those convictions were discussed which the reader carried to the work, retained throughout, and used almost exclusively in the process of evaluation. Here the concern is with the reader who brings to the work a desire for insight, not a mind made up. He is a seeker, not a dogmatist. Such a reader will ask such questions as: How effectively does this work re-create experience for me? How accurately does it mirror the personality of the author and the temper of his age? How consistently does it handle the necessary elements?

Psychological Insight

By this yardstick a literary work is valuable and good to the extent that it provides new and profound psychological perceptions. In this sense it is different from the yardstick of real life, which demands only that the characters act in accord with what the reader already knows about human behavior.

Potentially, almost every literary work is rich in psychological insights. The key word here, however, is "potentially" since obviously not every work in actuality does provide new knowledge of men's motives, of their actions and reactions. The reasons for their failure to do this are various. Frequently it is because the author has used hackneyed situations and conflicts. Sometimes it is because he has sacrificed his characters for a moral or a thesis. Sometimes it is because he has sacrificed them for his plot or story formula. Even Henry James admitted that in *The American* he had some of his characters act in poorly motivated ways because of the demands of his plot. No work, it seems clear, is likely to be rich in psychological perceptions unless the author is first of all interested in his characters and faithful to them. He must allow them to act as real people would act under similar circumstances.

This last statement should not lead one to suppose, however, that a work must be highly realistic in every respect in order to rank high when measured by this yardstick. Only psychological verity is required. For example, Hawthorne's tales and romances have many non-realistic elements in them. Yet few writers have given such thoughtful and probing analyses of what happens to the human mind and emotions when a human being commits what he considers to be a sinful act. Even Poe's wild tales of horror cast light on what could happen to anyone in a moment of abnormal stress.

Possibly the chief danger in the use of this yardstick is the tendency to place a higher value upon fresh perceptions of abnormal behavior than on equally fresh perceptions of normal behavior. A probing treatment of a psychotic seems much more significant, because the material is more lurid, than a conscientious treatment of an average American businessman. This is a tendency that needs to be fought because it can skew evaluations by this yardstick badly. In a chapter on a method of criticism he calls "Formism," Stephen C. Pepper in his provocative *The Basis of Criticism in the Arts* identifies human value with what is normal in human behavior. The greatest literature, he says, is that which deals with norms, which penetrates to actions and traits that count, dwelling seriously on what is serious and laughing at what is silly. Psychological insight for most readers, in short, is most likely to result from those works which cast light upon the normal in human behavior.

Sociological Insight

That literature can be a criticism of life in a sociological sense is a relatively new idea. It became strongly apparent in England when Dickens' novels brought home to thousands the wretched conditions in London slums and prisons. In this country, as early a writer as Cooper touched upon economic matters, but it was not until Twain, Howells, Norris, and Dreiser that social problems began getting widespread treatment in imaginative literature. Today, it would be no exaggeration to say that such problems are the prime concern of our major writers. Readers have come to expect that literature will go beyond the personal problems of a few men to the more general problems of man. What is the effect on man of his environment? of his economic system? of his political system? of his institutions, folkways, and mores?

Ethical Insight

According to Matthew Arnold, the great English critic, the desire of great writers is to "educe and cultivate what is best and noblest in themselves."

This is not to be construed, however, as a selfish objective. "They do not talk of their mission, nor of interpreting their age, nor of the coming Poet; all this, they know, is the mere delirium of vanity; their business is not to praise their age, but to afford men who live in it the highest pleasure which they are capable of feeling." With Arnold and this method of criticism, therefore, we come back to the conviction that literature has a dual role: it must be pleasurable and it must be instructive (i.e., ennobling). The most effective blending of these two elements results in the profoundest literature.

Traditionally, the finest blending of the two has been associated with the ancients, particularly the Greek poets. In their works, many readers have felt, man's best thoughts appear in their simplest and most moving form— simplest because they deal only with basic truths and primary emotions; most moving because the human actions they depict are elemental, the personages noble, and the situations intense. For the Greeks, meaning and structure were far more important than phrasing. Readers can learn from them, Arnold points out, "how unspeakably superior is the effect of one moral impression left by a great action treated as a whole, to the effect produced by the most striking single thought or by the happiest image."

Metaphysical Insight

Metaphysical insight, as the term is used here, is insight into the nature of being, into the fundamental causes and processes of things. More specifically it is insight into the relation of man to nature, to the cosmos, and to God. A term frequently used today for this kind of insight is "mythical," the word calling to mind, of course, the myths of classical times, which dealt not only with relations among men but relations between men and the gods. To rank high by this standard of judgment, a work must raise and attempt something of an answer to such ultimate questions as: What is life? Why am I here? What is man's eventual destiny? Is there a God? What is his nature? Is there purpose to our universe?

The chief danger in this yardstick lies in its current popularity. Myth-hunting has become a favorite indoor sport, with the result that many fine books which were never intended to be metaphysically significant have been assigned superfluous and sometimes bizarre meanings. Thus *Huckleberry Finn* has been transformed by some critics into a kind of huge allegory with the Mississippi being the river of life carrying Huck and Jim down toward the endless sea of death. Probably no one would have been more surprised by this interpretation than Mark Twain! But the fact that this yardstick has been overused and misapplied is no argument for avoiding it when a literary work clearly provides perceptions of a metaphysical sort. Indeed it would be unfair to an author who attempts to deal with such difficult considerations not to take them into account in making a judgment about his work. This is the most demanding of all yardsticks, and a work that measures up well to its demands is likely to be one of the finest products of the human genius.

Index of Titles and Authors